George F. Kennan

ALSO BY JOHN LEWIS GADDIS

The Cold War: A New History

Surprise, Security, and the American Experience

The Landscape of History: How Historians Map the Past

We Now Know: Rethinking Cold War History

The United States and the End of the Cold War:
Implications, Reconsiderations, Provocations

The Long Peace: Inquiries into the History of the Cold War

Strategies of Containment: A Critical Appraisal
of Postwar American National Security

Russia, the Soviet Union, and the United States: An Interpretive History

The United States and the Origins of the Cold War, 1941–1947

George F. Kennan

AN AMERICAN LIFE

JOHN LEWIS GADDIS

THE PENGUIN PRESS
New York
2011

THE PENGUIN PRESS
Published by the Penguin Group
Penguin Group (USA) Inc., 375 Hudson Street, New York, New York 10014, U.S.A. •
Penguin Group (Canada), 90 Eglinton Avenue East, Suite 700, Toronto, Ontario, Canada M4P 2Y3
(a division of Pearson Penguin Canada Inc.) • Penguin Books Ltd, 80 Strand, London WC2R 0RL, England • Penguin
Ireland, 25 St. Stephen's Green, Dublin 2, Ireland (a division of Penguin Books Ltd) • Penguin Books Australia Ltd,
250 Camberwell Road, Camberwell, Victoria 3124, Australia (a division of Pearson Australia Group Pty Ltd) • Penguin
Books India Pvt Ltd, 11 Community Centre, Panchsheel Park, New Delhi – 110 017, India • Penguin Group (NZ),
67 Apollo Drive, Rosedale, Auckland 0632, New Zealand (a division of Pearson New Zealand Ltd) • Penguin Books
(South Africa) (Pty) Ltd, 24 Sturdee Avenue, Rosebank, Johannesburg 2196, South Africa

Penguin Books Ltd, Registered Offices:
80 Strand, London WC2R 0RL, England

First published in 2011 by The Penguin Press,
a member of Penguin Group (USA) Inc.

LIBRARY OF CONGRESS CATALOGING IN PUBLICATION DATA

Gaddis, John Lewis.
George F. Kennan : an American life / John Lewis Gaddis.
p. cm.
Includes bibliographical references and index.
ISBN 978-1-59420-312-1
1. Kennan, George F. (George Frost), 1904–2005. 2. United States—Foreign relations—1945–1989. 3. World
politics—1945–1989. 4. United States—Foreign relations—Soviet Union. 5. Soviet Union—Foreign
relations—United States. 6. Cold war—Diplomatic history. 7. Diplomats—United States—
Biography. 8. Ambassadors—United States—Biography. I. Title.
E748.K374G34 2011
327.730092—dc23
[B] 2011021786

Printed in the United States of America
1   3   5   7   9   10   8   6   4   2

Designed by Meighan Cavanaugh

In memory of

Annelise Sørensen Kennan

1910–2008

without whom it would not have been possible

PREFACE

"I HAVE SOMETIMES WONDERED WHETHER YOU WOULD BE ABLE TO see your way to going through with it," George Kennan wrote me in 1995, fourteen years after I became his biographer, sixteen years before the book would appear. "But," he added, "I comfort myself with the reflection that I have, after all, deservedly or otherwise, become something closer to a national figure in recent years. . . . I do not expect to live to see the results of your efforts; and I am not sure that I ought to see them, even if I lived to do it. But write them, if you will, on the confident assumption that no account need be taken of my own reaction to them, either in this world or the next."[1]

Kennan had, of course, already secured an international reputation as a diplomat, grand strategist, historian, memoirist, cultural critic, and antiwar activist when, in 1981 at the age of seventy-eight, he agreed to cooperate in the writing of this biography. We both assumed that it would appear a few years after his death. Neither of us foresaw how far into the future that would be: Kennan would not die until March 17, 2005, at the age of a hundred and one. Characteristically, he blamed himself for the delay.

He saw no signs that the biography was in progress, Kennan wrote in his diary after I paid him a visit in 1997, but "I don't find this surprising. [Gaddis] would no doubt have preferred to write it when I am dead, as I should, in the natural order of things, long since have been." Perhaps "I should do him the favor of dying immediately." His failure to do so did not diminish the guilt he felt. "My unnatural longevity is now becoming a serious burden to others," he lamented in 2003. "Poor John Gaddis has seen his undertaking being put off for years while he waits for me to make way for it."[2]

I assured Kennan, on many occasions, that I didn't mind, that I had other things to keep me occupied, and that I would make the biography my chief priority, apart from teaching, after his death. Our strange relationship went on long enough, though, for my students—who tend to see anyone over forty as having a foot in the grave—to begin speculating somberly about which of us might go first.

From my perspective (assuming survival), the relationship could not have been better. Kennan granted me unrestricted access to himself, his papers, and his mostly handwritten diaries, which alone fill twelve of the 330 boxes of Kennan materials now open for research at Princeton University's Seeley G. Mudd Manuscript Library. With Kennan's encouragement, many of his friends and most of his family talked with me soon after I began this project—fortunately, as it happened, because he outlived almost all of them. I saw him for interviews, and later less formal visits, about once a year for a quarter of a century: he found it a relief, he once told me, that "you're not always around and under foot."

Kennan also gave me, from the outset, the greatest gift an authorized biographer can receive, which was the complete freedom to say what I pleased. The only portion of this book he ever read is a single paragraph in the Epilogue, drawn from a talk I delivered when Princeton opened its centennial exhibition on his life in November 2003. Would it be all right, he asked me that morning, if he afterward saw a copy of what I was going to say? Of course, I replied, I would send it to him. He thanked me, but added that I shouldn't do so if I felt this to be in any way an attempt to "influence" the biography.[3]

He and I originally thought of the book as more political than personal, but when we explained this to George's wife, Annelise, she strongly objected. His writings, she reminded us, were full of gloom and doom: I must get to know him well enough to see that he was not always this way. That, in turn, allowed me to glimpse the stabilizing role she played in his life. It first became clear to me one evening in Princeton in 1983. The Kennans were just back from Norway, and when I asked how it had been, George started complaining about dissolute youth hanging around the docks. Annelise put an end to that: "George, you're always worrying about docks!" All docks everywhere had dissolute youth. That, along with tying up boats, was what they were for. And then, turning to me: "He worries too much about the docks."[4]

Annelise had her way with this book, and that's why I have dedicated it to her memory. It's by no means the first, though, about George Kennan. I've learned from, and respect the work of, my predecessors, especially C. Ben Wright, Barton Gellman, Walter Isaacson and Evan Thomas, David Mayers, Walter Hixson, Anders Stephanson, Wilson D. Miscamble C.S.C., John Lamberton Harper, Richard L. Russell, John Lukacs, Lee Congdon, Nicholas Thompson, and Frank Costigliola, who will now be editing the Kennan diaries. But I've made no systematic effort to compare their conclusions—or even some of my own previous ones—with what this book contains. I want it to be a fresh look at Kennan himself, not at the scholarship he has inspired.

This is also, despite its length, a selective life. I've given more attention to some episodes than to others, and I've left out a lot. I've done so partly because I think that character emerges more clearly from the choices biographers make than from the comprehensiveness they attempt; partly also out of compassion for my readers. Kennan once recommended to me, as a model, Leon Edel's monumental biography of Henry James. He had in mind, though, Edel's psychological insights, not the five volumes required to convey them.

Finally, a note on names. First ones are necessary when writing about family, as an older sister of George's pointed out when I began an early interview with the question: "What was Professor Kennan like as a baby?" At the same time it seemed inappropriate to write, in later chapters, of "George's" long telegram, or his "X" article. So I have used "George" within the context of family, and "Kennan" elsewhere. I have also, following the custom of Kennan and his generation, occasionally used the term "Russians" when discussing the inhabitants of the Union of Soviet Socialist Republics. I am fully aware that a substantial minority were not Russians, but I also know how cumbersome it would be to have to remind readers repeatedly of this fact. I ask their indulgence in being reminded here.

George Kennan's willingness to entrust me with a biography he would never read was, from the beginning, an extraordinary expression of confidence. How much so came through all over again in 2002, on one of the last visits my wife Toni and I paid to the Kennans at their Princeton home. George showed me a stack of loose-leaf binders containing the only copy of his diary from 1970 until that moment. "They go with you," he said, to my astonishment. "But I guess you wouldn't be interested in this," he added, indicating a single smaller volume. "What is it?" "Oh, just my dream diary." "Take it too," Annelise insisted. I didn't argue. Never have I driven more carefully back to New Haven.

Whether I have merited the trust both Kennans placed in me I do not know. They were my companions, though, through a considerable portion of my life, and that, for me, was a great privilege. Now that we have reached, with the completion of this book, the point of parting, I can see how much I will miss them.

John Lewis Gaddis
New Haven, Connecticut
July 2011

CONTENTS

Part III

Part IV

Part V

Part I

ONE

Childhood: 1904–1921

"THE GREATEST TRAGEDY OF HUMAN EXISTENCE," GEORGE F. KENnan told me when we first talked of this biography, "is that we do not all die at the same time as those we love." It might seem odd to begin a life by invoking death, but in this instance it was appropriate, for the tragedy Kennan saw in death was not the oblivion it brings but the separations it causes: the way it rends relationships without which there can be no life. And death severed the most important relationship in young George's life just as it began.

Throughout much of his childhood George believed that his mother, Florence James Kennan, had died giving birth to him in Milwaukee on February 16, 1904. She had not. The death occurred on April 19, and the cause was peritonitis from a ruptured appendix, a mishandled but completely separate medical problem. The effect, though, was much the same: the rending of a relationship so brief that it could not even exist in memory. "Whether she nursed him or not, I don't know," George's sister Jeanette recalled eight decades later, "but I suspect she did. What a tragedy." Florence died at home, painfully and protractedly. The older children were brought in to kiss their mother goodbye, while baby George, held by an aunt in the next room but hearing everything, was "so quiet."[1]

In his memoirs, written when he was in his sixties, Kennan acknowledged having been "deeply affected, and in a certain sense scarred for life," by his mother's death.[2] But he was not then prepared to reveal where the evidence lay, in the realm of visions and dreams:

March 1931. A young diplomat at a Swiss winter resort suddenly finds himself dancing with tears in his eyes, not because the girl he's with isn't the one he wants, but because, as he notes bitterly in his diary, he misses someone else: "You had better go out into the open air and realize that Mother is far away and that no one is ever going to understand you and that it is not even very important whether anyone ever does."[3]

February 1942. An older Foreign Service officer, married now and a father, writes an unsent letter to his children from internment in Nazi Germany, wondering whether they would remember him were he not to return: "I myself grew up without a mother; and there are so many times that I have wished I had known what she was like—that I could have had at least one conversation with her."[4]

January 1959. A middle-aged historian, retired temporarily from diplomacy, dreams for the first time of meeting his mother. "She showed no recognition of me; she was plainly preoccupied with something else; but she accepted with politeness and with an enigmatic smile my own instantaneous gesture of recognition and joy and tenderness. She was, for the moment, the main thing in my existence; I was not the main thing in hers."[5]

July 1984. An aging brother, now eighty, writes his surviving sisters on the day he learns that their eldest has died: "I think of what desperation our mother must have felt as she faced death with the realization that she was being torn away relentlessly from four small children and abandoning them to a wildly uncertain future. And I think, of course, of the crushing blow this must have been to our poor father—who, God knows, had enough blows in this life without this crowning one."[6]

June 1999. A distinguished elder statesman, at ninety-five failing physically but fully in command mentally, suddenly sheds tears as he recalls Anton Chekhov's haunting story "The Steppe," about a boy of nine traveling with a group of peasants across a vast Russian landscape. The boy misses his mother, "understanding neither where he was going nor why," trying to grasp the meaning of stars at night, only to find that they "oppress your spirits with their silence," hinting at "that solitariness awaiting us all in the grave, and life's essence seems to be despair and horror."[7]

How to weigh the pain of loss when it occurs so early in life that one lacks the words, even the concepts, to know what is happening? When one accepts such pain at first as the normal condition of human existence, only to learn—yet another loss—that it is not? George Kennan provided an answer of sort in his memoirs: "We are, toward the end of our lives, such different people, so far removed from the childhood figures with whom our identity links us, that the bond to those figures, like that of nations to their obscure prehistoric origins, is almost irrel-evant."[8] But a biographer can, perhaps, be pardoned for not believing everything that the subject of his biography says.

I.

Sisters, most immediately, filled the void. Jeanette, only two years older than George, remembered holding, comforting, and occasionally disciplining him. Despite the proximity in their ages, she became as much substitute mother as sibling through-out his childhood and adolescence, and for the rest of her life would remain the member of his Milwaukee family to whom he was closest: "I could talk more with Jeanette than almost anyone in the world." Constance, who was six when her mother died, found her baby brother quick to learn in eliciting sympathy. Sitting on a blanket, he would topple over, bump his head on the floor, and pretend to cry. "We three sisters would all descend upon him and love him, comfort him. That was all he wanted, poor little thing." It did not take long, though, for identity to begin to emerge and for the cuddling to become constraining. George's senior sister Frances, eight at the time of his birth, remembered that as he grew older, "he didn't care for that at all. If we would try to put our arms around him he would push us away."[9]

George and Jeanette shared a room on the third floor of what he later described as their "dark, strange household." Located just north of downtown Milwaukee on a strip of land between Lake Michigan and the Milwaukee River, 935 Cambridge Avenue was built in just the wrong way, with the living room windows facing the house next door, while the blank side obscured an open lawn. There were, how-ever, a cook, a maid, and for young George a nurse, hired to take care of him for several months after his mother's death. This made an impression: "A woman in a nurse's uniform has for me a dangerous attraction," he admitted many years later. "I'm sure that this comes from the fact that the first mother I had was probably this nurse with the white uniform."[10]

George and Jeanette would wake early in the morning, she remembered, "as chil-dren are apt to do. We would run down in our bare feet into my father's room. He had a bed that had a footboard, and [we] used to get on the footboard and then somersault over into his arms. And then he would put his arms around both of us and cuddle us down and sing Civil War songs." The maid would come downstairs and rap at the door: "'Are the children there?' 'No,' my father would say, 'I haven't seen any children.' [He] loved babies. And of course, this baby George was very special."[11]

Father was Kossuth Kent Kennan, a prominent but not wealthy Milwaukee tax attorney who had been fifty-two years old at the time of George's birth and his wife's death. Mourning was no new experience for him. His first wife, Nellie McGregor Pierpont Kennan, had died in childbirth in 1889 along with a baby daughter, after only four years of marriage.[12] But Florence and Kent had four healthy children after theirs, which took place in 1895. Saddled, following her death, with the unexpected responsibility of managing a young family alone, Kent tried to maintain a semblance of stability, but there was always sadness surrounding it. Jeanette recalled him staying home in the mornings to supervise George's bath and returning early in the afternoon. "I also remember my father's tenderness—his taking us on his lap when we were little and reading to us—'The Pied Piper of Hamlin' I particularly remember. And 'The Little Match Girl.' Oh, dear! He'd cry too. The tears would come into his eyes."[13]

Kent had to provide financial as well as emotional support, however, which meant entrusting his children, most of the day, to nurses and maids while he was at the office. "They were a problem," Constance pointed out, "because if they liked children they weren't such good housekeepers, and if they were good housekeepers, they didn't care so much for the children." So Kent's second cousin Grace Wells, a young kindergarten teacher from Massachusetts, moved to Milwaukee and took up residence as a second mother for the Kennan children—the first George knew apart from his nurses. "She was really only with us for three years, but it seemed like a long long time because we were so happy. And of course she adored George—he was her baby. We all adored Cousin Grace."[14]

But this, too, was not a stable situation, for in 1908 Kent announced his intention to remarry, and Cousin Grace had to go. Jeanette never forgot getting the news. She and her sisters burst into tears, ran upstairs, and found Grace weeping also. For George, it meant losing yet another mother. Louise Wheeler, who grew up in Michigan, had been a preceptress in Latin and Greek at Ripon College, Kent's alma mater, where they had met. "When they were first married," Jeanette speculated, "they must have been a little romantic about each other, although we never thought they were in the later years—and when they wanted to say something that they didn't want us children to hear, they'd say it in Latin or Greek." The children resented Louise for supplanting Cousin Grace: she was, behind her back, "the kangaroo from Kalamazoo."[15]

"We felt that she wasn't always very nice to our father," George later explained. "We doubted, I think, how much she really loved him." Jeanette saw a different problem, which was that "my stepmother never really understood little boys. She wasn't at all an earthy person. She couldn't understand, for instance, why little boys would want to eat so much. How they could be so ravenous. . . . She was a very nervous woman, and any little thing that [George] did that was awkward— you could see her wince."[16]

Four years after the marriage, Louise unexpectedly became pregnant: her husband was then sixty-one. So in 1913 George found himself with a half-brother, also named Kent, who took most of his stepmother's time and diverted the attention of his older sisters. George "took a back seat," Jeanette remembered. "All of us loved the baby, [but] I don't know whether George loved him as much as the three sisters did." The younger Kent later acknowledged that George "did not feel at ease with my mother. He said to me that he'd never had a mother. I think she tried, she did the best she could to understand him, but I don't think he felt she was getting through to him."[17]

George's father found it difficult to provide consolation. He was, Frances pointed out, "a very sensitive man, but the fact that he was sensitive made him awkward. I never did get close to my father in any way at all." Emotional but distrusting emotion, Kent senior prided himself on having learned early in life "to do a thing which ought to be done, *when* it ought to be done and *as* it ought to be done, whether I *felt* like doing it or not." Such stoicism was little comfort to a son from whom his father concealed his softer side. "When we went abroad the first time," Jeanette explained, "we were on the ship just before we sailed, and they played the 'Star Spangled Banner,' and 'All ashore that are going ashore.' My father put his arm around me and I started to cry. He said: 'I always do, too.'" But "as George got a little older, he didn't put on that side for him. He thought it wasn't manly."[18]

"It was a very straight-laced family," the younger Kent remembered. "No movies or card-playing on Sunday, never a swear word. For example, 'darn' was considered too strong to use, and 'damn' was completely out. Once when I was taking French in high school I said 'Mon Dieu' and my father scolded me for it." Jeanette was even reprimanded for discussing the birth of puppies at the dinner table. The children were brought up in the Presbyterian Church, and their father made a point of reading the Bible all the way through several times. The girls learned to play the piano, but only for the purpose of accompanying hymns on Sunday evening.

Even here George was left out, for although his half-brother was also taught piano at an early age, that instrument was not thought appropriate for George, who proceeded to learn it on his own. He was, to his disgust, dispatched to dancing school, an indignity to which he responded with "sullen rages and sit-down strikes." Musical talent was there, though, and it showed up at unexpected moments, as during the summer task of picking strawberries with Jeanette. "George would harmonize with me, knowing what I was going to sing, because it was so obvious. But it wouldn't have been obvious to anybody who didn't have a great deal of music in him."[19]

The Kennans were also literary. His father had collected a large library, from which George read extensively: "I had nothing else to do." Writing and speaking were also important, Kent junior remembered: "When I would write letters home, I would sometimes get misspellings corrected in the letters I received back." Jeanette recalled "the speech in our house [as] very, very correct." While still little, she and George would have supper together at five o'clock, and "we carried on some wonderful conversations. We liked big words, and so when we'd find a new big word, we'd use it." One was "reputation." They weren't sure what it meant, "but we brought it into every sentence, while we ate our cream of wheat with maple sugar on it."[20]

Still, something was missing in family life on Cambridge Avenue. When the children were older and allowed at the dinner table, George and his siblings would flee at the first opportunity, preferring the company of books to that of grown-ups. "It's unusual for a family, I think, to disperse like that," Jeanette pointed out. "But we just never played games together, or sat around. I don't recall any real merriment when we were just ourselves." George recalled "daydreams so intense and satisfying that hours could pass in oblivion of immediate surroundings." His intensity became a family legend when an aunt, traveling with the brooding boy, felt obliged to tell him: "Stop thinking for a little while!"[21]

Jeanette would later reflect on how little home life George had. He lost his mother without ever getting to know her. He loved Cousin Grace but lost her too. He gained a stepmother, but never regarded her as a real mother. His father, George himself later admitted, "was so much older, and I still remained so shy that I seldom really talked with him." How much did all of this matter? "I sometimes wondered," George recalled in his old age, "whether all the grown-ups were not really deceiving me, and whether one day they would not come out and say: 'You little goose. Did you really think that we cared anything about you?' "[22]

II.

They never did, of course. Many children fear rejection, most of the time it doesn't happen, and it certainly did not to young George. Despite the losses with which he grew up, he was hardly bereft of adults who cared. Milwaukee and its environs were full of grandparents, aunts, uncles, cousins, and friends to whom the Kennan children could look for sympathy and support. "Everybody felt so sorry for [us]," Jeanette recalled, that at Christmas "we were showered with things."[23] And next door there were even surrogate parents.

Edward and Ida Frost were wealthy and well educated, owned a large house at 945 Cambridge Avenue, and lacked children of their own. The middle name Florence had picked for her son reflected the Frosts' friendship: he was George Frost Kennan. After her death, Constance remembered, "they had us over there and would read aloud to us. They were just second parents to us, always." "They were so close to our family," George added, "that we called them Uncle Edward and Aunt Ida." No fence separated the two houses, so the Kennan children always had a large yard available for baseball games and other activities. The Frosts even installed a special telephone line so that the families could keep track of one another. They remained, in young Kent's memory, "very strong, charming people, more outgoing and convivial than either my father or my mother."[24]

So too was Florence's family, the Jameses, with whom George spent a great deal of time. "They were *socially* elite, which the Kennans weren't," Jeanette observed. Their wealth came from the insurance business: Florence's father and brother both served as presidents of the Northwestern National Life Insurance Company. "They were not at all like my father's family," George commented. "They had none of the intellectual ability that my father obviously had. They were tough, handsome, but not intellectual."[25]

There was uneasiness between the Kennans and the Jameses. George's father made a point of recording, long after Florence's death, that her mother had not looked favorably on his attentions toward her daughter and had even sent Florence off to Europe in an unsuccessful effort to head off the marriage. The Jameses "set great store by charm," Frances explained. "I don't think Papa fulfilled it." And then there was the matter of finances. "Kent Kennan is a very good lawyer," Florence's brother Alfred was said to have observed, but "[he] is a very poor businessman."[26]

The Jameses paid for the house on Cambridge Avenue into which Florence and

Kent moved after their marriage, and Florence's bequest to her children included a second house in the James family compound on Lake Nagawicka, some thirty miles west of Milwaukee. It was, George remembered, "where the doors and windows of life were opened." The Kennan and James children spent joyous summers there, swimming, boating, fishing, riding ponies, playing in haystacks, staging amateur theatricals, watching fireworks go off over the lake on the Fourth of July. Short nights provided other impressions: the wind rippling the trees, the waves lapping gently against the shore, the hooting of owls, the croaking of frogs, the droning of insects—and then off in the distance, growing nearer, then fading away, the rumble, rush, and lonely whistle of the great trains on the mainline of the Chicago, Milwaukee, St. Paul and Pacific Railroad, just north of the lake, hurtling through the darkness, on the way to crossing a continent.[27]

The trains at Nagawicka were not the only connection to a wider world. Just a short walk from Cambridge Avenue were McKinley and Juneau parks, which looked out over Lake Michigan. For a boy who loved boats, the oceans that lay beyond were not difficult to imagine. Lake steamers lined the docks along the Milwaukee River, even as bicycles, electric streetcars, and automobiles were crowding horses off the streets. Milwaukee had about 300,000 inhabitants at the time of George's birth, three to four times the number when his father had settled there in 1875. A large percentage were recent immigrants: there were German, Irish, Scandinavian, Polish, Italian, Hungarian, Slovakian, Serbian, Croatian, Slovenian, and Russian Jewish neighborhoods. Foreign languages were spoken and read throughout the city. It even had a Social Democratic Party that, drawing heavily on the immigrant vote, elected a socialist mayor in 1910, the first in the United States.[28]

Nor was there anything provincial about George's family. The Jameses traveled widely, were knowledgeable about art, and supported it locally. George's aunt on his father's side had married a Frankfurt German, Paul Mausolff, who impressed his nephew with his goatee, his pince-nez, and his knowledge of languages. And George's father's first name honored Louis Kossuth, the failed Hungarian revolutionary who had been touring the United States at the time of Kent's birth in 1851. Kent knew Europe well, having spent two years there during the early 1880s recruiting immigrants for the Wisconsin Central Railroad, and spoke German, French, and Danish. He had then worked as a mining engineer in the western United States and in central Mexico. Appointed tax commissioner for the state of Wisconsin in 1897, Kossuth Kent Kennan made himself an internationally recognized expert on income tax law and in 1910 published a widely circulated book on that subject. Two years later he took his family back to Europe, where he studied the German tax system while his children learned the language.[29]

And then there was the other George Kennan, who had no middle name but whose life in many other ways prefigured that of George Frost Kennan. Born in Norwalk, Ohio, in 1845, fifty-nine years to the day before his namesake, this Kennan was a cousin of George's grandfather, Thomas Lathrop Kennan. His first trip abroad had come in 1865, when he accompanied the Russian-American Telegraph Expedition to Siberia in a spectacular but unsuccessful effort to link Europe with North America via Alaska and the Bering Strait—the effort fell through when the Atlantic cable began operating the following year. Subsequent journeys to Russia followed, and by the 1890s the first George Kennan had become the most prominent American expert on that country.

Through his books, articles, and speaking tours, this Kennan did more than anyone else to shape the image of Siberia—and to a considerable extent that of tsarist Russia itself—as a prison of peoples. He delivered more than eight hundred lectures on the regime's persecution of Jews and dissidents between 1889 and 1898, reaching roughly a million people. When the Russo-Japanese War began in 1904, six days before George Frost Kennan's birth, President Theodore Roosevelt turned to the elder Kennan as one of his chief Russian advisers.[30] Four decades later the younger Kennan held hopes—mostly unfulfilled—that another Roosevelt would similarly listen to him.

The parallels, George Frost Kennan reflected in his memoirs, went well beyond sharing the same name and being born on the same day:

> Both of us devoted large portions of our adult life to Russia and her problems. We were both expelled from Russia by the Russian governments of our day, at comparable periods in our careers. Both of us founded organizations to assist refugees from Russian despotism. Both wrote and lectured profusely. Both played the guitar. Both owned and loved particular sailboats of similar construction. Both eventually became members of the National Institute of Arts and Letters. Both had occasion to plead at one time or another for greater understanding in America for Japan and her geopolitical problems vis-à vis the Asian mainland.

With no mother and a distant father, it was only natural for young George to identify with this famous relative, who had no surviving children of his own. "He used to send me, on each of our common birthdays, something—one of his books on a couple of occasions—which he signed for me."[31]

"[Y]ou have a son who bears my name," George Kennan wrote to Kossuth Kent Kennan in December 1912. "It would be a great satisfaction to me if I could feel that certain things which have personal or historical interest and which have been closely associated with my work could be transferred to him when he becomes old enough to understand them and take an interest in them." Kent's son was "still very young, and I don't know him at all, but I have confidence in his parentage, and in the training that you and your wife will give him. . . . If I live to be as old as your father, I may see your boy grown to manhood, but life is more or less uncertain after 65."[32]

Even here, though, there was rejection. George Frost Kennan met George Kennan only once, shortly after this letter was written, when Kent took his son for a visit. Young George interested the old man, but his wife Lena resented the boy's sharing her husband's name, as well as that of their only son, who had died at birth. "She didn't like my coming. She thought that this was another branch of the family trying to horn in on his fame." Years later George learned that Mrs. Kennan had taken his thank-you note as an indication of inadequacy: "'Any boy who writes such a stupid letter, nothing's ever going to come of him. We should never see him again.' And indeed they didn't. So he never knew that I was going into Russian studies."[33]

"How sad it was," Jeanette would later reflect, "because George Kennan died in 1924, and George would have been twenty, so that he would have been old enough to have been interesting." It's not clear that the rejection affected George much at the time, although he would surely have been aware of it. As he grew older, though, and as his own career in Russian studies began to develop, identification with his famous but inaccessible relative became unavoidable. Despite the memory of his own father, "whose son I recognize myself very much to be, I feel that I was in some strange way destined to carry forward as best I could the work of my distinguished and respected namesake. What I have tried to do in life is, I suspect, just the sort of thing the latter would have liked for a son of his to try to do, had he had one. Whether he would have approved of the manner in which I have done it, I cannot say."[34]

III.

Some solace came, therefore, from these extensions of George's immediate family across space: from the Frosts next door and the Jameses at the lake to another

George Kennan and the wider world he inhabited. As the young George grew old enough to place his family in time—to understand that he had ancestors he would never know—their legacies provided a kind of refuge. "I wonder whether you will ever feel that panic[k]y urge to run for help," George wrote his daughters while interned in Nazi Germany in 1942, to "dim, gnarled, pioneer forefathers. They would have received us unceremoniously, made us work from morning to night, ascribed all our sorrows to dyspepsia, and driven us to distraction. But they would never have disowned us or thrown us out."[35]

Of Scotch-Irish extraction, the Kennans had emigrated to New England in the early eighteenth century. Like most Americans at the time, they were farmers, digressing occasionally into other professions—the Presbyterian ministry, Revolutionary War military service, the Vermont state legislature, ownership of a sawmill and tavern—but "[t]here was not one who did not work long and hard with his hands." Moving through upper New York and northern Ohio, they had settled, by the mid-nineteenth century, in rural Wisconsin. Kossuth Kent Kennan had been born in Oshkosh and had grown up on a farm near Packwaukee, which was still functioning when George visited it, a few years after his father's death. "I lay there through the summer night, in the guest bedroom, listening to the chirping of crickets in the grass outside, and breathing the smell of hot, warm hay and manure from the barn; and I felt closer to home than I have ever felt before or since in my wandering life."

The Kennans shared a certain temperament, George believed, an almost mystical self-awareness, across generations. They lacked the capacity for "gaiety, phantasy, humor, the courage to be honest with yourself, and the self-discipline to learn to sin gracefully and with dignity, rather than to try unsuccessfully not to sin at all." They passed neuroses along "like the family Bible." But they never begged, cheated, lost their pride, or were mean, "except to themselves." Indifferently educated, they were nonetheless intelligent; "[t]errified . . . of beauty, they were not impervious to it." And there was somewhere deep within them a tenderness "which will take them all, I hope—and myself included—to the heaven they always believed in."

It was important to George that, although the Kennans were often poor, "they never became proletarianized." They had come closest, he thought, during his father's generation, when several of Kent's siblings had "disappeared into suicide, madness, or the romantic dissolution characteristic of the American west." Kent himself, however, did not give up. He began life as a plowboy, educated himself, and became "a cultured, though painfully shy, gentleman."

Florence's family had been more colorful. They had emigrated from Scotland early in the nineteenth century, settling first in Massachusetts, and then in Illinois. George's grandfather, Alfred James, ran away from home at thirteen, became a barge hand on the Erie Canal, and in a series of hair-raising adventures as a sailor worked his way around the world. It fascinated young George that when Alfred returned, seven years later, his family did not at first recognize him. Alfred built an insurance career in Chicago following the great fire of 1871, and then moved to Milwaukee to run the Northwestern National. Still vigorous when George's older sisters were growing up, Grandpa Alfred would row them out on Lake Nagawicka, have them write messages to Neptune to be dropped over the side, and then regale them with sea chanteys. George was too small to have remembered the old man, who died a year after he was born. But he heard all the stories, developed a lifelong fondness for boats, and when in middle age he got one of his own, he named it *Nagawicka*.

The Jameses, he thought, were "more dashing, and more full of fight," than the Kennans. They lacked sentimentality, a good thing because the Kennans had too much of it. They were self-confident aristocrats, whereas the Kennans saw their worth "in the obscurity of their own consciences," demonstrating it only "in the eye of their relentless God." James family loyalties "were few but fierce and passionate." If feudal lords, they "would have gone down fighting for their privileges in the face of the rising power of kings." They might not survive "if the coming order of society demands the subordination of the individual to the mass."[36]

IV.

That was the family, and as the much younger George was coming to know them, he was himself becoming an individual. This was often a matter of figuring out how things worked. One of his earliest memories was of receiving, on his third birthday, the gift of a locomotive molded out of ice cream. But locomotives, he had been told, were very hot: how could this one be cold, and how could he be expected to eat it? On another occasion, George saw his cousin Charlie James fall into the lake at Nagawicka. Instead of trying to rescue him, George ran to announce tearfully to the grown-ups that "Charles is drowned," only to have them laugh as the sopping sputtering Charlie staggered up the hill behind him. Milk delivery horses, George discovered, had to be anchored with heavy weights, like boats, to keep them from straying. Bicycles required falling off in order to learn to stay on.[37]

Another mystery, for young George, had to do with relieving himself. He recalled being astonished, upon entering first grade, at seeing "little boys piddle standing up." His trousers had no fly, so he cut his own slit, and his stepmother was furious: "I think she spanked me for it, or scolded me very severely." The injustice would rankle for decades to come. So too did the discovery, two years later in Germany, that mothers there allowed little boys to pull their pants down and go, on the grass in the park. He remembered thinking "how wonderful it would be if you had a mother to whom you would admit—you would tell her—when you wanted to do this."[38]

A weightier matter that worried Jeanette and George was how you would know that a war was about to break out. Kassel, where they spent six months in 1912, was a military town, and the children had picked up rumors of naval buildups, war scares, even the possible need for an early return to the United States. They were alone in their room one day when a military band marched up the street. "We were sure," Jeanette recalled, "that this was the way a war would start.... Would we ever get home? We had heard a lot about Germany's wars and even about one called the Thirty Years War. I don't know how long we waited until Mother and the girls came in and said the band was serenading a General and his bride. We felt a little silly then."[39]

Self-confidence slowly came, though. Both children learned German easily: George would pride himself on his fluency for the rest of his life. German boys would occasionally harass him for being an American but he held his own, "flailing away with my fists." Faith in Santa Claus fell victim to the absence of a fireplace in the pension where the family was staying: "I knew damn well he couldn't come down the stove." And George asked his father's permission, "when I am big," to join the United States Navy.[40] After returning with his family to Milwaukee, George wrote his first surviving poem, entitled "My Soldier":

I had a big cloth soldier;
Just made for a little boy;
His arms and sword came off, you know,
But he is the funniest toy.

He belonged to the German Army;
But that doesn't matter to me;
I brought him back to America,
Way across the sea.

He can lift his feet right up to his eyes,
And up to his cap, that's more;
He can't salute 'cause his arms are off,
And he couldn't salute before.

It was a respectable literary effort for a child of nine, and George carefully preserved it—it remains the earliest document in his papers.[41]

George portrayed childhood, in his memoirs, as existing along an "unfirm" boundary between external and internal reality. He lived in a world "peculiarly and intimately my own, scarcely to be shared with others or even made plausible to them. I habitually read special meanings into things, scenes, and places— qualities of wonder, beauty, promise, or horror—for which there was no external evidence visible, or plausible, to others." At the end of Cambridge Avenue was a grimy brick building with a gloomy entryway, behind which lurked something with "a sinister significance all its own." There may, or may not, have been fairies in Juneau Park. And George was "absolutely scared green" of his grandfather Kennan's Victorian mansion on Prospect Avenue: when left alone there one day, he turned all the gaslights on and cowered in the corner, where nothing could get behind him until rescuers arrived.[42]

Jeanette, who knew him better than anyone else, thought him preoccupied with death when he was little. She did not find it funny when George and his cousin Charlie took to jumping off the porch at the Nagawicka house, joking that they might die, then rolling on the ground laughing. Even more disturbing was a conversation on a sleepy afternoon under a tree overlooking the lake. Jeanette was nine and George was seven, but what he said stuck in her mind so clearly that she could repeat it word for word decades later:

George: [A] person wouldn't have to live if he didn't want to, would he? He could kill himself.

Jeanette: But that wouldn't be nice at all. Why would you want to do that?

George: Well, you could shoot yourself, or maybe drown yourself in the lake.

Jeanette: But we don't have any guns, and how could you make yourself stay under water?

George: Papa has. He has his hunting gun in the closet in his room. You know that.

Jeanette: Yes, but it's so big. And if you tried to drown how would you keep yourself down?

Jeanette later understood this conversation as a brother trying to spook his sister by discussing the practicalities of committing suicide, but she did not take it that way at the time. George was insisting then, she thought, on "the freedom to die if one really wanted to." It was "too awful to talk about."[43]

And yet George did not recall his boyhood as being unhappy: "I was a very normal boy." Among his fondest memories were the wrestling matches with Charlie: "two grubby little fellows, grunting, pushing, straining, and squirming—both being too stubborn (after all, we were both Scots) to admit defeat, and both of us returning, mussed and dirty, for dinner, only to be sent upstairs first . . . and told to make ourselves more presentable." George remembered being "a little bit timid, a little bit of a sissy," but this did not show up in the diary he began keeping on New Year's Day 1916, at the age of eleven.[44] It opened with another poem:

In this simple, little book,
A record of the day, I cast;
So, I afterwards may look
Back upon my happy past.

What followed reflects, on the whole, an average boy's life—including the tendency to treat ordinary and extraordinary events in much the same way:

January 6: This morning Cary Jones and his father plunged over the railroad bridge in a limousine and were both killed instantly. I walked around there this afternoon only all that I could see was a busted railing and a lot of splinters. Then I went down to the Town Club to peek at the dancing class.

January 9: Right before supper Jeanette, Kenty (in pajamas) and I had a big pillow fight on Mother's bed.

January 28: We started baseball practice today. I made a bungle of it but so did nearly everyone who played.

January 31: We didn't have any school this afternoon because of the President's visit. I went to hear him speak at the Auditorium . . . only it was packed full. Then, in going to Uncle Alfred's office . . . , I watched his auto go past only never knew it. At last I saw him standing on the observation platform of his train with Mrs. Wilson behind him. My room is being painted over.

February 20: I went to the patriotic service at the church tonight and was very much pleased with Dr. Jenkins sermon on "Preparedness."

March 2: I went down to Dr. Taylor's office to be vacsinated for tyfoid. It isn't supposed to hurt, only on me he struck a blood vessel and it burned like fire. There are 244 cases of tyfoid and 5 deaths from it in the city.

March 3: Censored by G. K.

April 22: Papa said that I can't go up to camp this summer and that I have to work in the garden instead, ding bust it!

May 6: [After watching a baseball game] I guess I've had about as much fun as I ever had today.

George did have one physical reminder of "unfirm boundaries" between external and internal reality. He was color-blind, a fact that showed up in school drawings, to the amazement of his classmates. And the onset of puberty left other boundaries uncertain: "If at that time I'd had a mother to help me, I think it might have been easier."[45] On the whole, though, George's childhood was, considering the sadness with which it began, cheerfully unremarkable.

V.

George and Jeanette were fortunate to attend Milwaukee State Normal, a grade school used to train teachers. Founded in 1885, it had moved in 1909 into a new and well-equipped building two miles north of the neighborhood where the Kennan children grew up. George entered first grade the following year, making his way back and forth chiefly by streetcar, a mode of transportation he found "thrilling." His 1916 diary records him also doing so, however, by bicycle, roller skates, and on foot, the latter being the only method when it snowed too much for the streetcars to run, but attendance was expected anyway. After classes were dismissed in the afternoon, George would often stop off at one of the other boys' houses to play: "As long as I got home by suppertime it was all right."[46]

The school was progressive, requiring no homework, but "we were fully as

prepared as any other children." Grammar was emphasized, especially the dia-
gramming of sentences, and German was taught from the first grade. There was
also theater: George played an elf, in *Rumpelstiltskin*, when he was nine. Both
children had, as their fourth-grade teacher, the formidable Miss Emily Strong.
She was, as George described her, "a great big strong New England woman, who
had no difficulty keeping discipline in her class." Jeanette thought she "looked
like—and excessively admired—Theodore Roosevelt."[47]

George also had the memorable experience, during these years, of falling in
love for the first time. The girl was in his class, and he only admired her from afar,
"but oh! It was like intimations of heaven." He would walk an extra mile home to
pass her house, although he never called on her: "[O]nce I wrote her a note or a
Christmas card . . . and went through agonies of indecision over whether to send
this." George's sisters knew something was up when they discovered a manicure
set in his room: it was astonishing, Constance remembered, because "we'd always
had to make him take Saturday night baths." But when queried on the matter, he
responded with dignity: "Con, I never asked you anything about your life and I
don't expect you to ask anything about my life." "By the time I went to military
school," George recalled, "I was really quite a husky little boy getting much more
confidence in myself."[48]

The school was St. John's Military Academy in nearby Delafield, Wisconsin,
and George entered it at the age of thirteen, having been allowed to skip the eighth
grade at Milwaukee Normal. It was—and still is—a fortresslike institution located
just across Lake Nagawicka from where the Kennans and Jameses spent their summers. The other members of the family were not at all clear why George's father
decided to send him there, instead of to a high school in Milwaukee, in the fall
of 1917. Jeanette guessed that it had something to do with the fear "that George
wouldn't be masculine enough, growing up with sisters." If so, St. John's was the
right place. "There were so many boys who were sent there because they were
obstreperous," Constance recalled, "and their parents couldn't deal with them.
They used to play all sorts of tricks, and [George] felt sorry for the teachers!" But
George liked being in the country and had an enthusiasm for things military: he
had been on a drill team while at Milwaukee Normal, and since April 1917, the
United States had been at war.[49]

St. John's, George recalled, was good for him. There was hazing, but he tolerated it: "All of us toughened up." He found in the discipline a compensation for
loneliness: "[t]here was no harm at all to be woken up at six o'clock in the morning
and then have ten minutes to get dressed and get in ranks, and then to go back and

20

GEORGE F. KENNAN

make your bed and clean your room and then go to breakfast." There was pride:
when marching in parades, "[we felt] a certain superiority over the boys on the
curbstones, who led what seemed to us the incredibly soft and indulgent life of the
juvenile civilian." There was a kind of freedom: each Monday the students were
kicked off campus and told that they were on their own. "[W]e were the terrors of
the countryside," raiding apple orchards, building dugouts, "tobogganing on the
hill back of our dormitory and [fighting] enormous snow battles." There was also
refuge, on weekends, at the Frosts' nearby lake house, where George would arrive
"in my grubby, god-damned uniform, and [be] given a bath and put in a beautiful
bed with white sheets."[50]

It was a life without many choices to make, but "we did have the pleasures of
being promoted and getting command if we did things right." One test of patience
was drilling rookies, a trial Job never had. "I wonder what he would have done,"
George wrote to Jeanette. He later added, for his stepmother:

My corporal's lot is plenty hot,
And hasn't many joys,
For now I'm chief, (much to my grief)
Of eight unruly boys.

George made cadet lieutenant but handled his platoon so badly on maneuvers that
the Army colonel in charge chewed him out in front of two companies, announcing "that if I had done that in the regular army in wartime, I would have been shot
at sunrise." He was then transferred to the staff and discouraged from the further
pursuit of a military career.[51]

Teachers imprinted themselves indelibly. There was a burly Alsatian, once a
waiter, who hurled cadets out of the classroom if they acted up, but he was fine for
French verbs. George's Latin instructor, in contrast, never got upset: he had "an
amused recognition of me, of what I could do." The school's founder and head-
master, Dr. Sidney T. Smythe, an Episcopal clergyman who had been a boxer in
his youth, terrified the students but also inspired them in chapel: "I've never forgotten his reading of the Gospel of St. John: 'And the Word was made flesh and
dwelt among us, and we beheld his glory, the glory as of the only begotten of the
Father, full of grace and truth.' I've often thought that's the most beautiful sentence
in the English language."[52]

And then there was a young, handsome English teacher who "was very nice to a group of us," serving ice cream in his apartment and arranging school-sanctioned theater trips to Chicago. He introduced George to Oscar Wilde and Bernard Shaw, then "frightfully avant garde," and also to Princeton by having him read F. Scott Fitzgerald's recently published *This Side of Paradise*. But after George graduated, there came an invitation to stay overnight in Chicago, and "it turned out he was a homosexual. He made passes at me in the middle of the night, and I got up and fled and never saw him again. I felt sorry for him. I didn't want to hurt him. But I felt I just couldn't stay there. He later committed suicide."[53]

George was well aware, by then, of homosexuality. "What could you expect? These were boys in ages from 13 to 18 and obviously during this period the sexual powers ripened." He himself had been attracted to an older boy who played on the basketball team, and "I'm sure that had I remained in an all male environment any longer, I like all of us would have developed homosexual tendencies simply because of the lack of other objects." But "it was never in any way natural to me, and the moment I had an interest in women I never had anything like that."[54]

"I went there as innocent as an angel," George recalled of St. John's, "and emerged from it, four years later, not much more sophisticated than I was when I had entered it." Perhaps. But he was sophisticated enough, by his senior year, to send Jeanette, who preserved it, this slightly salacious poem:

Now student A has started
On a pleasant little snooze
And soon he dreams of holidays
And country clubs and booze;

. . . .

Flappers that have passed him by,
Flappers that have made him sigh,
Flappers that drink bonded rye,
        At any time they choose.

One flapper is particularly
Kind to him it seems,

. . .

So he leads her through the palm trees,
And he talks in happy streams,

Streams, -
　　　　Streams, -
While the maiden nods and beams;

His attentions are requited,
And the flapper so delighted
That the poor boy gets excited
　　　And proposes in his dreams.[55]

George's dream now was acceptance at Princeton—Fitzgerald's novel having eclipsed the Navy's attractions—and the St. John's dean, Henry Holt, excused him from classes to allow preparation. Jeanette helped also, tutoring George in chemistry: she knew nothing about the subject, "but I had the book." Even so, admission was no sure thing: George failed the entrance examination and resigned himself to a year of preparatory school. He tried again at the last moment, and this time he passed: as he remembered it, he was the last student admitted. No one else from St. John's made it into an eastern college.[56]

The 1921 St. John's Military Academy *Yearbook* shows a smiling and self-confident young man in a track suit in the front row of the team, having taken athletic honors in that sport as well as in football, hiking, and tennis—he was also, by then, an accomplished swimmer and diver. He played in a jazz band. His record as a cadet—whatever he remembered about his blunders on maneuvers—showed steady promotions from private through corporal, sergeant, and lieutenant. There were scholastic honors for Latin, French, English, and "Caesar." He was, unsurprisingly, class poet, although his commencement poem is much less interesting than the one he sent Jeanette. His favorite author is recorded as Bernard Shaw, his disposition as "vascillating," and his "pet peeve" as "The Universe."[57] And because he had skipped his final year at Milwaukee Normal, he was still only seventeen.

TWO

Princeton: 1921–1925

BY THE TIME HE ARRIVED AT PRINCETON IN 1921, GEORGE KENNAN had made his way through a difficult childhood. He was healthy, handsome, clever, and even if he had scraped by on his entrance examinations, at least as well educated as most of the other freshmen who enrolled that fall: the university was still decades away from admitting students chiefly for academic excellence. Fitzgerald was not far off when he described Princeton, in *This Side of Paradise*, as "the pleasantest country club in America."[1]

But even he acknowledged that the place was more than this. Fitzgerald has his hero, Amory Blaine, lying on the grass one night, surrounded by halls and cloisters "infinitely more mysterious as they loomed suddenly out of the darkness, outlined each by myriad faint squares of yellow light. . . . Evening after evening the senior singing had drifted over the campus in melancholy beauty, and through the shell of [Amory's] undergraduate consciousness had broken a deep and reverent devotion to the gray walls and Gothic peaks and all they symbolized as warehouses of dead ages." Kennan read these words at St. John's, and they shaped his expectations. "The taxi carried me up University Place and down Nassau Street . . . and as I discerned, through its windows, the shapes of the Gothic structures around Holder Hall, my penchant for the creation of imaginative wonders reached some sort of a crescendo. Mystery and promise, glamour and romance seemed to glow, like plasma, from these dim architectural shapes."[2]

And yet Kennan went on to portray Princeton in his memoirs in such bleak terms that readers have recoiled ever since. "I knew not a soul in college or town. I was given the last furnished room in the most remote of those gloomy rooming houses far off campus to which, at the time, late-coming freshmen were relegated. . . . I remained, therefore, an oddball on campus, not eccentric, not ridiculed or disliked, just imperfectly visible to the naked eye." He was careful to blame himself, not the university: "I was fairly treated at its hands; I respected it intellectually; I took pride in it as an institution." But "Princeton was for me not exactly the sort of experience reflected in *This Side of Paradise*."[3]

It is worth noting, though, that Kennan wrote this depressing account of his years at Princeton in the town of Princeton, having chosen to return a quarter-century after he graduated: he would live and work there for another half-century. Young George's experience, however he may have remembered it, began a trajectory that would bring him back to the place where he began a life away from home—and it would in time become home.

I.

"I suppose you've heard that I got into Princeton safely," George wrote Jeanette on September 28, 1921. He meant that he had arrived not knowing whether he would be admitted to the university itself, or would have to take remedial courses at one of the tutoring schools just off campus. He was a year younger than his classmates. His course of study would be daunting: English, French, Physics, History and Economics, Hygiene, Physical Training, and remedial Latin. But, he assured Jeanette, "I like Princeton quite well." The honor system especially surprised him, extending not only to unsupervised examinations but to credit in local stores. "[I]f a student buys something and then finds he hasn't the money to pay for it, the store-keepers insist on his taking the goods, paying when he wants to, and they won't even take his name."[4]

By October, when his father came to visit, George was more measured in his enthusiasm and a bit shaken in self-confidence: "I believe he was more impressed with Princeton than I myself have been." "Make good. I know you will," Kent senior said, adding only "that I should not cease entirely, now that I was away from home, to go to church." George knew how his father would feel if he failed, "and besides there's another reason—you know her name," he wrote Jeanette. "She got me into Princeton and it wouldn't be quite playing the game to flunk out, without a hard struggle."[5]

Thanksgiving found George succumbing to introspection, which was "like looking through a window into a dark and dirty old shack when you have a myriad of nice views to look at in the other direction." He asked Jeanette to try to stop the family from worrying about his lack of friends: "It honestly doesn't bother me in the least, except that I wish the lack were greater." The letter contained an apology for not writing earlier, because he had not been able to afford a stamp.[6]

George probably embroidered the truth a bit, but he was very cautious—as he had been at St. John's—about spending money: "I felt I mustn't make it too hard for my father." Florence Kennan had left her children a fund for college, but he had never asked his father how much it was. "I rather assumed that it was barely enough." This led George to conclude that if he was going to make it back to Milwaukee for Christmas, he would have to earn the train fare. He did so by taking a temporary job as a postman in Trenton, slogging through slushy streets for days until he had earned the necessary $28. In doing so, he contracted scarlet fever.[7]

George arrived home sick and was promptly quarantined on the third floor at the Cambridge Avenue house, with a trained nurse brought in to care for him. Because there was no penicillin, "I came within an inch of dying." His sisters were sent back to their colleges wondering whether they would ever see him again. But he slowly recovered and toward the end of his isolation even began "falling a little in love" with his nurse. He would not return to Princeton until the beginning of March, having lost much of his second semester. The physical effects, Jeanette thought, were permanent: "When he was at St. John's, he was a very healthy young boy," but "he was never as well after that." And it had all been unnecessary, because there was enough money. He just hadn't known it. "I was a junior in college when I found out," Jeanette recalled, so she "went out and bought new clothes!"[8]

Back on campus, George found his teachers sympathetic and the amount of work to be made up less than he had expected. He found a place in the freshman commons orchestra and tried out for—but did not stay with—the *Daily Princetonian*. He even began to have fun, breaking into the Junior Prom with other freshmen to steal sandwiches, helping a friend get out of a lease by harassing a landlady with as much noise as possible at four A.M., and pursuing a new hobby of shooting at magazines, in the fireplace, with a revolver. Money, however, continued to worry him. His friends treated him well, "considering my lack of personality. . . . But I just can't go much with their set unless I spend a little more money." It was worth doing this, "because if there's any one thing that isn't good for me it is to be alone, and it's a choice of going with them or with no one."[9]

With April came "soft days, and still softer nights." Victrolas played through open windows each evening. The campus was overrun with girls on weekends, making it impossible to play tennis "because we can't swear." But he did get himself to a prom without doing anything "absolutely wrong, outside of wearing the same soft shirt with a borrowed tuxedo, two nights in succession. I got along on about $31, having that amount when I started and three cents when I ended."[10]

And then there was—alluringly—New York. George's oldest sister, Frances, who had long since left Milwaukee to become an actress, lived there and generously offered the use of her sofa on occasional weekends. "I was absolutely neurotic with [the] excitement of this city," George recalled many years later, "to me it seemed just like fairyland." But Frances and her friends weren't interested in college students. She remembered it differently: "I'll tell you what my friends thought: 'Oh, how darling! Pink cheeks!'"

George did seem shy, though, so on one visit Frances and her roommates brought home a girl they thought he would like. "I think they expected more to happen than did because I wasn't prepared to go to these lengths yet." Sensing that he had disappointed, "I wrote her afterwards a passionate love letter and she wrote me very sensibly back and said that that wasn't the way it was." He did, however, fall in love with New York. "I thought it was absolutely marvelous."[11]

II.

George did not recall being depressed at Princeton, but he was indeed shy, and if anybody did talk to him, he tended to talk too much: "I think many Middle Western boys had this experience when they went East to college." There weren't many at Princeton in the 1920s: the university drew its students chiefly from wealthy families and elite prep schools on the East Coast. There were no women, no blacks, few Jews, and—somewhat surprisingly for an institution strongly shaped by its former president Woodrow Wilson—few foreigners. The emphasis in admissions was on "homogeneity," but that did not mean democracy: Princeton was as class-ridden as the society from which most of its students came.[12]

"[I]f you were from some place that you didn't think was 'the' place to be from," a friend recalled many years later, "you felt like a hick. You didn't think your clothes were right, and you didn't think what you said was right, and you didn't know the right people, and you held back in a corner and tried to hide all that part of yourself." George himself, half a century later, remembered asking a fellow freshman at the first student assembly what time it was. The young dandy took a puff on his cigarette, blew some smoke, and then walked away, searing himself into George's consciousness: "I was just proud enough not to suck up to those boys. And wouldn't have known how to do it anyway."[13]

For this reason, getting into Princeton was not nearly as difficult as *fitting* into Princeton once he was there. During his first year, of course, all freshmen were inferiors. They wore beanies ("dinks") and were banned from walking on certain sidewalks or patches of grass. The class stood disgraced if one or more of its members did not, at some point during the year, steal the bell-clapper from atop Nassau Hall. They expected to be photographed in front of Whig Hall while sophomores pelted them from above with unpleasant substances. This form of class consciousness was good-natured enough, though, and when George got to be a sophomore, he himself harassed freshmen. "We certainly did those boys up right," he wrote Jeanette, "with water, flour, eggs, tomatoes, fish, green paint, cement, alabaster, and every other conceivable concoction."[14]

There was, however, a more complex consciousness of class at Princeton, to which George alluded early in his sophomore year. "Last Sunday I was [at a] dinner in Trenton. . . . The other Princeton boy down there was a man who plays varsity football, is on the senior council, and belongs to Ivy, so you can see the eliteness."[15] "Ivy" was the Ivy Club, and George's boast reflected multiple meanings of the word *class*. It referred not only to individual courses, or to the collective experience of a common graduating year; it also signified membership—or lack of it—in Princeton's distinctive eating clubs, and that for many of its undergraduates was the most important thing of all.

Princeton had abolished fraternities in 1875 but neglected to replace them with adequate dining facilities for upperclassmen. This encouraged the construction and generous endowment of privately owned clubs, mostly along Prospect Avenue, which offered elegant dining, ample drink, and opulent facilities for parties, dances, and alumni reunions. Admission was by the vote of the members, and with few other places to socialize on campus, getting into a club became the prevailing preoccupation from the moment freshmen arrived. Since not all clubs were equal in prestige, joining the "right" one was at least as vital. Everything depended on "bicker," the critical spring week when sophomores waited anxiously for the all-important knock on the door that would tell them they had made it in—which is to say, that they had been deemed to have *fit* in. It all amounted, one professor later complained, to "a religious frenzy over the choice of a restaurant."[16]

By the time his own bicker week rolled around, George had decided that the process was beneath him: "In a veritable transport of false pride, self-pity, and thirst for martyrdom, I absented myself every afternoon from the campus, lest somebody ask me to join a club." In the end, though, somebody did. Bill Oliver, whose sister had roomed with Constance at Vassar, sought George out: "You're making a great mistake. This is going to damage your upper-class years—you'll be happier if you join." Moved that anyone had taken the trouble, he accepted membership in Key and Seal, which he described to Jeanette as "neither the best nor the worst" but "the wildest club in Princeton." He then took a job as assistant manager there to cover the costs.[17]

Even in his own club, though, George was uncomfortable. Its chief vice was drinking, but "since I don't like to drink, I'm not in fear of temptation on that score." He later acknowledged not having many friends in Key and Seal. By the end of his junior year, he was brooding about the "super-sensitiveness" that had led some of his classmates to "make social prestige during undergraduate years the sole aim of life." So he resigned when he returned to campus.[18]

He thereby saved, George wrote his father, $300. But it had been "no small sacrifice," because "[a] non-club man is quite generally snubbed and looked down upon, takes a very small part in college life, and misses out on practically all of the things that men have in mind when they talk about 'the grand old college days.'" For the rest of his senior year there was no choice but to eat with the "rejects," the students who had gotten into no club, and that, George later recalled, was terrible. Each of them "was afraid that the fellow next to him would think that he couldn't take it and was trying to butter him up to make friends, so we usually ate in a sort of proud silence."[19]

George drew from this unhappy experience the lesson that "one had to make one's own standards, one could not just accept those of other people; there was always the possibility that those others, in the very rejection of us, had been wrong." But it had been he who had rejected his fellow club members, not the other way around. George captured his own contradictions in a letter to Jeanette: "My hardest job is to be conventional, for that is something which self-respect and blood often tell [me] not to do," even though "I believe [conventionality] brought me to Princeton."[20]

"There was . . . a curious strain of weakness running crosswise through his makeup," it was once said of another student who wound up at Princeton. "[A] harsh word from the lips of an older boy . . . was liable to sweep him off his poise into surly sensitiveness, or timid stupidity. . . . [H]e was a slave to his own moods."[21] That student was Fitzgerald's Amory Blaine *before* he entered Princeton: he eventually got over it. George, for whatever reason, never quite did.

III.

Academics, fortunately, came more easily than social life. George's most challenging freshman course was Historical Introduction (known to the students as "hysterical interruption"), which sought to show the effects of climate, geography, and resources on civilizations. The professor was the young Joseph C. Green, "a stern, vigorous, and relentlessly conscientious scholar, placing no demands on us that he did not meet to the fullest degree himself." Young George had this course in mind when he wrote his father that "my future rests chiefly on how much studying I do in the next week and a half." But he passed everything—no small achievement given his bout with scarlet fever—although he did have to repeat freshman English literature in his sophomore year.[22]

That requirement provoked an early outburst of intellectual independence. George disliked the course and began cutting classes. He thought it silly to have to identify plots and climaxes in Shakespeare—"you either felt these plays as aesthetic and intellectual experiences or you did not." Called in by his instructor, who wanted to know, "bluntly but not unkindly, what the hell was the matter with me," George professed repentance. He then submitted a paper on what was wrong with the teaching of English in American colleges. It got the highest grade possible, and "I was taught an unforgettable lesson in generosity and restraint."[23]

George knew none of his teachers well, but he appreciated what some of them did. Like several generations of Princeton undergraduates, he relished the legendary Walter P. "Buzzer" Hall—so called for the sound his hearing aid made—who would arrive in a horse and buggy to teach modern European history, thunder through his lectures, and then end the semester with a masterpiece on Garibaldi that pulled in students from all over the campus. There was a philosophy professor who gained George's respect by allowing students to argue with him after his lectures: "Anyone who can ex[c]ite three or four hundred blasé easterners so that they emerge from their frigid cells . . . has got to be good." And then there was a German professor, short, stout, with close-cropped hair and a red mustache: "When he starts to speak German, he swells up, raises his head, glares at the class, draws a deep breath, and then bursts out in stenatorian [sic] tones, punctuated by a full measure of the spluttering and gurgling [which] accompanies the pronunciation of good German."[24]

Literature, inside and outside of class, sparked the greatest interest, especially contemporary American novels: "I was thrilled with these books." Princeton may not have lived up to the reputation Fitzgerald had given it, but Sinclair Lewis's *Main Street* put George back in touch with his midwestern roots. "[I]t was an enormous eye-opener to me that one could look at our lives and see drama." And then, as George was graduating, *The Great Gatsby* came out, "went right into me and became part of me."[25]

History, apart from "Buzzer" Hall, was disappointing. Too many instructors contented themselves with assignments like: "Read Chapter Twenty-Three, and be prepared to recite on it next week." It made a difference when the students encountered what *they* found interesting. Charles Seymour's *Woodrow Wilson and the World War* was "fortunately small enough to be read conveniently in chapel," where attendance was mandatory, "and I covered some fifty pages of it during that ceremony, this morning." Only one other history teacher held George's interest: he was Raymond J. Sontag, then a preceptor but later a distinguished diplomatic historian. "[S]keptical, questioning, disillusioned without being discouraging," he left an indelible impression. Many years later, having himself entered the profession, George recalled of his Princeton years: "I didn't realize how interesting history was!"[26]

So too, in a way, were current affairs. George carefully recorded the consensus reached in a Clio debate on Japanese exclusion. He composed, but did not send, a sardonic letter to the *Princetonian* on the Veterans' Bonus Bill. He wrote an essay on plans for construction of the St. Lawrence Seaway. He wrestled, in his international law class, with a case involving Soviet claims to property in the United States—an issue he would return to in an official capacity a decade later. He participated in a student discussion on German reparations, which veered off into wild plans for joining the French Foreign Legion, and then ended in "a general row on international politics" lasting much of the night. Princeton left him with "a vague Wilsonian liberalism; a regret that the Senate had rejected American membership in the League of Nations; a belief in laissez-faire economics and the values of competition; and a corresponding aversion to high tariffs." Otherwise, there were few "settled opinions, conclusions, or certainties in the field of public affairs."[27]

There was, however, a mounting concern that his undergraduate years might be his best: "I can readily see how, after one gets out into the world, regardless of what he may have intended, he will never learn anything again, and his interests will be absolutely limited to what he has learned." Time spent on courses was therefore precious—but not so precious that it prevented George from writing this letter to Jeanette in an English class, where he was supposed to have been taking notes on the lecture.[28]

IV.

Much about Princeton was exciting—even if English lectures were not—and in more ways than his memoirs suggest, George was becoming fond of the place. "I'm devilish busy," he wrote early in his sophomore year. He was taking six courses, had a job addressing envelopes for an Italian tailor, and felt like a swimmer trying to keep his head above water. "But I've become quite a stoic: I play not; neither do I smoke; yet the Phoenix in all his glory never took any colder baths than I do in the mornings."[29]

He now had a room on campus and was facing distractions that tested stoicism. When Princeton beat Chicago in football that fall, Nassau Street filled with celebrating students, "acting as if they had lost all semblance of intelligence." George was one of them. "I don't often get drunk, but I do think that was a worthy occasion." Then came an unexpected free trip to the Harvard game in Cambridge, causing George to write Jeanette exuberantly: "I just sort of bubble over. Can you imagine that? Last year I felt so lonely." There were even theater parties in New York, requiring excuses for why he had to return to Princeton "when I was asked to stay all night."[30]

George was a bit stoic when it came to women. He assured Jeanette that he had not arrived at Princeton "a prude." But he later could recall asking only one girl to a dance there, and it turned out to be an unhappy experience because nobody else danced with her. When George revealed one day that he thought he was in love, his junior-year roommate assured him "that a man can have any woman he wants, if he only wants to take the trouble." George reported this to Jeanette with scarcely concealed envy: he "sleeps until noon if I don't wake him; . . . writes to fifteen girls, and knows fifteen more; has two invited down to the Junior prom and still doesn't seem the least bit worried about it; and believes in Prohibition but can hold half a pint of gin with perfect sobriety. . . . Only a southerner could carry that off."[31]

Whatever the state of his love life, spring in Princeton could make it hard to study. Seniors singing on the steps of Nassau Hall moved him so deeply that he wanted to ban all phonographs, automobiles, and other recent inventions from the campus, "because they mar the effect." But when a classmate abandoned it all to become a sailor, "Lord, how I wanted to go with him." George did not expect Jeanette, "being a girl," to understand that the world beyond Princeton, now colorful and romantic, would by the time he graduated be drab and meaningless. He wanted to see it, even if penniless. He didn't go, though, because "I have too much regard for Father." At least "I'm not so impressionable as I was at this time last year."[32]

"Took the history quiz this morning," George wrote on May 24, 1924, in the diary he was now keeping again. "Also had my picture taken for a passport." It was George's first, since they had not been required when his family took him to Germany in 1912. The photograph shows a serious young man in coat and tie with a thick head of hair, close-cropped above the ears. Most striking are the eyes, which are large, almost haunted, and suggestive of vulnerability. Which perhaps accounts for another comment George wrote in his diary that evening: "They [his classmates] laugh at me, I know, but I don't mind being laughed at as much as I used to."[33]

V.

The passport was for a summer trip to Europe, a compromise remedy for George's wanderlust. He did not do it penniless, but he came close. He did do it with a Princeton friend whose "uninhibited Greek hedonism was a good foil to my tense Presbyterian anxieties." Constantine Nicholas Michaelas Messolonghitis routinely hitchhiked from his home in Ohio without apparent effort or worry. He had resigned from Key and Seal before George did. "His wide-eyed innocence about the East was even more staggering than my own; . . . [and] in the easy glow of his provincial garrulousness (he was a character, in reality, from Thomas Wolfe) I softened and felt at home." Traveling with Nick would mean "toil, trial, trouble, and tribulation—but still human nature is so unreasoning that I look forward to it."[34]

The trip was unremarkable in one sense: Europe was full of young Americans bumming around in the summer of 1924. What was remarkable was the hand-written account of over ninety pages that George kept and preserved. It was the first of many travel diaries he would compose throughout his life, and it opens a window into who he was at the age of twenty, still an adolescent, soon to cease to be one.

The journal begins, predictably, with a list of traveler's check numbers and addresses of adults to be contacted if something went wrong. It then describes hitchhiking from Princeton to New York, and an exhausting trek up and down docks on both sides of the Hudson in an unsuccessful search for a ship in need of inexperienced hands. June 24–25 became an odyssey, with George and Nick spending most of the day on the waterfront in Hoboken; then crossing back to Manhattan but failing to find friends with free beds, couches, or floors; then running into an acquaintance of Frances's who did at least provide tickets to the midnight show at the Hippodrome; then being turned away from the YMCA at four A.M.; and finally sleeping for the rest of the night in Central Park—all the while dragging along the necessary baggage for a summer in Europe. By eight A.M. the boys were up and at Battery Park, "about the seediest looking persons [there], which is saying something: soiled, wrinkled clothes, two day beards, unkempt, hot as usual, and tired to death. Our morale was utterly shot."[35]

But there was a ship, the SS *Berengaria*, which offered third-class passage at $97.50 apiece. " 'Nick,' sez I, 'on board that boat there must be a bath and a bed.' With that thought our reason fled, and we bought tickets forthwith," an extravagance that, before they had even sailed, exhausted more than half their funds. On board were some of the most "scurvy, seedy, filthy, low-down, diseased, wrecked, ignorant, miserable human beings that God ever made a bad job on." But there were also baths and beds, the sea was calm, and there were a couple of "nice girls" from Mount Holyoke and Wellesley with whom to lounge in deck chairs, compare notes on the fellow passengers, listen to the quartermaster's yarns about the Battle of Jutland, enjoy ice cream provided by a bribed steward, and peer through a window at a fancy-dress ball in first class.[36]

Landfall was at Southampton on July 2, and George's first sight of England amazed him. The taxis were "antiquated, fantastic, ancient hacks," the streetcars were double-decked, most of the houses were old, none of the buildings were high, and some of the male inhabitants dressed in a way that would "cause a good riot in the U.S.A." The boys spent the next few days hiking north of Exeter—George, reading *Lorna Doone* at the time, liked the moors—and occasionally hitching rides: one was unauthorized on the back of a slow moving bus, another was on a two-wheeled dog cart driven by an amiable woman to whom they attempted, without success, to explain the virtues of free trade. They celebrated the Fourth of July in Dunster by splurging on sauterne, but found on reaching London that sympathetic waitresses were sometimes willing to shave a few shillings off their bills. Efforts to find work failed, provoking poetry, first from George:

> *Dear God, who got us in this town*
> *Without a solitary crown*
> *For Christ's sake, get us back again,*
> *And make it snappy, God, Amen.*

and then from Nick:

> *Oh Lord, it gives us both a pain*
> *To eat this rotten London hash;*
> *Please ease up on the goddam rain,*
> *And send us down a little cash.*

After worrying for days about funds, George concluded that they should cross
the Channel, make their way across France to Marseilles, and persuade the consul there to send them home. "[T]o hell with finances. . . . Nick was of course
charmed with the idea."[37]

They arrived in Paris on July 17. "I have never seen any city even remotely
resembling it," George wrote. "It has all the 'magnificent distances' of Washington,
the boulevards of Philadelphia, the metropolitan freedom and gaiety of New York
(but more so), the time-honored mellowness of London"—and the taxis disre-
garded speed limits, "just as they do in Chicago." The Arc de Triomphe seemed to
Nick "quite satisfactory," although "I was so shot I wouldn't have known it from a
hitching post." The Eiffel Tower's elevator was rotten "in comparison to the Wool-
worth Bldg." There were visits to the Louvre, the Moulin Rouge, and Versailles, the
last of which reminded George that ceremonies could be comic opera: he had first
seen this at the unveiling of the Revolutionary War battle monument outside of
Princeton, with "poor Harding sitting there in a glaring sun on the white concrete
steps, mopping his brow with a handkerchief, and caring more for a glass of good,
cold beer, than [for] all the heroes of history."

July 26 brought an unexpected windfall at the American Express office: $100
from Frances, with instructions to ask for more if required. "[S]he evidently got
scared by the letter I wrote to her from London, and told the whole tale to Father,
who, of course, gritted his teeth, boiled with rage, and assured her he would send
me all [I] needed." Priding himself on his independence, George professed to be
appalled: "She couldn't have meant better; she couldn't have done worse." It would
be a while before he could show his face in Milwaukee again.[38]

But the cash made it possible to get to Italy, where George was afflicted by "terrible and weird dreams" about his family. There were, he thought, two kinds of
dreams: random impressions "flashing around in the brain at will, with no semblance of order," and, less frequently, dreams in which "we see and hear clearly
interesting things which we know we have never heard or seen in real life. . . . It
seems to me that the only possible explanation for these lies in the action of some

kind of mental telepathy." The dreams in Turin were of the latter variety, and they left him "very much depressed."

It was a signal, perhaps, that it was time to go home, so George and Nick proceeded to Genoa, where they began again "the sad parade of the water-front. If there be anything . . . more discouraging than trying to get a job on a boat I have yet to find it." They sought out, as planned, the American consul: "We lied to him about how much money we had and he lied to us in return about our chances of working away from this dump." It was, he insisted, "utterly impossible. . . . He won't help us out until we're flat broke or until he's convinced that we couldn't be scared into wiring for money." But "when we go broke we go to jail. . . . Then, the question is, must he send us home or can he let us stay in jail as long as possible?"[39]

Increasingly desperate and with George suffering from dysentery—"Nick kindly informs me that people die from it"—they did accept another $130, wired this time from Milwaukee. With it they were able to make it to Paris, where George found a doctor and where "Nick was a nervous wreck, as jumpy and fidgety and weak as an old woman," and then on to Boulogne-sur-Mer, where they had booked passage on a new Holland-America ship, the SS *Veendam*. She was, riding at anchor, "the most cheering sight I have seen for some time," even in third class "a revelation of comfort and cleanliness." George and Nick disembarked in New York on August 23 with $2.25 apiece, "the proceeds of one pound we had saved and cashed on the boat."[40]

Here they separated, and George, unsure what to do next, decided to hitchhike to Schenectady, where Constance and her husband lived. He arrived at about midnight, and "[t]hey pretended to be real glad to see me." "Oh, I'm so glad you're home, Connie," she remembered him having said. "I thought I'd have to sleep in the park." Fed, clothed, and refinanced, George took a Hudson River boat to New York and then went on to Princeton, closing out his diary: "Here ended, by exhaustion, the account of the European trip of George F. Kennan."[41]

VI.

"The only thing I'm really qualified for," George had written Jeanette during his first year at Princeton, "is to play in a dance orchestra." He had, by then, mastered the piano (despite being denied lessons at home), the cornet (an outgrowth of bugling at St. John's), the banjo, the guitar, and—to the amazement of his

half-brother Kent, who would become a distinguished musician and composer—
the French horn, "a fiendishly difficult instrument." George played in orchestras
and dance bands throughout his college years, with the latter generating badly
needed income. "Marvelously peppy party," he noted of one dance. "[E]ven I
enjoyed myself—profitable too." But as he had pointed out to his sister, this was
not a profession "as a rule, followed by Princeton men, as a life occupation."[42]

There had also been a succession of physically demanding summer jobs—
cherry-picking, tree-trimming, even working on a railroad during a strike and
having to cross picket lines—but these were not right for a Princeton graduate
either. There was, to be sure, his father's profession, the law, and at the end of his
sophomore year George had "fairly definitely" decided on that path. But Kent
senior was "too modest and honest, too conscious of his remoteness from the
modern age and his inadequacy as a guide," to press his son to follow his example:
George recognized him as "a shy, lonely, and not very happy person." Perhaps
with their father in mind, he lamented to Jeanette at about this time that "[w]e all
run along with our heads in the clouds, most of our lives, hoping for some kind
of great thing, until we suddenly realize that we've almost come to the end of our
rope and nothing great has happened at all. It must be sort of a disappointment."[43]

Like most college students, George sought in his summer travels something
great, even if neither he nor Nick had much of a sense of what that might be. In a
way, he found it: the weary young man who arrived back in Princeton at the end of
August was not the one who had happily hitched rides out of it the previous June.
The trip had been both a flight from and an assumption of responsibility—a liberation but also a test. It occasioned his first sustained descriptive writing: George
found words to reflect what his eyes had seen and his body had experienced, a
skill he would never lose. And like most such trips, this one explored an inner
self as well as a wider world. "I am making a strong effort," he wrote at one point,
"to be more equable in temper and disposition, by restraining myself when I find
myself too congenially inclined."[44]

George came back from Europe with firmer views about himself and his future.
He resigned from Key and Seal, thereby resigning himself to his bleak, though
principled, senior year. He had also decided against law school. "I will probably
disappoint you," he wrote his father, but "three more expensive years of education and another long period of time required to 'get headway'" did not seem to
make sense. "I have learned a *few* things, and one of them is that I don't want to
be poor. . . . [T]he ordinary money-making games don't particularly appeal to me
[but] the results of them do, and I have enough confidence in myself to think that

I can make a fair success at almost anything (except salesmanship) if I go into it for all it's worth." The only scheme that suggested itself, however, was well ahead of its time: "I figured it all out how I can make my millions by starting an airplane express company in the United States; I'll be the Harriman of commercial aeronautics."[45]

The best argument George made against law school, however, was one that Kent senior, who had himself traveled and worked abroad as a young man, could hardly question: "Very few of my ancestors, if any, can have been living such a restrained and quiet life at the age of twenty-one . . . it makes me very restless. I don't fit well in a leisurely life." The European trip, for all its travails, had demonstrated that. George made few references to home in his diary that summer, but when the harbor at Genoa reminded him of Milwaukee, he pointedly added that it would be a "misfortune" if he had to go back there.[46]

So what to do? Foreign languages came naturally: George's family and Milwaukee Normal had equipped him with German, and he had taken Latin and French at St. John's and Princeton. Professors Green, Hall, and Sontag had had their influence as well: "I had enjoyed the study of international politics and had prospered in it." George recalled having studied history and politics "with increasing enjoyment and success." It made sense, therefore, one day in January 1925, to drop in on his international law professor, Philip M. Brown, to ask about becoming a diplomat. Brown was encouraging and discouraging. On the one hand, the recently passed Rogers Act, which consolidated the Department of State's diplomatic and consular functions into a single new United States Foreign Service, had raised standards and ensured adequate salaries. Law school, on the other hand, would be a prudent backup, since ministerial and ambassadorial appointments could still be given to political appointees. A career officer might "work for years in the service and then suddenly find himself entirely out of it."[47]

George decided to accept the risk and to seek direct entry into the Foreign Service after graduation. "My decision . . . was dictated mainly, if memory serves, by the feeling that I did not know what else to do." His academic advisers did not object. Green thought George "well fitted" for diplomacy: "If you succeed in getting into the Service I am sure that you will find the work both interesting and valuable." Brown was "confident you will succeed in entering and in more than making good." George's own sense was that "[s]ome guardian angel must have stood over me at that point. It was the first and last sensible decision I was ever deliberately to make about my occupation."[48]

George Kennan graduated from Princeton in June 1925 with a respectable but not brilliant academic record: he ranked eighty-third in a class of 219. He resisted, to the end, fitting in. Convinced that commencement was just "an attempt to tele-scope, in a symbolic and over-simplified form, something which *was* of impor-tance," he skipped all the ceremonies "except the one at which I got my diploma. My high principles did not go quite far enough for me to forego attendance at that particular occasion." The Class Day edition of the *Nassau Herald* recorded him as "undecided as to his future occupation," and George promptly went off to work as a deckhand on a steamer operating between Boston and Savannah: "We received forty-eight cents an hour, worked up to sixteen hours straight on the days we came into port, and were quite happy."[49]

Princeton had, however, provided something of importance. It had guided George, along with his classmates, through the limbo that separated the constraints of childhood from assertions of independence and assumptions of responsibility. He left the university less of a chameleon than he had been while there, or before he had arrived—and he knew something about the world that lay beyond. Prince-ton had, he later acknowledged, "prepared the mind for future growth." And what was the task of a university, after all, if not to ready its students for "the formation of *their* prejudices, not to impregnate them with its own"?[50]

THREE

The Foreign Service: 1925–1931

THE GUARDIAN ANGEL THAT GUIDED GEORGE KENNAN TOWARD THE newly established Foreign Service had insufficient influence to gain him entry. That he had to accomplish on his own, by passing the formal examination the 1924 Rogers Act had mandated. It had two stages: a written test based on factual knowledge, and an oral interview before senior officers that was meant to determine whether the applicant would "fit in." The purpose, Kennan recalled, was to provide a way to "exclude you even though you passed the written." This dual structure reflected tensions within the Foreign Service itself. It was now a professional organization, with specified standards for admission, salary, benefits, promotion, and evaluation. But it was still run by a small group of career diplomats from wealthy families, educated at East Coast preparatory schools and Ivy League universities. They belonged to, and were determined to preserve, what one of them described at the time as "a pretty good club."[1]

Standard preparation for Foreign Service examinations involved enrollment at a Washington tutoring school taught by Angus MacDonald Crawford, whom Kennan remembered as "a big old Scot, . . . terribly interesting when he wasn't drunk." The emphasis was on memorization, not thought. Princeton history courses had allowed stretching a little knowledge into a lot of opinions, George wrote Jeanette, but "there is as much demand for free love advocates in the 'Bible belt' as there is for opinions in Washington." Style counted as much as substance. There wasn't much chance for "poor white-hosed, gold-teethed Elks and civil-service hounds from your Midwestern 'bad-lands' who . . . expect to get in, without ever having so much as seen a dress-suit, unless it were on a vaudeville magician."[2]

George lived, while studying for his examinations, in a boardinghouse on Church Street. The other residents were young Foreign Service aspirants like

Kennan, and although they worked hard, there was time for bridge parties, dances, and even a few grand dinners. Health continued to be a problem: George was hospitalized with fever soon after he arrived, but recovered sufficiently to have fun with his nurse, who liked being spanked by interns. "If I hadn't been so helpless I would have done it myself," he confided in Jeanette, "because she washed my mouth out with soap for saying 'goddam.'"[3]

"Professor" Crawford prepared his students well, and Kennan passed the written examination easily enough. But the oral interview, presided over by the formidable under secretary of state, Joseph C. Grew, was terrifying: "In my first words—to the effect that I was born in Milwaukee, Wisconsin—my voice broke into a falsetto on the second syllable of Wisconsin and set the board roaring with laughter." The examiners accepted him anyway, leaving Kennan to wonder whether it had been his performance that got him in, or the fact that Grew had met him a few nights before at a dinner given by the wealthy mother of one of the more socially acceptable candidates.[4]

However it happened, Kennan was appointed to the rank of "Foreign Service Officer, Unclassified" on September 9, 1926, at an annual salary of $2,500. He was given a loose-leaf book of instructions, some drafted before the Civil War, and a tremulous greeting by Secretary of State Frank B. Kellogg. His first assignment was to the new Foreign Service School, then a single room in the extravagantly ornate State, War, Navy Building (now the Executive Office Building), with a view of the White House and occasionally its occupant, Calvin Coolidge, next door. The lectures, which focused on passports, visas, and notarials, provoked a poem:

> *The steady flow of words*
> *Rises and falls with dull vacuity. . . .*
> *We sprawl in stolid patience on our chairs, . . .*
> *Read papers, surreptitiously. . . .*
> *We are a joint, slumbering animal,*
> *And if you prod one part,*
> *With a question,*
> *It twitches, verbally,*
> *Then it falls asleep again.*

But the training was useful, and there were opportunities to apprentice in the State Department itself, where Kennan's first formal report, on a British Commonwealth conference, received high praise. The students were also expected to participate in Washington high society: "It was like a coming-out."[5]

Society had been important at Princeton too, but George had hardly bothered with it: the rituals required to "fit in" there repelled him. The Foreign Service, however, was a profession, not an eating club. It had a function, and he had a role. He realized this for the first time the summer of 1927 when, just graduated from the Foreign Service School and newly installed as vice-consul in Geneva, he found himself, resplendently attired, greeting guests at the official Fourth of July reception: "There on that summer day, with the orchestra playing on the terrace and the great lake shimmering beyond, . . . I suddenly became aware that I had a reputable and appointed place in the proceedings." He was no longer "a species of naked intruder on the human scene."[6]

I.

Or so his memoirs say. But Kennan's diary that day has him "sour and sleepy," still suffering from the effects of a bad lunch the day before. Dragging himself to the reception at the Hotel Beau Rivage, he found the women fresh and flouncy, the men bored, and a few sleek students on tour gawking at the celebrities. Unimpressed, Kennan escaped to the lobby to read a magazine until tea was served and the guest of honor was ready to speak. He was Admiral Hilary P. Jones, the U.S. representative at the Geneva conference on naval arms control. What they were hearing was "conference fodder," Kennan explained to a British friend, but then it occurred to him that his superiors might not appreciate his candor. There were still things to learn about not having opinions.[7]

Kennan had arrived in Switzerland six weeks earlier and almost at once suffered a nightmare. He dreamed of being a consular officer surrounded by two gigantic clerks, evaluating an applicant for something. Upon discovering that the man was guilty of a despicable crime, he ordered the clerks to throw the culprit out of the office, which they did with such force that he hit the pavement with a thud and was unable to rise, while perspiration poured from him. "Does any man deserve that?" Kennan asked himself, horrified, in his dream. And then he woke up, bathed himself in sweat, with a soft rain falling outside, and the only sound that of a locomotive's shrill whistle as it switched cars off in the distance.[8]

It's hard not to see in this an inverted replay of the day, less than three years earlier, when George and Nick Messolonghitis tried to impose their indigence on the American vice-consul in Genoa. Now George had the same job, if in a different city, and he would soon come to loathe "any and all ragged students" seeking refuge "from the predictable consequences of their own improvidence."[9] Perhaps the dream marked a passage from irresponsibility to its opposite, a process never completely free from anxiety, regret, and projected guilt.

This, though, was the Foreign Service: it forced young men to grow up. It offered Kennan a new personality behind which to hide his earlier one. There were moments, to be sure, when "the silly student [would] reappear—pouting, resisting, posing, refusing to be comforted," but authority provided a welcome mask. Diplomacy was theater, and like an actor, "I have been able, all my life, to be of greater usefulness to others by what, seen from a certain emotional distance, I seemed to be than by what, seen closely, I really was."[10]

Geneva itself was a theater. Mont Blanc faded out one evening, to be replaced by a brilliant full moon emerging dramatically from a bank of clouds, "a great, strident, sexless disc of light, that mounted the sky with the assurance of a star actor making his appearance on the stage." The Genevese were spectators, eternally watching something, whether boats departing, policemen directing traffic, or buildings being torn down: "I have a suspicion that as they stood up here on their mountain tops and watched the rest of Europe fight, they had that same solemn air of attentiveness on their faces . . . , and I think they must have enjoyed it just as much."[11]

Kennan's consular duties did not rise to the level of war and peace. He forced himself, after interviewing an American who sold lamps, to develop an astounding interest in all things "electric and bulbous." Unlike Kennan, he had no disappointments, disillusionments, or longings, just an uncluttered belief that his product was good for humanity. "He may be right. Yet tonight, after dinner, I walked up and down the terrace, smoked a pipe, and wondered about it." A single star hung frozen, in the twilight, "and brooded on the world."[12]

On the day Swiss newspapers announced the impending execution of Sacco and Vanzetti, the wife of the consulate concierge intercepted Kennan, quivering with rage, expecting him, apparently, to cable the president immediately to demand their release. Acknowledging it as a "*mauvaise* affair," Kennan slunk shamefacedly out of the building, "but I couldn't help feeling that there was something glorious in the fact that that poor little dried-up woman, who putters around all day in the dirty basement of a Geneva office building, should . . . want to assault a vice-consul because she considered that somewhere, thousands of miles away, human beings were going to be cruel and unjust to two of their fellows."[13]

Kennan's Geneva assignment was temporary—he was, in effect, summer help while the arms control conference was under way—and at the end of August he reported for duty at the U.S. consulate in Hamburg, where the State Department had originally intended to send him. It was one of those places that quietly spread tentacles of both beauty and evil. There was a melancholy loveliness in its boulevards and a thrilling strength in the machinery of its harbor. But there were also "dismal, sooty streets" that looked like West Pittsburgh or South Milwaukee, and "unutterable horror [in] the lurid, repulsive alleys of St. Pauli," from which American seamen too frequently found their way to the consulate to "inflict their lives on mine."[14]

These juxtapositions left Kennan attuned "to all the struggle and tragedy and discord of the world as well as to all its harmony." An expatriate wedding caused him to conclude gloomily that "we are all expatriates" from another, more kindly world, "the memories of which fade from us with our childhood." But other days found him enjoying the beer halls, relishing the harbor lights as darkness set in, or sleeping until nearly noon on a clear, brisk autumn Sunday. An evening at the theater had him wanting "to lay my head on the expansive shoulder of the fat lady ahead of me and heave vast blubbers. Only the sense of my consular dignity . . . restrained me." On another evening he marveled at the exquisite taste and incredible technique of a young pianist named Horowitz, said to be near death from tuberculosis, whose "nervous spidery fingers trembled on the keys," while his "whole body [vibrated] tensely to every note of the music."[15]

As did Kennan himself, it seemed, to whatever he happened upon. A walk to the post office on the tenth anniversary of the Bolshevik Revolution caught him up in a communist demonstration: thousands of people marching with red flags in the rain behind sickly fifes and drums, singing the "Internationale," listening to speeches from soapboxes, protesting the fate of Sacco and Vanzetti. Fully aware of communism's "falseness and hatefulness," he nonetheless felt "a strange desire to cry." The experience hinted at "the real truth upon which the little group of spiteful Jewish parasites in Moscow feeds— . . . that these stupid, ignorant, unpleasant people were after all human beings—that they were, after centuries of mute despair, for the first time attempting to express and to assert themselves."[16]

Meanwhile, the European political scene was a world of its own, which most people knew nothing about. One minister could denounce another, provoking counterdenunciations, but underneath this "prattling of bitter little men," the great forces of nations and classes made their own unaffected way. And so, at the great fall fair in front of the cathedral, "[m]en yell . . . wheels revolve . . . lights blink . . . whistles blow . . . people laugh . . . people eat . . . human life flows along in all its variety and in all its monotony . . . and behind it all . . . the gods themselves dance on, in high indifference!"[17]

Kennan wrote in his memoirs that the Foreign Service had steadied "a young man by no means ready yet for complete personal independence." Maybe later, but not at this point. Six months abroad had left him with increasingly unsettling mood swings, and by November he was close to the breaking point. While at a charity dance on a new passenger liner in the harbor one afternoon, Kennan saw a tramp freighter glide past and felt a sudden urge to exchange his cutaway for a sailor's dungarees. He would sail

> into the darkness and the night rain, down the long black aisles of twinkling chan-
> nel buoys on the river, past the clustered harbor lights . . . at the mouth, [and] on
> beyond, to where . . . the revolving beams from the light-houses cut sweeping great
> circles around the black line of the horizon, . . . to where the wind, coming sharp and
> cold and salt-tanged from the North Sea, sang an ecstatic low song in the stays and
> the wireless aerial, and the bow of the freighter rose almost imperceptibly to the first
> long swell of the sea.

But then the orchestra struck up, he drank some more champagne and found someone to dance with. "Perhaps it was just as well." Ten days later George F. Kennan sat down and, in the formal language he had been trained to use, addressed a letter to the secretary of state. "Sir," it read, "I have the honor to submit herewith my resignation from the Foreign Service of the United States."[18]

II.

"Mr. Kennan gives no reasons for the tender of his resignation," a puzzled State Department official noted, although he did record that William Dawson, who had taught George at the Foreign Service School, thought health might be the explanation. An efficiency report from Geneva had described the new vice-consul as physically "rather delicate." After pondering the matter, the Office of Foreign

Personnel offered a compromise: sixty days of leave in the United States, with the opportunity for "consultation" before making the resignation final. "Don't be a damn fool, George," Dawson admonished him. "Take [the leave], and then resign." Kennan agreed and left Hamburg in mid-January 1928. Spurning the comfort of a passenger liner, he signed on as a supercargo on an American tanker, enjoyed a stormy four-week passage to Norfolk, and suffered the embarrassment, upon arrival, of having a suitcase stolen containing his copy of the *United States Consular Regulations.* The volume, he tried to assure his superiors, would probably be of no value to the thief.[19]

Kennan had in fact cited "urgent and unalterable personal reasons" in his resignation letter, but he had not elaborated on them. His memoirs say only that living in Geneva and Hamburg convinced him, given his "spotty" education so far, of the need for postgraduate study.[20] There was, however, a more pressing priority: George had fallen in love and was engaged to be married.

She was Eleanor Van Someren Hard, the daughter of William and Anne Hard, Washington journalists and pioneering radio commentators. They lived in one of the Georgetown houses where students from the Foreign Service School were invited to parties, and that is probably where George met Eleanor. "She was not inhibited at all," he remembered. "Come and meet these people," she would insist. "This was very good for me." The family appeared to be unconventional: Mr. Hard had been thought, during the war, to be a radical; Mrs. Hard favored women's emancipation; Eleanor "wrote poetry and patronized queer people." But at a deeper level, they were conservative individualists: their proximity to the opposite camp had hardened their allegiance. They struck George as thoroughly American, "accepting material prosperity as the just due of a spotless conscience." He was enthralled, began dating Eleanor, and "either I fancied myself in love or I thought I ought to [be]." There was no physical intimacy: "This was innocent, according to the ways of those times." But before leaving for Geneva, "I did bring myself to ask her to marry me, and she said she would."[21]

Eleanor confirmed, decades later, what George remembered. Despite having "the Charleston as our lamamba, the hip pocket flask as our pot," they were to the right of most young people even then: "How close to the Edwardians we were!" Flappers flourished, but under "our minimal dresses beat hearts not too far from Little Women." George was serious and self-disciplined, she was easily distracted and dependent on fun. Both were bright, but "we had absolutely nothing else in common." Eleanor's mother disapproved, convinced that George "would never amount to anything." And so when he arrived back in the United

States, he found that he would not be marrying Eleanor after all. "Very late in life," she recalled, "my mother asked me if she had made a mistake—she was utterly surprised by George's success. I could assure her that we would have been totally incompatible."[22]

"I went through the usual melodramatics of a person of that age when such things happen," a much older George acknowledged, "but it lasted about three days. I was over it at once. I don't blame her at all. . . . I don't know what the hell I was doing, to tell the truth." Jeanette, however, saw that the effects had been substantial. One reason was the engagement ring, which had belonged to their mother and was never returned: "That was quite a blow to him."[23] And although George himself did not record—or if he did, failed to preserve—anything about the engagement in his diary, he did write Jeanette a long letter about it after he returned to Europe. "[T]hese last few months," he began, "have witnessed far greater and more important experiences in the life of G. F. Kennan than have been described in his letters to his parents. Since I saw you last I have finally passed the big turning-point, and I feel, for the first time in my life, that I have just about found my place in the world."

There were, as he saw it, "two vitally contrasting ways of life." One was as lived in most of Milwaukee, almost all of Princeton and the Republican Party, and certainly the drawing rooms of northwest Washington. "There were splendid girls, in this America." Falling in love with and marrying one of them could be the greatest experience of life: one built one's home in the rock of the country. "Oh Netty, don't think that I didn't feel the force of all this." So "when Eleanor took me in hand, . . . it was no wonder that it struck deep." George realized, for the first time, "that I could beat the people I had always envied at their own game. I saw that I could become both respected and powerful—that I, too, might someday make the very pillars of the State Department tremble."

But "I would never have been happy in the life I so nearly entered. I am too much of an extremist, and there are other factors in connection with an unfortunate youthful environment which would have marred the picture." George did not explain what those were; however, there was no choice but embrace fully the other way of life. That would involve, bleakly, "the renunciation of all individualistic hopes," even if some might be realized accidentally:

> I will probably never be vastly admired; I shall never achieve much personal dignity; my wife, if I ever have one, will doubtless be in no sense ideal and will generally be spoken of as an impossible person. Far from becoming wealthy, I will probably . . .

lose what money I have. . . . Worse than all of these things—for me: I will doubtless cause considerable pain to all persons who love me but are themselves not able to understand what I am doing (Father for instance).

George would stick with the Foreign Service for a few more years, but it would have to realize "that I am a queer duck, and that it can't demand too much." During working hours, "I belong to it body and soul. . . . But when the last visa applicant has left, and the accounts are done, and the door of the Consulate closes behind me, I am George Kennan, and if the government doesn't like it, it can whistle long and loud."

As to alternatives, only time would tell. George sensed potentialities, among them "a moderate talent for words," but he would need to have something to say and hoped that he might one day. In the meantime, he must select from currents of life those that seemed to be flowing in the right direction and align himself with them, "faulty and imperfectible as I may be." "Poor Netty," he concluded, "you draw all the melodramatic letters, because you are the only person before whom I may safely act melodramatic. As long as you and I both live you will probably continue to be the butt of epistulary [sic] histrionics."[24]

III.

Histrionics there certainly were. "For on this night," Kennan wrote portentously in his diary on March 26, 1928, "I make my last reluctant obeisance to the obscure gods of Washington—to the cool, derisive deities, who have taken without compensation the two best years of my life." He would miss "the hurdy gurdy man in Church Street, on hot summer evenings, . . . grey and white buses streaming along Sixteenth Street, in the shadows of the shuttered Russian Embassy . . . charity balls in the Willard Hotel . . . where the softness of the atmosphere and the subdued lilt of the music contrasted so cruelly with the cheapness and vulgarity of the guests . . . shady streets in Georgetown, where the old brick houses sung [sic] to themselves the songs of a still, deep past . . . [and the] cool, dark corridors in the State Department." But now the train had begun to move, and the Capitol dome loomed above the lights of the switchyard, then faded from view: "These and a thousand other memories return now to taunt me for the homage I have done them. They sear like fire, for in every one of them lies the glow of failure!"[25]

It's hard to know, reading passages like this one, whether George was using his diary to substitute for not having anyone close at hand in whom to confide, or whether he was simply practicing to become a writer: a few passages show critical appraisals from a Princeton friend to whom George showed them.[26] What's clear is that he was not leaving Washington having failed professionally. Instead the Foreign Service had gone out of its way to show that it wanted to keep him on.

Dawson played the critical role. The State Department, he pointed out, would finance three years of graduate study at a European university if Kennan would seek proficiency in Chinese, Japanese, Arabic, or Russian. Despite the absence of formal diplomatic relations with the Soviet Union, Kennan chose Russian, supposing that there would someday again be official Americans there. "But I also had a mind to the family tradition established by the elder George Kennan." And so on March 29, three days after his despairing farewell to Washington, the younger George was accepted into a new Foreign Service program for "language assignments" in "Eastern Europe."[27]

The last American ambassador to Russia, David R. Francis, had left that country in November 1918, a year after Vladimir Ilich Lenin had seized power. The last Russian ambassador to the United States, Boris Bakhmeteff, represented the Provisional Government that Lenin had overthrown: he finally resigned in 1923, leaving the embassy on Sixteenth Street dark. By that time Woodrow Wilson's last secretary of state, Bainbridge Colby, had announced the policy of the U.S. government toward the new regime in Moscow: that it was not possible to maintain diplomatic relations with a government "based upon the negation of every principle . . . upon which it is possible to base harmonious and trustful relations, whether of nations or of individuals."[28]

Nevertheless, American contacts with the Union of Soviet Socialist Republics flourished. Despite the revolutionary aspirations of the first state in history to be run by a communist party, the United States sent desperately needed famine relief in 1921–22, and prominent businessmen—among them Henry Ford and the young W. Averell Harriman—quickly found opportunities for trade and investment. By 1930 the Soviet Union imported more from the United States than from any other country: the staunchly Republican senator William Borah described it as "the greatest undeveloped market in the world."[29]

The absence of diplomatic relations, therefore, became increasingly difficult to justify. Within the State Department there was deep hostility toward the Soviet Union and the international communist movement; but there was also the sense that nonrecognition could not last indefinitely, and that there ought to be experts in place when that policy shift took place. Russian studies became a priority, and in 1927 Robert F. Kelley, the new and energetic chief of the Division of Eastern European Affairs, began recruiting Foreign Service officers from its "unclassified" ranks for that purpose. This was the program Dawson recommended to Kennan, and it was one of the things that persuaded him—the breakup with Eleanor was surely another—to rescind his resignation. A career-minded guardian angel had again appeared on the scene, and as Kennan would say in his memoirs, "I have always been grateful."[30]

IV.

Officers selected for the program were first sent to perform consular duties in the region in which they were to specialize: only after a probationary period would they begin the promised postgraduate study. Kennan's assignment was Tallinn, in Estonia, one of the three Baltic republics that had broken away from the Russian empire after its demise. As had been the case the previous year, though, he was temporarily diverted, this time to Berlin, a city Kennan had visited briefly in the summer of 1926 after passing the Foreign Service examinations. If his diary entries are any indication, his mood had brightened somewhat: "I walk to work in the morning," he wrote soon after arriving, "and delight in the Berlin of the young day."[31]

There was, to be sure, the tedium of passports, visas, and accounts, but there were also receptions to attend and interesting people to watch: Berlin, the largest and liveliest city in Germany, was no backwater post. At one such event the German foreign secretary Gustav Stresemann held forth, "swaying his portly figure back and forth as he talks . . . One wonders at the secrets of Europe which must lie within that broad, shaven head." Should a man with such responsibilities laugh and joke? More pitiful were the Russian émigrés. "Alive they are," but "they move like lost phantoms in a world which is, and always will be, a distorted and gilded memory of the past." Meanwhile, at the communist theater, capitalists strutted around in top hats, brutal soldiers martyred proletarians, musicians played the "Internationale," and individuals offstage provided the mighty voice of the oppressed masses. It was all "doctrinaire tommy-rot," but under it "one feels the heat of a brightly burning flame."[32]

Crowded buses full of tired people passed beneath the Brandenburg Gate, where Napoleon's army had once marched: what was the bond between that day and this? Along the Wannsee, on a brilliant Sunday, people "ride, boat, walk, eat, wander, buy, stare, and make love," before returning, sunburned, to the city's slavery. Communists and nationalists competed in noisy political demonstrations, but more impressive were the less pretentious Social Democrats, who had unwittingly carried "the idealism of the German character through the horrors of war and revolution and economic collapse."[33]

George soon fell in love with one of them. Her name was Charlotte Böhm, and her story—which he sent to Jeanette—reflected what had happened to Germany in recent years. She had grown up in Berlin, the daughter of a businessman, and in 1914 had watched her brother march off to a war in which "it seemed that men had become gods and participated in incredible, awe-inspiring adventures." But one night the boy's guitar inexplicably fell off the wall. Charlotte's mother knew instantly that "*der Junge war tot.*" But when the war ended and the troops marched home, Charlotte could not help watching day after day for her brother: "There might have been some dreadful mistake; it might have been all a bad dream; he might march back, as he had marched away."

Of course he didn't. Impoverished by war and inflation, her mother gave up her apartment and moved to the country. Charlotte became a secretary, had love affairs that did not last, and "slowly the girlishness went out of her face," to be replaced by the signs of "a joyless, purposeless, solitary existence." That was how she was when he met her. Charlotte "literally blossomed out during the time we were together; it was like a rebirth." But he could not marry her, he had to go to Tallinn, and now "all that I had accomplished is undone again." This was why, George explained to Jeanette, "it is hard to live in Europe and see things of this sort and then come home and feel boundless optimism in perpetual prosperity and the general righteousness of things." It was also "why I am probably always going to be considerable of a radical."[34]

V.

June 1928. "The attractiveness of a blond German girl [not Charlotte] sitting beside me [on a train] is heightened almost unbearably by the fact that she pays no attention to me. I wish to hell Sherman [a friend] were not so drunk. He keeps starting to whistle, whereupon I look up from my Russian grammar in a startled fashion." Despite the fact that he was not to begin language training for another year, George used his time in Berlin to master the Russian alphabet and to begin learning—whatever the distractions—the rudiments of grammar. By mid-July he was in Tallinn serving as the second and very junior member of the two-person American diplomatic and consular office there. A single minister represented the United States in all three Baltic republics, but he operated chiefly out of Riga, in Latvia, with only occasional visits to Estonia and Lithuania. Kennan's work in Tallinn was varied and at times amusing: "I rather loved it."[35] But the real excitement was that the Baltic states were as close to the Soviet Union as it was possible to get without going there—an opportunity open to most Americans at the time but not, paradoxically, to the Foreign Service's young "experts" on that country, the existence of which their government had not yet officially recognized.

The Riga legation was the principal American "listening post" for Soviet affairs, just as Hong Kong would be during the 1950s and 1960s prior to the establishment of diplomatic contacts with the People's Republic of China. Kennan was not yet entrusted with such responsibilities, but he used his free time in Tallinn—of which there was plenty—to prepare himself for them. He hired a Ukrainian tutor who knew no English, and between them they studied Russian as best they could, unable to communicate in any other language. They used first-grade readers, and it was from these "that I conceived . . . a love for this great Russian language—rich, pithy, musical, sometimes tender, sometimes earthy and brutal, sometimes classically severe—that was . . . an unfailing source of strength and reassurance in the drearier and more trying reaches of later life."[36]

Kennan's fluency became sufficient that he could spend Christmas at the remote fifteenth-century monastery of Pskovo-Pechorsky, then located on the Estonian side of the Soviet border. "I damn near died of hunger, because these monks didn't have anything to eat, except barrels of salted herring and black bread. [But] they were nice to me." In Narva, farther north, he found equally ugly Orthodox and Lutheran churches glowering over the miserable huts that surrounded them: a clash of Russian and Scandinavian cultures. The same was evident in Helsinki, a strikingly more modern city than Tallinn, where within the magnificent new railroad station stood "the box-like passenger cars of the old Russian railway system, with their crazy, chimney-like ventilators protruding from their roofs," a reminder that "for hundreds of miles beyond there stretches the bleak melancholy expanse of northern Russia . . . ageless . . . unconquerable."[37]

While trying to fathom what lay to the east, Kennan brooded about Europe's fragility and his own superficiality. "Americanism, like Bolshevism, is a disease which gains footing only in a weakened body," he concluded with youthful certainty. "If the Old World has no longer sufficient vitality, economic and cultural, to oppose these new barbarian invasions, it will have to drown in the flood, as civilizations have drowned before it." The only escape lay "in *depth* rather than *breadth*," for in a world in which anyone with health and persistence could travel anywhere, the only unexplored territory lay "deep[e]r down in our own selves, about which we know everything, and understand nothing." That was a lofty way of addressing a lower problem: George's own self-absorption, from which flowed intellectual accomplishment and—increasingly—the ability to write compelling prose, but also still behavior echoing "my neurotic student youth."[38]

There was, for example, the August weekend he spent at the dacha of Harry Carlson, the American consul in Tallinn and his only immediate superior. He began it in a bad humor: "I hate the world, and the world hates me." While sharing a train compartment with a British officer who had also been invited, they quickly decided that they disliked each other and needed to make no effort to conceal the fact. Their host was well-meaning, earnest, and nervous, yet what right did he have to "force on me" his "timorous, middle-class standards?" George sulked through dinner, refused to play bridge, and woke the next morning "stuffy and bilious." Sensing this, Mrs. Carlson suggested "that I amuse myself as I see fit." So he hired a boat and set off rowing vigorously across the bay against the wind: after a while, with blistered hands, it was time to turn back. Upon his arrival, however, the British officer proposed a paddle-boat outing, during which both were drenched by a large wave. But both were stubborn. "He is not going to complain, and [n]either am I." So they grimly made their way to the other side and back, chilled, soaked, aching, and miserable. Aware at once that he had not been a good guest, George remorsefully recorded the details of the unhappy weekend. Long afterward he would remember his bad manners as having merited "the general ostracism I received thenceforth in the little diplomatic-consular community."[39]

Kennan moved to a larger community—the Riga legation—early in 1929. That city resembled, as none other did, prerevolutionary St. Petersburg: "The copy had survived the original." He also had colleagues now whose job it was to watch the Soviet Union. He listened carefully to their endless arguments "rising and falling with the hours." He was not in the "Russian Section," but his reports—mostly on Baltic issues—were winning respect. Four days after George's twenty-fifth birthday, a visiting State Department inspector noted that

Mr. Kennan . . . studies well all of his subjects and treats them intelligently, comprehensively and at times almost with brilliance,—certainly with flashes that indicate considerable promise as to his development into a reporting officer of considerable ability. He has assurance, a far-seeing eye, follows details unerringly and is usually on the lookout for anything that may turn up. His alertness is commendable, [but] his assurance may, until mellowed by further experience, lead him afield.[40]

There were few signs now of the petulance Kennan had displayed in Tallinn. He still patronized elders, but in the company of youthful contemporaries, and with self-critical empathy.

"Poor M——," he wrote in his diary of an older colleague who was leaving Riga, "always dignified even in his weakness, and now we assemble on this winter night, to bid him farewell." Each shook M—— by the hand, talking volubly "to conceal our uneasiness," trying to "make him feel that we like him, that we are sorry to see him go." But the train stood still, and the minutes dragged on. "We are not accustomed to playing the part of solemnity for more than a few moments." Suddenly the train started to move. "Like a group of hysterical children, we laugh, we shout 'Hurry up, M——, hurry up,' and we push him to the door of the car." Standing there, "waving his arm, smiling his sad, courteous smile, M—— disappears and leaves us . . . , a trifle embarrassed to find ourselves all together at this late hour, waving senselessly at the black emptiness of the Baltic night."[41]

Kennan's diaries were not available to the inspector from Washington, but his comments about alertness to detail, promising "flashes," occasional "brilliance," and a "far-seeing eye" could well have characterized the writing George was now regularly doing in his spare time:

Riga, February 2, 1929: A furtive, fitful wind, smelling of dirty snow, and deserted wharves, sneaks in from the harbor. It rushes aimlessly through the empty streets, muttering and sighing to itself, seeking it knows not what, crazed and desperate, like a drunken man, lost in the dawn.

Dorpat (Tartu), Estonia, March 29: From the sight of these drab peasants, staring at the ikons, crossing themselves, shuffling the balsam twigs under their feet, as they wait for the commencement of the service, on[e] can sense the full necessity for their presence here. . . . They do not understand the service, but they see the gilt and the robes and the candles; they hear the chanting and the singing; and they go away with the comforting feeling of there being a world . . . somewhere and somehow . . . less ugly than their own.

Kovno (Kaunas), Lithuania, April 9: Threads of Fate, leading to all parts of Europe and America, are responsible for the fact that this scrawny Jewish village lying by its frozen river in the morning sun, may call itself the capital of the muddy, impoverished country-side which stretches out around it. It has accepted [this] . . . as a hungry animal accepts an unexpected meal. When the tide of fortune turns, when the officials and diplomats go away, leaving the government buildings as empty as the shops of the little Jewish merchants, there will be snarling and recrimination, but there will be no real sadness, for there has been no real hope.

But why this profusion of extracurricular prose? Maybe to practice observation, a useful skill in a diplomat. Probably in imitation of the German journalist, poet, and playwright Alfons Paquet, whose travel writings had made a deep impression on Kennan. Certainly out of an extraordinary sensitivity to landscapes, environments, and moods, in a way that he found difficult to explain. Kennan speculated, late in life, that he might have done better as a poet or a novelist, but only at great cost, "because art is open-ended, and I didn't have a balanced enough personal life to have gone into this expression of the emotional without being torn to pieces by it."[42]

Kennan's life seemed sufficiently balanced, by the spring of 1929, for his superiors to send him on to greater things. From Tallinn, Carlson, despite the unfortunate weekend at his dacha, praised Kennan as "unquestionably the most gifted of any of the subordinate officers who have been under my supervision." He had applied himself assiduously to learning Russian, had high moral standards, and was in good health, even though his only exercise appeared to be "long walks with his dog." F. W. B. Coleman, the minister in Riga, endorsed this assessment, adding that while "Mr. Kennan might [earlier] have been charged with being too serious, too loath to leave his books and to make social contacts, . . . [the] charge is no longer sustained. He . . . commands the confidence of all people whom he approaches." These accolades were enough for the Department of State, which in July congratulated Kennan "on the successful conclusion of your probationary period for language assignment. It is hoped that an equal measure of success will attend your studies at Berlin."[43]

VI.

In the midst of a conversation, one evening in Riga, someone mentioned Berlin. "In a flash," George recorded in his diary, "I see the Leipzigerstrasse, every detail of it, as clearly as though I were standing in the traffic tower on Potsdamer Place." There were the cold, hard buildings, the boulevards swept shiny by the automobiles and the streetlamps, the shop windows spilling confused light onto jostling pedestrians, the huge buses with blinking signal-arms roaring through intersections, the yellow streetcars with ventilators spinning on their roofs, grinding to a halt before the corners. The vision was tactile in its intensity: "I feel the whole vibration and excitement of the city . . . and all the cruelty and fascination and adventure with which it throbs."[44]

Kennan's assignment was to enroll in Russian-language courses at the Seminar für Orientalische Sprachen at the Friedrich Wilhelm University of Berlin, and to take advantage of other opportunities in that city, as might be practicable, to study the geography, history, and institutions of Eastern Europe. The State Department would pay for tuition, textbooks, and living expenses. The seminar's two-year curriculum, designed chiefly to train Russian translators and interpreters for the German courts, was of limited use. Having taught himself conversational Russian while in Tallinn and Riga, Kennan was able to pass the required examination at the end of his first year, "barely skimming through." The rest of his time was spent more profitably, studying Russian history at the University of Berlin, as well as Russian language and literature with private tutors. Kelley had instructed his young protégés to equip themselves with an education similar to that which an educated Russian of the prerevolutionary era would have received. Exposure to Soviet affairs could come later.[45]

Just as important for Kennan, however, was the experience of living in Berlin at a remarkable moment in its history. The city had "surprised both itself and the rest of the world by becoming the centre of a cultural explosion," one of its historians has written. Suddenly it "threw off the Prussian imperial mantle, emerging as the capital of modernism and the undisputed centre of the 'Golden Twenties.'" It became, for Kennan, "the nearest thing I had known to an adult home."[46]

Soon after he arrived, George sought to rekindle his relationship with Charlotte Böhm, but she was seeing another man and probably understood "that I was too young for her, really." Disturbed nonetheless, he consulted a psychiatrist, who recommended a breakup: "My dear fellow, you're just a *Pantoffelheld*. You're a slipper-hero; you're under the domination of this woman. You'd better get out of it." And so, as George wrote Jeanette early in 1930, "I must put the idea out of my mind."[47]

There were other women: "Hello. Miss L——? This is the American you talked to the other night at the Russian opera. . . . I'd sort of like to go out and paint the town red, and I wondered if you'd come along." "Very red?" "Well, pretty red. Besides, I haven't been out with an American girl for pretty nearly two years." "All right, I'd be glad to." So they tried the Femina, famous for its table telephones and pneumatic tubes, but found it full. Then the Kakadoo, where the orchestra played far too fast. "I drink my whiskey-soda, she her cocktail, and we leave the bottle of Rheinwein standing on the table." And then home, alone, where "I drink another whiskey-soda, . . . at the same time wondering what it is that forces me to act like a gentleman, when I am with an American woman."

The next diary entry is titled "Fantasia." A man in a fur coat walking along the Kurfürstendamm at five o'clock on a Sunday morning meets a polite prostitute and goes to bed with her between bare blankets. The woman's legs are cold, as though she were dead. Afterward he is back on the street where, if listening closely, one might hear "a sudden, unexpected, half-suppressed sob, above the whining of the wind." What the man demanded of life was unbearably greater than what he had received, all of which might move one to pity someone "so utterly lost, in the cold winter dawn, in the forest of stone and steel which is called the city." But sympathy is a dangerous thing, so he should be allowed "to turn into a side-street and to seek his rest where he can. . . . (wicked, degenerate man, he must be, coming brazenly home at this hour, from the whores)."[48]

All diaries entangle fiction with truth, so there's little point in seeking to sort out here which was which. George did admit to Jeanette shortly thereafter, though, that "I had a very bad bringing up . . . (you needn't tell Father)." He had learned "to look for all sorts of things in the world, which aren't in it at all, and the few good things which the world has to offer, are things which I have never learned to see." As was often the case, the mood did not last: two weeks later George was back from nine days on the French Riviera, feeling "like a new man. I hope to work hard at Russian and play a lot of tennis . . . and forget that life is supposed to have other, more significant experiences."[49] And he had, by then, a new family.

"January 19, 1930. . . . Young Russian émigré to lunch. Burning eyes, deep pride, resentment and mistrust. Reputedly a tendency to tuberculosis. We discuss language, perfunctorily, he commenting on the fact that translations of foreign books into Russian are natural and veracious, whereas Russian novels, translated into foreign languages, lose all their Russian character." He was Vladimir (Volodya) Kozhenikov, who with his mother and sister eked out a precarious existence in a cellar in Spandau. George met Volodya through Cyrus Follmer, then serving as vice-consul in Berlin, and "we became good friends." On the day George took his final examination in Russian at the Oriental Seminar, Volodya had wanted to stand outside ready to whisper him answers. Still mindful of the Princeton honor code, George refused, but he became an adopted member of the Kozhenikov family.[50]

The Kozhenikovs survived "only by a series of those miraculous last-minute rescues that God reserves for the truly innocent and utterly improvident." George and Cyrus did what they could to keep them afloat. "They are a tremendously proud family and it's not easy for them to take help," George explained to Jeanette. The spontaneity of their devotion embarrassed him: "enthusiastic visits at unexpected hours, elaborate gifts they couldn't possibly afford." But he was pleased to be accepted as a Russian. "Sharing their woes and crises, I felt like a Russian myself."[51]

George understood later—whether at the time is less clear—that Volodya was homosexual. "I always had these curious friends," he would recall many years later, "people who are a little unusual—the *Bohème*—they understand me, better than do the regular ones. This has nothing to do with physical relations." Meanwhile Shura, Volodya's younger sister, had fallen in love with George, something she didn't admit to him until after her brother's death· her mother had ruled out the relationship on the grounds that George was too *pozhivzhie*—he had "lived a little too much." "I was much more sophisticated," he admitted, "and I had had my ladies, too."[52]

VII.

By early 1931 Kennan's professional success seemed assured. The Russian language, he explained to Walt Ferris, a Foreign Service friend, had come "so naturally (if not easily) that I hope in time to know it about as well as my own." Given the family interest—the first Kennan—becoming a specialist for that part of the world "fits in very conveniently with my preferences." More significantly, George was developing his own views on the country in which he lived, and the one he would spend most of his life studying.

The Germans, he wrote Ferris, were "a strong, coarse people, with a tremendous capacity for physical and intellectual labor and a total inability to comprehend the finer and the (for them) stranger elements of human psychology. Their only god is personal strength, and their only conception of the relation between human beings in essence that of slave and master." All of their thinking on love, friendship, enmity, education, and politics proceeded from this; even their humor was "obscene without being witty," and their language "involved without being delicate." Their sentimentality was dangerous because it contained no smile: "They are the final hope. . . . they are now the final despair of western European civilization."

As for the Soviet Union, its system was unalterably opposed to that of the United States. It followed, therefore,

> that there can be no possible middle ground or compromise between the two, that any attempts to find such a middle ground, by the resumption of diplomatic relations or otherwise, are bound to be unsuccessful, that the two systems cannot even exist together in the same world unless an economic cordon is put around one or the other of them, and that within twenty or thirty years either Russia will be capitalist or we shall be communist.

This was not, Kennan was careful to add, a judgment on the respective virtues of either ideology. It was simply to say that the two, like oil and water, could never mix. And if they ever came to blows, American liberals, "who now find the Soviets so pleasant, will be the first ones to be crushed in the clash."[53]

But he soon abandoned this neutrality on ideology. He found himself developing to Volodya "certain ideas which I had not formerly known were in my own mind." Communists, George now saw, combined "innate cowardice" and "intellectual insolence." They had "abandoned the ship of western European civilization like a swarm of rats." Having done so, they had grasped for a theory with which they could leap across the gulf through which the rest of mankind had been foundering. They "credited their own intelligence with powers far greater than those of all previous generations." They regarded their forefathers, and most of their contemporaries, as "hopeless fools."

This struck George, "not a religious man," as a form of "cultural and intellectual sacrilege." Maybe communism would work as a purely Russian phenomenon. For the West, though, it could only mean retrogression, and that required resistance. "Was it for us to stand aside and stop fighting because things were going against us? Did a football player leave the field when the score turned against his team?

Did a real soldier stand anxiously watching the tide of battle, in order to decide whether or not to fight?" There were principles of decency in individual conduct which offered hope for the human race. They required defense, not abandonment just because they were in danger. It was a stirring rejection of realism, as George himself recognized: "Enter Kennan, the moralist."[54]

With all that was going on, he wrote Jeanette, it seemed almost criminal to complain about his own situation: "A young man of twenty-six, with fundamentally good health, tolerable appearance, plenty of money, an incomparably advantageous official position, an active mind and an adaptability to every known form of culture, and a knowledge of English, French, German and Russian, has no right to be bored in the very vortex of the most intense intellectual and cultural currents of the world."

And yet he was bored: a raucous Christmas with American friends in Riga left him despairing of accomplishing anything "until I bring some peace and order into my private life." If he were a private citizen, he could "become a Boheme and attempt to think." Being a Foreign Service officer, he could only choose "between marriage and stupidity on the one hand, and nervous exhaustion, boldness and futility on the other." He would seek the first, "as soon as I can." But "I shall never be completely happy at it, for I shall never be able to do much thinking myself— and I have been just clever enough, in my youth, to mistrust everyone who tries to think for me."

By April he was losing patience with Volodya, who was failing to keep appointments, patronizing "hermaphrodite" dance performances, and taking opium— although George was still lending the Kozhenikovs money. "Essentially," he explained to Jeanette, "it is nothing more or less than my puritan origins rising in relentless revolt against the non-puritan influences of the last few years." So what would happen? "Perhaps I'll get religion. Perhaps I'll fall in love, for the first time in my young life. Or perhaps I'll get broken on the wheel, like Hemingway and others of the expatriates." One thing was clear: "Prolonged and intimate association with the devil does not lie in the Kennan character." Perhaps the tale should be titled "The story of the man who tried to sell his soul and couldn't."[55]

Three months after writing this last letter, Kennan wrote another to the secretary of state in Washington, using the formal language in which he had been trained: "Sir: . . . I should like to request that I be allowed to take 6 weeks leave of absence beginning approximately August 10, 1931." He had been in poor health for some time and needed several weeks of complete rest in order to get back into shape. "Furthermore, I am expecting to be married."[56]

FOUR

Marriage—and Moscow: 1931–1933

"COME RIGHT ON. LOVE, ANNELISE." THE TELEGRAM FROM KRIS-tiansand reached George in Berlin on August 5, 1931. Three days later he boarded a ship that would take him—along with his elegant but unreliable Nash roadster—on the first leg of a journey to Norway. Volodya Kozhenikov and his sister Shura came to Stettin to see him off, laden with flowers they could ill afford: "They take it very seriously, this departure," their benefactor wrote in his diary. "Instinct . . . tells them that while we may meet again soon, this day and this departure mark the termination of my residence in Berlin and that this is the real good-bye." He assured Jeanette, though, that "I am very happy, and am entering marriage with none of the qualms which I understand to be usually attendant upon this stage of development."[1]

Anna Elisabeth Sørensen, who had just turned twenty-one, had only a few qualms herself. "I am afraid you will have to be very patient in bringing me up to be an American girl," she wrote from Kristiansand, "they are all so clever, in all directions." She was, however, sure of herself. "I am glad I came here to think things over, but even here I miss you every minute. . . . Just can't help it. . . . I know you understand me as I understand you." She had shared news of the engagement with her astonished mother, who would need time to get used to the idea. "Have not had opportunity to tell daddy yet. I am curious to know what he will say." She had, however, let a former boyfriend know: it was strange that "when people lose a thing they realise how much they liked it."[2]

Annelise was born on July 23, 1910, in Kristiansand, where her father, Einar Haakon Sørensen, ran a building materials business. In a country facing the sea young people were expected to leave home, and at the age of seventeen Annelise went to Paris to study language, literature, and history. She had already learned English and, after several more months of tutoring, was speaking it well. There had been talk of becoming a doctor, but "I knew myself well enough to know that I didn't have seven years in me just to study." She expected to marry before that.³

After more schooling in Kristiansand, Annelise went to Berlin, "ostensibly to learn German." It was there that she encountered George Kennan, at a Sunday lunch arranged by a cousin who had hoped to rent him an apartment: the date was March 22, 1931. The plan succeeded, and that allowed them to meet from time to time at parties. George struck Annelise as "rather serious." On one early date, he brooded about America. "It was hardly the kind of thing that you'd think you would sit and talk to a young girl about—your worries about a country which I had never been to." They decided to marry after only a few weeks, a fact Annelise kept from her parents. Even so, "they were not pleased." But she was determined. "I finally just put my foot down and said that if I heard another sigh from my mother, I was going to scream!"⁴

George left for Kristiansand exhausted from overwork: Annelise had asked him to try to get there "without the black rings around your eyes!" He had planned to rest for a few days in Copenhagen, but the Nash needed work and he caught a cold. He left there "a complete wreck." Sitting miserably in the driver's seat of his car, which was lashed to the deck, he nursed his fever by reading Tolstoy until the islands of the Norwegian coast came into view. George later wondered what impression "the thin, slightly uncouth, very nervous, and rather unwell apparition of an American" must have made—the Sørensens' feelings, he sensed, "had not been exactly those of confidence or elation." But he spent several weeks with them before the wedding and that helped, as did Annelise's steely resolve. "So I don't think that it was really very awkward."⁵

The wedding took place in the Kristiansand cathedral on the afternoon of September 11, 1931: Annelise noted the event in her appointment book with the single Norwegian word "Bryllup." Cyrus Follmer came from Berlin to be best man, and the Kennans honeymooned in Vienna, where—Annelise's passport not corresponding with his—George labored to persuade the hotel porter that they were really married, only to have him look paternally over his spectacles to say, "We understand." A few weeks later George wrote Jeanette to say that concerns he had had six months earlier were all now nonexistent. "I might almost say that this letter comes from a completely new brother and not the one you have known before."⁶

I.

The marriage coincided with the end of Kennan's postgraduate studies in Berlin and his first assignment as a fully qualified Russian specialist. The Foreign Service sent him back to Riga—still, in the absence of diplomatic relations, the chief American observation post for the Soviet Union—and Annelise accompanied him. But his illusions of glamour as an unattached bachelor faded with a young wife. George made it no easier by warning Annelise that this or that colleague didn't like him. "[I]t wasn't really quite true," she recalled, "but I had to discover it in my own way."[7]

The Kennans chose not to live downtown among inquisitive diplomatic colleagues but instead leased the top two floors of a factory owner's house in the suburb of Tornakalns. It was cheap enough for them to have a cook and a chauffeur, who doubled as a butler. Unfortunately, though, there was a park across the street with a summer bandstand whose brass ensemble knew only five songs, endlessly repeated for months at a time: "You could retire to the innermost clothes closet of the house and bury your head in the clothes, it made no difference—the sound reached you."[8]

It was, George explained to Jeanette, a "new and strange world." For despite the fact that he was well trained, generously paid, and in no danger of losing a job that was sometimes interesting, "I, together with my wife, am lonely." The problem was not that marriage precluded thinking, as he had thought it might before meeting Annelise. It was rather that having a wife magnified his uneasiness with the lifestyle of his Foreign Service friends. People who once seemed interesting "stand before me now in a state of complete moral nakedness, and I see all the selfishness and cruelty and cowardice and emptiness which lies beneath their cordiality and their veneer of culture."

Loneliness, to be sure, could not be too serious for a married couple in love and living comfortably. But the future was very uncertain. The worsening economic crisis was worrying: George had not "the slightest faith in my money and property" because too many fortunes had already been lost "through inflations, revolutions, and confiscations." The Soviet frontier was only a hundred miles away, which meant that the Red Army could overrun Latvia whenever it wished. If that were ever to happen, "I think I should prefer to dispose of myself and my family in my own way before they got here. I have seen too many photographs of the corpses they left here twelve years ago."

But even if these dire events did not happen, "I don't want to stay in the Foreign Service." The United States had no foreign policy, only the reflections of domestic politics internationally. There was no satisfaction in representing that. The country was succumbing to a consumerism in which people equated charm with the absence of halitosis, balanced competing claims about toothpaste, and fretted about whether their refrigerators ejected ice cubes or required an ice pick.

> The America I know and love and owe allegiance to is Father's America—the America of George Kennan the elder, and John Hay and Henry Adams and Roosevelt and Cleveland and the Atlantic Monthly and the Century. That is the world we were brought up in on Cambridge Ave., after all, and it stood for certain ideals of decency and courage and generosity which were as fine as anything the world has ever known.

"I am not expatriated, Netty," he added. "I am very homesick—for the autumn in Wisconsin, for football games, for Sunday morning waffles, for loyal, generous people, and for a thousand memories of the U.S." If only Americans "could have their toys taken away from them, be spanked, educated and made to grow up, it might be worthwhile to act as a guardian for their foreign interests in the meantime. But when one can do none of these things?"

So he would stick with the Foreign Service for another two or three years, then become a student again and eventually "a pedagogue." Professors could survive almost anywhere: even the Bolsheviks had killed only a few. He would do Russian history seriously, writing something "so dull and so specialized that no one will ever dare to try to read it and everyone who sees it will be convinced that I know something about it." George ended this long letter, contradictorily, with a consumerist plea: could Jeanette please send a toaster, three cans of maple syrup, a dozen boxes of graham crackers, a dozen pairs of silk stockings, and subscriptions to Good Housekeeping and The Yale Review?[9]

Annelise, in the meantime, had become pregnant. "I can hardly believe it myself," she wrote Jeanette. "A year ago and I did not even know George!" She had already caused a "scandal" by fainting at a dinner given by the Belgian ambassador, just as dessert was being served. "They say I did it very nicely, and poor George took it like a man, but you can imagine what a shock he got!" The young husband had to carry his wife out, before the astonished guests, "as though I were abducting her." Grace Kennan—named for George's surrogate mother, "Cousin Grace" Wells—arrived, in Riga, on June 5, 1932: "The nights were again white, and the river," George recalled, "lay bathed in the golden reflections of an early sunrise as I drove back from the clinic."[10]

The rearing of Grace, as was customary in those days, was left to her mother. "Never mind George," she wrote him from Kristiansand, "it is not more boring than I expected it to be." George, for his part, juggled fatherhood with other concerns. His sister Constance remembered him pushing Grace in a baby carriage one day, thinking about everything but her, when he hit a bump, and she bounced into a snowbank: "It's so typical of George." But Annelise, when asked about this, doubted the story: "I have no recollection of George ever pushing the baby carriage."[11]

There was, in George's defense, much to think about, because the global financial catastrophe had by then hit home. His father, who had never accumulated much wealth, had seen his legal practice dwindle and an iron mine in which he invested shut down: by the early 1930s, he was struggling to pay for young Kent's education at the University of Michigan, and Louise was taking in boarders so they could keep the Cambridge Avenue house. In January 1932, shortly after his eightieth birthday, Kent senior sent a sad letter advising George to save as much money as possible and "hold fast to your job, for it might be a long time before you could get another." These recommendations came, he acknowledged, "with a poor grace from your old father who never saved anything and hasn't even made any provisions for his old age. Let us hope that the younger generation will profit by the mistakes of their elders!"[12]

Two months later Eugene Hotchkiss, Jeanette's husband, sent George "the most difficult letter I have ever written." George and Jeanette had entrusted Gene, a bond salesman at the respected investment bank Lee, Higginson, with managing the inheritance they had received from their mother. The money was in Northwestern National Life Insurance stock—the James family firm—but Gene had used it as collateral to buy shares on margin in Kreuger and Toll, the international holding company run by the Swedish "match king" Ivar Kreuger. George's father, Jeanette recalled, had advised against this on the grounds that matches were "unsafe," and so they turned out to be. With bankruptcy looming, Kreuger committed suicide on March 12, 1932. Eight days later Gene had to inform George that both his and his sister's inheritances were lost. Gene's job followed when Lee, Higginson also went under. "My first mistake," he admitted, "was to ever start to speculate, but my greatest was to ever speculate for you. . . . [M]y optimism . . . has been a curse rather than a blessing."[13]

George handled the shock with extraordinary graciousness. "Not only did he forgive it," Jeanette remembered, "but he apparently, as far as we knew, forgot it." There were no recriminations, and for fear of hurting Gene's feelings, no one said much about it. Many people were suffering financial reverses, George consoled his sister, but it was not worth worrying about them. "If one is fed, housed, and healthy, then debts, pride, conscience, standards, dignity, and what you will, will have to be laughed off. . . . We can't let ourselves go to pieces because we live in a cock-eyed economic system." The family was like his Berlin friends. "We must not all sink," Volodya had insisted, "trying to help each other." Jeanette knew, though, that George had wanted to leave the Foreign Service, and now he couldn't afford to do it.

The news came as "quite a blow," Annelise acknowledged. It was, she remembered, the first time she had seen George cry. No longer able to afford the Tornakalns house and its servants, the Kennans first moved into one of the diplomatic apartments downtown, and then, the following summer, to a tiny and very cheap dacha on the Riga Strand.[14]

The world was "falling to pieces," George confided in his diary a week before his daughter was born. As a single man, he might have adapted. As a married man and a father, it was out of the question. The only thing protecting him from unemployment was "[a]n accident, a freak": the fact that the State Department still provided its agents with a living standard few people anywhere else enjoyed. This was not likely to change, because Russian specialists were going to be needed. But there were no alternatives now, and even the Foreign Service carried the risk of purges brought about by Washington politics. The only defense was complete political neutrality, which would mean a long, quiet life as a minor official. "As one who had certain intellectual aspirations, I find this a blow to my pride, hopes, and egotism. As a father and a husband, I find it an undeserved blessing."[15]

II.

Over the next year and a half, George Kennan's character began to take on much of the shape it would retain for the rest of his life. It's best to think of it as triangular, held taut by tension along each of its sides. Professionalism was one of these: it was during this period that Kennan established his reputation, within the Foreign Service, as the best of its young Russian specialists. He would maintain that preeminence throughout his diplomatic career, and then transfer it successfully to the vocation of history. A second side was cultural pessimism: Kennan had begun to doubt whether what he thought of as "western civilization" could survive the challenges posed to it by its external adversaries and its internal contradictions. He never wholly reassured himself that it would. The third side was personal anguish: where did he as a husband and a father and a professional and an intellectual—but also as an individual tormented by self-doubt, regretting missed opportunities—fit into all of this? As happens with triangles, adjustments on one side could not help but affect the others.

Personal anxieties were not new, but they now had a new context. The date is June 13, 1932, the place Riga. A young man who has just become a father trudges home along the river after an excruciatingly boring day of work. The weather has cleared, and the late, low northern sun lights his way. A familiar temptation appears in the shape of a small, freshly painted Swedish passenger steamer, due to sail that evening for the Baltic island of Visby. "Why should I not go on board and ask to be taken along as a guest?" It is only a dream, but the details are vivid enough to fill a diary page when he records them. "Just now," though,

> we must walk home—one foot before the other—along the uneven cobble-stones of the quai, over the dust and manure. . . . Past the dirty tenements, which remind one so of Russia. Across the flats [where people] are working in their vegetable gardens. The sun catches a string of freight cars up on the embankment. This aggravates me. Why this silly lavishness? . . . Darkness would be a more proper setting for our actions and our thoughts and our creations.

And so he reaches home, with his mind circling through thoughts like these as if some kind of rosary. "There is only responsibility and self-sacrifice; all else is meaningless, all else is vanity, all else is not even interesting; adventure, mystery, even justice do not exist. Learn it, repeat it, comprehend it, wrestle with it, embrace it, cling to it."[16]

Most young fathers have felt such urges and suppressed them; few, however, take the trouble to write them down. Kennan claimed at the time that his "notes" were a protest against pointlessness. He always felt, he explained years later, "that there should be greater things happening in life than I could see around me, wherever I was." Diaries provided a private place to write about them: they were "a protective exercise for myself. . . . When I was happy and busy, I wasn't writing." Annelise confirmed this. "When you read his letters, you would think he was always just so blue." Even Jeanette, from a distance, at times thought so. In daily life, though, as Annelise knew better than anyone else, "he can be so gay." He had, she was sure, a "dual personality," and what he wrote tended to reflect only the morose side of it.[17]

The diary entries, therefore, should be read with this in mind. On June 14, for example, George followed up his fantasy about sailing to Visby with the appalling observation—by today's standards but by that day's as well—that "[w]omen are like the leaden centerboards on sailboats. They keep the boat upright and on its course, but they are not the motive power which makes it go." To "go fast before the wind, you have to eliminate them at all times. And one of them is all you can use; any more pull you down."[18] But Annelise, had she read this, would probably have been more indulgent than insulted, for this was a young man's backward bad-tempered glance in the direction of the independence he had chosen to give up. It did not mean that George was about to turn his fantasies into reality and sail away, unstabilized, from his wife and daughter. The marriage would last for seventy-three and a half years.

"One might well dream of the past," George admonished himself a few months later. One might "watch life outside, through the bars." But one could not participate in it. Pride and spirit were inconsistent with responsibility for other people, so he had become the model married man, faithful "in the ordinary sense as well as in the intellectual." Promiscuity was not sinful, "it was merely sloppy." Confusion, disorder, and uncertainty always accompanied it. And if monogamy was unhealthy, then a certain amount of physical discomfort was the price one paid for dignity.[19]

These outbursts of despair over ordinary life provide a clue, then, as to what to make of the self-described "complaints against civilization" that were beginning to pepper George's diaries:

April 7, 1932: There is, in this world, a preponderance of filth and cruelty and suffering. Cannot something be done to alleviate this situation? Yes, but not by the bourgeois. Why not? . . . Because he cannot be a leader. And the demand of our age is not for followers but for leaders.

July 13: Nothing good can come out of modern civilization, in the broad sense. We have only a group of more or less inferior races, incapable of coping adequately with the environment which technical progress has created. . . . No amount of education and discipline can effectively improve conditions as long as we allow the unfit to breed copiously and to preserve their young.

August 4: The world is at the end of its economic rope. I am at the end of my mental one. . . . I am beginning to comprehend that I am condemned (I know not whether by circumstances or by my own shortcomings) to a rare intellectual isolation. Be it a compliment or a reproach—the fact remains: my mental processes will never be understood by anyone else.[20]

A literal reading of these rants might lead to the conclusion that the third secretary of the U.S. legation in Latvia was becoming a dysfunctional fascist—an Ezra Pound of diplomacy. But this side of Kennan existed alongside his stable marriage and, even more strikingly, his professionalism: two weeks after insisting that he was at the end of his mental rope, he came closer than anyone else of his generation to predicting the Soviet Union's economic and social development over the remainder of the twentieth century.

He did so in response to a query from Robert P. Skinner, the American minister in Riga, as to whether the population of the U.S.S.R. was content with its government. Kennan replied, a bit pointedly, that in a country where millions of people had been killed in military operations, exiled to prison camps, or forced to emigrate—"where the ideals, principles, beliefs and social position of all but a tiny minority have been forcibly turned upside-down by government action"— and where that same regime harbored an ideologically driven hostility toward the rest of the world, "it is scarcely to be expected that most of the people should be as happy as those in other countries." Nevertheless the army, the factory proletariat, and urban youth had benefited from Bolshevik rule: young communists in particular were "as happy as human beings can be," having been relieved to a large extent "of the curses of egotism, romanticism, day-dreaming, introspection, and perplexity which befall the youth of bourgeois countries."

Still, this situation could not last. If the materialist phase of development succeeded, then consumerism—"autos, radios and electric ice-boxes"—would drain away ideological zeal. If it failed, anger over unkept promises would paralyze the regime. Either way, the artificiality now sustaining Soviet self-confidence would evaporate.

Totally untrained to think for himself, unaccustomed to . . . facing his own problems, guided by neither tradition, example, ideals, nor the personal responsibility which acts as a steadying influence in other countries, the young Russian will probably be as helpless and miserable as a babe in the woods. . . . From the most morally unified country in the world, Russia can become over-night the worst moral chaos.

Kennan's analysis went to Washington, but apparently no one read it. He himself forgot about it, and when shown the report sixty-eight years later, he wondered whether it had been "a dream or a premonition."[21] It was neither, but it was as good an illustration as one might hope for of how his triangular personality operated.

A professional who was nothing more than that might have replied to Skinner's query with what could be gleaned from Soviet newspapers and magazines, radio broadcasts, or interviews with émigrés and recent travelers to the U.S.S.R. But Kennan added cultural pessimism to his professionalism: he had developed it in criticizing American consumerism, but he now applied it to a system based on "dialectical materialism" to show how it might someday succumb to a different materialism: too many automobiles and ice-boxes could crash it, but so could too few. To this "no-win" prognosis, Kennan brought another, drawn from pessimism about himself: young people, when cast adrift from the stabilizing influences of tradition, principles, and personal responsibility, were apt to founder.

What this report reflected, therefore, was indeed the "far-seeing eye" that the State Department inspector in Riga three years earlier had sensed.[22] What Kennan's diaries reveal, however, is the personal tension that lay behind his professional accomplishments, and that would in the future endanger them.

III.

"Election day today," Annelise wrote George from Kristiansand on November 8, 1932. "I expect Roosevelt will win. . . . I wonder what they will do about Soviet Russia."[23] So did many others, not least the Russian specialists the Foreign Service had been training. It had done so because it anticipated, even if it did not want, diplomatic recognition. The State Department continued to hold out against the establishment of formal ties long after most other government agencies, business organizations, academics, journalists, and politicians had come to favor it: a persistent opponent was Robert F. Kelley himself, who began the program from which Kennan benefited. Kelley and his colleagues knew, however, that the Soviet regime was not going to disappear anytime soon, that the pressures to deal with it would become irresistible. Franklin D. Roosevelt had given no clue during the campaign as to what his attitude might be, but his willingness to jettison ineffective policies—whatever their purview—was clear enough. So there were expectations, by the time he took office in March 1933, that the department's young

Russianists would soon have more to do than simply watch events from a distance in Riga.[24]

Life there, in the meantime, had become more difficult. The Foreign Service had begun to reduce pay and allowances. George was tired from working too hard, Annelise reported to Jeanette: "He isn't gloomy at home or with me. I know you must think he is from his letters." Even on a shoestring, they were still entertaining. And they were planning a winter break in Norway.[25]

It took place against the background of Hitler's coming to power, and here Kennan's "far-seeing eye" failed him. He found Germany "pitiable and slightly repulsive in its sleep, loud-mouthed and obstreperous in its waking hours. God knew which condition was preferable." The Nazi revolution was not "a real awakening," though, but "only a nightmare." So the month in Kristiansand, which the Nazis would occupy seven years later, was idyllic. There were days of skiing and sledding, nights of eating and drinking, and at the end of the visit he wrote Jeanette with a sense of contentment that must have astonished her:

> [T]he Sørensens' home is a castle, and when I sit there in an arm-chair by the radio, and hear the preparations for supper, and watch Mosik (Annelise's younger sister and a very sweet girl) doing her lessons, and hear the younger boy (Per Sven) come in from skiing, and know that Mr. Sørensen and the older boy are finishing a day's work in the office down below, I drink in all the charm (which we never quite knew) of a permanent home, unaffected by wars and crises, where the generations come and go, and where nastiness and mistrust are unknown.

There were, he added, no great hopes in such a life, but also no great horrors. So why go on storming heights, frazzling nerves, and beating wings against the limitations of human existence when a person could live like this, "reconciled to death and oblivion, but sure of the comfort and security of his measured days"?[26] It was as if Kristiansand had become the ship on which the younger George had more than once dreamed of sailing away.

Back in Riga, he wrote one weekend in May, the baby had been put to bed, they didn't want any supper, the evening sun was shining horizontally into the living room, and the shouting of children playing outside mingled with the clock's ticking to complete the day's boredom. "I am 29 years old and presumably in the prime of life." Weekdays were busy: "I'm still enough of a kid to become absorbed in my work, when I have to do it." Relaxation allowed thinking about the future.

The real priority, "timid government clerks that we are," was to hang on until another career became possible. The Foreign Service had yet to decide what to do with him: "We may stay on here indefinitely. We may very well be transferred tomorrow." Where? The chances were as good for Moscow as for Peking, Berlin, or even Washington.[27]

It was not up to Kennan to decide such matters, but his superiors in the State Department had begun to notice him—despite neglecting his prophecy on the Soviet Union's future. A report on Moscow's gold and foreign currency accounts, prepared in the fall of 1932, elicited praise from Under Secretary of State William R. Castle, Jr. And a study of Soviet commercial treaties, prepared in April 1933, with the possibility of recognition in mind, made its way through the State Department to the White House itself. This was, however, an inauspicious initiation into the Washington policy-making process, because while negotiating terms of recognition with Soviet foreign minister Maxim Litvinov the following November, President Roosevelt suggested precisely the language—relating to the treatment of foreign nationals inside the U.S.S.R.—that Kennan had advised against using.[28]

The Kennans were back in the United States by then, having left Grace with the Sørensens in Kristiansand. They had planned the trip chiefly for family reasons. Kent senior was eighty-one and in precarious health. "As one year after another is sliced off from our allotted span," he had written George with mournful formality the previous winter, "we may well look with some misgivings at the diminished balance which remains." It would be Annelise's first visit: "To see America which I have heard and read so much about and to meet you all," she wrote Jeanette, "will be 'grand.'" The trip almost didn't happen because the State Department grumbled about Kennan's leaving the Riga legation understaffed, but Felix Cole, who ran the Russian Section, stood up for George, citing his family obligations together with the fact that he and Annelise had already given up their dacha, stored their furniture, and made all of their preparations.[29]

Many years later Loy Henderson, a longtime Foreign Service colleague, insisted that Kennan had asked for leave and rushed home knowing that the Roosevelt administration was about to recognize the Soviet Union: "George never misses an opportunity." This seems unlikely: the trip was authorized before anyone knew that Litvinov would be traveling to Washington. Kennan did spend three weeks in the Division of Eastern European Affairs helping to prepare for the upcoming talks, but he was no enthusiast for recognition, having convinced himself through his Riga research that the U.S.S.R. would violate whatever agreements were made with it. During the critical phase of the Roosevelt-Litvinov negotiations in mid-November, Kennan was not on the scene at all, but back in Milwaukee.[30]

George had sent Annelise ahead of him to save money—Washington hotels were expensive. So, he wrote Jeanette, he was "entrusting my youthful wife to your care." "[I]t's a shame that you aren't here to see the furor your wife is causing," she replied a few days later. Men were commenting: "That young sister-in-law is certainly a peach." George's father, pleased that Annelise had come five thousand miles to see him, met her at the door and embraced her without a word. Louise did too, and "we all wiped our eyes." She gave a tea that afternoon for the daughter-in-law she had just met, an occasion unusual enough to rate coverage in the *Milwaukee Journal.* Jeanette was "amazed at the amount of wisdom her sleek young head holds." She was equally astonished "at what a good husband you're making. I really thought you'd be quite a rotten one." Then she added: "She'll keep you from becoming 'queer.' And people who are too queer are neither happy nor effective as a rule."[31]

George's own visit was brief. He found the house overheated, probably because the vitality of its occupants was so low. Kent senior received his son in bed, in a room that darkened as they talked. One of the old man's legs kept sliding off onto the floor: George wanted to raise it to make him comfortable, but "some Kennan-ish repression made it impossible for me to follow even that little tender impulse, just as it has always made it impossible for me to tell him any of the things I should liked to have told him, throughout a number of years." "When you bade me good bye last Saturday," Kent wrote George on November 24, "whole waves and billows of sadness passed over me, . . . in view of my age, that I might never see you again."[32] The premonition proved accurate: Kossuth Kent Kennan died, not unexpectedly, on December 9. But by that time his son, quite unexpectedly, was on his way to Moscow.

IV.

"The ranks of American diplomatists have included, over the decades, many unusual people," George F. Kennan wrote in 1972. Among the most striking, "both in his virtues and in his weaknesses," was William C. Bullitt. A Philadelphia

aristocrat and a Yale graduate, Bullitt had been an ardent supporter of Woodrow
Wilson but also of the Bolshevik Revolution. The president's principal adviser and
confidant, Colonel Edward M. House, sent him to Moscow early in 1919 to try
to establish contacts with the new Soviet government, but Wilson—ill and preoccupied with the Paris Peace Conference—ignored Bullitt upon his return. So
he turned on Wilson publicly, bitterly, and unforgivingly. In 1924 Bullitt married
Louise Bryant, widow of the radical journalist John Reed, but divorced her
six years later. By then he had become a patient of Sigmund Freud, with whom he
collaborated on a highly critical psychobiography of Wilson—fortunately still
unpublished when, in 1932, Bullitt met Franklin D. Roosevelt. The new president made Bullitt his unofficial agent on the issue of Soviet recognition. Shortly
after signing the agreement establishing diplomatic relations, on November 17,
1933, Roosevelt nominated Bullitt to become the first U.S. ambassador to the
U.S.S.R.[33]

Now back from Milwaukee, Kennan was walking through the corridors of the
State Department one day with a friend, who suggested that he ought to meet
Bullitt: "Let's see whether we can find him." The new ambassador was in his office,
asked Kennan some questions about Soviet transportation and finance, which he
was able to answer, and then inquired as to whether he spoke Russian well enough
to interpret. Kennan replied that he did, whereupon Bullitt said that he was leaving in a few days for Moscow: "Could you be ready in time to come along with
me?" "The room," George recalled, "rocked around me." The offer was "a thunder
stroke of good luck" after years of preparation, and the Kennans were ready to sail
on the following Monday. They traveled with Bullitt on the SS *President Harding*,
from where George wrote his family: "Bullitt is a splendid man; it is an education
just to have him around. Besides that, . . . I can't forget that it is a rare feather in
my cap to be included on this expedition at all."[34]

"Oh, he was so excited," Annelise remembered. But the passage was rough, so
much so that Bullitt ruled out drinking red wine at dinner—"it's been shaken up
too much"—and insisted on providing everyone with champagne. George, who
spent much of the voyage in his cabin nursing a cold, remembered vividly the
afternoon Bullitt came in, sat on his bunk, and began to talk. "I was naturally
curious about the character of this brilliant and fast-moving man who had so suddenly become my immediate superior." He conveyed an impression of "enormous
charm, confidence, and vitality," but George also detected sensitivity, egocentric-
ity, and pride, as well as "a certain dangerous freedom—the freedom of a man

who, as he himself confessed to me on that occasion, had never subordinated his life to the needs of any other human being."[35]

Upon arrival at Le Havre, Annelise went on to Kristiansand to see Grace and await instructions, while the new ambassador and his entourage proceeded to Paris. There Kennan was surprised to be warmly welcomed by "fair-weather"— and no doubt envious—Foreign Service friends. The Bullitt group then went by train to Berlin, and from there through Poland to the Soviet border. A solemn representative from the Ministry of Foreign Affairs was waiting, and a banquet was served "with a touching Russian mixture of good will and inefficiency."

> Soon we were off again, in one of the big wide Russian sleeping cars. I shared a [compartment] with a Russian newspaper man [who] stripped to his underwear, lay down in the upper berth and snored healthily, but I was too excited to sleep, and bobbed up continually during the night, everytime the train stopped, to look at the little Russian stations, the snow-covered platforms, the booted citizens from the cars up ahead running through the icy cold with their little tea-pots to the boiling water tap which is the prime necessity of every station.

The next morning in Moscow there was a mix-up, with Bullitt and the official greeters going in one direction and the secretaries, servants, and baggage going in another. It fell to Kennan to reconnect them, which he did with sufficient efficiency "that we ended up with several more bags than we had when we started."[36]

That was December 11, 1933. On December 13 the new U.S. ambassador and his party were driven through the walls of the Kremlin to present credentials to the Soviet "president," Mikhail Kalinin. While the ceremony was under way, an Associated Press photographer sneaked a shot of the coatrack outside, with five hats lined up on a shelf above it. The caption identified three, a derby, a fedora, and a military cap, as belonging to Foreign Minister Litvinov and his aides. The other two were shiny silk top hats, said to have been worn by William C. Bullitt and his "secretary George Kennan." This was Kennan's first experience with inaccurate journalism, for in fact "I was too cheap to buy one." He did, however, appear in the official photographs, a tall, thin young man, standing politely behind the dignitaries in a cutaway and striped pants, ready to translate for them when needed. Even without his own top hat, it was the high point so far of his diplomatic career: "I almost fainted . . . to think where I was and what I was doing."[37]

V.

There was another reason to feel faint, though, because on December 12 George had received, through State Department channels, Jeanette's telegram conveying the news that his father had died. "It is somewhat to my own horror," he wrote her on the fourteenth, that he had been able to carry on "almost as though nothing had happened." The shock was not the death so much as "the inadequacy of our last visit, and the feeling that he may never have realized how much I loved him." It was the final episode of the tragedy that had begun when their mother died.

> I would like to hope that God is now satisfied with his handiwork—and I like to picture Father in a Heaven like the country place at Nagawicka thirty-five years ago, with himself no longer only a Kennan and our mother no longer only a James, but both of them full, complete beings, and ourselves as the group of understanding children we should have been—and then the breeze coming off the lake on summer afternoons, and the sounds of the grasshoppers and the crickets and frogs and the barking of the dogs across the lake on the long summer nights.

During the past few days in Moscow, George told his sister, he had been through "the most interesting and absorbing things I have ever experienced," but they seemed nonetheless trifling and foolish. "I have no heart to write about them now."[38]

He did write later about the "kaleidoscopic" ten days Bullitt had spent in Moscow. Kennan went to the ballet with the Litvinov family, and then to a performance of Chekhov's *The Cherry Orchard* accompanied by, improbably, Harpo Marx: there is unfortunately no record of what, if anything, they talked about. Backstage, however, they met the playwright's widow—a thrill because Kennan already had in mind someday writing Chekhov's biography. He called at the Foreign Office and other diplomatic missions, and then with Keith Merrill, the State Department's specialist on overseas buildings, drove to the outskirts of the city to pace off prospective embassy construction sites, with the temperature at twenty below zero. Too excited to go to bed when the day's activities were done, the Americans would sit around and talk until four or five in the morning. Kennan remembered it as a wonderful time, an example of "what Soviet-American relations *might*, in other circumstances, have been."[39]

He had Bullitt to thank for it all. "When I came back to Washington last fall,"

Kennan wrote him at the end of December, "I was—like a number of other young men in the service—pretty well beaten down by the bureaucracy. I despaired of ever getting work of any genuine significance." Bullitt could well understand, therefore, that "the events of the last few weeks took my breath away." Kennan was grateful "for the confidence and responsibility you've given me. They've done me more good than anything could have, . . . [and] the beneficial effect will wear for a long time to come." Bullitt too was pleased. "The men at the head of the Soviet Government," he wrote President Roosevelt, "are extremely eager to have contact with anyone who has first-rate intelligence and dimension as a human being. They were, for example, delighted by young Kennan."[40]

Part II

FIVE

The Origins of Soviet–American Relations: 1933–1936

"THE BLOW HAS FALLEN NOW, WITH A BANG," GEORGE WROTE Annelise from Riga on December 29, 1933: "It is a mean one, but we'll make the best of it." He had gone there to collect their possessions while Bullitt returned temporarily to the United States; but now the State Department had ordered Kennan back to Moscow to set up the new American embassy. However thrilling the previous weeks had been, this was not a task he welcomed. He would not be, as he had hoped, *chargé d'affaires.* The salary and benefits would be minimal, and his status would be "full of dangers and responsibilities." Should Annelise choose to join him, she would be the only Foreign Service wife in town, and because conditions were difficult, Grace would have to stay in Kristiansand. "You'll hate the hotel, and there won't be much for you to do there." He would leave it to her: "If you don't want to do it, you don't have to." But "I am damned anxious to have you with me again as soon as possible. After all, darling, we are man and wife, aren't we?"[1]

The assignment had come about because Bullitt insisted on it. He wanted Kennan in Moscow until the full embassy staff arrived, supervising building activities "and other urgent matters." The State Department questioned Kennan's training for such duties, but Soviet officials had asked specifically for him because of his linguistic fluency. They also associated him with the first George Kennan, who had exposed the Siberian prison conditions under which some of them, as young revolutionaries, had once been held. Bullitt took the issue to Roosevelt himself: without someone like Kennan to deal with authorities at the top, the staff could arrive in February to find their accommodations half finished, creating "extreme inefficiency and possibly . . . endanger[ing] life." Faced with this onslaught, the department capitulated. Kennan was "detailed for purpose outlined."[2]

He arrived in Moscow on January 3, 1934, and Annelise joined him two weeks later. "There is nothing I want to do more dear," she had replied to him. "I don't think it will be bad. . . . As long as we are together I don't care." She found George, still a month shy of his thirtieth birthday, the sole responsible representative of the United States of America in the Union of Soviet Socialist Republics.[3]

I.

They lived, for the moment, in the National Hotel, just off Red Square. With restaurants slow and the food bad, Annelise cooked for George in their room, using a hot plate on a whiskey case behind a screen. Under construction next door was the Mokhovaya, named for the street on which it was located, the building that was to be the temporary embassy chancery. Spaso House, the American ambassador's future residence, stood on a side street a mile west. Constructed by a wealthy merchant in 1914, it had been seized by the Soviet government, which used it for offices and apartments and was now leasing it to the Americans, along with the Mokhovaya, until a new residence and chancery could be built on a bluff in the Sparrow Hills, overlooking the city. Bullitt had proposed the location—it could be, he argued, a "Monticello in Moscow"—and Josef Stalin agreed at the end of a vodka-fueled Kremlin dinner, sealing the pledge by kissing the astonished ambassador. But the diplomatic climate soon cooled, and the compound never got built. Spaso House and the Mokhovaya were still the principal American facilities in Moscow when Kennan himself became ambassador in 1952.[4]

Kennan's job was to negotiate the leases, oversee construction and remodeling, arrange gas and telephone service, and clear shipments of office supplies and furniture through customs so that Bullitt and his staff would have places to live and work. Helping out were a male stenographer, the State Department architect Keith Merrill, and Charles W. Thayer, a young West Point graduate who had shown up in Moscow hoping to acquire Russian and a position in the Foreign Service. Kennan hired him; Thayer found a Harley-Davidson and was soon zooming around town on official business, "the ear tabs of his Russian fur cap flapping wildly in the wind." This bare-bones establishment operated without codes, safes, security, couriers, or even at first an office. Contrary to Bullitt's expectations, it had no access to the highest authorities: instead it dealt with a ponderously inefficient bureaucracy, the respective parts of which usually did not connect. "Nevertheless," Kennan recalled, "I felt that we, with our absence of bureaucracy, accomplished more in a few weeks than did the full embassy staff, when it arrived, over the first year of its existence."[5]

"All this had to be done," George wrote his cousin Charlie James, "in a place which has the world's craziest financial system," on behalf of a government—his own—"which has the world's craziest system of expenditure control." The State Department provided only minimal instructions, so Kennan meticulously documented every meeting, phone call, and disbursement of funds. He was attempting to master Soviet laws on insurance—such as they were—translating tortuously worded contracts, juggling the intricacies of currency exchange, assigning space in the still-uncompleted Mokhovaya, urging the eviction of Spaso's recalcitrant tenants, even bargaining on hotel rates for the incoming staff. The manager of the National agreed with Kennan that any Western European establishment would happily give official Americans a 25 percent discount, but that was because "the capitalist world had an economic crisis and Soviet Russia did not."

Kennan was also becoming an expert on menu planning, interior decorating, trade promotion, tourism, emigration, marriage counseling, and mortuary science. He spent hours one day trying to explain the concept of a "quick lunch" to the kitchen staff at the Savoy Hotel, where the Americans had relocated because the National would not budge on its room rates: he could provide recipes for "light, simple dishes," to be prepared "at very low cost." With his assistants, Kennan was measuring the rooms in Spaso House for rugs and draperies, while trying to meet the demands of Americans already in the Soviet Union who had hitherto lacked an embassy to which to turn: there were export-hungry businessmen, tourists with lost passports, requests for help with exit visas, questions about divorce proceedings, and in one instance the dilemma of whether to disinter and photograph a corpse in Chelyabinsk in order to persuade its widow in Wisconsin that it indeed had expired.

On the night before Bullitt's return, it fell to Kennan, Thayer, and Merrill to wrestle the ambassador's bed up the grand staircase at Spaso. They also had to tell him that, for several more months until the Mokhovaya was ready, his residence would double as the embassy chancery. Bullitt was "steaming with fury." There were evenings, Kennan remembered, when he and the other official Americans in Moscow, "assembled in my hotel room, gloomily sipping our highballs and watching the mice play hide-and-seek along the base-boards," were on the verge of admitting defeat, fearing that they would soon have to "give it up and sneak shame-facedly away, the laughing-stock of Europe."[6]

"The honeymoon atmosphere had evaporated completely," Bullitt reported to Roosevelt a few weeks after his arrival back in Moscow on March 7. The Soviets' hostility toward all capitalist countries, muffled during the negotiations leading to recognition, was now coming out. The only way to deal with them would be to offer carrots but to make it clear that if these were refused, "they will receive the club on the behind." The embassy staff was the only "bright spot in the murky sky. . . . I am delighted with every man."[7]

They were impressive. Loy Henderson, who went with Bullitt to Moscow as second secretary, understood that he wanted "dash, brilliance, imagination and enthusiasm," and this he got. For in addition to Kennan and Henderson, the embassy now had three other Foreign Service officers whose careers would shape Soviet-American relations well into the Cold War. One was Elbridge Durbrow, who followed Soviet economic affairs and would serve with Kennan again in Moscow during the mid-1940s. A second was Bertel E. Kuniholm, a Kelley protégé who had studied Russian in Paris, and would later report on Soviet activities in Iran. A third, Charles E. (Chip) Bohlen, also trained with Kelley, became Kennan's closest colleague, and would succeed him as ambassador to the Soviet Union in 1953. "In numberless verbal encounters, then and over ensuing decades," Kennan recalled, "our agreements and differences would be sternly and ruthlessly talked out, sometimes with a heat so white that casual bystanders would conclude we had broken for life." But "no friendship has ever meant more to me than his."[8]

Those debates started in Moscow, and Annelise witnessed them. Because of the housing shortage, Bullitt had initially prohibited wives from accompanying his staff, but she was already there and in much demand. She found the life exhilarating: "We were young, and gay; we danced all night; but we would also talk all night." Like the other Americans, the Kennans now had a room at the Savoy, where almost everyone was cooking on the hot plates Annelise had pioneered—when the electricity worked. Telephones functioned erratically, often with only labored breathing at the other end. Owing to ill-conceived State Department economy measures, there was no embassy automobile, so Intourist provided chauffeured Lincolns at rates that Kennan believed soon would have paid for one. With taxis scarce, the only alternative was motorcycles: Annelise recalled riding to one dinner in the sidecar dressed in a long formal gown, while George, in white tie, hung on precariously behind the driver. But the other embassies threw great parties, and as Durbrow recalled decades later: "You made better and closer friends in Moscow than any post I've ever heard about or been in."[9]

There were also opportunities for George—within the limits the secret police allowed—to begin to feel himself Russian. "Just to ride on a street-car, if you can understand the conversation, is an experience," he wrote Jeanette. One Sunday in May, with summer having suddenly arrived, the Kennans and several friends picnicked as close as they could get to Stalin's dacha. "[W]e did not see the big boy," but skirting the walls of his estate, they found a bluff overlooking the Moscow River filled with families making themselves at home, "with all the delightful informality which is the charm of the Russian countryside." Security men appeared, "asked where we 'citizens' might be from and what we were doing there, and subsided from view just as abruptly upon learning that we were not 'citizens' at all, but only a bunch of bourgeois from the American Embassy."[10]

From such daytime excursions and late-night discussions, Kennan gained some preliminary impressions of the Soviet experiment. He expressed these most clearly in a handwritten letter, sent by diplomatic courier, for his sister's eyes only:

> I find myself continually torn between sympathy for a nation which, within the limitations of its own character and an imported dogma, is trying to reconstruct its life on a basis finer and sounder than that of any other country anywhere, and disgust with the bigotry and arrogance of its leaders, who not only refuse to recognize their own mistakes and limitations but pretend that they have found the solution of all the problems of the rest of the world in their crude interpretation of a worn-out doctrine.

"I realize," George admitted, "that no revolution is entirely discriminate, or ever could be, but it could, at least, make its aim an intelligent discrimination." He would prefer one that "would raise the best elements of society—and not the worst—out of the futility and tragedy which unfortunately surrounds their existence. And this is the sort of revolution which Moscow has not got to offer!"[11]

Meanwhile Bullitt was worrying about the physical toll Moscow life was taking on his staff. There was, he advised the State Department, a form of acute indigestion, caused by the excessive use of canned food, that mimicked the symptoms of angina pectoris. One of his subordinates had already suffered such an attack. Russian cuisine was no solution, for even when "obtained at great expense in the best hotels, [it] produces digestive upsets dignified by purple blotches." If his young men were to stay healthy, they would need more frequent leaves than the department normally provided.[12]

The afflicted staff member was Kennan, who had been on duty in Moscow longer than anyone else. Leave was accordingly granted, allowing George a few days in Leningrad for the first time, while Annelise remained behind to set up the Mokhovaya apartment, into which they were finally now able to move. Peter the Great's capital, George wrote Jeanette, had been erected atop the poverty and suffering that Gogol, Dostoyevsky, and Chekhov had described, "like a flower on a manure-heap." The Bolsheviks had made no effort to clean up the mess. One of the unhealthiest in the world, the city should never have been built and would perhaps one day sink back into the swamp from which Peter had raised it.

George went on from Leningrad to Norway, where Annelise was to join him. As the mail boat from Oslo approached Kristiansand, having called at each small, freshly painted town along the way, he felt the contrast between Soviet and Scandinavian life that would always move him: "It is wonderful to see the young people all out here on vacation, clean and tanned and so strong and well-built as to put our own younger generation to shame." Soon "we will pass the island where the Sørensen family have their summer house, and some of the family will probably stand on the rocks and wave handkerchiefs and my little daughter will stare solemnly at the white boat and wonder what it's all about.... [W]hen she finally sees me, I'm sure she'll draw a wry face and clutch her grandmother's skirts for protection."[13]

II.

Kristiansand provided protection for George as well. It reunited his family: he had not seen Grace since leaving for the United States the previous September. She was, he wrote Bullitt, "so absurdly healthy" that he hated to take her away from "this paradise of cleanliness, order, and well-fed respectability." His own health had improved: "I feel perfectly well again now." And he had bought a seagoing sailboat. The experienced Norwegians, he added in a letter to Charlie James, had been "waiting for me to turn turtle in one of their numerous local squalls or bust up on one of their numerous local reefs." But he had come through the first four weeks without incident: "I regard my responsibility as a matter of national prestige."[14]

George would still be sailing Norwegian waters well into his eighties. In the summer of 1934, though, he was developing a higher ambition: he wanted to become a writer. The Kennan children had grown up in a house filled with books. George and Jeanette shared poems with each other and later a passion for novels.

Reading good fiction, he had written her from Riga the year before, "leaves me tingling with excitement and dissatisfaction." Lives throb with beauty and pathos, and "I am instinctively certain that if my poor intelligence was put into the world for any purpose, it was to act as a reflector and magnifier . . . to drag it out of the corners where it lurks and flash it to a world which sees too little of it."

The key to the greatness of novelists, though, had always been their limitations: "They knew one thing—one country, at the most—and were saturated with it." George envied Chekhov his ignorance of all but Russia, Hemingway his war and its relics, Sinclair Lewis his American Midwest.

> But what can a man do whose life has been lived in a hundred different places, who never had a home after he was thirteen and never noticed anything before, who speaks three languages equally easily? There has been nothing which hung together, nothing coherent, nothing even representative or symbolic about my life from the beginning. . . . [My] attention has been scattered around and wasted like the leaves of a tree, and I have only a hopeless hodgepodge of fading, incoherent impressions.

He could of course write about colleagues. If Chekhov could describe Russian villagers so clearly that American readers gasped, "how perfectly true," why couldn't the Moscow diplomatic community be written up in the same way? But literature was also a kind of history: it portrayed "a given class at a given time, with all its problems, its suffering and its hopes." Diplomats' lives, he finally concluded, were "too insignificant, too accidental, to warrant description."[15]

So too, in George's opinion, was sex. He read *Lady Chatterley's Lover* that summer but found it "not a very good book." Its frankness went nowhere and proved nothing: happiness in life was not contentment in bed. Lawrence's characters shared only a shallow and transitory compatibility. Sex, George insisted, was "not a field for introspection." It should be "only incidental," for people "who spend as little time contemplating its pleasures as they do worrying about its results. . . . [T]here are other things vastly more important."[16]

Perhaps so, but what were they? There was of course the world itself. George had seen more of it than most people and since his 1924 European trip had been filling his diaries with descriptive impressions. Now he hoped to get some of them published. One such piece, "Runo—An Island Relic of Medieval Sweden," did come out in 1935 in the *Canadian Geographical Journal* after having been turned down by *The National Geographic Magazine*: it was George's first appearance in print.[17] But travel writing was not likely to establish a reputation, or to provide an income.

Biography, however, might be an alternative. It allowed seeing beauty, pathos, class, sex, and scenes through someone else's eyes, an attractive possibility for George, who preferred functioning, as he himself put it, "from a certain emotional distance." That brought him back to Chekhov. Late in 1932 he sought State Department clearance to send an essay on "Anton Chekhov and the Bolsheviks" to *The Yale Review*. George's mentors Robert Kelley and Joseph Green (who had moved there from Princeton) liked the article, and the chairman of the department's publication committee allowed that "[i]f Yale can stand it, I can." Yale could not, however, and the piece was never published.[18]

There was, though, another possibility: could George F. Kennan write the life of the first George Kennan? The idea originated in Moscow, where he had found a lively interest in his ancestor: even Kalinin had asked about the connection. It had been awkward, George wrote Jeanette, "having the same name and nationality and having so much the same interests, to explain that I know little more of him than the average reader of his works and have never had any association with his branch of the family." So at some point in the spring of 1934, he asked her to see the elder George Kennan's widow at her home in Medina, New York, and to raise the question of a biography with her.

The visit went badly. Mrs. Kennan, now eighty, remembered George's inadequate thank-you letter, written at the age of seven after his only meeting with his famous namesake. She also resented George's name: convinced, erroneously, that the "Frost" had been meant to honor George A. Frost, the difficult traveling companion her husband had endured in Siberia, she had, she revealed, tried unsuccessfully after young George's birth to get it changed. "Because George Frost Kennan can speak Russian is no reason that he can do full just[ice] to a man who had spent a large part of his life stud[y]ing different races," Mrs. Kennan wrote Jeanette. "You see, my dear, you don't know anything of . . . our life, the world we knew, or our tastes, so extremely different from your father's or any of the [other] Kennan's." The current George Kennan had not fitted himself to be a writer, having neither style nor originality nor personality in expression. "[H]e may get all these things later in life after more experience," but if the first George Kennan's life were ever to be written, it would have to be by an "experienced biographer."

George was stung by the brush-off. "It is no fault of mine—nor is it very important—that my middle name is Frost," he complained to Jeanette. "I can also not feel apologetic about letters I may have written as a boy. Anyone who can remember the anguish of a child who is forced to try to write letters to grown-ups whom he scarcely knows will not take too seriously the products of these unnatural efforts." As for not understanding that branch of the Kennan family, he had, after all, managed to understand "many other sets of tastes and ideas and acquaintances." But with Mrs. Kennan convinced "that we are a strange crowd of backwoodsmen," and that "we would like . . . to ride into fame on the coattails of an illustrious cousin," there was little point in pursuing the matter. "I should prefer to make my progress as a Russian specialist independently."[19]

Whether because of this rejection or not, George admitted to Jeanette at the beginning of August that—despite his summer in Kristiansand—he had been through "a spell of the most miserable nervous depression, which almost made me physically ill." It had to do with his career, his marriage, and reaching the age of thirty.

> I have no illusions about the significance of my petty bureaucratic success nor the qualities which have helped to bring it about. I could take more pride in one page of decent writing than in being an Ambassador. And there are times when I see myself as a spineless, somewhat infantile, futile little man, passively growing older in the bonds of matrimony—missing dreams which grow fainter and fainter, and farther and farther from realization as the years go by.

George had been struck to learn that Jeanette was having similar problems. "We *are* so alike. It's almost embarrassing." And it was "ridiculous" that neither of them had been able to discover what their shared symptoms meant. Perhaps "thwarted ambitions" were "only the scapegoats on[to] which our . . . subconscious minds divert dissatisfaction." They probably reflected the family inheritance "of repression and sacrifice," or perhaps "a strange, stiff, motherless childhood."

The night before, George added, he had written in his notebook of a man sobered by scrapes with catastrophe who was willing to sacrifice much to save a little. There was humor and enjoyment in this, but no great elation: "No fantastic vistas gleam momentarily through the shifting mists." A price had been paid for peace of mind. It brought him "courage and a concentration of strength which he lacked before. His eyes are clear and his nerves are steady." However, "I disrigged my sailboat today and it was very sad."[20]

III.

Bullitt asked Kennan not to hurry back to Moscow. There was a long, hard winter ahead, and the work to be done there was less important than his health. But by the end of July George was ready to return: "I really feel that I have gotten all I can get out of my vacation here, and that to stay longer would only mean to get rusty and lazy from inactivity." The entire family—including Grace and a Norwegian girlfriend of Annelise's who served as a nanny—were back in Moscow by the end of August. "Kuniholm, Kennan, and Bohlen are all working admirably," Bullitt reported to the State Department a few weeks later. "[W]e could run this Embassy with the assistance of these three boys and no superior officers whatever."[21]

Kennan would have blanched at this after going through the previous winter, but he and his family were at least reasonably comfortable in their apartment on the fifth floor of the Mokhovaya. They shared the building with some forty other Americans who lived and worked there, mostly free of friction, with an intimacy and informality unusual in a Foreign Service post. Grace spoke a mixture of Norwegian and English that George found "fluent for this peculiarity." She was, he wrote Jeanette, "a sweet, happy child, and a good companion" who enjoyed family activities, including "the scrubbing of my back, whenever she is allowed to." Dividing her attention between Americans in the Mokhovaya and children in the Kremlin park, Grace "commanded communists and capitalists alike with a queenly contempt for ideological differences."[22]

Annelise had a Russian cook and maid, although it was a mystery to her how they could work so slowly. She had bought George a guitar and was herself learning Russian. "I understand a lot when I hear people speaking, even more when I read." One book on her list was Trotsky's autobiography: "He is a brilliant man, but also very vain." Family finances were better than they had been for some time, with George having received a promotion and a salary increase—the apartment came free. He was even considering co-purchasing, with Annelise's father, the island off Kristiansand where they had spent the summer: "It might provide for little Grace—as Nagawicka did for us—the symbol of a home, something which she will otherwise lack sadly as long as we continue our wandering existence."[23]

In the privacy of his diary, however, George was as gloomy as ever. He could not help but contrast the Soviet experience with "the neurotic unreality of our own." Russians lived life "in the raw, . . . good and evil, drunk and sober, loving and quarreling, laughing and weeping—all that human life is and does anywhere—but all the more simple and direct and therefore stronger." Their revolution, like nature, was lavish and careless. "Its victims are no more to it than the thousands of seeds which are cast to the wind, in order that one tree may grow." The survivors, though, possessed a healthy, earthy vitality that attracted him despite the fact that it would quickly crush him, "as it crushes all forms of weakness." So much for Kennan's confidence, two years earlier in Riga, that the Soviet system carried within itself the seeds of its own self-destruction.[24]

One visitor to Moscow that fall was George's half-brother Kent, then twenty-one, who spent a month in Bohlen's temporarily vacant apartment. Kent got to practice on the Spaso House grand piano while the ambassador was away. He relished seeing opera and ballet at the Bolshoi—"lavishly mounted, frequently with a good deal of gimmicky stage business like rising moons and setting suns (in which the Russian audiences seemed to take a certain naïve delight)"—and even managed to get into a performance of Dimitri Shostakovich's controversial *Lady Macbeth of Mtsensk* before Stalin shut it down. Annelise found it alarming, though, that Kent was even thinner than George, and George worried about his shyness. "I see in him," he wrote Jeanette, the "restless ghost (and a very gaunt ghost it is) of my former self." Kent remembered the visit as an exciting experience, with George and his colleagues constantly dropping into each other's apartments, confusing the maids and the hidden microphones with code words, expecting GPU eavesdropping—that was the current acronym for the secret police—on every telephone call.[25]

On November 7, the seventeenth anniversary of the Bolshevik Revolution, the Kennans watched the six-hour military parade in Red Square from their apartment windows. The next day George and Annelise attended their first Kremlin reception, mounting a terrifyingly high straight staircase that "made us feel like ants" to enter the great ballroom where Ivan the Terrible had once received foreign emissaries. "America," Annelise wrote, "seems far away." Life in Moscow was getting strenuous again, George complained later that month, as much because of social obligations as office work. In a single week the Kennans went to three dinners, three parties, and an impromptu luncheon, while giving another dinner and a tea. One event, hosted by the Russians, began at eleven in the evening and lasted until three-thirty in the morning. "I sometimes have misgivings as to how long I can stand it."[26]

Not long at all, as it turned out. George wrote that letter on December 2, 1934. Ten days later he fell ill with severe stomach pains, together with the inability to keep food down. "Poor boy," Annelise wrote Jeanette on the twenty-first: "He hadn't had anything to eat for 40 hours." As a consequence, George missed the most famous party ever held at Spaso House: the Christmas Eve celebration at which Thayer, responding to Bullitt's instructions to "make it good," brought in trained seals from the Moscow Circus to slither across the ballroom balancing champagne glasses on their noses. Annelise did not miss it: "I remember that very well." But George lay in bed at the Mokhovaya, entertained only by Grace, the two of them one "in our preoccupation with the present, our indifference to past and future."[27]

"He looks pretty bad to me," the embassy counselor, John C. Wiley, reported to Bullitt, who was in Washington. Soviet doctors had recommended a sanatorium in Germany or Austria. "Private means zero," but "Kennan is a valuable asset to the Service." Bullitt needed no prompting. "I am so fond of that boy and have such confidence in him that I hate to see him leave Moscow," but he knew from his own experience the agonies of ulcers. Could Kennan come to Washington for free treatment at the Naval Hospital? "[T]he President's physician . . . is a good friend of mine and would see to it that you had every possible care." But George's Foreign Service superiors decided instead to keep him in Europe, temporarily assigning him to the nearest post so that he would not have to take sick leave. They had been "magnificent," he wrote Jeanette. "I could embrace the old State Department for that, columns, conservatism, intrigues, and all."[28]

As for himself, "I am not unpleased at this turn of events." After months of feeling miserable while being told that he was suffering from an imaginary ailment, or perhaps "the lack of another drink," convalescence would be welcome. And so one night in mid-January 1935 his friends put him on the train to Warsaw. "Many of them, I was later told, never expected to see me again." He was still sick enough to have to be nursed through the night by the sleeping car porter—all the more so for discovering that he had failed to pack passport, visas, and other necessary papers. That required an extra day at the border and further treatment by the village doctor: the station was the one through which he and Bullitt had passed, with much greater ceremony, a little over a year before. Kennan finally made it to Vienna, where duodenal ulcers were confirmed, probably aggravated by inadequate treatment of the amoebic dysentery that had laid George low on his European trip with Nick Messolonghitis a decade earlier. He was sent off to Sanatorium Gutenbrunn, in the town of Baden on the edge of the Wienerwald and at the foot of the Alps, with firm instructions: "rest and diet."[29]

IV.

George knew European "cures" too well, he assured Jeanette—and, he might have added, his Thomas Mann—to see any *Magic Mountain* glamour in the Gutenbrunn. His treatment was "a beneficial form of torture." Except for his doctor's visits and the delivery of scanty meals, George was left alone and required to stay in bed, a jarring contrast to the hyperactivity of the past year. "Just think of it. Who else could contrive in these harassed days to set aside [even] one hour . . . to no further purpose than the contemplation of three walls, a ceiling, two cupboards, a washbowl, a mirror, a coat rack, and the fading, shifting universe of his own memory?"[30]

The doctor was Frieda Por, a Hungarian Jew who became a lifelong friend. "Believe me," George later recalled, "for a Jewish woman to become a staff physician in Gutenbrunn in those days—a very conservative old Austrian sanatorium with all the other doctors real Viennese—that was quite an achievement." Her therapy was as much psychological as physical. Whether at her behest or on his own, George read Freud for the first time. "I talked with her many times about this," the debates extending "high and wide" into the night. She defended the power of human will and the possibilities for happiness, but only, he suspected, as someone who was neither free nor happy and "dares not admit it." He complained that "your idea of what to do with a patient who has problems like [mine] is to wrap them in soft blankets and tell them not to be ashamed of anything they ever did. That it's all their parents' fault." George preferred the grimmer Puritan tradition, which was "that you jolly well bite the bullet if you have problems. . . . I think will power has got something to do with it." But his diary shows him wrestling with himself:

George #1: You feel the need of unburdening your soul to the Frau Doktor. You are anxious to tell her that you are depressed. You had not, after all, coped with life successfully in the past. That was clear enough from the very fact that you, a young man, in the prime of life, should be lying in this sanatorium together with a lot of old syphilitics and anemic women.

George #2: Whence this urge to confession? Did you really think that she could help you? You know she couldn't. You know no woman could, unless she were beyond the last trace of femininity and treated you with the unsparing frankness and the contempt which you deserve.

George #1: Well, after all, she is in charge of my treatment. Should she not know the state of mind of her patient?

George #2: Oho, you goddam hypocrite! None of that stuff! No sir! None of your limp excuses! You are in a sanatorium, not a psychopathic clinic. It's your stomach that is being treated, not your head. If you think your head needs treating, then go to a psychiatrist, but don't come sneaking around to lady stomach doctors with your little intimate confidences. Learn to take it, Kennan. It's your problem.

George did acknowledge, though, at least some relationship between his stomach and his head. "I must lack independence of character," he wrote Bullitt, "because I react so strongly to the confidence or mistrust of others." Loy Henderson, who supervised his work in Moscow, saw a direct connection between Kennan's ambition and his health: when things got difficult, he would get sick. Years later Kennan saw the connection as well: "I was too tense, too anxious to please my superiors and to measure up to the responsibilities I had. I noticed that when I left government, the ulcers stopped, because I was no longer responsible to anyone but myself."[31]

For the moment, though, George was using his Gutenbrunn time for self-analysis. Physical sickness, he thought, might provide a path to spiritual recovery. But he had no normal spiritual life, only the pressures of responsibility. So "I dare not relax. . . . I am like a man on a bicycle: as long as I keep going, I can balance; if I stop, I fall." What if the body could not stand it? What if there were more physical collapses, each worse than the other? There might be refuge in sleep, sport, and spartan life, but where would that leave Annelise? "Who is going to give her companionship in youth, gaiety, and human society?"

Communion with the past might be another way to heal. George's diary from these months contains detailed accounts of being dragged in sullen stubbornness to dancing school as a child, of being lonely at St. John's and looking forward to the liberation of holidays, of then spending them by himself at home sulking, reading "the dirty poems" in his father's edition of Robert Burns, snatched furtively from the living room bookshelf. Perhaps he had been trying to warn the grown-ups that they were raising "an unruly, neurotic child," who was appealing for help. George sent Jeanette a sixteen-page unfinished account of his life as a fledgling diplomat in Geneva and Hamburg, "the unhappy little adjustments of a scared young American, who cracks up now and then with a loud thud." And he wrote elegiacally to Cyrus Follmer about "associations of other days" in Berlin, where there were "rare friends in whose eyes and words the world and life were once so nicely mirrored." There had been none like that in Moscow or Riga. "Never since has life glowed so richly and so deeply. It probably never will."

Dreams became vivid enough to record, if not to analyze. The Foreign Service, irritated by George's messy accounts, tells him it has no further need for his services. Thinking of his family, he pleads for his job, offers if necessary to become a typist, but finds that his superiors have only been giving him "a good scare." Jews parade along the Riga Strand holding coffee cups to their mouths—but they could also be thermometers. A Doberman follows George out of a St. Petersburg restaurant where the murdered tsar lies on a bier, surrounded by his security men sitting at tables. The animal rears as if to attack, but then turns to show a sign on his back indicating that he is "an imperial watch-dog, with full official status." George bows in acknowledgment, introducing himself formally as "Kennan, . . . of the American Embassy."[32]

By mid-February, Annelise and Grace had joined George in Baden. "They take too much time," he groused to Jeanette in a letter on March 6. "Don't idealize our marriage. It's been near enough the rocks on more than one occasion." But the same letter devotes four pages to a rhapsodic description of the island off Kristiansand that he and Annelise's father hoped to buy. And when his wife and daughter left in April for a visit to Norway, George wrote wistfully, in his diary, of their departure:

> Annelise and Grace leaned out of the [train] window. . . . Annelise tried hard and unsuccessfully not to cry. Grace ran her lips dreamily along the metal rim of the window. I stared hard, for a while, into the blue glaze of the side of the car. Annelise could not reach down far enough to kiss me, so she gave me her hand, and I kissed it. Then Grace took off her woolen glove and held her hand out, too, for the same purpose. That saved the moment—if not the day.

"You can't come back to[o] soon for me," George wrote Annelise on the twentieth. A few days later he told Jeanette that "we are just sentimental enough to abandon our brave plan of staying separated until July." The family would be back in May.[33]

George was still searching out paths—however tortuous—to recovery. He must "pretend" to be interested in life and work: "It is the only way you can beat down your own ego and at the same time save your family." Or maybe he could arrange to "be a martyr by getting well." If someone could convince him that recovery was such a difficult and strenuous process that he should not attempt it—"if people shook their heads with disapproval and concern at every meal I ate, every hour

I rested, and every pound I put on"—then he might get well right away. He was at least trying to be "*vernünftig*" (sensible, judicious, reasonable) about his health, he assured Bullitt: "With these words I sound exactly like my Puritan father, but I can't help it: I *am* that way."[34]

Bullitt, in Moscow, insisted that he not rush things. "I want to have Kennan but not kill him," he explained to the State Department. "He is the best officer I have had here." So after being released from the sanatorium in April, Kennan was assigned light duty at the American consulate general in Vienna and later at the legation under the sympathetic supervision of the minister, George Messersmith. The idea was to see whether he could work without losing weight. There were setbacks, but Bullitt, passing through in June, was pleased to find that George had gained twenty-two pounds. "We are both homesick for Russia," Annelise wrote Jeanette. That seemed incredible to their friends. It had been "glorified in our memory and we will be disappointed when we go back." For the moment, though, George's stomach still needed a holiday.[35]

George, for his part, was learning "that you can't change human beings radically, all of a sudden." In a horticultural metaphor that would stick with him, he concluded that "[t]he best you can do is to influence them, like plants, over a long period of time, by gradual changes in their environment." The State Department had allowed him time, but it would ultimately want him back, and he would need to adapt. Diplomacy in most places required

> a facile tongue, unhampered by any sincerity; you must have a great capacity for quiet, boring dissipation: not great brawls, but continual rich food, irregular meals, enervating liqueurs and lack of sleep; you must have a deep interest . . . in golf and bridge, in clothes and other people's business; you must have an utter lack of conscience for the injustices of the world about you and not the faintest intention of ever doing anything about them; you must, in fact, be able to rid yourself of every last impulse to distinguish between right and wrong.

Diplomacy in Moscow was different, however, for Soviet society lacked the cynicism and listlessness found elsewhere: it "deludes itself into believing that it is going somewhere." George hastened to assure Jeanette, quite unnecessarily, that "I am no Bolshevik." But "some of the visions of the more intelligent communist leaders are the most impelling and inspiring human conceptions which it has been my lot to encounter—and my experience in this respect has not been small."

Of course diplomacy required selling one's soul "for a mess of very meretricious ministerial dignity." But the price of souls, like everything else, was subject to the law of supply and demand: "Probably it is better to sell one's soul . . . than to let it dry up in its own bitterness and get nothing for it whatsoever." It was like hanging on too long to virginity, which "only too soon comes to be worth nothing at all." And so in early November the Kennans were on their way back to Moscow: "I am looking forward to my return probably more than I should," George wrote Bullitt, "more, in any case, than I can justify through any amount of rationalization—and don't let anyone tell you I'm not."[36]

V.

But while Kennan was balancing the competing claims of body, mind, family, and profession in Vienna, the Soviet Union had changed. Although hardly free from difficulties, the political atmosphere throughout most of 1934, he recalled, had been "far more friendly, pleasant, and relaxed than anything Russia was to know for another two decades." The mood disappeared overnight, with the assassination, on December 1, of the Leningrad party boss, Sergei Kirov. It remains unclear, to this day, whether Stalin ordered the murder. But he used the provocation to consolidate absolute power through a wave of arrests, imprisonments, and executions that would terrorize the country for the next five years and would haunt it long after that. It was, as Kennan saw it, "one of the major catastrophes of Russian history . . . the revenge of the Revolution upon itself."[37]

By the time the Kennans returned to Moscow in mid-November, George had to admit to Jeanette that the life to which he had looked forward was not likely to be possible. Foreign friends were leaving, and Russian friends were vanishing, "even the doctors and dentists who are bold enough to treat us." Embassy life went on, but under the scrutiny of a staff riddled with spies. "Our position is precisely that of enemy negotiators in a hostile camp in time of war." The Soviet government was behaving, indeed, "as if the war were already here."[38]

There were still opportunities to travel, but only under strict police supervision. In mid-December Kennan attempted to visit Leo Tolstoy's country home, Yasnaya Polyana, as an ordinary tourist, without seeking special privileges. The trip was exhausting, though, and he became ill on the way: Russia was still "a bad place for weak stomachs." The GPU, which had been tailing him, intervened sympathetically to provide an overnight hotel room in Tula, a taxi to the estate the next day, and a guided tour, leaving Kennan with a rare feeling of gratitude to his minders—but also with the inescapable sense of being minded. The place reminded him of the Frosts' country house, near Delafield, where he used to hike from St. John's in the winter. "There was the same smell of apples and wood fires, the same chill in the corners away from the stove, the same sense of snow-covered fields outside."[39]

Kennan devised a more ambitious challenge to his own stamina—and to GPU ingenuity—when he risked a journey to the Caucasus in March 1936. Official timetables promised regular air service from Moscow: "I insisted on putting it to the test and asked for a ticket." Rather than admit that the flights did not exist, the authorities "placed a couple of ancient crates at my disposal." One of them, assigned to fly Kennan from Kharkov to Rostov-on-the-Don, was an open monoplane. He arrived too frozen to speak, "to the consternation of a girl guide sent out to meet me, who saw her linguistic talents confronted with ignominious failure." After thawing out, Kennan went more sensibly by train to the Black Sea, where he found tsarist hotels that were now proletarian "pig-sties," and then to Georgia, where the air at least felt freer than in Russia. He returned by slow train from Tiflis, after which Moscow seemed "a haven of civilization, culture, and comfort." Bullitt, who had suggested the trip, watched it carefully. His young aide arrived healthier than he had been for some time, he reported to the State Department. Perhaps there had been "no organic defect" at all, but "merely a general nervousness."[40]

Bullitt was in his final months of service in Moscow: he would spend the summer and fall working for Roosevelt's reelection, with the understanding that the president would then appoint him to some less demanding overseas post. With help from Kennan and his colleagues, the ambassador prepared a series of valedictory reports on what two and a half years of diplomatic relations had accomplished. The record was sparse: trade remained unimpressive, negotiations on debts and claims had broken down, there had been no further progress on the new embassy chancery, and the previous summer the Communist Party of the Soviet Union had hosted a meeting of the Third International, the organization dedicated to spreading revolution throughout the world. American communists attended, a blatant violation, Bullitt believed, of Litvinov's promise to Roosevelt, in 1933, that the Soviet Union would refrain from interfering, in any way, in the nation's domestic affairs. "[I]t must be recognized," the ambassador warned dramatically in what the staff referred to as his "swan song" dispatch, that "communists are agents of a foreign power whose aim is not only to destroy the institutions and liberties of our country, but also to kill millions of Americans."[41]

"People have sneered at Bullitt for the enthusiasm and optimism with which he approached his task in Russia, and for the meagerness of the results obtained," Kennan wrote in 1938. That was, he thought, not fair: "It was a gallant try, . . . in a profession where risks are unavoidable." He himself, however, had never shared Bullitt's optimism: Kelley's training had left him without illusions as to what diplomacy could accomplish in Moscow. Kennan also knew, from Russian history, that hostility toward the outside world was not new. To make this point, he prepared a report taken wholly from the dispatches of Neill S. Brown, the U.S. minister in St. Petersburg from 1850 to 1853. They had been found, Kennan claimed, in a pile of rubbish in what was left of the American legation there. "Secrecy and mystery characterize everything," Brown had written, of the reign of Nicholas I. "Nothing is made public that is worth knowing." The Russian government possessed, "in an exquisite degree, the art of worrying a foreign representative without giving him even the consolation of an insult."

Delighted, Bullitt forwarded Brown's observations to the State Department as an accurate picture of life in the Soviet Union in 1936: "*Plus ça change, plus c'est la même chose.*" Kennan saw in them the need to regard Bolshevism, "with all its hullabaloo about revolution," not as a turning point in history, but as only another milepost in Russia's "wasteful, painful progress from an obscure origin to an obscure destiny." Nothing in Brown's dispatches or in Kennan's training, however, anticipated the horrors of Stalinism. If the purges continued, he concluded in another study written for Bullitt, "there would be nothing left of the Soviet system of government but rule by a small irresponsible group" whose authority rested only on "bread and circuses" and repressive police power: "in short, fascism."[42]

This did not mean, though, that relations with the U.S.S.R. were useless. Bullitt's "swan song," in which he warned of the Soviet desire to "kill millions of Americans," concluded on a wholly different note: "We should neither expect too much, nor despair of getting anything at all." There is no way to know who drafted which portions, but the recommendations that followed—a patient balancing of competing pressures over a long period of time with a view to producing growth in desired directions—sounded more like Kennan's methods for achieving physical health and psychological stability than like Bullitt's emotional volatility:

We should take what we can get when the atmosphere is favorable and do our best to hold on to it when the wind blows the other way. We should remain unimpressed in the face of expansive professions of friendliness and unperturbed in the face of slights and underhand opposition. We should make the weight of our influence felt steadily over a long period of time in the directions which best suit our interests. We should never threaten. We should act and allow the Bolsheviks to draw their own conclusions as to the causes of our acts.

The future of Soviet-American relations would therefore depend chiefly on the United States. "[W]e should guard the reputation of Americans for business-like efficiency, sincerity, and straightforwardness. We should never send a spy to the Soviet Union. There is no weapon so disarming and effective in relations with the communists as sheer honesty. They know very little about it."[43]

Whoever drafted it, the conclusions of Bullitt's "swan song" anticipated with eerie precision the most famous essay Kennan ever published: his briefly anonymous 1947 "X" article, in *Foreign Affairs*, on "The Sources of Soviet Conduct."[44] Bullitt, more than anyone else, launched Kennan on the trajectory that led to that achievement. He gave Kennan his first big break by asking him, on the spur of the moment, to help open the Moscow embassy. He nursed Kennan through a year-long health crisis that, without steady behind-the-scenes support, could easily have ended his career. He consistently praised Kennan's work in reports to the State Department: Bullitt's critical personnel assessments spared no other member of the Moscow embassy staff. "Nothing but Mr. Kennan's health," he concluded in the last of these, "can prevent him from becoming one of the most valuable officers in the [Foreign] Service."[45]

Kennan knew what Bullitt had done for him. His generation of Foreign Service officers, he wrote his former boss after his ambassadorship to France was announced in September 1936, had been trying to save themselves "from the comfortable philistinism or the decadent estheticism which are the refuges of most of our older colleagues." Bullitt had understood and sympathized with these efforts. It would seem "very strange not to have your guidance in the Moscow work—especially for me, who can recall our associations in this work from the very beginning." The Americans there would "plug along," but "the last vestiges of the novelty of opening up a new territory are gone. Our work is routine—and no longer adventure."[46]

SIX

Rediscovering America:
1936–1938

SHORTLY AFTER HIS DECEMBER 1935 TRIP TO TOLSTOY'S HOME AT Yasnaya Polyana—with its unexpected assistance from the GPU and its unanticipated evocations of boyhood winters in Wisconsin—Kennan asked the State Department for permission to return to the United States. He had not been there for over two years, he pointed out, and on that visit he had taken only seventeen days of leave before departing with Bullitt for Moscow. Annelise and Grace would be traveling to America in February: it would be Grace's first trip there. Moreover, "my wife expects another child to be born in April. I should naturally like to join her soon after the child has been born."[1]

There were legal as well as sentimental reasons for the request. A new law had raised the possibility that children born abroad might be denied American citizenship if one parent lacked that status. Annelise was not yet a citizen, so there was little choice, George recalled, but for her to make the long winter voyage back before the baby arrived, after which "I had to come over and fetch them all back to Russia." The trip would strain finances, he told Jeanette, but with luck there would be enough "to see Annelise and Grace to the United States and the next youngster into the world. Then we'll see where we stand."[2]

Joan Elisabeth Kennan was born in April at Jeanette's home in Highland Park, Illinois, and George got there in mid-May. The expanded family vacationed for a few weeks at the Hotchkiss cottage on Pine Lake, just north of Nagawicka— the family compound there had long since been sold. George read Charles Beard's *The Open Door at Home*, listened to radio coverage of the Republican national convention, and wrote a letter to Bullitt "wishing that there were another opportunity—just at this time—for one of those high and wide discussions which we have had on only too rare occasions." What he wanted to talk about, though, was not Russia, but America.

The journey home, Kennan reported, had been a reintroduction to capitalism, of which he had seen little recently except Norway and Austria, which had been too idyllic and too depressing, respectively, to be representative. Germany, as he passed through it, had been a "great garden, well-kept and blooming, . . . populated by clean and healthy people." London had been full of business activity but striking for its social stability: he had forgotten that such a thing existed. So "I got back to this country almost a complete convert to the horrors of capitalism, ready to forgive even radio advertising, . . . and the Saturday Evening Post."

Once home, however, his optimism began to fade. He acknowledged the high living standard, the political liberties, the freedom of expression. But there was also chaotic municipal growth, an increasingly spoiled countryside, and an absence of public regulation, all of which left "little for the future but retrogression."

> It seems to me that this country doesn't want government. . . . It will suffer unlimited injustices and infringements on liberty from irresponsible private groups, but none from a responsible governing agency. Its people would rather go down individually, with quixotic courage, before the destructive agencies of uncontrolled industrialism—like Ethiopian tribesmen before Italian gas attacks—than submit to the discipline necessary for any effective resistance.

Geography insulated the United States from the international consequences of ineffectiveness, but "no oceans can spare us the internal consequences." Only "strong central power (far stronger than the present constitution would allow)" could rescue individuals from economic hardship and social injustice. "And I'm afraid that's what's coming."[3]

Kennan's letter set forth concerns about his country that would remain with him for the rest of his life: anxiety over the way unrestricted capitalism eroded community; a sense of environmental dangers that was well ahead of its time; frustration over the extent to which domestic political pressures, responding to private interests, shaped public policy; fear that this would weaken the United States in a world dominated by more purposeful states; and finally a striking lack of faith in the health and durability of democratic institutions. "I hate the rough and tumble of our political life," George had written Jeanette the previous year. "I hate democracy; I hate the press . . . ; I hate the 'peepul;' I have become clearly un-American."[4]

The problem, he conceded many years later, was "not just that I had left the world of my boyhood, . . . it was also that this world had left me." It had of course left everyone else too, but the process had been so gradual that most Americans hadn't noticed. Only expatriates, returning after years spent abroad, could really see what was happening. "Increasingly, now, I would not be a part of my country, although what it had once been would remain a part of me." Allegiance would be "a loyalty *despite*, not a loyalty *because*, a loyalty of principle, not of identification."[5]

The Kennans sailed for Europe in mid-July 1936, sharing the SS *Manhattan* with the "gum-chewing supermen" and "hefty amazons" who would represent the United States at the Berlin Olympics. Upon arrival in Hamburg,

> [t]he athletes lined the rail of the ship and light-heartedly shouted their locker-room banter at the people on shore. It did not occur to them that these people would not be apt to understand much of it. They failed to notice that the country before their eyes was a country different—excitingly, provocatively different—from their own. To myself, for whom these transitions from one world to another had never ceased to be momentous, awe-compelling experiences, . . . this was a little sad.

George, Annelise, Grace, and Joan went by way of Kristiansand, Oslo, Copenhagen, and Helsinki to Leningrad, where the fortress of Kronstadt at the harbor entrance provided a grim welcome. Getting to the Moscow train was an ordeal, followed by terror when family, luggage, and George got separated in the midst of huge crowds. Reunited, they arrived the next morning in a rainstorm with no one to meet them, and so made their own way to the Mokhovaya, "drenched, disorganized, and entirely happy to be again among the people whose friendship and understanding still made Moscow the nearest thing in the world to home."[6]

I.

Home, to be sure, had its problems. The Mokhovaya, constructed only of brick, wood, and plaster, was already falling apart, leaving cracks from which there emerged, according to an American inspection report, "countless moths, which feed upon the insulating material within the walls," along with "roaches and other insects against which a constant battle must be fought." Varying gas pressure made cooking uncertain, while electricity remained erratic. The building was poorly

heated in winter, but when the weather was hot and the windows were open, lay-
ers of oil, soot, and dust blew in from the traffic on the street outside. Bathrooms
doubled as laundry facilities, and servants slept in kitchens and halls. "Our friend
Durby [Durbrow] had fought with our cook and fired her," George wrote Jeanette.
"We hunted for another one but couldn't find any, and finally had to take the old
bitch (she is generally referred to in this manner) back. We still have no nurse."[7]
Nonetheless the living quarters were better than those of most other foreigners in
Moscow, and the work that went on in the offices below was remarkable.

"It is not an exaggeration to say," Kennan noted with pride the following year,
"that by the beginning of 1937 the American Embassy at Moscow, which had
started from scratch three years before, had become one of the two or three best-
conducted and best-informed missions in the city." He and four other Foreign
Service officers sent the State Department 329 dispatches of an "original informa-
tive or reportorial" character in 1936, comprising 3,857 pages. Topics ranged from
Soviet relations with the United States and other countries through the operations
of the Communist International, Stalin's first purge trials, the successes and shortcomings of the Soviet economy, the new draft constitution, and the activities of
Americans living in the U.S.S.R. There were also reports on slum clearance, fish
exports, fur auctions, sausage casings, and the All-Union Conference of Engi-
neers' Wives. At the department's request, Kennan himself produced a 115-page
analysis of Russian documents relating to the purchase of Alaska in 1867.

The embassy library received over a hundred Soviet and foreign newspapers
daily, subscribed to between 350 and 400 periodicals, and maintained a collection
of over a thousand books while forwarding additional copies to the legation in
Riga and to the Division of Eastern European Affairs library in Washington. However moth-ridden and roach-infested it may have been, the Mokhovaya was now
a major research center on Soviet affairs—so much so that department officials
were beginning to grumble about the number of dispatches they were receiving,
some of which seemed "unnecessarily voluminous."[8]

The work was "very hard, very delicate, and quite thankless," George wrote. "We
don't try to see anything of the Russians any more, except for a few official parties.
It's too risky for them." The isolation of foreigners had never been greater, and
the group that remained got smaller, more ingrown, and increasingly bored with
each other. Social life within the embassy was, if anything, more intense. "Have
been out every single night [except] last night," Annelise added on January 2—
George was back in Vienna for a medical checkup.

On the 30th Durbie had a few people in for dinner. At about 2 o'clock we were having such a good time that we decided we were celebrating New Years Eve in advance. I got home at 4:00, and 3 of the boys sat talking afterwards until 6. On New Years Eve I was first at the Hendersons, afterwards at the Metropole and finally ended at Durbie's. Got to bed at 6, slept to 12, and felt fine. It always seems fatal when George is away about getting to bed at any reasonable hours.

It helped that there was now, for recreation, an American dacha outside Moscow, which several of the embassy bachelors had purchased. Not far from Stalin's own country retreat, it had a log house, a tennis court, a garden, horses to ride, and a high wooden fence. There was something very comforting, Charlie Thayer remembered, "about driving through those big wooden gates after a long hard day trying to understand the Russians. . . . [T]he GPU seemed to disappear from existence."[9]

The Kennans used the place regularly. "We had the feeling we could go out at any time," Annelise remembered. Surrounding the dacha, George explained, was "the most wonderful riding country you can imagine. We make a point of saying good-day to all the peasants. They look as though they were seeing a ghost, and grope uncertainly for their hats. They think maybe the Revolution was all a bad dream, and that the masters are back in the saddle." On one memorable occasion, George, Grace, and Stalin drove back from their respective dachas on the same road at the same time. As his limousine passed, the dictator "stared gloomily out of his window at Grace and myself and we stared back."[10]

Still, Moscow was a difficult place to raise children. When Grace fell ill with bronchial pneumonia, no nurse dared enter a foreign embassy. A Russian doctor did come, but only after receiving permission from the Foreign Office, which also had to approve the use of a portable X-ray machine. "For one whole day," George admitted, "I literally didn't dare to hope that she would live." He worried that "we wouldn't even be able to find a priest to bury the little girl." Grace recovered dramatically, however, and was soon sitting up and pestering everyone, being as naughty as one can be with "feet firmly on this earth."

"I feel that I am ripe for a transfer," Kennan confessed wearily at the end of this December 1936 letter to Jeanette. For in addition to the hardships of life in Moscow, he and his colleagues were developing "a doctrinaire skepticism which cannot be a good thing. We know so thoroughly the limitations of our job that it seems hard to see its possibilities. . . . [W]e have the psychology of old men." The time had come to turn things over to people "whose experience is less and whose enthusiasm is greater. It will do us all good."[11]

II.

That opportunity came quickly enough. Bullitt's successor, Joseph E. Davies, arrived on January 19, 1937, with ample enthusiasm but no experience whatever. He was, like Bullitt, a friend of Franklin D. Roosevelt, but there the similarities ended. A lawyer, campaign contributor, and the new (but third) husband of Marjorie Merriweather Post, one of the richest women in the world, Davies was in every sense a political appointee. He was sleek, self-confident, hungry for publicity, and proud of *not* being a diplomat. He knew nothing of the Soviet Union but was sure that powerful men were the same everywhere and that he could, through the force of his own personality, get through to its leaders. All of this placed Davies at odds with the disillusioned Bullitt and the staff he had left behind. Davies "drew from the first instant our distrust and dislike," Kennan recalled. "We doubted his seriousness. . . . We saw every evidence that his motives in accepting the post were personal and political and ulterior to any sense of the solemnity of the task itself." At the end of the new ambassador's first day in Moscow, Kennan and several other young career officers gathered in Henderson's rooms to consider "whether we should resign in a body from the service."[12]

They did not, but the State Department was sufficiently concerned that it sent one of its most trusted investigators, J. Klahr Huddle, to assess the situation. "It is difficult to express just what happened to the staff of the Moscow Embassy when Mr. Davies arrived," Huddle reported back. One problem had been the difficulties of importing into the country all that the Davieses had wanted to bring. This included an entourage of sixteen aides, servants, and relatives, as well as a phalanx of freezers filled with the food they would consume while in residence at Spaso House. They demanded transportation on private trains—a concept unfamiliar to the Soviet railway authorities—together with Leningrad docking facilities for Mrs. Davies's yacht, the *Sea Cloud*. The ambassador showed up at his Mokhovaya office only twice before returning to the United States in March, but he left behind three thousand envelopes to be stamped, sealed, and mailed: these contained fund-raising appeals for the Mount Vernon Girls School in Washington, of which Mrs. Davies was a trustee.

A man of broad knowledge in many fields, Davies was reluctant to acknowledge, Huddle noted, "his lack in the present one." Soon after arriving he asked Henderson to produce, on two days' notice, briefings on all the other European states, specifying their leadership, population, culture, religion, economy, alliances, and the status of their relations with the U.S.S.R. He quickly developed a dislike for Kennan, Huddle reported, which was unfortunate, "because Kennan prides himself on his knowledge of Russia, is very sensitive, and does his best work with a little encouragement and praise." Overall, Huddle concluded, the ambassador in his first two months at Moscow had "very seriously" imperiled the morale of the embassy staff, and "when I arrived, [it] was almost at the breaking point."[13]

George confirmed this to Jeanette: it would be some time before the effect wore off, and "I can take my profession seriously again. If I had had a little money, you would probably already have seen me trooping back to Wisconsin to start life over again." Annelise added that the Davieses "are just awful. . . . I am trying to calm [George] down as best I can and just laugh it all off," but "[i]t is worse than I ever could dream it to be." The problem, Kennan later explained, was that men like Davies required underlings "to cover up their mistakes, to toss them meaningless baubles to keep them occupied, [and] to go on doing the important things under the surface." By March, the staff could at least look forward to the temporary departure of the "Davies ménage," at which point, Kennan predicted, "the sun will begin to shine, the flowers to peep through the ground, and the little birdies will arrive from the South and tell us what a nice world it is after all."[14]

The second of Stalin's purges was going on that winter, which made the atmosphere all the more oppressive. "[E]verybody was so scared," Annelise remembered. Davies gave a dinner for thirty-six people, of whom six were soon executed, "including the man who sat next to me." The ambassador insisted on attending the trials, but before doing so asked Kennan to

> go through the testimony and make for me a brief topical abstract of all of the various crimes recited, giving the name of the perpetrator, [and a] description of the crime in general terms not to exceed a sentence for each; as, for instance, "Three mine explosions, by blank, blank, blank." I should like to have that soon.

He then brought a furious Kennan along to whisper translations of the proceedings: "During the intermissions I was sent, regularly, to fetch the ambassador his sandwiches, while he exchanged sententious judgments with the gentlemen of the press concerning the guilt of the victims."

Davies assured the State Department that the trial had established "a definite political conspiracy to overthrow the present Government." He was careful to point out, though, that the trials had not been fair by American standards, because the accused had been denied counsel, were forced to testify against themselves, and their guilt had been assumed from the start. He also saw to it that the department got another perspective. Noting that "Mr. Kennan has been here a great many years and is an exceptionally able man, thoroughly familiar with Russia," Davies took the unusual step of forwarding his interpreter's assessment of the trials, along with his own.

They were not that far apart. Kennan's report emphasized the ease with which confessions could be coerced but acknowledged that the defendants had "probably done plenty, from the point of view of the regime, to warrant their humiliation and punishment." What really happened might never be known: "[t]he Russian mind, as Dostoevski has shown, . . . sometimes carries both truth and falsehood to such infinite extremes that they eventually meet in space, like parallel lines, and it is no longer possible to distinguish between them." In a significant acknowledgment of Kennan's expertise, Robert Kelley, now the director of the Division of Eastern European Affairs, sent both reports to the secretary of state, Cordell Hull: they represented, he observed neutrally, "two points of view based on different methods of approach," differing "only in degree" in their conclusions.[15]

Embassy security was another of Kennan's concerns. While the Davieses were back in the United States, Thayer discovered a crude listening device—lowered on a fishpole in the Spaso House attic—in the wall behind the ambassador's desk. Intrigued, the staff tried to catch the culprit, a project that required the rigging of trip wires, alarm bells, and in one instance Kennan's spending an uncomfortable night in the billiard room with a nonfunctioning flashlight and an empty revolver. The results, in the end, were inconclusive. Davies was "displeased that we had ever inaugurated them," fearing that they would compromise his public image of popularity with the Soviet leadership. It hardly mattered, for the ambassador "was not in the habit of saying things of any consequence, either in the bugged study or anywhere else."[16]

"[Q]uite frankly I think that [Kennan] has been here quite long enough—perhaps too long for his own good," Davies had by then written the State Department. "He is of a rather high-gear, nervous type" and had been ill "ever since I have been here." Given his health along with the difficulties of raising a young family in Moscow, it would be good for all concerned if Kennan could be transferred to a post where living conditions were easier. The loss to the embassy would be serious, but it was "not fair to Kennan not to give him a chance to get well."[17]

Kennan, for his part, was ready to go: as his comments about the "psychology of old men" suggest, he had been ready even before the Davies "ménage" appeared on the scene. "This has been, for me, the most unhappy winter on record," he wrote Jeanette at the end of March from Yalta, where he had taken a few days off to visit Chekhov's last home. But winter was coming to an end, "and with it, I hope, will end my sojourn in Russia. Life has its ups as well as its down[s], and we'll see what a new post, a new chief and new surroundings will bring."[18]

He was not displeased, therefore, when the State Department informed him in June that he would be reassigned to the American consulate in Jerusalem: "I sent to London for a bunch of books on the Palestine Mandate and prepared to forget, for a time, that Russia had ever existed." But Kennan was horrified to learn, almost simultaneously, that the department had eliminated the Division of Eastern European Affairs, his administrative and intellectual home in Washington. Kelley, its chief, was as surprised as everyone else, and the library he had assembled was broken up—although not before Bohlen had rescued several hundred of its most valuable books and hidden them in an attic. "I was shocked," Bullitt wrote R. Walton Moore, the State Department counselor. "[T]he division which Kelley built up was the most efficient in the world in its handling of these highly complicated questions."[19]

The official explanation was efficiency. Eastern European Affairs was to be merged, along with its Western European counterpart, into a single Division of European Affairs. Moore confirmed rumors, however, that the White House had ordered the change: someone had persuaded the president, perhaps unwisely. Just who was unclear. Kennan suggested long afterward that if there ever had been "the smell of Soviet influence" within the government, this moment was more plausible than any that Senator Joseph McCarthy's followers had identified. There is no conclusive evidence for this allegation, but it is reasonable to assume, from the fact of Davies's appointment, that Roosevelt wanted a new approach to Moscow. It's certainly possible, then, that the new ambassador had at least some role in shaping this new arrangement.[20]

However it happened, Kennan saw that Soviet-American relations were henceforth to have "the outward appearance of being cordial, no matter what gnashing of teeth might go on under the surface. . . . [N]ot only were we career officers in Moscow an impediment, but so was the Division of Eastern European Affairs." The president, it appeared, knew nothing about, or cared nothing for, what they had accomplished. "We could never forgive F.D.R. that he had done this to us." And so "I could only conclude that my approach to Russia had outlived its usefulness."[21]

III.

"At first I thought it was awful," Annelise wrote Jeanette of the Jerusalem assignment, but she soon changed her mind. At least the climate would be warmer, the roads would be better, and there would be the chance to study biblical history. George had even begun learning "the Yiddish language." Kennan's transformation into a Middle East expert was not to be, however, for on August 13, 1937, while on leave in Paris, he received an unexpected cable signed by the secretary of state himself: "Your work in Moscow has been so useful in character that Department is considering advisability of assigning you to the European Division to deal with Soviet affairs. While your personal preference may not be controlling, it would be gratifying to know before the assignment is actually made that it would be agreeable to you."[22]

Kennan's superiors, former and current, had quietly arranged this. Bullitt had insisted, after learning that Eastern European Affairs was to be abolished, on the need to strengthen Soviet analysis in Washington: Davies "cannot be counted on to handle the Russian situation in a serious manner." Henderson, from Moscow, strongly seconded the idea and suggested Kennan. It would be a waste to send him to Jerusalem: "George has developed a lot during the last two years." Meanwhile Messersmith, Kennan's chief during his Vienna recuperation, had conveniently become assistant secretary of state for administration and could oversee the change in plans. Finances would still be tight, and his rank would still be unimpressive, George wrote Jeanette, but "some of my best friends" had come out on top in the "palace revolution." So he replied to Hull that an assignment in Washington would indeed be agreeable.[23]

After a quick trip to the Riviera to see Kent, who was studying there, the Kennans picked up their children in Kristiansand, and by early October George was back in the city he had left, with bitter disillusionment, a decade earlier. His diary recorded a mixture of moods:

October 17: Out to Mount Vernon. . . . Bracing cool air; cloudless sky; warm autumn sunshine. Shapeless, droopy people—stuffy from Sunday morning waffles and funny papers, tired from not walking—staggered out of shiny automobiles and dragged themselves around the grounds of the old mansion. . . . Grasshoppers flicked themselves around before us. An occasional late bird sang from the hard, many-colored foliage. The corn was stacked in the fields. . . . It was very nice and encouraging, but in the distance the roar of the Sunday traffic on the big turnpike was never lost, and it was never clearer that man is a skin-disease of the earth.

October 24: Lunch [with Annelise, at the Raleigh Hotel]. The dance band wore flowers in their button-holes, and dark suits. Most of them ground out their stuff sleepily and mechanically. Only the piano player, the leader, spun delicate webs of improvisation around the melodies, in a nonchalant, dreamy manner, looking restlessly around at the guests as he played, and only occasionally giving a glance to his instrument or a gesture of command to his men.

October 25: A day of despair, in the middle of such a horribly senseless city, and of wondering whether there were not still—somewhere in America—a place where a gravel lane, wet from the rains, led up a hill, between the yellow trees and past occasional vistas of a valley full of quiet farms and woodlands, to a house where candles and a warm hearth defied the early darkness and dampness of autumn and where human warmth and simplicity and graciousness defied the encroachments of a diseased world and of people drugged and debilitated by automobiles and advertisements and radios and moving pictures.

Washington reeked of cigar smoke and automobile exhaust, rang with shrill voices and the slapping of backs, and it seemed that "[n]obody stayed there very long."²⁴ Still, there were compensations.

Despite their limited budget, the Kennans managed to rent a comfortable eighteenth-century house in Alexandria: largely unfurnished except for its own roaches. It was a step up, nonetheless, from the Mokhovaya. Thayer's wealthy relatives gave George and Annelise a "horsey" fall weekend outside Philadelphia, and they even attended a Christmas reception at the White House: "Very dull, of course," Annelise reported, "but it was fun to see the place, its occupants and the other guests." It had been, George acknowledged, a happy time.

We are getting used to the feeling of not having any pocket cash and even the general condition of bankruptcy failed to detract from the Christmas spirit. . . . We spent the last farthings on a grand big tree and things for the kids' stockings, a vase of flowers and a bottle of New York State claret, charged a turkey and a plum pudding at the corner grocer's, and had a real celebration.

Two months later George got a promotion that raised his salary to $5,000. This was not much, he explained, but "[o]nly one man who entered the service when I did has gotten as high, so there's a certain amount of satisfaction involved."[25]

George had arrived in time to help Bohlen, who would replace him in Moscow, retrieve the hidden books from Kelley's library and place them in the State Department office he would now occupy. It was, in effect, the "Russia desk" in the newly constituted Division of European Affairs, and Kennan was the resident specialist on that country. Relishing the old building's "solid cool corridors, its unruffled placidity, . . . its distinct distaste for anything which smacks of exaggeration, haste, or excitement," Kennan used his position to try to balance Davies's reports—still misleadingly optimistic, he thought—on what the life in the Soviet Union was really like.

The authorities, he emphasized, had restricted the activities of foreign diplomats, with the expectation that, "like well-trained children," they should be "seen and not heard." Officials once friendly to the embassy had disappeared in circumstances suggesting "exile, imprisonment, or disgrace, if not execution." Soviet citizens entering the United States should be watched with a view to determining "where they were and what they were doing." Kennan tried to explain to a puzzled Secretary of State Hull—it was the only meeting they ever had—why Russian communists were arresting American communists who happened to be in the Soviet Union. He prepared a brief report on Comintern activities, spent a fair amount of time on Soviet-American trade, and devoted very little to explaining why the moment was not right to seek Moscow's cooperation in demarcating the Alaskan boundary in the Bering Sea.[26]

The spring of 1938 brought Kennan two professional recognitions, only one of which he knew about. The latter was an invitation to lecture at the Foreign Service School, where he had been a student twelve years before. He spoke on "Russia," quoting Neill Brown's dispatches from the 1850s to show how little had changed since tsarist times. He found it "almost impossible to conceive of our being Russia's enemy," but "I cannot see that the possibility of our being Russia's ally is much greater." The United States must simply show patience: in a close paraphrase of Bullitt's 1936 "swan song," Kennan insisted that "[w]e must neither expect too much nor despair of getting anything at all."[27]

The recognition of which Kennan was unaware came by way of espionage.

On April 22 he drafted an internal memorandum, not meant for circulation beyond the State Department, questioning Davies's optimism about the future of Soviet-American relations. "According to the theories on which the Soviet state is founded," Kennan pointed out, "the *entire* outside world is hostile and *no* foreigner should ever be trusted." Davies's dispatch found its way into the official compilation of documents on U.S. policy toward the Soviet Union for this period, published in 1952. Kennan's commentary did not. But thanks to the enterprise of Aleksandr Troyanovsky, the Soviet ambassador in Washington, both documents wound up, in the summer of 1938, on the desk of Josef Stalin.

Troyanovsky had got them "by conspiratorial means," he explained, and "absolutely no one" in the Washington embassy or at the Soviet Foreign Ministry knew that he had done so. Davies, "a typical bourgeois," had both positive and negative things to say about the Soviet Union, but he had to contend with hostility in the State Department, led chiefly by Kennan. He "speaks Russian well and is a nephew [*sic*] of the celebrated George Kennan, who in the 1880s [*sic*] wrote the well-known book, 'Siberia and Hard Labor,' which we all read at one time or another." Kennan's attacks on Davies showed that he was "trying to turn Roosevelt personally against us," but despite these efforts the president and Secretary of State Hull "have not lost their equilibrium and in general take a comparatively acceptable position toward us."[28]

The security breach would have appalled Kennan, had he known of it, but the notoriety might have pleased him: Stalin personally underlined the most significant sections of Troyanovsky's report. Kennan could not have disputed the Soviet ambassador's assessment of his intentions, or his lack of success, for the moment, in seeing them realized. Stalin, no doubt, filed the information in his capacious memory, for future use.

IV.

There were also, that spring, two quietly personal gratifications. After Hitler annexed Austria in March, George helped his Jewish "Frau Doktor," Frieda Por, emigrate to the United States. "That saves my life," she wrote in an unpublished memoir she prepared four decades later. "It is almost unbelievable that you are now in America," Annelise wrote Frieda after George met her in New York. "I only hope that you will like it and that you will be able to work as you wish."

And then on June 13, 1938, in Milwaukee, Annelise herself became an American citizen.[29]

She and the children were spending the summer at Pine Lake, leaving a self-pitying George in Washington, bereft of family, car, or money, busing home each night along an avenue of filling stations, advertising signboards, hot-dog stands, junked automobiles, and trailer camps, to dine on a bowl of cereal and then to sit for an hour or so on the front steps. So it was a relief for him to get to Wisconsin in June. While there, he rented a bicycle for a few days with a view to discovering whether there was still a house at the end of some country road where "human warmth and simplicity and graciousness defied the encroachments of a diseased world."[30]

He found the highways deserted, except for the people traveling them encased in metal machines: in a hundred miles he met no other cyclist, pedestrian, or horse-drawn vehicle. The drivers and their passengers had no more of a link with the landscape than if they had been on an airplane flying over it. They were "lost spirits," for whom "space existed only in time." The roads were a far cry from "the vigorous life of the English highway of Chaucer's day." But there were inns and taverns along his route, with helpful people willing to provide directions.

As a consequence, George was able to find the farm, near Packwaukee, that his grandfather had once owned and where his father had grown up. The old house was gone, but there was a new farmer with a house of his own who insisted, despite George's unexpected arrival, that he stay the night. This he did, washing up in the kitchen, eating with the family and the farmhands, occupying the guest bedroom, and rising early the next morning for a breakfast as hearty as the supper had been. The farm, unlike the highway, was a community, with the only intimation that it might not survive coming in the arrival of a college-educated daughter, "smart, well-dressed, confident, blooming with health and energy, . . . a breath of air from another world." It seemed unlikely that she would wind up on the farm: the city, "at once so menacing and so promising," had claimed her for its own.

George saw the future himself when he spent the next night in a college town where the streets were empty except for automobiles, each containing a couple or two "bent on pleasure—usually vicarious pleasure—in the form of a movie or a dance or a petting party." Anyone unlucky enough not to be among these "private, mathematically correct companies" would be alone. "There was no place where strangers would come together freely—as in a Bavarian beer hall or a Russian amusement park—for the mere purpose of being together and enjoying new acquaintances. Even the saloons were nearly empty."

All of this convinced George that the technology industrialization had made possible—automobiles, movies, radio, mass-circulation magazines, the advertising that paid for them—was creating an exaggerated desire for privacy. It was making an English upper-class evil a vice of American society. This was

> the sad climax of individualism, the blind-alley of a generation which had forgotten how to think or live collectively, of a people whose private lives were so brittle, so insecure that they dared not subject them to the slightest social contact with the casual stranger, of people who felt neither curiosity nor responsibility for the mass of those who shared their community life and their community problems.

Americans had in the past, to be sure, subordinated personal interests to collective needs in the face of floods, hurricanes, or great wars. Perhaps some new cataclysm would force them to do so again. Kennan looked forward to it much as Chekhov, in the 1890s, had anticipated the "cruel and mighty storm which is advancing upon us, which . . . will soon blow all the laziness, the indifference, the prejudice against work and the rotten boredom out of our society." Whatever might be sacrificed in years to come, Kennan concluded, "the spirit of fellowship, having reached its lowest conceivable ebb, could not fail to be the gainer."[31]

The bicycle trip and the essay it inspired amplified the anxieties about America that he had raised with Bullitt two summers before, but they added the idea that challenges—cataclysms of some kind—could be a good thing. This idea too would stick in Kennan's mind, reappearing, nine years later, in the carefully read pages of *Foreign Affairs*:

> The thoughtful observer of Russian-American relations will find no cause for complaint in the Kremlin's challenge to American society. He will rather experience a certain gratitude to a Providence which, by providing the American people with this implacable challenge, has made their entire security as a nation dependent upon their pulling themselves together and accepting the responsibilities of moral and political leadership that history plainly intended them to bear.[32]

As with Kennan's 1932 vision of the Soviet Union's decline and fall, concerns about himself and his country had produced a grand strategic insight—with help, this time, from Chekhov. But what if the United States, in the face of great challenges, could not pull itself together? What if its internal institutions were not up to the task?

V.

Kennan suggested, in his 1936 letter to Bullitt, that a new form of government might be necessary, capable of wielding "strong central power (far stronger than the present constitution would allow)." At some point in 1938—it is not clear when—he began developing his ideas on this subject, apparently with the intention of producing a short book. He never finished the project, but the surviving drafts, entitled "The Prerequisites" and "Government," suggest the direction of his thinking.

The problems confronting the United States, Kennan believed, resulted from the fact that its constitution was a century and a half old. It worked well enough for its time but had now come up against uncontrolled industrialization, a malfunctioning economy, a declining agricultural population, and ugly problems of urbanization. The American people, hence, no longer had "its old fiber or its old ideals." Instead it was afflicted by crime and corruption, along with the antagonisms of class and race. Some saw government as having created these problems; others believed that only government could solve them. But both groups accepted democracy, abhorring "fascism" or "dictatorship." Both were wrong, Kennan insisted: the only solution lay along a path that few Americans were willing to contemplate, extending "through constitutional change to the authoritarian state."

There were, after all, no absolute democracies or dictatorships. Democracies taxed their citizens, allowed the police to use force, and tolerated unemployment: surely a government in the hands of political machines and lobbyists was not really majority rule. Dictatorships could not operate without the cooperation of those who administered them and without the acquiescence of those subject to them: why did dictators go to such lengths to shape public opinion through propaganda? If truly "absolute," they would have no need of it. And then there were regimes, like those in China, Japan, Eastern Europe, and Latin America, which were neither democracies nor dictatorships but fell somewhere in between. Both terms, then, were vague clichés: it was time to drop "the angel of democracy" as well as "the bogey-man of dictatorship."

The task of government was to provide its people with adequate living standards, to ensure their humane behavior toward one another, and to give them a sense of contributing toward the general improvement of their society. Beyond that, objectives need not be specified: "We leave to the communists the detailed description of distant millenniums." But what kind of government—if neither democracy nor dictatorship as generally understood—could best achieve these objectives?

Only one entrusted, Kennan was sure, to the right kind of people. They would have to be, of course, a minority, but not the conglomerate of professional politicians and powerful special interests that currently controlled the country. Leaders instead should be selected "from all sections and classes of the population . . . on the basis of individual fitness for the exercise of authority." Fitness would reflect "character, education and inclination," but because not everyone could be trusted to recognize it, there would have to be "a very extensive restriction of the suffrage in national affairs."

Three groups in particular would lose the right to vote. The first were "aliens" and "naturalized citizens," whose political influence, exercised through ethnic groups and the bosses that dominated them, had become disproportionate. They would be happier as the wards of a government they could respect than as "fodder for the rent-sharks, ward-heelers and confidence men of the big cities." The second was nonprofessional women, who were turning the country into a matriarchy through their domination of families, the economy, and national culture. They had failed to live up to the responsibilities their power entailed, placing it, rather, in the hands of "lobbyists, charlatans and racketeers," while themselves becoming "delicate, high-strung, unsatisfied, flat chested and flat-voiced." Finally, there were "negroes," for whom seventy years of the "nominal" right to vote had provided no benefits: their condition was "the outstanding disgrace of American public life." Removing the franchise from them would induce a greater responsibility for them on the part of the white population, because "we are kinder to those who, like our children, are openly dependent on our kindness than to those who are nominally able to look after themselves."

With these restrictions, political power would gravitate to people with the qualifications to exercise it "intelligently and usefully." Their leaders would organize themselves independently of all political parties or vested interests. They would be "profoundly indifferent to the size of [their] popular backing and unhampered by the necessity of seeking votes." They would thereby command the confidence of their followers. And they would train their successors, by recruiting young people willing "to abandon the attractions of private life, the prospect of making money and of keeping up with the Joneses," in order to subject themselves to the discipline that would be required of them "if they entered a religious order."

Kennan's elite would have no need to seize power, for "[i]f the present degeneration of American political life continues, it is more probable that power will eventually drop like a ripe apple into the hands of any organized minority which knows what it wants and which has the courage to accept responsibility." He was not trying to create such a leadership vacuum, for it was already on the way. He was only trying to anticipate it, with a view to ensuring that "there should be at least one competitor with a sense of decency and responsibility."[33]

VI.

Left incomplete, filed, and apparently forgotten, Kennan's essay resurfaced and became famous, after he opened his papers for research in the 1970s, as an egregious example of political incorrectness. Embarrassed, he withdrew it from further scrutiny, explaining to the historian who most carefully analyzed the draft that it stood in relation to his later thinking as "an *esquisse* does to an artist's final painting. It was to be modified, polished, pushed in other directions." More privately, he complained that he had never meant what he had written for publication. "They were scraps of diary material. I could just as well—if you asked me to write in the diary the next day—have written contrary to that." It was inappropriate to excavate this "stuff" as evidence "of my mature thinking and compare it with things that I wrote in later years."[34]

In one way, this makes sense. The essay abounds in gaffes that, one hopes, would never have made their way into print. Aliens could not have been denied the vote, because they had never been granted it. Fears of "flat-chested" women colluding with "racketeers" were, to say the least, bizarre. Insisting that African Americans would be better off deprived of even "nominal" voting rights brought Kennan perilously close to paternalist arguments advanced, before the Civil War, to defend slavery. It was not clear how narrowing representation would produce a government selected "from all sections and classes of the population." Nor were young people likely to prepare for leadership by becoming—even if temporarily—monks. "Buried in the papers of even the most enlightened men are, no doubt, some rather wild notions," two other historians who saw this 1938 essay commented, with philosophical resignation.[35]

But these were not, as Kennan claimed, just diary scraps. They were the beginnings of a book, and although he took it no further at this point, some of his arguments would show up again, softened, in later writings.[36] They also reflect, at this relatively early stage in Kennan's career, one of his most persistent paradoxes: that he understood the Soviet Union far better than he did the United States.

Kennan's analyses of the U.S.S.R. were as sophisticated as anything available at the time. By the end of his first decade in the Foreign Service, he was explaining Russian society far better than Russians were doing for themselves. He had proven himself a worthy successor to the first George Kennan, a point not lost on Soviet officialdom at the highest level. And yet the second Kennan's writing about the United States showed no sophistication at all. He portrayed an America devoid of leadership, riddled with corruption, engulfed in pollution, beset with boredom, and pervaded by such loneliness that the entire country seemed populated by refugees from Edward Hopper paintings. It was as if the New Deal had never happened.

In an unpublished memoir also composed in 1938, Kennan made a point of describing how a committee of experts under Austria's chancellor Kurt Schuschnigg had revised that country's social insurance system three years earlier: the government had been authoritarian, yet it had shown that an "intelligent, determined ruling minority" could act more responsibly than most democracies. Had Nazi Germany not taken over Austria, the scheme would have been "a model of foresight and thoroughness." But in 1935, the same year that Schuschnigg's experts submitted their recommendations, the Roosevelt administration established from scratch, through constitutional processes, a social security system far more robust than its Austrian counterpart. Kennan seems not to have noticed this, or the more general fact that an American *democratic* revolution was taking place in the 1930s that would, for all its shortcomings, shape world history at least as decisively as what was happening in the authoritarian states of Europe.[37]

To be sure, the Department of State did not expect Kennan to write professionally about the United States. His "reporting" on America was to himself and—occasionally in a sanitized form—to Jeanette and Bill Bullitt. He was free to indulge in impressions, omissions, even inconsistencies. But the same was true of his letters and diary entries about the Soviet Union, which also were not meant for publication. It's clear from reading these that Kennan knew what he was writing about. It's clear from reading his writings on the United States that he did not.

One explanation is that he had not lived there for more than a few months since being sent to Geneva in 1927. He had never traveled as extensively in the United States as he had in Europe. He had read more American literature than American history, and he appears to have had no interest at all in American politics. He viewed the country through a series of snapshots that were, to him, extraordinarily vivid; but they focused on small scenes at particular moments. They offered little sense of the country as a whole, or of its evolution through time. They provided a poor basis for grandiloquent generalizations about where the United States had been and where it was going.

Another difficulty was that Kennan romanticized what he did know. He could remember an America in which travel was by train and boat, automobiles were a novelty, not a curse, and country roads were elongated communities, like Chaucer's highways. Something of value had indeed been lost. But that same America had lacked antibiotics: hence his mother's death from a ruptured appendix, and his own near-death from scarlet fever. It was as if Kennan filtered his past through a gauzy screen, blurring or even eliminating the bad parts, while exaggerating those he saw in the present.

That led him, in turn, to turn personal grievances into national problems. He blamed capitalism for having left him on the verge of poverty in 1932, but he was hardly alone in this and as a result the domestic political system had brought about reforms. But it had also brought Joe Davies to Moscow in 1937, so there was little to be said for it: "Was the Foreign Service really supposed . . . to place itself at the disposal of each successive administration as a nurse-maid to its patronage creditors? If so, we were really nothing but high-paid flunkeys."[38] Kennan's view of the United States lacked a sense of proportion: displacement failed to produce the detachment that characterized the perspectives of foreign interpreters like Alexis de Tocqueville, James Bryce, and Alistair Cooke.

The problem, fundamentally, was patriotism. "I wonder whether anyone who has not lived abroad can understand the hypersensitiveness which expatriate Americans can develop toward their own country," Kennan wrote in another unpublished memoir composed in the early 1940s. Their information was necessarily based more on past memories than on present knowledge, yet faith in the United States was a spiritual necessity. "Were it to be otherwise—were it not to be possible to rely on the basic worthiness, the decency, the justice and the soundness of one's own country—then the Foreign Service officer would indeed be a lost soul." So Kennan came back to America "glowing inwardly at everything which . . . is sound and right and refreshing, and wincing at everything which offends a taste rendered more discriminate than the average by its ability to draw comparisons." His sensitivity was that of a musical instrument, vibrating to the "most minute phenomena," for "[t]hat which he represented having been judged for years by him, he can now do no other than to judge himself by that which he represents."[39]

"I think it's so extraordinary," Chip Bohlen later recalled. "He really sees things in a somber light, particularly as far as the United States is concerned." And yet "I don't mean for one minute the slightest suggestion that he wasn't a patriotic government servant. Indeed he was." Kennan viewed himself as *so* American that he had trouble distinguishing his own character from that of his country: he had always found it difficult, Bohlen remembered, to "divorce his visceral feelings from his knowledge of facts."[40] Because he was by nature a pessimist, he took a pessimistic view of the United States. Whatever inward glow he may have felt appeared rarely in what he wrote, but the winces—and worse—were always there. Faith in America left him doubting democracy: an American-bred authoritarianism, hence, was the only alternative.

Wisconsin was an exception. Despite the loneliness of its highways and the bleakness of its small-town life, it was, Kennan believed, a "compact commonwealth" with an admirable balance between industry and agriculture, a sturdy population, and a tradition of humaneness and good nature. Could it not become, like some of the small neutral countries of Europe, a refuge for decency and common sense? But this too was personalizing the country: Wisconsin was home and therefore his own refuge. It was a place where he could "conceivably be content," confident that he was doing something worthwhile. Salvation lay in smallness, whether of government, avocation, or aspiration.

The time for that, however, had not yet come. Kennan was "much too broke and in debt" to contemplate retirement from the Foreign Service. Moreover, Europe was heating up, what with Hitler's annexation of Austria in March and his demands for Czechoslovakia's German-speaking Sudetenland: "I did not want to miss the climax." So Kennan made his plea to his friends in the State Department, and they responded, in August, with instructions to depart as soon as possible for Prague.[41] It would be, also, a "compact commonwealth," but one surrounded, unlike Wisconsin, by Nazi German authoritarianism.

SEVEN

Czechoslovakia and Germany: 1938–1941

"ALL IN ALL, I THINK IT IS AN EXCELLENT SOLUTION," KENNAN wrote Bullitt in August 1938. The assignment to Prague was "eminently satisfactory." He would be the only secretary in the American legation. He knew German, "and I find that I can read Bohemian with little difficulty, after the effort I've put in on Russian." His time in Vienna had given him an interest in Central Europe. The only disappointment was that "I cannot have another chance to work with you."[1]

The timing could hardly have been better—or worse. On September 12 Hitler threatened military action against Czechoslovakia if it did not give up the Sudetenland. The resulting war scare led British prime minister Neville Chamberlain, on the fourteenth, to request a meeting: it took place the following day at Berchtesgaden, the dictator's mountain retreat. That same day *The Washington Post* ran a photograph of George and Annelise with Grace and Joan, aged six and two, under the headline "Alexandrian and Family Headed for Danger Zone." The editorial cartoon that day showed a skeletal finger turning the clock back from 1938 to 1914. The Kennans sailed from New York aboard the SS *Washington* on September 21, only to run into the great hurricane that would, when it hit Long Island and New England later that evening, kill some seven hundred people. "It was a fitting and ominous beginning," George recalled, "to the coming tour of duty in Europe."[2]

The ship's radio allowed its passengers to follow the developing crisis, but only sketchily. They did get the news that Chamberlain had met Hitler again at Bad Godesberg on the twenty-second, that Hitler had rejected the compromise Chamberlain proposed there, and that war was rumored to be only days away. Alarmed, the State Department advised George by radiogram that "[y]our family should not proceed to Prague at this time." They landed at Le Havre on the twenty-eighth, where they learned that Hitler and Chamberlain would hold a third meeting at Munich the next day with the Italian prime minister, Benito Mussolini, and the French premier, Édouard Daladier. With no way to know whether to expect war or peace, the disembarkation took place in "almost complete pandemonium." "For me," George remembered, "the war really began on that day."[3]

Despite the confusion, he managed to telephone the American embassy in Paris, which told him to bring himself and his family there. They arrived by train that evening, driving to the hotel through blacked-out streets, to find an airplane ticket to Prague for George only—the family would go to Norway.

> I got up alone the next morning in the darkness, and kissed my children good-by as they lay asleep in their beds. . . . [F]or the first time there was brought home to me a tiny part of that vast human misery summed up under the term of war-time separations. During the next four years, I was destined to see my children only on rare and brief occasions; and it was a loss which no victories, no reparations, no acquisitions of power could ever make good.

Kennan's plane, the last one for weeks from Paris to Prague, departed shortly before the one that would fly Daladier to Munich. Bombers were visible on German airfields, ready to take off. Czechoslovakia looked more peaceful, "[b]ut there were hundreds of thousands of men, down there, poised to shoot at each other, or not to shoot, depending on the outcome of the events of the day."[4]

The silence in Prague, when Kennan arrived, was unsettling for someone so recently in New York. It seemed implausible "that this quiet spot, where the swallows wheeled in the sunshine over roofs of Spanish tile and the sound of church-bells drifted down the hillsides, [could be] the center of world attention, and might within twenty-four hours be laid waste by German bombers." But the city was packed with people snapping up newspapers, while correspondents clustered around radios in the hotels, waiting for word from Munich. As rumors of the settlement began to come in, "horror and bitterness" swept the city. Kennan had to be careful, walking through the darkened streets, not to speak English loud enough to be overheard. The next day the Czechs listened to the official announcement "with all the excruciating sadness of a small people" who had tried to preserve their independence, "only to be cheated at last of the fruits of their efforts." They faced a future over which they had no control, seeking solace where they could while "the hand of misfortune—ponderous and relentless—smashed one after another of their most cherished creations."[5]

I.

"Prague is wonderfully beautiful," George wrote Frieda Por in mid-October, "but it is a sad time that I have experienced here." With the Germans occupying Czech territory to the north, west, and south, the city was almost completely cut off. It had, hence, a museumlike atmosphere.

> The old streets, relieved of motor vehicles by an obliging army, had recovered something of their pristine quiet and composure. Baroque towers—themselves unreal and ethereal—floated peacefully against skies in which the bright blue of autumn made way frequently for isolated, drifting clouds. . . . And the little groups of passers-by still assembled hourly in the market place, as they had for centuries, to watch the saints make their appointed rounds in the clock on the wall of the town hall.

But the world had bid farewell, it seemed, to the civility these monuments represented: this was a new and more brutal age. In the church near the City Hall, a priest instructed his congregation on how they should respond to the Munich betrayal. "Let them turn their faces from it. Let them abandon all hope of the virtue of the human race and seek their solace in a just, unbending, and stern God." Meanwhile, on the square outside, "[f]at Jews sat gloomily over their coffee cups and German papers."[6]

George's legation duties were light. "The work—after all the headaches of Moscow and the Department's Russian desk—seems like child's play," he wrote Cousin Grace. The minister, Wilbur J. Carr, was "as nice and kind as he can be." But there were, as always, irritating Americans to deal with. One was "an attractive young lady," indignantly tossing "a most magnificent head of golden hair," who demanded to know what the legation staff of eight proposed to do about the thousands of refugees from the Sudetenland who would be descending on Prague in the next few days. "We relegated her . . . to the category of ignorant, impractical do-gooders, and were relieved to get her out of the office." She turned out to be the journalist Martha Gellhorn, later a close friend, and George realized in retrospect that both had lessons they could have taught each other.

Even more exasperating was "young Kennedy" whose father, the American ambassador in London and another of Roosevelt's political appointees, had sent him on a "fact-finding" mission. The kid was "obviously an upstart and an ignoramus," so with the "polite but weary punctiliousness that characterizes diplomatic officials required to busy themselves with pesky compatriots," Kennan got him to Prague through German lines and back out again. It was a shock when the memory suddenly returned while Kennan was ambassador to Yugoslavia in the early 1960s, the kid having appointed him to that position. "By just such blows, usually much too late . . . , is the ego gradually cut down to size."[7]

Kennan was living, for the moment, in a flat presided over by an unpleasant German woman "whose stupidity is counter-balanced by a most amazing meticulousness and efficiency." She had fixed his few clothes "as they have never been fixed in their lives. Yesterday she even discovered that I had a book with uncut pages and spent half an hour indignantly setting that matter to right." With no car, he was hiking regularly in the countryside, sometimes fifteen or twenty miles a day, although he had to stop doing so in an improbable Abercrombie and Fitch outfit—a red mackinaw coat with matching breeches—because it made him look German: peasants muttered angrily whenever they saw him. Like the resentment of city-dwellers on hearing English, these were small, if misdirected, signs of defiance.[8]

Meanwhile the German army—"those gray-clad figures which were to become so familiar to all of Europe during the coming three years"—was ominously near. Traveling north through the Sudetenland at the end of October, Kennan found the officers he met receiving long lines of Czech, German, and Jewish refugees with equal courtesy. It was the first of many occasions on which he would wonder about "the strange qualities of that vast organization . . . , which has so stern a conscience for the correctness of its own behavior toward those who have submitted to its authority, and then—once its military work has been done—turns over its helpless charges without a quiver to the mercies of the National Socialist Party and the Gestapo." Already "Jews not wanted" signs were showing up in shabby Sudetenland hotels, but a young German soldier with whom Kennan shared a train compartment was "filled with childish confidence that a better life had come for all concerned in that unhappy district."[9]

George was making that trip to meet Annelise, who was driving their American car south—it had, with the family, crossed the ocean on the SS *Washington* and then taken refuge in Norway. The plan had been to rendezvous at the Hotel Flensburger Hof on the German-Danish border, but the police had taken it over, so George went on into Denmark, stationing himself on the outskirts of a town through which Annelise would have to pass. As tended to happen at tense moments, he was coming down with a bad cold that not even the warmth of aquavit could alleviate.

Finally, just as I was beginning to despair, she showed up—tearing like a bat out of hell and armed with that determined look, in the face of which neither time nor tide nor sleet nor rain are of any particular avail. When she saw me she stopped with a screeching of brakes that brought the village to its feet and the doughty Danes were treated to the sight of what they must have considered one of the quickest and most successful pick-ups on record.

They got back to Flensburg that evening, and "I subsided into bed with a fever of 101° and teeth rattling like a machine gun."

After a long wet drive the next day the Kennans checked into the Bristol Hotel in Berlin, where they ran into old Moscow friends, the journalists Demaree Bess and Walter Duranty. It was a new experience to find themselves there "at the peak of Germany's amazing development of strength, [recognizing] that here was at last a power—in a sense Moscow's own monstrous progeny—prepared to meet the Kremlin on its own terms." The Kennans lunched with Cyrus Follmer the next day, had tea with the Kozhenikovs, "who hadn't changed a bit," and then dinner with Charlie Thayer, now stationed in Berlin. After dinner, in his apartment, they sat up most of the night listening to Russian music while "talking, talking, talking as I suppose only people can who have lived in Russia and felt that strange, direct need for human communication which seizes everybody in that vast, drab country."

The car broke down on the way back to Prague, requiring its temporary abandonment in a village next to a new industrial plant—a project of the Luftwaffe chief Hermann Goering—where "[g]reat chimneys faded up into the night sky and enormous spurts of red flame lit the dark countryside." But on the third-class train into Dresden, tired German workmen sat silently, heads in hands, saying nothing about National Socialism. Dresden mechanics, "whose urban prestige demanded that they outdo their provincial colleagues," got the car going again, and it got the Kennans to Prague without further incident.[10]

They found there an apartment in a seventeenth-century palace. With walls a foot thick and nothing symmetrical, "you had a feeling of security as great as though you had been in an air raid shelter." It didn't matter that the Czech army was auctioning off its horses in the courtyard. The animals, at least, were indifferent to their fate. Grace and Joan arrived in time for Christmas, along with the handmade red cribs that had accompanied them to Moscow and Alexandria. "[F]or a few brief months, while the clouds of war and desolation moved steadily closer and an uneasy lightning played on the horizons of Europe, we again had the luxury of a home."[11]

There was still a diplomatic community, and although social life was not very cheerful, "it is quite enough as far as we are concerned," Annelise wrote Jeanette, "George particularly!" There were opportunities for tennis, horseback riding, ice skating, even dancing: "The other night I found myself having scrambled eggs and sausages at 5 o'clock in the morning. I hadn't been up so late since we were in Russia." Nonetheless, she noticed, the world outside was making itself known. "One Sunday we visited at an estate which is now in Germany. While we had tea the Gestapo was announced. Queer feeling." George urged his sister to visit while there was still time. Prague had been preserved "only by a damn thin margin."[12]

II.

Despite his sympathy for the Czechs, Kennan's first reaction to Munich had been one of relief. Their country's fortunes, he was sure, lay in the long run "with—and not against —the dominant forces of this area." The Allies had erred in breaking up the Austro-Hungarian Empire after World War I, and certainly in leaving three million Germans within Czechoslovakia's boundaries. No state could have survived as a democracy under those circumstances. At least Munich had preserved "a magnificent younger generation—disciplined, industrious, and physically fit— which would undoubtedly have been sacrificed if the solution had been the romantic one of hopeless resistance rather than the humiliating but truly heroic one of realism."[13]

That view assumed, though, that the Munich settlement would stick. Kennan's travels around the country quickly convinced him that it would not. The Germans were demanding what amounted to extraterritoriality, with jurisdiction over everyone of their nationality in Czechoslovakia. They were building no customs houses or passport control facilities along the new borders. Their businessmen were avoiding long-term deals with Czech counterparts. The army was under pressure to yield to German control. And the authorities in Slovakia and Ruthenia, which made up the eastern half of the country, had been completely won over by the Germans. "They are making awful fools of themselves; dressing up in magnificent fascist uniforms, flying to and fro in airplanes, . . . and dreaming dreams of the future grandeur of the Slovak or Ukrainian nations."[14]

Germany's racial policies also threatened the status quo. If left alone, Kennan reported in February 1939, Czechoslovakia would treat its Jews relatively humanely: there was not, in itself, "the basis for a really serious and widespread anti-Semitic movement." Yet German demands were already forcing Jews out of government, university, and other professional positions, and there were calls for more radical measures to eliminate Jewish influence. Because the Czechs on their own would be reluctant to go that far, meeting those requirements "might very well necessitate readjustment in the Prague government."[15]

The final blow to the truncated Czechoslovak state came early in March when the Slovaks, with German approval, demanded complete independence. Hitler then executed long-standing plans to occupy all remaining Czech territory. Kennan got the word at four-thirty on the morning of the fifteenth. "Determined that the German army should not have the satisfaction of giving the American Legation a harried appearance, I shaved meticulously before going to the office." He and the staff spent the morning burning their records on the American Jewish Joint Distribution Committee, which was helping Jews escape from Central Europe, lest the Nazis seize them. Meanwhile, ashen-faced applicants for asylum were lining up outside, but there was no authority to grant it, and there would have been few facilities for providing it. "Their faces were twitching and their lips trembling when I sent them away."

"People were caught like mice in a trap," Annelise wrote to Jeanette a few days later. "The Jews are panic-stricken. Our Consulate is swarmed with them. We have heard about many suicides already. I feel sor[r]y for them, but not half as sorry as for the Czechs." One Jewish acquaintance, who George knew had worked with the Americans for many years, showed up at the apartment. "We couldn't possibly keep him." The legation was about to be withdrawn, in which case American diplomatic privileges would probably be revoked, and "[h]e'd only have been in worse shape for having been found in our place." Besides, there were ten thousand others: "I told him that I could not give him asylum, but that as long as he was not demanded by the authorities he was welcome to stay there and to make himself at home."

For twenty-four hours he haunted the house, a pitiful figure of horror and despair, moving uneasily around the drawing room, smoking one cigarette after another, too unstrung to eat or think of anything but his plight. His brother and sister-in-law had committed suicide together after Munich, and he had a strong inclination to follow suit. Annelise pleaded with him at intervals throughout the coming hours not to choose this way out, not because she or I had any great optimism with respect to his chances for future happiness but partly on general Anglo-Saxon principles and partly to preserve our home from this sort of an unpleasantness.

"I was very worried," Annelise acknowledged, "that he was going to commit suicide with my two children there." But George advised him and other Jewish friends to go straight to the German army and apply to emigrate: "It's going to be easier than when they have the SS in." This worked, and they made their way safely out of the country.

By noon the Germans had taken the city: there were hundreds of vehicles plastered with snow, the occupants' faces red with what some thought was shame but what George feared was mostly the cold. Annelise noted that many of the Czechs "hissed, showed their fists, and shouted pfui." On the next day Hitler arrived, and the Kennans watched him pass by. "One thing which rather pleased me," Annelise commented, "was the quiet in the streets. They marched the Germans up to cheer for Hitler, but it was might[y] few and seemed like a drop in the bucket to what he was accustomed to." George too found the silence striking. "Hitler rode quietly past our front door, without even a crowd on the side-walk to impede the view."

With the extinction of Czechoslovak independence, most foreign embassies and legations left Prague. But the State Department kept the American consulate general open, making Kennan responsible for political reporting from what was now the German "protectorate" of Bohemia and Moravia. "The job," he explained to Jeanette, "is, all in all, an enviable one. I have my own office and staff, . . . and am more or less independent." He and Annelise would keep their apartment but would be ready to send the children to Norway at any moment if that seemed necessary. And George had to recommend, reluctantly, that Jeanette defer her trip, because "the whole situation is now too shaky for anyone to make any plans for more than a few days."[16]

III.

With Czechoslovakia the first non-German state the Nazis had taken over, their policies might well set a precedent for what to expect elsewhere in Europe, now that Hitler's intentions were clear. Kennan's job would be to convey this preview to Washington. Berlin, he thought, should want "peace, quiet, and a minimum of bad feeling," because Czechoslovakia was incidental to more distant objectives. Even Hitler had to worry about public opinion. Here Kennan was echoing one of the few shrewd insights in his 1938 "Prerequisites" essay: that dictators, "having deprived themselves of all legal means of retreat, have the bear by the tail." He now could watch how this dictator handled that problem.[17]

The Czechs, at first, did not seem bearlike. "Toward their rulers they show— like the 'brave soldier Švejk' of Czech literary fame—a baffling willingness to comply with any and all demands." They coupled this, though, with "an equally baffling ability to execute them in such a way that the effect is quite different from that contemplated by those who did the commanding." Beneath the surface, they were bitter indeed—so much so that they were the only Europeans who wanted a great war, because only that could liberate them. Clandestine political groups were already forming, ready to become resistance movements as soon as hostilities commenced. Nor would the Czechs, if victory came, treat their tormentors gently: "Retaliation will be fearful to contemplate."[18]

If the Germans were to have a trouble-free occupation, therefore, they would have to show tact and restraint, for which they were not noted. Their failure to do so appeared quickly. The military authorities allowed the Czechoslovak president, Emil Hácha, to retain his position and his residence in Hradčany Palace but rendered him honors in ways that suggested ridicule rather than respect. It was small recompense to have Hitler as an unannounced houseguest whenever it suited his convenience. Berlin appointed Konrad Henlein, the leader of the Sudeten German separatists, to administer all of Bohemia, but then removed him. Since nothing could have done more to harden Czech hostility, it was difficult to see why he had been selected in the first place. By the end of May, arrests were increasing, prisons were filling up, and old ones were reopening. Reports of brutality were all too well authenticated. Terror had now begun, and the Czechs "are quite powerless to oppose it."[19]

Meanwhile, the Slovaks' "independence" was turning out to be that "of a dog on a leash." Their leaders were mismanaging their economy, the Hungarians were openly coveting their territory, and the Slovaks themselves, who were hardly pro-Czech, were beginning to realize that they were not apt to fare as well as they had before dismantling their former shared state. If war broke out, the Bratislava regime would prove too undependable to be of use to the Germans, and they would take it over as well.[20]

Jews had even less to hope for. There had been no Jew-baiting in the streets of Prague, as had followed the *Anschluss* in Vienna, Kennan reported at the end of

March; still, Jews could hardly expect a fate much different from those in Nazi Germany. In Ostrava, near the Polish border, he found Jews being excluded from all public places. "One doctor, I am told, has attended thirty-three Jewish suicides since the occupation." And in Slovakia, legislation had relegated Jews to the status of "thieves, criminals, swindlers, insane people, and alcoholics." None of this made any sense in countries still dependent on Jewish capital.[21]

The Czechs, being realists, might have reconciled themselves to German rule had it been "firm in its purposes, conscious of its responsibilities, integrated in its activities, and incorruptible in the performance of its duties." But it had been none of these things; instead the Germans had given the impression "of a regime in an advanced state of moral disintegration." All of this had implications for the future of Europe, because until the Nazis developed greater maturity, they would stand little chance of successfully managing responsibilities borne for centuries—"and at times not uncreditably"—by the Roman Catholic Church and the Hapsburg Empire.[22]

Although Messersmith praised Kennan's reports, there is no evidence that they went beyond the State Department, or that they had any impact on American foreign policy in the final months of peace in Europe. They did reflect, though, a conviction that would grow stronger in Kennan's mind, the more he saw of the Germans over the next few years: "that even in the event of a complete military victory the Nazis would still face an essentially insoluble problem in the political organization and control of the other peoples of the continent." The reason was that Nazi ideology had nothing to offer apart from "glorification of the supposed virtues of the German people," an argument that had "no conceivable appeal" to anyone else.[23]

That conclusion, in time, would also shape Kennan's view of the country that eventually defeated Nazi Germany and sought its own domination of Europe. For the moment, though, the Soviet Union was moving toward an uneasy alliance with Hitler, the surprise announcement of which, on August 24, 1939, made possible Germany's attack on Poland a week later, and the beginning of the Second World War.

IV.

For all of his skill in analyzing Russia and Germany, Kennan failed to anticipate the Nazi-Soviet Pact. He had noted, in 1935, the Soviet Union's propensity to seek "non-aggression" treaties with capitalist states while building up its military strength for an eventual confrontation with them. He had wondered, after Hitler extinguished Czechoslovakia's independence in 1939, why the Germans were discouraging the Ruthenians' ambitions to make themselves the nucleus of a Nazi Ukraine. But Kennan did not put these two things together, assuming instead that if the Soviet Union aligned itself with anyone, it would be Britain and France. He did not know that an old Moscow acquaintance, Hans-Heinrich (Johnnie) Herwarth von Bittenfeld, a part-Jewish German diplomat, was using tennis matches and horseback rides at the American dacha to pass along top-secret information to Bohlen on the negotiations leading up to the Hitler-Stalin accord. But Bohlen hedged his reports to Washington, and when the State Department did at last alert the British and French ambassadors, their governments did nothing.[24]

Kennan, still in German-occupied Prague, had no espionage service to draw upon. The only people "who could tell us things," he explained to Messersmith in April, were no longer people worth trusting—presumably Germans. The best alternative was to attempt to guess, from an understanding of the past and an analysis of the present, what they might be planning. But his reports could go only by courier, and by May he was not even sure that he could continue sending those out. "[A]t the moment," he acknowledged, "it is a rather lonely job."[25]

Grace and Joan stayed in Prague through the first months of German occupation; in June, though, George and Annelise sent them to Kristiansand while treating themselves to a brief vacation in England. The sailing from Hamburg, he wrote, was "the saddest I have ever seen," with only a few forlorn passengers present as the ship's band tried to cheer things up with "Deutschland über Alles" and the "Horst Wessel Lied." London was disconcertingly normal, as equestrians rode badly in Hyde Park, while a fascist heckled a communist at Speaker's Corner. George got to meet Anna Freud, "a very fine psychologist in her own right," and then went off on his own for a few morose days on the Isle of Wight, where the food was "unimaginative beyond belief."[26]

There was time, after returning to Prague, for an automobile trip through Slovakia to Budapest, and then in early August for a family visit in Norway. George got back in midmonth and on the nineteenth sent his last long prewar dispatch, describing the summer as a strange and unhappy one: "Everything is in suspense. No one takes the initiative; no one plans for the future." Annelise arrived on the day the Nazi-Soviet Pact was announced, only to be sent back, "in high indignation," on what turned out to be the last train from Berlin into Sweden. "I didn't want to leave as I didn't think there would be immediate danger in Prague, but G. thought

I ought to." After a few days in Oslo, she arrived in Kristiansand on September 3, the day of Great Britain's declaration of war against Germany. "I hope all the time that this war is just a nightmare and that I'll wake up soon and find that it isn't true."

George was still in Prague when the war began. The State Department decided to transfer him to Berlin, and he drove himself there on empty highways in mid-September, carrying extra supplies of gasoline since there was none to be bought along the way. Embassy wives and children had departed, strict rationing was in place, and "I am settling down," he wrote Jeanette, "to what is bound to be a nasty assignment." Berlin had become provincial and dreary. "If there are any nice Germans left, it is practically impossible to have any normal association with them. . . . But it's all experience and it's what we're paid for."

During the past few weeks, he added, "I have felt myself overcome by wave after wave of sheer patriotism and gratitude to our poor old country for the relative quantity of good humor and decency which, thank God, it still contains." This was unlikely in itself to be enough, however: "If we are unwilling to make any serious move toward the prevention of the disintegration of Europe, I wish that we would at least start now on a rearmament program which would make everything we have done before look like child's play. Because if Europe disintegrates much further we may need it."[27]

V.

The State Department expected Kennan to continue the kind of political reporting he had been doing from Prague, but it soon became clear that the embassy in Berlin was overwhelmed. Having taken over British and French interests in Germany, it was keeping track of prisoners of war, assisting civilian nationals left behind, managing diplomatic properties, and arranging exchanges of official personnel. Out of sympathy for Alexander Kirk, the *chargé d'affaires*, Kennan volunteered his services as administrative officer and continued in that capacity throughout most of the time he was there.[28]

Annelise joined George after a few weeks, leaving the children in the comparative safety—and certainly the easier life—of neutral Norway. The fear of bombs in Berlin, she wrote Jeanette, was not great, since it was far away, well defended, and "the British seem to content themselves by throwing pamphlets." The blackout, however, was extreme. Going home each evening, George recalled, involved groping in pitch blackness from column to column of the Brandenburg gate, feeling my way by hand after this fashion to the bus stop; the waiting for the dim blue lights of the bus to come sweeping out of the obscurity; then the long journey out five and a half miles of the "east-west axis"; the dim, hushed interior of the bus, lightened only by the sweeps of the conductor's flashlight; the wonder as to how the driver ever found his way over the vast expanse of unmarked, often snow-covered asphalt . . . ; the eerie walk home at the other end, again with much groping and feeling for curb- stones; [and finally] the façade of what appeared, from outside its blackout curtains, to be a dark and deserted home; and the ultimate pleasant discovery, always with a tinge of surprise, on opening the door that behind the curtains was light, at least a minimal measure of warmth, . . . a wife, and a coziness all the more pronounced for the vast darkness and uncertainty of the war that lay outside.

The Kennans had rented a house they could ill afford, George explained to Jean- ette, in order to have a place where they could do something for friends: "At least give them a meal or a bed when they need one most."[29]

One guest was a German Baltic woman George had known in Riga, who now had three children. Terrified that the Soviet Union was about to absorb the Baltic states—it did in 1940—she and her family had fled to Germany with one suitcase each on three hours' notice. All they could expect, George believed, was resettle- ment in the apartment of "some miserable Pole who had himself been kicked out on three hours' notice." They would take over that family's belongings in compen- sation for their own, and then be expected to begin life over again "surrounded by the fanatical hatred and resentment of the neighbors." If George went broke putting up such friends for a few days at a time, he wrote his sister, then "I'll come back to Wisconsin and you can all support me . . . until I learn how to make bas- kets or breed cows or something." The family stayed with the Kennans for three months.[30]

Meanwhile the office routine was demanding—"people have stupidly neglected to provide any holidays in the prosecution of wars"—but rewarding: "My tasks and responsibilities are such that if I cope with them successfully I need have no qualms about running even the largest of our Foreign Service establishments, in the future." The years ahead would be full of difficulty, with an element of danger thrown in. There was at least the comfort, though, that if he had any belief left in the value of living when he came home, "it will not be for want of contact with the seamier aspects of human nature."[31]

There was, of course, still Norway. George and Annelise rejoined the children in Kristiansand for the Christmas of 1939, walking around the tree holding hands, opening presents, and attending amateur theatricals, while relishing "peace, lights, shops, food, smart clothes, smiling faces, mountains, snow, and normalcy." More Norwegian seamen than French soldiers had died as a result of military action, George reported to Jeanette on the last day of the decade, but the war was still, "as for you at home, a matter of voices on the radio and headlines in the papers. Let's hope that it will long continue to remain so."[32]

VI.

Apart from proclaiming neutrality and establishing a western hemispheric security zone, President Roosevelt's first significant diplomatic initiative after the war broke out came in February 1940, when he sent Under Secretary of State Sumner Welles on a mission to Rome, Berlin, London, and Paris. The purpose of the trip was left vague, but Roosevelt probably meant it to show that he had neglected no possibility, however remote, of helping to settle the conflict. Welles was not to visit Moscow—FDR was still angry about the Soviet attack on Finland two months earlier. But on the assumption that Welles might want information on the U.S.S.R., Kennan was assigned to meet him in Italy and accompany him through Switzerland and Germany. Welles asked for none, leaving Kennan with little to do but follow him around and help with the travel arrangements. Nothing came of the mission, but George did get himself, or at least part of himself, photographed in *Life*: everyone else was in the picture, he wrote Jeanette, "but all you could see of me was a hump in the table cloth, which denoted my knee."[33]

The visit to Rome did provide a chance to compare Mussolini's regime with Hitler's. Kennan thought the Italian dictator wise to have preserved the monarchy. The future of Europe, he wrote in a paper he finished while on the trip, might well lie in the survival of an aristocracy "pliable enough, irrational enough, and at the same time stable enough, to bridge all the delicate contradictions of the continent." Hitler was well on the way to unifying it, but he was doing so without any sense of responsibility for European culture as a whole. Monarchies, for all their foibles, at least had that. One ought not to shrink, therefore, "at the restoration of the Mozart court and the chocolate soldier. It is the real soldiers that are dangerous."[34]

Kennan saw plenty of them on both sides of the Rhine while escorting the

Welles mission from Berlin to Basel. They were not shooting at each other, but that was unlikely to last, at which point the war was bound to take its toll, even in Scandinavia. For the moment, though, George wrote Jeanette in February, "the little rascals will have to stay in Norway and take their chances along with several hundreds of thousands of Norwegian kids." Annelise joined them there in March.[35]

On April 4 George, back in Berlin, got information that changed his mind: "I had reason to call her long distance and ask her to bring the children back at once." He met them in Copenhagen on the sixth: Gracie and Joan were dressed in twin blue coats, with Happy Hooligan bonnets. The family returned by train to Berlin and on the eighth learned that a German ship had been torpedoed off Kristiansand. Mounting rescue efforts with characteristic thoroughness, the Norwegians wondered why the survivors all seemed to be young men of the same age with military haircuts. The next morning the Germans announced the occupation of Denmark and Norway. "At noon, Annelise and I heard together, with a feeling of sickness and horror, of the bombing of Kristiansand and the shelling of the town from the sea." She had taken it all with "composure and dignity," George wrote Jeanette on the fifteenth, "[b]ut it is naturally a cruel strain on her, and it is something which I am afraid neither of us will ever quite get over, however it turns out."

Kristiansand, he added, had always seemed a little unreal: "So much decency and comfort and health [existing] side by side, within a few hundred miles distance, with such overpowering forces of nastiness and perversion and brutality." But now at least things were clear. "The worst has happened, and there are no more questions to be asked . . . no more wondering about who is right and who is wrong." It would be, henceforth, a simple matter "of who gets whom, as Lenin put it. And we know only too definitely which side we are on."

What was not clear was where the family would go next. The embassy did not want wives with children staying in Berlin. The Kennans owned no home in the United States. George suggested France, but Annelise wisely objected: "I would be just two steps ahead of the German army with two children. I don't think this is a very realistic idea from somebody who is very smart." So they decided, in the end, on Highland Park. "We knew that we could stay with [Jeanette] for the summer. And that was as far as we thought."[36]

George was able to get everyone to Genoa—the port where, sixteen years earlier, he and Nick Messolonghitis had thrown themselves on the mercy of a harried

American vice-consul—and on May 4, 1940, Annelise, Grace, and Joan boarded the SS *Manhattan,* the ship they had shared, four years earlier, with the American athletes on their way to the Berlin Olympics. It was supposed to sail at eight o'clock that evening, but after dinner George went back to the dock, suspecting the ship might still be there. It was, although the gangplank had been taken up.

> A friend on deck kindly went below and summoned Annelise to the porthole, which was just at the level of the dock but some eight feet away. There, separated by those eight feet which were already just as effective and as irrevocable as eight thousand miles, we stole a half an hour from the semi-eternity of separation which had already begun.

At last the ship began to move, and soon "there was only a very tiny arm, waving with frantic despairing cheer, to indicate the particular cubby-hole of floating steel to which I had entrusted my only treasure of reality and permanence."[5]

VII.

On May 6, while on his way back from Genoa, Kennan heard radio reports of increasing tension in the Mediterranean: "I reflected with smug satisfaction that my family must by that time be somewhere west of Gibraltar." On the eighth, in the train to Berlin, he got into a conversation with a German American, now a Nazi, full of boasts about Germany's strengths and the weaknesses of the United States. Kennan consoled himself with the thought that if his country did harbor strengths, they would be of the kind that his traveling companion would be "unable to comprehend anyway." On the tenth he got word that the long-expected German invasion of Holland and Belgium was about to begin: "I rode to the office breakfastless, clutching my shaving articles."

On the fourteenth he dined with a German friend who would be off the next day to join the army. "As a reasonable and patriotic and loyal man, it was the only honorable thing to do, and I understood him. A sense of it being the end of all things hung over us, but our training stood us in good stead; we had a few drinks, and we were a gay little company." On the seventeenth—the Norwegian national holiday—Kennan took his dogs for a walk, let them chase rabbits in vacant lots, and came home "in complete depression, reading of the advance of the German armies in Belgium and France, and wondering how I could adapt myself to a world where Europe lived under the domination of Germany."[38]

Early in June, with France on the verge of defeat, rumors began circulating that the Italians were about to declare war. Kennan walked to the Italian embassy on the afternoon of the tenth, joining a cheerful, indifferent, obedient crowd the German authorities had ordered up, "like the Moscow proletarians bound for a parade." On the veranda were some of the staff, with their wives. The women were dressed as though for a garden party. "I knew most of them and slunk around in the crowd to avoid their seeing me." The sound trucks boomed out Mussolini's speech from Rome, and the Germans, understanding nothing, applauded politely. Later that evening Kennan sat with American friends on his own veranda, drinking highballs and listening to antiaircraft fire in the distance, while another more distant radio voice—Roosevelt's—proclaimed that "the hand which held the dagger had thrust it into the back of its neighbor."[39]

Four days later, equipped with a German permit, Kennan traveled into the Netherlands to reestablish communications with American diplomats there. The train passed boxcars taking prisoners of war east. Their pale faces and bewildered eyes made him wonder whether the day had not passed when free peoples made the better soldiers. Now, in an age of the machine, slave peoples had the advantage, for it was the machine that counted, and "the machine—in contrast to the sword—was best served by slaves."

As the train entered Holland, a Nazi businessman and a Dutch fifth columnist were congratulating each other. "I had to grip the cushion of the first-class compartment to keep from butting in and attempting to blast some of the complacency and hypocrisy of the conversation." In the end, Kennan could not resist, warning the Dutchman that

> he would indeed have a hard time creating a Dutch national-socialist movement: for either it would be truly Dutch, in which case it would be only an unsuccessful competition for the German movement, or it would be pan-Germanic, in which case all the values of Dutch nationalism would be sacrificed and the adherents, instead of being superior Dutchmen, would only be inferior Germans.

At the moment, though, the contradiction meant little. In The Hague, he found a German military band playing to a sizable audience of "placid, applauding Dutchmen," not far from a place where German bombs had wiped out most of a city block. In Rotterdam, shops were open, trains were running, and the streets were crowded with busy people. But suddenly, "with as little transition as though someone had performed the operation with a gigantic knife, the houses stopped, and there began a wide, open field of confused bricks and rubbish." Meanwhile, "the imperturbable Dutch rode along on their bicycles as though nothing had happened."[40]

Two weeks later Kennan was off to occupied France. War damage in Belgium was greater than in Holland, but there was no evidence anywhere of much resistance. With no other way to get to Paris, he offered to hitchhike, complete with diplomatic pouch, perhaps remembering his 1924 trip. But since the only vehicles on the road were those of the German army, embassy officers frowned on this idea and instead lent him a car with enough gasoline to get there, in the company of an American ambulance driver who had been caught behind the lines by the *Blitzkrieg*.

The devastation south of the Belgian frontier was horrendous. All the towns were damaged, and several of the larger ones were "gutted, deserted, and uninhabitable." The odor persisted, in places, of decomposing bodies. German sentries guarded the debris, as though it mattered now who stood before shattered houses and stinking corpses. French refugees were "seared with fatigue and fear and suffering." One girl, riding atop a cart in torn dirty clothes, made a particular impression on Kennan: "Just try to tell her of liberalism and democracy, of progress, of ideals, of tradition, of romantic love." She had seen the complete breakdown of her own people. But she could also see German soldiers, handing out food and water at crossroads, setting up first-aid stations, transporting the old and the sick. "What soil here for German propaganda, what thorough ploughing for the social revolution which national-socialism carries in its train."

In Paris, though, the Germans seemed strangely at a loss: the city was intact but dead. Policemen stood on the corners, without traffic to direct or pedestrians to guard. At the Café de la Paix, six German officers sat at an outside table with "no one but themselves to witness their triumph." It was as if Paris had been "too delicate and shy a thing to stand their domination and had melted away before them just as they thought to have it in their grasp." When the Germans came, its soul disappeared, leaving only stone. "As long as they stay—and it will probably be a long time—it will remain stone."[41]

VIII.

After returning to Berlin early in July 1940, Kennan settled into a lonely bachelor's existence. British air raids were hitting the city regularly now: shrapnel was ripping through the leaves of the trees in his garden, then clanking onto the street. It was more of a nuisance than anything else. Soon he was sleeping through the raids, and there was little evidence that they were having much effect. Hitler's military successes were expanding Kennan's embassy responsibilities as the Americans took over the "interests" of each new country the Germans had invaded, but he was growing more confident that they could not win the war.

September 11 was the Kennans' ninth wedding anniversary, but Annelise was not in Berlin to celebrate. George spent it, instead, arranging a clandestine midnight meeting in a limousine driving around the Grunewald forest. With him was a friend, Hubert Masarik, one of the two Czech diplomats who had been present but ignored at the 1938 Munich conference. Speaking only for himself, Kennan ventured a bold set of predictions: that within a year the United States and the Soviet Union would be at war with Germany, and eventually also with Italy and Japan; that it would take them through 1944 to defeat Hitler, but that victory was certain; that the Czechs should therefore conserve their strength, so that they would never again have to rely on British protection. At Kennan's request, Masarik passed this message on to General Alois Eliás, the Czech prime minister of the German "protectorate." It was, Eliás commented, the best news he had yet received—he expected the Germans to execute him, however, before it could be confirmed. This they did, a year later.[42]

Kennan's optimism was in part psychological warfare: he admired the Czechs, understood their fatalism, and hoped that they would not lose hope. But he had stronger reasons for saying what he did, one of which had to do with what was happening in Czechoslovakia itself. If the Germans' occupation of that country was indeed a hint of how they would run the rest of Europe, then they were already in trouble. Back in Prague in October to close down what was left of the American diplomatic establishment, Kennan found that the Germans had stripped the region of its economic assets, setting off serious inflation: the cost of living had soared by some 50 to 60 percent. Czech universities were closed completely or open only to Germans, and all major industries were now under German control. Their authority might be physically unchallengeable, but morally it did not exist.

"Whatever power the Germans may have over the persons and property of the Czechs, they have little influence over their souls."[43]

A second source of optimism came from souls of a different sort: those of Germans opposed to Hitler. Kirk, the retiring *chargé d'affaires*, had been meeting quietly with Count Helmuth von Moltke, one of several Prussian aristocrats who had always viewed the Nazis with disapproval and now were convinced that Hitler was leading Germany into disaster. After Kirk's departure, Kennan took over this contact, although because he feared leaks, he never reported his conversations to Washington. Another acquaintance with similar views was Gottfried von Bismarck, grandson of the Iron Chancellor, whom Kennan remembered refusing to rise at the opera when Nazi officials came in. Still another was Johnnie von Herwarth, who had leaked the information to Bohlen about the Nazi-Soviet Pact. These connections, however, involved only listening: Roosevelt was not about to authorize negotiations with the conservative German opposition. The conversations did, though, provide evidence of yet more friction within the Nazi machine: the fact that Hitler drew his support from the lower middle class and the nouveau riche, while the old Prussian nobility opposed him.[44]

Finally, it was now clear to Kennan that the Germans were losing military and diplomatic momentum. There were official acknowledgments that the war would not end that winter. The promised invasion of Britain had not materialized. Reports of German bombers raining ruin on English cities became so repetitive that newspaper readers began joking about them. And Kennan was picking up evidence of increasing tension in Soviet-German relations: "All the glowing references to this subject seem to come from Berlin; whereas the Russian expressions of opinion, as far as I see them, are marked by a very obvious dryness, and are interspersed with occasional sharp cracks of the Russian ruler over the German knuckles." By November, there were rumors that Soviet foreign minister Vyacheslav Molotov was about to pay an official visit: "That, if true, would really enliven things." Molotov did come and the meetings were difficult, not least because the last one had to take place in an air raid shelter. The Germans assumed that they had won the war, the acerbic Russian told his German counterpart Joachim von Ribbentrop, but it was the British who seemed to be fighting to the death.[45]

Life in Berlin, George wrote Jeanette, had not been easy: "You will probably find me distinctly older when and if I get back." But there had been no health crises: "Happily I still feel that I am gathering rather than losing strength as these months—some of which are like years—go by. Only I don't know what to use my strength on, when this is all over." He was rising high enough in the Foreign Service to expect significant future appointments but still doubted the American capacity to craft a real foreign policy. The alternative was "to stay home and do something useful." Who, though, would want him? "For good or for bad, I *am* Europeanized." "Thanks for the news about my children," George added. "I just lapped it up."[46]

The first months of 1941 were spent getting back to the United States to see the family, who were now renting a house in Milwaukee. This was not easy in wartime. George left Berlin on January 10, sailed from Lisbon on the seventeenth, and arrived in New York on the twenty-ninth: he then spent three weeks in Wisconsin, where early in February the *Milwaukee Journal* interviewed him as "[o]ne of the leading diplomatic representatives of the United States dealing with the German government." Had he heard Hitler's speeches? "No, I've been too busy at the embassy. . . . As a matter of fact, I don't think I've ever seen Hitler." "Yes you have, daddy," Grace piped up. "Remember we saw him together riding down the street in Prague." "Grace," George admitted, "it seems you remember things better than I do."[47]

The trip back, with Annelise, took five weeks: they did not reach Berlin until April 12. "I don't know how I can thank you enough for taking my little girls," she wrote Jeanette from the ship. "I miss them like hell—it was terribly hard to leave." But "George is not the kind of person who is happy alone and I think he needs me more than the children do (as long as they can stay with you)." Jeanette later admitted to having felt imposed on. "I at the time had [my] three boys and the two girls and I was running a nursery school, and there were times when I felt: 'Oh! It's much easier to go back to Germany with George!' But it wasn't that much easier for her."[48]

Annelise had gone back for several reasons. Her family in Norway had survived the German invasion and was for the moment safe. George had even been allowed to visit the Sørensens briefly before traveling to America. She hoped to do the same, but the Germans refused to allow this: "It is a great disappointment." She also worried about the "Kennan depression" she saw in the letters George had written from Berlin. "I know now that he really did have a bad time and that there were many things which I could have helped him with," she explained to Jeanette. "What a life! It may be exciting in spots, but it almost tears one to pieces. (If I don't stop soon I'll sound as gloomy as George!)"[49]

Something else concerned her as well. Annelise had discovered, by this time, that George's bachelor existence in Berlin had not been celibate: "Our personal life was also very difficult at that time." He had always, he admitted when he was seventy-eight, had a roving eye: "'Thou shalt not covet thy neighbor's wife.' My God, I've coveted ten thousand of them in the course of my life, and will continue to do so on into the eighties." Who this one was, how long the relationship lasted, and how Annelise found out about it remain unclear. Her resolve, however, was firm. When asked decades later why she had left her children to return to a war zone, she cut off further discussion with a single sentence: "To save the marriage."[50]

As the summer wore on, this arrangement too began to unravel. Despite Jeanette's willingness to provide a home for Grace and Joan when they had no other, the burdens on her were growing, but there was no way for both George and Annelise to make another long trip home. He was now the second-ranking officer in the embassy, with no one under him qualified to take over his responsibilities. So Annelise would return alone in September. "We have been so touched by what you have told about the children," George wrote Jeanette. "Poor little things, I wonder if they are destined always to bat around from one place to another with at best half of the normal parent complement."[51]

The need for roots was much on his mind that fall. Plans to purchase part of the island in Kristiansand had fallen through, probably fortunately in the light of the war. Now, though, George had another idea, even if Jeanette thought it "mad": he wanted to buy a farm somewhere in the United States: "I have thought this over very carefully and know what I am doing." After a series of rapid promotions, he was at last relatively well off. American farms were less expensive than Berlin houses, and after all how many other people made $8,000 a year? He had lived for too long with no home at all. He had seen too many places "where every form of existence except that of the small land-holder has been pretty thoroughly shattered." Wisconsin looked like the best bet: it was where the Kennans had lived longer than anywhere else. So might Jeanette and Gene sound out the owner of their grandfather's old farm near Packwaukee?[52]

IX.

"Dined at the Hoyos' to meet an American couple, the George Kennans," Marie Vassiltchikov, a young White Russian living in Berlin who kept a remarkable diary, noted on May 26, 1941. "He has highly intelligent eyes but does not speak freely, but then the situation is of course ambiguous, as the Germans are still allies of Soviet Russia." Kennan faulted himself and his Berlin colleagues, years later, for not having foreseen the abrupt end of that alliance less than a month later. Enough indications of trouble had accumulated, however, for the embassy to warn the State Department, which in turn tried to alert the Kremlin. None of this had any effect, and on June 22 the invasion began. Two days later Kennan sent Loy Henderson, now back in Washington, his views on this major turning point in the war.

He could see the advantage of extending material aid to the Soviet Union "whenever called for by our own self-interest." But there should be no attempts to identify politically or ideologically with the Russian war effort, because to do so would also associate the United States with

> the Russian destruction of the Baltic states, with the attack against Finnish independence, with the partitioning of Poland and Rumania, with the crushing of religion throughout Eastern Europe, and with the domestic policy of a regime which is widely feared and detested throughout this part of the world and the methods of which are far from democratic. It is, I believe, no exaggeration to say that in every border country concerned, from Scandinavia—including Norway and Sweden—to the Black Sea, Russia is generally more feared than Germany.

The Soviet Union was in the war because it had collaborated with Hitler, thereby playing "a lone hand in a dangerous game." It must now take the consequences alone. Sharing no principles with the Western democracies, it had "no claim on Western sympathies."[53]

It was a typical Kennan memorandum, relentlessly clear-sighted in its assessment of European realities, yet wholly impractical in its neglect of domestic political necessities in Washington and London. For how were Roosevelt and the new British prime minister, Winston Churchill, to persuade their democracies to aid the Soviet war effort without identifying politically and ideologically with it? On this point Kennan's nemesis Joseph E. Davies provided more useful advice, insisting in the face of State and War Department skepticism that the Russians would survive the Nazi onslaught, while offering to lead a publicity campaign to convince an equally doubtful American public that the U.S.S.R. would be a worthy ally. FDR listened to Davies, encouraged his efforts, and—given the circumstances—was right to do so.[54]

Kennan's attention remained focused on German-dominated Europe, where by the fall of 1941 the disaster confronting Jews was becoming obvious. "We didn't know about the gas chambers," he recalled. But "we had no optimistic feelings about the fate of the Jewish community. We thought they were in for it." One striking indication of this, George wrote Annelise in October, was the new requirement that the Jews wear yellow stars:

> That is a fantastically barbaric thing. I shall never forget the faces of people in the subway with the great yellow star sewed onto their overcoats, standing, not daring to sit down or to brush against anybody, staring straight ahead of them with eyes like terrified beasts—nor the sight of little children running around with those badges sewn on them.

Most Germans, he sensed, were "shocked and troubled by the measure." Perhaps as a result, "the remaining Jews are being deported in large batches, and very few more stars are to be seen."[55]

"We went to great lengths in the embassy in Berlin," Kennan remembered, "to try to rescue the Jewish children and get them out." The staff had difficulty, however, getting accurate information about the number of children from their parents and from the Jewish community. "[T]hey would falsify their statistics, they wouldn't come clean about things." Perhaps, Kennan later acknowledged, that was how the Jews had survived for centuries in Europe: "Wherever they met authority they had to try to get around it. But all I can say is that we were jolly well fed up with them."[56]

Kennan sensed, during the final months of 1941, "that things were now out of control—not only out of *our* control (we, after all, in our poor overworked embassy, had never at any time had any influence on the course of events), but out of everyone's control." As the Germans advanced into Russia—following the direction and the timing of Napoleon's invasion in 1812—relations with the United States, "never better than frigid at any time since the beginning of the war," continued to deteriorate. "No one knew how the end would come. But many of us sensed it to be near."[57]

With this in mind, Kennan sent a ten-page letter to the State Department on November 20, summing up what his three years in Czechoslovakia and Germany had taught him. It was, in a way, his own "swan song" dispatch. He began with calendar and climate: winter operations in Russia were now inevitable, and that in itself was a defeat for Hitler. "It means that none of the original aims of the Russian campaign has yet been achieved." Despite all their "gushing" about a "New Order," the best the Germans could hope for was a stalemate in the east while attempting to keep an increasingly restive Europe under control. Anything worse could be much worse,

> for Germany still has much to gain but very little that it can afford to lose. The German people themselves are abnormally sensitive to the movements of the barometer of their military fortune. Its general upward climb has come to be taken as a matter of course; but the slightest jog in the other direction sends waves of panic and foreboding running through the country.

Compounding the problem was the fact that Southern and Eastern Europe were "full of desperate little adventurists" who were holding their own people in check with repeated admonitions that the Germans were bound to win the war. If the impression ever took hold in those countries that the tide was running in the other direction, "there is going to be a scurrying for cover such as the world has rarely witnessed."

Even if none of this happened and the Germans achieved their objectives, what would they do next? Could they really restore order and peace in Europe? Their exploitation of conquered countries was "consuming the goose that lays the golden egg." They could not "go on indefinitely borrowing and re-borrowing the capital of their countries." Only abnormal war conditions allowed such a system, and these would not continue indefinitely. Any attempt to get back to normal "would split it wide open."

In the meantime, rationing was ineffective, black markets were thriving, and people in the occupied territories were working only as hard as they had to. Within Germany, civilian administration was chaotic, while the Nazi leadership was riddled with intrigues as the jockeying began to succeed Hitler: "The life of a single man, after all, is a weak reed on which to pin the difference between great personal power and violent death." Only the army seemed stable, which was why the elements opposed to Hitler were gathering there.

Hitler himself did not seem alarmed by any of this: to the contrary, he appeared ready to authorize a new wave of terror, designed to sweep away the slightest manifestations of independence. Either the gods were "making mad a man whom they would destroy," or Germany's future, and that of Europe, "is destined to be more gruesome than any of us have ever conceived. . . . Everything or nothing. Either we win or we pull the whole house down."[58]

X.

Kennan acknowledged, in retrospect, that "perhaps those of us who served in Moscow were not quick enough to understand the whole Nazi phenomenon, because we couldn't imagine that there could be any regime as nasty as the one with which we were confronted." There is something to this when it comes to the period before Kennan was sent to Czechoslovakia and Germany. He had, after all, found the latter state to be a "great garden" when he traveled through it in the spring of 1936, after two and a half years in the Soviet Union. What he saw in Prague in 1938–39, however, dispelled whatever illusions he may have had about the Nazi regime. His analyses of it from then on were at least as critical as his earlier assessments of its counterpart in Moscow. He certainly believed that Germany posed a greater threat than the U.S.S.R. to the balance of power in Europe, and hence to the security interests of the United States. And through Annelise's family, he had a personal stake in resisting the Nazis: "I was married to a woman whose father was tortured and nearly killed in Norway by these people."[59]

He was by no means anti-German. He relished the language, respected the culture, and recognized repeatedly that not all Germans shared the brutality of their leaders. He dealt with Germans professionally and met them socially: that was part of his job. He wrote, and years later published, sympathetic sketches of German women forced to survive by granting or selling sex.[60] He acknowledged acts of mercy on the part of the German troops that had just invaded France. He was fully aware that the German army—Hitler's principal weapon of destruction— also harbored such resistance as there was to him. He also saw, however, the selective morality of that organization, not least in the fact that it could treat Jews and Czechs no differently from Sudeten Germans, but then with equal ease hand the former over to the Gestapo. He caught the compulsive efficiency of Germans in small things like mending clothes or cutting book pages, but also their gross inefficiency in managing their own country as well as an occupied continent. And he understood that there would have been a "German problem" even if Hitler had never appeared on the scene: the Germans "were never a problem for the rest of Europe until the country was united."[61] Kennan's views on Germany, in short, were as complex as the Germans themselves.

The same was not true of his attitude toward Jews. He had a few Jewish or partly Jewish acquaintances, among them Frieda Por, Anna Freud, and Johnnie von Herwarth. He did more than he acknowledged in his memoirs to rescue Jews:

he got Por out of Austria in 1938; he and Annelise did the same for the Jewish friend who took refuge in their apartment in Prague on the day the Germans took over; he worked hard while in Berlin to arrange the exodus of Jewish children. He knew little, however, of Jewish culture. He found Jews as a class exasperating: hence his anger at the parents of Jewish children in Berlin. And like most members of their own generation and the many that preceded it, the Kennans often made references—"fat Jews," for example—that would today seem anti-Semitic. Even worse was Annelise's comment—no doubt George shared this view—that while she felt sorry for the Jews on March 15, 1939, she felt "not half as sorry as for the Czechs."[62]

Biographers have an obligation, however, to place their subjects within the period in which they lived: it is unfair to condemn them for not knowing what no one at the time could have known. What could the Kennans have anticipated, for example, about the respective fates of Czechs and Jews on March 15, 1939? That the Czechs had lost their independence was clear. That the Jews would have a hard time at the hands of the Germans was also obvious: the violence of Kristallnacht four months earlier left no doubt about that. But that over the next six years Hitler would seek to kill *all* the European Jews—and would succeed in murdering six million of them—was not at all apparent on the day he invaded Czechoslovakia, even to himself. As his most thorough biographer has pointed out, the Holocaust did not get under way until late 1941, and even then "there was as yet no coordinated, comprehensive program of total genocide."[63]

The problem with the future is that it isn't as clear as the past. That's why the writing of history generally—and the writing of biography particularly—requires empathy, which is not the same as sympathy. It asks a very simple question: What exactly would I, knowing what they knew then, have done differently?

EIGHT

The United States at War: 1941–1944

"THUS FAR BERLIN HAS BEEN AS SAFE AS HIGHLAND PARK," GEORGE wrote Jeanette on October 29, 1941. He was not sure how long that situation would last, but he wasn't worried. "The only real chance of my suffering any difficulties (and those would be more of a comic than a tragic nature) would be in the event that we were to enter the war, in which case I should probably be interned by the Germans for a number of weeks, if not months."[1]

He was the first American embassy official to hear the news, by shortwave radio on Sunday evening, December 7, that the Japanese had attacked Pearl Harbor. Four days of "excruciating uncertainty" followed, with the German government cutting off cable and telephone links. By Wednesday none remained. Embassy staffers began burning codes and classified files, so thoroughly that ashes drifted over the neighborhood, raising fears for the safety of adjoining buildings. On Thursday the eleventh, sound trucks and a crowd began to gather outside as Hitler prepared to speak in the Reichstag. An inoperative telephone abruptly rang, with word that a car would take the *chargé d'affaires*, Leland Morris, to a meeting with Foreign Minister Joachim von Ribbentrop. Kennan entertained the Foreign Office escort while Morris got ready: "A stiffer conversation has never transpired." At the Wilhelmstrasse, Ribbentrop kept Morris standing, subjected him to a tirade, and then handed him Germany's declaration of war on the United States.

The Foreign Office was as unsure as the Americans of what would happen next. Two more days of limbo followed, with the staff free to work and move about the city. Then, on Saturday the thirteenth, orders came to have everyone ready to leave Berlin the next morning. Embassy personnel would share a special train with remaining American journalists in the city. It fell to Kennan to organize the departure, working with an SS Hauptsturmführer, Valentin Patzak, who would be the Americans' keeper for the next five months. On Sunday all assembled at the embassy, "only to find the building, inside and out, already guarded by members of the Gestapo, and ourselves their prisoners."

The group knew nothing of their destination until menus appeared, in the otherwise threadbare dining car, labeled "Berlin—Bad Nauheim." The latter was a spa north of Frankfurt, where the young Franklin D. Roosevelt had stayed several times with his family. The Americans would be lodged in Jeschke's Grand Hotel, a once-elite establishment closed since the European war had broken out, but now hurriedly reopened. Furniture was in storage, pipes had burst, staff had scattered, and the manager had gotten twenty-four hours' notice that he would be housing more than a hundred Americans indefinitely. Morris, nominally Kennan's superior, left him in charge: "I personally bore the immediate responsibility for disciplinary control of this motley group of hungry, cold, and worried prisoners, as well as for every aspect of their liaison with their German captors. Their cares, their quarrels, their jealousies, their complaints, filled every moment of my waking day."[2]

I.

Years later Kennan would complain that historians—and some of his early biographers—had failed to acknowledge his organizational skills: they gave the impression "that I was a totally impractical dreamer, and could never do anything that was worthwhile in an administrative or practical sense." He had a point. He had, after all, almost single-handedly set up the American embassy in Moscow in 1934. He ran the Berlin embassy between 1939 and 1941, which by the end of that period was providing diplomatic representation for most of German-occupied Europe. And in 1947–49 Kennan would create the first Policy Planning Staff in the Department of State: that organization would never again be as effective as it was under his direction.[3]

None of these tasks, however, were as difficult as Bad Nauheim. The internees included Foreign Service officers, Army and Navy attachés, journalists and radio correspondents, several wives, a few children, five dogs, one cat, and three canaries. Logistics were a constant worry, the group having encumbered itself with forty tons of baggage, in some 1,250 pieces. They had no way of knowing how long they would be there, and no means of communicating with families and friends in the United States. They were totally dependent on the Germans, who were in turn constrained only by the knowledge that their own diplomats were interned—under much better conditions—at the White Sulphur Springs resort in West Virginia. The Grand Hotel offered greater comfort than that allowed prisoners of war or concentration camp inmates, to be sure. But the food was rationed and mostly unpalatable, the rooms were cold, and recreational facilities were limited. "The boredom, the lack of space, the distance from home and family, and the inevitable friction between people" were bound to cause strains, the principal historian of the internment has written. With Morris having declined the responsibility, "Kennan provided the direction, coordination, structure, and rule enforcement for the entire community."[4]

Collaboration with the Germans sounded objectionable in principle, but there was nothing to be gained in practice, Kennan believed, by refusing cooperation with Hauptsturmführer Patzak to make the internment run as smoothly as possible. Withholding it would invite punishment, forcing the Americans to treat their interned Germans similarly and delaying everyone's repatriation. Honesty required openness about what the Swiss—the intermediaries between the Americans and the Germans—were doing to get the group home. Information was unreliable, however, and even scraps could set off rumors, giving rise to false hopes and subsequent disappointment. So Kennan at times imposed censorship, in one instance even confiscating an issue of the internees' newspaper, the *Bad Nauheim Pudding*—named for a grimly ubiquitous dessert.[5]

Leadership also involved being an instantly available ombudsman. On January 25—an unusual day only in that he happened to keep a list—Kennan recorded thirty-two tasks performed. They included accounting for lost luggage, obtaining stationery, determining whether photographs could be taken from hotel balconies, drafting memoranda to go to or through the Swiss, discussing the issue of tips with the hotel management, clearing up several misunderstandings with Patzak, reporting a lady's missing powder case, and placating a husband who came in "to say that he did not want representations made about his wife." Later, as the weather warmed up, it fell to Kennan to negotiate the use of a nearby field for baseball. The bat was an improvised tree branch. The ball was a champagne cork wrapped in a sock. Kennan played catcher for the "Embassy Reds" against the "Journalists," under the puzzled supervision of the Gestapo. "I would never reveal George Kennan's batting average," Associated Press reporter Angus Thurmer replied when asked half a century later, "nor would I expect him to reveal mine. Gentlemen in this club don't do that."[6]

Through all of this, Kennan found the time to become a professor. The setting was "Badheim University," the school the internees organized to keep themselves busy. Kennan offered a "course" on Russian history, for which he prepared over a hundred pages of lecture notes, some of them scrawled outlines, others typed and finished presentations. They began with the establishment of Christianity and extended—although more thinly toward the end—well into the Stalin era. Apart from his lecture at the Foreign Service School in 1938, these were the first he had ever delivered. They attracted sixty "enrollees," almost twice the number as the next most popular lecturer. Kennan, the "university" organizers concluded in a written appreciation of his efforts, had "a natural gift for presenting material vividly and interestingly while meeting the highest standards of scholarship."[7]

The lectures stressed historical continuities—geography, climate, soil, ethnicity, culture—as the best way to understand the Soviet Union now that it had become a wartime ally. One in particular stood out for its application of Freudian psychology: in contrast to his skepticism while in Vienna six years earlier, Kennan was now convinced "that the theory is not without foundation." The "childhood" of peoples was just as important in determining their character as it was for individuals.

The first five centuries of Russian history had produced an "adolescent" nation with a primitive system of government, a crudely organized society, and an uneducated religious leadership. Beginning with Peter the Great, the tsars embraced modernization but their subjects did not. Industrialization and war in the late nineteenth and early twentieth centuries widened this gap, so that when revolution came, "the mighty tree of Tsardom, which had lost its roots in the people, could not stand the force of the gale." It fell with "a suddenness and impact that shook the world."

Russians at that point "shed their westernized upper crust as a snake sheds its skin," appearing before the world as a seventeenth-century semi-Asiatic people, with "all the weaknesses of backwardness and all the strength and freshness of youth." They moved their capital back to Moscow, and an "Oriental" despot—Stalin—installed himself in the Kremlin, bringing with him "the same intolerance, the same dark cruelty, the same religious dogmatism in word and form, the same servility, . . . the same fear and distrust of the outside world," that had characterized the premodern tsars. The only difference now was that the Russians made weapons and could use them "with the best of us." That raised the question, then, when the time came to make peace with Germany, "of whether Russia is to be the confusion or the salvation of the Western European continent."[8]

Kennan's image of a tree with thin roots came close to describing his own condition after weeks of confined hyperactivity. In one sense, he recalled, the responsibility of looking after other people from morning to night kept him from brooding too much about himself. But by February he was contemplating the possibility that he might never see his family again. That was when he drafted his long letter to Grace and Joan—never finished—in which he tried to explain what it would be like to grow up with a missing parent. The Kennan and James families, George warned his daughters, were susceptible to depression, even tragedy, but there was "something placid and gay and healthy in your mother's nature which is a good corrective for all that, and which I hope you have inherited."[9]

As the days dragged on with no end in sight, Kennan later admitted, "I had moments of real neurosis." One came on a Sunday when he lunched alone, in "gloomy dignity," then found in the lobby the luggage from the latest group of Americans to arrive from the latest country swallowed up by the Axis. The hotel had no one to move the bags upstairs, and none of the internees volunteered. So he himself performed the task, shaming a few other Americans into helping him load the elevator. At that point he remembered that his cocker spaniel Kimmy—"an unfortunate beast which [I] had been unable to get rid of in the last harried moments before internment" —had been left alone longer than was wise. Abandoning helpers, luggage, and elevator, George dashed to his room to find the dog surrounded by the shredded remains of the only photographs he had of Annelise, Grace, and Joan. Using the third person, he described what happened next:

With a gasp of horror, [he] fetched the puppy a whack which sent it flying across the room to the corner, where it promptly made a puddle. Then, to his own dismay, [he] burst into unmanly tears, for the first time in all the months of confinement. Knowing that he could never expect two minutes' peace from the responsibilities of his position, he quickly locked the door . . . , and then set about laboriously and with streaming eyes . . . attempting to fit the snapshots together. There were several knocks on the door, while this was in progress, repeated indignantly after puzzled pauses; but he ignored them all until finally there was a great thumping and rattling of the door handle. Knowing, with the intuition of a prisoner, that this last visitor could be none other than [Morris] himself, [he] pulled himself together and opened the door.[10]

That, however, was not the worst experience. Something else happened in April, and it was serious enough for Kennan to resume—briefly—keeping his diary:

April 19: [O]ne cannot go through life as a general ascetic, merely to exert control over one particular urge. That is only acknowledging one's slavery to it. . . . There is only one solution. . . . It is to acknowledge one's self as old and beyond those things. My God, man, you are no youngster any more. What do you expect?

April 20: What I have been guilty of was in my eyes a folly, to be sure, but a minor one; and there were plenty of ameliorating circumstances. That it should have been punished in so grotesque and humiliating a manner is what sets me back. . . . I cannot face these people now. . . . To think that I, George Kennan, should be in the position of having to conceal anything. If I go among them and lead a normal life, and the thing later comes out, I have made myself a double-hypocrite. . . . I have been thwarted, as I was when I was a boy. . . . But what are the "real things" you can't have? Women, that's one thing. Liberty is another. Peace of mind's a third. Isn't that enough? Yes, I suppose it is.

April 22: For a man to feel himself young in my circumstances means that he must of necessity be very tough of heart, very gay, very well-balanced in his human relationships, and relatively irresponsible. I am none of these things. I cannot therefore be young successfully. Nor can I continue to be young unsuccessfully. The resultant fiascos would soon be too much for me and would affect not only me but likewise the people I love.[11]

So what was this all about? Another sexual indiscretion? An exposure of irresponsibility in some other form? Perhaps even an overblown reaction to having lost his composure and locked himself in his room over the depredations of a dog?

What occurred was less important than what it showed, which was how precariously Kennan balanced leadership against fragility. Both were in evidence on May 5, 1942, the day he got confirmation that the internment was to end: the group would depart by train for Lisbon in a week, and thence by ship home. Kennan drafted the notice, got Morris to sign it, posted it in the empty front hallway, and then walked away. It had required months of work to bring this about, and he was sure that his fellow internees, for the most part, would be ungrateful.

I am utterly worn out by the strain of living uninterruptedly for 5 months under one roof with 135 other people among whom I have no single intimate friend, and of trying to save them from dangers for which they had no appreciation. My own personal life and strength have been so neglected that I have felt during the last few days something close to an incipient disintegration of personality: a condition of spirit devoid of all warmth, all tone, all humor and all enthusiasm.

There were complaints about being limited to a single carry-on bag on the train, this on a day "when thousands of people are dying . . . for what they conceive to be important issues." Kennan was so disgusted "that I couldn't bring myself to go down to dinner and have locked myself in my room for the evening."[12]

He was also, by this time, fed up with his own government. There had been no communication from the State Department, even through the Swiss, until shortly before the departure. At that point two messages arrived, neither of which boosted morale. One announced that the Foreign Service officers would not be paid for the period of their internment, since they had not been working. A second raised the possibility of sending only half of the internees back on the *Drottningholm*, the designated Swedish repatriation ship, in order to make room for refugees, presumably Jewish. "Mr. Morris and I succeeded in warding off both of these blows." It was not, Kennan explained years later, that "you didn't want the Jews to come." But "my God, this was an exchange ship." If half the Americans hadn't come, half of the Germans wouldn't have been repatriated either. "We didn't know anything about [the Holocaust], and obviously being prisoners we didn't learn anything about it."[13]

The Americans arrived in Lisbon on May 16, a day on which Kennan indulged himself in two long-postponed pleasures. One was a hearty breakfast at the Spanish-Portuguese border station, which he, as the internees' official representative, was able to enjoy while they remained, enviously hungry, on the train. The second was a poem composed—it showed—on a full stomach:

From you, embattled comrades in abstention,
Compatriots to this or that degree,
Who've shared with me the hardships of detention,
In Jeschke's Grand and guarded hostelry—

From you, my doughty champions of the larder,
Who've fought with such persistency and skill,

Such mighty hearts, such overwhelming ardor,
The uninspiring battle of the swill—

From you, my friends, from your aggrieved digestions,
From all the pangs of which you love to tell,
Your dwindling flesh and your enraged intestines,
Permit me now to take a fond farewell. . . .

The world might choke in food-restricting measures;
Chinese might starve; and Poles might waste away;
But God forbid that you—my tender treasures—
Should face the horrors of a meatless day.

The *Drottningholm* sailed, well supplied, on the twenty-second, with the ship's name and the word "DIPLOMAT" painted in huge black letters against its white sides to ward off submarine attacks. It arrived safely arrived in New York on the thirtieth.[14]

II.

Annelise had rented a house in Bronxville, New York, shortly before Pearl Harbor, and was there with the children when she learned of George's internment. The State Department told her not to expect him back before March: "I just keep praying that nothing will happen to make it more complicated than it is." Beyond that, she had no information: "I never had heard a word about him. No communication whatever." Shortly before his release, George was able to send a message through the department asking about his family. It reached Annelise as a telegram from the secretary of state. "I was sure he was dead," she recalled. "I was so furious. I sat down and wrote a telegram [that] said: 'I'm glad for the first opportunity to tell where we are and the welfare of the children.' He never got it."[15]

Frieda Por, who examined George soon after his return, found that he had lost fifteen pounds, his stomach problems had returned, and it had been only "through the exercise of great willpower that he was able to continue carrying out his heavy responsibilities." On the basis of her report, the State Department authorized a forty-five-day leave.[16] The Kennans used it, not to relax, but to buy a farm.

"I am a great believer in the power of the soil over the human beings who live above it," George had told his Badheim University "students" in one of his lectures on Russian history. His private reasons for wanting a farm were more complicated. A happy personal life, he had concluded while interned, would never be possible. Professional satisfaction was out of reach because Americans, "biologically undermined and demoralized," had a broken political system. The solution, then, was "the sort of glorified gardening called gentleman farming, . . . the only form of playing with toys which is not ridiculous in elderly men." (George was thirty-eight at the time.) But he could not ask his wife and children to give up "the advantages of education and all personal amenities." The ideal thing, therefore, would be to combine agriculture and diplomacy, "[f]or the same sort of catastrophe is not likely to hit both of them simultaneously."[17]

The Kennans had no farming experience: only a book, called *Five Acres and Independence*. They would not be able to manage a farm alone, but they could, Annelise pointed out, rent it to a resident farmer: "I'm always a little more realistic than George." Wisconsin was out as long as he remained in the Foreign Service, so the farm would have to be near Washington. They began looking, then, in the Gettysburg region of southern Pennsylvania. "It is lovely rolling country, with beautiful rich soil," George wrote Jeanette.

> I'm sure you would love the houses. They are all, I think, well over a century old, and have great potential charm. The farms themselves are also beautiful: with plenty of timber and springs and streams and comfortable quiet old lanes. I am quite surprised at the values, because although they are not much more expensive than the farms we looked at in Wisconsin, the buildings and equipment are better beyond comparison.

By the last week in June, the Kennans had given up the Bronxville house, stored their furniture, and set off "after the fashion of modern pioneers: the whole damned family, including the dog [the disgraced Kimmy, now forgiven], the phonograph and the typewriter, in an old Ford car—and with no home on the face of the globe." Their address, for the near future, would be simply "General Delivery, Gettysburg, Pa."[18]

"[W]e haven't bought a farm yet," Annelise added a few days later, but despite the temptation "to say to hell with it all, let's go somewhere nice where we can swim and sail and loaf," they were still at it "with all the perseverance that a Scott [*sic*] and a Norwegian can muster." They had seen one promising possibility: a 238-acre farm with an enormous three-story house, a smaller one for a tenant farmer, a tobacco barn, and a three-car garage, owned by the children of a Jewish emigrant, Joseph Miller, who had used it as a temporary refuge for Jews fleeing Nazi Germany. The house was ugly, awkward, filled with junk, and had not been cleaned since the old man's death: "It was just like the Cherry Orchard without the orchard." The price was $14,000, which would require, Annelise worried, "such a big mortgage." A few days later, she wrote again: "Jeanette, hold on tight— yesterday we bought it!"[19]

On July 21, 1942, George reported to his sister that the family had spent its first night in their own house. There had been cobwebs everywhere, "and I had no idea what sort of beasts or ghosts would emerge." Only a few doors had banged, though, and "we are starting on our first full day of country life." The motor for the pump had rusted and the well had silted up, but "never mind, we'll make it." By the next morning, he was relishing

> the horses munching and stamping, the cows giving voice, the pidgeons cooing in the loft, the roosters crowing, and the flies buzzing. I even enjoy having to chase the ducks out from under my car every time I want to drive it away. In short, I really do enjoy these things, and I don't much care that I have to work hard from morning to night to do so.

It was not clear "whether we'll be able to swing it financially, or whether [the farm] will gradually eat us up and ruin us, too." But he had no regrets. "I have the sense of having my hands on something really solid. . . . I can see the results of my own handiwork, and they are results that last." On the door frame leading into the house the Kennans discovered—and thought it right to keep—a mezuzah, the Jewish acknowledgment of the blessings of life.

That evening George took Grace, one of the tenant farmer's children, and Kimmy on a walk through towering stalks of corn. While the dog flushed pheasants and chased rabbits, George climbed a cherry tree to survey his estate. It was astonishing, he explained to his sister,

> to have so much land that you can take an hour's walk just in one direction without getting off your own property. To me it was such an enjoyment that I sometimes think if it only lasts a year or two it will have been well worth it, and I can return again to vagabondage, strengthened and refreshed by the mere reminiscences.

Located just outside the village of East Berlin, Pennsylvania, the farm allowed at least one economy. Beginning with this letter, and continuing until the supply ran out, the Kennans used stationery George had brought back from the other Berlin, scratching out the German street address and adding a carefully placed "East" and "Pa."[20]

The *East Berlin News-Comet* reported on July 24 that the Miller farm had been sold to "a Mr. Kennedy of New York and Washington, D.C.," who with his wife and two children would use the property for leisure activities and as their summer home. The editor, Harriet Tierney, had gotten the news from the town barber, Lavere Burgard, who later corrected the story to say that the name was more like "Cannon" and that the buyer "had something to do with the government." The George Shetters, who owned the local restaurant, confirmed this information, noting that the gentleman in question had made a long-distance phone call from there. East Berlin had little experience with important outsiders, and so the rumors began to fly. Mrs. Tierney then took it upon herself to settle the matter by driving out to the Miller place to find out who the newcomers were. Satisfied, she wrote another story introducing the Kennan family to East Berlin.[21]

III.

The psychological distance between the two Berlins was even greater than the physical distance, so for the moment—uncharacteristically—George Kennan was happy. But he was still in the Foreign Service and there was still a war on; hence on September 8, 1942, George loaded his family into the back of a borrowed milk truck, leaving Kimmy—who was to stay behind on the farm—racing desperately after them. Grace went to Washington, where she would spend the year in boarding school, while Annelise and Joan accompanied George back to Lisbon: his new assignment was to be counselor at the American legation in Portugal. The trip this time was by air. "It is just surreal to go so far so fast," Annelise wrote of the three-day flight via Bermuda and the Azores. "Somehow it doesn't seem right." She regretted leaving so soon. "Little by little my roots have fastened in the States," she assured Jeanette. "I like the country and love the people—in spite of what George thinks of them."[22]

George, for his part, accepted the wartime obligation of overseas service but envied those who could perform it in uniform. Military life carried risks, but survivors would return with the laurels "simply by virtue of their participation." Diplomacy too had its dangers, but there would be no rewards.

> In the task they have given me, I cannot succeed. I can hope to do better than other, less experienced men. But what I can do will be known to very few people, and appreciated by fewer still; and the effort will probably end in personal catastrophe for myself and the family.

Internment had at least taught him that "there is nothing worse than a vacillation between hope and despair." Strength came from having one or the other—"possibly they are the same thing." Kennan recorded these gloomy thoughts because "I feel that if I hold them constantly before me I shall be able to do my job with greater detachment, greater humor, less nervous wear-and-tear, and, paradoxically, greater enjoyment."[23]

"I am neither happy nor unhappy," he wrote Jeanette from Lisbon. He could never feel at home in a place, however beautiful, "where it never snows, where the hot summer is the dead dormant season, and where the grass gets green and the crops are put out in the fall. But I'm doing my job as best I can and—hell—it's war." Finances were again a problem: "We are broke, as usual." Portuguese living costs were high, Grace's school fees were a drain, and income from the corn crop had been slow to show up: "I hope the people in East Berlin won't get too excited about our arrears." Annelise was helping out by working in the legation press office. She found it "fun to get into a field which the Germans have had very much to themselves and see the results." Nevertheless, she added, "[w]e almost turn handsprings to save 15 dollars a month."

With the Anglo-American landings in North Africa on November 8, the war news was better. But Annelise's family in Norway was having a hard winter, and early in 1943 she learned that her father had been arrested. "He will take it," George told Jeanette, "just about the way our father would have, in similar circumstances." It was, though, Annelise emphasized, a grave, even life-threatening situation, made all the more frustrating by the fact that there was nothing they could do to help. Meanwhile George's job offered "no triumphs, no glory, no recognition—not even the satisfaction of physical hardship and combat. When the war is over, I won't even want to talk about it."[24]

There was one unexpected drama, though. On February 22, 1943, the Pan American Airways *Yankee Clipper*, a long-distance seaplane that set the standard for luxury transatlantic air travel at the time, crashed in the Tagus River as it was landing in Lisbon. Rushing to the scene, Kennan found, among the survivors, his Princeton classmate and fellow Foreign Service officer W. Walton Butterworth, who despite being in shock had managed to swim to shore with a briefcase of classified documents. George got him to a hotel and into a hot tub, filled him full of brandy, and pinned the papers on a clothesline to dry. The clothes, presumably, were left to dry on their own.[25]

Portugal, with Spain, had maintained an uneasy neutrality in the war. But whereas Generalissimo Francisco Franco had tilted his country toward the Axis, the Portuguese, honoring the spirit if not the letter of their ancient alliance with Great Britain, had inclined in the opposite direction. Politics and geography attracted intelligence services from all sides: Kennan estimated that eleven operated in Lisbon simultaneously, several of them employing double agents. "There were so many spies," the British diplomat Frank Roberts recalled, "that they completely obliterated each other." One of Kennan's unannounced tasks was to try to straighten out at least some of the confusions.[26]

There were many. The Office of War Information was portraying the Portuguese prime minister, Dr. António Salazar, as a Franco-like fascist. The Board of Economic Warfare was withholding food and arms in an effort to discourage the Portuguese from providing wolfram and other strategic commodities to the Germans. The Office of Strategic Services was organizing a rebellion against Portuguese rule in the Azores. The British were stockpiling fuel there with a view to securing air and naval bases for the forthcoming invasion of Western Europe. Meanwhile Bert Fish, the amiable but placid American minister in Lisbon— Roosevelt appointed him as a favor to a Florida senator—had made no effort to reach any agreement with Salazar on overall Portuguese-American interests. "Ah ain't goin' down there and get mah backsides kicked around," Kennan recalled him explaining. "He's too smart for me."[27]

Sorting this out required that Kennan focus for the first time on grand strategy. What, exactly, did the United States want from Portugal? To what extent were its practices consistent with its priorities? Were those priorities consistent with one another? Did any single agency or official know everything that was going on, or care? How did all of this relate to winning the war, or to what would happen when peace returned? The problem was not just that of a right and left hand failing to communicate. The more appropriate analogy would have been a confused Hindu deity with multiple arms, each appendage busily at work on projects of which the others were unaware.

Kennan's first approach was a traditional one: he studied the situation and, in

February 1943, drafted a long analysis, sent under Fish's name to the State Department, which specified, as the critical American interest, obtaining the Azores bases. It suggested letting the British negotiate the arrangements, justifying them under the Anglo-Portuguese treaty of 1373. Any other course, it warned, risked destabilizing the Salazar regime, perhaps even provoking German intervention. When the department did not respond, Kennan followed up with another dispatch pointing out that Salazar seemed inclined toward an alliance with the Western powers. This elicited no reply either, just "that peculiar and profound sort of silence which is made only by the noise of a diplomatic dispatch hitting the Department's files."[28]

By early April, Kennan was complaining privately about having to clean up the messes inexperienced people had made, while coping with lack of interest and confidence on the part of bosses. The frustrations were such that his ulcer—"that modern mark of distinction"—had returned, requiring a trip home for treatment. He was not as ill as he had been in Moscow, he told Jeanette, but "an ulcer is an inexorable sort of thing. You just have to let down." George got to Washington in June, retrieved Grace from her school, and spent a few weeks with her on the farm: "I simply love the place." Both then sailed for Lisbon on July 21, giving George the time, while at sea, to reflect on his country, and its capacity to lead the world.[29]

IV.

He did so in a ten-page single-spaced typed letter, intended only for Jeanette, which began with all the forebodings about America that his encounters with it—however brief—tended to set off. There had been a "retrogression" in civilian life "no less inexorable than our military advance.... I sometimes wonder whether, as in the case of declining Rome, its pace is not the price we are paying for the victory in arms." Familiar worries followed about industrialization and urbanization, compounded now by the question of where ten million veterans would find jobs after the war. Hundreds of intellectuals were planning the future of postwar Europe. "Is there no one with sufficient leisure to contemplate a postwar America?"

Here, though, there was a shift in Kennan's thinking. In 1938 he had seen authoritarianism as a solution for the nation's problems. Since that time he had witnessed European authoritarianism and worse: the greatest danger to the United States, he now believed, could come from a homegrown dictatorship. The cause would be the "petty-bourgeois jealousy which resents and ridicules any style of life more dignified than its own—a phenomenon of which we saw much in Nazi Germany."

> The entire experience of mankind indicates that it is always the few, never the many, who are the real obstacles in the path of the dictator. Equalitarian principles are the inevitable concomitants of dictatorship. They produced Napoleon as inevitably as they produced Hitler and Stalin. The powers of sovereignty, as Gibbon observed, will inevitably "be first abused and afterwards lost, if they are committed to an unwieldy multitude."

It followed, therefore, that some "enlightened and responsible" minority—not necessarily one of wealth—must gain power "if anything is to impede in our country the organic progress of political form from demagoguery to dictatorship."

Only in this way could two more vulnerable minorities be protected. One was blacks, "a gentle and lovable people" who had never adjusted to urban life, followed "every sort of quack or extremist," and thus were fanning "a racial antagonism from which no one except the outright enemies of our people could possibly profit, and which may have the gravest of consequences to the negroes themselves." Jews were the other endangered group. Twenty centuries of experience had shown that they would never assimilate, but Hitler had made it impossible even to mention this problem: instead "our leftist press [howls] down as a fascist and anti-semite anyone who suggests that it might be officially recognized and given governmental consideration." Both issues needed to be resolved if "[b]eat the negroes" and "beat the Jews" were not to become the slogans "for the solution of difficulties utterly unconnected with those unfortunate groups."

With respect to foreign policy, the aftermaths of wars were decisive moments when lines were drawn that could last for generations. The United States had had the opportunity to do that after World War I but "muffed" it. "If we muff this, too, can we be sure that we will be given a third?"

> Heretofore, in our history, we have had to take the world pretty much as we found it. From now on we will have to take it pretty much as we leave it, when this crisis is over.

Without an American effort to set postwar standards of international conduct, they would find their own level—probably that of the "rising masses" of Asia—at which "no humane, well-meaning people like our own could exist. Our position—and with it all that we prize in internal liberty—is one that can be maintained only by the firm, consistent and unceasing application of sheer power, in accordance with a long-term policy."

That would require professionalism: a state, like a business, must, if it wished to survive, find the courage to select "a few people in whose intelligence and integrity it has confidence" and to delegate to them over long periods of time not only responsibility for the execution of policy but also its formulation. In fact, though, the United States was approaching the postwar era with no such vision. Diplomacy was not "improvisation" or "exhibitionism" or "missions-to-Moscow"—here Kennan was slamming Joe Davies's recently released movie by the same name, which dramatized his Moscow experiences in a way that even sympathizers with the Soviet Union thought whitewashed the Stalin regime.

"Against the pageant of history we cut a small and distinctly episodic figure," George concluded. "Ignorant and conceited, we now enter blindly on a future with which we are quite unqualified to cope." He assured Jeanette, at the end of these "lugubrious" observations, that he had not lost hope. There were in the American character great reserves of decency and humor and good nature. But if these assets were to yield a return, "then new forms must be found, new ideas must gain currency, new associations of collective effort must come into being."[30]

"Don't take it too seriously," he added in a postscript from Lisbon, written before sending off this long screed.[31] Jeanette knew him well enough not to. She understood her value to George as a confidante, as a therapist, and even—as in this letter—as a soapbox. He had long relied on, and benefited from, her patience: she provided a mirror in which he could, from time to time, examine himself.

This particular reassessment showed Kennan beginning to connect his obtuseness regarding America and his astuteness with respect to the world. His experiences in Czechoslovakia and Germany had purged him of the simpleminded view, expressed in the "Prerequisites" essay of 1938, that a dictatorship might be good for the United States. He was not so sanguine as to assume, however, that one could never arise there: he understood how it had happened in Germany and refused to rule out the possibility that American reserves of decency and good nature might be exhaustible. However exceptional his own views of it were, he never believed that his country could exist as an exception to what was happening elsewhere.

Kennan's most significant argument, however, was that the United States, for better or for worse, had gone beyond discovering the world: whatever it did now would shape the world. That was a task, he believed, for which the nation was unprepared, and his Portuguese experiences had done nothing to reassure him. He began to develop, as a result, a new sense of responsibility within the duties assigned to him: at several points over the next few years Kennan took risks that jeopardized his own Foreign Service career because he thought that the *national* interest demanded that he do so. Obliged to operate for the first time at the level of grand strategy, he found the rules of his profession falling short. He chose, successfully but dangerously, to violate them.

V.

"It was a good thing that I returned when I did," George wrote in his postscript to Jeanette, "for the Minister here died . . . when I was on the boat, and it was high time I was getting back to my little parish." Fish's death left Kennan in charge of the legation at a critical moment. The British, he learned, had concluded a secret agreement with the Portuguese on August 17, 1943, allowing them to use the Azores bases. They had informed the State Department, but it had given the Lisbon legation no guidance as to what the American response should be. "We have no idea of the views of our Government," Kennan complained on September 9, despite the fact that this development "is of the greatest importance for the future correlation of military and political power in the whole Atlantic area." James C. Dunn, the department's adviser on political relations, replied lamely that the Anglo-Portuguese negotiations had been handled "in the highest quarters" and that "we have no clearer picture than you of the general plan."

Finally on October 8, the day the British landed on the islands, the department instructed Kennan to assure Salazar that the United States respected Portuguese sovereignty "in all Portuguese colonies." No further explanation was provided. Minutes before he was to meet Salazar on the tenth, however—the prime minister having returned to Lisbon to receive Kennan's message—the department rescinded the instruction. At this point, exasperated but thinking quickly, Kennan decided to exceed his instructions. He reminded the puzzled Salazar that there had been no general discussion of the Portuguese-American wartime relationship and proceeded to conduct one. He then told the State Department what he had done, only to receive an equally puzzled reminder that it had always been American policy to "promote our trade and have pleasant relations with the Portuguese people."[33]

Then, on the sixteenth, another department cable arrived instructing Kennan, "by direction of the President," to "request" the *American* use of Azores facilities on a scale far larger than anything the British had asked for or obtained. Convinced that such an unexpected communication would provoke Salazar's wrath—if not his resignation—Kennan took a second unusual step: he refused to carry out a White House order and asked permission to return to Washington to explain why, if necessary to the president himself: "I am willing to take full personal responsibility for this position."[34]

That message made its way back to FDR, who asked for Kennan's reasons in writing and, when given them, replied that he would "leave to your judgment and discretion the manner of approach to these negotiations." Vastly relieved, Kennan went to the Foreign Office in Lisbon and told "a whopping lie": that the State Department had now authorized him to extend a previously contemplated but delayed acknowledgment of Portuguese sovereignty over all Portuguese possessions, including the Azores. This elicited an appreciative message of gratitude from the Portuguese minister in Washington "for the guaranty thus given." But it in turn puzzled the State Department, causing the under secretary of state, Edward R. Stettinius, Jr., to tell a colleague that the Portuguese diplomat had thanked him "for some damn guarantee, and said that he always knew we would want facilities in the Azores. Now what in the name of hell did he mean by that?"[35]

Kennan himself—revealing nothing—witnessed that exchange, having been abruptly and without explanation ordered back to Washington. The trip took five days, flying by way of South America and Bermuda, so there was plenty of time to worry: he arrived "unnerved, overtired, jittery, not myself." Stettinius hustled him off to the Pentagon, where he found himself facing General George C. Marshall, the Joint Chiefs of Staff, Secretary of the Navy Frank Knox, and Secretary of War Henry L. Stimson, who was in a particularly bad humor that day. All were angry about the delay in securing Azores base rights. A confused discussion ensued, which Stimson ended by telling Stettinius that the State Department needed "a full-fledged ambassador" in Lisbon who could "give proper attention to our affairs at this important post. Will you see to that, Mr. Secretary?" Kennan was then told to leave.[36]

Angry with himself for having failed to explain the situation adequately, convinced that he knew more about Portugal than anyone else in Washington, Kennan took yet another unorthodox step: he got in touch with the president's chief of staff, Admiral William D. Leahy, who had been a fellow passenger the year before on the *Drottningholm*. Leahy arranged a meeting with Roosevelt's top aide Harry Hopkins, who then took the surprised Kennan to see the president himself. FDR listened cheerfully to the whole story, told Kennan not to worry "about all those people in the Pentagon," and drafted a personal letter to Salazar recalling that as under secretary of the Navy after World War I, he had been responsible for dismantling Azores bases used by the Americans and returning them to Portuguese control. "I do not need to tell you the United States has no designs on the territory of Portugal and its possessions. . . . I do not think our peoples have been in close enough touch in the past."[37]

That, Kennan recalled, produced the desired results: "I went back with that letter and opened negotiations with Salazar. . . . [W]e spent many hours in conversation, [and he] agreed to our use of the British facilities." Afterward Kennan was able to reconstruct what had happened. The Pentagon had seen only his refusal to execute Roosevelt's order, but not his explanation or FDR's approval of it. The State Department, "accustomed to sneezing whenever the Pentagon caught cold," had simply transmitted its demand for Kennan's recall, without attempting to clarify the matter. The episode illustrated how poor communication had been within the American government, so much so that four years later Kennan turned it into a case study, at the newly established National War College, on the need for closer political-military coordination. It was, one of his students commented, "a hell of a way to run a railroad."[38] But the episode also showed—for all his nervousness—a growing self-confidence on Kennan's part.

During the Azores base negotiations, Kennan violated at least four rules, any one of which could have got him sacked from the Foreign Service. He exceeded his instructions in a conversation with a foreign head of government. He refused to carry out a presidential order. He lied, to another government, about the position of his own. And he went over the heads of his superiors in the State Department—as well as the secretary of war and the Joint Chiefs of Staff—to make a direct appeal to the White House. He turned out to be right in the end and so enhanced rather than ruined his reputation: he even received, from the secretary of state, personal congratulations for "the rapid and substantial progress made." In this sense, Kennan passed his own test of hoping "to do better than other, less experienced men." There were, however, many more experienced men in the department who viewed Kennan's Azores "adventures," despite their favorable outcome, "with a disapproval bordering on sheer horror." They considered him, Kennan's British friend Frank Roberts guessed, "very foolish, and rather lucky to get away with it."[39]

VI.

Kennan's next assignment—there having been no enthusiasm on his part or the department's for his staying in Lisbon—did little to reassure him about Washington's coordination of military operations with political objectives. The new job was that of political adviser to the American ambassador in Great Britain, John G. Winant, who would be representing the United States on the recently established European Advisory Commission. Created by the British, Americans, and Soviets late in 1943, this organization's chief responsibility was to settle the terms of Germany's surrender and to agree on plans for the postwar occupation of that country. But Washington had reached no consensus on how to handle these matters: as a consequence, the EAC could accomplish little. "So far as I could learn from my superiors in the department," Kennan remembered, "their attitude toward the commission was dominated by a lively concern lest the new body should at some point and by some mischance actually do something."[40]

The inactivity might have been harmless had the British and Russians remained similarly inactive, but they did not. By February 1944 both had submitted draft surrender documents, and they had even agreed on occupation zone boundaries. Under their plan, the British would control the northwestern third of Germany, the Americans the southwestern third, and the Russians the eastern third. Berlin, deep within the Soviet zone, would be jointly occupied. Winant pressed Washington for a reaction, but for several weeks received no response. The State Department then forwarded, on March 8, a completely different plan, approved by the Joint Chiefs of Staff, that awarded the United States 46 percent of Germany's territory and 51 percent of its population, while pushing the Soviet zone far to the east. The proposed boundaries broke up existing German administrative districts but did not extend all the way to the Czech border, leaving control of that region undetermined. No explanation accompanied this plan: Winant was told simply to put it before the EAC as the American position.[41]

Kennan's Azores bases experience left him in little doubt about what had happened. Once again the Joint Chiefs had elevated military convenience above all else, and the State Department had unquestioningly passed along their plan. This time Kennan did not have to offer to return to Washington to explain the plan's deficiencies: his chief, Winant, sent him. The flight, by way of Iceland and Newfoundland, was the worst yet. The plane's heating system failed halfway across the Atlantic, and while landing at Gander its brakes froze, causing it almost to slide off the runway into the sea. Kennan arrived in Washington again "dazed and unnerved by the vicissitudes of wartime intercontinental travel." His reception, however, was considerably warmer than it had been the previous fall.[42]

"The President was kindly, charming, and talked to me at some length," Kennan reported to Bullitt, with whom he stayed. When shown the Joint Chiefs of Staff proposal, FDR "laughed gaily and said, just as I had expected him to say: 'Why that's just something I once drew on the back of an envelope.'" The president agreed that the proposal made no sense and authorized Winant to accept the British-Russian alternative. He spent most of the interview fretting about the British occupation of northwestern Germany—FDR wanted the Americans there—but he showed no concern about Berlin lying within the region the Russians would control. Kennan was relieved to have the confusion cleared up but irate that it had again fallen to him to do it. "Why it should have been left to a junior officer such as myself to jeopardize his own career by going directly to the president on these two separate occasions—why the Department of State could not have taken upon itself this minimal responsibility was a mystery to me at that time." It remained so when Kennan wrote that passage in his memoirs more than two decades later.[43]

Apart from their speed, one of the few benefits of long, uncomfortable transatlantic flights—Kennan took seven between September 1942 and March 1944—was that they allowed time to read: the noise level made conversation impossible. So his traveling companion was Edward Gibbon. It's not clear how much of *The Decline and Fall of the Roman Empire* he got through, but it was enough to influence his thinking on the problems of occupying the territories of defeated adversaries. One passage particularly stuck in his mind. "It is incumbent on the authors of persecution," Gibbon had written, "to reflect whether they are determined to support it in the last extreme." If they did so, they risked "excit[ing] the flame which they strive to extinguish; and it soon becomes necessary to chastise the contumacy, as well as the crime, of the offender."[44]

That, Kennan believed, was what the policy of unconditional surrender, agreed upon by Roosevelt and Churchill at the Casablanca conference in January 1943, was likely to do. It suggested no concern over "the amount of responsibility we are assuming in Germany." It reflected "no desire, and no real plan, for acquiring allies and helpers among the German people." It implied taking the harshest measures possible "short of actual physical extermination." It would demand "a ruthlessness now foreign to our troops," giving them "the worst possible lessons in the practices of government." And, he added, "[i]t will certainly require, to be successful, a far greater degree of unity of purpose and method than can conceivably be achieved at this time between the Russians and ourselves."[45]

So what to do? "We must keep quite separate in our minds our program for the treatment of Germany, and the type of surrender document we want. The latter should serve the former." That meant focusing on the military defeat of Germany, the removal and punishment of "the most conspicuous and notorious Nazi leaders," and the elimination "of all possibility for further oppression and aggression." It did not mean thorough denazification:

> There is no thornier or more thankless task . . . than that of trying to probe into the political records and motives of masses of individuals in a foreign country. It is impossible to avoid injustices, errors, and resentment. It involves the maintenance of a huge, and necessarily unpopular, investigative apparatus. . . . We will eventually get caught up in a round of denunciation, confusion, and disunity from which none but the Germans would stand to profit.

Such an approach would leave no Germans running the country, for "[w]hether we like it or not, nine-tenths of what is strong, able, and respected in Germany has been poured into those very categories which we have in mind."

Leaving some Nazis in power would not be popular. But the German resistance to Hitler had shown itself to be weak and disorganized, and even if it were stronger, "the worst service we could render to the liberal and democratic elements in Germany would be to saddle them with public responsibility at the moment of catastrophe and humiliation." Far better, then, to let lesser Nazis bear that burden under restrictions the Allies imposed and leave the German people eventually to kick them out. That would be "a profoundly democratic approach."

The fundamental American interest in Germany, Kennan concluded in a memorandum he sent Admiral Leahy at the White House, was "to see that no European power acquires the possibility of using Europe's resources to conduct aggression outside the continent of Europe." In a broader sense, it was also an American objective "to see that western Europe survives and prospers as a major cultural force in the world." This would require "patient, persistent and intelligent" efforts over a considerable period of time, with the goal of achieving "the maximum degree of federation in Europe." That, in turn, would depend upon enlisting German resources in the rehabilitation of European life. And what if the Soviet Union—also an occupier of Germany—should disagree? In that case, "we will be right and they will be wrong, and we will have to find ways of persuading them to accept our view."[46]

Kennan unburdened himself, while in Washington, to his fellow Soviet expert Bohlen, an increasingly influential adviser to Roosevelt and Hopkins, now back from his own internment in Japan: "Chip was very distressed if I didn't agree with him, and viewed it almost as a betrayal." He always seemed to be defending "what the Department did, what the government did." Bohlen pointed out that "we didn't have the tradition of fighting a war with an eye on the future." Kennan, not reassured, was sure that demanding unconditional surrender was dangerous, putting "too much weight on our future relationship with the Soviet Union. We ought to keep our hands free." For what? Bohlen wondered: "We've always wanted to win like a boxing match and get the hell out." The two friends tried to convince each other through most of the night. Kennan went home weeping with anguish. "I suppose, in a way, I loved him like a brother, . . . and this is why we argued so."[47]

Service on the European Advisory Commission confirmed Kennan's conviction that the U.S. government was woefully deficient at grand strategy, if by that term one meant the ability to coordinate *all* available means with fundamental policy ends. Military planners were not qualified to take political considerations into account; but the Department of State—which was qualified—refused to take that responsibility. Strategy was emerging, then, from a confusing mix of competing initiatives, false starts, wasted energy, and as he himself had experienced, emergency appeals to the president himself. It was indeed a hell of a way to run the state that was likely to be running the postwar world. In thinking about these problems, Kennan found himself deriving lessons from the running of other worlds; hence his airborne interest in ancient Rome. He had no position yet in which he could apply this approach, which echoed his argument in the Bad Nauheim lectures that the study of history was the most reliable guide to the making of policy. But one would soon come.

VII.

"Mostly, I was unaware of the war that raged around us," Joan recalled of the two years she spent in Portugal. "We took in some refugee Jewish children for a while, but I didn't know anything about Hitler's campaign against the Jews." Only seven at the time, though, "I must have understood something." One day, while the family was picnicking, some airplanes flew over. George and Annelise exchanged uneasy glances, enough for Joan to ask: "Are those German bombers?"

Her parents carefully kept whatever marital problems they were having from her, "[b]ut there are always little clues that children pick up." One day "[m]y mother threw something at my father, either a vase or a lamp. Naturally, this made an impression." Whether for this reason or not, Annelise and the children spent the Christmas of 1943 in Lisbon without George, who had flown back to Washington for the initial consultations on his EAC assignment: "Terribly disappointing," she cabled him, but "[w]ill carry on in the best tradition." He then went directly to London, where Annelise joined him: Joan realized only later how "blissfully ignorant" she had been of the danger they faced from the continuing German bombing of the city.[48]

Soon the stress he was under caused George's ulcer to flare up again, forcing a brief hospitalization in January. While he was back in Washington at the end of March, Navy doctors advised him "to discontinue all work for a period of time." Having received this news with "what I suspect to have been some relief," the State Department "urged me to make the vacation a good long one, and assured me that I had no need to worry further about the affairs of the EAC—another officer would be sent at once to take my place."[49]

Kennan's Foreign Service colleagues suspected him, one of them recalled, of using his illnesses to get out of boring jobs and back into the center of things. Certainly he did not stop working—he simply shifted the nature of it. He went to the farm, exhausted himself with physical labor, and as he explained to Bullitt, recovered remarkably quickly:

> I have painted rooms, built a culvert, hauled gravel, taught the farm boys how to plough on the contour, set out over a hundred and fifty trees all by myself, cleaned and heated and cooked for myself. I have had poison ivy and a sore back and torn fingers and mangled shins and a cold and sinus infection; and I am nevertheless so well that you will not know me when you see me.

"Excuse the sloppiness," George added in a letter to Gene Hotchkiss. "Getting cal-louses on your hands seems to raise hell with the more delicate capacities, such as letter-writing." Early in April, still unsure of his next assignment but relieved that it would not be London, George cabled Annelise in Lisbon to suggest that she pack things up and await further word: "Love to yourself and children. Hope we can soon be together." Three weeks later he was able to add: "Everything fine feeling much improved."[50]

Life at the farm allowed a brief reversion to bachelor life: George invited his old friend Cyrus Follmer—himself a Bad Nauheim internee, now working at the State Department—to East Berlin for a visit. They reminisced about the other Berlin and the Kozhenikovs, while Cyrus got enlisted in planting more trees. Some of the walnuts, George wrote several weeks later, were "thrusting themselves up with the most uninhibited abandon" while others were "hiding away in the deep grass." But "to them that last shall be given gifts that no extrovert can boast of: inner strength, and the fortitude born of suffering, and great persistence." "That my dear Cyrus," George concluded, "ends my little Sunday morning sermon. . . . I am apparently going abroad again soon: very far, and for a long time; and I am sad to think how little I am leaving behind in this country, beside these neglected acres, which could draw me back again."[51]

NINE

Back in the U.S.S.R.: 1944–1945

"I AM STILL ENTIRELY IN THE DARK ABOUT WHAT THE STATE DE-partment will assign me to next," George wrote Gene Hotchkiss from the farm in mid-April 1944. But he added: "I suspect that it will be Moscow; and if it is I am inclined to accept it and go. I spent so many years on Russia that I don't want them to be wasted. And I feel that . . . I must live there once more, before I retire from this form of life." Kennan's appointment as counselor, the second-ranking position in the U.S. Embassy to the Soviet Union, came through on May 22. It had been in the works long before that.[1]

W. Averell Harriman, the American ambassador since October 1943, was as remarkable as his predecessor, Bill Bullitt. The son of the railroad magnate E. H. Harriman—whose biographer, curiously, had been the first George Kennan—young Averell was a Union Pacific shareholder while still a Yale undergraduate and rowing coach. He became a company vice president at the age of twenty-four, five years later founded the bank that became Brown Brothers Harriman, and by the mid-1920s was running one of the first foreign mining concessions in the U.S.S.R. An avid skier, polo player, and racehorse breeder, Harriman was also a high-level fixer, which is why Roosevelt made him Lend-Lease administrator to Great Britain in 1941. There he formed a close friendship with Winston Churchill and an even closer one with the prime minister's daughter-in-law Pamela, who became his lover and, when he was seventy-nine, his third wife. With aid to Britain flowing smoothly after two years, FDR persuaded the reluctant Harriman to take the even more demanding job in Moscow. Like Bullitt a decade earlier, the new ambassador was determined to have good help.[2]

"Before I went to Moscow," he remembered, "I investigated who were the two best Russian experts. They were George Kennan and Chip Bohlen." But Kennan was handling the Azores bases negotiations, and Bohlen—then head of the State Department's Soviet desk—was becoming indispensable to Roosevelt as a policy coordinator and Russian-language interpreter. The president therefore promised Harriman, at the Tehran conference in November, that Moscow would be Kennan's next post. Characteristically, though, he failed to tell the State Department, which instead sent Kennan to London to work on the European Advisory Commission. It took until mid-January 1944 to sort out the confusion, by which time Kennan's ulcers had made it too risky to send him back to the city that had first provoked them.[3]

Kennan's "rest" at the farm brought a rapid recovery, however, and in May Bohlen arranged for him to meet Harriman—a fellow ulcer sufferer—in Washington. The two hit it off immediately, agreeing that Kennan would run the civilian side of the Moscow embassy. Harriman knew of Kennan's objections to Roosevelt's policies, but these did not bother him. Secure in his access to the president, self-confident enough to respect expertise he did not have, Harriman appreciated Kennan's candor: "I never considered a difference of opinion as something objectionable. It was something that I expected, and hoped for, to bring out the facts and establish a sound judgment."

"Averell Harriman was an operator," Kennan recalled. "He had a direct line to Stalin, which he thought was the only important thing. I don't think he attached great importance to our analyses of Russian society." But by encouraging his counselor to provide real counsel, Harriman gave Kennan the freedom to speak his mind without risking his career, as he had had to do in Portugal and on the EAC. Kennan used the opportunity to mount a sustained assault on Roosevelt's approach to the Soviet Union.

Most of Kennan's criticisms remained within the precincts of Spaso House and the Mokhovaya, although Harriman occasionally passed sanitized versions to Washington: "I would change the telegrams he'd drafted, and that sometimes upset him." Kennan had little sense at the time of whether his "anxious Needlings" were getting through to his boss. Harriman's own views on the U.S.S.R. were changing, though, and Kennan helped him find his way. He became, in turn, Kennan's channel to the highest levels of the American government. Through his official actions Harriman showed, Kennan later acknowledged, that he had not been oblivious to what "caused me such concern." This was, he was sure, a better way for Harriman to indicate agreement "than by verbally holding, so to speak, my intellectual hand."

Kennan regarded Harriman as "a towering figure on our Moscow scene, out-

wardly unassuming but nevertheless commanding in appearance, without petty
vanity, intensely serious but never histrionic . . . , imperious only when things or
people impeded the performance of his duties. The United States has never had a
more faithful public servant." Of Kennan, Harriman said simply: "I've never been
able to work with anyone as closely as I did with him."[4]

I.

The journey from East Berlin (Pennsylvania) to Moscow required the entire
month of June 1944, partly because wartime travel was complicated, but also
because the State Department allowed George to stop off in Lisbon to see his family. While he was there, the D-Day landings took place, a long-awaited military
breakthrough that made it possible to begin implementing the postwar planning
he had witnessed—and worried about—in London and Washington. In response
to a request from Henry Norweb, the new minister to Portugal, Kennan laid out
the implications for the Lisbon legation staff, making no effort to conceal his
qualms.

There was no doubting the heroism or the fighting ability of the men sacrificing their lives for faith "in the ultimate righteousness of our society and in the
wisdom of those who lead it." Americans at home had organized "an amazingly
successful war effort, which puts to shame all the predictions about the softness
and lack of fibre of our people." But the Roosevelt administration's strategy for
postwar Europe was ill-conceived, and there was cause for concern that war veterans, when they returned, would find their country a changed and perhaps unsettling place.

Without specifying the details, Kennan portrayed the American approach to
the European Advisory Commission as "shallow and often unrealistic." Washington was proceeding "not from what Europe is, but from what we would wish it to
be." It assumed extreme territorial changes without anticipating the tensions these
would create. It was proposing a new international organization, along the lines of
the old League of Nations, which would freeze that settlement in place. The resulting repression would "force the vanquished peoples to new feats of inventiveness
and organization," until finally they reached the point at which they could sell
their collaboration "to the highest bidder among the erstwhile victors." It would
be, in short, the post–World War I settlement all over again.

Meanwhile the men fighting the war would have to compete for jobs after it, with workers "spoiled by high wages" secured through collective bargaining. Veterans who had faced death on meager pay would have little sympathy for labor unions. When combined with growing racial tensions and increasing juvenile delinquency, it would be "a miracle if we could survive this crisis without violence and disorder." Americans should not think "that we can avoid at home the appearance of those same forces of ugliness and cruelty and timidity and intolerance which we are now fighting abroad." This was the clearest expression yet of an idea Kennan had been wrestling with—at times with erratic results—since the late 1930s: that there were no distinct boundaries between domestic and foreign affairs. Americans could not insulate themselves from forces that had disrupted other societies. How they handled these would largely determine what the United States could do in the postwar world.[5]

On June 15 George deposited his baggage at the airlines office in Lisbon, sat with Annelise for an hour at an outdoor café watching Portuguese passersby, and then drove with her to the airport, where "we said another of those tearing wartime goodbyes" that had become so familiar. "Don't worry about me," she wrote of this latest separation while he was still en route, "because I am feeling quite different about it." (George had arranged, this time, for Annelise and the children to follow him to his new post.) "But even so, I don't like it and never will." Getting to Moscow was more difficult than it had been in peacetime: George's trip required a circuitous routing across the Mediterranean, the Middle East, and the southern U.S.S.R. by whatever air transport was available. It took two weeks, giving him time to read more Gibbon, to keep a detailed diary, and to reflect on the Americans—and Russians—he met along the way.[6]

The journey provided Kennan's first close look at the U.S. military, and he liked what he saw. On the flight from Gibraltar to Algiers, "I sat proudly side by side with the pilot." He had never before been on an operational mission, "and I could not have been more pleased." The next day he found Naples full of "slouching, impassive young American kids" who were running it "pretty damned well." An Army Air Force general four years younger than he seemed "as efficient as any officer I ever saw." Kennan spent the night in an Army tent, then used the next morning to reread Gibbon's account of the Byzantine general Belisarius's conquest of Naples in A.D. 536. It was a rare opportunity for historical comparison "which only the fortunes of war and the settings of antiquity can provide."

Most of the Americans with whom he lunched that day, Kennan discovered, agreed with the great historian's warning that there was nothing "more averse to nature and reason than to hold in obedience remote countries and foreign nations in opposition to their inclination and interest."[7] For the moment, this was reassuring. If there was anything "more hopeful than the skill with which our military men pursue the responsibilities of conquest, it is the alacrity with which they again drop them, once their possession is no longer in dispute." Empires were not their avocation.

The Germans were still much on Kennan's mind. Prisoners of war, he learned, had been claiming that the Americans were destroying Europe's cultural values and turning it over to Bolshevism, "that we understand nothing of the continent, and have no plan for its future." The charge sat strangely, Kennan thought, against discoveries "of SS torture instruments, of bodies without fingernails or toenails, of tons of high explosives hidden in the German Embassy." But even if accurate, "the fault is still with the Germans for having provoked our intervention."

> We are bound to come over here every time anyone threatens the security of England; and if continental peoples do not wish to bring down upon their heads this dread plague of ununderstanding Americans, they must learn to leave the English alone. Let the Germans take a lesson from this, and not repeat their folly.

This thought too would stick with Kennan: that the national security of the United States was inseparable from the balance of power in Europe. Beyond that, though, the Americans were novices. "The French know exactly what they want, and are quite unreasonable about it. We are the soul of reasonableness and have only the dimmest idea of what we are after."

No one could say the same of the Soviet Union. "Whoever would understand Russia today should study . . . the great mass of women of the educated officer class," Kennan concluded after meeting one of them in Naples. For such women, "work is not a decoration to private life but a stern duty to the state. And independent thought is, as in Nazi Germany, a form of self-corruption, unnecessary, dangerous, immoral." Nor was the tendency confined to women: it was what Bolshevism had done to Russia. Kennan thought it "the most terrifying and discouraging difference from our own mentality."[8]

The next few days, which involved stops in Cairo, Baghdad, and Tehran, exposed Kennan for the first time to the Middle East. Overwhelmed by its heat, dust, and languor, repelled by the "religious bigotry" that—in contrast to the Russians—kept the feminine half of society under "indefinite house arrest," he found little in the region to recommend it. The trip left Kennan with an aversion to what would later be called the "third world" that he did little, in his own later life, to overcome.[9]

In Baghdad, Kennan stayed with Loy Henderson, exiled there by Roosevelt, Henderson believed, for his anti-Soviet views. Stuck in the legation because it was too hot to go out during the day and too dangerous at night, Kennan persuaded himself that the very bleakness of the place might someday tempt Americans into trying to fix it: "If trees once grew here, could they not grow again? If rains once fell, could they not again be attracted from the inexhaustible resources of nature? Could not climate be altered, disease eradicated?" His countrymen would do better to return, "like disappointed but dutiful children, to the sad deficiencies and problems of their native land."[10]

Kennan flew from Tehran to Moscow by way of Baku and Stalingrad on July 1, 1944. In the latter city, everything except the airport seemed to have been destroyed. Lunch was served in a dining hall with few chairs and only one glass, but everyone was good-natured about it: "How deeply one sympathizes with the Russians when one encounters the realities of the lives of the people and not the propagandistic preten[s]ions of their government." On the final leg into Moscow, "I sat glued to the window, moved and fascinated to see before me again this great, fertile, mysterious country which I had spent so many years trying to understand." Harriman had a car waiting at the airport, insisted on putting Kennan up at Spaso House, "and with that a new life began."[11]

II.

Kennan found the Soviet Union less wracked by fear than it had been when he left it in 1937. Stalin's purges had long since ended. Hitler's attack and the brutality that followed had "pulled regime and people together, in a process for which the former, at any rate, can be highly thankful." Soviet diplomats, to be sure, were still uneasy at social events with their Western counterparts, trying to imagine how what they said might sound "if repeated by an accusing comrade." But national self-confidence as a whole had been greatly strengthened, for the Russian people had "repelled the invader and regained their territories in a series of military operations second in drama and grandeur to nothing else that the history of warfare can show."[12]

Life in Moscow, if anything, was harsher than during Kennan's earlier tour of duty. American embassy personnel had been evacuated to Kuibyshev after the Nazi invasion, leaving Spaso House and the Mokhovaya empty. By 1943, when they returned, both buildings had deteriorated, and not much had been done since to fix them. "All is as well as it could be in our little world," Kennan wrote Bohlen in September 1944. By that he meant that "the building is falling to pieces, the majority of our cars don't run, . . . [and] the mouse population is increasing fast after its war-time vicissitudes." A State Department report, completed that summer, cataloged with grim precision what anyone assigned to Moscow should bring, keeping in mind weight limitations on airplanes: full dress evening attire with white tie, winter and summer clothing, overshoes and galoshes, socks and stockings, electrical appliances with adapters, radios and phonographs, extra eyeglasses, dental plates and prostheses. It warned not to expect drinkable tap water, fresh fruit, safe milk, palatable eggs, or recreational facilities: "There are no golf courses in the Soviet Union." And it strongly advised against sending anyone with "chronic, relapsing or recurrent diseases," such as "gastric or duodenal ulcer[s]."[13]

Despite the vicissitudes, Kennan was happy to be back. "Russia seems something poignantly familiar and significant to me," he explained to Jeanette, "as though I had lived here in childhood." Wandering the streets of Moscow and rambling through the nearby countryside left him with "an indescribable sort of satisfaction to feel myself back again in the midst of these people—with their tremendous, pulsating warmth and vitality." He sometimes felt that he would rather be sent to Siberia with them, "which is certainly what would happen to me without delay if I were a Soviet citizen," than to live among the "stuffy folk" on Park Avenue.

> On the other hand, the knowledge that I will never be able to become part of them, that I must always remain a distrusted outsider, that all the promise of the white nights, of the lovely birches, of the far-flung rivers, and of a thousand other things that have meaning for me in Russia will never be realized—this knowledge was harder than ever to swallow this summer.

Having forced himself to acknowledge that he could never become a Russian— "for at the age of forty one cannot afford to be unrealistic"—George had the sense of having passed the point "before which one still hopes for some unfolding of the mystery and after which one settles down to derive such modest comforts as one can from the remaining years of life."

By the time he wrote this, in early October, Annelise and the children had arrived, by much the same route that George had taken. "I have really enjoyed having the family here," he wrote Jeanette. "They couldn't be sweeter, and we have a lovely home life in the little apartment which we inhabited seven years ago." Grace and Joan were adapting to the life of diplomatic children in Moscow, playing regularly in the Spaso House garden, the closest equivalent to an American backyard. Both girls were learning Russian, and Grace was attending a Soviet school, where she was treated well by her teachers despite the ideological requirements they had to follow. The Kennans visited one day when gifts from America were being handed out. The teachers gave party-line speeches, but George noticed that while these were going on, "little hands were reaching out" attempting to open the packages. These were locked up after the ceremony, and the children never saw them again.

Grace pleased George, one day that fall, by praising him as a father: "I replied that I wasn't gay enough to make a really good Daddy." Joan at that point chimed in: "Oh Daddy, that's all right. With a little forcing, it would do. And if you wouldn't work in that office all the time." There were evenings, Joan recalled, when "my father told me wonderful stories that he made up himself, each installment being invented on the spot—they were so good that I wish he had written them down." He also read from *Grimm's Fairy Tales*: "It was one of my father's lesser known gifts, reading aloud." Diplomacy made its demands, though: her parents went out a lot, and "my mother would come in and say good night to me before they left."[14]

"George has put on weight since we came," Annelise reported to Jeanette, "so it looks as if it agrees with him!" But he was working hard, there were plenty of things to "upset a nervous tummy," and they all missed the farm, as well as the warmth and fresh food of Portugal. Annelise had no formal job in Moscow but spent much of her time introducing Foreign Service wives at other embassies: a whiz at languages, she also acted as their interpreter. That role could be tedious, but there were compensations. "Churchill is here," she wrote Jeanette in October, "and the big shots are busy and the smaller ones wish they were in on it." The Kennans fell somewhere in between. British ambassador Archibald Clark Kerr did not invite them to the dinner he gave for the prime minister, which Stalin attended, but they were allowed in afterward to gawk at the great men. "We waited for hours. . . . [A]t least I can tell my grandchildren that I have seen some of the people who [have] made history."[15]

The American diplomatic community was still small and closely knit. Dorothy Hessman, who became Kennan's secretary in Moscow and remained with him for almost two decades, recalled little consciousness of rank: "Everybody came to all the parties, and we had a good time together." There was even an embassy orchestra in which George played the guitar and the double bass: it called itself "The Kremlin Krows" until Soviet officials grumbled about the name, after which it became "The Purged Pigeons." The American dacha was still in use, there was swimming in the river that ran nearby, and in the winter even a tame form of skiing in the low hills outside of Moscow. "[W]e all saw each other too much," Patricia Davies remembered. "We didn't have any choice." There were feuds and rivalries, "but by and large, people seemed to get along pretty well." "It was something like a cruise ship," her husband, John Paton Davies, added, "a rather macabre cruise ship."[16]

Parties, under such circumstances, could become legendary. With Harriman out of town in November 1944, it fell to George and Annelise to organize a Thanksgiving dinner and dance at Spaso House for, as she put it, "the lonely souls in town." One was Lillian Hellman, the stridently left-wing playwright who with Roosevelt's support—but to the alarm of the FBI—had recently shown up in Moscow, ill after a harrowing two-week air trip across Siberia. Worried about her health, George arranged accommodations at Spaso, and she had recovered sufficiently by Thanksgiving to join the festivities. That evening Hellman fell dramatically and decisively in love with the embassy third secretary, John Melby. "Whatever might have happened that first night was postponed," their biographer has written, because Annelise insisted that Melby come back downstairs and dance with her. "But the next morning, at breakfast, they found the magic still held." The affair, a famous Cold War romance, would continue off and on for the next three decades.[17]

A few days before Christmas that year, two American journalists in Moscow, William Lawrence of *The New York Times* and John Hersey of *Time*, decided that they would like to have the holiday dinner with, as Hersey wrote his wife, the "Kennons." But "we couldn't think of any reason in the world why they should want us." So why not invite them to dine at the Metropole? "But then we decided that they'd want to have Christmas with their girls and we'd better not do that. We dropped the whole Kennon idea—until about five that afternoon. Then, without any prompting except what she must have gotten by mental telepathy, Mrs. Kennon called me first, and then Bill, and invited us to Christmas dinner! Both of us practically sang into the phone when we accepted."[18]

"There is no telling how long I'll remain here," George had written Jeanette that fall. "Presumably at least until both wars are over. But one never knows. . . . A single wrong word—a single mistake—can only too easily ruin a person's usefulness in any atmosphere as delicate as this, and among people so hyper-sensitive." Harriman, however, was "a truly exceptional man, of great courage and competence. I genuinely admire him and have learned a good deal, working for him." George's own job was important, "[t]o the extent that Russia's relations with the United States are important. . . . That might mean anything, depending on how you look at it."[19]

III.

"Our new minister has arrived so Ave's thrilled," Harriman's daughter Kathleen, who served as his official hostess in Moscow, wrote on July 3, 1944. "The new counselor speaks in Russian perfectly freely," an aide reported to Molotov a few days later, "quite willingly entering conversation, although in his manner he seems at first reserved and dry." By then Kennan had already spent hours talking with his new boss: as Harriman's aide Robert Meiklejohn noted, "[t]he Ambassador put him to work at once." The topic was probably Poland, for Kennan followed up with the first of many memoranda on that subject.[20]

History had shown, he wrote, that Germany and Russia tolerated a strong and independent Poland only when they themselves were weak. "Otherwise, Poland inevitably becomes a pawn in their century-old rivalry." With the Red Army nearing Warsaw, independence looked extremely unlikely. The alternative would not necessarily be communism, but it would involve "extensive control of foreign affairs, military matters, public opinion, and economic relations with the outside world." As a consequence, the United States should be very careful not to promise the Poles "a prosperous and happy future under Russian influence. Prosperity and happiness have always been, like warm summer days, fleeting exceptions in the cruel climate of Eastern Europe."[21]

"All interesting," Harriman commented, "especially last para[graph]." It was indeed, because Great Britain had gone to war in 1939 on Poland's behalf, and Roosevelt and Churchill had publicly pledged, two years later in the Atlantic Charter, to restore "sovereign rights and self-government . . . to those who have been forcibly deprived of them." Stalin, however, had paved the way for the German invasion of Poland with the Nazi-Soviet Pact, and the Red Army had occupied the eastern third of the country shortly thereafter. Hitler's attack in 1941 placed the Soviet Union nominally on the side of the Polish government-in-exile in London, but the relationship remained wary because Stalin was determined to keep the territorial gains the U.S.S.R. had made, as Germany's ally, at Poland's expense.[22]

Then in 1943 the Germans revealed that they had found the graves of some fifteen thousand Polish prisoners of war, allegedly shot by the Russians three years earlier, at Katyn Forest, near Smolensk. When the London Poles called for an investigation, Stalin broke diplomatic relations with them and began preparations to set up a Polish government of his own design. At Harriman's request, Kathleen and John Melby inspected the site early in 1944, after the Russians had recaptured it. They reported that the Germans had killed the Poles, and Harriman accepted their findings. Kennan, still in London, had his doubts—correctly as it turned out—but with no evidence of his own, he fell in "with the tacit rule of silence which was being applied at that time to the unpleasant subject in question."[23]

Meanwhile Roosevelt was running for reelection. With a large, politically active Polish American community in the United States, the last thing he wanted was controversy over Katyn or anything else that had to do with Poland. On his instructions, Harriman told Soviet Foreign Minister Molotov, a month before Kennan's arrival in Moscow, that "the Polish-Soviet question must not become an issue in the forthcoming presidential campaign." The president was doing what he could to restrain the London Poles and hoped that "whatever the Soviet Government publicly stated would be on a constructive side. . . . It was time to keep the barking dogs quiet."[24]

With that objective in mind, Roosevelt arranged for Stanisław Mikołajczyk, the prime minister of the London Polish government, to visit Moscow at the end of July. He was coming, Kennan warned Harriman, at a moment when pride and elation over Soviet victories had "almost reached the point of hysteria." The Russians were less worried than ever before about controlling Eastern Europe and would not go out of their way to meet the wishes of émigré Poles. But Harriman refused to pass this depressing conclusion on to Washington. "The Russians have a long-term consistent policy," Kennan complained in his diary. "We have—and they know we have—a fluctuating policy reflecting only the momentary fancies of public opinion in the United States." Given this disparity, Americans should stop "mumbling words of official optimism" and instead "bow our heads in silence before the tragedy of a people who have been our allies, whom we have saved from our enemies, and whom we cannot save from our friends."[25]

On August 1, 1944, the day Kennan wrote those words, resistance fighters linked to the London Poles seized large portions of Warsaw, in the expectation that the Red Army, which had reached the eastern suburbs of the city, would come to their assistance. But, as he noted on the sixth, "there is some suspicion that the Russians are deliberately withholding support, finding it by no means inconvenient that the Germans and the members of Mikołajczyk's underground should destroy each other." These fears seemed confirmed on the fifteenth when Harriman and Clark Kerr asked that British and American planes dropping supplies to the Warsaw insurgents be allowed to refuel at Soviet bases. Deputy Foreign Minister Andrey Vyshinsky turned them down flat, denouncing the uprising as "ill-advised, . . . not worthy of assistance." Harriman returned from this conversation, Kennan recalled, "shattered by the experience." The ambassador informed Roosevelt later that evening that "[f]or the first time since coming to Moscow, I am gravely concerned by the attitude of the Soviet government."[26]

Years afterward Kennan claimed to have concluded that this was the moment for an Anglo-American showdown with the Soviet leadership. They should have been given the choice "between changing their policy completely and agreeing to collaborate in the establishment of truly independent countries in Eastern Europe or forfeiting Western-Allied support and sponsorship for the remaining phases of the war." The second front had been established. Soviet territory had been liberated. The West had the perfect right to divest itself of responsibility for what their "ally" would now do. The time had come to "hold fast and be ready to drive a real bargain with them when the hostilities [were] over."[27]

Kennan's recommendations at the time, however, were less drastic. Stalin and his subordinates, he reminded Harriman, had "never ceased to think in terms of spheres of influence." They expected support in such regions, "regardless of whether that action seems to us or to the rest of the world to be right or wrong." This was not, he admitted, an unreasonable position, because they would surely have respected Washington's predominance in the Caribbean. The problem was that the American people, "for reasons which we do not need to go into," had not been prepared for such a postwar settlement, but instead had been led to believe that the Soviet Union was eager to join an international security organization with the power to prevent aggression: "We are now faced with the prospect of having our people disabused of this illusion." The United States should therefore warn the Kremlin leaders that their actions were making it difficult "for this or any other American administration to do for the Russian people the things which all of us would like to be able to do." The choice would then lie with Moscow: "If this position is adhered to and if repercussions in American public opinion are unfavorable, Russia has only herself to blame."[28]

Roosevelt quickly made it clear, though, that he did not wish to alter his Soviet policy in the light of the Warsaw Uprising, and Harriman followed his lead: "We had to fight the war. Hitler was our main enemy. We shouldn't let divergence interfere with that." Kennan, angrier now, suggested that an international force administer postwar Poland. If that were not possible, then the United States should abandon its interests there altogether rather than "to try to defend them in circumstances over which we will have no real influence." Harriman wrote back bluntly: "George—These are two extremes, and much 'too extreme.'"

"I didn't blame Averell for it," Kennan recalled. "Averell was the President's personal representative, and he couldn't join me in these criticisms." Isaiah Berlin, who knew both men well, explained that Harriman believed in negotiation, "whereas George believed in principle. Those two things could never quite be reconciled. There was no open hostility or tension between them that I know of. But they were very different." Harriman remembered respecting Kennan's judgments: "They were accurate but sometimes too impractical to be acted upon." When he disagreed with Kennan, though, "I simply didn't bother to waste the time to argue. It didn't amuse me to do so."[29]

IV.

While the Polish crisis was developing that summer, Kennan composed a long essay—the final version came to about twelve thousand words—in which he sought to compress what he knew about Russia generally, and Stalin's Russia in particular. He submitted it, with some diffidence, to Harriman's aide: "The Ambassador may want to glance over it. I doubt that he would care to read the whole thing. It is just what he would call 'batting out flies.'" But Kennan's hopes for the paper were higher than that: "Conscience forced me . . . to make this statement at least available to whose who had responsibility for the formulation of American policy. It would be up to them, then, to draw the logical conclusions, if by chance they should be interested."[30]

Entitled "Russia—Seven Years Later," the essay began by pointing out that the residents of a country, like sailors at sea, had little perception of the currents upon which they were floating. "This is why it is sometimes easier for someone who leaves and returns to estimate the speed and direction of movement, to seize and fix the subtleties of trend." Kennan had used this argument to justify writing about the United States after visiting it—even if briefly—from abroad. It was also why "no foreign observer should ever be asked to spend more than a year in Russia without going out into the outside world for the recovery of perspective."

The war, Kennan acknowledged, had left the Soviet Union weakened, with some twenty million of its people killed and the destruction of perhaps 25 percent of its fixed capital.[31] Those losses would be offset, however, by the absorption of new populations to the west—the territorial gains Stalin had demanded and his allies had tacitly granted—together with the relocation and massive expansion of heavy industry required to repel Hitler's invasion. When set against the coming collapse of Nazi Germany, these would make the U.S.S.R., whether for good or ill, "a single force greater than any other that will be left on the European continent when this war is over."

That gave its internal configuration international significance. In seeking to map this, Kennan considered first "the spiritual life of the Russian people," at once "the most important and the most mysterious of all the things that are happening in the Soviet state." No shepherd ever guarded a flock more carefully than the Kremlin watched "the souls of its human charges," and they responded with amiable acquiescence: "Bade to admire, they applaud generously and cheerfully. Bade to abhor, they strike a respectful attitude of hatred and indignation." There was nothing new in such dissembling: Russians had long considered it "a national virtue." It meant, though, that Soviet leaders could never really know what their people were thinking. "The strength of the Kremlin lies largely in the fact that it knows how to wait. But the strength of the Russian people lies in the fact that they know how to wait longer."

Culture, in the meantime, was stagnating. The Bolsheviks' triumph had stimulated creative minds, especially those of Jewish intellectuals: "It was their restless genius which contributed most to the keen and analytical quality of Soviet thought and Soviet feeling in the years immediately following the revolution." But the Jews suffered disproportionately from Stalin's purges, and now their influence was almost gone. In its place was a chauvinistic "cult of the past" that smothered innovations connected with the freedom of the spirit, the dignity of the individual, and the critical approach to human society. Only when Soviet power waned would Russian culture again give off those "effervescences of artistic genius" with which it had once "astounded the world."

Politics, in such a society, could hardly exist: as in most authoritarian states, there was only a struggle to reach the ruler and to control his sources of information. Yet Stalin's advisers knew little more than he about the outside world. Their judgments might occasionally correspond with reality, but these people were as often as not "the victims of their own slogans, the slaves of their own propaganda. . . . God knows what conclusions they draw from all this, and what recommendations they make on the basis of those conclusions."

For this reason, Western concepts of collective security could only seem "naïve and unreal" in Moscow. Soviet leaders paid lip service to these principles when they wanted military assistance from the United States and Great Britain, but with the second front in place, they no longer needed to observe "excessive delicacy." Their own priorities now took precedence, and these amounted simply to power. The form it took and the methods by which it was achieved were secondary issues: Moscow didn't care whether a given area was "communistic" or not. The main thing was that it should be subject to Moscow's control. The U.S.S.R. was thus committed to becoming "the dominant power of Eastern and Central Europe" and only then to cooperation with its Anglo-American allies. "The first of these programs implies taking. The second implies giving. No one can stop Russia from doing the taking, if she is determined to go through with it. No one can force Russia to do the giving, if she is determined not to go through with it."

Understanding the Soviet Union, Kennan insisted, would require living with contradictions. Russians were used to "extreme cold and extreme heat, prolonged sloth and sudden feats of energy, exaggerated cruelty and exaggerated kindness, ostentatious wealth and dismal squalor, violent xenophobia and uncontrollable yearning for contact with the foreign world, vast power and the most abject slavery, simultaneous love and hate for the same objects." Their life, hence, was not one of harmonious, integrated elements but an ever-shifting equilibrium between conflicting forces. No proposition about the U.S.S.R. could make sense "without seeking, and placing in apposition, its opposite." It would also be necessary to realize that for the Soviet regime there were no objective criteria of right and wrong, or even of reality and unreality. Bolshevism had shown the possibility of making people "feel and believe practically anything." Even an outsider, thrust into such a system, could easily become "the tool, rather than the master, of the material he is seeking to understand."

Few Americans, Kennan was sure, would ever grasp this. Most would continue to wander about in a maze of confusion, with respect to Russia, not dissimilar to that confronting Alice in Wonderland. For anyone who did penetrate the mysteries, there would be few rewards. The best he could hope for would be "the lonely pleasure of one who stands at long last on a chilly and inhospitable mountaintop where few have been before, where few can follow, and where few will consent to believe that he has been."

What Harriman thought of Kennan's essay is not clear, although he carried a copy with him when he returned to Washington in October 1944. Probably as a result, other copies wound up in the State Department files and in the papers of Harry Hopkins. Kennan was "puzzled and moderately disappointed" by Harriman's silence. He could understand why the ambassador might not wish to comment on content, since it was "politically unacceptable if not almost disloyal, in the light of the public attitude of our own Government." But "I did think he might have observed, if he thought so, that it was well written. I personally felt, as I finished it, that I was making progress, technically and stylistically, in the curious art of writing for one's self alone."[32]

That was a shrewd assessment. "Russia—Seven Years Later" was impressive for the way it used the past in order to see the future. Contrary to what almost everyone else assumed at the time, Kennan portrayed the Soviet Union as a transitory phenomenon: it was floating along on the surface of Russian history, and currents deeper than anything Marx, Lenin, or Stalin had imagined would ultimately determine its fate. Decades before the documents opened, Kennan anticipated what they would reveal about the leadership's ignorance of the outside world. His list of the intellectual adjustments Americans would have to make to understand the U.S.S.R. foreshadowed George Orwell's dramatization of them, five years later, in his great novel *1984*. And the essay was indeed well written.

But as policy prescription, the paper failed. It was far too long and hence too discursive: if Harriman did try to slog through its twenty single-spaced legal-sized typed pages, his eyes probably glazed over when Kennan meandered off into Byzantine influences on Russian architecture, or nineteenth-century Russian music, or the complaint that "the last good novel was written—let me see—at least a decade ago." Nor was Kennan's argument always clear. For all the space he gave to it, he failed to explain how Russian culture affected Soviet behavior. He contradicted himself by claiming at one point that Kremlin leaders could never know what their people were thinking, while warning elsewhere of their ability totally to control that thinking. There were no clear recommendations for what the United States should do: this surely would have disappointed anyone who read the essay through to the end. They would have found there, instead, a self-indulgent self portrait—the lonely expert atop the chilly and inhospitable mountain—which seemed to suggest that only Kennan was qualified to stand on that pinnacle, and that no one would take his conclusions seriously if he reached it. When conveyed in this form, he was correct.

V.

"This is my sixth winter in Moscow," George wrote Jeanette on January 25, 1945, "and I'm getting pretty well used to them. We are taking things pretty easy and just praying that they will really relieve me here in time to let me get home before the whole spring season is over." The main subject of this letter—Jeanette having sent Betty MacDonald's best seller *The Egg and I*—was chickens: "If we have any of our own on the farm, I'm afraid they'll have to live by the survival of the fittest." Jeanette knew her brother well enough to doubt, though, that he would ever take things easily, or that his principal preoccupation was poultry.[33]

She would have been right, for on the next day Kennan completed his sharpest attack yet on American policy toward the Soviet Union. It took the form of an eight-page personal letter to Chip Bohlen. Kennan wrote it knowing that Roosevelt, Churchill, and Stalin would be meeting at Yalta on February 4, and that Bohlen—the president's interpreter—would literally have his ear. He sent it four days after Harriman had left to supervise preparations: Hessman, who typed it, remembered that the ambassador's absences seemed to liberate Kennan. This document too failed to achieve its purpose: given its startling contents, he could hardly have expected otherwise. But it did, with uncanny foresight, prescribe policy. By the middle of 1947 the U.S. government had agreed to almost everything Kennan had recommended. He was still lonely and unappreciated at the beginning of 1945, but that was only because he was two and a half years ahead of everyone else.[34]

Kennan began by reminding his old friend of a claim Bohlen had made the previous summer: that if Kennan had not been limited by "the narrow field of vision provided by Lisbon and the EAC, . . . I would have had more confidence in the pattern of things to come." Six months in Moscow had expanded Kennan's horizons, but without changing his conviction that Soviet political objectives in Europe were not consistent "with the happiness, prosperity or stability of international life on the rest of the continent." Stalin and his subordinates viewed with suspicion "any source of unity or moral integrity" that they could not control. Rather than allow these to exist, there was no evil they would not be prepared to inflict, "if they could."

A basic conflict is thus arising over Europe between the interests of Atlantic sea-power, which demand the preservation of vigorous and independent political life on the European peninsula, and the interests of the jealous Eurasian land power, which must always seek to extend itself to the west and will never find a place, short of the Atlantic Ocean, where it can from its own standpoint safely stop.

No one was to blame for this: the situation was deeply rooted in Russian history and in European geography. Nor did Kennan question the need for Moscow's assistance in defeating Nazi Germany: "We were too weak to win [the war] without Russia's cooperation." Nor could anyone doubt that the Soviet war effort had been "masterful and effective and must, to a certain extent, find its reward at the expense of other peoples in eastern and central Europe."

He did wonder, though, "why we must associate ourselves with this political program, so hostile to the interests of the Atlantic community as a whole, so dangerous to everything which we need to see preserved in Europe." Why not instead divide Europe "into spheres of influence—keep ourselves out of the Russian sphere and keep the Russians out of ours?" That would allow honesty in dealing with Moscow, while "within whatever sphere of action was left to us we could at least [try] to restore life, in the wake of the war, on a dignified and stable foundation."

Instead, the Roosevelt administration was refusing to specify American interests in Europe, while going ahead with plans for a new League of Nations with "no basis in reality," a course that could only accentuate differences with the Soviet Union while giving the American public "a distorted picture of the nature of the problems the postwar era is bound to bring." As that was happening, political and territorial settlements were being made that would leave the food-producing regions of Germany in Soviet hands, the American and British zones flooded with refugees, and no realistic prospect for cooperative tripartite administration of that country. American influence would be confined "to the purely negative act of destroying Nazi power."

So what to do? "We should gather together at once into our hands all the cards we hold and begin to play them for their full value." Plans for the United Nations should be set aside "as quickly and quietly as possible." The United States should abandon Eastern Europe altogether. And Washington should accept Germany's division into a Soviet and a consolidated Anglo-American zone, with the latter integrated as much as possible into the economic life of Western Europe. Each of the victors would take reparations from its zone only, on a "catch as catch can" basis. Kennan admitted that this "bitterly modest" program would amount to a partition of Europe. "But beggars can't be choosers."

Bohlen received Kennan's letter at Yalta. He wrote back hurriedly that although its recommendations might make sense in the abstract, "as practical suggestions they are utterly impossible. Foreign policy of that kind cannot be made in a democracy. Only totalitarian states can make and carry out such policies." What Bohlen meant, he explained in his memoirs, was that democracies

> must take into account the emotions, beliefs, and goals of the people. The most carefully thought-out plans of the experts, even though 100 percent correct in theory, will fail without broad public support. The good leader in foreign affairs formulates his policy on expert advice and creates a climate of public support to support it.

More privately, Bohlen remembered worrying about Kennan's "damn-it-all-the-hell-with-it-let's-throw-up-our-hands" attitude. "Obviously you couldn't do that." Roosevelt understood that Americans, who had fought a long, hard war, deserved at least an attempt to make peace. If it failed, the United States could not be blamed for not trying. Or as Bohlen put it in his reply to Kennan at the time: "Quarreling with them would be so easy, but we can always come to that."

Kennan's letter went nowhere because he destroyed all copies of it—or thought he had—at Bohlen's request: "That it was written to him while he was at Yalta challenged what the President was trying to do." But Hessman quietly kept a copy, and as it happened Bohlen did also, even publishing portions of it years later in his memoirs, to Kennan's surprise. Despite all of Roosevelt's efforts to get along with Moscow, Bohlen acknowledged, Stalin did "exactly as Kennan had predicted and I had feared." Even so, Bohlen could not agree "that we should write off Eastern Europe and give up efforts to cooperate with the Soviet Union"—at least not yet.[35]

VI.

John Paton and Patricia Davies arrived in Moscow, after years of Foreign Service duties in China, at the end of March 1945. They found Harriman functioning at the level of Roosevelt, Stalin, and their respective advisers, mostly from his Spaso House bedroom, where the ambassador would review dispatches late into the night in a dressing gown, in front of the fireplace. "We'd sit around there and chat," Patricia remembered, while Harriman would feed the fire. "There was something about the way he did it that drove George absolutely up a tree! You could just see him holding himself back, and his eyes, those large eyes, practically popping out of his head." Kennan would whisper, when Harriman could not hear: "That man doesn't know how to build a fire!"[36]

The risk that Harriman might incinerate Spaso House was not Kennan's only source of anxiety. *New York Times* correspondent C. L. Sulzberger found him resentful that Harriman had concealed everything from him connected with Yalta. Martha Mautner, who had just joined the embassy staff, saw that Harriman had "both ears to the ground—he was very sensitive to political considerations." Frank Roberts, now serving in the British embassy in Moscow, recalled Kennan as insisting to Harriman: "You must get home to the president what a terrible villain Stalin is, what awful things he has done." Harriman's reaction was: "We're allies, and we're fighting the war together. There is a moral consideration which obviously you're quite right to put to me, but I don't think I need to put it now to the president." John Paton Davies remembered Harriman as "a great team player." He felt "that Kennan was too skeptical, not really at all with the Roosevelt point of view." Kennan, in turn, "suffered agonies of frustration" over his inability to influence Washington.[37]

No doubt Kennan was frustrated: that was his normal state. His differences with Harriman, however, were not as great as they appeared to Roberts or Davies—or probably even to Kennan—at the time. The ambassador had been advocating a tougher line toward the Soviet Union since the Warsaw Uprising. "Unless we take issue with the present policy," he had written Harry Hopkins in September 1944, "there is every indication the Soviet Union will become a world bully wherever their interests are involved." Harriman did not always confide in Kennan, so he may not have realized the extent of his boss's support for a firmer stance. And they did differ over how quickly such a shift could happen. Kennan, who resented domestic political influences on foreign policy, wanted it to take place at once. Harriman, like Bohlen, knew that this was impossible: "We couldn't shock people in Washington because we would lose our influence." It was, therefore, Harriman's patience that worried Kennan, not any significant disagreement over the postwar intentions of the Soviet Union, or how the United States should handle them.[38]

The key to changing American policy, Harriman knew, was changing the mind of the president himself. Roosevelt's declining health—obvious to all who saw him at Yalta—made this difficult: exhausted leaders tend not to embrace new initiatives. Even so, the gap between Stalin's promises of "democratic" regimes in Eastern Europe and the practices of Soviet officials there was becoming too large even for Roosevelt to ignore. When, at the beginning of April, Stalin interpreted a

German surrender offer in Italy as evidence of an Anglo-American plot to divert the remaining fighting to the Eastern front, the president was furious. Had he lived, Kennan later speculated, subsequent history "might have been quite different." But he was dying, and so he never saw Harriman's request for permission to tell the Soviet leader that if his government continued its policies, "the friendly hand that we have offered them will be withdrawn and to point out in detail what this will mean."[39]

On the morning of April 13, Joan Kennan, then nine, was lying quietly in bed in the Mokhovaya apartment, playing with a kitten. "My father came into the room and said, 'Joanie, the President is dead,' and then sat on my bed looking so serious and so sad that I knew this was something very significant." She could not recall her father ever speaking to her about world affairs, so "I was rather pleased that he thought me old enough to comprehend, at least partly, the significance of such a major event."[40]

Harriman had been planning a trip to Washington when the news reached him earlier that morning. Knowing the importance of being in the right spot at the right time, he accelerated his departure and so was on hand to advise an inexperienced Harry S. Truman on what he should do. With Bohlen present taking notes, Harriman warned that Stalin had interpreted American restraint as weakness: the view had developed in Moscow that "the Soviet Government could do anything that it wished without having any trouble with the United States." That left the West facing a "barbarian invasion of Europe."[41]

It's not clear what Kennan would have said if given the opportunity, but what Harriman said was close enough. He had not been oblivious to the concerns of his anxious subordinate, and now he had the ear of a president with no firm views of his own. The effect on policy, however, was for the moment minimal. Truman gave Molotov a tongue-lashing when he passed through Washington on April 23—even Harriman, who was there, thought it excessive—but the president did not immediately give up on his predecessor's efforts to enlist Stalin's cooperation in shaping the postwar settlement.[42]

There were several reasons for this. One had to do with Molotov's destination: he was en route to San Francisco, where the conference establishing the United Nations—Roosevelt's most cherished project—was to open on April 25. With hopes for the new organization as high as they had ever been, the United States could hardly undercut it before it had begun to function. A second reason was military: Pentagon planners, unsure whether the top-secret program to build the atomic bomb would produce a usable weapon, still counted on Soviet assistance in defeating Japan. Finally, Truman had other close advisers to whom he listened. One was Joe Davies, whose persistent desire to give the Soviet Union the benefit of every doubt countered Harriman's determination to do the opposite.[43]

From Moscow, Kennan saw little that encouraged him. Taking advantage of Harriman's absence, he peppered the State Department with an almost daily litany of complaints about Soviet behavior:

April 20, 1945: One of the fundamental tenets of Soviet control is that the people shall be exposed to no propaganda influences except those of the Soviet propaganda apparatus.

April 23: Words mean different things to the Russians than they do to us.... In official Soviet terminology the Warsaw Provisional Government and even Soviet Estonia are "free."

April 27: All information reaching Embassy indicates that Russians are seizing and transporting to Soviet Union without compunction any German materials, equipment or supplies which they feel could be of use to them.

April 28: Personally I believe that the Soviet Government actually wishes to discourage the maintenance here of large diplomatic staffs, believing that most of the functions they perform are more to the advantage of the foreign governments than of the Soviet Government.

April 30: It is now established Russian practice to seek as a first and major objective, in all areas where they wish to exercise dominant influence, control of the internal administrative and police apparatus, particularly the secret police ... [A]ll other manifestations of public life, including elections, can eventually be shaped by this authority.

May 3: If we feign ignorance or disbelief of a situation [the unilateral transfer of German territory to Poland] which ... is common knowledge to every sparrow in eastern Europe, ... [this] could only mean to the Russians that we are eager to sanction their unilateral action but we are afraid to admit this frankly to our own public.

May 8: More than thirty hours after signature of the act of surrender [by Germany to Allied forces in France], there had still been no recognition in Moscow of the fact that the end of the war was at hand. . . . For Russia peace, like everything else, can come only by ukase, and the end of hostilities must be determined not by the true course of events but by decision of the Kremlin.

Expecting the official announcement, Kennan and Roberts accepted invitations to a gala performance at the Bolshoi Theater that evening, only to find that it celebrated Aleksandr Popov, the alleged Russian inventor of radio.[44]

When the authorities did finally announce the end of the war, on May 9, they and everyone else were unprepared for what happened. The first spontaneous demonstration anyone could remember in Moscow broke out in front of the Mokhovaya, where Soviet and American flags were flying, and it would not disperse. "We were naturally moved and pleased by this manifestation of public feeling," Kennan recalled, "but were at a loss to know how to respond to it." Anyone venturing into the street "was immediately seized, tossed enthusiastically into the air, and passed on friendly hands over the heads of the crowd, to be lost, eventually, in a confused orgy of good feelings somewhere on its outer fringes. Few of us were willing to court this experience, so we lined the balconies and waved back as bravely as we could."

Sensing that more was expected, Kennan climbed precariously onto a pedestal at the base of a column in front of the building to make his first and last public speech in Russian before the walls of the Kremlin: "Congratulations on the day of victory. All honor to the Soviet allies." This was about all, it seemed, that "I could suitably say."[45]

VII.

Kennan could, however, write—and the essay he composed that month was neither contradictory nor self-indulgent nor impractical. Entitled "Russia's International Position at the Close of the War with Germany," it expressed the hope that peace would not resemble the Russian summer, "faint and fleeting, tinged with reminders of rigors that recently were and rigors that are soon to come." Reality, though, was likely to be just that. The war was ending with the defeat of two totalitarian states, but a third was poised to dominate much of the postwar world.

This was hardly an original insight. Bullitt had made the same point in a long letter to Roosevelt as early as January 1943. Harriman had been worrying about the war's outcome since the summer of 1944 and now had influential supporters in Washington: by May 1945, for example, the new secretary of the Navy, James V. Forrestal, had concluded that Soviet ideology was "as incompatible with democracy as was Nazism or Fascism." That same month Winston Churchill used the phrase "iron curtain" for the first time in seeking to alert Truman to the risks inherent in the way the war was ending.[46]

What set Kennan's essay apart was not the alarm it expressed but the optimism it reflected: the Soviet Union's position, he argued, was more likely in the long run to weaken it than to strengthen it. The reasons went back yet again to Gibbon, ancient Rome, and "the unnatural task of holding in submission distant peoples." The U.S.S.R. had taken over, or incorporated within its sphere of influence, territories that even the tsars had never controlled. The peoples affected would resent Russian rule. Successful revolts "might shake the entire structure of Soviet power."

Much would depend, therefore, upon the skill with which Stalin's agents managed their new empire. They had the advantages of geographical proximity, experience in running a police state, and the disorientation the war had left behind. No one could expect popularity, though, "who holds that national salvation can come only through bondage to a greater nation." The "naked bluntness" with which the Red Army had occupied these territories would make the task of running them even more difficult: in this sense, the Kremlin had been better served by the revolutionaries of the interwar era than by the generals and commissars "whose girth is no less and subtlety no greater than those of the Tsarist satraps of a hundred years ago."

Nor could Moscow provide economic assets to offset political liabilities. Land reform would not put more food on people's tables. Trade with the capitalists would undermine self-sufficiency. Heavy industry would drain resources from consumers, forcing them to accept a Soviet standard of living. There would of course be claims of economic success: "Russians are a nation of stage managers; and the deepest of their convictions is that things are not what they are, but only what they seem." Non-Russians to the west were not likely to buy such arguments.

The Kremlin's greatest difficulty, however, would come in administering its new empire. None of its peoples spoke Russian, and only 60 percent used other Slavic languages; few Russians knew any tongue other than their own. If Moscow sought local assistance, it would risk "disaffection, intrigue, and loss of control." If it tried to train Russians in the appropriate languages and customs, they were likely to be "corrupted by the amenities and temptations of a more comfortable existence and a more tolerant atmosphere." If it kept its agents isolated, or sent them only for brief periods of time, then they could hardly be effective either.

Curiously, Soviet leaders expected help from the West through recognition of the "independence" of states within their sphere, as well as help in repairing the economic damage their own policies were inflicting. They knew how often the Americans and British had been told that the only alternative to cooperation was another world war, in which civilization would face "complete catastrophe." As long as the West believed this, it would not challenge Soviet policy, and Soviet policy would not change.

Should the West, contrary to expectations, muster up "political manliness," the U.S.S.R. would probably not be able to maintain its hold on "*all* the territory over which it has today staked out a claim." Communist parties throughout Western Europe would bare their fangs, and Molotov would no doubt threaten withdrawal from the United Nations. But the Soviet Union "would have played its last real card." Further military advances would only increase responsibilities already beyond its capacity to meet. And it had no naval or air forces capable of challenging any position outside of Europe. No one in the Kremlin, however, believed that the West, "confronted with the life-size wolf of Soviet displeasure standing at the door and threatening to blow the house in," would stand firm. "And it is on this disbelief that Soviet global policy is based."[47]

This essay, Kennan recalled, "set forth for the first time—indeed, the writing of it evoked for the first time—thoughts that were to be basic to my view of Russia and its problems in future years." It laid out the key assumption of what later became the strategy of "containment": that the Soviet Union's self-generated problems would frustrate its ambitions if the West was patient enough to wait for this to happen and firm enough to resist making concessions. "I didn't say war was inevitable. I said we had to stand up to them. Time will have its effect, and . . . this is going to affect the regime."

Kennan gave the paper to Harriman, who returned it without comment. Harry Hopkins may have read it when he visited Moscow in late May and early June. Otherwise, as with Kennan's earlier efforts to "pluck people's sleeves, trying to make them understand the nature of the phenomenon with which we in the Moscow embassy were daily confronted," there was no response: "So far as official Washington was concerned, it had been to all intents and purposes like talking to a stone."[48]

VIII.

With the war over, George Kennan sent himself to Siberia. He had requested permission to go soon after arriving in Moscow the year before, and following months of delay the approval, to his surprise, came through. The ostensible reason for the trip was to visit the new industrial complex at Stalinsk-Kuznetsk (now Novokuznetsk), a massive steel production facility southeast of Novosibirsk where few if any foreigners had ever been. But there was also a personal motive, which was "the example of my distinguished nineteenth century namesake. I wanted, before leaving Russia again, to see at least a small portion of the vast Siberian territory where so many of his travels had taken place and with which his name was so widely associated."[49]

The first George Kennan had crossed Siberia by horse-drawn carriages and sleighs because the railroad to Vladivostok would not become fully operational until 1905. Four decades later, on June 9, 1945, the second George Kennan boarded the Trans-Siberian Express in Moscow, relishing the opportunity to relax and to watch the country and its inhabitants go by. He had a compartment to himself but shared a washroom with two taciturn secret police agents, stationed next door. Two good-natured car attendants, Zinya and Marusya, kept a samovar going with scraps of wood collected at frequent station stops along the way, while shooing away anyone trying to hitch an unauthorized ride.

> There, on the black cinder-track, hard-trodden and greasy with the oil and the droppings from the trains, under the feet of the milling crowds of passengers, train personnel and station hangers-on, without regard for the clouds of soot and dust, a thriving business was done: milk was cheerfully poured from old jugs into empty vodka flasks or army canteens; greasy cakes were fingered tentatively by hands black with train soot; arguments ran their course; bargains were struck; passengers pushed their way triumphantly back to the cars, clutching their acquisitions; and timid little girls with bare feet, who had not succeeded in selling their offerings, stood by in sad and tearless patience, awaiting with all the stoicism of their race the maternal wrath which would await them when the train had gone and they would return home with their tidbits unsold.

At one stop a soldier accused an old woman of cheating him. "'You'd better be careful, little mother,' he said gaily, 'not to run across me in the other world. The archangels are all my friends.' To the crowd's delight, the old girl crossed herself anxiously; and the incident ended in general laughter."

The trip took four days. Fellow passengers were pleasant but wary: "We didn't talk much." One evening, however, Kennan passed around copies of the American embassy's Russian-language magazine, provoking a lively corridor discussion on the transition from Roosevelt to Truman. "Then everybody began to look guiltily over his shoulder and the meeting quickly dispersed." With traffic on the line heavy,

> we were only one link in the long chain of trains, tiny trains against the surrounding distances, crawling eastward like worms, haltingly and with innumerable interruptions. . . . We stopped more than we moved; and when we stopped, we could see the freight trains piling up behind us, and hear them whistling for the right of way with the deep throaty voice which only trains in Russia and America have, and which brings nostalgia to every American heart.

The waits were long enough for the passengers to get off and pick flowers: at one point, "when the train stopped among the swamps, we climbed down the embankment, took off our shirts, splashed off the yellow scum from the surface . . . , and washed our heads in the cool dark liquid from underneath." Toward Novosibirsk, the prairie became "completely flat, treeless, shrouded in streaks of ground-mist; and the dome of the sky stretched out to tremendous distances, as though vainly trying to encompass the limits of the great plain."

Kennan arrived weary, wilted, and without an appetite after ninety-eight hours on the train, to be greeted with the usual Russian dinner accorded visiting dignitaries. It included of course vodka, as well as "river fish, salmon, cold meat, radishes, cucumbers, cheese, hard boiled eggs, bread and butter, soup, beer, steak, fried potatoes, fried eggs, cake, and tea." Each refusal was "an indication that the respective dish was not good enough," which served only "to stimulate my host and the waitress to new feats of hospitality." Upon recovering, Kennan felt well enough to inspect an airplane factory and an experimental farm, to attend a football match, the circus, and the Jewish theater—evacuated from Minsk early in the war, and "still playing on odd nights in Yiddish to a full house"—and to take in an opera in an enormous new theater, the largest in the Soviet Union, for which the funds had been raised locally, in wartime, with the streets surrounding it "still those of a Siberian village." There could be "no more flamboyant a repudiation of the past, no more arrogant expression of confidence in the future, than the erection of this almost mystical structure on the remote banks of the Ob."

After several days Kennan continued by train to Stalinsk-Kuznetsk, a city that fifteen years earlier had been a swamp. It now contained thousands of workers and their families, as well as one of the largest steel mills in the Soviet Union. Obviously it had required "a great feat of willpower and organization to build and put into operation at all an establishment of this size in a place so remote from the other industrial centers." Perhaps the sacrifices had been worth it if the plant had helped to win the war, but it had clearly cost far more to build and to operate than a comparable facility in the United States. State-sanctioned "labor unions" placed production ahead of the safety, health, and welfare of the workers. A nearby collective farm provided the state with a reliable supply of agricultural commodities, but its peasants seemed "as effectively bound to their place of work as were the Russian serfs of the period before emancipation."

Banquets continued to be a challenge. "I am having an extremely interesting and enjoyable trip," George wrote Jeanette on a postcard he mailed from Stalinsk-Kuznetsk. "I am constantly reminded here of G. K. the elder and his travels. Fortunately for me, I have none of his physical hardships to cope with; but I face a culinary hospitality before which I think even he, in the end, would have wavered." The police, if curious about the identity of "G. K.," failed to pursue the matter, and the card made it safely to Highland Park.

Back in Novosibirsk on a hot day, Kennan suggested to one of his handlers that they take a swim. They chose the river, surely a site known to the first George Kennan, but now with the great railroad bridge and the gigantic opera house looming in the distance. Still, "[l]ittle naked boys poked along the shore in a leaky old row boat as boys will do everywhere." The scene led Kennan to wonder whether Russian dreams of grandeur would not at some point "cut loose from all connection with reality and begin some fantastic colossus of a project, build part of it hastily and with bad materials, never to finish it, and then leave the beginnings to rot away or be used for utterly incongruous purposes." If so, the Ob would remain, flowing quietly toward the Arctic Ocean. "And probably, regardless of what marvels had or had not been constructed on shore, for countless summers naked little boys would continue to find leaky old boats and to pole their way up and down the stream . . . , shouting and splashing, cutting their feet on the rocks, and making astounding discoveries about the nature of rivers and the contents of river bottoms."

Kennan returned to Moscow by air, a trip that itself required three days, several stops, and considerable improvisation. On the flight to Omsk, an illiterate old woman regaled him with observations on life reflecting "all the pungency and charm of the mental world of those who had never known the printed word." Kennan shared his lunch with her under the tail of the plane after they landed, began reading Tolstoy aloud, and soon had half of their fellow passengers as an audience. Stuck overnight in Sverdlovsk with no continuing flight scheduled, Kennan watched gratefully as the local party secretary, shouting loudly over the phone, commandeered one. In Kazan, the police for once lost track of him, allowing Kennan the "pleasant and homelike, if slightly vulgar" experience of "sauntering on the streets of a Volga River town of a summer evening," philosophically eating sunflower seeds and spitting out their husks. It provided "the same sense of bovine calm and superiority as chewing gum. For a moment I could almost forget that I was a foreigner in a country governed by people suspicious and resentful of all foreigners. But not for long."

Flying to Moscow the next day, Kennan sat on a crate, looked out the window, and tried "to gather together into some sort of pattern the mass of impressions which the past fortnight had left upon me." The Russians, he concluded, were "a talented, responsive people, capable of absorbing and enriching all forms of human experience." They were "strangely tolerant of cruelty and carelessness yet highly conscious of ethical values." They had emerged from the war "profoundly confident that they are destined to play a progressive and beneficial role in the affairs of the world, and eager to begin to do so." How could Americans not sympathize with them?

Their government, however, was "a regime of unparalleled ruthlessness and jealousy, . . . determined that no outside influence shall touch them." As long as it was in place, outsiders could do little. Generosity would only strengthen it. Blows aimed at it would excuse further repression. The wise American, therefore, would try neither to help nor to harm but instead to "make plain to Soviet acquaintances the minimum conditions on which he can envisage polite neighborly relations with them, the character of his own aspirations and the limits of his own patience." He would then "leave the Russian people—unencumbered by foreign sentimentality as by foreign antagonism—to work out their own destiny in their own peculiar way."[50]

TEN

A Very Long Telegram:
1945–1946

SHORTLY BEFORE KENNAN LEFT ON HIS SIBERIAN TRIP, HE MOVED his family into a new Moscow apartment in the former Finnish legation, now empty because Finland and the Soviet Union had been on opposite sides during the war. The Finns had arranged, through the Swedes, to rent the building to the American embassy, which badly needed the space. The "Finnsky Dom," George wrote Jeanette, was "vastly preferable" to the Mokhovaya, with its cacophonous street outside and an equally noisy elevator inside. "Here we have a garden, and a balcony, and peace and quiet at night, and a room for each of the children; and the servants are tucked away where you don't stumble over them every day." George's career continued to prosper: on June 1, 1945, the Foreign Service promoted him to its Class I rank, at a salary of $9,000. He still worried, though, about the pre-cariousness of his position: "You can easily imagine how delicate a job [this] is in these particular days, when the public eye is focused on Russian-American relations to an extent where one false step or unwise word could attract attention everywhere."[1]

Some of the delicacy was Kennan's own doing, given his repeated objections to his government's policies. "I couldn't be the sort of smooth, self-contained type of Foreign Service officer who advanced because he'd made no waves. It's a wonder to me that I got along as well as I did." It is indeed, but there were safeguards. One was the State Department's respect for professional expertise. Having gone to the trouble to train Soviet specialists, it did what it could to protect them; Kennan, for all his prickliness, had long been regarded as the best of the group. Harriman too provided cover. He wanted a heretic working for him—although he rarely reassured the heretic—and Harriman usually got his way: "I was quite an arbitrary fellow in those days." Finally, Kennan had a good track record. He had been right on the Azores bases and while serving on the European Advisory Commission. As the months passed in Moscow, Soviet behavior further enhanced his reputation by vindicating his pessimism about its future course.[2]

Shifting Washington's policy, however, was more difficult than simply objecting to it. There were limits to what even a respected professional could do from a distance when hardly anyone outside his profession had ever heard of him.[3] Kennan's personal views were clear: he wanted to end any pretense of shared interests between the U.S.S.R. and the Western democracies. There should be an outright division of Europe into spheres of influence, with each side doing as it pleased in the territory it controlled. The term "Cold War" had not yet been invented, but its features had formed in Kennan's mind. He thought it folly not to reshape strategy to fit them: to do anything less was to risk what remained of Europe. "We were . . . in danger of losing, like the dog standing over the reflecting pool, the bone in our mouth without obtaining the one we saw in the water."[4]

Despite Truman's tough talk in his first meeting with Molotov, neither he nor his advisers were prepared to go that far. Hopes persisted that differences with the Soviet Union reflected diplomatic failures, not fundamentally divergent visions of the postwar world. Not even Harriman, now gravely concerned about Stalin's intentions, was ready to abandon negotiations, if only to show the American public that they had been given every chance. "I plagued whosoever might be prepared to listen, primarily the ambassador, with protests, urgings, and appeals of all sorts," Kennan remembered, but to little avail. Even Harry Hopkins was getting impatient with him. "Then you think it's just sin, and we should be agin it," he admonished Kennan, after hearing his objections to the attempts Hopkins was making, on Truman's behalf, to settle the Polish question through talks with Stalin in Moscow. "That's just about right," Kennan responded. "I respect your opinion," Hopkins replied. "But I am not at liberty to accept it."[5]

Faced with conflicting advice about what to do, Truman convinced himself that Stalin's subordinates were to blame for the deterioration in Soviet-American relations that followed the Yalta conference. Like his predecessor, the new president sought a solution in another face-to-face meeting with the Kremlin boss—who seemed to him much like an American big city boss. It took place at Potsdam, just outside Berlin, during the last two weeks of July 1945. Midway through, the British electorate removed Churchill from office, leaving Stalin the only one of the original Big Three still in power. He had focused, since the war began, on how its conduct would determine the postwar settlement. Truman and Churchill's successor, Clement Attlee, had hardly had time even to think about this.[6]

For Kennan, such thinking was fundamental. He had never understood how the fighting of the war could fail to affect the nature of the peace. He had always doubted that talks around big tables, whether at Tehran, Yalta, or Potsdam, would change much. With no one having listened, with the war at an end, with the agreements reached at Potsdam—as Kennan saw it—having once more papered over cracks, he saw no reason to remain in the Foreign Service. On August 20, 1945, he again submitted his resignation. He had long been contemplating this step, Kennan explained to H. Freeman (Doc) Matthews, the State Department's director of European affairs. The reasons were personal—Moscow was no place to raise children—but also political: "a deep sense of frustration over our squandering of the political assets won at such cost by our recent war effort, over our failure to follow up our victories politically and over the obvious helplessness of our career diplomacy to exert any appreciable constructive influence on American policy at this juncture."[7]

I.

Despite the distinction he attained within it, Kennan had rarely found the Foreign Service rewarding. "He was never satisfied," his friend and British embassy counterpart Frank Roberts recalled, "either with what he was doing or with what policy was [or with] what his effect on that policy could or should be." His first resignation had come in 1927, only a year after he entered the service: Kennan's superiors had persuaded him to stay on by offering the training that made him a Soviet specialist. No sooner had he become one than George was floating alternative possibilities—writing, teaching, farming—with his sister Jeanette. Losing his inheritance in 1932 ruled these out, and by the time the Kennans were again reasonably solvent, the war had started. George felt the obligation to see it through to the end, but he continued to write frequently—often wistfully—about doing something else. The farm made the prospect all the more alluring. George's back-to-back letters to his sister and to Chip Bohlen in January 1945 showed that one part of his brain was thinking about chickens, while another was dividing Europe.[8]

Annelise was certainly ready to return to the United States. George cabled the news of his resignation while she was returning from Norway where, with Grace and Joan, she had been visiting Kristiansand for the first time since the Germans occupied it in 1940. "My heart gave a jump," she replied. "It is a little scary, but only a little. We'll make out all right, but it will be quite a change." Her family had been well, but Norway no longer felt like home. "Maybe I took too readily to my adopted country." Annelise suspected, though, that it was better that way: having "a longing in you for another country makes it impossible to be happy anywhere else."[9]

George himself was longing for countries, or at least cities, other than Moscow. He welcomed the opportunity, therefore, to escort a group of American congressmen to Leningrad and Helsinki in September 1945. In contrast to his first visit, in 1934, the old capital evoked nostalgia, even a sense of coming home. Vivid images crowded his mind, and hence his diary:

> of Pushkin and [his] companion leaning on the embankment looking at the river; of Kropotkin exercising with his stool in the Fortress of St. Peter and St. Paul; of Alexander I looking out of the Winter Palace during the flood of 1823; of Prince Y[u]supov throwing the body of Rasputin into the Moika; of the crowd making across the square toward the Winter Palace on the night the place was stormed; of the generations of music teachers and pupils going in and out of the Conservatory; of the Italian opera of one hundred years ago; of the night of the grotesque flop of Chekhov's "Chaika"; of the unhealthy days of Leningrad's spring thaws, with little groups of black-clad people plodding through the slush behind the hearses to the muddy, dripping cemeteries; of the cellar apartments of the gaunt, dark inner streets, full of dampness, cabbage smell and rats, and of the pale people who manage to live through the winters in those apartments; of the prostitutes of the Nevski Prospect of the Tsarist time; [of] the people cutting up fallen horses in the dark, snow-blown streets during the [German] siege.

Somehow in that city, "where I have never lived, there has nevertheless by some strange quirk of fate—a previous life, perhaps?—been deposited a portion of my own capacity to feel and to love, a portion—in other words—of my own life."

From Leningrad, the trip was by train across former Finnish territory where the war had left few buildings standing. The gulls wheeling overhead mocked ruins below; healthy vegetation concealed land mines. At the new border, everything changed. There was a new station, simple, clean, and in good repair. Newspapers were on sale at a freshly painted kiosk. A fat, sleek horse pulled a peasant cart "with a happy briskness which no Russian horse possesses." Sidings were full of freight cars hauling neatly packed war reparations east, leading Kennan to wonder whether these might induce "pangs of shame among the inhabitants of the great shoddy Russian world into which they were moving. But on second thought I was inclined to doubt this very strongly."

The Finnish locomotive at last arrived, coupled onto the cars, and started off at a speed that seemed "positively giddy after the leisurely lumbering of Russian trains." A diner offered good if scanty food. The other passengers were friendly and unafraid. The scene suggested "the efficiency, the trimness, the quietness and the boredom of bourgeois civilization; and these qualities smote with triple effect on the senses of a traveler long since removed from the impressions of [a] bourgeois environment."[10]

The youthful Kennan had, from time to time, shown a certain disdain for that environment. Part of the fascination of Weimar Berlin—even more so of the Soviet Union when he first arrived there—had been that some other society seemed under construction, however harshly, inefficiently, and idealistically. Siberia still offered hints of that, but Stalinism had long since smothered such experimentation in the rest of Russia, leaving only a depressing seediness. The Finnsky Dom, hence, had been a relief after the Mokhovaya: seediness wears one out. And now Finland itself—a bourgeois horizon lying just across the Karelian isthmus—took on an almost mystical appeal, as it would for so many other foreigners in the U.S.S.R. over so many years.[11] It was time to leave—but that did not happen quite yet.

II.

"Dear Averell," Kennan had written while Harriman was still at Potsdam in July: "Gibbon stated in the 'Decline and Fall' that the happiest times in the lives of peoples were those about which no history was written." Moscow was quiet, with only the usual annoyances over staffing, housing, and courier services. "Compared to the questions you [are] discussing, . . . these problems seem small."[12] Perhaps so, but Kennan by then was beyond seeing anything as insignificant. His dispatches to Washington—on matters large and small—continued to be filled with portents of trouble to come.

An agreement between Soviet and Polish tourist agencies would restrict the free travel and residence of foreigners. A visiting journalist's sympathetic news-paper story revealed how the cultivation of novices could undercut the reporting of professionals. The Kremlin would regard any withdrawal of American troops from western Czechoslovakia—which they had occupied at the end of the war—as a sign of weakness, despite wartime agreements that had assigned that territory to the Red Army. Soviet requests for postwar economic assistance were meant to sustain wartime levels of arms production. An Anglo-French plan to consult Moscow on the future of Tangier would provoke "a colorful revolutionary pro-nunciamento denouncing all interference in Morocco by great powers and calling on Moroccan proletariat to arise and eject them."[13]

This last warning reflected a larger concern: that the international commu-nist movement—which Stalin had appeared to disavow when he abolished the Comintern in 1943—remained in place and subject to his authority. Paris was the operational center for the European democracies, as were Cuba and Mexico for Latin America. The West had yet to grasp that some of its own citizens could be trained, like pets, "to heel without being on the leash." To be sure, managing this network required finding the "almost imperceptible line which divides fancied independence of political action from the real thing." But Soviet leaders had a great deal of experience in doing that.[14]

On August 8, 1945, with Harriman back in Moscow, Kennan accompanied him to the Kremlin for a meeting with Stalin. Despite his short stature, scrawny mustache, discolored teeth, pocked face, and yellow eyes, the "Generalissimus," as he now styled himself, struck Kennan as having "a certain rough handsomeness," like "an old battle-scarred tiger."

> In manner—with us, at least—he was simple, quiet, unassuming. There was no striv-ing for effect. His words were few. They generally sounded reasonable and sensible; indeed they often were. An unforewarned visitor would never have guessed what depths of calculation, ambition, love of power, jealousy, cruelty, and sly vindictive-ness lurked behind this unpretentious façade.

The subject that day was the Soviet Union's declaration of war against Japan, with Harriman expressing pleasure at being once again allies. There was no avoiding the implications of the American atomic bomb, however, used two days earlier at Hiro-shima. It must have been "a very difficult problem to work out," Stalin acknowl-edged, and "very expensive." It would bring victory quickly, and it would mean "the end of war and of aggressors. But the secret would have to be well kept."[15]

Kennan could not have agreed more, except that it was the Soviets from whom he wanted to keep the secret. "My first reaction was: 'Oh God, if we've got something like this, let's be sure that the Stalin regime doesn't get it.'" He warned Harriman that "it would be a tragic folly for us to hand over the secrets of atomic energy production to the Russians." More formally, he cautioned the new secretary of state, James F. Byrnes:

> There is nothing—I repeat nothing—in the history of the Soviet regime which could justify us in assuming that the men who are now in power in Russia, or even those who have chances of assuming power within the foreseeable future, would hesitate for a moment to apply this power against us if by doing so they thought that they might materially improve their own power position in the world.

It was, thus, "my profound conviction that to reveal to the Soviet Government any knowledge which might be vital to the defense of the United States, without adequate guaranties for the control of its use in the Soviet Union, would constitute a frivolous neglect of the vital interests of our people." Unusually, Kennan asked that the State Department make his view "a matter of record," and to see that it was considered in "any discussions of this subject which may take place in responsible circles of our Government."[16]

The Generalissimus, in the meantime, had paid Kennan a compliment. The occasion was the congressional visit in mid-September. To Kennan's surprise, Stalin agreed to see the American legislators, probably with the hope of speeding action on a $6 billion postwar reconstruction loan Molotov had requested the previous January. With Harriman away again, it fell to Kennan to escort the delegation to the Kremlin, and to serve as interpreter. Several members arrived tipsy from having enjoyed "tea" somewhere in the Moscow subway, and just before entering Stalin's office one asked: "What if I biff the old codger one in the nose?"

> My heart froze. I cannot recall what I said, but I am sure that never in my life did I speak with greater earnestness. I had, as I recollect it, the help of some of the more sober members of the party, [and] our companion came meekly along. He sat . . . at the end of a long table, facing Stalin, and did nothing more disturbing than to leer and wink once or twice at the bewildered dictator, thus making it possible for the invisible gun muzzles, with which the room was no doubt studded, to remain sullenly silent.

Oblivious to this near-disaster, Stalin greeted his visitors politely and at the end of the meeting went out of his way to praise Kennan—with whose views espionage had already familiarized him—for the excellence of his Russian. Deputy Foreign Minister Vyshinsky added dutifully: "Yes, damn good."[17]

Byrnes and Harriman were at that time attending the first postwar conference of Soviet, American, British, French, and Chinese foreign ministers, held in London in mid-September. It was not a success. Molotov was difficult, no agreements were reached on the principal agenda item, peace treaties with former German satellites, and the meeting broke up without even a public communiqué. Harriman was pleased that Byrnes had held firm: there had been, he assured the Moscow embassy staff, no more "telling the Russians how much we love them." Kennan, for once, was also content. The Kremlin would have to face the fact, he cabled Byrnes, "that if it has not been thrown for a loss, it has at least been stopped without a gain." This was in effect a reversal: the first serious one, for Soviet diplomacy, since the war began. Whether there would be recriminations within the leadership remained to be seen. Byrnes took the trouble to reply personally, saying that he had found Kennan's dispatch "highly illuminating," with "much food for thought."[18]

The football metaphor failed to impress Dana Wilgress, the Canadian ambassador in Moscow, with whom Kennan shared it. He had great respect for Kennan, Wilgress reported to Ottawa, "but he suffers from having been here in the pre-war days when foreign representatives became indoctrinated with anti-Soviet ideas as a result of the purges and subtle German propaganda." With "only one down to go," it was the Anglo-Saxons who were "in a huddle about what formation to try next." That might be, Lester Pearson, Wilgress's counterpart in Washington, commented, but Byrnes had made it a point, at a meeting with Truman, Attlee, and Canadian prime minister William L. Mackenzie King, "to express great respect for Kennan's judgment and wisdom. . . . There is no doubt that whatever Kennan says carries great weight in the State Department."[19]

The Truman-Attlee-King meeting, held in mid-November, focused on the international control of atomic energy and what the Soviet Union's relationship to that process might be. Whether Kennan knew of Byrnes's praise is not clear, although he was in Washington at the time: having received his resignation, Kennan's superiors had called him back for consultations, just as they had done almost two decades earlier. "I took up with Mr. Kennan the question of his resignation," a State Department official noted in a memorandum he left unsigned. "I made it clear to him that I did not think that this was the time for any of our capable senior officers to quit; their services were too badly needed." Perhaps encouraged by the sense that the Washington mood was shifting and that his voice was beginning to be heard, Kennan agreed that "no action would be taken on his resignation . . . , that it would simply be held in abeyance."[20]

III.

One of the curiosities of Moscow life during this period, Roberts remembered, was that he and Kennan had found themselves in charge of their respective embassies longer than the actual ambassadors were. With Harriman and Clark Kerr often away, Kennan and Roberts collaborated closely: "We were constantly having to compare notes, not merely on how the Soviets were going to carry out Potsdam, but [on] what the Soviets were up to in the Middle East, or wherever." Both warned their governments that cooperation with Moscow "wasn't going to be very easy."[21]

Ernest Bevin, the former dockworker who had become British foreign secretary, understood this clearly, Roberts assured Kennan. He regarded the failure of the foreign ministers' conference as a healthy development: it would be a mistake for either government to show haste in trying to resolve the difficulties that had arisen. Harriman had already detected in Bevin a considerable difference from his predecessor, Anthony Eden. Where that "suave diplomat" would dodge Molotov's blows, the stolid Bevin, like Byrnes, had "simply faced up to them."[22]

It soon became clear, though, that Byrnes—more slippery than stolid—was no longer prepared to do so. He relished the plaudits his hard line had won him but hoped to earn more now by breaking the diplomatic stalemate. Making the most of the free hand Truman had given him, fancying himself a wily negotiator, convinced that Molotov lacked the authority to make decisions on his own, the secretary of state decided to deal with Stalin himself. In early December, shortly after Kennan's return to Moscow, Byrnes announced an agreement with Molotov to hold another foreign ministers' conference in that city just one week hence. Bevin, not consulted, was furious: he had no choice, though, but to attend.[23]

He could hardly have been more upset than Kennan, for whom Byrnes's self-appointed mission to Moscow—reminiscent of Joe Davies—exemplified all that was wrong with American foreign policy. "Those of us who have spent years in diplomacy appreciate better than anyone else the necessity for compromise and for flexibility," Kennan commented in his diary after commiserating with Roberts. "But when anyone is not able to exude more cheer and confidence than I can put forward at this time about the diplomatic undertakings of our Government . . . , I am sure that it is best that he should not be concerned with them."[24]

For the moment, though, concern was unavoidable. Accompanied by Bohlen— who had also not been consulted—Byrnes and his entourage landed in the middle of a Moscow blizzard on the afternoon of December 14. Confusion prevailed from the start, with Harriman having been told to meet the plane at the wrong airport. Kennan rushed to the right one just in time to greet the secretary of state, who spoke standing in snow with no overshoes, while the wind howled through the little group that had welcomed him. Byrnes was then driven to Spaso House to thaw out, but Kennan was given no significant role in the proceedings that followed: whatever respect Byrnes had accorded Kennan's views in Washington, he chose not to draw upon them in Moscow.[25]

Kennan was allowed to observe a single short session on the nineteenth. He found Bevin looking disgusted while Molotov presided with "a Russian cigarette dangling from his mouth, his eyes flashing with satisfaction and confidence as he glanced from one to the other Foreign Minister, obviously keenly aware of their differences." Byrnes was negotiating "with no clear or fixed plan, with no definite set of objectives or limitations." Relying entirely on his own agility, "his main purpose is to achieve *an* agreement."

> The realities behind this agreement, since they concern only such people as Koreans, Rumanians, and Iranians, about whom he knows nothing, do not concern him. He wants *an* agreement for its political effect at home. The Russians know this. They will see that for this superficial success he pays a heavy price in the things that are real.

Afterward Kennan and Roberts dined with Doc Matthews, who had also flown in with Byrnes. "By the end of the evening, [Matthews] looked so crestfallen at the things that he had heard from Roberts and myself [that] I felt sorry for him and had to try to cheer him up."[26]

One compensation was the lively presence, in Moscow, of Isaiah Berlin, whom Kennan quickly found to be the best informed and most intelligent foreigner in the city. A dinner conversation, joined by Bohlen, stretched on until two in the morning, with Berlin convinced that the Soviet leadership saw conflict with the West as unavoidable. Did they not realize, Kennan wondered, that if a conflict

George Kennan (born February 16, 1845)
in 1903
(CORBIS)

ABOVE: Kossuth Kent Kennan
(Joan Kennan Collection)

RIGHT: Florence James Kennan
(Eugene Hotchkiss Collection)

George Frost Kennan (born
February 16, 1904) in 1904
(Joan Kennan Collection)

George and Jeanette
(Joan Kennan Collection)

935 Cambridge Avenue, Milwaukee
(Joan Kennan Collection)

Lake Nagawicka
(Joan Kennan Collection)

Opposite side: house of Kent K. + Florence James Kennan, on Nagawicka Lake, near Hartland, Wis. Time – probably about 1905.

George with bike, ca. 1916
(Joan Kennan Collection)

George as cadet, St. John's Military
Academy, 1917
(Joan Kennan Collection)

The Kennan Family, ca. 1918 (from left, Frances, Kent senior, George, Kent junior, Louise, Constance, Jeanette) *(Joan Kennan Collection)*

George, at Princeton, while still fond of automobiles *(Joan Kennan Collection)*

Passport photo, May 1924 *(Joan Kennan Collection)*

George, on left, Princeton graduate and deckhand, 1925
(Joan Kennan Collection)

The young diplomat, probably in Estonia, late 1920s
(Joan Kennan Collection)

Annelise Sorensen Kennan, early 1930s
(*Joan Kennan Collection*)

Presenting credentials, Moscow, December 1933
(from left, Bullitt, Kennan in background, Kalinin)
(*Princeton University Library*)

George, third from left, brooding in Norway; Annelise, second from right
(*Joan Kennan Collection*)

THE WASHINGTON POST: TH

Alexandrian and Family Headed for Danger Zone

Associated Press Photo.

George F. Kennan, shown with his family above at their home in Alexandria, Va., will sail soon for Prague, Czechoslovakia, where Kennan will take up his duties as second secretary of the U. S. Legation. Following four years in Moscow, Kennan spent the past year in the State Department here.

The Washington Post, September 15, 1938 (from left, Joan, George, Grace, Annelise)
(Joan Kennan Collection, used by permission of the Associated Press and The Washington Post)

George in wartime Berlin, ca. 1940–41
(Joan Kennan Collection)

George, closely supervised, visiting collective farm, probably in Siberia, June 1945
(Joan Kennan Collection)

came about, it would be because of their own belief in its inevitability? Berlin thought not: "They would view it as inevitable through the logic of the development of social forces." Friends would discover in time that they were enemies, "even though [they] did not know it at the moment."[27]

Byrnes, to whom this would soon happen, left Moscow proud of what he had accomplished. Stalin had agreed to token concessions that in no way weakened his control over Eastern Europe, while winning symbolic involvement in an occupation of Japan that left American predominance in place. Both sides would continue to recognize Chiang Kai-shek's government in China; both would participate in a U.N. effort to control the atomic bomb. Stalin made no promises to remove Soviet troops from northern Iran; nor did he withdraw demands on Turkey for territorial concessions and a naval base in the Dardanelles. From Kennan's perspective, nothing had changed: all Byrnes had done had been to revive the pretense of common interests, to paper over still more cracks.

Profoundly discouraged, Kennan undertook yet another essay—never completed—to explain why this would not work. Unlike Americans, Russians throughout their history had faced hostile neighbors. As a result, they had no conception of friendly relations between states. There was no use "referring to common purposes to which we may both have done lip service at one time or another, such as strengthening world peace, or democracy, or what you will." Such "fatuous gestures" would only lead Kremlin officials to think "that they should have been demanding more from us all along."

It should be American policy "to accompany every expression of our wishes by some action on our part proving that Russian interests suffer if our wishes are not observed." That would require imagination, firmness, and policy coordination, precisely the qualities lacking in Byrnes's hastily arranged Moscow trip. There should be no top-level appeals over the heads of knowledgeable subordinates. Sledgehammers should be used, when necessary, to swat flies: "[W]e must be prepared to undertake a 'taming of the shrew' which is bound to involve a good deal of unpleasantness." The Soviet system was designed "to produce the maximum concentration of national energies. We cannot face them effectively unless we do all in our power to concentrate our own effort."[28]

Reflecting on the outcome of the Moscow conference, Wilgress assured his Ottawa colleagues that he had not intended "to question in any way the integrity or ability of Mr. George F. Kennan." The fact that he was so highly regarded explained "the *temporary* ascendancy of the tough school shortly after the taking over of office by Mr. Byrnes." But recent events had shown its repudiation. It was true that "American college teams usually have two or more quarterbacks," but "the rules of the game do not permit them to use more than one at a time."[29]

Kennan might well have agreed, had he been able to read Wilgress's dispatch. On January 21, 1946, he wrote to remind his old friend Elbridge Durbrow, now in the State Department, that he wanted to come home. "I have been abroad 18 of the last 19 years. I owe it to myself and particularly to my family not to delay longer in establishing roots in the United States." He did not wish to leave the Soviet field, since "our country is decidedly short of people who can speak of Russian affairs with any authority, objectivity and courage." But the Foreign Service was not the place to do this: "There is little that a person like myself can accomplish within the walls of a diplomatic chancery or in subordinate positions in the Department of State."[30]

IV.

George F. Kennan would be forty-two on February 16, 1946. Tall, thin, half bald now, with strikingly expressive blue eyes, he had spent all of his professional life in the Foreign Service. He had become, within the Moscow embassy, almost as compelling a figure as Harriman himself. "I was, in a way, astonished," Berlin recalled of his first meeting with Kennan. "He was not at all like the people in the State Department I knew in Washington during my service there. He was more thoughtful, more austere, and more melancholy than they were. He was terribly absorbed—personally involved, somehow—in the terrible nature of the [Stalin] regime, and in the convolutions of its policy." John Paton Davies was struck by Kennan's intuitive but creative mind, "richly stored with knowledge, eloquent in expression, and disciplined by a scholarly respect for precision."

> It was a delight to watch him probe some sphinxlike announcement in *Pravda* for what might lie within or behind it, recalling some obscure incident in Bolshevik history or a personality conflict within the Party, quoting a passage from Dostoevsky on Russian character, or citing a parallel in Tsarist foreign policy. His subtle intellect swept the range of possibilities like a radar attuned to the unseen.

Patricia Davies regarded Kennan quite simply as "a giant among the dwarves." But he remained a puzzle, even to his closest friends.[31]

Durbrow, for example, thought him cool, calculating, and ambitious: "George, in his not too pushy a way, was going to get ahead, by golly, if it was the last thing he did." He was "very sure of himself. I never saw him fly off the handle. I fly off the handle all the time, myself, so I would have noticed that." Loy Henderson agreed about the ambition but not the self-control. Kennan was emotionally fragile: "It was difficult for him to take unpleasant things." Perhaps as a result, ulcers still plagued him, although drinking milk helped. So did physical activity, for which the dacha outside Moscow substituted at least in part for the farm outside East Berlin. Henderson also remembered Kennan tending "to look down in a patronizing way on people whom he didn't consider as intellectuals. He would make little remarks now and then indicating that the person was not in his class."

Martha Mautner, however, had a different impression. Kennan "liked to have disciples—people who would sit at his feet, [but he] tended to treat everyone on an equal basis, even the most junior people. He used to talk with us a good deal, I guess as a way of blowing off steam. I thought at the time that it was unusual for someone in his position to be unloading this kind of thing on people like me." William A. Crawford, a young Foreign Service officer who arrived just as the war was ending, found Kennan very accessible. He ran "informal little confabs" on whatever he thought worth discussing. His personal interest extended beyond professional work: "You felt a very close relationship to him."[32]

Dorothy Hessman, who knew Kennan as well as anyone outside his family, saw that his apparent aloofness concealed shyness. He was "very approachable, if you made the first move. He didn't want to give the impression that you had to respond to any gesture of friendliness that he would make." There were no Valentine's Day cards in Moscow, so on one such occasion she and another secretary sent him a little verse. Fond of rhyming, he sent one back. The Kennans regularly hosted sing-alongs in the Finnsky Dom, with George playing the guitar: that was the rehearsal site, also, for Christmas carols. Patricia Davies thought him "very gentle, really, even with rather tiresome people." Mautner remembered him serving as a crown-bearer, with Frank Roberts, at an Orthodox wedding for two friends: "I can still see them to this day, holding these crowns during this long service, Kennan very tall and Roberts quite short, their arms getting tireder and tireder."[33]

Roberts thought Kennan an idealist and a realist at the same time. He was always "trying to find the morally best solution, while at the same time not ignoring the realities of the situation." Berlin sensed piety: he could not help feeling himself "in the presence of a dedicated preacher, in front of whom one can't tell off-color jokes. You can't enjoy yourself too openly. No boisterous laughter permitted. To some extent, he casts a lampshade over the room. Bright lights have to be dimmed a little."[34]

Kennan's Russian, Crawford remembered, evoked respect even among native speakers for its fluency and elegance. Bohlen's was that of the street, "colloquial, expressive, pungent," while Kennan's was "the Russian of Pushkin." He "loved the Russians," Berlin insisted. "He responded to Russian books, and the Russian character. I had long conversations with him about Moscow versus Petersburg, the Slavophiles, the Westerners, the development of Russian art." But Kennan had no illusions about the Soviet Union. "I think that maybe Harriman did, or chose not to look." Berlin saw Kennan as much more appalled by evil than Bohlen, who liked to regale listeners with accounts of the Big Three meetings, all of which he had attended. "The cynicism of Roosevelt, the bellicosity, the insensitivity, of Churchill, and the cunning of Stalin" shocked Kennan, "whereas for Chip, it was a play with various characters." It was not his habit to think "about the spiritual awfulness of it."[35]

With Bohlen in Moscow for the foreign ministers' conference, the Davieses got to watch him argue with Kennan. American policy was still off limits—at least before witnesses—but as Patricia recalled: "Oh, boy, on the Soviet Union!" No one struck physical blows, but "the verbal blows were very very heavy." Given their ferocity, John found it remarkable that the conversations remained friendly: "There were no nasty personal attacks." But as Patricia pointed out, "They had a very different outlook, my goodness." Berlin specified, in his characteristic rapid-fire diction, what set Kennan apart from Bohlen:

> Interest in ideology. Intellectualism of a certain kind. Ideas. Deep interest in, and constant thought, in terms of attitudes, ideas, traditions, what might be called cultural peculiarities of countries and attitudes, forms of life. Not simply move after move; not chess. Not just evidence of this document, that document, showing that what they wanted was northern Bulgaria, or southern Greece. But also *mentalités*.

For Kennan, communism was "an enemy to everything one believed in. He was a grave observer of spiritual phenomena, some white, some black. Nothing much in between. One was either with us or against us. At that time, it certainly felt like that."[36]

Annelise monitored George's intensity closely. "She [held] him down to earth," Patricia Davies recalled. He could be "rather impractical in many ways, maybe even slightly grandiose," but Annelise had ways "of pricking bubbles." It was difficult for him to get a big head, or even "the slightest little swelling. The prick would be there." She was "an extraordinary person, very strong," and with a good sense of humor. And George relied on her in all kinds of ways. Embassy colleagues could tell when Annelise was away, because he would come down to the office "in the darndest getups." Patricia wouldn't say anything to George about the weird combinations of socks, shirts, and ties, but she did mention it to Annelise one day, after she got back: "I just thought you ought to know." "Oh, of course," she explained, "I always lay everything out because you know he's color blind."[37]

That was George Kennan on the eve of becoming famous: he saw what others saw, but in different colors. He had always done so, whether because of loneliness, sensitivity, ambition, intelligence, imagination, impatience, or patriotism. He had a historian's consciousness of the past, which gave him a visionary's perspective on the future. Within the mundane present, however, he could come across—like his selections of socks, shirts, and ties in Annelise's absence—as a bit weird. How did it feel, Patricia Davies asked him one day toward the end of 1945, to be so much more of a hard-liner than anyone else? "I foresee that the day will come," he replied somberly, "when I will be accused of being pro-Soviet, with exactly as much vehemence as I am now accused of being anti-Soviet." She thought it then "one of the silliest things I'd ever heard," but years later after this had indeed happened, "I brought it up with him. He had forgotten, although it was no surprise to him that he had said it."[38]

V.

"I am insisting on leaving here this spring," Kennan wrote Bill Bullitt on January 22, 1946, the day after he asked Durbrow to expedite his return to the United States. "I hope to publish after I get home a book on the structure of Soviet power. . . . I have had exceptional opportunities to learn about things here, and I would like to feel that I had justified them." Moreover if, "like everyone else who has been bitten by this bug, I am destined to spend the rest of my life reading, talking, and arguing about Russia," he might as well establish his credibility.[39] Precisely one month later, in a final exasperated attempt to awaken Washington, Kennan sent the State Department a very long telegram. After that, nothing in his life, or in United States policy toward the Soviet Union, would be the same.

Like most legends, the Kennan "long telegram" of February 22, 1946, has become encrusted with certain inaccuracies, two of which originated with the author himself. The telegram was not, as he described it in his memoirs, "some eight thousand words" in length: the actual total was just over five thousand. Nor was it a response to "an anguished cry of bewilderment" from the Treasury Department over the U.S.S.R.'s refusal to join the World Bank and the International Monetary Fund, despite having participated in the wartime Bretton Woods conference that designed them. Kennan's explanation of that development had gone out early in January, with the pointed reminder that the Kremlin leadership considered "ultimate conflict between Soviet and Capitalist systems [to be] inevitable."[40]

Rather, it was Stalin himself who provoked the "long telegram" by making a speech meant, superfluously, to win him an election. He delivered it, with great fanfare, in the Bolshoi Theater on February 9, the eve of the first postwar balloting for the entirely symbolic Supreme Soviet. Districts throughout the country had all nominated their candidates by a unanimous vote. "Since prevailing local philosophy rules out hand of Divine Providence as origin of such singular uniformity of inspiration," Kennan cabled the State Department, "it must be attributed and is to a more earthly and familiar agency." Stalin used his address to congratulate the army, party, government, nation, and—by implication—himself for winning the war. He mentioned American and British allies, but only perfunctorily. He said nothing about foreign policy, but he did call for a peacetime level of industrial production three times what it had been before the war. He justified the sacrifices this would require with a turgid analysis—straight out of Marx and Lenin—of capitalism's tendency to produce conflict: it had happened in 1914 and 1939, and it was sure to happen again. The Soviet Union sought only peace, but it would have to be prepared.[41]

No one familiar with Stalin's thinking would have found much new in the speech: it reflected what he had long believed and often said. Kennan thought the address so routine that he simply summarized it for the State Department. Having analyzed hundreds of Moscow events over the past year and a half, he saw little need to exert himself over this one. He would, after all, be leaving soon, and at just this moment he was getting sick: "I was taken with cold, fever, sinus, tooth trouble, and finally the aftereffects of the sulpha drugs administered for the relief of these other miseries." Bedridden and in a bad humor, he was coping with the daily flood of dispatches and other embassy business as best he could.[42]

But the situation in Washington was far from routine. Truman had reprimanded Byrnes, on the secretary of state's return from Moscow, for failing to report to him regularly: as a self-taught student of ancient history, the president was especially worried about Stalin's ambitions in the Near East. He had also begun to share suspicions—long held by several of his other advisers and by congressional critics—that Byrnes's pride in his negotiating skills was really an addiction to appeasement. Always a weathervane, Byrnes quickly swung back to his tougher line from the previous fall. Stalin's repudiation of Bretton Woods had ended whatever chance there might have been for American economic assistance to the U.S.S.R., and there was now evidence—soon to become public—that Soviet intelligence had been running espionage operations in the United States and Canada aimed at stealing information on the atomic bomb. Within this context, Stalin's February 9 speech had something of the effect of a shot on Fort Sumter. "All the things we did to work out Lend Lease and gosh knows what else during the war, the efforts made by F.D.R. at the various meetings, the San Francisco conference and all that sort of business—it was just unbelievable the way he threw it all out the window," Durbrow remembered. Stalin's speech had said "to hell with the rest of the world."[43]

Kennan's silence puzzled Durbrow, and he was not alone. Matthews, his immediate superior, asked: "Durby, have you had anything from George Kennan on this Stalin speech?" "No, God, I expect it any day. He must be working on a real deep one, one of his better efforts." Still nothing. "Doc, I've looked at all the telegram take, and there's not a damn line. Maybe it's coming by pouch." "Why don't you send him a little friendly reminder?" As it happened, Matthews himself drafted the message, which went out over Byrnes's signature on February 13. Stalin's speech, it pointed out, had evoked a response with the press and the public "to a degree not hitherto felt." With the pronouncements of Stalin's subordinates, it had seemed "to confirm your various thoughtful telegrams. We should welcome receiving from you an interpretive analysis of what we may expect in the way of future implementation of these announced policies."[44]

Harriman, by then, had left Moscow for the last time as ambassador. "Now George," he claimed to have said, "you're on your own. I want you to express your opinions and send them in." He could say anything he wanted "without my dampening hand." So with the State Department also having encouraged him, Kennan could hardly remain silent. Sick or not, "[h]ere was a case where nothing but the whole truth would do."

> I reached, figuratively, for my pen (figuratively, for the pen was in this case my long suffering and able secretary Dorothy Hessman, who was destined to endure thereafter a further fifteen years studded with just such bouts of abuse) and composed a

telegram of some eight thousand words [*sic*]—all neatly divided, like an eighteenth-century Protestant sermon, into five separate parts. (I thought that if it went in five sections, each could pass for a separate telegram and it would not look so outrageously long.)

It was Kennan's habit to write out rough drafts, then call in Hessman to type as he dictated from a horizontal position: "He always said he could think better [that way]." Still nursing his ailments, this was his posture when he summoned her on February 22, which "was officially a holiday, so I wasn't all that thrilled." After she finished the final version, Kennan dragged himself out of bed to take it personally to the Mokhovaya code room, where Mautner was on duty: "This has to go out tonight." "Why tonight? I've got a date." "They asked for it—now they're going to get it!" So she found a Navy communications officer to help, and they sent it off.[45]

The mode of transmission was critical. A pouched dispatch would not have been read "until it got to the desk officer or some of the guys up the line," Durbrow pointed out. But a telegram—the longest ever sent in the State Department's long history—was sure to attract attention. Moreover, "we were wondering why George didn't send us something. Everybody was waiting for it. They'd say: 'Gee, has anything come in?' 'No, it hasn't come in yet.' So by the time it got there it was something." And "it was such a beautiful job to begin with." The department, Kennan was relieved to learn, had not been at all disturbed by his "reckless use" of its telegraphic channel. Kennan's number 511, Matthews cabled him on the twenty-fifth, was "magnificent. I cannot overestimate its importance to those of us here struggling with the problem. Heartiest congratulations and best wishes." Two days later Byrnes himself added that he had read 511 "with the greatest interest. It is a splendid analysis."[46]

Now back in Washington, Harriman found the telegram "fairly long, and a little bit slow reading in spots." But it did contain what Kennan "hadn't been allowed to say before." Harriman shared it with Secretary of the Navy Forrestal, who had long been looking for an analysis of this kind. Forrestal, in turn, had the telegram reproduced and circulated all over Washington, including to Truman himself. As Kennan recalled:

Six months earlier this message would probably have been received in the Department of State with raised eyebrows and lips pursed in disapproval. Six months later, it would probably have sounded redundant, a sort of preaching to the convinced.

This was true despite the fact that the realities which it described were ones that had existed, substantially unchanged, for about a decade, and would continue to exist for more than a half-decade longer.

It all showed, Kennan concluded, that the real world was less important than the government's "subjective state of readiness . . . to recognize this or that feature of it." Harriman did not find this surprising. "That was one of the things," he later recalled, "that I couldn't get George to understand—that our timing had to be right." It was "why I didn't want a lot of [his] stuff to go in, because I knew it would have gone in the files and died. But this was just the critical time. It hit Washington at just the right moment. It was very fortunate."[47]

VI.

Like Stalin's speech, Kennan's "long telegram" reiterated much that he had said at other times and in other ways. But by breaking the rules once again—this time the State Department's restrictions on the length of telegrams—he got the attention of his superiors, just as he had twice during the war by going to Roosevelt himself. "I apologize in advance for this burdening of telegraphic channel," he had written at the beginning of 511, dropping an occasional article in at least a gesture toward communications economy, "but questions involved are of such urgent importance, particularly in view of recent events, that our answers to them, if they deserve attention at all, seem to me to deserve it all at once."

There were from the Soviet perspective, he explained, two antagonistic "centers of world significance," one socialist, the other capitalist, with the latter beset by insoluble conflicts. The greatest of these divided the United States from Great Britain, and it would in time lead to war. This might take the form of an Anglo-American clash, but it could also involve an attack on the Soviet Union by "smart capitalists" seeking to ward off their own war by fabricating a common foe. If that happened, the U.S.S.R. would prevail, but only at great cost: hence the importance of building its strength while seeking simultaneously to deepen and exploit conflicts among capitalists, even to the point if necessary of promoting "revolutionary upheavals" among them.

That position did not, Kennan emphasized, reflect the views of the Russian people, who were for the most part friendly to the outside world, eager to experience

it, and hopeful now "to live in peace and enjoy fruits of their own labor." Nor did it
make sense: capitalists had not always fought one another; capitalism was not now
in crisis; the idea that capitalists would provoke a war with the Soviet Union was
the "sheerest nonsense." Soviet leaders, however, respected neither public senti-
ment nor logic. Instead, history and ideology shaped their actions in a particularly
insidious way.

The history was that of Russian rulers, whose authority had always been
"archaic in form, fragile and artificial in its psychological foundation, unable to
stand comparison or contact with political systems of western countries." The ideology was Marxism, made "truculent and intolerant" by Lenin, which provided
the Stalinists with the perfect justification

> for their instinctive fear of outside world, for the dictatorship without which they did
> not know how to rule, for cruelties they did not dare not to inflict. . . . Today they
> cannot dispense with it. It is fig leaf of their moral and intellectual respectability.
> Without it they would stand before history, at best, as only the last of that long suc-
> cession of cruel and wasteful Russian rulers who have relentlessly forced country on
> to ever new heights of military power in order to guarantee external security of their
> internally weak regimes.

Uneasy Russian nationalism, a centuries-old movement that had always blurred
distinctions between defensive and offensive actions, was now operating under
the cover of international Marxism, "with its honeyed promises to a desperate and
war torn outside world."

This dual character caused the Soviet regime to function on two levels: a visible
one consisting of its official actions, and an invisible one for which it disclaimed
responsibility. Both were coordinated in "purpose, timing and effect." On the visible plane, the U.S.S.R. would observe diplomatic formalities and participate in
international organizations to the extent that those facilitated its interests. On
the invisible plane, it would make full use of communist parties throughout the
world, as well as such other groups as it could penetrate and control, to undermine the influence of the major Western powers. This would involve efforts to
"disrupt national self confidence, to hamstring measures of national defense, to
increase social and industrial unrest, to stimulate all forms of disunity."

The problem, therefore, was a daunting one: "We have here a political force
committed fanatically to the belief that with US there can be no permanent modus
vivendi, that it is desirable and necessary that the internal harmony of our society

be disrupted, our traditional way of life be destroyed, the international authority of our state be broken, if Soviet power is to be secure." Controlling great resources and a great nation, it could draw upon "an elaborate and far flung apparatus of amazing flexibility and versatility, managed by people whose experience and skill in underground methods are presumably without parallel in history." Nor was its leadership subject to reason: "The vast fund of objective fact about human society is not, as with us, the measure against which outlook is constantly being tested and re-formed, but a grab bag from which individual items are selected arbitrarily and tenaciously to bolster an outlook already preconceived."

Coping with this adversary was "undoubtedly greatest task our diplomacy has ever faced and probably greatest it will ever have to face." It would require "the same thoroughness and care as solution of major strategic problem in war, and if necessary, with no smaller outlay in planning effort." But it was within the power of the United States to solve it, and it could be done peacefully. The Soviet Union, unlike Hitler's Germany, had no fixed timetable, was not inclined to take unnecessary risks, and would, when resisted, retreat. It was still much weaker than the West. It had no orderly mechanisms for replacing its leaders. It had swallowed territories that had severely weakened its tsarist predecessor. Its ruling party dominated but did not inspire the Soviet people. Its propaganda was negative and destructive: it should be "easy to combat it by any intelligent and constructive program." For these reasons, "I think we may approach calmly and with good heart problem of how to deal with Russia."

That would mean, however, educating the American public to the seriousness of the problem, for "[t]here is nothing as dangerous or as terrifying as the unknown." It would involve maintaining the "health and vigor of our own society," because international communism was "like malignant parasite which feeds only on diseased tissue." It would demand putting forward "a much more positive and constructive picture of the sort of world we would like to see than we have put forward in the past." Europeans, exhausted and frightened in the wake of the war, were "less interested in abstract freedom than in security. . . . We should be better able than Russians to give them this." Finally, "we must have courage and self confidence to cling to our own methods and conceptions of human society. After all, the greatest danger that can befall us in coping with this problem of Soviet Communism, is that we shall allow ourselves to become like those with whom we are coping."[48]

Kennan regarded the "long telegram," years later, as resembling "one of those primers put out by alarmed congressional committees or by the Daughters of the

American Revolution, designed to arouse the citizenry to the dangers of the Communist conspiracy." But if the task at hand was to shift Washington's policy from afar—and Kennan had been trying to do that since the summer of 1944—then his "outrageous encumberment of the telegraphic process" was just the right instrument. The "long telegram" expressed what Kennan knew, in a form suited for policy makers who needed to know, better than anything else he ever wrote. No other document, whether written by him or anyone else, had the instantaneous influence that this one did. "My reputation was made. My voice now carried."[49]

Part III

ELEVEN

A Grand Strategic Education: 1946

"I WAS PERMITTED TO READ A VERY LONG AND WELL-WRITTEN DIS-patch from Moscow from Kennan of our Embassy staff there," David E. Lilienthal, soon to become the first chairman of the U.S. Atomic Energy Commission, recorded in his diary on March 6, 1946. "When he says that the position of the U.S.S.R. . . . presents the greatest test of diplomacy and statecraft in our history, he certainly does not overstate the matter." With his own responsibility for managing the American atomic arsenal in mind, Lilienthal added: "I didn't sleep well last night, and little wonder. I find myself in the midst of wholly strange and fearsome things."[1]

Lilienthal wrote this a day after Harry S. Truman sat next to Winston Churchill on a stage at Westminster College in Fulton, Missouri, nodding approvingly as the former prime minister warned of an "iron curtain" that had descended across the center of postwar Europe. No speech of that era—not even Stalin's a month earlier—more clearly proclaimed the demise of the wartime grand alliance. Churchill's address in that sense paralleled Kennan's telegram, a more closely held obituary that was still top secret when Lilienthal read it.[2] Both texts became iconic in Cold War history. Neither, however, brought about the shift in U.S. policy toward the Soviet Union that took place during the first three months of 1946.

That was happening, J. C. Donnelly of the British Foreign Office noted on March 5, because circumstances had forced the Truman administration at last to give the world "some measure of the leadership which the United States ought to be providing."[3] The events in question were those Kennan had been reporting since arriving in Moscow in 1944. They showed the Soviet Union defining its postwar security requirements unilaterally, without taking into account those of the United States, Great Britain, and their democratic allies. That finding would have shocked most Americans while the war was going on, as Harriman and Bohlen were well aware: Kennan had been almost alone in insisting on it. The coming of peace, however, accomplished the only objective—military victory—that the U.S.S.R. shared with anyone else. The disillusionments that followed made balancing hopes against fears increasingly difficult, and Stalin's "election" speech on February 9, 1946, ended the effort altogether for all but his most abject apologists.

It was within this context that Truman took control of foreign policy, having for the most part delegated it, during his first months in office, to his secretary of state. There would be, the president insisted, no further concessions like the ones made at Moscow. Byrnes swung into line with an address of his own in New York on February 28: "We will not and we cannot stand aloof," he warned, "if force or the threat of force is used contrary to the purposes of the [U.N.] Charter. . . . If we are to be a great power we must act as a great power, not only in order to ensure our own security but in order to preserve the peace of the world."[4]

The secretary of state had seen Kennan's "long telegram" before delivering this speech, but most of it had already been drafted by then. What 511 did do, Doc Matthews explained to his friend Robert Murphy, was to provide the rationale for the course upon which the administration had already embarked. With pardonable pride—he and Durbrow having elicited it—Matthews confirmed that Kennan's analysis, "to my mind the finest piece of analytical writing that I have ever seen come out of the [Foreign] Service . . . , has been received in the highest quarters here as a basic outline of future Soviet policy. That goes for the Secretary [of State], the Secretaries of War and Navy, our highest Army and Navy authorities and also across the street." Across the street for the Department of State in 1946—as when Kennan trained there in 1926 and in moments of boredom could look out the window to monitor the comings and goings of Calvin Coolidge—was the White House. "I am very much impressed," Murphy replied. "I think that you deserve a large bouquet of orchids for having engineered this process."[5]

I.

Donnelly had expressed doubt, in his March 5 assessment from London, that the new policy would stick: "It is unlikely that even the most ideal American administration imaginable would achieve what we should regard as a high standard in clarity of thought and consistency."[6] Kennan would not have disputed that view.

Nothing had prepared him for the possibility that his country might devise and carry out a coherent grand strategy, much less one based on his own thinking. Yet this is what happened: the "long telegram" became the conceptual foundation for the strategy the United States—and Great Britain—would follow for over four decades. How then did a single dispatch sent from a distant post by a relatively unknown diplomat produce such a result?

One way to answer this question is to compare Kennan's telegram with a review of policy toward the Soviet Union that had been under way in the State Department since the fall of 1945. Authorized by the new under secretary of state, Dean Acheson, its principal authors were Bohlen and Geroid T. Robinson, a Columbia University historian of Russia who had worked in the Office of Strategic Services during the war. The Bohlen-Robinson report was meant to reflect both Foreign Service and academic expertise on the U.S.S.R., but it differed from Kennan's analysis in several ways.

It began by questioning its own authority: theirs was "a doubtful and uncertain enterprise," Bohlen and Robinson lamented, because "it is impossible to grasp the total situation fully and to describe it in a set of coherent and well-established conclusions." Mindful of this, they presented a matrix of options while avoiding specific claims. The report identified three probable "periods" in the future Soviet-American relationship in which it might be possible to apply a "Policy A," a "Policy B," or a "Third Alternative Procedure." They composed the paper over several months, while handling other responsibilities. The final draft, dated February 14, 1946, reflected these limitations, concluding inelegantly that

> the best and indeed the only general policy which would offer any chance of success in the achievement of our objective is to induce the Soviet Union in its own interest and in the interest of the world in general to join the family of nations and abide by the essential rules of international conduct embodied in the United Nations Charter, without abandoning the principle for which this country stands or surrendering any physical positions essential to United States security in the event that the Soviet Union refuses to cooperate.

Coming five days after Stalin's speech, which *Time* magazine described as "the most warlike pronouncement uttered by any top-rank statesman since V-J Day," this was not quite rising to the occasion. Despite its authors' credentials, the Bohlen-Robinson report was a bureaucratic soporific, hedged with qualifications, uninspiringly written, overtaken by events.[7]

Kennan's telegram, in contrast, projected fierce self-confidence in clear prose with relentless logic. It qualified nothing, advanced no alternatives, and made no apologies for seeing everything in a single snapshot. It was the geopolitical equivalent of a medical X-ray, penetrating beneath alarming symptoms to yield at first clarity, then comprehension, and finally by implication a course of treatment.

The clarity came from Kennan's demonstration—it was more than just a claim— that victory in war and security in peace required different strategies. The United States and Great Britain could have defeated Nazi Germany only by allying with the Soviet Union; their postwar safety, however, would depend on resisting the Soviet Union. Kennan drove the point home by placing wartime cooperation within the stream of time and the realm of ideas. The roots of Soviet policy lay not in that brief experience but much further back in Russian history and much more deeply in Bolshevik ideology. It was to these centers of gravity that Stalin was now returning. The Grand Alliance could not be a blueprint for the postwar world because the U.S.S.R. had never been, and as currently constituted would never be, a normal state, willing to work with others to establish a mutually satisfactory international order.

Comprehension followed, for if—as Kennan insisted—the Soviet regime *needed* external enemies to justify its internal rule, then this would account for the wariness with which it had regarded its wartime allies, as well as for the ease with which it turned them into enemies once victory had been achieved. Diplomacy would be of little use in this situation. The United States faced new and profound dangers, against which a mobilization of political, economic, ideological, intellectual, and moral resources would be as necessary as in the war just ended.

That grim prognosis, paradoxically, relieved most of those who saw it, because Kennan left open the possibility that military mobilization might not be required. Stalin's offensives would rely on agents and ideologies but not armies; he had no deadlines; there was time to construct fortifications. The most important of these would be a revival of European self-reliance, something the United States should want even in the absence of a Soviet threat. Hence, Kennan was saying, Americans could secure their interests by meeting their responsibilities. The tautology was oddly comforting.

After reading the "long telegram," Bohlen philosophically abandoned his own review. "There is no need," he wrote his State Department colleagues on March 13, "to go into any long analysis of the motives or the reasons for present Soviet policy." Kennan's telegram had provided that. It was clear now that the Kremlin saw a world "divided into two irreconcilably hostile camps." Provided neither contested the other's sphere, they might coexist: the problem was "(a) to convince the Soviet Union of this possibility and (b) to make clear well in advance the inevitable consequence of the present line of Soviet policy based on the opposite thesis."[8]

Kennan's dispatch, by then, had gained an unusually large audience for a classified document. The State Department sent summaries to major foreign posts, and the Army and Navy forwarded it to overseas commanders, one of whom—significantly for Kennan's future—was General George C. Marshall, then on a presidential mission to try to end the civil war in China. Accolades soon reached the author. A typical one came from Henry Norweb, now ambassador to Cuba, who had known Kennan in Lisbon during the war: "I am sure every chief of mission who read it has been made wistful—wishing such a report could emanate from his office." It was "a masterpiece of 'thinking things out,' [of] realism devoid of hysteria, of courageous approach to a problem." Norweb's staff had returned it with comments like "Astonishing!" "[A]n answer to prayer." "Suggest you tell the Department how good this is." Kennan's presence in Moscow had been "one tremendous, undeserved piece of good luck for the United States of America."[9]

Frank Roberts saw Kennan's telegram soon after he sent it and, with his permission, forwarded a summary to London. The Foreign Office response was "Please will you send us yours?" Roberts obliged with three dispatches—not cables—that went by pouch in mid-March. Much longer than Kennan's, Roberts's messages placed less emphasis on persuasion—his foreign secretary, Ernest Bevin, needed none when it came to suspecting Stalin's intentions—and more on how Soviet ambitions might affect the British Empire. Nonetheless, Roberts faithfully echoed Kennan's main points. "George was the great expert," he later acknowledged, "and I benefited enormously from this."[10]

The "long telegram" also had unauthorized readers. Kennan assumed, correctly as it turned out, that reports of the document, if not the full text, would quickly reach Moscow. It took a few months for its significance to sink in, but at some point in the summer of 1946, Foreign Minister Molotov ordered Nikolay Novikov, the Soviet ambassador in Washington, to follow suit. Kennan enjoyed imagining how Molotov might have put it: "Why haven't you produced anything like this?"

Sent by pouch on September 27, the Novikov dispatch began with, and at no point departed from, the proposition that the foreign policy of the United States, reflecting "the imperialist tendencies of American monopolistic capital," was one of "striving for world supremacy." It would seek this objective in collaboration with Great Britain; but Novikov also claimed—contradicting his own logic but aligning himself with Lenin's—that as capitalist rivals the British and the Americans regarded each other as their greatest enemy. "These poor people, put on the spot, produced the thing," Kennan concluded, but "it was only a way of saying to their masters in Moscow: 'How true, sir!' "[11]

Kennan's "long telegram" set an international standard for analytical reporting, and it was not just contemporaries who envied it. Future diplomats would dream of accomplishing what he did with a single document, but no one ever managed it: the dispatch remains unique. It set out no fully conceived grand strategy, but it was a start, and in that sense it met a need. "I now feel better about things than I have for some time," Kennan admitted to a friend two months after sending his famous message. "[S]ome of the most dangerous tendencies in American thought about Russia have been checked, if not overcome. If we can now only restrain the hot-heads and the panic-mongers and keep policy on a firm and even keel, I am not pessimistic."[12]

II.

Kennan still wanted to come home. "I feel I must get away this spring," he cabled Durbrow on March 7, and "if Dept can not take some action in near future I am afraid I will have to submit telegraphic resignation and ask to be relieved by May 1." Byrnes himself replied, noting that Harriman's successor as ambassador, General Walter Bedell Smith, would soon arrive in Moscow, but that Durbrow, who was to replace Kennan, would not be able to get there until July. Could not Kennan stay on until that date? "You have been doing a wonderful job, for which we are all very grateful." Smith followed up: "The most important single thing to me in connection with this mission is that I have the benefit of your experience and advice. . . . I request most urgently that you remain until about July first."[13]

"It is a source of great satisfaction to me that I have been able, with the loyal and effective support of the other officers here, to assist you in your heavy responsibility at this difficult period," Kennan replied to Byrnes. "I have been associated with this Mission on and off since its inception, and no one—I think—has its interests more keenly at heart." If the department really wanted him to stay through June, he would do so to the extent that his health permitted. But he warned Durbrow that it might not. He had been sick for weeks, and in "this sunless and vitaminless environment," recovery had been slow. With other departures and persisting staff shortages, "we are operating here under tremendous pressure and on absolutely no margin."[14]

That left Durbrow looking for a solution. "George wanted to get out of the Service [to go] into the academic world. I didn't want George to get out of the Service. Chip [Bohlen] didn't, and Loy Henderson didn't. We had a guy that had a wonderful analytical mind, and we needed him." Fortunately for all concerned, Durbrow enjoyed Washington cocktail parties. At one he ran into General Alfred M. Gruenther, a distinguished Army officer who had just been appointed deputy commandant of the new National War College. "You know George Kennan, don't you?" "Very well, yes." "We need somebody with background on the Soviet Union, who's brilliant." Behind the inquiry, Durbrow suspected, was "*the* telegram*,*" which Gruenther had probably read. "He's in Moscow, isn't he? Any chance of getting him back?" After hearing what the job would entail, Durbrow thought it perfect: "George will love that. It'll get him in the academic world to a certain extent. It'll get him out of the rut of routine business." Kennan too, when Durbrow wrote him, jumped at the opportunity. "Am interested in National War College job mentioned in your letter," he cabled back. "What would be "[n]ature of duties, salary, title, etcetera?"[15]

The title, it turned out, would be Deputy Commandant for Foreign Affairs; Kennan would retain his Class I rank in the Foreign Service; and his assignment would be to help design and teach the curriculum at the first school for grand strategy that had ever existed in the United States. Located in the former premises of the Army War College at Fort McNair in Washington, the National War College was an early response to the widespread conviction, emerging from World War II, that the nation could no longer afford to separate military operations from political objectives. Although he played no role in establishing it, the school was another vindication of Kennan's thinking. He was, Ambassador Smith had to acknowledge, "unquestionably the best possible choice that could be made from the State Dept." The students would be mid-career Army, Navy, and Foreign Service officers destined for higher responsibilities; classes would start early in September. The job suited Kennan for many reasons, not the least of which was that the task of preparing for it would get him and his family home sooner. They needed to leave right away, he wrote Bohlen on April 19. "[O]nly ex-Muscovite could understand."[16]

The Kennans departed on the twenty-ninth, traveling with Smith by plane to Paris, where George spent a week with the U.S. delegation to the Council of Foreign Ministers, which was meeting there. They sailed for New York on May 10, and by the twenty-first were back at the farm in East Berlin. "We are as usual frightfully busy getting settled," Annelise wrote to Frieda Por. "I wonder if we are ever going to get out of that state." The State Department, in the meantime, had authorized George's transfer, even if it was not quite sure where: "You are hereby assigned to duty at the Naval War College."[17]

Feeling guilty that he had abandoned Smith as the new ambassador was taking up his duties in Moscow, Kennan wrote him a long letter on June 27, explaining how he had used the past five weeks. Most of his time had been spent working with Gruenther and his colleagues on the war college curriculum. But there had also been "many demands" to talk about the Soviet Union:

> I gave a full-fledged lecture to the representatives of over forty national organizations. . . . I gave a similar lecture to a packed house of officials from all parts of the State Department. I went over to the Navy Department, lunched with Admiral [Chester] Nimitz and the highest officers on duty there, and then talked for an hour and a half with a larger group of naval officers. I had similar sessions at the War Department, both with the operations and the intelligence people. I had an evening with Secretary [of the Navy James] Forrestal out on his yacht. I had a luncheon with General [Carl] Spaatz and sat in on the sessions of the Russian committee of SWIN [probably SWNCC, the State-War-Navy Coordinating Committee]. I talked to the assembled economic experts of the [State] Department (I think this was the least satisfactory of all the conferences I have had). I spent one lunch hour trying to warn Mr. [Harold] Ickes about the Communist front organizations which he is frequently associated with. I had appointments with Mr. [Donald] Russell [Assistant Secretary of State for Administration] and General [John] Hilldring [Assistant Secretary of State for Occupied Areas], with the heads of personnel and the director of [the] Foreign Service and the acting head of the Foreign Buildings Office. I talked at length with the officers of the USSR section of the Research and Analysis Branch of the [State] Department. I spent an evening with [Assistant Secretary of State] Spruille Braden and the Department's leading Latin American experts. There was the usual number of unavoidable luncheons and dinners with press people. Finally, I had made arrangements (this should not go beyond you and the top officers in the Embassy) to give certain help to the new National Intelligence Agency now headed by General [Hoyt] Vandenberg.

There would now be three weeks at the farm until July 20, when Kennan would begin a speaking tour of the western United States. It was a State Department experiment in public outreach: "I hope it will be profitable to the victims."

Kennan was grateful for the confidence Smith had shown in him by allowing his early return: the pressure would have been much greater had he had to remain in Moscow through most of the summer. He and Annelise hoped that the Smiths were beginning to feel "some of the ineffable and implausible, but nonetheless real compensations which life [in Moscow] has to offer." The ambassador would probably say, "with a snort," that these were apparent "only to those who have left and are reposing comfortably in the arms of capitalism. And to that retort, I have no reply."[18]

III.

When he began designing a course on grand strategy in the summer of 1946, Kennan had to start from scratch: "This was the first time I had personally ever had occasion to address myself seriously, either as a student or as a teacher, to this subject." But it was also the first time the U.S. government had ever prescribed its study. Apart from Alfred Thayer Mahan, whose work at the Naval War College half a century earlier had focused exclusively on that form of power, no American had written anything worth reading on the relationship of war to politics. There were, to be sure, the great European strategists, conveniently analyzed in Edward Mead Earle's recently published collection of commissioned essays, *Makers of Modern Strategy*. But "in no instance was the thinking of these earlier figures . . . adequate to the needs of a great American democracy in the atomic age. All of this, clearly, was going to have to be rethought."[19]

The rethinking, for Kennan, began with the bomb. His initial reactions to Hiroshima and Nagasaki had been a jumble—relief that the war was over, regret at the destruction employed to bring this about, alarm at the possibility that the Soviet Union might obtain its own weapon, whether through espionage or the Truman administration's naiveté in prematurely embracing the principle of international control.[20] None of these thoughts cohered, however, until Kennan read another book of essays, edited by Bernard Brodie, just off the press in June 1946. Entitled *The Absolute Weapon: Atomic Power and World Order*, this volume, together with Earle's *Makers*, gave Kennan a crash course in the field he was about to teach. The notes he took suggest what he learned.

Kennan began with Brodie's book, grasping at once the paradox it posed: "Best way to avoid atomic war is to avoid war; best way to avoid war is to be prepared to resort to atomic warfare." He recorded detailed information on the destructive capabilities of the new weapon, on the resources necessary to build it, and on the possibility that the Baruch Plan, then being proposed by the Truman administration, might provide a way for the United Nations to manage it. He was, however, skeptical: "Soviets would not hesitate to promise to forego production & proceed nevertheless to produce." One essay claiming that only the world organization could handle the bomb caused Kennan to stop taking notes: "Remainder just rot."[21]

The real significance of atomic weapons, he concluded, lay not in the need to bolster international institutions but in the realization that "if we are to avoid mutual destruction, we must revert to strategic political thinking of XVIII Century." The complete annihilation of enemies no longer made sense, because:

> (a) in the best of circumstances (i.e., that the Russians lack atomic weapons or facilities for employing them against us) it implies on our part a war against the Russian people and the eventual occupation of Russian territory; and

> (b) in the worst of circumstances, the virtual ruin of our country as well as theirs.

It followed, then, that American objectives should be limited to:

> (a) preventing the power of the Sov. Gov't from extending to point vital or important to US or British Empire; and

> (b) without forfeiting the confidence & friendship of the Russian people, to bring [ab]out the discrediting of those forces in Russia who insist that Russia regard itself as at war with the western world.[22]

And how might the eighteenth century help? Here Kennan drew on Earle's volume, which contained essays on two post-Napoleonic grand strategists who had also rethought their subject in the aftermath of a total war.

The first, by the historians Crane Brinton, Gordon Craig, and Felix Gilbert, discussed the Swiss strategist Antoine-Henri Jomini, whose writings, the authors conceded, were outdated and little read. But Jomini had considered the central problem in warfare to be determining "correct lines of operation, leaving to enemy choice of withdrawing or accepting combat under unfavorable conditions." Kennan saw a lesson for the United States:

Our task is to plan and execute our strategic dispositions in such a way as to compel Sov. Govt. either to accept combat under unfavorable conditions (which it will never do), or withdraw. In this way we can contain Soviet power until Russians tire of the game.

The note is undated, but it appears to be Kennan's first use—in a geopolitical context—of the verb that became associated with his name.[23]

By far the greater impression, however, came from Hans Rothfels's article on Carl von Clausewitz—the best study available in English at the time on the much-misunderstood Prussian strategist. Kennan was struck by Clausewitz's emphasis on *psychologically* disarming an adversary: finding the point at which "the enemy realizes that victory is either too unlikely or too costly." Hence the need to pinpoint the "center of gravity"—an army, a capital city, an alliance, even public opinion—against which minimum pressure might produce maximum results. The defense would, thus, lure the offense into overextension: "Assailant weakens himself as he advances." (Kennan thought it significant that both Jomini and Clausewitz had fought on the Russian side when Napoleon invaded in 1812.) Once the "culminating point" of the offensive had been reached, the enemy could only shift to defense without its advantages: "The best he can do is to demonstrate that, if there is no longer any chance of his winning, his opponent cannot reach this aim either."[24]

Most important, for Kennan, was Clausewitz's claim that war is a continuation of policy by other means. Kennan correctly understood this to imply not that politics are suspended during war, but just the opposite: "For[eign] pol[icy] aims are the end and war is the means." Violence therefore could never be an objective: "Even in case of Germany it is questionable whether a war of destruction was desirable." It would certainly not be possible against the Soviet Union: the only possibility was "a political war, a war of attrition for limited objectives."

We are in peculiar position of having to defend ourselves against mortal attack, but yet not wishing to inflict mortal defeat on our attacker. We cannot be carried too far away by attractive conception of "the flashing sword of vengeance." We must be like the porcupine who only gradually convinces the carnivorous beast of prey that he is not a fit object of attack.

Not the least of Clausewitz's attractions was that he provided ammunition for arguments with Bohlen: "Chip says that [a war of destruction] could not have been otherwise: that the U.S. cannot fight a political war." Perhaps so, in World War II, but in the coming conflict Kennan—and Clausewitz's ghost—were insisting that it would have no choice but to learn to do so.[25]

What Clausewitz taught him, Kennan recalled years later, was that the United States had no peacetime political-military doctrine, only a set of obsolete traditions—isolationism, neutrality, the Open Door. There was, thus, the need to clarify the uses of military power: "what we could expect to do with it, what we could not expect to do with it, and how it should fit in with diplomacy and political aims." Kennan's war college teaching, he hoped, would "build an intellectual structure which could act as a guide to policy makers, and which could find acceptance gradually through the academic world in the country at large."[26]

IV.

In the meantime, though, the State Department had given Kennan an unusual opportunity to assess opinion in the country at large. He had called, in the "long telegram," for educating Americans to the "realities of the Russian situation: I cannot over-emphasize [the] importance of this." That passage particularly impressed William Benton, the new assistant secretary of state for public affairs, who pushed hard for giving Kennan part of that responsibility. The National War College appointment precluded any full-time commitment, but Kennan had been working with the department to find ways of "off-setting misleading and inaccurate propaganda." The "experiment" of a speaking tour was one such effort.[27]

Surprisingly for someone who had traveled so extensively elsewhere, Kennan had never been west of the Mississippi River until the State Department sent him there late in the summer of 1946. Accompanied by Annelise, George spoke in Chicago, Milwaukee, Seattle, Portland, San Francisco, Berkeley, and Los Angeles, concluding his trip with a talk to the Adams County Bankers' Association of Gettysburg, Pennsylvania. He prepared no texts, relying "on a few scribbled notes, on the resources of memory, and on the inspiration of the moment." The tour, for Kennan, was yet another discovery of America, although this time under official auspices, and with no bicycle.[28]

Businessmen, he reported to the department, were his best audiences. Possessing few preconceived ideas on the Soviet Union, with no personal positions at stake, they were "friendly, curious, and generally anxious to be enlightened." They were almost all male, and Kennan found that it was easier to hold their interest than when he was speaking to mixed audiences. Women, he still believed, were ill equipped to discuss international relations, because their clubs focused too earnestly on that subject. These organizations were a way of escaping "the boredom, frustration and faintly guilty conscience which seem to afflict many well-to-do and insufficiently occupied people in this country." Russia—"mysterious and inviting, with just enough of wickedness and brutality to complete the allure"—was easier to talk about than the problems of race, slums, and labor unions at home. Having been told so often that only cooperation with Moscow could ensure peace, it was a shock for them to hear that peace would be possible "only through a long, unpleasant process of setting will against will, force against force, idea against idea."

Professors were also difficult, because many of them had taken positions in public that were not in accord with what Kennan had to say. Their reputations were at stake, their pride was affected, they had made "rosy forecasts" in the hope of enhancing "their own glamour, prestige and importance." The tendency showed up most clearly in California, where university faculties also seemed to have "a geographical inferiority complex," resentful of the fact that foreign policy was still an East Coast product, confident that if given the chance they could handle it better, convinced that the future lay as much with countries bordering the Pacific as the Atlantic, certain that the Soviet Union, especially Siberia, fell within that realm.

Two West Coast groups particularly aroused Kennan's concern. One was atomic scientists at Berkeley, who seemed to have "an unshakeable faith" that if they could only meet Soviet scientists and enlighten them about atomic weapons, all would be well. It had not occurred to them that, far from frightening Kremlin leaders, the bomb's destructive potential might "whet their desire to find a way of using it." Kennan also worried about San Francisco intellectuals, among whom he saw signs of communist activity: "I have been connected with Russian affairs for too many years not to know the real thing when I see it." Everything he said, he was sure, was dutifully reported to the Soviet consul. (Kennan was right about this. A summary of his San Francisco remarks went off to the Foreign Ministry in Moscow on August 28.) Nothing he said was confidential, but if the State Department intended to send speakers on more sensitive topics, "it had better exercise some check on who is admitted to the meetings."

By the time Kennan reached Los Angeles, another intelligence organization, without his knowledge, was tracking his movements. The local office of the Federal Bureau of Investigation reported that a "Mr. George Kennan," whose name had appeared in left-wing publications in connection with activities taking place at the U.S. embassy in the Soviet Union, was soon to speak in that city. Did FBI headquarters wish "to ascertain the nature of his lecture"? J. Edgar Hoover's office failed to respond, so an agent took it upon himself to attend Kennan's talk on August 9, after which he sent in seven pages of notes and apologized for having earlier misspelled the speaker's name, which should be "Kennon." This did elicit a crisp reply: "For your information, George Frost Kennan has held many positions in the foreign service of the State Department, . . . is considered a foremost authority on Russian affairs, and his recent assignment to Moscow furnished considerable basis for our present foreign policy."

Kennan ended his trip report with an affectionate tribute to his Gettysburg neighbors, who had come to his lecture "unencumbered—bless their hearts—by any pretensions to knowledge of the subject or by any inordinate sense of responsibility about it." He had been warned that they might drift off, but this did not happen. They asked few questions, because they were shy, unaccustomed to that sort of thing, and "they don't think that fast." But they were "probably the most representative—and for that reason the most important—of the people I reached."

The speaking tour, Kennan concluded, had been "generally successful," in that he had been able to convey "a clearer, more realistic, less extreme and less alarmist view of Soviet-American relations" than his audiences had previously been exposed to, as well as "a greater confidence in the sincerity and soundness of the State Department." Decades later he explained what he meant. He had found, on returning from Moscow, that if he warned people "that we couldn't have the sort of collaboration we'd hoped for with the Russians," this would cause them to conclude: "Well, then, war is inevitable." So he had tried to say, on his trip, just the opposite: "You don't have to have a war. Just don't let them—if you can help it— expand their influence any further."[29]

"Boy, you missed your calling," a Milwaukee minister told Kennan after hearing him in his hometown. The tour showed that he could speak extemporaneously to diverse audiences, that he enjoyed doing so, and that he would like to keep it up. Perhaps it might be possible, he wrote Acheson, "for someone who, like myself, is not too far from the Department of State and at the same time not too near it, to accomplish something valuable." Acheson readily agreed: "I would like to have you accept as many invitations to speak as you can. . . . I appreciate the extra burden your generous offer places on you; nevertheless, I hasten to take advantage of it."[30]

V.

The National War College welcomed its first class, made up of forty-five Army and Army Air Force colonels, forty-five Navy captains, and ten State Department and Foreign Service officers, on September 3, 1946, a year and a day after the Japanese surrender. Vice Admiral Harry W. Hill, the commandant, warned the students that their wartime experiences would bear little relevance to what they would be studying: the atomic bomb might well require "a complete reorientation of old ideas." It was important, therefore, "that you keep your minds flexible." The purpose of the new institution, *The New York Times* reported the next day, was to integrate thinking "at the highest levels of the War, Navy, and State Departments." The setting matched the mission, for from the old Army War College, situated at the confluence of the Potomac and Anacostia rivers, the students and their professors could see the Washington Monument, the Capitol, the Pentagon, and the new building just north of the Lincoln Memorial that the State Department would soon be occupying. The view was comprehensive, and the course that began that day was also meant to be.[31]

The students attended the same lectures and worked on the same problems, regardless of the positions they held or the uniforms they wore. They would graduate not only with "mutual respect and understanding," Kennan explained, "but also a common approach to the major problems of our country in the field of foreign affairs." Future leaders rubbed elbows with current leaders, who frequently visited. Navy Secretary Forrestal, who had helped to establish the college, came most often, but "[o]ther officers of Cabinet rank, generals, and Senators sat at our feet as we lectured." The college became an "academic seminar for the higher echelons of governmental Washington generally."[32]

"Gentlemen; Admiral Hill. The question we have to consider this morning is a question of the relations between sovereign governments, and it pertains to the measures that they employ when they deal with each other for the main purposes for which states have to deal with each other." That is how Kennan began his first lecture on September 16, 1946, prosaically titled "Measures Short of War (Diplomatic)." On stage alongside him was a chart listing "Diplomatic Measures of Adjustment for the Redress of Grievances or for the Pacific Settlement of Disputes." There is no way to know how many inadequately caffeinated students—or policy makers—came close to dozing off at that point, but they soon woke up. For within five minutes Kennan had tossed traditional methods of conflict resolution onto a historical ash-heap.

Great-power clashes in the contemporary world, he insisted, did not take place within any agreed-upon framework of international law: rather, they pitted democracies against totalitarians prepared to employ "varieties of skullduggery . . . as unlimited as human ingenuity itself, and just about as unpleasant." These included "persuasion, intimidation, deceit, corruption, penetration, subversion, horse-trading, bluffing, psychological pressure, economic pressure, seduction, blackmail, theft, fraud, rape, battle, murder, and sudden death. Don't mistake that for a complete list." Restrained "by no moral inhibitions, by no domestic public opinion to speak of and not even by any serious considerations of consistency and intellectual dignity," states like Nazi Germany and the Soviet Union were limited only by "their own estimate of the consequences to themselves of the adoption of a given measure."

That left the question, then, of whether democracies could deal with such states by any means other than all-out war. Kennan had no definitive answer: the course they were taking, he reminded the students, was meant to develop one. But he did have suggestions, the first of which echoed Clausewitz. It was that psychology could itself become a strategy. The past decade had made it clear that everything the United States did produced psychological effects internationally. There had been no sustained effort, though, to tie these together in such a way as to serve a purpose.

Another suggestion had to do with economics, because democracies for the foreseeable future—he meant chiefly the United States—would possess a disproportionate share of the world's productive capacity. Given the Soviet Union's reliance on autarchy, that advantage might not produce immediate benefits, but the students should consider its cumulative effect "when exercised over a long period of time and in a wise way." It could be especially useful among satellites with little to gain from Soviet domination: economic pressure might well provoke "discontent, trouble, and dissension within the totalitarian world."

Finally the students should not neglect an important political weapon, which was "the cultivation of solidarity with other like minded nations." In this respect, Kennan acknowledged, the United Nations had been more helpful than he had expected, because it provided a way to connect power with morality. Without that link, competition over spheres of influence in Eastern Europe and the Near East might have come across simply as power politics. With it, the United States had been able "to build up a record for good faith which it is hard for anyone to challenge."

Each of these "measures short of war" fell within the realm of international affairs, which must now embrace all forms of power, even military capabilities: "You have no idea how much it contributes to the general politeness and pleasantness of diplomacy when you have a little quiet armed force in the background." Power, in turn, reflected the nation wielding it: "We are no stronger than the country we represent." Hence no one could afford indifference "to internal disharmony, dissension, intolerance and the things that break up the real moral and political structure of our society at home." Integrating force with foreign policy did not mean "blustering, threatening, waving clubs at people and telling them if they don't do this or that we are going to drop a bomb on them." But it did mean maintaining "a preponderance of strength" among the democracies: this was "the most peaceful of all the measures we can take short of war because the greater your strength, the less likelihood that you are ever going to use it."

What was required, therefore, was coordination across each of the categories of available power: "We must work out a general plan of what the United States wants in this world and we must go after that with all the measures at our disposal, depending on what is indicated by the circumstances." The nation needed in peacetime a "grand strategy no less concrete and no less consistent than that which governs our actions in war." If applied wisely, then "these measures short of war will be all the ones that we will ever have to use to secure the prosperous and safe future of the people in this country."

Kennan finished with that but got a tough first question: was it possible for the United States to have a grand strategy? "[W]e don't aspire to anything particularly except what we have; [so] what, mainly can our grand strategy consist of?" The point was well taken, Kennan acknowledged. "What has the United States got really to offer to other people?" Thinking quickly, he improvised an answer that raised a larger question:

[W]e have freedom of elections, freedom of speech, freedom to live out your life politically; but a great many people in this world would say that is not enough; we are tired; we are hungry; we are bewildered; to hell with freedom to elect somebody; to hell with freedom of speech; what we want is to be shown the way; we want to be guided. [You] don't believe in abstract freedom but only in freedom from something or freedom to something; and what is it you are showing us the freedom to?

Kennan would not attempt a reply. "I am going to let you try to think it out for yourself. I am still trying to think it out." But he did offer a place to start: "Perhaps it is better that we don't come to people with pat answers but say, instead, 'You will have to solve your own problems, we are only trying to give you the breaks.'"[33]

It's unlikely that anyone dozed, therefore, through Kennan's opening National War College lecture. It redefined international relations in an ideological age, it assessed totalitarian strengths and weaknesses, it sketched out democratic responses, it stressed the multiple forms that power can assume, it called for diplomacy to become grand strategy, and it concluded with Kennan's imaginative leap into the minds of those for whose allegiance the United States and the Soviet Union would be competing. It was a satisfactory start, not least because of the work it left for his students—and for Kennan himself—still to do.

VI.

Kennan had long liked the idea of becoming a teacher. He had regularly raised it with Jeanette as an alternative to the Foreign Service, and his Bad Nauheim lectures had revealed unexpected pedagogical skills. That was hardly the ideal environment, though: the war college came closer. "I am enjoying the work very much," George wrote Kent early in October. "It is the first time in years that I have been relatively free from administrative duties and able to give a good portion of my time to purely intellectual pursuits." He was supervising four civilian professors—one was Brodie, on leave from Yale—while giving occasional lectures and listening to many more. He was consulting on foreign policy in Washington and speaking to audiences elsewhere, as Acheson had encouraged him to do. He was getting, from all of this, a stimulus, as well as a degree of appreciation, "which I haven't experienced anywhere else. In consequence, I feel quite bucked up." Dorothy Hessman, who had followed Kennan from Moscow, thought the situation ideal for him: "There was no ambassador or Secretary to say 'he can't say that.'"[34]

By his count, Kennan composed seventeen lectures or articles, each about the length of the "long telegram," between September 1946 and May 1947: the list did not include occasions on which he spoke extemporaneously or from rough notes. He gave most of the lectures at the National War College but also spoke at the Naval and Air War Colleges, at Carlisle Barracks, Pennsylvania (where the Army War College would soon relocate), at Yale, Princeton, Virginia, Williams, at the annual convention of the American Political Science Association, and—as it turned out, famously—at the Council on Foreign Relations in New York. The indefatigable Hessman kept up, typing as many as three drafts for some of the lectures while managing a proliferating correspondence. This "veritable outpouring of literary and forensic effort" was meant to educate audiences on the nature of the postwar world and what the American response to it should be; but like all good teachers, Kennan was also educating himself along the way.[35]

His chief concern, in the fall of 1946, was still that too few Americans saw anything between diplomacy and war: if the first failed, the second must follow. Henry A. Wallace, Roosevelt's former vice president, now Truman's secretary of commerce and a leading Democratic Party liberal, dramatized the polarity in a New York speech on September 12, warning that "'[g]etting tough' never bought anything—whether for schoolyard bullies or businessmen or world powers. The tougher we get, the tougher the Russians will get." The president, he insisted, had read his speech and agreed with it. A confused week followed, at the end of which Truman made it clear that he did not agree and demanded Wallace's resignation. Everywhere he went, Kennan complained while the controversy was still raging, "I find people with their faces buried in their hands and an air of tragedy about them saying collaboration with Russia has proved to be impossible and, therefore, all is lost." When would the war start?[36]

Kennan used his first appearance before a university audience—an off-the-record lecture at Yale's Institute of International Studies on October 1—to take on Wallace. The result was an evisceration, arguably unnecessary since the target by then had largely eviscerated himself. The talk was a response, though, not just to Wallace but to a succession of Kennan's superiors—Bullitt, Davies, Harriman, Byrnes, and Roosevelt himself—all of whom had assumed, at one time or another, that if offered friendship the Soviet Union would reciprocate. If Wallace believed, like "many vain people" before him, "that the golden touch of his particular personality and the warmth of his sympathy for the cause of Russian Communism would modify in some important degree the actions of the Soviet Government," then he was not only ignoring the way states worked, but he was also "flying in the face of some of the most basic and unshakeable of Russian realities."

Stalin and his associates would not thank Wallace for implying that "they, the guardians of the Revolution, are a group of neurotic, wistful intellectuals, to be swept off their feet and won over from their holiest articles of faith by an engaging smile, [and] a few kind words." They had committed acts that, in the absence of an ideology to justify them, would have to be considered among "the most stupendous crimes in the history of mankind." They had built a regime in the image of that ideology. They had corrupted a generation:

> The official who wields the disciplinary power of the Communist Party; the worker of the secret police who has sacrificed his family relationships to the grim dictates of his profession; the army officer whose wife has become accustomed to the new fur coat, the larger apartment and the war-booty Mercedes; the economic administrator whose one talent is to force the pace of armaments developments; all these, and many others besides, have sold their souls to the theory that the outside world is threatening and hostile.

They resembled the village misfits Dostoyevsky had described in *The Demons*, "already caught up in the toils of the revolution," unable "to escape from its relentless demands." But now they controlled a nation.

It was clear, then, that the fears and suspicions so prevalent in Moscow related not to the Truman administration's policies but "to the character of the Soviet regime itself." They would not be dispelled by "fatuous gestures of appeasement," which could only lead "to the capitulation of the United States as a great power in the world and as the guardian of its own security." There was, however, no reason to despair: Americans should see the situation instead "as a narrow and stony defile through which we must pass before we can emerge into more promising vistas."

That promise resided in the Russian national character, more deeply rooted even than the Stalinist state or the ideology that animated it, yet visible in Russian literature. Kennan cited, as an example, the provincial governor in Gogol's *Dead Souls* who one day acknowledged, in "a typically Russian burst of honesty," that "perhaps I have, by my excessive suspiciousness, repelled those who sincerely wished to be useful to me." He also recalled the Chekhov heroine who had tried to befriend peasants, got nowhere with them, walked away sadly, but was followed by a sympathetic blacksmith:

> "Don't be offended, Mistress," said Rodion. . . . "Wait a couple of years and you can have the school, and you can have the roads, but not all at once. . . . [I]f you want to sow grain on that hill, first you have to clear it and then you have to take all the stones off and then you have to plow it up and then you have to keep after it and keep after it . . . and it is just the same with the people. You have to keep after them and keep after them until you win them over."

People, Kennan was suggesting, could indeed shape governments, but this would take time. And circumstances, not sentimentality, would shape people. Therein lay the key to what American strategy should be.

The United States could alter the circumstances in which the Soviet government operated "only by a long term policy of firmness, patience, and understanding, designed to keep the Russians confronted with superior strength at every juncture where they might otherwise be inclined to encroach upon the vital interests of a stable and peaceful world, but to do this in so friendly and unprovocative a manner that its basic purposes will not be subject to misrepresentation." The objective would be Clausewitzian: to shift the psychology of an adversary. The manner, however, would be Chekhovian.[37]

Was there reason to think that this might work? Kennan's Naval War College lecture, delivered on the same day he spoke at Yale, addressed this issue. The Russians, he pointed out, were "the most un-naval of peoples," but they understood naval strategy. Lacking easily defended borders, unable to count on domestic loyalty, Kremlin leaders would not willingly engage an adversary stronger than themselves. "They cannot afford to get into trouble." They respected, therefore, one of "the great truths of naval warfare," which was "that a force sufficiently superior to that of the enemy will probably never have to be used. Its mere existence does the trick."

That was where the United States, with superior force, had the advantage. It ought to be possible "for us to contain the Russians indefinitely" and perhaps eventually "to maneuver them back into the limits within which we would like them to stay." This would not "solve" the Soviet problem. "You never really solve problems like that; you only learn to live with them after a fashion and to avoid major catastrophe." But if the United States followed such a strategy consistently enough over a long enough period of time, then "I believe that the logic of it would enter into the Soviet system as a whole and bring about changes there which would be beneficial to everyone."

As currently configured, the American government was not equipped to do this. Its policies proceeded along separate tracks; there was no common concept. But it should be possible to secure such coordination. It would involve setting up "some formal organization for decision and action at the Cabinet level." It would demand closer liaison with Congress. It would require educating the public on the "powers and prerogatives of government in the field of foreign affairs" and on the need for its own "restraint and self-discipline." And there would have to be "more sheer courage" in defending policies from domestic critics.

The Soviet challenge, therefore, was really to "the quality of our own society, . . . [to] how good democracy is in the world of today." If it could "force us to pull ourselves together," then "perhaps we may call our Russian friends a blessing rather than a plague." Shakespeare's Henry V had anticipated that possibility long ago:

> There is some soul of goodness in things evil,
> Would men observingly distil it out;
> For our bad neighbor makes us early stirrers,
> Which is both healthful and good husbandry;
> Besides, they are our outward consciences
> And preachers to us all: admonishing
> That we should dress us fairly for our end.[38]

With these two lectures, given on the same day, Kennan found his voice as a teacher. He connected current events with his years of experience in the Soviet Union, his summer crash course on grand strategy and the atomic bomb, the impressions derived from his speaking tour, Admiral Hill's mandate to rethink the requirements of national security, and his own sense that literature could inspire statecraft.[39] He did all of this with an eloquence that existed nowhere else in the government: he understood—as his friend Bohlen did not—that rhetoric persuades, and that style instructs. It's no wonder that he attracted students, some of them highly placed.

The State Department sent Kennan to Ottawa in December to present the new American policy, on a top-secret basis, to Canadian officials worried about defense of the Arctic. It was "virtually certain," he assured them, that Stalin planned no surprise attack, there or anywhere else. Miscalculation, however, might lead to unplanned hostilities, so the United States and its allies must leave no doubt, in his mind, of their resolve. They would have to be as firm as they were patient: the goal should be "to 'contain' Russian expansionism for so long a time that it would have to modify itself." And how long might that take? Kennan guessed "10 or 15 years."[40]

VII.

"I seem to have hit the jackpot as a 'Russian expert,'" George wrote Jeanette on Christmas Day 1946. "You'd be amazed, what seems to be coming my way."

Harvard, Princeton, and Yale had all asked him to join their faculties. "As far as I can see, I can write my own ticket." The State Department was willing to keep him on the payroll while "loaning me out" for research: he would soon be promoted to the rank of "minister" with a salary rumored to be $15,000. It was "almost too good to be true, and I really doubt that it will materialize; but it all goes to show that nothing succeeds like success."[41]

The Kennans had been living, since September, in a graceful three-story brick house on "General's Row" at Fort McNair, courtesy of the U.S. Army. Facing the parade ground with a view of the Potomac out the back, it was large, well staffed, and came with full commissary privileges, which George noted "considerably reduce the cost of living." There were tennis courts, a golf club, a swimming pool, an officers' club, and it was all within reach of the East Berlin farm on weekends.

> Saturdays flew by in veritable orgies of labor on various "projects." The energies of guests were employed no less enthusiastically and no less inefficiently than our own. Then, on Sunday mornings, there would be the sad cleaning up . . . , followed by the long trek back amid Sunday-afternoon traffic; and finally—the sudden confrontation with the . . . fat stacks of the waiting Sunday paper and the insistent phone calls of people who had been trying to reach us ever since Friday noon.

The farm, George believed, kept him healthy: "When, for one reason or another, I omitted these weekend expeditions to the country, I fell ill." And his Pennsylvania neighbors provided not only practical advice but "a shrewd, reassuring common sense . . . that gave new, and sometimes healing, perspective to the trials, excitements, and disappointments of a hectic official existence."[42]

The disappointments, that fall and winter, were remarkably few. The children loved living in their Army house and, to their parents' relief, liked their Washington schools, to which a bus delivered them every day. Grace, now fourteen, had been to several local dances; Joan, however, missed ballet classes in Moscow. Hearing *The Nutcracker Suite*, her father noticed, caused her to go "through all the dances as she remembered them. . . . She certainly has it in her blood." George, for his part, was coming to see in his children something that he and his siblings had missed. "I hope you will get married," he wrote Kent, "if only because you—like the rest of us—did not have a normal family life in childhood; and the re-living of it in one's own family helps to overcome the effects of that." The war college allowed as "normal" an existence as the Kennans had yet managed.[43]

George was "terribly happy" at the National War College, Annelise remembered. "You must think me a little dotty," he would come home and say, but "this was said, and this was discussed, and this is wonderful." There had been eighty-five lectures that fall, he explained to Kent, probably the best series on international affairs that had ever been given. The contacts were "like manna to me after many years of the philistinism of American foreign colony life." He was not sure now that he would want to return to diplomacy: "I have found such generous appreciation . . . among the academicians for what little I know about Russia and have had such tempting offers to continue working with them that I am sorely tried." That knowledge now was "a chance aggregate of odds and ends, gathered without system and in large part without purpose." If he could spend a year or two in systematic study, "I might really be able to do something more worthwhile in scholarship than in diplomacy."

The months since his return from Moscow had also allowed a reacquaintance with his own country, but here Kennan's conclusions—admittedly tentative— were more measured.

> At work, it is certainly admirable. At play, it could hardly be worse. Its liberal intellectuals are in large part below criticism. Its emotional strength lies largely in the smaller and quieter communities, where intellectual life is least developed. I have no doubt that as a people we have tremendous latent power of every sort. But it is buried behind so much immaturity, such formidable artificialities in manner of living, such universal lack of humility and discipline, and such strange prejudices about the organization of human society that I am not sure whether it can be applied . . . successfully in another crisis, as it was in this last.[44]

Having educated himself in grand strategy, and having shown that he could educate others, he would get a chance to answer that question, sooner than he could have expected.

TWELVE

Mr. X: 1947

"THE REAL CONSEQUENCES OF STATESMANSHIP," KENNAN ONCE OB-
served, citing the historian Herbert Butterfield, "are always ironic in their relationship to what the statesman thought he was achieving."[1] What Kennan had
hoped to do, during his time at the National War College, was to lay the intellectual foundations for an American grand strategy that would counter the Soviet
Union's challenge to the postwar international system, without resort to war or
appeasement. No one has a better claim to having accomplished just that. As
Henry Kissinger observed with professional admiration in 1979: "George Kennan
came as close to authoring the diplomatic doctrine of his era as any diplomat in
our history."[2]

But Kennan took little pride in this achievement. If indeed he originated the
strategy of "containment," he wrote bitterly in his memoirs, composed as the Vietnam War was escalating, then "I emphatically deny the paternity of any efforts to
invoke that doctrine today in situations to which it has, and can have, no proper
relevance." Even after the Cold War had ended and the Soviet Union was itself history, Kennan regarded the "success" of his strategy as a failure because it had taken
so long to produce results, because the costs had been so high, and because the
United States and its Western European allies had demanded, in the end, "unconditional surrender." That outcome had been "one of the great disappointments of
my life."

Kennan made this complaint, strangely, at a birthday party. The date was
February 15, 1994—the eve of his ninetieth—and the celebration took place
at Harold Pratt House on East 68th Street in New York, long the home of the
Council on Foreign Relations. The organization had meant to honor Kennan's

accomplishments, but he used the occasion to lament them. He did so with a dejected felicity, reminding his audience of another event that had taken place in the same building almost half a century earlier. It had been then and there, he believed, that the consequences of his actions first began to diverge significantly from his intentions.[3]

When a younger Kennan, not quite forty-three, arrived at Pratt House on January 7, 1947, to address the Council's discussion group on "Soviet Foreign Relations," he did so with considerably less fanfare. The talk was one of dozens he had given since returning from Moscow. The audience would be small, and as was customary for Council events, everything said would be on a "not for attribution" basis. Like many speakers who have heard themselves repeat themselves too often, Kennan did not bother to prepare a text: the rapporteur's notes are the only record of what he said.

Marxist-Leninist ideology, he told the group, did not guide the actions of Soviet leaders, but it was "a sort of mental eye or prism" through which they viewed the outside world. It justified an amorality little different from that of Russian rulers as far back as Ivan the Terrible; this was, however, at odds with the strong moral sense of the Russian people. Stalin and his subordinates saw enemies, therefore, within and beyond their country's borders: they needed those on the outside, who were mostly imaginary, to excuse their brutality toward those on the inside, who were real enough. But Russians would outlast the regime that now governed them. That made it possible for the United States and its allies to "contain" Soviet power, "if it were done courteously and in a non-provocative way," for a long enough time to allow internal changes to come about in Russia. When they did, no one would be more grateful than the Russians themselves. Nothing could be accomplished, though, as Wallace wished to do, "by the glad hand and the winning smile." Americans would have to recognize that they were dealing "with the driving force of a great idea and a method of looking at the world which is anchored in the experience of centuries."

Like many Council discussions, the one that followed meandered. The author Louis Fischer doubted that Russians were looking for new leadership: perhaps not, Kennan replied, but he had noticed a "weariness and lassitude" among them. Journalist Joseph Barnes pointed out that during the past several years more Russians had come into contact with foreigners than ever before: yes, Kennan noted, but there were at present hardly any foreigners inside the U.S.S.R. George S. Franklin, Jr., of the Council staff, wanted to know what within the Soviet leadership gave Kennan grounds for optimism: its flexibility, caution, and unwillingness to allow commitments to exceed capabilities, he responded. International banker R. Gordon Wasson wondered why, if xenophobia was so pervasive in Russia, agents of International Harvester and the Singer Sewing Machine Company had found warm receptions there in the nineteenth century. Russians themselves were friendly to foreigners, Kennan explained; it was their governments, tsarist and Soviet, that had tried to curb that tendency. Geroid T. Robinson, the Columbia history professor who had coauthored the Bohlen-Robinson report, observed that if force was necessary to maintain the Soviet government in power and if Soviet leaders needed to exaggerate outside dangers to justify the use of that force, then it was those dangers that kept them in power and they could not afford more conciliatory policies. But that was what Kennan had said in the first place.[4]

Kennan could have been pardoned, then, for leaving Pratt House vaguely dissatisfied: he did not appear to have made much of an impression. Wasson, however, liked the talk well enough to suggest revising it for publication in the Council's journal, *Foreign Affairs*, and its longtime editor Hamilton Fish Armstrong—who had not been present—followed up on January 10 with a similar request. He had seen a copy of Kennan's lecture at Yale, "which means that you not only have your ideas well in mind, but also have put them in preliminary written form." Kennan might be under some constraints as to what he could say, "but I wonder whether the substance of your point of view as a whole isn't so fair and constructive, and does not tend so much in the direction of a really mutual understanding between the Soviets and ourselves, that you would be warranted in undertaking to lay it before the public."

Armstrong too, it seemed, had not quite gotten the point, and Kennan took his time in replying. When he did, on February 4, he observed that because he was still in the State Department, "I really can not write anything of value on Russia for publication under my own name. If you would be interested in an anonymous article, or one under a pen name, . . . I might be able to make the necessary arrangements." In no hurry either, Armstrong waited until March 7 before agreeing "that the interest of the projected article more than outweighs from our point of view the disadvantage of anonymity." Perhaps the piece would enable Kennan "to make effectively your one hopeful point which revolves around the liking that most Americans seem to have for most Russians." This appeared to leave a door open, "whether to a blind alley or not, no one can say."[5]

I.

While these leisurely and somewhat astigmatic exchanges were going on, a lot was happening elsewhere. On the evening Kennan spoke at the Council, President Truman announced the unexpected resignation of Secretary of State Byrnes and, in an even greater surprise, nominated as his replacement General George C. Marshall, the austere but highly respected wartime Army chief of staff, now back from his unsuccessful mission to China. Byrnes had written Kennan the previous day to confirm his promotion to career minister, and in his response Kennan expressed "keen disappointment" that Byrnes would be stepping down. The regret was probably real, for however much Byrnes might have irritated Kennan at the December 1945 Moscow foreign ministers' conference, he had since stuck to a policy of what he called "patience with firmness" with respect to the Soviet Union. When the Wallace controversy broke out the following September, Byrnes made it clear that if the president did not fire his secretary of commerce, his secretary of state would quit. Truman backed Byrnes, but their relationship soured, and so three and a half months later, ostensibly for health reasons, Byrnes did resign.[6]

Kennan's only previous contact with Marshall had been inauspicious: the general attended his unfortunate Pentagon briefing on Azores bases in the fall of 1943. But Marshall had, while in China, read several of Kennan's dispatches from Moscow, including the "long telegram." He would have heard more from Secretary of the Navy Forrestal, who had taken a special interest in advancing Kennan's career, as well as from former military colleagues now at the National War College. An especially convincing accolade came from Walter Bedell Smith in Moscow, who had been one of Marshall's wartime aides:

> George Kennan . . . knows more about the Soviet Union, I believe, than any other American. He speaks Russian better than the average Russian. And not only has he served here under four different ambassadors, but he has had about equally valuable service in Germany. . . . I know all of the Russian experts, here and in Washington, and they are all good, but Kennan is head and shoulders above the lot, and he is highly respected in Moscow because of his character and integrity.

Smith suggested including Kennan on the American delegation to an upcoming Moscow foreign ministers' conference, but Marshall had a larger responsibility in mind. As secretary of state, he was determined to achieve the policy coordination that had been missing during the war and, in his view, during the first year and a half of peace. Kennan, he thought, could help. "I was very close to Marshall then," Bohlen recalled. "The telegram from Moscow was the thing that put George in the Policy Planning Staff."[7]

Marshall took office on January 21, and three days later Under Secretary of State Acheson, acting on his new boss's instructions, asked Kennan whether he might be interested in running a new State Department organization "for [the] review and planning of policy." The group's function, Acheson later recalled, would be

> to look ahead, not into the distant future, but beyond the vision of the operating officers caught in the smoke and crises of current battle; far enough ahead to see the emerging form of things to come and outline what should be done to meet or anticipate them. In doing this, the staff should also do something else—constantly reappraise what was being done.

Despite his hopes to retire from the Foreign Service after completing his National War College duties, Kennan accepted the offer while wondering how to make the transition. "Mind you, I was dying to do this work," but he couldn't take time from his war college duties without Admiral Hill's permission, and yet "I had no authorization to tell him about these plans." Acheson and Kennan agreed, in the end, that he would take the job at an undetermined date in the spring. But Kennan had "no very clear understanding of what was involved; I am not sure that Mr. Acheson had gained a much clearer one from General Marshall."[8]

"Well, gentlemen," Loy Henderson remembered Acheson telling his staff, "we're going to have a new office—an office of Policy Planning. George Kennan's going to be brought in to take care of it. Loy, don't you think that's a good idea?" Henderson said that a man like Kennan would be excellent for the job. "A man like Kennan?" Acheson responded. "There's nobody like Kennan." The most important requirement for the new unit, Bohlen explained to Sir John (Jock) Balfour, the well-informed British chargé d'affaires, at a dinner party late in January, would be to ensure that all levels of the State Department understood official policy and the motives that lay behind it. People "like Kennan" might also give some talks on this subject. Acheson, also present, had already heard this once too often: "I am constantly being told that 'people like George Kennan' should give the boys the low-down about Russia," he grumbled. "Unfortunately there is only one George Kennan."[9]

Certainly there was only one Acheson. Trained as a lawyer, the dapper, defiantly

mustachioed under secretary of state had surprisingly little foreign policy experience when Truman appointed him to that position in August 1945. Preoccupied
at first with the international control of atomic energy, Acheson had been one
of the last of the president's top advisers—apart from Wallace himself—to give
up on postwar cooperation with the U.S.S.R. Kennan's "long telegram," Acheson
later acknowledged, had had a "deep effect on thinking within the Government,"
but it made little impression on him. When Acheson did finally change his mind
about Stalin's intentions, in August 1946, he did so for different reasons, totally
and almost overnight.

The provocation was Soviet demands on Turkey for boundary concessions and
bases in the Dardanelles. Stalin backed down when Truman sent the Sixth Fleet
into the eastern Mediterranean, but Acheson did not back off. The crisis, however
belatedly, caused him to connect dots: he suddenly saw how Soviet ambitions,
American complacency, and British weakness might combine to upset the balance of power in Europe. Acheson went from assuming the best to suspecting
the worst: it was shortly after that he began encouraging Kennan to speak openly
about the Soviet danger. His "predictions and warnings could not have been better," Acheson later acknowledged. "We [had] responded to them slowly."

But Kennan's recommendations for American policy had been "of no help."
They amounted to exhortations "to be of good heart, to look out for our own
social and economic health, to present a good face to the world, all of which the
Government was trying to do." Composed in the 1960s after he and Kennan had
disagreed about many things, Acheson's complaint may not have reflected what he
thought in 1947. His contemporary comments, however, mix respect for Kennan
with just enough acidity to suggest that one of the things about which Acheson
was unclear, regarding the planning staff job, was whether the Soviet expert that
Kennan had been could function equally successfully as the policy adviser Marshall wanted him to become.[10]

The question became more than hypothetical on February 21, when the British
embassy informed the State Department that the British government, staggering
under the burdens of postwar recovery and beset by one of the worst winters ever,
could no longer provide military and economic assistance to Greece and Turkey.
The news shocked Truman and most of his advisers, but Acheson had seen it
coming and was ready with a response. A Foreign Office official caught its substance when he reported a growing conviction in Washington "that no time must
be lost in plucking the torch of world leadership from our chilling hands." With
Marshall new in his job and about to depart for Moscow, Acheson took the lead in

determining how this might be done. And on February 24 he brought Kennan—
still at the war college—into the planning process.[11]

The forum was a committee convened that day under Henderson's chairman-
ship to draft recommendations for the president and the secretary of state. Kennan remembered arguing that the United States had to replace the aid the British
would now be withholding: "I returned to my home late that evening with the
simulating impression of having participated prominently in a historic decision
of American foreign policy." But the minutes of the meeting failed to record his
remarks, and Kennan later learned that Truman, Marshall, and Acheson had
already decided to extend assistance. "If, on this occasion, I somewhat overrated
the effectiveness of my own voice, it would not be the last time that egotism,
and the attention my words seemed often to attract on the part of startled colleagues, would deceive me as to the measure of my real influence on the process
of decision-taking."[12]

The problem now was to defend this departure from traditional noninvolve-
ment in European affairs before Congress and the American people. Acheson
improvised a solution at a meeting with the president and congressional leaders
on February 27 after Marshall—never rhetorically adept—fumbled his own presentation. The world was now divided into two hostile camps, Acheson warned, a
situation unprecedented since the days of Rome and Carthage. If Greek communists, with Soviet support, won the civil war the British had so far kept them from
winning, the infection—like the rot from bad apples in a barrel—could spread
from Iran in the east to France and Italy in the West, with devastating consequences for American interests. The Soviet Union was poised to reap great gains
at minimal costs. Only the United States stood in the way.[13]

That shook the skeptical legislators, and by early March drafts of a presidential
speech were circulating justifying aid for both Greece and Turkey in terms of an
American obligation to secure "a world of free peoples" against the imposition of
dictatorships "whether fascist, nazi, communist, or of any other form." Kennan
read one of these on the sixth and objected to it strongly: "What I saw made me
extremely unhappy." He favored assisting Greece but not Turkey, where there was
no civil war. He worried about provoking the Soviet Union, whose ambitions in
the region he thought were limited. And why should a crisis in a single country
become the occasion for an open-ended commitment to resist oppression everywhere? After complaining to Henderson and Acheson, Kennan produced a less
sweeping draft and waited to see what the results would be.[14]

Two nights later the Achesons hosted a dinner party. The Kennans attended, as did David Lilienthal, still chairman of the U.S. Atomic Energy Commission and one of the best diarists in Washington. Having read and been much struck by the "long telegram" a year earlier, he was meeting Kennan for the first time:

> A quiet, rather academic-looking fellow. . . . Bald, slight, not impressive except for his eyes which are most unusual: large, intense, wide-set. . . . He is the first man I have talked to about Russia who seems to have the facts that support my essential thesis: that Communism isn't what Russia stands for; it is rather simply a political machine with vested interests.

Acheson was anything but quiet that evening: "Dean spent a good deal of the time bubbling over with enthusiasm, rapture almost, about General Marshall," who had entrusted him with "a historic change in American policy." Kennan, however, was uneasy, brooding about how to aid the Greeks without their resenting it, anxious that Truman not play up the affair too much, "so that prestige isn't too deeply involved." It had been a particularly good moment, Lilienthal concluded, "to have an evening's talk with these two men."[15]

But Truman played up Greece—and Turkey—for all they were worth when he addressed Congress on March 12: the choice the world faced, he insisted, was between governments based on the will of the majority and those that denied it. In what quickly became known as the Truman Doctrine, the president announced "that it must be the policy of the United States to support free peoples who are resisting attempted subjugation by armed minorities or by outside pressures." Achesonian hyperbole had prevailed, while Kennan's cautions had been ignored. He had approached the edge of policy making at a critical moment, but had got no further.[16]

Kennan consoled himself by rewriting the president's speech two days later in a war college lecture. The need to act did often leave little time to think, he reminded the students: "You have to take a deep breath and decide, for better or for worse." Truman had decided to ensure that people who wished to achieve national security "are not deprived of the possibility of doing so through lack of our support, when the measure of that support is within reasonable limits." This final qualification, however, was Kennan's, not Truman's.

Greece, Kennan thought, lay within American capabilities. It was small but accessible, and the amount the president had asked for—$400 million—was roughly what New Yorkers spent on consumer goods in a single day. The stakes were high, though, because reports indicated "that unless something was done to instill confidence in us" among the Greeks, "there would be no halting of the advance of Communism in that country, not because people wanted it but because they are hungry, they are tired, they haven't anything, . . . [t]hey are afraid." Without some hope, they would reluctantly make peace with the other side, and so might desperate people elsewhere in Europe. If that happened, the Soviet Union would not need to mount a military invasion: it would instead work through "subterranean penetration" to make it look as though communism were taking hold spontaneously.

Turkey was different. Its strategic importance was obvious, but the Turks had staunchly resisted Soviet pressures. They had turned their country into a bowling ball without holes, leaving Moscow looking in vain for a grip. If they kept their nerve, "it is going to be awfully hard for the Russians to find a pretext for monkey business there." The same was true in the Middle East: was it really likely, given the region's psychology and its "patriarchal" system, that the Soviet Union could take it over? And then there were regions "where you could perfectly well let people fall prey to totalitarian domination without any tragic consequences for world peace in general." China was one: feeding it, clothing it, and resolving its social problems would probably be "beyond the resources of the whole world put together."[17]

Kennan, thus, dismantled the Truman Doctrine immediately after the president proclaimed it—a risky move, one might think, for a new policy planner. Again, though, the agile Acheson was ahead of him: he had quietly assured congressional leaders the day after Truman spoke that the United States would act only in areas "where our help can be effective in resisting [Soviet] penetration." So why the grandiose rhetoric in the first place? Kennan concluded years later that the Truman Doctrine reflected an American urge "to seek universal formulae or doctrines in which to clothe and justify particular actions." It seemed not to have occurred to anyone that the better approach might be simply "to let the President, or the Secretary of State, use his head."[18]

But democracies never allow their leaders the total freedom to use their heads. "He really had a childlike quality in such matters," Dean Rusk, who would later become secretary of state, recalled of Kennan. "He was an elitist. . . . He took the view that the function of Congress was to keep the public off the backs of the foreign policy professionals." Administrations have to act within boundaries, and the Truman Doctrine was meant to expand those that existed at the time. Its purpose was not simply to frighten Congress into aiding Greece and Turkey, although it had that effect and was meant to. It also set a goal for the future, however unattainable it might for the moment be. It was the geopolitical equivalent of a navigational beacon, pointing the way toward a destination beyond the visible horizon.

Machiavelli would have approved: four centuries earlier he had advised his prince to follow the example of "prudent archers" who, "knowing how far the strength of their bow carries, . . . set their aim much higher than the place intended, not to reach such height with their arrow, but to be able with the aid of so high an aim to achieve their plan." Acheson's arrow flew right over Kennan, but as a policy planner he would benefit from its trajectory, nonetheless.[19]

II.

On March 7, 1947—the day Armstrong agreed to publish Kennan anonymously in *Foreign Affairs*—Acheson, now acting secretary of state, formally asked the National War College to find a new deputy commandant for foreign affairs. Having authorized the creation of a "planning board," Marshall had found Kennan to be "by far the best qualified man in our Service to fill the top post." Appropriately, Kennan was lecturing that day on his 1943 Azores bases experience. He had chosen the case, he told his students, because it provided "a rather striking test-tube example" of the dangers that could come from lack of coordination within the government.[20]

No date was set for Kennan's return to the State Department, so he continued to teach while helping shape the policy Truman had set in motion. The *Foreign Affairs* article, never a top priority, now became less of one: having agreed to do it, Kennan lacked the time to write anything new. Armstrong had anticipated this when he suggested the Yale lecture as a suitable text, but Kennan had recently finished another essay he thought would work better. He had written it for Forrestal, whom Kennan remembered "as a man of burning, tireless energy, determined . . . to take both time and problems by the forelock." One of the first Washington officials to sound the alarm about Soviet behavior, he had been "much concerned that we should get to the bottom of this problem as soon as possible and find out what it was we were dealing with."[21]

Forrestal's first guide had been Edward F. Willett, a Smith College professor who had sent him an analysis of "Dialectical Materialism and Russian Objectives" several weeks before Kennan's "long telegram" arrived. The Navy secretary found Willett's essay impressive and shared it widely. Kennan, however, thought it abstract and alarmist, and when Forrestal asked for his opinion on Willett, Kennan dodged the request, offering instead his own ideas. They took the form of a six-thousand-word paper on the "Psychological Background of Soviet Foreign Policy," forwarded to Forrestal at the end of January 1947. Forrestal acknowledged it on February 17 as "extremely well-done," and promised to pass it on to Marshall. It was safe to assume that the distribution would not stop there.[22]

"Now that [the] article has been noted in official circles," Kennan asked one of Forrestal's aides on March 10, would the Navy secretary object to its being published anonymously in *Foreign Affairs*? Forrestal did not, and on April 8 the State Department's Committee on Unofficial Publications also approved the plan. "I then crossed out my own name in the signature of the article, replaced it with an 'X' to assure the anonymity, sent it on to Mr. Armstrong, and thought no more about it." Kennan made only a few handwritten corrections in the text. He also suggested a note, which Armstrong chose not to use: "The author of this article is one who has had long experience with Russian affairs, both practically and academically, but whose position makes it impossible for him to write about them under his own name."[23]

Kennan's essay was much less casual than its publication arrangements. He began it, as he had the "long telegram," with an explanation of how Marxism-Leninism shaped the beliefs and behavior of Soviet leaders. But ideology was now no longer just the "fig leaf of their moral and intellectual respectability": it was also the "pseudo-scientific justification" by which Stalin and his subordinates clung to power despite their failure to find popular support at home or to overthrow capitalism elsewhere. Convinced that they alone knew what was good for society, they recognized "no restrictions, either of God or man, on the character of their methods." That meant, paradoxically, that they could never be secure, because their "aggressive intransigence" had already provoked a backlash: the Kremlin leaders were finding it necessary, in Gibbon's phrase, "to chastise the contumacy" their own actions had generated. "It is an undeniable privilege of every man to prove himself right in the thesis that the world is his enemy," Kennan reminded his readers, "for if he reiterates it frequently enough and makes it the background of his conduct he is bound eventually to be right."

"Canonized" by the excesses it had committed, the Soviet system could not now dispense with its own infallibility. Stalin would always be right, for if truth were ever found to reside elsewhere, no basis would remain for his rule. As a result,

the leadership is at liberty to put forward for tactical purposes any particular thesis which it finds useful to the cause at any particular moment and to require the faithful and unquestioning acceptance of that thesis by the members of the movement as a whole. This means that truth is not a constant but is actually created, for all intents and purposes, by the Soviet leaders themselves.

With the party line prescribed, the Soviet governmental machine "moves inexorably along the prescribed path, like a persistent toy automobile wound up and headed in a given direction, stopping only when it meets with some unanswerable force." People within this system would not respond to persuasion from the outside sources. "Like the white dog before the phonograph, they hear only 'the master's voice.'"

It followed that the Russians would be difficult to deal with for a long time to come. It did not follow, though, that they had "embarked upon a do-or-die program to overthrow our society by a given date. The theory of the inevitability of the eventual fall of capitalism has the fortunate connotation that there is no hurry about it." Like the church, the Kremlin could afford to wait. It would retreat in the face of superior force: "Its main concern is to make sure that it has filled every nook and cranny available to it in the basin of world power." That made Stalin's ambitions more sensitive to resistance than those of Napoleon or Hitler. Resistance could not arise, though, from sporadic acts reflecting "the momentary whims of democratic opinion." What was needed instead were strategies "no less steady in their purpose, and no less variegated and resourceful in their application, than those of the Soviet Union itself." The main objective must be "a long-term, patient but firm and vigilant containment of Russian expansive tendencies."

Containment could be made to work, Kennan insisted in unusually convoluted prose, "by the adroit and vigilant application of counter-force at a series of constantly shifting geographical and political points, corresponding to the shifts and manœuvres of Soviet policy, but which can not be charmed or talked out of existence." This would produce results, with the passage of time, because the Soviet people were exhausted, the Soviet economy remained in many respects primitive, and the Soviet government had yet to evolve any orderly way of selecting a successor once Stalin had passed from the scene. Any one of these difficulties could disrupt discipline, and if that were ever to happen—here Kennan echoed the prediction he had made from Riga in 1932—"Soviet Russia might be changed over night from one of the strongest to one of the weakest and most pitiable of national societies."

Its condition, then, resembled that of the Buddenbrooks family in Thomas Mann's eponymous novel: a formidable facade concealed internal enfeeblement.

The light of distant stars, after all, "shines brightest on this world when in reality [they have] long ceased to exist." No one could know for sure whether this would happen, but "Soviet power, like the capitalist world of its conception, bears within it the seeds of its own decay, and . . . the sprouting of these seeds is well advanced." The United States could embrace with reasonable confidence, then, "a policy of firm containment, designed to confront the Russians with unalterable counter-force at every point where they show signs of encroaching upon the interests of a peaceful and stable world."

If Americans could create the impression of a country that knew what it wanted, was coping successfully with its internal problems, and could hold its own amid the geopolitical and ideological currents of international affairs, then the hopes of Moscow's supporters would wane, and there would be added stress on its foreign policy. The ultimate result could be "either the break-up or the gradual mellowing of Soviet power. For no mystical, messianic movement—and particularly not that of the Kremlin—can face frustration indefinitely without eventually adjusting itself in one way or another to the logic of that state of affairs." The Soviet challenge, therefore, required only that Americans live up to their own best traditions. "Surely, there was never a fairer test of national quality than this."[24]

It's hardly surprising that Forrestal liked the piece, or that Armstrong was eager to publish it. Like the "long telegram," Kennan's "Psychological Background" essay riveted readers in a way no one else in Washington had managed to do—certainly not Willett, whose report now followed that of Bohlen and Robinson into obscurity. Kennan had combined objectivity with eloquence, Armstrong wrote him: "It's a pleasure for an editor to deal with something that needs practically no revision. . . . I only wish for your sake as well as for ours that it could carry your name."[25]

Kennan claimed later to have written the paper for Forrestal's "private and personal edification," and to have sent it to Armstrong only because he had it on hand.[26] That's not how it reads, though: the tone is that of a stem-winding sermon and preachers normally seek out pulpits. Armstrong provided one, but not right away. Because *Foreign Affairs* was a quarterly, the piece would not appear until late June, five months after Kennan had finished writing it. With such minimal revisions, the article ignored all that had happened during that time: there was no mention of the Greek-Turkish crisis, the Truman Doctrine, or their consequences for American foreign policy. It was as if Kennan had shot off an arrow of his own on a high trajectory, and then somehow forgotten about it.

The best explanation is that he saw the *Foreign Affairs* essay as ending an assignment, not beginning a new one.[27] It completed the task Durbrow, Gruenther, Hill,

Forrestal, and Acheson had devised for him after his return from Moscow, which was to disseminate his insights about the Soviet Union as widely as possible, and to reflect—but only in general terms—on their implications for the United States in the postwar world. Marshall had now asked him to devise a grand strategy, a very different responsibility. Kennan's perspective henceforth would be Washington's, not Moscow's; the demands on him would be organizational, not instructional; and Marshall would expect invisibility, not publicity. "The Sources of Soviet Conduct"—the title Kennan's article carried—reflected his thinking as of January 1947 but not beyond. The only thing he did to connect it with his new job was to replace his name on the first page with an "X."

III.

The National War College, Kennan assured a Foreign Service friend in mid-March, was achieving its purpose. Each year it would be sending a hundred graduates into the top ranks of their respective services. His own teaching had given him a closer acquaintance with this new generation of military leaders than anyone else in the State Department. That in itself should avoid many of the political-military confusions of the last war, for then there had been no civilian official with "the prestige and the guts" to challenge the military. Now that Marshall was secretary of state and Kennan would be running his Policy Planning Staff, the relationship should be even closer. Whether the staff would improve the conduct of foreign policy remained to be seen, but Marshall was not likely to put up with it if it did not. By starting quietly but with a small and select group, Kennan wrote another friend, "we may be able to avoid some of the pitfalls which have beset the careers of more ambitious and grandiose undertakings."[28]

Mindful of grandiosity, Kennan was still dissecting the Truman Doctrine—but with some significant shifts in his views. He had come to see the need for aiding both Greece and Turkey, he explained to his students on March 28, even though neither was in danger of becoming a Soviet satellite. The reason was psychological: a failure to act might convey the impression that "the Western Powers were on the run and that international communism was on the make." Such a "bandwagon" mentality could cause Europeans to *choose* communism, in the belief that they had better climb on board while there was still time. That could shatter American prestige in the Near East, East Asia, and elsewhere.

This was a different and direr Kennan from the one who had lectured at the war college two weeks earlier. He was now approaching Acheson's view that everything was at risk: the danger, though, was not from rotten apples but from cultural despair. The first barbarians to sack Rome had not held it; nevertheless the blow had begun the end of the Roman Empire. There was no reason to assume that Europe, "as we know it—and as we need it—would ever recover from . . . even a brief period of Russian control." Floodwaters always receded, but was that a good reason not to build dikes? To abandon Europe would be to sever the roots of culture and tradition, leaving the United States with fewer safeguards against tyranny than one might think:

> The fact of the matter is that there is a little bit of the totalitarian buried somewhere, way down deep, in each and every one of us. It is only the cheerful light of confidence and security which keeps this evil genius down at the usual helpless and invisible depth. If confidence and security were to disappear, don't think that he would not be waiting to take their place.

Retaining their freedoms in a hostile world would require Americans, therefore, "to whistle loudly in the dark." That might not be enough to save them.

None of this meant, however, that they had to oppose totalitarianism everywhere all at once. Because means were limited, there had to be standards for determining when and how to act. The Truman Doctrine, with its promise "to support free peoples" wherever dictators threatened them, had failed to provide these. Kennan's criteria, in contrast, were explicit:

> A. The problem at hand is one within our economic, technical and financial capabilities.

> B. If we did not take such action, the resulting situation might redound very decidedly to the advantage of our political adversaries.

> C. If, on the other hand, we do take the action in question there is good reason to hope that the favorable consequences will carry far beyond the limits of Greece itself.

Anyone trying to concentrate troops everywhere would be dismissed as "a military ignoramus." Why that should not be true in foreign policy was a mystery. After all, bandwagoning could work both ways. There was "a very fair possibility" that, with a relatively small expenditure of money and effort in Greece and Turkey, "we might turn a critical tide and set in motion counter-currents which would change the entire political atmosphere of Europe to our advantage."

Such a strategy would depart from decades of isolationism extending back to the Monroe Doctrine. But that pronouncement had not been some "higher truth," divorced from the circumstances surrounding it: indeed the first drafts of Monroe's message to Congress in 1823 expressed sympathy—little else was possible at the time—for the Greeks' campaign for independence from the Ottoman Empire. What was happening now was that the United States was being asked defend principles too long admired only on "the comfortable plane of generality."

> Here we can no longer hide behind language, behind any international pooling of responsibility, or behind that smug sense of disentanglement that animates us whenever we dispense pure charity. Here we have to bite and chew on the bitter truth that in this world you cannot even do good today unless you are prepared to exert your share of power, to take your share of responsibility, to make your share of mistakes, and to assume your share of risks.

Kennan concluded his lecture with what he acknowledged *might* be an apocryphal story about an American consul in Finland after World War I who had requested permission to fly the U.S. flag over premises he was occupying. After deliberation and delay, the reply came back from Washington: "No precedent." The consul responded with equal brevity: "Precedent established."[29]

IV.

Marshall returned from the long and fruitless Moscow foreign ministers' conference on April 28, 1947, determined to set precedents. During the weeks he had been away, it had become clear to him that the European crisis went well beyond the British withdrawal of aid to Greece and Turkey. The clearest warning had come from Stalin himself: when the secretary of state called on him in the Kremlin, the old dictator assured his guest that he did not see the situation as at all "tragic," while at the same time doodling wolves on his notepad—a favorite tactic for disconcerting visitors. That was enough for Marshall, who ordered Acheson to get the Policy Planning Staff organized. On the day after his arrival in Washington, Marshall summoned Kennan for their first face-to-face conversation.

Something must be done, he insisted, otherwise others would seize the initiative: "I don't want to wait for Congress to beat me over the head." Kennan was to leave the war college immediately, review the whole question of Europe's future, and tell him "what you think I ought to do." He would have two weeks. Were there any other assignments? Kennan asked. Marshall's reply became legendary: "Avoid trivia." And so, "with this instruction and the weight of the world on my shoulders," Kennan set to work.[30]

Neither he nor Marshall nor any other individual invented the Marshall Plan. Its roots went back to the early 1920s, when American bankers, with quiet support from the Harding and Coolidge administrations, had helped to stabilize the post–World War I European economy. Roosevelt's New Deal expanded the government's responsibility for the domestic economy, and World War II made this a matter of international security, for if—as the experience of the 1930s strongly suggested—depressions made wars likely, then prosperity would be a prerequisite for peace. By the spring of 1947, however, the institutions designed to revive the global economy—the United Nations Relief and Rehabilitation Administration, the International Monetary Fund, and the World Bank—were faltering. Meanwhile Stalin, tutored by Lenin to expect crises among capitalists, was doodling wolves, waiting for history to follow its prescribed path.[31]

Calls for action converged from several sources. Marshall himself had discussed the European crisis with his British and French counterparts, Ernest Bevin and Georges Bidault, while still in Moscow. Acheson had a State-War-Navy Coordinating Committee report ready for Marshall upon his return. The secretary of state's economic advisers made their concerns clear, influenced by alarming reports from their chief, William L. Clayton, who was traveling in Europe. Well-informed columnists, notably James Reston and Walter Lippmann, were writing about the issue; their stories pushed officials who had supplied them with information into acting upon it. What Kennan did was to pull all of these threads together into a coherent policy.[32]

He did so almost single-handedly: there was no eagerness among Kennan's Foreign Service colleagues to join the new and as yet vaguely defined Policy Planning Staff. Nor was Acheson always helpful. With no background of his own in economics, Kennan had tried to recruit Paul H. Nitze—later to succeed him as staff director—but Acheson blocked the appointment on the grounds that Nitze was "a Wall Street operator," not "a long-range thinker." There was not even, for a while, assigned office space. The State Department was moving from its ornate but cramped quarters next to the White House to a spare but more spacious building—vacated by the War Department when it built the Pentagon—in the "Foggy Bottom" section of Washington. The name, Reston explained to his readers, was "not an intellectual condition but a geographical area down by the Potomac."[33]

When the staff formally began its operations, on May 5, it had only two other members: Joseph E. Johnson, a Williams College professor with no plans to remain in government, and Carlton Savage, a longtime aide to former secretary of state Cordell Hull. These were not heavy-hitters. It was under these circumstances, Kennan recalled, that

> I was supposed to review the whole great problem of European recovery in all its complexity, to tap those various sources of outside advice which we would never be forgiven for not tapping, to draw up and present to the Secretary the recommendations he wanted, and be prepared to defend these recommendations against all government critics, including ones unavoidably more deeply versed in the details of the subject matter than myself, and ones who could be expected to show no charity or mercy toward a man who came as an invader of their hitherto private bureaucratic premises.

He was staggering "under a terrible burden right now," George wrote his cousin Charlie James, but he was happy to have the sense "that perhaps I can leave a mark in the conduct of our international business." This was only the beginning, though, "of a long and hard fight and I think I better not do much talking at this stage."[34]

The staff soon grew to include more qualified members: Jacques Reinstein, who supplied the economic expertise Kennan had hoped to get from Nitze; Ware Adams, a Foreign Service officer with a background on German and Austrian issues; Charles (Tick) Bonesteel III, an Army colonel assigned to the State Department who supplied a military perspective; and later that summer, at Kennan's special request, his former Moscow colleague John Paton Davies, who handled East Asian affairs. Kennan was also fortunate to have Dorothy Hessman follow him into yet another job that generated an "endless torrent of prose."[35]

He took three weeks—not two—to propose a response to the European crisis, a pardonable delay given the scale of the problem. On May 23, after many late nights and much anguished discussion, he sent Marshall PPS/1, "Policy With Respect to

American Aid to Western Europe," the first paper to emerge from the Policy Planning Staff and certainly the most influential. Kennan drafted almost all of it, a practice he generally followed. The format, however, met Marshall's specifications: there was an opening summary of main points, a statement of the problem, a set of proposals for short-term and longer-term solutions, and a conclusion—in this case, a particularly pointed one.

The problem confronting Europe, as Kennan identified it, was not the Soviet Union itself, or international communism, but rather an "economic maladjustment" that had made European society vulnerable to exploitation by totalitarianism. It had arisen from "a profound exhaustion of physical plant and of spiritual vigor," brought about by the effects of war and the postwar division of the continent. Further communist successes would endanger American interests, a situation that should be "frankly stated" to the American people.

The immediate need was for "effective and dramatic action" to show Washington's determination to reverse the situation. The objective would be psychological: "to put us on the offensive instead of the defensive, to convince the European peoples that we mean business, to serve as a catalyst for their hope and confidence, and to dramatize for our people the nature of Europe's problems and the importance of American assistance." It would be, in short, an application of *leverage*, designed to accomplish a lot with a little. Kennan was vague on just what this might be: perhaps getting coal from the Rhine Valley to wherever else it was needed, possibly providing additional economic aid to Italy. His weakness in economics was showing here: the staff, he explained, would have to study this matter more fully.

Kennan did better when he turned to long-term solutions: the Europeans, he insisted, would have to design their own recovery. In language Marshall himself used in announcing the plan that bore his name, Kennan proclaimed it

neither fitting nor efficacious for this Government to undertake to draw up unilaterally and to promulgate formally on its own a program designed to place western Europe on its feet economically. This is the business of the Europeans. The formal initiative must come from Europe; the program must be evolved in Europe; and the Europeans must bear the basic responsibility for it.

The American role would be to finance such a program and to help the Europeans set its priorities. But they would have to act together. The United States could not respond to "isolated and individual appeals." The goal would be self-sufficiency: a "reasonable assurance that if we support it, this will be the last such program we shall be asked to support in the foreseeable future."

The question then was how to define "Europe." Great Britain would have to be included. Germany was nowhere mentioned, but by mentioning Rhine Valley coal and by citing the Americans' responsibilities in the territories they occupied, Kennan implied its inclusion. He made the point explicit in a war college lecture on May 6, while PPS/1 was still being drafted: reviving productive capacity in western Germany "should be the primary object of our policy." An equally sensitive issue was whether to invite the Soviet Union and its satellites to participate in the plan. Here Kennan recommended extending an offer, but in such a way that they would either "exclude themselves by unwillingness to accept the proposed conditions or agree to abandon the exclusive orientation of their economies."

The paper's conclusion was pure Kennan, although he had reason to know by then that Marshall would approve: "Steps should be taken to clarify what the press has unfortunately come to identify as the 'Truman Doctrine', and to remove in particular two damaging impressions which are current in large sections of public opinion." These were, first, that the United States was responding defensively to communism and would not be acting in the absence of that danger; and, second, that the Truman Doctrine was "a blank check to give economic and military aid to any area in the world where the communists show signs of being successful." Instead the United States must act "only in cases where the prospective results bear a satisfactory relationship to the expenditure of American resources and effort."[36]

Marshall convened top State Department officials on May 28 to discuss PPS/1. Kennan was present, as were Acheson and Will Clayton, just back from Europe and able to describe in startling detail the conditions he had seen. Bohlen was also there to support Kennan's recommendation that the United States "play it straight," offering aid to the Soviet Union and its satellites with the expectation that Stalin would refuse and thus take onto himself the responsibility for Europe's division. Marshall, as was his habit, listened carefully but said little: he did ask, however, what would happen if the Russians accepted. Kennan suggested reminding them "that you like ourselves are a raw material producing and food producing country. We are contributing. What are you going to contribute?" Marshall nodded at this point but said nothing. He sent word to Harvard that day, though, that he would speak briefly a week hence when the university would be awarding him an honorary degree. Bohlen drafted the speech while Acheson, anticipating Marshall's laconic manner, alerted the British that something significant was in the works.[37]

The secretary of state's address, unspectacularly delivered on June 5, 1947, left its audience unaware that they had heard something historic: like Lincoln's at Gettysburg, it got polite but not enthusiastic applause. Kennan learned that Marshall had drawn on PPS/1 only when he saw the final text. The American media were unsure what to make of the "Marshall Plan," as Truman insisted on calling it, but thanks to Acheson's tip, Bevin was ready to act: he and Bidault invited Molotov to Paris to discuss Marshall's proposal. The Soviet foreign minister arrived there on June 27 with a large group of economic experts, leading the Americans to worry briefly that Stalin had decided to participate in the plan. If he had, he soon changed his mind, ordering Molotov to walk out. The Eastern Europeans were at first told to accept aid with a view to sabotaging the Marshall Plan from within, but Stalin then countermanded those instructions as well.[38]

It had all gone as Kennan expected. "Strain placed on communist movement by effort to draw up plan for European rehabilitation," he wrote in a set of briefing notes for Marshall on July 21. "Communist parties in West[ern] Europe forced to show their hand. Russians smoked out in relations with satellite countries. . . . Events of past weeks the greatest blow to European Communism since termination of hostilities."[39]

What, then, was Kennan's role in designing the Marshall Plan? The secretary of state himself credited PPS/1 as its basis and with characteristic understatement—all the more valued for that—found ways to show his appreciation.[40] Kennan's contributions beyond that, though, are more difficult to sort out. Great Britain and Germany would have been included in the plan even if he had not recommended this: it would have made no economic sense without them. Kennan's argument that the European crisis was psychological in character and could be reversed by psychological means was more original, although he framed that recommendation as a long-term solution: it was Marshall, Bohlen, and Acheson who saw that a speech made on short notice could accomplish the same thing.

Two features of the Marshall Plan, however, were particularly Kennan's, one of them a success, the other a failure. The success was offering aid to the Soviet Union and Eastern Europe. Had Stalin agreed to take it, he could have killed the program by ensuring that the U.S. Congress would never vote the necessary appropriations. But Kennan was sure—in a way that no one else in Washington except Bohlen could have been—that Stalin was not that clever and that the offer would catch him off guard. That was what happened: the offer lured him into displaying his own confusion, a devastating blow in a system that claimed infallibility. It was a lot to have accomplished with very little.

Kennan's other priority—explicitly stated in the conclusion to PPS/1—was for the Marshall Plan to supplant the Truman Doctrine, with its implied obligation to act wherever Soviet aggression or intimidation occurred, without regard to whether American interests were at stake or the means existed with which to defend them. Unfortunately for Kennan, however, the literary arrow he had shot into the air before he had even heard of the Truman Doctrine or the Marshall Plan was now, in the wake of Marshall's speech, about to make its unexpected impact.

V.

The State Department announced the Policy Planning Staff's establishment, along with Kennan's appointment as its director, on May 7. He combined "great strength of character, not to say toughness, with high-minded idealism," Jock Balfour informed London, but this was "tempered by a healthy respect for the practicability of any given course." Kennan had thought the Truman Doctrine an "unnecessary and perhaps even dangerous" overdramatization of the need to aid Greece and Turkey. He knew a great deal about the Soviet Union but had not "given way to the hysteria which colours the views of so many of his countrymen." Balfour even reported on the Kennans' living arrangements: he would continue some lecturing at the National War College because his family wanted to hang on to the house it provided for as long as possible.[41]

Kennan became even more visible a few weeks later when the columnists Joseph and Stewart Alsop ran the first public story on the "long telegram," identifying him as its author. It was, they claimed, highly significant that Marshall had given this new responsibility to the man who had produced "the most important single state paper on the Soviet Union." Worried that the still-secret document had leaked, Kennan hastened to assure Acheson that he had not been the source. He pointed out, however, that the telegram contained little "which has not subsequently been stated as American policy on many occasions and by many other people."[42]

"Keep an eye on George F. Kennan," *The Christian Science Monitor* advised its readers a few days after the Alsops' column appeared. *United States News* ran a brief biography stressing Kennan's qualifications for the new job and noting—inaccurately—that while serving in Moscow, he had organized a dance band called "Kennan's Kampus Kids." He was "tall, lean, smooth-shaven and bald," *The*

Baltimore Sun reported early in June, alongside an improbable photograph from the 1920s showing an anxious young man with a full head of hair. Meanwhile, the Policy Planning Staff was posing for *The Washington Post*. Its photograph showed an older and more confident Kennan, elegant in a three-piece suit, leaning back in his chair with his chin in one hand and a pen in the other, legs crossed, a notepad balanced on his knee, as if waiting. The staff, journalist Ferdinand Kuhn noted, was as new and as sensible as the air-conditioned Virginia Avenue building where the State Department now had its headquarters. Its members would operate with a "passion for anonymity."[43]

That was the intention, but late in June the July issue of *Foreign Affairs* came out. With its somber cover and stolid contents, the quarterly made no effort to reach a mass audience: it cost $1.25 a copy, a lot in 1947, and its circulation was just over 19,000. There were articles that month on peacemaking, trade charters, international law, self-government in U.S. territories, Latin American population problems, and the Dutch-Belgian economic union. These raised few eyebrows, but one that did—at least in Moscow—was an essay by Yevgeny Varga, one of Stalin's economic advisers, that cited the Greek-Turkish crisis and the Truman Doctrine as evidence that Washington and London were cooperating to preserve capitalism. Varga seemed to be challenging Leninist orthodoxy about capitalist contradictions, and he got into trouble at home for having done so. Immediately preceding his article was one that made no reference at all to those recent events. Its title was "The Sources of Soviet Conduct," and its author was listed, without explanation, as "X."[44]

No one paid much attention until July 8, when *New York Times* columnist Arthur Krock pointed out that its argument was "exactly that adopted by the American government after appeasement of the Kremlin proved a failure." Obviously the author had studied the Soviet Union for years "at the closest range possible for a foreigner." His analysis had been so accurate that the State Department had used it to predict how Molotov would respond, at the Paris conference the previous week, to the American offer of Marshall Plan aid. The views of "X," Krock concluded, "closely resemble those marked 'Top Secret' in several official files in Washington."[45]

This set off a scramble for copies of *Foreign Affairs*. Krock had not named Kennan, but he knew who he was writing about because Forrestal had let him see the draft, with Kennan's name still on it, that had gone to Armstrong. By the end of the day, the United Press was reporting "X" 's identity: the tip-off was not just the argument but also the prose. "If Kennan didn't write that article," one diplomat commented, then it was done by someone who could "imitate his writing style." No one else, Hessman later confirmed, would have quoted from Gibbon's *Decline and Fall*. The State Department did not deny the rumor, and on July 9 the *Daily Worker*, the organ of the Communist Party of the United States, exposed the plot: "'X' Bared as State Dep't Aid [*sic*]: Calls for Overthrow of Soviet Government." That clipping made its way into Grace Kennan's scrapbook. "The first nasty article," she noted carefully, "but it's about Mr. X who may or may not be Daddy."[46]

The next issue of *Newsweek* treated the "X" article—and Kennan's ascent within the State Department—as a long-delayed vindication for the Soviet specialists Kelley had begun training two decades earlier. This "tightly knit little career group," having survived "the appeasement and war years," had concluded from them that dealing with Stalin was impossible. The "X" article, reflecting their thinking, explained the reasons behind the Truman Doctrine and the Marshall Plan, while charting "the course that this country is likely to pursue for years to come."[47]

Far from being anonymous, Kennan was now extremely conspicuous: "Feeling like one who has inadvertently loosened a large boulder from the top of a cliff and now helplessly witnesses its path of destruction in the valley below, shuddering and wincing at each successive glimpse of disaster, I absorbed the bombardment of press comment that now set in." Equally unsettling was what Marshall might say. He had been pleased to see Kennan's appointment publicized, because it suggested seriousness within the State Department about constructing a postwar grand strategy. He was not at all happy, however, to find what purported to be that strategy—along with its alleged author—emblazoned across the pages of national newsmagazines.

> He called me in, drew my attention to this anomaly, peered at me over his glasses with raised eyebrows (eyebrows before whose raising, I may say, better men than I had quailed), and waited for an answer. I explained the origins of the article, and pointed out that it had been duly cleared for publication by the competent official committee. This satisfied him.

Marshall never mentioned the matter to Kennan again, "[b]ut it was long, I suspect, before he recovered from his astonishment over the strange ways of the department he now headed."[48]

Kennan might soon have faded back into the anonymity he and Marshall wanted, had it not been for another unexpected event: Walter Lippmann brought his copy of *Foreign Affairs* with him to his summer fishing camp in Maine. When he returned to his home in Washington, *Time* magazine reported, America's "best-known pundit" had no fish, but he did have a juicy target at which he now took aim: "Two secretaries hovered beside him. Western Union stood by to pick up his copy daily at 1 o'clock and transmit it to New York, while Mr. Lippmann, in red silk Chinese trousers and a grey-&-black silk shirt, sat at his antique desk and wrote." And wrote, and wrote.

Lippmann produced fourteen columns on "Mr. X" for the *New York Herald Tribune*, the first of which appeared on September 2, 1947. Widely syndicated and republished as a short book entitled *The Cold War*—one of the first public uses of that term—they argued that Kennan had spawned a "strategic monstrosity" that would relinquish the initiative to Stalin, exhaust the United States, and force it into dependency on "a coalition of disorganized, disunited, feeble or disorderly nations, tribes and factions." Only a miracle could make "containment" work: that concept assumed a competition in which "the Soviet Union will break its leg while the United States grows a pair of wings to speed it on its way."

The basis for Lippmann's complaint was his certainty that Kennan had inspired the Truman Doctrine, a conclusion he reached by reasoning backward. Had not Truman claimed the need to assist victims of totalitarianism everywhere? Had not Kennan insisted that the United States must "confront the Russians with unalterable counterforce at every point where they show signs of encroaching upon the interests of a peaceful and stable world"? It followed, in Lippmann's mind at least, that the "X" article was "not only an analytical interpretation of the sources of Soviet conduct. It is also a document of primary importance on the sources of American foreign policy—of at least that part of it which is known as the Truman Doctrine."[49]

This could not have been more wrong. Kennan's "Psychological Background" paper, completed at the end of January 1947, had indeed preceded Truman's March 12 speech, but there is no evidence that it influenced the drafting of that address and abundant evidence that Kennan had sought to remove the language in it to which Lippmann later objected. Kennan had made his own objections to the Truman Doctrine clear in his National War College lectures, and in PPS/1 he recommended scrapping the idea altogether. Those positions were not public, but Lippmann had excellent sources within the government: Kennan had even consulted him, on Forrestal's recommendation, with respect to the Marshall Plan. Lippmann later acknowledged having found Kennan upset by the Truman Doctrine. "[W]e were in pretty good agreement, I thought."

Then the "X" article came out. Lippmann interpreted it as representing a faction within the State Department—opposed to the Marshall Plan—that favored the "military encirclement of the Soviet Union." They were using Kennan to promote that objective. Hence Lippmann's public attack: Kennan had either misled him or been captured by hard-liners. Lippmann could have cleared up the matter with a single phone call, but unlike Reston, Krock, and the Alsops, he was not an investigative reporter. It was not his habit to seek out information but rather to wait for it to come to him. When it did, he pronounced on its significance. And what he had, at his fishing camp in the late summer of 1947, were two apparently parallel texts: Truman's speech and Kennan's article. That was sufficient.[50]

"Mr. Lippmann," Kennan recalled ruefully, "mistook me for the author of precisely those features of the Truman Doctrine which I had most vigorously opposed." Privately, Kennan suspected a more personal reason for Lippmann's anger. Armstrong had banished Lippmann—and any mention of Lippmann—from the pages of *Foreign Affairs* after the editor's wife left him to marry the columnist in 1938. Lippmann in turn, Kennan believed, resented the fact that he had published the "X" article in Armstrong's journal, the only one in which Lippmann could not appear.[51]

Armstrong, pleased with all the attention, could not resist a bit of needling. "I see that Mr. Lippmann, having gone to Europe saying that the policy of containing Russia was based on fallacies and would fail, comes back saying that it has succeeded so well that it should be abandoned," he wrote Kennan in November. Kennan, by then, was resigned to Lippmann's inconsistencies: "I have never doubted that in the end the paths of Mr. Lippmann and myself would meet," he replied. "History will tell which was the more tortuous."[52]

Whatever motivated Lippmann, Kennan also bore—and later acknowledged—responsibility for what had happened. His language did imply relinquishing the initiative to the Kremlin: it was difficult to read any other meaning into "the adroit and vigilant application of counter-force at a series of constantly shifting geographical and political points, corresponding to the shifts and manœuvres of Soviet policy." He failed to say where the United States would find the means to do this, apart from maintaining its own self-confidence. He neglected to revise his draft in the light of the questions the Truman Doctrine had raised in his mind, which he in turn had raised with his war college students. He had time to do this: his final draft did not go to Armstrong until April 11, a day short of a month since Truman had made his speech. His insistence on anonymity secured the article a level of scrutiny it might not have received had he used his own name. And even after that anonymity had evaporated, Kennan continued to seek refuge in it: when Lippmann pounced, Kennan interpreted his own official responsibilities as precluding a public response, preferring instead to suffer in silence. Kennan's "containment" therefore became synonymous, in the minds of most people who knew the phrase, with Truman's doctrine.[53]

Herbert Butterfield, whom Kennan read later in life, wrote of "the tricks that time plays with the purposes of men, as it turns those purposes to ends not realised." Time played a trick on Kennan just as he was attaining national and international prominence. His Council on Foreign Relations talk, his essay for Forrestal, and its subsequent publication in *Foreign Affairs*, all looked backward to the despair of 1946 when war or appeasement appeared to be the only alternatives open to the United States. Kennan's criticisms of the Truman Doctrine, however, looked forward to the purposefulness of 1947: having decided to resist the Soviet Union, how might the United States do that with maximum effectiveness at minimal cost?[54]

But time does not tolerate such Janus-like postures. However distinct *visions* of the past and the future may be, conclusions drawn from them coexist in the present, intertwine, and often surprise. That was what happened to Kennan. He did indeed, as Kissinger acknowledged, come closer than anyone else to authoring the diplomatic doctrine of his era. But after 1947 he could never regard the doctrine with which he was credited as his own. That produced a dejection extending over dozens of Kennan birthdays to come.

THIRTEEN

Policy Planner: 1947–1948

KENNAN RETURNED TO THE NATIONAL WAR COLLEGE FOR WHAT he described as a farewell lecture on June 18, 1947. It seemed like centuries, he told his former students, since he had gone to work at the State Department. His months of teaching were now a lost age of youth and innocence. He could no longer sit in his office at Fort McNair, look out over the elm trees and the golf course, and encompass the world within "neat, geometric patterns" that fit within equally precise lectures. Policy planning was a very different responsibility, but explaining just how was "like trying to describe the mysteries of love to a person who has never experienced it."

There was, however, an analogy that might help. "I have a largish farm in Pennsylvania. The reason you never see me around here on weekends (or rather, the reason you *would* never see me around here if *you* were here on weekends) is that I am up there trying to look after that farm." It had 235 acres, on each of which things were happening. Weekends, in theory, were days of rest. But farms defied theory:

> Here a bridge is collapsing. No sooner do you start to repair it than a neighbor comes to complain about a hedge row which you haven't kept up half a mile away on the other side of the farm. At that very moment your daughter arrives to tell you that someone left the gate to the hog pasture open and the hogs are out. On the way to the hog pasture, you discover that the beagle hound is happily liquidating one of the children's pet kittens. In burying the kitten, you look up and notice a whole section of the barn roof has been blown off and needs instant repair. Somebody shouts from the bathroom window that the pump has stopped working, and there's no water in the

house. At that moment, a truck arrives with 5 tons of stone for the lane. And as you stand there hopelessly, wondering which of these crises to attend to first, you notice the farmer's little boy standing silently before you with that maddening smile, which is halfway a leer, on his face, and when you ask him what's up, he says triumphantly, "The bull's busted out and he's eating the strawberry bed."

Policy planning was like that. You might anticipate a problem three or four months into the future, but by the time you'd got your ideas down on paper, the months had shrunk to three or four weeks. Getting the paper approved took still more time, which left perhaps three or four days. And by the time others had translated those ideas into action, "the thing you were planning for took place the day before yesterday, and everyone wants to know why in the hell you didn't foresee it a long time ago." Meanwhile, 234 other problems were following similar trajectories, causing throngs of people to stand around trying to get your attention: "Say, do you know that the bull is out there in the strawberry patch again?"[1]

So how good a planner was Kennan? That he pioneered the process goes without saying: he was the first and remains the most respected of all Policy Planning Staff directors. Nor could he complain about access. Marshall gave him an office next to his own, with the implied invitation to walk through the door connecting them whenever he felt the need.[2] There was no competition: grand strategy was a new concept in Washington, and Marshall's prestige was such that the State Department—for the moment at least—took the lead in shaping it. The conditions for planning, then, were as good as any planner could expect to get. The world, however, defied theory as much as the farm did. Kennan relished and in many ways rose to the challenges his new job posed. In the end, though, he failed to master them—thereby setting the pattern for all the policy planners who would succeed him.

I.

Kennan delivered his June 18 lecture extemporaneously: there wasn't time to do more than sketch out rough notes. For that reason, though, it—together with a more formal lecture he had given on May 6—provides a good sense of what was on his mind as he was setting up the Policy Planning Staff. They show that even as he was helping to design the Marshall Plan, he was looking beyond it in search of general principles to guide the strategy of containment. He shared these first with his war college students.

One such principle was self-restraint. Kennan had argued in PPS/1 that it would be "neither fitting nor efficacious" for the United States to design a European recovery program: the Europeans should do this themselves. Marshall incorporated that language into his June 5 Harvard speech, but neither he nor Kennan had explained the reasoning behind it. Why should Americans allow Europeans to decide how Americans would spend their money?

Kennan's answer began with the communist parties of Western Europe, who on Moscow's orders would do all they could to frustrate any workable recovery program: "They will fight it everywhere, tooth and nail." But because they lacked the backing of the Red Army or the Soviet secret police, those parties depended on popular support. Their hard core of "violent, fanatical extremists" had to attract a wider circle of "muddled, discontented, embittered liberals." If the latter ever abandoned the former, then Stalin's strategy for dominating the rest of Europe would be in trouble. It made sense, therefore, to let the Europeans take the lead in shaping the Marshall Plan, because this would encourage unity among them while simultaneously undermining the agents through which Moscow had hoped to take control. Neither the Soviet Union nor its communist allies could credibly denounce a *European* initiative as "American imperialism."

Behind Kennan's argument were two larger ideas that had long shaped his thinking. One was Gibbon's conviction that conquered provinces—whatever the means of conquest—were sources of weakness: the Soviet Union, Kennan believed, was already overstretched. The other, closely related, was that international communism had itself become a form of imperialism: this was "the weakest and most vulnerable [point] in the Kremlin armor." It followed, then, that the Americans had time on their side and could afford to be patient. They could best secure their influence in Europe by not appearing too obviously to want it.

A second principle derived from the first: that containment meant contracting American aspirations, not expanding them. The resources available to the United States—material and intellectual—were more limited than anyone had understood them to be at the end of the war. As a result, a serious gap had developed between intentions and capabilities.

Perhaps we should never have tried to organize all the world into one association for peace. . . . Perhaps the whole idea of world peace has been a premature, unworkable grandiose form of daydreaming; perhaps we should have held up as a goal: "Peace if possible, and insofar as it effects our interests."

That interest lay in balancing power within the existing international system. If the United States was to avoid the overextension that was already afflicting the Soviet Union, then it should bolster the strength of allies in such a way as not to deplete its own.

The Marshall Plan's purpose, therefore, was not to create American satellites. Rather, it sought to encourage the Europeans to make maximum use of their resources, before drawing upon those of the United States. This approach would promote self-reliance, distinguish Washington's policy from Moscow's, and respect the interests of American taxpayers, who would be footing the bill for whatever assistance the Europeans did receive. Independence, not dependence, was to be the goal, and the effort expended in seeking it should be as little as possible.

That meant rethinking relationships with defeated enemies. The American occupation of part of Germany and all of Japan, Kennan reminded his students, was still focusing on prosecuting war criminals, dismantling industrial facilities, extracting reparations, restricting trade, and reeducating formerly authoritarian societies. There had been little coordination with the strategy of containment: the United States would need German and Japanese allies in resisting the Soviet Union. Even if that were not the case, to impose one's will on a conquered people "means eventually that you fall heir, unless you are very careful, to all the problems and responsibilities of that people." Americans were not equipped "to handle successfully for any length of time [those] other than our own."

Beyond Western Europe and Japan, there was little the United States could or should do. Marshall had spent all of 1946 trying to mediate the civil war between the Nationalists and the Communists in China, Kennan pointed out, but the country was probably still going to fall under Mao Zedong's control. "If I thought for a moment that the precedent of Greece and Turkey obliged us to try to do the same thing in China, I would throw up my hands and say we had better have a whole new approach to the affairs of the world." A communist China would not necessarily be a Soviet satellite. The more likely prospect—here Kennan reflected the views of John Paton Davies, his mentor on all things Chinese—was that "if you let the Russians alone in China, they will come a cropper on that problem just as everybody else has for hundreds of years."

A third principle, consistent with Kennan's emphasis on self-restraint and the contraction of responsibilities, was that expectations themselves could be a form of power. Stalin's self-confidence, which had so alarmed Marshall, rested on the belief that capitalism faced a new crisis. The task for the United States, then, was to rebuild self-confidence in those parts of the world most vital to it, while shaking that of the Soviet Union. Truth and reason, combined with economic assistance, were the only weapons available with which to do this. Employed effectively, they would "strengthen the resistance of other people to the lure of unreality, so power-ful in its effect on those who are confused and frustrated and who see no escape from their difficulties in the formidable mass of reality itself." Their use, however, would require planning, and it was not at all clear that the American political sys-tem was up to that task: "Great modern democracies are apparently incapable of dealing with the subtleties and contradictions of power relationships."

A fourth Kennan principle, therefore, was that—given the gravity of the situation—"there can be far greater concentration of authority within the operat-ing branches of our Government without detriment to the essentials of democ-racy." This would be federalism, not fascism: had not Hamilton pointed out that "the vigour of government is essential to the security of liberty"? Containment required "a more courageous acceptance of the fact that power must be delegated and delegated power must be respected." As a consequence, "many of our ideas about democracy may have to be modified."

Kennan concluded his June 18 lecture by thanking the students for the confi-dence they had shown him: "This experience has given me much more than many of you suspect."[3] The National War College had been—and with less frequency would continue to be—a place that allowed floating ideas before bright people on a confidential basis without worrying about Lippmann-like public critiques. But there was a greater distance than maps might indicate between neat geometric weekdays at Fort McNair and crisis-ridden weekends at the Pennsylvania farm: now, for Kennan, all the weekdays were weekends.

II.

The distance between theory and reality revealed itself almost at once as Kennan's insistence that the Europeans design the Marshall Plan began to run into diffi-culties. Representatives from the sixteen states expecting American assistance—minus the Soviet Union and the Eastern European satellites whose participation Stalin had forbidden—convened in Paris on July 12, 1947, to work out the amounts required and how the program would be administered. Washington's plan, Kennan reminded Marshall, was to "have no plan." But the United States did have certain requirements.

It should consider only proposals that would enable the Europeans to exist without charity so that "they can buy from us" and "will have enough self-confidence to withstand outside pressures." More fundamental, however, was the traditional concept of American security, which had assumed a Europe of free states subservient to no single great power. "If this premise were to be invalidated, there would have to be a basic revision of the whole concept of our international position," which might demand sacrifices far beyond those required by a program for European reconstruction. "But in addition, the United States, in common with most of the rest of the world, would suffer a cultural and spiritual loss incalculable in its long-term effects." It was of course important to respect European autonomy. The American people, however, were "bound to be influenced by whether the European nations are doing a good job of helping themselves."[4]

By the middle of August, it was becoming clear that they were not. The Paris conferees estimated that their countries would need $29.2 billion over the next four years—a figure well above what the Americans thought reasonable—and probably more after that. Even worse, there was no common plan for spending the money: the Europeans had simply added up each state's projected recovery costs without considering the efficiencies to be gained, or the political benefits to be achieved, by integrating their economies. These deficiencies led Under Secretary of State for Economic Affairs Will Clayton to conclude that "there is no other way to deal with this situation than to impose certain necessary conditions."[5]

But Robert M. Lovett, Acheson's replacement as under secretary of state, still hoped to salvage something of the idea that the Europeans should take the lead, so he sent Kennan on a quick trip to Paris to see what might be done. "I was very interested to meet him," Sir Oliver Franks, who headed the British delegation, recalled. "What struck me was the combination of rational, lucid exposition with controlled passion." Having "agonized within himself," Kennan came to a view "which I regarded as essentially intuitive, and then proceeded to argue with great elegance from the premises he had intuited."[6]

Geopolitical and economic interests precluded abandoning the Europeans altogether, Kennan believed, while limited resources and domestic political constraints ruled out giving them everything they wanted. Within those boundaries, there was room to maneuver. The State Department could work behind the scenes to reshape the Europeans' report. It could then treat that document as a basis for discussion, while deciding for itself what recommendations to make to the president and Congress. And it could include among these a program of interim aid without conditions, even as the conditions for a larger four-year plan were being worked out. In short, "we would listen to all that the Europeans had to say, but in the end we would not *ask* them, we would just *tell* them what they would get."[7]

Self-restraint, then, had turned out to be neither "fitting nor efficacious." In recommending its temporary abandonment, Kennan was acknowledging a paradox of planning: that short-term actions can proceed in opposite directions from long-term objectives and still be consistent with them. Only telling the Europeans what they would get would allow them to know what they should request. Only unconditional emergency aid would make extended conditional aid possible. Only by respecting European viewpoints could the Americans hope to change them.

The Paris trip had been an eye-opener: a collision of theory with reality. But it was also, in a way, exhilarating. Kennan composed a poem on the long flight home that suggested why:

> From out this world of stars and mists and motion
> The dawn—impatient of the time allowed—
> Probes sharply down the canyons of the cloud
> To find the fragments of an empty ocean.
> Let not this growing hemisphere of light
> Seduce the home-bound pilgrim to elation:
> He may not hope—against the dawn's inflation—
> To see his *darkness passing like the night.*
> The endless flight on which his *plane is sent*
> Will know no final landing field. Content
> Be he whose peace of mind from this may stem:
> That he, as Fortune's mild and patient claimant,
> Has heard the rustling of the Time-God's raiment,
> And has contrived to touch the gleaming hem.

The usual pessimism and self-pity were there, but so too, at the end of the poem, was a new theme, echoing something Bismarck had once said: "By himself the individual can create nothing; he can only wait until he hears God's footsteps resounding through events and then spring forward to grasp the hem of his mantle—that is all."[8]

Franks had it right: Kennan's performance in Paris was intuitive as well as passionate, but it fit, nonetheless, within a set of grand strategic priorities. The most important one, as Kennan described it a few weeks after his return, was to ensure that "elements of independent power are developed on the Eurasian land mass as rapidly as possible, in order to take off our shoulders some of the burden of 'bi-polarity.' To my mind, the chief beauty of the Marshall Plan is that it had outstandingly this effect."[9]

III.

The Europeans presented their report—scaled down now to $22 billion—on September 22. "We have as yet no cause to triumph," Kennan cautioned an audience at the Commerce Department two days later. But there was reason to believe that the tide of postwar extremism had peaked and was beginning to recede. The basis for Kennan's optimism lay less in the Europeans than in the confusion the Marshall Plan had caused among Soviet leaders.

Marshall's speech had "laid bare, as if with a scalpel," their inability to contribute to economic recovery. Stalin and his advisers had "tossed about on the horns of this dilemma, hoping that they could avoid a final impalement"—that was why Molotov had appeared briefly in Paris with his bevy of economic experts. Soon enough, though, the "iron logic" of the situation became clear, and the Soviet delegation fled "in the middle of the night." In ordering them to do so, Stalin divided Europe, an outcome he had hoped to avoid: it was, however, the lesser of the evils he now confronted. The Marshall Plan had forced him to choose between cooperating with a program whose success would discredit communism, or openly seeking that program's failure—a course that could, by a different route, produce the same result. It was a no-win situation: "The repercussions of it are still reverberating through the Kremlin."[10]

One became apparent in late September, when the Soviets convened a conference of East European, French, and Italian communists in Poland. In his opening address, Leningrad party boss Andrey Zhdanov acknowledged Europe's division into "socialist" and "capitalist" camps: all communists everywhere must now work for the triumph of the former over the latter. To facilitate that task, the old Communist International or Comintern—abolished during the war—would be revived as the Communist Information Bureau, or Cominform.[11]

What this meant, Kennan advised Lovett, was a tightening up of discipline within the Soviet bloc, regardless of its effects in "the left-wing liberal world." To do otherwise was to run the risk that communist parties in Western Europe, as well as in the Eastern European satellites, might evolve into a series of nationalist movements with which Moscow would eventually come into conflict. As a result, it now saw greater dangers than opportunities in European communism: "We should be able to capitalize effectively on this situation."[12]

But how? Kennan went back to the war college to work out an answer. He spoke there three times in five weeks after returning from Paris, using his lectures—still mostly extemporaneous—to clarify in his own mind what policy toward the Soviet Union should now be. He also took the opportunity to reply, off the record, to a conspicuous critic. "Our speaker this morning is Mr. X," the students were told on the first of these occasions, "the man who made Walter Lippmann famous."

Containment, Kennan insisted, did not mean preparation for war, because "it is not Russian military power which is threatening us; it is Russian political power. . . . Since it is more than a military threat, I doubt that it can effectively be met entirely by military means." But containment was not diplomacy either, because the United States and the Soviet Union shared no common interests: no Soviet diplomat was likely to return to Moscow and say, "I have just talked to these fellows and I think they have a case." Nor did containment require the "application of counter-force at a series of constantly shifting geographical and political points, corresponding to the shifts and manœuvres of Soviet policy"—the language Kennan had used in the "X" article that had so aroused Lippmann.

Instead, Kennan now spoke of selectively applied "counter pressure"—of deploying strengths against weaknesses with a view to producing a *psychological* change in the mind of the adversary. It would be like playing chess, disposing of pawns, queens, and kings "in such a way that the Russian sees it is going to be in his interests to do what you want him to do." The game would require patience as well as perseverance, but "[i]f they see that you are sufficiently determined, that you are sufficiently collected, and that you know exactly where you are going, you can sometimes put the fear of God in their hearts; and they will move."

Soviet leaders were less confident than they looked. They knew that their empire in Eastern Europe was unstable: why otherwise would they tighten their control over it? They would do so next, Kennan predicted, in Czechoslovakia, still a relatively free country from which Western influences could spread if allowed to take root. But was it really plausible to believe that 140 million Russians, who already had a third that number of minorities within their own country, would be able to take over and handle indefinitely an additional 90 million in Eastern and Central Europe?

Another reason for unease in the Kremlin went back to the differences Kennan had long perceived between Stalin's regime and the people it ruled. Three decades after the Bolshevik Revolution, the country remained what it had been for centuries, "a sea of mud and poverty and cruelty." The Russians didn't talk about this because it was dangerous to do so. They didn't do much about it, because that was even more dangerous. "But they know it in their hearts; and they are not happy about it. That I can assure you."

What, then, should the United States expect? Not that Russia would become a democracy: Americans who hoped for that were "quixotic fools," because it would never happen. But a change in the Soviet Union's international behavior could very well take place if it "gets its knuckles sharply rapped." That could stabilize the international system until—in a more distant future Russians overthrew communism for failing to keep its promises. They were "still potentially our friends. . . . I believe we still have a possibility of bringing [them] over to our side."[13]

By the end of October, Kennan could see some correspondence between his planning and the results American policy had begun to produce. Whatever difficulties the Paris conferees were having in drafting an aid request that would satisfy Washington, the very fact that the effort was under way and that Moscow could make no competitive offer had shifted the gravitational field in Europe. The center of attraction now lay in the West, a contingency for which Stalin's planners had made no provision: in time, Kennan suggested, it could pull not only European communists and satellite states from the Soviet Union's orbit, but ultimately the Russian people themselves. By persuading Marshall that he should invite *all* Europeans, east and west, to decide how Americans should spend their money, Kennan had pulled off a classic Clausewitzian maneuver: a minimal effort—the making of a single short speech—had reversed expectations in what Lippmann was calling the "Cold War," with consequences that, if managed wisely, might well determine its outcome.

IV.

On November 4, 1947, Marshall asked Kennan to prepare a brief résumé of the world situation for his use at a cabinet meeting three days later. Completed on the sixth, PPS/13 turned out to be the first comprehensive statement of U.S. grand strategy since the end of World War II. Marshall was impressed enough to read a summary aloud when the Cabinet convened on the seventh, and President Truman, in turn, requested a copy of the full paper. Kennan's views on *American* policy had now made their way to the top.

PPS/13 began with a lesson in geopolitics. The simultaneous defeats of Germany and Japan had left power vacuums into which the Soviet Union had tried to move, with a view to extending its "virtual domination over all, or as much as possible, of the Eurasian land mass." That offensive had now come to a standstill, partly because the postwar radicalism that fueled it was diminishing, but mostly because the United States had surprised the Kremlin by delaying its own military withdrawal from former enemy territories, by offering economic assistance to demoralized Europeans, and by using the United Nations to rally resistance. The question now was what to do next.

Kennan's answer was less, not more, for these accomplishments had "stretched our resources dangerously far in several respects." Americans still occupied portions of Germany, Italy, Austria, and Korea, as well as all of Japan: that task could only become more difficult as time went on. However effective the Marshall Plan was proving to be, it set no precedents: it was probably the last major effort of that kind that the United States should make.

> [I]t is clearly unwise for us to continue the attempt to carry alone, or largely single-handed, the opposition to Soviet expansion. It is urgently necessary for us to restore something of the balance of power in Europe and Asia by strengthening local forces of independence and by getting them to assume part of our burden.

That meant making allies of defeated enemies: to continue punishing the Germans and the Japanese would only perpetuate the power vacuums that had encouraged Soviet ambitions in the first place. But restoring the balance would also require abandoning actual and potential allies whose defense would now be too costly. Czechoslovakia fell into that category, as did Nationalist China and noncommunist Korea: where territories were "not of decisive strategic importance to us, our main task is to extricate ourselves without too great a loss of prestige."

The Soviet Union would attempt to exploit discontent in France, Greece, and especially Italy, where American forces would soon withdraw, while keeping its own hand concealed so as "to leave us in the frustrated position of having no one to oppose but local communists, or possibly the satellites." The United States "should be free to call the play," determining whether action was to be directed against the U.S.S.R. or only its stooges. The latter would be strongly preferable and would not necessarily lead to war. That danger was "vastly exaggerated in many quarters."[14]

Kennan's was, then, a minimalist strategy, at least as noteworthy for what it rejected as for what it endorsed. It contained none of the Wilsonian idealism that had shaped American foreign policy during and immediately after the two world wars. There was no Truman-like commitment "to support free peoples" wherever freedom was under attack: instead Kennan called for casting some adrift, while defending others who only a few years earlier had grossly violated freedom. The atomic bomb was nowhere mentioned in PPS/13, which stressed the limits of American power and the consequent need to distinguish vital from peripheral interests. The task would be to deploy strengths against weaknesses: "victory" would not be unconditional surrender, but rather a shift in the minds of Soviet leaders that would reverse their expectations about success.

Six days after Marshall presented these recommendations to the president, Kennan sent the secretary of state a report evaluating the Policy Planning Staff's accomplishments during its first six months. Consisting of five members—two others would soon be added—the staff had sought to remain small, flexible, and unencumbered by administrative problems. It had prepared, during this period, thirteen formal reports, eleven of which made recommendations that had "found some reflection in subsequent operations." If work continued at this level over the next six months, the result should be a collection of staff papers relating to all major areas. Together they would constitute "something like a global concept of United States policy."

Kennan acknowledged suspicions about his organization elsewhere in the State Department, where no such "uniform framework of thought" was possible. But the Policy Planning Staff was meeting a broader requirement, for with the establishment of the National Security Council in July 1947, the department needed a unit that could function as a counterpart to the Pentagon's planning units "in matters affecting *policy as a whole.*" If the staff did not already exist, something like it would have had to be created. And with Marshall having appointed Kennan as his representative on the NSC staff, "a desirable symmetry" had been reached in coordinating diplomatic with military strategy.[15]

What Kennan could not yet say was how critical that appointment would turn out to be. Over the next two years the Policy Planning Staff became the principal source of ideas for the National Security Council. Papers prepared under a PPS prefix were routinely renumbered, with little modification, as NSC papers, and if approved by the president—most of them were—they became national policy. Since Kennan so dominated his own staff, this arrangement had made him, by the beginning of 1948, not just the State Department's but the nation's top policy planner.[16]

V.

He was not generally available to the press. His name was not on the directory in the cold marble lobby. To reach his office, you had to pass portentous murals, lengthy corridors, private dining rooms, and watchful guards. "The buzzers buzz, a door opens, and here he is: Mr. X—George Frost Kennan, of Milwaukee and Moscow."

> He is tall—about six feet—slender, and good-looking in a refined and sensitive way. His eyes are blue, his chin well-formed, his mouth highly expressive, chilling or charming as its owner decrees. His smile, when used, melts an aloof expression into a surprising surge of warmth and friendliness. Nevertheless, [he] is not the type of man one would call "Georgie." Some, finding him distant, are tempted to address him by his middle name.

The job he held defied description. It could involve preparation for next week's squabble with the Russians, or something that might not happen for fifteen years. His decisions could affect everything from the cost of living to whether there would be war or peace. Prepared for whatever problem might wind up in its lap, the Policy Planning Staff met in a room without a phone, an intercom, or baskets marked "incoming" and "outgoing"—just a long table and eight green leather chairs. A connecting door led to Marshall's office.

The profile, by Philip Harkins, appeared in the *New York Herald Tribune* magazine on January 4, 1948, accompanied by an austere but (this time) current photograph of its subject. Entitled "Mysterious Mr. X," it was based on an interview with Kennan, although he was still not acknowledging the pseudonym. He would not have allowed access, however, without the State Department's approval: anonymity, it seemed, was no longer expected, and the "X" article appeared not to have been such a catastrophe after all.

Despite Harkins's ponderously mixed metaphors—Kennan was "the prize package in the deep freeze that the security-conscious State Department has installed for 'the cold war' "—the article did contain some shrewd insights. Kennan wore no cloak, carried no dagger, did not smoke, drank little, and ate judiciously, "out of respect to a dormant ulcer." He loved the guitar and with graceful gestures liked to imitate playing it. Circles might show under his eyes at the end of a long day, but he was still ready to draw on Dostoyevsky for insights into the Russian mind. He could even act out scenes from *Crime and Punishment* to show that although the Soviet government might believe that ends justified means, the Russian conscience shouted "No!" And what of Kennan's own conscience? It was, Harkins noted, Protestant, midwestern, and hence "baffling to Europeans and Orientals," but it had driven a young man from Milwaukee to Moscow and back again. Now it had conspired (more metaphors) "with a terrifying whirlwind of outside forces to put [him] at a radioactive chessboard opposite skillful and determined opponents."[17]

It's not clear what Kennan thought of the Harkins piece—he probably cringed—but his family was impressed: the clipping wound up in several scrapbooks. It felt strange, Jeanette recalled, "to have somebody so close to you and that you love so much, suddenly so important." Annelise remembered George's fame as having emerged more gradually: "I really can't say that I suddenly felt that I was the wife of an important man." But "I wasn't stupid." Invitations started arriving "to dinner here, and to dinner there. People are quick." Especially "the ambassadresses."

With George now no longer at the war college, the Kennans were renting a house at 4418 Q Street in the Foxhall Village neighborhood just west of Georgetown. "I was always the one who did everything about the house," Annelise explained. "And with the children, except if there was something important, I was the one who had to do it. He was very busy." George lacked the strength "to be social every day of the week," so the farm became all the more necessary. Weekends at East Berlin were "absolutely sacred," not least because those were the only days he could spend with Grace and Joan. The Kennans, at one point, even declined a dinner at the Achesons': "Whatever they felt, they were very nice about it." The farm had one other advantage, which was to substitute for summer camp: "We couldn't afford that."[18]

Weekdays normally began with the Policy Planning Staff members arriving at their desks to find stacks of overnight telegrams, distributed by areas of responsibility. There would be only an hour or two to read them before Kennan would call a meeting. "We'd all gather around the table, and George would start talking," Ware Adams recalled. "Very often none of us would say a word, but we'd just be looking at him. And he, by watching us, seemed to know just what we were think-ing." Robert Tufts, the staff's economics specialist, confirmed that

> Kennan was a very dominant personality, and he certainly did lead those seminars. The rest of us kept our remarks much briefer. But I didn't have the feeling, and I don't think others had the feeling, that Kennan was overdoing it. We listened, and we lis-tened carefully, and we thought carefully about what we had to say. We kept it rather brief, not because we thought we would annoy Kennan if we were long-winded, but we tried to make sure what we had to say was to the point.

John Paton Davies thought Kennan handled the staff well. As Foreign Service officers, they were not used to such seminars: "George was operating at an intel-lectual level several degrees above theirs. Nevertheless, he was most gracious and considerate of the feelings of these people."

The important papers, Davies added, originated with Kennan and were drafted by Kennan: "We sat by in some awe and tried to make intelligent comments about them. He invited the comments. He welcomed the criticism." That was a good thing, because "George does have a tendency to go sailing off, and he has to be brought back to earth." The Policy Planning Staff, he thought, functioned some-what as Annelise did. Someone would say: "Well, George, that's going a little far, isn't it?" He would then "tone it down and it would come into place." Kennan needed "a backboard against which to play his game. He's got to bounce it off of somebody who will react against it."[19]

One person who did was Dorothy Fosdick, recruited by Kennan in 1948 to help with United Nations affairs. "We were not equals," she stressed. "Kennan was the prince, and we were the advisers to him." Being female, however, gave her a special status:

> Kennan once told me that women throughout history had been confidential advis-ers to monarchs. Their role was to listen sympathetically, to provide comfort, to give private counsel. I didn't see this as demeaning. I've never been a self-conscious femi-nist. He certainly didn't see me as a threat of any kind. And I could always speak very frankly to him and say exactly what I thought about issues.

When crises would arise, Kennan would take Fosdick to lunch at J. Edgar Hoover's favorite restaurant, the Allies Inn. With the FBI director and his partner Clyde Tolson usually seated nearby, Kennan would "pour out his heart to me." That was what he saw as a woman's role: "to listen, to console, to quietly advise—and I regarded it at the time as a very high compliment. He knew he could trust me not to repeat what he'd said."[20]

Chip Bohlen, another confidant, was never a member of the staff—his official title now was Counselor in the State Department—although he participated frequently in its discussions. If inclined during the war to be optimistic about relations with Moscow, the British embassy in Washington noted, Bohlen had for some time shared the harsher view of Soviet policy "which the less career-minded and more profound Kennan has always expressed." Adams nonetheless found the contrasts fascinating. "They were both thinkers, but in different ways": Kennan was the dreamer, Bohlen the practical one. "It was interesting to see two people so unlike agreeing as much as they did," something that had not been true in the past and would not be in the future.

As Kennan had hinted to Marshall, others in the State Department doubted the Policy Planning Staff's usefulness. "I think it was all right," Loy Henderson observed neutrally, "but it was kind of a paper thing. It had no way of enforcing itself. The geographic bureaus were where the real power was." Henderson and the other assistant secretaries, Davies explained, resisted planning. They felt that "you had to ride like a bush pilot on the seat of your pants. You couldn't anticipate how things were going to go, therefore you took your cues from what was happening right in front of you. That was real. The rest was day-dreaming, or speculative, and therefore did not contribute very much." But Marshall respected Kennan and was used to working with planners. Kennan's assignment was to provide a broad outlook, which Marshall valued because he understood that "you can't proceed from 1A to 1B to 1C and so on down. You had to have an overview."[21]

That was how Kennan understood his responsibilities. "Look," he remembered telling the staff, "I want to hear your opinion. We'll talk these things out as long as we need to. But, in the end, the opinion of this Staff is what you can make me understand, and what I can state." There was, he believed, no such thing as a collective document, because "it has to pass, in the end, through the filter of the intelligence of the man who wrote it."

I knew that I could not go to [Marshall] and say to him: "Well, you know, this paper isn't a very good one. I didn't really agree with it, but the majority of the Staff were of this opinion." The General would not have accepted this from me. He would have said: "Kennan, I put you there to direct this staff. When I want the opinion of the staff, I want your opinion." So, I did insist that the papers had to reflect my own views.

Kennan recalled listening to the staff with respect and patience. He quickly discovered, though, that when "people get to talking, they talk and they talk. But they don't talk each other into conclusions." He once admonished them:

> We are like a wrestler who walks around another wrestler for about three minutes and can never find a place where he wants to grab hold. When you get into that situation, you then have to take the imperfect opportunity. There's going to come a time in each of these discussions when I'm going to say: "Enough." And I will go away and write the best paper I can.

At such moments, Tufts remembered, Kennan would disappear, and a paper would soon appear. "He could dictate a better paper than most of us could write, even after editing."

Having worked with Kennan since 1944, Dorothy Hessman knew how to keep up with him, even when his intensity caused him to lose track of time, place, and posture: "I was sitting by the desk one day, and he was pacing back and forth behind me, and suddenly his voice sounded a little strange. So I turned around and looked and he had sat down in the leather armchair with his feet over one arm and his back over the other and then stiffened up—so that he lay there across this chair." On other occasions, however, he needed an audience. Marshall Green, a young Foreign Service officer who went with Kennan to Japan early in 1948, found that one of his jobs was to "look intelligent." Kennan would speak to Green, while Hessman took it down. This gave his writing a conversational flavor, and "when he was through, he didn't have to change a word of it."[22]

During the two and a half years that Kennan ran the Policy Planning Staff, it produced over seventy formal papers: the complete set came to more than nine hundred single-spaced pages. "The world was our oyster," he later wrote, "there was no problem of American foreign policy to which we could not address ourselves—indeed, to which it was not our duty to address ourselves—if we found the problem serious enough and significant enough to warrant the effort." Kennan meant the papers to serve, not as a theoretical framework for the conduct of international relations, but rather as applications of certain "methods and principles" to "practical situations." No other office in the State Department produced so many papers on so many issues over so many months, "from a single point of view."

That was, if anything, an understatement. Kennan's Policy Planning Staff papers were the most thorough specification of interests, threats, and feasible responses that anyone had yet worked out within the U.S. government, and it would have been difficult to find anything comparable in any other government at the time. They were an intellectual tour de force: an extraordinary attempt to devise a global grand strategy. But they were also, as Kennan acknowledged, "one man's concept of how our government ought to behave and by what principles it ought to be guided."[23] They rested on the premise that a single policy planner (Kennan) could suggest to a single policy maker (Marshall) what he, and hence the nation, ought to do. They were, in this sense, strikingly solipsistic.

Kennan's strategy would depend, therefore, on the extent to which he could embed it in the minds of others. His policy papers, like his lectures, were a starting point, for strategies require coherence. But they must also inspire confidence, overcome resistance, and adapt to the unexpected. If they fail to take root, they wither. Kennan's task was now as much cultivation as conception: the farm had prepared him for it, arguably, about as well as the war college had.

VI.

The next set of issues the Policy Planning Staff faced, after getting the Marshall Plan under way, arose as aftershocks of the British withdrawal from the eastern Mediterranean. That unexpected development had left a new power vacuum in an area of strategic importance to the United States, not as the result of an enemy's defeat in war but from an ally's weakness in the first years of peace. The danger was the one Kennan had warned of in Western Europe: that the Soviet Union, working through the international communist movement, might fill the void, bringing southeastern Europe and potentially also the Near East within its orbit. The test for his strategy was whether minimalism would meet this threat. Could the Truman administration limit its response chiefly to economic assistance, while waiting for internal contradictions within the Soviet empire to halt its expansion? Or would something more be required?

Lovett posed the question bluntly in the late summer of 1947: what would happen if communists took power in Italy or Greece? The staff papers Kennan produced acknowledged the seriousness of the situation. The Italian Communist Party, now the strongest force in Italian politics, would, if it came to power, menace the interests of the United States in Western Europe, the eastern Mediterranean, even in South America, where there was a large Italian emigrant population.

A communist victory in the Greek civil war would produce similar results in Europe. In either instance, the Soviet Union would have extended its political and military control "beyond the high-water mark" it had reached at the end of the war. But constraints on American power limited what might be done: the United States could not, for example, send troops to fight the communists inside Greece or Italy, for that would require deploying forces it did not have to battle-fields it would not have chosen. It could, however, secure air and naval bases in those countries while strengthening the Sixth Fleet, which already dominated the Mediterranean.

The idea, Kennan explained, would be to make it clear "that extensions of Soviet military power, by means of concealed aggression, . . . will be countered by corresponding advances of the bases of U.S. strategic power." This is what he had in mind when he spoke to the National War College students of "counter-pressures." These would not, as the "X" article had implied, correspond precisely to those undertaken by Moscow; rather, "concealed aggression" would produce "corresponding advances" in *overall* American military strength in the region, which could then be used to exploit Soviet weaknesses. Local communists might destabilize a country internally, but only at the cost of attracting greater U.S. air and naval power into the region, something Stalin could hardly favor. The strategy would require patience and steady nerves, for getting Kremlin leaders to see that their ambitions endangered their interests might take months or even years. It would, however, remain within the limits of American capabilities. It was, in this sense, still minimalist.[24]

So too was another Kennan recommendation for containing national communist movements. The Central Intelligence Agency's legal advisers were not sure that Congress, when it established that organization in the summer of 1947, had meant for it to engage in covert activities. "[W]e are handicapped," Kennan told presidential aide Clark Clifford in August, "by the lack of ability to use the techniques of undercover political operation[s] which are being used against us." Kennan admitted to Forrestal, now the first secretary of defense, that the American people would probably never approve of policies relying on such methods: "I do feel, however, that there are cases where it might be essential to our security that we fight fire with fire." Italy and Greece were among them.[25]

For the most part, the Truman administration followed Kennan's advice. Italy was the first topic the National Security Council took up when it met for the first time on September 26, 1947, and PPS/9—Kennan's paper—provided the basis for discussion. NSC 1/1, "The Position of the United States with Respect to Italy," incorporated with only minor revisions the arguments he had made, and in December Truman approved it. When American troops were in fact withdrawn, Kennan suggested a presidential warning that the United States would not allow the overthrow of Italian democracy. Truman issued the statement on the thirteenth: if it became apparent that the freedom and independence of Italy were being threatened, directly or indirectly, the United States would be "obliged to consider what measures would be appropriate for the maintenance of peace and security."[26]

Five days later the president authorized the CIA, "within the limit of available funds," to conduct "covert psychological operations designed to counteract Soviet and Soviet-inspired activities which . . . are designed to discredit and defeat the United States in its endeavors to promote world peace and security." Kennan had not been alone in favoring this—pressures to undertake disavowable or "black" measures were converging from within the new agency and from Forrestal as well. It was at Kennan's insistence, however, that the NSC was given the authority to review all such operations: "We would want to examine the situation in all its aspects in case of any suggested operation, and to judge each case strictly on its merits." And Kennan was the State Department representative on the NSC staff.[27]

Meanwhile Kennan was battling his former superior Loy Henderson—now director of the Office of Near Eastern and African Affairs—over what to do about Greece, where the war against the communist guerrillas was going badly. Henderson wanted to send American troops to show "that we will, if necessary, resort to force to meet aggression." Kennan objected strongly: "We might find ourselves in a difficult position from which it would be hard to withdraw and equally hard to keep other nations from withdrawing the contingents they had contributed." The argument extended into January 1948, with Marshall in the end settling it in Kennan's favor by ruling that before any commitment of troops could be made,

> we would have to have a definition of the purpose of any action involving armed forces, an assessment of what would be required in the way of forces, and of what logistical support would be needed, an estimate of the probable effects on [the] domestic economy and on public opinion in this country, and a judgment as to whether we would be prepared to accept these implications.

The language was tough enough to have been Kennan's, as indeed it was: he took the notes in the NSC meeting at which Lovett presented Marshall's views.[28]

On the future of the British mandate in Palestine, however, Kennan agreed with

Henderson. Awarded by the League of Nations after World War I, it had placed Great Britain in the position of mediating between the Arab and Jewish inhabitants of the region—never an easy task, but an especially difficult one in the wake of World War II and the Holocaust because the international Zionist movement was determined at last to establish a Jewish state. Frustrated and overstretched, the British turned the issue over to the United Nations in February 1947, at the same time that they announced their decision to withdraw from Greece and Turkey. The General Assembly, the following November, voted with American support to partition Palestine between the Arabs and the Jews, but the Arabs immediately rejected this two-state solution. The question confronting the United States, then, was whether to help the United Nations impose partition against the will of the Arabs—a decision that might well require the use of military force—or to seek some other outcome.

Kennan and Henderson adamantly favored the latter approach. "Any assistance the U.S. might give to the enforcement of partition," the Policy Planning Staff concluded on January 20, 1948, would produce "deep-seated antagonism" throughout the Muslim world over many years. That could endanger military base rights and access to oil, which might in turn threaten the success of the Marshall Plan. The Soviet Union, whether it supported the Arabs, the Jews, or both at once, could only gain as a result. Unless this policy was reversed, Kennan added in his diary a week later, there would be no alternative to taking over major military and police responsibility for maintaining a state of affairs in Palestine "violently resented by the whole Arab world." Americans could not be "the keepers and moral guardians of all the peoples in this world."[29]

Here, too, Kennan prevailed, although not easily. Dean Rusk, director of the State Department's Office of United Nations Affairs, thought him too pessimistic about partition. Marshall and Lovett advised caution, aware of the objections supporters of Zionism would make to any change in policy. Kennan persisted, however, and on February 11 he produced a revised staff paper that boiled the options down to three: full support for partition, whatever the international consequences; a shift to neutrality, which would make it hard to justify existing commitments in Greece and Italy; or some form of international trusteeship for an undivided Palestine, a decision that would preclude the formation of a Jewish state but "would regain in large measure our strategically important position in the area." Boxed in by unpalatable alternatives, Marshall took the third recommendation to Truman, who approved it early in March—or, at least, appeared to have done so.[30]

With respect to Italy, Greece, and Palestine, then, Kennan maneuvered skillfully. He fought off pressures to send troops to these regions, while showing how the careful expansion of American naval and air capabilities might cause the Soviet Union to restrain the activities of local communists. He encouraged the CIA to develop its own covert means of countering those activities, while arranging to supervise how this would be done. And he retained throughout the Marshall Plan's focus on economic recovery as the principal instrument of containment. It was—or, at least, it seemed to be at the time—an impressive performance.

VII.

There was, nevertheless, an improvisational character to most of the Policy Planning Staff's work in 1947. Because it had inherited existing crises in Western Europe, the Mediterranean, and the Near East, there had not been time, Kennan acknowledged, to "come up for air, look around us, and attempt to take stock of America's world position as a whole."[31] He tried to do that hastily in the global survey he prepared for Marshall in November, but the first region for which the staff was able to initiate its own planning was East Asia, a part of the world not yet fully caught up in the emerging Soviet-American rivalry. Once again Kennan dominated the planning process, but the process refined his own thinking as it progressed.

When Kennan wrote of the need to develop independent power on the Eurasian landmass as quickly as possible, he was echoing an anxiety felt by British and American strategists since the completion of the Trans-Siberian Railway in the early twentieth century: the possibility that a single hostile state—whether German or Russian—might someday control all the territory from the English Channel to the Pacific Ocean. That would neutralize the advantages maritime strength had long given Great Britain and the United States. It was one of the reasons Kennan worried so much about the war having left power vacuums along the periphery of the Soviet Union.[32] But as he thought more about this, he began to see that not all such vacuums were dangerous. The critical issue was how territory might be used, not how much an enemy might rule.

Kennan came to this view by way of China, which he regarded as more likely to suck in power than to be a base from which to project it. The Joint Chiefs of Staff had called, in June 1947, for a major effort to rescue Chiang Kai-shek: Mao Zedong's forces were "tools of Soviet policy," the chiefs insisted, and if the Truman

Doctrine was to be effective, the administration must apply it consistently wherever Soviet expansionism was occurring. Skeptical but still sensitive about his mediation mission in China having failed, Marshall took no position on the proposal, suggesting instead that Truman send General Albert C. Wedemeyer, who had served as an aide to Chiang during the war, to assess his current prospects. Upon his return, Wedemeyer endorsed the chiefs' views, so Kennan volunteered to have the Policy Planning Staff do its own study. Marshall, with relief, accepted the offer.[33]

On November 3, Kennan advised him that while a Chinese Communist victory would be a serious setback, it would "not be a catastrophe." Mao could hardly rule all of China while deferring to Moscow; and only massive American assistance—more than was contemplated for all of Western Europe—could save the Nationalists. China was not the place, then, to confront the Soviet Union, despite the fact that Chiang's highly vocal supporters in the United States would demand doing so. The Truman administration should extend only the aid necessary to appease these domestic critics and, if possible, to prevent any immediate collapse of the Nationalist regime. It should not go beyond that point.[34]

Marshall presented this recommendation to Truman, who quietly accepted it. Early in 1948 the president asked Congress for $570 million in nonmilitary assistance for China, only slightly more than what he had requested a year earlier for Greece and Turkey, and much less than the $17 billion he was seeking for the Marshall Plan. After reducing the appropriation still further, Congress approved the China Aid Act in April. Kennan's role in cutting off aid to the Chinese Nationalists—for that was what these decisions amounted to—had been pivotal. He seized the initiative after Marshall passed it to him, he stood up to the Joint Chiefs and to Wedemeyer, and in doing so he carried his opposition to the Truman Doctrine from the realm of theory into that of policy. Most important, he did it with Truman's approval.[35]

Kennan's rationale for what he admitted was a "plague on both your houses" strategy reflected a new calculation: that hostility, divorced from capability, posed no danger. The United States must never again be threatened from Asia, he told a Pentagon audience in January. But only the industrial regions of Siberia, Manchuria, northern China, and northern Korea could provide bases from which to mount an attack. All were already under actual or probable Soviet control. Politically immature, economically desperate, no other mainland peoples—including the rest of the Chinese—could, by themselves, pose any danger. The Truman administration could, therefore, safely abandon Chiang Kai-shek. It could even remove American occupation forces from southern Korea unless that territory was deemed "of sufficient strategic importance to retain." Kennan doubted that it would be.

Japan, however, was different. It had shown itself to have dangerous capabilities, but these were now under American control. Disarming this former enemy was of course necessary, but it was just as vital to see that a demilitarized Japan did not fall within a Soviet sphere of influence: that would require "a stable, internally strong Japanese government." Current occupation policies had focused too much on punishment and not enough on what was to follow. Adjustments were therefore necessary: the United States should commit itself to defending the country while strengthening its economy. It should "dispense with bromides about democratization" in Japan and in "the island world generally."[36]

Herein lay the origins of what later became known as the "defensive perimeter" strategy: that the United States would use its air and naval strength to hold islands, while liquidating positions on the Asian mainland. "[W]e are greatly overextended . . . in that area," Kennan explained in PPS/23, a comprehensive review of commitments he completed for Marshall in February 1948. Americans had clung too long to the idea of remaking China, an end far beyond their means. The Policy Planning Staff should determine what parts of East Asia are "absolutely vital to our security," and the United States should then ensure that these remain "in hands which we can control or rely on."

Kennan framed this recommendation within the need to choose between universal and particularist approaches in foreign policy. Universalism sought to apply the same principles everywhere. It favored procedures embodied in the United Nations and in other international organizations. It smoothed over the national peculiarities and conflicting ideologies that confused and irritated so many Americans. Its appeal lay in its promise to "relieve us of the necessity of dealing with the world as it is." Particularism, in contrast, questioned "legalistic concepts." It assumed appetites for power that only "counter-force" could control. It valued alliances, but only if based on communities of interest, not on the "abstract formalism" of obligations that might preclude pursuing national defense and global stability. Universalism entangled interests in cumbersome parliamentarianism. Particularism encouraged purposefulness, coordination, and economy of effort—qualities the nation would need "if we are to be sure of accomplishing our purposes."[37]

Kennan had not set out to become a philosopher, but his job was turning him into one. He was making the point, in PPS/23, that while ideals existed in people's minds, capabilities determined what states could do. Ends for this reason were infinitely expandable; means could never be. Calculating relationships between ends and means required calibration: there was no place here for the untethered aspirations Americans had traditionally floated above the world, before they took over the responsibility for running the world. Now they would have to learn to operate like everyone else. The argument paralleled Hans Morgenthau's in his classic text, *Politics Among Nations,* the first edition of which appeared in the fall of 1948. Within the government, Kennan was ahead of him.[38]

VIII.

He was still enough of a Foreign Service officer, though, to distrust desk-bound perspectives. "The Director and members of the Staff must do more travelling and get about more," Kennan advised Marshall late in 1947. There was real danger that their isolation might separate them from reality in their work and cause them to "cease to have their feet on the ground."[39]

Japan offered an opportunity. The country anchored Kennan's East Asian strategy, but he had never been there. He knew that the first George Kennan, who had spent time in Japan, regarded its people as the Asians with whom Americans had the most in common. The second Kennan wondered whether it had been necessary to risk war with Japan while on the verge of war with Nazi Germany: the diplomat John Van Antwerp MacMurray, Kennan liked to point out, had argued as early as 1935 that such a course could only benefit the Soviet Union. From the moment he joined the Policy Planning Staff, Davies encouraged Kennan to challenge the punitive aspects of American occupation policy in Japan and to oppose any premature peace treaty that might leave the country unable to defend itself against the U.S.S.R. "Of all the failures of United States policy in the wake of World War II," Kennan wrote in his diary at the end of January 1948, "history will rate as the most grievous" the mismanagement of defeated enemies forced to surrender unconditionally. He had Japan chiefly in mind.[40]

Shifting policy, however, would require taking on General Douglas MacArthur, the supreme commander for the Allied powers in Japan: so far neither the president, nor the State Department, nor the Pentagon had dared to attempt it. MacArthur had gone from winning the war in the Pacific—as he liked to think of it—to running the most successful military occupation—as he also liked to think of it—since Caesar invaded Gaul and Britain. Determined to remake Japan from top to bottom, MacArthur compensated its victims, purged its government, broke up its big industries, redistributed land, secured votes for women, and demanded the teaching of democratic values. His reforms went beyond anything progressivism or the New Deal had accomplished in the United States, even though MacArthur considered himself a right-wing Republican.[41] The intoxications of power and the satisfactions of exile overrode ideological consistency and political practicality in the general's mind: he had, by his own choice, not set foot in the United States since 1939, but in the spring of 1948 he was eagerly awaiting a draft from his party—which never came—for its presidential nomination.

With little interest in Europe, less knowledge of the Soviet Union, and no inclination at all to defer to Washington, MacArthur cultivated a shogunlike remoteness that made it seem disrespectful, even impertinent, to ask how Japan might fit into the strategy of containment. He was, in Kennan's view, a major threat to its success: MacArthur's policies seemed almost designed "for the purpose of rendering Japanese society vulnerable to Communist political pressures and paving the way for a Communist takeover."[42]

Tutored by Marshall on what to expect, Kennan left for Japan on February 26, 1948, only two days after submitting PPS/23. He felt, he later recalled, as if he were establishing diplomatic relations with a suspicious foreign government. Accompanying him were a Pentagon representative, General Cortlandt Van Rensselaer Schuyler, Marshall Green, and Dorothy Hessman. The Seattle-Tokyo leg of the flight, which required thirty hours and two refueling stops, was as hair-raising as any of Kennan's wartime transatlantic journeys, and even more exhausting. Upon arrival he was received, it seemed to Green, as a spy from the State Department. Kennan was told later that MacArthur, furious at his being sent, had said: "I'll have him briefed until it comes out of his ears."

MacArthur began by subjecting his guests to an interminable lunch: "We were so weary we were falling off our chairs." The general turned his back on Kennan, giving Schuyler a two-hour table-pounding monologue on the occupation's accomplishments. It concluded with the claim that the great events of the next thousand years were sure to take place in "the Orient," and that Americans now had the opportunity, in Japan, to plant the seeds of Christianity and democracy throughout the region, thereby "fundamentally alter[ing] the course of world history."[43]

The general was a universalist in need of tethering, and that is what Kennan—once he had recovered—set out to do. After a day of uninformative briefings by

MacArthur's staff, Kennan sent a polite reminder "that I had questions of some moment which I was under instructions to discuss personally with him." There was no direct response, but an aide soon arrived to conduct an audition. Satisfied, he extended an invitation for Kennan to lecture, on the next day, to a group of senior officers. It was a second tryout, in which Kennan's improvisational skills served him well: having had much greater exposure to Soviet developments than any of them, "I think I was able to add to their knowledge and to clarify some of their impressions." MacArthur was not present, but Kennan got the sense "that he was, in some way or other, excellently informed of what I had to say." Green, who did attend, found the talk "absolutely brilliant," like an eye "piercing into eternity." A summons then arrived for Kennan to spend the evening of March 5 alone with the great man.[44]

They could have started the conversation—no record confirms that they did— by reminiscing about Milwaukee: MacArthur's father's family was from the city, and young Douglas had spent two years living with his mother in a local hotel while preparing for the examinations that would get him into West Point in 1899.[45] A second shared interest turned out to be the defensive perimeter strategy. MacArthur had no intention of using American troops to Christianize Asia, favoring instead the creation of an arc of island bases running from the Aleutians and Midway through Okinawa and the Philippines. His reforms, he claimed, had not weakened Japan's economy or compromised its security, but "academic theorizers of a left-wing variety" had influenced some of them. Changing priorities might make sense: this would require, however, the consent of the Far Eastern Commission, the international body established upon Japan's surrender to oversee the occupation. Inconveniently, its membership included the Soviet Union.

Knowing the "flealike agility" with which MacArthur had used this argument in the past when asked to align his policies with Washington's, Kennan was ready for it. The commission's mandate, he pointed out, extended only to supervising surrender terms, not to determining Japan's postwar future. The FEC could not be abolished, but making this distinction would leave it with little to do. MacArthur liked the idea, slapping his thigh in enthusiasm and telling Kennan this was "exactly the right line for us to take." The rest of the conversation proceeded smoothly, and they parted amicably. Green admired the way Kennan handled MacArthur. The State Department, he was saying, wanted the general to remain in charge, but without the nuisance of the FEC: "[T]his appealed to MacArthur, because MacArthur was an intelligent man."[46]

Kennan's lengthy report, however, called for an end to MacArthur's reforms, a reduction in his authority, a revival of the Japanese economy, and the eventual transfer of political control to the Japanese themselves. It was the East Asian equivalent of the Marshall Plan's requirement that western Germany be included in any program for the recovery of Europe. With strong support in Washington, Kennan's recommendations sailed through the NSC at the end of September 1948, and on October 9 President Truman approved them. The shift in Japanese occupation policy came to be known as the "Reverse Course": the course reversed was the one MacArthur had set.[47]

It was Kennan, in this instance, who had shown agility. He had concealed his resentment of MacArthur's arrogance, as well as his contempt for the sycophantic establishment that surrounded him. He had won the general's trust by impressing his aides, found commonalities upon which he and MacArthur could agree, and then *appeared* to expand the supreme commander's authority by proposing to emasculate the FEC. In fact, this constrained it, for with the FEC effectively out of business, MacArthur could no longer switch the administrative hats he wore— one international, the other American—when the actions he was instructed to take under one or the other displeased him. From this point on his orders came only from Washington, leaving the outmaneuvered general no excuses for ignoring or evading them.[48]

Kennan regarded his role in the tethering of MacArthur as, after the Marshall Plan, "the most significant constructive contribution I was ever able to make in government." On no other occasion did he make recommendations of such scope that met with such widespread acceptance: "I turned our whole occupation policy."[49]

IX.

Fixing policy in Japan, however, was like repairing a bridge on the farm: a lot could happen behind your back while you were concentrating on the task at hand. On February 25, 1948, the day before Kennan left for Tokyo, President Eduard Beneš of Czechoslovakia reluctantly agreed, under pressure from Moscow, to the formation of a communist government. Kennan for months had been predicting such a development. It would be, he insisted, a *defensive* response to the success of the Marshall Plan, requiring no action on the part of the United States. Czechoslovakia, after all, had been within the Soviet Union's sphere of influence since the

Red Army liberated it in 1945. An end to multiparty rule there would simply consolidate the status quo. It would not be part of a plan for "an unprovoked Soviet
military conquest of Western Europe."[50]

But Kennan failed to anticipate the emotional response to the Prague "coup"
in Western Europe and the United States. Less than a decade earlier the British
and the French had forced the same Beneš to accept the Munich agreement, now
universally regarded as having led to World War II. It was difficult to watch a
similar tragedy unfold without thinking about World War III—especially when,
on March 10, the broken body of the Czech foreign minister, Jan Masaryk, was
found sprawled in a courtyard beneath his office. Whether he died from murder
or suicide hardly mattered: he was the son of Tomáš Masaryk, who with Woodrow Wilson's encouragement had founded the state of Czechoslovakia after World
War I. His death symbolized the suppression, yet again, of the only democratic
regime in Central Europe.

An immediate effect was to strengthen a case British foreign secretary Ernest
Bevin had begun to make in December 1947: that Great Britain, France, and the
Benelux countries should form the "Western Union," a political and military alliance directed ostensibly against any resurgence of German aggression but in fact
against the Soviet Union. Kennan had been skeptical, warning Marshall that any
military buildup would divert the countries involved from the more important
task of economic recovery. The Russians had no intention of attacking anyone.
What they wanted instead was to take control from within, through "stooge political elements." The Marshall Plan was the best way to keep that from happening.[51]

By the time the Policy Planning Staff got around to analyzing Bevin's proposal,
however, the Czechoslovak coup had occurred and Kennan was in Japan, unable
to guide its deliberations. George Butler, its deputy director, was a Latin American specialist, so he asked a temporary member, Kennan's former Riga colleague
Bernard Gufler, to take on the assignment. Gufler, no expert either, sought help
from the Office of European Affairs, whose director, John D. Hickerson, not only
shared Bevin's concerns but wanted to go one step further: the time had come,
he believed, for a formal U.S. commitment to the defense of Western Europe.
PPS/27, completed on March 23, reflected Hickerson's reasoning. Fears of Soviet
aggression, it concluded, were now so strong that assurances of military support
from the United States were needed. Kennan was not consulted: "I was shocked
to learn, on my return, that . . . my deputy had produced a Planning Staff paper
blessing this idea."[52]

This had happened, as Kennan remembered it, because the State Department had panicked. There were indeed grounds for concern. On March 1 a Policy Planning Staff consultant, Yale professor Arnold Wolfers, warned on the basis of a just-concluded trip to Italy that the communists could win the upcoming elections there, and if that happened, the rest of Europe might follow the Italian example. Then on March 5 General Lucius D. Clay, MacArthur's counterpart in American-occupied Germany, alerted Army intelligence to "a subtle change" he had detected in Soviet behavior suggesting that war might now come "with dramatic suddenness." Clay's cable leaked, causing a war scare in Washington, and summaries of both pronouncements finally caught up with Kennan on March 15, while he was on a side trip to Manila. Startled, he tried to evaluate their significance in a hastily composed telegram to Marshall and Lovett. It conveyed the impression, however, that Kennan had panicked.[53]

He began by reminding his superiors that he had never foreseen Soviet military action unless Kremlin leaders became "dizzy with success" or feared a collapse of their authority in Eastern Europe. But now, strangely, both things seemed to be happening. Possibilities of success at the polls had excited European communists, while Stalin and his associates were becoming increasingly fearful that the Marshall Plan might succeed. This combination of euphoria and desperation posed new dangers: "We must be prepared for all eventualities."

Italy was the key: if it went communist, then the whole American position in Europe would be at risk. It would "be better that elections not take place at all than that [the] Communists win in these circumstances." So should the Italian government not outlaw their party prior to the elections? Civil war might follow, but that would give the United States the excuse to reoccupy whatever Italian military facilities it might wish. Such a course would "admittedly result in much violence and probably a military division of Italy." That would be preferable, though, "to a bloodless election victory, unopposed by ourselves, which would give the Communists the entire peninsula . . . and send waves of panic to all surrounding areas."[54]

If a long telegram from Moscow two years earlier had made Kennan's reputation, then this short one from Manila diminished it. The analysis was contradictory: how, if European communists were relishing their successes, could Soviet leaders be worrying about the success of the Marshall Plan? How could Kennan so suddenly withdraw his assurances about Moscow's reluctance to risk war, as well as his warnings against using American troops in the eastern Mediterranean? How, in a larger sense, could policy be planned if the top planner abruptly repudiated his own analyses? Hickerson, no admirer of Kennan, consigned his Manila dispatch to bureaucratic oblivion with a crisp comment, scribbled at the bottom of it:

1. Action to outlaw C.P. before election or to postpone election would be certain to cause civil war.
2. Non-communist parties have a good chance of winning election without any such drastic steps.
3. Therefore action recommended by GFK seems unwise.

Privately, Hickerson concluded that Kennan, when drafting this cable, could only have been "roaring drunk."[55]

That seems unlikely. Alcohol was not a problem for Kennan, but solipsism was, and in March 1948 it was beginning to catch up with him. He had built a staff around himself, producing analyses remarkable for their clarity, coherence, and depth; its members depended so much on Kennan's guidance, though, that they drifted in his absence. Designed to resist what he regarded as parochialism in the State Department's geographical bureaus, the Policy Planning Staff succumbed to just that malady when it accepted Hickerson's advice on Bevin's proposal: it embraced an Atlantic perspective but not a global one. Kennan had planted seeds but neglected their cultivation. "My mistake lay in my failure to realize that . . . , despite all that had been said in the reporting from Moscow, in the X-article, and in innumerable private conversations in the State Department, [my views] had made only a faint and wholly inadequate impression on official Washington."[56]

Solipsism showed up as well in Kennan's conviction that only he could reverse MacArthur's course in Japan: perhaps one reason the two hit it off is that each regarded himself as indispensable. Having insisted that all lines of authority over foreign policy go through him, Kennan assigned himself a task that would take him away from Washington for at least a month. He had no way of knowing that the month he chose would be as crisis-ridden as it was. But even in normal circumstances, it would have been unrealistic to assume, as Kennan seemed to, that all the crises except the one he was working on could wait until he got back. It's not even clear that the trip was necessary. Other pressures to shift his policies were converging on MacArthur: Kennan affected the timing but not the outcome.[57] By doing so in such a labor-intensive way, he fell into a parochialism of his own. He became, however briefly, Asia-centric—and in that too he resembled MacArthur.

Kennan also failed to allow for his own dependence on the staff he dominated. If Davies was right that his Policy Planning colleagues served as a backboard against which Kennan could bounce ideas—if, to use another metaphor, they tethered him, somewhat in the way that Annelise had always done—then this was another good reason for not leaving town. Deprived while on his trip of his staff's feedback, of his lunches with Fosdick at the Allies Inn, and of Annelise's sturdy common sense, Kennan fell into a funk if not a panic, with results embarrassingly apparent in the Manila "short telegram." It was not the first time, nor would it be the last, when loneliness got the better of him, upsetting the precarious balance between his emotions and his avocation.

"George is far away at the moment," Annelise wrote Frieda Por on March 8, 1948. "I hope he is enjoying it. If it isn't too strenuous, I know he will." But the trip was strenuous, and the delicate relationship between Kennan's head and his stomach now also suffered. Since his frustrating service on the European Advisory Commission four years earlier, his ulcer had given him little trouble. Now, though, it flared up again: by the end of his Japan trip, Kennan was sick in bed, where he began dictating his long report for Lovett and Marshall. Upon his return to Washington at the end of March, he and Hessman spent two days finishing off that document, and then Kennan checked himself into the Bethesda Naval Hospital. He was there for two weeks, followed by several more days of recuperation at the farm. Kennan had left his office on February 26. He was not back at work until April 19.[58]

By then, much had changed. On March 17 Great Britain, France, Belgium, the Netherlands, and Luxembourg signed the Brussels Treaty, a fifty-year defensive military alliance. President Truman welcomed it in an address to Congress on the same day, promising that the Europeans' determination to protect themselves would be matched by an American determination to protect them. On March 22 Hickerson began secret talks on behalf of the State Department with British and Canadian representatives, looking toward associating the United States and Canada with the Brussels Treaty signatories. On April 3 Congress, spurred by the coup in Czechoslovakia, at last approved the Marshall Plan, and Truman signed the bill into law. And on April 7 Lovett took a revised version of PPS/27 to the president, with a view to securing his permission—which Truman readily granted—to sound out congressional leaders on the possibility of a North Atlantic treaty that would formally link the military security of Western Europe to that of the United States. Kennan could only watch these events take place. He had nothing to do with shaping them.[59]

Meanwhile, another of Kennan's recommendations had caused a painful split between Truman and Marshall. On March 19 Warren Austin, the U.S. ambassador

to the United Nations, presented the American plan for an international trusteeship over an undivided Palestine. But on the previous day the president—despite
having approved the abandonment of partition—had assured the Zionist leader
Chaim Weizmann that there had been no change in policy. Embarrassed, Truman
blamed the State Department: there were people there, he complained, "who have
always wanted to cut my throat." That was an exaggeration, but Kennan had failed
to consider the humanitarian implications of withdrawing American support for
a Jewish state only three years after the world had learned of the Holocaust. Nor
had he taken into account the impact on Truman's reelection prospects in the fall,
an omission the White House staff quickly remedied. By the end of March the
State Department had lost control of U.S. policy in the Middle East. In deciding to
recognize the new state of Israel, an uncharacteristically angry Marshall told the
president a few weeks later, he had indulged in a "transparent dodge to win a few
votes." Truman replied coolly that he knew what he was doing.[60]

"The greatest mystery of my own role in Washington in those years," Kennan
wrote in his memoirs, "was why so much attention was paid in certain instances . . .
to what I had to say, and so little in others." The answer, he concluded, was that

> Washington's reactions were deeply subjective, influenced more by domestic-political
> moods and institutional interests than by any theoretical considerations of our inter-
> national position. It was I who was naïve—naïve in the assumption that the mere
> statement on a single occasion of a sound analysis or appreciation, even if invited
> or noted or nominally accepted by one's immediate superiors, had any appreciable
> effect on the vast, turgid, self-centered, and highly emotional process by which the
> views and reactions of official Washington were finally evolved.[61]

But surely policy planning in a democracy, if it is to be effective, must allow for
domestic politics, institutional interests, vastness, turgidity, self-centeredness, and
emotion. These are not mysteries to most people. That they were to Kennan—that
he expected theory to trump subjectivity—was in itself a solipsism that led to
failure.

FOURTEEN

Policy Dissenter: 1948

ENSCONCED ON THE SIXTEENTH FLOOR OF THE BETHESDA NAVAL Hospital in Washington through the first half of April 1948, Kennan recalled being "very bleak in spirit from the attendant fasting . . . made bleaker still by the whistling of the cold spring wind in the windows of that lofty pinnacle."[1] But the enforced rest provided an opportunity, as the doctors treated his physical ulcer, for him to alleviate the pain of a mental ulcer that still persisted. From his usual horizontal position (there being no choice this time), Kennan summoned Hessman and began dictating a lengthy letter to Walter Lippmann.

"You have chosen, for some reason, to identify the policy of containment with the 'Truman doctrine,' which you deplore," he admonished the pundit, "and to hold up the Marshall Plan, by way of contrast, as an example of constructive action." Had Lippmann forgotten their lunches together the previous May, at which Kennan advanced his ideas for the latter initiative? Contrary to what Lippmann claimed, he had never called for resisting the Russians wherever they challenged Western interests. "I do not know what grounds I could have given for such an interpretation." (Here Kennan ignored—or had repressed—his call in the "X" article for applying "counter-force at a series of constantly shifting geographical and political points, corresponding to the shifts and manœuvres of Soviet policy.") He did point out, accurately, that he had written "The Sources of Soviet Conduct" to counter "puerile defeatism" among American intellectuals who thought that firmness toward the Soviet Union could only bring war.

In fact, firmness had restored stability. "Has Iran gone? Or Turkey? Or Greece?" Not one would have remained independent had the Americans not acted. "Has Trieste fallen? Or Austria?" Italy was admittedly a weak spot, but that weakness had arisen from not stiffening the Italians soon enough. To be sure, Finland, Czechoslovakia, Manchuria, and North China had wound up on the wrong side of the "iron curtain." That was to be expected, given the military realities existing at the end of the war. Communism might indeed prevail in the rest of China: "What of it? I never said we would—or should—be able to hold equally everywhere." The point had been to hang on "in enough places, and in sufficiently strategic places, to accomplish our general purpose." That, for the most part, had been done.

Containment would not require the United States to arm itself to the teeth, defending overextended positions indefinitely. The Russians, made also of flesh and blood, had their own vulnerabilities. Afflicted by "internal contradictions," they would eventually defeat themselves. If capitalism bore within itself the seeds of its own destruction, why were they seeking so desperately to bring about its collapse? What was to be done, then, lay chiefly "within ourselves."

> Let us find health and vigor and hope, and the diseased portion of the earth will fall behind of its own doing. For that we need no aggressive strategic plans, no provocation of military hostilities, no show-downs, no world government, no strengthened UN, and no pat slogans with a false pretense to international validity.

The day would come—sooner than one might think—when their own weaknesses would convince Soviet leaders "that they cannot have what they want *without* talking to us. It has been our endeavor to assist them to that conclusion."

And what of European allies? Lippmann had argued that the United States, having provided them moral and material assistance, now also owed them military protection. This was "preposterous." The Russians much preferred conquest "by concealed methods, with a minimum of responsibility on their own part." The Marshall Plan was countering that strategy. Should it not satisfy the Europeans, "I can only shrug my shoulders." For the United States could not, by itself, sustain hope. But Kennan saw little faint-heartedness among recipients of Marshall Plan aid: they "have shown themselves ready enough to take risks as long as there is a reasonable indication that we are behind them and will do our best for them."

So what was Lippmann worried about? A year ago fear had hung over everything. Since then, however, "no fruits have dropped." Moscow had been forced to isolate the East from the West, where recovery was progressing rapidly:

"Admittedly, the issue hangs on Italy; but it hangs—in reality—on Italy alone. A year ago it hung on all of Europe—and on us." Lippmann should, then, "leave us some pride in our own legerdemain." The saddest part of the past year's experience was not the realization of how hard it was for a democracy to conduct a successful foreign policy. It was rather that if it did, "so few people would recognize it for what it was."[2]

Kennan's letter to Lippmann was roughly the length of a war college lecture. On reading it over, it seemed "plaintive and overdramatic," so he never sent it. He did corner Lippmann on a train a few months later and subject him to some of its arguments; no portion of the letter itself reached its intended recipient, however, until 1967, when excerpts appeared in Kennan's memoir. He blamed himself, after Lippmann's death, for having been "too arrogant" during his first months on the Policy Planning Staff to have accepted criticism as patiently as he might have. But something else was going on then as well: for once in his life—despite his ulcer—Kennan was optimistic about the future.[3]

Hardly anyone else was, however. Kennan's long Asian trip and the illness that followed prevented his seeing how pessimistic the mood in Washington and in allied capitals had become. As a result, the job to which he returned in mid-April was not the one he had left in late February. A year into his Policy Planning Staff directorship, Kennan found himself becoming a policy dissenter once again. He had, he discovered, lost his footing. He never quite regained it.

I.

The problems began with a recommendation that went awry. However much Kennan may have doubted himself over the years, he had never lacked confidence in his ability to explain—and even predict—the behavior of the Soviet Union. These skills had made his reputation in the Foreign Service, brought him to the National War College and the Policy Planning Staff, and inadvertently earned him, as "Mr. X," celebrity status. Whatever else he might have been wrong about, he had a habit of being right about the U.S.S.R.

Kennan's colleagues took him seriously, therefore, when he suggested in PPS/23, completed on February 24, 1948, that the Marshall Plan's success might soon compel Soviet leaders to negotiate. Once this had happened—probably after the November presidential election in the United States—the talks should be entrusted to someone who

> (a) has absolutely no personal axe to grind in the discussions, even along the lines of getting public credit for their success, and is prepared to observe the strictest silence about the whole proceeding; and

> (b) is thoroughly acquainted not only with the background of our policies but with Soviet philosophy and strategy and with the dialectics used by Soviet statesmen in such discussions.

Lest there be any doubt as to whom he had in mind, Kennan also insisted that the negotiator be fluent in Russian. Containment, in his mind, was meant to end the Cold War, not to freeze it into place. He meant to play as large a role in completing that effort as he had in initiating it. In the meantime, it might be worth seeking "some sort of a background understanding" with the Stalin regime.[4]

The Czech coup, which Kennan had predicted, took place on the next day, so he departed for Japan on the twenty-sixth with his prestige as high as it would ever be. Shortly after arriving in Tokyo, he told an off-the-record press briefing that "within six months [a] spectacular retreat of Soviet and Communist influence in Europe may be expected." The head of the Canadian mission in Japan reported Kennan's comments to Ottawa, where they set off expressions of incredulity. From London, the Foreign Office assured the Canadians—who had passed on the account—that there must have been a mistake. "I can hardly believe that Mr. Kennan can have been accurately reported," R. M. A. Hankey, head of the Northern Department, commented. It all seemed "so very much too optimistic." Kennan's former Moscow colleague Frank Roberts ventured another explanation: concerned by Lippmann's criticisms "that containment is a fruitless policy," he now "must prove that it can lead to positive results."[5]

But Kennan was not freelancing. Worried that Stalin might overreact to Truman's tough speech on March 17, the Policy Planning Staff had supported Kennan's call for a quiet approach. "We have no way of knowing what appraisal Stalin is receiving of American intentions," Davies pointed out. It was important to ensure that if war broke out, it would not have been through a misunderstanding. Bohlen seconded the suggestion, and on April 23 Lovett secured Truman's permission to go ahead. Marshall asked Ambassador Smith, in Moscow, to convey the message. The British and the Canadians were not informed: indeed the British embassy in Washington reported that the Truman administration *feared* conciliatory signs from Moscow, lest these strengthen Soviet "apologists," among them Wallace, now running for president on a third-party peace platform.[6]

Smith sent Molotov a carefully worded note on May 4, stating that while the United States would defend its interests, "the door is always wide open for full discussion and the composing of our differences." The two men then met on the tenth, with each professing his country's peaceful intentions. But on the eleventh, the Soviet news agency TASS released an edited version of this supposedly secret conversation: its apparent purpose was to imply that the United States had proposed a European settlement without consulting its allies. That unexpected development raised "very grave doubts in the minds of His Majesty's Government as to what may have been intended," Bevin cabled Marshall, in words more restrained than the anger he felt. Queries from other alarmed Europeans followed, as did a cacophony of excited press commentary.[7]

"I was appalled at what I had done," Kennan later recalled. "For two evenings, I walked the streets of Foxhall Village, trying . . . to discover where the error had lain." Finally he asked to see Marshall, for what he expected to be a reprimand. "I think we were right," he said, "and that the critics are wrong. But where there is so much criticism, there must be some fault somewhere."

> General Marshall put down his papers, turned ponderously in his chair, and fixed me penetratingly over the rims of his glasses. I trembled inwardly for what was coming.
>
> "Kennan," he said, "when we went into North Africa, in 1942, and the landings were initially successful, for three days we were geniuses in the eyes of the press. Then . . . for another three weeks we were nothing but the greatest dopes.
>
> "'The decision you are talking about had my approval; it was discussed in the Cabinet; it was approved by the President.
>
> "The only trouble with you is that you don't have the wisdom and perspicacity of a columnist. Now get out of here!"

The implications of what had happened, however, were not as reassuring. The Soviets had in the past respected confidentiality, Kennan reminded Marshall, but that could no longer be assumed: "The diplomatic channel to Moscow is really eliminated." As long as Molotov remained foreign minister, there could be no communication "without making it to the world."[8]

That was underestimating the problem, for Stalin himself had read Smith's note, scribbling a sardonic "Ha, Ha!" next to the passage about an open door for diplomacy. He then ordered the release of the edited exchange and compounded the mischief by inserting himself into the American presidential campaign. On May 12 Wallace published an open letter to Stalin closely paralleling the TASS version of the Smith-Molotov conversation. Stalin responded on the seventeenth, welcoming Wallace's letter as a possible basis for the peaceful resolution of differences. It was a transparent attempt, Durbrow reported disgustedly from Moscow, to "lend the appearance of substance to the vacuity of Wallace's declarations . . . and thus to emasculate American policy."[9]

The timing did seem more than coincidental. The State Department had evidence, Kennan explained to Smith, that Wallace had known what Stalin was going to do: "We unwittingly ran head on into a neat little arrangement between the Kremlin and some of the people in the Wallace headquarters." Wallace was indeed coordinating his actions with Moscow, but Kennan chose not to pursue the possibility that a former vice president of the United States had become a Soviet agent. What chiefly concerned him was that something had been "seriously wrong with my own analysis of events."

It was clear now that Stalin and his subordinates had no intention of dealing with Marshall and the other architects of containment. This was, in one sense, flattering: "They know very well that to us they would have to make real concessions, that we would not be put off with phony ones." But the situation was also dangerous, for they would use every opportunity to confuse public opinion and to build up Wallace. Kennan had been "horrified," he admitted to Smith, "by the ease with which the press and other groups interested in foreign affairs were taken in by this Russian maneuver."[10]

He was still seething when he traveled to Canada late in May. The invitation had come about because the Canadians, for whom Kennan had become a kind of Delphic oracle, were still trying to figure out what he had meant weeks earlier when he had expressed optimism about relations with Moscow in his Tokyo press conference. What they got now, however, were grim warnings about the naïveté of such a view. Speaking at the National Defence College in Kingston, Kennan summoned a long list of witnesses to Muscovite perfidy, extending all the way back to the emissaries of Queen Elizabeth I: "One can search in vain through the annals of Russian diplomacy for a single example of an enduring, decent and pleasant relationship between Russia and a foreign state."

Like early Christians in the late Roman Empire (Gibbon echoed loudly here), the international communist movement was hollowing out Western civilization from within, taking advantage of its "self-flagellating conscience." Such penitence ignored Russian history and Soviet ideology, encouraging the illusion that Stalin's behavior depended solely upon whether he was "pleased or irritated or impressed" with Western actions. The Smith-Molotov exchange had made it "terrifyingly clear" that "the Russians are able to raise or lower at will the temperature of American political life."

The United States and its allies could no longer expect, therefore, any reconciliation with the Soviet leaders, after which "we would all go away and play golf." The Cold War would continue, "probably through our lifetimes." The task now must be to manage it, and that would require an approach as "profoundly dialectic" as its Soviet counterpart. It would have to contain "conflicting elements of persuasion and compulsion." It would be "partly one and partly the other." It would require allowing what might appear to be "complete and arbitrary inconsistency." This capacity to "blow hot" one day and "blow cold" the next would be vital, for if "one or the other of these possibilities is denied to us, I assure you with the deepest conviction that we are lost."[11]

All of this may have clarified things for the Canadians, but Kennan's vehemence suggested how much the Smith-Molotov episode had shaken him: for the first time since the Nazi-Soviet Pact of 1939, he had failed to anticipate what Stalin would do. With a single sleazy trick, the old dictator had undermined Kennan's credibility as a Soviet expert. Kennan had let himself become too hopeful too soon. Even worse, he had transformed that hope into a failed policy initiative. His career did not suffer, because he still had Marshall's support. But his faith in himself did, along with the reputation his expertise hitherto had earned him.

II.

He had already been wrong about Italy. The prospect of a communist takeover there had so haunted Kennan that in his ill-conceived "short telegram" from Manila on March 15, he raised the possibility of canceling the upcoming elections and outlawing the communist party, even at the risk of civil war and an American reoccupation of military bases on the peninsula. The situation was still worrying him as he finished his letter to Lippmann on April 6: Italy was, he wrote, the only remaining weak spot in Western Europe. On the day after Kennan got back to the office, however, it became clear that the Italian Communist Party had suffered a decisive defeat in the April 18–19 elections. Alarmed by events in Czechoslovakia, encouraged by the prospect of Marshall Plan aid, the Italians had turned back a Moscow-inspired conquest from within, on their own and by democratic means. Or so it seemed.

In fact, Italy had been the site, over the past few weeks, of the CIA's first major covert operation. It's difficult, even today, to assess the importance of the secret funding the agency cobbled together for the Christian Democrats as against other influences on the election outcome: the Vatican's implacable anticommunist offensive; the massive Italian American letter-writing campaign warning that a communist victory would end economic assistance from the United States; the extent to which the Czech coup discredited the Italian communists. Those who knew about the CIA's intervention, however, considered it a great success. Although Kennan had pushed for the agency's involvement in Italy the previous fall, his Manila telegram and the Lippmann letter suggest that he did not know the full extent of what was going on. When he found out, he rushed to get ahead of what he had not seen coming. From having warned, in mid-March, that Washington was getting Italy horribly wrong, he went to arguing by the end of April that it had gotten Italy brilliantly right—so much so that its actions there should become a model for the future.[12]

"Political warfare," Kennan argued in a closely held and therefore unnumbered Policy Planning Staff paper completed early in May, was Clausewitz in peacetime. It employed all means short of war to achieve national objectives. These included overt initiatives like alliances, economic assistance, and "white" propaganda but also the clandestine support of "friendly" foreigners, the use of "black" psychological warfare, and even the encouragement of underground resistance in unfriendly states. The British had long relied on such methods, and Lenin had so synthesized the teachings of Marx and Clausewitz that the Kremlin's conduct of political warfare had become the most effective in history. Americans, in contrast, had traditionally viewed war as an extension of sports, free from any political context at all.

Now, facing global responsibilities and an intensifying conflict with the Soviet Union, the United States could no longer afford such innocence. It should not again have to scramble "as we did at the time of the Italian elections." The Policy Planning Staff had been studying possibilities: secret support for refugee organizations that might become liberation movements if war broke out; strengthening indigenous anticommunists in countries threatened by Moscow's political warfare; and, "in cases of critical necessity," direct action to prevent the sabotage of facilities or the capture of key personnel by Kremlin agents. Tight control would be necessary: "One man must be boss." And he would have to be "answerable to the Secretary of State."[13]

What Kennan was proposing now was a sustained covert complement to the Marshall Plan. The United States required an organization that could "do things that very much needed to be done, but for which the government couldn't take official responsibility." The model, Davies added, would be something like the British Special Operations Executive or the American Office of Strategic Services in World War II, but it would operate in peacetime, chiefly in Western Europe. Otherwise, "the Marshall Plan would be undone."[14]

Where to put such a unit, though? Kennan knew that the State Department could not handle it. He worried that the CIA might act too independently. Could not the NSC provide cover for such a program, perhaps under the leadership of Allen Dulles, an OSS veteran who had been conducting a review of CIA effectiveness? But Dulles wasn't interested, and the director of central intelligence, Admiral Roscoe Hillenkoetter, wasn't about to relinquish the agency's jurisdiction. If State would not "go along with CIA operating this political warfare thing," he snapped at one point, then "[l]et State run it and let it have no connection at all with us."[15] Which, of course, would mean no program at all.

The National Security Council, in mid-June, approved an unwieldy compromise. An Office of Special Projects within the CIA would take over the responsibility for covert operations, but Marshall would nominate its head with Hillenkoetter's assent. Hillenkoetter would ensure political and military coordination, working through an advisory committee made up of representatives from the Departments of State and Defense. Kennan was skeptical: the new organization, he worried, would be too remote from the conduct of foreign policy, and it would be hard to find the right person to run it. Nonetheless, he advised Marshall to accept the plan. "It is probably the best arrangement we can get at this time."[16]

At Kennan's suggestion, Marshall nominated Frank Wisner, another OSS alumnus now in the State Department, to run the OSP. "I personally have no knowledge of his ability," Kennan was careful to say, despite the fact that he and Annelise were regular guests at the Wisners' potluck dinners in Georgetown, and the Wisners were occasional visitors at the Pennsylvania farm. Kennan, in turn, became the State Department representative on the OSP's advisory committee. He made it clear, at a meeting with Wisner and Hillenkoetter early in August, that he would want "specific knowledge of the objectives of every operation and also of the procedures and methods employed in all cases where those procedures and methods involve political decisions." By the end of the month, Kennan had approved his first covert operation: it was Project Umpire, a program of clandestine radio broadcasts from the American zone in Germany, beamed toward Eastern Europe and the Soviet Union. He had done so not on State Department stationery but on plain paper, he explained to Lovett: "This means that I am ostensibly acting in a personal capacity, and can, if necessary, be denied by the Secretary."[17]

In this way the Policy Planning Staff became—officially at least—the overseer of all covert activities: perhaps with Kennan's concerns in mind, the Office of Special Projects was renamed the Office of Policy Coordination. "If effectively conducted," he wrote in a letter drafted for Lovett, "the new organization's activities might well enhance possibilities for achieving American objectives by means short of war." But the fundamental premise behind the OPC, Kennan reminded his superior a few weeks later, had been that "while this Department should take no responsibility for [Wisner's] operations, we should nevertheless maintain a firm guiding hand." As late as January 1949, Kennan was encouraging Wisner to think expansively: "Every day makes more evident the importance of the role which will have to be played by covert operations if our national interests are to be adequately protected."[18]

Kennan had few if any moral or legal qualms about such activities. He had maintained contacts with the anti-Hitler resistance in Germany before the United States entered the war, and had helped the OSS monitor espionage activities in Lisbon during it. He facilitated the immigration of German diplomats and spymasters who might have useful information about the U.S.S.R., even if they had worked for the Nazis: to leave them in Germany, he believed, risked having Soviet agents kill or co-opt them. He had been advising the Washington intelligence establishment since returning from Moscow in 1946, emphasizing particularly the need to work closely with Russian expatriates. He had called, in his first National War College lecture, for the pursuit of strategic objectives "with all the measures at our disposal," and he had acknowledged, shortly after the formation of the CIA in 1947, that it might be essential to "fight fire with fire." When he spoke to the Canadians about a "dialectical" approach that would appear to reflect "arbitrary inconsistency," he had Lenin's example of political warfare in mind. Setting up the OPC, therefore, was more a continuation of past practices than a dramatic innovation for him.[19]

It was also one of many Policy Planning Staff responsibilities: after the OPC was established, "I scarcely paid any attention to it." That, Kennan was sure in retrospect, was "probably the worst mistake I ever made in government." The plan had been, Davies recalled, that secret operations should not be entrusted to an enormous bureaucracy: "Well, O.P.C. went the other way." By 1952 it had forty-seven overseas stations, its budget was seventeen times what it had been in 1949, and it employed twenty times the number of people. Convinced that he had created a monstrosity, Kennan came to regret "all part that I or the staff took in any of this. I should never have accepted for the PPS the duty of giving political advice to Wisner's outfit. The fact that we are all prone to error does not comfort me greatly when I think about it."[20]

Kennan's regrets, in retrospect, seem disproportionate. He did propose giving the CIA a covert action capability, but it seems unlikely, had he not done so, that someone else would not have suggested this, or that the agency would not have thought of it on its own.[21] "The feeling in Washington," Dean Rusk recalled, was that "the Soviet Union was already operating with such methods. It was a mean, dirty, back-alley struggle, and if the U.S. had stayed out it would have found out what Leo Durocher [the legendary manager of the Brooklyn Dodgers] meant when he said 'nice guys finish last.'" That said, there was one aspect of Kennan's CIA involvement that made no more sense then than it does now. This was his continuing belief that he could do everything himself—that he could run covert operations against the Soviet Union, while conducting overt negotiations with the same country if they ever got under way, while planning all other aspects of American foreign policy. Annelise, as usual, was more practical: "There isn't the possibility in one man to do all this."[22]

III.

One of the reasons Kennan pushed so hard for control over covert activities may have been his sense that he was losing control of the rapidly evolving U.S. relationship with Western Europe. The minimalist strategy he advocated in 1947 had rested on two interlocking assumptions: that (a) the promise and provision of Marshall Plan aid would be all that was necessary to reassure the Europeans, because (b) the Soviet Union had no intention of attacking them. The first proposition depended upon the second, for if the Red Army ever did strike, then American economic assistance, however generous it might be, would do the Europeans little good. They had no means of defending themselves; nor had the United States offered them any.

These assumptions, in turn, depended on Kennan's proficiency as a mind reader. They would hold up only if he had accurately sensed what European and Soviet leaders were thinking. If the Europeans began to show nervousness, or if the U.S.S.R. began to exhibit aggressiveness, all bets would be off. Both developments had occurred by the time Kennan returned to his office at the end of April 1948. "As you know, I came in late on the work which is being done," he wrote Marshall and Lovett on the twenty-ninth. But he had now familiarized himself with the situation and consulted Bohlen, who agreed with what he had to say. The problem was not doubt about American support if the Soviet Union attacked— the presence of U.S. occupation forces in Germany left no reason for Europeans to worry about that. Rather, it reflected uncertainty about what to do if that happened. All that was needed were "realistic staff talks" to reassure them.[23]

By this time, though, top-secret negotiations on the possibility of a North Atlantic collective defense treaty had already taken place with the British and the Canadians. Meanwhile Marshall had secured the agreement of Senator Arthur H. Vandenberg, the Republican chair of the Senate Foreign Relations Committee, to sponsor a "Vandenberg Resolution" confirming congressional approval. Kennan's proposed reconsideration went nowhere. His frustration showed while he was in Ottawa at the end of May: did the Europeans not realize that "if the United States gave this guarantee, it would be doing something which would be in the interests of Western Europe but not necessarily in the interests of the United States, since the United States could, at any time, make a deal with the Soviet Union?" "We naturally took him up on this and he withdrew from this exposed position," Escott Reid, the Canadian assistant under secretary for external affairs, reported to his superiors. It was indeed exposed, with the Smith-Molotov exchange having failed. The exchange left Reid with the uneasy sense "that if you scratch almost any American long enough, you will find an isolationist."[24]

Kennan was no isolationist, but as Sir Oliver Franks, now the British ambassador in Washington, recalled, he did tend to see things from an "Anglo-Saxon" perspective: "All those other chaps were rather more difficult. Therefore stick with what you know." The planning process, in Kennan's absence, had gone well beyond that. "I have always reproached myself," he later admitted, "for not taking my own views to the General and making more of an issue of it." His door still led directly into Marshall's office, but "I'm afraid I didn't use it enough. I was always so afraid of abusing this privilege. . . . I think that I may have been too hesitant [and] that I should have."[25]

So what might Kennan have said, had he been bolder? "Look, for goodness

sake, let well enough alone, nobody is going to attack you," he remembered wanting to tell the Europeans.

> Don't talk about this, we'll get at the question of your military weakness as soon as
> we can, but give the Marshall Plan a chance to [work]. It's a field in which we are
> strong—the economic field—the military one is the field where we are weak. Let's not
> call attention to our weakness by making a big splash about the military situation now.

With his State Department colleagues, he would have been blunter:

> All right, the Russians are well armed and we are poorly armed. So what? We are
> like a man who has let himself into a walled garden and finds himself alone there
> with a dog with very big teeth. The dog, for the moment, shows no signs of aggres-
> siveness. The best thing for us to do is surely to try to establish, as between the two
> of us, the assumption that the teeth have nothing whatsoever to do with our mutual
> relationship—that they are neither here nor there.

Finally, he would have questioned the cultivation of Vandenberg. The Republicans
were jealous, Kennan believed. They had supported the Marshall Plan but now
wanted a plan of their own upon which they could put their stamp. Such people
did not deserve "admiring applause every time they could be persuaded by the
State Department to do something sensible."[26]
   As far as we know, Kennan made none of these arguments—at least not
openly—within the department. It's safe to assume, though, that they lay behind
the questions he did raise while participating in talks with British, French, Canadian, Belgian, and Dutch diplomats in Washington during the late summer of
1948. Might not the building of military strength distract attention from European economic recovery and the eventual unification of the entire continent?
Could there not be two loosely linked alliances—a dumbbell arrangement—made
up of the Americans and Canadians at one end, and the British, the French, and
the Benelux countries at the other? If there had to be a single alliance, should its
membership not be limited to those countries? If it were not, how many countries could the United States afford to defend? There was more than a hint of desperation in these queries, and Hickerson, the principal American negotiator, had
no trouble deflecting them. "I consider that a compliment," he responded when
told years later that Kennan considered him the State Department colleague with
whom he had disagreed most. "Thank you."[27]

IV.

There were still moments, though, when the policy process worked as Kennan thought it should. One came in late June 1948, after members of the Cominform, meeting in Bucharest, openly denounced the Yugoslav Communist Party. Under Josef Broz Tito's leadership, they claimed, the Yugoslavs were pursuing a policy unfriendly to the U.S.S.R. and in violation of Marxist principles. Because Stalin controlled the Cominform, the complaint carried weight. Kennan had been predicting trouble in Eastern Europe for some time, but he thought it would come in the north, not in the Balkans. He missed the hints of Tito's heresy conveyed in American diplomatic reporting from the region but rallied quickly, taking only two days to complete PPS/35, "The Attitude of This Government Toward Events in Yugoslavia." It was the most immediately effective policy paper he ever produced.[28]

Unusually for Kennan, it was brief—only four and a quarter typed pages—but it compressed a lot into that space. It placed the Cominform's condemnation of Tito within a historical perspective, while projecting its significance into the future. At one point Kennan distilled into just three sentences his Gibbon-inspired doubts about the stability of empires, his belief that an internationalist ideology could not indefinitely command national loyalties, and his conviction that Stalin, for all his craftiness, had overreached:

> A new factor of fundamental and profound significance has been introduced into the world communist movement by the demonstration that the Kremlin can be successfully defied by one of its own minions. By this act, the aura of mystical omnipotence and infallibility which has surrounded the Kremlin power has been broken. The possibility of defection from Moscow, which has heretofore been unthinkable for foreign communist leaders, will from now on be present in one form or another in the mind of every one of them.

The United States should not jump to Yugoslavia's defense: that would be undignified, and Tito remained a dedicated communist. It should acknowledge, though, that "if Yugoslavia is not to be subservient to an outside power [then] its internal regime is basically its own business," and ought not to prevent a normal diplomatic and economic relationship. In the meantime, "the international communist movement will never be able to make good entirely the damage done by this development."[29]

PPS/35 set forth several propositions that, in varying ways at various times, would guide American foreign policy through the rest of the Cold War. One was that communism need not be monolithic: the Soviet Union was likely to have as much trouble controlling its ideological allies as it would resisting its geopolitical adversaries. A second was that the United States should therefore cooperate with some communists to contain others: dividing enemies by driving wedges might now be feasible. A third was that the domestic character of a government was less important than its international behavior. The idea had long been implicit in Washington's support for authoritarian regimes in Latin America, in its wartime alliance with the U.S.S.R., and more recently in the extension of Marshall Plan aid to socialist regimes in Western Europe. Kennan made it explicit.

The paper was also unusual in that it instantly became official policy. Lovett sent its conclusions to all diplomatic missions and consular offices on June 30, the day he received it. Marshall approved it the next day, after which he forwarded it to Truman for his information: the president's endorsement was not thought necessary. PPS/35 eventually gained the status of an NSC document, but only for reasons of bureaucratic tidiness. Kennan's Yugoslavia planning had made policy in record time, leaving him with every reason to be pleased.[30]

Kennan then used Tito's defection to defend the China policy he and Davies had been advocating. The Joint Chiefs of Staff had never reconciled themselves to abandoning the Nationalists, and with the prospect of a communist victory looming, they called once more, in the summer of 1948, for a major effort to save Chiang Kai-shek. Mao Zedong, they still claimed, was as much a puppet of the Soviet Union as the Eastern European satellite leaders had been, but now Tito had proven not to be a puppet. With Davies's help, Kennan exploited that opening with PPS/39, "United States Policy Toward China," completed early in September.

It acknowledged that the U.S.S.R. would *appear* to benefit from a triumph of communism in China. But "the edifying truancy of comrade Tito" must already have raised doubts in the minds of Kremlin leaders about their ability to dominate Mao, who had been running the Chinese Communist Party far longer than Tito had controlled its Yugoslav counterpart. "[A]n exceedingly shrewd judge of his fellow Chinese," Mao knew that subservience to the Soviet Union would provoke resentment among them.

> It is a nice piece of irony that at precisely the time the Chinese Communist leadership is most likely to wish to conceal its ties with Moscow, the Kremlin is most likely to be exerting utmost pressure to bring the Chinese Communists under complete

control. The possibilities which such a situation would present us, provided we have regained freedom of action, need scarcely be spelled out.

It followed, then, that "we must not become irrevocably committed to any one course of action or any one faction in China," for there were operating in that country "tremendous, deep-flowing indigenous forces which are beyond our power to control."[31]

When his mentor and patron Forrestal protested that this was not a policy, Kennan responded firmly. Noninterference in the internal affairs of another country was, after all, a long-standing principle of American diplomacy, "deeply sanctioned in practice and in public opinion." Whoever proposed abandoning it now would have to show

(a) That there is sufficiently powerful national interest to justify our departure in the given instance from a rule of international conduct which has been proven sound by centuries of experience and which we would wish others to observe with respect to ourselves, and

(b) that we have the means to conduct such intervention successfully and can afford the cost in terms of the national effort it involves.

Neither of these claims held with respect to China, where "powerful 'Tito' tendencies" were likely to develop. It would, therefore, be "frivolous and irresponsible" to waste any more economic or military assistance on the Chinese Nationalists. They regarded the United States as a dairy cow, one end of which "can do you a lot of good" while the other "is incapable of conferring any damage."[32]

Kennan went so far as to draft a presidential statement, at the end of November 1948, warning that what was happening in China would not now be affected "by any measure of aid which the United States could feasibly make available." Not wanting to appear to be administering a final blow to Chiang Kai-shek, Truman decided against using it. But he reserved the right to do so in the future, thereby departing from Kennan's advice only on the question of when he should announce publicly that he was following it.[33]

In planning policy for Yugoslavia and China, Kennan combined fast footwork with modest objectives. He was arguing, in these two instances, for letting existing trends run their course, while taking advantage of whatever opportunities they might present. His China policy, he admitted, was one of acting "on a day by day basis in accordance with the changes of the moment. It cannot be explicitly defined on paper in a form which can serve as a guide for months or years ahead."[34] Curiously, this was the kind of improvisation Kennan had criticized in the past. It echoed Roosevelt's resistance to planning in World War II. It sounded like Byrnes making it up as he went along in Moscow at the end of 1945. It was how, in Kennan's view, the United States had drifted into a commitment to the military defense of Western Europe, regardless of the consequences for a European-wide settlement. Kennan was succeeding in shaping policy—or so it was beginning to seem in the last half of 1948—only where he could allow himself *not* to plan. Forrestal, who sensed this, was onto something.

V.

With good reason, for Kennan had failed to provide him with policy guidance on a more important issue when he desperately needed it. As secretary of defense, Forrestal faced the daunting task of ensuring that military capabilities were adequate to secure national interests, whether in peace or war. Worried that commitments were exceeding these, under pressure from Truman to stay within tight budget limits, beset by rivalries over scarce resources among the armed services, denied any assurance about the possible use of the atomic bomb, Forrestal was hoping for answers from his preferred Soviet expert to a big question: should the United States be preparing for a "peak period of danger" from the U.S.S.R., or for an extended but static threat? In either case, what proportion of American resources should be devoted to military purposes?[35]

Kennan doubted the Policy Planning Staff's ability to produce this information. It was not possible to predict when war might come, he explained to Marshall and Lovett, or which objectives might be achieved by military or nonmilitary means: "These things are hopelessly intertwined." The Soviet Union's capabilities, even when known accurately, would not necessarily shape its intentions: "We cannot calculate with precision the political imponderables."[36] The skeletal NSC staff was unable to answer Forrestal's question either, though, so Kennan reluctantly took it on. By the middle of August, he had finished a thirty-nine-page analysis that sought to reconcile the American tradition of distinguishing sharply between war and peace with Clausewitz's warnings about the impossibility of doing so. It was not quite what Forrestal had in mind.

PPS/38, "United States Objectives With Respect to Russia," pointed out that Soviet objectives had remained much the same, in both war and peace, from Lenin through Stalin. Planning for peak danger, therefore, made little sense. But a democracy would never find sustained planning easy, because its aversion to war would always tempt it to shift objectives in peacetime. The task, therefore, was to define present peacetime objectives and hypothetical wartime objectives in such a way as to diminish the gap between them.

Peacetime objectives were to reduce the Soviet Union's external power, while bringing about change in the theories that drove its use. Both tasks were well under way. The Marshall Plan had reversed the Soviet Union's appeal in Western Europe, while Tito's defection had shown that Eastern Europeans could challenge Soviet domination. Stalin's regime remained committed to the *idea* that conflict with the capitalist world was inevitable, but it was also capable of acting pragmatically, as when it cooperated with the United States and Great Britain to defeat Nazi Germany. It was prepared "to recognize *situations*, if not arguments." If such situations could be re-created and sustained long enough to allow changes to take place within the Soviet Union, then these might modify the way it dealt with the rest of the world. Wartime objectives would not be needed, because there would be no war.

None of this would be likely, though, in a permanently divided Europe. On the contrary, the danger of war would be greater if the continent remained split than "if Russian power is peacefully withdrawn in good time and a normal balance restored to the European community." With this call for a peaceful rollback, several aspects of Kennan's thinking fell into alignment: his pride in the Marshall Plan's accomplishments, his insistence on the need for covert operations to complement them, his quick exploitation of Tito's defection, his abortive effort to keep open the possibility of negotiations with Moscow, and his attempts to derail the North Atlantic Treaty, which he was sure would solidify Europe's disunity for decades to come. The dots, for Kennan at least, all connected.

Not for Forrestal, though. His peacetime objective was to be sure that the United States could win a war, and on this issue Kennan had nothing to offer. The last third of PPS/38 simply assumed victory, without saying how it would come about. Kennan made no effort to connect his political analysis with Pentagon war planning or with White House budgeting. Instead he focused on the terms a triumphant West should impose upon a defeated Soviet Union. These would not include unconditional surrender—the country was too big to occupy—but they might well require the detachment of certain non-Russian republics: Kennan specified which ones in some detail. All of this brought PPS/38 to over ten thousand words, twice the length of the "long telegram." Forrestal had found in that earlier document just what he needed to understand Moscow's behavior. This one, in contrast, turned out to be useless. His problem was that inadequate military resources might *lose* a war—not what to do after winning one.[37]

Drastically cut, PPS/38 became NSC 20/4, which Truman approved on November 24, 1948. Despite the effort Kennan put into it, the paper had little impact on actual policy. The reasons reveal Kennan's shortcomings as a planner, one of which was prolixity. Without the discipline imposed by time constraints, as in his Yugoslav paper, or by mode of transmission, as in the "long telegram," or by tough-minded subordinates, which he did not have, Kennan tended to ramble. He had done so in "Russia—Seven Years Later," the 1944 essay of which he had been so proud which no one else read. PPS/38 repeated that pattern. Another problem was shallowness in economics: neither Kennan nor his staff knew enough about that subject to answer Forrestal's question about sustainable levels of peacetime military spending. Finally Kennan, as always, was self-absorbed. He was finding it easier to connect dots in his head than within the U.S. government. He was writing increasingly, once again, for himself.[38]

VI.

In Kennan's defense, he had a lot on his mind while preparing PPS/38. For on June 24, 1948, Stalin cut off land access to the British, French, and American sectors of West Berlin, which lay over a hundred miles inside the Soviet occupation zone. He had been slowly restricting access to the city since March, presumably in response to talks the Western allies had been holding in London looking toward the establishment of a separate West German state. But by finally completing the process—ostensibly to stop circulation of the *Deutschmark*, the new West German currency, in the Soviet sector of the city—he created the gravest threat of a new war since the last one had ended.

Kennan had given relatively little attention to Germany since calling for its partition just prior to the Yalta conference in February 1945. He still lamented the Anglo-American insistence on unconditional surrender that had left the Red Army controlling almost half the country. He doubted the victors' ability to reform it, or even to agree on a plan for doing so. He saw in General Clay the same obliviousness to geopolitics—and to instructions from Washington—that MacArthur had shown in Japan. Kennan had argued strongly for including the western zones of Germany in the Marshall Plan; nor had he opposed their political consolidation when that idea was first broached. Now, though, the blockade forced him to focus on the German question, and within weeks he had repudiated most of his own thinking about that country since the end of the war.

His first response was to call for firmness. "[W]e are in Berlin by right," he wrote a friend, "and we do not propose to be ridden out by any blackmail or other forms of coercion." When the Joint Chiefs of Staff, concerned about the exposed position of American troops in the city, suggested withdrawing them out of "humanitarian consideration" for the West Berliners, Kennan reacted angrily: "The world would know well enough that we were turning 2,400,000 people over to all the rigors and terrors of totalitarian rule." The United States should risk war if necessary, he advised Lovett, to retain its position in Berlin. Still Kennan could not conceal from Smith, in Moscow, a growing concern "that our Soviet adversaries may be now too over-extended—at once too weak and too terrified of their own weakness—to behave rationally." If that was the case, "then I am afraid no one can save them, even for the sake of the peace of Europe, and that their regime will have to go down in violence, no matter how strongly the rest of us work to prevent this issue."[39]

It was with a view to avoiding that grim prospect that Kennan asked the Policy Planning Staff to take a fresh look at the German question in late July. Any peaceful end to the Berlin blockade, he assumed, would have to be arranged through the Council of Foreign Ministers, which still represented the four occupying powers in Germany; but what should the Americans seek in such negotiations? By August 12, working under intense pressure, Kennan had completed PPS/37, "Policy Questions Concerning a Possible German Settlement." Unlike his Yugoslavia and China papers, it argued for *not* allowing existing trends to continue but rather for making a bold effort to reverse them.

Continuity would mean carrying on with a divided Germany while strengthening Western Europe. That, though, would ensure a divided continent, which could hardly be the long-term goal of the United States. Stalin had blockaded Berlin because he feared the formation of a West German government. If that process proceeded, he would set up a rival regime in East Germany, and "the fight would be on for fair." Half of Europe would form a military alliance with Washington, precluding any rollback of Moscow's influence over the other half. Germans would resent the breakup of their country, the collapse of east-west trade would cripple European recovery, and the Truman administration would face the costs of an indefinite military occupation at a time when Congress could at any point cut the necessary appropriations: "From such a trend of developments, it would be hard—harder than it is now—to find 'the road back' to a united and free Europe."

The alternative was "to press *at this time* for a sweeping settlement of the German problem which would involve the withdrawal of Allied forces from at least the major portion of Germany, the termination of military government and the establishment of a German Government with real power and independence." This was, after all, what the United States supposedly had wanted since the end of the war. By showing how much Stalin feared a divided Germany, his blockade had advanced the prospects for reunification further and faster than anyone had expected. If handled imaginatively, the Berlin crisis could be an opportunity to mitigate—if not to end altogether—the European standoff.

Stalin would find it hard to resist an offer to substitute, for an independent West German state aligned militarily with the United States, a unified demilitarized Germany linked to no alliance—or so Kennan insisted. This would solve the Berlin problem, for if occupation forces were to leave the country, there could be no humiliation in withdrawing them from the city. The possibility that a reconstituted Germany might tilt toward Moscow was now vanishingly small, given the extent to which Stalin's blockade had angered most Germans. And Kennan's plan would remove the need to keep a large American military establishment in the middle of Europe, thereby placating Congress while alleviating Forrestal's concerns.

What if a unified Germany, even if anti-Soviet, again threatened the peace of Europe? The four occupying powers could prevent unauthorized rearmament, Kennan maintained, by each retaining a military base on German territory, even as they relinquished responsibility for civil affairs to the new German government. The American, British, and Soviet bases would be supplied by sea, leaving the U.S.S.R. with no justification for continuing to occupy Poland. Disengagement from Germany, hence, would also advance the liberation of Eastern Europe.

And what of the plans, now well under way, for a North Atlantic Treaty? Kennan said nothing about this in PPS/37, but his logic was clear enough. If the Europeans' military insecurity had led them to seek such a guarantee in the first place, would their anxieties not diminish as Soviet forces withdrew from Germany and even from Eastern Europe? The Americans would not go home: their bases on German soil, along with those of the British and the French, would allow watching the Germans, but also the Russians. So what would be left to fear?

Boldness, Kennan acknowledged, was more difficult than timidity: "The course of action and change is harder than the course of inaction." But disengagement would become no easier as time passed.

> [I]f the division of Europe cannot be overcome peacefully at this juncture, when the lines of cleavage have not yet hardened completely across the continent, when the Soviet Union (as I believe) is not yet ready for another war, when the anticommunist sentiment in Germany is momentarily stronger than usual, and when the Soviet satellite area is troubled with serious dissension, uncertainty, and disaffection, then it is not likely that prospects for a peaceful resolution of Europe's problems will be better after a further period of waiting.

The ultimate answer to the German question was a federated Europe into which all parts of the country could be absorbed. A divided Germany would prevent that. It followed, then, that "Germany must be given back to the Germans," for the reconstitution of Europe could not await the resolution of east-west differences. At a minimum, by putting forward such a proposal, "we shall at least have made the gesture, which is important."[40]

PPS/37 demonstrated, better than anything else Kennan ever wrote, his ability to look beyond processes to the structures they were creating, and to propose alternatives. Clausewitz, borrowing from the French, would have described this as a *coup d'oeil*: an integration of experience, observation, and imagination that constructs the whole out of the fragments the eye can see. The method, he suggested, was that of a poet or a painter, involving "the quick recognition of a truth that the mind would ordinarily miss or would perceive only after long study and reflection."[41]

The truth Kennan recognized in this instance was one his own mind had missed until this point: that the division of Germany, which he had been advocating since 1945 as a way of *restoring* a balance of power *in* Europe, was in fact *removing* power *from* Europe, concentrating it instead in the hands of the United States and the Soviet Union. The Cold War would go on indefinitely unless this trend was reversed. PPS/37 began Kennan's effort to do that: it was a Clausewitzian *coup d'oeil*, aimed at rescuing the Germans, the Europeans, the Americans, and ultimately even the Russians from the consequences of a course he had previously recommended. It was Kennan reversing himself.

VII.

The difficulty with *coups d'oeil*, however, is that they are more likely to be regarded as art than policy. PPS/37 was indeed "bold and imaginative," Hickerson wrote Kennan on August 31, 1948, but it would be dangerous to try to unite Germany until Western Europe was economically and militarily stronger. That was the first of many objections. Too many people, Kennan recalled—not just Hickerson and his State Department colleagues, but also Clay, the British, and even the French—had locked themselves into creating a West German government. They feared that any dealing with the Russians would cause confusion in Germany, leading to the suspicion "that we were about to sell some of these people out." From their point of view, though, Kennan was *too* inclined to negotiate. "The problem with that approach," Dean Rusk recalled—he was then running the Office of United Nations Affairs—"is that it allows you to be nibbled to death, like ducks. Kennan couldn't see that." All responses received opposed his conclusions, Kennan reported to Marshall and Lovett on September 8. "I think them worthy of careful attention. . . . I disagree with them all."[42]

Marshall nonetheless supported Kennan's effort to think broadly about a German settlement. He authorized the Policy Planning Staff to convene a group of consultants to discuss the issue—among them were Hamilton Fish Armstrong, still the editor of *Foreign Affairs,* and Dean Acheson, soon to replace Marshall as secretary of state. They endorsed Kennan's position as a long-term objective but doubted that Moscow would accept such a plan anytime soon: the United States should, therefore, proceed with the formation of a West German state. Kennan accepted their advice philosophically. "We will continue to work on this program," he assured Marshall on September 17. The consultants had at least agreed that "time is on our side, that we must not yield in Berlin, and that we must continue to sweat it out there as best we can."[43]

As it happened, Kennan was lecturing that morning at the National War College. There were, he told the newly arrived students, "only five centers of industrial and military power in the world which are important to us from the standpoint of national security." One, obviously, was the United States. The other four—Great Britain, Germany, the Soviet Union, and Japan—lay on or alongside the Eurasian landmass. Nowhere else did climate, population, tradition, and industrial strength allow developing the kind of military power that could endanger American interests. Only the Soviet Union was completely hostile. Japan could fall under Moscow's influence if the United States mismanaged its transition to full sovereignty, but that was now unlikely. Germany, however, was contested territory, the only point upon which the global power balance could now pivot. That was why its future was so important.

The ideal would have been to make a united Germany the centerpiece of a united Europe, but the allies were far from ready for such an arrangement: "Oh, it is very easy for you to talk," they would say to any American who proposed this. "You are strong and sleek and fat and you are three thousand miles away, and you can do this backseat driving perfectly safely, but it is a different thing for us up here." They were more interested in the guarantees they could extract from Washington, therefore, than in reuniting the Germans. A divided Europe, whatever its implications for the international system as a whole, would not much bother them.

Americans faced, then, a tough choice. Was it better to do alone what was right, or to do in company of allies what was wrong? The State Department had concluded that "come what may, we simply must hold with the French and the British, . . . because if we let disunity creep in we may have lost the whole battle anyway." For if the United States ever abandoned its allies, then it would have become cynical, a change that was bound to affect the nation's character: if "we cease having ideals in the field of foreign policy, something very valuable will have gone out of our internal political life." There was no alternative, then, but "to bind our friends to us with the proverbial Shakespeare's hoop of steel." This was "our worst problem of foreign policy today," because "what appears to be the sensible thing to do about Germany is the thing our own Allies are most reluctant to do."[44]

The Policy Planning Staff continued to work on "Program A," as Kennan's plan came to be called, and by mid-November he had a revised version ready for use if the United States should wish to specify terms for a comprehensive German settlement. It would be put forward, however, only with assurance of "a wide enough degree of British and French acquiescence to maintain basic three-power unity." Even then, the Russians probably would not accept it. The plan would at least show the Germans that Moscow, not Washington, was dividing their country: that would "place us in a more favorable position to continue the struggle both in Berlin and in Germany as a whole."[45]

A similar resignation informed Kennan's final report to Marshall on the North Atlantic Treaty, completed on November 23, 1948. It was too late now to prevent such a development, "but I was, after all, still the head of his planning staff, and I thought he should at least have available to him the view I took personally of the entire NATO project." PPS/43, "Considerations Affecting the Conclusion of a North Atlantic Security Pact," carried with it the warning "that there will be adverse views in the European office." Marshall did not need the reminder: this document, even more than Program A, would be art for art's sake.

A security guarantee, Kennan acknowledged, might stiffen the Europeans' self-confidence, in itself a desirable outcome. But their insistence on it was "primarily a *subjective* one, arising in their own minds as a result of their failure to understand correctly their own position." Their best course would still be to achieve economic recovery and internal political stability. Rearmament could easily divert such efforts. That would particularly be the case if the view took hold that war was inevitable and that therefore "no further efforts are necessary toward the political weakening and defeat of the communist power in central and eastern Europe"— in short (Kennan did not need to make this explicit), what covert operations were meant to accomplish.

If there had to be a military alliance, its members should include only the North Atlantic countries, where there was "a community of defense interest firmly rooted in geography and tradition." To go further would invite still further demands for protection: there would then be "no stopping point in the development of a system of anti-Russian alliances until that system has circled the globe and has embraced all the non-communist countries of Europe, Asia, and Africa." By then, one of two things would have happened: the alliances would have become meaningless, like the Kellogg-Briand Pact of 1928, or the United States would have become hopelessly overextended, in which case it would have ignored warnings about the increasing discrepancy between its resources and its commitments.

The fundamental issue was what kind of Europe the United States wanted. Official policy looked toward the eventual withdrawal of both American and Soviet forces and, accordingly, "toward the encouragement of a third force which can absorb and take over the territory between the two." But an alliance including most Marshall Plan recipients would mean "a final militarization of the present dividing-line through Europe." It would not only prevent a German settlement: it would also impede the satellites' ability to throw off Russian domination, "since any move in that direction would take on the aspect of a provocative military move." The United States should not do anything to make the status quo unchangeable by peaceful means. Process should not define purpose.[46]

But perhaps his strategy—with respect to both Germany and NATO—had asked too much of the Europeans, Kennan admitted to a Pentagon audience that same month. The Marshall Plan's success had provoked Moscow into *appearing* to be aggressive: "We knew that there would be . . . a baring of the fangs designed to scare us." By asking the Europeans to put economic recovery before military security, "we were in effect asking them to walk a sort of a tight-rope and telling them that if they concentrated on their own steps and did not keep looking down into the chasm of their own military helplessness we thought there was a good chance that they would arrive safely on the other side." The problem was that too many people in Europe—but also in Washington—had looked down. That was leaving the Soviet Union with no way out: it was making the division of Europe "insoluble by any other than military means."[47]

This was a shrewd assessment, not just of the Europeans, but also of Kennan himself. To mix his own metaphors, he had been asking them to ignore the snarling dog with which they shared a continent, even as they walked, unperturbed, across the tightrope the Marshall Plan had thrown to them. They could do this only with self-confidence, but he had taken it upon himself to *tell* them when they had reached that state. If, as Kennan had often noted, fear was a subjective condition, then surely self-confidence was too: he believed, however, that his objective view of Soviet intentions should override European subjectivity. He was after all, or at least he had been, the expert. His strategy amounted, in the end, to saying: "Trust me."[48]

VIII.

"George has been much better this fall," Annelise wrote Frieda Por late in 1948. "I am keeping my fingers crossed. He looks better too, and I think he has put on a little weight." His workload had by no means diminished. Since returning from the hospital in April, he had prepared major policy papers on the Soviet Union, Germany, China, Japan, Yugoslavia, the proposed North Atlantic Treaty, and covert action, some of them in several versions. He delivered four lectures at the National War College, and one each at the Pentagon, the Naval War College, and the Canadian Defence College. He found the time to do public lectures in Milwaukee, Detroit, Birmingham, and New York, as well as informal presentations for Air Force officers, the Harvard faculty, Princeton alumni, Louisville newspapermen and bankers, and his Pennsylvania neighbors. He continued to run the Policy Planning Staff and to serve as its representative on the National Security Council—although he gave up the latter responsibility at the end of the year. And all the while he was deeply involved in Berlin crisis management: the only diary entry Kennan made during these months recorded a sleepless night spent coordinating communications among American officials in that city, Paris, and Washington.[49]

Psychologically, though, he was more depressed than he had been when his physical ailments laid him low. For it was becoming clear that his grand strategy was no longer to be that of the United States. Kennan had suffered setbacks on seeking a "background understanding" with the Soviet Union, on managing covert operations, on heading off the North Atlantic Treaty, on calculating the relationship between military means and national ends, and—most significantly for him—on clearing the way for a European settlement based on German reunification. Only on Yugoslavia and China had he had his way.

If Kennan had been, in the eyes of the Canadians, a Delphic oracle in the spring of 1948, he was by the end of the year a beleaguered and increasingly bypassed oracle. His gloom was hard to miss when he returned to the war college on December 21 to deliver the final lecture of the semester. He promised the students "a completely unvarnished and unsparing picture of what appears to me personally to be our present international position." The underlining in the transcript was his own.

One thing not easily forgiven in life, he told them, was "to be elevated many times above the level of your fellows in privilege and riches and comfort and power. The rich man is rarely loved and never pitied." The United States had 50 percent of the world's wealth, but only 6 percent of its population. The remaining 94 percent included people who "would not hesitate to tear us limb from limb figuratively, or perhaps even physically, if they would thereby get a share of our wealth or reduce the power we hold." They would do this despite the fact that "never before in its history has the world known, or is it likely to know, a great power which has conducted itself more decently and more moderately in its foreign relations." The United States was "a misunderstood country throughout the world."

There was no more dangerous sense, Kennan cautioned, than that of being a victim. This was how persecution manias began. Practiced on a national scale, they could lead to fanaticisms like those of the Nazis and the Communists. Nevertheless, the world really was filled with jealousy and devoid of pity. The prevailing view was that "we have been favored by the Gods, . . . and that it is high time that the Gods shifted their favor and that our faces were ground into the dirt."[50]

It's hard not to see projection happening here. Kennan's letter to Lippmann, written in April at the height of his influence as Policy Planning Staff director, portrayed a world in which events were aligning themselves with American intentions. But by December, with Kennan's authority significantly diminished, the world had become a dark and dangerous place. The *objective* position of the United States could not have changed that dramatically in so short a period of time. What had changed was Kennan's *subjective* understanding of it: because Washington was no longer going his way, the world was no longer going Washington's way.

One of Kennan's most striking characteristics as a diplomat, as a strategist, and as a policy planner was an inability to insulate his jobs from his moods. Throughout his career he had taken things personally. He was "never able to detach himself emotionally from the issues we had to consider," Dorothy Fosdick remembered. "He could go into a bad slump when he thought he was not being listened to." He viewed the world through himself, not as something apart from himself. That could lead to great insights: Kennan's understanding of the Soviet Union and how to contain it grew largely out of his own self-analysis. But it could also produce volatility: no sooner did the Truman administration reconcile itself to the division of Germany—something Kennan had been advocating since 1945—than he began pushing for reunification. It was as if he were allergic to orthodoxy. "I have the habit," he acknowledged years later, "of seeing two opposing sides of a question, both of them wrong, and then overstating myself, so that I appear to be inconsistent."[51]

That raised a question, then, about how useful the policy planning process, as Kennan conceived it, really was. He never meant the hundreds of pages he and his staff produced to serve as a systematic *philosophy* of American foreign relations, although at times they read like that. He did see them, though, "as one man's concept of how our government ought to behave and by what principles it ought to be guided."[52] But what if that concept—and the principles that lay behind it—changed, whether in response to what was happening in the world or, more disconcertingly, in response to Kennan's own unstable emotions? Reconsiderations are reasonable enough in government. When emotions amplify them, though, they can come across as erratic behavior—even if, by general acknowledgment, brilliance still lies behind it.

FIFTEEN

Reprieve: 1949

"IN THE FACE OF THESE DIFFICULTIES, A DETACHED PHILOSOPHER might not give us a very good chance for avoiding real trouble," Kennan told the audience he had spoken to at the Pentagon on November 8, 1948. "But strange things have been known to happen. And who are we, in the face of the experiences of the past week, to say that theoretically unfavorable odds should be a source of discouragement?" The event he had in mind was President Truman's surprise reelection four days earlier. Kennan knew that Marshall, whose health had been deteriorating, would be stepping down at the end of Truman's first term: like almost everyone else, both expected it to be Truman's only term. The prospect of a Republican administration, together with the discouragements of the past few months, had Kennan thinking again about resigning from the Foreign Service and accepting an academic position. As it happened, though, it was Truman who got to select the next secretary of state. At the end of November, he asked Dean Acheson to take the job.[1]

Acheson had played an important role, as under secretary of state, in advancing Kennan's career. He encouraged the author of the "long telegram" to speak publicly about its contents, he facilitated Kennan's move from the National War College to the Policy Planning Staff, and the two cooperated closely in designing the Marshall Plan. They differed only on the public justification for aid to Greece and Turkey, but Acheson, preoccupied with getting the bill through Congress, hardly noticed Kennan's objections to the Truman Doctrine. Having left government to replenish his finances in the summer of 1947, Acheson could watch Kennan's subsequent policy planning only as a well-informed outsider. But he thought highly enough of it—after learning that Truman wanted him now to run the State Department—to ask Kennan to defer any decision about retiring. That led Kennan, on January 3, 1949, to send Acheson an unorthodox offer to stay on.

"We all have our egos and ambitions," he acknowledged. "But the shadows which fall on each of us, these days, are so huge and dark, and so unmistakable in portent, that they clearly dwarf all that happens among us individually, here below." The disclaimer that followed must have raised an Achesonian eyebrow: "I really have no enthusiasm for sharing with the people I have known—Kerensky, Bruening, Dumba, or the king of Jugoslavia—the wretched consolation of having been particularly prominent among the parasites on the body of a dying social order, in the hours of its final agony." Acheson was not to think it "implausible modesty"—there was little danger of that after reading this—when Kennan wrote that he wished to remain only if he could feel that "we are not just bravely paddling the antiquated raft of U.S. foreign policy upstream, at a speed of three miles an hour, against a current which is making four."

One problem was the State Department. It was drifting away from Marshall's concept of a planning staff that met regularly, avoided functional or regional parochialism, and conveyed its recommendations to a secretary of state who patiently awaited them. Nor was the department adequately publicizing its policies: the "X" article at the time had "shocked people to tears," but Kennan now wished there had been twenty like it. Byrnes and Marshall had spent too much time away from Washington: the secretary should not be "an itinerant negotiator," shuttling from one overseas meeting to another "in order to demonstrate our devotion to the principle of international organization." Nor should there be further "lofty pronouncements about peace and democracy." What was needed instead was "hard work, concentration, discipline, and an inner silence."

"There—dear Dean—are some of the things which I think would have to be done to the hull of the ship of state, if it is to be restored to a really buoyant condition." Without them, there was no point in anyone trying "to blow wind into the sails of the old hulk. . . . I'd rather be at Yale, or where-you-will—any place where I could sound-off and talk freely to people—than in the confines of a department in which you can neither do anything about it nor tell people what you think ought to be done."[2]

Kennan claimed, in a postscript, to have written this letter before he knew that Acheson would become secretary of state, but it did not read that way. Its tone was one of Kennan interviewing Acheson, rather than the other way around. It sounded like an effort to press the new secretary into the mold of the previous one, thereby restoring the Policy Planning Staff to its rightful place within the

State Department hierarchy. This, Kennan must have known, was going to be a
stretch.

Acheson had the highest respect for Marshall, so much so that he wrote one
of the best short descriptions of how the great man operated: "All elements of the
problem were held, as it were, in solution in his mind until it was ready to pre-
cipitate a decision." That was not, however, Acheson's style. He lacked Marshall's
modesty, self-discipline, and procedural restraint. He was incapable of commanding quietly: of not commenting on competing positions until he had chosen one.
Acheson paraded his wit, his wardrobe, and especially his mustache—the latter
ornament, the journalist James Reston wrote, was itself "a triumph of policy planning." Oliver Franks, the British ambassador, recalled that Acheson "*bathed* in
talk." The idea of "having your thinking done for you, which is what the Policy
Planning Staff stood for, was alien to Dean." The new secretary of state so loved
debate, in fact, that at one contentious NATO meeting, having exhausted the British and French foreign ministers, he took over and performed their parts after
they had gone to bed.[3]

"You have to remember this about Acheson," Kennan pointed out a few years
after the older man's death. "He was basically a Washington lawyer, not a diplomat. The fact that he looked like a diplomat confused people, but it didn't make
him one. He had never lived abroad, knew no foreign languages, knew nothing
about the outside world." Acheson was chiefly, Franks remembered, "a man of
action. He wanted actually to get things done. I think he felt that Kennan wasn't:
that he sat in his cell and thought major thoughts, but was not particularly concerned with their application to things as they are now." Kennan focused on the
long term. Acheson wanted to know: "What do I do now?"[4]

Why, then, did they think they could work together? One reason was that they
were good friends: the Kennans and the Achesons saw each other regularly, while
the Marshalls determinedly avoided the Washington social scene. "I enjoyed his
company, and profited constantly from exposure to the critical discipline of his fine
mind," Kennan recalled. "He was a lovely person." Acheson's sharp tongue, John
Paton Davies remembered, could not conceal "a great gentleness" in him—"a great
gentlemanliness." It was also the case that Acheson respected Kennan's accomplishments, whereas other secretaries of state—John Foster Dulles was widely assumed
to be the Republican alternative—might not have. Finally, Acheson returned to the
State Department with a relatively open mind. Having been out of government for
a year and a half, he had no position on several of the issues with which Kennan
had been wrestling, and so was ready to listen to him, even if only as one of several

voices. Kennan, for his part, was sure that the ship of state would crash into the rocks unless his could again become the dominant voice in setting a new course—but that could only happen now, if it was to happen at all, through Acheson.[5]

Shortly after receiving Kennan's letter, Acheson asked him to stay on as Policy Planning Staff director. Kennan readily agreed. And so one of the thinnest skins in Washington went to work for one of the thickest. Both men remembered it, years later, as a difficult relationship. But it seemed like a good idea at the time.

I.

"General policy meeting on Germany in the morning. Smaller one in afternoon. Packed in evening." That was all Kennan wrote, in the diary he had begun keeping again, about March 9, 1949, a day on which the prospects for Program A suddenly brightened. The next day's entry read simply: "Took off at 2:00 p.m. for Germany in General Clay's plane." Stranded overnight in Bermuda, Kennan did something he had not done for some time: he wrote a poem.

> Frown not, fair pilgrim, on this magic isle
> Where unseen fairies toll the bells of night.
> Dismiss not lightly, nor with scornful smile
> The things that strike the ear and meet the sight
> In this implausible, unlikely land:
> Fresh lawns, dark cedars, picture-postcard sky,
> A limpid sea, strange objects on the sand,
> White roofs in moonlight; and the aching cry
> Of strings of lights along a distant shore
> Across a darkened sea. Do not deplore
> These things—and others—just because they lie
> Amid the vast dread ocean of a dream.
> The island's real; and real—I trust—am I.
> The distant continents—
>   are what they seem.

Addressed to a fellow passenger—an unnamed lady—the lines hinted at liberation, whether from conventionality, or from being stuck in Washington, or from the sense of having reached a dead end in his job. Or maybe it was just a poem. The lady responded, in any event, with a dash of reality.

What seem to you the frown, the smile of scorn,
Dismissal, the deploring of a dream,
Are none of these. The islands are forlorn
Not for their magic or because they seem
Unreal, but just because one cannot stay
More than an instant in such happy air
Before each is impelled upon his way—
Aware of loss but saying "I must not care."
This is the sadness of a bitter time,
And this the final, but unfinished, rhyme.

Nevertheless, looking back over the past few weeks, Kennan had reason to be glad that he had not resigned.[6]

In his January 3 letter, he had advised Acheson to finish a task Marshall left uncompleted: bringing the military administration of occupied Germany and Japan into line with State Department planning on the future of those countries. They would be two of the five power centers that would shape the postwar world, and yet the establishments of Clay and MacArthur were so inflexibly top-heavy that the connection between objectives and actions was being lost: "I cannot tell you how serious this is." Kennan had already accomplished a partial course correction in Japan, but on Germany, after several months of effort, hardly anyone seemed to be supporting Program A.[7]

Except, from outside the government, an old but prominent adversary: on December 30 Walter Lippmann had published a column criticizing the rush to form a West German government. Such a regime, he insisted, would combine toxic irredentism with an indefinite dependence on the United States. Acheson was no fan of Lippmann: he had gone out of his way in a National War College lecture a few months earlier to ridicule the journalist's "somewhat tiring" attacks on Kennan's "X" article. But the incoming secretary of state had been briefed on Program A as a consultant to the Policy Planning Staff and would have connected it with what Lippmann had now written. Shortly after taking office, Acheson got Truman's permission to take a fresh look at the German problem, and then asked Kennan to chair an NSC working group assembled for that purpose. In the meantime, Kennan had shared the substance of Program A—still a classified

document—with Lippmann, who agreed that the liquidation of military government and a gradual withdrawal of occupation forces should be "a real and present
objective, not a remote and theoretical one." There was thus a Kennan-Lippmann
convergence on Germany, which in turn converged on Acheson.[8]

Was Kennan, as Frank Roberts suggested, trying to win Lippmann's approval?
Kennan had always believed that containment should lead to a settlement with
the Soviet Union, but Lippmann's criticisms may have induced him to advance
the timetable. Kennan would not have written his long unsent letter in April 1948
had he not taken Lippmann seriously, and from the time he returned to work later
that month, he was pushing simultaneously on several fronts—in a way that he had
not done before—to keep the diplomatic channels to Moscow open. The Smith-
Molotov exchange had been an effort to do this, but the same objective lay behind
Kennan's opposition to NATO and his support for Program A. Processes, he
believed, had to *reflect* purposes—here Kennan certainly agreed with Lippmann—
and ending the Cold War was what the purpose of conducting it should be.[9]

The Kennan-Lippmann-Acheson convergence gained added significance on
January 31, 1949, when Stalin, in a cryptic set of answers to a newspaperman's
questions, hinted at a willingness to lift the Berlin blockade on the condition
that the foreign ministers of the occupying powers meet to discuss Germany's
future. He did so without mentioning an earlier insistence that the *Deutschmark*
be withdrawn from circulation in the city. Discreet inquiries established that the
omission had been no accident. This raised the prospect, then, of a conference at
which the United States would have to reveal, once and for all, its intentions for
Germany. Program A was the clearest blueprint available.[10]

The controversy surrounding it, however, had not diminished. Robert Murphy,
Clay's political adviser, complained that if Stalin really had been serious, he would
have used confidential communications, not a newspaper, to explore a settlement.
Where Kennan stressed the need to avoid a division of Europe, Murphy retorted
that the line had already been drawn "through no fault of the Western Powers." If
the West Germans lost confidence in the Americans, the Truman administration
would soon be worrying about a new line that would leave all of Germany on the
wrong side. Murphy's views had support elsewhere in the State Department, the
Defense Department, and of course within Clay's command, where doubts about
Program A were as strong as ever.[11]

Kennan's committee was being whipsawed, he complained to Acheson early in
February, but the choices it was considering would shape the future for decades

to come. So in an effort to break the stalemate—and no doubt with his Japan trip in mind—Kennan offered to go to Germany to see the situation for himself. He was, Franks reported to London, a powerful influence in Acheson's State Department. "I regard his mission to Germany as likely to be of particular importance." Nonetheless, Kennan admitted on the day before he was to leave, it was probably too late to change the American position on the establishment of a West German government.

What followed surprised and gratified Kennan, for, in the words of the meeting minutes, taken by Murphy himself,

> The Secretary said that he was sorry to hear Mr. Kennan say this because he had been almost persuaded by the cogency of Mr. Kennan's argument. . . . [H]e did not understand . . . how we ever arrived at the decision to see established a Western German government or State. He wondered whether this had not been the brainchild of General Clay and not a governmental decision.

Acheson deferred any decision on Germany until after Kennan's return. He then asked Kennan to follow him home that evening to continue the discussion, and there expanded his assignment to include talks with American and allied diplomats elsewhere in Europe. This gave Kennan a broader mandate than he had ever received from Marshall to pursue Program A. Murphy, deeply worried, sent word ahead to Clay that "Kennan is as luke warm as ever toward the establishment of a Western German government. . . . I am most eager for him to obtain a better understanding of the actual German conditions."[12]

Still stuck in Bermuda on the night of March 10, Kennan made his way to the officers' club, where a bingo game was in progress. It seemed to exempt the players "from the necessity to think and speak." Outside a breeze was blowing, "unceasing and slightly sinister," while in the distance a B-29 was revving its engines for takeoff. Most Americans on the island were coming from, or going to, Germany: how had it been in the old days? one of them wanted to know. "It was awful now," he continued, without waiting for an answer. After another stop in the Azores— well known to Kennan as a place and as a problem in World War II—he flew into blockaded Berlin on March 12 and was able to see it for himself: "The city seemed dead—a ghost of its former self." For the ever-impressionable Kennan, who had always regarded Germany, along with Russia, as an expatriate home, it was as if he were seeing his own ghost as well.[13]

II.

Which is probably why he went back to keeping a diary, his first sustained effort to do so since returning to Washington in the spring of 1946. That city rarely inspired, or left time for, the kind of writing he had done in the past. Nor had his 1948 trip to Japan produced such an account, perhaps because the setting was too alien. But when Hessman finished typing what Kennan had written during the eleven days he spent in Germany in 1949, she had thirty-four pages. Kennan had permitted himself again—as if with relief—to filter a diplomat's observations through an artist's eye, a historian's ear, and a poet's emotions. He wrote of

Once fashionable Berlin suburbs, where people camped out in the surviving dark cold houses "like barbarians in the palaces of Italy."

Tall bare poplars, "which had waited and watched through the final years of the Weimar Republic and the Nazi era and the war and the bombings and the arrival of the Russian army," now standing "alone again through another night, until the battered cars of the first early subway train came clattering past."

Ruins, which still stood "in awful and imposing desolation: the piles of rubble flowing down to the sidewalk, twisted iron beams and the remnants of walls standing out above them, portions of rooms hanging giddily in the air like stage settings."

Chauffeurs, outside a brightly lit American club, "stamping up and down and muttering in the cold night air, . . . like an evil caricature of the bundled Russian coachmen of olden times, waiting for their masters outside the night-clubs of St. Petersburg and Moscow."

Occupiers, who in the midst of devastation were unable to stop "handing each other drinks and discussing through the long evenings the price of antiques, the inadequacies of servants, and the availability of cosmetics in the PX."

But also kids, with no memory of a different Berlin, who treated the devastated city as an immense playground: "What other children had infinite supplies of bricks and other building materials for building dams in the flowing gutters [or] such magnificent settings for hide-and-seek? Where else could you, if the policeman wasn't looking, detach one of the little steel dump cars on the rubble-removal tracks and roll it down

whole city blocks to a make-believe railway station far away? Who else
had such natural embattlements and redoubts for conducting snowball
fights?"

The planes landing every three minutes were keeping the city supplied, but that
was an improvisation: "We had no answer, yet, to the great political insecurity that
hung over this area." Whatever vision did exist was clouded by "our habits, our
comforts, our false and corrupting position as conquerors and occupiers."

Why was it, for example, that in their meetings with Germans, Clay's staff was
still seating them at the far ends of tables, as if to replay surrender negotiations?
Why couldn't the Americans understand that their "childish" reliance on ice cream
and Coca-Cola revived the Germans' old sense of superiority? Why relieve them
of responsibility by managing—often mismanaging—their daily affairs, while at
the same time "bloating their morbid delusions" by assuring them that the future
of Europe depended on them?

Too many Germans regarded defeat as a kind of automobile accident, allowing them to forget what they had done to bring it about. And yet denazification
was doing more harm than good. How could one ever acknowledge enough guilt
to compensate for the crimes? a half-Jewish editor asked Kennan. Balancing that
scale was a task for another world, not this one. Some Germans, however, welcomed having their occupiers cram down their throats things they would never
voluntarily have swallowed. They might not like living under the Americans, but
they didn't want them to leave. They were, on the whole, better than the British,
who ran their zone with a condescension imported from their empire, and certainly the predatory French, who seemed bent on stripping their zone bare. All
were preferable to the nearby Russians.

And yet it was André François-Poncet, the chief French diplomat in Germany
and a spokesman for the new foreign minister, Robert Schuman, who proposed to
Kennan a plan to end military government, place the three western zones under
civilian commissioners, and give those Germans as much control over their own
affairs as possible. The Soviet zone was gone, a German friend warned Kennan.
The Russians had imposed a social revolution of such thoroughness and brutality
that any attempt to reunify Germany would risk a civil war worse than the one
Spain had suffered. A reunited Germany, should that nonetheless prove possible,
would probably be "indigestible" for the rest of Europe: "We should, therefore,
make a virtue of necessity and cling to the split Germany as the only hope for the
consolidation of Europe."

Kennan's visit to Hamburg, where he had served in the late 1920s, hit him especially hard. Berlin had always been a cold imperial city, haughty and pretentious. Such places "invited the wrath of gods and men." But "poor old Hamburg"—it had been comfortable and good-humored, with no greater ambitions than "the common-sense humdrum of commerce and industry." Its center had been obliterated in just three nights of incendiary raids in 1943. Seventy-five thousand people had died; three thousand still lay buried in the rubble.

> [H]ere for the first time I felt an unshakeable conviction that no momentary military advantage—even if such could have been calculated to exist, could have justified this stupendous, careless destruction of civilian life and of material values, built up laboriously by human hands, over the course of centuries, for purposes having nothing to do with war.

It was not enough to excuse this with "the screaming non-sequitur: 'They did it to us.'" For if the West was to claim superiority over its adversaries, then "it had to learn to fight its wars morally as well as militarily, or not fight them at all." This might seem, at first, naïve. What it really required, though, was for the United States "to be militarily stronger than its adversaries by a margin sufficient to enable it to dispense with those means which can stave off defeat only at the cost of undermining victory." It was a nebulous early anticipation of nuclear deterrence.

With all of this, Kennan found some things little changed. There was the Elbe, the harbor, and its hinterland. There were the same stolid commuters, engrossed in their newspapers and smoking bad cigarettes as they took ferries to work: only the seagulls, riding the waves as they always had done, seemed "to rejoice in the wind and the water and the first premonitions of spring." Saint Pauli had in part survived: the facades of famous beer halls, the narrow streets stretching off into obscurity, "and at one point, under an archway, with the traditional uniform of fur neck-piece, short skirt and shiny handbag, . . . one of those merry damsels who once contributed so much to the life and lure of this port."

A final day left time to visit a few villages outside Frankfurt, near where Kennan had been interned seven years earlier. They were mostly intact, but the burghers who inhabited them—once the backbone of Nazism—were now grotesque: they were like "awkward, aging beetles, who had survived some sort of flood and catastrophe and were still stubbornly crawling around the haunts from which they were supposed to have been removed." They were throwbacks, however: they were not the future. On the train to Paris that evening,

I thought of the whole bizonal area stretching off behind us in the dusk; and it seemed to me that you could hear the great low murmur of human life beginning to stir again, beginning to recapture the rhythm of work and life and change, after years of shock and prostration. Here were tens of millions of human beings, of all ages and walks of life, reacting, as human beings always have and must, to the myriad of stimuli of heredity and education and climate and economic necessity and emotion. Whatever we did, they would no longer stand still in thought or in outlook.

Kennan did not cite Gibbon on this trip, but the historian's warning about conquered provinces, which had so often raised doubts about the ability of the Nazis and the Soviets to control the territories they had taken, must have haunted him. For now, Kennan did write, the "ironic dialectics of military victory and defeat" were constraining what the Americans and their allies could do—or, at least, what he thought they should do:

> [T]he victor, having taken upon himself all responsibility and all power, has nothing more to gain and only things to lose and is therefore enslaved by his own successes, whereas the vanquished, having nothing more to lose and only things to gain, . . . is free of responsibility, can afford to be clear-sighted and unpityingly realistic, and has only to wait, in order that things may again go his way.[14]

What Kennan saw on his trip provided little reason to think that a reunification of Germany, along the lines of Program A, could be imposed from the top down. A division of Germany was already taking place, with the consent of most Germans, from the bottom up. It was, Kennan thought, a Bismarckian moment, "when you hear the garments of the Goddess of Time rustling through the course of events. Who ignores this rustling, does so at his peril."[15]

III.

Acheson, however, was keeping his options open. His immediate priority was the upcoming visit of the British and French foreign ministers, who would be in Washington for the signing of the North Atlantic Treaty early in April. Nothing had been said to them about Program A, and Acheson did not think this the right occasion to raise it. He was still worried, though, about being rushed too quickly into a division of Germany, and he was not yet ready to write off Kennan's plan. Acheson's first concern was process but he had not given up on purpose: what kind of Europe did the United States really want?[16]

NATO answered one part of that question: there was now an American commitment to defend the western portions of Europe against a Soviet attack and, by implication, an acknowledgment that the eastern parts would remain, for the foreseeable future, under Soviet domination. That made it hard to see how Germany—already divided into Soviet and western zones—could reunify anytime soon. Acheson had little choice but to proceed with Anglo-American-French planning for an independent West Germany. The purpose the new state would serve, however, was still unclear in his mind. Would it become an end in itself—a final nail in the coffin of a unified Europe—or would it be the means by which that idea might revive?

The issue had to be settled quickly, because the American, British, and French foreign ministers would be discussing the German question with their Soviet counterpart in Paris at the end of May. Acheson asked Philip Jessup, ambassador at large in the State Department, to supervise preparations, and Jessup unexpectedly endorsed Program A as a set of "optimum" proposals, not to be discarded either "in anticipation of possible Soviet objections [or] for fear that they might be accepted by the Soviet Union and thus be translated into reality." Whatever happened, Kennan made it clear that Program A should be put forward *only* if there had been careful prior consultations with the British and the French.[17]

Acheson approved this procedure, got Truman's permission to present these ideas to the allies, entrusted Jessup and Bohlen with the assignment, and on May 11 dictated instructions on how it should be done: "Just as the unification of Germany is not an end in itself, so the division of Germany is not an end in itself." The test would be whether unification advanced the goal of a free Europe. The price for a Red Army withdrawal might well be too high, but

> [a] possible regrouping of troops which would have the effect of removing Russian troops eastward and possibly ending their presence in and passage through the Eastern European countries may have important advantages. It deserves the most careful study. . . . No outcome—even a good one—is free from objection. Any decision will have some dangers. But this is not a time for avoiding decisions.

Kennan himself could have written this. But then, on the next morning, James Reston published a simplified version of Program A on the front page of *The New York Times*. The headlines alone were shocking—

Big 3 Would Withdraw to Ports in the North Under Proposal.
French Would Go Home.
Presentation of Suggestion Will Depend on Soviet Stand in
Paris Talks.

—but the text was worse: "The screen of United States, British and French troops now standing between the Soviet Army and Western Europe . . . would be withdrawn."[18]

The impression given the British and the French, Kennan immediately realized, could only have been that the United States was considering pulling its forces out of Germany, had kept this from them, and was about to spring it on them. Bohlen and Jessup—now in Paris—tried to calm the resulting furor by disavowing any intention to remove or redeploy American forces. Acheson still was not ready to give up, however: he reminded Bevin and Schuman that Germany could not remain permanently occupied. Some "gradual reduction and regrouping" of forces would have to occur. At this point, though, the Russians put an end to the discussion. "The Germans hate us," General V. I. Chuikov, the Soviet high commissioner for the eastern zone, told Bohlen after Acheson asked him to propose Kennan's plan. "It is necessary that we maintain our forces in Germany."[19]

So who killed Program A? Reston never revealed his source, but there were plenty of possible culprits: Clay, who had moved from discouragement to satisfaction to outrage as Program A reappeared, disappeared, and reappeared again; Murphy, now in an influential position as acting director of the State Department's Office of German and Austrian Affairs; Hickerson and his colleagues in the Office of European Affairs, who had long seen NATO as a way to bind the western zones of Germany to Western Europe and the United States; the Joint Chiefs of Staff, who thought the idea militarily unfeasible. And Chuikov certainly had not helped. Whoever did it, Kennan ruefully acknowledged, had administered "a spectacular *coup de grace*" to Program A.[20]

A year earlier Stalin had killed another Kennan initiative by publicizing it: this was the supposedly confidential Smith-Molotov exchange. But that at least had been the act of an adversary, aimed at compromising the United States in the eyes of its allies. The Reston leak came from one or more American officials, who targeted Kennan while seeking to lock Acheson—and, through him, the United States—into an irreversible commitment to a West German state and hence to a divided Germany that would ensure a divided Europe. Acheson could do no more. "Interest in this approach waned," he wrote blandly in his 1969 memoir of over seven hundred pages, which devoted only three sentences to Program A.[21]

Kennan took it all badly. The past few days, he wrote the secretary of state, had eliminated any possibility of Germany's reunification under the auspices of its occupiers: there now appeared to be "*no* conditions on which we would really find such a solution satisfactory." This would surely embitter the Germans, raising the possibility of "some violent manifestation" by which they might unify themselves, demanding the departure of all occupying powers. At least as disturbing was what all of this implied about the American planning process:

> [W]e spent eight weeks last fall working out what we felt would be a logical program for advance toward the unification of Germany. Piece by piece, . . . the essentials of this program have been discarded, and the logic broken up. Some modification was necessary; but the program emerging from the Paris talks now bears no logical connection with the original concept.

Under these circumstances, Washington might as well let the British and the French solve the German problem, while acknowledging "that we have deferred extensively to their views."[22]

Which Acheson indeed had now done. What Kennan failed to point out, though, was that most *American* officials had long since given up on German reunification—as he himself had done between 1945 and 1948—so this was hardly a matter of blindly empowering allies. Nor did the Soviet Union want reunification if it could not be on Moscow's terms. Program A had always been a long shot: even Kennan had not been optimistic about its prospects. Why, then, was he so upset now?

Probably because Program A, for all its enemies, had won more support in Washington than his views on NATO ever did. There was never much chance of reversing the movement toward a military alliance, but his plan for Germany was a cat with multiple lives: it kept reviving after being declared dead.[23] To have it finally buried by a newspaper leak after all of these resurrections was infuriating. It was also alarming, for Kennan had convinced himself that the future of Europe would depend on what was done about Germany. Now, it seemed, that future had been determined by a fluke, rather than by the months of planning Kennan and his staff had devoted to it.

But it was not really a fluke, because it was not at all clear that even the West Germans would have accepted Program A. Kennan thought he understood Germans as well as any American, but he had not lived among them since 1942. He was aware, but only from a distance, of what they had since endured. As a consequence, he overestimated the Germans' resentment of their American, British, and French occupiers, and—strangely—underestimated their fear of the Russians. He objected especially to the signs he saw of American consumer culture, but there was only a single reference in his 1949 trip diary to the far more radical transformations that Soviet authorities were imposing in their part of Germany. Kennan acknowledged, two decades later, that he had worried more than most Germans about "the iniquities and inadequacies of our occupational establishment." These had been, on his part, "grievous miscalculations."[24]

Program A's fate also upset Kennan because it confirmed what he should already have known about his new boss. It was Acheson's habit, when circumstances forced him to change his mind, to do so quickly, without regret, often without acknowledgment that the reversal had even taken place. That had happened in August 1946 when, in response to the Turkish Straits crisis, he had gone from being a Henry Wallace sympathizer to a George Kennan publicist almost overnight. Acheson's shift on Germany in May 1949 was equally abrupt, but Kennan took it as a repudiation. He lacked the skill, as Acheson would put it in another context, of "graciously" conceding what one "no longer had the power to withhold."[25]

Acheson was conceding now, as Kennan saw it, any prospect of resolving Cold War differences within the likely lifetimes of either of them. If Acheson lost sleep over this, there is little evidence of it. Kennan—who could never avoid looking back, or reconsidering, or regretting what might have been—lost a lot.

IV.

He could hardly claim, though, that Acheson had not listened. Program A was a grand scheme that ran up against blunt realities, one of which was the secretary of state's lack of enthusiasm for the pursuit of lost causes. Where the cause was more promising, he would pursue it, even in the face of controversy. That became clear with respect to another Kennan idea, which was that not all communists everywhere were equally dangerous. The very success of communism beyond the Soviet Union, he had long believed, would corrupt it with nationalism, so that Moscow could only assume the loyalty of its ideological followers where they had not yet seized power—or where, as in Eastern Europe, the Red Army was keeping them in power. China was Kennan's prime example: under Davies's tutelage, he had been arguing since 1947 that a victory for Mao Zedong would not necessarily be one for the Kremlin. He had no word then for what he was describing, but Yugoslavia's defection in 1948 provided one: it was "Titoism," and one of Kennan's priorities in 1949 was to persuade Acheson of its importance.

"Tito's heresy is of the type unlikely ever to be forgiven," he wrote in an updated Policy Planning Staff paper on Yugoslavia, completed on February 10. By successfully defying the Kremlin, Tito had compromised Moscow's control of its remaining satellite empire. The repercussions would extend not only through Eastern Europe but also among communist parties in France, Italy, and especially China, where Mao "might already be infected with the Tito virus." The United States should do all it could, therefore, to ensure Tito's survival, without at the same time endorsing the nature of his regime.[26]

The Chinese Communists were "deeply suspicious" of the United States, Kennan added on February 25. But any further aid to Chiang Kai-shek would only alienate the Chinese people, perpetuating the illusion that China's interests lay with the U.S.S.R. Mao would discover that this was not the case: the Soviet Union would have no more success shaping events in China than had the United States. Eventually a new revolution would either overthrow the Communists or change their character. That would take time, but the Americans could afford to wait: "We are under no Byzantine Tartar compulsion to shackle as our own captive the revolution which we seek to release."[27]

Implied in all of this was another homage to Bismarck, who after unifying Germany in 1871 had turned its enemies' animosities upon themselves. "Our safety depends," Kennan told the war college students in his lecture the previous December, "on our ability to establish a balance among the hostile or undependable forces of the world." Adversaries should

spend in conflict with each other, if they must spend it at all, the intolerance and violence and fanaticism which might otherwise be directed against us, [so] that they are thus compelled to cancel each other out and exhaust themselves in internecine conflict in order that the constructive forces, working for world stability, may continue to have the possibility of life.

Such a strategy would achieve containment without overcommitment, and Titoism—the first tangible evidence of hostility among communists—made it seem possible. Smith, now back from three years as ambassador in Moscow, caught

Kennan's meaning precisely when he reminded the Policy Planning Staff, on March 1, that "the Russians fear Titoism above everything else. . . . [T]he United States does not fear communism if it is not controlled by Moscow and not committed to aggression."[28]

But as Davies, together with his staff colleague Ware Adams, reminded Kennan, acting on Smith's assumption would require shifting the official portrayal of international communism. The Truman administration had been describing it as "a single, coherent, unitary, self-consistent doctrine," and no doubt Soviet leaders wished that it were. But not all communists were Moscow's agents. By treating them all as such, Washington's rhetoric was forcing them into that position. If it could distinguish communism from Russian imperialism, "we would thus . . . remove from the communists in China and elsewhere throughout the world a strong force tending to compel them to collaborate with the Soviet Union." This would give the United States a much more effective weapon "than is the blunderbuss of primitive 'anti-communism,' aimed against a vaguely defined, out of date, self-contradictory, and possibly dying, set of political theories."[29]

Kennan's response is not on record, but shortly after returning from Germany at the end of March, he did tell the staff that the United States should do everything possible "to increase the suspicion between the Kremlin and its agents abroad." Titoism was a "disintegrating force" within international communism and "should be stimulated and encouraged by all devices of propaganda."[30] The problem would be to make this work in a domestic political climate that was growing more hospitable, not less, to rhetorical blunderbusses.

Defending communists of any kind had never been popular in the United States, and the onset of the Cold War had made it much less so. The Truman Doctrine was widely regarded as a declaration of war against communists everywhere. During the 1948 presidential campaign, the president denounced "Henry Wallace and his communists," while former State Department official Alger Hiss—an old friend of Acheson's—was charged with spying for the Soviet Union, raising fears that communists had infiltrated the U.S. government. Meanwhile, the pro-Nationalist "China Lobby" was whipping up support for Chiang Kai-shek in Congress and the media: Mao's triumph, it insisted, would be a disaster for the United States. Acheson had dropped Program A because it unsettled allies. To what extent would he support an even riskier Kennan strategy that—at least in the eyes of domestic critics—attempted to distinguish "good" communists from "bad" ones?[31]

V.

As it happened, Acheson did just that. It was an "obvious interest" of the United States, he commented in February, that Tito survive. Once it became clear that Yugoslavia had stopped assisting the Greek communists, Acheson favored relaxing restrictions on trade with that country, even to the point of allowing the sale of a militarily significant steel mill. That got him into trouble with the new secretary of defense, Louis Johnson—Forrestal had resigned after suffering a nervous breakdown, and then committed suicide. When the word got out that the United States was selling steel mills to communists, Johnson fumed, the resulting furor might sink the Democratic Party's chances in the next election. Acheson stood his ground, however, won Truman's approval for the sale, and to Kennan's relief it went through. The American objective, he suggested at the end of August 1949, should not be to promote democratic revolutions in Eastern Europe but rather to encourage other communists like Tito to follow a nationalist line. Acheson got the point. The Yugoslav dictator might be a son-of-a-bitch, he observed the following month, but he was "*our* son-of-a-bitch."[32]

Nor did Acheson object to less public methods of undermining Soviet authority in Eastern Europe. Kennan had been content at first to let Tito's example do that, but with Wisner's Office of Policy Coordination available, it was hard to resist the temptation to speed the process. By 1949 Kennan was helping to set up an ostensibly private National Committee for a Free Europe—actually funded through the OPC—to provide financial support and employment opportunities for Eastern European émigrés, as well as anti-Soviet broadcasts to their homelands through its subsidiary, Radio Free Europe. The OPC was also collaborating with "defectors, deserters and escapees" from the region: they were, a Policy Planning Staff paper noted in June, the "most effective agents to destroy the communist myth of the Soviet paradise." When asked, several months later, about more aggressive initiatives, Kennan replied that "some covert operations should be applied at the appropriate time," perhaps in Poland even immediately.[33]

Did these include the possibility of assassinations? Kennan acknowledged years later that a unit had existed within the OPC "specifically charged with this sort of activity *if and when* we ever decided to conduct it." But its chief, Boris Pash, an Army colonel whose military intelligence career went back to the Manhattan Project, had been vague about his authority: "If any such responsibility was written into his charter (and [Pash] couldn't remember that it was), it was because the list of dirty tricks with which they *were* charged had been taken over, practically verbatim, from the list of responsibilities of the corresponding division of the wartime O.S.S., which apparently did not preclude this sort of thing." Kennan was sure "that no assassinations were conducted during our time on the Planning Staff, and [that] the very idea of such a thing was decisively put down by higher authority."[34]

The OPC was already at work in Albania. Kennan had endorsed an operation there the previous April but remained unsure about its objectives. Should the United States, working with the British, seek to overthrow the regime of Enver Hoxha, still loyal to Moscow but caught between Tito's Yugoslavia and the failing communist insurgency in Greece? Should Tito be encouraged to do that? What might the Soviet reaction be? But when Bevin asked Acheson, in September, whether the United States would agree to "bring down" Hoxha, the secretary of state replied—cautiously—in the affirmative. Caution would have been advisable, for over the next three years the OPC and the British secret intelligence service MI6 tried repeatedly to infiltrate agents and even paramilitary forces into Albania, with unvaryingly disastrous results. The principal reason was not Kennan's insufficient oversight of the OPC, but the fact that MI6's liaison officer to Wisner's organization was the spy Kim Philby, who exposed each of the Albanian expeditions to Soviet intelligence and, through them, to Hoxha. Kennan had reason to regret his role in these activities, but the responsibility for their failure went well beyond him.[35]

Long before the extent of the debacle became known, Kennan had made it clear that such operations should not be the primary instrument with which to roll back Soviet influence in Eastern Europe. That should be Stalin himself, who would accomplish the objective by continuing to insist that the interests of the satellite states must never conflict with those of the U.S.S.R.

Power, even the taste of it, is as likely to corrupt Communist as bourgeois leaders. Considerations of national as well as personal interest materialize and come into conflict with the colonial policy pursued by the Soviet interests. When this happens, satellite officials may still remain, by force of other factors, Kremlin captives; but at least they are not entirely willing ones.

The optimal strategy, then, would not be to try to overthrow communist regimes in Eastern Europe, but rather to encourage their nationalism: "to foster a heretical drifting-away process on the part of the satellite states." In this way, the United

States might begin to operate "on the basis of a balance of forces in the Communist world, and to foster the tendencies toward accommodation with the West implicit in such a state of affairs."[36]

On the whole, Kennan's strategy of sustaining Tito succeeded. It survived the increasing tendency within the United States *not* to distinguish between communists: Acheson's help here was vital. No other Eastern European state openly defied Stalin, but his fear that one or more of them might rattled him sufficiently that he launched devastating purges, over the next few years, eliminating many of his own loyalists in the region. The covert operations Kennan supported at the time—even though he later repudiated them—increased the Soviet Union's insecurity about its empire. Their purpose, as he put it in August 1949, was to provoke a quarrel "between the Kremlin and the Communist Reformation." Whether because of these activities or in spite of them, that is exactly what eventually happened.[37]

VI.

Acheson shared Kennan's hopes that Titoism would take hold in China as well. Late in February 1949 he asked Truman to approve a Policy Planning Staff recommendation that the United States seek "to exploit through political and economic means any rifts between the Chinese Communists and the USSR," and the president readily did so. To say that the Russians controlled China and that "we might just as well die or give up," the secretary of state assured the Senate Foreign Relations Committee the following month, was "a very distinct exaggeration of the whole matter." The Nationalists were "washed up," Acheson told Bevin in April, but Chinese inertia and corruption would soon absorb the Communists. It was difficult to say so publicly, but the United States would henceforth pursue "a more realistic policy respecting China."[38]

There were, however, important differences between China and Yugoslavia. One was that Tito headed a government already in power that wanted Washington's help to stay there; Moscow offered only extinction. Mao led a movement about to take power that expected the Americans to try to stop it. Why, otherwise, were they still aiding their longtime ally Chiang Kai-shek? Moscow, from Mao's perspective, offered ideological legitimation—something Tito did not need—but also protection against American efforts to overthrow him. That the Truman administration was aiding the Nationalists as a way of extracting itself from China while deflecting the China lobby's wrath was a subtlety wholly lost on Mao. That he needed, for the moment at least, to align himself with Moscow was equally lost on the Americans. When Mao announced, at the end of June 1949, that the new China would "lean" to the side of the Soviet Union, it seemed to Acheson, Kennan, and Davies that he failed to follow the script. On that point, at least, they were right: Mao had been assuring Stalin that he would *not* become an Asian Tito.[39]

Mao's attitude made it difficult to portray him within the United States, therefore, as a "good" communist. Fed up with the Nationalists, Kennan and Davies had been overseeing the preparation of a voluminous "White Paper," meant for public release, that would document the failures of Chiang's government. Acheson endorsed the project, overriding objections from Secretary of Defense Johnson and the Joint Chiefs of Staff. But by the time this 1,054-page volume finally came out in August, relations with Mao had soured: the secretary of state's letter of transmittal—to which, strangely, neither Kennan nor Davies objected—denounced the communist leaders for having "forsworn their Chinese heritage." This put Acheson, his biographer has commented, "in the remarkable position of trying to divide Chinese from Russian communists by describing the former as fanatics subservient to the latter." In the meantime, the hundreds of declassified documents in the White Paper had insulted the Nationalists, while handing the China lobby enough ammunition to keep Acheson on the defensive through the rest of his term.[40]

Kennan, at the time, was worrying about Taiwan, where Chiang was planning to move his government after being ejected from the mainland. But could Washington afford to leave that island, strategically located between Okinawa and the Philippines, in the hands of the incompetent Nationalists, who would surely soon lose it to the Communists? Kennan proposed, in July, a dramatic solution: that the United States move with "resolution, speed, ruthlessness, and self-assurance" to evict the 300,000 Nationalist troops already on the island, in "the way that Theodore Roosevelt might have done it." This would have "an electrifying effect in this country and throughout the Far East." The recommendation electrified somebody, because Kennan withdrew it on the day he submitted it. Years later he attributed the idea to Davies, who, when asked about it, denied responsibility for such a "totally implausible" plan. "I imagine that anyone, even of the intellectual eminence of Kennan, is entitled to some mad acts."[41]

Davies was pulling his interviewer's leg here, for however bombastic Kennan's language was, his Taiwan proposal was no aberration. There had been discussions within the State Department, the Pentagon, the CIA, and MacArthur's headquarters in Tokyo, of how the United States might persuade Chiang Kai-shek to step down, or remove him from power, or even foster a Taiwanese separatist movement that would deny the island to *both* the Chinese Nationalists and the Communists. The idea would have been to incorporate Taiwan within the "defensive perimeter" strategy that Kennan had been advocating, without having the United States take sides too obviously in the Chinese civil war. Kennan's eviction scenario grew out of a Policy Planning Staff study Davies had helped prepare, and as he reminded Kennan, "God knows what the OPC may have been up to."

But it was now too late for such maneuvers. Chiang was consolidating his authority over Taiwan, and his increasingly vociferous supporters in the United States were determined to keep him there: for them, the island was the base from which the Nationalists would one day eject the Communists from China itself. The Joint Chiefs of Staff, concerned about a growing gap between political commitments and military capabilities, had never liked the idea of using American forces to secure Taiwan. "We didn't have the forces to throw Chiang off," Rusk recalled, "and the domestic political ramifications would have been overwhelming."[42]

Kennan's China policy showed that he was no China expert. All that he knew about it, he often acknowledged, had come from Davies. And Davies, in the summer of 1949, was suffering from an occupational hazard of experts: what happens when your country doesn't do what you expected it to? Stalin had surprised and angered Kennan by revealing the Smith-Molotov exchanges. Now Mao had surprised and angered Davies by embracing Stalin, not splitting with him. Surprises, for experts, can be unsteadying, and on China both Kennan and Davies were staggering. Thanks to them, Acheson was too.

"It is dangerous to talk about a Chinese Tito-ism," Kennan admitted in September 1949, a few days before Mao, in Beijing, formally proclaimed the People's Republic of China. "What happens in China is not apt to be a replica of what has happened in Yugoslavia or anywhere else." Still, Soviet leaders would have to watch the situation with great care, because their authority over China hung only on "the slender thread of a . . . tortuous and undependable ideology." If differences did develop, they would be very serious for Moscow. It was entirely possible "that Russian Communism may some day be destroyed by its own children in the form of the rebellious Communist parties of other countries. I can think of no development for which there would be greater logic and justice."[43]

VII.

Kennan's principal focus, however, was never on China: his attention to that issue was, at best, sporadic in 1949. What most concerned him, as Acheson's China policy was falling apart, was how Europe might come together now that Program A had foundered. Was the continent to be divided indefinitely into Soviet and American spheres of influence, or could it regain an identity of its own? If the latter—decidedly Kennan's preference—what identity might that be? The question was simple, he told the Policy Planning Staff on May 18: were there to be "two worlds or three"?[44]

The answer was not simple. Europe's most formidable war-making facilities—the Rhine-Ruhr industrial complex—lay within the boundaries of a country that had used them to start two great wars, the latter of which had left not only it but also Europe divided and for the moment powerless. That situation could not last: the Germans would sooner or later recover their strength, while the determination of their occupiers to control them would wane. At that point Germany would be in a position to dominate Europe again, a frightening prospect if, as Kennan suspected, the aggressive tendencies of the Germans had not changed. For Europe to remain split, though, would also be frightening: the Europeans were "almost the only modern, reasonable—if you will, tired—peoples with whom we can live. If they cease to be that . . . we would be a lonely nation. That terrifies me."[45]

Program A had proposed resolving this problem by negotiating a withdrawal of occupation forces from Germany, but then embedding the reunified state within a European federation: European values, in this scenario, would contain German ambitions. Now, however, the United States and its allies had given up on German reunification, leaving European integration in limbo. Could the United States, Great Britain, and France incorporate the new West German state within a sufficiently robust system to keep it from cutting its own deal on reunification with East Germany and the Soviet Union? That danger also alarmed Kennan, for if the Germans again linked up with the Russians, as they had in 1939–41, then "we might as well fold up."[46] That's why the future of Western Europe was so important to him in the summer of 1949. If the United States and its allies could not agree on how to reunify Germany in cooperation with the Soviet Union, then they should at least have a plan to keep the West Germans from doing that on their own.

Devising one became a final test, for Kennan, of what planning could accomplish. The past year—particularly the implosion of Program A—had given him many reasons for pessimism. But what if one were to approach the German problem, by way of European federation, in consultation *with* the British and the French? A British Foreign Office friend, Gladwyn Jebb, had suggested talks on what role Germany might play—or at least West Germany—in any future "United Western Europe." That was all Kennan needed to assign his staff another big task: to devise the optimal federal structure for the noncommunist portions of Europe.[47]

He was determined, this time, to do it right. He got Acheson's approval for the exercise. He met with other top State Department officials—among them Hickerson—to let them know the direction of his thinking. He convened consultants of near-Olympian stature: they included former ambassador to Moscow Walter Bedell Smith; John J. McCloy, soon to depart for West Germany as the first U.S. high commissioner there; J. Robert Oppenheimer, the physicist who had run the Manhattan Project to build the atomic bomb and was now the director of the Institute for Advanced Study at Princeton; Hans Morgenthau, rapidly emerging as the most influential academic theorist of international relations; and the equally influential theologian Reinhold Niebuhr, who was then reviving, as Christian doctrine, the obligation to resist tyranny, whether of the fascist or the communist variety. "Let us proceed," Niebuhr recalled Kennan saying, "as if there was no Russian threat." That struck Niebuhr as like saying: "Let us proceed as though there was not sex in the world"—but did at least stimulate discussion.[48]

As Robert Tufts recalled of the Policy Planning Staff consultants, though, "[w]e were often surprised to find how really ill-informed these people were on matters on which we'd expected them to provide some insights." The meetings were "much more interesting for [them] than they were for the rest of us." That happened in this instance: the heavyweights pontificated but reached no consensus, leaving Kennan free to construct his own.[49]

It took shape as PPS/55, not a formal staff paper, but an outline of what he might say during the next stage of the planning process, a trip to Paris and London to consult the allies. There was no point, Kennan insisted, in trying to force the British into any political or economic union with Europe: they would always prefer alignment with the United States, Canada, and what remained of their empire. But only a European union, Kennan also believed, could control the Germans. That left France in a critical role. With some form of "Franco-German understanding and association, . . . Germany could conceivably be absorbed into [the] larger European family without dominating or demoralizing others." The United States should retain its commitment to defend its NATO allies, plus West Germany and the western occupation zones of Austria, for as long as Europe remained divided. The Franco-German "association," however, would seek over time to end that division: like the Marshall Plan, it would attract the Soviet Union's satellites, filling the void left by the failure of Program A to reunify Germany and to reconstitute Europe.[50]

But the French officials Kennan consulted, fearing exclusion from any Anglo-American relationship, seemed singularly unreceptive. They showed none of the willingness to think creatively about Germany that he had picked up from François-Poncet a few months earlier. The British were less anxious, although more inclined than Kennan had expected to value their ties to the Western Europeans. They were also on the verge of a major financial crisis, which left little room for thinking on Kennan's grand scale. He returned to Washington, he recalled, "with empty hands." Acheson was noncommittal, but "I was under no doubt that he viewed the concept I had presented, closely integrated as it was with my view of the German problem, skeptically and without enthusiasm."[51]

With Britain's trade imbalance draining its gold and dollar reserves at an alarming rate, Kennan shifted the staff's attention, in August, to that problem. Never confident of his own economic expertise, he renewed a request that Acheson, as under secretary of state in 1947, had turned down: for Paul H. Nitze, then working in the department's Office of Economic Affairs, to join the Policy Planning Staff. Kennan had known Nitze since 1946. He had a formidable reputation as a prewar investment banker, as a wartime economic analyst, and as vice-chairman of the postwar Strategic Bombing Survey. Nitze's State Department work had focused chiefly on trade policy and administering the Marshall Plan, but he agreed with Kennan on Program A and had even helped draft the proposal. Now, with Acheson's approval, Kennan made him deputy director, on the understanding that Nitze would eventually become his successor.[52]

The sterling-dollar crisis showed, with almost textbook clarity, why planning was so difficult. Washington officials since before World War II had seen Anglo-American cooperation as a vital national interest, but Truman entrusted these negotiations to the secretary of the treasury, John W. Snyder, a Missouri political crony who made no secret of his contempt for the Labor government's "socialism." That upset Kennan, who knew that a major objective of the Marshall Plan—and even of several CIA covert operations—had been to strengthen the "noncommunist left" in Europe: Snyder seemed determined to rescue the British only if they dismantled their planned economy. James E. Webb, another Truman confidant who had replaced Lovett as under secretary of state, explained that because Acheson was under attack in Congress, it was necessary to give Snyder and Secretary of

Defense Johnson a larger foreign policy role. Kennan shot back that the president should be backing up his secretary of state—and should realize "how terribly difficult it would be to find anyone with comparable qualities for this position." Perhaps Snyder or someone else in the president's "entourage" should take the job?[53]

With Acheson's support and after much effort, Kennan was able to shift the administration's position, allowing the negotiators to work out a mutually acceptable plan to devalue the British pound in return for American concessions on trade and investment, but without any attempt to undo British socialism. After all of the "fireworks" for the benefit of Congress, Kennan grumbled, the president did exactly what he had advised doing: "But I got no credit for it. My name was never mentioned. I was disgusted with this. Acheson, however, being much more of a domestic political character than I was, found it all in order." He was there, after all, "to serve Harry Truman's political interests as well as his interests as head of state. I couldn't have cared less about his political interests."[54]

A few weeks later Webb took Kennan to a meeting at the White House: it was one of the few occasions on which he actually met Truman. "The President looked slightly tired, but was his usual likeable self," Kennan wrote in his diary that evening. "I could understand how such strong loyalties could develop between him and his associates." But

> I was glad, upon reflection, that I had had so little contact with him; for I would not like to be in a position where personal loyalty and affection forced me to close my eyes to the obvious deficiencies in the conduct of foreign policy in this period and to profess enthusiasm for what must remain a confusing and ineffective method of operation.

Two days later, on September 28, 1949, Kennan told Webb that he wanted to go on leave from the State Department the following June. He also asked—sooner than that—to be "relieved of the title and responsibilities as Director of the Planning Staff."[55]

VIII.

Acheson had not eased him out: indeed he had just promoted Kennan. Having spent seven years in Washington, Bohlen was eager to go abroad again, so Acheson asked Kennan to replace him as State Department counselor while continuing to run Policy Planning. Kennan made it clear, though, that this would be a temporary arrangement: "I am very conscious of the increasing complexity of government," he wrote his old mentor George Messersmith, "and sometimes wonder whether that complexity is not growing beyond the nervous and intellectual and physical strength of even the greatest human individuals."[56]

Webb, who was now in charge of State Department administration, thought that it was exceeding Kennan's strength. He had entered the Foreign Service, Webb later pointed out, "when brilliant individual action" was possible. Now, though, diplomacy required a large, complicated organization in which execution and feedback were at least as important as planning: "High-level statements simply do not implement themselves." Kennan's resignation arose, most immediately, from an effort by Webb to address that problem. He had instituted a new procedure by which Policy Planning Staff papers were to pass through his own staff, consisting of assistant secretaries for regions and functions, before going to Acheson. That more than quadrupled the distribution list, proliferating possibilities for objections. A paper on Yugoslavia came back with some on September 16, leaving it, Kennan believed, "in a state of suspended animation." He took this to mean that Policy Planning would henceforth be "a sort of drafting secretariat for the Assistant Secretaries' group."

> The whole *raison d'être* of this Staff was its ability to render an independent judgment on problems coming before the Secretary or the Under Secretary through the regular channels of the Department. If the senior officials of the Department do not wish such an independent judgment, or do not have confidence in us to prepare one which would be useful, then I question whether the Staff should exist at all.

Webb had, in effect, closed Kennan's door into Marshall's office, and Acheson, who now occupied that space, had done nothing to reopen it. This changed little in an operational sense: Kennan had always been one of several advisers to Acheson, who would have tolerated no other arrangement. Symbolically, though, Webb's requirement rankled—and it provided cover for the larger reason that lay behind Kennan's resignation.[57]

This was his sense that, even if the door to the secretary's office had remained open, Acheson was no longer listening to him: indeed, on the issue of European integration, Kennan believed, no one was. Hickerson had expressed "grave doubts" as to whether Germany could be absorbed into any Western European association to which the United States and Great Britain did not belong. Any effort to form an

"Anglo-American-Canadian bloc," Bohlen warned from Paris, would mean that "we will not be able to hold on to the nations of Western Europe." A meeting of U.S. ambassadors in that region concluded unanimously in late October that no European integration would be possible without British participation because the continental powers would otherwise fear German domination.[58]

"That you were right in your premonitions about . . . talking to the British about European union I gladly concede," Kennan wrote Bohlen early in November. "The path of lesser resistance and lesser immediate trouble in this matter would have been to keep silent." Nor did he have any intention of challenging the ambassadors: "Even if the Secretary agreed one hundred percent with my view, I would not ask him to move in the face of such a body of opinion." But the existing policy, Kennan warned,

> (a) gives the Russians no alternative but to continue their present policies or see further areas of central and eastern Europe slide into a U.S.-dominated alliance against them, and in this way makes unlikely any settlement of east-west differences except by war; and

> (b) promises the Germans little more in the western context than an indefinite status as an overcrowded, occupied and frustrated semi-state, thus depriving them of a full stake in their own resistance to eastern pressures and forfeiting their potential aid in the establishment of a military balance between east and west.

"You may have your ideas where one goes from here on such a path and at what point it is supposed to bring us out on the broad uplands of a secure and peaceful Europe," Kennan added, with some bitterness. "If so, I hope you will tell the Secretary about them. . . . I find it increasingly difficult to give guidance on this point."[59]

Bohlen responded angrily: "I had hoped we could profitably correspond on such subjects, but frankly I am not interested in polemics." "You should not have been offended at my letter," Kennan replied. "We have always argued warmly, and with gloves off. You know me well enough to take into account my polemic temperament." There was no point, however, in continuing the debate. "A decision has fallen. . . . Perhaps it was the right one. None of us sees deeply enough into the future to be entirely sure about these things." But the depths of these disagreements had diminished his usefulness, he was sure, "and I will be happier than ever if, as I hope, it will be possible for me . . . to subside quietly into at least a year or two of private life."[60]

"My planning staff, started nearly three years ago, has simply been a failure," Kennan wrote in his diary in mid-November. The State Department's operational units would reduce to meaninglessness any recommendation they did not originate. They would sabotage anything the secretary of state might decide on his own, knowing that no one could review every aspect of their work, and that the people who were trying to get action would soon be gone. Even if Acheson shared Kennan's views, "he would not be able to find others who did." The only way out would be to have a doctrine that could be "patiently and persistently pounded into the heads of the entire apparatus, high and low." But since no such mechanism existed within the government, the only alternative was "an intensive educational effort," conducted through the great universities, to reshape public opinion in the broadest sense. "All of this impels me to the thought that if I am ever to do any good in this work, . . . it must be outside the walls of this institution and not inside them."[61]

IX.

For once, Kennan was keeping a Washington diary: it was the only time he did so for more than a few days while serving as Policy Planning Staff director. He began it in August 1949, shortly after bringing Nitze onto the staff. He knew, even then, that he would be leaving and seemed to think it important to record the reasons why. In addition to Kennan's daily schedule, the diary documents the sterling-dollar crisis, his organizational disagreements with Webb, his growing sense of isolation over Western European integration, and hints at his future. It also shows, despite their differences, Kennan's continuing respect and affection for Acheson, which the secretary of state fully reciprocated.

Acheson was grateful to Kennan for having rescued the British negotiations from the Anglophobic Snyder. They shared a dislike, soon to become a loathing, for Secretary of Defense Johnson. And they still enjoyed each other's company: Acheson too had a farm—his was in Maryland—to which he invited the Kennans for an overnight visit on September 1. When, on the next morning, Joseph and

Stewart Alsop reported that Kennan had drafted key paragraphs of a recent Truman speech on Anglo-American relations, Kennan feared that Acheson might suspect him of leaking that information to the two journalists. "Dear George, Don't worry about," Acheson reassured him. "Nobody can both know you and suspect you. This is life in a disorderly democracy."[62]

Kennan and Acheson had the pleasure—if it could be called that—of hosting the notoriously prickly Indian prime minister, Jawaharlal Nehru, at the State Department on October 13. A few days earlier Kennan had entrusted to his diary the undiplomatic lecture he would *like* to deliver on that occasion; a few days later he recorded a Bill Bullitt prediction that any country allocating 30 to 50 percent of its food to sacred animals would never develop economically. On November 7 Acheson observed the anniversary of the Bolshevik Revolution by receiving Andrey Vyshinsky, the former prosecutor in the Moscow purge trials, now Molotov's replacement as Soviet foreign minister. Kennan sat in on the conversation, concluding from it that Vyshinsky was really a bourgeois at heart and would secretly prefer to work for Acheson: "It is much too late for this, of course." That evening Kennan attended the celebratory reception at the Soviet embassy, the first time he had been invited since returning from Moscow: "It was all the same—if anything, more false and grotesque than ever."[63]

With Acheson's encouragement, Kennan was still maintaining a regular schedule of public speaking. In New York, on November 10, he addressed the Academy of Political Science on the subject of American history. He chose as his text Secretary of State John Quincy Adams's Fourth of July address from 1821, which had proclaimed that the United States "goes not abroad in search of monsters to destroy." It would become Kennan's favorite quotation, and it reflected the shift in his thinking while on the Policy Planning Staff: the danger was now not that Americans would attempt too little internationally but that they would try to do too much. If that happened, Adams had warned, the United States could become "the dictatress of the world," but no longer "the ruler of her own spirit." Kennan was proud of this excursion into the past, but it got no publicity whatever. "You speak off-the-record," he complained, "and worry for weeks about the resulting leaks. Speak publicly, and it is as secure as a safe. No one knows what you said."[64]

On November 16 Kennan spent the day in Princeton. He was there to talk with Oppenheimer about an issue weighing heavily on them both: the recently announced news that the Soviet Union had successfully tested its first atomic bomb, and the still-secret possibility that the United States might respond by building a "super" bomb, a weapon far more powerful than the ones that had devastated Hiroshima and Nagasaki. There was time, though, that afternoon, to walk around the university. "The early dusk was already falling on town and campus. It was Princeton as I remembered it from the moments of my greatest loneliness as a student."

A light was on in his old window in the house where he had rented a room as a freshman. "Perhaps some other student was now there, much like myself, in many ways," and yet with the "subtle, undefinable differences" that distanced generations. The dormitory windows let light, voices, and radio sounds into the night air. The swimmers in the gymnasium were plowing dutifully through the water. "Far below, on the athletic fields, football teams were working out under flood lights, the bright uniforms of the tiny figures gleaming like armor." All of them regarded the people like himself at times as nuisances, at best as "regrettable and temporary necessities." In their minds, "we were already consigned to the ash-heap of history." Kennan and his contemporaries, however, would not be pushed.

> There is plenty of space where we stand—space to the point of loneliness and terror. And any who work themselves into our vicinity . . . will soon feel the protective covering of the generations falling ominously away from them and they will huddle together with us and with the curious ones of all times and ages, seeking warmth and company before the coldness and the endlessness and the silence that confront them.

Despite these intimations of mortality, Princeton still appealed. Oppenheimer and Kennan also discussed the possibility of his spending his leave from the State Department at the Institute for Advanced Study. And although Kennan declined when President Harold Dodds proposed a permanent university appointment, he did acknowledge that "I would like to live in Princeton and am thinking seriously of doing so."[65]

For the moment, though, there was another preoccupation: Grace and Joan had a little brother. "The wonder is to be officially known as Christopher James Kennan," George wrote Charlie James early in December, thus giving him "an opportunity to immortalize both our names." For weeks prior to his arrival, however, he had been referred to as "pumpkin," and "he honored this title by appearing in this world on Thanksgiving Day." That was still his nickname, but "I hope for his sake that it will not outlive his babyhood." It was true, George added, that he would soon be leaving the State Department. "The reasons are many—but mostly private. I want to see what it feels like to be a free man."[66]

Meanwhile the rumors were flying in Washington. "I got so blue that I got out of there as fast as possible," Lovett wrote Bohlen, on hearing that Kennan would be leaving. "I am equally disturbed at George's plans," Bohlen replied, but "a breathing spell for a year or so would not be at all a bad thing." The news became public on December 10, leading to careful analyses of its significance from the British embassy. "We have had the impression for some time past that Kennan was not feeling very happy in the State Department," F. M. Hoyer Millar informed London. Roger Makins of the Foreign Office, who had seen Kennan recently, confirmed this: with his views having "aroused keen and deep controversy in the State Department and Administration," Kennan doubted "whether this was a desirable state of affairs." Nitze would be the replacement, but although "hard-working and clear-headed and well thought of, . . . he is hardly of the stature of George Kennan."[67]

On December 21, 1949, the lucky students at the National War College got back-to-back lectures from Acheson and Kennan. The secretary of state took the opportunity to pay his subordinate a handsome tribute. The prospect of Kennan's departure had at first "filled me with despair. . . . I have rarely met a man the depth of whose thought, the sweetness of whose nature combined to bring about a real understanding of the underlying problems of modern life." Upon reflection, though, Acheson had concluded that a sabbatical was "the right and good thing" for Kennan. He had served the United States since the age of twenty-two, and the pressures were beginning to catch up with him. It would not be easy to have him gone, and "we will eagerly welcome him back." "Dear Dean," Kennan wrote that evening:

> As one who was tempted, day before yesterday, to go into the baby's room and say: "Go on, get up. You're going to work today. I'll get into the crib"—and who has since existed only on the reflection that "this, too, will pass"—I find no words to say how deeply moved I was by what you did and said this morning. Based on the past, you did me too much honor. Perhaps the future can correct some of the disparity.

Kennan's lecture that day summed up, with uncharacteristic modesty, what he thought he had learned as a policy planner. It had to do with the limitations of knowledge: just as it was not given to human beings to know the "totality of truth," so no one could see anything as unlimited in its implications as "the development of our people in their relation to their world environment." One could only fall back on Saint Paul's reminder that "[w]e know in part and we prophesy in part."

That made methods as important as objectives. Civilization best prospered when men stopped preoccupying themselves with purpose and began to apply restraints and rules on the means by which purposes were sought. From that perspective, strategy became "outstandingly a question of form and of style." Because "few of us can see very far into the future," all would be safer "if we take principles of conduct which we know we can live with, and at least stick to those," rather than "try to chart out vast schemes."[68]

X.

Kennan had set up the Policy Planning Staff, in the spring of 1947, with vast schemes in mind: had not Marshall told him to "avoid trivia"? The Marshall Plan was the first and most successful of these, but Kennan intended that others would follow. The papers he and his staff produced, all nine hundred pages of them, set courses for great destinations. They were to have been the navigational system for the ship of state—Kennan's own metaphor—in the postwar world. And he was to have been chief navigator.

In the long run, the ship reached the destinations specified: a secure and still-democratic United States; a peaceful and prosperous Germany and Japan; a reunified Europe capable of choosing its own future; a fragmented and ultimately moribund communist ideology; and a great-power peace more durable than any since the founding, three centuries earlier, of the modern state system. But it was, from Kennan's perspective, a *very* long run: these objectives looked no closer at the end of 1949 than they had been at the beginning of 1949, when he had accepted Acheson's invitation to stay on. That is why Kennan lost faith in himself as a navigator: the nation appeared to be as adrift as it had been before he took over.

Acheson agreed with Kennan on destinations but favored more flexible course settings. He didn't care how long the voyage would take, what it would cost, or whether deviations might occur along the way. Preferring action to brooding, he distrusted perfectionism, tolerated contradictions, and was determined to enjoy the trip. "Even if it was an emotional situation," Acheson's daughter Mary recalled, he would still say: "What can you do about it? And if you can't *do* anything about it, just stop *thinking* about it, and get on with something!" The secretary of state himself told the war college students, on the morning he shared the platform with Kennan, that "the more difficult a situation is, the more challenge there is to our powers, [and] the more keenness there is in life."

No one would have said of Acheson what Joe Alsop—a collector—wrote to Kennan on the last day of 1949: that he was "a flawless piece of Soong eggshell ware. . . . I hardly know how things will go on without you."[69]

SIXTEEN

Disengagement: 1950

KENNAN'S NATIONAL WAR COLLEGE LECTURE ON DECEMBER 21, 1949, was one of the last to be delivered from that platform during the first half of the twentieth century. It was certainly his last as Policy Planning Staff director. It reflected, appropriately enough, some personal planning: having arranged at least a temporary disengagement from the Department of State, he was trying to decide how to use it. His topic that day was a question: "Where Do We Stand?" The answer, Kennan told the students, depended on where "you think we have come from, and where you think we are going." Finding it required remedying an inattention to history—the tendency to view all problems "as though the world, like ourselves, had been born only yesterday."

He then took the students on a time machine trip, with stops at half-century intervals. It began in 1749 with Russia confined to the edge of Europe just as the British colonies occupied the edge of North America. Only half of the Empress Elizabeth's courtiers could read and write, while the future site of Washington was a wilderness plagued by wolves. France dominated Europe, and Europe ruled the world, although a few far-sighted advisers to Louis XV were shifting their attention from the Bourbons' longtime rivals, the Austrian Hapsburgs, to the rising but still peripheral kingdom of Prussia.

Half a century later a revolution in France had swept away its monarchy, setting off wars that brought Russian armies into the heart of Europe. Great Britain now had a global maritime empire, diminished only by the defection of the Americans, who had established their own frontier republic. It had practiced, under the Federalists, a foreign policy of "great dignity and reserve," but Jeffersonian idealists would set the nation—with no sense of irony—on the path of conquest and empire. Still, territorial acquisitions stayed within the continent: the United States refrained from involvement in European affairs.

By 1849, the Americans had expanded south to the Rio Grande and west to the Pacific, sowing the seeds of a civil war to be fought over slavery. Russia appeared stagnant under the despotism of Nicholas I, although revolutionary ideas had infected its intellectuals, artists, and the army officers who had fought the French. The European great powers had suppressed a new wave of revolutions in 1848, but a young Prussian called Bismarck was plotting ways to use the nationalism those upheavals had generated to make a unified Germany the strongest state in Europe.

The German Empire had reached that point by 1899 and was beginning to challenge British naval supremacy. Japan was now a comparably dominant power in Asia, while Russia, about to finish its Trans-Siberian Railway, was coming under pressure from both rivals even as it was hoping, like them, to carve up China. The United States, having built its own navy, defeated Spain, and taken the Philippines, was seeking to secure its interests by invoking the Open Door, the first of a series of unilaterally proclaimed principles that demanded the displacement of power politics by "juridical norms." Meanwhile Lenin, from the obscurity of exile, was constructing a movement in which ends justified means, convinced that only out of "the bloody, violent destruction of the old order could anything positive be expected to emerge."

These trends alarmed two Americans, Brooks and Henry Adams, the great-grandsons and grandsons, respectively, of John and John Quincy Adams, in different but complementary ways. Brooks was warning, as early as 1900, that rapid industrialization over the past half-century might now allow some combination of power on the Eurasian continent to end the British hegemony that had so far shielded the United States. Henry, even farther-sighted, was worrying about a scientific revolution that might someday harness the atom itself: infinite power, he suggested in 1905, could soon rest in the hands of finite men. It was just as well, Kennan concluded, that neither had lived to see 1949, by which time both of their visions had become realities.

"Gentlemen, reflect [for] a moment on what that means," he admonished the war college students. Most of them, like him, had been born into the "Booth Tarkington innocence" of America prior to World War I: "the shady streets and the wooden houses and the backyards in which the kids played at cowboys and Indians." Debilitated by decades of effortless security, American thinking about foreign policy had become "childish and naïve," something the nation could no longer afford.

> We are today . . . like a young person from a wealthy family who has suddenly lost his parents after a sheltered bringing-up, and now finds himself on his own for the first time in an unmerciful and inconsiderate world. . . . The problems of maturity have caught us ill prepared. We have to grow up, fast.

The crisis had come, not from the world wars or the Cold War, but from "the growing disproportion between man's moral nature and the forces subject to this control." Solutions, therefore, would have to begin at home: by showing that men could govern themselves somewhere without destroying themselves and their environment. Only then would Americans qualify to take on the great issues of international affairs.

That was why *style* was so important. Ends might justify means, but the reverse was also true: means could corrupt ends and, if carelessly chosen, even annihilate them. Care came from what the students had been doing: applying "the sober and undramatic process of scholarly analysis to all the intangibles, all the imponderables, all the elusive, shifting relationships of national policy." They had probably been tempted, at various points in their course, to toss the political scientists into the Potomac: "Ah, to hell with it. Let's have a war." They should recall, however, what Thoreau had written: "Our darkest grief has that bronze color of the moon eclipsed. There is no ill which may not be dissipated, like the dark, if you let in a stronger light upon it."

Kennan's had been a profound, impressive, "and, I must admit, somewhat disturbing presentation," General Harold Bull, the new commandant of the war college, concluded in thanking him. He had, the previous September, provided the kickoff for the course, "and now he has run ahead and caught his own punt. . . . I am very grateful to you, sir."[1]

I.

The lecture suggested much broader concerns than those with which Kennan had taken up policy planning two and a half years earlier. Then his focus had been on geopolitics, ideology, and recent history: on devising a strategy that would contain the Soviet Union and international communism in the aftermath of World War II. Now his perspective had expanded backward in time and forward in portent, drawing on Brooks Adams's insistence that industrialization was realigning politics, as well as Henry Adams's fear that technology was outpacing morality. The development of nuclear weapons confirmed both premonitions, with implications that would haunt Kennan for the rest of his life.

His early thinking about the bomb had been unsystematic. Although Kennan conceded, after reading Brodie's *The Absolute Weapon* in 1946, that great wars were now unlikely, he also believed in preserving American military superiority for as long as possible. He warned Acheson—still at that point under secretary of state—that the Soviet Union would consider the international control of atomic energy only if the United States maintained the capacity "to absorb atomic attack and to effect instant retaliation." There could be no greater protection, Kennan claimed in a rare public lecture on national defense in January 1947, "than the deterrent effect of overwhelming retaliatory power in the hands of this country." He went further in classified comments at the Air War College a few months later. Soviet industry was sufficiently concentrated that, if a war did break out, "ten good hits with atomic bombs" would probably destroy it. He even acknowledged the possibility of preventive war: it would be justified, however, only if the U.S.S.R. was undertaking more rapid industrial mobilization than the United States, and there was no sign of that: "I think we and our friends have a preponderance of strength in the world right now."[2]

"What a fiery hard-liner I was, in those days!" Kennan later admitted. "However, it *was* the Stalin era." The Soviet regime was "dizzy with success" after winning the war and after "the complacent abandonment to it, by the Western powers, of half of Europe." He did acknowledge, early in 1948, "the suicidal nature of atomic warfare in a world in which more than one country has bombs." But he was not yet ready to think about that: like most Washington officials at the time, he saw the new weapons as enhancing the strategic bombing capabilities of World War II, not as the revolution in warfare Brodie had predicted. PPS/38, completed in August 1948, discussed the terms the United States might impose upon a defeated Soviet Union without saying anything about the use of atomic bombs. Even Kennan's tour of Hamburg in March 1949—from which he concluded that nothing could have justified the devastation he saw—failed to shake his conviction that the best way to avoid another such catastrophe would be to stay stronger than all potential adversaries. That included maintaining the American advantage in atomic weaponry.[3]

But Kennan had no sense of what that advantage was. He lacked access to Pentagon war plans; nor did he know how many atomic bombs there were. Nor would he have seen the top-secret study, commissioned by the Joint Chiefs of

Staff, which concluded in May 1949 that even if the United States used *all* available atomic weapons—about two hundred—against a Soviet Union with none of its own, this would not in itself ensure victory. That led the Defense Department to propose building more, and on August 2 Acheson called a meeting at the State Department to discuss the matter.

It took place within an informational fogbank, because the participants did not know—or if they knew, could not say—how large the increase would be. As far as Kennan was concerned, the current number of atomic bombs could as easily have been two thousand as two hundred. That may explain why he shocked Acheson—and perhaps surprised himself—by confessing, according to the minutes of the meeting, to

> an uneasy feeling that we were traveling down the atomic road rather too fast. He went on to state his own personal feeling that it perhaps would be best for this country if it were decided that atomic bombs would never be used. He for one was glad that no final decision to use the weapon had as yet been made.

One can imagine, at this moment, a bewildered silence. Then Acheson pointed out that it would be difficult to justify such a strategy, "particularly if our failure to use atomic weapons meant a great loss of lives or a defeat in war."[1]

It would indeed, so much so that one wonders where Kennan's latest heterodoxy came from. Maybe it was "worst case" worries about what the Pentagon was proposing. Possibly it was a delayed reaction to what Kennan had seen in Hamburg. Certainly it was another of his prophetic leaps: it was not the first time he had startled colleagues by projecting policy much further into the future than they were able to do. The problem was never the desirability of what he wanted. Who could object to the prospect that nuclear weapons might exist for decades without the United States having to use one? Who could oppose, for that matter, a peacefully reunified Germany, or an epidemic of Titoism within the international communist movement, or a Soviet Union collapsing under the weight of its internal contradictions? The difficulty, as Acheson's response suggested, was that Kennan so rarely specified the steps that would be necessary—over the next days, months, or years—to bring about these auspicious outcomes.

Two weeks later, on August 16, 1949, the Policy Planning Staff completed PPS/58, a paper whose title, "Political Implications of Detonation of an Atomic Bomb by the U.S.S.R.," appeared to reflect an immediate prophetic insight. For thirteen days later, on August 29, the Soviet Union did in fact test its first atomic bomb. PPS/58, however, was less impressive than it looked. Only two pages in length, it focused on the importance of being able to *detect* a Soviet test if and when one took place. It made no prediction that one was about to happen. It acknowledged—unspectacularly—that such a development might require rethinking the American position on the international control of atomic energy, and it suggested—unhelpfully—that the existence of a Soviet bomb might or might not cause other states to cooperate more closely with Washington. Questions relating to the vulnerability of the United States if it should lose its nuclear monopoly were best left, the paper concluded, to the National Military Establishment. "The document in question was plainly not drafted by me," Kennan commented, with some disdain, many years later.[5]

Kennan learned of the Soviet test on September 13, two weeks after it had taken place. After receiving confirmation, Truman decided to make the news public, overriding Acheson's initial inclination—which Kennan opposed—to let it leak out gradually: Stalin had as yet said nothing. The president's announcement came on September 23. "Bedlam," Kennan recorded in his diary that day, but on the next he noted that "for the most part, people took it calmly and the press did a good job of placing the event in the proper perspective."[6]

Calm, however, was hard to maintain. Kennan had hoped for a continuation of wartime cooperation with the British and the Canadians in building atomic weapons: that was one of the reasons he wanted to keep them and the United States out of any Western European federation. But the Joint Congressional Committee on Atomic Energy had grown increasingly concerned about security, and now, in the wake of the Soviet test, Kennan concluded that international collaboration would have to end altogether, apart from a few agreements on the allocation of raw materials. Congressional fears, it turned out, were well founded. Donald Maclean, the British representative on the committee overseeing atomic bomb production, was a Soviet spy: thanks to him, Stalin knew more than Kennan did about the size of the American arsenal. Maclean's treachery was not yet known in the fall of 1949, but the FBI did have evidence that Klaus Fuchs, a British scientist who worked on the Manhattan Project, had also leaked critical information to Moscow. That revelation explained to most people at the time—as it has to most historians since—how the U.S.S.R. got its own bomb so much sooner than anyone had expected.[7]

As it happened, Fuchs had also been present at a 1946 Los Alamos meeting during which the builders of the atomic bomb discussed the possibility of a thermonuclear, or hydrogen, or "super" bomb, based on the fusion of atoms instead of their fission, theoretically thousands of times more powerful than existing atomic weapons. Nothing had been done since to develop such a device, but when the news broke of the August 1949 Soviet atomic test, pressures began to mount, among the few scientists who knew that a "super" might be feasible, for the United States to build one. Who could say that a Soviet "super," with Fuchs's help, was not already under construction? Lewis L. Strauss, the most bellicose member of the Atomic Energy Commission, shared the scientists' concerns, and on October 6 he conveyed them to Truman—for whom the concept of a hydrogen bomb was as unfamiliar as that of an atomic bomb had once been.[8]

It's not clear when Kennan learned that thermonuclear weapons might be possible. But he met on October 12 with a group of Pentagon officers who favored greater reliance on atomic, biological, and chemical "weapons of mass destruction," and the "super" was probably among the options discussed. What he heard, Kennan thought, reflected an overestimation of Soviet capabilities and a misunderstanding of Soviet intentions: "But I cannot prove this conviction, and the matters in question are too important for anyone to dare acting on a hunch." By November 3, his position had become clearer. The United States, he told a Policy Planning Staff meeting attended by Acheson, was so far behind the Soviet Union in conventional military strength that its whole policy might soon be "tied to the atom bomb." The question, then, was what the "super" bomb would accomplish.

Acheson acknowledged this, but then surprised Kennan, as he had done several months earlier on Program A, by thinking out loud. Could there be a two-year moratorium—"bilateral if possible, unilateral if necessary"—on the development of "super" bombs? Might that open possibilities for agreements on the international control of atomic weapons, on German and Japanese peace treaties, and maybe even on forgoing the use of "subversive tactics"? At least the Americans and the Soviets would be "attempting to do something constructive rather than just sitting and exchanging glassy stares." If at the end of this "vacation" no progress had been made, then "go ahead with the overall production of both [atomic and thermonuclear weapons], backed up by your economy and your people, having made your best effort to do otherwise."

This was, Acheson's biographer has written, "a remarkable ball of wool" for him to have gathered, but the secretary of state's mind was not normally woolly. His openness on this issue probably reflected his friendships with Oppenheimer and David E. Lilienthal, soon to retire as chairman of the Atomic Energy Commission. All three had worked, in 1946, on the imaginative Acheson-Lilienthal Plan for the international control of atomic energy: Truman had converted it, over their objections, into the more forbidding Baruch Plan, which the Soviet Union rejected. None now wanted a quantum leap in the lethality of weaponry when so little had been done, as yet, to limit the effects of the last one. Kennan liked what Acheson was suggesting, but Nitze did not, insisting that the burden of proof should fall on those who saw no power advantages in building the "super" bomb. He added tactfully, though, that the secretary of state's question—whether "we would really be at a disadvantage if they developed it and we did not and why"—required further study.[9]

Kennan brought up Acheson's idea of a "super" moratorium when he met with Oppenheimer in Princeton on November 16, only to have the physicist—still passionately opposed to developing such a weapon—throw cold water on it. However reasonable the plan might be, he wrote Kennan the next day, it would not seem so to those who demanded safeguards "of rigid and absolute quality." Undaunted, Kennan on November 18 produced a draft presidential announcement that the United States would unilaterally forgo constructing thermonuclear weapons: they could serve no military purpose apart from mass destruction, they would add nothing to American security, and "for us to embark on such a path would certainly not deter others from doing likewise, and probably quite the contrary."[10]

Truman, however, was not about to be rushed into any hasty decision. On the next day he ordered the formation of a special NSC committee, made up of Acheson, Lilienthal, and Secretary of Defense Johnson, to advise him on the matter. Since Johnson strongly supported the "super" and Lilienthal equally adamantly opposed it, Acheson's would be the swing vote. To help him decide, he asked Kennan and Nitze to prepare separate reports on the matter, knowing that they would disagree. Acheson's sympathies were with Kennan: his affectionate tribute at the National War College came only a few days after he read an early version of what Kennan was going to recommend. But Acheson's political instincts told him that the decision would go the other way. For that reason, he put Nitze on the working group that advised the NSC committee.

Nitze's report, completed on December 19, was short and to the point. Although fission weapons were likely to remain of primary importance in the military strategies of both the United States and the Soviet Union, there was at least a 50 percent chance that either country could achieve a thermonuclear reaction. Weapons of mass destruction—the hydrogen bomb apparently qualified, the atomic bomb did not—would serve American interests in neither peace nor war, and the Soviets would probably not initiate their use. Nevertheless, "it is essential that the U.S. not find itself in a position of technological inferiority in this field." Accordingly, the president should authorize the Atomic Energy Commission to *test* the possibility of a thermonuclear weapon, reserving any decision to produce and deploy it until the results were known. In the meantime, the NSC should review American security requirements in the light of the Soviet atomic bomb, and the prospect that a thermonuclear bomb might be feasible.[11]

Kennan, characteristically, wrote much more. He had begun composing a "super" bomb paper before Acheson asked him to, and he was determined to do justice to the secretary of state's mandate. "Remarkable man," Lilienthal noted, after watching Kennan read a draft: "Peeled off his coat, exhibiting farm-type galluses over his thin and bent shoulders. Then he nervously started rolling back his sleeves, folding them back by stages till they were way above his elbows." Kennan submitted his final version, which came to seventy-nine pages, on January 20, 1950: he remembered it as "one of the most important, if not the most important, of all the documents I ever wrote in government." Entitled "The International Control of Atomic Energy," it called for nothing less than an end to reliance on nuclear weapons as instruments of offensive warfare.

Its reasoning echoed Henry Adams's concern that morality was lagging behind technology. There was no way, Kennan argued, in which weapons of mass destruction could be made to serve rational ends beyond deterring the outbreak of hostilities. War, after all, was a means to an end, not an end in itself; it might imply an end "marked by submission to a new political will and perhaps to a new regime of life, but an end which at least did not negate the principle of life itself." Nuclear weapons lacked these characteristics. "They reach beyond the frontiers of western civilization, to the concepts of warfare which were once familiar to the Asiatic hordes. They cannot really be reconciled with a political purpose directed to shaping, rather than destroying, the lives of the adversary. They fail to take account of the ultimate responsibility of men for one another." Shakespeare had seen how thin this thread was:

> Take but degree away,—untune that string
> And hark what discord follows: . . .
> Then everything includes itself in power—
> Power into will, will into appetite,
> And appetite, a universal wolf,
> So doubly seconded with will and power,
> Must make perforce a universal prey
> And at last eat up himself.

It was vital therefore, Kennan argued, "that we not fall into the error of initiating, or planning to initiate, the employment of these weapons and concepts, thus hypnotizing ourselves into the belief that they may ultimately serve some positive national purpose."

He was not arguing here for any unilateral relinquishment of nuclear weapons. Some such devices would have to be retained "for purposes of deterrence and retaliation." What he was advocating was, in peacetime, a posture of what would come to be called "minimum deterrence"—restricting the number and power of bombs in the American arsenal strictly to "our estimate as to what it would take to make attack on this country or its allies by weapons of mass destruction a risky, probably unprofitable, and therefore irrational undertaking for any adversary," and should war come, a strategy of "no first use." Such an approach, he admitted, would require consultation with allies and a considerable upgrading of conventional capabilities. But it might obviate the need to build a hydrogen bomb, and it would place the United States in a better position from which to negotiate seriously with the Soviet Union on controlling all nuclear devices. Even an imperfect agreement would be less dangerous than leaving "the shadow of uncontrolled mass destruction weapons" lying across the world.

Now no longer Policy Planning Staff director—he had passed the job to Nitze on January 1—Kennan sent his memorandum to Acheson as a personal paper. "Paul and the others were not entirely in agreement with the substance," he explained, in a considerable understatement. "I was afraid that this report might be embarrassing to have on record as a formal Staff report." The course it recommended, he added, was filled with obstacles, so much so that "there is extremely little likelihood, judged by present circumstances, that we would ever successfully make our way to the end of it." But the nation must see "that the initial lines of its policy are as close as possible to the principles dictated by its traditions and its nature, and that where it is necessary to depart from these lines, people are aware that this *is* a departure and understand why it is necessary."[12]

Kennan later doubted, correctly, that the paper was seriously considered. Nor could he remember the secretary of state's reaction: "It was probably one of bewilderment and pity for my naïveté." Years afterward Acheson claimed to have said that if it was really Kennan's recommendation that the United States not build the hydrogen bomb, then "he ought to resign from the Foreign Service and go out and preach his Quaker gospel." There is no evidence, however, that Acheson said anything like this at the time: he was himself deeply troubled by the advice he was going to have to give, and Kennan would not have forgotten such an outburst if it had occurred.[13]

On January 31 an ambivalent Acheson, an enthusiastic Johnson, and a reluctant Lilienthal recommended to Truman, much as Nitze had suggested, that the United States "proceed to determine the technical feasibility of a thermonuclear weapon." Johnson, in turn, reluctantly agreed to another Nitze proposal, insisted on by Acheson and Lilienthal: that the State and Defense departments reexamine national objectives in war and peace "in the light of the probable fission bomb capability and possible thermonuclear bomb capability of the Soviet Union." Truman agreed on the spot and publicly announced his decision on the "super" that same day.[14]

The contrasts in the ways Kennan and Nitze had advised Acheson were striking. Nitze, balancing scientific evidence against military, political, and moral considerations, came up with a crisp recommendation, capable of being read in two minutes, which Acheson, Johnson, Lilienthal, and ultimately Truman could all accept. "I thought that the most important role of the Policy Planning Staff was not just creating a paper," Nitze recalled. It was "to *affect* today's decisions, and to do so in a way which would create or expand the margins of freedom for the future."[15]

Kennan's memorandum, more than thirty times the length of Nitze's, was the most serious effort by any American at the time to grapple with the implications of the nuclear revolution. The ideas it developed—especially "minimum deterrence" and "no first use"—would shape the strategic debates of the 1970s and 1980s, some of which Kennan conducted with Nitze himself. "George was a sensitive, imaginative fellow," Dean Rusk recalled. "He had the ability to look some distance down the trail, and to see the awesome consequences of the development of these weapons. But to look away from the problem we faced was not the way to prevent war." As far as the Truman administration was concerned, Kennan's memorandum was, as Nitze suggested, just a paper: it was of little use in shaping immediate policy. He had become prophetic but no longer relevant. Hence the equanimity with which his indulgent boss reconciled himself to the idea that Kennan needed a break. As Acheson reminded the war college students on the day they both appeared there, "it was not by chance that the Prophets used to go up in the mountains and fast and think and be in solitude."[16]

II.

Kennan chose instead to go to Latin America. As had been the case with Japan, he had never been there. The Policy Planning Staff had produced only three papers on the region under his directorship, all narrowly focused. And yet Marshall, while in Bogotá for a conference in April 1948, had run into rioting so severe that for a time he had been literally under siege: the only life-threatening situation he encountered as secretary of state came in a part of the world his planners had largely ignored. Kennan may have had that episode in mind when he warned the war college students a few months later that, with half the earth's wealth but only 6 percent of its population, the United States faced enemies willing "to tear us limb from limb figuratively, or perhaps even physically." He was less dire in his December 1949 lecture, but he did—unusually—go out of his way to link the civil rights struggle at home with the credibility of American efforts to cooperate with "colored peoples in other parts of the globe." So he was ready, at the beginning of 1950, not just to remedy his own inattention to problems of race, class, and inequality but to see them for himself.[17]

Feeling slightly guilty for abandoning his family, Kennan left Washington on February 18, taking advantage of the opportunity this time to avoid the discomforts of air travel and to indulge his love of trains. With a change in St. Louis, it was possible then to take a sleeping car all the way to Mexico City. The three-day journey allowed time to write:

> about passing in the night within a few miles of the Pennsylvania farm, where "the old drake would be standing, motionless, on the concrete water trough in the barnyard, . . . contemptuous of the cold, of the men who had neglected him, of the other birds and beasts who basked in the warmth of human favor—contemptuous even of the possibility for happiness in general, human or animal."
>
> about the fellow passenger who, having inspected his luggage labels, could not help asking: "Say, are you the fellow who . . . ?" Confused associations followed, "too close to reality to be wholly denied, too far from it to be flatly admitted."
>
> about St. Louis, which like many American cities had grown too fast to clean up after itself. "The new is there before the old is gone. What in one era is functional and elegant and fashionable survives into the following era as grotesque decay."
>
> about the canned music in the lounge car on the train to Texas: what of the person "who doesn't like *The Rustic Wedding* or *Rose Marie* or *Ave Maria*, or who has heard them too often, or who doesn't like music at all through loud speakers, or who doesn't like music?"

about trying to write while crossing northern Mexico trapped by an Indiana
voice, which boomed, with "unquenchable loquaciousness," through
the cars: "What-cha carryin' that ink around fur?"

Nevertheless, the trip was a welcome respite. With a steam engine helping, the
diesel ascended a mountain pass, wound its way down the other side, and brought
the train on time into Mexico City on the evening of the twenty-first. The American embassy, where Kennan stayed, was preparing for its Washington's birthday
reception the next day.

The event, held on the veranda, required routine skills: clutching drinks in
the left hand to keep the right one dry for shaking others; looking for places to
stash empty glasses so they wouldn't get stepped on; being patient with the wife
of a senior colleague who wanted to know about the Russians: "They're all slaves
aren't they? Why don't we *do* something about it?" Outside there were magnificent monuments, handsome boulevards, and frenetic traffic, but in the adjoining neighborhoods people were "living, eating, and begging on slimy sidewalks."
Bearing little relation to its surroundings, the city was an "ostentatious, anxious
demonstration of wealth by an ever-changing *nouveau riche*," boiling up "like
foam to the surface of a society that calls itself revolutionary."

A weekend in Cuernavaca placed Kennan in a simulated Moorish palace
owned by American friends, where the ceiling, wall paneling, furniture, and art—
all imported from Europe—were not simulated. "I lay sleepless, through the long
night, under the huge crimson draperies which had once served a prince of the
Church and still bore his insignia—while mosquitoes buzzed around my pillow."
Outside the night breeze flitted aimlessly among the cloisters: the wind "of exiled
royalty, of the hopelessly rich, of the tortured intellectuals," of people like himself
who had wandered in, amid "unhappy antiques, crowded together, like creatures
in a zoo." Kennan's host, the next morning by the swimming pool, was also curious about the Russians: "I don't see why we don't go right over there and drop the
bomb on those fellows. What are we waiting for?"

Four forest fires were visible on the road back into Mexico City, a frequent
occurrence because the mountains were badly eroded. Water tables were sinking
at an alarming rate. Population pressures were overtaking improvements in agriculture, industrial productivity, and public health. Mexico would remain inhospitable to earthly hope, which was why the Virgin of Guadalupe shrine, a brief
stop on the way to the airport, moved Kennan deeply. There were of course hus-
tlers outside the cathedral, and there was oppressive ostentation within. But who

could doubt the need for "*some* moral law, even an imperfect one"? And how did this Mexican display of faith and corruption differ from Ilya Repin's unforgettable painting of a religious procession outside a Russian village in an earlier century?

After several short stops in Central America, Kennan flew on to Caracas, a city that defied even his descriptive powers. So he instead wrote its history: how the Spanish had located it at a comfortable elevation inland, connected to its port by a wagon track; how the British had replaced this with a narrow-gauge railroad; how the Americans had arrived to pump oil out and to pump wealth back in; how the city was now so expensive that this particular American wanted to hide in his hotel, fearing "the financial consequences of any contact with the shops or the taxi drivers." All the evils apparent at home from imposing a new technology on an unprepared people were magnified a hundredfold in Venezuela. One day the "morphine" would be withdrawn, and "a terrible awakening" would follow.

Perhaps because the culture was Portuguese and hence familiar, Kennan liked Rio de Janeiro better. The Brazilians had inherited a gentleness "for which one can only bear them respect and affection." It was striking on the beaches, which displayed every shade of color, "a vast panorama of racial tolerance and maturity which could stand as a model for other peoples." Still, it was depressing to sense "the gulf between the rich and the poor, the desperation with which people seek to leap over that gulf, and the lack of imagination they show in the enjoyment of their new emoluments when the leap has been successfully completed." His reputation, by now, had caught up with him: Rio was plastered with "To Death With Kennan" signs, put up by local communists, and he had been accorded four mock funerals. Only in São Paulo, though, where the security was exasperatingly thorough, did he began to feel "like a hunted beast, and to ask myself whether it was really possible that I was as sinister as all this."

There were further stops in Montevideo, Buenos Aires, and Lima—the Argentine president, Juan Perón, somehow mistook Kennan for the head of the CIA—but the trip by this time was tiring him out, teaching him little, and making him homesick. He was impressed by a demonstration, in Panama, of how the canal locks worked and, upon arrival in Miami, by the "relaxed, unemotional but utterly objective and self-respecting attitude" with which a railroad ticket clerk explained to a trainee how to change a reservation: "I went out onto the station platform with a sense of deep gratitude and of happy acceptance of this American world, marked as it is by the mediocrity of all that is exalted, and the excellence of all that which is without pretense."[18]

Back in Washington, Kennan wrote a long report and submitted it to Acheson on March 29. He acknowledged the imprudence of generalizing about so vast a region, because differences in Latin America were often more significant than similarities. Nevertheless, some patterns were clear. One was location: human development was harder than in North America, with its broad plains, unifying rivers, and temperate climate. Compounding this problem had been the arrival, "like men from Mars," of the European conquerors: "History, it seems to me, bears no record of anything more terrible having been done to entire peoples." Slavery followed, as did the splendor and pretense of Latin American cities, built to compensate for the squalor of the countryside from which they sprang. All of this had produced a culture of "exaggerated self-centeredness and egotism," conveying the illusion "of desperate courage, supreme cleverness, and a limitless virility where the more constructive virtues are so conspicuously lacking." This was a world "where geography and history are alike tragic, but where no one must ever admit it."

So what was Washington's responsibility in an era in which Latin American communists, even if only loosely linked to Moscow, might seek to exploit the hopelessness that surrounded them by seizing power? That part of the world was of little military significance to either the United States or the Soviet Union, but there was a bandwagon psychology in international relations: multiple victories for communism could be demoralizing. One such victory somewhere, however— Kennan thought Guatemala the most likely possibility—might have an inoculating effect, shattering complacency about communism elsewhere. The problem, in any event, would be for the Latin Americans to handle: the United States could not return to the military interventions of the early twentieth century. It might, at most, apply economic pressure quietly. In public, its hands would have to be clean.

The United States could afford to relax, therefore, in managing its hemisphere, for the Latin Americans needed it more than it needed them. That meant tolerating rule by whatever means local rulers considered appropriate: they should not be held to the standards of American domestic democracy. It meant respecting their sovereignty, cooperating with them only when they wanted it. It meant that they, in turn, could not make their countries "the seats of dangerous intrigue against us." No great power would ever have shown such restraint in dealing with neighboring smaller powers. If the Latin Americans liked it, fine. If not, the responsibility would be theirs for forfeiting its advantages. This was the best Washington could expect to do, Kennan concluded, in a region where problems would always be "multitudinous, complex and unpleasant."[19]

The term "politically incorrect" had not yet been invented, but Edward G.

Miller, the assistant secretary of state for inter-American affairs, acted as if it had when he read Kennan's report. Appalled by its candor, worried about leaks, he persuaded Acheson not to circulate it. "I am not sure that he required much persuading," Kennan remembered. As a consequence, all copies were "hidden from innocent eyes," except for the one Kennan kept and quoted from in his 1967 memoir. The full document would not be published until 1976, after which historians treated it either as an example of Kennan's insensitivity to "third world" issues, or as a blueprint for what the United States would do in Latin America for the rest of the Cold War.[20] Neither interpretation makes much sense.

Kennan in fact focused on the historical, cultural, economic, demographic, and environmental problems afflicting the region: he came closer to getting Latin America right in 1950 than he had Germany—a country he knew much better—in 1949. Nor was he unsympathetic to the Latin Americans. The rich and the poor, he repeatedly stressed, shared tragedies not of their own making. Nor did his memorandum affect what later transpired: it could hardly have done so, since nobody read it. If they had, they would have found it recommending a far more cautious policy than those carried out by the Eisenhower, Kennedy, Johnson, Nixon, and Reagan administrations, each of whom intervened in Latin America in ways well beyond anything Kennan recommended. It's hard to see how the policy he suggested would have produced worse results.

Two things made Kennan's report unacceptable, though, even by the standards of his own day. One was his outsider's perspective, which upset the State Department's Latin American experts, much as he would have been upset if forced to read a report from one of them on the Soviet Union or Germany. Crude looks at the whole[21] generally unsettle specialists who spend their lives scrutinizing parts of it. The other problem was Kennan's honesty about Latin America's tragedies and his call for restraint in attempting to alleviate them. His pessimism was consistent with his own view of life. But it was—to use another term just coming into vogue at the time—deeply un-American.

III.

"I am not one of those who have been attacked," Kennan assured a hometown audience in Milwaukee on May 5. However, "I must tell you that the atmosphere of public life in Washington does not have to deteriorate much further to produce a situation in which very few of our more quiet and sensitive and gifted people will be able to continue in government." What worried him was not the reception of his Latin American report but rather the emergence of something that was coming to be called, in honor of the junior Republican senator from Wisconsin, "McCarthyism."[22]

It began as a backlash against the apparent "loss" of China. Mao Zedong had completed his conquest of the mainland the previous October, and then spent two months in Moscow. The State Department seemed not to care. It had discredited the Chinese Nationalists, now established on Taiwan, through the White Paper Kennan and Davies had helped to produce in the summer of 1949. On January 12, 1950, Acheson announced in a National Press Club speech that the United States had no plans to defend Chiang Kai-shek's regime, despite a "defensive perimeter" strategy—which he was announcing publicly for the first time—of protecting other offshore positions including Japan, Okinawa, and the Philippines. The secretary of state's comments reflected the conclusions of a top-secret paper, NSC 48/2, endorsed by Truman at the end of December, that distilled a series of Policy Planning Staff studies, written mostly by Davies, dating back to 1948. Using American forces to prolong the civil war in China, all of these had concluded, would be a disaster. Nor was it clear, even now, that Mao would be a Soviet puppet. The very fact that he had spent so long in Moscow, Kennan believed, meant that problems already existed in the relationship.[23]

This was not the best time, however, to try to explain these subtleties to the American people. Acheson had won few friends in Congress when he characterized his China policy, shortly after taking office, as one of waiting "until the dust settles." Then on January 25, 1950, Alger Hiss was convicted of lying under oath about his involvement with Soviet intelligence: the secretary of state further inflamed his critics by telling a press conference that day that he would not "turn my back" on his old friend. Six days later Truman announced that the United States would try to build a hydrogen bomb. Four days after that the news broke of the Fuchs atomic espionage case. It was predictable, therefore, that someone would soon claim that the Department of State had knowingly harbored traitors who had sold out the Chinese Nationalists, given the Russians the atomic bomb, and who knew what else? The only thing unpredictable about the speech Senator Joseph R. McCarthy did in fact make on February 9 was the forum he chose for it: the Ohio County Women's Republican Club of Wheeling, West Virginia.[24]

Kennan read the reports on McCarthy while on his Latin American trip, naïvely expecting the outrageousness of the senator's claims to discredit him immediately. Just the opposite happened, however, with results that would wreck the career of Kennan's closest Policy Planning Staff colleague and one of his closest friends. Still assigned to liaison duties with Wisner's Office of Policy Coordination, John Paton Davies had found himself being questioned, in November 1949, by two "very low-powered characters" from that organization about a plan he had suggested to recruit American China experts who had retained some credibility with Mao's regime to advise on psychological warfare operations against it. "It's all very well to have white propaganda phrased as a direct attack against the Communists," Davies later explained, "but one has to have some people whose view is more acceptable, who have a standing in China, who can give some guidance as to what might be done under OPC control."

Davies's interrogators, however, turned out to be counterintelligence agents searching for spies within the government. "So they misconstrued what I said and passed it on." Hillenkoetter, still the director of central intelligence, professed to be shocked and turned the information over to the FBI. That meant that Davies would have to go before one of the loyalty review boards the White House had established to investigate such allegations of subversion.[25]

"We have no protection against this happening again," Kennan warned Webb shortly after returning to Washington in March 1950, "and no assurance that any one in this Department will even be aware of it when it does happen." It had not been Wisner's fault, but until the matter was clarified, there should be no further State Department cooperation with the OPC. The idea of covert operations had been "largely my own," and Kennan remained convinced of its importance. Anything that interfered with such work—like the harassment of Davies—"seems to me to diminish the chances for defeating communist purposes on a world-wide scale."[26]

It was with Davies in mind that Kennan chose to challenge McCarthy—although not by name—in the state they shared. He could do so, he told his Milwaukee audience, because "I am leaving the Government for a long time in the near future." He had chosen that city because "[m]y boyhood was spent here." Whenever he returned to talk about international problems, he had the feeling of "rendering an accounting" to people who had a right to expect it and whose understanding "is somehow basic to the success of what we are trying to do." So what should the State Department have recommended, given the obvious incompetence of the Chinese Nationalist government? He could conceive of "no more ghastly and fateful mistake" than to try to prop up with "our own blood and treasure a regime which had clearly lost the confidence of its own people. Nothing could have pleased our enemies more."

The speech was courageous: few Foreign Service officers were saying such things openly at the time. But the size of the audience was disappointing, and the publicity was minimal. Kennan was irked to have provoked the wrath, not of McCarthy's supporters, but of local "communists" who passed out handbills linking "Mr. X" to the development of the hydrogen bomb. The trip, he complained to State Department colleagues upon his return, had been a waste of his time.[27]

IV.

Despite the investigation of him, Davies had taken on a new responsibility. "Paul Nitze apparently discovered that he couldn't get along without him," Annelise wrote George on February 23, while he was still in Latin America. She had had dinner the night before with the Nitzes, after which they had seen *All the King's Men,* starring Broderick Crawford, a cinematic evocation of Huey Long that eerily anticipated McCarthy.[28] Nitze had delayed Davies's next assignment, which was to have been Germany, to enlist him in an extraordinary effort to triple or quadruple defense spending in the United States—over the violent objections of its secretary of defense, Louis Johnson. It was a strange thing for someone suspected of sympathy with communists to be doing.

The idea, in a way, had originated with Kennan. He had long seen the need for a credible military deterrent but assumed that the American atomic monopoly could provide this. As long as it lasted, the Soviet Union would not attack: conventional defense could be entrusted to small, well-trained units like the Marine Corps, capable of responding rapidly in limited conflict situations. The capacity for massive mobilization would have to be in place, of course, but an actual mobilization should not be necessary in peacetime. The Soviet atomic bomb, however, shook Kennan's confidence. He admitted to Acheson and the Policy Planning Staff, at a meeting in October 1949, that it might now be impossible "for us to retaliate with the atomic bomb against a Russian attack with orthodox weapons."

Nitze at that point asked an important, if delicate, question: might this situation require increasing the conventional military forces of the United States and its Western European allies? Otherwise, what peacetime deterrent would there be? The delicacy lay in the fact that such armaments—and armies—would be considerably more expensive than atomic bombs and the bombers needed to deliver them. The costs could lower living standards in Europe while unbalancing budgets at home. Neither was a palatable alternative, given the Marshall Plan's accomplishments and Truman's determination to keep defense spending under tight control. The problem, Acheson acknowledged, was "what peoples and governments *will* do rather than what they *can* do."²⁹

The hydrogen bomb debate distracted everyone over the next few months, but Nitze kept the idea of a conventional buildup alive by skillfully coupling his call for developing thermonuclear weapons with a recommendation to review *all* national security requirements. That won Acheson's support for the "super" and ultimately even Lilienthal's. Neither Truman nor Johnson understood what Nitze had in mind, but Acheson saw it clearly, and Kennan had a sense of it. If the United States was ever going to reduce its dependence on nuclear weapons, he wrote on the eve of his departure for Latin America, then this might require "a state of semi-mobilization."³⁰

Acheson later implied that he had sent Kennan south to get him out of town while Nitze's review was getting under way. That's unlikely, because Kennan had been planning his trip for well over a year. He also sympathized with Nitze's objective, which was to strengthen nonnuclear as well as nuclear means of deterrence. Kennan did believe, however, that this could be done only by drastically reducing "the exorbitant costs of national defense." In this respect, he shared the views of Truman, Johnson, and other fiscal conservatives. Nitze, drawing on domestic policy studies undertaken by White House economic advisers, took a different approach. He pointed out that increased expenditures would create new jobs, generating the additional tax revenue that would allow balancing the budget at a higher level while correcting the American deficiency in conventional arms. It was a posthumous enlistment, in the Cold War, of John Maynard Keynes.³¹

It's also unlikely, though, that Acheson or Nitze regretted Kennan's absence as they developed this line of argument. Kennan had opposed the presidential decision that allowed Nitze's review to proceed. He knew little about economics, Keynesian or otherwise. His preference for prophecy was isolating him within the government. And he was becoming increasingly wary of policy papers whose content had to reflect a consensus and whose implementation he could not control: "You understand how hard this was for someone like myself, who felt that what you do has to be flexible, according to the situation of the moment." Kennan's real problem with the new initiative, Nitze believed, was that it was to be "a group paper, not his."³²

NSC 68, "United States Objectives and Programs for National Security," prepared mostly within the Policy Planning Staff, went to Truman on April 14, 1950.

It was worthy of Kennan in several ways. One was length: the report came to sixty-six legal-size pages. A second was style: although classified top secret, it read as if meant to be proclaimed, even preached—its most memorable phrase, which Davies contributed, was the need to "frustrate the Kremlin's design." A third was its acceptance of containment: there need be neither appeasement of the Soviet Union nor a war fought with it. A fourth was the imprint of a distinctive personality: despite Nitze's claim, he dominated the drafting, much as Kennan had always done. A final similarity was historical significance: since its declassification in 1975, historians have regarded NSC 68, alongside Kennan's "long telegram" and "X" article, as a foundational statement of United States grand strategy in the Cold War.[33]

But both Kennan and Bohlen objected to NSC 68, when they finally read it, for much the same reason that Kennan had opposed the Truman Doctrine. In order to "sell" the idea of a major military buildup—in this case, to Truman himself—the document exaggerated the threats the United States confronted. It portrayed a Soviet Union resolved to risk war as soon as its capabilities exceeded those of the Americans and their allies: that point would come, it claimed, if nothing was done, as early as 1954. It rejected distinctions between vital and peripheral interests, emphasizing instead the damaging psychological effects of losing even remote regions to communism. It saw all parts of the world as equally important because all threats were equally dangerous. And because it ruled out both appeasement and all-out war, it called for responding to aggression wherever and at whatever level it might take place. At Acheson's suggestion, NSC 68 contained no estimate of what all this would cost. The amounts would be huge, though, which led Bohlen to conclude, shortsightedly, that "there was absolutely no chance that [it] would be adopted."[34]

Acheson was unrepentant. Of course NSC 68 exaggerated, he admitted in his memoirs. Its purpose was "to so bludgeon the mass mind of 'top government' that not only could the President make the decision but the decision could be carried out. . . . If we made our points clearer than truth, we did not differ from most other educators and could hardly do otherwise." There were times, his great mentor Oliver Wendell Holmes, Jr., had said, when "we need education in the obvious more than the investigation of the obscure." Kennan, when asked about this shortly after Acheson's account came out, had his own Holmes reference ready: the great man had also observed "that he couldn't write out his philosophy of the law; he could express it only as it applied to specific cases." Documents like NSC 68, Kennan argued, "assume a static world. They freeze policy, making it impossible to respond to external changes."[35]

The issue, fundamentally, was the tension between planning policy and executing it. Kennan's approach, one historian observed, relied heavily on the "noncommunicable wisdom of the experienced career official" and had little patience with the "rigidities, simplifications, and artificialities" involved in administering large organizations. Acheson, in turn, had to think about exactly this: "I recognized and highly appreciated the personal and esoteric skill of our Foreign Service officers, but believed that insofar as their wisdom was 'non-communicable,' its value, though great in operations abroad, was limited in Washington." Davies, on this point, sided with Acheson. "Kennan and Bohlen thought that NSC-68 was an extreme reaction and a misreading of Soviet intentions," he recalled, "because it was so schematic. As indeed it was. It was highly schematic, it was a counter to the Communist Manifesto." The Soviet Union "was a growing threat to the United States that had to be met. Whatever it cost, we had to do it."[36]

V.

The Kennans, at the beginning of 1950, were renting a house at 3707 33rd Place NW, a cul-de-sac in the Cleveland Park section of Washington, not far from the National Zoo. Grace was seventeen, Joan was thirteen, and Christopher was just over a month old: he was "very healthy and good natured," George wrote a friend, "and vegetates quite normally." Meanwhile Annelise had written to Kent, now a professor of music at the University of Texas, to thank him for a basket of grapefruit. These became regular Christmas gifts, and the appreciative letters back to Austin—sometimes from Annelise, more often from George—would over the next several decades chronicle family life. Apart from the children, the main topic in Annelise's first grapefruit letter was George's upcoming sabbatical: "We haven't decided where to go yet, but the chances are pretty much in favour of the Institute for Advanced Studies at Princeton. They have asked him to come." In the meantime George had taken up carpentry. He had built himself a workshop, was repairing old things, and making new ones. He would love to get some classical guitar music. Having taught himself to read it, "he struggles along in his spare moments."[37]

Finances were also a struggle. "My mother was a very feminine woman who greatly enjoyed pretty clothes," Joan recalled, "but not to the point of ever neglecting what was most important. She could make do when she had to." One day a

Washington policeman stopped her because the car she was driving had Pennsylvania plates. When asked where they lived, Annelise was about to say East Berlin when Grace blurted out: "Oh, we live just around the corner." This got them a fifteen-dollar fine, which meant that Annelise wouldn't be able to buy the new dress for which she'd been saving money. She surprised her daughters by—uncharacteristically—bursting into tears.[38]

The Institute appointment was definite by the middle of February, although Harvard, the Massachusetts Institute of Technology, and Dartmouth, as well as Princeton and Yale, had also tried to recruit Kennan. He would receive the equivalent of his Foreign Service salary, which he would be free to supplement through occasional lecturing and perhaps part-time teaching. Kennan would leave his job as State Department counselor, as he had requested, at the end of June. What he would do at the Institute was left vague, although he had hinted at an agenda a few days after his November 1949 meeting with Oppenheimer, when he wrote of the need for "an intensive educational effort directed toward our public opinion in general and particularly toward the work of our universities."[39] For the moment, though, he had a more immediate objective: this was to write, for the widely circulated *Reader's Digest*, an updated "X" article.

The idea came from Paul Palmer, senior editor of the magazine, who had approached Kennan the previous September about critiquing the "preventive war psychology" that he saw sweeping the country. Kennan agreed, knowing that news of the Soviet atomic bomb was about to break. Acheson approved the idea, but the need for State Department clearances delayed the article's appearance: it had been "plucked and torn," Kennan wrote Palmer, by people more interested in reducing its vulnerability than in improving its legibility. The original "X" article, "happily, though fortuitously," had avoided such pitfalls and appeared "in all its helpless innocence." The new piece finally came out in late February 1950, under Kennan's own name, with the title: "Is War with Russia Inevitable? Five Solid Arguments for Peace."

The subtitle answered the question. War was always possible, Kennan argued, but highly unlikely. Soviet imperialism had bitten off more than it could chew. The end of the American atomic monopoly had not significantly shifted the military balance. A strong defense was necessary, but not "a morbid preoccupation with what *could possibly happen if.*" Americans should avoid "vainglorious schemes for changing human nature," while cultivating "Christian humility before the enormous complexity of the world in which it has been given to us to live." For all the effort that went into it, the article fell flat, confirming Kennan's suspicion that publicity was more a matter of accident—an exasperated telegram, a mysterious pseudonym, a malicious leak—than of design.[40]

Disappointed by this, and by the tepid response to his Milwaukee speech, Kennan hoped to cheer himself up by attending the twenty-fifth reunion of his Princeton class: he had, he wrote Oppenheimer, "succumbed to some very decent and considerate letters from fellow alumni." On June 8 he, Annelise, and Jeanette drove there from the farm. An undergraduate "checked my name off the list, and coolly asked me for $75.00. I was horrified. I was head over heels in debt. I couldn't have raised $75.00 by any stretch of the imagination. I fled, and repaired in panic to the Institute." Oppenheimer offered to cover the cost, but Kennan refused and arranged instead for a telegram to be sent—from his Washington office—conveying regrets that he would not be able to attend after all. The three disheartened celebrants then slipped quietly out of town, driving to Dartmouth where, on the eleventh, George received an honorary degree. Another, from Yale, was awarded on the next day, "as a gesture of respect," Kennan was told, "for the Department of State in the face of MacCarthy's [sic] attacks."

On June 14 he was back in Washington, where Webb wanted to talk about his future. His plan, Kennan told the under secretary of state, was to be away for at least an academic year: what happened after that depended on "what use [the department] could make of me." If no one else qualified, perhaps ambassador to Great Britain? Webb said he had already spoken with Acheson about that post, which was "so expensive that I would not be able to afford it." Kennan sat in for Nitze at one last meeting of the Policy Planning Staff, spent a gloomy afternoon griping to Joe Alsop about the hopelessness of conducting coherent policy in a democracy, and then went back to the farm. While he was driving to a nursery a few days later to pick up some trees, inspiration struck, so he pulled over and composed a poem.

From: G. F. Kennan
To: The Members of the Policy Planning Staff
Subject: Their Peculiar Fate

Friends, teachers, pupils; toilers at the wheels;
Undaunted drones of the official hive,
In deep frustration doomed to strive,
To power and to action uncommitted,
Condemned (disconsolate, in world of steel and glass confined)

To course the foggy bottoms of the mind,
Unaided, unencouraged, to pursue,
The rarer bloom, the deeper hue,
The choicer fragrance—these to glean
And, having gleaned, to synthesize
And long in deepest reticence to hide . . .
Until some distant day—perhaps—permitted,
Anonymous and unidentified,
The Great White Queen
*   at last*
*   to fertilize.*

. . . .

Who knows?
*   Perhaps in moment unforeseen*
The Great White Queen,
Made fruitful by your seed,
*   may yet create*
So dazzling and so beauteous a brood
That worlds will marvel, history admire.
And then the scorned, no-longer-wanted sire,
From bondage loosed, from travail freed,
Basking beside the rays these progeny exude,
May find the warmth to which all souls aspire
*   in autumn late.*

He meant it to be his last Policy Planning Staff paper.[41]

VI.

Perhaps it would have been, had it not been for Stalin, Mao, and the North Korean leader Kim Il-sung, who found a way, on June 25, 1950, to frustrate this and many other American designs. Korea, like Germany, had remained divided at the end of World War II. Unlike Germany, however, neither the United States nor the Soviet Union regarded the country as a vital interest. They were thus able to agree, if tacitly, on a mutual withdrawal of occupation forces, what Kennan had long hoped for in Germany. United Nations–sponsored elections south of the 38th parallel—the dividing line hastily drawn at the end of the war—had by then established the Republic of Korea; and the Soviet Union, without U.N. sanction, had set up the Democratic People's Republic of Korea in the north. It was no satisfactory solution, but by Cold War standards it looked like a relatively untroublesome one, which was why Acheson felt comfortable excluding South Korea from the "defensive perimeter" he publicly announced in January 1950. The only difficulty was that Stalin, Mao, and Kim read his speech—and probably also, courtesy of British spies operating in Washington at the time, NSC 48/2, upon which it had been based.[42]

There had been indications, Kennan later recalled, that military operations might begin soon somewhere in the communist world, but the intelligence was not site-specific and MacArthur's analysts in Tokyo discounted it. As a result, North Korea's attack on South Korea, undertaken with the full knowledge and support of Stalin and Mao, caught the rest of the world by surprise. It came on a Sunday: President Truman was at his home in Independence, Missouri; Acheson was at his Maryland farm; Nitze was fishing in New Brunswick miles away from the nearest road; and Kennan was spending a quiet weekend with his family in East Berlin (Pennsylvania). He knew nothing of the invasion until they returned to Washington late that afternoon and saw the newspaper headlines: "Nobody had thought to notify me, and perhaps there was no reason anybody should have; but I could not help but reflect that General Marshall would have seen that this was done."[43]

Kennan had asked to be relieved of policy responsibilities. As with most things he did, however, there was a certain ambivalence about this. "It never occurred to me that you [and Acheson] would make foreign policy without having first consulted me," Nitze remembered him saying sometime in the summer of 1950. Now, with Nitze stuck in the wilds of Canada—the first leg of his trip back had to be by canoe—Acheson welcomed Kennan's offer to help. The next two months were an extraordinary moment in Kennan's career: at no other point did he operate nearer to the top levels of government in a major crisis, or with greater freedom to provide advice. Remarkably—but with an eye to history and perhaps biography—he found the time to keep a detailed diary of those crowded days. It showed what he meant about the inadequacies of grand strategic documents that sought to embed, as if in amber, the complexities of a rapidly shifting world. At the same time it revealed several of these inadequacies as having been his own.[44]

The first and most obvious one had to do with the "defensive perimeter" strategy, which reflected Kennan's principle that because some interests were more important than others, not all needed to be defended. That sounded good in theory; in practice, however, it conflicted with another principle in which Kennan believed strongly—that psychology was as important as industrial-military capability in shaping world politics. Having excluded South Korea from American protection because it was militarily insignificant, he now concluded along with almost everyone else in Washington that it was psychologically vital. So too, he insisted, was the defense of Chiang Kai-shek and the Chinese Nationalists. Kennan's first recommendation upon arriving at the State Department on the evening of June 25—it was probably the first on this subject from anyone in government— was to ensure "that Formosa did not fall to the communists since this, coming on top of the Korean attack, would be calamitous to our position in the Far East."[45]

With the approval of the U.N. Security Council—the Soviet representative, protesting the organization's failure to seat the People's Republic of China, had not been present to cast a veto—President Truman announced on June 27 that American troops, under MacArthur's command, would be coming to the defense of South Korea. Meanwhile, the Navy would begin patrolling the Taiwan Strait. Asked on short notice to brief the NATO ambassadors that day, Kennan acknowledged that the United States was acting not because of the strategic importance of the territory at risk but because "of the damage to world confidence and morale which would have been produced had we not so acted." The effects could have extended throughout East Asia and even into Europe. He then added—without authority, since the issue had not yet been decided—that the war would be limited: "We had no intention to do more than to restore the *status quo ante* and no intention to proceed to the conquest of northern Korea."[46]

That evening the Kennans attended a long-planned dinner party. On their way in, they met Joe Alsop. "Although he regards himself as a total contemplative," the columnist wrote of this encounter, "I have always observed that George makes his best sense as a man of action, when there is a good, loud, cable machine at his elbow clacking out horrible problems all over the world. When George broods, he becomes a little silly."

On this day, the cable machine had been clacking madly, and George was dancing on air because MacArthur's men were being mobilized for combat under the auspices of the United Nations. He was carrying his balalaika, a Russian instrument he used to play with some skill at social gatherings, and with a great, vigorous swing, he clapped me on the back with it, nearly striking me to the sidewalk.

"Well, Joe," he cried, "what do you think of the democracies now?"

No matter how well intended, it is never pleasant being knocked about, and I replied quite crossly, "I think about democracy exactly what I always have, but not what you thought when you came to see me."

Two days later, still elated, Kennan attended a meeting of the NSC staff in the former State Department building next to the White House. Nostalgic for its cool, calm, and spacious interior, Kennan joked to his old friend "Doc" Matthews that the crisis would never have happened if they hadn't moved to the new headquarters in Foggy Bottom. "To my surprise the colored elevator woman turned around and said with great firmness and enthusiasm: 'That's right, sir.' "[47]

A second shift in Kennan's thinking related to NSC 68. He had not questioned its call to spend more on conventional forces—how else could reliance on nuclear weapons be reduced?—but he and Bohlen had objected to Nitze's portrayal of a worldwide Soviet threat. Now, though, by authorizing the attack in Korea, Stalin had made Nitze look prophetic. "I stated it as my deep conviction that the U.S. had no choice but to accept this challenge," Kennan wrote of a meeting with Acheson and his advisers on June 26. It would have to commit whatever was required for the completion of the task. The fighting in Korea was likely to spread, and it was "absolutely essential" to mobilize for that purpose. If, in World War II, "our commanders had been told [that their only task] was to cope with an army of 90,000 Koreans with 100 tanks and small air support and to occupy Korea to the 38th Parallel, they would have considered it a small operation indeed." So the question was one of will, not capability.

When told, on July 12, that the Council of Economic Advisers had seen no need for drastic mobilization measures, Kennan was furious. The problem, he complained to an equally worried Nitze on the seventeenth, lay in the president's failure himself to take responsibility, and to require that *all* of his subordinates do so. Key portions of the executive branch had been left "to wallow around in the cluttering impediments of the committee system, complicated by the presence of such personalities as Mr. Johnson and Mr. Snyder and his own White House political advisers." If this continued, "our world position might well be lost . . . for lack of the horse-shoe nail of real executive direction." Its vigorous exercise, in contrast, would "electrify the Government into an entirely different style of action." It would certainly impress the Russians, he added a few weeks later, who would see how little of the American national income was going to military spending compared with themselves. The United States would not go bankrupt "even if we were forced to shell out three times as much for defense."[48]

Kennan did not give up on his strategy of seeking to strain Sino-Soviet ties, but the Korean conflict made it much harder to sell that idea in Washington. He was wondering as early as June 29 whether it might be the Russians' intention "to keep out of this business themselves . . . but to embroil us to the maximum with their Korean and Chinese satellites." If so, why not offer the Chinese Communists an inducement not to cooperate? Would it not appeal to them and embarrass Moscow, he asked on July 11, "if we were suddenly to favor and achieve the admission of the Chinese Communists to the U.N. and to the Security Council?" Kennan's proposal reflected no greater sympathy for Mao Zedong than he had for Chiang Kai-shek: like the decision to deploy the Navy in the Taiwan Strait, this would be a strategic maneuver, not a conciliatory gesture. China, he told the British ambassador Oliver Franks, "would never, in my opinion, be dependable from the standpoint of western interests."[49]

But when Kennan mentioned this plan to John Foster Dulles—who would have become secretary of state had the Republicans won in 1948 and was now the principal Japanese peace treaty negotiator—"I was shouted down." It would look to the American public, Dulles insisted, "as though we had been tricked into giving up something for nothing." Kennan saw the problem and abandoned the idea, but he hoped that history would someday record this as an example of the damage done "by the irresponsible and bigoted interference of the China lobby and its friends in Congress." A few days later he learned what Dulles was telling newspapermen: "that while he used to think highly of George Kennan, he had now concluded that he was a very dangerous man: that he was advocating the admission of the Chinese Communists to the United Nations, and a cessation of U.S. military action at the 38th parallel."[50]

The latter charge oversimplified Kennan's position. He had argued from the first days of the fighting that MacArthur should be free to conduct military operations anywhere on the Korean peninsula, as long as these advanced the *political* objective of liberating South Korea. What he did oppose, on both military and political grounds, was occupying all of North Korea. Kennan was sure that MacArthur would soon take the offensive, despite defeats that were pushing U.N. forces into a tight perimeter around Pusan. When he did,

the further we were to advance up the peninsula the more unsound it would become from a military standpoint. If we were actually to advance beyond the neck of the peninsula, we would be getting into an area where mass could be used against us and where we would be distinctly at a disadvantage. This, I thought, increased the importance of a clear concept of our being able to terminate our action at the proper point, . . . [to] make sure that we did not frighten the Russians into action which would interfere with this.

Kennan knew how hard it had been to control MacArthur in Japan. Any insensitivity now to instructions from Washington could lead the Soviet Union to commit its forces. Nitze and Bohlen also worried about this, as did Davies, who stressed the additional danger of Chinese intervention. Even if these worst cases did not materialize, Kennan asked on July 31, what chance would there be of getting Soviet help to end the war if MacArthur was approaching "the gates of Vladivostok"?[51]

Restraint had few other advocates in Washington, however, as the planning for MacArthur's offensive advanced. The Joint Chiefs of Staff disliked having diplomacy constrain military operations, and even within the State Department there were vigorous objections to Kennan's argument, notably from John Allison, director of the Office of Northeast Asian Affairs, who attacked it as "a timid, half-hearted policy designed not to provoke the Soviets to war." Meanwhile the administration's critics had become no less vehement. "This noisy and violent Republican minority in Congress [is] paralyzing . . . an intelligent and courageous approach," Kennan wrote on August 14. Never before had there been such confusion with respect to foreign policy.

> The President doesn't understand it; Congress doesn't understand it; nor does the public, nor does the press. . . . Only the diplomatic historian, it seems to me, working from the leisure and detachment of a later day, will be able to unravel this incredible tangle and reveal the true aspect of the various factors and issues involved.

Kennan could not resist, however, making one last effort to sort it all out. On the twenty-third, he sent Acheson some parting recommendations before leaving for Princeton: "I am afraid that, like so many of my thoughts, they will be too remote from general thinking in the Government to be of much practical use to you."[52]

This proved to be true. For as Kennan detached himself from the clacking cable machines and began to contemplate what had happened over the past two months, the euphoria he had felt during the early days of the Korean conflict gave way to a more characteristic pessimism—some of it merited, much of it not—about what the United States could hope to accomplish in East Asia. The immediate problem was MacArthur: "We are tolerating a state of affairs in which we do not really have full control over the statements that are being made—and the actions taken—in our name." But there were larger long-term issues as well.

One had to do with Korea's future once the fighting had stopped. It had been necessary to resist the invasion, since the "psychological radiations" from a failure to do so would have been so devastating. But did the United States really wish to commit itself, indefinitely, to keeping the Korean peninsula outside of the Russian and Japanese spheres of influence within which it had historically been included? The latter would obviously be the better option, but defeat in war and occupation by the Americans had so weakened Japan that it could no longer play that role. Was there any alternative, then, to tolerating Soviet control, as long as it was not manifested "in ways calculated to throw panic and terror into other Asian peoples and thus to achieve for the Kremlin important successes going far beyond the Korean area"?

The war in Korea had led the Truman administration, in addition to ordering naval patrols in the Taiwan Strait, to increase economic and military assistance to the French in Indochina: this amounted to "guaranteeing the French in an undertaking which neither they nor we, nor both of us together, can win." Would it not be preferable "to permit the turbulent political currents of that country to find their own level, unimpeded by foreign troops or pressures, even at the probable cost of an eventual deal between Viet-Nam and the Viet-Minh, and the spreading over the whole country of Viet-Minh authority"?

Finally, and most controversially, Kennan insisted that the United States could not indefinitely, using its own strength, keep Japan resistant to Soviet influence. Only the Japanese, through their own choices, could do that; yet how could they exercise that freedom if the Americans kept troops there? Any peace treaty anchored to a continued military presence would never have legitimacy in the eyes of the Japanese. The implied duress would divert their attention to the problem of "how to get United States troops out" rather than "how to meet Soviet pressures against Japan."

The best solution, then, would be to seek a comprehensive settlement with the Soviet Union—partly explicit, partly tacit—that would terminate hostilities in Korea, admit Communist China to the United Nations, allow a plebiscite to determine Taiwan's future, bring about the neutralization and demilitarization of Japan, and reduce American military capabilities to a "mixed combat force, commanded and operated as a unit, capable of dealing a sharp blow on a limited front almost anywhere in the world on short notice." None of this could be left to MacArthur: "It would take a real diplomatic envoy, backed by Presidential authority but instructed to operate quietly, patiently and inconspicuously."

Kennan admitted that such a project would provoke "violent and outraged opposition." It would pour oil on fires already kindled by Republican charges "that our Far Eastern policy has been over-lenient to Communism and therefore neglectful of our national security." But all of that, he too grandly concluded, "is not really my competence, and I do not think I should discuss it in this paper." It was, as Acheson later summarized it, "a memorandum typical of its gifted author, beautifully expressed, sometimes contradictory, in which were mingled flashes of prophetic insight [with] suggestions . . . of total impracticality."[53]

VII.

Precisely so, which raises the question of what Kennan was trying to say, or do, or mean. He did not deliberately set out to irritate his boss, who was at the time and even in retrospect surprisingly restrained in his response to this document, which was yet another demonstration, or so it seemed, of Kennan's volatility. Acheson saw him as "not a very useful policy adviser," Nitze answered crisply years later, when asked what the secretary of state really thought of Kennan. "But there did seem to be a certain affection on Acheson's part for Kennan, and vice versa," Nitze's interviewer protested. "There was," he acknowledged. Isaiah Berlin, like Joe Alsop, saw in Kennan a dual personality, one part professional, the other elsewhere:

> Provided he had before him the machine, whatever it is, which encodes the tele-grams, he behaved like an exceptional State Department official. His famous dis-patches were concrete, clear, useful and truly important. Once he got away from that, he was in the empyrean, a mystic and a visionary, you see. You couldn't tell which way he would turn. In short, a kind of Jekyll and Hyde.

Most people have mood swings, if not that extreme: few, however, turn theirs into prophetically impractical policy memoranda. Toward what empyrean, then, was Kennan drifting?[54]

One way to answer that question is to return to Kennan's December 1949 National War College lecture, which focused on the underlying *systems* of inter-national relations: over the past two centuries, he argued, states and statesmen had been carried along by structural shifts that few of them fully understood. Kennan's distinctiveness lay in his ambition, as a policy planner, to detect such evolutions in international systems and to align statecraft with them. It was another Bismarckian reach for the hem of history.

He reached, however, just as the international system was undergoing its most radical shift in centuries. Kennan's frame of reference was the balance of power system of the eighteenth, nineteenth, and early twentieth centuries, in which several great powers—most recently the United States, Great Britain, Germany, Russia, and Japan—had balanced one another. This was, for him, the default: the gravitational center to which world politics must sooner or later return, however drastic the disruptions of recent decades. That those disruptions had themselves altered that structure—that bipolarity had replaced multipolarity—was not, and in some ways would never be, visible to him.

He was hardly alone in this. Who would have anticipated, in 1950, that a divided Germany could form the basis, over the next four decades, for a peaceful Europe? That despite devastating regional wars that left Korea divided and unified Vietnam, there would be no world wars? That the United States and the Soviet Union, soon to have tens of thousands of thermonuclear weapons pointed at one another, would agree tacitly never to use any of them? That the only empires of consequence left anywhere in the world would be those run from Washington and Moscow? That China and Taiwan, still under separate regimes and without admitting it, would half a century later share a common *capitalist* ideology?

The answer, obviously, is that no one did. What set Kennan apart from his contemporaries was not his failure to see this future, but rather his constant concern for how policies and structures related to one another. With the latter shifting in ways that not even Kennan understood, his anxieties came across as contradictions, volatility, even to Alsop and Berlin as a dual personality disorder. Acheson paid little more attention than they did to grand international systems. But he did know, from his legal training, that decisions—however expedient, hasty, or ill informed—built practices, which established precedents, which over time made law, which then *became* structures. It was enough, he believed, to have some vague sense of the destination toward which you were stumbling, to be of good cheer, and not to look back. The hyperconscientious Kennan could never reconcile himself to such an attitude. Which was why he now chose to depart, at last, for his own empyrean.

Part IV

SEVENTEEN

Public Figure, Private Doubts: 1950–1951

KENNAN'S EMPYREAN WAS THE INSTITUTE FOR ADVANCED STUDY, one of the first American think tanks. Founded in 1930, located on a large tract of meadows and woods outside of Princeton, the Institute—never a part of Princeton University—made itself famous by creating a position for Albert Einstein when he left Germany after the Nazis came to power. He remained there for the rest of his life. During its early years, the Institute recruited mostly mathematicians: like its model, All Souls College, Oxford, it had no students and hence no teaching responsibilities. Its fellows' only obligations were to ponder, research, occasionally publish—and to stay out of each other's way. How did Kennan get along with Einstein? "I never went to see him," he admitted rufully, half a century after the great physicist's death. "This was partly a reflection of my youthful arrogance. I felt I knew nothing about his subject and knew it. Einstein knew nothing about my subject, and didn't know it."[1]

Oppenheimer became the Institute's third director in 1947, determined to broaden the diversity of its fellows without changing what was expected of them. This led him to offer Kennan a visiting appointment, over objections from several mathematicians who wondered what contribution a Foreign Service officer with no advanced degree and no scholarly publications would be able to make. Kennan accepted it despite the continuing efforts of Princeton's president, Harold Dodds, to give him a university professorship. "I want to make sure," Kennan wrote, "that I do not move from a sphere in which I have occasionally . . . accomplish[ed] things despite a great number of diversions to one where I keep the diversions and dispense with the accomplishment."[2]

Kennan and Oppenheimer had first met at the National War College in the fall of 1946. "He shuffled diffidently and almost apologetically out to the podium," Kennan remembered,

> a frail, stooped figure in a heavy brown tweed suit with trousers that were baggy and too long, big feet that turned outward, and a small head and face that caused him, at times, to look strangely like a young student. He then proceeded to speak for nearly an hour, without the use of notes—but with such startling lucidity and precision of expression that when he had finished, no one dared ask a question—everyone was sure that somehow or other he had answered every possible point. I say "somehow or other," because, curiously enough, no one could remember exactly what he said.

They then become consultants to one another. Oppenheimer advised Kennan on European federation—not very successfully—when the Policy Planning Staff considered that issue in the summer of 1949. Kennan advised Oppenheimer, in turn, on what the U.S. Atomic Energy Commission should recommend with respect to the "super" bomb: Oppenheimer chaired its General Advisory Committee. Despite his reservations about Acheson's suggested moratorium, Oppenheimer found the new weapon as abhorrent as Kennan did, and strongly opposed building it. Kennan's long January 1950 report, Oppenheimer's biographers have observed, might as well have been coauthored with him.[3]

"Could there be," Kennan wrote of Oppenheimer after his death, "anyone harder to describe than he? . . . [P]art scientist, part poet; sometimes proud, sometimes humble; in some ways formidably competent in practical matters, in other ways woefully helpless: he was a bundle of marvelous contradictions." To many, he seemed abrasive.

> The shattering quickness and critical power of his own mind made him, no doubt, impatient of the ponderous, the obvious, and the platitudinous, in the discourse of others. But underneath this edgy impatience there lay one of the most sentimental of natures, an enormous thirst for friendship and affection, and a touching belief—such as I have never observed in anyone else—in what he thought should be the fraternity of advanced scholarship.

Thanks to Oppenheimer, the Institute for Advanced Study became Kennan's professional and intellectual home for the next half century: he would spend twice as many years there as he did in the Foreign Service. Oppenheimer saw in Kennan—as Kennan saw in Oppenheimer—something of himself.

I.

The Kennans arrived in Princeton on Sunday, September 10, 1950, unpacked their belongings in the house they had rented, and stashed young Christopher in a playpen. There he stood, George recalled, "leaning his head idyllically on his arm (belying, in this peaceful pose, . . . the more frantic tendencies of later years)." Outside, mists rose on the meadows, while crickets soothed with their dreamlike drone. On Monday Kennan spent his first day at the Institute. A gentle rain was falling, "an English sort of rain," as though deferring "to the quiet green of the place."

Oppenheimer welcomed him with two pieces of advice. One was not to try to write anything immediately, but rather to use his first months at the Institute for unsystematic reading, to broaden what Kennan knew to be "an intense but narrow educational experience." The other was to learn "that there is nothing harder in life than to have nothing before you but the blank page and nothing to do but your best." Savoring the suggestion, impressed by the admonition, "I installed myself in my new office, with windows looking out over the fields to the woods, and had a sense of peace and happiness such as I have not had for a long time."[4]

Kennan promised Acheson that he would rule out distractions: he could hardly seek refuge from Washington without accomplishing things he could never have done while there. But he was already swamped with invitations to speak, write, and consult. Most he could decline and did: his diary records seventy-seven between July and October; six more arrived on a single day, November 1. Others were more difficult to reject, whether because they came from people too prominent to put off, or from friends, family, even the children's schools. Miss Fine's in Princeton, where Joan was enrolled, got a carefully prepared lecture the following spring on the past and future of Soviet-American relations. Finally, there were the flattering ones that promised to amplify "one's own voice and with it one's possibilities for usefulness."[5]

Outstanding obligations also ensnared him. Kennan had agreed to write a new article for *Foreign Affairs*, in yet another effort to update and clarify what he had said four years earlier as "X." He had accepted, "with staggering frivolity," invitations to give two series of lectures, one at Northwestern University and the other at the University of Chicago. He was participating in a Council on Foreign Relations study group on aid to Europe. He was reading book manuscripts: the historian S. Everett Gleason got five pages of single-spaced comments on a single draft chapter of *The Challenge to Isolation,* the semiofficial history of pre–World War II American foreign policy he was coauthoring with William L. Langer. And Kennan had assured Dodds that he would participate in university affairs, even if not as a professor. So he ran, successfully, for alumni trustee in 1951—despite having fled his own class reunion a year earlier because he couldn't afford the fee.[6]

But he turned down an invitation to join the advisory board of the Woodrow Wilson School's new Center for Research on World Political Institutions, which was seeking to apply social and behavioral sciences to the making of public policy. "[U]seful thought in the political sciences," Kennan explained to a Columbia professor who had tried to interest him in these techniques, "is the product not just of rational deduction about phenomena external to ourselves but also of emotional and esthetic experience and of a recognition of the relationship of 'self' to environment." He was more candid with Edward Meade Earle, the wartime editor of *Makers of Modern Strategy,* now a historian at the Institute. Such people seemed to think "that all you have to do is put these problems in the hopper of a group of qualified social scientists and the proper answers [will] emerge from the other end, along the lines of the Institute's computer."[7]

There really was a computer at the Institute in 1950, or at least the mathematician John von Neumann was building one. Located in the basement of Fuld Hall, beneath Kennan's new office, it was enormous and unreliable but the first in the world. Its processing capabilities would prove good enough to speed development of the American hydrogen bomb and later to form the basis for the discipline of game theory. Kennan had already opposed the first invention; he would come to despise the second. His coexistence in space but not in sympathy with von Neumann reflected the Institute's failure to foster the "rich and harmonious fellowship of the mind" that its director hoped for. "[M]athematicians and historians continued to seek their own tables in the cafeteria," Kennan recalled, while Oppenheimer remained largely alone "in his ability to bridge in a single inner world these wholly disparate workings of the human intellect." For the moment, though, this did not matter.[8]

II.

Joe Alsop went to see the Korean War for himself two weeks after his June 1950 run-in with Kennan's balalaika. Forgivingly, he had allowed George and Annelise to camp out amid the Soong eggshell ware in his Dumbarton Oaks house—the lease had run out on the more modest quarters they had rented in Cleveland Park. "Your battle accounts were the best I have seen in our press," Kennan wrote, thanking him. "Like Tolstoy, you are an artist and should write about what you see and perceive rather than what you think. For the latter, I have respect too, but not as much." With that barb implanted, Kennan admitted to having been "startlingly wrong" in some of his views about Asia, "and you, it would seem, much righter." But "not necessarily" for the right reasons. "I can't help but feel that you over-rate my descriptive powers and perhaps just slightly underrate my poor intellect," Alsop responded, "but you and I will argue as long as we are friends."[9]

Once out of Washington, Kennan watched with admiration as MacArthur landed American and South Korean forces at Inchon on September 15, and then with foreboding as they swept into North Korea at the beginning of October. No less a figure than George C. Marshall, recruited by Truman to replace the hopeless Louis Johnson as secretary of defense, had cabled MacArthur that he was "to feel unhampered strategically and tactically" in operating north of the 38th parallel. Meeting little opposition, United Nations forces advanced rapidly through the narrow neck of the Korean peninsula and toward the much longer border with China at the Yalu River. Mao Zedong ordered his armies to cross into North Korea on October 19. A week later they attacked South Korean units, but MacArthur kept going. As he neared the Yalu on November 25, the Chinese surprised him with a massive counteroffensive, which soon had his forces retreating in disarray and Washington in a state of panic.

Kennan had indeed been wrong about some things and right about others. He had warned of intervention, but it was the Soviet Union that worried him: he hardly mentioned the possibility that the Chinese might enter the war. He opposed trying to occupy all of North Korea, but Chinese sources suggest that Mao might have attacked even if United Nations forces had remained south of the 38th parallel. There were strains in the Sino Soviet relationship, but they originated more from Stalin's uncertainty about how to handle MacArthur's advance than from Mao's determination to assert his independence from Moscow. Still eager to show his loyalty to the Soviet Union, Mao welcomed a war with the Americans, partly for ideological reasons but chiefly because the Truman administration had accepted Kennan's recommendation to deploy the Seventh Fleet in the Taiwan Strait. That, as Mao saw it, was intervention in the internal affairs of China.[10]

But none of this was known then. What was clear was that official Washington—having spent the past five months experiencing despair, and then euphoria, and then despair again—was badly rattled. Asked at a press conference on November 30 whether he had considered using the atomic bomb in Korea, Truman acknowledged that he had, and then alarmed everyone by adding that "the military commander in the field" would decide when its employment would be appropriate. The White House quickly backtracked, insisting that only the president could make such a decision, but British prime minister Clement Attlee invited himself to Washington anyway to try to figure out what was going on. The next morning Bohlen called Kennan from Paris to point out that there was now no one in the State Department with "a deep understanding" of the Soviet Union. Kennan must volunteer his services once again.[11]

He immediately did so, received thanks from Acheson, and caught the next train. He spent the evening of Saturday, December 2, with the Davieses and on Sunday morning reported for duty. With the secretary of state tied up at the Pentagon and the White House, it fell to Webb to brief Kennan. Military planners required a decision within thirty-six hours as to whether to withdraw completely from Korea. Attlee would be arriving the next morning. The State Department needed an urgent assessment of what the prospects might be for negotiating something—just what was left unclear—with the Soviet Union.

Kennan, Davies, and their colleague G. Frederick Reinhardt produced, within four hours, four pages of what Kennan remembered as "the bleakest and most uncomfortable prose that the department's files can ever have accommodated." There had never been a worse time to approach Moscow, they concluded. There was "not the faintest reason why the Russians should wish to aid us in our predicament." Diplomacy would work only when there were "solid cards in our hand, in the form of some means of pressure on them to arrive at an agreement [which would be] in their own interests." Acheson, looking exhausted, was leaving his office when Kennan brought the report to him. Could he come home for dinner? Kennan did, saving the depressing news for the next morning.

Acheson unburdened himself that evening. He joked about a new portrait that seemed to show him impervious to criticism. He spoke "of the strangeness of his position" as if he were the only person in Washington who understood the seriousness of the situation. He sounded, at that moment, like Kennan, who recalled years later that "I had often disagreed with him—our minds had never really worked in the same way; but never for a moment could I deny him my admiration for the manner in which he bore this ordeal." So Kennan went back to the Davieses, sat up into the early morning of December 4, and wrote out in longhand this letter for his embattled superior:

Dear Mr. Secretary:

On the official level I have been asked to give advice only on the particular problem of Soviet reaction to various possible approaches.

But there is one thing I should like to say in continuation of our discussion of yesterday evening.

In international, as in private, life, what counts most is not really what happens to some one but how he bears what happens to him. For this reason almost everything depends from here on out on the manner in which we Americans bear what is unquestionably a major failure and disaster to our national fortunes. If we accept it with candor, with dignity, with a resolve to absorb its lessons and to make it good by re-doubled and determined effort— starting all over again, if necessary, along the pattern of Pearl Harbor—we need lose neither our self-confidence nor our allies nor our power for bargaining, eventually, with the Russians. But if we try to conceal from our own people or from our allies the full measure of our misfortune, or permit ourselves to seek relief in any reactions of bluster or petulance or hysteria, we can easily find this crisis resolving itself into an irreparable deterioration of our world position—and of our confidence in ourselves.

George Kennan

Both Acheson and Kennan included this document in their memoirs—but only Acheson, who found it "wise and inspiring," quoted it in full.[12]

It would be too much to claim that this note, together with Kennan's advice over the next few days, reversed the mood of desperation gripping Washington. He was not alone in pointing out that, as the Chinese Communists drove south, they would outrun their supply lines: it ought to be possible to stabilize the front somewhere in the vicinity of the 38th parallel. That became the consensus on the course to be followed, and ultimately—despite MacArthur's increasingly erratic mood swings—this is what happened. Kennan's intervention was important enough, though, for Acheson to read his note aloud at a State Department staff meeting the next day, and to convey his argument against negotiations to Truman and Attlee.[13]

What must have impressed the secretary of state was that Kennan, for once, was *not* advocating diplomacy. Instead he agreed with Rusk, who evoked the example of the British in the two world wars. "They held on," Kennan added, "when there was no apparent reason for it." If there was any validity to the idea of negotiating from a position of strength, then this was "clearly a very bad time for an approach to the Russians." Acheson may have sounded like Kennan the previous evening, but Kennan now sounded like Acheson. He was even more vehement about the Chinese Communists, with the department's note-taker struggling to keep up:

> He said the Chinese have now committed an affront of the greatest magnitude to the United States. He said that what they have done is something that we can not forget for years and the Chinese will have to worry about righting themselves with us not us with them. . . . He said we owe China nothing but a lesson.

Kennan went back to the Institute satisfied that the week had been well spent. On December 17 he sent Alsop a Christmas card: "You must not be offended that I could not see you in Washington recently. I was there very briefly—and it was better that way. On the rare occasions when I can push the ubiquitous present out of the way, I am greatly enjoying my associations with the past—i.e., diplomatic history. But the present is a fearful nuisance."[14]

III.

"I am enjoying Princeton and my work here immensely," George wrote Kent on the second day of 1951, "though I am still harried by outside demands on my time. . . . I seem to get less done than under the pressures of the State Department." Nevertheless, the Institute was the ideal place for him now, "and all I would ask would be that I might be left alone to work there. . . . [T]hanks awfully for the grapefruit. They are delicious."[15]

Kennan was getting a lot done, although the results did not begin to show until January. Between then and the end of April, he completed his article for *Foreign Affairs,* submitted a forty-page study on American participation in international organizations to the Woodrow Wilson Foundation, and began studying the relationship between population growth, industrialization, and diminishing water reserves in the eastern United States, while preparing ten original lectures, each of them different, none to be delivered extemporaneously. He was trying, he said in the first of these, given in New York on January 27, "to disentangle the snarled skeins" of contemporary American foreign policy, "to bring order out of the chaos." But he was also clarifying his own thinking, most successfully in the two lectures he gave—little noticed at the time and less remembered since—immediately afterward at Northwestern University.

He began with a universally known piece of World War II graffiti. Anyone attempting to lead, he observed, encountered relics of those who had gone before. Wherever you looked, the scribbles would appear: "Kilroy—Kilroy the statesman, Kilroy the historian, Kilroy the policy maker—was here." Ahead was the future, shrouded in silence, mystery, and probably danger, all the greater if one advanced without looking back. For there was in the past a fund of human wisdom to draw upon. The wording might be cumbersome, or the imagery unfamiliar, but "a lot of people have thought very hard about human affairs for a long time, and may have done a lot of work that we need not repeat." It was vital, therefore, to use this "credit balance of experience and wisdom," because that was the only way to locate the point beyond which "we are really on our own."

Human nature had hardly changed since humans first evolved. What had changed was the environment surrounding them, not because of any alteration in biological cycles of growth and decay, or rhythms of climate, or even global warming—Kennan was looking into that problem then—but because of the population explosion that had taken place over the past two centuries. Martians with good telescopes and long life spans might note this: "These little microbes have suddenly begun to multiply at the most tremendous rate." The planet earthlings occupied was exhausting its empty space.

Some had sought to solve that problem by turning their homelands into workshops, buying what they needed by selling what they produced. Mercantile in their habits, mostly maritime in their capabilities, these people had accumulated enough wealth to dominate much of the rest of the world—for the moment. But the vast majority of its inhabitants were reproducing themselves without getting richer: this was tragedy for which the mercantile states had no answer. That being the case, it behooved the United States to refrain from offering one: "It is never easy for a rich man to talk with conviction to a poor man."

Meanwhile, the great wars of the twentieth century had disrupted the balance of power among the workshops. Few Americans realized it, but Germany and Japan had once contributed to their safety. With their defeat, the Soviet Union—a state neither mercantile nor maritime—had won most of Eurasia. Once this would not have mattered, because large territories were difficult to control. Now, though, technology had given totalitarians the capacity to monitor and hence to manage everything that was happening within their boundaries. That endangered civilization, for wars among land powers tended to leave behind "devastation, atrocity, and bitterness." Sea power had always been "more humane, more tempered, less drastic and less final in its objectives."

The danger for Americans lay less in another Pearl Harbor than in what they might do to themselves because they feared one. For confronting totalitarians required, in many respects, emulating them. The leader who would attempt this "must learn to regiment his people, to husband his resources, to guard against hostile agents in his midst, to maintain formidable armed forces in peacetime, to preserve secrecy about governmental decisions, to wield the weapons of bluff and surprise, to wage war in peacetime—and peace in wartime. Can these things be done without the selling of the national soul?"

That raised a larger problem, which was that Americans no longer saw, as clearly as they once had, their own self-interest.

> Whereas at one time the individual citizen swam in a relatively narrow stream, the banks of which were clearly visible to him, and could therefore measure easily his progress and position, today he is borne on vast expanses where too often the limits are not visible to him at all, and where he is incapable, with such subjective criteria of judgment as he possesses, to measure the rate and direction of the currents by which he is being borne.

The nation was thus vulnerable to "powerful trends of thought that promised clarity." Marxism, of course, was one. Another was "modern psychology," which saw behavior as dominated by influences of which people were unaware. A third, Kennan added—not with tongue in cheek—was advertising, which found thousands of ways daily to convince consumers that their material existence depended on "almost every sort of reaction except the direct and rational one."

Isaiah Berlin had recently suggested that there were two kinds of freedom. One was that of Dostoyevsky's Grand Inquisitor: "We shall persuade them that they will only become free when they renounce their freedom and submit to us." The other appeared in the Declaration of Independence, which sought to secure freedom without prescribing its nature. This, Kennan believed, was the great contest of the age. The great enemy was abstraction, which promised perfection while denying the imperfections of human nature. Left to itself, it would construct "an international Antarctica, in which there would be no germs because there would be no growth, in which there would be no sickness because there would be no people, in which all would be silence and peace because there was no life."

What, then, was a policy maker to do? Here Kennan returned to what he had learned as a policy planner: that *how* one did things was as important as *what* one did.

> Our life is so strangely composed that the best way to make ourselves better seems sometimes [to be] to act as though we were better. The man who makes it a point to behave with consideration and dignity in his relations with others, regardless of his inner doubts and conflicts, will suddenly find that he has achieved a great deal in his relations with himself.

The same was true of nations. "Where purpose is dim and questionable, form comes into its own." Good manners, which might seem "an inferior means of salvation, may be the only means of salvation we have at all."[16]

Kennan managed, in these Northwestern lectures, to make sense out of much that had puzzled colleagues—sometimes even himself—over many years: his pessimism about human nature; his growing concerns about ecology and demography; his despair about what was coming to be called the "third world"; his nostalgia for the international system that had preceded the two world wars; his distrust of land power and respect for sea power; his suspicions of Marx, Freud, McCarthy, and advertising; his admiration for Isaiah Berlin, the great classics of Russian literature, and the American Founding Fathers; his enlistment of elitism in defense of democracy. It was as if Oppenheimer's institute had given him the opportunity, at last, to resolve his contradictions.

IV.

It certainly allowed him to rebuild his finances. Oppenheimer had used his discretionary funds, together with a grant from the Rockefeller Foundation, to match Kennan's $15,000 State Department salary when he first arrived at the Institute, but those were temporary arrangements. On February 19, 1951, the new president of the Ford Foundation, Paul G. Hoffman—formerly director of the Economic Cooperation Administration, which had run the Marshall Plan—announced that the former director of the Policy Planning Staff was to become a "consultant" while remaining at the Institute for Advanced Study on leave from the State Department. Ford offered $25,000 plus expenses: Kennan in turn would advise the foundation on how to spend some of the $25 million its endowment generated each year. "[Y]ou are [the] master," Hoffman assured him, "of all arrangements affecting you or your activities for the Ford Foundation."[17]

This was a sufficiently good deal for Kennan to resign from the Foreign Service again, thereby greatly upsetting Bohlen. Arthur M. Schlesinger, Jr., witnessed the argument they got into, after dinner one evening in New York. "Chip, growing increasingly heated, began to denounce George for having left." The Foreign Service had made him: he could not desert the country in an hour of crisis. "George, much more composed and clearly aware that Chip was hurt and a bit drunk, tried to mollify [him], but did not retract his position." Big businessmen, Bohlen retorted, could not be trusted. "I hope you have an ironclad contract, boy. . . . One day Paul Hoffman will decide that it is all over—and you'll be swept out with the leavings."

> George said that he couldn't get anyone to listen to him in Washington. Chip said that he gave up too easily; that you just have to keep plugging away. . . . George said that he felt that his intellectual integrity was being compromised. . . . Chip said to hell with his intellectual integrity; that if George had been on the spot in Washington [last] fall, US policy might not have got into its present mess.

They struck Schlesinger as "a marvelous pair. . . . They loved each other and were enthralling company together." In the end, Kennan withdrew yet another resignation, explaining to Hoffman that State Department colleagues had "called me in the middle of the night" pleading "that I not take this step at this time—that it would be taken as another blow to Dean Acheson."

So Hoffman agreed to pay his salary for as long as the department would permit Kennan to be away, with the understanding that the job would become permanent as soon as he qualified for his Foreign Service pension and could gracefully retire. Ford also promised the Institute $225,000 over the next five years to fund whatever projects Kennan wished to undertake there. It was all "somewhat complicated," George wrote Kent, "but by and large it is as favorable a setup as I could wish for. I enjoy the life of a scholar and have little wish to return to government."[18]

Kennan had two major projects in mind beyond his own writing and public speaking. One was to set up a study group, at the Institute, that would "suggest a *rationale* for foreign policy and a set of premises and principles by which we could all be guided in our thinking on this subject." It would be a Policy Planning Staff operating independently of the State Department. The second project, to be run from Ford, would—in Kennan's mind at least—follow the example of the first George Kennan by helping exiles and refugees from the Soviet Union establish themselves in the United States. The foundation announced the formation of the Free Russia Fund, with a $200,000 annual budget and with Kennan as its president, on May 17, 1951.[19]

There was more to this initiative than met the eye. Hoffman had maintained close connections with Wisner's Office of Policy Coordination while administering the Marshall Plan, and he wanted the Ford Foundation, under his direction, to do the same. That made Kennan particularly useful to him. Kennan, in turn, kept Acheson, FBI director J. Edgar Hoover, and the new director of central intelligence, Walter Bedell Smith, informed about the Free Russia Fund—which, to avoid confusion with other CIA projects, changed its name a few months later to the East European Fund. The new organization operated openly, relying on Ford Foundation support, but it coordinated its activities with other refugee support groups that received, or were hoping to receive, secret CIA funding. Their purpose was to collect recent intelligence on the U.S.S.R., to ensure that defectors did not re-defect, and to build a community of exiles who might one day return to Russia to form the nucleus of a post-Soviet government.[20]

One beneficiary was the Tolstoy Foundation, established in 1939 by Leo Tolstoy's youngest daughter, which ran a farm in upstate New York where it welcomed, trained, and helped resettle Russian refugees. The organization was running out of money by 1951, so Kennan arranged an initial grant through the East European Fund, and after the Ford trustees had second thoughts—perhaps because of the group's monarchist tendencies—he persuaded the CIA to subsidize it. "[W]hat the hell was wrong with this?" Kennan demanded years later, after this information became public. "There were Russian professors working as janitors in seamy New York buildings, because nobody had made any effort to tap their knowledge, to help them learn the language, to put them to some use, something useful for them and for us. It was things like this that I had supposed we could do with an outfit for secret operations."

Kennan was even prouder of his role in helping to publish cheap editions of Russian literary classics—in the original Russian—that could never have appeared in the Soviet Union. This project originated as an initiative of the banker R. Gordon Wasson, the man who persuaded Kennan, in 1947, to contribute what became the "X" article to *Foreign Affairs*. Kennan asked Ford to take over the responsibility four years later by setting up the Chekhov Publishing House. They agreed to do so "as sort of a sop to me, but they didn't understand it." Ford supported Chekhov until 1956, at which point Kennan was unable to convince the CIA to continue its funding, and the company folded. It did manage to publish over a hundred books, relying almost entirely on the support Kennan had arranged. "We really, for the first time, broke the monopoly of the Soviet government on current literary pub-lication in the Russian language."

The Ford Foundation appointment, however, left Kennan with less time for his own work than he had expected. It required several trips each year to California, never a preferred destination, where Hoffman ran the organization from Pasa-dena. The émigrés Kennan tried to help often disagreed about what was needed. The foundation's trustees continued to fret about Hoffman's—and Kennan's—ties to the intelligence community. The whole effort required so much attention, Ken-nan complained in the fall of 1951, that it was "mak[ing] ridiculous my continued presence here at the Institute under the pretense of being a scholar."[21] Meanwhile Kennan was undergoing one of the gravest personal crises that ever afflicted him.

V.

Hans Morgenthau had arranged for Kennan to deliver a second set of lectures, in April at the University of Chicago, under the sponsorship of the Charles R. Wal-green Foundation. The topic would be U.S. foreign relations during the first half of the twentieth century. By early 1951 he had prepared rough drafts on the Spanish-American War, the Open Door Policy, and East Asia through the outbreak of war with Japan in 1941. He also had notes for a lecture on Woodrow Wilson and World War I, and these he casually showed to Earle, who tactfully suggested bringing in a few diplomatic historians to comment on Kennan's conclusions prior to their delivery. He agreed. It was easy to forget, he admitted to Hoffman, "how serious a matter scholarship can be, and how implacable its requirements."[22]

The historians included Dexter Perkins, Gordon A. Craig, Richard W. Leopold, and Wilson's biographer, Arthur S. Link. The seminar took place at the Institute on March 10. "Most of us were pretty appalled," Link remembered. The lectures were "ahistorical, very presentist and personal, lacking even the semblance of what we would ordinarily think of as historical scholarship." Kennan showed no resent-ment of the criticisms he got: "Quite the contrary, he seemed very grateful." He kept assuring the group that "of course I'm not a professional historian." But the experience shook his self-confidence about doing history, only a month before his public debut as a historian. "They took me to pieces, quite properly." Dean Rusk, now a trustee of the Rockefeller Foundation, heard that Oppenheimer called Kennan in to give him "a shirt-tail lecture on the standards that were expected in the world of scholarship. George's later books reflect the influence of that lecture."[23]

Something else, simultaneously, was causing Kennan to take himself to pieces. Were it not for the diary in which he could atone for "the damage I have done," he wrote in it on April 2, "the situation would indeed be desperate." For he had placed the happiness of others in jeopardy. Unsure "that the blow would not still fall, I would continue to feel myself half a murderer, to have horror of myself, and to place limitations, in my own mind, on my ability to be useful to anyone else in any physical intimacy." He was "like a person who has placed poison in one of two glasses before a person he loves—looks back upon his act with horror and incredulity—but still does not know from which glass the person will drink." The next day he added: "It is right and necessary that I should become much older in a short space of time."

He found some solace in the daily rhythms of work, "where people wear their professional personalities like uniforms." During the past two days, he noted on April 5, he had rewritten one lecture, finished a new one, consulted Earle, talked with a student, lunched with Oppenheimer, "and done a dozen necessary and unavoidable little things." But these didn't alleviate the nightmares. Perhaps

> the subconscious mind, like the workings of history, is often years out of date in its causality. Even were I to bow before the suggestions that the dream contained—were I to say to the subconscious: you are right, you are unanswerable, I will cut all the fateful knots and follow you—none of it would work out. Ten years ago—it would have; not today. How dangerous a guide, in later age, is then that which is most powerful—or nearly the most powerful (for that remains to be seen)—within us.

On April 7, he would be leaving for Chicago, where "there will be all the things that are difficult for me":

> a strange city, a hotel, solitude, boredom, strange women, the sense of time fleeting, of time being wasted, of a life pulsating around me—a life unknown, untasted, full of mystery—and yet not touched by myself. . . . Let us see whether, if I can stand the first day, the next will not be easier. It will be a real test, an opportunity for a real triumph—no—that is an exaggeration—there are no triumphs—an opportunity to inch a tiny bit along the road.

He had another nightmare before he left, which had to do with concealment: "Unquestionably, there is an abnormality here: a dread of being found out. This can probably be repaired only by making my life such that there is genuinely nothing to conceal and that means making it such that it will no longer, in a sense, be my life at all."[24]

Kennan opened his lecture series on the afternoon of April 9. It would, he told his audience, examine the record of the past half century in search of lessons "for *us*, the generation of 1951, pressed and hemmed in as we are by a thousand troubles and dangers." Before giving it, he had attempted to rest in his hotel room. But

> [w]hen I try, as I did then, to bring the spirit to a state of complete repose, shutting out all effort and all seeking, I become aware of the remnants of anxieties and desires still surging and thrashing around, like waves in a swimming-pool when the last swimmer has left; and I realize in what a turmoil the pool of the soul usually is, and how long it must lie untroubled before the surface becomes clear and one can see to the bottom.

The newspapers that day were reporting public disagreements between Truman and MacArthur over Korean War strategy, and on the eleventh—the day of Kennan's second lecture—the president fired the general. Kennan might have been pleased had he received the news within the familiar surroundings of Princeton or Washington, but the reaction in Chicago frightened him.

> For the first time in my life I have become conscious of the existence of powerful forces in the country to which, if they are successful, no democratic adjustment can be made: people . . . who have to be regarded as totalitarian enemies. . . . [M]y homeland has turned against me. . . . I am now in the truest sense of the word an expatriate.

He was glad he had not gone to Milwaukee: "I hope never to go there again until McCarthyism has burned itself out there and people are thoroughly ashamed of it." Even Jeanette and her family, in Highland Park, could offer no refuge. The day would soon come when they "will be afraid and embarrassed to have me in the house, when my presence will bring unpleasantness and danger to them, when—if I came—they would want me to sneak in and out in the middle of the night."[25]

That was hardly the response, however, of his University of Chicago audience: "Respectable at the start, attendance grew most alarmingly." By the third lecture, students were sitting on the floor and in the aisles, requiring that the fourth be moved to an auditorium, where Kennan worried that he was only "a remote silhouette and a canned, electrified voice." But they still kept coming: "I was surprised, delighted, and yet in a sense sobered, by the success of the undertaking." One cause for concern was that he had not yet written the final lecture, scheduled for April 20. On learning of this that morning, the editors at the university press, which would be publishing the series, summoned him to "a great office clattering with a dozen typewriters, and with my letter of acceptance lying reproachfully before me, I was put to work to produce some sort of publishable document."

> Only one who has faced many lecture audiences knows . . . that peculiar sense of tension and desperation that can overcome the unprepared lecturer as the hour of the lecture inexorably draws nearer and his mind is whipped by the realization that within so and so many minutes he must get up there and say *something*, but he does not yet know what he wants to say.

The panic seared itself so deeply into his consciousness, Kennan recalled two decades later, "that I continue even now to relive it as a recurring nightmare." But a young professor who attended the lectures detected no signs of unease. Kenneth W. Thompson remembered Kennan's "marvelous melodic flow." Listening to him was "like an experience on the road to Damascus." One evening, at a fraternity house, Kennan sat talking with students until the early hours of the morning. It was "an absolutely elevating experience for everyone."[26]

Except Kennan. By April 16—the day his lecture was moved to accommodate the hundreds who wanted to hear it—he had concluded that with his combination of personal and public problems, it would be a miracle if "anything remained for me personally in life. . . . This will be a time for leadership or for martyrdom or for both. I may as well prepare myself for it." And on the seventeenth:

> Myths and errors are being established in the public mind more rapidly than they can be broken down. The mass media are too much for us. . . . McCarthyism has already won, in the sense of making impossible the conduct of an intelligent foreign policy. The result is that there is no place in public life for an honest and moderate man. . . . I should not have signed up with the Ford Foundation. . . . I should not have started the enterprise to help Soviet fugitives. Some day we will have to give it up out of sheer embarrassment and humiliation over the conduct of our country. . . . I should not be speaking out here in Chicago. It will do no good—any of it. I must stop this public speaking, this writing for publication.

Farming would be the only salvation. He would finish his work at the Institute "for consistency's sake" and to get Joan through school. He would retire from the Foreign Service as soon as his pension was earned "or forfeited"—here he had in mind the plight of his colleague Davies, whose loyalty investigation was still under way. But all of these plans were problematic because war would probably break out within two years: "Except for the little boy, the best thing that could happen would be that I should go with the services and get myself killed."[27]

Kennan never said, explicitly, what lay behind all of this, but diary fragments provide hints:

June 19, 1951: More and more I feel myself becoming a receptacle for the confidence of other people. Am I not deceiving them all? . . . . [They] believe that I am an honest man and are thereby relieved. Have I any right, in these circumstances, to accept their confidence?

August 3, 1951: I was annoyed with myself for my habit of staring after women. What could they give me? Nothing but trouble and disillusionment and dissipation of valuable strength. I must teach myself to remember that I do not really want them: that this habit is a sort of echo of youth, and a very misleading one at that. In this endeavor, . . . I have the best of all possible allies: increasing age.

Undated: Physical desire, in a man my age, is often like the experiment the teachers of psychology used to use as an example: where a finger pressed to the brow for a time is removed, but the sensation, and the illusion of its presence, lingers after.

September 5, 1951: I am ill, of course, with the old malady which is a condition and not a disease. But I am resolved that this time I will not cure it by flying from reality—by running away to the phoney protectedness of a hospital bed and a nurse's uniform. . . . Let the damned sore do its worst, burn through to the surface if it must. Perhaps then we will finally get some clarity and harmony into this warring combination of flesh and spirit.

Also September 5, 1951 (contradicting what he had told himself in April): Write, you bastard, write. Write desperately, frantically, under pressure from yourself, while God still gives you the time. Write until your eyes are glazed, until you have writer's cramp, until you fall from your chair for weariness. Only by agitating your pen will you ever press out of your indifferent mind and your ailing frame anything of any value to yourself or anyone else.[28]

Given Kennan's tendency to blame himself for so much, the offense could have been almost anything: a covetous glance, a casual dalliance, a full-blown affair. Did Annelise know? Nothing in George's diary confirms that she did, but she didn't miss much. If she suspected something, or even if she knew a lot, she would not have let whatever it was imperil the marriage or hurt the family. That was the way of a wife who saw no contradiction in simultaneously loving her husband and anchoring him.

George, at this point, badly needed anchoring, for the upheavals of April 1951 had come close to overwhelming him. He was lecturing on history in Chicago, having been told, by historians, that he was not yet one. He was carrying the weight of a personal crisis as wrenching as the ones he had gone through in Vienna in 1935 and at Bad Nauheim in 1942. His audiences were expanding as his texts were diminishing. He spoke at a moment when the part of the country from which he came seemed to be sinking into dementia. And he was filling his diary with despair: perhaps his ability to do that, together with Annelise's anchoring, was what got him through this bad month—although never beyond the bad dreams.

VI.

One of Kennan's better dreams had been the possibility that he might represent the United States—alone, on a top-secret basis, using his knowledge of the Russian language and of the Soviet system—in some form of direct negotiations with the U.S.S.R. looking toward a relaxation of Cold War tensions. Stalin's sabotage of the Smith-Molotov initiative killed any chance of this while Kennan was on the Policy Planning Staff, and he himself opposed approaching Moscow after the Chinese intervened in Korea at the end of 1950. By May 1951, however, the situation had changed. Truman had sacked MacArthur. The new U.N. commander, General Matthew B. Ridgway, had halted Mao's offensive in the vicinity of the 38th parallel. And an opportunity for diplomacy had arisen—strangely—from a high-level hitchhike.

With the permanent headquarters of the United Nations still under construction alongside New York's East River, the Security Council had been meeting in temporary quarters at Lake Success, on Long Island. The drive into Manhattan could take almost an hour, and at the end of a session on May 2, two American diplomats, Thomas J. Cory and Frank P. Corrigan, found themselves without transportation. A large Chrysler drove up, stopped, and its occupants offered a ride. They turned out to be Jacob Malik, the chief Soviet representative at the United Nations, and Semyon K. Tsarapkin, his deputy. The Russians were in an unusually good humor, and after pleasant exchanges about American automobiles, military bases, imperialist ambitions, capitalist profiteers, and warmongers, the conversation turned to how the Korean War might be settled. The four men agreed that some sort of Soviet-American consultation would have to take place, whereupon Malik, returning to the theme of warmongers, asked what had become of George Kennan.

Cory explained that Kennan was "engaged in advanced study at Princeton." Kennan had had "a great and unfortunate influence," Malik observed: no doubt his voice was still heard in Washington. When Cory protested that Kennan admired the Russian people and hoped to write Chekhov's biography, Malik was unimpressed. But by the normal standards of Soviet diplomacy, the two Americans reported to their superiors, he had been "a charming and cordial host."[29]

Their account set off speculation within the State Department as to whether the pickup had been deliberate. Cory thought not but added that he had suggested dinner sometime and that Malik had agreed. "The question," Davies wrote Nitze, "is whether we should follow up on Malik's evident willingness to talk about American-Soviet relations. I think we should." Stalin might be planning another trick, but the risks would be minimal "if our representative is someone [who] . . . although not a high American official, is in a position to speak with authority and in confidence for the Government. That person is Kennan."[30]

As Davies probably knew, Kennan was thinking similarly. He had advised Acheson in March that as the military front stabilized in Korea, the time would come to deal with the Russians. The talks should take place "through informal channels" and in "complete secrecy," using "some intermediary who could be denied in case of necessity." They would acknowledge a simple reality: that the situation in Korea was unsatisfactory to both the Soviet Union and the United States. There should be, then, "a mutuality of interest" that might make a settlement possible.[31]

That made sense to Acheson, who had come through the difficult winter of 1950–51 with renewed admiration for Kennan. And so, when the Malik report came in, the secretary of state accepted Davies's suggestion. "On Friday, May 18," Kennan wrote in his own report of the events that followed,

> having been called to Washington by P, I talked with O in the presence of P and two other persons. O asked me whether I would be willing to undertake the project in question, and I told him that I would. It was agreed that arrangements would have to be made by E in New York, and that I should see him when I was up there the following week.

P was Doc Matthews, then serving as deputy under secretary of state. O was Acheson. E was Malik's passenger, Tom Cory. E agreed to suggest to X—not Kennan, who had given up pseudonyms, but Tsarapkin—that it might be useful for him to talk with the former Mr. X, but there was no reply. Whereupon Kennan wrote to Tsarapkin on the twenty-sixth, asking him to tell Malik that it might be useful "if he and I could meet and have a quiet talk some time in the near future. I think that my diplomatic experience and long acquaintance with problems of American-Soviet relations should suffice to assure you that I would not make such a proposal unless I had serious reasons to do so."[32]

Three days later Kennan's secretary at the Institute received a cryptic telephone message informing her that the "gentleman Mr. Kennan had asked to see" could receive him on the afternoon of the thirty-first at a Long Island address. This turned out to be the Soviet U.N. delegation's dacha, an estate in Glen Cove, to which Kennan drove himself alone. Malik began the conversation nervously, upsetting a tray of fruit and wine. After each man had expressed regret about the isolation of diplomats in the other's country, Kennan explained that he had come to explore the possibility of a Korean cease-fire, roughly along the current line of military operations, to be supervised by some international authority. Malik said he would think about it, which Kennan took to mean consulting Moscow. When asked if it would be useful to meet again, Malik replied "that it was a good thing in general for people to talk things over and that he would always be happy to receive me and to pass the time of day."[33]

They did meet again, at Glen Cove on June 5, and Malik was ready with an answer: the Soviet Union wanted to end the Korean War at the earliest possible moment, but because its forces were not involved it could take no direct part in any cease-fire negotiations. The United States should contact the North Koreans and the Chinese Communists. Kennan promised to pass this message to Washington, noting however that it would be difficult to rely on anything those adversaries might say. The Soviets, in contrast, "took a serious and responsible attitude toward what they conceived to be their own interests." Malik deflected this compliment with the complaint that a Wall Street conspiracy dominated American life. "You see our country as in a dream," Kennan replied. "No, this is not [a] dream," Malik insisted, "this is the deepest reality."

Kennan concluded from these meetings that the Soviet leadership did indeed want a cease-fire, that it had instructed the North Koreans and the Chinese Communists to accept an American proposal for one, and that it was willing to see the talks proceed without bringing in such wider issues as the future of Japan or Taiwan. "I hope that we will not hesitate to grasp at once the nettle of action. . . . We may not succeed; but I have the feeling we are moving much closer to the edge of the precipice than most of us are aware, and that this is one of the times when the dangers of inaction far exceed those of action."[34]

The precipice he had in mind, Kennan wrote Acheson in a personal letter on June 20, was the possibility of war with the U.S.S.R. While Stalin had no appetite for such a conflict, he would view with "mortal apprehension" any U.S. military presence along the Soviet or the Chinese border with North Korea. That was why he had encouraged Mao to cross the Yalu and hurl MacArthur's forces back. Now that the Chinese offensive had stalled, the Russians feared another American drive north. If that happened, they would have no choice but to intervene themselves, and a catastrophe would result. The whole Korean experience had been, for the Kremlin leaders, "a nerve-wracking and excruciating experience, straining to the limit their self-control and patience." That explained Malik's response, which the United States should not reject. For even though it might not seem so at the moment, "our action in Korea, so often denounced as futile, may prove to have . . . laid the foundation for the renewal of some sort of stability in the Far East."[35]

Three days later, as if on cue, Malik made his cease-fire suggestion public. Talks began in July between the opposing military commanders in Korea, even as the fighting continued. It would take two years to achieve an armistice, partly because of disagreements over repatriating prisoners of war, partly because Stalin, reassured now that the war would be limited, was in less of a hurry to see it end. When it did finally in July 1953, shortly after his death, the terms were close to what Kennan had suggested.

His role in the Korean War, Kennan wrote later, had been "relatively minor," but that was an understatement. For on several issues—his recommendation to deploy the Seventh Fleet in the Taiwan Strait, his concerns about crossing the 38th parallel, his warnings about MacArthur, his advice against negotiating after the Chinese had intervened, his reversal of that advice after the Chinese had been contained, and his delicate conversations with Malik—he won a degree of respect within the government that he had not enjoyed since 1947.[36] Which is probably why Acheson asked Kennan, on July 23, 1951, if he would like to become the next U.S. ambassador to the Soviet Union.

VII.

"I did not turn it down cold," George wrote Annelise from Washington—she and the family were in Kristiansand. "I said I would not be available, in any case, before completion of the next Institute term." He would write Acheson a fuller response, "but [I] want to talk to you first." The Kennans had sailed to Norway on the SS *Oslofjord* in late June, with George traveling on Ford funds since, as he had explained to Hoffman, "I would otherwise not be able to go at all." He would use the opportunity to make contacts useful to the foundation. He had remained depressed through most of the voyage, despite his recent diplomatic achievements. "My children would laugh at me," he wrote in his diary while still at sea, "but it is true. The adult world is a broken-hearted world, . . . because there is no leadership in it, and no inspiration."[37]

As the ship neared the Norwegian coast, however, George's mood brightened On the Fourth of July, he watched children parading around the deck waving American flags, listened as the ship's orchestra played "The Star Spangled Banner," and at the captain's invitation made a speech, linking what had happened in his country 175 years earlier with what Annelise's had experienced at the hands of the Nazis: who could really appreciate the value of freedom "who hasn't seen it attacked by a foreign invader and occupier on his own soil"? He even praised NATO—Norway had been a founding member. The alliance's commitment to interdependence, he reminded the ship's passengers and crew, meant that there was "really no such thing as a purely *national* independence day any more in this area."[38]

The ship called at Bergen early the next morning, and then navigated the rugged coastline to the south. "Norway simply took my breath away," George recorded,

> not just, or even primarily, the colors of the mountains and sea and sky, but rather the places where the hand of man had softened and ordered this hard nature: the little docks, the villages at the foot of the rocks, the white cottages, the hay drying on

fences around the tiny green pastures, the old stone monastery-church on the tree-less, rocky island near the sea—stubborn, hard, defiant, braving century after cen-tury, the long winter bleakness, the gales, the loneliness, the rain and the cold—living the poetry of wind-swept rock and sky and only that.

They reached Kristiansand at about midnight, with a midsummer glow on the horizon reminiscent of Riga "in other days." At the Sørensens', after the children had gone to sleep, "[w]e sat up with the old people and drank vermouth with brandy until near four o'clock. Then A. and I dragged ourselves back to the little cottage, in the morning light, and went to bed."[39]

George had little time to enjoy Norway, though, because he insisted on flying back to Washington, at his own expense, to testify on behalf of Davies before the State Department's loyalty board on July 23: that was where Acheson raised the possibility of a return to Moscow. "I believe the hearing went well," George wrote Annelise, "but have not yet heard the final result." The case had stirred enough indignation, however, that the secretary of state had promised to rethink proce-dures for such investigations. "I am very pleased about this, as it makes it unneces-sary for me to pursue the matter further."[40]

So he returned to Europe by way of Portugal—which Kennan found little changed since he was last there in 1944—as well as Italy, Austria, West Germany, France, the Netherlands, and Great Britain. It was his first European trip in a pri-vate capacity since the one he and Nick Messolonghitis had made in the summer of 1924. The Norwegians had been unsure of his status, so Kennan asked the State Department to inform other governments along his route that he required "no official courtesies or attentions beyond those that would be extended to the ordi-nary traveler." "I dream about you all, including Christopher, with the greatest regularity," he wrote Annelise from Lisbon. And, from Rome: "If you would like to join me [in Basel], wire to Vienna."[41]

An English weekend at the beginning of September gave Kennan a chance to respond to Acheson, in longhand and at length, about Moscow as well as what might follow. Many opportunities had arisen over the past year: this came, he sup-posed, with "being a public figure."

[A]fter going over all the familiar categories of rich man, poor man, beggar man, thief, etc., I concluded that the Potter, in addition to establishing the obvious predes-tination to poverty, had probably moulded this clay in the slightly doubtful hope that it would some day prove serviceable in the capacity of scholar and teacher—one of those teachers whose teachings rarely please people, and are no doubt often wrong, but of whom it is sometimes said, when they are gone: "It is useful that he taught as he did."

It made sense, then, to return to government long enough to retire with a pension, and then to resume work at the Institute with "academic life as my normal pursuit from that time on."

The position should be an overseas mission not associated with the formulation of policy. For it was only right to acknowledge "the full measure of divergence" between his views and those of the Truman administration.

> I say that quite without bitterness, and in full realization that in many of these differences . . . I may be the one farthest from wisdom. I also realize that there may be a feeling that it is useful from time to time to have around the place a sort of intellectual gadfly whose benevolent questionings and dissentings can sting gently and stimulate, without destroying. But it is a difficult position for the gadfly.

Moscow might be feasible, therefore, for the work there involved the analysis of Soviet policy, not the making of policy in Washington. Commitments at the Institute and elsewhere, however, would keep him from going until well into 1952. Perhaps Admiral Alan G. Kirk, the current ambassador, could stay on; if not, the mission could probably be left under a *chargé d'affaires*.[42]

The Kennans sailed for home on September 5, with George worried that the children had enjoyed Europe less than he had. "My friends," he wrote them gravely one day at sea,

> *with stoic mien, with patience grim,*
> *With martyr's silence, with impassive stare,*
> *You have now coursed the chambers of the past,*
> *The crooked climbing street, the boulevard,*
> *The pavement where the scaffold stood, the scenes*
> *Of valor and of battle and the spots*
> *Where once, in verse or note or stone,*
> *The idle muse lent mystery and grace*
> *To drab old life.*
> *   Now these and other things*
> *That in past ages caused the simpler human heart*

To stir have passed unanswered, unsaluted,
Before your glazed impassive orbs; and I
Have been allowed to sense that I should not
Have dragged you thither.

He also composed, for himself, a bucolic poem about flies—which could also have been State Department gadflies:

How long before the unctuous fly
—Its love for mammals still undaunted—
Will learn from swats and slaps and flails,
From sticky traps and swishing tails,
That its attentions are unwanted?

Kennan decided not to send Acheson a four-page summary of "points of difference" with the State Department that he had prepared. It listed disagreements over the United Nations, nuclear weapons, the future of Europe, the Near and Middle East, East Asia, Latin America, relations with Congress, and the administration of foreign policy. "This is, in my opinion, important," he wrote across the top, presumably with historians and maybe even a biographer in mind. It was certainly comprehensive: when he finished, it was hard to find a policy with which he did agree.[43]

"It is reasonable that I should look forward with a sense of relief to the prospect of being an ambassador," Kennan commented in an undated diary fragment that summer. "It is just about the only profession one can have these days in which nothing—but really nothing—is either expected or required of you." But there was more to it than that. He was still a Foreign Service officer: "I did not feel it proper to decline any assignment given to me." It would be difficult to pass up an appointment to the Soviet Union, "a task for which my whole career had prepared me, if it had prepared me for anything at all." Finally, Bohlen had urged him to take the job, on the grounds that Stalin might be more open than in the past to negotiations, particularly on Germany. So with Acheson having assured him that the president really wanted him in Moscow, Kennan agreed to go.[44]

There was, however, one last effort to derail the appointment. It came from Annelise, who knew how bleak conditions there would be, and how reluctant George was to disrupt his work at the Institute. She surely had some sense, from the spring and summer, of how precarious his psychological balance had become. And she had just learned that she was again pregnant. So she took it upon herself—without asking George—to go to Washington and talk with their old Moscow friend Elbridge Durbrow, then in charge of State Department personnel assignments. "I told him that I thought this was a very bad time, that he should send somebody else, and then we could go afterwards in a couple of years."

> Well, they gave me this lovely run-around—how wonderful it would be to have George there, they didn't want to change it. I still remember, I was furious! I was livid! I mean, for somebody I knew very well—Durbrow—to give me this little song and dance. It was not necessary.

She never doubted that George should return to Moscow. "I felt very strongly that he was a specialist and he should go back, [and] at that time one still felt pretty young." It was also "a nice honor to go as an ambassador, because we don't have so many career ambassadors in the major countries. It was just that the timing was not so good."[45]

Annelise had still one other reason for not wanting to go to Moscow at that moment: the Kennans had just bought a house of their own in Princeton. The all electric one they had rented, Patricia Davies recalled, had become barely inhabitable the previous winter when a blizzard knocked out the power: the family survived by huddling around the fireplace, which contained a hook from which Annelise could cook, "in her proper Norwegian fashion." The new house—old enough to match George's age, having been built in 1904—was located on a large lot at 146 Hodge Road, a tree-lined street half a mile from the university and a mile from the Institute. George was soon bicycling to both destinations and would continue to do so for decades.

Apart from the farm, it was the first permanent residence the Kennans had occupied during their twenty years of marriage. The first floor contained large living and dining rooms, a library, a kitchen, and a breakfast nook. Upstairs there were seven bedrooms, some meant for maids, one in a third-story tower. There was even a separate apartment over the garage, useful for visiting family and, at times, for renters. "We lack beds now," George wrote Jeanette in October 1951, "but I am sure we will have them by Thanksgiving." The Ford Foundation salary had made the purchase possible, he explained to Kent, even though "we haven't saved any money." The house was "friendly and receptive in a relaxed way," George wrote in his memoir two decades later, "but slightly detached, like a hostess to a casual guest—as though it did not expect us to stay forever." The Kennans did stay for a long time: George and Annelise would each die in the house, fifty-four and fifty-seven years, respectively, after they moved into it.[46]

VIII.

"A book by George Kennan is an event in Washington," James Reston wrote in *The New York Times* on September 30, 1951. The relentlessly efficient University of Chicago Press had rushed Kennan's Walgreen lectures into print as *American Diplomacy: 1900–1950*. To flesh out the thin volume, Kennan added the 1947 "X" article, as well as the essay he intended as its successor, "America and the Russian Future," which had appeared in the April issue of *Foreign Affairs*. But the first piece was familiar and the second looked too far into the future to attract much attention: it was an unclassified update of PPS/38, the 1948 study in which Kennan had tried to specify American objectives for a post-Soviet Russia. The lectures, however, enthralled their readers, just as they had packed the room—and then the auditorium—in which he delivered them. It was Kennan's first book, but it sold better than anything else he ever wrote.

Characteristically, he did not enjoy this triumph. He didn't like the idea of publishing lectures, he grumbled to Alsop, who wrote to congratulate him: "Either you write or you talk, but you don't do both together." He had been heartened, but also shamed, by the favorable reaction. Hostile reviews would have made him miserable, Kennan admitted to Oppenheimer; nevertheless the complimentary ones "leave me with a sense of discomfort," because the lectures were not nearly as good as he could have made them. There was, however, the satisfaction of having produced a book, "if only by inadvertence."

American Diplomacy succeeded for several reasons. It was, as Reston noted, the most critical account of U.S. foreign policy produced by any government official since the end of the war. Not "ghost-written," it was "straight Kennan," and he was "perhaps the most reflective of the young American professional diplomats." The author himself, more modestly, would later attribute the book's success to its shallowness, for it met the needs of teachers eager to find easy reading for their students. His foreword, however, had promised more: he would show why the United States, which in 1900 could not have imagined threats from abroad to its prosperity and way of life, had reached the point by 1950 "where it seemed to think of little else."[47]

Kennan's explanation was short but shocking: the insecurity the United States faced resulted less from what its adversaries had done than from its own leaders' illusions. Forgetting their forefathers' warnings, American statesmen in the twentieth century had come to prefer the proclamation of principles to the balancing of power. The pattern began with John Hay's Open Door notes, announced as an afterthought in the wake of the Spanish-American War and the American occupation of the Philippines, with a view to discouraging China's division into European, Russian, and Japanese spheres of influence. Hay accomplished little for the Chinese, but he set a style for his own country's diplomacy: it manifested itself, with more serious consequences, in Wilson's Fourteen Points, in Roosevelt's Atlantic Charter, and in the World War II demand for the "unconditional surrender" of Germany and Japan, which had opened the way for Soviet domination of half of Europe and much of Asia. Far from securing its interests, the "legalism-moralism" with which the United States had conducted its diplomacy had left it in grave peril.

It had encouraged toothless treaties like the 1928 Kellogg-Briand Pact, which between the two greatest wars in history had outlawed war as an instrument of national policy. It had caused hopes to be invested in, and time to be wasted on, the League of Nations and the United Nations, which could act only if the great powers had already settled their differences. It had led to long periods of inattention, punctuated by spasms of senseless violence. "I sometimes wonder," Kennan wrote, in the book's most memorable passage,

> whether in this respect a democracy is not uncomfortably similar to one of those prehistoric monsters with a body as long as this room and a brain the size of a pin: he lies there in his comfortable primeval mud and pays little attention to his environment; he is slow to wrath—in fact, you practically have to whack his tail off to make him aware that his interests are being disturbed; but, once he grasps this, he lays about him with such blind determination that he not only destroys his adversary but largely wrecks his native habitat.

Kennan's imagery—the dinosaur in particular would pursue him for decades. It dramatized, but vastly oversimplified, what he had been trying to say since studying Clausewitz at the National War College in 1946: that while war must always be subordinate to policy, alternatives to war can always fail. Hence, the need for grand strategy *in peace as well as in war*.[48]

Hastily composed, passionately written, brilliantly if not deliberately timed,

American Diplomacy became Kennan's "long telegram" to the American academy: it insisted on the need to see the world as it was, not as professors of international relations might like it to be. For the young Kenneth Thompson, who had studied with the University of Chicago legal and institutional scholar Quincy Wright, Kennan opened "a whole new world. I'd never really heard a 'realist' interpretation of foreign policy." One grateful reader wrote to *Time* magazine that, having read Kennan, he could now retire his well-worn copy of Machiavelli's *The Prince.* To be sure, Morgenthau, Niebuhr, and Lippmann had all warned, in their writings, against relying on principles while neglecting power. They, however, had done so from outside the government. Kennan was still, to most of his audience, an insider, and that—together with his flair for the dramatic—was what made his argument so compelling.[49]

It was also, to careful readers, unsettling. He had *not* meant to say that Americans should abandon "decency and dignity and generosity," he assured the historian Arnold Toynbee. His point, rather, had been that the United States should refrain from claiming to know what was right or wrong in the behavior of other societies. Its policy should be one of avoiding "great orgies of violence that acquire their own momentum and get out of hand." It should employ its armies, if they were to be used at all, in what Gibbon called "temperate and indecisive contests," remembering that civilizations could not stand "too much jolting and abuse." There was no room, in the modern world, for moral indignation, "unless it be indignation with ourselves for failing to be what we know we could and should have been." He should have said all of this at Chicago, but "the material had to be compressed, I was dilatory, the last lecture was written in the publishers' office on the day it was delivered, and there I was, before I knew it, making myself out an amoral cynic for all time."[50]

Father Edmund A. Walsh, the legendary founder of the Georgetown University School of Foreign Service, certainly saw it that way: he publicly attacked Kennan in July 1952 for having abandoned "the concept of right and wrong in judging the actions of a foreign state." That logic led "straight back to the jungle" and had even been "used as a defense for Hitler's extermination of 6,000,000 Jews." Kennan was in Moscow by then, but Walsh's excoriation worried him enough that he drafted—but wisely did not send—a letter to *The New York Times* restating the explanation he had given Toynbee. It would not have been the moment, while trying to run an embassy in a forbiddingly hostile state, to get into an open argument with the most formidable American Jesuit.

"[T]he reaction in academic circles is really intense," Philip Jessup warned the

Policy Planning Staff in September, "and I think it is doing some harm." Morgenthau's hefty *Politics Among Nations* had already become a standard university text, but Kennan's brief book, which was about to appear in a thirty-five-cent reprint, would surely compete with it. And yet, "as I have gathered from talking with him, it is not a final and profound statement of his thinking. . . . It is by no means the complete negation of law and morals which many people think it is."[51]

As if to confirm the fears of Toynbee, Walsh, Jessup, and even Kennan himself, the American Political Science Association had already by then named *American Diplomacy* "the best book of the year in the field of international relations." And so its author—told by diplomatic historians that he was not yet ready to join their guild—found himself enshrined instead within a "realist" theoretical tradition that dated back to Thucydides—whom Kennan had not yet even read. Meanwhile his Northwestern lectures, a far more careful exposition of his thinking, had appeared unheralded in the *Illinois Law Review*, where they have languished in obscurity ever since. It was yet another example of Kennan's strange tendency to be remembered more for what he said in haste than for what he took the time to ponder.[52]

IX.

The well-informed Reston broke the news of Kennan's ambassadorship on November 20, 1952, before the Soviet foreign ministry had provided the necessary *agrément*. A delay of several weeks followed, along with a *Pravda* complaint about Kennan's association with the East European Fund—he had by now resigned as its president. This convinced Harrison Salisbury, the *New York Times* Moscow correspondent, that Stalin was about to veto the appointment. Kennan was well known, after all, as the author of the "long telegram" and the "X" article; moreover, Ralph Parker, a left-leaning British journalist, had been allowed to publish a book in Moscow in 1949, entitled *Conspiracy Against Peace*, claiming that at the victory celebration outside the Mokhovaya four years earlier, Kennan had turned away cynically from the cheering crowds to predict a new world war. By December 26, Salisbury had a story ready on the impending rejection, but the censors refused to clear it.

Andrey Gromyko, the wartime Soviet ambassador in Washington, had advised Stalin that "it is hardly conceivable that the USA government at present may appoint a more acceptable candidate." Whether for that reason or some other, the Kremlin boss then gave his approval, allowing the White House to confirm that Kennan was indeed Truman's choice. Salisbury, for once, was grateful to the censors: "By killing my adverse speculation [they] spared me an embarrassing error."[53]

A week later, in bed at the Princeton house with a sprained back from having fallen off his bicycle, the ambassador-designate wrote out in longhand, for his future embassy counselor Hugh Cumming, what he hoped to accomplish:

> It seems to me that the best an ambassador can hope to do in Moscow is to reside there patiently, cheerfully, and with a reasonable modicum of dignity, burdening the rest of the Mission as little as possible with his household and his presence, holding himself available for such chores of negotiation as may come his way, gaining what understanding he can of the local scene from such fragmentary evidence as the regime finds it impossible not to divulge to him, keeping himself prepared to give advice on Soviet-American relations whenever it can be useful to the Government, and helping himself and his associates to remain of good heart and bear themselves with confidence and dignity in an atmosphere of hostility and insults, of suspicion and misinterpretation of their every action, of attempts to belittle their world and their beliefs—an atmosphere of lies and distortions, in other words, of which the very essence is the unceasing effort to induce people to abandon the evidence of their senses and of all objective criteria and to accept as valid a version of reality artificially created, unconnected with objective fact, and calculated to reduce them to a state in which no reactions are operative but those of fear and respect for the mysteries of Soviet power.

This might seem an "overly modest set of aspirations," Kennan added, "but I think you will agree with me that it is job enough for any man; and if I am able to acquit myself of it with as few mistakes and as much distinction as have my immediate predecessors, I shall be satisfied."[54]

Cumming would probably also have agreed—a very long telegram once having made its way from Moscow—on the appropriateness of a very long sentence now making its way back.

EIGHTEEN

Mr. Ambassador: 1952

"GEORGE F. KENNAN, THE STATE DEPARTMENT'S 'MR. X,' IS LEAV-ing for Moscow this spring to take over a job for which he has been preparing for 25 years—and which he doesn't want." This is how the journalist Louis Cassels introduced the new U.S. ambassador to the Soviet Union to the readers of *Collier's* in March 1952. Based on a conversation with Kennan at the farm on the day after Truman announced the appointment, the article portrayed an envoy who "prob-ably knows as much about Russia's history, literature, and national characteristics as many members of the Politburo." He would be the first since the opening of relations with the U.S.S.R. to need no interpreter when meeting Stalin. He "cer-tainly ought to know his way around," the president was said to have commented. Even *Pravda* had honored the ambassador-designate by awarding him "its highest decorations for Western statesmen—'spy,' 'warmonger,' and 'tool of Wall Street.' "

Why, then, did Kennan *not* want the job? The "deep dark truth about Mr. X," Cassels revealed (not quite accurately), "is that he has never had any great ambi-tion to be ambassador to Russia, or anywhere else." What he wanted instead was "to write a dozen or so books that have been stillborn in his wide-ranging mind during his hectic two and a half decades as a public servant." The Institute for Advanced Study had given Kennan that opportunity, so why had he agreed to go to Moscow? Because, Cassels suggested (not inaccurately), Kennan believed in predestination.

He was, after all, the son of three men. One was his real father, a stern Scotch Presbyterian with a strong sense of duty and—owing to his youthful travels in Europe—an international outlook rare in turn-of-the-century Wisconsin. Kos-suth Kent Kennan would not have wanted George to decline the job for which the Foreign Service had trained him, at public expense, over so many years. "I've never had the opportunity of serving in the armed forces," the younger Kennan added. "I don't think any man has the right to refuse to serve his country in any position where he might be useful."

A second "father" was the first George Kennan. When given the choice, in 1928, of studying Chinese, Japanese, Arabic, or Russian, young George had chosen the last out of deference to his famous ancestor. The many parallels in their lives, down to sharing the same birthday, "almost makes me believe in astrology," the mature George admitted. Then, while studying Russian in Berlin, he had encountered a third "father," Anton Chekhov, whose plays and short stories Kennan came to regard "as Russia's and perhaps the world's greatest literature." Trained in medicine, Chekhov made his reputation as a writer—a trajectory Kennan envied as he weighed his professional obligations against his literary inclinations. And it had been Chekhov, he believed, who had posthumously persuaded him to buy the farm. George knew he had to do it when Annelise compared the place with the run-down Russian estate in *The Cherry Orchard*.

No visitor could regard its owner as an aloof intellectual after seeing him tramping around "in torn khaki trousers, plaid cotton shirt, heavy leather boots and a Russian-style fur hat." Kennan did much of the work himself to hold down expenses: "He is not independently wealthy, as some people suppose." Finances, not fame, preoccupied him on the day the newspapers reported his appointment: "Well-wishers found him behind a paper-strewn desk in the parlor of the farmhouse, struggling with 'the books' and trying to make out his income-tax return."

Cassels concluded his profile by reporting one further step Kennan had taken to put down roots: in a "full-cycle return to the faith of his fathers," he had recently joined the First Presbyterian Church in Princeton. "I drifted away from the church when I was a young man," Kennan explained. "But I have come back to it. I still see much in formal religion that is imperfect, but I know now that a man with no religion is a very hideous character. I have a great horror of people who have no fear of God."

Arthur Link, who knew Kennan well, was certain of his belief in predestination: "He was reared a Presbyterian, but he's been much more influenced by Russian Orthodoxy: the acceptance of things as they are, without getting too high expectations; [the view] that the world is fundamentally evil and that really there's not a great deal that you can do about it." Kennan himself, recalling his stay as a young man at the Pskovo-Pechorsky monastery in Estonia, assured a Russian Orthodox bishop late in 1951 that "I have never felt anything but the deepest respect for the grandeur of [the Church's] spiritual tradition, the power and beauty of its ritual, and the warm current of human feeling that flows through all of its life."

Princeton was a long way from Pskovo-Pechorsky, however, so First Presbyterian would have to do. He worried that he would be "a very imperfect Christian," Kennan wrote its pastor on accepting membership early in 1952, but he would be bearing a burden "far away and in loneliness." The Soviet Union was

> the most impressive example of hell on earth that our time has known—and to reside there as the leading representative and exponent of the world with which the Christian faith is today most prominently identified . . . is surely a heavy and unusual task for any Christian: . . . perhaps this one may be forgiven if he concentrates his attention at this time on the problem of how he can best cleanse himself and brace himself spiritually for the ordeal.

One model, he thought, might be the Prince in Dostoyevsky's *The Idiot*: "To make one's self as pure of heart as one is capable of becoming, to put fear and cynicism and craftiness behind one, and to abandon one's self to the reflection that if the simple truth will not do, then nothing will." He would have to remind himself, however, that what he would be managing was "not the encounter of George Kennan with the phenomenon of Soviet power but the encounter of the political entity known as the Government of the United States of America."

Had he not already spent enough time in that awful place? Kennan stared into the fire for a long time before answering: "[F]ate pushed me into the diplomatic service. A man has to do what fate calls him to do, as best he can."[1]

I.

His task, Kennan told guests at a dinner given by Paul Hoffman early in February, would be exploit possibilities for "continuing to exist in the same world with Soviet power and yet avoid the calamities of a third world conflict." Americans must not conclude that war was inevitable "just because we find the absence of it to be unpleasant and difficult." Diplomacy was not disloyalty: "It is tragic that in the course of recent events we have permitted not only valuable people, but also valuable words to be deprived of their usefulness." Harriman, Smith, and most recently Kirk had all served with self-effacement in Moscow under difficult circumstances. "[I]f I can meet the requirements of the job with as much competence and dignity as they did, and make no more mistakes, I will be pleased enough."[2]

Meanwhile, Kennan was winding up his affairs at the Institute. The study group he had hoped to make a Policy Planning Staff in exile became the first casualty: after "considerable anguish," he told the assistants whom he had recruited to work on the project that he would have to drop it. He could not resist, however, sending a long letter to Acheson—at some three thousand words, it could have been a paper from the original planning staff—complaining about the indulgence of emerging nationalism in Asia and the Middle East. There was little to be gained, Kennan insisted, from trying to win the goodwill of its leaders, "on whose bizarre frames the trappings of statesmanship rest like an old dress suit on a wooden scarecrow." But Washington policy making, he cautioned himself in his diary, was now beyond the control of any individual: people were spending most of their time in "a dream-like futile battle against the folds of [their] own bureaucratic clothing." He "shuddered inwardly at the prospect of going into the lion's den" as the representative of such a place.[3]

Few forebodings were apparent, however, when Kennan appeared before the Senate Foreign Relations Committee for his confirmation hearing on March 12. Moscow was "a hard city to live in," he acknowledged. "You are surrounded with hostility and hatred and meanness on every side." But war was unlikely, and relations with the Soviet Union deserved "to be handled with the greatest of circumspection and care and self-control." The senators treated Kennan respectfully, if ramblingly. The only reference to ongoing loyalty investigations came when Theodore Francis Green, Democrat of Rhode Island, asked facetiously whether previous associations with Kremlin leaders might be taken as evidence that Kennan was a communist. "I assume, Senator," the ambassador-designate responded, "that I must have been investigated quite a number of times." The Senate confirmed the nomination unanimously on the next day.[4]

Would attacks by Soviet propagandists affect his ability to do his job? He didn't think so, he told reporters in an off-the-record press conference at the State Department on April 1. Totalitarian regimes "always enlist hatred against individuals." After the "X" article came out, he and Forrestal had been called "cannibalistic hyenas." But being insulted "does not necessarily mean that you're not respected. It may mean almost the contrary." He would be happy simply "to see the diplomatic amenities observed and not too closely connected with emotions."[5]

The new ambassador met that same day with the president of the United States, who had just announced that he would not be running for reelection. Truman agreed that Stalin did not want war, and asked Kennan to write from time to time, saying that he liked getting personal reports from overseas representatives. "Beyond this, he gave me no instructions of any kind." The same thing happened when Kennan lunched with Acheson the next day: "He, too, was cordial but very reserved; and he said nothing that could give me any clue to the basic line of policy I was to follow in my new capacity."

Courtesy calls on Soviet officials in Washington and New York were no more instructive. Ambassador Aleksandr Panyushkin and his staff seemed worn down by the hostility they had encountered in the United States. Jacob Malik, with whom Kennan had had useful conversations about a Korean War cease-fire a year earlier, was now "much more bitter and sour." The Soviet Union was being threatened, he complained, at the end of their talk. "Are you sure," Kennan asked, "that your Government does not prefer to be threatened?" "Positively," Malik answered.

Soviet attitudes were no surprise, but Kennan did find the State Department's silence unsettling. So he arranged, through Bohlen, another meeting with Acheson on April 18: "It was left entirely to me to set the trend of the discussion." His reputation and the publicity surrounding his appointment, Kennan tried to point out, meant that

> anything I said in that city would be listened to with great eagerness and interest; and that even statements made to other diplomats, correspondents or visitors would get back to the Soviet Government in the majority of cases; that these . . . would be scrutinized with intense curiosity by the Soviet leaders and might well have the result of affecting their attitudes.

Should he not have, then, a clear understanding of policy on such issues as Germany—did the United States really want reunification? Or Korea—what kind of a settlement should follow a cease-fire? Or disarmament—did this not require, first, a reduction of tensions? Kennan got no answers to any of these questions: "Our position seemed to me to be comparable to the policy of unconditional surrender in the recent war."

A private conversation with Bohlen was even more disturbing. He appeared to have embraced "the flat and inflexible thinking of the Pentagon," which privileged "the false mathematics of relative effectiveness" regarding weapons of mass destruction over all other considerations that might attend their use.

The philosophic difference between this view and my own was so profound, and the hour of our conversation so late, that I could not even bring myself to argue with him about it, but it shocked me deeply for he and I have been closer than any other people in Washington, I think, in our views about Russia generally, and I realized that the difference of view implicit in his remarks would go very deep and would really prevent any further intellectual intimacy on the questions of American policy between the two of us.

Kennan returned to Princeton "feeling extremely lonely." No one in Washington sympathized with his views, and no one in Moscow was likely to. It seemed "that I was being sent on a mission to play a game at which I could not possibly win and that part of my obligation consisted of . . . taking upon myself the onus of whatever overt failures were involved."[6]

What Kennan expected remains unclear. Exhausted from constant crises and furious criticism, Acheson knew that his term would soon end. This was no time for new initiatives, and Kennan had disagreed, over the past several years, with most of the old ones. He still harbored hopes of redesigning the Soviet-American relationship: the fact that "a friend of the Russian tradition" would be representing the United States "might not be lost" among Moscow's artists and intellectuals, Kennan explained, a bit forlornly, to Richard Rovere of *The New Yorker* on the eve of his departure. Even Stalin was not "irretrievably provincial, doctrinaire, and inflexible in his outlook on the rest of the world." But with Truman leaving office, the Korean War still raging, and the old dictator's rule not likely to last much longer—he had just turned seventy-three when he agreed to Kennan's appointment—breakthroughs seemed less than likely.[7]

On April 24, 1952, the *New York Herald Tribune* ran a picture of a smiling Ambassador Kennan, departing for Europe the day before with Annelise and Christopher on the *Queen Elizabeth*—Grace and Joan, still in school, were to follow later. He shared the page, for they shared the ship, with the comedian Jimmy Durante and the Indian film star Sabu, known for playing characters from Rudyard Kipling novels. Kennan's mood, however, was darker than the photograph suggested. A few nights earlier, at the farm, he had written out on the back of an envelope this valedictory:

> Old house and pleasing slopes, who have received us all these years like a warm, relaxed, motherly host, you have given us many things: your walls have echoed the Christmas hymns sung by childish voices; young people have danced the polka

through the ground floor rooms; many evenings of talk have been spent around the fire; the gurgling of the little stream has many times lulled people to sleep who were tired and troubled from the cares of the city; we have all had health and enjoyment and hope and reassurance from your wordless, patient, kindly and mysterious influence.

Perhaps tonight I am sleeping here for the last time, and all this has gone, as in a dream. And therefore I ask you now—you who have been so mysteriously benevolent to me, let your spirit come into me on this night and enter my dreams; tell me something of your past and your meaning; tell me to what end you have been so kind to me and given me so much, that I may have strength to accept as past that which is past and go, strengthened and unregretful, into the future.[8]

The words were Kennan's, but the tone, as he knew well, was that of Chekhov's Madame Ranyevskaya, standing surrounded by suitcases in the final act of *The Cherry Orchard*, listening to the sound of it being cut down.[9]

II.

After an uneventful voyage, the Kennans spent a few days in London before meeting their own Air Force plane, which came equipped with a colonel—Annelise, "highly pregnant," would have preferred a midwife. It flew them to Wiesbaden, where she was impressed to see George get the military honors of a five-star general. They then drove to Bad Godesberg, where she was to have the baby, while John and Patricia Davies, recently posted to Bonn, would help take care of Christopher. George proceeded to Berlin and after that Moscow, arriving there on the afternoon of May 6, having arranged to avoid the May Day celebrations with their inevitably anti-American character.[10]

It was his first trip back since 1946. A building boom was under way: massive wedding-cake structures were rising around the city, each thirty to forty stories high, all to be topped off with spires supporting garishly illuminated red stars. In contrast to what Kennan remembered from the war, urban transit was working: "They have traffic regulated within an inch of its life." Off the main streets, there were still log cabins with no indoor plumbing, "but they are making progress." At Spaso House, a few servants he remembered were there to greet him, including two elderly Chinese, who retained "a concept of their calling somewhat higher than that by which the Russians were animated." All appeared to be under orders to show no pleasure at his arrival, however, and to do as little as possible to help him move in. Setting out for a walk the next day, he found his "angels"—the plain-clothesmen assigned to follow him everywhere—waiting at the gate. Hugh Cum-ming and Elim O'Shaughnessy, the embassy's second- and third-ranking officers, gave him lunch in the Kennans' old apartment at the Mokhovaya. Dinner that evening was on a tray, "and here I am," George wrote Annelise, "alone at night in the vast recesses of an empty Spaso."

Recently redecorated, the house looked good on the inside, but the servant problem was serious: "I wish you were here to help, for I think you are the only person who can do anything." He was already missing his family: "It seems like years, instead of just four days, since I said goodby to you." Finding a bag filled with Christopher's cloches had almost caused him to weep. But the little park in front of Spaso was full of children, "and I have hopes that if he is not too con-spicuously dressed he will be able to play there normally." There were hundreds of things to say, but it was hard to know where to begin, "and I am sleepy, so I will close now."

"So you have had your baby!" he wrote on the eleventh, after the communi-cations officer awakened him at three A.M. with the news. Because there were no direct telephone connections between Moscow and Bonn, he knew nothing other than that Annelise and her daughter were well, and that she was to be called Wendy. He was "mad with curiosity. What a feeling of frustration." Nevertheless, "three girls and a boy now. . . . Just like my own mother's family."[11]

The new American ambassador presented his credentials to the figurehead Soviet president, Nikolay Shvernik, in a carefully scripted Kremlin ceremony on May 14. Speaking in Russian from a memorized text, Kennan expressed hope that his actions in Moscow would "meet with the understanding and collaboration of the Soviet Government." Shvernik promised "collaboration" in his reply but said nothing about "understanding." The event took place in the same ballroom where eighteen and a half years earlier a younger Kennan—having learned the night before of his father's death—had stood behind a self-confident Bullitt, trying very hard not to faint. It had all gone like clockwork this time, George wrote Annelise: at least "what little potential value the position might have has not been dimin-ished by anything that has happened so far." Meanwhile "[w]e have gotten a veg-etable garden worked up—lettuce, radishes, and dill already planted—tomatoes and beans to go in, with luck, this weekend."[12]

Annelise's first letter, written two days before the baby's birth, reached Moscow via diplomatic pouch only on the fifteenth. By that time George was deeply into the round of calls he was expected to make on Soviet officials and members of the diplomatic corps. There would be, he estimated, fifty or sixty of these: he, in turn, would host return calls at Spaso House, a process that would go on for weeks. The mood, he warned her, "has become grim in a way it never was before." Reinforcing it was a propaganda campaign that exceeded "in viciousness, shamelessness, mendacity and intensity" anything he had experienced before in the Soviet Union, or even in Nazi Germany. The purpose, he reported to the State Department on the twenty-second, appeared to be "to arouse hatred, revulsion and indignation with regard to Americans," who were said to be using bacteriological weapons in Korea while torturing prisoners "with red hot irons, hanging them upside down, pouring water into their noses, forcibly tattooing them, forcing them to sign treasonable statements in blood, etc." The vilification was "on a scale hardly excelled in human history."[13]

Managing Spaso was still an ordeal. Burobin, the Central Bureau for Services to the Diplomatic Corps, supplied a staff of twenty-two, all of whom presumably reported to the secret police. They were under orders not to do anything other than what they had been told to do, to remain on the premises for as short a time as possible, "and above all never to permit themselves to enjoy, or feel a part of, the family in which they are working." It was like being served by "tight-lipped ghosts." Determined to make a point, Kennan fired the night watchman, who was showing up only occasionally. But that left him alone every evening, wandering around like a ghost himself. Guards outside followed his movements from room to room by watching the lights go on and off: "Somehow or other, it doesn't seem to get me down; but I really wonder whether we can or should be asked to live this way." Spaso was safe enough: no one would dare break in. But the atmosphere— Annelise would not have missed the allusion to Bad Nauheim—"is more like a sort of a prison-hotel than like a home."[14]

"Anneliesschen sweetheart," George wrote her early in June: "If there has been a gap in these letters, it has been because I did not send the one I wrote to you on Sunday." It had seemed too depressing: "Letters are unsatisfactory things." But there were less than three weeks left. "That's not so terrible, though it seems a long time." He would travel to Leningrad, he added a week later, and then "only five days will remain before this separation is over. Dreamed the other night that I saw Christopher, but he had grown quite big and didn't recognize me."[15]

The opportunity to see his wife, son, and new daughter in Bad Godesberg arose from an Acheson trip to London. Kennan would meet the secretary of state, update him on Soviet-American relations, and then bring all of the family—Grace and Joan would be out of school by then—back with him to Moscow along with their own small staff, a modest declaration of independence from Burobin. There was, however, a strangely sinister aspect to this visit. On June 25 Samuel Reber, the political adviser to the U.S. high commissioner in Bonn, John McCloy, passed the word to Frank Wisner, at the CIA in Washington, that Kennan could meet briefly in London the next day with the "Representatives."[16]

There turned out to be only one, Peer de Silva of the CIA's Clandestine Service, who had been sent to discuss assigning an undercover agent to work out of the Moscow embassy. Kennan opposed the idea, as had Bohlen when consulted on it earlier. De Silva noticed, though, that "the ambassador was very tense and nervous." At the end of the meeting, he said he had something to ask of the agency. As de Silva remembered it, Kennan handed him an envelope, which he said contained a letter to Pope Pius XII. He wanted it passed to Allen Dulles, the deputy director of central intelligence, with the request that it reach the Vatican by secure means. There was "a good possibility that I will wind up someday before long on the Soviet radio," Kennan explained. "I may be forced to make statements that would be damaging to American policy. This letter will show the world that I am under duress and am not making statements under my own free will." Did the CIA not have "some sort of a pill that a person could use to kill himself instantly"?

De Silva acknowledged that it did: small glass vials containing cyanide, which, when bitten, would release the chemical with lethal results. "I think I must have two of these," Kennan told him. De Silva promised to pass the request along—if Dulles approved, the pills could be sent by diplomatic pouch. There was a long puzzled silence when de Silva conveyed this to Dulles after flying back to Washington, but he finally decided that the agency could not deny Kennan the pills if he really wanted them.[17]

When asked about this in 1987, Kennan pointed out that the prospect of war was very real at the time. He had no confidence that the Soviets would observe "the amenities," as the Germans had done in 1941–42, and that internment had been bad enough: "If they had decided to sacrifice their mission [in the United States], they wouldn't have hesitated to arrest us and then to put me in solitary confinement." Having held senior positions in the State Department, he had information his interrogators might try to extract by torture: "If that was what I had to face, I was quite prepared to—I asked for this." But he had asked to be provided "with pills that you could easily conceal. . . . God knows what Stalin would have done."[18]

Elbridge Durbrow, who read de Silva's account shortly after it appeared in

1978, had a different explanation: "Something got to George. I don't know what it was, [maybe] the KGB got to him and said: 'We've got the goods on you.'" After all, "they tried to screw up every ambassador there the best they could one way or another." Hugh Cumming was more specific. Kennan had gotten into trouble "with some 'dame' and thought the Russians might in some way publicize it." They did not do this, "and he's been grateful ever since."[19]

III.

Kennan was lonely during his first six weeks in Moscow, and there was an opportunity for romance. The American embassy still maintained a dacha outside of the city, but it had become so run-down that he was reluctant to use it. He preferred a smaller one rented by correspondents Harrison Salisbury, Thomas P. Whitney, and Whitney's Russian wife, Juli Zapolskaya—soon he had his own key. "There is a sound of hammers, dogs barking, chickens, children's cries, and distant trains," George wrote Annelise from the front porch one afternoon at the end of May, "a relief from the old beat between Spaso and Mokhovaya." The dacha was a refuge for a temporary bachelor: he could go on walks (accompanied by angels, to be sure, but they allowed him a sympathetic distance), indulge in long late conversations in rapid Russian with the Whitneys (Salisbury, still learning the language, struggled to keep up), and accompany songs that they all could sing (Russian and American) on his guitar. The atmosphere, Kennan recalled, was one of "health and simplicity and subdued hope which I drank in, on my brief visits there, as one drinks in fresh air after long detention in a stuffy room."

He described Juli, in his memoirs, only as "a musician and *chanteuse* of talent." Salisbury, in his, went further. She had, he was certain, fallen in love: "No one who saw Juli's face light up and her eyes glow in George's presence could mistake the feeling." He was, to her, "a character out of not Chekhov but Turgenev, sophisticated, wise, urbane, gifted with a philosophy and emotion close to the Russian heart. He was Russian but not Russian, American but a special kind of American. She could talk to him all day and all night." Only wife and country kept George from reciprocating: "He was an extraordinarily happily married man, and strongly as he was drawn to this most Russian of relationships, he was not prepared to venture on an excursion down that path." He told Juli, according to Salisbury, that he had made a decision of principle; he had placed himself at the service of his country, and this service came ahead of personal desires and inclinations. His life, in a sense, was no longer at his disposal; it was his country's. This declaration, so similar to that of a priest's in dedicating himself to the service of God, might have sounded presumptuous in another man. But from the lips of the serious and solemn Kennan, one could only respect it.

Salisbury believed Juli did. "She smiled at him, she gave him her most tender looks, but she made no effort by the arts of her coquetry to woo him from his resolve."[20]

To be sure, Salisbury—and Whitney, for that matter—may not always have been present. But angels were, and as George was well aware, they reported on his activities in the country as carefully as they tracked his movements within the gloomy precincts of Spaso House. "The great good earth of Mother Russia," he wrote a friend later that summer,

> seems to exude her benevolent and maternal warmth over man and beast and growing things together; and only, perhaps, an American Ambassador, stalking through the countryside with his company of guardians to the amazement of the children and the terror of the adults, is effectively isolated, as though by an invisible barrier, from participation in the general beneficence of nature and human sociability.[21]

It was hardly the setting for an affair, however lonely Kennan may have been. So what else could have caused him to request suicide pills in the same week that he rejoined his family and first met his new daughter?

Kennan kept no diary during this period, probably for fear that it might fall into the hands of the Soviet authorities. Major General Robert W. Grow, the Army attaché in Moscow while Kirk was ambassador, had suffered just that misfortune in 1951 and had been court-martialed as a result. Kirk's wife, Lydia Chapin Kirk, had committed a less serious indiscretion by rushing a gossipy account of Spaso House life into print in the United States before her husband had formally resigned. George was not about to risk adding to "the follies of our predecessors," he wrote to Annelise early in June 1952. Because of them, she should "not be surprised at the coolness of the reception that awaits you in Moscow . . . I am not."[22]

Nonetheless he was surprised. Sir Alvary Gascoigne, the British ambassador, found Kennan unprepared for how differently foreign missions were treated from when he had last served in the U.S.S.R.: "This came as quite a shock to him."

Cumming remembered Kennan returning from a walk one day soon after his arrival, so subdued that he seemed ill. "Hugh, I am shocked to discover [that] the Soviets regard me as such a dangerous person." I said: "What do you mean?" "Why, this outbreak of anti-American posters all over the town." "George, those damn things have been there for months! I honestly don't think that they have anything personally to do with you." But Kennan wasn't listening: he got "that rather distant, misty look in his eyes," which showed that he was composing a dispatch. Calling in a secretary—not Hessman, who would only later join him in Moscow—he "lay down on the sofa to dictate, almost like a patient in a psycho-analyst's office. I envied him the ability," Cumming recalled, "to do that."[23]

The result was a long letter to Doc Matthews, pouched to Washington to ensure security. There were, Kennan suggested, four possible reasons for the Kremlin's propaganda offensive. The first was to boost sagging morale in the Soviet Union and the rest of the communist world, where there was "widespread political apathy and skepticism." With the exception of the wartime years, however, that disillusionment had been present since the purges of the late 1930s—alone it could not account for what now was going on. A second explanation was mobilization for war: Kennan had never believed, though, that Stalin would deliberately unleash one. A third was some kind of leadership struggle, but there was no hard evidence for this. That left a fourth possibility, which was that the campaign "might have something to do with my own appointment and arrival."

Kennan was known to Stalin and his associates, after all, as someone who was *not* "bloodthirsty and boorish, . . . lacking in good will, ignorant and contemptuous of Russian cultural values, [or] obtuse to developments in the world of the Russian spirit." Because of his prior service in the country and his knowledge of the language, they might have interpreted his appointment as an indication that the U.S. government was ready for "real" discussions on significant issues. Why, then, the anti-American campaign? To the normal mind, it could hardly be a less fitting prelude for diplomacy. But Stalin's mind was not normal:

> Let us remember that it has been the policy, and apparently sometimes the secret delight, of Stalin, before adopting a given course, to eliminate or force into an embarrassing position all those who might be suspected of having themselves favored such a course.

It was also important to the Kremlin leaders, when on the verge of making even minor concessions, not to seem to have been pressured into doing so.

This might have particular relation to myself if they felt that my personality and presence here tied in in any way with the neurotic uneasiness which besets a large number of Soviet artists and intellectuals in present circumstances in connection with their extreme isolation from the main cultural currents of the world.

If Stalin did see any possibility of a Cold War settlement, then, he might think it useful "to remind a new and somewhat inscrutable American Ambassador . . . that if he is going to talk to anyone around here it is going to be to Papa—that the other members of the family know their places and are well in hand."

But an invitation to talk with Papa would have thrilled Kennan, even though he had resolved—given his lack of instructions from Washington—not to ask for one: why did he still feel threatened? He now came up with a fifth explanation, which was that the Soviet authorities had developed a "reckless contempt for whatever values and safeguards might conceivably still lie in the maintenance of the normal diplomatic channel." That had not happened during Kennan's previous service in Moscow. Now, though, the restraint was gone. There was, in its place, "the excited, uncertain bravado of the parvenu who thinks that his fortunes have advanced to the point where he need no longer pretend to be a man of correct behavior or even a man of respect for correct behavior." It was

the swaggering arrogance of the drunken peasant-speculator Lopakhin in the last act of Chekhov's *Cherry Orchard*, when he has just purchased at auction the estate on which he grew up as a serf, and now loses control of himself in his excitement and stamps around, reveling in his triumph, impervious to the presence of the weeping family who are leaving the place forever, confident that never again will he need their respect, their help, or their solicitude.

If this was right, "then we have a bitter problem on our hands." Restoring sobriety and decorum among such people would take "real thought and skillful action on our part, and probably luck as well."[24]

The contradictions in this letter can only have bewildered its readers. Kennan portrayed a Soviet leadership that both needed a settlement and did not need one. He hoped for diplomacy in a state that, he insisted, had given up on diplomacy. He described anti-Americanism as a shocking development, but he had been arguing, as far back as the "long telegram," that Stalin's regime required a hostile outside world. He placed himself at the center of the aging dictator's concerns despite having noted, before leaving for Moscow, that successful ambassadors there practiced self-effacement. Kennan cast himself in the role of someone Stalin might enjoy eliminating, or at least forcing into an "embarrassing position," but with whom he would be eager to negotiate. None of these claims were necessarily implausible: they could hardly all be plausible, however, at the same time. "George is an egocentric person, a highly emotional person," Cumming explained years later. "It's a strange combination of a well-drilled mind, a fine command of the English language, and yet shot through all of this is this emotional response to external stimuli, which somehow or another his well-drilled mind doesn't seem to be able to control."[25]

The problem was evident in a second letter Kennan pouched to Matthews two weeks later, complaining about the intelligence-gathering activities of American military attachés in Moscow. These involved the use of cameras, radio receivers, and listening devices to collect information from embassy buildings and vehicles. A favorite opportunity was Aviation Day, in July, when the Americans would invite their British and Norwegian counterparts to the roof of the Mokhovaya to photograph the planes flying over, and then downstairs for drinks. It was done so openly, Kennan pointed out, that the Soviets had their own photographers documenting the activity, apparently with a view to compiling a dossier. Like the Grow diary and Mrs. Kirk's book, these provocations encouraged retaliation: their continuation placed in jeopardy "the physical security of the members of the [American] mission and their families." Diplomatic immunity could only extend so far: if relations ruptured or if war broke out, it was entirely possible that the staff "might suffer seriously by virtue of these activities that have been conducted in the past."

So he had ordered a halt to them—despite warnings from the attachés that their superiors would not welcome the prohibition—and he would stick to that policy unless otherwise instructed from Washington. Cumming thought this naïve: "The Russians would do it in [the United States] if they didn't have other ways of getting things." And Kennan knew, from his own experiences dating back to the days of Joe Davies, how thoroughly the Soviets had compromised the immunity of Spaso House by installing their own bugs, as well as servants who were also spies. "We never talked, really, very much, even in the privacy of [our] bedroom," Annelise recalled. "It makes you absolutely tongue tied." By 1952 there was even a microwave beam aimed at the windows in Kennan's Mokhovaya office, presumably in an effort to pick up conversations there.[26]

Kennan became even more worried about provocations when Joseph and Stewart Alsop published a series of alarming columns, in mid-June, reporting in rapid succession on American reconnaissance flights into Soviet airspace, on similar Soviet flights over Alaska, on progress in developing the hydrogen bomb, on rumors of a new Berlin blockade, and—most disturbing—on his own confidential reports to the State Department about the anti-American campaign in the U.S.S.R., which had caused Kennan to reconsider earlier assurances that its leaders would not risk war. Their reports in turn alerted Henry Luce, whose correspondents hounded Kennan while he was in Bonn and London, trying to confirm the story. Could Bohlen not plead with the *Time-Life* editors to spare the American embassy in Moscow "the spotlight of further press curiosity"?[27]

All of this, then, puts the suicide pills episode in a broader context than that of "some dame." Kennan's loneliness had led to affairs in Berlin in 1940–41, probably at Bad Nauheim in 1942, and surely somewhere in 1951. He had even admonished himself, in his most recent agony over infidelity, that were it not for his youngest (at that time Christopher), he should go into the military and get himself killed in a war.[28] What concerned Kennan now, though, if war broke out, was the risk of internment, torture, and the compromise of state secrets: taking a pill under these circumstances would be an act of patriotism, not just an escape from embarrassment. There are, then, multiple explanations for his behavior in late June 1952: it need not have been the fear of blackmail. And the letter to the pope, if de Silva's account is to be believed? Kennan was indeed egocentric, and he was becoming deeply religious. Not so much so, though, that he would have sought absolution, from the supreme pontiff, for a dalliance with a dame. He had worse things than that on his mind.[29]

IV.

The severely functional office of the U.S. ambassador to the Soviet Union, Salisbury reported to the readers of *The New York Times Magazine* shortly after Kennan arrived, was less impressive than what a deputy price administrator in Washington might occupy. There was a desk in one corner, a table for books and out-of-date American magazines in a second, and a couch, some armchairs, and a coffee table in a third. The fourth corner was empty. The only decorations were photographs of Presidents Roosevelt and Truman, the latter slightly larger. The view, though, was spectacular: swiveling in his chair, Kennan could look out across Manege Square to the walls of the Kremlin, only a two-minute walk away. Thanks to the acquisition of the Mokhovaya in 1934, no foreign embassy was closer. And should

Stalin seek to see Kennan, few men were better qualified to explain American policy "in terms and language which have real meaning to Soviet minds."

Apart from ceremonial occasions like the presentation of credentials, however, visits to the Kremlin had become rare for American ambassadors in recent years. Kirk had met Stalin only once, shortly after arriving in 1949. It was not at all clear when, or even whether, Kennan would be received. The Mokhovaya's proximity therefore could be frustrating: as if to illustrate this, Salisbury's article carried a photograph of Kennan staring expectantly from his window at the Kremlin's dark towers, as if waiting for the invitation.[30]

In one sense life was easier: "The world's most efficient police system protects me from my old enemies—the telephone and the visitors." Knowing that he would not soon return to the United States, Kennan could see his own country "with detachment, with charity, with serenity—as I imagine the dead look back on life." There was consolation also in the "comfortable consciousness, underlying all government work, that it was someone else besides yourself who decided that . . . you should be where you are and doing what you are doing." Duty relieved guilt, "and in its soothing influence lies, I am sure, something of the appeal of totalitarianism."[31]

Still, he could not help looking for signs and portents. The Moscow theater offered Kennan proximity to the Soviet artistic community: its members, he felt, must have been aware of his presence, if for no other reason than that his angels bumped anyone seated around him. Attending a performance of Tolstoy's *Resurrection* one night with Robert C. Tucker, a young Foreign Service officer who would become a distinguished professor of Soviet studies at Princeton, Kennan was startled to see the leading man advance to the footlights, appear to address him directly, and say: "There is an American by the name of George, and with him we are all in agreement." Kennan and Tucker rushed back to the embassy to check the text, only to find that the line referred to Henry George, the late nineteenth-century proponent of the single tax. "But was the actor aware of the play on words? And did he enjoy it as much as we did?" Like astronomers listening for life on other planets, "we were forced to try to gain our feeling for the Russian cultural world" by such indirect means, despite its "presence and vitality . . . all around us."[32]

Exasperated by the silence, Kennan called in Cumming one day in mid-June to ask if the embassy staff had run across anyone who might have known him earlier in Moscow. Cumming suggested Boris Fedorovich Podserob, a former secretary to Molotov, now secretary general of the Foreign Ministry, with whom Kennan

had had reasonably good relations during the 1930s. "If you find yourself talking with Podserob," Kennan replied, "I wish you'd tell him that I regret that there
is no person here in the entire apparat with whom I could occasionally come
together and have a cup of tea and talk." Cumming had no Russian and Podserob
little English, but they did both have French, so at the next opportunity—a diplomatic reception at the Moskva Hotel—Cumming conveyed the message, bringing
O'Shaughnessy along as a linguistic backup: Kennan was picking up his family
in West Germany at the time. Podserob appeared interested, remained with the
Americans long enough to make sure that he understood, and then departed.

Kennan returned to Moscow on July 1, and an invitation to talk soon followed,
although not in the form he had expected. A young Russian appeared inside the
Mokhovaya, having somehow got past the Soviet militia who controlled access to
the building. "I was startled," Cumming recalled. "Is this a joke or something?"
"No, it's not a joke." So he went out and talked to the man. "He looked vaguely
familiar, but I couldn't quite identify him. His clothes looked good, but dishev-
eled. He wanted to see the ambassador." "Don't you recognize me?" he said. "I
have interpreted for you a number of times on your calls to the Foreign Office. I
have asked to see you so you can identify me." Cumming then remembered him,
asked a colleague to keep an eye on the visitor, and went in to inform Kennan.

"Do you think I should see him?" "I don't know, George. It's entirely up to
you. He has either broken through the militiamen outside, or they've allowed him
to enter." But the American Marines guarding the embassy reported no scuffle.
"So it was obvious to me that the militia had let him come in." Part of Kennan's
office was exposed to the microwave beam, but the corner with the sofa and the
armchairs was not. Kennan asked his visitor to sit there and to speak in English,
so that Cumming could follow the conversation. He then identified himself as
the son of Viktor Semyonovich Abakumov, the minister for state security, who
he said had been arrested. "That was the first knowledge that any of us had that
Abakumov had disappeared." Kennan recalled what came next: "Like the sons of
other high figures here, I think what's going on is very dangerous. We know the
comings and goings of the leaders here, and we would be in a position to mount
an action to remove them."

"Look here," Kennan replied. "I did not come here to violate the laws of the
Soviet Union, or to encourage anyone else to do it. I think you'd better leave this
room and this building immediately." The young man protested that he would be
arrested as soon as he stepped outside: "They saw me come in here." Could the
Americans not smuggle him out in a car, or allow him to leave through one of the

steam tunnels that connected the Mokhovaya to the central heating plant? "No," Kennan insisted, "you'll have to go out the way you came in." He was escorted to the front entrance. Cumming, with Kennan, watched from the window as the militiamen seized him. "One crooked his arm up behind his back, they put him in a car with the curtains down, and they drove off. The interesting thing was that there were crowds moving back and forth on the street. Nobody even turned a head to look at this. You don't do that in the Soviet Union."

Kennan concluded that this was a message to him from Stalin: "I know, you son of a bitch, what you're here for. I'll send the fitting sort of fellow to you. Let's see what you do." Cumming was at first more skeptical, because "George always tended to regard things personally, as a provocation of some kind." There had been other incidents of Russians trying to break into the Mokhovaya: one, at just this time, involved a demented man who ran past the militia, stationed himself in the commissary, seized a hammer, demanded asylum, and threatened to kill himself if he did not get it. With Kennan's approval, the Soviet authorities were allowed into the embassy to remove him. That intruder, however, had not proposed an assassination plot. This one did, and the fact that he was a Foreign Ministry interpreter—Cumming confirmed this by finding him in a photograph, taken a year earlier, of the ceremony at which Gascoigne, the British ambassador, had presented his credentials—lent plausibility to Kennan's hypothesis. No genuine conspirator would have used so conspicuous a method of signaling his intentions, without any prior assurance of how he would be received.[33]

The intruder was in fact Nikolay Nikolayevich Yakovlev, the son not of Abakumov but of a Soviet marshal who had just been arrested—so too had young Nikolay. A third Nikolay, General Vlasik, the head of Stalin's security detail, "came to see me in my solitary confinement and offered a deal: my only chance to survive . . . was to go to the American Embassy, to see Kennan himself, and make him believe a story which had been prepared for me." Yakovlev was given no other information, "but the whole plot was clear to me even without that."

> I accepted the offer without much deliberation: by then I had been severely beaten several times and had many teeth broken; so, for me, there was not much of a choice. In a few days I was put back in shape and was fit enough to go to Kennan. I must have been very nervous, Kennan was very frosty, and gave me a nasty turn-around. I was taken back to [the] Lubyanka and never saw Vlasik again, but obviously he wasn't pleased with my performance, since though the beatings ceased I was let out only after Stalin's death.

Yakovlev later became one of the first Soviet historians of the Cold War, well known for his criticisms of U.S. foreign policy (based only on American sources, no Soviet documents being available at the time), his attacks on prominent dissidents, including Aleksandr Solzhenitsyn and Andrey Sakharov (which he probably had no choice but to make), and his tortured ambivalence about George F. Kennan.[34]

Was the Yakovlev intrusion a test Stalin devised? Salisbury thought so at the time, and there is some evidence to support this possibility. It emerges, circuitously, from an interview the Kremlin boss granted to the Italian socialist Pietro Nenni, a recent recipient of the Stalin Peace Prize, on July 17, 1952. Such meetings were rare enough to send embassies all over Moscow scrambling for information, and in a report to Acheson on the twenty-fifth, Kennan summarized what he had learned about this one. His source was the Italian ambassador, Mario Di Stefano, an old friend from earlier service together in the U.S.S.R. Stalin had been in good health, Nenni told Di Stefano, had shown a keen interest in Italian politics, and had reconciled himself to the indefinite division of Germany. Nenni then asked about Kennan: "whether I really entertained friendly feelings toward Russia." Di Stefano replied "that I had come here in the hopes of bettering the situation and of getting some idea of the thinking of the Kremlin on present international problems."[35]

Kennan made no immediate effort to assess this query, although it would not have struck him as an idle one: had Stalin asked Nenni to make it? Salisbury, who also talked with Di Stefano, concluded that he had: "I wish Kennan and I had known each other better in those times and had been able to talk more freely." Salisbury had something else to regret, which was that the indefatigable Alsops scooped him. It was "at least conceivable," they wrote in their syndicated column on August 8, that "Nenni's questions about Ambassador Kennan . . . might mean that the men in the Kremlin are considering some sort of approach to the American Government through Kennan." Combined with the information about Germany, the Nenni interview "seems to hold out two rather small and quite possibly deceptive crumbs of comfort."[36]

The next day the Milan newspaper *Corriere della Sera* ran a front-page story with the headline: "Stalin Tries an Oblique Maneuver Aimed at a Relaxation of Tension With America: A Report of the American Ambassador in Moscow." He and Di Stefano were distressed by the leaks, Kennan cabled Acheson: "Suppose it quixotic to wish means could be found to make Alsop[s] understand how difficult they make my task here by reckless and needless references to personalities, particularly myself in their column." It turned out, though, that the French too had the story—probably provided by the garrulous Nenni—which strengthens the likelihood that Stalin had instructed him to mention Kennan's name.[37]

Then, on August 23, Stalin received the new French ambassador, Louis Joxe, for a twenty-minute visit. Kennan was furious. Joxe had not informed him that he was seeking the meeting: he had been "ill-advised" to proceed without receiving any indication that Stalin wished to see him. The "obvious purpose" was to drive a wedge between the French, the British, and the Americans, since neither Kennan nor Gascoigne had received an invitation. (Someone in Washington, on reading this telegram, scribbled in the margin: "Did GFK ever ask?") Joxe's reception "may have been . . . intended as a reproach to me or as a means of embarrassing me," Kennan wrote Doc Matthews, "by conveying the implication that had I made a similar request I also would have been received." But he professed to be content:

> What these people need is to be left alone for a while and taught that other people are capable of doing without them, and I am quite sure that when the proper time comes for me to see Stalin (and this might be at any time for any number of reasons) my usefulness on that occasion will be enhanced, rather than otherwise, by virtue of the fact that I have refrained from bothering him until I really had something to talk about.

After reading a similar complaint from Gascoigne, however, Sir Pierson Dixon of the British Foreign Office put a different spin on the situation: "There is a certain puckishness about Stalin, and I dare say he could not resist the temptation of setting the Chancelleries buzzing by seeing the new French ambassador on the eve of the latest Soviet note on Germany."[38]

The note on Germany restated a surprising proposal Stalin had first put forward on March 10, 1952. that the four occupying powers agree to hold free elections throughout Germany, looking toward the establishment of an independent, reunified, rearmed, but neutral state. This seemed to confirm Bohlen's sense, from the previous summer, that Stalin was ready to talk; it also echoed, remarkably closely, Kennan's Program A. Yet few historians today believe that Stalin was sincere, and Kennan at the time was skeptical. The Soviet initiative appeared to be a last-minute effort to split West Germany from its European and American allies on the eve of its integration into a European Defense Community closely linked to NATO. When it failed, as Stalin seems to have expected it would, he at last reconciled himself to the prospect that the Soviet Union would never control any more than the eastern third of its former adversary: short of war, Germany and Europe would remain divided. The Nenni interview gave Western diplomats their first hint of this shift in Stalin's thinking.[39] There is irony, nonetheless, in the fact that Stalin's ideas appear to have come closest to Kennan's—if only briefly—during a period in which Kennan was just a phone call, and a few minutes' walk, away. But neither picked up the phone: each may have been waiting for the other to do so.

Kennan, of course, had no instructions from Acheson to explore Stalin's intentions. The March 1952 note had initially intrigued the secretary of state—as had Program A—but he backed off when the British, the French, and the West Germans made it clear that they did not wish to pursue the idea. By late May, Kennan was dismissing the most recent version of Stalin's suggestion as having been prepared "by hacks supplied only with grudging, cryptic, and guarded instructions and told to make the best of it."[40] And by the end of August—after the Nenni leak and the Joxe interview—he was insisting that the Soviet leader must come to him, not the other way around, a tone more appropriate for a head of state than for an ambassador.

Stalin's behavior is more difficult to explain. He certainly knew who Kennan was, having read both the "long telegram" and the "X" article—as well as, through espionage, an unknown number of other Kennan dispatches and policy papers. He had made no effort to call off Soviet propagandists, who had been attacking Kennan for several years: Parker's 1949 book, for example, had denounced him as "the first and in some ways the most influential agent of America's warmongers," a man "of violent hatred not only of the Soviet Union but of all democratic mankind." The Foreign Ministry briefing prepared for Shvernik when Kennan presented his credentials in May 1952 claimed that he had shared the views of Nazi diplomats prior to World War II, called for the criminal prosecution of Soviet sympathizers in the United States, headed a foundation financing "reactionary organizations and political émigrés" from Eastern Europe, and was plotting war against the U.S.S.R. and the other "people's democracies." It concluded, as if this were an offense also, that Kennan "knows the Russian language well."[41]

And yet—Stalin did agree to accept Kennan as the new U.S. ambassador. It's possible that he was playing a game all along, first by delaying the *agrément* to the appointment, then by greeting Kennan with an intensified anti-American propaganda campaign, then by trying to compromise him within his own embassy, then by planting a tantalizing question about him with Nenni, then by snubbing him while receiving Joxe—all the while plaguing him with bad service in Spaso House. That's how it looked to Kennan, and that possibility would parallel the view most historians have of Stalin's March 1952 note on Germany: that the old man was trying to keep his enemies off balance.

Another explanation, though, is that he was simply an old man. It's at least as likely that Stalin had no coherent strategy, that his attention wandered from day to day, and that his subordinates were too terrified to point out the contradictions. It was during this period, after all, that Stalin unwisely launched a purge against his own doctors. Joxe, in contrast to Nenni, had found him showing his age. The French had the impression, Kennan reported, that Stalin "moved his left arm only with difficulty and that his bodily movements were in general labored and jerky." There had been a revealing moment, also, during the Nenni interview: Stalin suddenly informed his guest that the staunchly anticommunist American Francis Cardinal Spellman had been present at the 1945 Yalta conference—he had not—and that it had been he who had turned Roosevelt against the Soviet Union, thereby confirming the Vatican's hand behind every development unfavorable to Moscow.[42] Perhaps it was just as well that Stalin didn't know of Kennan's letter to the pope, if it ever existed. Or maybe, even if it didn't, he thought it did.

V.

"You should have seen us arrive in great style," Annelise wrote Cousin Grace and Frieda Por in mid-July, two weeks after all six Kennans had landed in Moscow on their four-engine U.S. Air Force plane: "I almost felt important." Accompanying them were a Danish couple to take over the Spaso House responsibilities of butler and cook, their three-year-old daughter who would be a playmate for Christopher, and a Danish nurse to manage all of the younger children—plus what seemed to Annelise a fortune in frozen meat, canned goods, whiskeys, and wines. Grace, on vacation from Radcliffe, took several embassy jobs, was pleased to get paid for them, but was not getting much sleep because "young girls are at a premium in the foreign colony." Joan, who had stayed briefly in Moscow, was now in Kristiansand, not a bad thing since "there was nothing for her to do and she would have been very bored." Full of energy but not as tractable as he used to be, "Tiffer Tennan" made sure that he was the center of attention: Wendy would "have to wait until she gets bigger." It was just as well that she had turned out to be a girl.

Unlike George, Annelise did not find Moscow to be as oppressive as it had been in the late 1930s. There were goods, albeit expensive, in the stores, and people were better dressed than during the war: "They seem pretty friendly in spite of the anti-American campaign that [is] going on. They don't dare have anything to do with us, but I am sure they would if the taboo was lifted." With Spaso's staff and her Danish helpers, Annelise could imagine spending a lot of time in bed, "but somehow it doesn't work out quite that way. The house is really big and I would like to put a speedometer on myself to see how much ground I cover [in] a day." Nevertheless, it seemed natural to be back in Moscow: "I'd been in Russia more than any other place since I'd been married."[43]

Things did get better, George acknowledged, after his family arrived. Under Annelise's supervision and with the assistance of the Danes—whom the police could not easily intimidate—Spaso became more hospitable. There was even an opportunity for George, with Grace, to revisit Tolstoy's home Yasnaya Polyana, where he had last been in 1935, sick, during a snowstorm, being nursed by the GPU. His ambassadorial angels again respected his privacy, allowing him a long talk with the great writer's last secretary, Valentin Fedorovich Bulgakov, whose Russian carried "the authentic accent—rich, polished, elegant and musical—of the educated circles of those earlier times. So, I thought to myself, must Tolstoi himself have spoken."[44]

But running the embassy continued to frustrate Kennan. It was, he believed, "absurdly overstaffed." The Soviet authorities were pressing for its relocation to a site more distant from the Kremlin. Meanwhile the younger Foreign Service officers were treating him, he complained to Bohlen, "with the same weary correctness which we reserved in our youth for chiefs whom we thought were hopelessly behind in their mental processes." Two in particular provoked Kennan's ire. They were Malcolm Toon and Richard Davies, later themselves ambassadors, respectively, to the Soviet Union and Poland, who after studying Russian at Columbia had been assigned to Moscow prior to Kennan's appointment. They had the reputation, Cumming remembered, of being brilliant but troublesome: this the new ambassador certainly found them to be.[45]

Toon and Davies had made the mistake, while still at Columbia, of entering an essay contest sponsored by the *Foreign Service Journal*. Without knowing that they would be working for Kennan, they decided to try their hand at a new "X" article, entitled "After Containment, What?" That strategy had been all right as far as it went, they argued, but it had done nothing to bring about "the destruction of Stalinism." This would require a sustained effort to detach the Eastern European satellites from Soviet control, beginning right away with East Germany. Admittedly this might risk a third world war, but they concluded—rather too grandly—that such an outcome was unlikely. It "may not have been," Davies later admitted, "the most judicious proposal" to have put forward at that particular time. "I may have been brash," Toon added, "but I wasn't stupid. I certainly would never have written this paper had I known [Kennan] was going to be our ambassador." He and Davies were "quaking in our boots as to what would happen to us."

"Friends" of the two arranged for Kennan to read their essay: soon thereafter the journal editors dropped it from consideration for a prize, indeed from publication in any form. Meanwhile the ambassador set about getting the miscreants out of Moscow. He requested early transfers—a cumbersome process—and approved unfavorable fitness reports that would plague the two for years to come. Three years earlier, however, Kennan himself had approved covert operations meant to bring about much of what Toon and Davies advocated. Some of his exasperation with them grew out of their open discussion of what should have been kept secret. Some of it may also have reflected concern over the 1952 presidential campaign: John Foster Dulles, no fan of Kennan's, had condemned "containment" publicly in May and was calling for "liberation" as an alternative.[46]

Kennan's chief concern, however, was that the very success of Western policies—overt and covert—was making the Soviet regime desperate. It was behaving, he wrote to Doc Matthews, like a "savage beast" that "hisses and spits and snarls at us incessantly." Only flimsy barriers deprived it of the pleasure, in the words of the Russian poet Aleksandr Blok, "of making our skeleton 'clatter in his fond embrace.'" That made it all the more important to avoid provocations like the Toon-Davies article, or efforts to publicize a recent congressional report that had linked Stalin and his subordinates to the 1940 Katyn Forest massacre. It was of course accurate: no "serious student" of Soviet affairs believed otherwise. The truth would not shame the perpetrators of that atrocity, however, since their victims *prior* to Katyn ran "into the hundreds of thousands and probably millions." Poking or prodding the beast made little sense, therefore, but perhaps someday, "if we keep cool and use our heads, we will manage to subdue him in such a way that he will cause us less trouble."[47]

Would the Americans, though, stay cool and use their heads? Late in the summer of 1952 Kennan learned, through a military attaché, of a plan he considered so shocking that he was unwilling to reveal its specifics for several decades to come: it involved preparations, if war broke out, to mine the Turkish Straits. The information convinced him that "the Pentagon now had the bit in its teeth." As had been the case during World War II, there was insufficient vigor "on the political side of the Potomac" to balance military considerations. The scheme hardly seems surprising in retrospect. Turkey had joined NATO a few months earlier, and even prior to its doing so the National Security Council had deemed it a vital American interest to deny the Soviet Union the use of the straits if hostilities occurred.[48]

Kennan was now hypersensitive, however, to the danger of blundering into a major war. Kremlin leaders did not *want* one, he still insisted, but NATO's actions might provoke one. He felt caught "between immense forces over which I have little or no control." His only hope was "to handle things in such a manner as to lessen the likelihood of the blindest and wildest sort of reactions on both sides." With that objective in mind, he pouched a dispatch to Washington on September 8—at ten thousand words, it was one of his longest—that tried to see the situation through Soviet eyes. It made him sound, he admitted years later, like one of the early "revisionist" historians of the Cold War.[49]

It was more sophisticated than that. Kennan portrayed a Soviet regime shaped by history and ideology, to be sure, but also subject to "considerable vacillation, doubt and conflict," not only between individuals and groups but also "within individual minds." Of course the system required the appearance of external hostility to justify its own internal oppression. That did not mean, however, that it always distinguished what it needed to see from what was really happening. Stalin and his associates combined rationality with its opposite. Because they were secretive and often erratic, "it is not easy to tell when you are going to touch one of their neuralgic and irrational points."[50]

Kennan wrote this document—or rather dictated it, since Hessman had now made it to Moscow—for a meeting of American chiefs of missions in Western Europe, to be held in London on September 24–26, 1952. These took place periodically, but it was unusual for the ambassador to the Soviet Union to be invited. That Kennan was asked to come suggests the seriousness with which his views were still taken, despite his having no instructions from Washington and no one to whom to talk in Moscow. The State Department would be remiss, one of Nitze's aides wrote of Kennan's lengthy dispatch, "if, in the light of this penetrating diagnosis of Soviet motivations and intentions, it did not review NATO objectives and activities." But Under Secretary of State David Bruce, who organized the event, was less impressed: he had reached the point, he later recalled, where he no longer read Kennan's reports "because they were so long-winded and so blatantly seeking to be literary rather than provide information."[51]

Two Spaso House incidents deepened Kennan's pessimism before he departed. One was the discovery that, during the mansion's recent renovation, a sophisticated listening device had been installed inside the wooden Great Seal of the

United States that hung in the ambassador's study, a "gift" the Soviet government had presented to Harriman shortly after the end of the war. The embassy's technicians found it by having Kennan dictate loudly to Hessman while they swept the room with their own detectors—a more sophisticated method than the ones he and Charlie Thayer had used in trying to fumigate Spaso against more primitive bugs during Joe Davies's ambassadorship. With a grim sense of history, Kennan used as his text his own compilation of Neill Brown's dispatches from the early 1850s, which Bullitt had sent to Washington in 1936: the State Department had just published these in 1952. The exposure of the new apparatus terrified the Burobin staff, while the guards at the gate scowled even more menacingly. "So dense was the atmosphere of anger and hostility," Kennan remembered, "that one could have cut it with a knife."[52]

The other incident was more innocent but, for him, more significant. It involved Christopher—not quite three at the time—and a late summer afternoon he spent playing in a sand pile in the front garden, while his father sat reading a book. Bored with this,

> the boy wandered down to the iron fence, gripped two of the spikes with his pudgy little fists, and stood staring out into the wide, semi-forbidden world beyond. . . . Some Soviet children came along the sidewalk on the other side of the fence, saw him, smiled at him, and gave him a friendly poke through the bars. He squealed in pleasure and poked back. Soon, to much mutual pleasure, a game was in progress

At this point the guards—presumably under orders now to be even more vigilant—shooed the children away. The revelation that the beast could not tolerate even this most minimal poking caused Kennan's patience to snap. Had he been a better ambassador, he later admonished himself, this would not have happened: "But give way it did; and it could not soon be restored."[53]

VI.

On the afternoon before his departure, Kennan asked to see Salisbury, Whitney, Eddy Gilmore, and Henry Shapiro, the principal American correspondents in Moscow. He was concerned about leaks in Washington, which seemed to suggest that his views of the Soviet Union were more critical than what he was saying publicly. Kennan assured the journalists, Salisbury recalled, that "he would say absolutely nothing while on this trip abroad; if he had something on his mind, he would call us in when he returned." Salisbury accompanied him to the airport the next morning, September 19, 1952. "He was in a silent, withdrawn mood."[54]

The ambassadorial plane flew Kennan to West Berlin, accompanied this time not by his family but by the gadget found in the Great Seal. Expecting reporters when he landed at Tempelhof, determined to have safe answers ready, Kennan conducted an interview with himself in a small notebook while still airborne:

> *Where are you going?* I am on my way to London to attend a meeting of some of our European chiefs of mission with the Under Secretary of State, Mr. Bruce.
> *Is the situation more hopeful than it was when you went in last spring?* The situation is not worse.
> *Have you seen Stalin?* There has been no occasion for me to ask to be received by Premier Stalin.
> *What do you think of the last Soviet note on Germany?* It shows that the Soviet leaders do not wish the discussion of precisely those matters which will have to be discussed first if there is to be a really free and united Germany.

Upon arrival, though, one of the questions caught him off guard: were there many "social contacts" with Russians in Moscow? "Why, I thought to myself, must editors send reporters of such ignorance to interview ambassadors at airports?" *The New York Times* reported what he said next:

> George F. Kennan, U.S. Ambassador to the Soviet Union, declared today that he and other Western diplomats resided in Moscow in an "icy-cold" atmosphere of isolation so complete that he could not talk even to his guides or servants except on simple business. . . .
>
> His isolation in the Soviet capital today is worse than he experienced as an interned U.S. diplomat in Germany after Pearl Harbor when the Nazis declared war on the United States, Mr. Kennan said.
>
> The only modification he offered about this statement was that in Moscow he and other Western officials were permitted to walk about the streets.

Kennan thought he had made the comment off the record. There was airplane noise, though, and if he did restrict it, he didn't do so loudly enough. "Correct or incorrect, accurate or inaccurate, it was an extremely foolish thing for me to have said."[55]

He saw at once that he had gone too far. "Don't be a boy, and don't feed the little ego," he scribbled in his notebook, just below his practice press conference, probably on the next leg of the flight to London—the shakiness of the handwriting suggests nervousness or turbulence or both. "Be deliberate. Learn not to mind pauses and silences. . . . Never be a raconteur unless you are desperate." Upon his arrival he met Cumming, who was returning from Washington with the suicide pills Kennan had requested from the CIA. "George, why in the hell did you make that remark at Tempelhof?" Cumming asked, after watching him pocket the package. "Particularly since one thing you've always drilled in on all of us was: never, never, never, never compare the totalitarian structure of the Soviet Union with that of Nazi Germany?"

The only explanation Kennan provided was the story of Christopher and his friends playing at the Spaso House fence. "There is no Iron Curtain between children," he claimed to have been thinking, until the guards corrected him. "I was still under that emotional strain when I made that statement." "You'll probably be 'png'd' for that [declared persona non grata]," Cumming warned. "Oh, no," Kennan protested, "they wouldn't dream of a 'png.'"[56]

For a week nothing happened. Kennan met with the other chiefs of mission, cautioned them that there was no longer a "diplomatic cushion between peace and war," and came away convinced that he had made no impression, either orally or in his long dispatch: "The NATO people, as well as our own military authorities, were completely captivated and lost in the compulsive logic of the military equation." Nor was there flexibility on Germany. No one had wanted to talk about reunification, or even a mutual withdrawal of occupation forces. The only option was to wait for Moscow's authority to collapse in East Germany and in turn over all of Eastern Europe—in short, the Toon-Davies plan. "[I]t was hopeless to expect the Soviet Government to agree to any such thing as this."

What, then, was an ambassador in the U.S.S.R. to say or do? Walking the streets of London afterward with his embassy counselor Elim O'Shaughnessy, Kennan concluded "that war had to be accepted as inevitable, or very nearly so." To think that he would have to return to confront more "foul, malicious, and insulting propaganda," knowing that there was just enough truth behind it to make it impossible to challenge, "seemed to me as bitter [a reflection] as a representative of our country could ever have had."[57]

It fell to *Pravda* to spare him that prospect, when on September 26 it furiously attacked him for his Tempelhof statement. "Kennan in ecstasy lied," it shrieked, by claiming that Americans had no social contacts with Soviet citizens: had not the vice president of the International Fur and Leather Workers Union praised the ease with which his delegation talked with Muscovites during their visit a year earlier? Such "truthful and sincere words . . . nail to the pillar of shame the American slanderer under the mask of a diplomat." But Kennan had committed a much greater offense by

> comparing the situation of Americans in Moscow with what he allegedly experi-
> enced when in 1941-42 he was interned by the Nazis in Germany. . . . [O]nly a per-
> son who cannot hold back his malicious hostility to the Soviet Union could talk thus,
> who not only does not want an improvement in American-Soviet relations but is
> making use of any opportunity to make those relations worse.

This was, after all, the same Kennan who, as related by "the English journalist Parker," had sneered at the crowds celebrating Hitler's defeat outside the American embassy in May 1945: "They think that the war has ended and it is just beginning."[58]

Kennan's first instinct was to defend himself. What he had said was not new, he assured the State Department—that was true as far as it went, but he failed to mention the comparison to Nazi Germany. Instead he cited his *conciliatory* attitude toward the Soviet Union to explain *Pravda*'s anger. It had alarmed "elements" who wanted him out of Moscow, because if he ever did talk with Stalin, the old man would realize the extent to which his subordinates had "consistently misinformed him about [the] outside world." The delay in Kennan's *agrément*, his protests over the propaganda campaign, the provocateur in the embassy, the prestige he enjoyed among foreign diplomats in the city, the fact that his experience in Soviet affairs went back "farther than it is wise for even Soviet memories and acquaintances to go"—all of this had made his ambassadorship an issue within the Kremlin hierarchy beyond what the "dominant group" was willing to allow.[59]

"Cannot anticipate Department's reaction," George cabled Annelise from London, "but think it quite possible they may wish me to return and brave it out. Meanwhile there is no change in my plans, and see no reason for any change in yours at the moment. . . . Lots of love, and don't worry." The attack on Kennan, Acheson did indeed announce, had been "wholly unjustified," since he had accurately described life in the Soviet Union. Nor was the State Department planning to recall him, its press spokesman commented on the twenty-ninth, noting that "we haven't had a peep" out of Moscow regarding his status.[60]

By that time, though, Kennan had begun to grasp the paradox that confronted him. He had given up on Washington for being too warlike, but now Moscow was giving up on him for just the same reason. "What the United States Government started on one day," he lamented in his diary, "the Soviet Government finished on the next." In this exposed position, with the world watching,

> I realized for the first time that . . . I was actually the victim of a loneliness greater than any I had ever conceived, and that it was up to me to brace myself for the prospect that nowhere would I be likely to find full understanding for what I had done . . . ; that there would never be any tribunal before which I could justify myself; that there would be few friends whom I could expect ever wholly to understand my explanations.

Then, on October 3, Moscow produced not a peep but a cannon blast: Andrey Vyshinsky, the foreign minister, summoned the American *chargé d'affaires,* John McSweeney, and handed him a note declaring Kennan persona non grata for having made "slanderous attacks hostile to the Soviet Union in a rude violation of generally recognized norms of international law." It demanded his immediate recall. Kennan thereby became the first—and so far the only   U.S. minister or ambassador to be so ejected in over 230 years of Russian-American diplomatic relations.[61]

This produced, however, no major crisis. Preoccupied by the heated presidential contest between Dwight D. Eisenhower and Adlai Stevenson, most Americans hardly noticed. Even Jeanette, writing from Highland Park, devoted three pages to the election but just two sentences to George's travails. The only significant demand for severing diplomatic ties came from a right-wing Republican senator, William Knowland of California: Acheson brushed it aside, with Kennan's approval. Despite his public support, the secretary of state blamed Kennan more than he did Moscow. Kennan's had been, Acheson wrote in the single paragraph he devoted to the affair in his massive memoir, an "unusual statement by an experienced diplomat." He held the barb for the end. "I sent . . . Bohlen to accompany Ambassador Kennan to Switzerland, there to await the arrival of Mrs. Kennan and their children with such patience and taciturnity as he could summon."[62]

In fact, Kennan was already in Geneva visiting Joan, who had just enrolled at the International School, when the news of his expulsion reached him. He took refuge in a movie theater to "make myself comprehend the whole incredible reality of what had occurred"—only to find, with disgust, that he was becoming absorbed "in the damned film." So he turned to copying out lines in his notebook from Shakespeare's *Henry VIII*:

> Nay then, farewell.
> I have touched the highest point of all my greatness;
> And, from that full meridian of my glory
> I haste now to my setting; I shall fall
> Like a bright exhalation in the evening,
> And no man see me more.

But Cardinal Wolsey offered little consolation for Kennan's personal and professional humiliations, and was of no help at all in resolving a major logistical difficulty, which was how to get the family out of Moscow.[63]

That task fell chiefly to Annelise, who had already had some difficult weeks. Accompanied by Toon, she had taken Grace to Leningrad, but the police harassed them throughout the visit. They then sailed to Stockholm on a Soviet ship that had not been much better: upon docking, "we were like two colts being let out in the spring after having been in the barn!" Grace went from there back to Radcliffe, while Annelise met Joan in Denmark and dropped her off in Geneva. Then in Bonn, visiting John and Patricia Davies, Annelise came down with ptomaine poisoning. After recovering, she flew back to Moscow on September 18, using the Air Force plane that was to take George out the next day. It "wasn't much fun," she recalled, being buzzed by a Soviet fighter on the descent, and upon landing "the first thing I heard about was the microphone they had found." But Wendy and Christopher could not be without at least one parent. "George flew to London this morning and I am left behind," Annelise wrote Jeanette on the nineteenth, in an unusual acknowledgment that she was beginning to feel sorry for herself: "It seems like a mistake."[64]

She learned from McSweeney, immediately after he saw Vyshinsky on October 3, that George had been declared *persona non grata*. As surprised as everyone else, Annelise now had to organize an abrupt departure. She had agreed to dine and attend a dance concert that evening with the wife of the British ambassador, who was also away. With the news still secret, "I felt like a fool—I couldn't tell her. I thought: 'This is the last time. I'm never going to do this again.'" By the time she returned to Spaso, the word was out. "They asked: 'When can you leave?' I said: 'I can leave as soon as that plane can get in!'"

It came on October 8. Annelise gave a party that afternoon for the entire embassy staff, the American journalists, the crew of the plane, and Father Louis Robert Brassard, a Catholic priest serving the diplomatic community in Moscow. He offered her a ticket for that evening's performance of Prokofiev's *Romeo and Juliet*. Annelise was reluctant to go by herself, so he came up with another one using his Belgian embassy connections, and she took Mrs. McSweeney. "That was my last night in Moscow."[65]

The next morning Annelise, the two children, and their three Danish servants left for Cologne, where George was to meet them, on the now ubiquitous Air Force plane. "Embassy staff and quasi totality of non satellite diplomatic corps were present at her departure," O'Shaughnessy cabled the State Department: the military attachés showed up in full uniform. "Whether or not I had been up to my job," George recalled, in admiration, "she had been up to hers."[66]

VII.

The postmortems began at once: how could so skilled a diplomat have said such a stupid thing? Kennan at first feigned insouciance. "I have a good conscience about the matter," he wrote his old Princeton classmate Bernard Gufler at the end of October. The Soviets would not have expelled him unless he was making them "uncomfortable" by "coming too close to the exposure of some of their frauds and outrages, which it seems to me it was my job to do." He was happy not to have to go back, and expected to spend another year and a half in Washington before becoming eligible for retirement.[67]

But had it indeed been his job, a British Foreign Office professional wondered, to deliver "an unforgivable insult to Soviet ears" and to do it, of all places, in Berlin? "As 'Mr. X', and perhaps as a too-penetrating observer, [Kennan] has never in reality been persona grata; once he stepped outside what the Russians consider the role of an ambassador, the Soviet leaders may have taken some malicious pleasure in making him look rather foolish." Kennan had weakened the position of all

Western diplomats in Moscow, Joxe complained. He would never be allowed back in the U.S.S.R. An Irish journalist called Kennan's Tempelhof outburst "one of the worse gaffes of postwar diplomacy."[68]

Given how often Kennan had stressed the need to avoid provocations, one of the Moscow embassy's junior provocateurs, Dick Davies, wondered if he had done it on purpose. Having built himself up as "the right man in the right spot at the right time," Kennan found it intolerable that Stalin had not received him and that the atmosphere in Moscow had been so hostile. "[T]here is a great hand pressing down on all of us," Davies remembered him saying one evening as they watched his angels—"goons," the younger man called them—insulating a theater audience from them during an intermission. Kennan believed that he had somehow failed, "both in terms of his own self-image and of the image he felt he had in the eyes of others." He could not resign: that would have been an admission of failure. "So how to get out of this? . . . [P]erhaps that was the way."[69]

Charles Burton Marshall, a member of Nitze's Policy Planning Staff who saw Kennan in Germany soon after his expulsion, was even more certain of this. If there were to be no contacts with the Soviet leadership, Marshall remembered him saying, then there was no point to remaining in Moscow, but there was a compelling reason to come home. Eisenhower would be elected president and would probably appoint John Foster Dulles as his secretary of state. Recognizing his own limitations, Dulles would make Kennan his under secretary. Kennan would agree, on the condition that Eisenhower and Dulles repudiate McCarthyism unequivocally. It was thus necessary to return to Washington, for there would be a lot to do in getting the new administration under way.[70]

The only source for this conversation is Marshall's memory three decades later. It's possible, though, that Kennan could have said something like this. He needed a better explanation for what had happened than that he had lost control of himself, as he had initially admitted to Cumming, over an interrupted children's game. And he was capable of erratic grandiosity. He had felt neglected in Moscow while simultaneously placing himself at the center of Stalin's concerns. Why should he not have assumed that Washington, which had also neglected him, was now eagerly awaiting his arrival?

Two pieces of contemporary evidence suggest that he did. Kennan had alerted the State Department back in July that he might have to resign if John Paton Davies were convicted of perjury. Both presidential candidates were busy, he knew, but it might be worth letting them know "that this cloud hangs over my own future," for "they will both find that the problem of replacing me [in Moscow] is not the simplest of problems." Then on October 7, four days after it had become clear, for a different reason, that he would have to be replaced, Kennan suggested to Bohlen that he be reassigned to the National Security Council to assess Soviet develop- ments for the president and the secretary of state. He did not specify which ones, but he knew that Truman and Acheson would not be there much longer. Bohlen responded positively, but—on Acheson's instructions—he did not encourage Kennan to hurry home.[71]

If Kennan had *not* meant to provoke his own expulsion, Paul Mason, the assis- tant under secretary in the British Foreign Office, observed, then "his lack of self control is extraordinary." So Adam Watson, of the Washington embassy, sought an explanation from Bohlen, now back from seeing Kennan in Geneva. Kennan had hoped to keep the Kremlin from grievous miscalculations like those of Hitler with respect to the British in 1939 or Stalin's in setting off the Korean War, Bohlen surmised. But the "Hate America" campaign, together with his own isolation, had quickly convinced Kennan that this would not be possible. Feeling "that sense of escape from prison which people have when they emerge from behind the Iron Curtain," he had spoken unguardedly at Tempelhof, believing his comments to be off the record. Kennan had not done so to "see whether they would throw him out," Bohlen insisted, but Watson could not help wondering "whether sub- consciously he did not feel inclined to take some risk."[72]

In fact, Bohlen himself was mystified. "Why he did it, I don't know," he recalled when asked about the incident years later. "George is certainly an experienced enough man . . . to realize that you can't make a statement [like that] without hav- ing it get in the papers." It had been "one of the most extraordinary things in George's career." But Bohlen was able to determine, to his satisfaction, why the Soviets responded in the way that they did. Two years after Eisenhower appointed him as Kennan's successor—Bohlen had arrived in Moscow in April 1953, five weeks after Stalin's death—he found himself in a conversation with Politburo members Anastas Mikoyan and Lazar Kaganovich at a diplomatic reception. All Kremlin leaders including Stalin, they assured Bohlen, had held Kennan in high regard "as a serious and intelligent student of Soviet affairs." They particu- larly respected ambassadors "who stood up firmly for their country's interest," as opposed to those "who attempt to ingratiate themselves with the Soviet Gov- ernment by hypocrisy or other means." They regretted the remarks that had led to Kennan's expulsion and were still not able to understand how he could have "departed from the accepted tenets of diplomacy."

Bohlen defended his friend, pointing out how "tricky" it was to deal with the press in impromptu settings, something with which Soviet officials had little expe-rience: the expulsion had been "far and away beyond the requirements of the situ-ation." But the problem, Mikoyan explained, was where Kennan had made his remarks: "In Berlin it was too much. That we should be insulted precisely from Berlin was intolerable." Both men seemed to be saying, Bohlen concluded, "that it was Stalin himself who had ordered George's expulsion."[73]

Kennan eventually acknowledged having provoked his own expulsion. All of his excuses, he admitted in his 1972 memoir, had been attempts to "salve the wounded ego. . . . At heart, I was deeply shamed and shaken by what had occurred." Had he really been fit for the job in the first place? He was a good reporting officer, he thought, and did not normally shatter crockery. He had not understood, to be sure, that he was simply to "keep the seat warm" in Moscow until the next administration took over: "A little more clarity on this point might have . . . helped me to accept more philosophically the irritations of the situation into which I had been placed." But even with such guidance,

> I was probably too highly strung emotionally, too imaginative, too sensitive, and too impressed with the importance of my own opinions, to sit quietly on that par-ticular seat. For this, one needed a certain phlegm, a certain contentment with the trivia of diplomatic life, a readiness to go along uncomplainingly with the conven-tional thinking of Washington, and a willingness to refrain from asking unnecessary questions—none of which I possessed in adequate degree.

The exposure of these inadequacies was painful at the time and would long remain so. "When I reflect, however, that it [caused a] change in my own life which I would never have encompassed on my own initiative, I realize that I must not protest this turn of fate too much. God's ways are truly unfathomable. Who am I to say that I could have arranged it better?"[74]

VIII.

George, Annelise, Christopher, and Wendy waited out the 1952 presidential election in the comfortable guest quarters of the U.S. high commissioner in Bad Godesberg. "Just what dangers my presence in the country would have added to the fortunes of the Democratic party I was unable to imagine," George recalled, "but I was thoroughly humbled by what had just befallen me, and was in no mood to argue." Following Eisenhower's landslide victory on November 4, the family sailed for home on the SS *America*, arriving in New York on the eleventh. All four Kennans rated photographs in the *New York Herald Tribune* and *The New York Times*, but George was wary about answering questions. "I would like to say something," he assured the reporters, but he refrained apart from observing, when asked whether the Moscow post was the most difficult an American diplomat could take, "I think your imagination will tell you as much as I could say."[75]

With the Princeton house rented in the expectation of a longer Moscow stay, the only place the Kennans could go was the Pennsylvania farm: not unusually, it was in need of repairs. As far as the U.S. government was concerned, George F. Kennan was still its ambassador to the Soviet Union: he would remain so until his replacement was named. But he spent these weeks negotiating only with plumbers, carpenters, and painters, while doing a fair amount of the work himself. The family were well and happy to be back, Jeanette wrote Kent after spending Thanksgiving with them, although "disappointed not to have been able to continue their good work in Moscow." It was just for that reason, she added, that the Soviets wanted "to get rid of them." The method chosen "was very harmless compared to what it might have been."[76]

Kennan saw Acheson shortly after his arrival and paid his respects to Truman early in December. Neither mentioned a future appointment: both had "the far-away look of men who know that they are about to be relieved of heavy responsibilities." Back in town on the eighteenth to deliver his customary end-of-term lecture at the National War College, Kennan avoided any discussion of recent events other than to acknowledge, regarding the challenge of communism, that "we have held our own." Mistakes had been made, but with proper attention to lessons learned, there was no reason why, fifteen or twenty years hence, "our children will still not be listening to the World Series and running around in Chevrolets and doing all the things we associate with the American way of life."[77]

By Christmas, the work at the farm was mostly done. Joan was home from Geneva, Grace had arrived from Radcliffe, and the Burlinghams—Annelise's sister Mossik's American relatives—were also there. "[Y]ou can imagine how very lively it was," Annelise wrote Frieda Por. "It is nice to be a large noisy family." Meanwhile George had thanked Kent for the grapefruit, "the like of which we never see locally." With fifteen people in the house, it had come in handy. The house was Chekhovian in a happier sense, then, than when they had left it in April: the Cherry Orchard outside East Berlin remained reassuringly distant from Moscow.

"I thought it was unfortunate what he said," Annelise replied many years later, when asked about George's Tempelhof embarrassment. "He should certainly never have said it, and I think he feels that way himself." She was sure, though, that if he had said nothing at all, "they would have tried to do something else. They had decided that they were going to get him out. I think they would have done something much worse."[78]

NINETEEN

Finding a Niche: 1953–1955

"I HAVE NO IDEA WHAT IS GOING TO HAPPEN TO ME AFTER THE 20th of January," George wrote Kent on Christmas Day 1952, "but think it doubtful that I shall be given any post of major political responsibility." One reason was that he had worked with Democrats, and that "my name has been prominently connected with the word 'containment,' which has gone out of style." Another was that "I have had the temerity to say things about the role of morality in foreign policy which sound disrespectful of some of the favorite poses of American statesmen." He had only a year and a quarter to go before becoming eligible for retirement, however. At that point, "I hope to leave government service altogether and contribute what I can, thenceforth, as a scholar, commentator, and critic."[1]

This bleak assessment reflected the fact that Eisenhower, as expected, had nominated John Foster Dulles to be his secretary of state. Kennan's relationship with Dulles had been strained since shortly after the outbreak of the Korean War, when they differed over the desirability of admitting Mao's China to the United Nations and of sending MacArthur's forces across the 38th parallel: Dulles had described Kennan at the time as a "dangerous man." With Dulles's encouragement, Republican demands to replace "containment" with "liberation" had dominated the 1952 presidential campaign, and on September 26—the day *Pravda* attacked Kennan for his Tempelhof statement—Dulles also attacked him in a St. Louis speech for having repudiated, in *American Diplomacy*, legal and moral principles. "I disagree and have long disagreed with his basic philosophy," Dulles explained to a friend who thought the criticism unfair, "and have repeatedly made this clear on many occasions."[2]

Nevertheless, he was careful to send Kennan, who was still in Bad Godesberg, a copy of what he had said: "As you will see, I took issue with . . . your recent book.

I hope you will not feel that I did so in any improper way." Kennan responded by forwarding his unpublished reply to Father Walsh's harsher denunciations, as a way of conveying "a somewhat clearer idea of how I feel about morality in foreign policy." Dulles acknowledged this as "clarifying" but insisted that "there are certain basic moral concepts which all peoples and nations can and do comprehend, and to which it is legitimate to appeal as providing some common standard of international conduct."[3]

The correspondence veiled changes of mind by both men. Dulles was distancing himself from "containment" despite the fact that he and his fellow Republicans had supported that concept when Kennan first articulated it: they raised no significant objections during the 1948 campaign. But in the aftermath of the Democrats' victory that year, the Soviet atomic bomb, the communist takeover in China, espionage revelations, the Korean War, and China's intervention in that conflict, Dulles had come to regard "containment" as fair game; hence his call for "liberation" as an alternative. Meanwhile Kennan was distancing himself from his own support, while running the Policy Planning Staff, for efforts to detach the Soviet Union from its satellites. Given the sensitivities he had witnessed in Moscow, Republican promises of "liberation" could, he worried, provoke a major war.[4]

Even if Kennan had not expected to become Dulles's chief foreign policy adviser, as Charles Burton Marshall would subsequently claim, he did assume that the new administration "would still attach value to my opinions and to the preservation of a mutual relationship of cordiality and understanding." Weeks passed without any word, however, "and I, over-proud and over-shy as usual, was reluctant to make the first move." That was the situation when George wrote Kent on Christmas Day. Friends and colleagues were beginning to treat him, he later recalled, "with the elaborate politeness and forbearance one reserves for someone who has committed a social gaffe too appalling for discussion. . . . It was as though my objective judgment had been somehow discredited with my discretion."[5]

There were, nonetheless, invitations to speak, most of which he declined. Kennan made an exception, however, for the annual meeting of the Pennsylvania State Bar Association in Scranton on January 16, 1953. "I am now a resident of Pennsylvania," he explained to the State Department, "but have had very little opportunity to take part in civic affairs here, and feel that this is one way I can show an . . . appreciation for the many kindnesses people have shown me." He had said nothing publicly about Soviet-American relations while serving as ambassador, and silence might also be necessary in any new appointment: "It seemed to me, therefore, that any statement I might make on this subject should be made during the incumbency of the old administration, in order that the new one might remain wholly uncommitted by what I had said." Kennan submitted his text for review, and Bohlen, in his capacity as counselor, cleared it.[6]

He was hardly the first American who had gone to Moscow with high hopes and disappointing results, Kennan reminded his audience: "My own recent experience was unusual in form, but not in content." Soviet hostility arose from "*their* necessities, not ours." It would give way eventually "to something more healthy, because Providence has a way of punishing those who persist long and willfully in ignoring great realities." The most prudent American response would be to stay strong and remain calm, while waiting for this to happen.

At this point, though, Kennan's rhetoric ensnared him yet again. He chose this moment—four days before Eisenhower's inauguration, one day after Dulles had reiterated his commitment to "liberation" before the Senate Foreign Relations Committee—to denounce that concept:

> It is not consistent with our international obligations. It is not consistent with a common membership with other countries in the United Nations. It is not consistent with the maintenance of formal diplomatic relations with another country. It is replete with possibilities for misunderstanding and bitterness. To the extent that it might be successful, it would involve us in heavy responsibilities. Finally the prospects for success would be very small indeed; since the problem of civil obedience is not a great problem to the modern police dictatorship.

There was no place in foreign policy for "emotionalism, the striking of heroic attitudes, and demagoguery of all sorts, . . . no place for impulsiveness, no place for self-seeking, no place for irresponsible experiments, and no place for the spotlight of sensationalism." It was as if he invited the front-page headline that ran the next morning in *The Washington Post*: "Dulles Policy 'Dangerous,' Kennan Says."

The story, by Ferdinand Kuhn, reported that "the foremost government expert on Russia" had "sounded a warning last night against the John Foster Dulles policy of encouraging the liberation of captive peoples in Europe and Asia." It didn't matter that Kennan had neither named Dulles nor used the word "dangerous." It appeared "that I had attacked a Secretary [of State] before he had even taken office. I hadn't meant to do that." Professing shock at what had happened, claiming that he had not had Dulles in mind and had no significant differences with him,

Kennan asked Doc Matthews to let the new secretary know that all he wanted was "to make myself useful in some capacity until I become eligible for retirement." Any job appropriate to his rank and experience would do.[7]

Dulles asked to see Kennan on January 23, listened to his explanation but promised no new appointment. That afternoon his press spokesman, Michael McDermott, announced that the secretary regarded the matter as "closed." Did that mean, a reporter asked, that Kennan "is in good standing and that everything is fine and dandy?" Dulles had been "too busy on other things" to think about Kennan's future, McDermott replied, but the Scranton speech would not jeopardize it. "Still not a single word or hint," Kennan fretted on the twenty-fifth; "nor has any one in the new administration [sought] my opinion about anything to do with the Soviet Union." Several weeks later he was still in a state of suspension, "the only advantages of which are that I continue to receive salary checks (as Ambassador) and am under no obligation to be in Washington."[8]

"[W]e still don't know any more about what we are going to do," Annelise complained to Jeanette, except that "with each appointment it seems to become clear that they are not going to use their top Foreign Service people for much." "To say that we are on tenterhooks," Jeanette commiserated, seemed slight "compared to what *you* must be feeling." Things were "going very badly indeed," George admitted to Annelise early in February. It was "not just that they have been too busy. There has been a decision that I am not to be consulted or used in any way in this country, but am to be 'sent away' as a sort of punishment for my association with the Truman administration." It might be Turkey or Yugoslavia, and under normal circumstances he would be happy to have either of those posts. In the current climate, though, he was inclined to retire if, as it now appeared, he might be allowed to do so. That would require "a pretty drastic financial readjustment," but "the more I see of the new administration, the less I wish to have anything to do with it."[9]

After learning that Eisenhower had asked Bohlen to replace him in Moscow, Kennan twice sought clarification of his status from Dulles: he was still the U.S. ambassador to the Soviet Union, and the president would at some point have to accept his resignation. But the secretary of state chose not to respond to either of these communications, despite the fact that the second one was written while Kennan was in Washington consulting with Bohlen and Allen Dulles, the new director of the CIA, on the implications of Stalin's death, which had occurred on March 5. The uncertainty finally ended on the twelfth with a call from William H. Lawrence of *The New York Times*, who let Kennan know that he would not be getting another post. Under Foreign Service rules, any ambassador not assigned to a new one within three months of leaving the previous one had to retire. Lawrence published his story the next day, revealing that Kennan's pension would be $7,000 annually, about $500 less than it would have been with a final ambassadorship.[10]

Only at that point—Friday, March 13, 1953—did the secretary of state call Kennan in to tell him "that he knew of no 'niche' for me in government at this time, and thought I would have difficulty getting confirmation by the Senate for any representative position, tainted as I am with 'containment.'" And then, as if nothing had happened, Dulles asked Kennan to assess the implications of Stalin's demise: "You interest me when you talk about these matters. Very few other people do." It was, Kennan thought, as if he had told Annelise that he was divorcing her but had added that "I love the way you cook scrambled eggs, and I wonder if you'd mind fixing me up a batch of them right now, before you go." The two men parted, Kennan reported to Oppenheimer, "in what was apparently a hearty agreement that I should now retire, although our reasons for this view were not identical."[11]

Kennan asked Dulles to announce the arrangement as soon as possible but another long silence ensued, until on April 6 he was shown a draft statement implying that he was retiring at his own request. He refused to approve it, so Dulles—claiming confusion—called him in again the next day to ask what he really wanted. That depended, Kennan replied, on whether the secretary of state and the president really wanted him. Dulles again dithered, so Kennan wrote the press release himself:

> Mr. Kennan expects to retire from the Foreign Service in the near future and to return to private activity in the academic field. He hopes to be able to . . . function, following his retirement, as a regular consultant to the Government. These plans are the result of discussions between him and the Secretary, and are agreeable to both.

It had been, Kennan admitted to Acheson, "a strange and chilling experience." His ambassadorship ended officially on April 29, but George remained on call in Washington for another three months, so he and Annelise rented a house on Quebec Street for the summer.

When his last day at the State Department came, Kennan spent the morning working in an empty office, had lunch, and then went looking for Hessman, who would be staying on for a few weeks. Not finding her, he left a note saying "that I was leaving and would not be back—ever." He was able to take leave of another secretary and the fifth-floor receptionist: "We all nearly wept." Then he rode the elevator down, "as on a thousand other occasions, and suddenly there I was on the steps of the building, in the baking glaring heat: a retired officer, a private citizen, after 27 years of official life. I was not unhappy."

Perhaps—but it was an inglorious conclusion to an illustrious career. No Foreign Service officer had advanced more rapidly within its ranks. None had more significantly shaped grand strategy at the highest levels of government. None had created, if inadvertently, a "school" of international relations theory. And yet Kennan walked out of the State Department on July 29, 1953, with hardly anyone noticing. He was not prepared to reflect, at that point, on how this had happened: "Someone else, I knew, would have to strike the balance, if one was ever to be struck, between justice and injustice, failure and accomplishment."[12]

I.

"Why hell," Senator Homer Ferguson of Michigan told Kennan, after learning that Dulles had denied him a new appointment, "you wouldn't have had any trouble getting confirmed." Ferguson had asked to see Kennan to get his opinion of Bohlen, whose Moscow nomination had run into trouble. The problem was Yalta, the wartime conference associated now, in the minds of Republicans eager for "liberation," with the alleged "sell-out" of Eastern Europe. Bohlen had attended as Roosevelt's interpreter and one of his advisers. So had Alger Hiss. That was enough to upset Ferguson, despite Kennan's reassurances. It infuriated Joseph McCarthy and his senatorial allies.

Eisenhower fought back: otherwise, he feared, he would be relinquishing his authority over the conduct of foreign policy. The battle, which consumed most of March 1953, was heated, public, and ultimately successful. It was the first time the White House had defended a Foreign Service officer accused of disloyalty—Truman had done little to assist John Paton Davies and others similarly accused. The victory was all the more important given Dulles's demands, which had offended many of his State Department subordinates, that they "positively" demonstrate their patriotism. But even as Eisenhower struggled to save Bohlen, he did nothing to retain Kennan who, as the Alsops pointedly noted in their column on April 12, would have accepted a position if one had been offered him. His "unequalled knowledge" and "intuitive brilliance" were assets "the American

Government cannot replace at any price." The *Chicago Sun-Times* ran an editorial cartoon a few days later showing Dulles in a baseball uniform winding up for a pitch, with an empty second base labeled "George Kennan's retirement" looming behind him.[13]

Kennan was the same age as Bohlen, similarly trained, and—in Ferguson's view, at least—less controversial. He had not been at Yalta and had made no secret of his objections to Roosevelt's policies. His "X" article had been an attack on Henry Wallace. He was, to be sure, the architect of "containment" and had spoken out against "liberation," but it would have been hard to portray the author of *American Diplomacy* as a dangerously naïve idealist. Nor would it have been easy to suspect him of sympathy for the Soviet Union, that country having just kicked him out. And even if Dulles did not think highly of Kennan, Eisenhower did: he knew Kennan from the National War College, the Council on Foreign Relations, and the Policy Planning Staff. "I respect the man's mind as well as his integrity and knowledge," he had written a friend in 1950. As president of Columbia University, Eisenhower even tried to recruit Kennan to run its Institute of War and Peace Studies. Why did he not, then, as president of the United States, insist that his secretary of state find Kennan a "niche"?[14]

The Bohlen nomination fight suggests one reason. Kennan was not as vulnerable, but Dulles had attacked him during the campaign and Kennan appeared to have struck back in his Scranton speech. Eisenhower didn't need another controversy just at this moment. Moreover, Kennan had mentioned retirement in the apology he asked Matthews to convey to Dulles: "This was foolish. I shouldn't have done it." Dulles was "a cagey, tricky man," with no appreciation of what lay behind this gesture: "He simply used this as a way of getting rid of me." Kennan could have "raised hell" by going to Eisenhower and saying: "Look here, I've [had] an honorable career. How can you let me be fired in this way?" But Dulles could have simply said: "I understood you'd wanted to leave the Service."[15]

There was, however, a deeper issue, which was that Kennan had made himself hard to place: it's revealing that Acheson, exasperated by the Tempelhof gaffe, had offered no new appointment either. Unlike Bohlen, always a smooth operator, Kennan had gained a reputation for brittleness. "He doesn't bend," Isaiah Berlin recalled. "He breaks." Years later Robert R. Bowie, who became Dulles's Policy Planning Staff director, suggested some reasons why.

Kennan had the intuitions and insights—but also the volatility—of a poet, Bowie thought: these made him too "reactive." Convinced that people in power were taking the wrong direction, he would simplify and thus dramatize his argument, as in his call for toughness toward the U.S.S.R. in the "long telegram" and the "X" article. That would persuade them, but Kennan would then worry that they had gone too far. They were now seeing the Soviets "as an implacable foe, not subject to change, and not open to the ordinary rules of Great Power rivalry." So Kennan would jump to the opposite camp, where once more he would exaggerate "because he feels it's so important to get things back into balance. And so it goes."

With constituencies to hold together and coalitions to maintain, Bowie pointed out, governments can't manage such fine adjustments. Acheson understood that, but "I don't think George feels those constraints, or if he does feel them I think he resists them. Getting it intellectually right is of very high value." Kennan had an "academic" mentality, in that he always wanted to reconsider things. He preferred committing himself not "to a course of action, but to a course of analysis, and therefore if he gets better insights later on, he not only feels free but feels obligated to modify it." In doing so, his empathy would "go deaf." That left Kennan surprised when people took what he had said or done in ways he hadn't anticipated. Of course the Soviets were going to expel him after he compared life in Moscow to internment in Nazi Germany, but he was "genuinely taken aback." Of course the Scranton speech was going to offend Dulles, but Kennan just "didn't visualize it."

Bowie saw one other problem, which was that the higher Kennan rose in the Foreign Service, the more he took things personally. However passionate his prose, the author of the "long telegram" had not seen himself as the target of Stalin's hostility. The recently expelled ambassador to the Soviet Union did see himself in this way. Kennan was convinced, his friend Bill Bundy added, "that they were deliberately doing nasty things to *him*, not just to the United States." His "extreme sensitivity" made it hard for him not to be affected even in situations "where there was nothing you could do about it." Success in government was a kind of "slavery," Berlin explained, because the more responsibility you wielded, the less freedom you had to say what you really thought. "The State Department dehydrates you."[16]

Eisenhower sensed without saying so that Kennan had outlived his usefulness as a diplomat: he made no effort to reverse Dulles's decision. At least one White House aide, though, believed that Kennan was being shabbily treated. The secretary of state's dislike for Kennan's "theorizing" was understandable, Emmet John Hughes, a presidential speechwriter, pointed out to Chief of Staff Sherman Adams. But there was a difference "between (a) the manifest right to 'ease out' a diplomat whose views are felt to be contrary to prevailing policy and (b) the use of this right in a way that is needlessly rude and perhaps offensive not only to one man but to the service he represents." Dulles had let two months pass without acknowledging Kennan's resignation. Now he was using "the crude—and silent—expedient of simply failing to offer him a diplomatic post," a procedure "designed for the dismissal of plain incompetents." It was a "singular and studied insult."

"I can appreciate and must respect your wishes [to retire]," Eisenhower wrote to Kennan on July 8, using a draft Hughes had prepared. "Your years of devoted work in the Foreign Service certainly entitle you to such a choice." It would have been a routine send-off, had it not been for the fact that, at just this moment and in a characteristically subtle way, the president was making Kennan his top, if temporary, policy planner. His assignment—of which Hughes knew nothing—was to liberate Eisenhower from the "liberation" strategy to which Dulles had tried to commit him during the 1952 campaign.

II.

Dulles's bluster had long made Eisenhower uneasy, but in a Republican Party still dominated by isolationists and McCarthyites, he seemed the only plausible possibility to run the Department of State. Despite the president's military background, it was not his habit to discipline subordinates: instead, he sought to *educate* his secretary of state and others within his administration about the probable risks, costs, and consequences of a more aggressive strategy. The mechanism was Project Solarium, an elaborate National Security Council exercise Eisenhower authorized in May 1953. Three "teams" would make the case, respectively, for "containment" as the Truman administration had understood it; for "deterrence," which would involve threatening nuclear retaliation if the Soviet Union or its allies attempted further gains anywhere; and for "liberation," which meant using political, psychological, economic, and covert methods to reverse the advances those adversaries had already made. The president asked Kennan, still on the State Department payroll, to chair the first group, "Task Force A."[17]

Consisting of seven members each, the teams met at the National War College from June 10 to July 15. They had access to everything, Kennan recalled, even the most sensitive intelligence information. "It was all highly secret. . . . I was not permitted—nobody was permitted—to say anything about it." The cover story, which Kennan used even in his private diary, was that the work involved updating the school's curriculum. "We all knew we couldn't expect to put our own personal opinion through pure, that we would have to come to some sort of a collective idea.... And that we did."[18]

Task Force A's report nevertheless reflected Kennan's thinking throughout its 152 pages. It identified three great principles, each consistent with what he had been arguing since returning from Moscow in 1946:

> First, the U.S. must avoid ... pursuing in time of peace aims which have essentially a wartime objective: namely, the complete destruction or unconditional surrender of the enemy. Accordingly, we must see to it that our negotiating positions vis-à-vis the Soviet Union appear sincere and reasonable, and that U.S. power appears everywhere as power for peace.
>
> Second, the U.S. must take great pains to create an impression of steadiness and reliability in the formulation and implementation of its foreign policy. This means that special emphasis must be laid on discipline and unity of approach, ... avoiding every indication of abruptness or erratic behavior.
>
> Third, the positive emphasis of U.S. policy must be placed on ... the creation generally within the non-Communist area of an atmosphere of confidence and hope. These efforts should not be openly related in each case to the winning of the cold war, but should be addressed in good faith primarily to basic and long-term problems ..., many of which would exist in important degree even if there were no Soviet Union.

Contrary to Dulles's claims, the United States and its allies were already stronger than their adversaries. With "the wise and flexible application of [this] integrated national strategy," that advantage would "bring about the diminution of Soviet-Communist external influence until it ceases to be a substantial threat to peace and security."

Two great temptations, Kennan warned, might deflect the nation from this course. One was resorting to war, a path "full of risk, empty of calculation, and unwarrantedly hazardous to the continued existence of the U.S." The other was succumbing to internal "totalitarian" pressures, for that would ruin the reputation of a nation seeking to lead the world in "the defense of free institutions." Within those limits, the United States could expect the "progressive retraction of Soviet control" from Eastern Europe and China; the "discrediting of Soviet power and Communist ideology" elsewhere; and an increase "in internal stresses and conflicts within the Soviet system," which would force its rulers "to accept the necessity of adjusting their objectives to those of peaceful co-existence with the Free World."

Kennan even got Task Force A to endorse his own Program A. The United States should seek "a reunified, sovereign, independent Germany with a democratic form of government." All foreign occupation forces would withdraw, or at least retreat to enclaves supplied by sea. The new state would have its own military establishment, except for "atomic or other weapons of mass destruction." And it would operate free from political control by either the Soviet Union or the West. If Stalin's successors accepted these proposals, they would have rolled back their own influence in Central Europe. If they rejected them, they would "bear the onus of remaining in East Germany solely on the basis of naked power." This policy would achieve beneficial results "under either eventuality."[19]

The Task Force A report easily overshadowed the others in the force of its logic and the quality of its prose. It showed that "containment" and "liberation" were not mutually exclusive, indeed that the first could bring about the second. It stressed the extent to which irresponsibility in choosing means—whether by too casually risking war or by too fecklessly indulging McCarthy—could corrupt the ultimate end, which was to preserve the American way of life. It was a far more effective attack on Dulles than Kennan's Scranton speech had been. And most important, it carried the authority of Eisenhower, who had entrusted him with preparing it in the first place.

All three task forces presented their recommendations to the president and his top advisers at a White House meeting on July 16, 1953. As Kennan began speaking, he was amused to find a "silent and humble but outwardly respectful" Dulles sitting in the first row: "I could talk, and he had to listen." Eisenhower, fully in charge, dominated the discussion that followed. What he said convinced Kennan that "he was prepared to accept the thesis we had put forward, that our approach to the Soviet Union, as it had been followed in the immediately preceding years, was basically sound." Some adjustments might be necessary, but "there was no need for a drastic change." If, therefore, Dulles had triumphed "by disembarrassing himself of my person, I . . . had my revenge by saddling him, inescapably, with my policy."[20]

Historians, on the whole, have sustained that judgment. Kennan would find much to criticize in the Eisenhower-Dulles strategy as it evolved over the next seven and a half years: his chief concerns were its reliance on nuclear retaliation as a way of minimizing containment's costs, and its refusal to seek a reunified Germany. But in its doubts that the Soviet Union would risk war, in its determination to apply Western strengths against Communist weaknesses, in its willingness to wait for contradictions within the latter system to shatter its unity while sustaining strength and self-confidence in the United States and among its allies—in all of these things, the "New Look," as it came to be called, was closer to Kennan's strategy than NSC 68 had been.[21]

Kennan's departure from government, therefore, was not as lonely as he made it look in his memoirs. For even though Dulles gave him no appointment, Eisenhower accepted the basic elements of the strategy Kennan had designed under Marshall's supervision: it was not irrelevant that Eisenhower worked for Marshall longer during the war than Kennan had after it. And so Kennan's final act as a policy planner was to explain all of this to a newly deferential secretary of state, as well as to the president and the vice president of the United States, the secretary of defense, the Joint Chiefs of Staff, the secretaries of the Army, Navy, and Air Force, and the director of the CIA. It may not have been a "niche," but it was a more prestigious platform than he had occupied before—or ever would again.

III.

"We reflect that you are a Member of the Institute for Advanced Study, and have much unfinished to do," Oppenheimer had cabled Kennan on October 6, 1952, three days after the Soviet Union declared him persona non grata. "We hope the time will come when you will be happy to reflect on this too." Kennan responded gratefully: "No mark of confidence received means more to me." It was not yet clear that he would be leaving government, but when he did, the best contribution he could make would probably be "the independent pursuit of truth . . . in the field of public affairs." His time away from the Institute had made him appreciate all the more its benefits. Oppenheimer renewed the invitation in March 1953, on the day he read in *The New York Times* that Kennan would be retiring: "I want you to be quite sure that in addition to the formal welcome, of which your membership here is a warrant, there is a deeper welcome that awaits you whenever and in whatever form you can accept it."[22]

There were, as usual, other opportunities. Freedom House wanted Kennan to become its president: he politely declined. The Johns Hopkins School of Advanced

International Studies hoped that he would help build a research center in Washington for refugees from government like himself: Kennan liked the idea but balked at having to do fund-raising. Allen Dulles made it clear that if his older brother did not wish to employ Kennan, he did; Walter Bedell Smith, the younger Dulles's predecessor at the CIA, enthusiastically seconded this proposal. Kennan respected both men, but the organization's increasing reliance on covert operations worried him; its cooperation with the Ford Foundation had not gone well; and it had, he believed, mishandled the Davies case, an unresolved issue for which he felt personally responsible. With one exception, Oppenheimer and Kennan's other Princeton friends all felt that he should make the break from government a clean one, "and not permit the situation to be obscured by getting loaned to the CIA. The more I thought about it, the more this seemed to me to be the correct answer, too."[23]

That left the Institute, Kennan's preference all along, and the arrangements were quickly made. Dean Rusk, the new president of the Rockefeller Foundation, had no problem persuading Robert Lovett, John J. McCloy, and his other trustees to approve a grant of $15,000 for Kennan's work during the 1953–54 academic year. "If he wanted to be at Princeton," Rusk recalled, "then this was the natural thing to do to make it possible." Oppenheimer added another $5,000, which with Kennan's Foreign Service pension brought his income close to what he had been making as an ambassador—a respectable but not munificent sum for someone maintaining a house, a farm, and a family. His responsibilities would be to seek a more "solid foundation" for his views on "utopian tendencies" in U.S. foreign policy, Kennan explained to Princeton University president Harold Dodds, and to study the internal politics of the Soviet Union during the Stalin era. "Curiosity has thrown me into contact with one, experience with the other. I would like to get both off my chest in a scholarly form before I turn to other things."[24]

The Institute appointment would not begin until the fall, though, so that left Kennan free to get other things off his chest. One was his worry that American universities were trying to teach international relations as if it were an extension of law, or some newly fashionable "social science." It was neither, he argued in the May issue of *The Atlantic Monthly*, whose editors put him on its cover. The world would never accept constitutional governance as it existed within the United States, while politics could never resemble physics because people were unpredictable. The only useful preparation for diplomacy came from history, as well as "from the more subtle and revealing expressions of man's nature" found in art and literature. Students should be reading "their Bible and their Shakespeare, their Plutarch and their Gibbon, perhaps even their Latin and their Greek." These alone would build those qualities of "honor, loyalty, generosity, [and] consideration for others" that had been the basis for effectiveness in the Foreign Service "as I have known it."

McCarthyism remained another concern. It fed on contempt for artists and writers, Kennan warned a University of Notre Dame audience in a well-publicized speech on May 15, "as though virility could not find expression in the creation of beauty, as though Michelangelo had never wielded his brush, as though Dante had never taken up his pen, as though the plays of Shakespeare were lacking in manliness." This "anti-intellectualism" flaunted its own virility, fearing that in the absence of such exhibitions, "it might be found wanting." Unchallenged, its practitioners would reduce the range of respectability to "only themselves, the excited accusers," excluding anyone not engaged in "the profession of denunciation." Having lived for years in totalitarian states, "I know where this sort of thing leads."[25]

The costs of confronting totalitarianism were on Kennan's mind two weeks later as he stood in a cemetery near East Berlin, delivering a Memorial Day address meant only for his Pennsylvania neighbors. He could hardly improve on what Lincoln had said almost ninety years earlier at a similar place only a few miles away, but he would try to reflect on the meaning those words still carried:

> Under each of these stones there lies the remains of a son of this township. Each had half a life behind him, and each should have had another half a life before him. Someone had guided each of them through the trials and illnesses of early childhood. Each of these boys had passed, before he died, through the wonder of adolescence. Each had felt in his hands, at one time or another, the same shale soil we know so well. The same winds blew. The same hills were visible to them in the distance. The same sky was overhead.
>
> When death finally faced them, each had to reconcile himself to the thought that all this should come to be as nothing, that all the love and sacrifice and hope others had placed in them should be in vain, that all the promise of life should suddenly be rendered, to all outward appearances, meaningless. With each of these deaths, some parent died a little bit, too. And to the agony of death, there must have been added the trial of knowing that many other young men did not die but were permitted to live on and complete their lives, as though nothing had happened.
>
> These young men did not die voluntarily or gladly. Like most men who die in war, they probably died in pain and misery and horror and bewilderment. The only

thought that could have helped them was that perhaps because of their death this country would be a tiny bit nearer to what they knew, and we know, it ought to be, than it would have been had they not died at all.

And for this reason the act of faith that they performed was not really complete with their passing. Part of its meaning remained to be written in by other people, and notably by ourselves. Every time we reply with selfishness and cynicism and cowardice to the demands which are placed upon us, we deal another blow to the men that lie here and to those who loved them. Every time we reply to these demands with generosity and faith and courage, we bring comfort and recompense to the souls of these people.

The point, then, was to respect "the suffering these stones tell us about," to ensure that "the dying of these men will come to make sense, as a part of the whole great story that found its supreme expression in the death of our Lord on the Cross."[26]

Kennan remained in Washington through the middle of August to run a seminar at the School of Advanced International Studies, while his family abandoned the city for the farm. Then, on the eighteenth, he emptied the Quebec Street house and drove slowly to East Berlin, "reminding myself repeatedly that there was no hurry." No one was at home when he arrived, so he spent much of the afternoon sitting quietly on the porch.

> Before me, literally, stretched the two fields: the first in wheat stubble, the second in corn, both parched and lifeless from the long drought. Behind me, figuratively, stretched 27 years of foreign service; and behind that an almost forgotten and seemingly irrelevant youth and boyhood. Ahead of me, figuratively, was only a great question-mark: somewhere between 1 and 30 years to live, presumably, and for what?

Seeking physical pleasures would be "nonsense" for someone his age. Eating and drinking invited obesity; "those of the flesh become ridiculous, unimportant, and hardly dignified." He would instead embrace "solitude, depth of thought, and writing." The first two would amount to nothing without the third, so "the great dictate" was to sit at a desk and begin. "The thoughts will come. They always do." The crickets were subdued that evening, there was a half-moon, and the night was "deathly quiet, as though waiting."[27]

IV.

On the twentieth Kennan repacked the car, tied his bicycle on top of it, and drove alone to Princeton. The Hodge Road house was "empty, battered, and barn-like," without electricity or telephone service but with poison ivy proliferating along the driveway, a broken tree branch hanging over an unkempt yard, rats in the basement, and cats in the garage. Rather than confront these crises, Kennan spent the rest of the day pondering a lay sermon he had agreed to give later that fall at the First Presbyterian Church. In search of inspiration, he went to the university bookstore, purchased John Calvin's *Institutes of the Christian Religion*, and sat on a bench outside reading it—although surely not all of it. "Very interesting," he noted, but with the family arriving soon, the rest of the month had to go to making the house habitable, a process "not conducive to theoretic thought."[28]

Oppenheimer's vagueness about Institute expectations allowed Kennan to set his own priorities. One was to answer the question he had left unanswered in *American Diplomacy*: could governments behave as individuals should? His preliminary conclusion, sketched out in his diary, was that politics, whether within or among nations, would always be a struggle for power. It could never in itself be a moral act. It followed that government was "a sad necessity and not a glorious one." Politics might, from time to time, draft moral men into government, but even they would never be "wholly unsullied," for although an individual might remain uncorrupted by power, he would have to surround himself with others who were.[29]

Foreign policy was not, therefore, a contest of good versus evil. To condemn negotiations as appeasement, Kennan told a Princeton University audience early in October, was to end a Hollywood movie with the villain shot. To entrust diplomacy to lawyers was to relegate power, "like sex, to a realm in which we see it only occasionally, and then in a highly sublimated and presentable form." Both approaches ignored the fact that most international conflicts were "jams that people have gotten themselves into." Trying to resolve them through rigid standards risked making things worse. Evil existed, to be sure: the Soviet regime reflected it, as had Nazi Germany. Sometimes you had to fight it, sometimes you had to deal with it. The important question was "what sort of compromises we make," not how to "escape altogether from the necessity of making such compromises."[30]

Dictatorships promised escapes from such dilemmas, he reminded the First Presbyterians when he delivered his sermon a few days later. Why not say "Why not?" when some Grand Inquisitor dangled relief from the discomforts of conscience and self-discipline? But that worked only until the approach of death, for which "there is no answer in the totalitarian book." In theory, there could be no grief because there was no soul, "just an accumulation of chemicals." In practice, "there is nothing more empty, nothing more mocking, than the trappings of a totalitarian funeral; for here we see the meaninglessness of life expounded and argued from the meaninglessness of death." It was easier, then, to be a Christian than not to be one; but that meant confronting "the full rigor and severity of the great ethical problems" of which the founders of that faith "were so acutely aware."[31]

Kennan spared the Presbyterians any detailed discussion of these, but when two Princeton seniors invited him to address a conference they were organizing on "Christianity Re-Examined," he could no longer evade the issue. "[W]hat they really want to know is: what I believe." He used his diary to make a list:

> Human nature not perfectible.
> Civilized life a compromise with nature.
> *Das Unbehagen in der Kultur* [which he later translated as "The Discomfort of Man in the Civilized Context"].
> No perfect human relationship.
> No perfect solutions in political matters.
> The dangers of romantic love: (love is at best a friendship and a practical partnership, complicated by an intensely intimate, impermanent and . . . unstable element that we call sex).

But was sex really sin? Had not biblical injunctions against adultery assumed polygamy, even the enslavement of women? It was hard to believe that human beings "are destined to rot in hell because their efforts to combine an animalistic nature with the discipline of civilization are not always successful." After all, it was God "who placed these dilemmas upon us."[32]

"I hope that nobody will think," Kennan cautioned the conference when it convened in December, that "I am exhorting the student body to immorality." But could it be that "the American male knows only one sexual object in life, namely the female with whom, at an appropriate age, he falls romantically and delightfully in love, whom he then marries and with whom he lives happily ever after?"

> Really, gentlemen, . . . ask yourself: "How silly can people get?" . . . [L]ook around you, among those of us who are your elders and your teachers, and I think you will find not one in a thousand of us who has met these touching and idyllic standards.

Christianity's value lay in its balancing of appetites against obligations, for Christ had shown that man could live tolerably with himself by taking responsibility for others. Only this could keep the conflict between nature and spirit from bringing disaster. The students should not brood, therefore, about whether life was worthwhile: "You might forget to live it."[33]

Kennan returned to diplomacy in four lectures—the Stafford Little series—delivered on the Princeton campus in late March 1954, with President Dodds himself in attendance. The site was Alexander Hall, "that curious relic of [the] 1890s," and "to my combined delight and consternation, the place was packed on each of these occasions to the last of its one thousand sixty uncomfortable seats." Once again, Kennan revised right up to the last moment. "Forgetting my age (like anyone just turning fifty)," he felt like "the daring young man on the flying trapeze."[34]

Despite their precarious composition, the lectures were less provocative than the ones at Chicago three years earlier, and the book they became—published by the Princeton University Press as *Realities of American Foreign Policy*—was less widely read. Kennan regarded it, nonetheless, as "the most comprehensive statement I ever made of my outlook on the basic problems of American foreign policy." Several of his themes were familiar: his respect for the Founding Fathers, his skepticism about international law and collective security, his criticism of World War II strategy, his analysis of the Soviet Union and international communism, his concern with concentrations of industrial-military power, his defense of "containment" over "liberation." There was, however, a new emphasis on material and moral ecology.

Americans could no longer afford economic advances that depleted natural resources and devastated natural beauty, Kennan insisted. Nor could they tolerate dependency, for critical raw materials, on unreliable foreign governments. Nor could they tear their democracy apart internally because threats to democracy existed externally. Nor could they entrust defenses against such dangers to the first use of nuclear weapons, for what would be left after a nuclear war had taken place? These were all single policies, pursued without regard to how each related to the others, or to the larger ends the state was supposed to serve. They neglected "the essential unity" of national problems, thus demonstrating the "danger implicit in any attempt to compartmentalize our thinking about foreign policy."

That lack of coordination ill-suited the separate "planes of international reality" upon which the United States had to compete. The first was "a sane and rational one, in which we felt comfortable, in which we were surrounded by people to

whom we were accustomed and on whose reactions we could at least depend."
The second was "a nightmarish one, where we were like a hunted beast, oblivious of everything but survival; straining every nerve and muscle in the effort to
remain alive." Within the first arena, traditional conceptions of morality applied:
"We could still be guided . . . by the American dream." Within the second, "there
was only the law of the jungle; and we had to do violence to our own traditional
principles—or many of us felt we did—to fit ourselves for the relentless struggle."
The great question, then, was whether the two could ever be brought into a coherent relationship with one another.

They could, Kennan suggested, through a kind of geopolitical horticulture: "We
must be gardeners and not mechanics in our approach to world affairs." International life was an organic process, not a static system. Americans had inherited
it, not designed it. Their preferred standards of behavior, therefore, could hardly
govern it. But it should be possible "to take these forces for what they are and to
induce them to work with us and for us by influencing the environmental stimuli
to which they are subjected." That would have to be done

> gently and patiently, with understanding and sympathy, not trying to force growth
> by mechanical means, not tearing the plants up by the roots when they fail to behave
> as we wish them to. The forces of nature will generally be on the side of him who
> understands them best and respects them most scrupulously.

Democracy had the advantage over communism in this respect, because it did
not rely on violence to reshape society. Its outlook was "more closely attuned to
the real nature of man, . . . [so] we can afford to be patient and even occasionally
to suffer reverses, placing our confidence in the longer and deeper workings of
history."

It was here, then, that Kennan's views on foreign policy cycled back through
his previous thinking on self containment, Russian literature (especially Chekhov), environmentalism, religion, and even sex. For if the issue, in the end, was
human nature, didn't survival require balancing appetites and obligations? "Only
too often in life we find ourselves beset by demons, sometimes outside ourselves,
sometimes within us," but they "have power over us only so long as they are able to
monopolize our attention." They lose that power "when we simply go on with the
real work we know we have to do." Nothing could be more shortsighted than "to
sacrifice the traditional values of our civilization to our fears rather than to defend
those values with our faith."[35]

V.

The particular demons Kennan had in mind were those of McCarthyism, which was not only deranging foreign policy but also ruining friends and former colleagues. Chief among them was John Paton Davies, who after being exonerated by the State Department's loyalty board in 1951 had been subjected to a long series of inconclusive investigations by the Senate Internal Security Subcommittee. Kennan worked hard to prevent these from leading to perjury charges, even to the point of threatening to withhold future consultations with the government if Davies should be prosecuted. He never was, but the ordeal ended Davies's Foreign Service career. John and Patricia spent the next decade living in Peru. Kennan blamed himself, but Davies did not blame him: "The forces against which he was struggling were far stronger than he."[36]

Similar fates befell other "China hands," among them John Stewart Service and O. Edmund Clubb, both of whom Kennan tried to help, and the fight over Bohlen's nomination showed that even Soviet specialists could be suspect. Meanwhile the FBI was investigating Oppenheimer for alleged ties to communists and for having opposed building the hydrogen bomb. His chief accuser was Lewis Strauss, now chairman of the Atomic Energy Commission and, ironically, a longtime trustee at the Institute for Advanced Study. So why not Kennan, who had spent years in the U.S.S.R., joined Oppenheimer in objecting to the new weapon, criticized the Republican strategy of "liberation," railed against McCarthy, and was now also at the Institute? "I was sometimes attacked, sometimes even called a 'socialist,' or a 'Marxist,'" he later recalled, "but the attacks made little impression." That was more "by luck than by any just deserts."[37]

Perhaps, but Kennan was also careful. He had "always been friendly to the Bureau," one of J. Edgar Hoover's aides reminded the director in 1951, "furnishing pertinent and helpful information when in the State Department." A former government employee, then in a mental institution, did raise questions about Kennan's loyalty a few months later, but Hoover chose not to pursue the matter. Before departing for Moscow as ambassador in 1952, Kennan let the bureau know that he would be calling on his Soviet counterparts in Washington and at the United Nations; after returning to the Institute the following year, he informed Hoover that he would be subscribing to *Pravda* for research purposes, unless the director thought this "undesirable or unwise." Hoover did not, passing the word to the Post Office Department that "the Bureau has had cordial relations with him."[38]

Did Kennan protect himself by reporting on others? He had done so on one or two occasions, he told the Oppenheimer investigators, but only in the case of "minor employees." Kennan had long been sure that Soviet espionage was taking place within the United States, but he was equally convinced that spies had never significantly influenced policy. It was on that last point that he differed with McCarthy and his supporters. Staying on the right side of Hoover may have made that possible: confronting evil did require compromises.[39]

Survivor's guilt, under these circumstances, was inescapable. It was one of the impulses that led Kennan early in 1954 to surprise himself, his family, his friends, and his funders by deciding—on the spur of an emotional moment—to enter politics. The story began when the East Berlin Veterans of Foreign Wars honored him on February 11 for distinguished national service. It was important, Kennan said in thanking them, that the country "show itself united and confident—not afraid of anyone else, and above all, not afraid of itself." What was happening, though, was just the opposite:

> The tone of political life has become sharper; the words have become meaner; the attempt is often made today to bring people to distrust other Americans—not on the grounds that they are dumb or selfish or short-sighted (that sort of thing has always gone on in our political life) but on the grounds that they are disloyal, that they are connected with hostile outside forces, that they are enemies to their own people.

Veterans had a special responsibility to avoid such hysteria: "Fellows, don't fall for this." It gratified him deeply that instead of suspecting someone, they had found an occasion "for announcing your trust."[40]

A few weeks later a young farmer and his wife rang the doorbell in Princeton, having driven there from Pennsylvania without knowing whether they would find the Kennans at home. Some of "us fellows" had gotten together, he announced, decided they didn't like the candidates being put up for the House of Representatives, and wondered if Kennan would agree to run. "Well, I was very much moved by this. I think it's a duty of citizenship, if your fellow citizens want you to represent them, that you don't turn it down." So he drove to Gettysburg to meet local Democratic leaders, who with the "marvelous brutality" of grassroots politics "picked me to pieces right in my presence." Kennan loved it. "These were such absolutely genuine people." Decades later he could still quote them: "He ain't even registered as a Democrat!" "Yeah, but his wife is." "Well, what would you say if you had to run here?" He said a few things. "Why, we could run him for the Senate!"

Kennan announced his candidacy on March 13. The next morning's *New York Times* quoted the Adams County Democratic Party chairman, Fred Klunk, who with his neighbors welcomed the idea "of George Kennan being our nominee."[41]

Had that happened and had he been elected, Kennan would have been the president's congressman, because Eisenhower's farm was just outside Gettysburg. But he wanted to run only if unopposed in the primary, on the grounds that his other responsibilities—which included finishing the Little lectures—left him no time to campaign. The other two candidates, unimpressed by an "outsider" who had only just declared himself a Democrat, refused to withdraw. Pennsylvania law limited the money Kennan could legally raise: he was not prepared, less than legally, to approach dairy owners, the usual way of getting around this problem. Finally Rusk and Oppenheimer let Kennan know that the generosity of the Rockefeller Foundation and the Institute for Advanced Study, ample though it was in other respects, did not extend to supporting candidates for public office.

The problem, Rusk later explained, was that as a tax-exempt foundation, Rockefeller—which provided most of Kennan's Institute funding—could not appear to be involving itself in politics. The only option would be a terminal grant, but when Oppenheimer suggested this, Kennan was not prepared to sever the Institute connection. "I could not afford to remain without regular income. . . . I do take seriously the commitments I have made in the academic world." And so, four days after he entered the race, he abruptly abandoned it. He was "full of agony over this. I felt I'd let down the people in the country. On the other hand, I couldn't see going deeply in[to] personal debt. I think I was quite right."[42]

So did almost everyone else, apart from the disappointed Pennsylvanians. Men qualified to serve in Congress were "not altogether rare," John V. A. MacMurray, the retired diplomat whose views Kennan had long respected, wrote him with stately delicacy, "but one who combines your integrity and intellectual grasp with actual experience . . . is of irreplaceable value [in] refining of its grossness the thinking of the American people." Others were franker. "I was horrified," Jeanette recalled. "Oh, goodness! That's the last thing in the world he could have done." But Kennan always regretted this path not taken. "All my friends laugh and say: 'You were never cut out for politics.' I think I could have done it if I'd wanted to throw myself into it. I might have gone on to a senatorial position."

The episode seems, at first glance, inexplicable. How could Kennan, supposedly a realist, expect to succeed in politics without competing in primaries or soliciting contributions? What of his insight, recorded in his diary only a few months earlier, that the moral man drafted into government would have to surround himself with

The "long telegram"
(Harry S. Truman Library)

The Policy Planning Staff, 1947.
From left, Kennan, Carlton
Savage, Joseph Johnson, Leroy
Stinebower (substituting
for Jacques Reinstein),
Ware Adams
*(Princeton University Library,
used by permission of The
Washington Post)*

President Truman, Robert M. Lovett, Kennan, and
Charles E. Bohlen at the White House, 1947
(Bettmann/CORBIS)

George C. Marshall and Dean Acheson, 1947
(Bettmann/CORBIS)

Kennan, dictating to Dorothy Hessman, 1949
(Joan Kennan Collection)

J. Robert Oppenheimer, John von Neumann,
and the Institute for Advanced Study
computer, 1952
(Bettmann/CORBIS)

Ambassador Kennan in his Mokhovaya
office, contemplating the Kremlin, 1952
(Princeton University Library)

Arriving in New York from
Moscow, November 1952
(from left, Wendy, Annelise,
George, Christopher)
(Bettmann/CORBIS)

George, just arrived (note pants)
in East Berlin (Pennsylvania),
vigorously pruning
*(Princeton University Library,
photo by Bob Motter)*

George, with Joan's horse Rusty,
at the Cherry Orchard, mid-1950s
*(Princeton University Library,
photo by Bob Motter)*

Kennan and Tito, Brioni, 1961
(Princeton University Library)

Senator J. William Fulbright
and Kennan, Senate Foreign
Relations Committee,
February 1966
(Bettmann/CORBIS)

George, soulfully, with guitar, 1975
(Bettmann/CORBIS)

Captain Kennan
(Joan Kennan Collection)

Kennan siblings reunion, October 1982 (from left, Kent, Constance, George, Frances, Jeanette) (*Joan Kennan Collection*)

George Kennan Pfaeffli (born February 16, 1984) in 2007 (*Wendy Kennan Collection*)

Annelise and George on their sixtieth wedding anniversary, at Hodge Road, Princeton, September, 1991 (*Joan Kennan Collection*)

Kennan outside Fuld Hall, the
Institute for Advanced Study, 1990s
(Joan Kennan Collection)

Ninetieth birthday, in New York,
February 1994 (from left, Joan, Grace,
George, Annelise, Wendy, Christopher)
(Joan Kennan Collection)

Elder Statesman, 1996
(Erik Freeland/Corbis 1)

immoral advisers? What of his elitism, which included a long-standing contempt for Congress itself? Shrewd observers of Kennan, without too much trouble, found explanations. One was Jeanette, herself a keen critic of McCarthyism: "He was so complimented by being asked." A second was a Princeton friend, the historian Cyril Black, who saw Kennan confusing the rough-and-tumble of American politics with the British tradition of invited "safe" seats. A third was his Hodge Road neighbor J. Richardson Dilworth: "George is ultra-conservative. He's almost a monarchist." And finally there was Isaiah Berlin, who detected more than a whiff of Tolstoy in Kennan's desire to be among but above his country neighbors: "Close to the soil, and simple views. Simple truths, shining out. The prophets of the world— you know, he wasn't too modest, Tolstoy." Would the two have gotten along? "Tolstoy would have approved of him. He'd have had a good time with Tolstoy."[43]

People who have "what you might call genius of some sort, intellectual or artistic," find it hard to arrange their relationships "in a manner which is wholly conventional." That was Kennan, speaking not of himself but of Oppenheimer in testimony before the Atomic Energy Commission's personnel security board on April 20, 1954. Such a person could be "profoundly honest and yet . . . have associates and friends who may be misguided and misled." Did this mean, one of the commissioners wanted to know, "that all gifted individuals [are] more or less screwballs?" Kennan would not go that far, "but I would say that when gifted individuals come to a maturity of judgment which makes them valuable public servants, you are apt to find that the road by which they have [traveled] may have had zigzags in it of various sorts."

Wasn't Kennan himself gifted? one of Oppenheimer's lawyers asked. How had *he* remained in government for so many years with so little suspicion? The answer, Kennan suggested, was that he had encountered evil at an impressionable age. As a young Foreign Service officer, he had visited the square in Riga where the Bolsheviks had executed their hostages only a few years earlier, for no better reason than that they were members of the bourgeoisie.

I was so affected by what I saw of the cruelty of Soviet power that I could never receive any of its boasts about social improvement with anything other than skepticism. I think that experience helped me a great deal at an early date, and helped me to avoid mistakes that I otherwise might have made.

Kennan's career, he acknowledged, had been no freer from blunders than anyone else's: his four-day congressional campaign, he did not have to say, had been a big one. But he had learned the value of discretion: he had managed "to conceal the difficulties on the intellectual road that I have gone through more than other people have been able to." His habit was "to keep them within myself and fight them out myself." And so, better than many, he had survived.[44]

VI.

Oppenheimer survived as the Institute's director, which allowed him to renew Kennan's appointment for another year with the understanding that he would stay out of politics. But in a devastatingly public humiliation, the Atomic Energy Commission withdrew Oppenheimer's security clearance, ending his ability to do further government work in nuclear physics. For Kennan, this meant that McCarthyism had claimed another close friend. Why, he wondered, did Oppenheimer not leave the United States, since universities throughout the world would have clamored to recruit him? "He stood there for a moment, tears streaming down his face." Then he stammered: "Dammit, I happen to love this country."[45]

Kennan did too, but as he admitted during the Oppenheimer hearings, he was more critical of his country than most people: this was yet another thing "I have had to fight within myself." He wasn't fighting very hard, his diary suggests, in the spring of 1954. Princeton was "lush and beautiful," but the university's reunion consisted of "gents" in ridiculous costumes looking "vaguely unhappy." The resident farmer at the Cherry Orchard was paying no attention to his instructions—Kennan would have seen the resemblance to Tolstoy's cheerfully dysfunctional peasants in *Anna Karenina*. Grace's graduation from Radcliffe required a drive through Connecticut, which had been taken over by scrub forest, Italians, Portuguese, and the Catholic Church. Cambridge was "sooty, overshaded, [and] dampish." Giving the commencement address was an obligatory drudgery, redeemed only by the unexpected presence of Joe Alsop, whose views Kennan attacked: Alsop protested, but was "actually very pleased by the personal attention." A visit to Washington found it overrun by the "great burly Babbitts" of the Eisenhower administration. A haircut for Christopher had his father marveling "at the combination of affection and irritation one can feel toward such a small person."

The Kennans sailed for Europe in June on a slow and seedy freighter like the ones George had traveled on in his youth. That continent did not seem much better, though. His lectures on Soviet-American relations, given in German at the University of Frankfurt, were, he was told, a great success, "but if I were to be asked . . . what had been accomplished, or whether it would have made any difference if I had never appeared, I would not know what to say." For most of those who heard him, "the highest spiritual aim seems to be a motorcycle. . . . One sees, today, how much the Jews added to Germany." Of the Americans in that country, "I will not speak," but he did anyway: "Their presence here infuriates me."

Moscow continued to haunt him: a dream had him returning as counselor in the Ethiopian embassy, a job he had taken because it seemed "a loyal and self-effacing and almost heroic thing to do." The ambassador, though, was an unhappy little man who left town on the day Kennan arrived, without having provided him a place to stay. Standing forlornly next to his suitcase, "I wondered whether I should call on _____ [probably Bohlen] and my other erstwhile colleagues at the American Embassy. Would they understand? Not likely."[46]

Whether because of his political misadventure, or Oppenheimer's ordeal, or the more general sense that he had not yet found his footing, whatever equanimity Kennan had gained by moving back to Princeton now seemed to have deserted him. A long diary entry, composed while still at sea, became almost a biblical lamentation:

1. So far as my own feelings and interests are concerned, I have nothing to live for, yet fear death.

2. I abhor the thought of any occupation that implies any sort of association with, and adjustment to, other people. This is particularly true in the U.S. Nowhere there can I share any of the group or institutional enthusiasms.

3. So far as I myself am concerned, I may as well live in Europe. . . . I am an exile wherever I go, by virtue of my experience.

4. I do not see any way in which I can use any of my own past in approaching the problems of the future. That has all got to die on the vine: the languages, the intellectual interests, the acquaintances. It makes no whole. It is a museum of odds and ends and left overs   and whatever value it had is declining day by day in geometric progression.

5. Intellectual life is barred for me, partly by the way of life forced upon me by the family whenever we are with other people, partly by the fact that intellectual exertion comes, with me, only from outside stimulus and constitutes a nervous and psychic strain; yet I have no means of relaxing from it and preserving the balance of life.

And so on, through seven other complaints, one of which involved teaching: "I should never be able to conceal my own intellectual despair, above all—the despair with U.S. society. But to reveal it would be inconsistent with the mythology of any American educational institution."

"It is not I who have left my country," he concluded early in 1955, not for the first time. "It is my country that has left me—the country I thought I knew and understood."

> I could leave it without a pang: the endless streams of cars, the bored, set faces behind the windshields, the chrome, the asphalt, the advertising, the television sets, the filling-stations, the hot-dog stands, the barren business centers, the suburban brick boxes, the country-clubs, the bars-and-grills, the empty activity, the competitiveness, the lack of spontaneity, the sameness, the drug-stores, the over-heated apartment houses, the bus terminals, the crowded campuses, the unyouthful youth and the immature middle-aged—all of this I could see recede behind the smoke of the Jersey flats without turning a hair.

And so, he now realized, "Mr. Dulles was quite right to fire me." People like himself had no role in government. Why, then, was he unhappy? "Here, of course, the trouble is with me. . . . I sometimes ask myself whether there is *anything* I am interested in—*anything* I would like to do."[47]

VII.

Dysfunctional peasants had nothing on Kennan, one might conclude from these entries, but that would be to miss the function his diary served. It allowed him despair in order to shield others from it. Family, friends, and colleagues saw some, but by no means all, of this inner turmoil. The diary, in turn, failed fully to reflect what Kennan's contemporaries could clearly see: that with Oppenheimer's help he was finding a niche, sufficiently satisfying that he would remain within it—or at least near it—for the last half of his long life. George's 1953 Christmas Day letter to Kent hinted at what was happening.

> I am just beginning to get my teeth into my work for this [coming] year, which is a beginning on what I suppose will eventually be a two-volume

history of Soviet-American relations. It is slow work, and laborious; but it is one way of earning a living, and it might just help to steady American thinking on the contemporary aspects of the subject—something which seems to me to be sorely needed.

Speaking of teeth, "[y]ou can't imagine how good the grapefruits taste to us. They are the first good fruit I have had this year."[48]

Why history? The immediate reason, of course, was that Kennan had promised Oppenheimer scholarship, and *American Diplomacy*—his first venture into the field—had not delivered it. Kennan was determined to do better. But history had always been a lodestone, attracting him when opportunities arose. He liked working as a research assistant for Professor Karl Stählin at the University of Berlin in 1930: his assignment had been a Kremlin librarian during Napoleon's invasion. He gleefully excavated Neill Brown's dispatches from the era of Nicholas I for Bullitt to resend to Washington. He exhausted the State Department with his exhaustive study of the Alaska Purchase. He lectured on Russian history while interned at Bad Nauheim. He discovered Gibbon while in flight during the war. And even if his own past might not be useful in solving the problems of the future, he had long believed that the *study* of the past could be: that was a recurring theme in Kennan's National War College lectures.

Now, thanks to the Institute, he could concentrate on history. His first impulse had been to survey all of Soviet-American relations, but "I immediately realized that the archival resources had never been properly touched, that anything I might say after reading what few memoirs there were would be superficial and maybe not even accurate. So I happily went to the sources." That meant immersion in the intricacies of the Bolshevik Revolution, a topic recent enough for there to be living—if unreliable—witnesses, close enough to Kennan's experience for him to use his linguistic and diplomatic skills, distant enough that he had not been personally involved. Would the world be different "when I have finished"? he wondered aloud in a talk he gave at the National Archives in the fall of 1954. Not much, he conceded, but "a few people may have been helped to understand some of our failures and failings today." At the top of his speaking notes, he wrote a single word: "Loneliness."[49]

He later explained what he meant. His work involved warming himself alongside fires kindled four decades earlier. Their heat was now as pale and faint as moonlight. If the era seemed remote, however, it was "because I was a poor historian, incapable of re-creating the flesh-and-blood images of the characters I was studying." Only through the deepest identification with the past could there be the "intimacy of acquaintance which permits historical personages really to become alive again." Being a good historian, then, required cutting one's self off from the present. Contemporaries rarely forgave that, because each age believed its own to be the most important that ever had existed, or ever would. What normal person would spend time with people suffering from "the obvious inferiority of not being alive"?

> The historian too often finds himself, I fear, in the position of the man who has left the noisy and convivial party, to wander alone on cold and lonely paths. The other guests . . . murmur discontentedly among themselves: "Why should he have left? Who does he think he is? Obviously, he doesn't like our company. He thinks us, plainly, a band of frivolous fools. . . . Let him sulk." So they say. And he does.

And so Kennan did. Because he disapproved of so much in the present, it was a party he was content to leave for "a never ending communion" with wax-museum figures "whose eyes never move and whose voices one never hears."

If they spoke at all, it was in words hovering above their heads "like the bubbles of utterance" that emerged from the characters in the comic strips of his boyhood. Context—those "elusive nuances of circumstances, of feeling, of environment, of intuition and telepathy"—was mostly lost. The relationship, for the historian, was not reciprocal.

> *He* takes an interest in *them*. He supports them. He becomes their posthumous conscience. He tries to see that justice is done them. He follows their trials and experiences, in many instances, with greater sympathy and detachment than any of their egocentric and jealous contemporaries ever did. But do *they* support *him*? Not in the least. They couldn't care less.

Historians, then, were disembodied spirits. Their task was to understand while remaining "unseen, unknown, unaided." That, for Kennan, was "loneliness."[50]

But if loneliness lay in both the present and the past, where was consolation? George worked out an answer of sorts while staying with Jeanette and her family in Highland Park one day in August 1956. He drove himself, alone, around Milwaukee. The Cambridge Avenue house was still there, looking as it always had despite taller trees and a deteriorating neighborhood. It struck him as "strangely serene and timeless," as though content to live by memories "and to await, without either complaint or haste, the day—which cannot be far off now—when it will disappear from the face of the earth and all that once transpired in it and around it will be swallowed up in the forgotten past."

A half hour later he was at the Forest Home cemetery, which he had visited for the first time only a year earlier: "I sat at the head of my parents' graves and wept my heart out, like a child."

> They seemed to say: we have reached a reality beyond all your strivings and sufferings; on your terms it is neither good nor bad; you cannot conceive of it; you cannot help us now, any more than we can help you; but we are serene and timeless and you are not; we have our secret, infinitely sad to your mind, no doubt, but in tune with Nature; we have known all the suffering you now know, and then some; we are beyond your sympathy, as you are beyond our pity; Look: we give you the breath of peacefulness—we are a part of the long afternoon of life; take the hint, go your way as best you can; do not ask too many questions; it will not be long before you join us.[51]

Kennan had lived with loneliness—but had found it difficult to accept—all his life. Being a historian required and even rewarded it, offering something like the reassurances he thought he heard on that day. History brought wholeness closer than anything else he had ever done. It was a way of coming home.

TWENTY

A Rare Possibility
of Usefulness: 1955–1958

ONLY THE INSTITUTE FOR ADVANCED STUDY COULD HAVE GRANTED
Kennan the freedom to live in the past with so few obligations in the present. Any
university appointment would have involved teaching, and Kennan—despite his
superb skills as a lecturer—had no desire to supervise students, grade examinations, or serve on faculty committees. "He had no conception of what academic
life is like," the Princeton historian Cyril Black recalled. "It's hard work, especially here. He wanted it to be like Oxford, I suppose: give a lecture or two a week
and then stay away as much as possible." The Institute was in fact better than
Oxford—or at least all parts of it except All Souls—since it enrolled no students,
required no lecturing, and specified no expectations for publication. So Kennan
was delighted when Oppenheimer called him in on a cold and rainy December
29, 1954, to say that the board of trustees "would be glad to have me there as a
member, and to help with the attendant financial problems, for some years to
come. Nothing could have been more gratifying to me."[1]

But the proposed Kennan appointment—which amounted to lifetime tenure—
became a test of Oppenheimer's authority as director. The man who built the
atomic bomb had found that task considerably easier than running the Institute.
Its faculty remained bitterly divided between the mathematicians, mostly past
their professional prime with plenty of time to make trouble, and their more productive colleagues in other fields. Oppenheimer favored the latter group while
cultivating friendships with sympathetic trustees. This was an unhealthy situation, board member Dick Dilworth thought, but it was from such conversations
that the idea of a permanent position for Kennan probably arose.[2]

Until this point in the Institute's history, the faculty had approved all such appointments unanimously. Kennan's, it quickly became clear, would break that precedent. The School of Historical Studies, weakened by the recent death of Edward Mead Earle and the impending retirement of the diplomatic historian Sir Llewellyn Woodward, was strongly in favor. Kennan was known at the Institute, had recently been asked to spend a year at Oxford as George Eastman Professor, and was at work on a book that, as one of the historians put it, was sure to earn "the highest praise [in] that it would not have to be done again." The School of Mathematics, however, protested vociferously. Its heavyweights, among them John von Neumann and Kurt Gödel, pointed out that Kennan had no advanced degree, no scholarly publications, and no reputation as a professional historian. He had, moreover, involved himself in "politics." Tenuring him would "debauch the standards of the Institute and set its feet upon a downward path." In no other instance had it taken such a risk.[3]

Anticipating objections, Oppenheimer solicited external assessments, but these were not reassuring. Joseph Strayer, the chairman of the Princeton history department, foresaw "surprise and adverse comment" if the Institute were to make Kennan a professor of history. "He simply does not have the standing." Strayer's colleague Gordon Craig agreed: "He is not a historian, although he has taken to writing history." Ray Billington, of Northwestern University, worried that Kennan's "knowledge of men in the field is limited." Philip Mosely, of the Columbia University Russian Institute, wondered whether he would apply "traditional academic standards in the selection of people and projects." Only Theodor Mommsen of Cornell University, among the historians consulted, regarded Kennan as qualified: even he, though, suggested that an Institute appointment might more appropriately rest on Kennan's strengths as a "humanist."

Isaiah Berlin, writing from Oxford, came vigorously to Kennan's defense. The Eastman electors had chosen Kennan unanimously: his had been the only name suggested by everyone consulted. He was "one of the most interesting and attractive human beings I [have] ever met." His books and articles contained "more ideas per page, and more freshness and directness of vision," than most academic publications.

> In short, he seems to me to be a man of unique distinction of mind and remarkable, sometimes rather mysterious, intellectual processes, leading to original conclusions of an arresting kind in any subject matter to which he applies himself. Moreover, he has that rarest of all possessions—something to say.

The Institute would perform a great service by allowing Kennan to do history there indefinitely. "I myself would ask no greater privilege than that of being able to communicate with him about such matters for the rest of my natural life."[4]

These mixed reviews emboldened the mathematicians, who demanded the right to make their case directly to the board of trustees. Fearing that this procedure would undermine Oppenheimer, the trustees rejected it in a contentious meeting on November 15, 1955: fortunately Lewis Strauss was not present. After summarizing the arguments for and against, Oppenheimer proposed that Kennan be made a professor of international relations, not of history. The board agreed with a single dissent, from a trustee concerned that for the first time "an appointment had been recommended by less than a unanimous vote of the faculty and [that] a substantial minority of the faculty seemed quite upset about this." Oppenheimer then amended his own compromise: Kennan's appointment, which took effect on January 1, 1956, was simply "professor" in the School of Historical Studies.[5]

How much Kennan knew of the controversy is unclear. His diary makes no mention of it, and Oppenheimer—knowing how easily he bruised—appears to have spared him the details. He explained only that certain colleagues had doubted Kennan's long-term commitment to scholarship, and that if he himself had doubts, he should not accept the position. "That seemed fair enough," Kennan recalled, grateful that he now had the means of supporting his family after his temporary appointment had ended. "The Institute took me," he wrote years later, "already a middle-aged man devoid of academic credentials, substantially on faith, gambling on the existence of scholarly capacities that remained to be demonstrated. . . . I can find no adequate words in which to acknowledge the debt I owe to this establishment."[6]

I.

Kennan worked throughout 1954 on *Russia Leaves the War*, the first of his projected two volumes—which soon became three—on the early American response to the Bolshevik Revolution. Arthur Link, who thought *American Diplomacy* "extraordinarily simplistic," became Kennan's tutor: "I advised him to go back and read some good manuals on how one goes about doing research. What is a primary document? What is a secondary document? How much reliance can you put on memoirs?" Kennan went to the National Archives, the Library of Congress, the New York Public Library, manuscript collections at Princeton, Harvard, Yale, and the University of Chicago, even to the state historical societies of Wisconsin and Missouri for the papers, respectively, of Raymond Robins, the American Red Cross representative in Petrograd in 1917–18, and David R. Francis, the American ambassador at the time. Hessman, still Kennan's secretary, accompanied him on most of these trips, copying out long passages from the materials he selected. He wrote (and dictated) as he researched, mixing narrative with analysis, resisting the temptation to stockpile notes. His speed, as a consequence, exceeded that of most academic historians.[7]

"It was my first major effort," Kennan later recalled, "and I was not quite sure what it was, actually, that I had produced." So he sought out readers as he neared completion. Despite differences over Woodrow Wilson, Link liked what he saw: "There's no question that he [had] learned a great deal." The most helpful comments, however, came from the Institute's medievalist Ernst "Eka" Kantorowicz, who had fought in the German army during World War I but afterward, like Einstein, fled the Nazis.

> He took the typescript home and read, at least, great parts of it. Then he asked me to dinner, alone. . . . Being not only a gourmet but also an accomplished cook, he prepared with his own hands a marvelous meal for the two of us, served it with the best of wines, and then, seating me in the living room over coffee and brandy, took out the typescript and said: "Now, my friend, we will talk about what you have done."

Whereupon he subjected it to "unforgettable criticism," not from the standpoint of factual accuracy or interpretive logic, but from that of style. "This, I thought, was the mark not just of a great scholar but of a great gentleman."[8]

By March 1955 Kennan was almost done. "The book is my diary," he wrote apologetically in his neglected diary. "My own life has been of no importance." On the tenth he delivered the manuscript, with great trepidation, to the Princeton University Press. The editors took their time, and Kennan continued to make revisions, so the book did not appear until the summer of 1956. One of the first reviews came from Harrison Salisbury, who sardonically credited Dulles with coauthorship: deprived of any current policy position, Kennan had had little choice but to turn to the past. "I thought of you many times as I wrote it," Kennan assured Acheson, who had read the book and praised it.

Only the stern censorship of my academic colleagues, who urged that I keep the editorializing to a minimum, restrained me from observing that in the strange conditions of 1917 people neglected to charge [then Secretary of State Robert] Lansing with treason for his "do nothing" policy, nor did they even think to blame him for the future course of the Russian Revolution—an inexplicable oversight [by] contemporary standards.

It meant a great deal, he added, to have Acheson's approval. "There is no one for whom I could more have wished that the tale would prove interesting and worth reading."[9]

Carefully researched and compulsively documented, *Russia Leaves the War* devoted over five hundred pages to just four months—the period from the Bolsheviks' seizure of power in November 1917 to their separate peace with Germany in March 1918. The book would become "the classic work in its field," Yale's Frederick C. Barghoorn wrote in the *Political Science Quarterly*, but it was "somewhat too detailed, considering the shortness of the period covered." Dexter Perkins, of the Cornell History Department, suggested that Kennan had tried too hard to follow the example of "scientific" scholarship, and Kennan acknowledged as much in a letter to Herbert Butterfield: "The amateur's lack of self-confidence—the fear of being criticized by professional historians," had certainly been one of the reasons "why I dredged up and hurled at the reader this appalling accumulation of detail."

The book's readability, however, made it anything but ponderous. Kennan had spent most of his life sketching scenes in his diary and correspondence, but he had never published anything like the opening paragraph of *Russia Leaves the War*:

> The city of Sankt Petersburgh—St. Petersburg, Petrograd, Leningrad, call it what you will—is one of the strangest, loveliest, most terrible, and most dramatic of the world's great urban centers. The high northern latitude, the extreme slant of the sun's rays, the flatness of the terrain, the frequent breaking of the landscape by wide, shimmering expanses of water: all these combine to accent the horizontal at the expense of the vertical and to create everywhere the sense of immense space, distance, and power. The heaven is vast, the skyline remote and extended. Cleaving the city down the center, the cold waters of the Neva move silently and swiftly, like a slab of smooth grey metal, past the granite embankments and the ponderous palaces, bringing with them the tang of the lonely wastes of forests and swamp from which they have emerged. At every hand one feels the proximity of the great wilderness of the Russian north— silent, sombre, infinitely patient.

Personalities, too, came alive, as in Kennan's characterization of the volcanically hyperactive Raymond Robins:

> His concept of diplomacy was a deeply personal one, in which understanding came to rest upon the fire of a glance or the firmness of a handclasp. He suffered, in his state of exalted and dedicated enthusiasm, from an inability to find with other men any normal middle ground of association between the extremes of passionate loyalty and dark suspicion.

Kennan seasoned his scholarship with his own Foreign Service experience. "Like many American diplomatists who had gone before, and many who were to come after," he wrote of Ambassador Francis and his perplexed subordinates,

> they were left to vegetate as best they could at their foreign stations, gleaning their understanding of the rationale of American policy from the press or from such cryptic hints as might from time to time be given them, sending their interpretive reports to a Department of State wrapped in a deep and enigmatic silence, endeavoring uncomfortably to conceal from the governments to which they were accredited the full measure of their helplessness and lack of influence.

The finest feature of *Russia Leaves the War*, Barghoorn concluded, was its "charitable spirit." Kennan revealed "follies and frailties" without being "harsh, intolerant, or dogmatic." In that respect, as in others, he had "set a splendid example."[10]

Kennan embedded substantive themes within his narrative. One contrasted the purposefulness of Lenin and Trotsky with its absence among the Americans, whose determination to keep Russia in the war missed the disillusionment with the war that had made the Bolshevik takeover possible. A second was their failure to see not only a distrustful regime but also an irreconcilably hostile ideology. A third, echoing *American Diplomacy*, was the irrelevance of Wilsonian idealism—particularly the Fourteen Points speech of January 1918—to the realities at hand. A fourth was the sheer confusion of the situation, no easy thing to reconstruct in retrospect. That, in turn, suggested that contrary to what Soviet propagandists had claimed ever since, U.S. policy had been too befuddled to have had any discernible effect on what was happening inside Russia at the time.

There was only one significantly sour review. It came from William Appleman Williams, then an obscure history professor at the University of Oregon, later the founder of American revisionist historiography on the origins and evolution of the Cold War. *Russia Leaves the War* was not serious history, Williams insisted, but rather an extended brief on behalf of Kennan's former profession, the Foreign Service. He had used no new sources, his employment of existing ones was incomplete, and he said little about the "social philosophies" of the individuals he discussed "or their systems of accounting for—and anticipating—the relationship between cause and effect." Williams himself would soon remedy this last omission: his dismissal of confusion as an influence on American foreign policy would spark debates among diplomatic historians for decades to come.[11]

For the moment, though, *Russia Leaves the War* was a triumphant success—and, to Kennan's astonishment, a prize-winner. "I can only hope that the judges were right," he commented on accepting the National Book Award for nonfiction in March 1957. He apologized for taking a year and a half to write the book, as if this were somehow excessive. Having come to history thinking it would be easy, he now knew how difficult—but also how important—it was. For

> [i]f we plod along with only the feeble lantern of our vision of contemporary events, unaided by history, we see—to be sure—a little of the path just under our feet; but the shadows are grotesque and misleading, the darkness closes in again behind us as we move along, and none can be sure of direction or of pace or of the trueness of action.

Only historians could confirm links between efforts and outcomes, providing the necessary corrective if, as Shakespeare had said—it was a favorite Kennan quotation—"we are to 'dress ourselves fairly to our end.' "[12]

Two months later, just after finishing his second volume of almost five hundred pages—*The Decision to Intervene*, which carried his account only through July 1918—Kennan learned that *Russia Leaves the War* had won the Pulitzer Prize. By then it had also received the Bancroft and the Francis Parkman prizes. "I cannot believe that the book was that good," he protested in his diary, "it must have been a dull year in the non-fiction field." Still, the honors rewarded "a love of language and writing which never found any appreciable recognition in government . . . I now have the ability to be widely heard, on my own merits." Deservedly or not, there was now "a rare possibility of usefulness," to be "cherished and protected, wholly aside from its chance relation to my own person."

And when, Link asked, would he finish his third volume? The first two had appeared, after all, under the series title "Soviet-American Relations, 1917–1920." "Oh, I'm never going to complete them," Kennan replied, a bit too casually for

Link, who devoted his entire career to Wilson's life and papers. "Well, why did you write them?" "I wrote them to establish my credentials as a historian."[13]

II.

Kennan did this in a way that vindicated, more thoroughly than either of them could have imagined, the risk Oppenheimer had taken in proposing him for tenure at the Institute for Advanced Study: Kennan now had "security for life." But the implications unsettled him as much as they reassured him. "Is it right," he wondered, "that one should become, when this side of fifty, suddenly without anguish?"

The "torture of the constant presence of the opposite sex" was abating, but what about other forms of anguish? Chekhov had been lucky to die so young having achieved so much. "I still have work to do, and am doing it; but it seems too easy. . . . Men—or at least such men as I—are no good unless they are driven, hounded, haunted, forced to spend every day as though it were the last they were to spend on earth." Old age must therefore become "a sort of self-torture—not driving one's self, as some do, to pretend to be younger than one really is, but forcing the muscles of body, intellect, and capacity for sympathy to work full time, even at the cost of shortening life."[14]

Physical self-torture came easily enough, as Kennan's Hodge Road neighbor Bunny Dilworth discovered one weekend at the farm. "George had no sooner got there," her husband Dick recalled, "than he rushed out and started the tractor to mow the lawn. Then he'd rush inside and go upstairs and type. He was typing on and off most of the night. But in the morning he was out again mowing the lawn." On another occasion, visiting the Kennans in Kristiansand, both Dilworths were awakened by the sound of a wheelbarrow. "Here was George, with really immense stones, bigger than a normal person could pick up, building a set of steps down to the water. He was incapable of just stopping and taking a few hours off." Kennan did much of his own yard work around the Princeton house, devoting several days in September 1956 to digging up a dead maple. On the morning of the twenty-third, the university awarded him an honorary degree, which Kennan accepted alongside Dag Hammarskjöld, the secretary general of the United Nations. That afternoon "I returned to my tree and exhausted myself in two or three further hours of hacking."[15]

Intellectual exertion—particularly when it involved empathy—was more difficult. Kennan achieved it in his histories: one of the most striking features of *Russia Leaves the War* and *The Decision to Intervene* was his ability to put himself in the position of the people he wrote about. He took pains to see things from *their* point of view, without imposing his own or those of a different age. He listened, but rarely judged. He showed respect for the dead.

But rarely for the living, or for the culture they had created. He loathed "this thin, tight, lonely American life." He acknowledged "a growing gap between my own outlook and that of my countrymen," but blamed their habits, not his, for it. He had a vision of what the country once was, Dick Dilworth sensed, "and what under better circumstances it could be." But it hadn't turned out that way. He was "like a rejected lover." If not for the family, Kennan told himself, he would have become "a recluse and an esthete," living somewhere on the west coast of Scotland, reading, traveling, studying "the beauty man has created," to the end that "I might someday create some of my own." What beauty was there, though, in the United States? "Before us stretches the whole great Pacific Coast," he wrote while on a flight to California,

> and my only thought, as we approach it, is: throughout the length and breadth of it not one single thing of any importance is being said or done; not one thing that gives hope for the discovery of the paths to a better and firmer and more promising human life, not one thing that would have validity beyond the immediate context of time and place in which all of it occurs.

Yes, but the people were happy, someone would say. Why not join them? "Forget that you have ever been a mature person. Learn to play and be amused, again, like a child." "Perhaps, perhaps," was the reply. But elsewhere "man has from time to time risen to great dignity and to immense creative stature. I have lived too long in the neighborhood of those evidences to forget them so easily."

Kennan tried to be polite to the people he met. He imagined how his mother would have wanted him to live: "unhurriedly, with grace and dignity, secure and relaxed in the consciousness of her love and her forgiveness, not pecking at myself for past faults nor worrying about present limitations." This required constant effort, though, for it meant acknowledging kindness and accepting hospitality while concealing from those providing these gifts all the things that "divide us so deeply." He was learning to live "in an inner world. I am utterly without relationship to this country and this age."[16]

Paradoxically, though, with every public statement, he had found wider and more appreciative audiences. Kennan's platform skills partly accounted for this: Princeton students not only applauded a lecture he gave there but surprised him by roaring with laughter, "which I trust was with me and not at me." With *American Diplomacy* required reading in university classrooms across the country, he was getting similar responses wherever he spoke. A Stanford instructor suggested that his students were finding, in Kennan's views, a way to rebel against those of their parents. That led him to worry that he had courted popularity, that he had "watered down my own thoughts, sweetened them with a lot of optimistic baloney." If his youthful admirers ever caught on to what he really believed, "they would probably hate me for it. If they approve of me, it is because I have been a hypocrite and have successfully disguised myself and my thoughts."[17]

And what of his own children? If American culture encouraged healthy physical, intellectual, and spiritual development, he could leave them to thrive within it, he wrote in the summer of 1956. It did, however, just the opposite.

> How can one sit by and see them become older without really maturing: socially uncertain, imitative, conformist, nervously over-wrought by too much television, exposed first to the false excitement of teen-age hot-rod adventure, then moving into some premature liaison with the opposite sex[?] . . . In this false life innocence is lost before maturity is achieved. To say nothing of the poverty of education, the incoherence of speech, the never-ending mumbling of stereotypes—the cult, in fact, of un-eloquence, of verbal awkwardness—the pretense of tough, disillusioned taciturnity.

Social adaptability required consigning children to mediocrity, "in order that they may feel comfortable in their time." He should therefore advise Christopher, now six, that "whatever I like, you learn to dislike; whatever I believe in, you distrust; whatever I am, you try to be the opposite." Only then could he have "the faintest chance of fitting into the new age."[18]

For all of his pessimism about culture in the United States, Kennan had not yet given up on its politics. He respected Eisenhower but thought him too inclined to defer to Dulles and to McCarthyite pressures in foreign policy. He had registered as a Democrat during his brief Pennsylvania congressional candidacy, but in terms of domestic affairs, "I am much closer to the Republicans." He opposed farm subsidies and distrusted labor unions while worrying increasingly about race relations, "still the most terrible . . . of our national problems." In the privacy of his diary, however, he regretted Lincoln's having kept the nation together during the Civil War: it would have been better off without the "Latin-American fringe" of California, Texas, and Florida. "I ought, in truth," he concluded, "to have nothing to do with either political party."

Politicians, however, could still attract him. Kennan admired Adlai Stevenson "as a sensitive, intelligent and valiant person" who ought to be running the country and "probably never will." Nevertheless, he agreed early in 1956 to co-chair the New Jersey "Stevenson-for-President" committee. He suggested saying little about foreign policy but sent Stevenson four single-spaced typed pages on what he should say. He even made a campaign speech in Princeton, "a task for which I am very poorly fitted," assuring his neighbors that Stevenson would bring an "intellectual and moral conscience" to government, would conduct "an exercise of national self-scrutiny," and would have the courage to tell Americans what they would not necessarily like to hear.[19]

Stevenson soon disappointed him. During an address to the Pittsburgh Foreign Policy Association on May 3, Kennan had described the situation in Eastern Europe as "a finality, for better or for worse." The United States should not be encouraging "liberation." This was no new position, but when James Reston quoted Kennan a few days later alongside a *New York Times* news story listing him as a key Stevenson adviser, an angry Democratic congressman, Thaddeus Machrowicz of Michigan, warned the candidate that he could lose the Polish-American vote unless he publicly repudiated Kennan. Stevenson wasted no time in doing so: he issued a press release "completely" disagreeing with Kennan, who "is in no way connected with my staff and never has been."[20]

Kennan was not consulted, nor was he even given a copy of the Stevenson letter. The brush-off cured him, or so he claimed, "of the illusion that I have any place whatsoever in American public life—even as an independent supporter of Mr. Stevenson. Serves me right for even messing in it." Kennan wrote that on August 20, during his visit with Jeanette in Highland Park. Three days later her phone rang with a message from the Democratic nominee himself: he had just learned that Kennan was nearby—could he come to dinner that evening at the Stevenson farm in Libertyville? George asked if he could bring Grace, who had just arrived. Of course, Stevenson replied. "So we drove over almost at once."

The meal took place to the sound of Republican rhetoric, for Eisenhower and Nixon were accepting their nominations that night, and the television was on in the next room. Stevenson assessed the speeches professionally, talked foreign policy briefly, and then George and Grace made their farewells.

Mr. Stevenson accompanied us out to the parking lot in back of the house. There was a bright moon, and the fields were in mist, and looked like a sea. We both felt intensely sorry for him: he seemed so tired and harassed and worn, he had so few people to help him; and his whole equipment for going into this battle was so shabby compared with the vast, slick, well-heeled Eisenhower organization. And not the least of his problems is to carry on his shoulders the whole miserable Democratic party; disunited, indisciplined, unenlightened, itself already having unconsciously imbibed and assimilated about half of the McCarthyism of the past few years.

Stevenson had rejected Kennan more abruptly and more visibly even than Dulles, but unlike Dulles, he found a gracious way to make amends. That, for Kennan, was style—a later generation would call it "class." It was a quality he struggled to find within himself, even as he drove, hounded, and haunted himself.

"I am living in the world my father despaired of, and rightly so," Kennan wrote on August 26, 1956, after returning to the archives in St. Louis. Why take it too seriously? It was, after all, late afternoon: "The main happenings of the day are over; not much more is going to happen." He, like his father, had been "passed by, and do not really mind too much—because the present is too uninteresting."[21]

III.

But the present, in fact, was very interesting. Six months earlier the new Soviet leader, Nikita Khrushchev, had secretly denounced Stalin before the Twentieth Soviet Communist Party Congress in Moscow. Two months earlier Polish workers had rioted in Poznań. One month earlier the Egyptian president, Gamal Abdel Nasser, had nationalized the Anglo-French Suez Canal Company after Secretary of State Dulles, retaliating for an arms deal Nasser had made with Czechoslovakia, cut off American funding for the Aswan Dam. Kennan had no involvement in any of these crises, but he could hardly avoid taking an interest in them. And as far as Soviet and Eastern European affairs were concerned, the CIA expected him to do so: despite Kennan's having declined the offer of a job there in 1953, Allen Dulles had been using him ever since as a confidential adviser.

Initially this meant membership on an advisory committee reviewing national intelligence estimates. Conveniently for Kennan, it met in Princeton with the CIA director frequently in attendance. After J. Edgar Hoover approved Kennan's

Pravda subscription, he was also able to monitor post-Stalin political maneuvering in the Kremlin, passing periodic analyses to his chief CIA contact, John Maury. The arrangement made sense on all sides. It gave the Eisenhower administration access to Kennan despite its having, in effect, fired him. It allowed Kennan the freedom to criticize policy openly while still seeking quietly to shape it. Because Kennan wished to avoid any impression "that he is seeking to intrude or in any way impose his views," Frank Wisner explained in 1956, agency documents referred to him only as "the expert."[22]

One of the first things Allen Dulles did after the CIA obtained a transcript of Khrushchev's speech was to send Maury to Princeton to show it to Kennan. His first reaction was that one or more of the new Soviet leaders must have arranged Stalin's death and were now trying to cover their tracks. He advised caution in releasing the text, but Dulles overruled him and, with the other Dulles's cooperation, the State Department published it on June 4. The Polish upheaval followed three weeks later, leading Kennan to admit that they had been right. Khrushchev had attacked the system that produced him far more effectively than the Americans could ever have done. They had only amplified what he said.[23]

By August, Kennan was worrying more about the Suez crisis. The Truman and Eisenhower administrations had made a great mistake playing up to "Middle Eastern tin-pot dictators," he told *New York Times* correspondent C. L. Sulzberger in an off-the-record interview. "These men are not our friends," but the British and the French were. The United States had traditionally favored self-determination, Kennan added in a speech at Johns Hopkins two months later, but was everyone equally ready to exercise it? Especially when doing so involved expropriating foreign property, along with the right to control an international waterway vital to the global economy? How strongly would Americans support Nasser if he cut off oil shipments from the Middle East at a time when they and their allies were increasing their dependence on that commodity?[24]

Meanwhile, Kennan was modifying his views on the "finality" of Soviet rule in Eastern Europe. Moscow's authority there was eroding "more rapidly than I had ever anticipated," he told the House Foreign Affairs Committee on October 11. The process had begun with Tito in 1948, and now, in the aftermath of the Poznań riots, Poland was showing signs of independence that Stalin would never have permitted. Khrushchev flew to Warsaw a week later to demand the resignation of Wladyslaw Gomulka, the recently installed reformist leader of the Polish Communist Party, but surprisingly, he failed to get it. Washington wanted him to come for "consultation," Kennan wrote in his diary on the twenty-second. Should he go? His relations with his government and even his country were approaching a crisis

> that will almost unquestionably end in my being driven further away rather than brought closer. Deep in my heart I have a feeling that I shall end either in exile or— well, better not to speculate on it. Too bad: I am just now beginning to like this country a little, as a place to live—better, at least, than I did. But I shall never be able to take its public life. And the coming election will seal my estrangement.

Kennan could claim, in a way, vindication, having insisted for over a decade that the Soviet Union could not indefinitely, as Gibbon would have put it, "hold in obedience" its satellites "in opposition to their inclination and interest." But Kennan's problem, his old Moscow boss Bill Bullitt had suggested in a public attack on him a few months earlier, was that his devotion to Gibbon had left him with "a pessimistic bent of mind for one so young." Kennan was "more captivated by declines and falls than by rises and achievements."[25]

Kennan did acknowledge, on October 29, that the situation in Eastern Europe was developing more favorably than if "we ourselves [had] tried deliberately to achieve this effect." Perhaps Titoism had been a precursor to "liberation." But the Hungarians were "running tremendous risks in trying to force so many issues at once." Encouraged by the Polish example, the new government of Imre Nagy had followed an anti-Soviet uprising in Budapest with the demand that the Red Army withdraw altogether from Hungary. It appeared to have done so by November 1, when Kennan again saw John Maury. "I think there is a hooker in this somewhere," he warned. "I cannot understand their accepting this kind of humiliation." Khrushchev was indeed wavering, but he soon stopped by ordering a full-scale invasion of Hungary on November 4, which brutally crushed the rebellion. The fighting killed some 2,700 people, and another 230, including Nagy, were eventually executed.

While all of this was happening, the British, French, and Israelis—with exquisitely bad timing and without having consulted the United States—had launched an ill-planned invasion of Egypt with a view to retaking the Suez Canal. That left Eisenhower wondering how to condemn one such action and not the other: he solved the problem by condemning both, while asking the United Nations to do the same. Under brutal pressure from Washington, the Anglo-French-Israeli forces had no choice but to accept a cease-fire and withdraw. Khrushchev and Nasser achieved their objectives, leaving NATO to face the worst crisis in its history. Nevertheless, on November 6, Eisenhower won reelection by a landslide.[26]

"The events of these recent days have been so shattering," Kennan wrote on the seventh, "that I am at a loss to know how to react to them." They had confirmed, "beyond my wildest dreams," his doubts about "liberation" and the appeasement of "third world" dictators. But the United States and its allies were now in a dangerous situation over which they appeared to have little control. Despite this, Americans had voted Eisenhower a second term with a huge majority. So of what use was Kennan's advice, even if anyone were willing to listen to it?

He was sure that in most instances he had been right. Almost alone, in 1945, he had foreseen "the horror of Russia's rule in the satellites, and the necessity of its eventual disintegration." He had accurately diagnosed the weaknesses of Stalin's rule. The Marshall Plan had been his idea, and he had correctly calculated what was needed for its success. Had he been listened to on Germany, that country would now have been reunited, free of communist control. He had urged, before the Korean War broke out, that Taiwan be placed under MacArthur's control: "no nonsense about returning it to China." He had warned against invading North Korea. He had opposed deferring to the United Nations rather than to allies with "a traditional stake in our future." So what should he do with insights like these? "Bury them? Hide them? Die with them? They are not wanted."[27]

IV.

The George Eastman Professorship in Balliol College, established in 1929 by the founder of the Eastman Kodak Company, was meant to bring to Oxford each year a senior American scholar "of the highest distinction," regardless of field. Kennan's 1955 appointment came at a good time, strengthening his case for tenure at the Institute for Advanced Study. Before accepting it, though, he checked with Loy Henderson to make sure that the secretary of state had no plans to recall him to duty, as Foreign Service rules would allow him to do until Kennan was sixty-five. Dulles assured Henderson that he had no such intention, so Kennan was free to go. The appointment required giving a set of lectures, an obligation he took seriously enough to propose writing between twenty-five and thirty on the history of Soviet foreign policy. "I think you rather overestimate the amount of care you ought to give to these," a former Rhodes scholar cautioned. Few people in Oxford spoke from full texts. As at Princeton, "notes would be all you need."[28]

Relieved by this advice, determined to finish *The Decision to Intervene* before departing for Europe in the summer of 1957, Kennan gave little further thought to his Eastman lectures, or to another series he had committed himself to in which speaking from notes would be impossible: these were the annual Reith lectures, to be delivered live over the national and international radio networks of the British Broadcasting Corporation. Perhaps, he suggested to his increasingly anxious producer Anna Kallin at the end of June, he might update the "X" article from a decade ago. "I have taken on far more than I can possibly do," he admitted to Kent. "I have no one to blame but myself. It . . . will be a miracle if I contrive to acquit myself creditably."[29]

Four of the six Kennans—Grace, now graduated from Radcliffe, had a job in Washington, and Joan was about to begin her third year at Connecticut College—sailed for Norway in late July on the SS *Stavangerfjord*. While at sea one day Christopher asked his moody and irritable father what he was interested in. "I couldn't answer him. What indeed? Boats, I said, vaguely." Maybe also growing things, but certainly not international affairs. That field had produced so many frustrations "that I have only pessimism left; and I am too healthy to be interested in what I am pessimistic about."

So Kennan amused himself by outlining a set of Reith lectures that would begin with the sterility of American society, point out the overpopulated nastiness of the rest of the world, and conclude by proposing a new country composed of Great Britain, Canada, and the healthy parts of the United States (the South, Texas, and California would go elsewhere), with its capital to be near Ottawa. Democracy would then save itself from itself by half a century of benevolent dictatorship. "How would all this sound over the BBC?" Miss Kallin, fortunately, was not on board to say, and after arriving in Kristiansand Kennan settled—or so he thought—for something less controversial. The series would be "Russia, the Atom, and the West," and he had rough drafts ready by the time he left for Oxford at end of August. But "damn poor lectures they are, by and large. This is no longer my *forte*. . . . What miseries I let myself in for when I accepted this invitation."[30]

"Oxford!" Kennan exclaimed in his diary. "Serene courtyards. Magnificent old towers, graceful but strong, seeming to swim against the background of the blowing clouds." But that was as far as romanticism went. Industrial plants bracketed the university, with grimly goggled motorcyclists shuttling noisily between them. Tourists dutifully dragged themselves among colleges and churches. Restaurant patrons whispered over menus that never changed. Sundays, with everything closed and children to be amused, seemed meant to "try men's souls." The parks were damp, the suburbs prim, and lovers huddled for warmth along riverbanks:

"Ah, love in England, so frail, so handicapped, so overwhelmingly without a chance, and so terribly poignant by consequence!" Michaelmas term would not begin until October, so there was hardly anyone to talk with beyond the family. And when dons and students did return, they brought viruses with them. All the Kennans came down with influenza.

Balliol housed them in a Merton Street flat that presumed servants no longer present. There was no central heating, so it fell to George to carry coal up two flights of stairs and ashes back down. "Your brother thinks he is quite a martyr," Annelise wrote Jeanette. The dining room doubled as his office, and he had to hire his own secretaries. The library system bewildered him. He was "vastly over-committed." Real work could only be done at night, in weariness, without inspiration, "getting something written, even if inferior." There was no point in trying to rest: strength would only be drained "by trivia or one sort or another, the following morning."[31]

Trivia infused the university itself. Kennan had imagined its colleges, Berlin was sure, "as grand, old, almost feudal institutions," in which distinguished men dined at high table, then lingered in common rooms over port, claret, nuts, and snuff, their conversation "polished by deep traditions, refinement, moral quality." What he found instead was "a lot of idle gossip about local affairs, academic tittle-tattle. He was horrified by that. Profound disappointment. England was not as he thought. An idealized image had been shattered." Attendance at a single Balliol fellows' meeting convinced Kennan never to return: "I've never seen such back-biting, such fury, such factions in my life." Oxford was "a tight, tough community," he wrote Oppenheimer at the end of October, and "few of its mysteries are to be penetrated in the course of a few months by the casual visiting professor." He had not had a serious discussion with a colleague since arriving, "except with Is[a]iah Berlin—where you can't help having it."[32]

The Kennans did, however, befriend two American graduate students, Anthony Quainton, later a career Foreign Service officer, and Richard H. Ullman, a historian of early Anglo-Soviet relations who would become a professor of international affairs at Princeton. The informality of Sunday lunches surprised Ullman: Wendy and Christopher roamed freely and even romped boisterously under the dining room table. "I was quite impressed by that. I thought [George's] relationship with the kids was terrific."

His lectures, delivered twice a week in the Examination Schools building on High Street, were also impressive. Kennan wrote out every word and read them beautifully, Ullman recalled. As had happened at Chicago, they quickly outgrew the assigned space and were filling the largest hall available. "The terrible thing,"

Kennan complained, was that they were "tremendously successful." Berlin's followed immediately, so hundreds of people came, staying for both. Dons were sitting on radiators and hanging from chandeliers, one attendee remembered. But Kennan was again drafting his lectures just prior to delivering them—about ten thousand words a week—while also carrying coal, getting sick, recoiling from common room banalities, helping to manage small children, and preparing for the Reith broadcasts that would begin on November 10, when he would have not hundreds but hundreds of thousands of listeners.[33]

With television in its infancy, radio still dominated the British airwaves, so the lectures were a major event. Delivered on six successive Sunday evenings, each required rehearsal as well as careful editing to fit within the time allotted. Kennan would drive himself to the BBC's London studios, make last-minute corrections while waiting for the nine o'clock news to end, and at nine-fifteen take his cue from the announcer's remorseless "Mr. Kennan."

> I knew, then, that for twenty-eight and a half minutes into the future I would be left alone—alone as I had never been before—alone as I had never hoped to be—alone to acquit or disgrace myself, as my capacities might determine—but alone beyond the power of any other human being to help me.

Anything unexpected—a botched sentence, a misplaced page, even a sneeze or a blown nose—would be a national embarrassment: "I felt a tremendous sense of responsibility. Half of England was listening to these things." Kennan sensed this shortly after the broadcasts began, when he stopped by his Oxford garage to pick up his car. "The man behind the parts desk, with his greasy hands, when he heard me speak, said: 'Where did I hear that voice before?'"[34]

V.

"Kennan Says Rule in Soviet is Shaky," *The New York Times* reported on the morning after his first Reith lecture. The next week's headline was a bit more startling—"Kennan Calls Talks with Soviet Futile"—but the story revealed that he was only questioning the need for high-level summitry. On November 25, however, the lead got more attention: "Kennan Offers Plan on Neutral Germany." Was it not "quixotic," he was reported as having asked, to be promoting "freedom" by consigning East Germans—and hence all of Eastern Europe—to indefinite Soviet domination? Only a mutual withdrawal of all foreign forces from Germany could bring about its reunification, and that would require its detachment from all Cold War alliances. "Kennan Calls Atom Race Suicidal," *The Washington Post* shrieked on December 2. NATO allies should therefore reduce their military establishments to militia levels, "somewhat on the Swiss pattern," for the Soviet challenge lay more in the realm of politics than on battlefields. It followed, then, both the *Times* and the *Post* reported on December 16, that Kennan had warned against seeing NATO as an end in itself. To strengthen it would risk war, to perpetuate it would delay peace, and its continental European members had no reason to fear an Anglo-Canadian-American special relationship.[35]

The stories oversimplified, but not by much. Kennan had made substantially these points. Curiously, neither newspaper picked up what turned out to be his most provocative suggestion: that Europe would be safe if each of its countries not now under Moscow's control could credibly promise resistance after occupation.

Look here, you may be able to overrun us, if you are unwise enough to attempt it, but you will have a small profit from it; we are in a position to assure that not a single Communist or other person likely to perform your political business will be available to you for this purpose; you will find here no adequate nucleus of a puppet regime; on the contrary, you will be faced with the united and organized hostility of an entire nation; your stay among us will not be a happy one; we will make you pay bitterly for every day of it; and it will be without favorable long-term political prospects.

Kennan was again, of course, channeling Gibbon on the difficulty of holding distant provinces. And how could he be sure that the Soviet Union had learned the great historian's lesson? "I think I can give personal assurance that any country which is in a position to say this to Moscow . . . will have little need of foreign garrisons to assure its immunity from Soviet attack."[36]

Each of these arguments had appeared over the past decade in Policy Planning Staff papers, war college lectures, correspondence, articles, and books. Never before, though, had Kennan pulled them together and broadcast them, quite literally, to the world. The hitherto "mysterious Mr. X," all the more so now for having been kicked out of both Stalin's Soviet Union and Dulles's State Department, appeared at last to be emerging from the constraints imposed by official secrecy, personal discretion, and the lack of an appropriate forum. He was, before an immense audience, baring his soul. The Reith lectures were "secular sermons," one listener recalled. "George Kennan was the best sermonizer I've heard, anywhere."[37]

Kennan had accepted the BBC's invitation because it further bolstered his scholarly reputation: Oppenheimer, Bertrand Russell, and Arnold Toynbee had been earlier Reith lecturers. But having done so with no particular topic in mind, and having misjudged how long it would take to prepare when he finally did choose one, he fell back on familiar concepts but was close to panic as he was conveying them. And as with the "long telegram," the "X" article, the Chicago lectures, the Tempelhof statement, and the Scranton speech, he gave little if any thought to what the *response* would be to what he said. The first hint of trouble came when a reporter asked John Foster Dulles at a press conference, after the fifth lecture, whether he might now bring Kennan back into the State Department to get the benefit of his thinking. "Well," Dulles replied, provoking laughter, "we have an opportunity to get his thinking anyway, don't we?"[38]

The timing, unplanned by Kennan, could hardly have been better: his final broadcast had long been scheduled for Sunday evening, December 15, 1957, but the NATO heads of government had only recently decided to convene a conference that would begin in Paris on the following morning. It was the first time they had all gathered since establishing the alliance in 1949. From their point of view, though, the content of Kennan's lectures could hardly have been worse.

NATO was reeling from the shocks of the Suez crisis, the Soviet suppression of the Hungarian uprising, and the unexpected launch, on October 4, of the first earth satellite, *Sputnik*, which appeared to confirm Khrushchev's claims to have developed intercontinental ballistic missiles. Dulles sought to reassure the allies with an offer of tactical nuclear weapons and intermediate-range missiles, but since these were meant for use on their own territory, this did little to diminish their anxiety. Eisenhower added to it when he suffered a mild stroke on November 25— coming after his 1955 heart attack and an emergency operation for ileitis in 1956, it was his third health crisis in as many years. Meanwhile West German chancellor Konrad Adenauer had not yet fully convinced his countrymen—especially his critics in the Social Democratic Party—that they should forgo reunification in return for American protection. The last thing any of the leaders in Paris wanted, therefore, was for the principal American strategist of containment, in the most public manner possible, to be calling on them to reconsider it.

That is why Adenauer complained to Eisenhower on December 17, "with some impatience" as the official record understated it, about "the recent lectures by George Kennan which unfortunately had made quite an impression." The opposition newspapers were "quick to pick up this kind of thing." Eisenhower agreed explosively—no small matter in a man upon whose blood pressure the fate of the West appeared to depend:

> The President said that nothing could be more wicked for Germany and the world than the neutralization of Germany. He could see only one result of such neutraliza-tion, namely, absorption by the communists. . . . [W]hat Kennan really proposes is the neutralization of all of Europe, which would be the actual result of his proposal for the neutralization of Germany. He described Kennan as a headline-seeker.[39]

Kennan knew nothing of this conversation, but other reactions reached him soon enough. The Reith lectures had "echoed around the world," the moderator of a special BBC broadcast noted, while introducing him for a follow-up discussion on December 20. The nineteen hundred journalists present in Paris seemed to be spending more time discussing Kennan's arguments than those of anyone else.

The other panelists were unimpressed. What Kennan had said, *Economist* editor Donald Tyerman told him bluntly, seemed dangerous. How could he be sure that the Soviet Union would not attack? The question had plagued Kennan since 1948, and he still had no answer. Soviet ideology, he pointed out, had never required the use of force to ensure communism's triumph, but Soviet leaders were "rubbery," and "infinitely flexible." Might they not try to terrify the Europeans, Tyerman persisted, employing what Kennan himself had called the "psychologi-cal shadow" of military superiority? No, Kennan replied, all they wanted was to get communist regimes in power. But wouldn't that have the same effect? Hadn't Britain declared war in 1914 and 1939 because it feared intimidation, not because it had been attacked? "There I fully agree with you," Kennan conceded, "and I think that the great danger today is that we will be put in a position where we would have to take the overt act." How, then, would a neutralized Germany and a nonnuclear NATO make war less likely? He had not suggested either, Kennan claimed. "I did not feel that any outsider like myself could propose a specific plan of disengagement."

So what *had* he proposed? the puzzled moderator asked. "You're not all that much of an outsider." He was, Kennan responded, in the sense that there were "military considerations" he didn't know about. And he did know, from his State Department service, the limitations of uninformed advice: "I was trying to tell governments what they ought to think about, not what they ought to do." But he proceeded to do that anyway: "I can see no solution to this present jam we're getting ourselves [into] . . . except by some sort of a disengagement of the forces of the great powers in Europe and perhaps later in the Far East."

All of this exasperated Sir John Slessor, of the Royal Air Force, who wondered how the Europeans would defend themselves in the absence of American and British forces "when we've got Sputnik whirling overhead." Was Kennan really proposing that the Europeans rely, as their only deterrent, on the prospect of local resistance after their countries had been overrun? Resistance groups had given the Germans trouble in World War II, Kennan replied, much too lamely, and NATO "obligations" would remain in place after American and British troops had been withdrawn. But a neutralized Germany would not *be* in NATO, the moderator pointed out. No, but it would have its own conventional forces, Kennan retorted. Wouldn't that frighten everybody else, all of the panelists wanted to know, including the Russians?

Kennan fell back, in the end, on something he had once condemned: reliance on "trust" in the conduct of international relations. The figurehead Soviet premier, Nikolay Bulganin, had formally offered to withdraw the Red Army from East Germany and the other Warsaw Pact countries in return for the removal of American and British troops from the European continent: he should be taken seriously. And Kennan himself was certain, on the basis of his residence in Germany as a little boy and as a young diplomat during the 1930s, that the Germans had changed, that they were now "on our side." How the two claims meshed—how the Russians could confidently leave a unified Germany to itself if the Germans were pro-American—he did not explain.

"My feeling now," Kennan wrote in his diary after this embarrassing exchange, "is that I have thoroughly exhausted the working capital of knowledge about international affairs with which I left government, five years ago." He wished "never to open my mouth about them again until I have some opportunity to learn all over again."[40]

VI.

The Kennans left Oxford on December 28 to drive, via an English Channel ferry, to the Swiss resort town of Crans for what they hoped would be a rest. But the weather-plagued hair-raising trip took five days, and when they arrived, George found the proofs of his Reith lectures waiting. "I haven't the faintest enthusiasm for this publication," he lamented, sensing the furor following him around like a baleful ghost. The respected *Neue Zürcher Zeitung*, unaware of his presence in the country, began a series of attacks on him two days after he arrived. At tea that afternoon, one of his hosts jovially credited Kennan with killing the NATO alliance. Just then a message came from an old friend, Gladwyn Jebb, who wanted Kennan to know that his lectures had greatly complicated Jebb's task as British ambassador in Paris. All of this worried Kennan, "because unless I can find some means of withdrawing from the discussion of contemporary affairs, I shall never be able to go successfully through the next term at Oxford."[41]

Much worse came, a week later, in an eruption of monumental proportions from an enraged Dean Acheson. "I am told," the former secretary of state announced in a widely publicized statement on January 11, 1958, "that the impression exists in Europe that the views expressed by Mr. George Kennan . . . represent the views of the Democratic Party in the United States. Most categorically they do not, as I'm sure Mr. Kennan would agree." Kennan could speak authoritatively "in the field he knows," which was Russian history and culture and Marxist-Leninist ideology. However, he "has never, in my judgment, grasped the realities of power relationships, but takes a rather mystical attitude toward them." Had he not provided his "personal assurance" that there was "no Soviet military threat" in Europe? "On what does this guarantee rest, unless Divine revelation?"[42]

The sarcasm was withering, as only Acheson's pen could have made it. As he got older, "he got more drastic," Arthur Schlesinger recalled. "He enjoyed being extravagantly dismissive." But he was doing so, in this instance, on behalf of the American Council on Germany, an influential pro-NATO organization headed by James B. Conant, the ex-president of Harvard who had also served as U.S. high commissioner and later ambassador in West Germany. With Conant's approval— and Nitze's encouragement—the group's vice-chairman, Christopher Emmet, had asked Acheson to reply to Kennan, lest the Europeans mistake him as a "semi-official spokesman and super brain-truster for the Democratic Party." Acheson did not simply jump at this opportunity: he pounced on it. He had written "more for European than American readers," he explained to Emmet, but "it won't hurt some of our Democrats to learn that they don't agree with George."[43]

Harry S. Truman accepted instruction quickly. "I do not agree with Kennan," he assured the press on the day Acheson's statement appeared. "He is not a policy maker." He had been a good ambassador, but only when he had Acheson "to tell him what to do." Conant went further, condemning Kennan's proposals as "a blueprint for the appeasement of the Soviet Union." *The Washington Post*, however, found Acheson's assault "savage" and "inexplicable," coming from someone who had himself been the target of unfair attacks: "He seems to regard Mr. Kennan as an adversary scarcely less dangerous than Mr. Khrushchev, and one to be demolished in entirety." That didn't faze Acheson, but congratulations from Dulles did. "I am getting too respectable to be safe," he wrote a friend. "Alice [Acheson] is already suspicious of me. When I got a letter from Foster thanking me for my attack on George Kennan she was about ready to leave me."[44]

Compliments arrived also from a couple who, had things worked out differently, would have had Kennan as a son-in-law. "Will you send me George Kennan's skin to hang up as a trophy on my office wall?" Eleanor Hard's father Bill wrote Acheson after reading his press release. "You took it off him completely." Anne Hard, who had vetoed the marriage, then added her own reflections:

> George, I thought when he was engaged to Eleanor, [had] integrity, and sweetness and kindness and a pedantic mind and I have seen no reason to alter that judgment in following his later career. . . . I think he is one of those personally lovable people who just can't bear to recognize that anything is ugly and when he gets a hint of it turns and flees or reaches for his kid gloves. I never thought he had great scope or imagination and he looks to me like a fish in water too deep for him.

"Your analysis of George's character seems to me wholly right," Acheson responded. "I had quite forgotten that he was engaged to Eleanor. What an interesting subject for speculation that is."[45]

Kennan was still in Crans when he saw newspaper stories reporting Acheson's assault and Truman's comment: there had been no warning. He was at a loss to account for "this sudden vehement outburst of malevolence" by people he had never publicly criticized "who had hitherto treated me only with cordiality." His difficulty in Moscow, after all, had been "that I *had* no instructions from Mr. Acheson." Quite apart from the personal implications, Kennan took the criticism as ruling out any discussion of a European political settlement within the Democratic as well as the Republican Party. That left only the option of plunging "blindly, recklessly ahead" with an arms race, "wherever it leads us." He was unsure whether even to reply: "The distortions of my thinking are so bad [that] I do not wish to let them ride; on the other hand, is there any use? . . . The die is now cast. . . . These people will have their war, on which they all seem so intent."[46]

Not surprisingly, Kennan's ulcer flared up again under the stress. The demands of the autumn had left him physically debilitated, and he had picked up a sinus infection on the arduous drive to Switzerland. Feeling miserable, he checked himself into a Zürich hospital in mid-January, while Annelise kept Christopher and Wendy busy with skiing lessons in Crans. That at least got George out of a further discussion of the Reith lectures, which the Congress for Cultural Freedom—the secretly CIA-funded organization for European intellectuals—had arranged in Paris. While Joe Alsop, Raymond Aron, Denis Healey, and Sidney Hook were dismantling Kennan's arguments, his doctors were probing his "ghastly digestive system." Sitting for hours one morning with a tube in his stomach, he reached the unsettling conclusion that Dulles might understand him better than Acheson did. "One would think," Kennan wrote of the chorus of critics singing to the tune of his former boss, that "I had caught them all doing something they were ashamed of."[47]

Discharged from the hospital with orders to avoid further tension, George packed the family into the car and drove it back across the Alps into France through a raging blizzard. Fighting snow and ice all the way, they crossed the Channel, this time in an automobile air ferry, and by the end of January were back in Oxford, where George was swamped with unanswered correspondence, demands for interviews, and the need to prepare a new set of lectures. The children, who had thrived in Switzerland, soon had severe coughs, and even Annelise, unusually, was depressed. "Between you and me we just loathe [Oxford]," she wrote Jeanette, and could easily "start chalking up the days until we can leave."[48]

VII.

"The way in which the Establishment set out to swat him down—the things that Dean Acheson said in print about him—wounded [Kennan] very much," Ullman recalled. Meanwhile well-meaning friends, dismayed by the rift, were trying to heal it. "I suppose it was necessary," Joseph C. Harsch, the National Broadcasting Company correspondent in London, wrote Acheson: "If he had to be destroyed only you could do it." But couldn't Acheson let Kennan know that there had been nothing personal in the "dissection"? Not yet, Acheson replied: Kennan's lectures had been not only silly but "extremely harmful."

> An appeal to the lotus-eating spirit in mankind, which urges him to relax just at the
> time when real effort might possibly cause a great improvement, could be disas-

trous. . . . I decided to let him have it, and the reports which have come to me from the continent indicate that it was well worthwhile.

Someday he would write George a friendly note. "For the present, I wish to God that he would devote himself to giving us a new volume on the period 1917–1920 as delightful as the last, and would leave the next forty years alone." Harsch tried again, pointing out that Kennan had been sick and was still convalescing. Acheson was unmoved: "One can hardly do as much damage as George has done," he grumbled to William Tyler, of the American embassy in Bonn, "and then rush off to immunity in the hospital."[49]

"Your January broadside was perfect as a bucket-full of cold water down George's neck and into the faces of the admiring throng," Tyler replied. "As soon as the Germans found out that George was unlikely to be the next secretary of state in a Democratic administration, (and you removed any expectations they may have had on that score) they lost interest in his arabesques." The "brawl" with Kennan had indeed pained their friends, but as Acheson reminded Philip Jessup, "I was not writing for our friends. . . . I was writing for the Germans to destroy as effectively as I could the corroding effect of what he had said and the belief that he was a seer in these matters." Kennan had been trotting out Program A as a "panacea" for every crisis since 1948. Of course it could be looked at again, "just as a loaded gun can be." But "I am against it."[50]

One prominent Democrat, however, chose not to let Acheson tell him what to think. Senator John F. Kennedy wrote Kennan on February 13 to say that he had read the Reith lectures, thought them excellent, and regretted the extent to which their contents had been "twisted and misrepresented"—nothing justified "the personal criticisms that have been made." He did disagree with Kennan on several points; still it was

> most satisfying that there is at least one member of the "opposition" who is not only performing his critical duty but also providing a carefully formulated, comprehensive, and brilliantly written set of alternative proposals and perspectives. You have directed our attention to the right questions and in a manner that allows us to test rigorously our current assumptions.

"It meant a great deal to me," Kennan responded, "to know that you were not among those who consider the Reith lectures to have been some kind of outrage."

Composed under difficult circumstances, they certainly had their shortcomings. Surely, though, NATO policy was sufficiently robust "to stand re-examination at this moment, which seems to me a very dangerous and crucial one."[51]

Unaware of this correspondence, Acheson had sent "Jacquie" Kennedy—whose family he had long known—a copy of a speech he had made objecting to her husband's attacks on French policy in Algeria. "Mr. Acheson" got back a handwritten note praising his "beautifully constructed prose," while wondering how someone "capable of such an Olympian tone can become so personal when attacking policy differences." Caught off guard, Acheson reminded her that the Olympians had been "a pretty personal lot," but he admitted that "[p]erhaps lawyers, who are always contentious fellows, are too hardened to be sensitive to these things. . . . So, you see, you have me very much mixed up." Two days later, on March 10, he asked a mutual friend to tell Kennan that although he would soon be restating his argument in *Foreign Affairs,* "[m]y disagreement does not involve any diminution of my affection for him." A direct letter, enclosing the article proofs, went off three days later: "I am more accustomed to public controversy and criticism than you are. So you are entitled to a few earthy expletives."[52]

Kennan wrote back immediately, claiming to harbor no bitterness but seizing the moment to indulge in a bit of it nonetheless: "I could have wished that your statement had not been so promptly and eagerly exploited by people for whose integrity of motive I have not the same respect I have for your own." He had also been "saddened" by Truman's outburst. "I did not thrust myself on General Marshall or yourself as head of a planning staff, nor on Mr. Truman as Ambassador to Russia, and the efforts I put forward, in all three instances, were the best of which I was capable." As for Acheson's *Foreign Affairs* article, he would answer it in the same forum. He could only say that "rarely, if ever, have I seen error so gracefully and respectfully clothed. One hates to start plucking at such finery; but I suppose that in one way or another I shall have to do so."[53]

"I think this leaves the honors to George," Acheson acknowledged to C. C. Burlingham, a distinguished New York lawyer, then ninety-nine, whom both men knew and revered. He had written to Kennan, Acheson assured the old man— the tone was more that of an apologetic schoolboy than of an aggrieved elder statesman—to say that "although we were engaged in committing mutual mayhem, I was still fond of whatever might be left of him."[54]

VIII.

Not much was. The Reith lectures controversy was really about Germany's place in postwar Europe, and Acheson easily prevailed. He did so because he knew when *not* to plan policy. He had supported Program A until leaks to the press ruled out its pursuit in the spring of 1949; then, to Kennan's bewilderment, he simply dropped it. "If you couldn't get it done you'd proceed another way, but you didn't agonize over things," Acheson's daughter Mary Bundy recalled. "[H]e was a lot tougher than George, and he was a lot more practical a person."

Kennan, in contrast, was constantly recycling, rearranging, and repackaging his ideas. The BBC broadcasts contained no proposals that Acheson hadn't heard before. He had never heard them all at once, though, or in so public a forum, or at such a critical moment. They made it seem as though Kennan, having lost the policy battle in Washington, was now appealing over the heads of elected NATO leaders to their domestic opponents, and even to the Soviet Union itself, the country he had once sought to contain. Acheson was "absolutely furious," Kennan admitted. Bundy remembered this as the moment her father lost confidence "in the stability of the man's thinking, really."

Stability was indeed the issue, but it applied to the entire postwar European settlement. For Kennan, who believed himself more an expert on Germany than Acheson and his supporters, it was absurd to seek safety in that country's indefinite division. "I had, after all, spent five years of my life in Berlin. I was bilingual in the language. What the hell [did] these people know?" No one in his right mind could have planned such an arrangement, which could fall apart at any moment under the combined pressures of German irredentism, Anglo-French anxiety, Eastern European irresponsibility, Soviet neocolonialism, and American militarism. Over it all loomed the unprecedented danger of nuclear war: any other course, Kennan was sure, would be better than that.[55]

Acheson, despite his fury, was more hopeful. He saw more clearly than Kennan that however illogical the division of Germany was, few people anywhere—not even most Germans—were seeking to overturn it. The very danger of war that Kennan regarded as destabilizing had, in Acheson's view, the opposite effect: it was "deterrence." A post–World War II order was *evolving* in Europe, much as legal precedents evolve, without anyone having *designed* it, as had happened with so little success after World War I. Trained as a lawyer, Acheson understood and respected this process, so much so that it became almost theology. Anything that might deflect NATO from its present path bordered on heresy—even the grand design of a former policy planner, the logic of which Acheson had once embraced.

Both men were right, but in different eras. Acheson's settlement kept the peace in Europe for the next three decades, and by the 1970s even Kennan could see its robustness. "[W]e might all have been spared a lot of trouble if someone in authority had come to me before these lectures were given and had said: 'Look here, George, the decision to leave Europe divided . . . has already been taken, even if it hasn't been announced; the talk about German unification is all eyewash; and there isn't the faintest thing to be gained by your attempting to change this situation.'" Or as he put it in 1984, "the right thing said at the wrong time is almost worse than saying the wrong thing at the right time."[56]

But by the end of the 1980s, the division of Germany was breaking down, as Kennan had predicted it would while on the Policy Planning Staff in 1948–49 and over the BBC in 1957. This was occurring, though, not through the negotiations he had envisaged with Moscow but because the Soviet system itself was breaking apart, something an earlier Kennan had foreseen from his vantage point in Riga in 1932 and in the "X" article of 1947. He had, his friend Oliver Franks pointed out, put the cart before the horse in making German reunification the prerequisite for ending the Cold War: the sequence, in fact, was the other way around. "It's very difficult," Franks added, "to distinguish between those insights of Kennan which are almost prophetic in their accuracy, and those which just aren't."[57]

IX.

Kennan resumed his Oxford lectures late, on February 18, 1958, delivering only five before Hilary term ended the following month. This disappointed his audience, because he had promised a history of Soviet foreign policy and got only as far as the Rapallo Conference of 1922. Health was cited as one of the reasons, but the Reith controversy was still a major distraction for Kennan, leaving little time for anything else. Late-winter Oxford was as depressing as ever, so much so that he now missed—however implausibly—the United States. Hearing an American accent made him realize "how much this period abroad has caused me to love my own people." To be sure, they faced great problems: they were destined "within my children's time to know unprecedented horrors and miseries and probably to pass entirely from the scene of world history." If he could do anything to keep them from that fate, "this would be the most useful purpose to which I could put the remainder of my life."

But what? The crisis he had been through had shown that scholarship and current events were "like oil and water; they have nothing to do with one another; attention given to one is given at the cost of the other." Nobody thought his historical writing relevant to the present, but giving it up for journalism or politics would require sacrificing the independence that the Institute for Advanced Study had provided him. "I am in some travail," he admitted to "Eka" Kantorowicz, over "how to reconcile the obligations of a historian with the maddening and unaccountable preference of the public . . . to hear what I have to say about contemporary events, concerning which I know almost nothing. If you have any suggestions, I should be grateful."[58]

The Kennans spent the Oxford spring break at Cascais, in their much-loved Portugal, where George finished his response to Acheson for *Foreign Affairs* and began pondering his future. The leisure, the sun, and the sea caused him to tell himself—most uncharacteristically—that he should lighten up:

> I see myself laughing at myself—even at my weaknesses—recognizing the latter for the anachronisms that they are—sketching and writing fiction when the alternative would be restlessness—trying harder than I have ever tried to taste and preserve in this way the texture of life, the flavour of each day, as though it were the last I had to live—inflicting a certain asceticism on the body (for what is worse than an aging body indulged), but doing so, by all means, gaily, ironically, without grimness, taking with a laugh and without fear the body's aches and pains, its desires, and its need for discipline.

The next evening he started Joseph Conrad's *Under Western Eyes*, couldn't stop until he finished it, and then was so excited that he got no sleep. The following morning found him "dead tired and full of remorse. Time to begin laughing at myself."

An excellent opportunity arose the following day when Kennan paid his respects to Dr. António Salazar, still Portugal's prime minister, whom he had first met during the Azores bases crisis of 1943. Then almost seventy, the durable autocrat was happy to see Kennan, but totally unsympathetic to his recent proposals. "Disengagement" made no sense because no one trusted the Germans or the Russians. Nuclear weapons were too terrible ever to be used and hence nothing to worry about. Intercontinental ballistic missiles had hardly even registered with

Salazar. Kennan had the good sense not to argue with the old man, or even to fall into a diary funk afterward—this was progress.[59]

The last months in England were far more relaxed than the fall and winter had been. Kennan lectured in London, Swansea, Aberystwyth, and Cambridge, the latter on a spring day, with punters on the Cam, tennis players in the Backs, under "such a wonderful mellow, shimmering light as one sees only in the French impressionist paintings." John Holmes, a Canadian diplomat who attended an off-the-record Chatham House discussion with Kennan, found him reluctant to disagree with any of his critics. "[W]ell beyond most mortals" in his sense of history but "incredibly naïve" about current policy, Kennan left Holmes wondering "if perhaps it was I rather than he who was blind. . . . I could see, however, why so many people have a great affection for him and why, at the same time, they all grow so exasperated with him."[60]

Kennan's last Oxford talk, on May 13, was to American students at Rhodes House. He told them, as he later summarized it,

> that neither our political system, nor the popular attitudes underlying it, were ade-
> quate to the solution of our national problems, but that one should nevertheless not
> hesitate to do whatever one could in public life, because (1) you could never tell; his-
> tory performed strange tricks on us, and I might be wrong; and (2) even if we were
> going down, that was no reason for deserting the ship: I had sometimes thought, in
> my blacker moments, that even if the things I cared about were disappearing, I could
> find satisfaction in the feeling that they would disappear more slowly, more stub-
> bornly, more majestically, for what I had done to invigorate them.

The young men, Kennan could see, were "interested but disturbed" by what he had said: coming from him, however, it was a rare expression of optimism.[61]

Three days later he traveled by rail to Cornwall to pick up a collection of Rus-sian revolutionary newspapers, with the last leg of the trip on a branch line little changed since the nineteenth century: "The little locomotive puffed furiously as it pulled us up and up through the forests to Bodmin. . . . It reminded me of my youth; and I was aware of experiencing, this one last time, a form of transporta-tion which the younger generation will probably never know." Feeling this loss yet mindful of the future, he rode back to Oxford with an imaginary companion.

At fifty-four, he told himself and his fellow traveler, he could assume perhaps another ten or fifteen years of active life. Both his government experience and his scholarly pursuits were wearing thin. So what would he lose, his companion asked, "by setting out, like the [M]arxists, to act upon life rather than to understand it?" Why not seek "real power," in the hope of accomplishing "at least one or two concrete things before turning [it] over entirely to the new generation?"

> I saw myself shedding the naïve sincerity I have worn on my sleeve throughout . . . my life; ceasing to be the wide-eyed child I have always been; becoming as wise as the serpent, and as lonely; taking no one fully into confidence; playing the game as others play it, but not for myself . . . , rather for the sake of what I represent and belong to, which is now in such urgent and mortal peril.

There could be, his friend whispered, great strength in choosing this path, for everything would fall into place: there would be "a rationale for all personal choices, as well as for professional decisions." It could "take up the strains created, and fill the gaps opened up, by increasing age." It could relieve personal frustrations—"the passage of sexual love, the growing up and weaning of one's children, . . . the decline of one's powers of imagination and perception"— allowing their acceptance "with a scornful smile." For as Goethe had written:

> *Bedenkt, der Teufel, der ist alt;*
> *Man muss alt sein, ihn zu verstehen.*
>
> *[Ponder this, the devil is old;*
> *one must be old too, to understand him.]*

Perhaps, Kennan concluded, Mephistopheles had something to offer.[62]

TWENTY-ONE

Kennedy and Yugoslavia: 1958–1963

"Never, I believe, have I parted with greater indifference from any place where I have lived," George wrote of Oxford after he and his family finally left it in June 1958 for a summer in Kristiansand, before returning to the United States. Norway was brighter, cleaner, and more congenial than Great Britain, yet even there youths had few interests beyond motorbikes, sailing was a dying sport, walking was a forgotten pastime, and adults were succumbing to "an anti-intellectualism, a cultural flaccidity, a complacent materialism worse than ours—plus a devastating secularism." If this was happening in Scandinavia, then did the West deserve to survive? Hadn't the time really come for the Russians to take over?

It was another descent into diary despair, although this time with a twist: "I cannot believe it." Once subject "to the wind of material plenty," Kennan predicted, the Russians would be "as helpless as the rest of us—even more so—under its debilitating and insidious breath." He had been forecasting the corruption of communism by capitalism since 1932, but his lack of faith in his own country had made it hard to see when or how that might occur. Now, though, having spent a year abroad, the United States was looking better to him.[1]

On June 27 Kennan flew to Copenhagen, where the State Department had opened a new embassy building. He found the male staffers "loose-jointed, casual, diffident, drawling, yet full of modesty and common sense"—qualities he had admired, during the war, in the young American occupiers of Italy. The women were crisp, controlled, and helpful, their voices as innocently unselfconscious as if "they had never left Kansas City." Suddenly—melodramatically—Kennan was homesick:

Oh my countrymen, my countrymen, my hope and my despair! What virtues you conceal beneath your slouching self-deprecation: virtues inconceivable to the pompous continental. How strong you are in all that of which you are yourselves not conscious; and how childish and superficial you are in your own concept of the sources of your excellence.

His frustrations about America were really frustrations about himself: "These are my people; it is to them, with all their deficiencies, that I, with all my deficiencies, belong. It is to them that I must return, after every rebellion, for punishment or forgiveness." Like distant but patient parents, their strengths were not to be underestimated:

Take heed, you scoffers, you patronizers, you envious and malicious detractors, you conceited and superior Europeans, you Nassers and Khrushchevs: if you continue with your efforts to tear us down, you will rouse us yet to maturity, to introspection, to disillusionment, to cunning in our own defense; and when you do, you will discover in us reserves of strength such as you never dreamed of; and then you, even more than we, will come to regret the passing of the days of our own innocence.

Kennan shared the next leg of his flight, to Warsaw, with an Air Force attaché, his wife, and their family. Despite heavy turbulence, he chewed his gum, read his magazines, and exuded complete confidence. Would he do so in the face of "atomic death"? Probably, Kennan concluded. "Great institutions create, for those who are within them, their own illusions of security; and the United States Air Force is now a great institution."

The Polish trip, arranged through Oxford friends, was Kennan's first to a communist country since the Soviet Union expelled him in 1952. Most of Warsaw had been rebuilt from its near obliteration, on Hitler's orders, during the war. Much seemed slavishly Russian: the tawdry apartment blocks rising from seas of mud; the Stalinist skyscraper on which Poles carefully did not comment; the Hotel Bristol, which with its "shoddy air of mystery," its "dreary, furtive corridors," its "intensive eyeing of people," even its delegations of visiting Chinese, Mongolians, and North Koreans, evoked the Metropole in Moscow.

But in the city center, a declaration of architectural independence had taken place: the Polish government was meticulously reconstructing the palaces and churches of the feudal and bourgeois eras. Had it tried to design anything more modern, Kennan was sure, the plans would have been ideologically incorrect and hence rejected. The Poles sensed, though, a respect on the Russians' part for prerevolutionary culture, the natural evolution of which their revolution had so brutally broken off. So the new buildings were safe because they *looked* old. They stood "a trifle sheepishly, as [though] surprised, and almost discomfited, to be thus resurrected from a past [to] which, after all, they can never return."

Kennan's hosts at the Institute of International Affairs were charming, urbane, and politically sophisticated. Not really communists, they treated recent history like Soviet architecture: one did not speak of the Katyn massacre, or of the Red Army's failure to prevent the crushing of the Warsaw Uprising, and "in this studied silence, there is a condemnation more devastating than in any words." The only committed communist Kennan met was trying to build something hopeful on a "dismal foundation of error and grim despotism." He felt sorry for her: she was "destined, unquestionably, for disillusionment and tragedy."

Knowing that he would be among scholars, Kennan had planned to lecture on American intervention in Russia after the Bolshevik Revolution. Upon his arrival, however, the head of the institute informed him, with some embarrassment, that the Soviet authorities had objected to this topic, but that he was to go ahead with it anyway. The lecture was readvertised as one on contemporary problems of U.S. foreign policy. Puzzled, Kennan asked if he should now switch to that subject. No, he was told, he was to give the original talk, *under* the newly announced title. This had been "the bargain" with Moscow.

So Kennan spoke, on July 1, to a hand-picked audience, received polite applause when he finished, and then waited, in awkward silence, for questions. Only one came: how he could have called World War I a "tragedy," since it had led to the formation of the modern Polish state? Kennan stumbled through an answer, and the session ended. The audience's reticence, he later realized, reflected the fact that *it* was being watched. But it had been happy for *him* to say whatever he wished.[2]

Kennan subsequently reported to the CIA on how much the Poles were departing from Soviet "socialism." If left unchallenged, the liberties they were taking would become rights, so deeply rooted that "any withdrawal of them would appear as a preposterous injury." A kind of "liberation" was occurring from within. Further rhetoric about "liberation" from without could only delay its development. "While I do not share the views of the writer on many subjects," Allen Dulles commented, in forwarding Kennan's analysis to the White House, "his report on Poland is the best summary I have seen on the evolving situation there. It is possible that the President would be interested in glancing it over." The initials "DE" on the document, together with underlinings and a distinctive doodle, show that he did.³

George could have felt some satisfaction, therefore, as he, Annelise, Christopher, and Wendy sailed for home in late July on a slow freighter, the MS *Texas*, whose principal cargo was cement, granite blocks, and a hundred Volvos. The European balance of power looked very different from what it had been a decade earlier. With American help, the Western Europeans had regained prosperity and self-confidence. It was now the Russians who were walking a tightrope in Eastern Europe, knowing how gleefully their "allies" would welcome a tumble into the abyss. Kennan had anticipated both possibilities, devised a strategy to bring them about, and for all of its parochialism, immaturity, and opportunistic politics, his country had broadly followed it.

In fact, though, Kennan made no further effort, on the long voyage home, to reflect on the relaxed Americans and resolute Poles he had met—or to wonder why the Russians, in Warsaw, had been so nervous about his presence. Instead, as the ship approached the New England coast, he was brooding about what lay ahead.

> [W]hat does one do with this contemporary America: with this great hive of bewildered people, now in such deep trouble, so anxious in some ways for the sort of help I can give, so resentful of it in others, so exhausting and competitive in its demands, so quick to pluck to pieces and destroy anything and anyone that engages its attention?

Should he try to help? Or should he admit the futility of doing so and retire to cultivate his garden, writing books that only a handful of people might read and that would "probably burn up, anyway, in the imminent atomic holocaust?" The *Texas* rounded Nantucket on August 2, "and just as we did so the moon rose, ominous and blood red, in the east. A strange evening, intensely beautiful, and slightly sinister."⁴

I.

The Kennans spent the rest of August 1958 at the farm, where George carefully chronicled his activities: ditch digging, fence building, buying a tractor, completing a survey of the property, arranging for a new tenant to manage the place. He also granted an interview—his first in over a year—to the *Harrisburg Patriot-News*, which celebrated its exclusive "Press Conference with Ex-Ambassador Keenan" by staging a "Mr. X Contest." Princeton, when the family returned to it in September, was "gloriously quiet, relaxed, comfortable," but George soon felt himself sinking back into "the false, tense, harried life of the American upper class—tightly organized, over-elaborate in all its arrangements, lacking in spontaneity, everyone living on the outward edge of their energies and resources, . . . attempting to meet standards which, being themselves survivals of the age of servants, are themselves exorbitant." So he resolved to seek refuge, for three hours each day, deep within the university's Firestone Library, "where no one knows where to find me." That would leave twelve hours for sleeping and meals, eight for activities apart from scholarship, and one for work around the yard and the house.[5]

George liked to joke that separating his older and younger children by thirteen years had been a triumph of policy planning: "We raised our baby sitters first." Now, though, they were leaving. Grace had married in March, while her parents and younger siblings were still in Oxford: the bridegroom was Charles K. McClatchy, a reporter and former Adlai Stevenson aide whose family owned a major newspaper chain in California. George and Annelise covered the costs of the event, which took place in Washington, but then could not afford to fly back for it. They met their new son-in-law when he and Grace came through London in May, and by the end of the year, there was a first grandchild.[6]

Joan, in the meantime, had announced her engagement to Larry Griggs, a rising senior at Brown University. Shortly after returning for her own final year at Connecticut College, she received a letter, in familiar handwriting and on Institute for Advanced Study stationery, purporting to be from the family dog Krisha. Life in Princeton was lonely, the poodle complained. Rations were meager. It was a relief to get Christopher and Wendy off for school each morning, because their idea of petting resembled Greek-Roman wrestling. And the neighborhood canines were either ancient or lascivious:

> [D]ear Joany, what does one do with the male sex? Why are they so single-minded? It's all very flattering; and I suppose one wouldn't be without it; but why can't they show a little imagination? . . . I heard Wendy tell your Dad, yesterday, that there was a wedding going on in the backyard, and I suppose that's one way of putting it.

Dismayed, on a trip to the farm, not to find Joan there, Krisha had to spend the weekend "in the scintillating company of her old man, with his muddy boots, his bills and workmen, his ditches and gutters, and his grim physiognomy—well, at least he takes a walk occasionally."[7]

The old man, that fall and winter, was grimly regarding his country, the world, the afterlife, and of course himself. He found Eisenhower's determination to defend Chiang Kai-shek's offshore outposts on Quemoy and Matsu to be tautological, since their importance lay only in the administration's assurances that they were important. He worried about Khrushchev's increasing unpredictability: a mature and "statesmanlike" enemy—Stalin?—was manageable, "but God save us from the erratic and distraught one." He was reading Henry Kissinger and Reinhold Niebuhr on nuclear weapons, finding the former unconvincing and the latter prophetic. Seeking safety in such devices, Kennan concluded, was like a child wandering through his father's house "with a faggot of burning papers in his hand." He wondered, on Christmas Day 1958, how there could be hope for earthly progress if Christ had been born "to save us in the next world, not in this." And on the following Easter Sunday, having exhausted himself with farm work, he lay down in the fading Pennsylvania light to ponder "the genuine dead-end" at which his life had arrived: "I haven't the faintest idea what now to do with myself."[8]

"Here I am: 55 years of age," Kennan wrote a few weeks later. "I have some talents and some strength. I have nothing to lose by dedicating myself to something," for without that, life would be "a gradual rotting and disintegrating in the warm, debilitating narcotic bath of upper-class American civilization." Anything would be better than that. "I am, after all, expendable," but for what? "Where is a vehicle, a framework, in which energy can usefully be expended?"[9]

Thanks largely to Acheson, Kennan had become persona non grata with much of the American—and Western European—foreign policy establishment. White House press secretary James Hagerty felt it necessary to assure reporters, when Kennan attended a conference there in January, that he would not be meeting alone with the president. "Why, hello Kennan," a startled Eisenhower said as they shook hands in the receiving line. "It's some time since I've seen you." Kennan showed up at a Council on Foreign Relations discussion in April but was made to feel "as if the Devil had been occupying a pew in church." It was clear, he acknowledged in July, that "[t]here is to be no disengagement.... The line of division in Europe is to be made steadily sharper, more meaningful, more ineradicable."[10]

Kennan continued to get compliments, however, from Senator John F. Kennedy, who, having read his reply to Acheson in *Foreign Affairs,* praised the way it avoided "the kind of *ad hominem* irrelevancies in which Mr. Acheson unfortunately indulged last year." Kennedy was always looking for negotiating possibilities with the Russians, Arthur Schlesinger remembered: also, he "admired Kennan as a historian." Another admirer, unexpectedly, was Richard M. Nixon, in whose company Kennan found himself at a Washington reception in July. The vice president greeted him warmly, insisted on being photographed with him, and went out of his way to explain, to a very surprised Loy Henderson, that "Kennan here has performed a great service in his lectures and writings. We need someone like this to stir things up." "Poor Loy, who probably thinks I ought to be shot at sunrise, had no choice but to agree," George wrote Annelise afterward.[11]

John Foster Dulles had resigned as secretary of state shortly before his death, from cancer, in May 1959. His successor, Under Secretary Christian A. Herter, harbored no particular animus toward Kennan but gave him no reason to anticipate an appointment during the remainder of Eisenhower's term. The Institute would expect Kennan to continue as a historian: having established his credentials in that field, however, he felt the need now only to deliver lectures, write periodic reviews, and encourage younger scholars. The promised third volume on early Soviet-American relations was less important than commentary on public affairs: "I owe it to people here who have confidence in me to write, in book form, the rationale of my despair with the country." At least in England there had been a community "to which I was civilly and fully admitted, during the period of my residence there."[12]

Kennan had not forgotten how much, only a year earlier, he had despised the place: the "community" he really missed was a great friend. "I sometimes think I would accept again all the asperities of English life," he wrote Isaiah Berlin, "for the delights of sheer conversation." He had even dreamed recently of trying to talk with Berlin, over "the roar and surge of some enormous cocktail party." Perhaps this reflected "the desperate intensity with which England seems to be trying to become like ourselves. . . . How the good old subconscious does go to the heart of things!"[13]

Never had he lived in any place "where the present did not seem to represent a deterioration as compared with the past," George realized in a flash of self-recognition that spring. This had been true of Riga, Berlin, Prague, Vienna, Moscow—the only exception, perhaps, had been Lisbon under Salazar. It was as if he blighted his own surroundings. If Christopher were to ask where, "in this world to which you have introduced me," he could have a rewarding life, "what could I say? Only at the ends of the earth: in the Arctic, perhaps; where almost no other men live; where Nature, not man, is your companion. For my own country, I have not a shred of hope, not one."[14]

And what of his own weaknesses? In Chicago, in April, "I took X to tea." Wandering around the lobby of the Palmer House, they found a quiet place to talk. She was "her old self: impulsive, warm, and very foolish." When they parted, her final word, "flung over the heads of the startled passers-by," was: "Sorry to have been so miserable." She thereby negatively illustrated a positive principle: "If you have tendencies which you know yourself are wrong, which you cannot control yet cannot leave, don't apologize for them—brave them out; they are, after all, a part of you."[15]

Joan's wedding took place in Princeton that June, just after her graduation, under unexpectedly dramatic circumstances. As the guests gathered, there was a screeching of brakes and Christopher came running to say that Krisha had been run over. George and Jeanette's son Gene rushed her to the veterinarian, who determined that she had been frightened but not hurt, while the rest of the family conspired to keep the news from Joan. Despite the near-tragedy, the wedding went off smoothly: "The present, at least, had been well lived through," George wrote with relief in his diary. "[T]he future would have to take care of itself."[16]

He sailed for Europe, where he would be attending a series of conferences, in early September. His family, this time, did not accompany him, so he spent most of the voyage in the company only of his diary. "I have been very heroic. . . . I have lived for a week in studied solitude among this crowd of people; I have had a drink with no one at the bar; aware of my age and dignity, I have let the ladies all pass me by; I have resisted the temptation to hear myself talk." Why make "such a fetish of my loneliness"? Why take such satisfaction "in a total abstention from contact with any one else?" Why, for that matter, at Oxford, had he never watched a crew race or dined at high table in Balliol, his host college? It was of course a neurosis, perhaps inherited: "I have an idea that my father was much the same way." But it was also "for myself that I do this. . . . I am determined that if I cannot have all, or the greater part, of what I want, no one is going to deprive me of the glorious martyrdom of having none of it."[17]

"I still think constantly about what we should do," George wrote Annelise from Rheinfelden, in Switzerland, where he was trying in vain to extract coherence from a meandering meeting of the Congress for Cultural Freedom. "I suppose we shall end up by continuing to do exactly what we have been doing." But "I have washed my clothes so regularly, and have acquired such expertise, that I could set up in the laundry business when I get back."[18]

II.

Strangely, the American political process, in which Kennan had so little faith, produced presidential candidates in 1960 who professed to admire him. As an Eisenhower administration exile, Kennan dismissed Nixon's praise as opportunistic flattery, probably unfairly. Kennedy, however, had impressed Kennan from the second time they met. That was in 1953, fifteen years after their unfortunate first encounter in Prague after Munich. "I was amazed," Kennan recalled, "to see anyone looking so young and so modest in [a] Senatorial position." Kennedy's support in the Reith lectures controversy had been a boost at a bad time, and while vacationing in Jamaica at the end of 1959, he sent another compliment—this time in his almost illegible handwriting—applauding the "dispassionate good sense" of a talk Kennan had given on the possibility of abolishing nuclear weapons, while wondering how in their absence the United States might contain the "endless" conventional forces of the Chinese. "I was much moved that you should have taken the trouble to write," Kennan replied, "for I know how tremendously burdened your time must be."[19]

Perhaps because of his 1956 disillusionments, Kennan took little part in the 1960 campaign. Citing Institute obligations, he rejected an effort by New Jersey Democrats to have him run for the Senate. Support was strong enough, though, for Governor Robert Meyner to insist on a face-to-face refusal. "I did my stuff," Kennan recorded, "and everyone, I think, was happy." Paul Nitze got a similar brush-off after asking—it seemed "with no great show of enthusiasm"—whether Kennan would join the Democratic Party Advisory Council's foreign policy committee: "This was not my dish."[20]

One other reason for avoiding politics was that Kennan had become, temporarily, a teacher. He spent five weeks at Harvard that spring drafting and delivering the rest of the lectures he had meant to give at Oxford two years earlier. Dick Ullman attended this series too, and found the response much the same: Kennan filled the largest hall available. "Without any concessions to the crowd, without any attempt to make the complex more palatable by oversimplifying or sensationalizing, by the mere force of his intellect and eloquence," the Russian historian Richard Pipes later wrote, Kennan's was "one of the most impressive rhetorical performances I have ever witnessed." Combined, the two sets of lectures became a survey of Soviet-American relations, *Russia and the West under Lenin and Stalin*, which appeared the following year. Meanwhile Kennan had agreed to teach a graduate seminar at Yale in the fall. "History Goes Big," the *Yale Daily News* excitedly editorialized. "It is the first time I have ever done anything of this sort," George wrote Kent, "and I am enjoying it very much."[21]

The Kennans had spent most of the summer of 1960 in Europe: Kristiansand, Berlin, Hamburg, Venice, and—most interesting for George—Belgrade, where his notes on what he saw in three days filled six single-spaced pages. The high point was an hour with Tito, "a Balkan communist of humble origin, tough and simple, no longer young; the personality [shaped by] endless battles and dangers; a trifle smug with success, yet also somewhat out of place in the white uniform and pretentious setting of a head of state." What interested him most about Yugoslavia, Kennan wrote Elim O'Shaughnessy, now *chargé d'affaires* there, was how delicately its leaders balanced the acknowledged absurdity of Marxism-Leninism against their need to preserve the ideology in whose name they had gained and retained power. China, Kennan predicted, would soon face the same dilemma.[22]

Out of the country during the Democratic and Republican conventions, Kennan returned in mid-August to find Kennedy and Nixon in a tight race. He quickly sent Kennedy an eight-page letter on how to regain the initiative in world affairs by curtailing existing commitments, strengthening conventional military capabilities, and encouraging a Sino-Soviet split through improved relations with Moscow, now "royally fouled up" as a result of the U-2 incident the previous May when an American reconnaissance plane had been shot down over the U.S.S.R. He ended with a reminder of Marshall's 1947 advice: "Avoid trivia."[23]

Disappointingly, Kennedy responded only through his aide, Theodore Sorensen, who wrote to welcome whatever other thoughts Kennan might have. Kennedy later explained to C. L. Sulzberger that Kennan's support for "disengagement" made it awkward "to mention his name at this time." He had been in touch with Kennan, though, and hoped "to get him back." Kennan, in the meantime, had tried to help by criticizing Nixon's refusal, in the second televised debate with Kennedy, to reconsider policy on Quemoy and Matsu or to express regret over the U-2. Shockingly, though, *The New York Times* declined to publish Kennan's full letter. If he could not look to the *Times* "as a channel for my own views," he complained angrily to James Reston, then this raised doubts "as to whether I can and should continue to try to contribute at all to the discussion of public problems in this country."[24]

Even if the Democrats won, Kennan warned himself, he would have little influence in the new administration, "partly because I am poor; partly because I have aroused jealousy; partly because I have said the right things too soon; partly because the appeal to the public, in our country, has to go through the mass media; and these media are incapable of appreciating or transmitting that which I have to offer." Therefore,

> having nothing of any importance to give my strength to, I shall do all possible to conserve and develop it;
> having nothing for which to be prepared, I shall try to act as though the next day, in each case, was the day of supreme challenge;
> having no audience, I shall try to act as though a million people were watching.

And how had he improved since leaving for England three years earlier? "The changes have been only chemical, and not to the good: like toenails growing on a corpse."[25]

III.

Nevertheless, Kennan got Oppenheimer's assurances, a few days before the election, that if asked to serve in the next administration, he could do so without giving up his professorship. On October 30 Kennedy finally wrote to say that he had "profited greatly" from Kennan's August letter, and to thank him for his support in the campaign. After Kennedy's narrow victory on November 8, Joe Alsop, still sensing caution in the president-elect, urged him to offer Kennan at least an ambassadorship: he was, next to Bohlen, "the Foreign Service's most distinguished member." Frieda Por sent George a new pair of gloves for Christmas, which Annelise took to mean that she expected an overseas appointment: "So far we have not seen any sign of it." And George, writing to thank Kent for the annual shipment of grapefruit, thought it "quite unlikely that I should be going back to government."[26]

He explained why, to himself, in a long, anguished diary entry on Monday, January 2, 1961: "[I]t is now nearly two months since the election, and I have heard literally nothing from anyone in Washington." All the senior foreign policy posts had gone to people "whom I thought of as friends: Dean Rusk, Adlai Stevenson, Chester Bowles, Paul Nitze, Mac Bundy." The newspapers were speculating about Bohlen's future but had said nothing about his. The silence was as profound as after Eisenhower's election. "Mr. Acheson and the others" who had worked to keep him out of the Kennedy administration had won. "I have lost." All that was left was to write his memoirs, after which "the shades of loneliness will really close in on me. . . . Never, I think, has there been a man so wholly alone as I have been in this time."[27]

But it was not 1953 all over again. On Tuesday the phone rang: Senator Kennedy's office wished to know whether Ambassador Kennan could meet him in New York on January 10, "which I agreed to do." Kennan found the Kennedy plane waiting at LaGuardia, and after the president-elect arrived, they flew to Washington, talking over lunch all the way. Kennedy asked brief questions, to which Kennan provided long answers. Why were the Russians so eager for a summit? How should he organize the White House staff? Could the Foreign Service be made more efficient? Should Llewellyn Thompson remain as ambassador in Moscow? Kennan thought Kennedy an excellent listener: he resisted the temptation to tell jokes or to make sententious statements, "a rare thing among men who have arisen to very exalted positions." He said nothing about an appointment, though, and after the plane landed, Kennan caught a train back to Princeton, arriving in time for dinner.[28]

But on Monday, January 23—three days after Kennedy's inauguration— Kennan checked his mail at Yale's Branford College. An ashen-faced undergraduate was on the office phone: "Seeing me, he jumped up in relief and said: 'Mr. Kennan, the President of the United States wants to talk to you.'" It was indeed Kennedy, calling to ask whether Kennan might agree to become ambassador to Poland or Yugoslavia: could he let Rusk, now secretary of state, know which it might be? Kennan was staying that evening with the George Piersons—he was the chairman of the Yale history department—and it was from their house, before dinner, that Kennan called Rusk to say that it would be Yugoslavia. "I am very enthusiastic about the way in which the new administration is taking hold," a more cheerful George wrote his half-brother a few days later. "This is one of the reasons why I go back to government so gladly."[29]

There was no delay this time about the *agrément*: the Yugoslavs were delighted with Kennan's appointment. They had liked his Reith lectures and were sure, despite his denials, that he had visited the country the previous summer "to case the joint." So Kennan spent the first week of February receiving briefings in Washington while delivering one of his own to the Policy Planning Staff and its new director, George McGhee. The topic was not Yugoslavia, about which Kennan as yet knew little, but the future of Soviet-American relations. It was the first time since the Solarium exercise of 1953 that anyone within the government—apart from the CIA—had sought his views.

Kennan saw no possibility now of ending the division of Europe. But the United States should seek points of agreement with the U.S.S.R.—particularly on commercial ties, to which the Kremlin leadership attached symbolic significance—while avoiding unnecessary irritants like the annual congressional resolution that called for liberating the "captive nations" of Eastern Europe: "Khrushchev with all his bluster is a sensitive man. We need patience and humor in dealing with him. We should not be worried by his statement that the Soviet Union intends to bury us—this was metaphorical, and the Soviet leaders know where their real interests lie." Kennan did not repeat his suggestion, made to Kennedy, that improving Soviet-American relations could sharpen Sino-Soviet differences. He did, however, revive his proposal—first made over a decade earlier—that the United States withdraw its military bases from Japan. And it would be helpful if the State Department could return "to the old practice of giving instructions to a newly-appointed Ambassador explaining the purposes and objectives of his mission."[30]

On February 11 Kennan, along with Rusk, Harriman, Bohlen, National Security Adviser McGeorge Bundy, and Vice President Lyndon B. Johnson, attended a briefing for President Kennedy at the White House from Ambassador Thompson, just back from Moscow. Kennan could not help noticing that Johnson sat "in what seemed to me to be a sulky silence." There was general agreement with Thompson's claim that Soviet military and economic strength was increasing but also with Kennan's reminder that Khrushchev and his colleagues expected to win "by the play of other forces." Among these were "third world" opportunities, as in Laos, the Congo, and Cuba. The Soviet leader was eager to resume talks with the United States, broken off after the U-2 incident, and would probably not react violently "to a possible swift action against the Castro government." Bundy's minutes failed to specify who made this last suggestion; nor did they record what Kennan recalled Bohlen and himself saying next to the president: "Whatever you feel you have to do here, be sure that it is successful."[31]

At his confirmation hearing on March 6, Kennan reminded the Senate Foreign Relations Committee that neither the Soviet Union nor Communist China controlled Yugoslavia: "We should be happy to see that country maintain maximum independence." The committee confirmed Kennan's appointment unanimously, the Senate quickly agreed, and he was sworn in on March 22. That afternoon Kennan again saw the president, who wanted to know what his new ambassador to Belgrade thought about the government to which he was now accredited.

The Yugoslavs, Kennan replied, accepted American economic and financial assistance, yet supported the Soviet position "on almost every important issue."

Tito and his associates were "too deeply affected by their early Communist training to be able to get away from it entirely." The best hope lay in the next generation
of Yugoslav leaders, who might welcome "normal and intimate relations with us."
Would it help, Kennedy asked, to invite Tito to the United States? Perhaps, Kennan replied, but only if the visit was likely to produce "*some* favorable effect of a
tangible nature" on the mutual relationship.[32]

The important thing for Kennan at the moment, though, was rehabilitation:
having despaired of any such possibility at the beginning of January, he now, at
the end of March, had regained his influence in Washington, had been given an
ambassadorship in a country he had long considered significant, and was serving
a president who sought and respected his counsel. "Kennedy was a fan," Bundy
recalled. He responded to "exactly the kind of unusual, sensitive, independent
intelligence" that Kennan possessed. The president had been "very kind," George
wrote in his diary on the evening of the twenty-second, and "my admiration continues undiminished."[33]

Back at the farm that weekend, he found "the house dank, the pump broken,
the furnace losing water—A. was very dispirited. However, by evening, I had the
house warm. And when Dorothy [Hessman], Wendy, and Krisha arrived from
Princeton, it seemed more like old times." The Kennans' final briefing on Yugoslavia came a few days later from a friend, Robert Strunsky:

The people are mainly Serbs and Croats
Who used to be at each other's throats.
But times have changed, and they've called it quits,
And now toast each other in slivovitz,
(A native brandy distilled from the prune
Which, when over-indulged in, can lead to ruin).

The language is difficult to determine;
The "j" is pronounced like the "j" in German,
But the "z" is pronounced like the "j" in French
(You set your jaw; and your teeth you clench).
. . . .

So much for the language . . . The People are gay,
And given to poetry, music and play.
The names of their cities are short and sweet,

Like Bled and Brod and Ub and Split.
On the other hand, you can also go
From Virovotica to Sarajevo.

So it looks as if there is much in store
For our friends who are off to this distant shore.
As eastward you turn with new bonds to forge
We wish you Godspeed, Annelise and George.[34]

IV.

Kennan's first significant act as ambassador took place before he left the United States. On April 19, 1961, he stopped by the Yugoslav embassy in Washington to warn his counterpart, Ambassador Marko Nikezic, of the "mischief" that could ensue if Belgrade "joined in anti-U.S. hysteria over the Cuban fiasco"—this was the CIA's failed attempt to overthrow Fidel Castro by landing Cuban exiles at the Bay of Pigs two days earlier, about which Kennan had expressed forebodings when he first learned of it at the White House in February. It was under that cloud—"not helpful" at the beginning of his assignment—that George, Annelise, Christopher, Wendy, and Krisha sailed for Cannes on the twenty-fourth.[35]

From there George flew with his son to London, where Christopher would be attending the nearby Sunningdale School: "This was really the end of the pleasant and affectionate association I had had, these past years, with the little boy, who would never be a little boy again." George rejoined the rest of his family in Milan, and after a weekend in Venice they arrived by train in Belgrade on May 8. Krisha had repressed all natural functions while on the last part of the journey, so "we feared complications for the red carpet." None occurred, but George was worrying about something else. Always slightly superstitious, he had noticed how closely these travel dates corresponded to those of 1952, when he had taken up the Moscow ambassadorship: "I hoped history was not preparing to repeat itself."[36]

Kennan presented his credentials to Tito on May 16, at the Yugoslav president's summer residence off the coast of the Istrian peninsula. Doing so required flying, with Annelise, to a military airfield, being ferried across to the Brioni islands, and staying overnight in the once-elegant Grand Hotel, now an almost-empty official guesthouse, surrounded by deer, pheasants, peacocks, and Roman ruins.

Wandering around, George found himself picking up a mosaic stone laid down in the time of Christ. It was, he wrote Grace and Joan, "as though only twenty days, not twenty centuries, had intervened." Transportation was by horse-drawn carriages, and that was how Kennan, in great solemnity, went to meet his host.

Despite his standing as a communist leader, Tito seemed comfortable in these imperial surroundings, and after the ceremony the two talked informally for an hour. Recent debacles like the U-2 affair and the Bay of Pigs landings had caused Tito to doubt American competence, but "we were beginning to learn from our past mistakes," Kennan assured him, and would not indefinitely accept passively "the undermining of our world position at the hands of the Russians and Chinese." It was a tough line with which to begin his ambassadorship, and Kennan was not at all certain that he had gotten through.

George and Annelise found the embassy's massive Cadillac—known to envious fellow diplomats as "the flagship"—waiting for them when they returned to the mainland. It drove them to Pula, a former Austro-Hungarian naval base, which evoked in George a sense of the past and, as it happened, a distant future:

> Strong touches of the Hapsburg atmosphere still hung over the place: over its wide, shady boulevards and its ponderous Viennese buildings; and one could easily picture in imagination the scenes of the first years of this century: the brilliant uniforms of the officers, the trailing skirts and high-necked blouses of their ladies, the elegant sidewalk cafes, the summer band concerts, the lassitude, the pretensions, the warning flashes of distant lightning, the uneasy premonitions of tragedy, and—all around—the disconcerting dissimulation or open bitterness of the Slavs who inhabited the surrounding countryside, seething with the suppressed resentments of centuries, biding their time for a day of bloody and terrible revenge.

The "flagship" then dropped the Kennans off at the port of Rijeka, where they picked up their own less imposing vehicle, a battered British Sunbeam left over from Oxford and shipped from New York. Leaking oil and missing parts, it nonetheless got them back to Belgrade across 350 miles of bad roads, the ambassador driving it all the way.[37]

Kennan's embassy subordinates were unsure what to make of the legendary figure under whom they were serving: "They viewed me, I suspect, with a certain amused astonishment, enjoyed the rhetorical melodrama of my numerous telegraphic conflicts with the Department of State, were intrigued by my unorthodox reactions to the work they performed and the experiences they reported to me, and were aware—as I like to think—of the genuine respect and affection in which I came to hold them." But he could not know for sure, given "that treacherous curtain of deference" that surrounds any ambassador. It parted only occasionally, as when, on "international night" at the American club, Kennan got out his guitar, propped a foot on a chair, and sang, to great acclaim, "Have Some Madeira, My Dear." A British embassy secretary whispered to Dorothy Hessman: "I can't imagine H[is] E[xcellency] doing anything like that!"[38]

V.

Having never seen Stalin during his months in Moscow, Kennan found Tito's accessibility striking: the Yugoslav leader received him three times within the next two and a half months, once in Belgrade and twice again at Brioni. Kennan briefed him on the Kennedy-Khrushchev summit, held in Vienna on June 2–4; they discussed escalating tensions over Berlin as well as decolonization crises in Africa; and Tito promised his guest that he would host an upcoming conference of "nonaligned" states without favoring either of the Cold War superpowers. The Americans, Kennan replied, would take "a very calm view." Their common language was Russian—Kennan was still learning Serbo-Croatian—and they found, if not in all respects common ground, then at least mutual respect. Tito had none of Stalin's "refined hypocrisy and cruelty," Kennan reported. Marxist prejudices still confused him, and his people's experiences had made him abnormally sensitive to the oppression of others. But he had "an excellent, pragmatic political mind" and had "gained both stature and mellowness with the years."[39]

Anticipating Yugoslav sensitivities, Kennan had urged before leaving for Belgrade that Kennedy *not* proclaim "Captive Nations Week" in response to the annual congressional resolution, which was sure to call for it. Among the "nations" regularly mentioned, Kennan pointed out, were "Ude-Ural" and "Cossackia," which had never existed except in the minds of Nazi propagandists during the war. And did the United States really want real nations like the Ukraine to seek their independence from the Soviet Union? The time had come to end the charade "as soon as this can be tactfully and quietly arranged."[40]

The resolution passed, as usual, in July, but the State Department promised that Kennedy would not endorse it. Kennan passed the assurance on to the Yugoslavs. Then, on the fourteenth, Kennedy did just that. It was "the most discouraging thing that has happened to me since my arrival at this post," Kennan complained to Bundy, for it conveyed the impression that the United States was seeking to break up the Soviet Union and perhaps Yugoslavia as well. Bundy, embarrassed, acknowledged the resolution's "foolishness" but explained that Kennedy could not ignore it "for political reasons [such] as the strength of support for foreign aid." So the president had issued his proclamation on a Saturday evening, "the quietest possible moment of the news week," in the hope that it would attract little notice. "It was a tactical judgment," Bundy admitted, but Kennan took it as a warning that the new administration would be no less inclined than its predecessor to resist the primacy of domestic politics over foreign policy.[41]

Khrushchev's threats against West Berlin, by then, were approaching a climax. Kennan had refrained from offering advice, he wrote Bundy, since he knew that Kennedy was consulting Acheson, which must mean "a considered rejection of my own views." Now even more embarrassed, Bundy replied, on the twenty-seventh, that Kennan had not been asked to rejoin the government "for the purpose of shutting you up." The president would think it "absurd that the cardinal should be quiet while the bishops are squawking." So Kennan should speak his mind, even if this meant bypassing the State Department. After all, "there are not many people in the current management who can hold their own, in purely stylistic terms, with Dean, and you are surely one of them."[42]

On the next day the other Dean—Secretary of State Rusk—asked Kennan to fly back to Washington with him from a meeting of American chiefs of mission in Paris that both would be attending early in August. The purpose would be consultations on Berlin, the general situation in Europe, and Tito's upcoming conference. Another of Rusk's passengers on that flight was the president's brother, Attorney General Robert F. Kennedy, with whom Kennan had a long talk. It had been "the easiest trip I have ever made across the ocean," George wrote Annelise from the farm on the evening of August 12. "Even I was not tired."[43]

But he was frightened. On the way from the airport, Kennan had stopped at the White House to see Arthur Schlesinger, now serving as a presidential aide—Kennedy was spending the weekend at Hyannis Port, Massachusetts. "You and I are historians," Schlesinger recorded Kennan as having said, "or rather you are a real historian and I am a pseudo-historian."

> We both know how tenuous a relation there is between a man's intentions and the consequences of his acts. . . . I have children, and I do not propose to let the future of mankind be settled or ended by a group of men operating on the basis of limited

perspectives and short-run calculations. I figure that the only thing I have left in life is to do everything I can to stop the war.

Kennan was in East Berlin when the Wall went up on the thirteenth, but this being the Pennsylvania village of that name, he was not inconvenienced. Nor was he upset, Bundy reported to Kennedy on the fourteenth: to the contrary, Kennan was relieved. His conclusions—which, for once, paralleled Joe Alsop's—were that

(1) this is something they [the Soviets and the East Germans] have always had the power to do; (2) it is something they were bound to do sooner or later, unless they could control the exits from West Berlin to the West; (3) since it was bound to happen, it is as well to have it happen early, as *their* doing and *their* responsibility.

The Berlin Wall, then, might ease the crisis, by means that did Khrushchev little credit. Kennan presumably conveyed this thought to Kennedy when he saw the president in an off-the-record meeting, upstairs at the White House, on the fifteenth, but Kennedy was already thinking similarly. Khrushchev's decision showed "how despised is the East German government, which the Soviet Union seeks to make respectable," he had written Rusk the day before. So the question was "how far we should push this."[44]

Acheson had strongly opposed negotiations over Berlin. "I never found in him at any time any enthusiasm for agreements that would meet the requirements of both sides," Bundy recalled. "I'm not sure he ever saw that animal." This had been the basis for Acheson's attack on Kennan in 1958: NATO's solidarity was more important than resolving the issues that had led to its formation in the first place. Any compromise now, the former secretary of state was sure, would shake the alliance. But Kennedy, who had admired the Reith lectures, was tilting Kennan's way.[45]

He flew back to Belgrade, therefore, reassured about his influence in Washington and at least cautiously optimistic about Soviet-American relations. There was "no compelling reason," Kennan wrote Oppenheimer in mid-September, why the world should now "tear itself to pieces" over Berlin. And his own morale was improving: his ambassadorship had "wrenched me out of established habits," refreshing "an expertise which was rapidly disappearing through neglect but which so many outsiders still expected me to be cultivating." Whatever contribution he could still make as a scholar would "be strengthened, even if it is delayed, by this feeding of the other side of my nature."[46]

VI.

Kennedy probably wanted to see Kennan secretly on August 15 to discuss the unsigned "personal and eyes only" instructions prepared the previous day in the Department of State: that upon his return to Belgrade, Kennan was to contact the Soviet ambassador, Aleksey Alekseyevich Yepishev, to suggest setting up a confidential channel about which no other governments, particularly Germans on either side of the wall, would know. "I had the opportunity," Kennan later explained, of talking "without an interpreter or anybody else present." All he would have to do would be to walk "from my home to the Soviet ambassador's home, and sit down with him in his own living room."[47]

Whether by coincidence or on orders from Moscow, it was Yepishev who asked to see Kennan on August 21. They met, not in Yepishev's living room, but in the garden of the Soviet embassy—to avoid detection devices, the ambassador whispered. Confining their first conversation to the relatively safe issue of how Laos might be neutralized, the two envoys agreed to meet again on the thirty-first, but on the previous day two Soviet correspondents tipped off the United Press representative in Belgrade to the fact that the meeting would be taking place. Fearing a repeat of the Smith-Molotov embarrassment of 1948, Kennan was initially inclined to cancel the talks altogether, but then decided to go ahead on the grounds that they might at least reveal something of Khrushchev's intentions. If exposed, Kennan could say that they were social visits. He would "take great care not to betray more than a general knowledge of our policies."[48]

They met, a day later than planned, on September 1. Khrushchev had jumped at the opportunity to use the Belgrade channel, Yepishev reported: any message that Kennan might want to send would go straight to the Soviet leader without passing through intermediaries. Meanwhile an agreement on Laos seemed possible. Kennan took this communication seriously, "since things more important than Laos were potentially involved." Chief among these was Khrushchev's surprise announcement, on the preceding day, that the Soviet Union would be resuming the testing of nuclear weapons, ending an informal moratorium that had been in effect since 1958. Why, Kennan demanded, had Khrushchev chosen this particular moment, "a most delicate one from [the] standpoint of progress toward negotiations over Berlin"?

Yepishev had no answer, but he went on to state Soviet preconditions for a Berlin settlement with such specificity that Kennan was sure he was acting under

instructions. They amounted to formal recognition, on the part of the United
States and its allies, of the fact that two German states existed and that their
boundaries could not now be changed. The West Germans would not have to
"take tea" with the East German leader, Walter Ulbricht, but they would have to
end efforts to subvert his government. In return, the Soviet Union would "dis-
interest" itself in West Berlin: its citizens could have whatever government they
wanted, secure communications with the outside world, and the continued presence of American, British, and French troops in the city to guarantee these rights.
Kennan responded, cautiously, that none of this seemed "beyond the borders of
what could conceivably be discussed if the right time and atmosphere and setting"
could be arranged. But if Moscow "continued the sort of behavior we had recently
witnessed that time might never come."

His assessment, for Washington, was that Khrushchev was balancing competing factions within his government. New initiatives on Berlin and Germany should
be pursued, therefore, "only with utmost prudence on our part." Nevertheless,
it would be unwise to shut down the Belgrade channel, for "I am quite satisfied
that it does indeed represent a means of private and earliest communication with
Khrushchev." As if to confirm this, Yepishev followed up with a ten-page unsigned
memorandum reiterating the points he had made orally. Kennan himself translated it for the State Department and sent it off by pouch: having cabled its substance, he had no need this time for a long telegram. He had no doubt, though, that
Khrushchev would regard any Kennan reply as coming from Kennedy.[49]

That message, Kennan advised, should stress the inconsistency of "provocations" like the resumption of nuclear testing with the peaceful protestations Yepishev had conveyed. It was important to remember, however, that Khrushchev, for
all his blustering, did not want a war. Washington's position, then, should also
reflect a readiness to negotiate, if necessary alone: "[W]e cannot let petty inhibitions of our allies, or even desire for moral support in unaligned camp, paralyze
our action in any of the great decisions." Rusk's response was curt. "Approve your
proposed reply on Berlin," he cabled, but then added that Ambassador Thompson would soon be seeing Soviet foreign minister Andrey Gromyko in Moscow
to make "tentative soundings on attitudes toward negotiations on Germany and
Berlin. Believe your channel should be kept open but not developed on Berlin at
this point."[50]

There were two more meetings with Yepishev, at which he seemed to be pleading for flexibility, but Kennan had no further instructions on how to respond.

By mid-September, the NATO ambassadors had met in Paris and complained about lack of consultation; meanwhile the State Department was reverting, as Kennan saw it, to "a sullen and passive refusal to discuss Berlin." That amounted to demanding "a unilateral Soviet military and political withdrawal from central Europe," he complained to Under Secretary of State Chester Bowles on the twenty-second. "[I]f this is the only alternative presented to the Russians, it is clear that they would prefer to make war." Acheson, it seemed, had prevailed after all.[51]

Khrushchev, with characteristic earthiness, had the last word. He had agreed, he wrote Kennedy on September 29, that Kennan and Yepishev should exchange views informally. "I never met Mr. Kennan," but he seemed to be a man "with whom preparatory work could be done." The two ambassadors were spending too much time, however, "sniffing each other." For the Belgrade channel to work, they would need instructions "to start talks on concrete questions without needless procrastination and not merely indulge in tea-drinking, . . . walk[ing] round and about mooing at each other." The instructions, from Washington at least, never came.[52]

Kennan acknowledged, in 1965, that his conversations with Yepishev on Laos had been useful: "I attribute the subsequent quietness of the Laotian situation, in part, to these discussions." But Rusk and his soon-to-be-appointed under secretary of state, George Ball, shut down the Berlin discussions, fearing that if news of them ever leaked, the West Germans would be horrified: "I always felt that it was a great shame that this channel was allowed to die, because they [would] not have found a better one." That might well have been the case, for Khrushchev had been following Kennan's thinking since the Reith lectures. "Many of Mr. Kennan's ideas would be acceptable to us and should be to the advantage of the US as well," the Soviet leader had told Harriman in 1959. Kennedy took a similar view, and in the wake of Kennan's visit to Washington in August 1961, there was serious talk within the National Security Council about what form a deal on Berlin might take. "I suspect that Kennan provided expert reinforcement for views Kennedy already had," Schlesinger later recalled.[53]

In the end, though, Kennedy was no more prepared to take on his own State Department, Adenauer, and of course Acheson, than he had been Congress on "captive nations." And so it would be left to a new generation of Germans a decade later, with the wary acquiescence of Richard Nixon and Henry Kissinger, to work out much the same Berlin settlement that Khrushchev, through Yepishev, had recommended in 1961 and that Kennan could have negotiated.

VII.

The White House gave Kennan one other assignment during his August visit, which was to cultivate Tito's guests at the September conference of "nonaligned" states. "[P]robably no American is more admired among the neutrals than George Kennan," Schlesinger reminded Kennedy. "Many of those coming to Belgrade would wish to see him." The American ambassador could hardly buttonhole delegates in the corridors, but he could attend receptions for them in other embassies, respond if they sought his views, and explain U.S. policy to them. "We would be depriving ourselves of one of our most powerful weapons at the conference if Kennan were told that he could have nothing to do with it." That did not happen.[54]

Now, however, Tito reneged on a promise. He had assured Kennan, during the summer, that he would host the conference in an impartial manner. But when he addressed the delegates on September 3, the Yugoslav leader said that although the timing had surprised him, he "could understand" Khrushchev's decision to resume nuclear testing, given the "incomprehensible policies pursued by some powers" who believed that rearming West Germany would enhance European security. "George absolutely hit the ceiling," Bill Bundy recalled. Khrushchev himself could have written the speech, Kennan reported with disgust. It looked, he later observed, "as though the Russians were in a position to make [Tito] say anything they wanted to."[55]

So instead of Kennan listening to the delegates, they—and the press—had to listen to him as he voiced his indignation: "The Yugoslavs didn't like this at all," but they had "chosen their road," he wrote the State Department. They could no longer be considered "a friendly or neutral nation." Tito had become a sycophant, it seemed, in a single speech. Ball detected in Kennan's telegrams a sense of personal affront: "I never saw that attitude on the part of any other ambassador." Most Foreign Service officers dealt with governments that behaved "like sons-of-bitches," Bill Bundy added. "George found [that] very hard to accept." Shocked, the Yugoslavs took to asking: "Is the Ambassador still angry with us?" But Kennedy backed Kennan: "I want you to know that I particularly like your insistence upon representing the interests and purposes of the United States Government, even when this involves abrasions with those to whom you are accredited."[56]

Since 1948 the United States had supported Tito's regime with economic and even military assistance, despite its communist character: Kennan, more than anyone else, had originated that policy. Sustaining it had been difficult, given the objections of anti-Tito exiles, skepticism about foreign aid of any kind, and the widespread belief that all communists were enemies, whether they had split with Moscow or not. Yugoslavia was thus a tempting target for congressional critics, and now Tito was behaving, Kennan believed, as though he could not care less about "the preservation of American, or indeed western, influence anywhere in the world." It was important that the Yugoslavs learn the "limits to American patience." They had cheered Kennan's appointment, the *New York Times* Belgrade correspondent reported, because they thought him a "big man." They still did, but now there were "no happy grins."[57]

Despite these strains in the official relationship, Kennan liked the Yugoslav people. He appreciated "their sweetness to children, their feeling for beauty, their intense suspicions and loyalties, their individuality and charm and sense of humor," he wrote Oppenheimer. His task was to reconcile three things: the lifelong ideological commitment of Tito's generation; American support for West German rearmament, which the Yugoslavs would "never understand or forgive"; and their continuing need for aid from the United States, which, "proud as they are, they hate to take." But perhaps he and their leaders were beginning to work out "what is possible and what is impossible in our relations."[58]

Kennedy asked Kennan to return for a review of Yugoslav policy in January 1962. After meeting with him twice, the president approved moderate amounts of food and development assistance, the sale of supplies for military equipment that the Yugoslavs had already obtained from the United States, and a continuation of trade on the same basis as with "non-Soviet bloc" nations. All of this required congressional approval, so Kennan presented the proposals to the Senate Foreign Relations Committee and the House Foreign Affairs Committee, encountering no significant objections. He would return to Belgrade, he wrote Annelise, with understandings that "should get us over the major humps and make possible the continuation of my own work on a reasonably favorable basis."[59]

At the president's request, Kennan had prepared a summary of administration policy, but on February 5 Rusk released a revised version of it which stressed—as Kennan had been careful not to do—that Yugoslavia was strengthening its Western ties at the expense of those with the East. The Chinese published Rusk's statement, embarrassing Kennan, who knew how much Tito resented being portrayed as a tool of the "imperialists." No one in the State Department was listening to him, Kennan complained to Schlesinger in March, despite the fact that Rusk and

the new ambassador to the Soviet Union, Foy Kohler, had once been his subordinates. Perhaps it was time to resign. He would not do this "precipitately," but he
wanted the White House to know.[60]

NSC staffer Robert Komer found in Kennan's reporting few "constructive ideas"
but thought the State Department reluctant to argue with an ambassador who had
the ear of the White House. That he did have, McGeorge Bundy assured Kennan:
the president "follows your reports with a personal interest that is matched only in
one or two places which, on their surface, are more troublesome than Belgrade."
So Komer hoped that "we're going to use Kennan's visit here for a long cool look
at what we could or should do to forestall or limit Tito's lean leftward."[61]

The occasion this time was a Washington trip by the Yugoslav foreign minister,
Koča Popović. Kennedy received his guest in the White House living quarters on
May 29 and from his rocking chair began gently questioning him on what ideology really meant in the modern world. Weren't other issues shaping relations
between Yugoslavia, the Soviet Union, Communist China, and Albania? If that
was the case, why should ideology affect Yugoslavia's relations with the United
States? There were, to be sure, still American isolationists who were "not sophisticated" about communism. But if the Yugoslavs could avoid episodes like the Belgrade conference, then there could surely be friendly relations, since the purpose
of American policy was to preserve Yugoslavia's independence.[62]

"I was full of admiration for the way the President handled him," Kennan
recalled. Kennedy's boyish courtesy, bordering on naïveté, reminded him of the
young Charles Lindbergh, perhaps even Lincoln: "There was something very
appealing about it." Kennan took the opportunity, nonetheless, to leave a letter
with the president and the secretary of state confirming his intention to spend
another year in Belgrade, and then to return to his academic responsibilities at
the Institute for Advanced Study. Were it not for these, "nothing would give me
greater satisfaction than to continue to serve . . . in any manner that was useful to
your purposes."[63]

VIII.

Nonsophisticates were much on the minds of Kennedy and Kennan during their
meeting with Popović, because two weeks earlier the House Ways and Means Committee had quietly approved an amendment to the trade expansion bill denying

"most-favored nation" status—meaning generally applied tariffs and quotas—to all communist countries. "This news fills me with consternation," Kennan had cabled from Belgrade. The Yugoslavs would interpret it as "a gratuitously offensive act." Bundy replied, soothingly, that the bill made no explicit mention of Yugoslavia, that the administration expected to obtain an "escape clause" in the Senate, and that the Ways and Means chairman, Representative Wilbur Mills of Arkansas, had promised not to oppose this maneuver in the conference committee that would reconcile the bills prior to final passage. "I have some official worries—not with the Executive Branch but with Congress—and I won't breathe easily until they are resolved," George wrote Annelise on the thirty-first. But when Kennan paid a call on Mills the next morning, he disclaimed responsibility for the offending language and seemed willing to have it removed.[64]

Then on June 6 Senator William Proxmire of Wisconsin, citing Tito's handling of the "nonaligned" conference, proposed an amendment to the foreign aid bill denying assistance in any form to Yugoslavia. This pleased his colleagues, who extended the ban to include Poland, and it passed by a vote of 57 to 24. Reminded that they had precluded agricultural exports, the senators then amended the amendment to allow these. The world's "greatest deliberative body," columnist James Reston fumed, had thereby insulted both countries, first by cutting off all aid, and then, as an afterthought, by making them "a dumping ground for farm surpluses." Kennan learned of this after returning to Belgrade. Nothing further was needed, he cabled despairingly, "to confirm Tito on his recent course and to discourage those who have argued in favor of [a] Western orientation."[65]

Caught off guard, Kennedy took the unusual step of releasing a paraphrased version of Kennan's telegram, as well as one from John Moors Cabot, the American ambassador in Warsaw. These congressional actions, Kennan was quoted as saying, reflected "appalling ignorance" about Yugoslavia and amounted to "the greatest windfall Soviet diplomacy could encounter in this area." His message read, reporter Max Frankel observed, as if Kennan were pleading to come back to try to save the situation. And so he was. The least he could do in Washington, Kennan wrote in his original cable, "would be more important than the most I could do, in present circumstances, at this end." Kennedy agreed, and after only two weeks in Belgrade, Kennan was on an airplane once again.[66]

"I am now launched, for the first time in my life, into the thick of a major Congressional struggle," George wrote Annelise from Washington on July 3. "Chances of success are poor; but one doesn't think of that in the heat of battle." Rusk seemed unsure of why he had come, and the State Department offered little help.

The president and his staff, however, arranged meetings with congressional leaders, lined up television interviews, and encouraged Kennan to state his position in *The Washington Post*. When he asked about trying to see Eisenhower, Kennedy instantly agreed: Kennan visited and secured the support of the former president at his Gettysburg farm, after which he stayed overnight at his own in nearby East Berlin. "I slept like a top, [and] woke up"—it was the Fourth of July—"feeling greatly refreshed."

The next day was "hell day." Kennan spent it "tramping from the office of one Texas or Arkansas congressman to another," but it all seemed futile: not one would be ashamed to vote for the Proxmire amendment. "I am now desperately tired, and must be off to bed." A second day of lobbying went better: the vote would probably be closer than it might otherwise have been. George took a bus from Washington that evening to the closest drop-off point for East Berlin, "where, in the late evening and in pitch-blackness, Joany and Larry miraculously found me by the roadside." His *Washington Post* piece appeared on July 8, and two days later George wrote Annelise to say that he had finished—he hoped—his Capitol Hill diplomacy: "I have done about all that I can do."[67]

Kennan's brief career as a lobbyist convinced him that the legislators were using Yugoslavia to demonstrate their anticommunism. It was harder to do this with the Soviet Union, because people were afraid of war. Everybody knew, though, that "Yugoslavia was not going to make war on us." This left him, as an ambassador, with little to say. The Yugoslavs would ask: "Why is this being done to us?" He could only reply: "I have no knowledge of why it's being done to you." They would then inquire: "What would we have to do to avoid this?" He could only say: "I don't know what you could do."[68]

The Proxmire amendment, in the end, fizzled: after Kennedy assured House and Senate conferees that the authority to aid Yugoslavia and Poland was one of his strongest Cold War weapons, they restored it on July 18. Kennan returned to Belgrade at the end of that month, assuming that the "most-favored nation" issue was also being resolved. But on September 27 the phone rang in the Belgrade embassy residence. The caller was Frederick G. Dutton, assistant secretary of state for congressional relations, with the news that the House-Senate conferees on the trade bill, to the surprise of the State Department, had voted to retain the denial of "most-favored nation" status to Yugoslavia and Poland. Wilbur Mills had reneged on *his* promise, or at least what Kennan understood it to have been. "There's only one thing that could stop it at this point," Kennan remembered Dutton as having said. "That would be if you would appeal personally by telephone directly to the President."

Because the phone line was not secure, Kennan assumed that the Yugoslavs were listening: "I had no choice, then, but to call the President." Rising to the occasion, the ambassador summoned his ancient Russian butler, Alexander, "the usual intermediary with telephone central," and instructed him, to his amazement, to place a person-to-person call to the president of the United States. This he did, and to Kennan's amazement, Kennedy immediately came on the line. Kennan stated as forcefully as he could what he saw as the implications of Mills's action, whereupon the president suggested that he talk directly to the congressman and had the call transferred. Kennan was amazed again when Mills picked up the phone, but he had his speech ready, delivered "in my official capacity as ambassador in Belgrade and against the background of thirty-five years of experience with the affairs of Eastern Europe." Denying "most-favored nation" treatment, he insisted,

> would be unnecessary, uncalled for, and injurious to United States interests. It would be taken, not only in Yugoslavia but throughout this part of the world, as evidence of a petty and vindictive spirit, unworthy of a country of our stature and responsibility. This judgment has the concurrence of every officer in the mission. If the amendment is adopted, it will be in disregard of the most earnest and serious advice we are capable of giving.

Mills's response was "cursory, negative, and offered no hope for a reversal of the action." But at least the point had been made, and Yugoslav intelligence had had an amazingly interesting evening.[69]

By a vote of 256 to 91, the House passed the trade expansion bill, with Mills's language unchanged, on October 4. The Senate approved it by acclamation on the same day. On the fifth Kennan cabled Kennedy and Rusk to say that his usefulness as an ambassador had come to an end, and that he would soon be stepping down: the Yugoslavs did not wish for him to leave, but they understood his embarrassment "after adoption by Congress of measures I have publicly opposed." This caused a flurry at the White House, where Bundy promised that Kennedy, in signing the bill, would make "emphatically plain" his objections to the language on Yugoslavia: "I feel sure that you would not want to do anything which might be construed, even by a few, as reflecting differences with the President." Kennedy himself weighed in on the ninth: "Bundy is right. You must stay in Yugoslavia since you understand better than anyone else what our policy aims to accomplish." Most convincingly, Annelise also opposed resignation: "You don't want to do that."[70]

Sadly, Kennedy himself, when he did sign the trade bill on the eleventh, reneged on Bundy's promise: he praised the legislation as the most important since the Marshall Plan, leaving it to an unnamed White House "source" to voice his dissatisfaction with the denial of "most-favored nation" status. "I want you to know that the matter is very much on his mind," Bundy apologetically cabled Kennan. "Fearful agonies of decision whether to resign or not," George recorded in his diary on the fourteenth. "Allowed myself finally to be persuaded (not just by A's remonstrations alone, but by these as [the] last straw of many) not to do so; but went off for a long walk, totally discouraged, feeling defeated as I have not felt since 1953."[71]

IX.

Kennedy learned, on the next morning, that there were Soviet missiles in Cuba: these gave him much more to worry about than Yugoslavia, Kennan, and Wilbur Mills. Kennan had cautioned the State Department by cable, on September 13, that it should not dismiss as "propaganda" Khrushchev's warnings about the island: "When Soviet Union threatens to intervene militarily and to unleash world war if we move to defend our security and peace of Western Hemisphere, this is profoundly serious matter." But he played no role in the crisis that followed, hearing of it only when the rest of the world did. "I recall vividly the strains of the last world war and the months that I was [separated] from any communication with the family," he wrote Joan on October 23 from Milan, where he and Annelise were on a brief holiday. Could she take responsibility for Christopher if they, with Wendy, should be interned somewhere? "I feel it is very serious," Annelise added, "but cannot work myself up to the same pitch as Daddy. . . . However, it is better to be prepared!"[72]

The chauffeur of the embassy "flagship" rushed the Kennans back to Belgrade—over five hundred miles—in eleven hours, from where they watched the Soviet-American confrontation unfold. Appalled by the risks Khrushchev had run and not particularly sympathetic to Castro, the Yugoslavs kept their heads down, protesting the blockade of the island only after the larger crisis had been resolved. Kennedy's handling of the situation had been "masterful," Kennan thought. Tito's colleagues quietly agreed, pointing out that if war had come, they would have had to come down on the Cuban side.[73]

With the assurance, then, that there would be a future, Kennan turned to an

analysis of where American policy toward Yugoslavia had gone wrong. The problem, he concluded in an eight-thousand-word dispatch pouched to Washington
at the end of November, had been "heroic struggles with ourselves." If the United
States could not do better, then it might as well "fold up our tents, before the Yugoslavs fold them up for us." Bundy passed Kennan's analysis to the president, who
ordered yet another review and again asked Kennan to fly back for it—his fifth
such trip since becoming ambassador.[74]

Meanwhile Tito was in Moscow, having been driven there, Kennan was sure,
by American obtuseness. He had to acknowledge, though, that the Yugoslav
leader was enjoying the "personal triumph of his life." Khrushchev received him
as an honored guest, with a deference that did not seem to expect subservience.
Strangely, Kennan thought this a sham and even proposed, early in January 1963,
that he begin cultivating Tito's domestic opponents. Washington should provide
no further food aid, and although Kennedy should seek the reinstatement of
"most-favored nation" treatment, he should do this as a point of principle and not
as way of luring Tito back to the side of the West.[75]

These suggestions bewildered the NSC staff. "The Ambassador is clearly on the
zag course now, having completed the zig with his [November] airgram," David
Klein complained to Bundy. No one in Washington or in the Moscow embassy
shared Kennan's suspicions of a Tito-Khrushchev plot. Clearly "matters of personality and intuition" were shaping Kennan's judgment, making it "difficult to
come to grips with the substance of the problem." As for standing on principle,
"[t]he President can do many things, but I doubt that even he could pull off this
kind of a gambit with the U.S. Congress in the year of our Lord 1963."[76]

"It is by no means certain that the President will do, at this time, what I should
like him to do," George wrote Annelise from Washington, "and if it is not done
now, I fear it will never be done." That proved to be prescient. Kennedy received
him on January 16 but ruled out any challenge to Congress for the foreseeable
future. All that he agreed to do was to answer a planted press conference question
a few days later, noting the importance of exploiting differences "behind the Iron
Curtain" and hoping "that the Congress would reconsider the action it took last
year."[77]

Bearing that crumb, Kennan saw Tito soon after returning to Belgrade. Tito
seemed uneasy but made it clear that Yugoslavia was not about to abandon its
independence. The Warsaw Pact no longer fitted "modern conditions." The word
"bloc" was losing its relevance. The other Eastern Europeans would soon follow Yugoslavia's example. Tito hoped no longer to have to rely upon the United

States, because "he never knew at what point they would get hit by some whim of the Congress." But the Americans had nothing to fear from his policy. The State Department and its Belgrade embassy should simply give them "a true picture of [the] situation as of today."[78]

The meeting left Kennan deflated, dispirited, and on the way to the hospital. The trouble this time, the American military doctors in Frankfurt determined, was not ulcers but a kidney stone that would plague him for years to come. From his bed, Kennan reverted to another habit: he completed an eight-page letter to Walter Lippmann, not unlike the one he had dictated from another hospital in Washington a decade and a half earlier. "Being myself inhibited from writing for publication," he wanted the Yugoslav situation to be known "to *someone* at home; and there could be no one better qualified than yourself to understand its complexities and implications."

The ultimate goal of the United States, Kennan argued, should have been to loosen the cohesion of the Marxist-Leninist world, which might be "the only means short of war by which we can ever make headway against the communist colossus."

> That this possibility, with all of its implications, should continue to be sacrificed to the passions of a few Ukrainian and Croatian exiles and the brutal demagoguery of a few violent temperaments here and there in our political life—and that this should occur without any appreciable protest on the part of American public opinion—is a situation so painful and lamentable, particularly to one who has tried to represent us in Yugoslavia, that it is my excuse for invading your privacy in this way, and for doing so at this outrageous length.

To John Paton Davies, Kennan added, a few days later, that his had been "a disastrously unsuccessful tour of duty." He would have accepted the blame had it not been for the fact that no one on either side had listened to him: "I am as remote from the counsels of the congressional and labor leaders who have made U.S. policy . . . as I am from the internal deliberations of the Yugoslav League of Communists." Their insults "go past my head like bullets past the head of one who sits between the battle-lines (and for the safety of whose head neither side could care less)." He would "leave U.S.-Yugoslav relations at an all-time low."[79]

X.

The White House announced Kennan's resignation on May 17, 1963. "We all knew George had been through a lot," Schlesinger remembered, "and there was no surprise or bitterness over his leaving." Seeking to dispel rumors to the contrary, Kennan claimed in his own statement to have had the support throughout of the president and the secretary of state, even though congressional actions regarding Yugoslavia had been "a great disappointment." In fact, Kennan complained in 1965, neither Rusk nor his under secretary of state, George Ball, had ever concerned themselves with his problems: they had seen his appointment as having been Kennedy's and "were not interested in what happened to me."

Kennedy too disappointed Kennan—by proclaiming "Captive Nations Week," by failing to keep open the Yepishev channel, by repeatedly promising a tougher line with Congress than he was willing to pursue—but Kennan bore him no grudge: "[T]he President completely understood what he did to me, and I, on the other hand, completely understood why he had to do it." Because he had so narrowly won the presidency, Kennedy's political position was weak. He could not afford to appear "soft" on communism. Taking a stand against Mills might have "gummed up" his civil rights program and other domestic legislation. "This was a tragic situation, and I think both of us came out of it entirely without bitterness. . . . I was sorry that it was myself whom he was obliged in a way to destroy."[80]

Kennan came around, as well, to a more charitable view of Tito. The Sino-Soviet split was in the open now, and neighboring Albania had sided with the Chinese. Tito knew how much credit he could get with Khrushchev by sticking up for him after his decision to resume nuclear testing: that accounted for the Belgrade conference speech, which had cost Kennan his ambassadorial equilibrium. The Moscow trip was Tito's payoff: the "prodigal son" returned, but on his own terms. He would make verbal concessions, but with "no intention of giving up his independence." As a consequence, Eastern Europe was safer for heterodoxy than it had been in 1958, when Kennan had detected some of the first signs of it in Poland. He and Tito, it turned out, had wanted much the same thing.[81]

Relations with Yugoslavia were therefore never close to collapse, but Kennan more than once was. As usual, he took too much personally. In contrast to colleagues like Rusk, Ball, and Bohlen, Kennan had never achieved the diplomatic equivalent of clinical detachment. Emotional fragility led to professional volatility, a problem that had afflicted him throughout his career and was still doing so in

Belgrade. "I am attached to the man as a person," Kennan's economic counselor, Owen T. Jones, wrote in his private diary: to his "kindness and decency, his brilliance, his reputation and stature, his access to people at all levels, the essentially long term soundness of his judgments." But "I am repelled by his self-centered egoism, . . . his mercurial moods, his meticulous arrogance." Kennan's "fixations," Jones concluded, "haunt any dealings with him."[82]

Kennan had his own explanation for his difficulties in Belgrade. Progress generally resulted from accumulations of small services, he reminded himself in a note written while on a flight back to the United States—*not* for consultations this time—at the end of May 1963. Those who performed such tasks tended to have little sense of the larger picture. He had been trying, in Yugoslavia, "to do one small thing," and he did not regret this: "It might have been worse if I had not been there." But as he returned now to wider perspectives, "I find myself little aided by two and a half years' immersion in the dust and heat."[83]

His first stop was a conference in upstate New York where gloom about his own country quickly resurfaced. His own speech had failed, while Oppenheimer's had been "too compact and subtle to be fully understood, and too impressive to be answered." A gang of sullen teenagers, encountered on an early morning walk, would have killed him "for kicks" if they not been exhausted from being up all night. There was nothing to do now but "stand by and watch the internal catastrophe . . . which will surely overtake us if the external catastrophe does not anticipate it."[84]

He was also having weird dreams. One moved the East Berlin farm to Nagawicka, where the Kennan children had spent their summers, which adjoined California, where Grace and her husband were living, which was just across the lake from Delafield, where George had attended St. John's and now was considering entering local politics. Another occurred while traveling overnight to Chicago on the 20th Century Limited. The train was somehow diverted into Canada, where George had to board a bus to another railroad station, located with the aid of Prime Minister Lester Pearson, from which he caught another train, settled himself in the club car without a ticket, but was sure "that if I, being who I was, explained my predicament, there would be no difficulty." The sugar bags in the real dining car the next morning read: "Have sweet dreams on the Century."[85]

George visited Jeanette and her family in Highland Park, spoke at the University of Wisconsin commencement in Madison, and helped Charlie James, now president and chairman of the board of the Northwestern National Insurance Company, open its new building in Milwaukee. He then picked up an honorary degree at Harvard, flew to Paris for a NATO meeting, and rescued Christopher from Sunningdale, where he had just finished his second and final year. They spent a day nostalgically in Oxford, drove from there to Harwich, and boarded a Channel ferry for Holland. Sitting on deck in the sun and out of the wind, George spent the afternoon reading Thurber aloud to his son, who "laughed until he got the hiccoughs."[86]

The Kennans' last full day in Belgrade, July 26, 1963, was a somber one because of the earthquake that had occurred that morning in Skopje, killing over a thousand people and devastating most of the city. The next day they flew to Brioni, where on the twenty-eighth Tito hosted a luncheon for all four Kennans, with George able to announce the arrival, near the disaster site, of an American emergency field hospital. The children comported themselves appropriately in the presence of the Yugoslav president, who toasted their father as a "nauchnik"—a scholar—just the right thing to have said. From there the family flew to Venice, Christopher having negotiated permission to keep his turtle.[87]

XI.

Kennan had one more ambassadorial duty to perform that fall, since Kennedy had not yet appointed his successor: this was to help host the long-planned Tito visit to the United States. Anticipating hostile demonstrations in Washington, the State Department had arranged to house the Yugoslavs within the controlled precincts of Colonial Williamsburg, and Kennan was dispatched there to welcome them. The horse-drawn carriages were a bonus, but also "a fitting answer," George thought, to those at Brioni. The Kennans were the only Americans at dinner that evening, where the conversation veered off, improbably, onto snakes. "I ask Koča [Popović] whether they were much bothered by such things during their life in the mountains, in the Partisan war." No, he replied, "for some reason, wild life avoided us." "That," Tito explained, "is because we never washed." The Kennans spent the night in an overheated room at the Williamsburg Inn, with George "assailed by gloomy premonitions, harder to bear than the exhalations of the burning radiators."[88]

They were well-founded. Demonstrators noisily picketed the White House when the Yugoslavs were received there the next day. Reporters noticed Kennedy's reluctance to be photographed shaking hands with his guest. The president explained to Tito that he had signed the Trade Expansion Act, despite its denial of the "most-favored nation" privilege, because it was "a very important measure." He hoped to regain presidential discretion in the matter, perhaps within the next few weeks. Tito should understand, though, that "every member of Congress wanted to avoid being called pro-communist," and it was hard for them "to distinguish among the Soviet Union, Communist China, Poland, Yugoslavia, and Albania." As for the pickets, he got them all the time himself.[89]

Worse was to come. When Tito arrived in New York to address the U.N. General Assembly, he and his entourage were literally besieged in the Waldorf-Astoria, with two young protesters almost breaking into his suite. Kennan was at least able to greet the Titos peacefully in Princeton, where, he reported with relief to Kennedy, the visit had gone well. But if New York was to continue to host the United Nations, it would have to take "greater responsibility than it now does for the protection of its foreign guests against insult and molestation."[90]

Some spirit told him, though, not to end his ambassadorship on a sour note. So Kennan added a handwritten compliment, reminiscent of one he had sent Acheson in even more trying times thirteen years earlier:

Dear Mr. President:

You get many brickbats; and of those who say approving and encouraging things, not all are pure of motive.

I am now fully retired, and a candidate for neither elective nor appointive office. I think, therefore, that my sincerity may be credited if I take this means to speak a word of encouragement. I am full of admiration, both as a historian and as a person with diplomatic experience, for the manner in which you have addressed yourself to the problems of foreign policy with which I am familiar. I don't think we have seen a better standard of statesmanship in the White House in the present century. I hope you will continue to be of good heart and allow yourself to be discouraged neither by the appalling pressures of your office nor by the obtuseness and obstruction you encounter in another branch of the government. Please know that I and many others are deeply grateful for the courage and patience and perception with which you carry on.

Very sincerely yours,
George Kennan

The date was October 22, 1963. The reply went out on the twenty-eighth:

Dear George:

    Your handwritten note . . . is a letter I will keep nearby for reference and reinforcement on hard days. It is a great encouragement to have the support of a diplomat and historian of your quality, and it was uncommonly thoughtful for you to write me in this personal way.

Sincerely,
John Kennedy

"Many thanks," the president added, in his own handwritten postscript. Kennan later recalled what Kennedy had said at the end of their last private conversation, on the day before Tito's visit to the White House: "George, I hope you'll keep on talking."[91]

Part V

TWENTY-TWO

Counter–Cultural Critic: 1963–1968

THAT HE DID. "OUR FOREIGN POLICY IS PARALYZED," LOOK MAGA-
zine had Kennan complaining, in an interview that ran under a large photograph,
showing him apparently wincing in pain. The causes, he insisted, lay in Congress,
where just a few powerful legislators could tie things up; in the bureaucracy, which
suffered from "ponderousness"; and among allies, who found it easier to demand
"everything but the kitchen sink, rather than take a real negotiating position."
There had been, thus, no "New Frontier" in diplomacy because Kennedy had no
latitude to construct one. Kennan had resigned his ambassadorship, not over differences with the administration but because he lacked credibility and authority.
It had not even been clear how much humanitarian assistance the United States
could legally provide after the Skopje earthquake. At least he had given blood: "No
Congressional committee could stop me from doing that."[1]

The article appeared in the November 19, 1963, issue. Kennan was with Oppenheimer three days later when they heard the news. "He said nothing, nor did I—
there was no need. . . . [B]ut we were both aware that it was more than just one
life that had been obliterated: that the world we cared about had been grievously
diminished, together with our own ability to be in any way useful in it." In the
sad days that followed, Kennan composed a eulogy for the only president under
whom he had served of whom he approved.

John F. Kennedy understood, Kennan wrote, two great principles of statecraft:
"First, that no political judgments must ever be final; and second, that the lack of
finality must never be an excuse for inaction." Blessed with "a clear mind, a quick
intelligence, an uncommonly retentive memory," Kennedy appraised dispassion-
ately the people and problems he confronted.

He had the rare quality of being sensitive without being vain; and when, as sometimes befell him . . . , he was faced with behavior on the part of others which seemed
to fall little short of outright deception, his reaction was less one of anger than of
wonder and of renewed curiosity as to what it was that had caused men to act in
this way.

Kennedy approached issues with an open mind, studied them carefully, and
embraced answers while asking further questions. He respected the past, never
assuming that those who had gone before "were idiots or men of bad will." Despite
setbacks, he never lost heart: he bore disappointments "in manly loneliness," seldom revealing them to others. An "extraordinarily gallant and gifted man," he was
only approaching his full potential when "the hand of the assassin reached him."[2]

The eulogy itself was extraordinary, given Kennan's disappointments over the
past two and a half years. Kennedy had repeatedly subordinated foreign policy
to the interests of Congress, the bureaucracy, and the allies, precisely the habits
Kennan had so often condemned, most recently in his *Look* interview. Survivors
rarely speak ill of the dead; but Kennan had spoken well of Kennedy before his
death, despite compromises that differed little from those Roosevelt, Truman, and
Eisenhower had made, toward which Kennan had been far less charitable.

Kennedy, however, consulted Kennan—indeed treated him almost as a
mentor—in a way no previous president had done. They met, after Kennedy's
election, at least fourteen times, an unusually large number for a serving overseas
ambassador. Their conversations softened, although they never removed, Kennan's bitterness over his defeats: "When I came home and saw him there in his
room—that bedroom of his upstairs in the White House—and realized the pressures that were brought to bear against him, realized even what it meant to him
to take an hour out to sit down in his rocking chair and talk with me, I always
was aware that I must not look at his position from the standpoint of my own
problems."

Kennan the historian understood that all presidents confront inadequate information and irreconcilable choices: his two volumes on Wilson and the Bolshevik
Revolution had portrayed these brilliantly. But Kennan the diplomat, the policy
planner, and the public intellectual rarely showed such sympathy. Kennedy, with
some success, brought the two Kennans together, perhaps because Kennan—self-
critical as always—saw in Kennedy what he himself should have been.[3]

I.

He had known, since October 1962, that he would be resigning: what to do next, however, was as usual unclear. There were, as always, invitations to teach, this time at Princeton's Woodrow Wilson School and at the Fletcher School of Law and Diplomacy. Yale asked him to replace its great diplomatic historian Samuel Flagg Bemis. Harvard offered a "university professorship," tied to no particular department. But these would involve "a disorderly, harried life," Kennan explained to Oppenheimer. "I would probably be pressed to speak too much; the voice would soon wear thin; nothing permanent or identifiable would remain to mark the effort."

The alternative was immersion in history, possibly the transition "from the clear and symmetrical concepts of 18th-century culture to the strange Victorian world of the latter half of the 19th century." He could try to become conscious of all "the currents and impulses to which men were exposed at that time—to let this work in me, and then to determine, as spirit and occasion might dictate, what I want to express, and what form to give it." Were he to take this course, he would return to the Institute, where "I would expect to detach myself completely from the public discussion of contemporary affairs (Dorothy [Hessman] smiles as I dictate this; but she is wrong)." Yet another possibility would be a memoir. "But what if it should be a success?" Could he really retire into the past? This was "the whirlpool of questions in which I rotate."[4]

"I cherish you as a colleague and neighbor far too much to trust my own objectivity," Oppenheimer replied, in a letter exquisitely attuned to these ambivalences. He went on to remind Kennan, though, that the Institute could allow all of these options. It would expect scholarship, but the topics pursued need not always be the same. Most of its faculty taught, from time to time, "in nearby campi." As for public commentary, Einstein, Earle, von Neumann, "and indeed I myself have not felt silenced, or even inhibited, by our attachment to this place." There need be no final commitment: Harvard could keep its chair warm while Kennan sampled life back in Princeton. He should say no to Yale. In the end, he ought to give "an appropriately small weight to what other people expect of you, and a very great one to what you expect of yourself."[5]

As Oppenheimer had hoped, that settled it. Kennan promised that he would be on hand for the Institute's fall term. The other offers had left him "much torn," George admitted to Kent, but returning to Princeton would give him the greatest flexibility, while not forcing another relocation upon his family. He and Annelise had moved, he later estimated, some thirteen times while he was in government. "I recognized her need for a permanent home." So the White House resignation announcement made it official: Ambassador Kennan would resume his duties at the Institute for Advanced Study, in accordance with "long standing plans."[6]

He would do so without Hessman, who had spent almost two decades with him. Now a Foreign Service employee, she decided to stay on to work for C. Burke Elbrick, Kennan's successor in Yugoslavia. Her own successor turned out to be Constance Moench (later Goodman), a Smith College graduate who had applied for a secretarial position in Oppenheimer's office but was assigned instead to Kennan. It was "a blind date," she recalled, "because the two of us agreed to this sight unseen." However, "I did know something about Professor Kennan. I'd been a government major, and I'd read the 'X Article' and *American Diplomacy*." She had also seen, in *The New York Times*, an account of the ambassador's last days in Belgrade. "I thought, well, if his staff is weeping when he's leaving, he can't be all that bad."

Moench found her new boss "slim, elegant, and rather young in the face, although balding—balding? He was bald." Kennan was shyer than she had expected, and sensitive to everything around him: "By that I mean his [capacity] to observe and to feel beauty, to drink it all in like a sponge, his caring for other people." His eyes, she noticed, resembled Oppenheimer's: "extraordinary eyes, just absolutely riveting, those clear blue eyes. I sensed a very real affection between the two men." Kennan was a man of many moods, "although I never felt terribly dragged down by them." He always treated her "with kindness and affection and respect."[7]

Princeton University made Kennan a "visiting" professor of history and international affairs in the fall of 1963. This was an unpaid position, in line with the Institute's policy on outside academic appointments, but the courses were for credit, and he welcomed the interaction with students. It would counter, George wrote Kent, "the unbroken loneliness of pure research and writing [which] is not good for me." His spring semester courses would include lectures on Russia in the era of Nicholas II, a seminar on recent diplomatic history, and a preceptorial, Princeton's version of a tutorial. Moench remembered his working hard on these, compiling bibliographies, searching out maps, even locating recordings of famous speeches. "It was very lively, there was a lot of wonderful discussion that went on, and he spent almost full-time making [it] exciting and interesting and rich for the students."

Kennan enjoyed teaching, although he soon realized that he would have to cut back his course load if he was to get anything else done. He preferred undergraduates to graduate students: the latter were too beaten down, too lacking in spontaneity, too worried about what he might think of them. Both groups wrote badly and were poorly prepared linguistically. Kennan agonized over grades but was generous when his own role in history came up. "I think he deserves an A," he wrote a few years later of a student who had turned in a paper on Harriman without discussing him. "Better people than ____ have failed to mention me in this connection."[8]

II.

Kennan was also working that fall on the Elihu Root lectures, a series of three to be delivered at the Council on Foreign Relations in early November. He would type out first drafts—embarrassingly, Moench found him to be faster than she was—then mark them up, rearrange passages using scissors and tape, and return them for further editing. He still dictated, at times horizontally, but chiefly for correspondence, or to relieve kidney stone pain. Published in 1964 as a short book, *On Dealing with the Communist World*, the lectures were Kennan's attempt to extract lessons from his Yugoslavia experience. He meant them "as a polemic" against the ill-informed anticommunism so evident within Congress. They were a Cold War primer: "Little steps for little feet." They were also, as it happened, little read. In the aftermath of Kennedy's assassination, Kennan's ambassadorial travails seemed inconsequential. The implications he drew from them, however, marked an important shift in his thinking about the postwar international system.

Owing to a sequence of events that began in 1948—Tito's defection, Mao's triumph, Khrushchev's de-Stalinization campaign, unrest in Poland, rebellion in Hungary, and now the Sino-Soviet split—it hardly made sense anymore, Kennan argued, to speak of "communism" as a unitary phenomenon. That opened opportunities, because by exploiting divisions within that ideology—by selectively extending support to or withholding it from regimes that still espoused one variety or another of Marxism-Leninism—the West could determine "whether the Chinese view, or the Soviet view, or perhaps a view more liberal than either, would ultimately prevail within the Communist camp." Capitalism, in theory at least, could shape communism's future.

In practice, though, this was not happening. Mindful only of mindless constituencies, Congress was indiscriminately legislating trade and aid policy. Deference to the West Germans precluded any disavowal of their irredentist ambitions in East Germany and Poland. These, in turn, prevented the Soviet Union from reducing its military presence in Eastern Europe, something it would have to do before "polycentrism" could flourish there. The great colonial powers, during the nineteenth century, had alienated millions through insensitivity toward those who were within their power. Weren't the United States and its allies offending "just as many more through lack of imagination and feeling toward those who were in the power of their ideological adversaries"?[9]

Kennan had based his call for "disengagement," in the Reith lectures, on his own assurances that Soviet ambitions were limited. That seemed, at the time, too thin an assumption upon which to risk so much. But if Moscow no longer controlled its satellites—if Titoism was becoming the norm and not the exception within the international communist movement—then what did it matter what Kremlin leaders thought? Perhaps ideology, for these old men, was like sex, Kennan explained to a puzzled Japanese audience in the summer of 1964: "I think men just like to exercise power over other people just as they have certain other things that they like to do."

They tended "to clothe this love for power in ideological terms, and sometimes they really believe them. I am sure that Lenin did." But as regimes aged, ideology declined, leaving only the more normal competition "for prestige with the public, for admiration, for respect, for all these things that make up a position of power." And what of their children? "They care about the twist and they care about certain types of hairdo for the ladies. They would like to hear the Beatles sing but they do not seem to be much interested in communism as an ideology."[10]

Kennan said nothing in *On Dealing with the Communist World* about what U.S. policy toward China ought to be. His Asia trip gave him a chance to think about this, though, and by November 1964—a few weeks after the first Chinese atomic bomb test and Khrushchev's almost simultaneous deposition by his Kremlin colleagues—Kennan had answers ready. He began, in *The New York Times Magazine*, with one of his portentous single sentences:

> The great country of China, forming the heart of Asia, a country which for many years we befriended above all others and in defense of whose interests, in part, we fought the Pacific war, has fallen into the hands of a group of embittered fanatics: wedded to a dated and specious ideology but one which holds great attraction for masses of people throughout Asia; finding in this ideology a rationale for the most ruthless exertion of power over other people; associating this ideological prejudice

with the most violent currents of traditional nationalism and xenophobia; linking their power to the arrogance and pretension traditional to governing groups in a country which long regarded itself as the center of the world; consumed with ambition to extend to further areas of Asia the dictatorial authority they now wield over the Chinese people themselves; sponsoring for this reason every territorial claim of earlier Chinese Governments for which history could show even the flimsiest evidence; and now absolutely permeated with hatred toward ourselves, not only because the ideology pictures us all as villains, but also because we, more than any other people, have had the strength and the temerity to stand in their path and to obstruct the expansion of their power.

But—the United States was not "the avenging angel of all humanity." It lacked the power or the will to rescue Mao's victims. It could not even defend allies along China's periphery "if we fail to find support in the temper of the inhabitants." The best Americans could do would be to assist other Asians in preserving their independence as long as the help they needed fell within the scope of what "we might reasonably be expected to give."

Meanwhile the Chinese leaders, for all of their brutality, were only human. They once had "mothers and children and affections." They were what circumstances had made them, and circumstances would determine what they, or their successors, would become. It was up to the West, therefore, to shape those "in such a way that the fruitlessness of some of their undertakings will become apparent to them," even as it held open "the possibility of negotiation and accommodation if their ambitions are moderated and their methods change." Not least among those circumstances was rivalry with the Soviet Union, an antagonism too deep to be resolved by Khrushchev's removal. The United States would be foolish not to take advantage of this. "We should be prepared to talk to the devil himself," Kennan had said in his *Look* interview the year before, "if he controls enough of the world to make it worth our while."[11]

III.

As had happened in Oxford six years earlier, illness complicated Kennan's teaching in the spring of 1964. He came down with infectious hepatitis, which kept him hospitalized for several weeks and left him debilitated for several more—although he did manage to write all of his lectures and deliver some, while continuing to dictate long letters. The sixteen points made in one of these, he assured its recipient, "are all views I held *before* the color of the world turned a jaundiced yellow." He was well enough by June, however, to risk the Asian journey as a guest of the International House of Japan. It was his first trip back since 1948, and Annelise's first ever. It gave him a chance to reassess a country he had long regarded, like Germany, as a Cold War anomaly.[12]

After formally making peace in 1951, the United States had taken on the responsibility of defending Japan and still had military bases there. Sooner or later, Kennan was sure, the Americans would make themselves so unpopular that they would have to leave. The constitution MacArthur had imposed prohibited rearmament, so Japan's only alternative would be an agreement with the Soviet Union to "neutralize" the country—Kennan's East Asian equivalent of European disengagement. Protests over renewing the bilateral security treaty had forced Eisenhower to cancel a visit in the summer of 1960, leading Kennan to revive his proposal to withdraw American forces when he briefed the Policy Planning Staff in February 1961. He gave little further thought to Japan's affairs, though, until he arrived there in June 1964.[13]

Kennan's lectures, chiefly historical, aroused no particular controversy, but shortly after returning to the United States, he published a *Foreign Affairs* article that did. Entitled "Japanese Security and American Policy," it stressed the "great schizophrenia of thought and feeling" he had encountered, induced by the shock of defeat, the humiliation of occupation, and the fear of nuclear war.

> The instincts, outlooks and needs of the Japanese people simply will not tolerate for long anything that appears to be an effort to enlist Japan as a passive instrument in an all-out cold war to which no one in Japan can see a favorable issue generally and which seems to imply the indefinite renunciation by Japan of all hopes for a better relationship with the mainland.

So had the time not come to seek Moscow's cooperation in guaranteeing Japan's security, under United Nations auspices, while leaving its government free to make its own arrangements with Beijing? Had not MacArthur himself once insisted, "if the writer of these lines understood him correctly," that Japan's most suitable long-term status would be "permanent demilitarization and neutralization"?[14]

Worried that the Japanese would regard a Kennan appearance in *Foreign Affairs* as an official trial balloon, the American ambassador in Tokyo, Edwin P. Reischauer, urgently arranged a rebuttal. The task fell to Bill Bundy, now assistant secretary of state for Far Eastern affairs, who while literally in flight across the Pacific had to turn a previously written speech into a repudiation of Kennan's article. Knowing little about Japan, Kennan had fallen victim, Bundy believed, "to a rather common syndrome of the liberally inclined American who finds liberally inclined conversational partners in a foreign country and concludes that's where opinion is headed."

"I feel guilty [for] having kicked up so much dust," Kennan contritely wrote one of his Japanese hosts. He saw now how few people, either in Washington or in Tokyo, hoped to improve Soviet-Japanese relations. That was unfortunate, because Japan's ability to manage the Chinese, "with whom an accommodation must sooner or later be negotiated," would be enhanced if it first settled its differences with the U.S.S.R. Unlike the Reith lectures, this particular Kennan heresy did little to shake prevailing orthodoxies. It did, however, Bundy recalled, reinforce the views of those in Washington, especially Secretary of State Rusk, who "didn't feel [that] George really knew a hell of a lot about Asia."[15]

IV.

Kennan had not returned to the Soviet Union since Stalin declared him persona non grata in 1952, but its diplomats had for some time been regularly approaching him, obviously with the permission of the Foreign Office, usually with a bottle of Caucasian brandy in hand, to ask: "Why don't you ever come to Russia?" The queries reminded Kennan of a line to a former lover in an Edna St. Vincent Millay sonnet: "I find this frenzy insufficient reason for conversation when we meet again." The frenzy of his expulsion need not now be discussed. He would be welcomed back.[16]

Knowing that he was to be in Japan, Kennan decided to test Soviet hospitality. He had taken the Trans-Siberian Railway from Moscow to Novosibirsk and Kuznetsk in 1945, he wrote Anatoly Dobrynin, the new ambassador in Washington, but he had never ventured beyond those points, despite the fact that the elder George Kennan, the author of "a well-known work" praised by the early Bolsheviks, had traveled extensively in eastern Siberia. So might it be possible, after his

Japanese visit, to travel to Norway by rail, seeing the rest of the Trans-Siberian and revisiting Moscow, "which has changed so much since I was last in the Soviet Union"?

The embassy's consular division replied curtly that Kennan should consult Intourist, the notoriously unfriendly Soviet travel agency. Dobrynin apologized a few weeks later, claiming a misunderstanding and offering to help with the arrangements, but by then Kennan had contracted hepatitis. The illness required a recovery not likely to be facilitated by a long Russian train ride, so he let the matter drop. Sadly, he never made the trip.[17]

Instead the Kennans flew from Tokyo to Oslo, by way of Bangkok, New Delhi, Tehran, Beirut, and Geneva. While Annelise waited for Christopher and Wendy to arrive from the United States, George traveled alone to Kristiansand to open the Sørensen house, empty in the wake of her parents' recent deaths. "The old, so-little-used Buick, . . . which no one else was allowed to touch, was now standing there," George wrote in his diary, "our property, officially."

> With the feeling of one who commits sacrilege, I drove it out to . . . the empty cottage; wept a tear and said a prayer for the peace of the souls of its erstwhile proprietors, whose absence seems so preposterous; went to bed in their bedroom, unoccupied since they died; and lay long awake, listening to the many night noises: the banging of the shutters and scraping of the [e]spalier tree against the wall in the night breeze, the chattering of the hot water heater and, with the advent of the early northern dawn, the cries of the gulls.

The family got there the next day, and after dinner George, Christopher, and Wendy walked to the boathouse, dragged the rowboat down to the water, and watched as it promptly sank.[18]

But there was a better boat waiting. On July 10, just outside Bergen, the Kennans took possession of *Nagawicka*, their new seagoing sailing vessel. "I was so excited," George recorded, that "I could scarcely pay the taxi-driver." After a few days of trials in a nearby fjord, they stocked up on supplies, took on a Norwegian deckhand, and set off for Kristiansand, a voyage of some 220 miles down the coast and around the southern tip of the country, partly in protected waters, partly in open ocean. They almost didn't make it.

On the second day out—the first beyond the shelter of islands—they ran into a strong headwind accompanied by stinging rain, an "uninterrupted shower-bath" that left Wendy, huddled against her mother, "barely recognizable under her heavy oilskins." The next afternoon, with fog approaching, they anchored near Stavanger, from where George had intended to put Annelise and Wendy on the train to Kristiansand, to spare them the long sea-exposed stretches that lay to the south. But the weather was fine the following morning, and there was another port with a rail connection—Egersund—on the way, so George decided, "influenced, I must say, by the common desire of the male contingent to continue to have the services of a cook," to proceed there.

They were off Egersund at five that evening, with another five hours of daylight left, when George changed his plans again: why not do another twenty or thirty miles? He quickly regretted this. The diesel engine quit, just as visibility diminished and a sudden storm began driving them toward the coast—the one portion for which he had neglected to bring a chart. Sturdy as she was, *Nagawicka* could not easily tack if forced into a confined harbor or a narrow fjord. With darkness approaching, George finally saw the beam from a distant lighthouse. He knew then that he was at the mouth of the Listafjord, into which he blindly sailed boat and family, finally locating, at around midnight, a secure anchorage. Annelise, imperturbably, had kept a stew simmering throughout the excitement, and they all now devoured it, relishing the implausibility of ever having been "in danger near so snug and peaceful a spot." Two days later, her engine repaired but unused, *Nagawicka* tacked "manfully" into the sound at Kristiansand. She had, on the whole, "behaved splendidly throughout—exceeded, in fact, our highest hopes. . . . If her master is able to develop qualities comparable to her own, she will go anywhere."[19]

It was the first of many such voyages with family and friends, some equally hair-raising. "George obviously responds to this sailing life," his Princeton neighbor Frank Taplin recalled of a trip they made together on a successor sailboat, *Northwind*. Sailing also brought out, as Kennan's guitar sometimes did, a ribaldry quite at odds with the his public image. Taplin preserved one example, recited gleefully by George while at sea:

> *Oh mistress Mary, we do believe,*
> *That without sin thou didst conceive;*
> *Oh mistress Mary, still believing,*
> *Teach us to sin without conceiving.*

George never allowed Annelise to take the tiller when sailing out of a harbor, Dick Dilworth noticed, "although she's fully competent to do so." So because *Northwind* had no winch, on at least one occasion—it happened to be July 4, 1976—the task of hauling up her heavy slimy anchor fell to this financial adviser to the Rockefeller family, trustee of the Institute for Advanced Study, member of the Yale Corporation, and chairman of the Metropolitan Museum of Art, while Captain Kennan kept his eye firmly fixed on the nautical horizon.[20]

V.

The Soviet Foreign Ministry was still trying to get Kennan back to Moscow, and in December 1964 Mikhail Smirnovsky, the head of its American desk, brought the matter to the attention of White House aide David Klein at a Washington dinner: why was Kennan so reluctant? "I said the reason was probably the obvious one," Klein wrote him, "the treatment you received in 1952." Smirnovsky insisted that the expulsion was "no longer valid," that Kennan would be received cordially. Dobrynin then followed up with another invitation. So Kennan finally decided to go, not as an official guest but as an ordinary tourist, and to bring Christopher with him.[21]

They left Budapest by rail on the evening of June 21, 1965, in a Soviet sleeping car on which George was relieved to hear Russian spoken—Hungarian being one of the few European languages to have eluded him. The rough roadbed irritated his kidney stone, but the car attendant did her best to make him comfortable. "I saw it in your eyes," she said of his pain. There was a late-night border crossing, after which George and Christopher slept through the Carpathians and spent the next day crossing the fertile plains of the western Ukraine. An Intourist guide took them around Kiev on the twenty-third—the cathedral, the university, the catacombs, the banks of the Dnieper, the deep but excellent subway. The next day they flew to Moscow.

Foy Kohler, the American ambassador, had invited them to stay at Spaso House, which to George's eyes looked "absolutely splendid—immensely improved." There was time that afternoon for a drive through the city, a walk around the Kremlin, and an evening at the Bolshoi, where the dancers conveyed simultaneous impressions of proficiency and of "something already done too often." The Soviet foreign minister, Andrey Gromyko, came to lunch at Spaso the following day, bringing only Smirnovsky with him—it was, *The New York Times* noted, "a special tribute." Positions were "stoutly maintained on both sides," Kennan recorded, but "I gained a new respect for our visitor, in whom I was obliged to recognize an able and sea-soned statesman, not unkind or unreasonable, nor devoid of a sense of humor." Gromyko was saying, in effect: "Please understand that the Foreign Office had nothing to do with your expulsion, and was not even informed about it. Therefore, I hope that we can have as pleasant relations as we would normally have, had this never occurred." It was Edna St. Vincent Millay, improbably channeled.

On the next morning a chauffeur drove George and his son to the ancient city of Novgorod, where they admired the local Kremlin, enjoyed the view of the Volk-hov River and Lake Ilmen, soaked in the long rays of the evening sunshine, felt the breezes blowing in from the Baltic, and savored the cheerful disorder of the Russian families picnicking, fishing, swimming, sailing, or just walking around. Following dinner in the hotel, they had an unexpected visit from two students, who wondered whether they might be willing to sell Christopher's only pair of shoes, "i.e., his ghastly loafers."

There were, then, two days in Leningrad, after which George took Christopher on another train ride, this time to Helsinki, from where they would go on to Nor-way. At the Finnish border, they watched "with more than a detached interest" the train's slow progress across the heavily guarded frontier zone. George had been there before, both in his diplomatic career and in his historical imagination: *The Decision to Intervene* ends with this description of the site, as it would have appeared to the last official Americans to leave Russia in the fall of 1918.

> The sky was leaden; a cold wind blew from the northwest. . . . The little stream, hur-rying to the Gulf of Finland, swirled past the wooden pilings and carried its eddies swiftly and silently away into the swamps below. Along the Soviet bank a tethered nanny goat, indifferent to all the ruin and all the tragedy, nibbled patiently at the sparse dying foliage. . . . The Finnish gate now clanked down behind them—one more link in that iron curtain that was to constitute through the coming decades the greatest and saddest of the world's political realities.

How had he known that there had been a goat? He couldn't prove it, he later admitted, but "I never saw such a scene in Russia *without* a goat," so it seemed safe enough to include one. Now he was there with Christopher, and perhaps even in the distance another goat. It was the end of a train trip George had hoped to begin in Vladivostok. This one didn't, but the border crossing brought a kind of closure, nonetheless.[22]

VI.

"I spent the day laboriously endeavoring not to think about the event," Kennan confessed on January 20, 1965, the day Lyndon B. Johnson was inaugurated for the full term he had won by defeating Barry Goldwater the previous November. "Is this just sour grapes—the fact that I am rejected by Washington? In part, perhaps." Probably "I would like, deep down, to be called upon to serve again," but "I know I should dread, on closer contact, having actually to do so." With Kennedy's death, Kennan had lost his chief listener in the White House. He expected no such relationship with Johnson.

> [W]hat this man represents—this oily, folksy, tricky political play-acting, this hearty optimism, this self-congratulatory jingoism, all combined with the whiney, plaintive, provincial drawl and the childish antics of the grown male in modern Texas—this may be the America of the majority of the American people but it's not *my* America.

"I had a horror of Mr. Johnson," Kennan recalled years later. "I think he did worthy things internally, but, my God!—he did them with such methods that I couldn't have lasted in his entourage."[23]

Johnson did, in the spring of 1965, attempt a connection to Kennan, or at least his aide, the historian Eric Goldman, did. In an effort to evoke Kennedy's style, Goldman had proposed a White House Festival of the Arts, but by the time Johnson got around to approving the idea, he had begun escalating the war in Vietnam and had ordered military intervention to prevent an alleged pro-Castro coup in the Dominican Republic. Goldman asked Kennan to speak, in his capacity as the newly elected president of the National Institute of Arts and Letters. The invitation came at an awkward moment, because Kennan's predecessor, Lewis Mumford, had used his departing speech to the organization in May to launch a vitriolic attack on Johnson. He had then "fled, leaving the meeting to me." Kennan's conscience would not have allowed such a thing, he wrote Mumford afterward, "but this implies no lack of respect on my part for the faithfulness with which you followed the dictates of your own."[24]

Convinced that he had to represent the National Institute at the White House event, Kennan flew back at his own expense from Europe, where he was preparing for his trip to the Soviet Union with Christopher. The festival took place on June 14 with extensive media coverage, much of it generated by the poet Robert Lowell's highly public rejection of the invitation he had received. Kennan addressed the luncheon, with Lady Bird Johnson in attendance. He defended the "eccentricities" of artists but cut from his prepared remarks a passage endorsing their right to address controversial issues: it would, Goldman had warned him, offend the president. "Are we his guests?" Kennan asked. Goldman said yes, and that settled it as far as Kennan was concerned. Mrs. Johnson thanked him for avoiding controversy, but reporters noticed the omission, obliging a presidential press spokesman to claim, lamely, that Kennan had run over his allotted time. Johnson, who had been in his office most of the day, appeared only for the concluding evening address and never bothered to greet Kennan: "That was my only contact with the White House in his time."[25]

Kennan's own doubts about Vietnam developed gradually. He had gone out of his way, while in Belgrade, to defend Kennedy's support for Ngo Dinh Diem against Yugoslav press criticism. But by the time of the *Look* interview in November 1963—which appeared just after Diem's overthrow and assassination—Kennan was advising caution: "When you have regimes of this sort, . . . [y]ou always have to be ready to get out." In Japan, several months later, he acknowledged uncertainty about Johnson's intentions but suggested that the domino theory did make sense. By March 1965, though, with American military involvement growing, Kennan was privately expressing deep concern "about what our people are doing in Southeast Asia. It seems to me that they have taken leave of their senses." And in May, writing to Annelise: "I am absolutely appalled at what is going on. It looks to me as if Mr. J[ohnson] had lost his head completely."[26]

Nevertheless, he kept these views to himself. When he saw Gromyko in Moscow on June 25, Kennan used the occasion, Ambassador Kohler reported, to mount an "able and effective" defense of American policy. That was a diplomatic facade: Kennan was in fact wondering how the United States could hope to exploit Sino-Soviet differences while fighting a major war in Vietnam. Washington had lost "almost all flexibility of choice not only in that particular area but in our approach to the communist world generally," he wrote Yale's chaplain, William Sloane Coffin. He saw no point, however, in speaking out. "I have had my day in court. My views are known. . . . I can do no more, it seems to me, than to fall silent."[27]

But he didn't. Kennan's first published criticism of Johnson's strategy appeared in *The Washington Post* on December 12, 1965. If victorious, he argued, the North Vietnamese and the Vietcong would surely impose a ruthless dictatorship: young Americans marching on their behalf were choosing "a very strange way" to support freedom. But the world contained much more oppression than the United

States could ever hope to remedy, some of it "closer to home than what transpires in Vietnam." A communist triumph there would not shift the global balance of power. Meanwhile the war was overshadowing everything else. "[E]nslaved to the dynamics of a single unmanageable situation," the United States was losing the initiative, "not just locally but on a world scale."[28]

Kennan was recovering, when the piece appeared, from yet another health crisis, this time a prostate operation, which laid him low through the Christmas holidays. "[T]he incomparable grapefruit," he assured Kent, "are already contributing to my recovery in a most welcome way." He was well enough by February 1966 to draft a statement on Vietnam for the Senate Foreign Relations Committee, whose chairman, J. William Fulbright, had invited him to testify. Kennan then traveled to Ohio for lectures at the College of Wooster and at Denison University. He took a late flight to Washington on the ninth, arriving sleep-deprived and exhausted— only to find himself, for five hours the next day, on national television.[29]

Angered by Johnson's decision to resume the bombing of North Vietnam after a five-week halt failed to produce negotiations, Fulbright and his staff director, Carl Marcy, had arranged live coverage of the hearings they had convened. Worried by this, Johnson tried to seize the spotlight by scheduling, on the spur of the moment, a "summit" conference in Honolulu with South Vietnamese president Nguyen Cao Ky. He also pressed the television networks to resume their normal programming. CBS executives obliged with *I Love Lucy* reruns on the day Kennan appeared, provoking the resignation of their respected news division director, Fred W. Friendly. NBC, however, carried Kennan's testimony in full.

"An unusual hush fell over the prelunch drinkers at the Metropolitan Club," *The New York Times* reported, "as members and guests, including Government officials, bankers, lawyers and journalists, grouped, glasses in hand, around a television set." What they and the nation saw, *Washington Post* columnist Murrey Marder added, was not the explosive drama of past congressional hearings, "only a bald, soft-spoken, well-tailored man just five days short of 62, . . . calmly and decorously surgically dissecting a whole concept of foreign policy [of] which he profoundly disapproved."

Ho Chi Minh was not Hitler, Kennan explained; nor would he be, if he won, a puppet of Moscow or Beijing. Defeating him, however, would cost civilian lives and suffering on a scale "for which I would not like to see this country responsible." The United States could not continue to "jump around" like "an elephant frightened by a mouse." Instead its standard must be that of John Quincy Adams: to sympathize with freedom everywhere; to fight for it only where feasible; and to "go not abroad in search of monsters to destroy." Kennan added, to this famous aphorism, one of his own: "There is more respect to be won in the opinion of this world by a resolute and courageous liquidation of unsound positions than by the most stubborn pursuit of extravagant or unpromising objectives."[30]

"Your testimony," Kennan's friend Louis Fischer wrote, "resembled a supersonic plane breaking the sound barrier; it ripped through the nation, and perhaps the world, breaking windowpanes of the mind." That was extravagant, but Johnson did find it necessary, in a press conference the next day, to deny significant disagreement with Kennan, or with retired Army general James M. Gavin, who had earlier made a similar argument. Privately, Johnson was fuming. "They both would just rather not be troubled with Asia," he complained to his aides. Why would Kennan even talk about Vietnam when he had never been there and knew nothing about the situation? But George Reedy, Johnson's former press secretary, pointed out that Kennan and Gavin were reasonable men, who had expressed their uneasiness from a moderate perspective and in a sensible tone. Perhaps they had a point in wondering whether the war was being conducted "as an integral part of an overall United States world strategy." Could Johnson meet with them and see that they got regular briefings? The president, now very much on the defensive, chose not to do so.[31]

Kennan had not sought this visibility. He had participated in no public protests against the war, he assured a former State Department colleague, not even university teach-ins. But he had felt it necessary, when asked by Fulbright, to make his views known. The response astonished him: "It was perfectly tremendous. I hadn't expected anything remotely like this." One woman wrote to say that when his testimony began, she had been ironing: "I ironed all day." She was not alone. CBS might have thought that the typical opinion maker didn't watch daytime television, humorist Art Buchwald wrote, "but in my house it happens to be my wife."

The other day I came home from the office and said casually, "What's new?"

"George Kennan made a very persuasive case against our present containment policy."

"Oh," I said, "that's nice."

"He differed in some respects from Gen. Gavin on the enclave policies, but he has come out for courageous liquidation of unsound positions rather than stubborn pursuit of extravagant or uncompromising [sic] objectives."

"That's fine," I said. "What's for dinner?"

One poll, shown to Johnson, revealed support for his handling of the war drop-ping from 63 to 49 percent in the single month that followed the Senate hearings. More than any other episode in Kennan's career, this one confirmed his long-standing belief that style was as important as substance. After seeing them on television, nobody could dismiss Kennan or Gavin as "irresponsible students or wild-eyed radicals," Fulbright's biographer has written. Their testimony "made it respectable to question, if not to oppose, the war."[32]

On the Sunday after he testified, Kennan gave the chapel sermon at Princeton University. His theme was "Why Do I Hope?" There were many reasons not to: the state of the world, the fallibility of human nature, the frailties of the human frame. And yet:

> Repeatedly, in my own life, occurrences which seemed at the time to be personal misfortunes, turned out later to have been blessings in disguise. And on those occa-sions when I have tried to be very clever and far-sighted in my own interests, and to calculate nicely the best approach to the gratification of this or that ambition or desire, a wise and beneficent hand has seemingly intervened in the current of events to frustrate these puny, silly efforts, and to make of me the fool that deserved to be made.

There was hope, then, in simply struggling, against whatever odds: "Churchill taught us that, in 1940." There was hope in "this marvelous earth around us." There was hope in professional dedication, which "like some gigantic spiritual ski-lift" overcame "the abysses of our true loneliness and helplessness." But the strongest reason for hope was love:

> love in the family, love for friends, love—in the sense of genuine personal affection— for persons of the opposite sex, love for people with whom we are associated as neighbors or in our work; and finally, for those who are strong enough and great enough for it, love for mankind at large.

No act of love, he was sure, "will not ultimately be given its true value in the settle-ment of the affairs of the human spirit—in ways, perhaps, that defy our powers of imagination, but fully and in such a way to make it a thousand times worthwhile."[33]

VII.

"Dearest Annelise," George wrote her from Geneva, where he had been lecturing at the Graduate Institute of International Relations, on May 5, 1965. "I have been thinking constantly about ourselves and our future. . . . I thought it might be easier to write some of this to you than to say it when I get home." They were approaching

> a serious crisis, not in our relations, which are unaffected, but a crisis brewed of the point of change to which my life, and partly our life, has come: with the growing up of our children, the exhaustion of my public usefulness, the passage of the farm beyond the limits of our mutual strength, and my own need for some steady and creative purpose, if I am to move cheerfully through the strains of advancing age.

There would be "more of Princeton, and more of the loneliness of the Institute," but this would raise problems. "We'll have to dream up something, I think, to prevent a complete drying-up of my personality . . . , and to make our life and home sufficiently interesting to hold some attraction for the children—as well as for ourselves." It wouldn't be easy, "for our taste in people and in recreations is not always the same." Annelise's reply, if she wrote one, is not on record, but the issue was one of which they were both aware. Marriages, like life, go through stages. Some survive the transitions; others don't. How this happens is often a mystery, since few couples document—and fewer outsiders witness—the inner workings of an intimate relationship.[34]

Of their love there can be no doubt: the marriage could not otherwise have lasted for as long as it did. How two people love, though, is—as George's letter gently suggested—not always the same. "I think they must have had a lot of hard times with each other," a close friend surmised. George acknowledged as much—also gently—in his Princeton chapel sermon: "The path of true love indeed never does run smooth, [given] the inevitability of jealousies, of unrequited affections, of separations and bereavements."

He had known, as a young man, that he must marry, but he also dreaded the prospect. "[O]nce married," George informed Jeanette before he had even met Annelise, "very few men ever think at all any more." Annelise wasn't his equal as a thinker and never tried to be. "I wonder what it's going to be like, living here with all these great brains," she teased Oppenheimer, on the day they were introduced in the spring of 1950. She had been living with George for a long time by then, though, and his brain was still functioning. Some other wife, facing his slides into self-absorption, might have given up on him, Jeanette speculated. But "Annelise would make him go out and buy her a birthday present! She wouldn't sit and sulk." She was, George's older sister Constance observed, totally unlike him, and therefore "[s]he couldn't have been a better wife for him."[35]

Annelise's resilience, their neighbor Dick Dilworth thought, reflected her Scandinavian origins: an American would not have had the patience. Another Princeton friend, Bill Bundy, admired her skill in getting George to relax: "One has seen matrimonial relations where you feel that it's too jangly, because they're both trying to show off to each other." Annelise had been a Washington wife when Mary Bundy first encountered her: "You talk about your husband. It's tedious beyond measure." In Princeton, though, "I began to see the other side, and to think she was just wonderful." But George might have found Annelise "a little boring at times," even there.[36]

"George is more apt to talk about himself with women than with men," Annelise herself acknowledged. "Much more so." Shrewdly, she used the plural. She could always discuss with him where to live and travel, what they could afford, and how to raise the children. But George never wrote her the kind of long, self-revelatory letters he sent to Jeanette. Annelise had seen some, and they made it appear "as if he were having absolutely the worst time. I knew it wasn't like this. I can't explain to you why always when he took pen in hand—" "Gloom and depression would set in?" "Yes."[37]

Dorothy Fosdick, with whom Kennan shared his troubles when they served together on the Policy Planning Staff, attributed his need to confide in women to "deep psychological considerations." Annelise agreed, pointing out that the loss of George's mother, and then of Cousin Grace after his father remarried, had changed "his whole feeling about women." George went even further: his relations with women, he wrote when he was seventy-seven, had been "unfortunately affected by the bewildering succession of female figures who flitted in and out of the house, each taking care of me in her way, through the years of my infancy and childhood."[38]

The stability of a long marriage never quite balanced this instability in his upbringing; hence his dependence on Jeanette, as well as on a succession of female friends from whom George sought solace, to one degree or another, at one time or another: Frieda Por, Dorothy Hessman, Juli Zapolskaya, Fosdick herself. Others— more secretly—became lovers in times of loneliness, lapses George explained in Freudian terms without absolving himself of Calvinist guilt.

I've noticed over the years what a tremendous difference there can be between what Freud calls the "persona"—the outward personality which we all have to put forward, but particularly to people dependent on us—and the real personality underneath. We all have vestiges of our animalistic existence in us.

The best you could do, when afflicted by such "emotional and instinctual chaos," was "to learn to act as though you weren't." But concealment too had its price: "There's no use pretending that it's anything other than what it is."[39]

That's why he used Russian, at times, to chronicle concealments. "I am ringing her up," George wrote under an English-language entry in his diary on February 14, 1965. "No one is answering. I am calling again. She has picked up but I can hear in the tone of her voice that she is not alone. Embarrassed, I am ending the conversation. I am absolutely devastated and driving home." Similar passages stretched across the bottom of pages for the next three months. They were to be understood, he explained to himself and to whoever would later read them, as "a story or novel based on fantasies flowing from my own life, representing its [switching back to English] *fictional extension.*" A few of these entries, however, also recounted dreams. "Enticing opportunities of getting intimate with particular women," he wrote of one, "which don't materialize because of the presence—the watchful presence—of my wife."[40]

He even left instructions for his son, not to be passed on "until I am dead," on how to manage such matters. Marriage could indeed provide "the deepest moments of happiness a man is capable of experiencing and the best conceivable background for the great constructive tasks of life." But not all marriages were successful, and even those that were did not always fully satisfy "the sexual instinct," second only to self-preservation in the demands that it made. So what about affairs? If conducted openly, the woman would become possessive, in an effort to demonstrate "her proprietary rights and the security of her status." If clandestine, the affair risked becoming "the source of endless gnawing shame and apprehension." If the woman was not married, "you may be fairly sure she wants to be, or will at some point want to be." If she was married, there was always the possibility "of a sudden and unwanted intimacy with her husband." If asked which was worse, "the friendship of an unsuspecting husband, or the resentment of a discerning one, I should not be able to tell you. God save you from them both."[41]

Domesticity, George griped in another "imaginary" letter, was "children, diapers, illnesses, relatives, tiresome questions of money, [and] the sex-destroying question: 'Have you remembered the key?'" He ought to be able to stroll, "sometimes alone, sometimes in company, through shady *allées*. There should be just enough of the female sex to ease the mind, not enough to destroy it. Can one have these things in Princeton?" He was not sure. It would require

> keeping in mind at all times that which is physically absent as well as that which is present: the people, dependent on you, whom you do not at the moment see; the responsibilities that do not at the moment impinge themselves on your life and consciousness; your past failures; the appalling acts of weakness of which you have been guilty; the injustices you have done to people; the tragedies that may not yet have happened, but do happen—and are bound to;—in short, the whole tragic bedrock of existence.

Tragic indeed—until one notes that George began this last diary entry in the transit lounge at the London airport and completed it hours later as his plane was landing in New York: air travel almost always drove him, with pen in hand, into sloughs of despond. During the three weeks he had been away on this trip, he had sent Annelise an affectionate letter every other day. "It will be good to get home," the last of them ended. "Love, G."[42]

George led multiple lives through most of their marriage, and Annelise knew that he did. What these were when—which were real, which imagined, which dreamt—is harder to establish and doesn't much matter. He was hardly alone, in this respect, among his contemporaries. He was unusual in taking responsibility for these affairs, whatever their nature, and in leaving behind an account of what they cost. He would hardly have done so had they not filled a void, the origins of which lay further in the past than he could remember. Annelise, missing little, understood much. George, in turn, understood how much greater his emptiness would have been without her.

VIII.

"Received this morning the proofs of some portrait photos I had taken for publicity purposes," George wrote one day in January 1965, "and was so appalled at the hideousness of my own visage that I went off . . . to the library and worked alone there, that others might be spared the ordeal of looking at me." So how could he expect female companionship to ease the mind if the body was so visibly advancing beyond middle age? In fact, it seemed to help.

"He's adorable," the journalist and novelist Martha Gellhorn had written another of George's admirers a few months earlier: "so naïve really, so gentle, so conscience eaten that he feels he ought to suffer every minute for the US." Gellhorn had not been so smitten when she stormed into the Prague legation in the fall of 1938, demanding that a younger Kennan "*do* something" about the German takeover of the Sudetenland. Now, though, she found him charming and began a passionate but one-sided correspondence about their mutual detestation of the war in Vietnam. George saw her less frequently than she wished and responded laconically to her letters: "What, you ask, does the private citizen do? If he is capable of it, I think he prays."[43]

A less needy friend was the formidable *Die Zeit* editor Marion Dönhoff, an East Prussian aristocrat who had joined the anti-Hitler resistance during the war and then, in 1945, escaped on horseback to the west, just ahead of the Red Army. George saw her as "a rare phenomenon in German life: a person who has preserved a real knowledge and understanding of the values of the past, a clear conscience, and a detached judgment, into the modern age." That she had done this without self-pity was the source of her strength, "now so widely recognized." When Dönhoff's nephew, Hermann Hatzfeldt, enrolled as a Princeton graduate student in the mid-1960s, the Kennans treated him as a surrogate son, and after inheriting Schloss Crottorf, the Rhineland family estate, he would host them there, along with his famous aunt, for many visits over many years.[44]

The most famous of George's female friendships, however, was one about which the father of the woman involved would have spun furiously in his grave, had it not been encased under tons of concrete just outside the Kremlin wall. She was Svetlana Iosifovna Alliluyeva, the only daughter of Josef Stalin, and on the evening of March 6, 1967, she appeared at the U.S. embassy in New Delhi to request political asylum. She had with her a memoir that, Ambassador Chester Bowles informed Washington, was likely to sell extremely well if published with "timely guidance from some American whom she trusts." Bowles arranged to fly her to Rome, and shortly after midnight on the tenth, Connie Goodman (as Moench was now, having recently married) got a phone call "from a gentleman I knew to be connected with the C.I.A." He was Donald "Jamie" Jameson: "I've been trying very hard to get in touch with Mr. Kennan. Can you tell me where he is?"

Upon learning that he was at the farm, Jameson waited until a more reasonable hour to call: "We have a tremendous defection." The agency had the manuscript. Could Kennan assess it, both for its intelligence value and with a view to possible publication? It arrived in Princeton on the sixteenth, by which time Kennan was in bed with the flu: "I read it through the night, and realized that this was not only publishable but also probably worth hundreds of thousands of dollars." After receiving this information, the State Department asked Kennan to meet Alliluyeva in Switzerland, where the authorities were now hiding her: the news was out, and journalists were on her trail. So he flew to Milan, and the Swiss smuggled him across their border. They were "very good at this sort of thing—don't ever underestimate the Swiss!"

"George Kennan was tall, thin, blue-eyed, elegant," Alliluyeva wrote of their first meeting, which took place at a safe house in Bern on the twenty-fourth. "That hour proved that fantasies and dreams could sometimes come true." She should indeed publish, he told her, and perhaps also emigrate to the United States. It would be unlike the Soviet Union, but she would have friends, not least his own family, who would welcome her to the Pennsylvania farm, a place like "your Zubalovo." That was the dacha outside Moscow where Alliluyeva had grown up, and "I knew then that he had read my manuscript very attentively." Kennan had already found her a lawyer, his Princeton neighbor and Institute trustee Edward Greenbaum, who in turn secured a publisher's advance that made Alliluyeva wealthy before she ever set foot on American soil. She did that on April 21, and *The New York Times* described the scene: "A vibrant figure danced down the steps of a Swissair jetliner," approached the microphones, and said cheerfully, in English, "Hello there, everybody!"[45]

Now a media sensation, Alliluyeva at first sought refuge on the Long Island estate of Stuart H. Johnson, whose daughter, Priscilla McMillan, was translating her memoirs: the Kennans went there to greet her, using young Hatzfeldt as their driver. "Annelise by nature was very calm," Svetlana recalled. Neither "a university professor, nor a writer, nor a historian," she would "give good advice." George, in the meantime, was trying to portray Svetlana not as a "defector" but "as a human being in herself. . . . She is a remarkable and courageous woman." The elder Kennans were about to leave for Africa and then Norway, though, so Joan offered to host—and hide—Stalin's daughter in East Berlin.

Svetlana spent two months incognito at the Cherry Orchard with Joan, Larry, and their two young sons. The house reminded her, as it had George and Annelise, of a prerevolutionary Russian country estate. She found something special in every room, especially George's study on the third floor: "full of sunshine, reflected in squares on the yellow parquet floor," it was "rather empty, and this was the most wonderful part of it." One wall was full of books, Russian newspapers, and journals. There was a big plain wooden table with no drawers, "so convenient for work, it seemed to invite one to settle down." By the window was a hard rock-ing chair, "polished by time," and nearby an old-fashioned typewriter, sitting on a stand "nailed together by the professor himself." Svetlana had confided in her, Joan wrote her father, "that she loved you very much, [and] missed you." This was "not to be interpreted in some overly emotional sense—it meant simply that you were the first person she met after leaving India, with whom she had an instant rapport."[46]

Soviet propagandists, by then, were trying to discredit Alliluyeva: she was, they claimed, psychologically unstable; her arrival in the United States had been a plot to divert attention from the upcoming fiftieth anniversary of the Bolshevik Revo-lution; Kennan had arranged it. So she retaliated, on a day when no grown-ups were present to try to stop her, by summoning Joan's and the farmer's children, their babysitter, and Christopher, then seventeen and just back from his spring term at Groton. She had him light the hibachi. On it went her Soviet passport, incinerated before small solemn American witnesses, its ashes then scattered in the Pennsylvania wind.[47]

After his return from abroad that fall, George introduced Svetlana to Prince-ton. They walked through the Institute's woods, toured the university campus, and visited the chapel, "leaving outside his black poodle [Krisha], who followed us everywhere. No one paid the slightest attention to us, and this was the best thing I could have wished for." She rented a house and became, for several years, a neighbor. Bill Bundy remembered a dinner, in 1975, to which the Dilworths, the Taplins, the Kennans, and Alliluyeva came. "Let's have some music," someone said. So "George started playing his guitar, singing these sad Russian songs, and, well, Svetlana brightened, she effervesced, in a way that I didn't ever see her do on any of the other half-dozen occasions we met her. Her devotion to George was very clear that evening."[48]

"Dear George," she wrote him the following year from California, where she had recently moved, "you are unhappy—and this is very obvious—because you constantly betray yourself." What followed was a bizarre form of poetic justice. Kennan, famously, had analyzed Stalin from afar three decades earlier. Now Sta-lin's daughter, from a shorter distance and in still slightly erratic English, was analyzing him.

> You constantly do not allow yourself to *be* yourself. You've put yourself—and all your
> life—into the position of (pardon me, please!) that deadly Presbyterian Righteous-
> ness which looks "good" only in pronouncements from the pulpit; which is based on

human experiences of different era; different people; different social millieu, than yours.

Like Lincoln, Walt Whitman, Henry David Thoreau, and Frank Lloyd Wright—Alliluyeva had lived briefly at Taliesin West, the late architect's compound—Kennan had been "*born* to be constantly misunderstood." She saw in him the aging Tolstoy, "trying to be an old homebody, a patriarch of all big family crowd; *so what?* You were never good in this role." He never would be, "no matter how much you might try—in full sincerity—to brake your own bones to fit *that* pattern." He needed "freedom; travel; opened sea; life on the boat and with the Nature; life on the farm, among trees, animals and manual work."

> You *are* a writer. *Not* that academic type of a historian who (no doubt about that!) collects awards every year from all important institutions of the world. Did those awards make you happier? . . . Because you are *not* a man of vanity. Only your own, *inner* satisfaction can make you really happy.

Changing one's life, however, took an effort. She had done it by leaving the Soviet Union. He could do it by separating himself "from that killing vanity of Hodge Road; from that depressing Norwegian narrow practicality; from constant calls from Washington, D.C. which only frustrate you, and remind you that you are a 'retired ambassador.' . . . Because, George, you deserve to be happy, you deserve more than anyone else to live *your way*." [49]

It's not clear whether George showed this letter—one of many he received from Alliluyeva—to Annelise. When later asked about her in his presence, however, Annelise succinctly said a lot: "George, you don't realize—there's something about that female! She gets a little jealous!" It was an unusual reprimand. For if Annelise resented George's need for female companionship—or the need of other females for George's—she rarely showed it. "Whatever difficulties she and my father might have had were never aired in public," their daughter Joan recalled. "She never spoke disparagingly about him, aside from the minor frustrations common to all married couples." With an even temperament and practical good sense, self-pity was not her style. "She had a healthy sense of herself. . . . She was like the rock of Gibraltar." George had been "extraordinarily lucky," Frank Taplin concluded. Annelise was "the greatest thing that ever could have happened to him." [50]

IX.

The Kennans went to Africa in the spring of 1967, George later explained, to "cure my ignorance, since I'd never been there." The trips—there turned out to be two of them—came about through his friend Harold Hochschild, an Institute trustee with extensive mining interests in the region. The United States–South Africa Leader Exchange Program and the African-American Institute sponsored the visits, drawing on help from the State Department to arrange an arduous schedule of tours, luncheons, receptions, dinners, press interviews, and meetings with public figures. Kennan also lectured on his historical research but found his audiences more interested in the Vietnam War and in the now-famous Alliluyeva.[51]

Determined to miss nothing, George kept an unusually detailed diary, employing undiminished descriptive skills to capture Johannesburg's sprawl and the aridity of the plain surrounding it; the California-like cultural sparseness of Pretoria; the stately elegance of the Blue Train to Cape Town; the excitement of standing at the windswept tip of the continent, where great swells from the Atlantic collided with smaller ones from the Indian Ocean. He noted jarring contrasts: modern universities, luxurious country clubs, and efficient mining operations, but also townships into which Bantus were being relocated against their will. Kennan had no objection in principle to the idea of separate development, having long believed that race shaped culture. Recent American efforts to pretend otherwise had even left him sympathetic to apartheid, he confessed to Dönhoff in 1965. But separation should not require humiliation, and that was what bothered him about South Africa.

> Took a walk to a park [in Johannesburg] where grown up "non-Europeans" were permitted to walk but their children could not play on the swings. Similarly, there is a beach, on the sea coast, where black fishermen may ply their calling and launch their boats but must not swim for recreation. I am told that a drawing appeared in one of the periodicals here showing a black man on his hands [and knees] scrubbing a church floor and a white overseer saying: "One prayer out of you, and out you go."

In the Transkei, the first of the "homelands" the white minority government had established, the Kennans visited a hut with a thatched roof and a dirt floor, surrounded by human and animal excrement because there were no sanitary facilities. It was, George guessed, how most of the territory's residents lived. He found it "heart-rending" to see how cruelly apartheid oppressed the people he met, "particularly the younger ones." He doubted, therefore, that it could last.

It was a relief, paradoxically, to arrive in the Portuguese colony of Mozambique, where Kennan saw fewer signs of "racial tension and artificiality." The chief excitement there was a visit to a game preserve near Beira. Lions appeared, as expected, but just at that moment the Kennans' Volkswagen minibus broke down, unexpectedly. "So there we stood" while the driver nervously attempted repairs, "with our heads sticking out above the roof . . . , surveying the scene, but powerless to move." A passing car at last rescued George and Annelise from the prospect of being eaten.

The next stop was Lusaka, in Zambia, on June 4, and here things began to fall apart. Arriving exhausted, George found that his hosts had lined up, beginning early the next morning, a long series of calls "on people I did not know, whose country I had never seen, and with whom I had nothing in common." One was President Kenneth Kaunda, to whom he was introduced as "Mr. Frost." Even worse, Kennan was asked to meet exiles from South Africa, Mozambique, and Rhodesia who were seeking to overthrow the governments of those countries. A set of book proofs he had needed to work on had not caught up with him. And then, on June 5, war broke out between the Israelis and the Arabs. If it escalated, "we would be stuck here for God knows how long."

"I was over-reacting," George knew, "not sleeping, not digesting, suffering—literally—from a touch of jaundice and viewing everything with a jaundiced eye." But to continue in that condition would be unfair to the organizers and to the remaining countries they had him visiting. So he proposed, and Annelise agreed upon, a quick escape to Norway. "I feel terribly about having to break off the trip," George wrote Joan from Kristiansand, but had it gone on it would have ended badly. He hoped to go back: for the moment, though, "I must go out and mow the lawn."[52]

The Kennans did go back, for two weeks in September, first to Zambia, and then on to Rhodesia, Malawi, Tanzania, Kenya, Ghana, and the Ivory Coast. What George saw strengthened his pessimism. He was used to having communist governments treat him as an enemy, while the people were friendly. In Africa, "everyone equivocates." But he did, this time, meet all of his obligations. On the last evening in Abidjan, "amour-propre thus partially restored," George was satisfied "that I had had just about as much enlightenment as I could absorb at my age in any concentrated dose."[53]

Apartheid, Kennan wrote the president of the African-American Institute shortly after returning to Princeton, was "not only offensive to our sensibilities, but clearly inadequate to South Africa's own needs and doomed to eventual failure." Any quick shift to majority rule there or elsewhere, though, would be "a disaster for all concerned." Blacks were not ready for it, and whites were determined to fight rather than yield. So did it make sense for the United States to be supporting "national liberation" movements? Was it prepared to liquidate the war in Vietnam to fight an even bigger one on their behalf? It was "not our business, nor does it lie within our capabilities," to compel changes in institutions and practices of other countries "when they do not meet with our approval." With the passage of time, South Africa's leaders would see that they could not continue to keep most of their population in "ignorance and civil helplessness." The greatest service Americans could provide to apartheid's victims would be to permit "the logic of that situation to work itself out."[54]

X.

The proofs pursuing Kennan around Africa were for his first volume of memoirs. Edward A. (Ted) Weeks, the Atlantic–Little, Brown editor who published *Russia and the West under Lenin and Stalin* in 1961, had long encouraged this project, but Kennan didn't begin working on it until the fall of 1966. With Goodman's help, he had finished a five-hundred-page book by mid-March 1967, at which point he checked to see who rejected the earlier autobiography he had prepared in the late 1930s, when "we were incredibly broke, and I [hoped to] make a couple of hundred dollars." It turned out to have been Atlantic–Little, Brown: both author and publisher had forgotten this previous disappointment with one another.

George wrote the memoir, he explained to Joan that summer, "primarily for you children, so that you would have some idea of what I did and tried to do." A few scholars might also find it useful. With the declassification of American documents on the early Cold War, and in response to the escalating Vietnam War, a new generation of scholars was questioning the premises of "containment": had the Soviet Union really been as dangerous as Kennan claimed? Some of their criticisms, he thought, reflected "lack of knowledge as to how I came by [my] views. . . . I ought to try to explain." Others he agreed with: the United States had made itself dangerous in attempting to "contain" the Soviet Union, and he wanted to account for that as well.

It was not enough simply to restate positions, as he had done in *Realities of American Foreign Policy*, and in the published version of the Reith lectures, *Russia, the Atom, and the West*. Few people had read those books, and they offered no biographical context. Kennan's histories, in contrast, described other lives vividly. Could he depict his own? "I rather hate it," George complained to Kent, as he began the task. "The best that can be said . . . is that it would be more unfortunate if I failed to write [it] than if I did." So he was grinding out pages, wincing at each use of the first person singular, constantly falling into "traps of vanity, distortion of memory, hindsight and pompousness." He had done the book "much too hastily," he admitted, and "of the excitement of authorship there is none."[55]

But by the time it appeared in October 1967, under the title *Memoirs: 1925–1950*, Kennan was ready for a little publicity. So he granted an interview, in his Institute office, to the *New York Times Book Review* editor Lewis Nichols. The younger Kennan might have had to settle for the last room in Princeton when he arrived as a student in 1921, Nichols wrote, having read George's account of his undergraduate years. But now, on the second floor of Fuld Hall, he had one of the best rooms in town. Its wide windows looked out on a forest in fall foliage. His desk was two tables, with a sturdy typewriter alongside. His sofa was "so comfortable that it is left with regret." Bookcases lined the walls, the volumes on Russia filling one side and those on diplomacy the other. The books Kennan had written—nine by Nichols's count—were stashed in a corner, battered from frequent use. One was *American Diplomacy*, which its author dismissed as "that old pot-boiler." When Nichols reminded him that *Russia Leaves the War* had won four major prizes, thereby bettering the Triple Crown in horse racing, Kennan smiled like a small boy who "not only had found the cookie jar but found it full."[56]

That was not the tone, however, of his memoir. In the alienation it expressed from his era, his country, and himself, it most closely resembled *The Education of Henry Adams*—with whose author the two George Kennans, eerily, shared a birthday. The second Kennan had read Adams and, like him, used autobiography for self-reproach. Both rejected the self-congratulation typical of the modern genre; both reflected an ancient prototype, Saint Augustine's *Confessions*. It was not an example Acheson would follow when he chose, as the title for his 1969 memoir, *Present at the Creation*.

Where Kennan differed from Adams was in the quality of his writing: he left indelible impressions in print. Thanks to him, there will always be fairies in Milwaukee's Juneau Park. Midwesterners will always find Princeton inhospitable. The Foreign Service will always have its roots in the cool, sleepy corridors of the venerable State-War-Navy building. Stalin will always be "an old battle-scarred tiger," with "pocked face and yellow eyes." Marshall will always peer, "penetratingly," over the rims of his glasses. Acheson will always treat Kennan as "a court jester, expected to enliven discussion, privileged to say shocking things."[57]

Unlike Acheson, but in the manner of Adams, Kennan underestimated his own influence. He credited himself with having sorted out wartime confusion over Azores bases, accurately sensing Stalin's intentions, organizing the Policy Planning Staff, designing the Marshall Plan, and realigning occupation policy in Japan. He made no claim, though, to having designed any long-term strategy of "containment." He said nothing about anticipating the Sino-Soviet split. And he devoted at least as much space to what he regarded as his failures: the Truman Doctrine; the "X" article; the Smith-Molotov exchange; the North Atlantic Treaty Organization; Program A; the idea of an integrated Europe apart from the United States and Great Britain; and the decision to build the hydrogen bomb.

Some issues were too delicate for Kennan to discuss. One was his ties to the CIA: *Ramparts* magazine had exposed the agency's secret funding of the Congress for Cultural Freedom—of which Kennan had long been aware—only months before his memoir appeared, but the full extent of his role in originating covert operations would not become apparent for years to come. He said little, beyond childhood, about his family, and certainly nothing about his affairs. He did, through the diary entries he quoted, suggest the complexities of his inner life, but some of his selections raised questions about his values. He gave four lines, for example, to an account of turning away a Jewish acquaintance from the Prague legation on the day the Germans occupied Czechoslovakia in 1939, then four pages to a sexless encounter with a Berlin prostitute a few months later, in an effort to show that not all Germans were Nazis. No reader would have known, from his memoir, of the efforts Kennan made to get Jews out, in both Prague and Berlin.[58]

The omission reflected Kennan's chronic insensitivity to impressions created by what he said and wrote: even his most charitable biographer found his portrayal of the Prague events, if not callous, then "self-consciously, cold."[59] But Kennan was using his memoir to establish a literary, not a moral, reputation. He had experimented with his writing since first beginning to keep a diary in the late 1920s. Now he was publishing excerpts for the first time, and at considerable length. He meant them to display descriptive skills, and this they did. The greatest surprise of the memoir was its novelist's eye—which is probably what earned it Kennan's second National Book Award and his second Pulitzer Prize, this time for biography.

These explorations in style, however, caused controversies over substance that would plague Kennan for years to come. Did his memoir reveal him to be pro-German? Anti-Semitic? Amoral? Contrite? A Cold War apologist? A Cold War revisionist? An evader of tough issues? A visionary who saw beyond them? Or simply someone who tried to write, for his children, a book that they might read, much as Henry Adams claimed to be writing one simply for his friends?[60] It's in the nature of classics that they defy categories. Among these is the distinction, so indistinct in Kennan's life, between what one sets out to do, and what one does.

XI.

It might come as a surprise, Kennan warned an audience at Swarthmore College on December 9, 1967, that having been invited to help dedicate its new library, he should choose to speak on a subject so remote from the spirit of silence with which libraries were associated: "the present state of mind of the radical Left on the American campus." But could the first be realized "without a drastic change" in the second? Did not education imply a voluntary withdrawal from contemporary life in order to achieve a better perspective on it? Was there not a "dreadful incongruity" between that vision and "the condition of mind and behavior in which a portion of our student youth finds itself today"?

Instead of withdrawal, there was intense involvement. Instead of calm, "transports of passion." Instead of self-possession, "screaming tantrums and brawling in the streets." Instead of rational discourse, "banners and epithets and obscenities and virtually meaningless slogans." And instead of hope, "eyes glazed with anger," as well as by "artificial abuse of the psychic structure that lies behind them." In saying all of this, Kennan knew he sounded parental, a prisoner of all the "seamy adjustments" to practicality that came with that status. He made no apologies, for without such compromises, children would not enjoy the privilege of "despising us for the materialistic faint-heartedness that made their maturity possible."

Behind the protests was legitimate outrage over racial injustice at home and an apparently endless war in Vietnam. If the young had a plan for resolving these issues, "then many of us, I am sure," could join them. But

> when we are offered, as the only argument for change, the fact that a number of people are themselves very angry and excited; and when we are presented with a violent objection to what exists, unaccompanied by any constructive concept of what,

ideally ought to exist in its place—then we of my generation can only recognize that such behavior bears a disconcerting resemblance to phenomena we have witnessed within our own time in the origins of totalitarianism.

As a consequence, "many of us who are no happier" would have "no choice but to place ourselves on the other side of the barricades."[61]

The speech, to put it much too mildly, was not well received. On being escorted to a reception at the president's house, Kennan found himself surrounded "by a number of bearded creatures who were absolutely hissing at me, like a crowd of geese!" His host, Courtney C. Smith, was also not pleased: "He was trying to appease these people." (Smith would later die of a heart attack during a student occupation of the college admissions office.) Having heard of the controversy, *The New York Times Magazine* published a revised version of Kennan's speech in January 1968. It brought in hundreds of letters, all of which he read, many of which he found impressive: "These people challenged me on things that were perfectly fair. I had to face up to this." So he did so in a short book, *Democracy and the Student Left*, which included the Swarthmore lecture, twenty-eight letters from students, and another eleven from members of "the older generation," together with a response six times the length of his original address. "A lot of people didn't like [it]. I didn't care."[62]

Several of the faculty letters were silly. One professor suggested that Kennan stage an emotional breakdown, in front of his own children, as an act of contrition. He could not believe, however, that they "would be greatly enlightened by such a spectacle, however much they might enjoy it for its unexpected dramatic aspects." How, another wanted to know, could a student pursue scholarship with Marines recruiting on campus? By "taking a book, going into the library, and reading," Kennan answered. "I doubt that the recruiter would follow him there." Still another, defending the students' objections to university parietal rules, wondered how Kennan would feel if he were in a room with someone about whom he cared deeply and was forced to leave the door open: "To this reproach, I freely confess myself devoid of any adequate answer."

The students he took more seriously, if no less critically. Their only apparent agenda, the 1962 *Port Huron Statement* of the Students for a Democratic Society, was social science "gobbledygook." Even more alarming was their absence of humor, their tendency to treat people impersonally, and their belief in "the total ubiquity of responsibility." Everyone, of a certain generation at least, was to blame for everything. Kennan's antiwar testimony on national television had not absolved him: "There should, I gather, have been more evidences of excitement and indignation on my part—more noise and less thought."

Whatever their chances of being drafted, the students had a point, Kennan acknowledged, when they complained of having to register for military service at eighteen, while not being allowed to vote until they were twenty-one. Nor was there any excuse for sending draftees into wars "of obscure origin and rationale," halfway around the world. If such conflicts were necessary, professionals ought to handle them. If there weren't enough to do so, then the wars shouldn't be fought. These were failures of *policy*, though, not of *institutions*. Democracy provided means of redress, even if not immediate. "But, the students will say, this is too slow. What you are talking about will take years. By that time, we will all be dead." As usual, Kennan observed, "they exaggerate. I shall be dead. They probably will not."

And what of civil rights? In their sympathy for oppressed blacks, the students reminded Kennan of that shown for peasants by the Russian populists of the late nineteenth century. In neither case had the sympathizers known much about those with whom they sympathized. In both they viewed the oppressed as "help-less" and therefore expected of them no accountability for their own behavior: "The American Negro is not going to be aided by an approach which treats him only as object and not at all as subject." Nor would apartheid's sufferers benefit from American universities withdrawing their South African investments, as the student left was demanding. The time had come for the academy to reclaim its authority from those who had "no experience of its past, no expertise for its present, no responsibility for its future."

It was characteristic of radicals to abhor being outflanked. This had led, in Russia, to the nihilism that undermined the old order, thereby opening the way for Lenin and the Bolsheviks, who allowed no defiance. That was not likely to happen in the United States, Kennan thought: with an end to the war, a phasing out of the draft, and the aging of students beyond thirty, things would settle down. But it was worth asking why the students had become radicalized in the first place.

The answer, Kennan insisted, went well beyond the immediate targets of protest. For the students reflected the "sickly secularism" of society as a whole: its shallow convictions; its preoccupation with gadgetry; its disconnection from nature; its lack of understanding for "the slow powerful processes of organic growth." These had created, in college youth, "an extreme disbalance in emotional and intellectual growth." In the end, then, the culture itself would have to change, and here Kennan fell back on familiar jeremiads: the evils of automobiles, advertising, and environmental degradation; the corruption of politics; the possibility that the country itself might be too big to solve its problems. Were the students gloomy about the American future? "[T]hey haven't seen anything yet. Not only do my apprehensions outclass theirs but my ideas of what would have to be done to put things to rights are far more radical than theirs."[63]

XII.

"George was somewhat shrill," Dilworth recalled, "at least we thought so, and our children thought so." It went beyond that. Kennan was getting FBI reports on student and black protests throughout this period, and at one point suggested that the government suppress them, in a manner "answerable only to the voters at the next election but not to the press or even to the courts." There should even be special prisons for "political offenders," to keep them apart from common criminals. "One may think what one will of the events of the last two or three years," he wrote the master of Yale's Branford College in 1970, asking to be removed from its roster of nonresident fellows, "but that they have impaired the ability of old and young to communicate with each other is something all of us, I think, must recognize."[64]

Kennan's anxieties—extreme even for him—arose from fears for his own children as much as for his country. Grace's marriage had broken up, and Joan's was about to. Christopher had found adjustment to Groton difficult. Wendy, her father worried, was growing up too fast. "[W]e have failed badly, somewhere, in the way we have brought these children up and the sort of life we have offered them," George complained after spending a Thanksgiving at the farm with slouchy, sullen teenagers—his two youngest, plus some of their friends. Soon they would be off to the great universities, which would quickly expose them to "the morbidity of the present student population. We are in a hell of a shape, here at home."[65]

Left to himself, he often claimed, he would have become an exile, even a hermit: the west coast of Scotland still beckoned. His family could hardly follow, though, so the next best choice was to avoid, as far as possible, "all confrontation with American life. . . . I must learn to live in it as though I did not live in it." But could his children? That seemed implausible, given their need for education, employment, love, and families. How could he shield them, then, from "this false life," as he had once described it, in which "innocence is lost before maturity is achieved"?[66]

The Kennans spent the summer of 1968, as usual, in Norway. Unusually—but as an expression of confidence—George allowed Christopher and three of his buddies to sail *Nagawicka* from Denmark to Sweden in early August, without adult supervision. On leaving them at the dock,

> I was suddenly seized with a great pang of love and concern for these young crea-
> tures: so helpless, so vulnerable, so endangered despite their changed voices, their
> incipient whiskers, and their great protective show of callous amusement over life—
> vulnerable and endangered not so much by the sea to which I was now entrusting
> them in my little boat, and not so much by the built-in tragic nature of the individual
> human predicament which men had always had to face, but rather by the enormity
> of what the human community was now doing to itself, with its overpopulation, its
> precipitate urbanization, its feverish hyperintensity of communication, its destruc-
> tion of the natural environment, and its cultivation of weapons too terrible for the
> wisdom and strength of any that might command their custody and use.

To George's relief, they arrived safely and flew home, a few days later, with Wendy and Annelise. He stayed behind to secure the Kristiansand house for the winter and spent his last evening there going through family photographs. "I think of the way that Fate has tied our lives together," he wrote Joan, "and how we struggle along, half knowing what we are doing, but with our destinies also largely formed by the accidents of birth and circumstance."

All depended, he could see, "on God's grace and on each other; and with this, the whole monstrous fragility and tragedy of our lives, and yet also their poetry and their occasional heroism, become visible and real to me. I wish I could cap-ture this moment of awareness and make it a part of my view of the world, instead of being absorbed and carried away, as I shall be tomorrow morning, by a thou-sand trivialities and vanities."[67]

TWENTY-THREE

Prophet of the Apocalypse: 1968–1980

J. ROBERT OPPENHEIMER DIED IN PRINCETON, OF THROAT CANCER, on February 18, 1967, at the age of sixty-two. A week later six hundred people crowded into Alexander Hall for the memorial service, at which Kennan delivered the final eulogy. He praised his friend's scientific mind, "rigorous but humane, fastidious but generous and powerful, uncompromisingly responsible in its relationship to ascertainable truth but never neglectful of the need for elegance and beauty in the statement of it." He deplored the official injustice inflicted upon Oppenheimer: the government had used his talents to exploit the destructive capabilities of nuclear physics, but denied him the opportunity to explore "the great positive ones he believed that science to possess." His life cruelly illustrated "the dilemmas evoked by the recent conquest by human beings of a power over nature out of all proportion to their moral strength."

Shakespeare's image of a "universal wolf" as a "universal prey" eating itself up had haunted Kennan ever since he incorporated it into his long but mostly unread January 1950 paper on the "super" bomb. The idea, however, was Oppenheimer's: it was he who first alerted Kennan to the *ecological* consequences of the nuclear revolution. "[N]o one paid any attention to us," Kennan recalled, "but that brought us together." Oppenheimer gave Kennan an institutional home after he left government. Kennan, in turn, spoke for Oppenheimer after allegations about the beleaguered physicist's loyalty effectively silenced him. A war fought with modern weapons, Kennan warned in his 1957 Reith lectures, would risk everything: "the kindliness of our natural environment to the human experience, the genetic composition of the race, the possibilities of health and life for future generations." In bidding Oppenheimer farewell a decade later, Kennan acknowledged that without his help "some of us—most of us, I suppose—would never have been quite where we are today. . . . [A]ny further progress we now make is in part his achievement."[1]

There were, at the time of Oppenheimer's death, about forty thousand nuclear weapons in the arsenals of the United States and the Soviet Union—three-fourths of them American. Most were thermonuclear warheads, designed for near-instantaneous delivery by land-based and submarine-launched missiles. The least powerful, intended for battlefield use, each approximated the strength of the bombs dropped on Hiroshima and Nagasaki in 1945. Kennan lacked access to these numbers, but he didn't need it to conclude that seeking security by these means was an absurdity.

Since the Cuban missile crisis, there had been fewer explicit threats to use nuclear weapons. Satellite reconnaissance was reducing the risk of surprise attack. Diplomacy had produced a Limited Test Ban Treaty in 1963, a Nuclear Non-Proliferation Treaty in 1968, and a Soviet-American agreement, that same year, to begin negotiations on limiting nuclear weapons delivery systems while restricting the deployment of defenses against them. The goal, it appeared, was no longer to *win* a nuclear arms race but rather to *stabilize* it by ensuring equal opportunities for destruction. Both superpowers seemed to have embraced Bernard Brodie's 1946 argument that the best way to avoid war was to make its prospect as horrible as possible.

Kennan did not doubt the proposition but wondered—with Oppenheimer— why it required retaining the capacity to end civilization so many times over. That was why he distrusted détente, which most people understood to mean something he should have favored: the use of diplomacy to secure peace by balancing power. Kennan saw it as applying outdated techniques to a world in which the relation-ship between war and politics had changed. The nineteenth-century view had been that "you really could win a war and gain something from it." Now, though, the destructiveness of weaponry had made such calculations meaningless. War and politics, in Kennan's mind at least, were becoming equally dangerous.

Where, then, did the strategy of "containment," which was to have bridged the gap between war and politics, fit into all of this? When Kennan described its objective, in 1947, as bringing about peacefully either the breakup or "grad-ual mellowing" of the Soviet Union, that country had no nuclear capability. By the beginning of the 1960s, its warhead and missile technology was qualitatively approaching that of the United States. By the end of the decade, it was doing so quantitatively. By 1986, when the number of nuclear weapons peaked at around seventy thousand, just under two-thirds belonged to the U.S.S.R.[2]

So did the risks of attempting to change that state now exceed the benefits? Was the danger to be contained no longer its behavior but nuclear war itself? If so, did that suggest accepting the Soviet Union and its satellites as permanent features of the international landscape? What would that mean for the future of Germany, and of Europe itself? None of these were new questions for Kennan: he had wrestled with all of them prior to Oppenheimer's death. In the years that followed, though, they took on a renewed urgency. It was as if Kennan felt an obligation to keep Oppenheimer's prophetic vision alive, whatever that might imply for the original concept of "containment."

I.

Late in 1967 Kennan was elected president of the American Academy of Arts and Letters. Established in 1898, limited to fifty members, and modeled on the much older *Académie française*, the organization's mission was to recognize distinction in literature, music, and the fine arts. Kennan had been invited to join five years earlier because of his accomplishments as a writer, sixty-four years after the first George Kennan was similarly honored. The academy's parent organization, the National Institute of Arts and Letters, had made the second Kennan its president in 1965, just in time for the ill-fated White House Festival of the Arts. He took all of these institutional responsibilities seriously. Kennan's sense of having been excluded as a young man, Arthur Schlesinger speculated, had left him with a love of ritual as an older man: "He believes strongly that the ceremonies of life are important. It's an endearing, interesting characteristic."[3]

Kennan addressed the academy for the first time in his new capacity on May 28, 1968, three months after the Tet offensive in Vietnam, two months after Johnson's announcement that he would seek a negotiated settlement of the war but not reelection, seven weeks after the assassination of Martin Luther King, Jr., and one week before that of Robert F. Kennedy. "[W]e are meeting," Kennan acknowledged, "in a very troubled time." The artist's duty was not to get involved in politics, which were always "polluted with the passions and the myopia of the moment." Nor was it to attempt to correct, in any immediate sense, "the manifold follies and stupidities to which man, in his capacity as a political actor, is prone."

Perhaps it might be, though, to "lend to the comprehension of the human predicament a deeper dimension of insight," through which "the tragic illusions of power and anger will lose their force." Had not Cranach and Grünewald painted during peasant rebellions and religious wars? Had not Goethe, Beethoven, and Schiller flourished alongside the upheavals of the Napoleonic era? Most moving of all was Boris Pasternak, "scratching out his poems through the night in that abandoned country house in the Urals during the Russian civil war, while each night the dark shadows of the wolves against the snow came nearer." It took forty years for his writings to appear, but they were now "an imperishable component of Russian literature." Much would have been lost if those artists had sacrificed their creativity "in order to throw themselves into political pursuits for which they were ill-prepared and in which, as Pasternak realized, they could do nothing comparable in importance to what they could achieve by the employment of their real talents."[4]

Kennan's luxury—but also his burden—was not having to be Pasternak. He spoke wistfully of wanting to detach himself from contemporary events, but no one forced him to do so. That left him resisting temptation, mostly unsuccessfully. It had seemed safe enough that summer, for example, to publish his 1938–40 dispatches from Prague, unearthed while preparing his memoirs. But on August 20–21, the Soviet Union and its Warsaw Pact allies invaded Czechoslovakia to suppress the growing reform movement there. The new Kremlin leadership of Leonid Brezhnev and Aleksey Kosygin had made "a colossal mistake," Kennan was sure, and *The New York Times* quickly connected that violation of sovereignty with his reports on another such event three decades earlier. Soon Kennan was calling for an additional hundred thousand American troops to be sent to West Germany as a show of force, to counter what he saw as an increasingly "adventuristic streak" in Soviet behavior.[5]

He was also still thinking, wistfully, about politics. "I think I could have been successful at it," he wrote Joan a few days before the 1968 presidential election. "I have never found it hard to communicate with people from a platform, and I rather love all the human and intellectual intricacies." But he could never have afforded to run for office; his views, moreover, were "light years ahead of the current drift of public opinion." If the next administration were to offer him a position like under secretary of state or ambassador to the United Nations, though, he might take it.[6]

Kennan called the office of Richard M. Nixon two days after his victory at the polls to offer whatever advice the president-elect might want. None was sought, but Nixon's appointment of Henry A. Kissinger as his national security adviser surprised and pleased Kennan. He had been reading Kissinger since the 1950s and now regarded him as "fully recovered from the militaristic preoccupations of earlier years"—his writings, presumably, on the "limited" use of nuclear weapons. Shortly after learning of his new job, Kissinger in turn assured Kennan of Nixon's regard for him as "a leading example of people whose possibilities were not being used by the last administration," the implication being that the new one might find a way to do so.[7]

That conversation took place at a Princeton cocktail party on December 4, 1968. The occasion was the inaugural conference of the International Association for Cultural Freedom, a privately funded reincarnation of the Congress for Cultural Freedom, exposed the previous year as having had CIA support. Other attendees included Schlesinger, John Kenneth Galbraith, Stanley Hoffmann, Zbigniew Brzezinski, Norman Podhoretz, Marion Dönhoff, and Kennan's old Moscow friend Lillian Hellman, but also a clamorous contingent of young black power advocates and white New Leftists. Understandably confused, the local Students for a Democratic Society chapter prepared an all-purpose poster: "Down With Racism, Imperialism, Genocide, Corporation Capitalism, Policy Planners, etc." (A stronger exhortation had been crossed out, at the last moment, on the advice of a university official.) Kennan, improbably, delivered the dinner address. With his "gray suit, silk tie, elegant gold chain across his vest, [and] dignified bearing," *The New York Times* reported, he personified a lifestyle "for which the young could muster little sympathy or understanding. He reciprocated completely."

The nation had many problems, Kennan told his audience, not the least of which was "the extremely disturbed and excited state of mind of a good portion of our student youth, floundering around as it is in its own terrifying wilderness of drugs, pornography and political hysteria." This was not Pasternak-like detachment, and a heated discussion followed. "Since when [are] youth not allowed to be asses?" Hellman demanded, prompting one young activist to announce that he had just fallen in love with an older woman. She was not amused. "He did a very brave thing," she said in defense of Kennan: "He refused to be a swinger."[8]

"The new administration must be given a fair opportunity to show what it can do," Kennan commented that evening. He got no invitation to work for it, though, and this time he didn't agonize over phones that didn't ring. He had decided to return to Oxford during the spring of 1969, and he had a new project in mind: he would write the first full English-language history of the Franco-Russian alliance of 1894. The logic of doing so was not immediately obvious, but Kennan's academy address provided a clue.

Unlike the artists he had cited, he was neither a painter nor a playwright nor a philosopher. His poetry was chiefly whimsical, his musicianship only companionable. But he could write history: his distinction lay in the skill with which he represented the past to the present and future. World War I, Kennan believed, had been the greatest tragedy of the twentieth century, having set so many subsequent tragedies in motion. No one in 1914, however, had foreseen any of this. Each belligerent had entered the war optimistically, even enthusiastically. If his new book could explain such miscalculations, perhaps it might dispel illusions out of which new tragedies could grow.

It would have to be thorough, he explained to Joan, for late-nineteenth-century European diplomacy was "a frightfully complicated subject with an enormous existing literature." It would have to be scholarly, because the Institute for Advanced Study expected that of him. It would take years to complete, and "since no one in this generation will be interested in it," it would be a lonely enterprise. And why the Franco-Russian alliance? Because it had replaced Bismarck's system of unilateral restraint, which reconciled Germany's neighbors to its post-1871 unification, with one of multilateral deterrence, which meant risking war to prevent war. It should have been obvious, even in 1894, that *any* great-power clash employing modern weaponry would be "a madness from which nobody [could] benefit." Kennan would be writing a cautionary history of wolves, preparing to eat themselves up.[9]

II.

With Connie Goodman on leave from the Institute to raise a family, Kennan had a new secretary, Janet Smith. She was not shy about questioning his priorities: did he really think he could isolate himself to write history? It was probably unrealistic, he acknowledged from Oxford in March 1969, to suppose "that anyone in my position—i.e., with my past, my reputation, and my connections—would be able to find the time, the privacy, and the peace of mind to do a really major, serious work of historical scholarship." He was now sixty-five, and demands for commentary on current events had not diminished. He had also come to realize, belatedly, the benefits of inadvertence: the fact that such influence as he had accumulated over the years had more often arisen unexpectedly than from his own plans.

So he must allow for opportunities like the "long telegram," the "X" article, the Chicago lectures, the disengagement debate, the Fulbright hearings, and the Swarthmore speech, even if such "unwithstandable approaches from the outside" didn't always produce the results he wanted. However much he might wish to be a prophet, life had burdened him with the role of pundit. "Let me then accept it and be prepared to play it with distinction."[10]

Oxford was friendlier than it had been in 1957–58. The Kennans' Iffley flat was adequately heated—no need to carry coal this time—and George had an office in All Souls College. He liked having his radio free of commercials, his roads uncluttered by billboards, and telephones that rang rarely "because the English don't phone—they send notes." He was dining occasionally with colleagues; even student life struck him as "relatively rich and gay and confused and happy." But he couldn't resist controversy. What was wrong with black power anyway? Kennan asked a startled assemblage of dignitaries at a Ditchley Park conference shortly after he arrived: why shouldn't Americans follow South Africa's example and give blacks their own state? It had taken that to satisfy the Jews, his friend Richard Crossman helpfully added. Having tossed these grenades, the two took their leave, under a full moon, cheered by the mayhem they had left behind.[11]

Kennan's chief task in Oxford was to deliver the Chichele lectures, a less demanding series than the two he had taken on twelve years earlier. He chose to analyze *La Russe en 1839*, the account of a trip through Russia by Astolphe Louis Léonor, the Marquis de Custine. Like Neill Brown's dispatches from St. Petersburg in the 1850s, Custine's book allowed viewing the recent past through a distant past, a perspective Kennan relished. Custine had been unfair to Nicholas I and his contemporaries, Kennan concluded in the published version of the lectures, which appeared in 1971, but he had accurately anticipated the Stalin regime and, to a lesser extent, those that followed. Another of Kennan's epic sentences specified the analogies:

> the absolute power of a single man; his power over thoughts as well as actions; the impermanence and unsubstantiality of all subordinate distinctions of rank and dignity—the instantaneous transition from lofty station to disgrace and oblivion; the indecent association of sycophancy upwards with brutality downwards; the utter disenfranchisement and helplessness of the popular masses; the nervous punishment of innocent people for the offenses they might be considered capable of committing rather than the ones they had committed; the neurotic relationship to the West; the frantic fear of foreign observation; the obsession with espionage; the secrecy; the systematic mystification; the general silence of intimidation; the preoccupation with appearances at the expense of reality; the systematic cultivation of falsehood as a weapon of policy; the tendency to rewrite the past.

These were traits, some active, some latent, the recognition and correction of which would be vital to the Soviet Union's future: "to its security, above all, not just against those external forces by whose fancied heretical will Russians of all ages have so easily seen themselves threatened, but [also] its security against itself."[12]

That sounded a lot like the "X" article: how could there be a normal relationship with such a country until its internal configuration—indeed its culture—had changed? But Kennan was writing about Custine in the nuclear era: didn't that require overlooking such issues? Wasn't the important thing now to balance power among states, rather than to await—or even to encourage—changes from within? The questions came from the editors of a new journal, *Foreign Policy*, who had noticed (as those of *Foreign Affairs* had not) that 1972 marked the twenty-fifth anniversary of Mr. X's memorable appearance.

Eager "to welcome Professor Kennan to the pages of this magazine," they published an interview with him in late May, a week before the first American presidential visit to the Soviet Union since Roosevelt had gone to Yalta in 1945. The Nixon-Brezhnev summit promised the greatest progress yet toward strategic arms control: an "interim agreement" limiting land- and sea-based missiles armed with nuclear warheads, and a treaty banning defenses against those that remained. It followed the even more surprising trips that Kissinger and Nixon had already made to the People's Republic of China. What did Kennan think?

Brezhnev's state, he acknowledged, was not Stalin's. It had long since lost ideological authority beyond its borders: "The façade of solidarity can be maintained, today, only by extensive concessions to the real independence of the respective Communist parties." It had stabilized, but not expanded, its control over half of Europe—perhaps NATO had been of some use, after all. And the Soviet Union now had its own "containment" problem in East Asia, where China posed at least as great a challenge as did the United States. All of this had left Kremlin leaders "no alternatives except isolation or alliance with the capitalist countries, which could undermine the legitimacy of their power at home." The geopolitical balance was obviously preferable to that of 1947.

The military balance, however, was another matter. Always ahead in manpower and conventional armaments, the U.S.S.R. now had such formidable nuclear strength that American concerns no longer focused on who was to dominate Eurasia but rather on a "fantasy world" of weaponry.

It has no foundation in real interests—no foundation, in fact, but in fear, and in an essentially irrational fear at that. It is carried not by any reason to believe that the other side *would*, but only by a hypnotic fascination with the fact that it *could*. It is simply an institutionalized force of habit. If someone could suddenly make the two sides realize that it has no purpose and if they were then to desist, the world would presumably go on, in all important respects, just as it is going on today.

How might that happen? Not through the intricate agreements to be signed in Moscow, for these would only clarify the rules in a continuing contest. What was needed instead were "reciprocal unilateral steps of restraint." If one could, by such means, shrink armed establishments to more reasonable dimensions, then the Soviet Union would pose no greater threat than had prerevolutionary Russia— even if it retained vestiges of the society Custine had described.

No one should expect such a state *not* to behave as its predecessor had done. It would want to preserve, and where possible expand, its spheres of influence. It might well build a blue-water navy. It would not, in its culture or politics, become a democracy. Why, then, should "the peace of the world [depend] on the ability of the rest of us to prevent the Soviet Union indefinitely from acting like a great power?" The priority now should be to reduce or even eliminate nuclear weapons, not simply to tinker, as Kennan had put it earlier in his diary, with "the wretched ABMs and MRVs and MIRVs and SALTs and what not."[13]

Kennan's reasoning reflected his thinking on the origins of World War I. For then, as now, great-power rivalries had existed. So too had diplomacy as a means of managing them. Nixon and Kissinger were following Bismarck's example by balancing power, a considerable improvement over Johnson's practice of expending it where no vital interests were at stake. But like the Europeans who came after Bismarck, the United States and the Soviet Union were simultaneously accumulating arms of such strength that any use of them would destroy what they were meant to defend. It had taken the belligerents of 1914–18 four years to accomplish this. In the nuclear age, it would take about forty minutes.

III.

"I could not be more pleased than I am by this appointment," Kennan wrote Kissinger on September 19, 1973, shortly after the beleaguered Nixon, now deeply enmeshed in the Watergate scandal, had nominated his national security adviser also to become secretary of state. Kennan's congratulations came, however, only in the last two lines of a long letter criticizing the novelist-historian Aleksandr Solzhenitsyn, the Soviet Union's closest contemporary equivalent to Tolstoy himself, and the nuclear physicist Andrey Sakharov, whose anguish over the bombs he had built paralleled Oppenheimer's. Both were "behaving very unwisely" by provoking a showdown over their alleged official mistreatment. Even worse, they were trying to enlist Americans in support of their cause. The United States could not sacrifice its entire relationship with the U.S.S.R. to satisfy "the grievances of these people."[14]

It was a surprisingly harsh tone for the self-regarded heir of the other Kennan, the most prominent nineteenth-century defender of Russian dissidents, and for George F. Kennan as well. He had made his reputation in 1946–47, after all, by *blurring* the distinction between domestic and foreign policy in the Soviet Union. He had worked for years afterward to help settle refugees from Stalin's regime in the United States, right down through the arrival, in 1967, of the most famous of them all, the dead dictator's daughter. He had gone out of his way to honor Pasternak in his May 1968 American Academy presidential address. "I wouldn't trust any so-called détente," he had told *The New York Times* after the invasion of Czechoslovakia three months later, "if it is not supported by free contacts between governments and peoples." And six months after his letter to Kissinger, Kennan publicly praised Solzhenitsyn's *Gulag Archipelago* as "the greatest and most powerful single indictment of a political regime ever to be leveled in modern times." Why, then, was Kennan becoming less sympathetic to the Kremlin's domestic critics as the attention they attracted, during the early 1970s, began to grow?[15]

One reason was that he was becoming more sympathetic to the conduct of American foreign policy. By the time Nixon relinquished the presidency to Gerald Ford in August 1974, his administration had reached agreements with the Soviet Union to limit strategic arms, brought China out of its long diplomatic isolation, negotiated an end to the war in Vietnam, contained an unexpected Arab-Israeli war, and endorsed the concept of a multipolar world that resembled in principle, if not in all its details, Kennan's thinking while on the Policy Planning Staff a quarter-century earlier. Kissinger "understands my views better than anyone at State ever has," Kennan acknowledged. It was a relief to know that he would stay on: "Henry's a fine person, and I think very highly of him," but at the same time "he scares me." For "with opportunists like Scoop Jackson around, he could go at any moment."[16]

"Scoop" was Senator Henry M. Jackson, a long-serving Washington State Democrat who, in the aftermath of the 1972 Nixon-Brezhnev summit, had taken it upon himself to dismantle détente. He wanted to return the Democratic Party—whose presidential nominee that year was the haplessly dovish George McGovern—to the tough foreign policy traditions of Truman and Acheson. Nixon and Kissinger, Jackson claimed, had ceded superiority in strategic weaponry to the Soviet Union through ill-conceived arms control agreements, while failing to condemn that country's growing harassment of dissidents and potential emigrants, chiefly Jews. Jackson would use his considerable influence in the Senate to demand numerical parity in any new strategic arms treaties. He would also withhold "most-favored nation" status and Export-Import Bank credits—both promised by Nixon in Moscow—until the U.S.S.R. relaxed its restrictions on emigration. Solzhenitsyn and Sakharov, as Kennan saw it, were cheering him on.

The intricacies of arms control mattered little to Kennan. With both sides possessing the capacity for "fantastic overkills," he had told the Senate Foreign Relations Committee several years earlier, all calculations of advantage and disadvantage were meaningless. Human rights, though, were a trickier issue. Like John Quincy Adams, Kennan doubted the feasibility of trying to right wrongs committed by foreign governments against their own citizens. He still hoped for change within the Soviet Union but had lost faith in the ability of American leaders to bring this about. He had long deplored the ease with which domestic politics could derail foreign policy—Scoop Jackson was hardly the first example—but now the stakes were higher: with weapons of mass destruction available in such numbers, even a slight miscalculation could produce universal destruction. What gave Soviet dissidents the right, then, even if they were the figurative descendants of the Russians the elder Kennan had tried to help, to place détente at risk?[17]

They would have replied, with good reason, that the Soviet leaders were using détente to suppress dissent. Following the crushing of the "Prague spring" in 1968, Brezhnev had proposed an international conference to confirm post–World War II boundaries throughout Europe, with a view to regaining, through diplomacy, the legitimacy his own and other Eastern European regimes had lost. For if the United States and its allies formally recognized the status quo, what basis would domestic dissidents have for challenging communist party rule? The persistence with which Moscow pressed this plan gave the Western Europeans and the Canadians—Washington, in this instance, paid little attention—the opportunity to attach a Jackson-like condition of their own: that all parties to any such agreement acknowledge "the universal significance of human rights and fundamental freedoms." Brezhnev, equally inattentively, accepted the compromise. So on July 31, 1975, thirty-five heads of government from the United States, Canada, the

Soviet Union, and all European states except Albania gathered in Helsinki to sign, on the next day, the "Final Act" of the Conference on Security and Cooperation in Europe.[18]

It was "a lot of nonsense," Kennan wrote privately, "two years of wrangling over language, most of it of a general nature, none of it committing anyone specifically to anything." The Americans and their allies had lost nothing, since none intended to reunify Europe—particularly Germany—in the first place. The Soviets had made some significant verbal concessions, subscribing to language that appeared to proscribe, in the future, what they had done to Czechoslovakia, but hardly anyone in the United States understood this. Nixon, Ford, and even Kissinger had promised too much, and now—with allegations from hard-line Democrats and right-wing Republicans that the United States had again, as at Yalta, sold out Eastern Europe—the reaction was setting in. As far as Kennan could see, Americans were "right back where we were in Mr. Dulles's time." If anyone should devise "really sound and brilliant diplomacy vis-à-vis the Soviet Union, the country at large would not recognize it and would call with great acclaim for its abandonment."[19]

Despite the Helsinki agreements, Kennan wrote in a bicentennial history of Soviet-American relations published in the July 1976 issue of *Foreign Affairs*, the Nixon-Kissinger approach to détente had, on the whole, improved them. President Ford, however, was finding it impossible to say so, having barely survived a challenge for the Republican nomination from a Kissinger critic, Ronald Reagan, and now facing another, the Democratic nominee, Jimmy Carter. "[N]ot unnaturally," Kennan noted, after lunching with Kissinger in late August, he was "somewhat dispirited, believing that he had failed in his effort to instill into American diplomacy some depth of concept and some subtlety of technique. . . . He is a wise, learned and agreeable man." His memoirs would be "worth the enormous price the publishers will offer for them."

And what of Solzhenitsyn, Sakharov, and the first Kennan's legacy? The second Kennan made no mention of them in *Foreign Affairs*, noting only that "[t]he Soviet authorities will no doubt continue to adhere to internal practices of a repressive nature that will continue to offend large sections of American opinion." But in an interview that summer, with unusual asperity, he did:

> [M]y namesake, George Kennan the elder, was busy for many years trying to whip up sympathy for the Russian revolutionaries, admittedly not the Bolsheviks but their moderate predecessors the Populists. The assumption behind all this was that if one

could only overthrow the old Czarist autocracy, something much better would follow. Have we learned anything from this lesson?

He had "the greatest misgivings about any of us, Americans or West Europeans,
taking upon ourselves the responsibility for trying to overthrow this, or any other,
government in Russia." Kennan's attitude earned him a stinging rebuke from a
sensitive source. She found it pitiful, Svetlana Alliluyeva wrote him, "that *of
all people* . . . it *is* George Kennan who surrendered, and forgot *his own* words,
[which] he said in 1952. It is *still* true, George—even though Stalin [is] 20 years
[*sic*] in grave, they are *all*—still—no better than Nazis. And you know this better
than I do."[20]

Containment, as Kennan had conceived it, never required action from the outside to change the internal character of the Soviet system: that was to happen from
within, in response to external circumstances the West should have wished to create in any event. Reforms would require visionaries—dissidents, if you will—who
would sense these new circumstances and would have the courage to respond to
them. Solzhenitsyn, Sakharov, and their allies met that standard. But by the time
they did, Kennan, fearing that disruptions of any kind could lead to nuclear war,
had come to regard them as dangerous enemies.

IV.

Kennan published the second volume of his own memoirs in 1972. "I don't think
it is my best work," he wrote after finishing it. This time he was right—his first
volume had set a high standard. Covering the years 1950 through 1963, the new
one focused on the Korean War, the Moscow ambassadorship and its aftermath,
Kennan's unsuccessful efforts to save the Foreign Service career of his former
subordinate John Paton Davies, the Reith lectures controversy, and service under
Kennedy in Yugoslavia. It was oddly uneven, treating these episodes in detail while
ignoring most of what Kennan was otherwise doing, notably writing history. "I
don't see how a memoir could be better," John Kenneth Galbraith observed in *The
New York Times,* before proceeding to show how it might have been. What the
book did reveal, he concluded accurately enough, was that Kennan "derives no
special pleasure—as I always do—from the feeling that everyone else is wrong."[21]

He certainly took no pleasure in the latest crisis at the Institute for Advanced

Study. After the ailing Oppenheimer resigned as director in 1966, the board of trustees appointed an economist, Carl Kaysen, to that position. A skillful fund-raiser, Kaysen upgraded the Institute's physical facilities but lacked Oppenheimer's tact in managing its prickly personalities. After he overruled a majority of the Institute's permanent professors to offer that status to a sociologist, Robert Bellah, in 1972, they demanded Kaysen's resignation. Soon both sides were attacking one another in *The New York Times*, which did not normally cover academic politics in such gruesome detail. "I am very, very much distressed about the dispute," Kennan himself told the *Times*. "A lot of it has been sheer misunderstanding of a tragic nature."

That was part of the problem, but the larger issue was one of governance: did authority reside with the trustees, the tenured faculty, or the director, and if all three, in what proportion? Diplomacy, Kennan ruefully recalled, had been much easier than trying to answer this question. For the most part, he avoided taking sides: the trustees even approached him, at one point, about becoming interim director if Kaysen was forced to step down. To Kennan's great relief, that didn't happen. Bellah decided to go elsewhere, and Kaysen stayed on until 1976, when he yielded the directorship to a historian of science, Harry Woolf. But the furor robbed Kennan of the calm the Institute had once provided him. "As far as I can see," he wrote one friend, "just about everybody here who has had any responsibility in this matter has done, with remarkable consistency, the wrong thing." And, to another: "What fools these mortals be."[22]

Kennan was hard at work, in the meantime, establishing an institute of his own, as a way of repaying "something of the debt I owe to those who once taught and inspired me." One was his Foreign Service mentor, Robert Kelley, who had insisted that the best way to understand the Soviet Union was to study Russian history and culture. Kennan's book on Custine reflected that principle, but there was no American center for Russian research independent of major universities. Kennan wanted one, to be located in Washington. "Of the necessity," he wrote his former Moscow boss (and later New York governor) W. Averell Harriman, "there can, in my opinion, be no doubt whatsoever." Only Harriman had "the position, the authority, and the institutional detachment"—Kennan was too tactful to mention the cash—"to carry things forward."[23]

Richard Ullman, now a Princeton professor for whom Kennan had been a mentor, found it fascinating that he still deferred to Harriman: "I'd never seen [Kennan] with anybody else with whom he had that junior relationship." Ullman watched it crack, briefly but revealingly, at a dinner Kaysen arranged shortly after

Alliluyeva's arrival. Harriman had been eager to meet her, but she found his questions about her father intimidating and refused to say much. Richard Holbrooke, Harriman's feisty young aide, came gallantly to her rescue: "Governor, you are the most impossible man to work with I have ever encountered." "Oh, I'm so glad you've said that," Kennan burst out. "I've always felt that. Averell, you really were impossible!"[24]

Now, though, he needed Harriman's help, and the old man had not mellowed. "I always distrust statements [like] 'of the necessity . . . there can be no doubt whatsoever,'" he grumbled to his secretary after reading Kennan's letter about the new institute. Why not expand existing centers at Harvard or Columbia? If a Washington site really was necessary, he advised Kennan, then "[t]he School of Advanced International Studies, started by Paul Nitze and associated with Johns Hopkins, might be a good home." But Kennan did not like this idea. "I am naturally disappointed," he responded to Harriman. The need for a Washington program that would not be an adjunct to something else was clear to "all the leading authorities in our country. I know that to find the money for it is not going to be an easy task."[25]

That proved to be correct, but with the help of two energetic young historians, James Billington (later Librarian of Congress) and S. Frederick Starr (later president of Oberlin College), Kennan was able to get a small "Institute for Advanced Russian Studies" established at the new Woodrow Wilson International Center for Scholars, a congressionally mandated memorial to the former president, housed in the old Smithsonian building on the Washington Mall. "[A]s you will see from this stationery," Kennan wrote Harriman again at the end of 1975, the new institute "bears, at the insistence of my younger colleagues, my own name and that of my great-uncle—the one who did all the travel in Siberia and wrote the book on your father." The Kennan Institute still needed help: might Harriman purchase a "modest" building nearby, to be known as "Harriman House," at which it could accommodate visiting scholars?[26]

Harriman did make a contribution, but the idea of a modest house named for him within the Kennan Institute carried no greater appeal than the idea of putting the latter in Nitze's school had carried for Kennan. He approached Harriman once more in 1978, asking for help in raising a $3–5 million endowment, but this time got a flat rejection: "My prior commitments are such that I cannot give the substantial sum that you speak of in your letter to your Institute." Kennan should approach the industrialist Armand Hammer, taking care to "give his name [sufficient] recognition to excite his interest." Four years later Harriman announced that he and his family were giving Columbia University $11.5 million to endow its Russian Institute, which would henceforth be the "W. Averell Harriman Institute for the Advanced Study of the Soviet Union."[27]

Knowing Harriman's ego, Kennan might have expected this. Having one of his own, he did not. Despite the two Kennans for whom his institute was named, the younger one had hoped through it, he later admitted, "to 'institutionalize' myself"—and had been bold enough to seek Harriman's help. Harriman liked the concept, but thought that a different person deserved the distinction. It was a contest of the vanities Kennan could not win. If he had been willing to name his institute for Harriman, the Princeton historian Cy Black speculated, "he might have gotten the money. But a man like Harriman doesn't give it to Kennan's institute."[28]

Kennan wondered, on getting the bad news, whether he should recommend liquidating his institute altogether, "the shattering of one more dream." In the end, though, he agreed to go on the Harriman Institute's advisory board, Harriman's wife Pamela went on his, and the Kennan Institute became the primary Washington center for research on Russia, as well as on the non-Russian territories of the former Soviet Union. Fund-raising was always difficult, though, and so it was never able to separate itself, as Kennan had hoped it might, from the Wilson Center. His institute remained "beautiful, valuable, full of promise, but, like a young lovely Victorian governess without fortune or family, at the mercy of the one who gives her meals, a roof, and a pittance of salary."[29]

V.

The Kennans celebrated their fortieth wedding anniversary on September 11, 1971. Their children surprised them with a dinner followed by a ball, featuring engraved invitations, guests brought in from all over, and an orchestra playing George's Dixieland favorites. "They organized it all by themselves, without a word to us. . . . All Princeton was impressed." Mortality, however, was intimating itself more regularly now. Chip Bohlen died after a long illness on the first day of January 1974. He was "closest to me in professional experience and interest," George wrote his widow, Avis. "I find it quite impossible to believe that he, who was so much a part of my world, is really gone. Perhaps, in one way, he is not."[30]

Six weeks later Kennan turned seventy, thereby becoming, in line with Institute for Advanced Study procedure, a professor-emeritus. To mark the occasion, he composed a poem, which he read aloud at his birthday dinner. It sounded play-ful, but it was not casual: he reworked it several times before he was satisfied, and then ensured its survival by saving it in several locations. As if to humiliate future biographers, he compressed much of himself within just fifteen stanzas.

> *When the step becomes slow, and the wit becomes slower,*
> *And memory fails, and the hearing declines;*
> *When skies become clouded, and clouds become lower,*
> *And you find yourself talking poetical lines;*
>
> *When the path that you tread becomes steeper and darker;*
> *And the question seems no longer whether, but when—*
> *Then, my friend, you should look for the biblical marker,*
> *The sign by the road that reads: Three Score and Ten;*
>
> *At this point you'll observe, if you care to look closely,*
> *You're no longer alone on the highway of life;*
> *For there trudges behind you, and glowers morosely,*
> *A bearded old man with a curious knife;*
>
> *At first you defy this absurd apparition*
> *(For it's old Father Time, with his glass and his scythe);*
> *You swear you were never in better condition—*
> *The body more jaunty, the spirit more blythe;*
>
> *And you laugh in his face, and you tell the old joker:*
> *"You must be mistaken; I'm feeling just fine,"*
> *But the wretched old scarecrow just picks up his poker*
> *And gives you a jab and says: "Get back in line";*
>
> *So you swallow your pride, and you march with your brothers;*
> *You do all the things you're instructed to do;*
> *But you're sure this compulsion, just right for the others,*
> *Could not have been really intended for you;*
>
> *And you turn to the thought of your erstwhile successes—*
> *How brilliant, how charming, how worthy of fame;*

'Til a small voice protests and the conscience confesses
What an ass you once were and how empty the claim;

Then the ghosts of the past find you out in your sadness,
And gather about, and point fingers of shame—
The ghosts of stupidities spawned by your madness—
The ghosts of injustices done in your name;

And you grieve with remorse for the sins you've committed:
The fingers that roamed and the tongue that betrayed;
But you grieve even more for the ones you omitted:
The nectar untasted, the record unplayed.

But the cut most unkind, and the cruelest teacher,
Is the feeling you have when, as sometimes occurs,
The wandering eye of some heavenly creature
Encounters your own, and your own catches hers;

And you conjure up dreams too delightful to mention,
And you primp and you pose, 'til it's suddenly seen
That the actual object of all her attention—
This burning, voluptuous female attention—
Is a fellow behind you who's all of nineteen.

So you swallow your pride, and you scurry for cover
In the solaces characteristic of age:
You tell the same anecdotes over and over,
Forget the same names, and reread the same page;

And at length you concede, though with dim satisfaction,
That it's not on yourself that your peace now depends—
That for this you must look to a different reaction:
To the weary indulgence of children and friends.

Yet, if given the chance to retread, as you've known it,
The ladder of life—to begin at the spot
Where the story picked up, and before you had blown it,

Would you take it, dear friends?
I suspect you would not;

So let us take heart; we are none of us friendless;
And fill up your glasses, and raise them again
To the chance that an interval, seemingly endless,
Will ensue
> *Before you*
>> *Become Three Score and Ten.*

Kennan also resolved, with posterity in mind, to keep his diary more conscientiously: "An occasional hour of intimate reflection will be no less useful—and have no smaller chances of usefulness—than anything else I might be doing," he wrote on the first day of January 1975. "And there is so little time left in which the real 'me,' as distinct from the mind alone or the various things I seem to mean to other people, can be expressed."[31]

A week later he was sitting under the great vault in Washington's National Cathedral—where his own memorial service would be held thirty years later—thinking "highly egoistic and improper, but very human thoughts" while the late Walter Lippmann's friends eulogized him. Why had Lippmann had more influence than he? Kennan's own education had been "broader, if less deep," his mind "no less powerful," his stylistic ability "fully as great," his insights "bolder, more penetrating and more prophetic," but his impact on American public life was "undetectable." So why not give up punditry altogether and concentrate on history? "Will it make any difference, several decades later, whether what I wrote about . . . was my own dreary time or the period of the 1880s?"[32]

Kennan spent the spring and summer of 1975 researching the Franco-Russian alliance in European archives. "I feel detached," he wrote late in April, just prior to the final collapse of South Vietnam. "I have done what little I could." He seemed strangely connected, however, to the departed. Walt Butterworth, another Foreign Service colleague and, in recent years, a Princeton neighbor, had also recently died. But Kennan dreamed, one night in Vienna, of a "visitation" from Butterworth, who

embraced me affectionately, we both being fully aware of the fact of his deadness, and allowed himself to be assured by me in the absurd, stammering language of dreams (for we were both much moved) of our continued companionship of the spirit, death notwithstanding. What to make of this I know not. . . . But that there was something in it more than just what is of this world—was clear.

Two weeks later, on a visit to Hermann Hatzfeldt's Crottorf, Kennan was left to work alone, as was his preference, in the castle's great library.

[I]t is of course haunted—not in a particularly sinister sense, although it does have a whiff of death about it, in all its loveliness. One is somehow aware of a recent, linger-ing, still significant presence. But then, I thought to myself, perhaps I, who work here and love the place and respond to its atmosphere, will join the company of spirits (or is it one, alone?) who inhabit it.

Until then, he needed "to quiet down, grow up, act my age, gather my strength," and it struck him that if he made the effort, "God will help me." Even God, though, would find it difficult "to teach this old dog new tricks." For as soon as he joined the company of others, "the old fool—Kennan the enthusiast—Kennan the entertainer—takes over before I can control him, and we are off again."[33]

While in Bonn early in May, Kennan walked through a hotel lounge, found the movie version of *South Pacific*—dubbed into German—playing on televi-sion, and was "suddenly obliged—to my own amazement and amusement—to repress tears." It was a relic from a lost civilization: "these fresh, boyish images of American sailors, the harmless inanities of the plot, the heroine's belief in a happy future." He could not say, with Oppenheimer, "Dammit, I happen to love this country," but "I can say that I loved, and love in memory, something of what the country once was. . . . [T]he young will never know it."[34]

Kennan was in Helsinki in July 1975, on the eve of the great thirty-five-nation conference, but his mind was on the archival remains of a late-nineteenth-century world a lifetime removed from his own: "Yet all of this has now faded into the shadows." Empires had disappeared. Names once "mountain-high in grandeur" were now known "only to a handful of historians like myself." Stepping out onto the streets, where preparations were under way to welcome the notables of his era, Kennan could see that within another lifetime they too would be "carried off with the wind into the obscurity of time." The present could only be captured "as in some old photograph, never to be recaptured as a living reality. Such is the dizzi-ness, with relation to time, that can, on occasion, seize the historian."[35]

God had not yet induced in Kennan the habit—also once recommended by Acheson—of "taciturnity." That became clear in an interview Kennan granted to the writer and broadcaster George Urban, which, when published in the September 1976 issue of the journal *Encounter*, filled thirty-three of its pages. "[T]ried to read it," Kennan admitted on the day his copy arrived, but "found it much too long, and so boring that I went to sleep, literally, before I could finish it." As with other Kennan pronouncements over the years, however, his critics found this one anything but boring.

He began with a bicentennial prediction for the United States: "This country is destined to succumb to failures which cannot be other than tragic and enormous in their scope." They would arise from the familiar evils of industrialization, urbanization, commercialization, secularization, and environmental degradation. The only remedy would be "a much simpler form of life, a much smaller population, a society in which the agrarian component is far greater in relation to the urban component.... In this sense I am, I suppose, an 18th-century person." Short of coercion, there was no way a nation the size of the United States could manage its affairs without never-ending compromises among self-centered constituencies. But if that was the only way the country could govern itself, then "this places certain limitations on what it can hope to do in the field of foreign affairs." Its policy should be "a very restrained one."

Had Kennan become, then, an isolationist? Not if that meant abruptly curtailing existing commitments. It should be possible, though, to reduce these gradually, with a view to "leaving other people alone and expect[ing] largely to be left alone by them." Would that not consign European allies to Soviet domination? Perhaps they deserved it, Kennan replied: they had grown far too self-indulgent under American protection. While recently cruising in the Baltic, he had happened upon a Danish youth festival "swarming with hippies—motorbikes, girlfriends, drugs, pornography, drunkenness, noise—it was all there. I looked at this mob and thought how one company of robust Russian infantry would drive it out of town."

But with an ideology "at least 70–80 years out of date," Kremlin leaders would not know what to do with Western Europe if they were to take it over. And if the moderate socialists of the region ever summoned the resolve to end their countries' dependence on the United States, the Soviet Union would have no plausible justification for continuing to control Eastern Europe. Disarray, therefore, "cuts both ways."

Kennan's most startling comments were on nuclear weapons. People would always find excuses to fight one another, so they had to be prevented "from playing with the worst kind of toys."

This is why I feel that the great weapons of mass-destruction—and nuclear arms are not the only conceivable ones—should never be in human hands, that it would be much better to go back, symbolically speaking, to bows and arrows which at least do not destroy nature. I have no sympathy with the man who demands an eye for an eye in a nuclear conflict.

Compared to the ecological and demographic consequences of a nuclear conflagration, Soviet domination of Western Europe would be only "a minor catastrophe."

After all, people *do live* in the Soviet Union. For the mass of people there, life is not intolerable. The same is true in East Germany; the same is true in Hungary. It is not what these people would like; but, still, it is a way of living, and it does not mean the end of the experiment of human civilisation; it leaves the way open for further developments.

Because there could be no recovery from a war fought with nuclear weapons, the United States should be "much bolder" in seeking their elimination, if necessary unilaterally. Was Kennan advocating unilateral nuclear disarmament? "Not all at once," he replied, "or not without reciprocation, but if no one takes the lead in imposing self-restraint in the development of these weapons, we are never going to get any reduction of them by negotiation."

Did this mean that Western civilization was no longer worth defending? "Of course not," Kennan retorted, but defense had to begin at home:

Show me first an America which has successfully coped with the problems of crime, drugs, deteriorating educational standards, urban decay, pornography, and decadence of one sort or another—show me an America that has pulled itself together and is what it ought to be, then I will tell you how we are going to defend ourselves from the Russians. But as things are, I can see very little merit in organising ourselves to defend from the Russians the porno-shops in central Washington.

This and much else in the interview was self-indulgent nonsense. It was Kennan's confirmation of Parkinson's Law: given space, he would fill it, wisely or not. Kennan the enthusiast, Kennan the entertainer, Kennan the old fool, had taken over yet again.

But so had Kennan the prophet. We do not demand, of such seers, that they be logical, proportional, or brief. It's their function to detect big dangers in little ones, to sense doom around each corner, to inflate admonitions, like balloons, to the bursting point. It's also their lot to be derided, and in that respect Kennan's bicentennial jeremiad could not have been better timed.[36]

VI.

"He's on their side," Paul Nitze wrote angrily on his copy of the *Encounter* interview, where Kennan had imagined the Red Army dispersing the Danish hippies. Meanwhile Kennan had taken on Nitze—without naming him—in his *Foreign Affairs* article: people like him required the *image* of an implacable adversary, to be displayed repeatedly like a ventriloquist's dummy, until to question its reality seemed frivolous or treasonous. Nitze was "a very good friend," Kennan later acknowledged, but he believed in "a fictitious and inhuman Soviet elite, whereas I am dealing with what I suspect to be, and think is likely to be, the real one." "George and I have always been good friends," Nitze confirmed. They had known each other since serving together on the Policy Planning Staff in the late 1940s and had never differed "except on matters of substance." Each was convinced, their joint biographer has written, "that the other's desired policies could lead the United States to the ultimate catastrophe."[37]

A week after Jimmy Carter's election in November 1976, Nitze and a bipartisan group of fellow détente critics announced the formation of a new Committee on the Present Danger—an earlier one, in 1950, had rallied support for increases in defense spending after the Korean War broke out. Nixon, Ford, and Kissinger, they insisted, had underestimated the threat posed by the Soviet military buildup over the past decade. Carter had made it clear that he would not seek to reverse the trend. The committee would therefore, as loudly as possible, sound the alarm.[38]

Kennan decided, that same week, to sound one of his own. He put aside his research on the Franco-Russian alliance and began writing a new book, to be called *The Cloud of Danger: Current Realities of American Foreign Policy.* The title left no doubt about its purpose: it would be a critique of Nitze and the movement he had started. With Connie Goodman's help—she had come back to work for Kennan in 1975—he finished it in three months. He dedicated it "[t]o my wife Annelise, whose lack of enthusiasm for this and my other excursions into public affairs has never detracted from the loyalty with which she supported these endeavors."[39]

The book was "a big disappointment," Goodman acknowledged. *The New York Times* thought it insufficiently newsworthy even to review. Philip Geyelin, who did review it for *The Washington Post*, found Kennan to have a "lamentably loose grip" on policy practicalities. Could the United States really restrain its military-industrial complex *and* achieve energy independence *and* correct the corruptions that afflicted its culture? Reduce its global commitments to the defense of Western Europe, Japan, and—in a rare Kennan bow to domestic politics—Israel? Abandon "obsolescent and nonessential" positions in Panama, the Philippines, and South Korea? Refrain from involving itself elsewhere in the "third world," especially southern Africa? Sympathize with Soviet dissidents while trusting the Soviet government? Acknowledge, with respect to nuclear weapons, that there was "simply no need for all this overkill," that both sides could "give up four fifths of it tomorrow," and that a unilateral reduction of 10 percent, "immediately and as an act of good faith," would hurt neither of them?

Each of these might be goals worth considering, but to propose them all without explaining how to achieve them—in what order, on what time scale, with what trade-offs—was to compile a catalog, not to suggest a strategy. *The Cloud of Danger* in this respect paralleled its author's complaints, to the *New York Times* columnist James Reston, about Carter's initial approaches to Moscow: that by pushing for deep cuts in strategic weaponry while simultaneously pressing the issue of human rights, his administration had already made "just about every mistake it could make." Kennan's mistake, in this hurriedly composed book, was to expand into 234 pages of large type what he had taken too many pages of small type to say in *Encounter,* without adding anything new. Meanwhile he was living with the frustration "of having no influence on the conduct of foreign policy and, at the same time, being invited and expected to talk about it on every conceivable occasion."[40]

One he could hardly avoid was the "X" article's thirtieth anniversary. Not wanting to be caught off guard, as the *Foreign Affairs* editors had been five years earlier, the Council on Foreign Relations invited Kennan to reflect on the event—he appeared somewhat belatedly in November 1977—at the organization's recently established Washington headquarters. Little was now left of Stalinism, he insisted: Brezhnev was a moderate, even conservative figure, "confidently regarded by all who know him as a man of peace." That made it hard to see why détente had become so controversial in the United States. Without specifying Nitze and the Committee on the Present Danger, Kennan blamed those who "lose themselves in the fantastic reaches of what I might call military mathematics—the mathematics of possible mutual destruction in an age of explosively burgeoning weapons technology."[41]

Nitze had been a banker, Kennan later explained. He liked statistics: "He was happier when he could take a blank sheet and do calculations than he was [with] the imponderables." Because an adversary's intentions could never be quantified, Nitze dismissed them as irrelevant. Capabilities did count, because they could be counted. Kennan had characterized him correctly, Nitze acknowledged. "When people say 'more,' I want to know how much 'more'? I can understand it a hell of a lot better if you can put it into numbers or calculus or something like that. Then you can be precise as to what you're talking about."[42]

Kennan was being imprecise, in Nitze's view, when he called Brezhnev a "man of peace." How did Kennan know this? What if he turned out to be wrong? Even if he was right, what did Brezhnev mean by "peace" in the first place? Why, if his intentions were peaceful, was his military so compulsively acquiring weaponry? Kennan had always found it difficult to answer questions like these, because he relied so heavily on his *intuitive* sense that the Russians were not going to start a war. When an interviewer for *The New York Times Magazine* asked him in May 1978 whether he accepted the principle "better red than dead," Kennan unwisely admitted that he did, although "I don't think there's any need for us to be red, because I don't think that war is the way the Russians would like to expand their power."

That was just the point, Nitze retorted, in an article the *Times* ran alongside Kennan's interview. Soviet leaders did not want a war, but they did want the "strategic nuclear preponderance," upon which "all other levers of pressure and influence depend." If allowed to achieve it, they would indeed expand their power, while containing that of the United States and its allies. Their goal was a world in which they would be "the unchallenged hegemonic leaders." It had been "little short of bizarre," Kennan complained, that the *Times* had felt obliged to balance him with "a good dose of hard-line conventional wisdom from Nitze." He could not understand why so many friends were now criticizing him "in this way."[43]

It got worse the following month when an enemy joined the chorus. Aleksandr Solzhenitsyn, expelled from the Soviet Union four years earlier, attacked Kennan in a widely publicized Harvard commencement address for having denied the applicability of morality in politics: "On the contrary, only moral criteria can help the West against communism's well-planned world strategy." With Kennan calling for "unilateral disarmament," even the youngest of Kremlin officials were laughing "at your political wizards." Kennan heard of this only when his mail caught up with his sailboat, appropriately enough, in a Danish port. "Abruptly yanked back . . . from the harsh but simple realities of the sea," he wandered disconsolately among a forest of "indifferent masts," but as the evening wore on, "the annoyances of life ashore, about which for the moment one could do so little, faded from consciousness. This, I suppose, is the therapeutic quality of cruising in small sailing craft."[44]

Kennan had criticized the Committee on the Present Danger "at length and with care," Eugene V. Rostow, one of the organization's cofounders and close friend of Nitze, wrote in *The Yale Law Journal* that summer. But as Kennan's *Memoirs* had shown, he had long suffered inner conflicts "about himself, his dream world, his work, his goals, and his relationship to the American nature and culture." These had brought him "perilously close to preaching that we don't really need a foreign and defense policy at all." He had, in this way, outdone the Old Testament prophets, for however sharply they scolded the ancient Israelites, "not even Jeremiah despaired of their survival." Kennan had no sense of what it would take to ensure that of the West, because his mind had "never moved along mathematical lines, and never will." He was "an impressionist, a poet, not an earthling."[45]

Having been called many things but never before an extraterrestrial, Kennan wrestled in his diary with how to respond. "Blast the stupidities? Expend, in this way, such authority as I possess?" In the end he wrote a long letter, typed it himself, and sent it off late in November 1978 to Reston. "I shall soon be 75 years of age," he pointed out. "[M]y means and energies are obviously limited. For me to try to involve myself in public disputes with Paul Nitze and others would merely mean to get myself chewed up in controversy, and I would soon lose what little value I may have as a force in public opinion."

He then went on to show how the skills of an impressionist or a poet—if not an alien—could be valuable. He did so by imagining himself in the position of Brezhnev and his closest associates, most of whom were approaching Kennan's age. They might "*like* to have everything under such perfect control that they could address themselves exclusively to schemes for our early undoing," as the Committee on the Present Danger had suggested, "but the fact is: they don't." Whatever their self-confidence, it had to be vastly overshadowed by their fears

of alarming declines in the rates of increase of national product and labor efficiency; of poor morale, expressing itself in cynicism, absenteeism and drunkenness in great portions of their population; of a developing labor shortage of truly spectacular dimensions; of disturbing demographic changes; of an extremely serious erosion of their moral authority and political position in Eastern Europe; of a Chinese ideological competition that threatens to deprive them of their position of leadership among the Marxist forces of the world; of a Chinese military competition that threatens them with a two-front war (the *bête noire* of every Russian strategist of all time) in the case of complications with the West; of their virtual isolation among the great advanced nations of the world; of the forthcoming difficulties of succession within their own party.

Now they had something else to worry about: the unexpected election of a Polish pope. To claim, in the light of all this, that the old men in the Kremlin could want anything more than to hang on to what they had was "to distort out of all verisimilitude their nature, their situation, and their interests."

But, Nitze and his friends would protest, weren't the Soviets busily exploiting "third world" opportunities? Had they not moved into Angola in the wake of the Portuguese empire's collapse? What about the "horn of Africa," where the superpowers were competing for influence in Somalia and Ethiopia? Or Afghanistan, where a Marxist revolution had taken place earlier that year? In fact, Kennan insisted, in each of these situations local Marxists had exploited the Soviet Union, whose leaders knew that if they failed to aid these causes, the Cubans or the Chinese would, and their own credibility would suffer. Far from opportunities, these were liabilities, depleting strengths needed to maintain the status quo.

Kennan was now, he reminded Reston, "the patriarch." No one else living, not even the Kremlin's long-serving foreign minister Andrey Gromyko, could draw on his half-century of diplomatic experience. He would not claim, in all respects, to speak for the dead—Bohlen, in particular, had "never encountered a statement of mine to which he could not take *some* exception"—but his late Foreign Service colleagues would share, he believed, his astonishment at how little respect their kind of professionalism commanded in the face of current frivolities, abuses, and misrepresentations: "There, Scottie, I have chosen you as the object for what I hope will be my last statement on Soviet-American relations. Make what you will of it."[46]

No one, not even Reston, made much of it at the time. But when Soviet archives opened after the Cold War ended, they showed Kennan's impression of a frightened, overstretched gerontocracy, desperately trying to regain the initiative lost by its own ineptitude dating back at least as far as the invasion of Czechoslovakia, to be much closer to reality than Nitze's calculation of a purposefully rising hegemon. The difference, to oversimplify, was between *what* and *why*. Nitze could see what the Brezhnev regime was doing and from this he concluded, inaccurately, that he knew why. Kennan sensed why, and so worried much less about what. Nitze seemed right in the short run, because only the long run could confirm Kennan's claim. But, with the passage of time, it did.[47]

VII.

"[I]t isn't easy being George Kennan," his friend Dick Ullman once observed. "I've always thought that that was a heavy weight to bear." Kennan seemed genuinely reluctant to get into policy debates, but he rarely resisted the opportunity. He appeared to regard himself as "an asset to be treasured," a historical figure whose life needed to be documented as thoroughly as possible. He was keeping more complete diaries now than ever before, and he had his research assistants— one was Ullman's wife, Yoma—filling scrapbooks with Kennan-related newspaper clippings in multiple languages from all over the world. "I'll bet you," Ullman commented, "that there is no Nitze scrapbook."[48]

Yoma Ullman was one of several assistants who worked with Kennan on his Franco-Russian alliance book. Connie Goodman, who still handled his correspondence, was another: she helped Kennan devise an elaborate system of color-coded note cards—pink for the French, blue for the Russians—which his color-blindness at times caused him to confuse. Mimi Bull, who had been Goodman's college roommate, also worked for Kennan in Princeton and later in Austria. "I was in awe and frankly terrified to begin with," she recalled, but soon "[t]he austere scholar diplomat relaxed and became a gifted raconteur with a delight in the absurd." She found him, on one occasion in Vienna, sporting an old beret, a new pencil moustache, and a radiant smile, "pleased with the wealth of material he realizes is here."[49]

In addition to the European and American archives he visited, Kennan returned to the Soviet Union several times during the 1970s to research the foreign policies of the last tsars, a privilege granted to few Western scholars. He learned to request specific documents, identified from previously published histories, whereupon the archivists would please him by producing entire files, with the explanation that they hadn't had time to find the individual items he had requested: "They can loosen up when they want to." They mostly did, for with Kennan's criticisms of dissidents, he was back in favor in the Kremlin. *Pravda* reviewed *The Cloud of*

Danger even if *The New York Times* didn't, pointing out that his views had evolved "in the direction of good sense."[50]

Kennan's "retirement" from the Institute for Advanced Study would normally have left him on half salary without the use of an office, but the trustees were well aware, Dick Dilworth recalled, that he had been "infinitely more productive and certainly more prominent" than anyone else there. So they allowed Professor-Emeritus Kennan to continue as a fully active professor in all but name, exempting him only from faculty meetings. To Kennan's embarrassment, the arrangement required raising the funds needed to support him, but the Institute found them easily enough from sources including Dilworth himself, the Rockefeller family, the Ford Foundation, the Carnegie Corporation, and because of his interest in nuclear issues, the legendary Omaha investor Warren Buffett.[51]

Continuing to write history, therefore, met his continuing obligation to the Institute, but Kennan still hoped to connect his research, in some way, to contemporary affairs. It was also, his friend Cy Black observed, a kind of hobby: "It is fun for him. It keeps him busy." Goodman agreed: "He enjoyed this so much more than any other work." Being Kennan, of course, he could hardly have fun without feeling guilty: his book had become "a pretence," he told himself as he neared completion of his first volume, "an excuse for existence." He should have recognized it years ago as "a quixotic undertaking."[52]

The Decline of Bismarck's European Order: Franco-Russian Relations, 1875–1890, came out from the Princeton University Press in the fall of 1979. It was not as meticulously documented as Kennan's volumes on early Soviet-American relations, but at over four hundred pages it was an impressive performance for a man of seventy-five. Paul Kennedy, a cheeky young historian less than half Kennan's age, congratulated him in *The Washington Post* for his "mature, warm, beautifully written book," although it was "not a little questionable" that Kennan had neglected the French military archives, the Bismarck family papers, and the monographs of Professors Hillgruber and Mueller-Link. Kennedy acknowledged, however, that these were points "about which the general reader will care little." One with a particular interest in Bismarck confirmed this. "I have enjoyed reading your book," Kissinger wrote Kennan. "Not that it fails to be depressing. If even Bismarck could not prevent what he clearly foresaw, what chance does the modern period have? That is the real nightmare."[53]

"Bismarck did all that he could, in his outwardly rough but essentially not inhumane way," Kennan replied. "What surprises me more is the failure of our own generation, with the warning image of the atom bomb before it, to learn from his example." This, of course, had been Kennan's point all along. Had he been born only a few years earlier, he noted in his introduction, he might have been among the millions of young men who fought in World War I. He would have done so, he imagined, with the same "delirious euphoria" most of them had felt: that an era of "self-sacrifice, adventure, valor, and glory" lay ahead. Having had the luck to avoid their experiences, he wanted now to focus in detail on the statesmen of that age, for in them "we can see, not entirely but in larger degree than is generally supposed, ourselves."[54]

"I don't think it explains anything," Black grumbled about *The Decline of Bismarck's European Order*, and he had a point. Kennan had enjoyed writing the book too much to make its message clear. He spent months, for example, tracking down information on a relatively minor figure, the French-Russian double agent Elie de Cyon, not because his role was in any way critical to the coming of the war, but because Kennan relished this kind of detective work. It was an all-weather form of recreation: the scholarly equivalent of summer sailing. But it left Kennan with another volume to write if he was even going to get to the alliance of 1894—and that event would still precede, by two decades, the outbreak of the conflict whose origins he had meant to explain, and whose consequences he had hoped to assess.[55]

Kennan had again rambled, as in his *Encounter* interview and in *The Cloud of Danger*. He produced, this time, a wonderfully readable history—it could almost be a novel, he thought[56]—but its literary and scholarly strengths made it ineffective as prophecy. Despite the pleasures it held for Kennan, using the past to instruct the future was a Sisyphean task: as his sources proliferated, his energy faded, and the distractions of the present, as always, demanded comment.

VIII.

Détente collapsed completely during the last half of 1979. After years of negotiations, Carter and a visibly enfeebled Brezhnev were able to sign the SALT II arms control treaty in Vienna in June, but a rapid succession of unexpected crises left it languishing in the U.S. Senate. The first occurred in August, when a CIA source leaked the news that the Soviet Union had placed a combat brigade in Cuba. Carter demanded its removal but had to back down after learning that the unit had been there since the missile crisis of 1962. He had never before seen "such dilettantism, amateurism and sheer bungling," Kennan complained: it had been "an artificially-manufactured domestic-political event if there ever was one." What he didn't know was that he knew the manufacturer. Nitze had helped arrange the leak with a view to delaying, perhaps preventing, the treaty's ratification.[57]

The second crisis broke on November 4, when Iranian students stormed the American embassy in Tehran and took sixty-six hostages, with the subsequent approval of the Islamist government that had recently deposed Washington's longtime ally, Shah Mohammad Reza Pahlavi. Furious at this violation of diplomatic immunity, recalling his own five and a half months of internment in Nazi Germany, angry that the Carter administration had let almost four months go by without securing the Americans' release, Kennan told the Senate Foreign Relations Committee on February 27, 1980, that the United States should simply declare war on Iran. This would allow detaining Iranians within its boundaries, while enlisting the aid of a neutral country in arranging an exchange of internees, as Switzerland had done for the Bad Nauheim "hostages" thirty-eight years earlier.

What made Kennan's testimony particularly striking, however, was his equally emphatic insistence that the Carter administration had *overreacted* to the third and most serious crisis that had developed in recent months: the Soviet Union's invasion of Afghanistan on Christmas Day 1979. Eleven years earlier Kennan had criticized the Johnson administration's tepid response to Czechoslovakia's occupation. Now, though, in the face of Carter's more vigorous retaliations—withdrawing the SALT II treaty from the Senate, embargoing grain and technology shipments to the U.S.S.R., calling for military draft registration, increasing defense spending, and demanding a boycott of the 1980 Moscow Olympics—Kennan claimed that the president had gone too far. Brezhnev had sent troops into Afghanistan in a desperate effort to save the imperiled Marxist government there, not—as Carter and his national security adviser Zbigniew Brzezinski had argued—with a view to beginning an offensive aimed at controlling the Persian Gulf. The Soviets would soon see that they had made a mistake, would be looking for a way out, and the United States should help them find one.[58]

There was a compartmentalized logic in Kennan's positions. Iran had, under a strict interpretation of international law, committed an act of war against the United States. The U.S.S.R. had indeed acted from a position of weakness, not strength, in Afghanistan. But Kennan's grand strategic logic—the ability to see how contents mix after compartments are opened—eluded him altogether in this instance. What would the implications have been of the first formal declaration of war by anybody since 1945? What was to prevent escalation? How might Kremlin leaders respond to the prospect of American military action in a country bordering their own and Afghanistan? What conspiracies might they see in the rise of the Solidarity trade union movement in Poland, the rapturous reception accorded Pope John Paul II on his first visit back after his election, and in the Polish-born Brzezinski's recent well-publicized trip to the Khyber Pass? It was not at all clear that Kennan's method of rescuing the hostages would reassure the aging officials in Moscow who now controlled half of the world's arsenal of nuclear weapons.

Kennan always had trouble keeping his emotions apart from his strategies, but as he grew older, the problem got worse. He commanded, as an elder statesman, increasing respect: there was supposed to be some kind of connection, he knew, between advanced age and wisdom. But "as one to whom these imputations would presumably be applicable, I am bound to say that this theory is at best complicated, and at worst questionable."[59] He had fewer contemporaries, now, who could insist that he reconcile his contradictions before publicly displaying them. Bohlen had most frequently played that role, but so too had Acheson, Lippmann, and Harriman—the last still living and selectively donating, but in no condition to set Kennan right, as he used to do in Moscow, on the limits of policy feasibility. Nitze, a personal friend, was a public adversary who delighted in pouncing (or having associates like Eugene Rostow pounce) on Kennan's lapses. No one had asked, with respect to his *Encounter* interview, *The Cloud of Danger*, the Bismarck book, or his remarkable appearance before the Senate Foreign Relations Committee: "George, how will all of this hang together?"

But in October 1980 one old friend tried. With events in Iran and Afghanistan having produced so much "confusion, bewilderment, and fuzzy thinking," Elbridge Durbrow wrote, he could not help but recall "how realistic, sound and prophetic" Kennan had been in the "long telegram" and the "X" article. "Practically everything you predicted has transpired," but hardly anyone in government was even aware of this. So did each new administration have to learn all over again "that the Soviet leaders since Lenin have not fundamentally changed their basic aims, goals, and methods of operation"? It was a polite way of asking, Durbrow later explained, "what the devil is the difference? I see them as still the same enemies we always had. Why does George see [them] differently?"[60]

"Mr. Carter's performance is only a bit of history," Kennan replied grimly on November 10, six days after Reagan's landslide victory. Foreign policy would now be in the hands of Nitze, Scoop Jackson, and other hard-liners. There would be no limits to the arms race, or to preparations for a military showdown. Kennan had tried, since the end of the last war, to find a way of dealing with the Soviet Union that would not require a new war: "[T]oday I have to recognize the final and irreparable failure of this effort." How all of this could please Durbrow—himself a hard-liner—Kennan could not understand, "but if it does—my congratulations. It is a small consolation to know that even if one cannot, one's self, see hope in a situation, one has friends who can."[61]

IX.

Kennan was just back from attending the annual meeting of Pour le Mérite, an elite eighteenth-century Prussian military order revived by the West German government to celebrate civilian achievements in the arts and sciences. He had become one of its thirty foreign members in 1976, regarding the honor at least as seriously as his membership in the American Academy of Arts and Letters. The German organization combined his love of ceremony with his affinity for that culture, and despite the fact that attendance required flying across the Atlantic instead of simply slipping into New York, he rarely missed its meetings. The 1980 convocation took place in Regensburg in late September, after which the Kennans went to Garmisch, where, on October 1, George was to give the principal address at the Second World Congress for Soviet and East European Studies.

Characteristically, he had put off finishing it until the last moment, so while waiting for it to be typed, he sat wearily on a park bench in the fading afternoon sunlight, envying other old people around him who seemed free of such weighty responsibilities. Could he ever be like them? Would anything come of it, if he tried, apart from physical and intellectual decay? Thirteen hundred people were present when he rose to address them that evening, and just as he came to the passage of which he was proudest, a woman in the audience let out a piercing shriek, as if to herald what he was about to say—which was what he wished he could say, simultaneously, to leaders in both Washington and Moscow:

For the love of God, of your children, and of the civilization to which you belong, cease this madness. You have a duty not just to the generation of the present—you have a duty to civilization's past, which you threaten to render meaningless, and to its future, which you threaten to render nonexistent. You are mortal men. You are capable of error. You have no right to hold in your hands—there is no one wise enough and strong enough to hold in his hands—destructive powers sufficient to put an end to civilized life on a great portion of our planet. No one should wish to hold such powers. Thrust them from you. The risks you might thereby assume are not greater—could not be greater—than those which you are now incurring for us all.

The outburst, he later determined, had no connection to the lecture. But the Slavicists, expecting neither a shriek nor a prophet, responded with only polite applause. And so Kennan was left "as uncertain of the suitability (not the truth) of what I had had to say as I had been before saying it."[62]

TWENTY-FOUR

A Precarious Vindication:
1980–1990

KENNAN HAD NEVER HEARD OF THE ALBERT EINSTEIN PEACE PRIZE when he got a phone call on March 9, 1981, informing him that he had won it. The prize was a new one, selection committee chairman Norman Cousins explained, established only a year earlier by the trustees of Einstein's estate. Kennan would be the second recipient. "I was, of course, in one way pleased over this news—a pleasure not diminished, I must confess, although not mainly occasioned, by the fact that the award carries with it a $50,000 check." He and Einstein had, after all, once been "colleagues of sorts" at the Institute for Advanced Study, even if they had never spoken. But in Kennan's continuing struggle between scholarship and prophecy, the award might tip the balance irrevocably in the latter direction. Accepting it would imply a commitment "to do what I can to bring people to their senses and to halt a wholly unnecessary and infinitely dangerous drift towards war—and all of this at a time when I would like to finish my historical study, really retire, work around the house and garden, etc. Oh dear!"[1]

While researching his second volume on the Franco-Russian alliance in Moscow the following month, Kennan received two other unexpected accolades. Jack Matlock, the American *chargé d'affaires*, gave a dinner at which he praised his guest in more generous terms than Kennan could ever remember hearing from anyone in government. The toast made up "for all the slights and rebuffs I have had from . . . J[ohn] Foster Dulles on down." Then at a luncheon the next day, Georgi Arbatov, the influential director of the USA and Canada Institute, offered an equally handsome tribute from the Soviet side, which also had not always passed out "posies and compliments." Moved by these honors, Kennan came home resolved to make the most of the Einstein award: "May God give me the insight to retain, in the light of my weaknesses, my humility, and the strength to do something useful in the remaining time."[2]

The ceremony took place in Washington on May 19 before an audience including members of the new Reagan administration as well as the longtime Soviet ambassador, Anatoly Dobrynin. Kennan used the occasion not to thunder dire warnings, as at Garmisch, or to descend into details, as in his recent historical writing, or to redesign America, as he had tried to do in *The Cloud of Danger* and in the *Encounter* interview. Nor did he contradict himself, as in his puzzling congressional testimony the previous year. Rather, he spoke softly, reasoned strategically, and put forward a single striking proposal, the logic of which swept aside conventional wisdoms almost effectively as the "long telegram" had done three and a half decades earlier.

Kennan began with the question he and Oppenheimer had often posed to each other: why, if nuclear weapons were so destructive, did there have to be so many of them? With the megatonnage of more than a million Hiroshima bombs between them, Soviet and American arsenals were "fantastically redundant to the purpose in question," which was supposed to be deterrence. The superpowers had no excuse for holding themselves hostage to such devastation, along with the rest of the northern hemisphere. Their leaders seemed hypnotized, "like men in a dream, like lemmings heading for the sea, like the children of Hamlin marching blindly behind their Pied Piper."

However well intentioned, the SALT agreements of the 1970s had worsened the situation by exaggerating the importance of intricate balances, so that even slight shifts could set off clamorous alarms. What was needed, instead, was an acknowledgment, on all sides, of lethal redundancies. This should then lead to

> an immediate across-the-boards reduction by 50 percent of the nuclear arsenals now being maintained by the two superpowers; a reduction affecting in equal measure all forms of the weapon, strategic, medium-range, and tactical, as well as their means of delivery: all this to be implemented at once and without further wrangling among the experts, and to be subject to such national means of verification as now lie at the disposal of the two powers.

A 50 percent cut would be more symbolic than systematic, but it would be a start. For if the superpowers could accept that arbitrary number, then why continue haggling over the complex calculations that had stalemated SALT? Why not cut the arsenals by half again, and then by half after that, until nuclear stockpiles were approaching the point at which, as President Reagan had recently and "very wisely" said, "neither side threatens the survival of the other"? Kennan concluded his address with an exhortation from Bertrand Russell, endorsed by Einstein just before his death: "Remember your humanity, and forget the rest."[3]

I.

"It was a radical proposal from a figure not known for radicalism," *Washington Post* reporter Don Oberdorfer aptly observed. Certainly it was no small thing for Kennan to have enlisted Einstein, Russell, and Reagan in an attack on SALT, the centerpiece of détente. His speech was not just a *challenge to* orthodoxy: it was a *scrambling of* orthodoxies, and it produced surprising responses. Nitze, when asked the next day, acknowledged that a 50 percent reduction might make sense, provided the cuts started with the heaviest multiple-warhead ICBMs. Eugene V. Rostow, who in 1978 had dismissed Kennan as "not an earthling," now told *The New York Times* that "[w]e are taking a careful look at [his] proposal." Reagan had nominated Rostow to run the Arms Control and Disarmament Agency, and at his confirmation hearing a month later, he suggested replacing the acronym SALT—Strategic Arms Limitation Talks—with START—Strategic Arms *Reduction* Talks: "Such proposals have been made from time to time—notably by Paul H. Nitze in 1971 and by George Kennan a few weeks ago. . . . No American administration could reject such a possibility out of hand."[4]

So how did Kennan, Nitze, and Reagan (for whom Rostow was speaking) wind up suddenly on almost the same page? The answer had to do with what the SALT process had become. Nitze had indeed proposed cuts of roughly 50 percent in ICBM launchers during the initial stages of the SALT I talks—the date was 1969, not 1971—on the assumption that the word "limitation" in the acronym meant reduction. His idea went nowhere, though, and "arms control" came to be seen as a way of stabilizing *existing* numbers of nuclear weapons and delivery systems. By the time Carter and Brezhnev signed the SALT II treaty in 1979, its provisions had become so arcane that only experts could understand them. That allowed Nitze, himself an expert but now also a vociferous critic, to claim that technocrats were squandering American assets while the Soviets were surging ahead. It ought to be possible, with a new and simpler approach, to do better.[5]

Kennan also saw SALT as having lost its way but worried more about its dependence on "mutual assured destruction." This was the idea, which had earned the acronym MAD, that each side's safety lay in its capacity to annihilate the other many times over. Costs would be cataclysmic if the slightest miscalculation should ever occur, as had indeed happened, Kennan knew well, with the outbreak of World War I. Unlike Nitze, he supported SALT II, not on its merits but out of fear for the effect on Soviet-American relations if it should be rejected. After Carter withdrew the treaty from the Senate, however, Kennan too was ready for something new: hence his Einstein Prize proposal.[6]

Reagan, it turned out, agreed with *both* Nitze and Kennan. He wanted a more straightforward approach to arms control that would complement his efforts to regain American strategic superiority: that put him in Nitze's camp. But his abhorrence of nuclear weapons went back at least as far as Kennan's. Throughout Reagan's slow shift from Hollywood liberalism to Goldwater conservatism, he had always believed that nuclear weapons should be abolished. They could be the means, he worried quite literally, by which the biblical prophecy of Armageddon might be fulfilled. Making no secret of his aversion to MAD, Reagan asked repeatedly during the 1980 campaign why there could not be "an honest, verifiable reduction in nuclear weapons." He opposed SALT II because it failed to provide that.[7]

Whether by accident or design, the State Department chose the day of Kennan's address to announce that the United States would no longer be bound by either SALT agreement, thereby ending twelve years of Soviet-American negotiations on "arms limitation." In the fall of 1981, however, Reagan proposed a new round of talks on a different problem: the upgraded intermediate-range ballistic missiles the U.S.S.R. had deployed against Western European targets during the late 1970s, against which NATO now planned a counterdeployment. Kennan saw an opportunity to "denuclearize" Europe, by exchanging a Soviet removal of IRBMs for an American withdrawal of tactical nuclear weapons from West Germany. Reagan did not go that far, but he came close. He put Nitze in charge of the negotiations, and then accepted a proposal from Assistant Secretary of Defense for International Security Policy Richard Perle to offer a "zero option"—not a 50 percent cut but a verifiable ban on *any* IRBMs aimed at European targets by either side.[8]

Reagan announced the plan in his first major "arms reduction" speech—his preferred term—on November 18, 1981. He called also for cutting conventional forces in Europe, while resuming talks on strategic weapons under the acronym START, the one Rostow had suggested, which Kennan and Nitze had inspired.

Reagan did so a day after Kennan, speaking at Dartmouth, had condemned the "systematic dehumanization" of the Soviet leadership in administration rhetoric, but the president was ready for that criticism too. He revealed that while recovering from an assassination attempt the previous spring, he had sent a handwritten letter to Brezhnev emphasizing the aspirations Americans and Russians held in common: "They want to raise their families in peace without harming anyone or suffering harm themselves." The juxtapositions were striking enough for *The New York Times* to suggest editorially that some kind of Reagan-Kennan dialogue must be under way.[9]

II.

Despite his gloomy postelection letter to Durbrow, Kennan had reconciled himself quickly to Reagan's victory, if only because the alternative would have been Carter. "I am hopeful that things will now be somewhat better," he wrote in a 1980 Thanksgiving note. When the new president shocked even his own advisers by claiming, at his first press conference, that the Soviet Union would "commit any crime" in the pursuit of "world revolution," Kennan warned publicly against "oversimplifications" without saying who had indulged in them. "It was an effort on my part to stake out a middle ground for myself between that sort of thing and its opposite: the sort of naïve pro-Sovietism of which I am so often accused by the hard-liners."[10]

In his diary, though, Kennan was already fretting about the "childishness and primitivism" of Reagan's advisers. Alexander Haig, now secretary of state, was so alarmed about Central America that one would think the Red Army was invading the region. Richard Pipes, the Harvard historian and Committee on the Present Danger member who handled Soviet and Eastern European affairs for the National Security Council, was insisting that war was inevitable unless the U.S.S.R. changed its system. Its leaders had behaved badly, Kennan acknowledged: their polemics were "as Russian as boiled cabbage and buckwheat kasha. But what about my own government and its state of blind militaristic hysteria?"[11]

Reagan evoked Kennan, also not by name, in his first significant speech after being released from the hospital, on May 17, 1981. Delivered at the University of Notre Dame, it came five days after an assassination attempt on Pope John Paul II, and two days before Kennan's Einstein Prize address. In words well suited to

the drama of the occasion, Reagan predicted that "[t]he West won't contain communism, it will transcend communism. It won't bother to . . . denounce it, it will
dismiss it as some bizarre chapter in human history whose last pages are even now
being written." Strangely, Kennan took no notice of what the president had said,
despite its resonance with his own—if more moderately phrased—prophecy in
the "X" article thirty-four years earlier.[12]

Another Reagan speech given at West Point on May 27, however, did provoke
a response. "It is a simple world picture that he paints," Kennan wrote in his diary.
"I ought to love it, as he sees it, and be thrilled by it. I cannot. I love certain old-
fashioned values and concepts, but not *his*." Kennan then *imagined* a conversation
with Reagan if they should ever meet, "which is most unlikely." Remembering
"my evil reputation," the president would "look me sternly in the eye and ask:
'Kennan, are you patriotic?'" If that meant loving the land, he would reply, he
had loved it the way it was when he was a boy, before its inhabitants had made
"a wasteland, a garbage dump, a sewer out of it." There would be little left once
Reagan's supporters had completed that process. If the president meant loving
the people, Kennan would have to reject any claim that their superior virtue and
strength entitled them to lead the world.[13]

Like many Kennan diary entries, this one demands discount. Reagan, always
a gentleman, would never have asked so pointed a question, and Kennan, equally
polite, would never have given such a harsh answer. The passage shows, though,
that despite his resolve to keep an open mind, Kennan was beginning to project
his anger about his country onto its new leader. Despite the credit he had given
Reagan, in the Einstein address, for wanting reductions in nuclear weaponry,
Kennan wasn't listening carefully to what he said. Throughout Reagan's presidency, Kennan would remain surprisingly inattentive to what he did.

"I have a foreign policy," Reagan wrote a friend in July 1981. "I just don't happen to think that it's wise to [tell] the world what your foreign policy is." Had Reagan had a chance to explain it to him, Kennan might have picked up additional
echoes of his own earlier thinking. The president was seeking to restore Western
self-confidence, not for the purpose of economic recovery, as in the Marshall Plan,
but by redressing the military imbalance created by actual increases in Soviet
strategic and conventional capabilities, as well as by psychological impressions
of American weakness in the aftermath of the Vietnam War. He hoped thereby to
prepare the way, not just for new negotiations aimed at reducing nuclear weapons, but also for sharpening the stresses under which the Soviet system operated.
Although Reagan had joined the Committee on the Present Danger, he had never

accepted its insistence that the U.S.S.R. was getting stronger. Instead, he would have agreed with what Kennan had written in his 1978 letter to James Reston: that Brezhnev's aging, frightened, and overstretched regime had no choice, if it was to survive, but to alter its course.[14]

Reagan's *reasons* for thinking this, however, puzzled his own advisers and would have appalled Kennan, had he known of them. Kennan had reached his conclusions after a systematic effort, over several years, to compile and compare statistical information on Soviet capabilities, gleaned from as many sources as he could find. The president, in contrast, based his view on the simple conviction that capitalism fit human nature better than communism—and on jokes about the Soviet economy. Both were right: Kennan's statistics were revealing, as were Reagan's anecdotes. But Kennan would have found them more frightening than funny.[15]

Meanwhile Reagan's determination to exploit Soviet weaknesses struck Kennan as dangerous. He had indeed recommended efforts to undermine Stalin's empire in 1947–48, but as the dictator's successors softened their rule while expanding their military capabilities, Kennan became almost protective of them, fearing that challenges might provoke war. He dismissed the dissidents as troublemakers. He portrayed the invasion of Afghanistan as a defensive maneuver, posing no threat to American interests. And when, in December 1981, General Wojciech Jaruzelski imposed martial law in Poland and arrested the leaders of Solidarity, Kennan saw the action as a realistic response to Moscow's concerns. Reagan's retaliatory sanctions, he insisted, were "driving the Soviet leadership to desperation by pressing it mercilessly against a closed door." Even the normally sympathetic *New York Times* found this to be too much: the "Kennan Doctrine," it editorialized, seemed to be "that might should at least define right in world affairs."[16]

"I think there is a good deal of latent discontent with the Brezhnev regime among younger members of the hierarchy," Kennan wrote Durbrow early in January 1982, "and that we could, and should, give greater encouragement to these people." But Reagan would get nowhere with human rights "agitation," because "Russia is not going to be 'democratic' in our time." Nor did it make sense to seek to destroy the Soviet system: "Our task is to accept it, for the moment, as it is; to try to avoid . . . an unnecessary and mutually disastrous war; and to see that the influence we exert on that country by our words and policies is one conducive to gradual change in what we would regard as the right direction."[17]

How, though, to exert that influence? He was beginning to feel "like a one-man His Majesty's royal opposition," Kennan wrote Charlie James. He could have avoided this isolation, he added in his diary, by becoming a politician. He would then have

> said a thousand things I did not mean, cultivated a thousand people for whom I had no respect, mouthed all the fashionable slogans, got myself—at least briefly—into a position of authority, and then—playing, as others do, on popular emotions and slogans—wheedled less perceptive people into doing useful things, the real nature of which they would not have understood at all.

That kind of leadership, however, was not his:

> My role, vain as this assertion may sound, [is] that of a prophet. It was for this that I was born. And my tragedy is to enact this part at a time when it becomes increasingly doubtful that there will, as little as ten or twenty years hence, be anyone left to recognize the validity of the prophecies, or whether, indeed, any record of these prophecies will have survived the conflagration to which nuclear war can lead, or any eyes would be there to read it, if it did.

The choice, then, was Reagan versus Kennan: the politician versus the prophet. Neither could become the other. Meanwhile "there is a bit of life still to be lived—a bit to be seen of the tragic beauty and poetry of this world—a bit, in short, to be witnessed, perceived, and recorded."[18]

III.

"I am only a small part of the resistance in the U.S. to the madness of the present Am[erican] administration," Kennan wrote on March 11, 1982. What he meant was the campaign then under way to achieve a "mutual, verifiable freeze" in Soviet and American nuclear capabilities. Originating within the peace movement, galvanized by the journalist Jonathan Schell's frightening *New Yorker* articles on the effects of a nuclear war, the freeze had won sufficiently widespread support by then for 139 members of Congress to have endorsed it. Kennan had too, but only because the freeze was the least controversial objective around which the largest "opposition" could rally. It would not be nearly enough, "and I would not like to appear to be suggesting, by associating myself with it, that it *was* enough." He had already gone beyond the freeze by calling for sharp reductions in nuclear capabilities, and he was now reviving a proposal he had first made in his 1950 "super" bomb paper: that the United States should promise never to initiate the use of nuclear weapons in fighting a war.[19]

"No first use" attracted no support at that point and for decades afterward because NATO depended on nuclear deterrence. The alliance had never matched the Warsaw Pact's conventional forces, so American nuclear superiority—in principle—was supposed to balance them. In fact, the Soviet Union had long since caught up with the United States in both categories of weaponry, which meant that NATO had a credibility problem: would Americans risk their own safety to defend Western Europeans, especially West Germans?

To show that they would, all administrations since Eisenhower's had deployed troops equipped with tactical nuclear weapons along the East German–West German border, where they would bear the brunt of any Warsaw Pact attack. Like "mutual assured destruction," however, this "rational" strategy assumed irrationalities: that armies could fight on battlefields their own armaments had made uninhabitable; that the enemy would not respond in kind; that there would be much left of West Germany if it had to be "defended" in this way. It was a strange sort of deterrence, Kennan pointed out: "If you dare to attack West Germany, we will destroy that country; and then where will *you* be?"[20]

NATO's nuclear doctrines "were marvelous instances of intellectual incoherence and practical success," former national security adviser McGeorge Bundy observed, for despite their illogic, there had been no European war. But could they survive the collapse of détente, a new race to deploy intermediate-range missiles, the Soviet crackdown in Poland, the Reagan administration's retaliations, and a harshness in official rhetoric on both sides not seen since the early Cold War? The president's "zero option" proposal of November 1981 had done little to allay these concerns: even his supporters believed it to be a negotiating gambit—a crafty bit of public grandstanding—not a serious proposal.[21]

Shortly after the president's speech, Kennan attended a Washington dinner hosted by R. Sargent Shriver, President Kennedy's brother-in-law, the founder of the Peace Corps, a former ambassador to France, George McGovern's running mate in 1972, and a devout Catholic. His other guests included former secretary of defense and World Bank president Robert S. McNamara; Gerard C. Smith, the chief American delegate at the SALT I negotiations; Paul Warnke, Smith's SALT II counterpart; and Father J. Bryan Hehir, who was drafting a statement for the National Catholic Bishops on the danger of nuclear war. A lively discussion ensued, during which someone—probably Kennan—brought up "no first use." To the surprise of all present, all now favored it.

Kennan agreed, therefore, to cooperate with McNamara and Smith in resurrecting the concept: they, in turn, decided that Bundy—who had not been present—should draft a proposal. Such collaboration was unusual for Kennan, but in this instance, he saw its value: "If I were to write [alone] about 'first use' people would say: 'What the hell does Kennan know about military matters? He doesn't know a damn thing about them.'" Bundy was initially skeptical but decided to go ahead because McNamara, who had originated the doctrine of "mutual assured destruction," and Kennan, who had always despised it, had found common ground. *Foreign Affairs* was alerted, and the article appeared as "Nuclear Weapons and the Atlantic Alliance" early in April 1982. Its authors quickly came to be known—in a quirky homage to the victims of Mao Zedong's last purge—as the "Gang of Four."[22]

The proposal, Kennan hoped, would "force" the Reagan administration to abandon "first use," but Secretary of State Haig ruled that out immediately. Such a shift, he claimed in a speech on April 6, would make Europe "safe for conventional aggression" while endangering "the essential values of Western civilization." No West German outdid Haig in hyperbole, but a spokesman for the ruling Social Democratic Party did point out that a long conventional war would be just as damaging as a limited nuclear war. A leading Christian Democrat called the idea "unusually dangerous, both politically and psychologically."[23]

So as a policy initiative, "no first use" died at birth. The episode was significant, though, because Kennan had allies, this time, in criticizing NATO strategy. With Bundy, McNamara, and Smith on his side, no one could claim, as had Acheson after the Reith lectures, that Kennan had a "mystical attitude" toward power relationships. Old orthodoxies, in the face of new tensions, were breaking up, winning Kennan at least a respectful hearing within the foreign policy establishment. Not, however, within the Reagan administration, which he now regarded as "ignorant, unintelligent, complacent and arrogant; worse still is the fact that it is frivolous and reckless." The president seemed blithely above it all. "A few public statements professing his love for peace, in principle, and one or two propagandistic proposals put forward publicly and so designed as to assure Soviet rejection, and the problem, so far as he is concerned, will be resolved."[24]

Kennan wrote that last diary entry on May 7, 1982. Two days later Reagan spoke at his alma mater, Eureka College, in Illinois. He began his discussion of arms reduction by quoting from Carl Sandburg's poem "Cornhuskers," which his own class had included in its 1931 yearbook: "Have you seen a red sunset drip over one of my cornfields, the shore of night stars, the wave lines of dawn up a wheat valley?" Then the president invoked, in words that could have come from Jonathan Schell, the "nightmarish prospect that a huge mushroom cloud might someday destroy such beauty." Despite difficulties in Soviet-American relations, therefore, his START negotiating team would propose a mutual reduction of one-third in strategic missile warheads, with further cuts in other categories to follow: "My duty as President is to ensure that the ultimate nightmare never occurs."[25]

Two days after that, Kennan spoke to a predominantly Catholic audience in Davenport, Iowa, just ninety miles northwest of Eureka. He celebrated "[t]his habitat, the natural world around us, . . . the house the Lord gave us to live in." No one had a right to deny it, "with all its beauty and fertility and marvelousness," to future generations. The very existence of nuclear weapons endangered it. The situation would not change until Americans came to see themselves *and* their supposed Soviet adversaries together as "God's creatures," embodying "the struggle between good and evil, which is the fundamental mark of all humankind."[26]

"I fire my arrows into the air," Kennan had written in a philosophical moment before Reagan took office. "Sometimes, they strike nothing; sometimes, they strike the wrong things; sometimes one or another of them strikes a bell and rings it, loud and clear." Despite wishful thinking in *The New York Times*, none of these categories fits the Kennan-Reagan relationship: there was never a direct dialogue between them. But arrows fired from different points, at different times, by very different archers, can nonetheless converge.[27]

IV.

"Louis and I have been talking, pleasantly, widely, and since we always ended up with the dilemmas, uselessly," Kennan noted on October 1, 1982, while visiting friends in Switzerland. Louis J. Halle served under Kennan and Nitze on the Policy Planning Staff, had written the best early history of the Cold War, and had taught for years at the Graduate Institute of International Studies in Geneva. A close observer of Kennan, he recorded the conversation more carefully, for it helped to explain "a public advocacy that does not, to my mind, stand up to reality."

Could two men pointing pistols at one another trust a "no first use" declaration? Kennan had no answer. Wasn't nuclear deterrence keeping the peace, so wouldn't abolishing nuclear weapons imperil it? Kennan conceded the point. Hadn't world government advocates foreseen a third world war if their advice wasn't followed? Kennan acknowledged that they had been wrong. He nonetheless showed Halle a page from his diary—claiming that it had slipped out of its ringbinder—in which he foresaw his own children's deaths within five years because no one heeded his warnings about a nuclear holocaust. He was a Christian, Kennan insisted, but in this situation God was helpless.[28]

Unwilling to let his friend off the hook, Halle wrote a few months later to express dismay when people whose minds he respected "take positions for which I see no adequate basis." It was wholly implausible to claim that the U.S.S.R. had recovered from Stalinism, a phenomenon whose roots, Kennan had once argued, went back through a thousand years of Russian paranoia. "I think you were right when you said the Soviet Union had to be contained, even if you had in mind something other than military containment." Kennan's reply rejected his younger self: Brezhnev's successors—the ailing autocrat had finally succumbed in November 1982—were men who calculated their interests rationally and would do all they could to avoid a war. The same could not be said of their Washington counterparts, who were deliberately destabilizing the nuclear balance: "That is, presumably, what Mr. Reagan and his associates really want."[29]

But if Kennan could have read NSDD-75, the administration's first top-secret review of policy toward the Soviet Union, approved by Reagan on January 17, 1983, he would have found still more echoes of "Mr. X." American goals, the document specified, should be:

1. To contain and over time reverse Soviet expansionism by competing effectively on a sustained basis with the Soviet Union in all international arenas—particularly in the overall military balance and in geographical regions of priority concern to the United States.
2. To promote, within the narrow limits available to us, the process of change in the Soviet Union toward a more pluralistic political and economic system in which the power of the ruling elite is gradually reduced.
3. To engage the Soviet Union in negotiations to attempt to reach agreements which protect and enhance U.S. interests and which are consistent with the principle of strict reciprocity and mutual interest.

It's not clear whether Reagan had read Kennan's famous *Foreign Affairs* article, but he did devote two 1977 radio broadcasts to an analysis of the recently declassified

NSC 68, which incorporated its fundamental points. Whatever Kennan's subsequent views on "X," Reagan's priorities were hardly those of a president bent on destroying the U.S.S.R. at the risk of ending life on the planet.[30]

He had fired the incendiary Haig the previous summer, replacing him with the less combustible George Shultz. With the president's approval, the new secretary of state quietly brought Soviet ambassador Dobrynin to the White House on February 15, 1983, for his first private meeting with Reagan. Neither the press nor the president's staff—who doubted their boss's ability to hold his own with the experienced diplomat—were informed. After talking for two hours "pretty nose to nose," Reagan wrote in his diary, he asked Dobrynin and Shultz to help him communicate regularly with the new Soviet leader, Yuri Andropov: "Geo. tells me that after they left, the ambas. said 'this could be a historic moment.'"[31]

Knowing nothing of it, Kennan arranged his own meeting with Dobrynin while visiting Washington on March 2. He wanted to show Dobrynin that "our country could do a bit better in this respect than the Soviet Union had done by me"—he meant his own isolation in Moscow in 1952, when an invitation from Stalin never came.

> So I marched bravely into the old embassy building on 16th Street, under the amazed eyes and furiously clicking cameras of God knows how many agents of the F.B.I. and others of the intelligence fraternity, was kindly and jovially received by my ambassadorial host, lunched and talked pleasantly with him for an hour or so, well aware that the recording devices of both governments were probably noting, for the benefit of posterity, every word of our rather innocuous conversation.

If Dobrynin mentioned his visit to the White House—this seems unlikely given its secrecy—Kennan made no note of it. He did meet Shultz at a dinner that evening and liked his imperturbability but thought that "it jolted him a bit when I gave him the name." Shultz was an improvement over Haig; nevertheless "I foresee something of [a] crisis between him and the fanatics . . . around the President, particularly if he tries to do anything sensible about relations with the Soviet Union."[32]

Shultz had some rough weeks ahead of him. Reagan gave him no warning before denouncing the Soviet Union, in an address to the National Association of Evangelicals on March 8, as "the focus of evil in the modern world," and only minimal notice prior to his announcement, on March 23, of the Strategic Defense Initiative, his plan to protect the United States by building an antiballistic missile system. But the secretary of state soon saw Reagan's logic in wanting to put both the U.S.S.R. and his own critics on the defensive. How could one reconcile religious faith with the political practice of "moral equivalency"? What was wrong with making nuclear weapons, as the president put it, "impotent and obsolete"?[33]

Kennan was vulnerable on both counts. He trusted Andropov—until recently the head of the KGB—more than he did Reagan. He opposed MAD and the first serious effort to move beyond it. He took these positions not just because he feared war but also because he allowed sensitivity to *style* and susceptibility to *emotion* to cloud his judgment. How could an apparent lightweight like Reagan have any strategy at all, much less one that echoed what Kennan's once had been? How could Kennan share aspirations with someone so unlike himself? The administration's attitude toward the Soviet Union, he claimed in a Washington speech that spring, was "simply childish, inexcusably childish, unworthy of people charged with the responsibility for conducting the affairs of a great power in an endangered world."

Delivered on May 17 under the sponsorship of the Committee on East-West Accord, Kennan's address was in other ways worthy of its author. It was his first in the city since his Einstein Prize speech two years earlier. He delivered it before an audience including diplomats from NATO and Warsaw Pact countries, as well as an eagle-eyed Harriman, now ninety-two. Soviet negotiating techniques, Kennan admitted, could be "stiff, jerky, secretive, unpredictable," lacking in "useful lubrication." But it was wrong to apply, to their practitioners, "an image of unmitigated darkness," as if they were the product of some "negative genetic miracle." Nor was there any point in threatening the use, against their country, of useless weaponry: the goal should be to reduce nuclear arsenals, "with a view to their total elimination." His fifty-five years of involvement in Soviet-American affairs— longer than that of anyone living—had never made him lose faith in constructive possibilities: "I wish I could convey some of that confidence to those around me here in Washington."

The seventy-nine-year-old Kennan, Stephen Rosenfeld wrote in *The New York Times,* was "a driven, concentrated man of an increasingly spectral appearance" whose warnings, however imbalanced, reflected the widespread anxieties felt about Reagan. One turned to Kennan now not for policy analysis but "for glimpses of an uncommon, even mystical prophetic power." There was "an old man's economy of truth in him." Kennan was, for once, pleased with his performance: "I came away with the impression that I had put one small barb into the complacent behind of the Administration."[34]

When Kennan published his speech in *The New Yorker* the following October, he had to make a few revisions. One was to acknowledge that Harriman's Soviet experience went back further than his own: the older man had put the younger in his place yet again. The other was to mention, if only briefly, the shooting down of a South Korean airliner that had strayed over Sakhalin on the night of August 31–September 1, 1983. Andropov and his subordinates should learn from this "what harm they do to themselves when they let military considerations ride roughshod over wider interests." Kennan should have stopped there.

Feeling the need for further explanation, though, he decided to provide one in *The Washington Post*. The incident should have surprised no one familiar with the "exaggerated sensitivity" of the Kremlin leaders, their inflexible ideology, and their inability to control their military. This was not as reassuring as Kennan had meant it to be. He went on to insist that the event would never have happened had it not been for the dangerous games intelligence agencies on both sides were playing, and for the Korean pilot's "inexplicable obstinacy" in flying at night through forbidden airspace. It was understandable, then, that Andropov had given up hope for anything other than "implacable hostility" from Reagan's administration.

Now even Annelise, to whom George had not shown the piece before submitting it, "rose in revolt." She was "a woman of good judgment," he told himself, obviously shaken. "And if it makes her intensely unhappy that I should, once or twice a year, speak my mind publicly, that in itself is a reason for not doing so." There was, however, such a thing as paralysis from frustration. "The people who experiment on rats know that. I, poor rat, am close to experiencing it."[35]

On November 15, 1983, the Woodrow Wilson Center—still the Washington home of the Kennan Institute—held a dinner to "celebrate" fifty years of diplomatic relations with the Soviet Union. Kennan was the main speaker, but the mood was noticeably subdued. A few other American ex-ambassadors attended, as did Dobrynin; the only Reagan administration official present, however, was Jack Matlock, who had recently replaced Pipes as the president's Soviet and East European adviser on the National Security Council. Kennan praised Franklin D. Roosevelt, a very rare thing for him. If *that* president still occupied the White House, he would not have fallen into cynicism and despair over the state of Soviet-American relations. He would be setting about, "with boldness and good cheer, to make things better." Why should anyone now accept anything less?[36]

Stalin's daughter was asking the same question. Desperately worried that war was about to break out, she demanded that Harriman and Kennan undertake a mission to Moscow to save the situation. "What are you going to do about it?"

Harriman asked. Alliluyeva was emotional, Kennan answered, "with certain oddities and disabilities of character that have been a great trial to all her friends." Like her father, though, she was at times capable of "penetrating insights." This was one, and Kennan would not reject the role if offered it. But that Reagan and Shultz might welcome such an initiative seemed doubtful, "and without their recognition and acceptance of it, I am not sure whether it could be of any value."[37]

V.

On Saturday, January 14, 1984, to Kennan's astonishment, he did get a call from the White House. It would have come a day earlier, but Annelise, still hoping for a less visible husband, had refused to disturb him. The caller was Matlock. He had no Moscow trip in mind, but he did want Kennan to know that on the morning of the sixteenth—timed for European television—Reagan would be making an important speech.

> He then told me very interesting things: that the President felt some regret over certain of the things he had said, in the early period of his presidency, about the Soviet Union; and that the reason why he had been unwilling to deal with the Soviet government at that time was that he had felt that we were too weak militarily for our word to have any weight. Now, he felt we were stronger, and that he was in a better position to deal with them.

Matlock, whom Kennan greatly respected, would not have called without authorization: that this had been granted was "extraordinary." But by whom? Shultz, rumored to have read the *New Yorker* article? The new national security adviser, Robert McFarlane? The president himself? "[I]t is assuredly a straw in the wind, and certainly a part of the significant change of policy toward the Soviet Union which Matlock assures me is taking place."[38]

The speech, one of Reagan's most memorable, deplored the possibility that "dangerous misunderstanding[s] and miscalculations" might wreck the hopes of parents everywhere "to raise their children in a world without fear and without war." In a peroration only he or FDR could have composed, the president envisaged a Soviet couple, Ivan and Anya, meeting an American couple, Jim and Sally. Finding how much they had in common, they would not have debated differences between their governments. Instead they might have gone out for dinner some-where, thereby demonstrating that "people don't make wars."[39]

Kennan was momentarily reassured. "I have a sense that respect for me has recently risen in White House circles," he wrote on January 29. The president's advisers were not consulting him directly, "but I suspect they listen, if apprehen-sively, to what I say." He had found three references, in Reagan's address, to the *New Yorker* article, although he didn't specify what they were. Given the presi-dent's strong position, given the mess Andropov and his associates had made of their relations with the Western Europeans—the West German Bundestag had voted to deploy NATO intermediate-range missiles in November—maybe Ken-nan should try to help Reagan.

> But then I thought of all of his other follies and of his unlimited commitment to a military showdown, and I also reflected on my own age and on the limitations that imposes; and I thought: no, the faintly more positive tone of his recent speech is surely no more than a minor tactical concession, he is a stubborn man who, precisely because his political position is a strong one, is unlikely to wander very far from the primitive preconceptions he has already formed. Better, I thought, for you, Kennan, to keep out of this.

So he was "effectively stymied." He should simply accept old age, and "let the trag-edy take its course."[40]

Unbeknownst to Kennan, it almost had. Andropov turned out to have been *less* capable than his predecessors of calculating interests rationally, and in his fear of nuclear war—which was real enough—had almost set one off. Convinced while still at the KGB that the Reagan administration was planning a surprise attack on the Soviet Union, he had ordered an intelligence alert that went on for two years, with agents throughout the world looking for evidence to confirm his suspicions. The Korean airliner incident occurred within that context, as did Andropov's sub-sequent denials that any error had taken place. Already on kidney dialysis at the time, he was in no condition to be running a superpower, much less exchanging ideas with Reagan on how to reduce tensions.[41]

Kennan had been right, then, to stress the hypersensitivity of Soviet leaders, but because he had been doing this for years while also emphasizing their com-mon sense, his warnings lacked the weight they might otherwise have had. What made the situation doubly dangerous was that Reagan too assumed rationality. He expected Andropov to take him at his word when he said, publicly and in private, that the last thing he wanted was a war. But Andropov, like Kennan, doubted Reagan's sincerity.

Both were wrong to do so. On October 10, 1983, the president previewed *The Day After,* an ABC television movie about the effects of a Soviet missile strike on an American city, Lawrence, Kansas. "It's very effective & left me profoundly depressed," Reagan acknowledged, hence the need to do "all we can to have a deterrent & see that there is never a nuclear war." On November 18—two days after Kennan demanded Rooseveltian reassurance—Reagan got his first full briefing on American war planning. Unlike previous presidents, he had postponed this as long as possible, apparently because he knew he would hate what he heard. "A most sobering experience," he now recorded. "I feel the Soviets are so defense minded, so paranoid about being attacked[,] that without being in any way soft on them, we ought to tell them no one here has any intention of doing anything like that." A subsequent briefing on December 9, covering Soviet war plans, left him wishing that "some of our pacifist loud talkers could have access to this information."[42]

The allusion was to probably the second most dangerous crisis—after Cuba in 1962—of the entire Cold War. NATO ran military maneuvers in the North Atlantic each fall, but it upgraded the 1983 exercise, code-named "Able Archer," to include top-level decision makers. Alarmed by this, Soviet intelligence analysts concluded that the surprise attack they had been told to expect was about to happen. Oleg Gordievsky, a British spy in Moscow, alerted his London handlers, who in turn warned Washington. Reagan found the reports hard to believe but immediately began efforts to defuse the crisis. The purpose of his upcoming speech, he wrote on January 6, 1984, would be to "reassure the eggheads & our European friends"—and presumably also the Kremlin—"that I don't plan to blow up the world."[43]

The idea for Reagan's globally televised "fireside chat" didn't come directly from Kennan. The president was no regular reader of *The New Yorker,* and *The Washington Post* buried its account of Kennan's Wilson Center speech at the end of an inconspicuous story on page B13. But Matlock read what Kennan had written, heard what he had said about Roosevelt, and happened to be drafting Reagan's speech—until the president himself took it over to introduce Jim and Sally to Ivan and Anya. There were again convergences, if not causes. "Reagan's Soviet policy had more in common with Kennan's thinking than the policy of any of Reagan's predecessors," Matlock later recalled, even if "the rhetoric that offended Kennan's sensibilities temporarily blinded him to the real substance of American policy."[44]

Andropov died on February 9. Kennan thought his successor, Konstantin Chernenko, the worst possible choice, exemplifying "all that the regime ought to be turning its back on." Subordinates who would have to work with him deserved sympathy, not reproach: "Whatever their inner doubts, they could not admit to recognizing the justice of anything you might be saying without entering, if only so slightly, into the realm of the wholly treasonable." Kennan might have been writing about Mikhail Gorbachev, but he hardly knew the name.[45]

And what of Reagan, now running for reelection? The president had become a peace candidate, Kennan explained to Dobrynin, because the antinuclear campaign and the public reaction to *The Day After*, which eighty million people saw, had left him no choice. Fearing that Reagan would revert to his hard line after his probable reelection, Kennan had his own choice to make. He could oppose the president openly, remaining true to his convictions but forfeiting any possibility of influence in a second term. Or he could "lie low," in the faint hope that the administration might seek his help in repairing the damage it had done: "I have, God knows, no admiration for Mr. Reagan, but if a certain amount of restraint, dissimulation, and self-abasement could be useful in sparing my children— and our civilization—the final catastrophe, there could be no question of what I should do."[46]

VI.

Reagan's November victory was no surprise, therefore, but Kennan had trouble accounting for its landslide proportions. If public opinion had forced the president, against his will, to resume arms reduction talks, then why had he gotten so many votes for so little progress? Kennan shifted to the argument that the antinuclear movement had failed miserably and would have to pull itself together in some more effective form of resistance. Bill Bundy saw a draft "statement" to this effect but thought it too pessimistic for publication, and so Kennan adjusted his position yet again: after all, "new faces might appear [in Moscow] with whom, for one reason or another, people in our government might find it easier to talk."[47]

As if to confirm that possibility, Chernenko died on March 10, and Gorbachev immediately succeeded him. After making his third trip up 16th Street in as many years to sign the Soviet embassy's "grief book," Reagan offered to meet with the new leader, as he had unsuccessfully with Brezhnev, Andropov, and

Chernenko. Gorbachev, at fifty-four, was of a new generation, Kennan told *The New York Times*, despite having risen through the old system. With economic problems at home, unrest in Eastern Europe, war in Afghanistan, and rivalries with both China and the United States, he had every reason to reconsider existing policies.[48]

Kennan had expected the *Times* to call, but not the State Department. He met there on April 2 with Under Secretary for Political Affairs Michael Armacost and his aides, who wanted to know what he thought of Gorbachev: "[T]his is the first time in many years that I have been consulted in this place. . . . I am mildly pleased to be given this attention." But the "smooth remoteness" of the questioning left Kennan uneasy. It was too close to Dulles's suggestion, after firing him in 1953, that he drop in from time to time when he had anything useful to say.

On April 11, however, Dulles's successor dropped in on Kennan. Secretary of State Shultz, speaking at Princeton on international economic policy, went out of his way to seek Kennan's advice, over lunch, on how to handle the new Kremlin leadership. Shultz's cordiality so surprised Kennan that he could only dispense bromides: that these were insecure people who required reassurance and respect; that both sides should agree on what the talks were to be about; that it was unwise to raise irrelevant issues. For Shultz, this was nothing he didn't know. For Kennan—himself an insecure person who required reassurance and respect—it was yet another reason to rethink his attitude toward the Reagan administration.[49]

He found this very difficult to do. He was shocked, while in Oslo in August, to hear a recent Norwegian ambassador to Moscow defend Reagan's firmness. "Was all diplomacy," Kennan wondered, "some sort of dance in which we demonstrated our 'resolve' . . . our unbending pursuit of our chosen course?" Where was the opposition? he asked himself in October: this "greatest escape artist since Houdini" had, with the help of the Democratic Party, "defeated us all. We are left powerless and unmanned." These were diary lamentations, not to be taken too seriously, but Kennan displayed his distrust openly in a *New York Times* op-ed on November 3. The upcoming Reagan-Gorbachev summit in Geneva, he insisted, should focus on slowing the arms race. It would be "tragic in the uttermost degree if *Washington* failed to make the effort."[50]

On November 7, 1985, the president met at the White House with a group of academic experts on the Soviet Union. Kennan was not among them. "It sounds to me like Reagan invited people who tell him things he likes to hear," an unnamed uninvited scholar grumbled to *The Washington Post*. By then, though, a senior presidential aide—also unnamed—had told the same newspaper that Kennan's

1981 proposal for a 50 percent cut in nuclear arsenals was likely to come up at Geneva: "We have for a long time proposed a reduction of about half in land- and sea-based ballistic missiles." This was indeed the first topic Reagan raised in his first substantive private conversation with Gorbachev, on November 19. When the Soviet leader hedged, citing concerns about the Strategic Defense Initiative, Reagan went further: why not get rid of nuclear weapons altogether, thereby removing any need for defenses against them?[51]

A few days later Kennan got an excited phone call from Congressman John F. Seiberling, an Ohio Democrat active in the peace movement. He had sent the White House, before the summit, a copy of the Einstein Prize address. Now Reagan and Gorbachev, in principle, had endorsed its chief recommendation. But Kennan was not prepared, yet, to accept the suggestion that he had, in any way, influenced the president, or even that the two had reached the same conclusions independently. "Mr. Reagan does not object to a certain amount of window-dressing in the field of academic, scientific, and personal exchanges," he acknowledged in December. But "behind it—in the fields that really count—stands a stone wall he has no intentions of dismantling."[52]

"I have no cheerful thoughts to offer as you leave this country," Kennan wrote Dobrynin in March 1986. His long Washington ambassadorship was coming to an end, and although "the future is full of surprises—sometimes even pleasant ones," Reagan, Kennan was sure, would not provide them. He saw the president at times as a sinister political wizard, at others as an amiable actor speaking lines sinister writers had prepared for him. Whatever he was, Reagan would never seek nuclear arms reduction. Thanks to him, "we love these apocalyptic devices; we have taken them to our hearts; and we would not give them up if the Russians had none at all."[53]

At the Reykjavik summit in October, however, Reagan and Gorbachev did agree to remove all intermediate-range nuclear missiles in Europe. They also endorsed the concept of a 50 percent cut in intercontinental-range missiles, and they even discussed the possibility of eliminating all nuclear weapons from the face of the earth. Only the president's unwillingness to dismantle the Strategic Defense Initiative brought the negotiations to an angry halt, but as Gorbachev was quick to acknowledge, Reykjavik had "created a qualitatively new situation. And nobody is now in a position to act the way he was able to act before."[54]

The New York Times ran Gorbachev's statement on the morning of October 15. Kennan read it, set aside another attack on Reagan—"a deeply prejudiced, ill-informed, and stubborn man, not above the most shameless demagoguery"—and after talking with McGeorge Bundy agreed that "we should try to be helpful and not just critical." He could not resist inflicting on Annelise, however, what he would like to have said to Gorbachev:

> You could give in to us on every point in our negotiations; you would still encounter nothing but a stony hostility in official American circles; and your concessions would be exploited by the President as evidence that he had frightened you into compliance, that the only language you understood was the language of force.

The problem was not just Reagan. Other powerful "elements" in American society felt the need for an inhuman enemy "as a foil for what they like to persuade themselves is their own exceptional virtue." Through no fault of his own, Gorbachev had been cast in that role.[55]

Fortunately, this communication went no further than Kennan's diary and his wife's seasoned discretion. For it sounded embarrassingly close to a dispatch, now published, that Kennan had sent from Moscow forty years earlier. "Some of us here," he had written the State Department then, had been trying to guess what the United States would have to do if it wished to win Stalin's trust. The list included unconditional surrender, complete disarmament, a transfer of power to the Communist Party, and even then "Moscow would smell a trap." Now, Kennan seemed to be saying, Gorbachev in his dealings with Reagan was facing an American Stalin.[56]

VII.

"Mr. Kennan," Gorbachev said to him, in an actual conversation that took place in Washington on December 8, 1987: "We in our country believe that a man may be a friend of another country and remain, at the same time, a loyal and devoted citizen of his own; and that is the way we view you." The tribute came at a Soviet embassy reception on the occasion of Gorbachev's first trip to the United States. "I was just standing on the fringes," George recalled, until Annelise took charge: "For goodness sake, go up and greet people." So he pushed his way past Kissinger, McNamara, McGeorge Bundy, and John Kenneth Galbraith, as well as less familiar luminaries— Billy Graham, Paul Newman, Joyce Carol Oates, Norman Mailer, Robert De Niro, and John Denver. Maybe, as Kennan approached Gorbachev, somebody whispered his name. Maybe they didn't need to. However it happened, he "recognized me, opened his arms, and embraced me." It was not what Kennan expected from the first successor to Stalin he had ever met.

Kennan had not expected either, though, the Intermediate-Range Nuclear Forces Treaty, which Reagan and Gorbachev had just signed at the White House. It was the "zero option" brought to fruition: the first abolition, by mutual consent, of an entire category of the "apocalyptic devices" Kennan so greatly feared. The day was full of surprises. Seated at Kennan's table while Gorbachev spoke was "a lady of most striking appearance, who chain-smoked Danish cigars and appeared to be rather bored with the whole performance. . . . I was later told that I should have recognized her—as the widow of a famous rock star." His name, strangely, was something like "Lenin." Gorbachev's "extraordinarily gracious and tactful statement," Kennan concluded, had brought a fitting end to his long involvement in Soviet affairs: "If you cannot have this sort of recognition from your own government . . . , it is nice to have it at least from the one-time adversary."

How, though, had Kennan's idea—that nuclear weapons should not be just "controlled" but reduced or even eliminated—taken hold in Reagan's administration? Perhaps it had to do with simplicity, Kennan suggested, when asked this question a few days after meeting Gorbachev. Stalin had known that "complicated things never wash in high politics." Reagan knew that too. He had wanted "some simple formula," and the Einstein Prize proposal provided it. "[T]he things that are done by great statesmen publicly have to be quite simple."[57]

As the comparison suggested, the "greatness" of which Kennan spoke was not meant as a compliment. Reagan's policies, Kennan had predicted at the beginning of 1987, were likely "to preclude the pursuit of any sensible policy towards [the Soviet Union] for years to come." When the president demanded, in June in Berlin, that Gorbachev "tear down this wall," Kennan, speaking two weeks later within sight of it, deplored "confrontational tactics." The time was "plainly not ripe," the onetime architect of "disengagement" now maintained, for German reunification, or for any shift in existing military alliances. "The approach of Mr. Gorbachev depresses me profoundly," Kennan had written before the December summit in Washington. "I cannot understand why he consented to come."[58]

Joe Alsop, now dying of cancer, hosted a dinner for some old friends just prior to Gorbachev's arrival. Kennan was startled to find everyone there more optimistic than he was. Might something more come out of the summit than the "zero option" treaty, which Reagan had obviously proposed in the belief that the Soviets would never accept it? Had Gorbachev done so out of weakness? Or perhaps out of cleverness? "There is nothing that so upsets the NATO commanders, Mr. Reagan among them, than a sudden and unexpected consent to their more outrageous demands." But *Kennan* had been demanding the removal of nuclear missiles from Europe for decades, and now *he* was upset that it was about to happen. His attitude itself bordered on the outrageous: how could he have loved John F. Kennedy, who repeatedly rejected his advice, and loathed Ronald Reagan, whose actions in this and other respects were consistent with it?[59]

Gorbachev's tribute to Kennan suggests one answer, for Reagan never offered one. There are no references to Kennan in any of Reagan's prepresidential radio broadcasts, in his speeches and press conferences as president, or in his voluminous White House diaries, which he kept more regularly, if less introspectively, than Kennan did his. Recognition was important to Kennan, whose vanity equaled his self-doubt. Kennedy's cultivation of Kennan softened the disappointments he inflicted. Reagan's failure to do so kept Kennan from seeing that his own vindication was taking place.

But even if the president had tried, he might not have succeeded, for he embodied what Kennan deplored about America. Reagan's roots lay in movies, television, and advertising. His political home was the Republican Party's right wing, where McCarthy had once resided. Reagan viewed the world through dangerous simplicities, not realist subtleties. He was not the first California president—Hoover and Nixon had preceded him—but he was the first happy one. With Kennan distrusting both happiness and California, he probably would have distrusted Reagan, even if the president had tried to win his trust. Shultz and Matlock did try but, perhaps sensing the pitfalls, did not persist. Nitze, another possible intermediary, did not even bother. Kennan's complaints about Reagan, he wrote at one point, were "entirely a red herring," followed by "a lot of drivel."[60]

Reagan, for his part, had little need of Kennan. Like Franklin D. Roosevelt, he was an instinctive grand strategist, fully capable of operating without policy planners. He saw more clearly than his advisers the *sequences* of actions, together with the *coalitions* of constituencies, necessary to get him where he wanted to go. He refused to let complications obscure destinations, or to make conventional wisdom a compass. And he understood that, in order to lead, he could never despair. Kennan saw destinations clearly enough, and he certainly defied orthodoxies. But he was bad at sequencing: as he himself admitted, he too often did the right things at the wrong times. He tended more often to shatter than to solidify coalitions. And he despaired constantly, whatever he was doing. So Kennan turned himself into a complication, leaving it to Reagan to bring his strategy to its successful conclusion.[61]

Eventually, grudgingly, and a bit wistfully, Kennan came to see this. When asked, in 1996, who had ended the Cold War, he predictably named Gorbachev. But then he added, watching carefully to see whether his interviewer, who came close, would fall off his chair: "also Ronald Reagan, who in his own inimitable way, probably not even being quite aware of what he was really doing, did what few other people would have been able to do in breaking this log jam."[62]

VIII.

When President George H. W. Bush took office in January 1989, it was not yet clear that the Cold War was over. Gorbachev, speaking at the United Nations the previous month, had announced a unilateral withdrawal of half a million Soviet troops from Central and Eastern Europe, but Bush nonetheless ordered a policy review, implying that Reagan had been too trustful. Kennan was glad to have "new and more intelligent people" at the White House. He worried, though, about loss of momentum in responding to Gorbachev and so resolved, by going public again, to make the case for regaining it. "If I don't say something now, and the new people go the wrong way, I will never know whether something I could have said and didn't would make a difference."

An avid fan of the Public Broadcasting System's *MacNeil/Lehrer NewsHour*, Kennan made himself available for interviews on it. He regretted, in *The New York Times Magazine*, the "reluctant, embarrassed, and occasionally even surly" American reactions to Gorbachev's concessions. As it had done three and a half decades earlier, *The Atlantic* again put him on its cover, this time to publicize *Sketches from a Life*, a forthcoming book of selections Kennan had made from his diaries. And he agreed to testify, on April 4, before the Senate Foreign Relations Committee: "I dare not be optimistic. . . . I don't think I do so well anyway, under this sort of questioning. But here we go."[63]

"Grandeur on Capitol Hill? Yes, it sometimes happens," an enthralled Mary McGrory assured her readers in *The Washington Post*. "Kennan is 85. His back is as straight as a young man's, his jaw as chiseled." He spoke "with such lucidity, learning, and large-mindedness that the senators did not want to let him go." Gorbachev, he told them repeatedly, had ended the Russian revolutionary experiment that had begun in 1917, with the result that the Soviet Union was now becoming a normal state. When Kennan did finish, after two and a half hours, everyone in the room—even the committee's stenographer—rose in an unprecedented standing ovation. The sense seemed to be, journalist Peter Jenkins wrote, that "[i]f anyone is entitled to call off the Cold War, it is George Kennan, the man who invented the Western strategy for winning it."[64]

On May 13 President Bush went to Texas A&M University to announce the results of his policy review. He began by praising the "wise men" who "crafted the strategy of containment," among them Marshall, Acheson, and Kennan. Because they had shown the way, the United States could now move "beyond containment" toward the Soviet Union's full integration into the community of nations. One source for the phrase, White House staffers revealed to columnist William Safire in "passionate anonymity," was the National Security Council's young Soviet specialist, Condoleezza Rice—the future secretary of state had recently met Kennan at a conference of Soviet and American Cold War historians. The slogan would serve as Mount Kilimanjaro, another Bush adviser explained, "something you can see in the distance as a goal."[65]

While in Kristiansand at the end of June, Kennan got the word that the president wished to confer upon him, in Washington the following week, the Medal of Freedom. "I am somewhat bewildered by this development," he wrote in his diary. Bush had indeed spoken favorably of him, as had others in recent months. But why this gesture on behalf of someone "whose views on a number of important subjects are known to be so little in accord with those that he represents?" Perhaps it was a consolation prize, "given in recognition not of my success but of my failure." Without the failure, "it would never have been accorded."[66]

The ceremony took place at the White House on July 6. The other honorees were retired Senator Margaret Chase Smith of Maine, an early critic of Joe McCarthy; General James Doolittle, aviation pioneer and war hero; former Secretary of the Treasury C. Douglas Dillon; and the late television comedienne Lucille Ball, for whose reruns CBS had bumped Kennan's 1966 congressional testimony on the Vietnam War. Once again Bush spoke not of failure but of "the successful strategy of containment which George Kennan did so much to develop." Responses were not expected, but Kennan could not help composing one silently, "[t]he usual disclaimers of merit seem[ing] no less invidious, in their obvious hypocrisy, than the more blatant evidences of self-satisfaction." It followed the example of Adlai Stevenson, who after hearing a comparably lengthy list of his many virtues, had assumed a noble pose and announced: "Right on target."[67]

By the time Kennan got his medal, the Hungarians had given Imre Nagy, the reluctant and subsequently executed leader of the 1956 rebellion, a belated state funeral; meanwhile they were tearing down the barbed wire along the Austrian border that had been their stretch of the Iron Curtain. In Poland, restrictions on Solidarity had been lifted, and its candidates had swept the first free postwar parliamentary elections. In the Soviet Union, Gorbachev had allowed contested candidacies for the Congress of People's Deputies and then television coverage of unconstrained debates within it. Antiauthoritarian protests had even reached Beijing, where the Chinese government, at Tiananmen Square on the night of June 3–4, forcibly suppressed them. But what struck Kennan, after returning to Kristiansand, was not "how much I read of the news from the outside world but how little of it. . . . I see nothing hopeful in any of it."

That was because none of these developments, in his view, diminished the nuclear danger—instability in Eastern Europe and the Soviet Union might even be increasing it. There was nothing more Kennan could do about this: "My own efforts to save civilization should be considered as substantially completed." He had another less cosmic grievance against all of this current history, which was that it kept him from doing earlier history. His second volume on the Franco-Russian alliance had appeared in 1984, but had only reached 1894. He would need to finish a third if he was going to connect his years of research to the outbreak of World War I, and at his age there could not be much more time left. It was a "publish before perishing" obligation, compounded by the fact that despite being "retired" from the Institute for Advanced Study for the past fifteen years, he still had an office there and was expected to make good use of it. But he should try to follow the news, "if only in order not to become entirely a bore to one's children."[68]

Kennan was in Princeton on November 9, 1989, the day the Berlin Wall came down. He had cleared his calendar that week for the writing of history, and "[p]recariously, almost desperately, I continued the struggle." Elizabeth Stenard, his current secretary, heroically fended off phone calls, but it was clear from their number and from the distinction of some of the callers that the battle was lost: there would be no third volume. "Put the books away," Kennan told himself. "Reconcile yourself to the inevitable. . . . [Y]ou are never again, in the short remainder of your life, to be permitted to do anything significant." So he dashed off a warning for *The Washington Post* that it was far too soon to be considering German reunification, and a few evenings later went for a long lonely walk.

He saw it as a metaphor for his future: he would become a mobile movie camera, recording impressions on this or that, for whoever wanted them. There would still be choices to make, but only among insignificances. He hoped biographers would see him "as one who, having indeed had the aptitude for it, had tried valiantly to live as a scholar, only to be prevented in the end from doing so." Now, though, he should get home to watch *MacNeil/Lehrer*, "for one has to keep up, you know."[69]

IX.

It was good that he did, because Kennan joined several other former ambassadors in the Oval Office two days later to brief the president, Vice President Dan Quayle, and National Security Adviser Brent Scowcroft on the implications of what had happened. Kennan had come to like Bush but regarded him as "not independently thoughtful." He did better adjusting to the views of others "in whom he sensed political influence and authority." Kennan had no sense that he fell into that category: nothing he had said or written, he believed, had made any impression on the president's mind. On his own mind, Kennan acknowledged sheepishly early in December, was—tennis. He had "grandly wasted" a weekend watching Becker, Edberg, and McEnroe play, "while the Communist domination of Eastern and parts of Central Europe was going up in flames."

He could fairly say that he had seen it coming: "I was trying to tell the government, as early as the late 1940s and early 1950s, that Russian Communism as an ideology had entirely lost its hold on the Soviet people." Years before Gorbachev, he had been arguing "that the structure of Soviet authority in Eastern Europe was seriously undermined, and would, if challenged, prove unable to stand up against any pressure." But he could not have foreseen when the collapse would come, and now it was happening too quickly. None of the "excited peoples" being liberated had yet learned, as the Finns had long ago, that "the only safe way to establish their true independence is to show a decent respect for Soviet security interests." If they failed to do that, they would destroy Gorbachev, who had given them their freedom.[70]

Kennan saw him briefly in another receiving line, this time at a White House state dinner, on May 31, 1990. Standing next to the president, the Soviet leader was again gracious, praising a recent Kennan statement with such warmth that he, overwhelmed, "failed to notice Mesdames Bush and Gorbachev, . . . and had to be yanked back by Annelise to greet them." Apart from his own faux pas, Kennan thought the event well managed, but he could not help worrying about the issues Bush and Gorbachev would have to discuss the next day.[71]

The most important was German reunification. Kennan had opposed it in 1945, but by 1949 had come to favor it, on the grounds that the Germans would not indefinitely accept the division of their country. Because the Soviet Union would never agree to the inclusion of a single Germany within NATO, however, the price of reunification would have to be neutralization. Those had been the premises of Program A, which Kennan had proposed while running the Policy Planning Staff, and he had controversially made them public in the Reith lectures. Now, though, President Bush and West German Chancellor Helmut Kohl were insisting that the unified German state—unavoidable now without the Berlin Wall—remain within NATO. With the Warsaw Pact crumbling and his own government facing secession threats from its non-Russian nationalities, Gorbachev no choice but to agree.[72]

The two Germanies became one on October 3, 1990, and the Kennans were in Berlin to witness the event: "We joined the tens of thousands of people shuffling along in two great streams, in opposite directions, on Unter den Linden." George took no pleasure in what he saw, not just because his aging legs made it difficult to keep up. For German reunification had come about, not from anyone's planning, but as a consequence of the spontaneous actions of thousands of young East Germans, motivated "by the hope of getting better jobs, making more money, and bathing in the fleshpots of the West." Of course everyone cheered, but "was this, over the long term, what we really wanted?"[73]

TWENTY-FIVE

Last Things: 1991–2005

HAVING ENCOUNTERED IT AT BIRTH, GEORGE KENNAN HAD MORE time than most people do to think about death. As he got older, the occasions—often dreams—became more frequent. One of these, in 1979, had him laid out in a hilltop temple, surrounded by mourners who believed him to be dying. Feeling fine, he was tempted to get up and walk away, but that would have disappointed his admirers. So he reconciled himself to his fate, except for one complication: "I needed to piddle." A pause in the proceedings allowed him to perform this act without anyone noticing, after which he returned to his bier, surrounded now by scrolls containing hundreds of written tributes. How would he ever respond to them all? Why, with Connie Goodman's help, of course, and so he cheerfully entered the afterlife, assured that the present would continue to provide secretarial assistance.[1]

He had long known, or thought he knew, the day on which he would die. It would be May 9, 1983, at which point he would have lived precisely seventy-nine years, two months, and twenty-three days. That was how old the first George Kennan had been when he died in 1924. Had both not been born on February 16, in 1845 and 1904? Had their lives not corresponded in too many ways for coincidence to explain? The fateful day, however, passed uneventfully: Kennan spent it in his Institute office preparing a speech, receiving visitors, and reading a set of conference papers by historians Michael Howard ("excellent"), Adam Ulam ("good in many ways"), and John Gaddis (no comment). That evening, at home with his family, there was "much animation"—although not, presumably, because he had alerted them to the significance of the day.[2]

Having survived it, he could see that what lay ahead was a kind of petrification: Kennan the public intellectual would become Kennan the public monument.

The process would resemble death, because while people on pedestals tend to be respected, even venerated, they're also beyond being listened to, or argued with—or invited to share lunch. He was eating alone regularly now, he noticed, in the Institute for Advanced Study cafeteria. Younger colleagues vigorously debated this or that at surrounding tables, but the great man was left to himself. None was any more inclined to intrude upon his privacy than Kennan had been upon Einstein's, decades earlier: "I am caught, like a fly in the spider web, in the golden filigrees of my wretched image; and there is no use flapping the wings too violently—it will not help."[3]

In Washington one evening a few months after the day his death did not occur, Kennan again dined alone and walked back to DACOR House, the F Street lodging for retired diplomats, accompanied only by a breeze, which swept indifferently over the White House and "its insignificant occupant." He had spent the day "weak, shaky, unstrung, devoid of composure, the voice high, hoarse, and cracking." Never had he played his part less well. "I despise the George Kennan that appears before other people—despise him not for being what he is, but for not appearing to be what he ought to appear to be. They should hire an actor in my place."[4]

They could not for his eightieth birthday party, held in Princeton a day late, on February 17, 1984. Nitze's was the most memorable toast: Kennan had long been for him "a teacher and an example," although "George has, no doubt, often doubted the aptness of his pupil." Kennan graciously declined the opportunity to agree. Dick Ullman was not alone, among those present, in wondering how two men who had disagreed about so much over so many years could retain such respect for one another: "This was really the Establishment rallying around, and I've never seen anything like it."[5]

As on his seventieth birthday, Kennan read a poem—not his own, this time, but his translation of one by Hermann Hesse. It portrayed a man who had returned from a long trip, found a stack of mail from admirers waiting, and burned the lot in the fireplace. Noting furrowed brows, Kennan explained that only a saint or a mystic could, from within, keep the flame of life fluttering. For anyone else, this required "the respect, affection, support, forbearance, and even forgiveness of those around him." Whose letters, unanswered, had just gone up in smoke. The poem meant something to him, Kennan wrote, a bit defensively, in his diary. "Whether to anyone else, I could not tell."[6]

Something else had happened on his and the first George Kennan's real birthday, though, that meant much more. For on February 16, 1984, the second Kennan's youngest daughter, Wendy, now the wife of a Swiss businessman, Claude Pfaeffli, gave birth to a son. "There was no way," his uncle Christopher recalled, "that that kid was not going to be named George Kennan Pfaeffli." And so, three weeks later in Geneva, George Frost Kennan held his own and his namesake's namesake in his arms and gave him a silent blessing, "persuaded, almost superstitiously, that his preoccupations will some day have some strange connection with my own."[7]

I.

Kennan's preoccupation now was to find a life within the limits imposed by an aging body and an enhanced reputation. It would have to be "unrelated to this epoch" and yet, "somehow or other, worthwhile." He would become a disembodied spirit, like the one haunting the gloomy great rooms of Spaso House in 1952. But he was thinking these thoughts in 1983, in Paris, in the spring. He was entering the Métro, and a train was approaching. He quickened his steps. In this new life of being old, though, why hurry? Then, distracted by an alluring female figure,

> I questioned myself again: You . . . profess to be seeing these women as though you were thousands of miles off in space; what possible difference could it have for you whether or not they are attractive? But then I thought to myself: even if a spirit is disembodied, it may still have yearnings.

It could at least sigh, as the aged Oliver Wendell Holmes, Jr., had once done: "Ah, to be seventy again!"[8]

He could offer his country little, Kennan believed, because those who ran it would not listen. He was living in a country—indeed a civilization—that was well on its way to catastrophe. His own and Annelise's physical decline lay ahead, as did anguish for their children, all of whom had faced, or were likely to face, disappointments greater than anything their parents had experienced. At the same time, his name evoked respect among thousands of people. He must not let his pessimism drive them to despair. He disliked the term "role model," but he had become one. So what to do?

Perhaps attempt to look "like what people believe me to be—to encourage them in the illusion that there really is such a person—and, by doing this, to try to add, just a little bit, to their hope and strength and confidence in life." Results were irrelevant, for these might be "burned in the rubble of a nuclear war." The

important thing was to hold up his end of his reputation, whatever the consequences or the costs: "Duty, then, as a dedication—as a means of redemption in
the final years—yes. But no hope; no fear; and, to the extent [that] the line is
firmly and consistently pursued, no apologies."[9]

That was, of course, easier to write than to accomplish. Demands on his time
were as great as ever: "Come here; come there; speak here; write these; attend
this conference; receive this visitor." Under no circumstances sit quietly, or read a
book, or "try to learn something." Kennan's body, however, was approaching the
point at which reading was one of the few things it would permit. "I feel like hell,"
he complained, in one of hundreds of such diary entries. "How hard it is to pace
one's self at this age. One is too old to try to win, too young to give up."[10]

His illnesses had long since earned him the right to hypochondria: appendicitis
and scarlet fever in his youth, amoebic dysentery followed by several hospital-
strength bouts with ulcers as a young man, a kidney stone that accompanied him
through much of his later life, periodic herpes zoster outbreaks, prostate difficulties, jaundice, arthritis, and beginning in his mid-eighties, debilitating heart
irregularities. Treatments often provoked new problems. Drug reactions were frequent; lithotripsy broke up the kidney stone but at the cost of uremic poisoning
in 1984, and by 1992 Kennan's heart problems had become serious enough to
require a pacemaker. His relationship with it was not amicable: "Mine is a body, I
suspect, that *should* be dead; but the pacemaker won't allow it to be."[11]

He was "a tough old bird," though, Annelise rightly observed. It upset George
when, at seventy-eight, protesting knees forced him to improvise a walking stick
at the farm. He was still, in his eighties, riding a one-speed bicycle around Princeton, pushing it up hills when he came to them. He was cutting his own firewood
in the Institute's forest, hauling it to the Hodge Road house, and stashing it in a
woodshed he had recently built. He remained agile on and around his Norwegian
sailboat, and he took literally Goethe's admonition that, when beset by old age,
one should "take a spade and dig." He tested poet, proposition, and pacemaker
one day in Kristiansand by trying, at eighty-eight, to uproot yet another dead tree.
For the first time in many such excavations, the tree won: "this, I clearly understand, is the beginning of my real and final old age."[12]

Kennan hated how he now looked. He hardly recognized "this strange, tall,
scrawny-necked apparition of an old man, clutching the marble of the lectern,
swaying back and forth like a bush in the wind, bending down occasionally to
peer through his glasses at the manuscript below," he wrote, after seeing himself on
television in 1982. He must never again appear before any group larger than could

"grace a drawing-room." But he continued to do so because duty demanded it. And in the eyes of others—as in his 1989 triumph before the Senate Foreign Relations Committee—he conveyed an antique gravity almost extinct in the modern age. A new generation had suddenly discovered his existence, Kennan concluded. That accounted for their enthusiasm. There was, after all, "not much competition."[13]

II.

Bill Clinton was as eager to align his administration with Kennan's image—if not his advice—as George H. W. Bush had been. Clinton had first encountered Kennan as a Rhodes scholar at Oxford in 1969, where he attended a talk that turned out to be an attack on shaggy students. Being one at the time, the future president was unimpressed. But in the White House one day in 1994, Clinton asked his deputy secretary of state, Strobe Talbott—his housemate and fellow Oxonian years before—why they didn't have a concept as succinct as "containment." Talbott, who had known Kennan since Oxford and still regularly consulted him, undertook to solicit suggestions from the source.

The opportunity arose at an October dinner in Kennan's honor given by the secretary of state, Warren Christopher. It had been forty-one years, Kennan could not help but recall, since John Foster Dulles had arranged his ignominious departure from the building in which he was now being feted. But when Christopher mentioned that he and Talbott had been trying to package post–Cold War policy in a single phrase, Kennan said they shouldn't. "Containment" had been a misleading oversimplification; strategy could not be made to fit a "bumper sticker." The president laughed when Talbott told him what had happened: "that's why Kennan's a great diplomat and scholar but not a politician."[14]

Clinton had another honor in mind for Kennan, however, which had to do with the fiftieth anniversary of the end of World War II. Would Kennan accompany him to the ceremony at Arlington National Cemetery and then—taking advantage of the fact that the Soviet Union had declared the war over a day later than its allies in 1945—fly with him to Moscow to celebrate the event there? Moved by the invitation, Kennan wanted to accept: "I was, after all, the senior American official present in Moscow on that memorable day." He would welcome returning "as an honored and friendly guest," not as "the dangerous enemy that I was always supposed to be."

Annelise was willing as long as she could go too. George's family thought it a fine idea, as did his doctors, who could find nothing wrong with him "except for the failing heart and arthritic knees." But every morning, when he got up, his body was telling him: "Never, never." He would be a burden to others, while making "a pathetic exhibit of myself." Clinton wanted him, he suspected, as a portable public monument. And he was not quite ready to give up being a public intellectual.[15]

The Clinton administration, since 1993, had been exploring the idea of expanding NATO to include Poland, Hungary, and the Czech Republic, against the wishes of the Russians. Kennan wondered why the alliance should even survive the end of the Cold War, much less grow. He kept his doubts to himself, though, until October 1996, when he heard Talbott make the case for expansion in a talk at Columbia's Harriman Institute. Kennan spoke first at the dinner that followed, denouncing the idea as a "strategic blunder of potentially epic proportions." With one exception, everyone else present agreed with him.

It was a "cold shower," Talbott remembered in his memoir, published six years later. In his diary five days later, Kennan expressed surprise that what he said had made "such a fuss," but he no longer worried "about the opinions of others concerning my conduct." Then in February 1997 he went public. Expanding NATO, he wrote in *The New York Times*, would be "the most fateful error of American policy in the entire post-cold-war era." The op-ed was on Clinton's desk the next morning. "Why isn't Kennan right?" he asked Talbott. "Isn't he a kind of guru of yours going back to when we were at Oxford?" He was, Talbott acknowledged, but Kennan had opposed NATO since its creation. The Russians would go along with expansion, whatever he thought. "Just checking, Strobe," Clinton chuckled. "Just checking."[16]

For Kennan, the episode evoked Shakespeare's dying John of Gaunt: "Where words are scarce, they are seldom spent in vain, / For they breathe truth that breathe their words in pain. . . . Though Richard my life's counsel would not hear, / My death's sad tale may yet undeaf his ear." Not very likely, though, Kennan had to admit. His words would have no more effect on Clinton and his advisers than had Gaunt's on "the foolish Richard II."[17]

III.

He was, Kennan had written a few years earlier, "the most elaborately-honored non-political and non-governmental person in the country, yet totally without influence where it counts."[18] What else could a disembodied spirit approaching his tenth decade expect, though, even if yearnings for lost causes did persist? Kennan had already disengaged from the writing of history—at least diplomatic history— so detachment from the making of history did not really surprise him, however much it frustrated him. Now, though, he faced a new problem, which was that history was attaching itself to him: he had lived long enough to become its subject. Adjusting to that process was not easy.

He accelerated it, without foreseeing the consequences, by opening his papers early. Most donors prohibit access while they are alive, but as Kennan finished each volume of his memoirs, he transferred the materials he had used to Princeton University, in the hope that "mature" scholars might also find them useful. He failed to review the files carefully, though; there was confusion about which portions were to be opened when; and determining "maturity" proved to be impractical. So rather than close the collection altogether, Kennan resigned himself to living uncomfortably alongside it—the Seeley G. Mudd Manuscript Library was only about a mile from his house—without control over who would go through his papers, what they would find, or how they might employ it. All he did was to forbid photocopying, by then a standard archival procedure. Kennan researchers took notes laboriously in longhand or on portable typewriters, therefore, while envying those working nearby on the duplicatable dead.[19]

When the dissertations, articles, and eventually books began to appear, their authors tended to be young. They were the most in need of fresh topics, and they had the stamina to survive the photocopying ban. Several, however, were also of the "student left" generation Kennan had so vociferously condemned. They generally respected, even admired him: he had, after all, opposed the Vietnam War. But their scholarship reflected revisionist historiography of the origins of the Cold War, of which Kennan strongly disapproved. Nor did they hesitate to highlight documents from his papers that he now found embarrassing. Some, like his 1938 "Prerequisites" essay, he had simply forgotten. Others he had deliberately passed over in his memoirs. Still others succumbed to political correctness: words unexceptional when written could shock when published half a century later.

Kennan had always lived alongside his own history: self-scrutiny came naturally, even compulsively, to him. Scrutiny by others, however—especially by the youth of the 1960s—was something else again. That became evident in 1976 when C. Ben Wright, a recent University of Wisconsin Ph.D., pointed out in a *Slavic Review* article that Kennan's original concept of "containment" had incorporated more of a military component than he had acknowledged in his memoirs.

Wright's dissertation had been the first serious biography of Kennan, based not just on his papers but on careful interviews with contemporaries, even his sister Jeanette. Now, though, Kennan was furious. "I stand, as I see, exposed," he wrote in a rejoinder the journal published. "Mr. Wright has stripped me of my own pretenses and revealed me as the disguised militarist he considers me to be." The attack was so devastating that Wright abandoned history altogether, and Kennan gained the reputation of devouring young scholars at dinner.[20]

It was not a sustainable situation. Kennan couldn't respond in print to every objectionable thing historians might write. But neither could he guide each one individually through his archives, providing context and commentary along the way: there were too many, and they would have insisted, entirely properly, on reaching their own conclusions. So Kennan's solution, in the end, was to authorize a biographer whose biography he would never read.

He had mostly approved of my *Strategies of Containment*, an analytical study based partly on the Kennan papers that appeared (at the cost of a worn-out portable typewriter) late in 1981. I wanted to continue working on Kennan but had no desire to repeat Wright's experience. Might there be the possibility, I gingerly asked Kennan, of a full biography, prepared with his cooperation and with access to all of his papers (including photocopying privileges), on the understanding that it would not appear for another ten to fifteen years? Kennan, seventy-eight at the time, replied—wholly implausibly—that he had never thought about a biography but would now do so. Delicate negotiations followed, in which neither he nor I used the term "posthumous," even though we both had it in mind. For me, the advantage would be access with independence. For Kennan, it was that designating one biographer would deter others. How did he know that I would treat him fairly? He didn't. We hardly knew each other. But Kennan did believe strongly in placing faith above reason.[21]

Despite the arrangement, the other biographers did not back off. Kennan at first found this irritating. "I ought really to be dead," he grumbled about a particularly persistent one, "it would all then be much easier." He could not resist reading what they wrote, though, and some of it he even liked. Walter Isaacson and Evan Thomas's *The Wise Men* (1986), a collective biography of himself, Acheson, Bohlen, Harriman, Lovett, and McCloy, was "a caricature gleaned from hasty oral interviews" but "not devoid of a certain amount of truth." Although relentlessly critical, Anders Stephanson's *Kennan and the Art of American Foreign Policy* (1989) was "truly a great work," addressed "to a subject unworthy of so impressive an effort." Wilson D. Miscamble's careful study of the Policy Planning Staff years, *George F. Kennan and the Making of American Foreign Policy, 1947–1950* (1992), left its subject sobered "by the number and extent of my failures"; nonetheless "I would rate it as the best thing that has been written about me in published book form."[22]

He did, however, despise inaccuracy. A prominent offender was Nitze, whose brief essay on Kennan in his 1993 book, *Tension Between Opposites*, contained so many errors "that I suspect Paul, although we view each other as friends, really knows very little about me." Even worse were attempts to impose the present upon the past. He was appalled to find himself criticized for publishing diary entries from the late 1930s and early 1940s that had not anticipated the Holocaust. Efforts to link his CIA involvement with the lenient treatment of German war criminals provoked lengthy, if unpublished, rebuttals: "I never knew I had such enemies." And when, in 1997, the *Journal of American History* ran an article entitled "'Unceasing Pressure for Penetration': Gender, Pathology, and Emotion in George Kennan's Formation of the Cold War," its ninety-three-year-old target wondered why previous scholarship had been so slow to discover his "true sexual and 'binary' nature," all of it permeated, whether he knew it or not, "with concealed desires to violate, to rape, and thus to dominate. Of such terrible motives the purer and more innocent spirit of [the author] was happily unbesmirched."[23]

IV.

The youngest of the Kennan scholars impressed him most. Barton Gellman was a twenty-two-year-old Rhodes scholar in 1983 when Kennan got around to reading his Princeton senior thesis, completed the previous year under Dick Ullman's supervision. *Contending with Kennan: Toward a Philosophy of American Power* was an attempt, Gellman explained in the book the thesis quickly became, to "cut and paste" Kennan into coherence, a project for which "the man himself has never had any taste." Yet shouldn't a person given to displaying his thinking in "bits and pieces" provide a more complete picture?[24]

Kennan had been asking himself the same question. He had always distrusted philosophical systems: they were too gray, he believed, to reflect the colors of life, much less to guide one through their complexities. But he feared having his ideas whisked into oblivion, "like a paper-handkerchief carried away by the wind from the deck of an ocean-liner." His diaries, usually written late at night, tended to

bury what was worth saving beneath long stretches of "sleep-dulled humdrum."
Unwilling to rely on some future editor's excavations, he felt the need "to clarify, to organize, and to state my general philosophy, before it becomes too late to
do so."[25]

Gellman showed him that it could be done, while convincing Kennan that
he could do it better. "I don't in the least mind the critical reflections," he wrote
the astonished young man. "I am grateful to you for having put forward such a
brilliant effort to make sense out of my scattered and so often cryptic utterances,
and congratulate you most heartily on the success of that formidable effort." But
Gellman had "cheerfully mingled" things said decades apart, Kennan admonished me, as though circumstances had not changed. He would not respond
directly, but he would try "to set forth, more systematically than I have done
in the past, my views, as of this stage of my life, on some of the questions he
raised."[26]

Around the Cragged Hill: A Personal and Political Philosophy appeared in 1993,
a rare example of a book inspired by a critic a fourth its author's age. The title
came from a passage in John Donne's third *Satyre*, a Kennan favorite:

> *On a huge hill,*
> *Cragged, and steep, Truth stands, and hee that will*
> *Reach her, about must, and about must goe;*
> *And what the hills suddenness resists, winne so;*
> *Yet strive so, that before age, deaths twilight,*
> *Thy Soule rest, for none can work in that night.*

As political philosophy, the book contained little Kennan had not said elsewhere.
There were predictable condemnations of advertising, automobiles, Congress,
consumerism, domestic politics, environmental degradation, juvenile delinquency, nuclear weapons, pornography, television, and even demands for unconditional surrender in World War II. Kennan proposed yet another revival of the
Policy Planning Staff, this time as a "Council of State," a presidentially appointed
body of senior notables like himself who, freed from the lures of personal gain or
political ambition, would determine long-term national interests. If philosophy at
all, these portions of *Cragged Hill* were a Platonic contemplation of ideal forms,
not an Aristotelian adaptation to practicality.[27]

But as personal philosophy, the book was something new: it was Kennan's
first full public profession of private faith. It began, unexpectedly, with sex, a

characteristic shared with the "lowest and least attractive" of mammals and rep-
tiles. In addition to progeny, sex produced great happiness, great art, and great
trouble, for "people's physical needs change even when their deeper affections do
not." The results included "jealousies, suspicions, conflicting loyalties, wounded
pride, and tragic unhappiness." That these *were* trouble, however, reflected a
higher aspect of human nature, which was the soul, the capacity "to perceive and
to hold in mind the distinctions between right and wrong." How had only one
species developed this?

Not by way of Original Sin, Kennan was sure: sex had preceded people, and
some Primary Cause—neither benevolent nor malevolent but indifferent—had
preceded both. Where, then, did the soul come from? Of that, Kennan was unsure,
but of the soul's existence, indeed its immortality, he had no doubt. For bodily
needs alone could not explain love or self-sacrifice. Those qualities constituted,
then, another Deity, neither omnipotent nor omniscient but sympathetic, from
whence came the strength, in the face of adversity, to endure, if not to prevail.

Each person's Deity was his own, but there were compelling examples to emu-
late. By far the greatest, for Kennan, was Christ, but not as the Son of a benevolent
God: there was too much evil in the world for such a Father to exist. Kennan
even suspected—he refrained from saying so in the book—that it was Christ who
conceived God, rather than the other way around. If so, it didn't matter: Kennan's
faith in Christ was unshaken.

Organized religion reinforced it but was not its source. Faith lay in an inner
voice that promised help, but only to the extent that one helped one's self. For
Kennan, that was Christ, but it was also the voices of the great poets, playwrights,
and novelists, who mingled their brilliance with responsibility for others. It was
the voices of dead parents and departed friends, which Kennan still sometimes
heard in his dreams. But it was also the voice of his own conscience, as he walked
the tightrope between selfishness and selflessness, beset by "little demons" at every
step of the way. One could not simply brush them away. One could, however, deny
them the satisfaction of having their existence acknowledged.

Salvation lay in forgiveness, a theme Kennan developed more clearly in his
diary than in his book. Why, other Christians might ask, could he not more easily
accept his inadequacies? "Your God is supposed, by virtue of Christ's intercession,
to be a forgiving God. Confess your sins and rely on His forgiveness."

My answer to that would be: "Yes, I can, no doubt, rely on his forgiveness. But that
does not mean that I should light-heartedly forgive myself. Is it not possible that He

will forgive me only precisely in the measure that I *decline* to forgive myself in those things I find unworthy of my own forgiveness?"

And so, with John Donne, Kennan went about, and around, and up and down his hill, in an uneasy soul's acknowledgment that it soon must rest, "for none can work in that night."[28]

V.

He dreamed again about death one night in 1995, this time horribly. His dread, though, came not from what afflicted or awaited him but from a vision of Annelise bidding him farewell outside a large dark Victorian house, entering it, putting on a black gown, and disappearing behind a closing door. She was a widow, she would be alone, and "I could not stand it." Should he not rush up, ring the doorbell, and ask for reconsideration: "Why don't we disregard all the circumstances of our lives that have led to this *dénouement* and start all over again?" But this, he knew, was not possible, and even if it had been, it might have frightened her more than the loneliness she now faced. So he had no choice but to wake up, "still shattered by what had happened, and desperate."[29]

To be sure, not all deaths were devastating. What everyone understood to be the last reunion of George and his siblings—Frances, Constance, Jeanette, and Kent—had taken place at the farm on a brilliant fall day in 1982. Frances, the oldest, thought it extraordinary that all were alive, even ambulatory: "Nobody had to be wheeled in!" But this final reunion was their first in six decades. They had long since ceased relying on each other to fend off loneliness, and so when they did occur in 1984, 1991, 1994, and 2003, respectively—these deaths did not drive George, the last to survive, into the despair he feared Annelise would face when he was gone.[30]

She did all she could to keep him going. After a protracted visit from a tedious friend, George made a point of acknowledging, in his diary, "the sweetness of my wife and of the loyalty with which she, still enjoying a relative robustness, looked after both of us tottering, shambling and tiresome old men." She, in turn, made her own point by acknowledging his infirmities as little as possible, a habit that at times exasperated him but that balanced the fretting with which he filled his diary:

July 1983: I stand now, presumably, within a year or two of my death.

May 1985: Would that . . . the young could cast us out and be done with us, as the animals do.

January 1988: I had [hoped] that the end of my life would precede the final filling up of the [tax] ledger, so that I would not have to buy another.

April 1994: I feel myself moving closer to the abyss; but everyone says: "Oh, you look so well."

April 1996: If I die in Norway? . . . What to do with the damned body?

He practiced death there once, when Annelise wasn't looking: "I simply collapsed on the stony path near the boathouse, lay on my back staring at the oak leaves silhouetted against a cloudy Norwegian sky, and thought to myself: this would not be a bad time and place to die. But Fate (which, as Donne wrote, God fashioned 'but doth not controul') decided otherwise."[31]

So did George's hyperactivity, which countered his hypochondria. His mostly handwritten diaries—carefully recording each ailment and its attendant indignities—were as voluminous and legible as ever. He published a new book of "reflections" in 1996, chiefly his lectures and articles since 1982. He was driving himself and Annelise over much of New England researching a long-planned history of the Kennan family: even she thought this to be too much. He was compulsively reading, or rereading, and taking notes: on Shakespeare, whose plays suggested experiences with women—some presumably painful—that had left him "with high respect" for them; on Saint Augustine, whose *Confessions* had taken up far too much of God's time; on Macaulay, who had made English "the most felicitous" of all languages for expressing "the higher ranges of thought and feeling"; on Saint Paul, whom Kennan found to be, disconcertingly, a Dostoyevskian "extremist." And he had wisely come to relish the great naval history novels of Patrick O'Brian.[32]

Major birthdays, now major events, also encouraged survival: it would have been irresponsible to die before the festivities had taken place. The Council on Foreign Relations celebration of his ninetieth in New York in February 1994 left Kennan, he claimed, "not only overwhelmed but unable to think of any even appropriately adequate response." In fact he spoke vigorously, regretting how much had been made of a certain talk on "containment" given there in 1947, cautioning against any comparable oversimplification of post–Cold War foreign policy. Shortly after returning to Princeton, he had a minor stroke and spent a few days in the hospital, but within a week of his release was rigging a sump pump in the basement and driving himself, alone, to the office.[33]

The Kennans were still traveling frequently, if to familiar destinations: Kristiansand for part of the summer, but also now regularly the island community of North Haven, Maine; Hermann Hatzfeldt's castle at Crottorf for Pour le Mérite meetings in the fall; Captiva Island in Florida for winter visits with the naturalists Bill and Laura Riley—George left behind, on one such occasion, a set of poems, addressed in stately formality to the resident birds. His research trips were over by the late 1990s, but their results appeared in his last book, *An American Family: The Kennans; The First Three Generations*, published when he was ninety-six. He had made his ancestors, one reviewer observed, into what he wanted them to be; but at that age, perhaps he had earned that right.[34]

The pace could not continue. "What a doctor!" George wrote with relief, when his primary physician, Dr. Fong Wei, ordered him in the spring of 1998 to stay at home for a week, not answer the phone, and watch whatever animals visited the backyard. George "wasted the time most grandly" and was grateful for having been told to do so. But he was having trouble walking by the time his book came out in 2000, and Annelise, now ninety herself, was becoming frailer. Worst of all, his ancient Royal typewriter broke down one day that fall, "initiating a very similar breakdown in him who does the writing." He continued the diary entry in a quavering hand, inscribing "the end is nearing." It almost came out "the near is ending." It made little difference: "the one, come to think of it, was no less true than the other."[35]

The summer of 2001 was the last George was able to spend in Norway. Reduced almost to immobility, he found a typewriter there that worked and so resumed his diary as his extended family came and went. "[C]rippledom," however, did not lead "to productive brilliance of the mind," for his thoughts would evaporate while waiting for his limbs to catch up. One of his final afternoons in Kristiansand was spent watching anxiously from the lawn as his young namesake, now seventeen, expertly windsurfed himself across the great sound and safely back. In Princeton that fall, George at last closed the Institute for Advanced Study office that Oppenheimer had given him half a century earlier. The Kennans' seventieth wedding anniversary fell, unhappily, on September 11, 2001—happily, though, Christopher, Joan, and her husband Kevin Delany had arranged a congratulatory dinner with a few Princeton friends the previous weekend. George and Annelise spent the terrible day quietly at home.[36]

I found him, a few months later, stretched out on a couch in his living room, his legs covered in a blanket, his hearing aids malfunctioning, his profile still strong from the side, but emaciated head-on. His mind, though, was undiminished: the conversation was a healthy mix of convictions firmly held and curiosity keenly expressed. Why did no one read Toynbee anymore? Because his books dealt with forces, not people: "You could spend your life reading Toynbee, but what would you have at the end of it?" Kennan did not find it necessary to say, as on several previous occasions, that his own life soon would be ending. He was beyond the need for denial, or reassurance.[37]

VI.

The Kennans had live-in help now in the Hodge Road house. A Portuguese couple, Tony and Ana Mano, cooked and gradually took over other duties as well: Tony even began bringing ocean water from the New Jersey shore to bathe George's arthritic knees. Betsy Barrett, who lived in the garage apartment, started as a housekeeper, became George's secretary, and wound up as his nurse. Days became indistinguishable, apart from a brief stay in a Washington "assisted living" facility in the fall of 2002, while the Manos were away. The word got out, reporters got in touch, and Kennan granted his last interviews, condemning President George W. Bush's plans to invade Iraq as well as the Democrats' timidity in not opposing him more vigorously.[38]

By the summer of 2003 Kennan could still read his correspondence but no longer reply: friends received messages, through Barrett, assuring them that silence did not mean negligence, or lack of regard. Meanwhile, preparations were under way for the grandest birthday of them all, George's hundredth. Princeton University's Firestone Library opened an exhibit on his life that fall, the centerpiece of which was every page of the "long telegram" displayed in a correspondingly long case. It was diplomacy's Bayeux Tapestry.

There were three celebrations of the real birthday, in February 2004. One was for family on February 16, when George eased his way downstairs for dinner, blew out an unrecorded number of candles on his cake, and wound up making three speeches. A second, on the eighteenth, was at the Institute for Advanced Study, which George's family, helpers, and Dr. Wei conspired to have him attend: it had been "a plot," he muttered. The third was a full-scale "George F. Kennan Centennial Conference" at the university, with the major address given by the secretary of state, Colin Powell. He did so with such respect, George's grandson Brandon Griggs commented on the way out, that one would never have guessed his grandfather's detestation of the administration in which Powell served. This enormous event was too much for Kennan to attend, so the secretary of state came to see him afterward, in his own bedroom. Tony Mano had ordered him to stay alive for the great day, George commented, and that had gotten him through it.[39]

He lived for another thirteen months, but with little life left. He could read newspapers and receive visitors, but his mind was fading. So was Annelise, whose decline seemed synchronous with his own. One of the last outsiders to see them together was George's old friend the historian John Lukacs: "His head, resting on a pillow, now had a kind of skeletal beauty; he could speak only a little, forcing out a few words with increasing difficulty; near the foot of the bed she sat huddled in a wheelchair at a table, uttering a few sensible words, not many." They still shared that bed, and one day in March 2005 Betsy Barrett heard George turn to Annelise and ask: "Are you content?" She didn't hear or perhaps didn't understand, but he said clearly: "I am content."[40]

VII.

George F. Kennan died peacefully of old age—he was 101—in his own bed, surrounded by his family, on the evening of March 17, 2005. Annelise followed, under similar circumstances, on August 7, 2008. His memorial service was held, a few weeks after his death, in the National Cathedral in Washington. Hers took place two days after she died, in Princeton's Trinity Episcopal Church. Both were appropriate, but funerals only faintly suggest lives. His inspired countless obituaries; hers as she would have thought fitting—very few. One of his best he composed himself when I asked him to do so, with no warning, one day in 1995:

> Giving full recognition to the fact that no one fully understands himself, that no one can conceivably be fully objective about himself, I would like to tell you—I'm now quite old, most of my life lies behind me—how I view myself, and my usefulness, or lack of it, in this world. I realize the delicacy of my nervous structure. I don't think I

would have been well qualified for a very high office, especially not a political one. I see, in other words, certain of my weaknesses.

Somebody once said to me: "George, you are by nature really a teacher." I think that there's a lot to that. I have certain [other] things going for me. First of all, that I am independent, and have always kept my independence. I've always revolted against trying to say things as a member of a collective group, simply because it's what the others said. I don't belong to any organization where I feel that I have to say things they decide they want said. That is a relatively rare quality for anybody who writes a lot and speaks a lot.

I think I have certain insights, from time to time. They are not organized. I've never tried to put them in the strait-jacket of an intellectual discipline of any sort. But they could have been more useful to people than they have been. How much that's my fault and how much theirs I don't know. I leave that alone.

And finally, I credit myself with having been honest all my life. This is a very simple virtue, but outside of that I see all my faults. How much it's going to mean, when looked back on, I have no idea. I hope that I'm right about these qualities. They exist on the surface of a great many which are no better than anybody else's, and sometimes worse.[41]

Greatness

LORD MOUNTBATTEN'S BIOGRAPHER, PHILIP ZIEGLER, BECAME SO enraged with his subject while writing his life that he found it necessary to place a sign on his desk: "Remember, in spite of everything, he was a great man."[2] I never felt the need to do that while preparing Kennan's biography, but the experience did convince me that "greatness" takes multiple forms. There may be as many definitions as there are subjects for biography: my own would be that greatness is *one* of the things that distinguishes immortality from mortality. It was not, for Kennan, the only thing, or even the most important thing. He was a man of deep faith, and when he spoke of immortality, he generally had in mind the kind God provides. Biographers must aim lower but can perhaps suggest qualities that might make a life, for mortals, memorable.

Begin with grand strategy, by which I mean the discipline of achieving desired ends through the most efficient use of available means. Its most memorable practitioners have attained that status by leaving behind examples—whether through their actions or their writing—of how to do this. These transcend time, space, and circumstance. Sun Tzu, Thucydides, Machiavelli, the American Founding Fathers, Metternich, Clausewitz, Lincoln, Bismarck, and Isaiah Berlin remain as relevant to the twenty-first century as to their own time. Students of grand strategy will study them well into the future. Will they study Kennan?

Henry Kissinger, himself a plausible subject of such study, made the case that they should when he credited Kennan with having come "as close to authoring the diplomatic doctrine of his era as any diplomat in our history."[3] Historians, to be sure, debated what that doctrine was, and Kennan more than once disavowed it. With the demise of the Cold War, however, these controversies faded in the light of a more important question: what did "containment" accomplish? More than any other idea, this one appears now to have illuminated the path by which the international system found its way from the trajectory of self-destruction it was on during the first half of the twentieth century to one that had, by the end of the second half, removed the danger of great-power war, revived democracy and capitalism, and thereby enhanced the prospects for liberty beyond what they ever before had been.

This outcome was by no means predetermined. To see why, go back to the moment in February 1946 when Kennan, sick in bed from the rigors of a Moscow winter and irritated as usual at the Department of State, summoned Dorothy Hessman and from his preferred horizontal position dictated a lengthy telegram. The world was not safe then from the scourge of great-power war: how could it have been, when in contrast to the previous world war, it had not even been possible to convene a peace conference? Nor was the world safe from authoritarianism, given the democracies' recent reliance on one such regime to defeat another. Nor was it safe from economic collapse, in the absence of any assurance that a global depression would not return. The world was certainly not safe from abuses of human rights, with one of the most advanced nations in Europe having just resorted to genocide on an unprecedented scale. Nor was it safe from the fear that in a future war no one would be safe. How could it have been, with atomic weapons now available, and with no guarantee that they would remain under one state's exclusive control?

What Kennan opened up, on that bleak day in Moscow, was a way out: a path between the appeasement that had failed to prevent World War II and the alternative of a third world war, the devastation from which would have been unimaginable. Might someone else have proposed the path, had Kennan not done so? Probably, in due course, but it's hard to think of anyone else at the time who could have charted it with greater authority, with such eloquence, or within so grand a strategic a framework.

Only Kennan had the credibility to show, at a time when too many Americans still viewed the Soviet Union as a wartime ally, that for reasons rooted in Russian history and Marxist-Leninist ideology, there could never be a normal peacetime relationship with it: Stalin's regime required external enemies. Only Kennan could have said this so compellingly as to command immediate attention in Washington. And only Kennan foresaw the possibility—Sun Tzu, Machiavelli, and Clausewitz would have approved—that the United States and its allies might in time get the Soviet Union to defeat itself.

Kennan came to this last conclusion through an improbable convergence of ideas. One source was Gibbon, on the Romans' difficulties in attempting to hold, indefinitely and against their will, conquered provinces. Another was the great Russian writers—Tolstoy, Dostoyevsky, Chekhov—who had shown their country's resistance, however subtle, to revolutionary redesign. A third was Kennan's sense that, being human, not even Soviet leaders could withstand repeated frustration; that if confronted with it consistently, they would eventually discover an interest in joining, rather than seeking to overthrow, the existing international order. Finally, Kennan's strategy reflected faith in the United States: if it remained true to its founding principles, it would provide a more attractive example for the rest of the world than the Soviet Union, which might itself not be immune. All that would be required was "a long-term, patient but firm and vigilant containment of Russian expansive tendencies." Anyone could have written that sentence. Only Kennan could have made it believable.

Others determined, to be sure, what "containment" required; hence Kennan's disillusionment with that strategy from the moment he ceased to make those determinations. By the mid-1970s, his dismay had grown to the point of seeing his own country, not the Soviet Union, as the principal threat to international stability; that shortsightedness in turn blinded Kennan to the extent to which Reagan's policies returned to his own. Kennan's ideas turned out to be transferable to an American leader so different from himself that he could never quite bring himself to believe what had happened.

Kennan's strategy, then, was more robust than his own faith in it. "Containment's" goal was not to achieve perfection but to distinguish lesser from greater evils. Its components—even those Kennan did not design—for the most part complemented the whole. It proved to be sustainable because it generally deployed strengths against weaknesses and, when it did not, corrected the error. With the help Kennan had predicted the Kremlin would provide, the world saw something worse, during most of the Cold War, than the wielding of American power. And Kennan's strategy aligned his country's interests, far more successfully than did his counterparts in Moscow, with long-term historical forces. For Kennan understood that in order to look forward you have to look back: that the only way you can know anything at all about the future is to know as much as you can about the past.

This brings up a second, if less striking, qualification for greatness, which is Kennan's career as a historian. He never trained formally for this profession— perhaps that's why he was good at it—but the study of history was at the center of his preparation for diplomacy and strategy in several ways: first, through his

696 GEORGE F. KENNAN

understanding of European and American history, acquired as a Princeton undergraduate; second, through his immersion in the history and culture of Russia as a
young Foreign Service officer; and finally, through his crash reading in the classics
of grand strategy while organizing the curriculum at the National War College in
1946–47.

Despite two National Book Awards, two Pulitzers, and a Bancroft Prize for
his historical and autobiographical writing, Kennan was for years more widely
thought of as a theorist of international relations—indeed, with Lippmann,
Niebuhr, and Morgenthau, as a founding father of post–World War II realism.
But Kennan disliked theory and never regarded himself as practicing that dark
art. What he did believe in was the capacity of those who have studied the past to
know themselves better for having done so. The "mechanical and scientific creations of modern man," he once wrote, "tend to conceal from him the nature of
his own humanity and to encourage him in all sorts of Promethean ambitions and
illusions." Reminders were needed, therefore, "of the limitations that rest on him,
of the essential elements, both tragic and helpful, of his own condition. It is these
reminders that history, and history alone, can give."[4]

Kennan's life as a historian, in turn, evokes a third quality for which he is likely
to be remembered, which is his skill as a writer. Not the least of the reasons Kennan succeeded as a strategist and a historian is that he used words well. There was
passion, luminosity, vigor, and originality in almost all of his prose, so much so
that its vividness at times obscured the meanings he meant for it to convey. Had
it not been for that—had Kennan written as most other Foreign Service officers
did—the world might never have heard of him, and his readers would not have
retained the phrases, sentences, and sometimes whole paragraphs he so indelibly
imprinted upon them.

So might Kennan also be remembered as one of the great American writers of
the twentieth century? He hoped for this in his youth, but as an essayist, perhaps a
novelist, and certainly as Chekhov's (if not the first George Kennan's) biographer.
Those things never happened: he attracted his readers, instead, through his official
dispatches, then through his lectures and articles, then through his books, and
finally through the selections he published from his letters and diaries. These last,
however, are fragments. Kennan's unpublished letters rival those of distinguished
literary contemporaries, and his diaries, which run, with gaps, from 1916 to 2003,
are arguably the most remarkable work of sustained self-analysis—and certainly
self-criticism—since *The Education of Henry Adams*.[5]

One reason for the diaries' importance is that they document yet another career for which Kennan should be remembered: that of philosopher. We usually understand this term to mean someone who has thought deeply about living a worthwhile life. Kennan did not attempt, until in his late eighties, to publish his conclusions (hence *Around the Cragged Hill*), but he had always used his diary to agonize over obligations to civilization, country, community, family, and himself. Not surprisingly, these were rarely compatible. And so, as the need to balance objectives and capabilities gave rise to a grand strategy at the level of geopolitics, in Kennan's diaries it produced, over many decades, a personal strategy for survival.

Its most distinctive feature was Kennan's detestation of the culture—at first American, but later European as well—that surrounded him. He claimed from time to time that he would have been happier living in the eighteenth century, an assertion to be taken with a large grain of salt; but he was always an outsider in his own time. His attempts to explain why have had less influence than his other writings, chiefly because he never found the right balance between careful criticism, of which there was some, and repetitive rants, of which there were many.

Something serious lay behind both, though: it was a profound uneasiness with complacency, or, to put it another way, a strong conviction that *we*—whoever "we" were at the time—ought to be able to do better than *this*—whatever "this" might turn out to be. That's why Kennan was never satisfied with the way "containment" was implemented during the Cold War. It's why the end of that struggle, the most thorough vindication imaginable of his strategy, gave him so little satisfaction. It's why he was so at odds with post–Cold War policies of the Clinton and Bush administrations. And it's why, had he been able to respond to the tributes that poured in on his one hundredth birthday, he would have taken himself to task for his failures.

All of which is why his self-composed obituary from nine years earlier makes a great deal of sense. When asked unexpectedly to sum up and connect the various careers of George Kennan, he placed them all under the heading of *teacher*: on understanding Russia; on shaping a strategy for dealing with that country; on the danger that in pursuing that strategy too aggressively, the United States could endanger itself; on what the past suggested about societies that had done just this; on how to study history; on how to write; on how to live.

It's a paradox, given all this teaching, that so little of it took place in conventional classrooms. I asked him about this once. Kennan's answer was that when he had tried it, he worried so much over assigning grades that he had given it up, because there wouldn't have been time for anything else. George Kennan was granted far more time to teach in unconventional classrooms than he could ever have imagined. He never wasted a moment; nor did he shrink from assessment, not least of himself. That's why he had no retirement. And it's where his posthumous greatness primarily resides: in timeless, transcendent *teaching*.

ACKNOWLEDGMENTS

This book has taken so long to finish that the debts I've incurred remind me of the national deficit. I'm sure that I've missed some of these in what follows, so let me begin with apologies to all not mentioned to whom I owe thanks.

My greatest debt, of course, is to George and Annelise Kennan, for the help they gave, the trust they showed, and the patience they maintained over so many years. I also owe much to my other interviewees—almost fifty of them—whose memories took me beyond what the documents showed. The younger Kennans, Grace, Joan, Christopher, and Wendy, have also in recent years assisted me with this project: I am particularly grateful to Joan for the family correspondence, photographs, and reminiscences she has provided, and to Christopher for his visits with my Yale undergraduate seminar on "The Art of Biography" when it focused on his father. Other members of the extended Kennan family shared stories, sources, and time, especially Eugene and James Hotchkiss, Douglas James, Ted Vogel, and—certainly not least—George's secretaries over more than half a century, Dorothy Hessman, Constance Goodman, Janet Smith, Elizabeth Stenard, Terrie Bramley, and Betsy Barrett.

Archivists and staff at Princeton's Seeley G. Mudd Manuscript Library have facilitated my work on Kennan since the mid-1970s. Hence my gratitude to that admirable institution and its directors, Nancy Bressler, Ben Primer, and most recently Daniel Linke, who organized the recataloging of George's papers after his death. Adriane Hanson, who prepared an excellent new finding aid, helped me reconcile old with new box and folder numbers, and locate photographs. Jean Holliday, the Mudd Library's receptionist and reading room supervisor for many years, made sure that we researchers got to know one another: I owe to her several friendships that I still cherish. For their responses to particular queries, I also should like to thank Tad Bennicoff, of the Mudd Library staff; Christine Di Bella and Erica Mosner, of the Institute for Advanced Study Archives; Michael Devine and Samuel Rushay, of the Harry S. Truman Library; Susan K. Lemke, of the National War College Archives; Gary Richert, director of alumni relations at St. John's Northwestern Military Academy; Tim Ericson, of the Wisconsin State Historical Society; Craig Wright, of the Herbert Hoover Library; and of course Judith Schiff, Diane Kaplan, William Massa, and their colleagues at Sterling Library Manuscripts and Archives, Yale University.

A generation of research assistants has, at one time or another, worked with me on this book. They include Anne Louise Antonoff, Ryan Floyd, Michael Gaddis, Victor Kaufman, Matthew Kennedy, Victor McFarland, Ned Mitchell, Michael Schmidt, and Andrew Scott: all have extended the biography beyond what it otherwise would have been. Igor Biryukov, Andrey Ivanov, Jeffrey Mankoff, and Adam Tooze have helped with translations, and I am also grateful to Rene Bystrom, Kimberly Chow, Jack Cunningham, Robert English, Barton Gellman, John Lamberton Harper, Mark Lawrence, Melvyn P. Leffler, Geir Lundestad, Douglas McCabe, Philip Nash, Christian Ostermann, Thomas Schöttli, Strobe Talbott, and Nicholas Thompson for passing along Kennan information obtained in their own research.

Institutional support has come, over the years, from the Guggenheim Foundation, Oxford University, the Norwegian Nobel Institute, and the Woodrow Wilson International Center for Scholars, as well as my "home" universities, Ohio and Yale. Fred Greenstein and Richard Ullman arranged a semester for me at Princeton University in 1987, where I was able to complete much of the early research for this book. Others have helped in more specific ways: Avis Bohlen spent a morning talking with me about her father; Mark Bradley showed me Milwaukee sites that I would write about; Mimi Bull sent me her correspondence with Kennan while she was working as his research assistant; Patricia Woolf shared reminiscences about the Institute for Advanced Study; and S. Frederick Starr, while president of Oberlin College, arranged for me to join the second George Kennan on a memorable visit to the house, in Norwalk, Ohio, where the first George Kennan had grown up.

Teaching, I discovered long ago, is how I learn, so the students I've had in my classes—especially my Yale biography seminar—have been my collaborators, whether they realize it or not. For his role in the early placement of this book, I should like to thank Gerald McCauley, then more recently Andrew Wylie, of The Wylie Agency, to whom I am grateful not just for his help with this book, but also for his willingness to support the scholarship of several of my younger colleagues and graduate students. Eamon Dolan, my editor at Penguin, gave the manuscript the bracingly critical final reading that it badly needed, while Emily Graff has carefully but tactfully overseen the production process, with the valuable assistance of Janet Biehl, Barbara Campo, Roland Ottewell, and Don Homolka. Scott Moyers, first at Penguin, then at Wylie, and now back at Penguin, has in every way made this project his own, and I am deeply grateful.

Friends and family sustain projects like this in ways less tangible but no less important. So my special gratitude, for contributions the nature of which they will understand, goes to Paul Kennedy and Cynthia Farrar, Charles Hill and Norma Thompson, Gaddis and Barclay Smith, Charles Ellis and Linda Lorimer, Sam and Sherry Wells, Henry and Nancy Kissinger, Susan Ferber, Vladimir Pechatnov, Bill Miscamble C.S.C., Nancy Stratton, Jack and Rebecca Matlock, Roger Hertog, Barbara Gaddis, Michael and Tina Gaddis, David Gaddis, Eliza Shaw Valk, and—it would take another book of this size even to begin to explain how much—Toni Dorfman.

—J. L. G.

ABBREVIATIONS TO NOTES AND BIBLIOGRAPHY

ASK: Annelise Sørensen Kennan

CIA: Central Intelligence Agency

CKB: Constance Kennan Bradt

DSR-DF: Decimal File, U.S. Department of State Records, Record Group 59, National Archives, Washington, D.C.

FBI: Federal Bureau of Investigation

FKW: Frances Kennan Worobec

FRUS: U.S. Department of State, *Foreign Relations of the United States*

GFK: George F. Kennan

GFK Diary: George F. Kennan Diary, Seeley Mudd Manuscript Library, Princeton University, filed chronologically in Boxes 230–39 and 325–26

GFK, *Memoirs*, I: George F. Kennan, *Memoirs: 1925–1950* (Boston: Atlantic–Little, Brown, 1967)

GFK, *Memoirs*, II: George F. Kennan, *Memoirs: 1950–1963* (Boston: Atlantic–Little, Brown, 1972)

JKH: Jeanette Kennan Hotchkiss

JEK: Joan Elisabeth Kennan

JLG: John Lewis Gaddis

KKK: Kossuth Kent Kennan

KWK: Kent Wheeler Kennan

NSC: National Security Council

OPC: Office of Policy Coordination

OSP: Office of Special Projects

OSS: Office of Strategic Services

PPS Papers: *The State Department Policy Planning Staff Papers, 1947–1949*. New York: Garland, 1983.

PPS Records: U.S. Department of State, Policy Planning Staff Records, Record Group 59, National Archives, Washington, D.C.

NOTES

PREFACE

1 GFK to JLG, April 18, 1995, JLG Papers.
2 GFK Diary, April 15, 1997; GFK to Eugene Hotchkiss, February 14, 2003, copy in JLG Papers.
3 JLG Diary, November 9, 2003, *ibid.*
4 JLG notes, August 24, 1982, and September 5, 1983, *ibid.*

ONE • CHILDHOOD: 1904–1921

1 Unless otherwise noted, the author conducted all interviews. Dates are repeated only for multiple interviews with the same individual. A key to abbreviations is on page 701. JKH interview, December 21, 1982, p. 3; CKB, interview by JEK, undated, p. 1. See also GFK, *Memoirs,* I, 4, and JKH, "Memoirs for Two."
2 GFK, *Memoirs,* I, 3–4.
3 GFK Diary, March 8, 1931, quoted in GFK, *Sketches from a Life,* pp. 20–21.
4 GFK to "my dear children," Bad Nauheim, Germany, February 1942, GFK Papers, 140:9. Here and henceforth, for the Kennan papers, the first number is the box, the second the folder. Where no folder is indicated, files are in alphabetical or chronological order. Locations of all manuscript collections are listed in the Bibliography.
5 GFK Diary, January 14, 1959. The Kennan diaries, hereafter cited by date only, are in the GFK Papers, boxes 230–39 and 325–26.
6 GFK to JKH and CKB, July 21, 1984, JKH Papers.
7 Chekhov, *Steppe and Other Stories,* pp.1, 47. My wife, Toni, and I witnessed these tears during a visit with GFK in Princeton, N.J., June 26, 1999.
8 GFK, *Memoirs,* I, 4.
9 GFK interview by JEK, undated, CKB interview, November 13, 1982, p. 2, and FKW interview, June 28, 1984, p. 3; also JKH interview, p. 4, and CKB interview by JEK, p. 14.
10 JKH interview, August 24, 1982, p. 4. See also Sanborn Map Company, *Insurance Maps of Milwaukee,* I, 61. The house was later renumbered as 309 Cambridge Avenue.
11 GFK interview by JEK, p. 8; CKB interview, p. 1; JKH interview, p. 2.
12 KKK handwritten reminiscences, no date but probably 1933, KKK Papers. I am indebted to Tim Ericson for bringing these materials to my attention.
13 JKH interview, p. 3.
14 CKB interview, p. 2.
15 JKH interview, p. 7; JKH, "Memoirs for Two," p. 8; CKB interview, p. 2.
16 GFK interview, August 24, 1982, pp. 4, 11–12; JKH interview, p. 4.
17 JKH interview, December 29, 1982, p. 5; JKH, "Memoirs for Two," pp. 17, 21; KWK interview, December 29, 1982, p. 1.
18 FKW interview, p. 3; KKK reminiscences, emphases in original; JKH interview, p. 3. See also GFK's own portrait of his father in his *Memoirs,* I, 7–8.
19 KWK interview, p. 2; GFK, *Memoirs,* I, 3; JKH interview, p. 23.
20 GFK interview, August 24, 1982, p. 13; KWK interview, December 29, 1982, pp. 3, 5; JKH interview, pp. 4, 11–12, 25.
21 JKH interview, pp. 1, 9; JKH to JLG, September 24, 1983; FKW interview, p. 13; GFK, *Memoirs,* I, 1.

22 JKH interview, p. 6; GFK interview, August 24, 1982, pp. 4, 12.
23 JKH interview by JEK, p. 2.
24 CKB interview, p. 3; GFK interview, August 24, 1982, p. 14; KWK interview, p. 5.
25 JKH interview, p. 1; GFK interview, August 24, 1982, p. 3.
26 KKK reminiscences; FKW interview, p. 4; JKH, "Memoirs for Two," p. 10.
27 GFK to JEK, November 12, 1972, JEK Papers. I have relied here also on the GFK Diary, July 9, 1927, and
    April 16, 1929, as well as on Seegert, *Oakwood Bay Centennial*. I am grateful to Jeanette's son Jim Hotchkiss
    for giving me a tour of the area in 1996.
28 Anderson and Olson, *Milwaukee: At the Gathering of the Waters*, especially pp. 46, 57–60; Orum, *City-
    Building in America*, pp. 88–90.
29 JKH interview, p. 1; FKW interview, p. 4; GFK interview, August 24, 1982, pp. 8–9; CKB interview, p. 5;
    KKK reminiscences; Gregory, *History of Milwaukee, Wisconsin*, p. 142; GFK interview by JEK, pp. 8–9. The
    book was KKK, *Income Taxation—Method and Results in Various Countries*.
30 Travis, *George Kennan and the Russian-American Relationship*, provides the fullest treatment of the first
    George Kennan's life; but see also Saul, *Concord and Conflict*, especially pp. 281–92. Kennan's most influ-
    ential book was *Siberia and the Exile System*, but he also described his earlier experiences in *Tent Life in
    Siberia*.
31 GFK, *Memoirs*, I, 8; GFK interview, August 24, 1982, p. 7.
32 George Kennan to KKK, December 30, 1912, typed copy in JKH Papers.
33 CKB interview, p. 6; GFK interview, August 24, 1982, p. 7. See also JKH interview, pp. 28–29; and Travis,
    George Kennan, p. 107.
34 JKH interview, p. 28; GFK, *Memoirs*, I, 9.
35 Unless otherwise noted, the quotations in this section come from GFK's letter to "my dear children," Bad
    Nauheim, Germany, February 1942, GFK Papers, 140:9. See also GFK, *Memoirs*, I, 5–6; and GFK, *An Amer-
    ican Family: The Kennans*.
36 For the James family, see, in addition to GFK's 1942 letter, Vogel, *Sauce for the Gander*, pp. 338–52; GFK
    interview, August 24, 1982, pp. 1–3; CKB interview, pp. 3–4, 7; FKW interview, p. 5; and Seegert, *Oakwood
    Bay Centennial*, pp. 42–44.
37 GFK interview by JEK, p. 1.
38 *Ibid.*, pp. 2–3; GFK interview, August 24, 1982, p. 11.
39 JKH, "Memoirs for Two," pp. 19–20.
40 GFK interview by JEK, pp. 16–17; GFK to KKK, November 5, 1912, JEK Papers.
41 GFK, "My Soldier," March 1913, GFK Papers, 183:6.
42 GFK, *Memoirs*, I, 3–5; GFK interview by JEK, pp. 17–18. After George mentioned the Juneau Park fairies
    in his memoirs, his irreverent cousin Ted Vogel pointed out that the park had been cited in the Milwaukee
    newspapers for harboring "fairies" of "a different life style." Vogel, *Sauce for the Gander*, p. 369.
43 JKH, "Memoirs for Two," pp. 11–12.
44 GFK interview by JEK, pp. 4–5; GFK to the sons of Charlie James, May 6, 1994, Eugene Hotchkiss Papers.
    The diary is in the JEK Papers, and the quotations that follow all come from it.
45 GFK interview by JEK, pp. 4–5.
46 GFK, *Memoirs*, I, 3; GFK 1916 diary, JEK Papers; GFK interview by JEK, p. 5. See also, for these and sub-
    sequent details about the school, Mitchell, *Quarter Centenary of the Milwaukee State Normal School*. The
    school building survives as Mitchell Hall, on the University of Wisconsin–Milwaukee campus.
47 GFK interview, December 13, 1987, pp. 2–3; JKH interview, pp. 24–30; JKH, "Memoirs for Two," pp. 13–14.
    Helen Hase Barnes, who played a fairy, sent the *Rumpelstiltskin* program to George seventy-seven years
    later, GFK Papers, 90:2. Another teacher at the school in George's final year was Golda Mabovitz, later to be
    known as Golda Meir, but George did not recall having taken courses with her.
48 GFK interview by JEK, pp. 18–19, and CKB interview by JEK, pp. 14–15.
49 JKH interview by JEK, p. 16; CKB interview, p. 3; GFK to KKK, November 5, 1912; GFK Diary, April 8,
    1916, JEK Papers.
50 GFK interview by JEK, pp. 19, 27–29; GFK interview, August 24, 1982, p. 14; also GFK, "The Value of a St.
    John's Education," commencement address, St. John's Military Academy, June 4, 1960, p. 3, GFK Papers,
    260:10.
51 GFK interview by JEK, p. 29; GFK to JKH, September 24, 1919, GFK Papers, 23:10, and to Louise Wheeler
    Kennan, undated, JEK Papers; GFK, "Value of a St. John's Education," p. 4; GFK interview, August 24, 1982,
    p. 12.
52 *Ibid.*
53 *Ibid.*, pp. 12–14; also GFK interview by JEK, p. 26.
54 *Ibid.*, p. 29.
55 GFK to JLG, May 13, 1996, JLG Papers; GFK to JKH, February 20, 1921, GFK Papers, 23:10.

56 GFK interview by JEK, pp. 20–21, 27; JKH interview, p. 14.
57 St. John's Military Academy *Yearbook, 1921,* courtesy of Gary Richert, Director of Alumni Affairs, St. John's Northwestern Military Academy. See also KWK interview, p. 7, and GFK interview, December 13, 1987, p. 5.

TWO • PRINCETON: 1921–1925

1 Fitzgerald, *This Side of Paradise,* p. 36.
2 *Ibid.,* pp. 53–54; GFK, *Memoirs,* I, 9.
3 *Ibid.,* pp. 10–11, 13, 15.
4 GFK to JKH, September 28, 1921, GFK Papers, 23:10; GFK, *Memoirs,* I, 9. For the tutoring schools and the honor code, see Axtell, *Making of Princeton University,* pp. 113, 181–82, 234.
5 GFK to JKH, October 30, 1921, GFK Papers, 23:10; GFK, *Memoirs,* I, 17.
6 GFK to JKH, November 24, 1921, GFK Papers, 23:10.
7 *Ibid.;* GFK interview by JEK, p. 20; GFK interview, August 25, 1982, p. 1; JKH interview, pp. 8–9; GFK, *Memoirs,* I, 10–11.
8 GFK interview, August 25, 1982, p. 1; JKH interview by JEK, p. 5; GFK interview by JEK; JKH interview, p. 13.
9 GFK to JKH, March 4, 8, and May 3, 1922, GFK Papers, 23:10.
10 GFK to JKH, April 1, May 13 and 20, 1922, *ibid.*
11 GFK interview by JEK, pp. 13–14; FKW interview, pp. 8–9.
12 GFK interview, December 13, 1987, p. 4; Axtell, *Making of Princeton University,* pp. 6–11, 115–19.
13 Mary Bundy interview, December 6, 1987, p. 4; GFK interview, August 24, 1982, p. 16. See also GFK interview by JEK, p. 21.
14 GFK to JKH, October 4, 1922 [misdated 1921], GFK Papers, 23:10; Axtell, *Making of Princeton University,* pp. 359–68.
15 GFK to JKH, November 1, 1922, GFK Papers, 23:10.
16 Quoted in Axtell, *Making of Princeton University,* p. 309. Axtell discusses the history of the clubs at pp. 291–309.
17 GFK, *Memoirs,* I, 11; GFK interview, December 13, 1987, p. 6; GFK to JKH, undated but probably April 1923, GFK Papers, 23:10. Key and Seal, long since defunct as a club, is now Adlai Stevenson Hall. While teaching at Princeton in 1987, I took Kennan to dinner there, the first time he had set foot in the place since 1924.
18 GFK to JKH, April 11, 1923, GFK Papers, 23:10; GFK interview, December 13, 1987, p. 6; GFK Diary, July 20 and 21, 1924, JEK Papers.
19 GFK to KKK, October 20, 1924, GFK Papers, 53:7; GFK interview, December 13, 1987, p. 6.
20 GFK, *Memoirs,* I, 11–12; GFK interview, December 13, 1987, p. 4; GFK to JKH, April 11, 1923, GFK Papers, 23:10.
21 Fitzgerald, *This Side of Paradise,* p. 19.
22 GFK to JKH, March 4, 1922, GFK Papers, 23:10; GFK, *Memoirs,* I, 14; GFK to KKK, May 26, 1922, and JKH, October 4, 1922 [misdated 1921], GFK Papers, 53:5.
23 GFK, *Memoirs,* I, 15.
24 *Ibid.,* p. 13; GFK interview, August 24, 1982, p. 15; GFK to JKH, October 4, 1922 [misdated 1921], GFK Papers, 23:10; Axtell, *Making of Princeton University,* p. 223.
25 GFK, *Memoirs,* I, 16; GFK interview, August 24, 1982, pp. 15–16.
26 GFK Diary, April 30 and May 4, 1924, JEK Papers; GFK, *Memoirs,* I, 14; GFK interview, September 8, 1983, p. 10.
27 GFK Diary, May 1, 3, 9, 20, 1924, JEK Papers; GFK to KKK, October 8, 1924, GFK Papers, 53:7; GFK to JKH, undated but later marked "1924," *ibid.,* 23:10; GFK, *Memoirs,* I, 16. Clio, with Whig, were venerable Princeton debating societies.
28 GFK to JKH, February 28, May 18 and 25, 1923, GFK Papers, 23:10.
29 *Ibid.*
30 GFK to JKH, November 1, 10, and December 6, 1922, *ibid.*
31 *Ibid.*
32 GFK to JKH, May 18, 1923, GFK Papers, 23:10.
33 GFK Diary, May 24, 1924. The passport, dated June 2, 1924, is *ibid.*
34 GFK, *Memoirs,* I, 12–13; GFK Diary, May 12, 1924, JEK Papers. The Key and Seal roster for 1925, showing George as an active member and Nick as having left, is in the *Princeton Bric-a-Brac* for that year, copy courtesy of Tad Bennicoff, Special Collections Assistant, Seeley G. Mudd Manuscript Library, Princeton University.

35 GFK European trip diary, June 19–25, 1924, GFK Papers, 230:16.
36 *Ibid.*, June 26–July 1, 1924.
37 *Ibid.*, July 2–16, 1924.
38 *Ibid.*, July 17–26, 1924.
39 *Ibid.*, July 27–29, 1924.
40 *Ibid.*, July 30–August 23, 1924.
41 *Ibid.*, August 23–15, 1924; CKB interview, p. 8.
42 GFK to JKH, March 8, 1922, GFK Papers, 23:10; JKH interview, p. 23; GFK interview, August 24, 1982, p. 5; KWK interview, p. 4; GFK Diary, May 9, 1924, JEK Papers.
43 GFK to JKH, incorrectly marked "1924," and May 1, 1923, GFK Papers, 23:10; GFK, *Memoirs,* I, 17–18; JKH interview, p. 20; KWK interview, p. 7.
44 GFK European trip diary, August 4, 1924, GFK Papers, 230:16.
45 GFK to KKK, October 20, 1924, *ibid.*, 53:7; GFK European trip diary, July 25, 1924, *ibid.*, 230:16. This Harriman was the railroad magnate E. H. Harriman, father of W. Averell Harriman, under whom George served in the U.S. embassy in Moscow during World War II.
46 GFK to KKK, October 20, 1924, GFK Papers, 53:7; GFK European trip diary, July 30, 1924, GFK Papers, 230:16.
47 GFK, *Memoirs,* I, 17; GFK interview, August 24, 1982, p. 9; GFK to KKK, January 19, 1925 [misdated 1924], GFK Papers, 53:7.
48 GFK, *Memoirs,* I, 17; Joseph C. Green to GFK, October 25, 1925, Philip A. Brown to GFK, November 27, 1925, both in JEK Papers.
49 GFK commencement address, Dartmouth College, June 11, 1950, GFK Papers, 299:40; GFK, *Memoirs,* I, 15, 18; *Nassau Herald,* June 15, 1925, p. 227. I am indebted to Daniel J. Linke, University Archivist and Curator of Public Policy Papers at Princeton, for providing me with a copy of Kennan's academic transcript.
50 GFK, *Memoirs,* I, 16. The chameleon image comes from Axtell, *Making of Princeton University*, p. 111.

THREE • THE FOREIGN SERVICE: 1925–1931

1 GFK interview by JEK, p. 24, JEK Papers; Heinrichs, *American Ambassador,* pp. 95–98; Weil, *Pretty Good Club,* pp. 46–47.
2 GFK interview by JEK, p. 24; GFK to JKH, December 3, 1925, GFK Papers, 23:10. See also, on the Crawford School, Bohlen, *Witness to History,* p. 5.
3 GFK interview by JEK, pp. 23–24; GFK to JKH, October 28, 1925, GFK Papers, 23:10.
4 GFK interview by JEK, p. 24; GFK, *Memoirs,* I, 18.
5 Joseph C. Grew to GFK, September 9, 1926, DSR-DF 1910–29, Box 548, 123 K36/orig.; GFK draft speech (unused) to Princeton alumni, February 5, 1953, GFK Papers, 252:11; GFK, *Memoirs,* I, 19–20; GFK poem copied in diary for January 18, 1930, GFK Papers, 230:20; GFK interview by JEK, p. 25.
6 GFK, *Memoirs,* I, 20–21.
7 GFK Diary, July 4, 1927.
8 *Ibid.*, May 20, 1927.
9 GFK, *Memoirs,* I, 13.
10 *Ibid.*, pp. 20–21.
11 GFK Diary, May 16 and 26, 1927.
12 *Ibid.*, May 24, 1927.
13 *Ibid.*, July 14, 1927.
14 *Ibid.*, October 30 and November 3, 1927.
15 *Ibid.*, September 10, October 9, 10, 30, November 5 and 28, 1927.
16 *Ibid.*, November 7, 1927. See also GFK, *Memoirs,* I, 22; and GFK, *Sketches from a Life,* p. 4, where he prints this passage but edits out the word "Jewish."
17 GFK Diary, November 1 and 30, 1927.
18 GFK, *Memoirs,* I, 20; GFK Diary, November 12, 1927; GFK to Department of State, November 22, 1927, DSR-DF 1910–29, Box 548, 123K36/19. See also GFK, *Sketches from a Life,* pp. 5–6.
19 EJN to the Foreign Service Personnel Board, December 7, 1927, DSR-DF 1910–29, Box 548, 123K36/19; State Department to GFK, December 9, 1927, *ibid.*; GFK to State Department, January 6 and April 24, 1928, *ibid.*, Box 1476, 123K36/22 and 25; Cassels, "'Mr. X' Goes to Moscow," p. 88; GFK, *Memoirs,* I, 23.
20 *Ibid.*
21 GFK interview by JEK, p. 26; GFK to JKH, September 3, 1928, GFK Papers, 23:10; GFK interview, December 13, 1987, p. 7.
22 Eleanor Lake to John Lamberton Harper, July 12, 1990, and June 1991, copies provided by Professor Harper. Eleanor's son, Anthony Lake, would serve during the Carter administration as director of the

State Department's Policy Planning Staff, the position Kennan was the first to fill when the staff was created in 1947.

23 GFK interview, December 13, 1987, pp. 7–8; JKH interview, p. 16. Eleanor Lake, in her July 12, 1990, letter cited above, says that her mother destroyed all of George's letters to her.

24 GFK to JKH, September 3, 1928, GFK Papers, 23:10.

25 GFK Diary, March 26, 1928.

26 See, for example, entries for December 4, 1927, and March 17, 1928, *ibid*. George mentions "Peck"—probably Howard F. Peckworth, who graduated from Princeton a year after he did—as his only other confidant in a letter to Jeanette, October 20, 1928, GFK Papers, 23:10, but adds that they have the "sensible" arrangement of corresponding just once a year.

27 GFK, *Memoirs*, I, 23; Wilbur J. Carr to GFK, March 29, 1928, DSR-DF 1910–29, Box 548, 123K36/25.

28 Saul, *War and Revolution*, pp. 318–19, 434, 437–40. The Colby note, dated August 10, 1920, is in *FRUS: 1920*, III, 463–68.

29 Gaddis, *Russia, the Soviet Union, and the United States*, pp. 98–104.

30 GFK, *Memoirs*, I, 23. See also DeSantis, *Diplomacy of Silence*, pp. 27–29; and Engerman, *Modernization from the Other Shore*, pp. 246–47.

31 GFK, *Memoirs*, I, 18–19, 24–25; GFK Diary, April 16, 1928.

32 *Ibid.*, April 16, 18, May 6, 1928.

33 *Ibid.*, April 16, May 6, 1928.

34 GFK to JKH, October 20, 1928, GFK Papers, 23:10.

35 GFK Diary, June 1928; GFK, *Memoirs*, I, 25–27.

36 GFK interview, August 24, 1982, p. 10; GFK, *Memoirs*, I, 28. See also, on the Riga legation, DeSantis, *Diplomacy of Silence*, pp. 30–31; Engerman, *Modernization from the Other Shore*, pp. 247–50; and, for an argument about the lasting influence of service in Riga for American Soviet specialists, Yergin, *Shattered Peace*.

37 GFK interview, August 24, 1982, pp. 10–11; GFK Diary, July 28–29, September 22, November 4, 1929.

38 GFK Diary, September 4, 6, 1929; GFK, *Memoirs*, I, 27.

39 GFK Diary, August 5, 1928; GFK, *Memoirs*, I, 27.

40 *Ibid.*, pp. 28–30; T. W. Wilson report on the American legation in Riga, Latvia, February 20, 1929, Department of State, Inspection Reports, 1906–39, Box 128, National Archives.

41 GFK Diary, January 20, 1929.

42 *Ibid.*; GFK interviews, August 24, 1982, pp. 10, 16, and August 25, 1982, p. 3.

43 "Report of Consul Carlson on Mr. George F. Kennan," enclosed in F. W. B. Coleman to the State Department, May 6, 1929, DSR-DF 1910–29, 123K36/49; Wilbur J. Carr to GFK, July 18, 1929, *ibid.*, 123K36/58.

44 GFK Diary, April 20, 1929.

45 Carr to GFK, July 18, 1929, DSR-DF 1910–29, 123K36/58; Raymond H. Geist to the State Department, August 4, 1930, DSR-DF 1930–39, 123K36/81; GFK, *Memoirs*, I, 31–33.

46 Richie, *Faust's Metropolis*, pp. 325, 331; GFK, *Memoirs*, I, 34–35.

47 GFK interview, December 13, 1987, p. 8; GFK to JKH, March 8, 1930, GFK Papers, 23:10.

48 GFK Diary, January 26, 1930. See also, for the Femina, Richie, *Faust's Metropolis*, pp. 459–60.

49 GFK to JKH, March 8 and 28, 1930, GFK Papers, 23:10.

50 GFK Diary, January 19, 1930.

51 GFK to JKH, January 3 and April 28, 1931, GFK Papers, 23:10; GFK, *Memoirs*, I, 34.

52 GFK interview, December 13, 1987, pp. 9–10.

53 GFK to Ferris, January 12, 1931, JEK Papers.

54 GFK Diary, May 30, 1931.

55 GFK to JKH, November 16, 1930, January 3, April 18 and 28, 1931, GFK Papers, 23:10.

56 GFK to State Department, July 29, 1931, DSR-DF 1930–39, 123K36/99.

Four • Marriage—and Moscow: 1931–1933

1 ASK telegram to GFK, August 5, 1931, JEK Papers; GFK Diary, included in entry for May 7, 1932; GFK to JKH, no date, GFK Papers, 23:10. See also GFK, *Memoirs*, I, 37.

2 ASK to GFK, three undated letters, JEK Papers.

3 ASK interview, August 26, 1982, p. 1; Alice Green certificate, Cours des Billettes, Paris, June 20, 1928, JEK Papers. The birth date is from a baptismal certificate attached to the American Consular Service Certificate of Marriage, *ibid*.

4 ASK interview, August 26, 1982, pp. 3–4; ASK Diary and Memorandum Book for 1931, JEK Papers.

5 ASK to GFK, undated, JEK Papers; GFK Diary, May 7, 1932; GFK, *Memoirs*, I, 38–39; ASK interview, August 26, 1982, p. 4.

6   GFK, *Memoirs,* I, 39–40; ASK Diary, September 11, 1931, JEK Papers; GFK to JKH, October 18, 1931, GFK Papers, 23:10. See also GFK Diary, October 3, 1932.

7   GFK, *Memoirs,* I, 40; ASK interview, December 14, 1987, p. 2.

8   *Ibid.,* p. 8; GFK to Jeanette and Gene Hotchkiss, November 1, 1931, GFK Papers, 23:10; GFK, *Memoirs,* I, 40–41.

9   GFK to JKH, October 18, 1931, GFK Papers, 23:10. See also GFK, *Memoirs,* I, 40.

10   ASK to JKH, January 28, 1932, JEK Papers; GFK, *Memoirs,* I, 41.

11   ASK to GFK, undated, JEK Papers; CKB interview, p. 9; ASK interview, December 14, 1987, p. 5.

12   KKK to GFK, January 14, 1932, JEK Papers. See also JKH interview, pp. 7–9, and KWK interview, pp. 2–3.

13   Eugene Hotchkiss to GFK, March 20, 1932, JEK Papers; JKH to JLG, July 8, 1983, JLG Papers. For more on the "match king," see *Economist* 385 (December 22, 2007), 115–17.

14   JKH interview, p. 10; GFK to JKH, June 24, 1932, and December 25, 1935, GFK Papers, 23:10; ASK interviews, August 26, 1982, p. 5, and December 14, 1987, p. 8; JEK to JLG, April 4, 2008, JLG Papers.

15   GFK Diary, May 29, 1932.

16   *Ibid.,* June 13, 1932.

17   *Ibid.,* March 24, 1932; GFK and ASK interview, December 13, 1987, pp. 13–15.

18   GFK Diary, June 14, 1932.

19   *Ibid.,* January 1933, otherwise undated portion titled "Pocket Notebook."

20   GFK Diary, April 7, July 13, August 4, 1932.

21   "Memorandum for the Minister," August 19, 1932, enclosed in dispatch #650 from Robert F. Skinner to the State Department, DSR-DF 1930-39, 861.5017 Living Conditions/510; GFK to JLG, February 12, 2001, JLG Papers. I am indebted to David C. Engerman for bringing this document to my attention. His own evaluation of it is in his book *Modernization from the Other Shore,* pp. 254–55.

22   GFK, *Memoirs,* I, 28–30; T. W. Wilson report on the American legation in Riga, Latvia, February 20, 1929, section III, Department of State, Inspection Reports, 1906–39, Box 128.

23   ASK to GFK, November 8, 1932, JEK Papers.

24   For the pressures leading to recognition, see Saul, *Friends or Foes?,* pp. 254–90; and, for the State Department perspective, Henderson, *Question of Trust,* pp. 213–29.

25   GFK, *Memoirs,* I, 41; ASK to JKH, February 8, 1933, JEK Papers.

26   GFK Diary, January 1933, otherwise undated portion titled "Personal Notebook"; GFK to JKH, March 21, 1933, GFK Papers, 23:10.

27   GFK to JKH, May 1 and June 3, 1933, *ibid.*

28   Skinner to State Department, September 10, 1932, enclosing GFK memorandum on "The Gold and Foreign Currency Accounts of the Russian Government," and Castle to Skinner, December 6, 1932, DSR-DF 1930–39, 851.51/2539; Skinner to GFK, *ibid.,* 123K36/128. See also GFK, *Memoirs,* I, 49–52, 58.

29   KKK to GFK, January 29, 1933, and ASK to JKH, August 4, 1933, JEK Papers; Cole to State Department, September 23, 1933, DSR-DF 1930–39, 123K36/134.

30   Henderson interview, September 25, 1982, p. 1; J. V. A. MacMurray to State Department, January 9, 1934, DSR-DF, 123K36/151. See also, for similar speculation on Kennan's motives for returning, Isaacson and Thomas, *Wise Men,* pp. 155–57.

31   ASK interview, August 26, 1982, p. 5; GFK to JKH, October 26, 1933, GFK Papers, 23:10; JKH to GFK, November 2 and 5, 1933, JEK Papers; "Daughter-in-Law Greeted at Tea," *Milwaukee Journal,* November 4, 1933, clipping in JKH Scrapbook.

32   GFK to JKH, December 14, 1933, KKK to GFK, November 24, 1933, JEK Papers.

33   GFK, "Introduction" [to Bullitt, *For the President*], pp. v–vi. For Bullitt, see Brownell and Billings, *So Close to Greatness,* and Cassella-Blackburn, *The Donkey, the Carrot, and the Club.* The Wilson biography did not appear until shortly before Bullitt's death in 1967.

34   GFK unpublished 1938 memoir, "Fair Day Adieu," p. 1, GFK Papers, 240:2; GFK to family, December 2, 1933, JEK Papers.

35   ASK interview, December 14, 1987, p. 15; GFK, "Introduction," p. xv.

36   GFK to JKH, January 6, 1934 [misdated 1933], JEK papers.

37   *Ibid.,* GFK to Charles James, July 29, 1934, GFK Papers, 22:4; GFK to JKH, January 25, 1934, *ibid.,* 23:10. The newspaper photos are in a family album in the JEK Papers. See also GFK, *Memoirs,* II, 119–20.

38   GFK to JKH, December 14, 1933, GFK Papers, 23:10.

39   GFK to JKH, January 6, 1934 [misdated 1933], *ibid.*; GFK, *Memoirs,* I, 59–60.

40   GFK to Bullitt, December 27, 1933, Bullitt Papers, 17:5; Bullitt to Roosevelt, January 1, 1934, in Bullitt, *For the President,* p. 65.

FIVE • THE ORIGINS OF SOVIET-AMERICAN RELATIONS, 1933–1936

1 GFK to ASK, December 29, 1933, JEK Papers.
2 Bullitt to State Department, December 16, 1933, DSR-DF 1930–39, 123K36/141; Wilbur J. Carr to William Phillips, December 20, 1933, *ibid.*, 124.61/54; Merrill to Carr, December 24, 1933, *ibid.*, 124.611/53; Bullitt to Roosevelt, Phillips, and R. Walton Moore, December 24, 1933, *ibid.*, 124.611/55; Phillips to Bullitt, December 27, 1933, *ibid.*, 124.611/53.
3 ASK to GFK, January 2, 1934, JEK Papers; GFK Moscow Diary, January 15, 1934, DSR-DF1930–39, 124.616/113.
4 GFK, *Memoirs*, I, 59; GFK 1938 memoir, "Fair Day Adieu," pp. 8–9, GFK Papers, 240:2; Bullitt to Roosevelt, January 1, 1934, in Bullitt, *For the President*, p. 69. The National still exists—in a different era—as Le Royal Meridien National. See also, for the history of Spaso House and the Mokhovaya, http://moscow.usembassy.gov/embassy/ embassy.php? record_id= spaso.
5 Thayer, *Bears in the Caviar*, p. 75; GFK, *Memoirs*, I, 59.
6 GFK to Charles James, July 29, 1934, Douglas James Papers; Keith Merrill telephone conversation with GFK, January 9, 1934, DSR-DF 1930–39, 124.611/94 [this copy undated, but date determined from "Mr. Kennan's Moscow Diary, 1934," *ibid.*, 124.616/113]; Thayer, *Bears in the Caviar*, p. 85; GFK to Rebecca Matlock, October 29, 1987, GFK Papers, 27:18; GFK 1938 memoir, "Fair Day Adieu," p. 11, GFK Papers, 240:2. See also GFK, *Memoirs*, I, 63–64; and Peter Bridges, "George Kennan Reminisces About Moscow in 1933–1937," *Diplomacy and Statecraft* 17 (June 2006), 283–93.
7 Bullitt to Roosevelt, April 13, 1934, in Bullitt, *For the President*, p. 83.
8 Henderson, *Question of Trust*, pp. 262, 301–5; GFK, *Memoirs*, I, 61–63.
9 Henderson, *Question of Trust*, p. 303; ASK interviews, August 26, 1982, p. 7, and December 14, 1987, p. 4; Durbrow interview, September 24, 1982, p. 1. See also GFK, *Memoirs*, I, 63–64; and Thayer, *Bears in the Caviar*, pp. 85–86.
10 GFK to JKH, April 15 and May 7, 1934, JEK Papers.
11 GFK to JKH, May 19, 1934, *ibid.*
12 Bullitt to State Department, May 9, 1934, DSR-DF 1930–39, 123K36/164. See also Thayer, *Bears in the Caviar*, pp. 85–86.
13 Robert F. Kelley memorandum, June 18, 1934, *ibid.*; GFK to JKH, June 24, 1934, JEK Papers.
14 GFK to Bullitt, July 6, 1934, Bullitt Papers, 19:8; GFK to Charles James, July 29, 1934, GFK Papers, 24:4.
15 JKH interview, p. 24; GFK to JKH, June 7, 1933, JEK Papers; GFK Diary, April 8, 1934.
16 GFK Diary, September 18, 1934, *ibid.*
17 GFK, "Runo—An Island Relic of Medieval Sweden," *Canadian Geographical Journal* 11 (November 1935), 255–64. See also JKH to GFK, December 2, 1932, JEK Papers; and C. Ben Wright, "George F. Kennan, Scholar-Diplomat: 1926–1946," Ph.D. Dissertation, University of Wisconsin, 1972, pp. 36–37.
18 GFK, *Memoirs*, I, 21, 49; Carr to Skinner, December 27, 1934, enclosing comments from Green, Kelley, and Edward C. Wynne, DSR-DF 1930–39, 123K36/123.
19 Mrs. George Kennan to JKH, June 7 and 27, 1934, JEK Papers; GFK to JKH, July 1, 1934, *ibid.* For George A. Frost, see Travis, *George Kennan and the American-Russian Relationship*, pp. 112, 123–24.
20 GFK to JKH, August 1, 1934, JEK Papers.
21 Bullitt to GFK, July 20, 1934, Bullitt Papers, 19:8; Bullitt to R. Walton Moore, September 22, 1934, *ibid.*, T12:13.
22 GFK to JKH, December 2, 1934, GFK Papers, 23:10; GFK 1938 memoir, "Fair Day Adieu," p. 17, *ibid.*, 240:2.
23 ASK to JKH, November 9, 1934, JEK Papers; ASK interview, August 26, 1982, p. 8
24 GFK Diary, September 3, 1934. Compare with GFK's "Memorandum for the Minister," August 19, 1932, enclosed in dispatch #650 from the Riga Legation to the Department of State, discussed in Chapter Four.
25 ASK to Louise Wheeler, October 12, 1934, and JKH, November 9, 1934, JEK Papers; KWK to JLG, January 9, 1983, JLG Papers; GFK to JKH, November 24, 1934, GFK Papers, 23:10; and KWK interview, pp. 11–13.
26 ASK to JKH, November 9, 1934, JEK Papers; GFK to JKH, December 2, 1934, GFK Papers, 23:10.
27 GFK 1938 memoir, "Fair Day Adieu," pp. 22–23, GFK Papers, 240:2; ASK to JKH, December 21, 1934, JEK Papers; ASK interview, December 14, 1987, p. 5. See also Thayer, *Bears in the Caviar*, pp. 106–14.
28 Wiley to Bullitt, December 27, 1934, DSR-DF 1930–39, 123K36/174; Wiley to Bullitt, January 2, 1935, Bullitt Papers, 21:5; Bullitt to Wiley, January 7, 1934, *ibid.*, T14:2; Bullitt to GFK, January 7, 1934, *ibid.*, 21:1; GFK to JKH, December 31, 1934, GFK Papers, 23:10.
29 GFK to JKH, December 31, 1934, January 20, 1935, and January 6, 1937 [misdated 1936], *ibid.*; GFK to Bullitt, February 12, 1935, Bullitt Papers, 21:1; GFK 1938 memoir, "Fair Day Adieu," pp. 25–27, GFK Papers, 240:2.
30 GFK to JKH, December 31, 1934, and February 10, 1935, *ibid.*, 23:10.

31 GFK interviews, August 25, 1982, p. 1, and December 13, 1987, pp. 12–13; GFK Diary, February 12 and April 11, 1935; GFK to Bullitt, February 12, 1935, Bullitt Papers, 21:1; Henderson interview, September 25, 1982, p. 4. I have slightly edited the diary passage.

32 GFK Diary, February 4, 6, 14, 15, 1935; GFK to JKH, February 10, 1935, *ibid.*, 23:10. The letter to Follmer is quoted in the diary entry for February 6.

33 GFK to JKH, March 6 and April 29, 1935, GFK Papers, 23:10; GFK Diary, April 8, 1935; GFK to ASK, April 20, 1935, JEK Papers.

34 GFK Diary, February 15, 1935; GFK to Bullitt, February 12, 1935, Bullitt Papers, 21:1.

35 Bullitt to R. Walton Moore, May 11, 1935, *ibid.*, T12:13; GFK to Bullitt, April 15, 1935, *ibid.*, 21:1; Bullitt to Thomas D. White, June 6, 1935, *ibid.*, 21:5; ASK to JKH, May 31, 1935, JEK Papers.

36 GFK Diary, April 20, 1935; GFK to JKH, June 28, July 30, September 11 and 30, 1935, *ibid.*, 23:10; GFK to Bullitt, November 4, 1935, Bullitt Papers, 21:1.

37 GFK, *Memoirs,* I, 64; GFK 1938 memoir, "Fair Day Adieu," pp. 14–15, GFK Papers, 240:2.

38 GFK to JKH, November 17, 1935, *ibid.*, 23:10. For a recent but still inconclusive account of the Kirov murder, see Simon Sebag Montefiore, *Stalin: At the Court of the Red Tsar* (New York: Knopf, 2004), pp. 143–52.

39 GFK to JKH, December 25, 1935, GFK Papers, 23:10; GFK to Charles James, December 16, 1935, *ibid.*, 24:4; GFK 1938 memoir, "Fair Day Adieu," pp. 36–38, *ibid.*, 240:2.

40 *Ibid.*, pp. 41–44; Bullitt fitness report on GFK, August 1, 1936, Bullitt Papers, T12:21. See also, for a detailed account of this trip, GFK, *Sketches from a Life,* pp. 27–33.

41 Bullitt to State Department, April 20, 1936, in *FRUS: The Soviet Union, 1933–1939,* p. 292. See also Bullitt, *For the President,* pp. 134–35, and Henderson, *Question of Trust,* pp. 319–85, 407–8.

42 GFK 1938 memoir, "Fair Day Adieu," pp. 13–14, 23–24, 38–40, GFK Papers, 240:2; GFK, *Memoirs,* I, 68–70. The Neill Brown observations were included in Bullitt to State Department, March 4, 1936, in *FRUS: The Soviet Union, 1933–1939,* pp. 289–91. GFK described their discovery in a lecture to the Canadian National Defence College on May 31, 1948, GFK Papers, 299:9.

43 Bullitt to State Department, April 20, 1936, in *FRUS: The Soviet Union, 1933–1939,* p. 296.

44 See "The Sources of Soviet Conduct," *Foreign Affairs* 25 (July 1947), especially pp. 580–82.

45 Bullitt fitness report on GFK, August 1, 1936, Bullitt Papers, T12:21.

46 GFK to Bullitt, June 9, 1936, *ibid.*, and September 4, 1936, *ibid.*, 20:17.

Six • Rediscovering America: 1936–1938

1 GFK to State Department, January 9, 1936, DSR-DF 1930–39, 123K36/213.

2 ASK to JKH, November 2, 1935, JEK Papers; GFK 1938 memoir "Fair Day Adieu," p. 41, GFK Papers, 240:2; GFK to JKH, December 25, 1935, *ibid.*, 23:10.

3 GFK to Bullitt, June 9, 1936, Bullitt Papers, T12:21.

4 GFK to JKH, May 13, 1935, GFK Papers, 23:10.

5 GFK, *Memoirs,* I, 77.

6 *Ibid.*; GFK 1938 memoir, "Fair Day Adieu," pp. 47–50, GFK Papers, 240:2; also GFK to JKH, September 8, 1936, *ibid.*, 23:10.

7 *Ibid.*; J. Klahr Huddle to State Department, April 17, 1937, Department of State, Inspection Reports on Foreign Service Posts, 1906–39, Box 102.

8 GFK 1938 memoir, "Fair Day Adieu," p. 66, GFK Papers, 240:2; R. Walton Moore to Bullitt, March 19, 1936, Bullitt Papers, T12:15. The information on embassy productivity is in the Huddle inspection report, April 17, 1937.

9 GFK to JKH, December 6, 1936, GFK Papers, 23:10; ASK to JKH, January 2, 1937, JEK Papers; Thayer, *Bears in the Caviar,* pp. 132, 135.

10 ASK interview, December 14, 1987, p. 6; GFK to JKH, September 8, 1936, GFK Papers, 23:10; GFK Diary, May 30, 1937.

11 GFK to JKH, December 6, 1936, GFK Papers, 23:10; also ASK interview, December 14, 1987, p. 19.

12 Henderson, *Question of Trust,* p. 414; Davies, *Mission to Moscow,* p. xviii; GFK, *Memoirs,* I, 82. See also, on Davies's background, MacLean, *Joseph E. Davies,* pp. 7–22.

13 Henderson interview, p. 3; Huddle inspection report, April 17, 1937.

14 GFK 1938 memoir, "Fair Day Adieu," p. 67, GFK Papers, 240:2; GFK to JKH, February 17, 1937, *ibid.*, 23:10; ASK to JKH, March 3, 1937, JEK Papers; GFK undated memoir, "Washington 1937–1938," GFK Papers, 240:3; GFK to Eugene Hotchkiss, undated but March 1937, *ibid.*, 23:10.

15 ASK interview, September 8, 1983, p. 4; Davies to GFK, February 2, 1937, Davies Papers, Box 3; GFK, *Memoirs,* I, 82–83; Davies to State Department, February 17 and 18, 1937, DSR-DF 1930–39, 861.00/11675–76; Kelley to Hull, March 13, 1937, *ibid.*, 861.00/11676. Davies's February 18 dispatch forwarded

Kennan's report, "The Trial of Radek and Others," dated February 13, 1937, subsequently published in *FRUS: The Soviet Union, 1933–1939,* pp. 362–69. See also MacLean, *Joseph E. Davies,* pp. 28–30.

16 GFK to Peter S. Bridges, September 20, 1963, GFK Papers, 57. See also GFK 1938 memoir, "Fair Day Adieu," pp. 71–72, *ibid.,* 240:2; Thayer, *Bears in the Caviar,* pp. 95–96; MacLean, *Joseph E. Davies,* p. 40; and, for official reports, Henderson to State Department, May 14 and August 10, 1937, in *FRUS: The Soviet Union, 1933–1939,* pp. 441–42, 445–46.

17 Davies to Kelley, February 10, 1937, Davies Papers, Box 3.

18 GFK to JKH, December 6, 1936, and March 31, 1937, GFK Papers, 23:10.

19 GFK 1938 memoir "Fair Day Adieu," pp. 68–70, *ibid.,* 240:2; GFK, *Memoirs,* I, 85; Bullitt to R. Walton Moore, June 15, 1937, Bullitt Papers, T12:16. For another version of the library story, see Bohlen, *Witness to History,* p. 41.

20 Moore to Bullitt, June 26, 1937, Bullitt Papers, T12:16; GFK, *Memoirs,* I, 84–85; also MacLean, *Joseph E. Davies,* pp. 37–38.

21 GFK, *Memoirs,* I, 82–83; GFK to Rebecca Matlock, October 29, 1987, GFK Papers, 27:18; GFK 1938 memoir "Fair Day Adieu," p. 70, *ibid.,* 240:2.

22 ASK to JKH, June 24 and July 28, 1937, JEK Papers; Hull to GFK, August 13, 1937, DSR-DF 1930–39, 123K36/246.

23 Bullitt to Moore, June 15, 1937, Bullitt Papers, T12:16; Henderson to Bullitt, September 3, 1937, *ibid.,* 22:10; GFK to JKH, September 14, 1937, GFK Papers, 22:10; GFK to Hull, August 16, 1937, DSR-DF 1930–39, 123K36/248. See also Henderson, *Question of Trust,* p. 397.

24 GFK, *Memoirs,* I, 85; GFK Diary, October 17, 24, 25, 1937, and February 11, 1938; GFK undated memoir, "Washington 1937–1938," GFK Papers, 240:3.

25 GFK to JKH, November 3, 1937, *ibid.,* 23:10; ASK to JKH, October 19 and December 20, 1937, JEK Papers; GFK to JKH, December 26, 1937, and February 8, 1938, GFK Papers, 23:10.

26 GFK undated memoir, "Washington 1937–1938," pp. 4, 15, GFK Papers, 240:3; GFK memorandum, "The Position of an American Ambassador in Moscow," November 24, 1937, in *FRUS: The Soviet Union, 1933–1939,* p. 446; GFK, *Memoirs,* I, 85–86; GFK and Edward Page, Jr., memorandum, "Comments on the Memorandum of Oral Conversation Left by the Soviet Ambassador," July 19, 1938, in *FRUS: The Soviet Union, 1933–1939,* p. 658; GFK memorandum, December 23, 1937, DSR-DF 1930–39, 711.61/628.

27 GFK lecture, "Russia," delivered at the Foreign Service School, May 20, 1938, GFK Papers, 298:1.

28 Troyanovsky to Stalin (from Washington), June 20, 1938, and a second undated report (from Moscow), Presidential Archive of the Russian Federation, Fond 3, Opis 66, Delo 362, ll. 140–211, translation by Jeffrey Mankoff. The Davies dispatch is in *FRUS: The Soviet Union, 1933–39,* pp. 542–51.

29 "Memoires of Dr. Frieda Por," enclosed in a letter to GFK and ASK, June 12, 1977, GFK Papers, 39:5; ASK to Frieda Por (in German), July 25, 1938, JEK Papers. See also, on the Frieda Por emigration, GFK interview, December 13, 1987, pp. 11–12; and ASK to GFK, undated but summer 1938, JEK Papers.

30 GFK undated memoir, "Washington 1937–1938," pp. 17–19, GFK Papers, 240:3. GFK, *Memoirs,* I, 75–76, misdates this trip as 1936.

31 GFK, *Sketches from a Life,* pp. 36–44; also GFK undated memoir, "Washington 1937–1938," GFK Papers, 240:3.

32 GFK, "The Sources of Soviet Conduct," *Foreign Affairs* 25 (July 1947), 582.

33 GFK, "The Prerequisites: Notes on the Problems of the United States in 1938," and "II. Government," GFK Papers, 240:4.

34 Mayers, *George Kennan and the Dilemmas of U.S. Foreign Policy,* p. 338n; GFK interview, January 30, 1991, p. 13. Wright, "George F. Kennan, Scholar-Diplomat," pp. 133–34, catalogs the political incorrectness with succinct precision.

35 Isaacson and Thomas, *Wise Men,* p. 172.

36 See, for example, GFK, *Around the Cragged Hill,* pp. 232–49.

37 GFK 1938 memoir, "Fair Day Adieu," pp. 29–31, GFK Papers, 240:2. See also, on the global significance of the New Deal, Hamby, *For the Survival of Democracy.*

38 GFK undated memoir, "Washington 1937–1938," p. 9, *ibid.,* 240:3.

39 *Ibid.,* pp. 1–2.

40 Bohlen interview by Wright, September 29, 1970. I have edited this passage for clarity.

41 GFK undated memoir, "Washington 1937–1938," pp. 31–33, GFK Papers, Box 19R.

SEVEN • CZECHOSLOVAKIA AND GERMANY: 1938–1941

1 GFK to Bullitt, August 15, 1938, Bullitt Papers, 4:12. See also GFK, *Memoirs,* I, 86.

2 GFK undated memoir, "Prague—Munich to Occupation, 1938–1939," pp. 1–3, GFK Papers, 240:3. The *Washington Post* clippings, dated September 15, 1938, are in the JEK Papers.

3 GFK undated memoir, "Prague—Munich to Occupation, 1938–1939," pp. 3–4, GFK Papers, 240:3; State Department radiogram, September 24, 1938, DSR-DF 1930–39, 123K36/272, National Archives.

4 GFK undated memoir, "Prague—Munich to Occupation, 1938–1939," pp. 4–6, GFK Papers, 240:3.
5 *Ibid.*, pp. 7–9.
6 GFK to Frieda Por (in German), October 15, 1938, JEK Papers; GFK personal notes, October 1938, in GFK, *From Prague After Munich,* pp. 3–4; GFK Diary, October 2, 1938.
7 GFK, *Memoirs,* I, 90–92; GFK Diary, October 13, 1938. Gellhorn drew on her experiences in her first novel, *A Stricken Field.* There is an encounter with an apparently insensitive diplomat—although she makes him British—on pp. 162–65.
8 GFK to Grace Wells, October 17, 1938, GFK Papers, 23:10; GFK Diary, October 23, 1938; GFK personal notes, October 1938, in GFK, *From Prague After Munich,* p. 4.
9 GFK undated memoir, "Prague—Munich to Occupation, 1938–1939," pp. 12–13, GFK Papers, 240:3; GFK to JKH, November 14, 1938, *ibid.,* 23:10.
10 GFK to JKH, November 14, 1938, *ibid.;* GFK undated memoir, "Prague—Munich to Occupation, 1938–1939," pp. 12–16, *ibid.,* 240:3.
11 *Ibid.,* pp. 16–19.
12 ASK to JKH, December 10, 1938, and February 6, 1939, JEK Papers; GFK to JKH, December 28, 1938, GFK Papers, 23:10.
13 GFK personal notes, October 1938, in GFK, *From Prague After Munich,* pp. 4–5.
14 GFK personal letters of December 8, 1938, and January 6, 1939, in *ibid.,* pp. 9, 11. See also Raymond E. Cox to State Department, January 12, 1939, and Wilbur J. Carr to State Department, February 1, 1939, both drafted by GFK, in *ibid.,* pp. 29–31, 38–39.
15 GFK to State Department, February 17, 1939, in *ibid.,* pp. 46–50, 56.
16 GFK personal notes, March 21, 1939, in *ibid.,* pp. 80–87; GFK interview, September 7, 1983, p. 6; ASK to JKH, March 18, 1938, JEK Papers; GFK to JKH, March 24, 1939, GFK Papers, 23:10; GFK undated memoir, "Prague—Munich to Occupation, 1938–1939," p. 45, *ibid.,* 240:3; ASK interview, December 14, 1987, p. 14.
17 GFK to State Department, March 29 and 30, 1939, in GFK, *From Prague After Munich,* p. 94; GFK, "The Prerequisites," pp. 4–5, GFK Papers, 240:4.
18 Irving N. Linnell to *chargé d'affaires* in Berlin (drafted by GFK), April 14, 1939, and to Department of State (drafted by GFK), May 23, 1939, in GFK, *From Prague After Munich,* pp. 117–18, 178.
19 GFK to State Department, March 29, 1939, Linnell to State Department (drafted by GFK), May 23, 1939, *ibid.,* pp. 98, 173–74.
20 GFK to State Department, May 1, 1939, in *ibid.,* pp. 135–38.
21 GFK to Robert Coe, March 30, 1939, GFK to State Department, April 26–27, 1939, Linnell to State Department (drafted by GFK), May 10, 1939, all in *ibid.,* pp. 103–4, 133, 150.
22 GFK to State Department, May 15, 1939, in *ibid.,* pp. 169–71.
23 Messersmith to GFK, June 27, 1939, GFK Papers, 140:10; GFK, *Memoirs,* I, 128.
24 GFK, "The War Problem of the Soviet Union," March 1935, GFK Papers, 250:1; Linnell to American *chargé d'affaires* in Berlin (drafted by GFK), in GFK, *From Prague After Munich,* pp. 88–91; Linnell to State Department (drafted by GFK), May 23 and June 6, 1939, *ibid.,* pp. 177, 183. See also GFK, *Memoirs,* I, 100–101. For the Herwarth affair, see Bohlen, *Witness to History,* pp. 67–87, and Herwarth and Starr, *Against Two Evils,* pp. 153–62.
25 GFK to Messersmith, April 7, 1939, GFK Papers, 250:4; GFK to Jay Pierrepont Moffatt, May 10, 1939, *ibid.,* 140:10.
26 GFK Diary, June 8–14, 1939. See also GFK, *Sketches from a Life,* pp. 57–58.
27 Linnell to State Department (drafted by GFK), August 19, 1939, in GFK, *From Prague After Munich,* p. 217; ASK to JKH, July 10, 1939 and to CKB, September 5, 1939, JEK Papers; GFK to JKH, September 16, 1939, GFK Papers, 23:10.
28 GFK, *Memoirs,* I, 105.
29 ASK to JKH, October 24, 1939, JEK Papers; GFK, *Memoirs,* I, 107–8; GFK to JKH, November 14, 1939, GFK Papers, 23:10.
30 *Ibid.;* ASK to JKH, February 18, 1940, JEK Papers.
31 GFK to JKH, November 14 and December 9, 1939, GFK Papers, 23:10.
32 GFK to JKH, December 31, 1939, *ibid.*
33 GFK, *Memoirs,* I, 115–16; GFK Diary, February 24, and March 4, 1940; GFK to JKH, April 15, 1940, *ibid.,* 23:10. For the Welles mission, see Gellman, *Secret Affairs,* pp. 166–202.
34 GFK untitled paper, February, 1940, GFK Papers, 240:5, GFK Diary, February 24 and 26, 1940. See also GFK, *Memoirs,* I, 116–19.
35 GFK to JKH, February 13 and March 7, 1940, GFK Papers, 23:10.
36 GFK to JKH, April 15, 1940, *ibid.;* ASK interviews, August 26, 1982, p. 9, and December 14, 1987, p. 22.
37 *Ibid.;* GFK Diary, May 4, 1940. GFK dates the departure incorrectly in his *Memoirs,* I, 123–24.

38 GFK Diary, May 6, 8, 10, 14, 17, 1940.
39 *Ibid.,* June 10, 1940.
40 *Ibid.,* June 14, 15, 16, 1940. See also GFK, *Memoirs,* I, 124–27; and GFK, *Sketches from a Life,* pp. 66–68.
41 GFK Diary, July 2, 3, 1940; also GFK, *Sketches from a Life,* pp. 70–74.
42 GFK Diary, August 26–September 6, 1940; GFK to JKH, November 5, 1940, GFK Papers, 23:10; Masarik, *Le dernier témoin de Munich,* pp. 417–18. I am indebted to my Yale student Rene Bystron for this reference.
43 GFK report, "A Year and a Half of the Protectorate of Bohemia and Moravia," October 1940, in GFK, *From Prague After Munich,* pp. 226–40.
44 GFK, *Memoirs,* I, 119–23; GFK to G. van Roon, March 14, 1962, GFK Papers, 56; GFK interview, August 25, 1982, p. 8; Herwarth and Starr, *Against Two Evils,* pp. 177–78.
45 GFK to Jacob D. Beam, October 17 and November 8, 1940, GFK Papers, 140:9. See also Miner, "His Master's Voice," in Craig and Loewenheim, *Diplomats,* p. 78.
46 GFK to JKH, October 21, 1940, GFK Papers, 23:10.
47 ASK interview, August 26, 1982, pp. 9–10; "Kennan Kept Busy in Berlin," *Milwaukee Journal,* February 6, 1941.
48 ASK to JKH, March 23, April 13, and June 5, 1941, JEK Papers; JKH interview, p. 19. The travel dates are from GFK's personnel file, DSR-DF 1940–44, 123K36/338, 342, and 345, but see also GFK to JKH, May 4, 1941, GFK Papers, 23:10.
49 ASK to JKH, April 13 and June 5, 1941, JEK Papers. See also GFK, *Memoirs,* I, 124.
50 ASK interview, December 14, 1987, p. 23; GFK interview, August 25, 1982, p. 6; JLG diary, December 14, 1987.
51 JKH to JLG, August 12, 1983; GFK to JKH, August 6 and September 5, 1941, GFK Papers, 23:10.
52 GFK to JKH, August 17, September 5, and October 29, 1941, *ibid.,* 23:10. For the island, see ASK to JKH, May 31, 1935, JEK Papers; ASK interview, December 14, 1987, p. 26.
53 Vassiltchikov, *Berlin Diaries,* p. 53; GFK, *Memoirs,* I, 130–34. For American warnings to the Soviet Union, see Heinrichs, *Threshold of War,* pp. 21–23, 56.
54 MacLean, *Joseph E. Davies,* pp. 71–79. See also Davies, *Mission to Moscow.* Davies had stepped down as ambassador in June 1938.
55 GFK interview, September 7, 1983, p. 9; GFK to ASK, October 21, 1941, in GFK, *Sketches from a Life,* p. 75.
56 GFK interview, September 7, 1983, p. 9.
57 GFK, *Memoirs,* I, 134.
58 GFK to James W. Riddleberger, November 20, 1941, GFK Papers, 140:8.
59 GFK interviews, August 25, 1982, p. 16, and December 13, 1987, p. 17; GFK to Bullitt, June 9, 1936, Bullitt Papers, T12:21.
60 See GFK, *Memoirs,* I, 109–12; GFK, *Sketches from a Life,* pp. 59–63.
61 GFK interview, September 7, 1983, p. 3.
62 ASK to JKH, March 18, 1938, JEK Papers.
63 Kershaw, *Hitler: Nemesis,* pp. 479–81.

EIGHT • THE UNITED STATES AT WAR: 1941–1944

1 GFK to JKH, October 29, 1941, GFK Papers, 23:10.
2 GFK, *Memoirs,* I, 134–36; Burdick, *American Island in Hitler's Reich,* pp. 8–11, 34–43; and GFK, "Report, the Internment and Repatriation of the American Official Group in Germany, 1941–1942," pp. 422–26, 456–59.
3 GFK interview, December 13, 1987, p. 1. See also Miscamble, *Kennan and the Making of American Foreign Policy,* p. xi.
4 Burdick, *American Island in Hitler's Reich,* p. 43. The information on luggage and pets comes from the internees' newspaper, *Bad Nauheim Pudding,* February 14, 1942, copy in GFK Papers, 231:9.
5 Burdick, *American Island in Hitler's Reich,* pp. 35–36, 39–40, 70–72.
6 List of activities, January 25–29, 1942, GFK Papers, 231:9; Stephen Turnham, "WWII Slugger Earns a Footnote in Baseball History," *Washington Post,* April 11, 1991.
7 "To Whom It May Concern" letter signed by P. W. Whitcomb, Louis P. Lochner, J. P. Dickson, and S. W. Herman, Jr., February 26, 1942, GFK Papers, 231:9. The lecture notes are in *ibid.,* 298:3–8.
8 Untitled, undated lecture notes, *ibid.*
9 GFK to "my dear children," February 1942, *ibid.,* 140:7. For more on this letter, see Chapter One.
10 GFK interview, December 13, 1987, p. 15; typescript marked "Unfinished Story," no date but probably late March or early April 1942.
11 GFK Diary, April 19–22, 1942.
12 *Ibid.,* May 5, 1942.

13 GFK, *Memoirs*, I, 139; GFK interview, December 13, 1987, pp. 16, 19.

14 GFK, *Memoirs*, I, 138; Burdick, *American Island in Hitler's Reich*, pp. 106–8.

15 ASK to Frieda Por, undated but December 1941, JEK Papers; ASK interview, August 26, 1982, p. 11. GFK's query, conveyed through the Swiss, is in the DSR-DF 1940–44, 123K36/368.

16 Frieda Por to State Department, *ibid.*, "123Kennan George F." folder; G. Howland Shaw to GFK, June 12, 1942, *ibid.*, 123K36/371.

17 Bad Nauheim Lecture 2, undated, GFK Papers, 298:5; GFK Diary, April 20, 1942.

18 ASK interviews, August 26, 1982, p. 11, and December 14, 1987, p. 27; GFK to JKH, June 12 and 21, 1942, JEK Papers. The book was M. G. Gains, *Five Acres and Independence: A Practical Guide to the Selection and Management of the Small Farm* (New York: Greenberg, 1940).

19 ASK to JKH, two undated letters, JEK Papers; ASK interview, December 14, 1987, p. 29.

20 *Ibid.*, pp. 29–30; GFK to JKH, July 21 and 22, 1942, JEK Papers.

21 "A Diplomat Moves Into the Joe Miller Place," *York* [Pennsylvania] *Dispatch*, June 13, 1964. Jeanette Hotchkiss and Kent Kennan both brought this story to my attention.

22 GFK Diary, September 8, 1942, ASK to JKH, September 30, 1942, JEK Papers.

23 GFK Diary, August 28, 1942.

24 GFK to JKH, December 1 and 2 [misdated], 1942, and January 31, 1943, GFK Papers, 23:10; ASK to JKH, November 14 and December 10, 1942, February 12, 1943, JEK Papers.

25 Blair Butterworth, "Fond Family Memories of an Extraordinary Man," *Seattle Times*, March 22, 2005. I am indebted to Blair Butterworth for sharing this story with me. See also "Clipper Crashes at Lisbon," *New York Times*, February 23, 1943.

26 GFK, *Memoirs*, I, 143; Robert Meiklejohn Diary, December 23, 1945, Harriman Papers, Box 11; Roberts interview, March 15, 1993, p. 2.

27 GFK, *Memoirs*, I, 143–45. See also GFK's National War College lecture, "Problems of Diplomatic-Military Collaboration," March 7, 1947, p. 7, GFK Papers, 298:29.

28 *Ibid.*, pp. 4–6.

29 GFK to JKH, April 30, July 2, and 20, 1943, GFK Papers, 23:10.

30 GFK to JKH, undated letter composed "at sea," *ibid.*, 23:10. The Gibbon quote is from *Decline and Fall of the Roman Empire*, I, 30. For the Davies film, see MacLean, *Joseph E. Davies*, pp. 91–93, 106–7.

31 GFK to JKH, August 14, 1942, GFK Papers, 23:10.

32 *Ibid.*; GFK to Dunn, September 9, 1943, Dunn to GFK, October 1, 1943, DSR-DF 1940–44, 711.53/31.

33 GFK, *Memoirs*, I, 147–50; GFK National War College lecture, March 7, 1947, pp. 9–13. See also the partial documentation in *FRUS: 1943*, II, 547–50.

34 State Department to GFK, October 16, 1943, GFK to State Department, October 18, 1943, *ibid.*, pp. 554–57. See also GFK, *Memoirs*, I, 150–53.

35 *Ibid.*, pp. 153–55, 163; also *FRUS: 1943*, II, 557–62.

36 GFK, *Memoirs*, I, 156–59.

37 Roosevelt to Salazar, November 4, 1943, in *FRUS: 1943*, II, 564–65. See also GFK, *Memoirs*, I, 159–62. For Leahy's presence on the *Drottningholm*, see Burdick, *American Island in Hitler's Reich*, p. 107.

38 GFK National War College lecture, March 7, 1947, Harlow and Maerz, eds., *Measures Short of War*, p. 151; GFK, *Memoirs*, I, 162–63.

39 Hull to Norweb and GFK, December 4, 1943, in *FRUS: 1943*, II, 576; GFK, *Memoirs*, I, 166; Roberts interview, p. 4. See also Bohlen interview by Wright, p. 4.

40 GFK, *Memoirs*, I, 164–66. See also, for background on the EAC, Gaddis, *United States and the Origins of the Cold War*, pp. 105–9.

41 GFK, *Memoirs*, I, 167–69.

42 *Ibid.*, pp. 168–70.

43 GFK to Bullitt, April 4, 1944, Bullitt Papers, 30:15; GFK, *Memoirs*, I, 171–74. See also the documentation in *FRUS: 1944*, I, 207–9. The map containing the JCS proposal is in *ibid.*, facing p. 196.

44 Quoted in GFK handwritten memorandum, no date but probably March 1944, GFK Papers, Box 1R, "1944" folder. The Gibbon reference is from *Decline and Fall of the Roman Empire*, II, 373. Kennan's airplane reading is confirmed in GFK to JLG, October 18, 1995, JLG Papers.

45 GFK handwritten memorandum, probably March 1944, GFK Papers, 231:12.

46 *Ibid.*; GFK paper on "The Treatment of Germany," enclosed in GFK to Bullitt, April 4, 1944, Bullitt Papers, 30:15; GFK to James W. Riddleberger, June 13, 1944, GFK Papers, 140:6. This memorandum is cited incorrectly in GFK, *Memoirs*, I, 175–78, as dating from 1943.

47 GFK interview, August 25, 1982, pp. 11–12; Bohlen interview by Wright.

48 JEK unpublished memoir, JLG Papers; ASK to GFK, December 24, 1943, DSR-DF 1940–44, 123K/463.

49 Winant to State Department, January 17, 1944, *ibid.*, 123K36/471; S. C. Jalecki memorandum, March 30, 1944, *ibid.*, "123Kennan, George F." folder; GFK, *Memoirs*, I, 171.

50 GFK to Bullitt, April 23, 1944, Bullitt Papers, 30:12; GFK to Eugene Hotchkiss, April 18, 1944, GFK Papers, 140:6; GFK to ASK, April 4 and 24, 1944, DSR-DF 1940–44, 123K36/489 and 495. For the speculation about GFK's ulcer, see Cumming interview, p. 2.
51 GFK to Follmer, May 14, 1944, GFK Papers, 140:6.

NINE • BACK IN THE U.S.S.R.: 1944–1945

1   GFK to Eugene Hotchkiss, April 18, 1944, GFK Papers, 140:6; G. Howland Shaw to GFK, May 22, 1944, DSR-DF 1940–44, Box 474, 123K36/507.
2   The fullest biography of Harriman is Abramson, *Spanning the Century;* but see also Harriman and Abel, *Special Envoy.* The first Kennan's biography is *E. H. Harriman: A Biography.*
3   Harriman interview, September 24, 1982, p. 1. See also Harriman and Abel, *Special Envoy,* p. 229n; and Bohlen, *Witness to History,* pp. 132–33, as well as the extensive correspondence regarding Kennan's Moscow assignment in his State Department personnel file, DSR-DF 1940–44, 123K36/470–81.
4   GFK, *Memoirs,* I, 180–81, 233–34, GFK to Thomas A. Julian, March 31, 1965, GFK Papers, 58:4–8; Harriman interview, pp. 1–3; GFK interview, August 25, 1982, p. 10.
5   GFK remarks to the officer staff of the American legation in Lisbon, June 1944 [specific date not given], GFK Papers, 298:9.
6   GFK Diary, June 15, 1944; ASK to GFK, June 25, 1944, JEK Papers. See also GFK, *Memoirs,* I, 181.
7   Gibbon, *Decline and Fall of the Roman Empire,* III, 49. The Belisarius account is in *ibid.,* II, 559–61.
8   GFK Diary, June 15–18, 1944; GFK to ASK, June 21, 1944, GFK Papers, 23:10.
9   GFK, *Memoirs,* I, 181–85.
10 GFK Diary, June 23–25, 1944; Henderson interview, pp. 4–6.
11 GFK Diary, July 1, 1944.
12 *Ibid.,* July 31, 1944; GFK memorandum, "Russia—Seven Years After," September 1944, in GFK, *Memoirs,* I, 504, 522.
13 "Post Report, American Embassy, Moscow, U.S.S.R.," July 11, 1944, Department of State, Record Group 84, Moscow 1944, Box 30, "124—Post Report." See also Abramson, *Spanning the Century,* pp. 351–52.
14 GFK to JKH, October 8 and November 18, 1944, GFK Papers, 23:10; ASK Interview, September 8, 1983, p. 3; GFK and ASK interview, December 13, 1995, pp. 8–9; JEK to JLG, April 7, 2008, JLG Papers.
15 ASK to JKH, October 6, 12, and November 24, 1944, JEK Papers; John and Patricia Davies interview, December 7, 1982, p. 3.
16 Hessman interview, September 24, 1982, p. 2; Mautner interview, September 24, 1983, p. 1; and John and Patricia Davies interview, December 7, 1982, pp. 4–5. See also Roberts interview, pp. 5–6, and Roberts, *Dealing with Dictators,* p. 94.
17 ASK to JKH, November 24, 1944, JEK Papers. See also Newman, *Cold War Romance of Lillian Hellman and John Melby,* especially pp. 21, 33–34. Hellman's own account is in her *Unfinished Woman,* pp. 125–65.
18 John Hersey to Frances Ann Hersey, December 25, 1944, Hersey Papers, Box 7. I am indebted to my Yale student Kimberly Chow for finding this letter.
19 GFK to JKH, October 8, 1944, GFK Papers, 23:10.
20 Kathleen Harriman to Mary Harriman, July 3, 1944, Harriman Papers, Box 173; GFK Diary, July 2, 1944; S. K. Tsarapkin to Molotov, July 7, 1944, Russian Federation Foreign Policy Archive, Molotov Fond, Opis 6, Papka 46, Delo 610, L 46; Meiklejohn Diary, July 3, 1944, Harriman Papers, Box 11.
21 GFK memorandum, "Comments on the Polish-Russian Question," July 3, 1944, Department of State, Record Group 84, Moscow 1944, Box 39, "711–Poland" folder.
22 Harriman handwritten notes, July 3, 1944, Harriman Papers, Box 173. Roberts, *Stalin's Wars,* pp. 31–117, provides a recent—if charitable—assessment of Stalin's intentions. For the importance of the Atlantic Charter, see Gaddis, *United States and the Origins of the Cold War,* pp. 1–31.
23 Abramson, *Spanning the Century,* pp. 361–63; GFK, *Memoirs,* I, 207–8. The Soviet government finally admitted its responsibility for the Katyn murders in 1990.
24 Harriman handwritten notes, July 3, 1944, Harriman Papers, Box 173; Edward Page memorandum, Harriman-Molotov conversation, June 3, 1944, Department of State, Record Group 84, Moscow 1944, Box 39, "711—Poland" folder.
25 GFK to Harriman, undated but late July 1944, Harriman Papers, Box 173, "July 26–31, 1944" folder; GFK Diary, July 27 and August 1, 1944.
26 GFK diary, August 6, 1944; Harriman to Roosevelt, two cables, August 15, 1944, in *FRUS: 1944,* III, 1374–77; GFK, *Memoirs,* I, 210–11. Kennan erroneously recalls Harriman and Clark Kerr as having been received on this occasion by Stalin himself.
27 *Ibid.,* p. 211; GFK interview, September 7, 1983, p. 18.

28 GFK to Harriman, September 18, 1944, GFK Papers, 140:6. GFK misdates this memorandum as December 16, 1944, in his *Memoirs*, I, 222.
29 GFK to Harriman, October 3, 1944, with Harriman annotation, Harriman Papers, Box 174; GFK interview, August 25, 1982, p. 19; Berlin interview, November 29, 1992, p. 1; Harriman to JLG, September 23, 1982, JLG Papers; Harriman interview, p. 5.
30 The full text, dated "September, 1944," is in DSR-DF 1940-44, 861.00/2-1445, although the date stamp shows that it was not received in the department until February 1945. It also appears in GFK, *Memoirs*, I, 503-31; and excerpts were published in *FRUS: 1944*, IV, 902-14. GFK's comments on the background of the paper are in a letter to R. Gordon Wasson, December 7, 1949, GFK Papers, 140:1; and in a note to Harriman's aide, Robert Meiklejohn, attached to the copy in the Harry Hopkins Papers, Box 217, "1st Russia" folder. I am indebted to Vladimir Pechatnov for this last reference.
31 The actual figure, it is now clear, was closer to 27 million.
32 GFK, *Memoirs*, I, 230-31; GFK to Wasson, December 7, 1949, GFK Papers, 140:1. See also note 30.
33 GFK to JKH, January 25, 1945, GFK Papers, 28:10; Betty MacDonald, *Egg and I* (Philadelphia: Lippincott, 1945).
34 GFK to Bohlen, January 26, 1945, Bohlen Papers, Box 1, "Personal Correspondence, 1944-46," National Archives; Hessman interview, September 24, 1982, pp. 2-3.
35 Bohlen's undated reply, together with his comments on the Kennan letter, are in *Witness to History*, pp. 174-77. See also *ibid.*, pp. 208-9; Bohlen interview by Wright; and GFK interview, August 25, 1982, p. 8.
36 John and Patricia Davies interview, December 7, 1982, pp. 1-2, 12.
37 Sulzberger Diary, March 23, 1945, in Sulzberger, *Long Row of Candles*, p. 250; Mautner interview, p. 2; Roberts interview, p. 5; John Paton Davies interview, December 8, 1982, p. 1; Davies, *Dragon by the Tail*, p. 390.
38 Harriman to Hopkins, September 10, 1944, in *FRUS: 1944*, IV, 988; Harriman interview, p. 2. See also GFK, *Memoirs*, I, 221.
39 GFK to Louis Fischer, October 4, 1954, GFK Papers, 13:8. Harriman's memorandum, drafted on April 10, 1945, is quoted in Miscamble, *From Roosevelt to Truman*, p. 83.
40 JEK to JLG, April 7, 2008, JLG Papers.
41 Bohlen notes, Truman-Harriman conversation, April 20, 1945, in *FRUS: 1945*, V, 232-33.
42 Bohlen notes, Truman-Molotov conversation, April 23, 1945, *ibid.*, pp. 256-58. See also Harriman and Abel, *Special Envoy*, pp. 453-54; and Miscamble, *From Roosevelt to Truman*, pp. 113-23.
43 Gaddis, *United States and the Origins of the Cold War*, pp. 205-15, 224-30; also MacLean, *Joseph E. Davies*, pp. 133-49.
44 GFK to State Department, April 20, 1945, Department of State, Record Group 84, Moscow Harriman Telegrams, Box 4, #111, OWI; GFK to State Department, April 23, 1945, *ibid.*, Box 1, #23 China; GFK to State Department, April 27 and 28, 1945, *ibid.*, Box 6, #155, Reparations Commission; GFK to State Department, April 30, 1945, *ibid.*, Box 1, #8 Austria; GFK to Elbridge Durbrow, May 4, 1945, *ibid.*, Box 5, #118 Poles; GFK to State Department, May 8, 1945, *ibid.*, Box 6, #161A Rumania. See also Roberts, *Dealing with Dictators*, pp. 85-86.
45 GFK, *Memoirs*, I, 240-41. See also C. L. Sulzberger, "Moscow Goes Wild over Joyful News," *New York Times*, May 10, 1945.
46 Bullitt to Roosevelt, January 29, 1943, in Bullitt, *For the President*, pp. 576-90; Forrestal to Homer Ferguson, May 14, 1945, in Millis, *Forrestal Diaries*, p. 57; Churchill to Truman, May 12, 1945, quoted in Gilbert, *"Never Despair,"* p. 7.
47 "Russia's International Position at the Close of the War with Germany," May 1945, in GFK, *Memoirs*, I, 532-46.
48 *Ibid.*, pp. 247, 251, 293; GFK interview, January 30, 1991, p. 5.
49 GFK, *Memoirs*, I, 271. GFK's first request probably came in a meeting with Foreign Ministry official Semyon K. Tsarapkin on July 6, 1944, at which he mentioned the elder Kennan's Siberian connection, as well as his popularity with the Russian revolutionaries of that era. See Tsarapkin to Molotov, July 7, 1944, Russian Federation Foreign Policy Archive, Molotov Fond, Opis 6, Papka 46, Delo 610, L 46.
50 "Trip to Novosibirsk and Stalinsk, June, 1945," GFK Papers, 231:13. See also GFK, *Memoirs*, I, 271-75; GFK, *Sketches from a Life*, pp. 91-110. GFK's postcard to JKH, dated June 18, 1945, is in the JEK Papers.

TEN • A VERY LONG TELEGRAM: 1945-1946

1 GFK to JKH, June 6, 1945, GFK Papers, 23:10. The Finnish legation rental agreement is summarized in GFK to State Department, April 26, 1945, Department of State, Record Group 84, Moscow Harriman Telegrams Box 3, #74 Housing. Kennan's promotion is confirmed in Julius C. Holmes to GFK, June 1, 1945, DSR-DF 1945-49, Box 786, "123 Kennan" folder.

2 GFK interview, August 25, 1982, p. 9; Harriman interview, p. 1. See also GFK, *Memoirs*, I, 293.
3 Kennan's name appeared in *The New York Times* only twelve times from the beginning of 1940 through the end of 1945, in each case in connection with stories on other subjects.
4 GFK, *Memoirs*, I, 256.
5 *Ibid.*, pp. 212–13. Robert Meiklejohn's diary for June 5, 1945, Harriman Papers, Box 11, contains a succinct summary of Kennan's thinking at the time of the Hopkins visit.
6 Miscamble, *From Roosevelt to Truman*, pp. 125–71, provides a comprehensive account of Truman's views and those of his key advisers during this period.
7 GFK to Byrnes, August 20, 1945, DSR-DF 1945–49, Box 786, "123 Kennan" folder; GFK to Matthews, August 21, 1945, GFK Papers, 140:5. For Kennan's objections to the Potsdam agreements, see GFK, *Memoirs*, I, 258–66.
8 Roberts interview, pp. 13–14; GFK to JKH, January 25, 1945, GFK Papers, 23:10; GFK to Charles E. Bohlen, January 26, 1945, Bohlen Papers, Box 1, "Personal Correspondence," National Archives.
9 ASK to GFK, July 29 and September 4, 1945, JEK Papers.
10 GFK Diary, "Journey to Leningrad and Helsinki, September, 1945," in GFK, *Sketches from a Life*, pp. 113–16. See also GFK, *Memoirs*, I, 275–78, 281–83.
11 An American diplomat with long service in Moscow admitted to me in the mid-1980s that he dreamed regularly of Helsinki, especially Stockmann's Department Store.
12 GFK to Harriman, July 25, 1945, Harriman Papers, Box 181.
13 GFK to State Department, July 11, 1945, Department of State, Record Group 84, Moscow Harriman Telegrams, Box 2, #35 Czechoslovakia; GFK to State Department, July 21, 1945, *ibid.*, Box 5, #119 Poles; GFK to State Department, July 21, 1945, *ibid.*, Box 5, #137 Press; GFK to Harriman, July 25, 1945, *ibid.*, Box 6, #167 Russia; GFK to State Department, August 2, 1945, in *FRUS: 1945*, VIII, 624.
14 GFK to State Department, July 15, 1945, Department of State, Record Group 84, Moscow Harriman Telegrams, Box 6, #167 Russia; GFK to Harriman, July 26, 1945, Harriman Papers, Box 181.
15 GFK, *Memoirs*, I, 279; GFK notes, Stalin-Harriman conversation, August 8, 1945, Harriman Papers, Box 181.
16 GFK interview, September 7, 1983, p. 12; GFK to Harriman, September 30, 1945, in *FRUS: 1945*, V, 884n; GFK to Byrnes, September 30, 1945, *ibid.*, pp. 885–86.
17 GFK, *Memoirs*, I, 275–78; Senator Claude Pepper notes on interview with Stalin, September 14, 1945, Harriman Papers, Box 182. Kennan's report on the meeting with the congressmen, sent to the State Department on September 15, 1945, is in *FRUS: 1945*, V, 881–84. For the origins of the "Russian loan" question, see Herring, *Aid to Russia*, pp. 144–78.
18 Transcript, Moscow embassy staff conference, October 10, 1945, Harriman Papers, Box 183; GFK to Byrnes, October 4, 1945, in *FRUS: 1945*, V, 888–91; Byrnes to GFK, October 8, 1945, *ibid.*, p. 888n.
19 Wilgress to the Ministry of External Affairs, Ottawa, November 14, 1945, Pearson to Norman Robertson, December 6, 1945, both in Record Group 25, Volume 5696, External Affairs Records, National Archives of Canada.
20 Unsigned memorandum, October 25, 1945, DSR-DF 1945–49, Box 786, "123 Kennan" folder. See also Bohlen to Harriman, October 5, 1945, *ibid.*
21 Roberts interview, pp. 3, 6. See also Roberts, *Dealing with Dictators*, pp. 92–93.
22 GFK to Harriman, October 12, 1945, Harriman Papers, Box 183; Transcript, Moscow embassy staff conference, October 10, 1945, *ibid.*
23 Messer, *End of an Alliance*, pp. 135–48, provides a good account of Byrnes's thinking. For the failure to consult Bevin, see Bullock, *Ernest Bevin*, pp. 198–99.
24 GFK Diary, December 10, 1945.
25 *Ibid.*, December 14, 1945.
26 *Ibid.*, December 19, 1945. Underlining in the original.
27 GFK Diary, December 17, 1945.
28 GFK draft, "The United States and Russia," winter 1946, in GFK, *Memoirs*, I, 560–65.
29 Wilgress to Norman Robertson, January 15, 1946, Record Group 25, Volume 5696, Ministry of External Affairs Records, National Archives of Canada. Emphasis added.
30 GFK to Durbrow, January 21, 1946, GFK Papers, 140:4.
31 Berlin interview, p. 1; Patricia Davies interview, December 7, 1982, p. 5; Davies, *Dragon by the Tail*, pp. 389–90.
32 Durbrow interview, p. 2; Henderson interview, pp. 3–4; Mautner interview, p. 1; Crawford interview by Wright, pp. 4, 22.
33 Hessman interview, p. 3; Mautner interview, pp. 1–2.
34 Roberts interview, p. 5; Berlin interview, pp. 26, 29.
35 Crawford interview by Wright, September 29, 1970, pp. 2, 23; Berlin interview, pp. 1, 3.
36 John and Patricia Davies interview, December 7, 1982, pp. 5–6; Berlin interview, p. 8.
37 John and Patricia Davies interview, December 7, 1982, pp. 9–10.

718

38 *Ibid.,* pp. 7–8.
39 GFK to Bullitt, January 22, 1946, Bullitt Papers, 32:3.
40 GFK to State Department, January 2, 1946, Harriman Papers, Box 185. Kennan's explanation of the circumstances surrounding the "long telegram" is in his *Memoirs,* I, 293. I myself have perpetuated these errors in several books and in far too many classroom lectures. I am grateful to Nicholas Thompson for actually counting the number of words in the "long telegram."
41 GFK to State Department, February 8, 1946, in *FRUS: 1946,* VI, 693. The text of Stalin's speech was printed in *Vital Speeches of the Day* 12 (March 1, 1946), 300–304.
42 GFK to State Department, February 12, 1946, in *FRUS: 1946,* VI, 694–96; GFK, *Memoirs,* I, 292–93.
43 Durbrow interview, p. 3. I have discussed the shifting Washington mood in *United States and the Origins of the Cold War,* pp. 282–302.
44 Durbrow interview, pp. 3–4; Byrnes to GFK, February 13, 1946, DSR-DF 1945–49, 861.00/2–1245.
45 GFK, *Memoirs,* I, 293; Harriman interview, pp. 5–6; Harriman to JLG, September 23, 1982, JLG Papers; Hessman interview, p. 4; Mautner interview, p. 2.
46 Durbrow interview, pp. 4–5; Matthews to GFK, February 25, 1946, DSR-DF 1945–49, 861.00/2–2246; Byrnes to GFK, February 27, 1946, *ibid.*
47 Harriman interview, pp. 5–6; GFK, *Memoirs,* I, 294–95. See also Harriman to Forrestal, February 26, 1946, Harriman Papers, Box 186; Millis, *Forrestal Diaries,* pp. 135–36; and Hoopes and Brinkley, *Driven Patriot,* pp. 270–73.
48 GFK to State Department, February 22, 1946, DSR-DF 1945–49, 861.00/2–2246. The "long telegram" also appears in *FRUS: 1946,* VI, 696–709.
49 GFK, *Memoirs,* I, 294–95.

ELEVEN • A GRAND STRATEGIC EDUCATION: 1946

1 Lilienthal Diary, March 6, 1946, in Lilienthal, *Journals of Lilienthal,* II, 26.
2 Miscamble, *Kennan and the Making of American Foreign Policy,* p. 27.
3 J. C. Donnelly minute, March 5, 1946, AN 587/1/45; British Foreign Office Records, FO 371/51606, National Archives, London.
4 Byrnes speech to the Overseas Press Club, February 28, 1946, *Department of State Bulletin* 14 (March 10, 1946), 355–58. See also, for the American policy shift as well as the background to Churchill's speech, Harbutt, *Iron Curtain,* pp. 151–82.
5 H. Freeman Matthews to Robert Murphy, March 12, 1946, Murphy to Matthews, April 3, 1946, Robert Murphy Papers, Box 58 (courtesy of Christian Ostermann).
6 Donnelly minute, March 5, 1946.
7 "Looking Outward," *Time* 47 (February 18, 1946), 29–30. The best account of the Bohlen-Robinson report is in Messer, "Paths Not Taken." The first section of the report, completed in December 1945, is *Diplomatic History* 1 (Fall 1977), pp. 389–99, and the final draft version is in DSR-DF 1945–49, 711.61/21446, Box 3428. See also Ruddy, *Cautious Diplomat,* pp. 57–59.
8 Bohlen memorandum, March 13, 1946, Bohlen Papers, Box 4, "Memos (CEB) 1946" folder, National Archives.
9 Matthews to Murphy, March 12, 1946, Murphy Papers, Box 58; Norweb to GFK, March 25, 1946, GFK Papers, 140:4.
10 Roberts interview, March 15, 1993, pp. 4, 10–12. See also Roberts, *Dealing with Dictators,* pp. 107–9. The Roberts dispatches are published in Jensen, *Origins of the Cold War,* pp. 33–67.
11 GFK, "Commentary [on the Novikov Dispatch]," 540–41; GFK interview, December 13, 1995, p. 12; Kondrashov interview by Pechatnov, May 29, 1999. The Novikov dispatch is in Jensen, *Origins of the Cold War,* pp. 3–16. For a confirmation of Kennan's guess about Soviet intelligence, see Pechatnov and Edmondson, "Russian Perspective," in Levering et al., *Debating the Origins of the Cold War,* p. 116.
12 GFK to Bruce Hopper, April 17, 1946, GFK Papers, 140:4.
13 *Ibid.,* GFK to Durbrow, March 7, 1946, Byrnes to GFK, March 11, 1946, Smith to GFK, March 12, 1946, DSR-DF 1945–49, Box 786, "123 Kennan" folder.
14 GFK to Byrnes, March 13, 1946, GFK to Durbrow, March 15, 1946, *ibid.*
15 Durbrow interview, p. 5; GFK to Durbrow, April 2, 1946, DSR-DF 1945–49, Box 786, "123 Kennan" folder.
16 Smith to Matthews, April 17, 1946, *ibid.;* GFK to Bohlen, April 19, 1946, *ibid.*
17 GFK to State Department, May 22, 1946, *ibid.;* ASK to Frieda Por, June 24, 1946, JEK Papers; Donald Russell to GFK, June 20, 1946, DSR-DF 1945–49, Box 786, "123 Kennan" folder.
18 GFK to Smith, June 27, 1946, JEK Papers.
19 GFK, *Memoirs,* I, 307–8; also Earle, *Makers of Modern Strategy.*
20 GFK interview, September 7, 1983, pp. 11–13; also GFK, *Nuclear Delusion,* pp. xiv–xv.
21 GFK 1946 National War College notebook, pp. 5, 14–15, GFK Papers, 231:14; also Brodie, *Absolute Weapon.* The article in question was by Percy E. Corbett.

22 GFK National War College notebook, p. 22.

23 *Ibid.*, pp. 20–21. See also Crane Brinton, Gordon A. Craig, and Felix Gilbert, "Jomini," in Earle, *Makers of Modern Strategy*, pp. 77–92, especially p. 88. Significantly, a July 1946 *Fortune* article on the Foreign Service mentioned a group of its officers who "think in terms of 'containing' Russia by a series of firm stands on specific points: Iran, Trieste, and so on." Kennan was mentioned separately—not in this context—as having written "shrewd and highly literate dispatches from Moscow; Byrnes calls him 'by far the best reporter' in the service." "The U. S. Foreign Service," *Fortune* 34 (July 1946), 81–86, 200–207.

24 GFK National War College notebook, pp. 23, 27. Clausewitz makes a cameo appearance in Tolstoy's account of the Battle of Borodino. See *War and Peace*, p. 774.

25 GFK National War College notebook, pp. 23–27. For background on Rothfels, see Bassford, *Clausewitz in English*, pp. 185–86.

26 GFK interview, August 25, 1982, pp. 20–21.

27 Benton to Henderson and GFK, March 7, 1946, DSR-DF 1945–49, 861.00/2-2246, Box 6462; GFK to Smith, June 7, 1946, *ibid.*, Moscow 1946, Box 106, 711 Russia.

28 GFK, *Memoirs*, I, 298–99; GFK to Smith, June 27, 1946, JEK Papers.

29 GFK interview, September 7, 1983, pp. 17–18. Kennan's report, dated August 23, 1946, is to Francis H. Russell, chief of the State Department's Division of Public Liaison, GFK Papers, 298:11. The Soviet summary is in Russian Federation Foreign Policy Archive, Opis 30, Papka 187, Delo 81, List 111-25. The FBI reports are from Kennan's file, 62-81548, obtained August 11, 2000, under Freedom of Information/Privacy Act request 410933/190-HQ1312163, copies in GFK Papers, 181:3–6.

30 GFK, *Memoirs*, I, 299; GFK to Acheson, October 8, 1946, Acheson Papers, Box 27, "State Department Under Secretary Correspondence, 1945–47" folder, Truman Library; Acheson to GFK, October 11, 1946, DSR-DF 1945–49, Box 786, "123 Kennan" folder.

31 Hill, "Opening Address to the First Class," September 3, 1946, National War College Archives, Washington, D.C. (courtesy of Michael Schmidt); "New War College Enters Atomic Era," *New York Times*, September 4, 1946. See also Harlow and Maerz, *Measures Short of War*, p. xiv.

32 GFK address to Princeton University Bicentennial Conference on University Education and the Public Service, November 13–14, 1946, GFK Papers, 251:6; GFK, *Memoirs*, I, 306.

33 Transcript, GFK National War College lecture and discussion, September 16, 1946, GFK Papers, 298:12. The lecture, though not the record of the question period, is published in Harlow and Maerz, *Measures Short of War*, pp. 3–17.

34 GFK to KWK, October 5, 1946, JEK Papers; GFK, *Memoirs*, I, 307; Hessman interview, pp. 5–6.

35 GFK, *Memoirs*, I, 307.

36 Transcript, Department of State off-the-record briefing by GFK and Llewellyn Thompson, September 17, 1946, GFK Papers, 298:13. For the Wallace controversy, see Blum, *Price of Vision*, pp. 612–32, 661–69.

37 GFK lecture, "'Trust' as a Factor in International Relations," Yale University Institute of International Studies, New Haven, Conn., October 1, 1946, GFK Papers, 298:15. See also Chekhov, "The New Villa," in Ford, *Essential Tales of Chekhov*, p. 303.

38 GFK lecture, "Russia," Naval War College, Newport, R.I., GFK Papers, 298:14. Kennan's thinking on naval strategy may well have been influenced by Margaret Tuttle Sprout's essay on Mahan in Earle, *Makers of Modern Strategy*, especially pp. 433–34.

39 I am indebted, on this point, to my Yale colleague Charles Hill, whose *Grand Strategies* brilliantly illustrates it.

40 Edward A. Dow, Jr., notes, Canadian–United States Defense Conversations, Ottawa, December 16 and 17, 1946, in *FRUS: 1946*, V, 70.

41 GFK to JKII, December 25, 1946, JEK Papers. President Truman had in fact approved Kennan's appointment to the rank of career minister on November 25. Byrnes to GFK, January 6, 1947, DSR-DF 1945–49, Box 786, "123 Kennan" folder.

42 GFK to Waldemar J. Gallman, March 14, 1947, GFK Papers, 140:3; GFK, *Memoirs*, I, 304–5.

43 ASK to Frieda Por, November 10, 1946, and February 10, 1947; GFK to Walter Bedell Smith, June 27, 1946; GFK to KWK, October 5, 1946, all in JEK Papers.

44 GFK to KWK, December 31, 1946 [misdated January 31], *ibid.*; ASK interview, August 26, 1982, p. 13. The fall lectures are listed in *Lecture Program, 1946–1956*, National War College Archives (courtesy of Michael Schmidt).

TWELVE · MR. X: 1947

1 GFK interview, December 13, 1987. Kennan probably had in mind Butterfield's *The Whig Interpretation of History*.

2 Kissinger, *White House Years*, p. 135.

3 GFK, *Memoirs*, I, 367; GFK, "Failure in Our Success," *New York Times*, March 14, 1994; JLG Diary, February 15, 1994, JLG Papers.

4 Council on Foreign Relations Discussion Meeting Report, "The Soviet Way of Thought and Its Effect on Soviet Foreign Policy," January 7, 1947, GFK Papers, 298:21. For background on the Council during this period, see Wala, *Council on Foreign Relations*.

5 Wasson to GFK, January 8, 1947, Armstrong to GFK, January 10, 1947, GFK to Armstrong, February 4, 1947, Armstrong to GFK, March 7, 1947, all in GFK Papers, 140:3.

6 Byrnes to GFK, January 6, 1947, GFK to Byrnes, January 8, 1947, DSR-DF 1945–49, Box 786, "123 Kennan" folder. See also Messer, *End of an Alliance*, pp. 195–216.

7 Pogue, *George C. Marshall*, p. 150; GFK, *Memoirs*, I, 354; Smith to Marshall, January 15, 1947, quoted in Miscamble, *Kennan and the Making of American Foreign Policy*, p. 10; Bohlen interview by Wright. See also GFK interview by Pogue, February 17, 1959, p. 2.

8 *Ibid.*, pp. 2–4; Acheson, *Present at the Creation*, p. 214; GFK, *Memoirs*, I, 313.

9 Henderson interview, p. 7; Balfour to Nevile Butler, January 31, 1947, British Foreign Office Records, FO 371/61045/AN633, National Archives, London.

10 Acheson, *Present at the Creation*, p. 151. For Acheson's shift on policy toward the Soviet Union, see Beisner, *Dean Acheson*, pp. 28–47.

11 Acheson, *Present at the Creation*, pp. 217–18; GFK, *Memoirs*, I, 313. See also F. B. A. Rundall minute, March 10, 1947, British Foreign Office Records, FO 371/61053/AN906.

12 GFK, *Memoirs*, I, 314. See also Acheson, *Present at the Creation*, pp. 217–18, and, for the minutes of the February 24, 1947, meeting, in *FRUS: 1947*, V, 45–47.

13 Acheson, *Present at the Creation*, p. 219. See also Beisner, *Dean Acheson*, pp. 56–57; and Jones, *Fifteen Weeks*, p. 141.

14 SWNCC-FPI 30, "Informational Objectives and Main Themes," undated but approved by SWNCC on March 3, 1947, in *FRUS: 1947*, V, 76; GFK, *Memoirs*, I, 315; Jones, *Fifteen Weeks*, pp. 154–55; Francis H. Russell, "Memorandum on Genesis of President Truman's March 12 Speech," March 17, 1947, in *FRUS: 1947*, V, 123; Henderson interview by McKinzie, June 14, 1973, p. 88.

15 Lilienthal Diary, March 9, 1947, in Lilienthal, *Journals of Lilienthal*, II, 158–59.

16 *Public Papers of the Presidents: Harry S. Truman, 1947*, pp. 178–79; GFK, *Memoirs*, I, 315.

17 GFK National War College lecture, "National Security Problem," March 14, 1947, GFK Papers, 298:30.

18 Acheson executive session testimony, Senate Foreign Relations Committee, March 13, 1947, U.S. Congress, Senate, *Legislative Origins of the Truman Doctrine*, p. 22; GFK, *Memoirs*, I, 322–23.

19 Rusk interview, December 9, 1982, p. 3; Machiavelli, *Prince*, p. 22.

20 Acheson to Hill, March 7, 1947, DSR-DF 1945–49, Box 786, "123 Kennan" folder; GFK National War College lecture, "Problems of Diplomatic-Military Collaboration," March 7, 1947, GFK Papers, 298:29.

21 GFK to John Osborne, July 31, 1962, GFK Papers, 56:5–7.

22 GFK, *Memoirs*, I, 354–55; Forrestal to GFK, February 17, 1947, GFK Papers, 251:7. Kennan did send Admiral Hill a detailed analysis of the Willett paper on October 7, 1946, GFK Papers, 140:4. See also Miscamble, *Kennan and the Making of American Foreign Policy*, p. 31n, and Millis, *Forrestal Diaries*, pp. 127–28; and Hoopes and Brinkley, *Driven Patriot*, pp. 273–76.

23 GFK to John T. Connor, March 10, 1947, GFK Papers, 140:3; Marx Leva to GFK, March 12, 1947, *ibid.*; E. Eilder Spaulding to GFK, April 8, 1947, *ibid.*; GFK to Byron Dexter, April 11, 1947, *ibid.* See also GFK, *Memoirs*, I, 354–55.

24 GFK paper, "Psychological Background of Soviet Foreign Policy," January 31, 1947, GFK Papers, 251:5.

25 Armstrong to GFK, May 15, 1947, *ibid.*, 140:3.

26 GFK, *Memoirs*, I, 355.

27 David Mayers suggests this in *George Kennan and the Dilemmas of U.S. Foreign Policy*, p. 113.

28 GFK to Waldemar J. Gallman, March 14, 1947, and Norris B. Chipman, March 18, 1947, GFK Papers, 140:3.

29 GFK National War College lecture, "Comments on the National Security Problem," March 28, 1947, GFK Papers, 298:31.

30 Bohlen, *Witness to History*, pp. 262–63; Pogue, *George C. Marshall*, pp. 189–90; GFK interview by Pogue, p. 6; GFK interview by Price, p. 1; GFK, *Memoirs*, I, 325–26.

31 For background on the Marshall Plan, see Cohrs, *Unfinished Peace After World War I*; Hogan, *Marshall Plan*; and Behrman, *Most Noble Adventure*.

32 Pogue, *George C. Marshall*, pp. 194–96; Miscamble, *Kennan and the Making of American Foreign Policy*, pp. 46–48; Behrman, *Most Noble Adventure*, pp. 53–62. See also Charles P. Kindleberger's memorandum, "Origins of the Marshall Plan," July 22, 1948, in *FRUS: 1947*, III, 242.

33 Miscamble, *Kennan and the Making of American Foreign Policy*, pp. 38–39; Nitze, Smith, and Rearden, *From Hiroshima to Glasnost*, pp. 50–51; James Reston, "New Role for the State Department," *New York Times Magazine*, May 25, 1947.

34 GFK to Charles James, May 8, 1947, Douglas James Papers.

35 Miscamble, *Kennan and the Making of American Foreign Policy*, pp. 37–39, 48–49, 70; GFK, *Memoirs*, I, 307, 326.

36 PPS/1, "Policy With Respect to American Aid to Western Europe," May 23, 1947, in *FRUS: 1947*, III, 223–30. Charles P. Kindleberger confirms Kennan's insistence on the Europeans taking the initiative in a retrospective memorandum, "Origins of the Marshall Plan," *ibid.*, p. 244. For Kennan's May 6 National War College lecture, see Harlow and Maerz, *Measures Short of War*, p. 186. Marshall's reservations about the Truman Doctrine are mentioned in Bohlen, *Witness to History*, p. 261.

37 Acheson, *Present at the Creation*, pp. 231–34; Pogue, *George C. Marshall*, pp. 208–10; GFK interview by Pogue, pp. 8–9; GFK interview by Price, February 19, 1953, p. 2. Kennan misdates the meeting as May 24 in his *Memoirs*, I, 342.

38 Pogue, *George C. Marshall*, p. 214; Behrman, *Most Noble Adventure*, pp. 71–90.

39 GFK notes for conversation with Marshall, July 21, 1947, in *FRUS: 1947*, III, 335.

40 Marshall interview by Price, February 18, 1953, quoted in Miscamble, *Kennan and the Making of American Foreign Policy*, p. 51; GFK, *Memoirs*, I, 344–45.

41 Balfour to Foreign Office, May 15, 1947, British Foreign Office Records, FO371/61047/AN1795.

42 Joseph Alsop and Stewart Alsop, "Kennan Dispatch," *Washington Post*, May 23, 1947; GFK to Acheson, May 23, 1947, GFK Papers, 140:3.

43 Neal Stanford, "Planning Staff for Foreign Policy" *Christian Science Monitor*, May 26, 1947; "Foreign Policy Planner," *United States News*, May 23, 1947, pp. 61–62; Paul W. Ward, "Diplomats, Historians in New 'Brain Trust,'" *Baltimore Sun*, June 8, 1947; Ferdinand Kuhn, Jr., "Five Thinkers Chart Foreign Policy Reefs for Marshall," *Washington Post*, June 15, 1947.

44 GFK, "The Sources of Soviet Conduct," *Foreign Affairs* 25 (July 1947), 566–82. For the unfortunate Varga, see Wohlforth, *Elusive Balance*, pp. 68–69, 77–87. The *Foreign Affairs* circulation figures come from the July 21, 1947, issue of *Newsweek*, p. 15.

45 Arthur Krock, "A Guide to Official Thinking About Russia," *New York Times*, July 8, 1947.

46 GFK, *Memoirs*, I, 356; United Press account quoted in *Daily Worker*, July 9, 1947; Hessman interview by Wright, October 1, 1970, p. 12; Ernest Lindley, "Article by 'X,'" *Washington Post*, July 11, 1947; Grace Kennan Scrapbook, JEK Papers.

47 "The Story Behind Our Russia Policy," *Newsweek* 30 (July 21, 1947), 15–17.

48 GFK, *Memoirs*, I, 356–57.

49 "Lippmann's 'Cold War,'" *Time*, September 22, 1947; Lippmann, *Cold War*, pp. 4, 6–7, 11, 14. See also Steel, *Walter Lippmann and the American Century*, pp. 443–45.

50 Lippmann interview by Allan Nevins and Dean Albertson, April 8, 1950, pp. 258–59, Walter Lippmann Papers, 123:2419. The British embassy was fully aware of Kennan's position. See Balfour to Bevin, May 15, 1947, British Foreign Office Records, FO 371/61047/AN1795.

51 GFK, *Memoirs*, I, 360; Steel, *Walter Lippmann*, pp. 342–66; GFK interview, February 2, 1977.

52 Armstrong to GFK, November 5, 1947, GFK to Armstrong, November 7, 1947, GFK Papers, 140:3.

53 GFK to Byron Dexter, April 11, 1947, *ibid.*; GFK, *Memoirs*, I, 360.

54 Butterfield, *Whig Interpretation of History*, p. 21; GFK, *Memoirs*, I, 364.

THIRTEEN • POLICY PLANNER: 1947–1948

1 GFK National War College lecture, "Planning of Foreign Policy," June 18, 1947, in Harlow and Maerz, *Measures Short of War*, pp. 207–8.

2 GFK, *Memoirs*, I, 345.

3 GFK's May 5 and June 18, 1947, National War College lectures are in Harlow and Maerz, *Measures Short of War*, pp. 175–216. For the Kennan-Davies relationship, see Miscamble, *Kennan and the Making of American Foreign Policy*, pp. 212–18.

4 GFK notes for Marshall, July 21, 1947, in *FRUS: 1947*, III, 335; PPS/4, "Certain Aspects of the European Recovery Problem from the United States Standpoint (Preliminary Report)," July 23, 1947, *PPS, 1947*, pp. 31–32, 50.

5 Clayton to Robert Lovett, August 25, 1947, in *FRUS: 1947*, III, 377–79. For background on the Paris Conference, see Hogan, *Marshall Plan*, pp. 60–73.

6 Franks interview, August 1, 1987, pp. 1–5.

7 GFK report, "Situation With Respect to European Recovery Program," September 4, 1947, in *FRUS: 1947*, III, 397–405.

8 "Homeward bound—at dawn over mid-Atlantic," GFK Diary, 1947, GFK Papers, 231:15; Pflanze, *Bismarck and the Development of Germany*, p. 80.

9 GFK to Cecil B. Lyons, October 13, 1947, PPS Records, Box 33, "Chronological—1947."

10 GFK talk to the Business Advisory Committee, Department of Commerce, September 24, 1947, GFK Papers, Box 17, "1947, June—December." See also GFK's notes for a conversation with Marshall, July 21, 1947, in *FRUS: 1947*, III, 335.

11   For the organization of the Cominform, see Mastny, *Cold War and Soviet Insecurity*, pp. 30–33.

12   GFK to Lovett, October 6, 1947, PPS Records, Box 33, "Chronological—1947."

13   GFK National War College lectures, "Formulation of Policy in the U.S.S.R.," September 18, 1947, "Soviet Diplomacy," October 6, 1947, and "The Internal Political System [of the Soviet Union]," October 27, 1947, in Harlow and Maerz, *Measures Short of War*, pp. 217–92.

14   PPS/13, "Résumé of World Situation," in *FRUS: 1947*, I, 770–77. For Marshall's summary, see pp. 770n–71n.

15   PPS/15, "Report on Activities of the Policy Planning Staff (May to November 1947)," November 13, 1947, in *PPS Papers*, I, 139–46.

16   For more on the PPS-NSC relationship, see Miscamble, *Kennan and the Making of American Foreign Policy*, pp. 76–78; and Nelson, "Introduction," in *PPS Papers*, I, xix.

17   Philip Harkins, "Mysterious Mr. X.," *New York Herald Tribune* magazine, January 4, 1948.

18   JKH interview, December 21, 1982, p. 26, and ASK interview, August 26, 1982, pp. 14–16.

19   Adams interview by Wright, September 30, 1970, pp. 5, 17; Tufts interview, February 5, 1987, p. 6; and John Paton Davies interview, December 8, 1982, p. 4.

20   Fosdick interview, October 29, 1987, pp. 1–2.

21   Henderson interview, pp. 7–8, and Davies interview, December 8, 1982, p. 5.

22   GFK interview, August 25, 1982, pp. 22–23; Tufts interview, pp. 1–2; and Hessman interview, p. 4; Green interview by Kennedy, March 2, 1995.

23   GFK, "Foreword" in *PPS Papers*, I, vii. I have discussed these papers at length in Gaddis, *Strategies of Containment*, especially pp. 24–86.

24   PPS/8, "United States Policy in the Event of the Establishment of Communist Power in Greece," September 18, 1947, in *PPS Papers*, I, 91–101; PPS/9, "Possible Action by the U.S. to Assist the Italian Government in the Event of Communist Seizure of North Italy and the Establishment of an Italian Communist 'Government' in that Area," *ibid.*, pp. 1027. For "counter-pressures," see GFK's October 6, 1947, National War College lecture, in Harlow and Maerz, *Measures Short of War*, p. 258.

25   GFK to Lovett, August 19, 1947, and Forrestal, September 29, 1947, PPS Records, Box 33, "Chronological—1947."

26   Truman statement, December 13, 1947, *Public Papers of the Presidents: Truman 1947*, document 234. NSC 1/1 is in *FRUS: 1948*, III, 724–27. For more on this episode, see Miscamble, *Kennan and the Making of American Foreign Policy*, pp. 84–87.

27   State Department memorandum, "Coordination of Foreign Information Measures (NSC 4) Psychological Operations (NSC 4-A)," and NSC 4-A, "Psychological Operations," both dated December 17, 1947, in *FRUS: Emergence of the Intelligence Establishment*, pp. 646–51. Truman's approval is noted on p. 650n. For more on the background of these documents, see the editorial introduction on pp. 615–17; see also the CIA's internal history, completed in 1953 but not declassified until 1989: Darling, *Central Intelligence Agency*, pp. 256–62.

28   Henderson memorandum, "Willingness of United States Government in Certain Circumstances to Dispatch United States Forces to Greece," December 22, 1947, in *FRUS: 1947*, V, 458–61; Memorandum of State Department meeting, December 26, 1947, *ibid.*, pp. 468–69; GFK memorandum, NSC meeting, January 13, 1948, in *FRUS: 1948*, IV, 27. See also Miscamble, *Kennan and the Making of American Foreign Policy*, pp. 87–93.

29   PPS/19, "Position of the United States with Respect to Palestine," January 20, 1948, in *PPS Papers*, II, 39–41; GFK Diary, January 28, 1948.

30   PPS/21, "The Problem of Palestine," February 11, 1948, in *PPS Papers*, II, 80–87. See also Miscamble, *Kennan and the Making of American Foreign Policy*, pp. 93–99.

31   GFK, *Memoirs*, I, 368.

32   See, on these anxieties, Mackinder, "Geographical Pivot of History"; Spykman, *America's Strategy in World Politics*, pp. 194–99; and Earle, *Makers of Modern Strategy*, pp. 148, 390–91, 404–5, 444–45, 452, 515, which GFK was reading in the summer of 1946.

33   Joint Chiefs of Staff to the State-War-Navy Coordinating Committee, June 9, 1947, in *FRUS: 1947*, VII, 838–48; GFK to Walton Butterworth, October 29, 1947, PPS Records, Box 33, "Chronological—1947" folder. See also Miscamble, *Kennan and the Making of American Foreign Policy*, pp. 218–20. GFK's National War College comments, delivered on May 6, 1947, are in Harlow and Maerz, *Measures Short of War*, pp. 198–99.

34   "The Situation in China and U.S. Policy," November 3, 1947, PPS Records, Box 13, "China 1947–8" folder.

35   Miscamble, *Kennan and the Making of American Foreign Policy*, pp. 220–23.

36   Notes, Secretary of the Navy's Council Meeting, January 14, 1948, GFK Papers, 299:3.

37   PPS/23, "Review of Current Trends: U.S. Foreign Policy," February 24, 1948, in *FRUS: 1948*, I, 523–29.

38   Morgenthau, *Politics Among Nations*. Joel D. Rosenthal tracks the parallels between GFK and Morgenthau in *Righteous Realists*.

39   PPS/15, "Report on Activities of the Policy Planning Staff (May to November 1947)," November 13, 1947, in *PPS Papers*, I, 146.

40 Travis, *Kennan and the Russian-American Relationship,* pp. 292–93; GFK interview, September 4, 1984, p. 18; Miscamble, *Kennan and the Making of American Foreign Policy,* p. 251; GFK Diary, January 30, 1948; GFK to MacMurray, September 19, 1950, *ibid.,* 139:8. GFK discussed MacMurray's warning in his first book, *American Diplomacy,* p. 48.

41 The best treatment of MacArthur's policies in Japan and of his political aspirations is James, *Years of MacArthur,* III, 1–217. The reference to Caesar is in GFK's report on his first conversation with MacArthur on March 1, 1948, in PPS/28/2, "Memoranda of Conversations with General of the Army Douglas MacArthur," in *PPS Papers: 1948,* II, 184.

42 GFK, *Memoirs,* I, 376.

43 GFK interview by Pogue; Green interview by Kennedy; GFK memorandum of conversation with MacArthur, March 5, 1948, in PPS/28/2, in *PPS Papers,* II, 186. See also GFK, *Memoirs,* I, 382–84; and Hessman interview by Wright, p. 20.

44 GFK, *Memoirs,* I, 384–85; Green interview by Kennedy.

45 James, *Years of MacArthur,* I, 63–66. Kennan family legend has it that one of MacArthur's teachers was Miss Emily Strong, who also taught Jeanette and George, but I have not been able to confirm this independently. JKH interview by JEK, November 2, 1972, p. 35; GFK interview, December 13, 1987, p. 2.

46 GFK memorandum of conversation with MacArthur, March 5, 1948, in PPS/28/2, in *PPS Papers,* II, 187–96; Green interview by Kennedy. See also GFK, *Memoirs,* I, 370, 386; and Schaller, *MacArthur,* pp. 150–51.

47 GFK, *Memoirs,* I, 386; Miscamble, *Kennan and the Making of American Foreign Policy,* pp. 264–68.

48 James, *Years of MacArthur,* III, 233. See also Schaller, *MacArthur,* pp. 150–51.

49 GFK, *Memoirs,* I, 393; GFK interview, September 4, 1984, p. 18.

50 GFK presentation to the Senate Armed Services Committee, "Preparedness as Part of Foreign Relations," January 8, 1948, GFK Papers, 299:1. Soviet sources confirm GFK's argument about the defensive objectives of the Czech coup. See Pechatnov and Edmondson, "The Russian Perspective," in Levering et al., *Debating the Origins of the Cold War,* pp. 134–35.

51 GFK to Marshall, January 6 and February 3, 1948, PPS Records, Box 33, "Chronological January–May 1948" folder. See also Miscamble, *Kennan and the Making of American Foreign Policy,* pp. 116–20.

52 PPS/27, "Western Union and Related Problems," March 23, 1948, in *PPS Papers,* II, 162; GFK to Louis Halle, April 20, 1966, GFK Papers, 59:1–4. See also Miscamble, *Kennan and the Making of American Foreign Policy,* pp. 113–23.

53 *Ibid.,* pp. 103–4. For Clay's message, see Smith, *Lucius D. Clay,* pp. 466–67.

54 GFK to Marshall and Lovett, March 15, 1948, in *FRUS: 1948,* III, 848–49.

55 Hickerson annotation, *ibid.,* p. 849n; Hickerson interview, November 15, 1983, p. 8.

56 GFK, *Memoirs,* I, 403. For GFK's moderate use of alcohol, see Black interview, November 24, 1987, p. 10.

57 James, *Years of MacArthur,* III, 221–26, discusses the other pressures converging on MacArthur at the time.

58 ASK to Frieda Por, March 8, 1948, JEK Papers. See also Miscamble, *Kennan and the Making of American Foreign Policy,* p. 264; Hessman interview by Wright, p. 21; and GFK, *Memoirs,* I, 404.

59 Miscamble, *Kennan and the Making of American Foreign Policy,* pp. 124–27. For Truman speech, see *Public Papers of the Presidents: Truman 1948,* Document 52.

60 Truman Diary, March 20, 1948, in Ferrell, *Off the Record,* p. 127; Marshall memorandum of conversation with Truman, May 12, 1948, in *FRUS: 1948,* V, 975. See also Miscamble, *Kennan and the Making of American Foreign Policy,* pp. 99–102; and Clifford and Holbrooke, *Counsel to the President,* pp. 3–25.

61 GFK, *Memoirs,* I, 403–4.

FOURTEEN • POLICY DISSENTER: 1948

1 GFK, *Memoirs,* I, 360–61.

2 GFK to Lippmann, April 6, 1948, GFK Papers, 299:7.

3 GFK, *Memoirs,* I, 361–63; GFK interview, September 7, 1983, p. 19.

4 PPS/23, "Review of Current Trends: U.S. Foreign Policy," February 24, 1948, in *FRUS: 1948,* I, 522–23.

5 E. Herbert Norman to Department of External Affairs, March 6, 1948, Pearson to Norman, March 11, 1948, Norman Robertson to Escott Reid, April 1, 1948, and May 11, 1948, all in Ministry of External Affairs, Record Group 25, Volume 5697, File 2AE(S), Pt. 2.1, National Archives of Canada. Hankey's minute, dated April 30, 1948, is in the British Foreign Office Records, FO 371/71671, National Archives, London.

6 Davies to George Butler, March 19, 1948, PPS Records, Box 23, "USSR 1946–1950" folder; Bohlen to Lovett, April 22, 1948, Bohlen Papers, Box 1, "Correspondence 1946–49: H" folder, National Archives; Lovett memorandum on April 23, 1948, cabinet meeting, dated April 26, in *FRUS: 1948,* IV, 834n; Marshall to Smith, April 29, 1948, *ibid.,* pp. 840–41; Inverchapel to Foreign Office, May 5, 1948, British Foreign Office

Records, FO 371/68014/AN1914. See also Miscamble, *Kennan and the Making of American Foreign Policy* pp. 186–88.

7 Bevin to Inverchapel, May 11, 1948, conveyed to Marshall on the same date, in *FRUS: 1948*, IV, 860–61n. See also Bullock, *Ernest Bevin*, p. 558.

8 GFK, *Memoirs*, I, 347; GFK to Marshall, May 12, 1948, PPS Records, Box 23, "USSR 1946–1950" folder.

9 Pechatnov and Edmondson, "The Russian Perspective," in Levering et al., *Debating the Origins of the Cold War*, p. 140; Durbrow to State Department, May 18, 1948, in *FRUS: 1948*, IV, 871. For more on the Wallace initiative, see White and Maze, *Henry A. Wallace*, pp. 262–64.

10 GFK to Smith, June 18, 1948, GFK Papers, 140:2. See also GFK to Lovett, June 9, 1948, PPS Records, Box 23, "USSR 1946–1950" folder; and, for the evidence on Wallace's collusion with Moscow, Pechatnov, *Stalin, Ruzvel't, Trumen*, pp. 527–57; and Zubok, *Failed Empire*, pp. 47, 76. Smith's own account of this episode is in his memoir, *My Three Years in Moscow*, pp. 157–66.

11 GFK lecture, "Russia and the Community of Nations," Canadian National Defence College, Kingston, Ont., May 31, 1948, GFK Papers, 299:9.

12 Miscamble, *Kennan and the Making of American Foreign Policy*, pp. 106–8; Weiner, *Legacy of Ashes*, pp. 26–29. Miller, *United States and Italy*, pp. 243–49, provides a good overall account of the election campaign.

13 PPS Memorandum, "The Inauguration of Organized Political Warfare," May 4, 1948, in *FRUS: 1945–1950: Emergence of the Intelligence Establishment*, pp. 668–72. The *FRUS* version of this document indicates that other proposed secret activities have been excised from it. The reference to the Italian elections has also been removed, but it appears in the Policy Planning Staff files and is quoted in Lucas and Mistry, "Illusions of Coherence," p. 52.

14 GFK interview, September 7, 1983, p. 21; Davies interview, December 8, 1982, p. 11. For the Marshall Plan connection, see Pisani, *CIA and the Marshall Plan*.

15 Hillenkoetter to James S. Lay, Jr., June 9, 1948, in *FRUS: 1945–1950*, p. 703. See also the CIA's internal history of these events, Darling, *Central Intelligence Agency*, p. 272.

16 GFK to Lovett and Marshall, June 16, 1948, in *FRUS: 1945–1950*, p. 709. NSC 10/2, "National Security Council Directive on Office of Special Projects," approved by the NSC on June 17, is *ibid.*, pp. 713–15.

17 GFK to Lovett, June 30, 1948, *ibid.*, p. 716; Wisner memorandum, meeting with Hillenkoetter and GFK, August 6, 1948, *ibid.*, p. 720; GFK to Lovett, PPS Records, Box 33, "Chronological July–December" folder. Hersch, *Old Boys*, and Thomas, *Very Best Men*, provide the best accounts of Wisner's life and career. For the dinners, see Weiner, *Legacy of Ashes*, pp. 20–21. Project Umpire is described in Corke, *U.S. Covert Operations and Cold War Strategy*, p. 51.

18 Lovett to Forrestal (drafted by GFK), October 1, 1948, in *FRUS: 1945–1950*, pp. 724–25; GFK to Lovett, October 29, 1948, *ibid.*, pp. 728–29; GFK to Wisner, January 6, 1949, *ibid.*, p. 734. See also Miscamble, *Kennan and the Making of American Foreign Policy*, pp. 109–10.

19 GFK National War College lecture, "Measures Short of War (Diplomatic)," September 16, 1946, in Harlow and Maerz, *Measures Short of War*, p. 17; D. M. Ladd to J. Edgar Hoover, April 18, 1947, FBI Records, 62-81548-4x1, GFK Papers, 181:3–6; GFK to Forrestal, September 29, 1947, PPS Records, Box 33, "Chronological 1947"; GFK Canadian National Defence College lecture, May 31, 1948, GFK Papers, 299:9. See also Chapters Seven, Eight, and Eleven, above.

20 GFK interviews, September 7, 1983, pp. 20–23, 27, and December 13, 1987, p. 21; Davies interview, December 8, 1982, p. 11; GFK to JLG, November 13, 1987, JLG Papers. See also Karalekas, "History of the Central Intelligence Agency," pp. 31–32.

21 A point missed by several secondary studies of Kennan's CIA connections, especially Corke, *U.S. Covert Operations and Cold War Strategy*, and Simpson, *Blowback*. Miscamble, *Kennan and the Making of American Foreign Policy*, pp. 199–205, provides the most balanced assessment.

22 Rusk interview, p. 5; ASK interview, August 26, 1982, p. 15. See also, on Kennan's failure to control OPC, Aldrich, *The Hidden Hand*, pp. 172–73.

23 GFK, *Memoirs*, I, 405–6; GFK to Marshall and Lovett, April 29, 1948, in *FRUS: 1948*, III, 108–9. See also Miscamble, *Kennan and the Making of American Foreign Policy*, pp. 128–29.

24 Reid to Hume Wrong, June 3, 1948, Ministry of External Affairs, Record Group 25, Volume 5800, File 283(S), Pt. 2.2, National Archives of Canada.

25 Franks interview, pp. 16–17; GFK interview by Pogue, pp. 23–25. See also Pogue, *George C. Marshall*, pp. 323–28.

26 GFK interview by Pogue, p. 25 (I have edited this passage slightly for clarity); GFK, *Memoirs*, I, 405–8. See also GFK to Louis Halle, April 20, 1966, GFK Papers, 57:1–4.

27 Hickerson interview, p. 11. The "Washington Exploratory Talks on Security," which ran from July 6 through September 10, 1948, are extensively documented in *FRUS: 1948*, III, 148–250. See also Miscamble, *Kennan and the Making of American Foreign Policy*, pp. 129–33; and Pogue, *George C. Marshall*, pp. 328–35.

28 R. Borden Reams to Marshall, June 30, 1948, in *FRUS: 1948*, IV, 1078. For background on the Yugoslav situation, see Lees, *Keeping Tito Afloat*, pp. 1–79. GFK's prediction of trouble elsewhere is in E. Herbert Norman's report to the Canadian Department of External Affairs on Kennan's Tokyo press briefing, March 6, 1948, Ministry of External Affairs, Record Group 25, Volume 5697, File 2AE(S), Pt. 2.1, National Archives of Canada.

29 PPS/35, "The Attitude of This Government Toward Events in Yugoslavia," June 30, 1948, in *FRUS: 1948*, IV, 1079–81. See also Miscamble, *Kennan and the Making of American Foreign Policy*, pp. 189–93.

30 *FRUS: 1948*, IV, 1079n, tracks the bureaucratic history of PPS/35. For the "wedge" strategy, see Gaddis, *Long Peace*, pp. 147–94; Mayers, *Cracking the Monolith*; and Selverstone, *Constructing the Monolith*.

31 PPS/39, "United States Policy Toward China," September 7, 1948, in *FRUS: 1948*, VIII, 146–55. See also Miscamble, *Kennan and the Making of American Foreign Policy*, pp. 223–26.

32 PPS/39/1, "U.S. Policy Toward China," November 23, 1948, in *FRUS: 1948*, VIII, 208–11; GFK comment, question and answer period, lecture to the Pentagon Joint Orientation Conference, November 8, 1948, p. 23, GFK Papers, 299:17. See also GFK to Marshall and Lovett, November 24, 1948, in *FRUS: 1948*, VIII, 211–12.

33 GFK draft presidential statement, in PPS/45, "U.S. Policy Toward China in the Light of the Current Situation," November 26, 1948, *ibid.*, pp. 219–20; Marshall to Lovett, November 26, 1948, *ibid.* p. 220.

34 PPS39/1, November 23, 1948, *ibid.*, pp. 210–11.

35 GFK to Lovett, June 23, 1948, in PPS/33, "Factors Affecting the Nature of the U.S. Defense Arrangements in the Light of Soviet Policies," in *PPS Papers* II, 281; Forrestal to the NSC, July 10, 1948, in *FRUS: 1948*, I, 591. For the budget battles of this period, see Leffler, *Preponderance of Power*, pp. 220–65; and Hogan, *Cross of Iron*, pp. 159–208.

36 GFK to Marshall and Lovett, August 5, 1948, in *FRUS: 1948*, I, 599–600; GFK to Marshall, August 25, 1948, PPS Records, Box 33, "Chronological July–December 1948" folder.

37 PPS/38, "United States Objectives With Respect to Russia," August 18, 1948, in *PPS Papers*, II, 372–411. See also Schilling, "Politics of National Defense," pp. 185–87.

38 NSC 20/4, "U.S. Objectives With Respect to the USSR to Counter Soviet Threats to U.S. Security," November 23, 1948, in *FRUS: 1948*, I, 662–69. See also Miscamble, *Kennan and the Making of American Foreign Policy*, pp. 197–99; and, for Forrestal's frustration, Hoopes and Brinkley, *Driven Patriot*, pp. 405–19.

39 GFK to Frank Altschul, July 20, 1948, GFK Papers, 140:2; GFK to Lovett, August 2, 1948, PPS Records, Box 15, "Germany 1947–8" folder; GFK to Lovett, August 3, 1948, in *FRUS: 1948*, II, 994n; GFK to Smith, August 20, 1948, GFK Papers, 140:2.

40 PPS/37, "Policy Questions Concerning a Possible German Settlement," August 12, 1948, in *FRUS: 1948*, II, 1287–97.

41 Clausewitz, *On War*, pp. 102, 109. For a more recent treatment of the phenomenon, see Gladwell, *Blink*. See also, for the analogy to painting, Churchill, *Painting as a Pastime*.

42 Hickerson to GFK, August 31, 1948, in *FRUS: 1948*, II, 1287n; GFK interview, September 8, 1983, p. 4; Rusk interview, p. 2; GFK to Marshall and Lovett, September 8, 1948, PPS Records, Box 33, "Chronological July–December 1948" folder.

43 GFK to Marshall, September 17, 1948, *ibid.* See also, for the consultants' meeting, Miscamble, *Kennan and the Making of American Foreign Policy*, pp. 148–49.

44 GFK National War College lecture, "Contemporary Problems of Foreign Policy," September 17, 1948, GFK Papers, 299:12. The Shakespeare reference is from *Hamlet*, Act I, Scene III, lines 62–63: "The friends thou hast, and their adoption tried, / Grapple them to thy soul with hoops of steel."

45 PPS/37/1, "Position to Be Taken by the U.S. at a CFM Meeting," November 15, 1948, in *FRUS: 1948*, II, 1320–38. See also GFK, *Memoirs*, I, 425–26.

46 *Ibid.*, 409–10; PPS/43, "Considerations Affecting the Conclusion of a North Atlantic Security Pact," November 24, 1948, in *FRUS: 1948*, III, 283–89.

47 GFK lecture to Pentagon Joint Orientation Conference, "Estimate of the International Situation," November 8, 1948, pp. 11–12, GFK Papers, 299:17.

48 I have made this argument at greater length in *Strategies of Containment*, pp. 82–83, 86.

49 ASK to Frieda Por, no date, JEK Papers; GFK Diary, September 25–26, 1948. The transcripts of GFK's lectures and speeches are in GFK Papers, 299:8–19. For his lecture schedule, see the list dated March 17, 1949, in PPS Records, Box 33, "Chronological—1949" folder. GFK's NSC staff resignation is in a letter to Sidney Souers, December 3, 1948, *ibid.*, "Chronological July–December 1948" folder.

50 GFK National War College lecture, "Where Are We Today?" December 21, 1948, GFK Papers, 299:19.

51 Fosdick interview, p. 2; Rusk interview, p. 2; GFK interview, September 7, 1983, p. 2.

52 GFK, "Foreword," in *PPS Papers* I, vii.

FIFTEEN • REPRIEVE: 1949

1 GFK lecture to Pentagon Joint Orientation Conference, "Estimate of the International Situation," November 8, 1948, pp. 11–12, GFK Papers, 299:17. For Acheson's appointment, see Acheson, *Present at the Creation*, pp. 249–50; and Beisner, *Dean Acheson*, pp. 82–83.

2 GFK to Acheson, January 3, 1949, Acheson Papers, Box 64, "Memos—conversations January–February 1949" folder, Truman Library. The references to defunct leaders were to Aleksandr Kerensky, prime minister of the Russian Provisional Government until its overthrow by the Bolsheviks in November 1917, Heinrich Brüning, chancellor of Germany from 1930 to 1932, Konstantin Dumba, the last Austro-Hungarian ambassador to the United States, expelled for espionage in 1915, and King Peter II of Yugoslavia, deposed in 1945.

3 Acheson, *Present at the Creation*, p. 141; Franks interview, p. 20; Beisner, *Dean Acheson*, pp. 88–89, 596.

4 GFK interview, October 31, 1974, p. 3; Franks interview, pp. 20–21.

5 GFK, *Memoirs*, I, 426; GFK interview, September 8, 1983, p. 5; Davies interview, December 8, 1982, p. 5. See also Miscamble, *Kennan and the Making of American Foreign Policy*, pp. 157–58, and Beisner, *Dean Acheson*, p. 119.

6 GFK Diary, March 9–10, 1949, GFK Papers, 231:17.

7 GFK to Acheson, January 3, 1949, Acheson Papers, Box 64, Truman Library.

8 Lippmann to GFK, February 1, 1949, Lippmann Papers, 81:1281. Lippmann's column, "The Dark Prospect in Germany," appeared in *The Washington Post* on December 30, 1948. See also Acheson's National War College lecture of September 16, 1948, Acheson Papers, Box 69, "Classified Off the Record Speeches, 1947–52" folder, Truman Library; also Steel, *Walter Lippmann*, pp. 458–59; and Miscamble, *Kennan and the Making of American Foreign Policy*, p. 159.

9 For the extent to which Lippmann's criticisms influenced Program A, see Miscamble, *Kennan and the Making of American Foreign Policy*, pp. 146–47.

10 The Stalin interview is in *FRUS: 1949*, V, 562–63. For Acheson's careful analysis of it and the clarifications that followed, see his *Present at the Creation*, pp. 267–70.

11 Murphy, "Memorandum for the Files," February 19, 1949, Murphy Papers, Box 77 (courtesy of Christian Ostermann). For a representative summary of arguments against Program A, see DRE SP-2, a State Department Office of Intelligence Research paper, "Effects of Postponement of the Western German State," in *FRUS: 1949*, III, 194–95.

12 GFK to Acheson and James Webb, February 8, 1949, PPS Records, Box 15, "Germany 1949" folder; Franks to Foreign Office, March 4, 1949, British Foreign Office Records, FO 371/74160; Murphy minutes, Acheson-GFK conversation, March 9, 1949, in *FRUS: 1949*, III, 102–3; Murphy to Clay, March 10, 1949, Murphy Papers, Box 57 (courtesy of Christian Ostermann). See also Miscamble, *Kennan and the Making of American Foreign Policy*, pp. 161–63; and Beisner, *Dean Acheson*, pp. 134–35.

13 GFK Diary, March 10–12, 1949.

14 GFK Diary, "Visit to Germany," March 10–21, 1949, partially published also in GFK, *Memoirs*, I, 429–42. GFK's account of his conversation with François-Poncet also appears in *FRUS: 1949*, III, 113–14.

15 GFK to Acheson (unsent), March 29, 1949, GFK Papers, 163:58.

16 Miscamble, *Kennan and the Making of American Foreign Policy*, p. 162.

17 Jessup to Acheson, April 19, 1949, in *FRUS: 1949*, III, 859–62; GFK memorandum, "Position of the United States at Any Meeting of the Council of Foreign Ministers on Germany That May Occur," April 15, 1949, *ibid.*, pp. 858–59. See also Miscamble, *Kennan and the Making of American Foreign Policy*, pp. 166–69; and GFK, *Memoirs*, I, 443.

18 Acheson to Lewis Douglas, May 11, 1949, in *FRUS: 1949*, III, 872–73; James Reston, "U.S. Plan Weighed," *New York Times*, May 12, 1949.

19 GFK, *Memoirs*, I, 444–45; Bohlen, *Witness to History*, pp. 285–86; Jessup to Acheson and Murphy, May 14, 1949, in *FRUS: 1949*, III, 878; Acheson to Truman, May 22, 1949, *ibid.*, p. 893; Nitze, *From Hiroshima to Glasnost*, pp. 71–72.

20 Reston, *Deadline*, p. 323; GFK, *Memoirs*, I, 444.

21 Acheson, *Present at the Creation*, pp. 291–92. See also Miscamble, *Kennan and the Making of American Foreign Policy*, pp. 169–70.

22 GFK to Acheson, May 20, 1949, in *FRUS: 1949*, III, 888–90.

23 The cat metaphor comes from Beisner, *Acheson*, p. 141.

24 GFK, *Memoirs*, I, 447. See also, on the larger context, Schwartz, *America's Germany*, pp. 35–40, 306–7.

25 Quoted in Beisner, *Dean Acheson*, p. 544.

26 PPS/49, "Economic Relations Between the United States and Yugoslavia," February 10, 1949, in *PPS Papers*: III, 14–24.

27 PPS/39/2, "United States Policy Toward China," February 25, 1949, *ibid.*, pp. 25–28.

28 GFK National War College lecture, "Where Are We Today?" December 21, 1948, p. 8, GFK Papers, 299:19; Minutes, Policy Planning Staff meeting, March 1, 1949, in *FRUS: 1949*, V, 10.
29 Draft Working Paper, "United States Policy Toward Communism," March 8, 1949, PPS Records, Box 8, "Communism 1947–51" folder. One of the few scholarly evaluations of the Davies-Adams paper is Selverstone, *Constructing the Monolith*, pp. 122–25.
30 PPS minutes, April 1, 1949, in *FRUS: 1949*, V, 12.
31 For a recent overview of American anticommunism, see Morgan, *Reds*. Truman's campaign attacks on Wallace are discussed in Hamby, *Man of the People*, pp. 453–54.
32 Acheson to U.S. embassy in Belgrade, February 25, 1949, in *FRUS: 1949*, V, 873; Willard Thorp memorandum of Acheson conversation with Paul Hoffman, February 19, 1949, *ibid.*, p. 872; Johnson-Acheson meeting memorandum, July 21, 1949, *ibid.*, p. 909; Minutes, Under Secretary of State Staff Meeting, August 31, 1949, Department of State Records, Executive Secretariat Files, Box 13; Eban Ayers Diary, September 15, 1949, Ayers Papers, Box 27, "Diary, 1949" folder.
33 GFK to Acheson, April 19, 1949 (drafted by Robert Joyce), PPS Records, Box 33, "Chronological 1949" folder; PPS/54, "Policy Relating to Defection and Defectors from Soviet Power," June 29, 1949, in *PPS Papers*, III, 80; Minutes, Under Secretary of State Staff Meeting, August 31, 1949, Department of State, Executive Secretariat Files, Box 13.
34 GFK to John Paton Davies, December 6, 1984, GFK Papers, 10:12 (emphases in the original). Kennan wrote Davies after receiving a query from the historian Bruce Cumings, who seemed "very anxious to stage an academic-journalistic coup" by showing that the CIA had planned assassinations "under the influence of the diabolic State Department. Since you and I appear to be almost the only survivors of that period who had anything to do with OPC, I would like to nip this firmly in the bud." The fullest account of Pash's activities is in Simpson, *Blowback*, pp. 152–55, which sees them as providing a justification for subsequent confirmed CIA assassination plots, but does not contradict what Kennan claimed in his letter to Davies.
35 Robert Joyce to Carlton Savage, April 1, 1949, in *FRUS: 1949*, V, 12–13; Minutes, Under Secretary of State Staff Meeting, August 31, 1949, Department of State, Executive Secretariat Files, Box 13; Acheson memorandum, conversation with Bevin, September 14, 1949, in *FRUS: 1949*, V, 316: GFK interview, September 7, 1983, p. 23. Corke, *U.S. Covert Operations and Cold War Strategy*, especially pp. 55, 75, 84, makes the case for GFK's culpability in the Albanian fiasco; for a less accusatory view, see Miscamble, *Kennan and the Making of American Foreign Policy*, pp. 207–9.
36 PPS/59, "United States Policy Toward the Soviet Satellite States in Eastern Europe," August 25, 1949, in *PPS Papers*, III, 130, 134. See also GFK Diary, October 4, 1949.
37 PPS/59, August 25, 1949, in *PPS Papers*, III, 133. For Stalin's purges in Eastern Europe, see Mastny, *Cold War and Soviet Insecurity*, pp. 72–74; Aldrich, *Hidden Hand*, pp. 172–79; and, for post-Stalin developments, Gaddis, *Cold War: A New History*, pp. 104–15.
38 NSC 34/2 (based on PPS/39/2), February 28, 1949, in *FRUS: 1949*, IX, 494–95; Acheson executive session testimony, March 18, 1949, U.S. Congress, Senate, Committee on Foreign Relations, *Historical Series*, p. 30; Jacob Beam memorandum, Acheson-Bevin conversation, April 4, 1949, in *FRUS: 1949*, VII, 1140–41.
39 Goncharov, Lewis, and Xue, *Uncertain Partners*, pp. 33–34; Sheng, *Battling Western Imperialism*, pp. 167–68.
40 Acheson to Truman, July 30, 1949, as published in *The New York Times*, August 6, 1949; Beisner, *Dean Acheson*, pp. 187–88. For GFK's suggestions on what Acheson should have said—not greatly different from what he did say—see GFK to Jessup, July 29, 1949, PPS Records, Box 33, "Chronological 1949" folder.
41 PPS/53, "United States Policy Toward Formosa and the Pescadores," July 6, 1949, in *FRUS: 1949*, IX, 356–64; GFK interview, September 8, 1983, p. 6; Davies interview, December 8, 1982, p. 8. Theodore Roosevelt, of course, never did anything like this.
42 Davies to GFK, December 12, 1984, GFK Papers, 10:12; Rusk interview, p 4 I have discussed the "defensive perimeter" strategy and the Taiwan independence movement in *Long Peace*, pp. 73–81; but see also Miscamble, *Kennan and the Making of American Foreign Policy*, pp 233–34.
43 GFK lecture, Fourth Joint Orientation Conference, September 19, 1949, GFK Papers, 299:30.
44 Minutes, PPS meeting, May 18, 1949, PPS Records, Box 32.
45 Minutes, PPS meeting, June 8, 1949, *ibid.*
46 Minutes, PPS meeting, June 13, 1949, *ibid.*
47 Jebb to GFK, April 7, 1949, in *FRUS: 1949*, IV, 290–91.
48 Minutes, PPS meeting, June 13, 1949, PPS Records, Box 32; Thompson interview, pp. 6–7. Miscamble, *Kennan and the Making of American Foreign Policy*, pp. 281–84, discusses the thoroughness with which GFK approached this problem.
49 Tufts interview, p. 6. For more on the use of consultants, see Miscamble, *Kennan and the Making of American Foreign Policy*, pp. 283–84.

50 PPS/55, "Outline: Study of U.S. Stance Toward Question of European Union," July 7, 1949, in *PPS Papers,* III, 82–100.

51 GFK Diary, July 18, 1949; GFK, *Memoirs,* I, 456–57.

52 Nitze interview by Wright, October 2, 1970; Nitze interview, December 13, 1989, p. 7; Nitze, *From Hiroshima to Glasnost,* pp. 85–86. See also Miscamble, *Kennan and the Making of American Foreign Policy,* pp. 286–87; and the biographical information in Thompson, *Hawk and the Dove.*

53 GFK interview, September 8, 1983, p. 2; GFK Diary, August 23 and September 7, 1949. See also Hogan, *Marshall Plan,* pp. 261–62, and, on the policy of supporting the noncommunist left in Europe, Gaddis, *Long Peace,* pp. 149–52.

54 GFK interviews, August 25, 1982, p. 13, and September 8, 1983, p. 2. See also Hogan, *Marshall Plan,* pp. 262–64, and Beisner, *Dean Acheson,* p. 81.

55 GFK Diary, September 26 and 28, 1949.

56 GFK to Messersmith, July 7, 1949, *ibid.,* 140:1. See also Bohlen, *Witness to History,* p. 288.

57 James E. Webb to C. Ben Wright, October 16, 1975, Wright Papers, Box 1; GFK Diary, September 16 and 19, 1949. See also GFK, *Memoirs,* I, 465–66.

58 Hickerson to GFK, October 15, 1949, PPS Records, Box 27, "Europe 1949" folder; Bohlen to GFK, October 6, 1949, Bohlen Papers, Box 1, "Correspondence 1946–49: K" folder, National Archives; David Bruce to Acheson, October 22, 1949, in *FRUS: 1949,* IV, 343. I have purloined portions of this paragraph and the next two from Gaddis, *Long Peace,* pp. 69–70.

59 GFK to Bohlen, November 7, 1949, GFK Papers, 140:1.

60 Bohlen to GFK, undated but November 1949, *ibid.;* GFK to Bohlen, November 17, 1949, *ibid.*

61 GFK Diary, November 19 and 22, 1949.

62 GFK Diary, August 30, September 1–2, 1949; Acheson handwritten comment on GFK to Acheson and Webb, September 2, 1949, PPS Records, Box 33, "Chronological 1949" folder.

63 GFK Diary, October 4, 13, 24, November 7, 1949.

64 *Ibid.,* November 12, 1949.

65 *Ibid.,* November 16 [misdated 15], 1949; GFK to Dodds, December 29, 1949, *ibid.,* 140:1.

66 GFK to Charles James, December 10, 1949, Douglas James Papers.

67 Lovett to Bohlen, October 21, 1949, and Bohlen to Lovett, December 19, 1949, Bohlen Papers, Box 2, "Correspondence 1949–July 1951: L" folder, National Archives; Hoyer Millar to Makins, December 10, 1949, Makins to Hoyer-Millar, December 15, 1949, British Foreign Office Records, FO 371/74160/AN3813; Hoyer-Millar to Makins, December 23, 1949, *ibid.,* FO 371/81614/AU1017/4. See also "Kennan Maps Rest from U.S. Duties," *New York Times,* December 11, 1949.

68 Acheson National War College remarks, December 21, 1949, Webb Papers, Box 20 (courtesy of Michael Devine and Sam Rushay); GFK to Acheson, December 21, 1949, Acheson Papers, Box 64, "Memos—conversations December 1949" folder, Truman Library; GFK National War College lecture, "Where Do We Stand?" December 21, 1949, pp. 32–33, GFK Papers, 299:32.

69 Mary Bundy interview, December 6, 1987, p. 10; Acheson National War College remarks, December 21, 1949, Webb Papers, Box 20; Alsop to GFK, December 31, 1949, Joseph and Stewart Alsop Papers, Part 1, General Correspondence, Box 5, "November–December 1949" folder. These paragraphs draw on Beisner, *Dean Acheson,* especially p. 654, as well as my review of it in *New Republic* 235 (October 16, 2005), 32.

Sixteen • Disengagement: 1950

1 GFK National War College lecture, "Where Do We Stand?" December 21, 1949, GFK Papers, 299:32. The Adams brothers' prophecies were in Brooks Adams, *America's Economic Supremacy,* and in *The Education of Henry Adams* (completed in 1905), especially p. 494. The Thoreau quotation is from *Week on the Concord and Merrimack Rivers,* p. 440.

2 GFK to Acheson, July 18, 1946, in *FRUS: 1946,* I, 864; GFK lecture to the National Defense Committee of the U.S. Chamber of Commerce, January 23, 1947, p. 4, GFK Papers, 298:23; question and answer transcript to GFK's lecture, "Russia's National Objectives," at the Air War College, April 10, 1947, pp. 13–14, *ibid.,* 298:32. Kennan's own account of his early thinking on atomic weapons is in *Memoirs,* I, 310–12, and in GFK, *Nuclear Delusion,* pp. xiv–xvi.

3 GFK to McGeorge Bundy, March 14, 1980, GFK Papers, 7:10; GFK untitled lecture to "Selected Leaders of Industry," January 14, 1948, p. 27, *ibid.,* 299:2; GFK Diary, March 18, 1949.

4 R. Gordon Arneson memorandum, "Tripartite Negotiations Chronology," undated, in *FRUS: 1949,* I, 506–7. The Joint Chiefs of Staff report, "Evaluation of Effect on Soviet War Effort Resulting from the Strategic Air Offensive," May 11, 1949, is excerpted in Etzold and Gaddis, *Containment,* pp. 360–64. Nuclear stockpile figures are from Norris and Kristensen, "Nuclear Notebook," p. 66. For GFK's lack of access to this information, see Bundy, *Danger and Survival,* p. 201.

5 PPS/58, "Political Implications of Detonation of an Atomic Bomb by the U.S.S.R.," August 16, 1949, in *PPS Papers: 1949*, pp. 122–23; GFK to JLG, October 1, 1993, JLG Papers.

6 GFK Diary, September 13, 19, 20, 23, 24, 1949.

7 *Ibid.*, September 27, 1949; Rhodes, *Dark Sun*, pp. 374–77. Botti, *Long Wait*, pp. 1–64, covers the history of these negotiations. For the significance of Fuchs's espionage for the Soviet bomb project, see Holloway, *Stalin and the Bomb*, pp. 220–23.

8 Rhodes, *Dark Sun*, pp. 252–54, 374–75, 381. In fact, the Soviet Union had been working on its own "super" since 1946. See Holloway, *Stalin and the Bomb*, p. 295.

9 PPS minutes, November 3, 1949, in *FRUS: 1949*, I, 573–76; Beisner, *Dean Acheson*, p. 230. See also GFK Diary, October 12, 1949, GFK Papers, 231:18. GFK's meeting that day was with "Eisenhower's colonels," a group of officers recruited by General Dwight D. Eisenhower, now the president of Columbia University but still a consultant to the Joint Chiefs of Staff, for the purpose of thinking about national security issues on a five- to ten-year time scale.

10 Oppenheimer to GFK, November 17, 1949, in *FRUS: 1950*, I, 222–23; GFK draft statement, November 18, 1949, Oppenheimer Papers, Box 43, "Kennan" folder. See also Bird and Sherwin, *American Prometheus*, p. 425.

11 Nitze to Acheson, December 19, 1949, in *FRUS: 1949*, I, 610–11. See also Nitze, *From Hiroshima to Glasnost*, pp. 87–91; and Miscamble, *Kennan and the Making of American Foreign Policy*, pp. 303–4.

12 GFK memorandum, "The International Control of Atomic Energy," January 20, 1950, extracts published in *FRUS: 1950*, I, 22–44. The Shakespeare is from *Troilus and Cressida*, Act I, Scene 3. See also the Lilienthal Diary, December 18, 1949, in Lilienthal, *Journals of Lilienthal*, II, 610; and GFK, *Memoirs*, I, 472. I have borrowed portions of the above paragraphs from Gaddis, *Strategies of Containment*, pp. 77–78.

13 GFK to Lucius Battle, January 24, 1950, in *FRUS: 1950*, I, 22, GFK, *Memoirs*, I, 474. Acheson's comment is from an April 9, 1963, interview by David McLellan, quoted in his *Acheson*, p. 176. GFK confirmed that Acheson never said this to him, in a letter to George Krol, February 9, 1981, GFK Papers, 1:2.

14 Report by the Special Committee of the National Security Council, "Development of Thermonuclear Weapons," January 31, 1950, in *FRUS: 1950*, I, 513–17. See also Miscamble, *Kennan and the Making of American Foreign Policy*, pp. 306–7.

15 Nitze interview, p. 3.

16 Rusk interview, p. 5; Acheson National War College remarks, December 21, 1949, Webb Papers, Box 20.

17 GFK National War College lecture, December 21, 1949, GFK Papers, 299:32, pp. 27–28. For the riots in Bogotá, see Pogue, *George C. Marshall*, pp. 385–93. GFK's 1948 National War College lecture is discussed in Chapter Fourteen, above.

18 GFK Diary, February–March 1950. See also GFK, *Memoirs*, I, 476–484, and *Memoirs*, II, 65–70. Ilya Repin's painting, *Easter Procession in the Region of Kursk*, is in the Tretyakov Gallery, Moscow.

19 GFK to Acheson, March 29, 1950, in *FRUS: 1950*, II, 598–624. I have also drawn, with reference to GFK's views on Guatemala, on an April 3, 1950, memorandum from Edward W. Clark, of the Office of Middle American Affairs, to Edward G. Miller, assistant secretary of state for inter-American affairs, describing GFK's views, DSR-DF 1950–54, Box 608, "123 Kennan" folder.

20 For the first interpretation, see Miscamble, *Kennan and the Making of American Foreign Policy*, pp. 316–17; Mayers, *Kennan and the Dilemmas of U.S. Foreign Policy*, pp. 261–66; Beisner, *Dean Acheson*, p. 571; Stephanson, *Kennan and the Art of Foreign Policy*, pp. 162–65; and Trask, "George F. Kennan's Report on Latin America." For the second, see Hixson, *George F. Kennan*, pp. 70–71; LaFeber, *Inevitable Revolutions*, pp. 107–8; and Smith, *Last Years of the Monroe Doctrine*, pp. 65–73.

21 I owe this phrase to the physicist Murray Gell-Mann.

22 GFK speech, "Current Problems in the Conduct of Foreign Policy," Milwaukee, May 5, 1950, GFK Papers, 251:13. Most of the speech was published in the *Department of State Bulletin* 22 (May 15, 1950), 747–61.

23 See, for example, GFK's off-the-record address to the Pentagon Joint Civilian Orientation Conference, April 17, 1950, pp. 12–14, GFK Papers, 299:39. Acheson's National Press Club speech of January 12, 1950, "Crisis in Asia—an Examination of U.S. Policy," is in *Department of State Bulletin* 22 (January 23, 1950), 111–18. It followed NSC 48/2, "The Position of the United States with Respect to Asia," approved by Truman on December 30, 1949, in *FRUS: 1949*, VII, 1215–20, which in turn grew out of the PPS/39 series, dating from September 1948.

24 Beisner, *Dean Acheson*, pp. 281–306, provides a vivid account of these events. For McCarthy's speech, see Oshinsky, *Conspiracy So Immense*, pp. 108–12.

25 Davies interview, December 8, 1982, pp. 12–13. See also GFK, *Memoirs*, II, 196–97, 200–203; Corke, *U.S. Covert Operations and Cold War Strategy*, pp. 78–80; and Kahn, *China Hands*, pp. 244–46.

26 GFK to Webb, March 30, 1950, in *FRUS: The Intelligence Community, 1950–1955*, pp. 5–8.

27 The lecture, delivered on May 5, 1950, is in GFK Papers, Box 2, "May 5, 1950" folder, along with the handbill. For GFK's complaint, see the Summary of Daily Meeting with the Acting Secretary, May 8, 1950,

Department of State, Summaries of the Secretary's Daily Meetings, 1949–52, E 393, Box 1 (courtesy of Thomas Schöttli).

28 ASK to GFK, February 23, 1950, JEK Papers.

29 PPS minutes, October 11, 1949, PPS Records, Box 32. For GFK's earlier thinking on conventional deterrence, see PPS/33, "Factors Affecting the Nature of the U.S. Defense Arrangements in the Light of Soviet Policies," June 23, 1948, in *PPS Papers*, II, 281–92; and GFK, *Memoirs*, I, 311–12.

30 GFK draft memorandum to Acheson (substance conveyed orally), February 17, 1950, in *FRUS: 1950*, I, 165; Hammond, "NSC-68," pp. 291–92.

31 Nitze to Acheson, December 19, 1949, in *FRUS: 1949*, I, 610–11; GFK to Acheson, February 17, 1950, in *FRUS: 1950*, I, 165; Acheson, *Present at the Creation*, p. 753; GFK to Ellis O. Briggs, November 2, 1948, GFK Papers, 140:2. See also Nitze, *From Hiroshima to Glasnost*, pp. 96–97, and Gaddis, *Strategies of Containment*, pp. 91–92.

32 GFK interview, August 26, 1982, pp. 1–2; Nitze interview, p. 6.

33 See May, *American Cold War Strategy*. For Davies's contribution, see Nitze, *From Hiroshima to Glasnost*, p. 94.

34 Hammond, "NSC-68," pp. 310–15; Bohlen, *Witness to History*, p. 291.

35 Acheson, *Present at the Creation*, pp. 374–75; GFK interview, October 31, 1974, p. 5.

36 Hammond, "NSC-68," pp. 317–18; Acheson, *Present at the Creation*, p. 347; Davies interview, pp. 9–10. This paragraph parallels closely one in my *Strategies of Containment*, p. 85. See also Nitze, *From Hiroshima to Glasnost*, p. 99.

37 ASK to KWK, January 3, 1950, JEK Papers; GFK to Ralph Jarvis, January 9, 1950, GFK Papers, 139:8.

38 JEK unpublished memoir.

39 GFK to Oppenheimer, February 13, 1950, Oppenheimer Papers, Box 42, "GFK" folder; GFK to Joseph H. Willits, February 16, 1950, GFK Papers, 139:8; GFK, *Memoirs*, I, 485; GFK Diary, November 22, 1949.

40 *Ibid.*, September 22, 1949; Acheson to GFK, October 17, 1949, GFK to Palmer, November 1, 1949, both in GFK Papers, 251:12; GFK, "Is War with Russia Inevitable? Five Solid Arguments for Peace," *Reader's Digest* (March 1950), 1–9. See also, on publicity, GFK Diary, November 12, 1949.

41 GFK to Oppenheimer, June 5, 1950, Oppenheimer Papers, Box 43, "GFK" folder; GFK Diary, June 10 and 15, 1950; JKH interview, p. 25; GFK, *Memoirs*, I, 469–70; Alsop with Platt, *"I've Seen the Best of It,"* pp. 306–7.

42 The best account of the origins of the Korean War is now Stueck, *Rethinking the Korean War*, pp. 11–83.

43 GFK, *Memoirs*, I, 484–85; Alsop, *"I've Seen the Best of It,"* pp. 306–7; Acheson, *Present at the Creation*, p. 402; Nitze, *From Hiroshima to Glasnost*, pp. 101–2. See also GFK interview by Paige, August 1, 1955, p. 1.

44 Nitze, *From Hiroshima to Glasnost*, p. 86; GFK, *Memoirs*, I, 486–87.

45 GFK Diary, June 25, 1950; GFK interview by Paige, p. 3. See also Gaddis, *Long Peace*, pp. 86–87.

46 GFK Diary, June 27, 1950.

47 Alsop, *"I've Seen the Best of It"*, pp. 308–9; GFK Diary, June 27 and 29, 1950.

48 *Ibid.*, June 26, 30, July 1, 10, 12, 17, 25, 1950; GFK background press conference, August 22, 1950, GFK Papers, 299:41. See also Bohlen, *Witness to History*, p. 291.

49 GFK Diary, June 29, July 11, 25, 1950.

50 *Ibid.*, July 17, 31, 1950.

51 *Ibid.*, June 28, July 21, 31, 1950. See also the PPS draft memorandum of July 22, 1950, in *FRUS: 1950*, VII, 449–54; Bohlen, *Witness to History*, pp. 292–93; and Nitze, *From Hiroshima to Glasnost*, p. 107.

52 Allison to Nitze, July 24, 1950, in *FRUS: 1950*, VII, 460–61; GFK Diary, June 29 and August 14, 1950; GFK to Acheson, August 23, 1950, Acheson Papers, Box 65, Memoranda of Conversations, "August, 1950" folder, Truman Library. See also, on the 38th parallel debate, Gaddis, *Long Peace*, pp. 97–99.

53 GFK to Acheson, August 21, 1950, in *FRUS: 1950*, VII, 623–28; Acheson, *Present at the Creation*, p. 446.

54 Nitze interview, p. 8; Berlin interview, pp. 12–13.

SEVENTEEN • PUBLIC FIGURE, PRIVATE DOUBTS: 1950–1951

1 Quoted in Adam Begley, "Lonely Genius Club," *New York Magazine*, January 30, 1995, 61-67. See also GFK, *Memoirs*, II, 17–18. Regis, *Who Got Einstein's Office?*, provides an informal history of the Institute but never mentions Kennan. The Institute prepared its own shorter unpublished history on its seventy-fifth anniversary in 2005, entitled simply *Institute for Advanced Study*.

2 Dodds to GFK, January 3 and February 14, 1950, GFK to Dodds, February 16, 1950, GFK Papers, 11:1. See also Bird and Sherwin, *American Prometheus*, pp. 371–72, 431–32.

3 GFK, *Memoirs*, II, 20; Bird and Sherwin, *American Prometheus*, pp. 371–72, 427, 432. See also Chapter Sixteen, above, and Herken, *Brotherhood of the Bomb*, p. 206.

4 GFK, *Memoirs*, II, 4, 9–10, 18–19; GFK Diary, September 11, 1950 [misdated September 10].

5 GFK to Acheson, September 12, 1950, Acheson Papers, Box 32, "Secretary of State Alphabetical: Kelley-King" folder, Truman Library; GFK, *Memoirs*, II, 4–7; GFK lecture to Miss Fine's School, May 23, 1951, GFK Papers, 300:6. The decline list is in the GFK Diary for 1950.

6 GFK, *Memoirs*, II, 8–9; GFK to Arthur Nevins, November 14, 1950, GFK Papers, 139:8; GFK to Gleason, October 6, 1950, *ibid*. For the reunion, see Chapter Sixteen, above.

7 GFK to Dodds, November 13, 1950, GFK Papers, 11:1; GFK to Earle, October 6, 1950, enclosing draft letter to James Russell, *ibid.*, 139:8.

8 GFK, *Memoirs*, II, 19. For Oppenheimer's assessment of von Neumann's computer, see Institute for Advanced Study, *Report of the Director*, pp. 9–13; also Poundstone, *Prisoner's Dilemma*, pp. 76–78.

9 GFK to Alsop, October 20, 1950, Alsop Papers, Part 1, General Correspondence, Box 5, October 1950.

10 Marshall to MacArthur, September 29, 1950, in *FRUS: 1950*, VII, 826. Chen, *China's Road to the Korean War*, provides the best account of Chinese decision making during the early months of the Korean War; but see also Stueck, *Rethinking the Korean War*, pp. 102–11.

11 GFK Diary, December 1950. For the events of that week, see Stueck, *Korean War*, pp. 130–32.

12 GFK Diary, December 1950; GFK, *Memoirs*, II, 28–31; GFK to Acheson, December 4, 1950, Acheson Papers, Box 65, "Memoranda of Conversations, December, 1950" folder, Truman Library; Acheson, *Present at the Creation*, p. 476.

13 Minutes, Truman-Attlee meeting, December 4, 1950, in *FRUS: 1950*, VII, 1367.

14 Lucius D. Battle memorandum, Acheson meeting with GFK, Rusk, Nitze, and others, December 4, 1950, in *FRUS: 1950*, VII, 1345–46; W. J. McWilliams memorandum, Acheson meeting with GFK, Rusk, Nitze, and others, December 5, 1950, *ibid.*, p. 1385; GFK to Alsop, December 17, 1950, Alsop Papers, Part 1, General Correspondence, Box 6, "December, 1950" folder.

15 GFK to KWK, January 2, 1951 [misdated 1950], JEK Papers.

16 GFK, "How New Are Our Problems?" and "The National Interest of the United States," delivered on January 29–30, 1951, at Northwestern University, later published in *Illinois Law Review* 45 (1951), 718–42. See also GFK's Roosevelt Day Dinner address to the Americans for Democratic Action, New York, January 27, 1951, GFK Papers, 251:17, reprinted as GFK, "Let Peace Not Die of Neglect," *New York Times Magazine*, February 25, 1951, pp. 10ff; and his report for the Woodrow Wilson Foundation, "American Participation in Multilateral Authority," March 15, 1951, *ibid.*, 300:3. GFK discussed his growing environmental interests in a September 8, 1983, interview, pp. 18–20. Berlin's article, entitled "Political Ideas in the Twentieth Century," appeared in *Foreign Affairs* 28 (April 1950), 351–85.

17 "Kennan Joins Ford Foundation," *New York Times*, February 20, 1951; Hoffman to GFK, March 12, 1951, GFK Papers, 13:18. The salary figures are from a memorandum GFK prepared for the State Department, January 23, 1951, *ibid.*, and from Bird and Sherwin, *American Prometheus*, p. 432. See also "Ford Fund Grants Emphasize 'Deeds,'" *New York Times*, June 3, 1951; and GFK to KWK, December 17, 1951, JEK Papers.

18 GFK to Hoffman, February 8 and March 8, 1951, GFK Papers, 13:18; Schlesinger undated diary entry, in Schlesinger to JLG, March 31, 1994, JLG Papers; Schlesinger interview, p. 1; Oppenheimer to Robert M. Hutchins, February 16, 1951, Lewis Strauss Papers, IAS Files, Box 108 (courtesy of Craig Wright); GFK to KWK, March 1, 1951, JEK Papers.

19 GFK to Hoffman, March 8, 1951, GFK Papers, 13:18; "Ford Found to Aid Soviet Refugees," *New York Times*, May 18, 1951. For the first Kennan's work with Russian exiles, see Travis, *George Kennan*, pp. 195–248.

20 Chester, *Covert Network*, pp. 43–53, provides a good account of the Ford Foundation's relationship with the CIA. See also Pisani, *CIA and the Marshall Plan*, pp. 46–52.

21 GFK interview, September 7, 1983, pp. 23–26; GFK to Nicholas Nabokov, October 18, 1951, GFK Papers, 32:13. See also Chester, *Covert Network*, pp. 49–51, 124–27; and GFK, *Memoirs*, II, 8–9.

22 *Ibid.*, pp. 72–73, GFK to Hoffman, March 8, 1951, GFK Papers, 13:18. For Morgenthau's role, see Thompson interview, p. 7.

23 Link interview, p. 1, GFK interview, September 8, 1983, p. 8; and Rusk interview, p. 6. See also Earle to Leopold, February 2, 1951, Richard W. Leopold Papers, 45:6.

24 GFK Diary, April 2–4, 1951.

25 *Ibid.*, April 9, 16, 1951. GFK's opening lecture, entitled "Introduction," is in the GFK Papers, 251:21.

26 GFK, *Memoirs*, II, 75–76; Thompson interview, December 6, 1982, pp. 1–2.

27 GFK Diary, April 16–17, 1951, GFK Papers, 232:2.

28 *Ibid.*, August–September 1951.

29 Corrigan and Cory memorandum, May 3, 1951, in *FRUS: 1951*, VII, 401–10.

30 Davies to Nitze, May 8, 1951, *ibid.*, pp. 421–22.

31 G. Frederick Reinhardt summary of GFK's views, sent to Acheson on March 17, 1951, *ibid.*, pp. 241–43.

32 GFK memorandum, undated, GFK to Tsarapkin, May 26, 1951, both *ibid.*, pp. 460–62.

33 GFK to Matthews, May 31, 1951, *ibid.*, pp. 483–86. See also Acheson, *Present at the Creation*, pp. 532–33.

34 GFK to Matthews, June 5, 1951, in *FRUS: 1951*, VII, 507–11.
35 GFK to Acheson, June 20, 1951, *ibid.*, pp. 536–38.
36 GFK, *Memoirs*, II, 37–38. Stueck, *Korean War*, pp. 204–347, covers the lengthy armistice negotiations in detail.
37 GFK to ASK, July 24, 1951, JEK Papers; GFK to Hoffman, March 8, 1951, GFK Papers, 13:18; GFK Diary, June 30, 1951.
38 *Ibid.*, July 5, 1951; GFK speech on the *Oslofjord*, July 4, 1951, GFK Papers, 300:8.
39 GFK Diary, July 10, 1951.
40 GFK to ASK, July 24, 1951, JEK Papers; GFK, *Memoirs*, II, 207. See also, on the Davies investigation, Ybarra, *Washington Gone Crazy*, pp. 564–65.
41 GFK to George W. Perkins, July 24, 1951, GFK Papers, 139:7; GFK to ASK, July 24, August 6 and 8, 1951, JEK Papers.
42 GFK to Acheson, September 1, 1951, GFK Papers, 139:7. The handwritten copy is in GFK's State Department personnel file, DSR-DF 1950–54, Box 608, "123 Kennan" folder.
43 Both poems, undated, are in the GFK Diary for the summer of 1951. The summary, dated only September 1951, is in GFK Papers, 164:27.
44 GFK Diary, undated but late summer 1951; GFK, *Memoirs*, II, 105–6; and Ruddy, *Cautious Diplomat*, p. 106, where Bohlen's suggestion is misdated as having been made in 1952.
45 ASK interview, September 8, 1983, pp. 1–2.
46 John and Patricia Davies interview, December 7, 1982, pp. 13–14; GFK to JKH, October 26, 1951, and to KWK, December 17, 1951, JEK Papers; GFK, *Memoirs*, II, 62.
47 James Reston, "Our Ways in Diplomacy," *New York Times*, September 30, 1951; GFK to Alsop, October 3, 1951, Alsop Papers, Part 1, Box 6, "October, 1951" folder; GFK to Oppenheimer, October 4, 1951, Oppenheimer Papers, Box 43, "Kennan" folder. See also GFK, *Memoirs*, II, 76–77; and GFK, *American Diplomacy*, pp. 6–7.
48 Despite the reference to "this room," the dinosaur did not appear in the text of GFK's Chicago lectures—although it's possible that he might have improvised it. The lectures are in the GFK Papers, 251:21–23, 252:1–3. The dinosaur is in *American Diplomacy*, p. 59.
49 Thompson interview, p. 1; *Time*, October 8, 1951. See also Lippmann, *U.S. Foreign Policy*; Niebuhr, *Children of Light and Children of Darkness*; and Morgenthau, *Politics Among Nations*.
50 GFK to Toynbee, March 31, 1952, GFK Papers, 139:5.
51 GFK to *New York Times*, August 16, 1952 (not sent), *ibid.*; Elim O'Shaughnessy memorandum, August 19, 1952, DSR-DF 1950-54, "123 Kennan, George F." file; GFK to Bohlen, August 21, 1952, GFK Papers, 139:4; Jessup to George Wadsworth, September 9, 1952, Philip Jessup Papers, 1:9. For Walsh's attack, see Warren Weaver, "'Dangerous' Views Charged to Envoy," *New York Times*, July 28, 1952.
52 GFK, "How New Are Our Problems?" The announcement of the American Political Science Association award is in *The New York Times*, August 27, 1952. Rosenthal, *Righteous Realists*, discusses GFK's place within the "realist" tradition. GFK acknowledged not having read Thucydides in a letter to Louis J. Halle, September 27, 1993, Louis J. Halle Papers, 4:1. I am indebted for this citation to Michael Schmidt, whose 2008 Yale History Department senior essay, "Present at the Creation: Thucydides in the Cold War," quotes it.
53 James Reston, "Kennan Is Slated for Post of Ambassador to Moscow," *New York Times*, November 20, 1951; Salisbury, *Journey for Our Times*, pp. 407–8; Gromyko to Stalin, December 12, 1951, Russian Federation Foreign Policy Archive, Fond 3, Opis 66, Delo 279, List 134–36. Parker's book was published as *Conspiracy Against Peace* in 1949. GFK's account of this episode is in his *Memoirs*, I, 243–46.
54 GFK to Cumming, December 31, 1951, GFK Papers, 139:7.

EIGHTEEN • MR. AMBASSADOR: 1952

1 Louis Cassels, "'Mr. X' Goes to Moscow," *Collier's*, March 12, 1952, pp. 19–20, 87–90; Link interview, p. 8; GFK to Bishop John of San Francisco, December 17, 1951, GFK Papers, 139:7; GFK to Dr. John Bodo, January 18, 1952, *ibid.*, 5:15; GFK to Nicholas and Patricia Nabokov, January 14, 1952, *ibid.*, 32:13.
2 GFK dinner speech, Pasadena, February 7, 1952, *ibid.*, 300:17.
3 GFK to Acheson, copy in GFK Diary, January 23, 1952.
4 Executive Session testimony, March 12, 1952, U.S. Congress, Senate, Committee on Foreign Relations, *Historical Series*, IV, 190–92; "Kennan Is Confirmed," *New York Times*, March 14, 1952.
5 Transcript, GFK State Department press conference, April 1, 1952, pp. 16–17, GFK Papers, 300:18.
6 GFK retrospective diary, April 22–23, 1952. See also GFK's account of his April 3, 1952, meeting with Panyushkin in *FRUS: 1952–54*, VIII, 968–70.
7 Richard Rovere, "Letter from Washington," *New Yorker*, May 17, 1952, pp. 122–33.

8 "Off to Europe for Business and Pleasure," *New York Herald Tribune*, April 24, 1952. The envelope, dated "probably April, 1952," is in GFK Papers, 232:3.

9 I owe this analogy to Toni Dorfman, whose November 2009 Yale undergraduate production of *The Cherry Orchard* caused me to see it.

10 ASK interview, September 8, 1983, p. 3; ASK to JKH, CKB, and Grace Wells, May 13, 1952, JEK Papers; John and Patricia Davies interview, December 7, 1982, p. 14; GFK, *Memoirs*, II, 112, which gives the date, incorrectly, as May 5.

11 GFK to ASK, May 7, 8, and 11, 1952, JEK Papers. See also GFK's presentation to the State Department's Division of Research for Europe, January 22, 1953, GFK Papers, 164:37; ASK interview, September 8, 1983, p. 3; and GFK, *Memoirs*, II, 112–15.

12 GFK to Acheson, May 14, 1952, DSR-DF 1950–54, Box 608, "123 Kennan" folder; GFK, *Memoirs*, II, 119–20; GFK to ASK, May 15, 1952, JEK Papers.

13 GFK to ASK, May 16, 1952, *ibid.*; GFK to State Department, in *FRUS: 1952–54*, VIII, 972–73, 976.

14 GFK to ASK, May 16, 22, 25, and June 3, 1952, JEK Papers; GFK, *Memoirs*, II, 116.

15 GFK to ASK, June 3 and 11, 1952, JEK Papers.

16 Reber to Robert Joyce, June 25, 1952, DSR-DF 1950–54, Box 608, "123 Kennan" folder.

17 De Silva, *Sub Rosa*, pp. 71–74. De Silva misdates the meeting as having occurred in June 1953.

18 GFK interview, December 13, 1987, pp. 27–28. See also Cumming interview, April 17, 1984, p. 17.

19 Durbrow interview, p. 13; Nancy Jenkins to Nitze, May 27, 1980, Paul H. Nitze Papers, 29:5. See also Thompson, *Hawk and the Dove*, p. 138.

20 GFK to ASK, May 11 and 31, 1952, JEK Papers; GFK, *Memoirs*, II, 125–26; Salisbury, *Journey for Our Times*, pp. 403–4, 413–14.

21 GFK to Matthews, July 15, 1952, in *FRUS: 1952–54*, VIII, 1024.

22 GFK to ASK, June 8, 1952, JEK Papers. See also Hoffmann, *Cold War Casualty*; and Kirk, *Postmarked Moscow*. GFK's dispatch to Matthews referred to the "Grew" diary, leading the editors of *Foreign Relations of the United States* to confuse it with the recently published diaries of his old Foreign Service examiner Joseph C. Grew. See *FRUS: 1952–54*, VIII, 973, 1007, 1011–12; and the comment on this in Hoffmann, *Cold War Casualty*, pp. 19–20.

23 Gascoigne to Sir William Strang, June 16, 1952, British Foreign Office Records, FO 371/100836/NS 10345/15; Cumming interview, pp. 4–5; Hessman interview, p. 14.

24 GFK to Matthews, June 6, 1952, in *FRUS: 1952–54*, VIII, 987–1000. Jacob Liberman's portrayal of Lopakhin in the November 2009 Yale production of *The Cherry Orchard* conveyed clearly to me what Kennan meant.

25 Durbrow interview, p. 13; Cumming interview, pp. 5–6.

26 GFK to Matthews, June 18, 1952, in *FRUS: 1952–54*, VIII, 1004–10; GFK, *Memoirs*, II, 153–54; ASK interview, September 8, 1983, p. 1; Cumming interview, pp. 9, 13. Microwave beams became a long-standing problem for the American embassy in Moscow. See Steneck, *Microwave Debate*, pp. 92–118, who correctly dates the beginning of the surveillance in 1952 but inaccurately claims that it was first deployed not at the Mokhovaya but at the new embassy facilities on Tchaikovsky Street. The embassy moved to that location only in 1953.

27 GFK to Bohlen, June 29, 1952, in *FRUS: 1952–54*, VIII, 1017–20. The Alsop columns appeared in *The Washington Post* on June 9, 11, 13, 18, and 20, 1952, and were widely syndicated elsewhere. *Time's* story on GFK's concerns, entitled "Russia: Report from Moscow," appeared in the June 30, 1952, issue.

28 See Chapter Seventeen, above.

29 Or so I surmise, after much wrestling with this puzzling episode. There are always a few things biographers neglect to ask their subjects about while they have the chance. This, unfortunately, is one of them.

30 Harrison Salisbury, "View from Mokhovaya Street," *New York Times Magazine*, June 1, 1952, pp. 7, 30–33.

31 GFK to Robert Strunsky, June 9, 1952, GFK Papers, 46:12.

32 GFK, *Memoirs*, II, 130–31.

33 My account of this episode comes from GFK interview, August 26, 1982, pp. 6–10, and Cumming interview, pp. 7–11, as well as a brief retrospective diary entry, dated September 29, 1952, GFK Papers, 232:3, and GFK, *Memoirs*, II, 146–50.

34 Yakovlev interview by Pechatnov, November 13, 1994. See also Arbatov, *System*, p. 44n. For a mild sample of Yakovlev's writing, see Sivachev and Yakovlev, *Russia and the United States*. Shortly after becoming Kennan's biographer—but without knowing Yakovlev's connection to the 1952 episode—I was treated to an opulent but bizarre dinner in his Moscow apartment at which he spent a very long evening alternately praising and bitterly denouncing "Georgi Frostovich."

35 GFK to Acheson, July 25, 1952, in *FRUS: 1952–54*, VI, 1584–87. I have edited this passage slightly to fill in telegraphic abbreviations.

36 Salisbury, *Journey for Our Times*, pp. 411, 416. For the Alsops' column, see "Stalin Speaks Again," *Washington Post*, August 8, 1952.

37 GFK to Acheson, August 16, 1952, DSR-DF 1950-54, 661.00/8-1652; R. L. Thurston to GFK, August 16, 1952, *ibid.*

38 GFK to Acheson, August 23, 1952, *ibid.,* 661.51/8-2352; GFK to Matthews, August 25, 1952, in *FRUS: 1952–54,* VIII, 1042–45. Dixon's minute of August 29, 1952, is in the British Foreign Office Records, FO 371/100830/NS1026/17.

39 I have discussed the 1952 Stalin "note" more fully in *We Now Know,* pp. 125–29; see also Zubok, *Failed Empire,* pp. 82–84.

40 GFK to State Department, May 25, 1952, in *FRUS: 1952–54,* VII, 252–53. See also Beisner, *Dean Acheson,* pp. 606–15.

41 Parker, *Conspiracy Against Peace,* p. 199; V. Bazykin to Andrey Vyshinsky, May 9, 1952, Russian Federation Foreign Ministry Archive, Fond 0129, Opis 36, Papka 247, Delo 23, L. 3.

42 GFK to Matthews, August 25, 1952, in *FRUS: 1952–54,* VIII, 1044; H. A. F. Hohler to P. F. Grey, December 15, 1952, British Foreign Office Records, FO 371/100826/NS 1023/34G. See also Brent and Naumov, *Stalin's Last Crime.*

43 ASK to Grace Wells and Frieda Por, July 18, 1952, JEK Papers; ASK interview, September 8, 1983, p. 4.

44 GFK, *Memoirs,* II, 118–19, 129–30. For GFK's previous visit, see Chapter Five.

45 GFK to Bernard Gufler, August 12, 1952, GFK Papers, 139:4; "U.S. Is Told to Move Offices in Moscow," *New York Times,* July 8, 1952; GFK to Bohlen, August 21, 1952, GFK Papers, 139:4; Cumming interview, p. 12.

46 Richard Davies interview by Jessup, November 9, 1979; Toon interview by Mattox, June 9, 1989; John Foster Dulles, "Policy of Boldness," *Life* 32 (May 19, 1952), 146-60. See also Bowie and Immerman, *Waging Peace,* pp. 75–77.

47 GFK to Matthews, August 8, 1952, GFK Papers, 139:4. See also GFK, *Memoirs,* II, 124–25.

48 *Ibid.,* pp. 136–37; GFK interview, December 13, 1987, p. 26. See also NSC 73/4, "The Position and Actions of the United States With Respect to Possible Further Soviet Moves in the Light of the Korean Situation," August 25, 1950, in *FRUS: 1950,* I, 380.

49 GFK to Barklie Henry, September 9, 1952, copy in Oppenheimer Papers, Box 43, "Kennan" correspondence; GFK, *Memoirs,* II, 137–38.

50 GFK to State Department, September 8, 1952, *ibid.,* pp. 327–51. The original is in DSR-DF 1950–54, 661. 00/9-852.

51 L. W. Fuller to Nitze, September 23, 1952, *ibid.,* Box 608, "123 Kennan" folder; C. L. Sulzberger Diary, April 1, 1954, in Sulzberger, *Long Row of Candles,* p. 987. See also, for the origins of the chiefs of mission meeting, *FRUS: 1952–54,* VI, 636–43, and "U.S. Envoys to Confer," *New York Times,* September 19, 1952.

52 GFK, *Memoirs,* II, 153–57; GFK to Rebecca Matlock, October 29, 1987, GFK Papers, 27:18; Bullitt to State Department, March 4, 1936, in *FRUS: The Soviet Union, 1933–1939,* pp. 289–91. See also, for the technology of the bug, Wallace and Melton, *Spycraft,* pp. 162–65. For more on the Brown dispatches, see Chapter Five, above.

53 GFK, *Memoirs,* II, 157–58.

54 Salisbury, *Journey for Our Times,* p. 414. Salisbury's cautious account of this conversation, passed through Soviet censors, appeared the next day as "GFK Sees View on Soviet Correct," *New York Times,* September 19, 1952.

55 GFK, *Memoirs,* II, 156–59; GFK notebook, GFK Papers, 232:3; Jack Raymond, "GFK Describes Isolation in Soviet," *New York Times,* September 20, 1952.

56 Cumming interview, pp. 17–19.

57 GFK Diary, September 29, 1952. See also GFK, *Memoirs,* II, 161–62, and, for the minutes of the chiefs of mission meeting, *FRUS: 1952–54,* VI, 643–65.

58 The *Pravda* statement appeared in the September 27 issue of *The New York Times.* Molotov, in prepublication editing, dropped a reference to the "X" article, "a vileful pasquinade against the Soviet Union" that Kennan had published "hiding under [an] alias." The draft is in the Russian Federation Foreign Policy Archive, Fond 3, Opis 66, Delo 279, List 46.

59 GFK to Acheson, September 26, 1952, in *FRUS: 1952–54,* 1048–51.

60 GFK to ASK, September 27, 1952, Department of State, Record Group 84, Moscow 1950–54, Box 167, "123 Kennan—personal" folder; Acheson press conference, September 26, 1952, in *FRUS: 1952–54,* VIII, 1048n; "Kennan to Return to Post," *New York Times,* September 30, 1952.

61 GFK Diary, September 29, 1952. For the communication to McSweeney, see *FRUS: 1952–54,* VIII, 1053.

62 JKH to GFK and ASK, September 28, 1952, JEK Papers; Acheson, *Present at the Creation,* p. 697.

63 GFK, *Memoirs,* II, 164; GFK notebook, GFK Papers, 232:3. The passage is from *Henry VIII,* Act III, Scene 2.

64 ASK interview, September 8, 1983, pp. 6–8; ASK to JKH, September 19, 1952, JEK Papers.

65 ASK interview, September 8, 1983, pp. 8–9.

66 O'Shaughnessy to State Department, in *FRUS: 1952–54,* VIII, 1052–53n; GFK, *Memoirs,* II, 165.

67 GFK to Gufler, October 27, 1952, GFK Papers, 139:4; Cloyce K. Huston to State Department, October 27, 1952, DSR-DF 1950–54, Box 608, "123 Kennan" folder.

68 H. T. Morgan minute, October 9, 1952, British Foreign Office Records, FO 371/100836/NS 10345/28; Sulz-
    berger Diary, October 24, 1952, in Sulzberger, *Long Row of Candles*, p. 784. See also Bohlen, *Witness to History*,
    p. 312.
69 Davies interview by Jessup.
70 Marshall's account is in "Memorandum for the File," July 9, 1981, Nitze Papers, 29:5.
71 GFK to Nitze, July 26, 1952, GFK Papers, 139:4; GFK to Bohlen, October 7, 1952, Bohlen to GFK, October
    8, 1952, DSR-DF 1950–54, Box 608, "123 Kennan" folder; GFK, *Memoirs*, II, 168.
72 J. H. A. Watson report, October 9, 1952, enclosed in Christopher Steel to Paul Mason, same date, British
    Foreign Office Records, FO 371/100836/NS 10345/33.
73 Bohlen interview by Wright, p. 12; Bohlen to Livingston Merchant, August 23, 1955, Bohlen Papers, Box
    36, "Correspondence—Special, George Kennan, 1951–70," Library of Congress. See also Bohlen, *Witness to
    History*, p. 312.
74 GFK, *Memoirs*, II, 165–67.
75 *Ibid.*, p. 168; "GFK Returns, Silent on Moscow Ban," *New York Herald Tribune*, November 12, 1952; "GFK
    Returns to See Acheson," *New York Times*, November 12, 1952.
76 GFK, *Memoirs*, II, 170; JKH to KWK, December 2, 1952, JEK Papers.
77 GFK Diary, March 13, 1953; GFK, *Memoirs*, II, 170; GFK National War College lecture, "Tasks Ahead in
    U.S. Foreign Policy," December 18, 1952, GFK Papers, 300:21.
78 ASK to Frieda Por, December 28, 1952, JEK Papers; GFK to KWK, December 25, 1952, *ibid.*; ASK inter-
    view, September 8, 1983, p. 11.

NINETEEN • FINDING A NICHE: 1953–1955

1 GFK to KWK, December 25, 1952, JEK Papers.
2 GFK, *Memoirs*, II, 170–71; GFK Diary, July 17, 31, 1950; "Dulles Says U.N. Being Slighted," *New York Times*,
   September 27, 1952; Dulles to Lewis W. Douglas, September 29, 1952, Box 59, "Douglas" folder, Dulles
   Papers. See also Dulles, "Policy of Boldness"; Dulles to the editors of *Commonweal*, September 5, 1952,
   Dulles Papers, Box 59, "Containment" folder; and, for GFK's differences with Dulles during the Korean
   War, Chapter Sixteen, above.
3 Dulles to GFK, October 2, 1952, GFK to Dulles, October 22, 1952, Dulles to GFK, October 29, 1952, Dulles
   Papers, Box 61, "Kennan" folder.
4 See, on this issue, GFK, *Memoirs*, II, 97–102.
5 *Ibid.*, pp. 170–71; GFK Diary, March 13, 1953. For Marshall's recollection, see Chapter Eighteen, above.
6 GFK to David Bruce, December 11, 1952, GFK Papers, 139:4; GFK Diary, March 13, 1953; GFK, *Memoirs*, II,
   171; Bohlen, *Witness to History*, p. 310.
7 Kuhn, "Dulles Policy 'Dangerous,' Kennan Says," *Washington Post*, January 17, 1953; GFK, *Memoirs*, II,
   174–75; GFK to Matthews, January 18, 1953, copy in GFK Diary, March 13, 1953. The Scranton speech is
   in GFK Papers, 252:10.
8 GFK, *Memoirs*, II, 175–76; State Department press conference transcript, January 23, 1953, GFK Papers,
   Box 252:10; GFK to Jacob Beam, January 25, 1953, *ibid.*, 4:11 GFK to John McSweeney, February 11, 1953,
   ibid., 139:1–3.
9 ASK to JKH, January 19, 1953, JKH to GFK and ASK, January 19, 1953; GFK to ASK, February 3, 1953, all
   in JEK Papers.
10 GFK Diary, March 13, 1953; William H. Lawrence, "Dulles Expected to Retire Kennan, Considered Top
    Expert on Soviet," *New York Times*, March 13, 1953.
11 GFK to Oppenheimer, March 15, 1953, Oppenheimer Papers, Box 43; GFK interview, August 26, 1982, pp.
    12–13; GFK, *Memoirs*, II, 176–77, 180. The latter page misdates the meeting as March 14. See also GFK's
    retrospective diary account, dated April 6, 1953.
12 Robert J. Ryan memorandum on GFK's retirement, June 17, 1953, DSR-DF 1950–54, Box 608, "123 Kennan"
    folder; GFK to Acheson, April 28, 1953, Acheson Papers, 17:222, Yale University; GFK Diary, July 29, 1953;
    GFK, *Memoirs*, II, 178, 181, 187–89. GFK mistakenly gives the month here as June.
13 Joseph Alsop and Stewart Alsop, "Kennan's Insight Will Be Missed," *Washington Post*, April 12, 1953;
    "Who's On Second?" *Chicago Sun-Times*, April 15, 1953. For the Bohlen controversy, see his *Witness to
    History*, pp. 309–36; and Ruddy, *Cautious Diplomat*, pp. 109–24. Ferguson's comment is in GFK, *Memoirs*,
    II, 180–81; see also the GFK Diary, April 6, 1953.
14 Eisenhower to Walter Mallory, March 4, 1950, and to GFK, November 3 and December 12, 1950, in Chan-
    dler et al., *Eisenhower Papers*, XI, 1000, 1403–4, 1474; also the transcript of GFK's Air War College lecture,
    April 10, 1947, GFK Papers, 298:32; GFK to George S. Franklin, February 2, 1949, *ibid.*; and GFK to Ache-
    son, November 24, 1950, Acheson Papers, Box 32, Truman Library.

15 GFK interview, August 26, 1982, pp. 12–13.
16 Bowie interview, December 10, 1987, pp. 1–4, 8–9, 15; Berlin interview, pp. 11, 17; William P. Bundy interview, December 6, 1987, p. 7.
17 Hughes to Adams, July 2, 1953, Eisenhower to GFK, July 8, 1953, GFK to Eisenhower, July 24, 1953, Dwight D. Eisenhower Papers, White House Central File: Subject Series, Confidential File, Box 67, Department of State Folder 9 (courtesy of Melvyn P. Leffler). See also Hughes, Ordeal of Power, p. 120n. For the origins of Project Solarium, see Bowie and Immerman, Waging Peace, pp. 123–27.
18 GFK comments at the Princeton University John Foster Dulles Centennial Conference, February 27, 1988, in Pickett, Kennan and the Origins of Eisenhower's New Look, pp. 17–19. See also GFK Diary, June 1, 1953.
19 "A Report to the National Security Council by Task Force 'A' of Project Solarium," July 16, 1953, pp. 13–14, 18, 22, 24, 57, Eisenhower Papers, NSC Series, Subject Subseries, Records of the White House Office of the Special Assistant for National Security Affairs.
20 GFK, Memoirs, II, 182; GFK comments at Dulles conference, February 27, 1988, in Pickett, Kennan and the Origins of Eisenhower's New Look, pp. 19–20.
21 For an extended comparison of GFK's thinking with that of Eisenhower and Dulles, see Gaddis, Strategies of Containment, pp. 125–96; also Immerman, Dulles and Diplomacy of the Cold War, p. 263.
22 Oppenheimer to GFK, October 6, 1952, GFK to Oppenheimer (telegram and letter), October 14, 1952, Oppenheimer to GFK, March 13, 1953, Oppenheimer Papers, Box 43.
23 GFK to Harry D. Gideonse, May 5, 1953, GFK Papers, 139:1–3; GFK to Harold Dodds, May 1, 1953, GFK Papers, 11:10; GFK Diary, April 6, 28, and June 1, 1953.
24 GFK to Dodds, May 1, 1953, GFK Papers, 11:10.
25 GFK, "Training for Statesmanship," Atlantic Monthly 191 (May 1953), 40–43; GFK Notre Dame speech, May 15, 1953, GFK Papers, 252:13. See also GFK, Memoirs, II, 224–26; and, for press coverage, "Kennan Upbraids Anti-Red Zealots," New York Times, May 16, 1953. For the social scientists' skepticism about GFK, see Engerman, Know Your Enemy, p. 3.
26 GFK address at the Joint Memorial Celebration of the Emmanuel Evangelical-Reformed and the St. John Lutheran Churches of Hampton, Reading Township, Adams County, May 27, 1953, GFK Papers, 300:24. I have compressed this talk to convey its structure within limited space.
27 GFK Diary, August 18, 1953. GFK's SAIS seminar outlines are in GFK Papers, 300:27.
28 GFK Diary August 18, 20, 31, 1953. GFK, Memoirs, II, 4–5, 187–89, confuses the dates of these episodes, an error repeated in Sketches from a Life, pp. 158–60.
29 GFK Diary, August 21, 1953. Kennan had obviously read Reinhold Niebuhr by this time, probably Moral Man and Immoral Society.
30 GFK address, "Basic Problems in the American Approach to Foreign Policy," Woodrow Wilson School, Princeton University, October 5, 1953, GFK Papers, 300:28.
31 GFK Laymen's Sunday sermon, First Presbyterian Church, Princeton, N.J., October 18, 1953, ibid., 253:7.
32 GFK Diary, October 28 and November 9, 1953, GFK Papers.
33 GFK address to Student Christian Association conference, Princeton University, December 6, 1953, ibid., 253:11.
34 GFK, Realities of American Foreign Policy, p. vii.
35 Ibid., especially pp. 29–30, 53, 84–85, 93–94, 102, 111–12, 118–19. GFK first used this horticultural metaphor, as noted in Chapter Five, above, in 1935. It's strikingly similar to one his fellow farmer Acheson frequently employed. See Beisner, Dean Acheson, p. 92.
36 GFK draft letter to Herbert Brownell, September 6, 1953, GFK Papers, 139:1–3; GFK notes on conversation with Robert Murphy, November 25, 1953, ibid., 253:12; Davies interview, December 8, 1982, p. 14. See also GFK's extended account in his Memoirs, II, 200–214.
37 Ibid., pp. 214–18, 228. The Oppenheimer case and the long series of events that led up to it are discussed thoroughly in Bird and Sherwin, American Prometheus, and in Herken, Brotherhood of the Bomb.
38 D. M. Ladd to Hoover, March 28, 1951; Ladd to A. H. Belmont, April 2, 1952; GFK to Hoover, October 20, 1953; Hoover to GFK, October 22, 1953, all in GFK's FBI file, 62-81548, GFK Papers, 181:3–6. The extensive but heavily sanitized exchanges on disloyalty allegations are also in this file.
39 See GFK's testimony on April 20, 1954, in U.S. Atomic Energy Commission, Matter of J. Robert Oppenheimer, pp. 354–55, 364; also his Woodrow Wilson School address of October 5, 1953, GFK Papers, 300:28.
40 GFK handwritten remarks, February 11, 1954, GFK Papers, 300:33.
41 "Kennan Will Run for House Seat," New York Times, March 14, 1954. See also GFK, Memoirs, II, 77–78; and GFK interview, September 8, 1983, p. 15.
42 Ibid., pp. 16–17; GFK to Wasson, March 23, 1954, GFK Papers, 51:2; Rusk interview, pp. 6–7; "Kennan Bows Out of Congress Race," New York Times, March 18, 1954.
43 MacMurray to GFK, March 27, 1954, GFK Papers, 138:6–7; JKH interview, p. 27; GFK interview, September 8, 1983, p. 16; Black interview, p. 11; Dilworth interview, p. 7; Berlin interview, pp. 29–30.
44 U.S. Atomic Energy Commission, Matter of J. Robert Oppenheimer, pp. 356–57, 368–69.

45 GFK, *Memoirs,* II, 21. See also Bird and Sherwin, *American Prometheus,* pp. 538–50.
46 GFK Diary, June 11–July 30, 1954. See also U.S. Atomic Energy Commission, *Matter of J. Robert Oppenheimer,* p. 369.
47 GFK Diary, July 8, 1954, January 3, 16, 1955.
48 GFK to KWK, December 25, 1953, JEK Papers.
49 GFK handwritten notes for National Archives talk, October 27, 1954, GFK Papers, 300:34. See also GFK, *Memoirs,* I, 32–33; and Chapters Five and Six, above.
50 GFK Diary, December 30, 1954, January 8, 1956; GFK American Historical Association lecture, "The Experience of Writing History," December 29, 1959, GFK Papers, 259:7, later published under the same title in the *Virginia Historical Review* 36 (Spring, 1960), 205–14.
51 GFK Diary, August 20, 1956, GFK Papers, 233:4.

TWENTY • A RARE POSSIBILITY OF USEFULNESS: 1955–1958

1 GFK Diary, December 29, 1954; Black interview, p. 3.
2 Dilworth interview, December 6, 1987, p. 10. For a useful analysis of Oppenheimer's relations with his board and faculty, see Bird and Sherwin, *American Prometheus,* pp. 382–90; also Mark Wolverton, *Life in Twilight.*
3 This paragraph relies on Oppenheimer's summary of the two schools' position for the Institute Board of Trustees meeting, November 15, 1955, Strauss Papers, IAS Files, Box 109. (This and the following citations from the Strauss Papers are courtesy of Craig Wright.)
4 The letters, written between March and October 1955, are in Von Neumann to Strauss, November 14, 1955, Strauss Papers, IAS Files, Box 109.
5 Minutes, Board of Trustees meeting, November 15, 1955, *ibid.*; Sidney A. Mitchell to Oppenheimer, June 6, 1956, *ibid.*; Erica Mosner, Institute for Advanced Study Archives, to JLG, November 9, 2010.
6 GFK Diary, January 30 and February 1, 1955; GFK interview by Labalme, August 30, 1989, p. 15; GFK, *Memoirs,* II, 15.
7 Link interview, p. 2; Hessman interview, pp. 12–13; GFK interview, September 8, 1983, p. 9.
8 Link interview, p. 2; GFK, *Memoirs,* II, 16–17. See also GFK to Kantorowicz, January 31, 1957, GFK Papers, 138:2.
9 GFK Diary, March 6 and 10, 1955; Harrison Salisbury, "When Russia's Revolution Was Young," *New York Times Book Review,* August 26, 1956, pp. 1, 18; GFK to Acheson, September 5, 1956, Acheson Papers, 17:222, Yale University.
10 Barghoorn in *Political Science Quarterly* 72 (June 1957), 306–8; Perkins in *American Historical Review* 62 (January 1957), 367 68; GFK to Butterfield, December 17, 1956, GFK Papers, 53; GFK, *Russia Leaves the War,* pp. 3, 29, 64.
11 Williams in *Wisconsin Magazine of History* 40 (Winter 1956–57), 133. See also his *Tragedy of American Diplomacy.*
12 GFK remarks at National Book Award ceremony, March 12, 1957, GFK Papers, 301:9. The actual line, from *Henry V,* Act IV, Scene 1, is "That we should dress us fairly for our end." See Chapter Eleven for another use of it.
13 GFK Diary, May 6 and 23, 1957; Link interview, September 8, 1983, p. 5.
14 GFK Diary, December 26, 1955, January 21, 1956.
15 Dilworth interview, pp. 1–2; GFK Diary, September 21, 23, 1956.
16 *Ibid.,* January 3, 30, February 1, March 19, 23, 1955; Dilworth interview, p. 8.
17 GFK Diary, March 15, 20, 25, 1955.
18 *Ibid.,* February 29, August 5, 1956.
19 *Ibid.,* January 27, 1956; GFK to Stevenson, March 28, 1956, GFK Papers, 53; GFK address to the Princeton Stevenson for President Committee, April 30, 1956, *ibid.,* 301:2. See also *New York Times,* January 31, 1956.
20 GFK speech to the Pittsburgh Foreign Policy Association, May 3, 1956, GFK Papers, 255:10; James Reston, "'Style' in Foreign Policy," and Richard J. H. Johnson, "Old Pros Heading Stevenson Staff," both in *New York Times,* May 7, 1956; Machrowicz to Stevenson, May 10, 1956, Stevenson to Machrowicz, May 26, 1956, both in "Stevenson Says Kennan Doesn't Speak for Him," *U.S. News & World Report,* June 29, 1956, p. 78. See also *New York Times,* June 9, 1956.
21 Sulzberger Diary, August 1, 1956, in Sulzberger, *Last of the Giants,* p. 309; GFK Diary, August 20, 23, 26, 1956.
22 William P. Bundy interview, pp. 15–16; GFK to Maury, April 12, 1954, GFK Papers, 138. GFK later described his post–State Department CIA connections in a letter to KWK, November 11, 1996, *ibid.,* 24:8.
23 Grose, *Gentleman Spy,* pp. 424–26; Frank Wisner to Allen Dulles, May 8, 1956, and to Robert Murphy, July 4, 1956, in *FRUS: 1955–57,* XXIV, 96–98, 125–27; GFK handwritten "Comment," undated, GFK Papers, 301:4.

24 Sulzberger Diary, August 1, 1956, in Sulzberger, *The Last of the Giants*, p. 315; GFK lecture at Johns Hopkins University, October 17, 1956, GFK Papers, 301:6.
25 GFK October 11, 1956, testimony, U. S. Congress, House of Representatives, Committee on Foreign Affairs, *Foreign Policy and Mutual Security*, pp. 170–71; GFK Diary, October 22, 1956; William C. Bullitt, "What Should We Do About Russia?" *U.S. News & World Report*, June 29, 1956, p. 71. The Gibbon quotation is in *Decline and Fall of the Roman Empire*, III, 49.
26 GFK to Brainard Cheney, October 29, 1956, GFK Papers, 138; Kennan-Maury telephone transcript, November 1, 1956, GFK Diary. For recent accounts of the Polish, Hungarian, and Suez crises, see the essays by Csaba Békés and Douglas Little in Leffler and Westad, *Cambridge History of the Cold War*.
27 GFK Diary, November 7 and 11, 1956.
28 GFK to Henderson, June 1, 1955, Henderson to GFK, June 18, 1955, Henderson Papers, Box 2, Folder "K"; GFK to Frank Aydelotte, February 24, 1955, Aydelotte to GFK, February 27, 1955, GFK Papers, 138:5. A brief history of the professorship and a list of its occupants appear in *American Oxonian* 87 (Summer 2000), 88–89.
29 GFK to Kallin, June 29, 1957, GFK Papers, 54:3; GFK, *Memoirs*, II, 230–31; GFK to KWK, July 20, 1957, JEK Papers.
30 GFK Diary, July 28 and August 28, 1957; GFK, *Russia, the Atom and the West*, p. vii.
31 GFK Diary, August 28, and September 7, 1957; GFK, *Memoirs*, II, 232–33, 262–63; ASK to JKH, September 24, 1957, JEK Papers.
32 Berlin interview, p. 20; GFK interview by Labalme, February 27, 1990; GFK to Oppenheimer, October 24, 1957, Oppenheimer Papers, Box 43. See also, on Michaelmas influenza, Gaddis, *We Now Know*, p. vii.
33 Ullman interview, September 30, 1987, pp. 3–5, 8; GFK, *Memoirs*, II, 231–32; GFK interview, August 25, 1982, p. 2; Von Oppen interview, August 27, 1982, p. 1.
34 GFK, *Memoirs*, II, 232–34; GFK interview, August 25, 1982, p. 2.
35 *New York Times*, November 11, 18, 25, December 2, 16, 1957; *Washington Post*, December 2, 16, 1957.
36 GFK Reith Lecture on "The Military Problem," December 2, 1957, in GFK, *Russia, the Atom and the West*, pp. 64–65.
37 Von Oppen interview, p. 2.
38 Dulles news conference, December 10, 1957, in *New York Times*, December 11, 1957.
39 C. Burke Elbrick memorandum, Eisenhower-Adenauer conversation, December 17, 1957, in *FRUS: 1955–57*, XXVI, 346–7.
40 Transcript, BBC symposium, December 20, 1957, GFK Papers, 257:7; GFK Diary, December 22, 1957. For Kennan's earlier pronouncements on "trust," see Chapter Eleven, above.
41 GFK Diary, December 28, 1957–January 5, 1958.
42 Acheson statement in *The New York Times*, January 12, 1958.
43 Schlesinger interview, December 17, 1983, p. 2; Christopher Emmet to Acheson, December 24, 1957, Acheson to Emmet, December 30, 1957, Acheson Papers, 9:123, Yale University. See also Thompson, *Hawk and the Dove*, p. 168, and, on the Council's role, Brinkley, *Dean Acheson*, pp. 79–80.
44 "Kennan in the Cold," *Washington Post*, January 14, 1958; Dulles to Acheson, January 13, 1958, Acheson Papers, 9:111, Yale University. See also *Washington Post*, January 13, 1958; *New York Times*, January 22, 1958; and Brinkley, *Dean Acheson*, pp. 83–84.
45 William Hard to Acheson, January 14, 1958, Anne Hard to Acheson, February 20, 1958, Acheson to Anne Hard, March 4, 1958, Acheson Papers, 15:192, Yale University.
46 GFK to Dorothy Hessman, copy to Oppenheimer, January 16, 1958, Oppenheimer Papers, Box 43; GFK Diary, January 12 and 21, 1958.
47 GFK, *Memoirs*, II, 250–51; ASK to JKH, January 13, 1958, JEK Papers; GFK Diary, January 21, 1958. The transcript of the Congress for Cultural Freedom discussion, which took place on January 18, 1958, is *ibid.*, 257:10. Paul Nitze later claimed, in a memorandum dictated in July 1982 (Nitze Papers, 29:5), in an interview with me on December 13, 1989, and in a subsequent book, *Tension Between Opposites*, p. 131, to have been asked by Acheson to meet Kennan in Geneva and seek a recantation. Kennan adamantly denied that any such meeting had taken place (GFK to JLG, October 1, 1993, JLG Papers), and his diary for this period, which is comprehensive, contains no mention of it.
48 GFK Diary, January 21–February 2, 1958; ASK to JKH, February 3, 1958, JEK Papers.
49 Ullman interview, pp. 6–7; Harsch to Acheson, January 28, 1958, Acheson to Harsch, February 4, 1958, Harsch to Acheson, February 12, 1958, Acheson Papers, 15:194, Yale University; Acheson to William Tyler, February 25, 1958, *ibid.*, 31:404.
50 Tyler to Acheson, March 4, 1958, *ibid.*; Acheson to Jessup, March 25, 1958, *ibid.*, 15:12.
51 Kennedy to GFK, February 13, 1958, GFK to Kennedy, February 19, 1958, John F. Kennedy Papers, PPP: Senate Files, Legislation Files 1958, Foreign Policy: General, Box 691.

52 Jacqueline Kennedy to Acheson, undated, Acheson to Jacqueline Kennedy, March 8, 1958, Acheson Papers, 18:223, Yale University; Acheson to Louis Halle, March 10, 1958, *ibid.*, 15:189; Acheson to GFK, March 13, 1958, *ibid.*, 17:222. See also McLellan and Acheson, *Among Friends*, p. 137n.
53 GFK to Acheson, March 20, 1958, Acheson Papers, 15:212, Yale University.
54 Acheson to Burlingham, March 25, 1958, *ibid.*, 4:53.
55 Mary Bundy interview, pp. 5, 12; GFK interview, September 8, 1983, pp. 5–6; GFK, *Russia, the Atom and the West*, p. 86.
56 GFK, *Memoirs*, II, 253–54; GFK interview, September 4, 1984, p. 19.
57 Franks interview, p. 24.
58 ASK to JKH, February 3, 1958, JEK Papers; Von Oppen interview, p. 1; GFK Diary, February 2, 3, 1958; GFK to Kantorowicz, March 13, 1958, GFK Papers, 138:1.
59 GFK Diary, March 28, April 9, 10, 11, 1958.
60 *Ibid.*, May 15, 1958; Holmes to R. A. D. Ford, May 30, 1958, Holmes Papers, D/II/3/a. I am indebted to Jack Cunningham for this reference.
61 GFK Diary, May 15, 1958. Kennan's notes for this talk are in GFK Papers, 301:22.
62 GFK Diary, May 27, 1958. Kennan garbled Goethe somewhat. The original quotation, from Act II of *Faust*, is "Bedenkt; der Teufel der ist alt, / So werdet alt ihn zu verstehen!" And I have of course dramatized this diary entry slightly.

TWENTY-ONE • KENNEDY AND YUGOSLAVIA: 1958–1963

1 GFK Diary, June 21, 1958; GFK to KWK, July 19, 1958, JEK Papers.
2 GFK Diary, June 27–July 3, 1958.
3 Dulles to Andrew Goodpaster, August 3, 1958, Eisenhower Papers, Whitman DDE Diary, Box 22, "August 1958—Staff Notes (3)" folder. The memorandum is in *FRUS: 1958–60*, X, 129 33.
4 GFK Diary, July 25–August 2, 1958.
5 *Ibid.*, August 5–September 10, 1958. The interview appeared in the *Harrisburg Patriot-News* on September 7, 1958.
6 "Minority Diplomat," *New York Times*, November 18, 1957; "Newsman Fiance of Grace Kennan," *ibid.*, January 5, 1958; ASK to JKH, January 13, 1958, JEK Papers; GFK Diary, May 27, 1958; ASK to Frieda Por, November 27, 1958, JEK Papers.
7 "Krisha" to JEK, undated, JEK Papers. Joan's engagement announcement appeared in *The New York Times*, September 7, 1958.
8 "George F. Kennan Assays Quemoy: Sees 'Excessive Commitment' to Chiang's 'Fortunes,'" *New York Herald Tribune*, September 21, 1958; GFK "Points for *New Leader* Meeting," September 25, 1958, GFK Papers, 301:23; GFK Diary, December 25, 1958, and March 29, 1959. GFK's reading notes on Kissinger and Niebuhr are appended to his 1958 Diary.
9 *Ibid.*, May 17, 1959.
10 Chalmers M. Roberts, "German Policy Change Denied," *Washington Post*, January 23, 1959; GFK Diary, February 6, April 13, and July [misdated June] 17, 1959.
11 John F. Kennedy to GFK, January 21, 1959, copy in GFK Oral History, John F. Kennedy Library; Schlesinger interview, p. 3; GFK to ASK, July 4, 1959, JEK Papers. See also GFK, "Disengagement Revisited," *Foreign Affairs* 37 (January 1959), 187–210.
12 GFK Diary, July [misdated June] 17–18, 1959.
13 GFK to Berlin, March 5, 1959, GFK Papers, 5:5.
14 GFK Diary, March 29, 1959.
15 *Ibid.*, April 17, 1959. Who was she? I don't know.
16 GFK Diary, June 30, 1958.
17 *Ibid.*, September 10, 1959.
18 GFK to ASK, September 22 and 26, 1959, GFK Papers, 24:5.
19 GFK interview by Fischer, March 23, 1965, Oral History Collection, John F. Kennedy Library; Kennedy to GFK, undated, GFK to Kennedy, January 4, 1960, copies *ibid.* GFK misdates this last exchange, in his *Memoirs*, II, 268, as having taken place in 1961.
20 GFK Diary, December 13, 1959; GFK Desk Calendar, January 10 and February 25–26, 1960.
21 Ullman interview, p. 5; Pipes, *Vixi*, p. 102; *Yale Daily News*, February 15, 1960; GFK to KWK, May 17 and December 30, 1960, JEK Papers. See also GFK, *Russia and the West Under Lenin and Stalin*.
22 GFK Diary, July 6–8, 1960; GFK to O'Shaughnessy, July 30, 1960, *ibid.* GFK described these summer travels at length in *Sketches from a Life*, pp. 190–202. His memorandum on his talk with Tito is in *FRUS: 1958–60*, X, 432–36.

23 GFK to Kennedy, August 17, 1960, copy in GFK Oral History Collection, Kennedy Library.
24 Sorensen to GFK, August 30, 1960, Pre-Presidential Correspondence, Box 469, *ibid.*; Sulzberger Diary, October 11, 1960, in Sulzberger, *Last of the Giants,* p. 698; GFK to *New York Times,* October 12, 1960, and to James Reston, October 19, 1960, GFK Papers, 55.
25 GFK Diary, August 10, 1960, and two undated diary fragments.
26 GFK Desk Calendar, October 27, 1960; Kennedy to GFK, October 30, 1960, copy in GFK Oral History Collection, Kennedy Library; GFK interview by Fischer, p. 135; Alsop, *"I've Seen the Best of It,"* pp. 432–33; ASK to Por, December 26, 1960, JEK Papers; GFK to KWK, December 30, 1960, *ibid.*
27 GFK Diary, January 2, 1961. GFK expressed himself similarly in a letter to Walter Lippmann, December 28, 1960, Lippmann Papers, Box 81, Folder 1202 (courtesy of Wilson D. Miscamble, C.S.C.).
28 GFK Diary, January 10, 1961; GFK interview by Fischer, pp. 34–35; GFK Desk Calendar, January 10, 1961.
29 *Ibid.,* January 23, 1961; GFK, *Memoirs,* II, 267; GFK to KWK, February 2, 1961, JEK Papers.
30 GFK interview by Fischer, pp. 55–56; Carlton Savage notes, GFK meeting with the Policy Planning Staff, February 8, 1961, in *FRUS: 1961–63,* V, 62–63. See also, on the "captive nations" resolution, GFK to McGhee, April 20, 1961, *ibid.,* 56. For the Yugoslavs' enthusiasm over Kennan's appointment, see "Yugoslavs Delighted," *New York Times,* January 26, 1961, and Foy Kohler to GFK, February 7, 1961, GFK Papers, 26:15.
31 McGeorge Bundy notes, White House discussion, February 11, 1961, in *FRUS: 1961–63,* V, 63–67; GFK interview by Fischer, p. 42.
32 "Kennan is Backed as Envoy to Tito," *New York Times,* March 7, 1961; Rusk to GFK, March 7, 1961, DSR-DF 1960–63, Box 321, "123 Kennan" folder; GFK memorandum, conversation with Kennedy, March 22, 1961, NSF Country Files: Yugoslavia, Box 209A, Kennedy Library.
33 McGeorge Bundy interview, December 17, 1986, p. 3; GFK Desk Calendar, March 22, 1961.
34 *Ibid.,* March 24, 1961. Strunsky's poem is in GFK Papers, 46:12.
35 GFK Desk Calendar, April 19, 1961; GFK interview by Fischer, p. 55.
36 GFK undated diary fragment, 1961; GFK, *Memoirs,* II, 269. The Kennans had indeed sailed on the same day, April 24, 1952, but George had arrived in Moscow on May 6.
37 GFK to Grace and Joan Kennan, May 17, 1961, GFK Papers, 325:1.
38 GFK, *Memoirs,* II, 274–75; Hessman interview, pp. 16, 19.
39 GFK memorandum of conversation with Tito, July 17, 1961, in *FRUS 1961–63,* XVI, 191–96. See also GFK's dispatches of June 8, 1961, and July 31, 1961, *ibid.,* pp. 189–90, 196–99.
40 GFK to McGhee, April 20, 1961, GFK Papers, 56.
41 "Kennedy Appeals on Captive Lands," *New York Times,* July 15, 1961; GFK to Bundy, July 19, 1961, NSF Country Files: Yugoslavia, Box 209A, Kennedy Library; Bundy to GFK, July 27, 1961, *ibid.*; GFK, *Memoirs,* II, 292–93.
42 GFK to Bundy, July 19, 1961, NSF Country Files: Yugoslavia, Box 209A, Kennedy Library; Bundy to GFK, July 27, 1961, *ibid.*
43 GFK to ASK, July 20 and August 12, 1961, GFK Papers, 24:5; Rusk to GFK, July 28, 1961, DSR-DF 1960–63, Box 321, "123 Kennan" folder.
44 Schlesinger Diary, August 12, 1961, in Schlesinger, *Journals,* p. 128; Bundy to Kennedy, August 14, 1961, in *FRUS: 1961–63,* XIV, 331; White House Diary, August 15, 1961, Kennedy Library; Kennedy to Rusk, August 14, 1961, in *FRUS: 1961–63,* XIV, 332. See also Schlesinger, *Thousand Days,* p. 397; and Beschloss, *Crisis Years,* p. 275.
45 McGeorge Bundy interview, p. 2. See also Brinkley, *Dean Acheson,* pp. 148–53; and Trachtenberg, *Constructed Peace,* pp. 325–27.
46 GFK to Bundy, August 15, 1961, NSF Country Files: Yugoslavia, Box 209A, Kennedy Library; GFK to Oppenheimer, September 21, 1961, Oppenheimer Papers, Box 43.
47 Rusk to GFK, August 14, 1961, DSR-DF 1960–63, 762.00/8-1461; GFK interview by Fischer, p. 120.
48 GFK to Rusk, August 31, 1961, NSF Country Files: Yugoslavia, Box 211A, Kennedy Library.
49 GFK to Rusk, September 2, 4, 1961, *ibid.* Kennan's translation of Yepishev's memorandum, completed on September 5, reached the State Department on September 16 and was immediately forwarded to the White House.
50 GFK to Rusk, September 4, 1961, NSF Country Files: Yugoslavia, Box 211A, Kennedy Library; Rusk to GFK, September 5, 1961, in *FRUS: 1961–63,* XXIV, 402.
51 GFK interview by Fischer, pp. 122–23; GFK to Chester Bowles, September 22, 1961, in *FRUS: 1961–63,* XIV, 436–37.
52 Khrushchev to Kennedy, September 29, 1961, *ibid.,* VI, 33–34.
53 GFK interview by Fischer, pp. 122–23; memorandum, Harriman-Khrushchev conversation, June 23, 1959, in *FRUS: 1958–60,* X, 276; Schlesinger interview, p. 3. See also Bird, *Color of Truth,* pp. 211–12.

54 Schlesinger to Kennedy, August 3, 1961, NSF Country Files, Yugoslavia, Box 209A, Kennedy Library.

55 GFK to State Department, September 3, 1961, in *FRUS: 1961–63*, XVI, 202; William P. Bundy interview, p. 6; GFK interview by Fischer, p. 66. For Tito's assurances, see GFK's dispatch of July 17, 1961, *ibid.*,192. Excerpts from Tito's speech appeared in *The New York Times*, September 4, 1961.

56 GFK interview by Fischer, pp. 53, 63, 71–72; GFK to State Department, September 15, 1961, in *FRUS: 1961–63*, XVI, 206; Ball interview, October 12, 1987, p. 2; William P. Bundy interview, p. 7; Raymond E. Lisle to State Department, in *FRUS: 1961–63*, XVI, 209; Kennedy to GFK, October 11, 1961, *ibid.*, p. 211.

57 GFK to David Riesman, October 3, 1961, and to Hamilton Fish Armstrong, November 2, 1961, GFK Papers, 56; Paul Underwood, "Belgrade Impressed by Kennan, But Finds Him a Tough Envoy," *New York Times*, January 5, 1962.

58 GFK to Oppenheimer, December 8, 1961, Oppenheimer Papers, Box 43, "Kennan" folder.

59 Lucius D. Battle to McGeorge Bundy, January 5, 1962, NSF Country Files: Yugoslavia, Box 210, Kennedy Library; National Security Action Memorandum 123, "Policy Toward Yugoslavia," January 15, 1961, in *FRUS: 1961–63*, XVI, 255–56; GFK to ASK, January 12, 1962, GFK Papers, 24:5.

60 Schlesinger Diary, March 31, 1962, in Schlesinger, *Journals*, pp. 149–50. For GFK's brief, completed on January 15, 1962, see NSF Country Files: Yugoslavia, Box 210, Kennedy Library. Rusk's February 5 statement is in *Department of State Bulletin* 46 (February 26, 1962), 346–48. GFK's report on the Yugoslav reaction, sent on February 14, is in *FRUS: 1961–63*, XVI, 257–58.

61 Komer to Bundy, May 25, 1962, NSF: Meetings and Memoranda: Staff Memoranda: Robert W. Komer, Box 322, Kennedy Library; Bundy to GFK, May 8, 1962, NSF Country Files: Yugoslavia, Box 210, *ibid.*

62 Memorandum, Kennedy-Popović conversation, May 29, 1962, in *FRUS: 1961–63*, XVI, 266–70.

63 GFK interview by Fischer, pp. 46–50; GFK to Kennedy and Rusk, May 31, 1962, NSF Country Files: Yugoslavia, Box 210, Kennedy Library.

64 GFK to Bundy, May 15, 1962, and Bundy to GFK, May 16, 1962, NSF Country Files: Yugoslavia, Box 210, Kennedy Library; GFK to ASK, May 31, 1962, GFK Papers, 24:5; GFK Desk Calendar, June 1, 1962.

65 "Senate Bans Aid to Red Nations; Rebuffs Kennedy," *New York Times*, June 7, 1962; "Aid Bill Voted by Senate: Red-Bloc Ban is Modified," *ibid.*, June 8, 1962; James Reston, "Greatest Deliberative Body in the World," *ibid.*, June 8, 1962; GFK to State Department, June 11, 1962, NSF Country Files: Yugoslavia, Box 210, Kennedy Library.

66 Max Frankel, "U.S. Envoys Warn on Cuts in Red Aid," *New York Times*, June 15, 1962; GFK to State Department, June 11, 1962, NSF Country Files: Yugoslavia, Box 210; "Kennan Leaves Belgrade," *New York Times*, June 24, 1962. See also GFK, *Memoirs*, II, 300.

67 GFK to ASK, July 3, 5, 8 and 10, 1962, GFK Papers, 24:5. See also GFK Desk Diary, July 2–10, 1962; also GFK, "U.S. Shouldn't Slam Door on Yugoslavia," *Washington Post*, July 8, 1962.

68 GFK interview by Fischer, pp. 71–72, 76–77.

69 "Conferees Grant Kennedy Leeway to Aid Red Lands," *New York Times*, July 19, 1962; GFK interview by Fischer, pp. 86–89; GFK, *Memoirs*, II, 303–5; GFK Desk Diary, September 27, 1962.

70 GFK to Kennedy and Rusk, October 5, 1962, Bundy to GFK, October 5, 1962, Kennedy to GFK, October 9, 1962, all in NSF Country Files: Yugoslavia, Box 210, Kennedy Library; GFK interview by Fischer, pp. 92–93.

71 "Trade Act Signed, Also Postal Bill," *New York Times*, October 12, 1962; Bundy to GFK, October 11, 1962, NSF Country Files: Yugoslavia, Box 210, Kennedy Library; GFK Desk Diary, October 14, 1962.

72 GFK to State Department and American Embassy, Moscow, September 13, 1962, NSF Country Files: Cuba, Box 39, Kennedy Library; GFK and ASK to JEK, October 23, 1962, JEK Papers.

73 GFK interview by Fischer, pp. 110, 124.

74 GFK to State Department, November 28, 1962, in *FRUS: 1961–63*, XVI, 292–309.

75 Bundy to Kennedy, December 13, 1962, *ibid.*, pp. 309–10; GFK to State Department, December 13, 1962, and January 3, 1963, *ibid.*, pp. 310–13, 315–19.

76 Klein to Bundy, January 4, 1963, NSF Country Files: Yugoslavia, Box 210A, Kennedy Library.

77 GFK to ASK, January 10, 1963, GFK Papers, 24:5; GFK memorandum, conversation with Kennedy, January 16, 1963, in *FRUS: 1961–63*, XVI, 326–27; Kennedy press conference, January 24, 1963, *Public Papers of the Presidents: John F. Kennedy, 1963*, Document 35.

78 GFK to State Department, January 30, 1963, in *FRUS: 1961–61*, XVI, 332–34.

79 GFK Desk Diary, February 5–11, 1963; GFK to Lippmann, February 8, 1963, *ibid.*, 56; GFK to Davies, February 19, 1963, *ibid.*, 10:12.

80 White House press release, May 17, 1963, *ibid.*, 57; Schlesinger interview, p. 5; GFK interview by Fischer, pp. 83–84, 94–95, 111–16.

81 *Ibid.*, pp. 67–70; GFK, *Memoirs*, II, 278–80.

82 Jones Diary, undated but pp. 62–63, Owen T. Jones Papers, Box 6, "August 18—December 31, 1962" folder (courtesy of Sam Rushay).

83   GFK Diary, May 31, 1963.
84   GFK Desk Diary, June 2, 6, 1963.
85   GFK Diary, June 1, 8, 1963.
86   GFK Desk Diary, June 9–22, 1963.
87   GFK, *Memoirs*, II, 311–12.
88   *Ibid.*, pp. 313–14; GFK notes on Tito visit, October 16, 1963, GFK Papers, 235:4.
89   "Tito's Whirlwind White House Visit Marked by Meetings and Protests," *New York Times*, October 18, 1963; memorandum, Kennedy-Tito conversation, October 17, 1963, in *FRUS: 1961–63*, XVI, 355–59.
90   GFK, *Memoirs*, II, 314–15; GFK to Kennedy, October 22, 1963, GFK Papers, 57. The New York Times covered the anti-Tito protests in a series of stories on October 21, 22, and 23, 1963.
91   GFK to Kennedy, handwritten, October 22, 1963, PDF Special Correspondence, "Kennan" folder, Kennedy Library; Kennedy to GFK, October 28, 1963, GFK Papers, 26:5; GFK interview by Fischer, p. 106.

TWENTY-TWO • COUNTER-CULTURAL CRITIC: 1963–1968

1   J. Robert Moskin, "Our Foreign Policy Is Paralyzed," *Look* 27 (November 19, 1963), 25–27.
2   GFK, *Memoirs*, II, 21; GFK untitled, undated typescript, published as "Sein Tod ist nicht allein Amerikas Tragödie," in the Zürich *Tages Anzeiger*, November 30, 1963.
3   GFK interview by Fischer, pp. 115–16. I am indebted to my research assistant Andrew Scott for compiling the number of meetings, based on Kennedy Library records.
4   GFK to Oppenheimer, November 16, 1962, GFK Papers, 56.
5   Oppenheimer to GFK, December 4, 1962, Oppenheimer Papers, Box 43.
6   GFK to KWK, February 8, 1963, JEK Papers; GFK interview by Labalme, August 30, 1989, p. 14; White House Press Release, May 17, 1963, GFK Papers, 57.
7   Hessman interview, pp. 1, 17; Goodman interview, December 10, 1987, pp. 1–4, 7, 15, 30. See also "Kennan Leaves Belgrade and Retires," *New York Times*, July 29, 1963.
8   GFK to KWK, February 8, 1963, JEK Papers; Princeton University press release, November 13, 1963 (courtesy of Cyril E. Black); Ullman interview, p. 11; Goodman interview, pp. 29–32; GFK interview by Labalme, February 27, 1990, pp. 19–22; GFK to Richard Challener, handwritten response to letter of May 25, 1970, GFK Papers, 4:12.
9   GFK, *On Dealing with the Communist World*, pp. viii–ix, 15, 45, 51. See also Constance Moench to Cass Canfield, July 2, 1964, conveying GFK's intentions regarding the book, GFK Papers, 57.
10 GFK lecture to the International House of Japan, June 19, 1964, published as "The Passing of the Cold War" in its *Bulletin* 14 (October 1964), 71–72.
11 GFK, "Fresh Look at Our China Policy," *New York Times Magazine*, November 22, 1964, pp. 27, 140–47; Moskin, "Our Foreign Policy is Paralyzed," p. 27.
12 GFK to David Mark, March 12, 1964, GFK Papers, 57.
13 Carlton Savage notes, GFK meeting with the Policy Planning Staff, February 8, 1961, in *FRUS: 1961–63*, V, 62–63. See also Chapters Thirteen and Sixteen, above.
14 GFK, "Japanese Security and American Policy," *Foreign Affairs* 43 (October 1964), 14–28. For evidence that MacArthur did at one time think this, see Gaddis, *Long Peace*, pp. 79–80.
15 William P. Bundy interview, pp. 21–23; GFK to Chihiro Hosoya, December 15, 1964, GFK Papers, 21:3. Bundy's address, delivered in Tokyo on September 29, 1964, is in *Department of State Bulletin* 51 (October 19, 1964), 534–42.
16 GFK interview, August 26, 1982, p. 10. Millay's sonnet is "I Being Born a Woman and Distressed."
17 GFK to Dobrynin, January 28, 1964, Dobrynin to GFK, March 3, 1964, GFK to David Klein, January 13, 1965, GFK Papers, 11:9.
18 GFK Desk Diary, July 6–7, 1964.
19 "Account of Trip from Bergen to Kristiansand," July 1964, GFK Papers, 236:2.
20 Taplin interview, December 5, 1987, pp. 3, 15; Dilworth interview, p. 2; GFK Diary, July 4, 1976.
21 David Klein to GFK, January 7, 1965, GFK to Klein, January 13, 1965, GFK to Klein, February 1, 1965, GFK Papers, 11:9; GFK interviews, August 26, 1982, p. 10, and September 4, 1984, pp. 1–2.
22 GFK Desk Diary, June 21–29, 1965; GFK interview, September 4, 1984, p. 2; "Kennan, Once Barred in Soviet, Feted There," *New York Times*, June 26, 1965; GFK, *Memoirs*, I, 281–83; GFK, *Decision to Intervene*, p. 469; GFK, "History as Literature," pp. 13–14.
23 GFK Desk Diary, January 20, 1965; GFK interview, September 4, 1984, pp. 12–13.
24 *Ibid.*, p. 12; GFK Desk Diary, May 19, 21, 1965; GFK to Mumford, June 5, 1965, GFK Papers, 149:5.
25 GFK Diary, June 14, 1965. See also Leroy F. Aarons, "Culture is King at Arts Festival; Lowell Controversy Mars Event," *Washington Post*, June 15, 1965; President's Daily Diary, June 14, 1965, Lyndon B. Johnson Library; and, for his own lengthy account, Goldman, *Tragedy of Lyndon Johnson*, pp. 495–563.

26 GFK to Joze Smole, February 15, 1962, GFK Papers, 56; Moskin, "Our Foreign Policy is Paralyzed," p. 27; GFK, "Passing of the Cold War," pp. 62, 69–70; GFK to Woodward, March 4, 1965, GFK Papers, 58; GFK to ASK, May 9, 1965, *ibid.*, 24:5.

27 Bundy to Johnson, June 26, 1965, in *FRUS: 1964–68*, III, 52; GFK to Coffin, August 27, 1965, GFK Papers, 58.

28 GFK, "An Authority on Communism Says We're Letting This One Area Disbalance Whole Policy," *Washington Post,* December 12, 1965, pp. E1, E4.

29 GFK to KWK, December 19, 1965, JEK Papers; GFK Desk Diary, February 7–9, 1966.

30 GFK's testimony is in U.S. Congress, Senate, Committee on Foreign Relations, *Supplemental Foreign Assistance Fiscal Year 1966—Vietnam,* quoted portions at pp. 333, 335–56, 380. See also "Scholarly Diplomat," *New York Times,* February 11, 1966; Murrey Marder, "Kennan's Testimony: A Profound Challenge," *Washington Post,* February 11, 1966; Flora Lewis, "CBS News Executive Morale Upset By Issues That Made Friendly Quit," *ibid.*; and for the origins of the Fulbright hearings, Woods, *Fulbright,* pp. 402–5.

31 Fischer to GFK, February 13, 1966, GFK Papers, 13:8; Johnson press conference, February 11, 1966, *Public Papers of the Presidents: Johnson, 1966,* Document 65; Johnson telephone conversation with U. Alexis Johnson, February 11, 1966, in *FRUS: 1964–68*, IV, 220–22; notes on White House meeting, February 26, 1966, *ibid.*, p. 261; Reedy to Johnson, February 17, 1966, *ibid.*, pp. 235–37.

32 GFK to Llewellyn Thompson, April 5, 1966, GFK Papers, 59; GFK interview, September 4, 1984, p. 10; Art Buchwald, "Audience Is Live, if TV Isn't," *Washington Post,* February 17, 1966; Woods, *Fulbright,* pp. 405, 409–10.

33 GFK sermon, "Why Do I Hope?" February 13, 1966, GFK Papers, 264:5.

34 GFK to ASK, May 5, 1965, GFK Papers, 24:5.

35 Mary Bundy interview, p. 35; GFK, "Why Do I Hope?" p. 3; GFK to JKH, January 3, 1931, GFK Papers, 23:10, further quoted in Chapter Three, above; JKH interview, pp. 18, 27; CKB interview, p. 10.

36 Dilworth interview, p. 3, William and Mary Bundy interview, pp. 34–35.

37 ASK interview, August 26, 1982, pp. 8, 16–17.

38 Fosdick interview, p. 2; ASK interview, December 14, 1987, p. 10; GFK Diary, April 19, 1981. See also, for some perceptive psychological speculation on these matters, Harper, *American Visions of Europe,* pp. 148–54.

39 GFK interview, August 25, 1982, pp. 4–6.

40 GFK Diary, February 13–May 12, 1965, translation by Igor Biryukov.

41 The letter, unfinished, is in the GFK Diary for November 1987 with a note: "evidently written (clearly by myself) at some time in the 1960's." GFK showed it to his editor, Ted Weeks, who thought it "searching and excellent," but it was never published.

42 GFK diary fragment, July 5, 1964 [misdated 1960]; GFK Desk Diary, June 10, 1965 [begun on blank pages running from May 17]. The letters to ASK are in the GFK Papers, 24:5.

43 GFK Desk Diary, January 14, 1965; Gellhorn to Nikki Dobrski, June 14, 1964, in Moorehead, *Selected Letters of Martha Gellhorn,* p. 310; GFK, *Memoirs,* I, 90–91; GFK to Gellhorn, May 21, 1965, GFK Papers, 16:6. Gellhorn's many letters are in this file.

44 GFK Diary, September 27, 1959. For Hatzfeldt, see GFK's dictated 1998 memorandum on their relationship, GFK Papers, 19:10; and GFK to Hatzfeldt, January 10, 1997, *ibid.*

45 Goodman interview, pp. 8–10; GFK interview, December 13, 1987, pp. 35–37; Alliluyeva, *Only One Year,* pp. 218–21. I have also relied, here, on the State Department documentation in *FRUS: 1964–68*, XIV, 462–63, 467–73; and the extensive coverage in *The New York Times,* especially "Short Cab Ride in India Began Her Odyssey," April 22, 1967.

46 GFK and ASK interview, December 13, 1987, p. 38; Alliluyeva, *Only One Year,* pp. 312–13, 327–29; GFK to Louis Fischer, April 24, 1967, GFK Papers, 13:8; JEK to GFK, July 23, 1967, JEK Papers.

47 "Pravda Denounces the U.S. Over Mrs. Alliluyeva," *New York Times,* May 27, 1967; also Foy Kohler's report of a conversation with Yuri N. Tcherniakov, the Soviet chargé d'affaires in Washington, May 31, 1967, in *FRUS: 1964–68*, XIV, 488–90.

48 Alliluyeva, *Only One Year,* pp. 435–36; William P. Bundy interview, pp. 17–18.

49 Alliluyeva to GFK, April 28, 1976, GFK Papers, 38:5. Nicholas Thompson first alerted me to this letter in *Hawk and the Dove,* pp. 257–58.

50 GFK and ASK interview, December 13, 1987, pp. 37, 39; JEK unpublished memoir; Taplin interview, pp. 21–22.

51 Lewis Nichols, "Visit with George Kennan," *New York Times,* October 29, 1967. What follows is from GFK's "Account of Trip to Africa, May–June, 1967," GFK Papers, 237:1. For Hochschild, see Hochschild, *Half the Way Home.*

52 GFK to JEK, June 28, 1967, JEK Papers. See also GFK to Dönhoff, March 15, 1965, GFK Papers, 58.

53 GFK "Account of Second African Journey," *ibid.*, 237:2.

54 GFK to Waldemar Nielsen, October 19, 1967, *ibid.*, 60. See also, for a fuller version of this argument, GFK, "Hazardous Courses in Southern Africa." *Foreign Affairs* 49 (January 1971), 218–36

55 GFK interview, September 5, 1984, p. 1; Goodman interview, pp. 20–21; GFK to JEK, June 26, 1967, JEK
    Papers; GFK to KWK, December 21, 1966, and October 16, 1967, *ibid.* See also, for an early comment on
    Cold War revisionist history, GFK to Gar Alperovitz, January 11, 1965, GFK Papers, 58.
56 Nichols, "Visit with George Kennan."
57 GFK to Arthur Schlesinger, Jr., February 17, 1993, handwritten, copy provided by GFK. John Lamberton
    Harper has emphasized the Adams-Kennan connection in his *American Visions of Europe,* especially chap.
    4. See also, for the suggestion that Kennan was the better writer, Lukacs, *Kennan: Study of Character,* p. 6.
58 The passages referred to here are in GFK, *Memoirs,* I, 98–88, 109–12. See also Chapter Seven, above;
    Thompson, *Hawk and the Dove,* pp. 237–38; and, for the *Ramparts* article, Saunders, *Cultural Cold War,* pp.
    381–90.
59 Lukacs, *Kennan: Study of Character,* p. 44.
60 See D. W. Brogan's introduction to Adams, *Education of Henry Adams,* 1946 reprint edition, pp. xi–xii.
61 GFK address, "The Library and the Student Radical," Swarthmore College, December 9, 1967, GFK Papers,
    265:3.
62 GFK interview, September 4, 1984, pp. 13–14; GFK, *Democracy and the Student Left.* See also "Head of
    Swarthmore Dies During Protest," *New York Times,* January 17, 1969.
63 GFK, *Democracy and the Student Left,* pp. 121, 124–26, 132–33, 136–37, 140–41, 153–54, 160–63, 190–93,
    199, 208.
64 Dilworth interview, p. 1; GFK to William C. Sullivan, October 22, 1968, and December 11, 1970, GFK
    Papers, 46:17; GFK to J. P. Trinkaus, November 9, 1970, *ibid.,* 52:19.
65 GFK to JEK, November 25, 1967, JEK Papers.
66 GFK Diary, August 19, 1968; *ibid.,* August 5, 1956.
67 GFK "Account of Cruise to Denmark, July 31–August 5, 1968," quoted in GFK, *Sketches from a Life,* p. 225;
    GFK to JEK, August 18, 1968, JEK Papers.

TWENTY-THREE • PROPHET OF THE APOCALYPSE: 1968–1980

1 GFK memorial service address, February 25, 1967, GFK Papers, 264:10; GFK interview by Labalme, August
   30, 1989, p. 3: GFK, *Russia, the Atom and the West,* p. 50. See also Bird and Sherwin, *American Prometheus,*
   pp. 3–5; and "600 at a Service for Oppenheimer," *New York Times,* February 26, 1967.
2 GFK interview, September 4, 1984, pp. 21–22; "Global Nuclear Stockpiles, 1945–2006," *Bulletin of the
   Atomic Scientists* 62 (July–August 2006), 66. GFK's early views on containment are discussed in Chapters
   Twelve and Thirteen, above.
3 Schlesinger interview, p. 6. Kennan's elections are reported in *The New York Times,* January 28, 1965, and
   December 9, 1967. For the history of the Academy, see its website, at www.artsandletters.org/about_history
   .php, accessed November 2010.
4 GFK Diary, December 21, 1967; GFK opening address, American Academy of Arts and Letters and
   National Institute of Arts and Letters, May 28, 1968, GFK Papers, 265:8.
5 GFK Diary, undated but August 1968, also October 4, 1968; Henry Raymont, "Kennan Book Recalls 1938–
   1939 Crisis," *New York Times,* August 25, 1968; "Kennan Decries Talk of Détente," *ibid.,* September 22, 1968.
6 GFK to JEK, October 31, 1968, JEK Papers.
7 GFK Diary, May 6, 1966, November 7 and December 4, 1968.
8 "Kennan Analysis Coolly Received," *New York Times,* December 4, 1968; "A Hit and Myth Gathering of Intellectuals," *ibid.,* December 8, 1968; Walter Goodman, "Liberal Establishment Faces:
   The Blacks, The Young, The New Left," *New York Times Magazine,* December 29, 1968. Excerpts from Kennan's speech ran in the December 4, 1968, issue of *The New York Times.*
9 GFK to JEK, September 21/22, 1968, JEK Papers; GFK interview by Labalme, August 30, 1989, pp. 13–
   14; George Urban, "From Containment to . . . Self-Containment: A Conversation with George F. Kennan,"
   Encounter 47 (September 1976), 43.
10 GFK Diary, March 6 and 29, 1969.
11 GFK to JEK, January 31, 1969, JEK Papers; Crossman Diary, January 31, 1969, in Crossman, *Diaries of a
    Cabinet Minister,* pp. 353–54. I owe this reference to Wilson D. Miscamble, C.S.C.
12 GFK, *Marquis de Custine,* p. 124.
13 GFK, "Interview with George F. Kennan," conducted by Charles Gati and Richard Ullman, *Foreign Policy* 7
    (Summer 1972), 5–21; GFK Diary, October 12, 1969. See also Bernard Gwertzman, "Kennan Now Advo-
    cates Closer Ties with Soviet," *New York Times,* May 28, 1972.
14 GFK to Kissinger, September 19, 1973, GFK Papers, 26:11. See also the transcript of a GFK-Kissinger tele-
    phone conversation, September 14, 1973, Kissinger Telephone Conversations KA 10845, Digital National
    Security Archive.

15 "Kennan Decries Talk of Détente," *New York Times,* September 22, 1968; GFK, "Between Earth and Hell," *New York Review of Books,* March 21, 1974; Robert and Evgenia Tucker interview, September 4, 1984, pp. 11–16.

16 GFK interview, October 31, 1974, pp. 6–7. See also GFK Diary, March 9, 1973. I have discussed the analogies between the Nixon-Kissinger strategy and Kennan's concept of five vital power centers in *Strategies of Containment,* pp. 278–79.

17 "Kennan Says ABM Could Peril Talks," *New York Times,* February 7, 1970. See also GFK, *Nuclear Delusion,* pp. xxiii–xxiv.

18 For background on the Helsinki Conference, see Gaddis, *Cold War: A New History,* pp. 184–88; also, much more thoroughly, Thomas, *Helsinki Effect,* and Morgan, "Origins of the Helsinki Final Act," Ph.D. dissertation, Yale University, 2010.

19 GFK to Patricia Davies, August 9, 1975, GFK Papers, 10:12.

20 GFK, "United States and the Soviet Union, 1917–1976," *Foreign Affairs* 54 (July 1976), 686–88; GFK Diary, August 30, 1976; Urban, "Conversation with George F. Kennan," p. 39; Alliluyeva to GFK, September 21, 1976, GFK Papers, 38:5.

21 Galbraith's review appeared in *The New York Times Book Review,* October 8, 1972.

22 GFK interview by Labalme, February 27, 1990, pp. 2–19; Dilworth interview, p. 13; GFK to Edwin O. Reischauer, March 12, 1973, and David Riesman, March 27, 1973, GFK Papers, 149:1. See also, Israel Shenker, "Dispute Splits Advanced Study Institute," and "Foes at Institute Dig In for a Fight," *New York Times,* March 2 and 4, 1973, and, for general background, John H. Elliott interview December 7, 1992. Kaysen's tenure as Institute director is briefly covered in Regis, *Who Got Einstein's Office?,* pp. 202–7.

23 GFK Diary, March 13, 1978; GFK interview, September 5, 1984, pp. 4–7; GFK to Harriman, October 8 and 28, 1972, Harriman Papers, Box 1012.

24 Ullman interview, pp. 19–20.

25 Undated Harriman note; Harriman to GFK, November 3, 1972; GFK to Harriman, November 18, 1972, all in Harriman Papers, Box 1012.

26 GFK to Harriman, December 4, 1975, *ibid.* On the elder Kennan's biography of the elder Harriman, see Chapter Nine, above.

27 GFK to Harriman, May 10, 1978, Harriman to GFK, May 22, 1978, *ibid.;* "Columbia Gets Harriman Gift of $11 Million," *New York Times,* October 22, 1982.

28 GFK interview, September 5, 1984, pp. 4, 6; Black interview, p. 28. See also Taplin interview, pp. 28–32. Of course if Kennan, half a century earlier, had followed through on his idea of starting an airborne express company—"I'll be the Harriman of commercial aeronautics"—the roles might have reversed. Chapter Two provides the context.

29 GFK Diary, January 28, October 12, 1982. See also McGeorge Bundy interview, December 17, 1986, p. 9.

30 GFK to Mimi Bull, September 21, 1971, Bull Papers; GFK to Avis Bohlen, January 20, 1974, GFK Papers, 5:16.

31 "Verses by G. F. Kennan on the Occasion of his Seventieth Birthday," February 16, 1974, *ibid.,* 325:5; GFK Diary, January 1, 1975.

32 GFK Diary, January 8, 1975.

33 *Ibid.,* April 24, May 4, 6, 7, 1975.

34 *Ibid.,* May 12, 1975.

35 "Trip to Helsinki," July 1975, GFK Papers, 24:6.

36 Urban, "Conversation with George F. Kennan," pp. 10–43; GFK Diary, August 23, 1976. Acheson's comment, relating to GFK's 1952 expulsion from the Soviet Union, is in *Present at the Creation,* p. 697.

37 Thompson, *Hawk and the Dove,* pp. 1, 247; GFK, "United States and the Soviet Union, 1917–1976," p. 682; GFK interview, August 26, 1982, p. 3; Nitze, *Tension Between Opposites,* p. 131.

38 Nitze, *From Hiroshima to Glasnost,* pp. 353–54; Thompson, *Hawk and the Dove,* pp. 262–63.

39 GFK Diary, February 3, 1977; GFK, *Cloud of Danger,* p. vii.

40 Goodman interview, p. 16; GFK to Mimi Bull, September 29, 1977, Bull Papers; Philip Geyelin, "A Grand Design for Peace," *Washington Post,* June 26, 1977; GFK, *Cloud of Danger,* p. 204, also pp. 3–26, 228–234; James Reston, "Kennan on Carter's Diplomacy," *New York Times,* April 3, 1977; GFK Diary, June 30, 1977.

41 The text of Kennan's November 22 speech appeared in *The Washington Post* on December 11, 1977.

42 GFK interview, August 26, 1982, p. 3; Nitze interview, p. 15.

43 Marilyn Berger, "An Appeal for Thought" [interview with GFK], *New York Times Magazine,* May 7, 1978; Paul H. Nitze, "A Plea for Action," *ibid.;* GFK to S. Frederick Starr, May 15, 1978, GFK Papers, 155:1.

44 Lee Lescaze, "Solzhenitsyn Says West Is Failing as Model for World," *Washington Post,* June 9, 1978; "Diary Notes, Summer, 1978," p. 13, GFK Papers, 239:4. An abridged text of Solzhenitsyn's address appeared in *The Washington Post* two days later.

45 Eugene V. Rostow, "Searching for Kennan's Grand Design," *Yale Law Review* 87 (June 1978), 1527–48.

46 GFK Diary, August 19, 1978; GFK to Reston, November 28, 1978, GFK Papers, 41:9.

47 Thompson, *Hawk and the Dove*, p. 313. For evaluations of the archival evidence, see Zubok, *Failed Empire*, pp. 227–64; Ouimet, *Rise and Fall of the Brezhnev Doctrine in Soviet Foreign Policy*; and Westad, *Global Cold War*, especially pp. 218–41, 250–88, 299–330.

48 Ullman interview, pp. 13–14.

49 Goodman interview, pp. 17–19; Bull to JLG, May 30, 2002, JLG Papers; Bull diary note, October 1–15, 1972, Bull Papers.

50 GFK interview, September 4, 1984, pp. 3–4; Gennadi Gerasimov, "From Positions of Realism," *Pravda*, July 12, 1977.

51 Dilworth interview, p. 13; Goodman interview, pp. 21–24.

52 Black interview, p. 16; Goodman interview, p. 18; GFK Diary, March 28, 1978.

53 Paul M. Kennedy, "Bismarck Bowing Out," *Washington Post Book World*, January 6, 1980; Kissinger to GFK, January 10, 1980, GFK Papers, 26:11.

54 GFK to Kissinger, February 2, 1980, *ibid.*; GFK, *Decline of Bismarck's European Order*, pp. 3–7.

55 Black interview, p. 16. For an earlier example of GFK's detective work, see his "The Sisson Documents," *Journal of Modern History* 28 (June 1956), 130–54.

56 Bull diary note, October 1–15, 1972, Bull Papers.

57 Schlesinger Diary, September 28, 1979, in Schlesinger, *Journals*, p. 474; GFK Diary, September 17, 1979; Thompson, *Hawk and the Dove*, pp. 273–74. For a detailed account that doesn't mention Nitze's role, see Garthoff, *Détente and Confrontation*, pp. 913–34.

58 Don Oberdorfer, "George Kennan Urges Tougher Stance on Iran," *Washington Post*, February 28, 1980; Charles Mohr, "George Kennan Says U.S. Magnifies Soviet Threat," *New York Times*, February 28, 1980; James Reston, "Some Hope for the Hostages," *ibid.*, March 14, 1980; GFK to Harrison Salisbury, December 23, 1968, GFK Papers, 43:2. See also Chapter Twenty-Two, above.

59 GFK undelivered draft speech, December 1979, GFK Papers, 325:7.

60 Durbrow to GFK, October 6, 1980, *ibid.*, 12:10; Durbrow interview, p. 13.

61 GFK to Durbrow, November 10, 1980, GFK Papers, 12:10.

62 GFK Diary, October 2, 1980. The text of the speech is in GFK, *Nuclear Delusion*, pp. 134–47. The actual figure for the combined American and Soviet nuclear arsenals in 1980 is approximately 54,000. "Global Nuclear Stockpiles, 1945–2006," p. 66.

TWENTY-FOUR • A PRECARIOUS VINDICATION: 1980–1990

1 GFK Diary, March 11, 1981 [misdated, in perhaps a Freudian slip, 1891].

2 *Ibid.* April 17, 1981.

3 The full text of the speech, partially published in *Washington Post* on May 24, 1981, is in GFK, *Nuclear Delusion*, pp. 175–82. For the occasion, see Don Oberdorfer, "Kennan Urges Halving of Nuclear Arsenals," *Washington Post*, May 20, 1981.

4 Don Oberdorfer, "George Kennan's 30-Year Nightmare of Our 'Final Folly,'" *ibid.*, May 24, 1981; Talbott, *Master of the Game*, p. 165; Barbara Slavin and Milt Freudenheim, "Kennan: Are We Nuclear Lemmings?" *New York Times*, May 24, 1981. The Rostow testimony, delivered on June 22, 1981, was excerpted in *ibid.*, June 23, 1981.

5 Nitze, *From Hiroshima to Glasnost*, pp. 302, 307–8, 363; Talbott, *Master of the Game*, pp. 157–59.

6 GFK interview, October 31, 1974, p. 6; GFK Diary, March 22, 1981.

7 Gaddis, *Strategies of Containment*, p. 352; Cannon, *President Reagan*, pp. 287–89; Lettow, *Reagan and His Quest to Abolish Nuclear Weapons*, pp. 3–41, 132–34.

8 Bernard Gwertzman, "U.S. Says It Is Not Bound by 2 Arms Pacts With Soviets," *New York Times*, May 20, 1981; GFK, "Denuclearization," *ibid.*, October 11, 1981; Talbott, *Master of the Game*, pp. 168–70.

9 Reagan National Press Club Speech, November 18, 1981, *Public Papers of the Presidents: Reagan, 1981*; "George Kennan Calls on U.S. to View Soviet More Soberly," *New York Times*, November 18, 1981; "Adding Up the 'Zero Option' Will Take Time," *ibid.*, November 22, 1981. See also Tom Wicker, "A Voice of Rationality," *ibid.*, December 1, 1981. GFK's Dartmouth speech is in *Nuclear Delusion*, pp. 192–207.

10 GFK to Charles James, November 27, 1980, Douglas James Papers; GFK, "A Risky Equation," *New York Times*, February 18, 1981; GFK Diary, February 20, 1981. Reagan's January 29 press conference is in *Public Papers of the Presidents: Reagan, 1981*. See also Hayward, *Conservative Counterrevolution*, p. 97.

11 GFK Diary, March 19, 22, April 16, 1981.

12 Reagan Notre Dame speech, May 17, 1981, in *Public Papers of the Presidents: Reagan, 1981*.

13 GFK Diary, May 27, 1981.

14 Reagan to John O. Koehler, July 9, 1981, in Skinner, Anderson, and Anderson, *Reagan*, p. 375. See also Gaddis, *Strategies of Containment*, pp. 349–53, and Matlock, *Reagan and Gorbachev*, pp. 3–26.

15 Pipes, *Vixi*, p. 193; GFK to Reston, November 28, 1978, GFK Papers, 41:9. For Reagan's jokes, as well as a summary of what more sophisticated indicators were showing about the Soviet economy, see Hayward, *Conservative Counterrevolution*, pp. 102–16.

16 GFK, "As the Kremlin Sees It," *New York Times*, January 6, 1982; "The Kennan Doctrine," *New York Times*, January 10, 1982. See also "George Kennan Says Sanctions Were Hasty," *ibid.*, January 4, 1982.

17 GFK to Durbrow, January 6, 1982, GFK Papers, 12:10.

18 GFK to Charles James, January 1, 1982, Douglas James Papers; GFK Diary, January 10, 1982.

19 GFK Diary, March 11, July 30, 1982; "139 in Congress Urge Nuclear Arms Freeze by U.S. and Moscow," *New York Times*, March 11, 1982; GFK interview, September 4, 1984, pp. 26–27. Schell's *New Yorker* articles became a best-selling book, *The Fate of the Earth*. For the "freeze," see Wittner, *Toward Nuclear Abolition*, pp. 313–15.

20 GFK to Louis Halle, March 7, 1983, GFK Papers, 18:4.

21 Bundy interview, pp. 12–13; Hayward, *Conservative Counterrevolution*, pp. 240–42.

22 GFK interview, September 4, 1984, pp. 24–25; Bundy interview, p. 13; J. Bryan Hehir to JLG, January 15, 2011, JLG Papers; McGeorge Bundy, George F. Kennan, Robert S. McNamara, and Gerard Smith, "Nuclear Weapons and the Atlantic Alliance," *Foreign Affairs* 60 (Spring 1982), 753–68.

23 GFK Diary, April 7, 1982; "U.S. Refuses to Bar Possible First Use of Nuclear Arms," *New York Times*, April 7, 1982; "2 Bonn Parties Cool to Ban on First Use of Atom Arms," *ibid.*, April 10, 1982. Haig's April 6, 1982, speech is in *Department of State Bulletin* 82 (May 1982), 31–34.

24 GFK Diary, March 28, May 7, 1982.

25 Reagan's May 9, 1982, speech is in *Public Papers of the Presidents: Reagan, 1982*.

26 "Nuclear Weapons and Christian Faith," in GFK, *At a Century's Ending*, pp. 69–71.

27 GFK Diary, February 28, 1980.

28 *Ibid.*, October 1, 1982; Halle memorandum, October 4, 1982, Halle Papers, Box 4, "Correspondence 1961 84—K" folder (courtesy of Wilson D. Miscamble, C.S.C.). See also Halle, *Cold War as History*.

29 Halle to GFK, February 9, 1983, GFK to Halle, March 7, 1983, GFK Papers, 18:4.

30 NSDD-75, "U.S. Relations with the USSR," January 17, 1983, at www.fas.org/irp/offdocs/nsdd/nsdd-075.html. See also, on the drafting of NSDD-75, Pipes, *Vixi*, pp. 188–202; and on Reagan's understanding of containment, Matlock, "George F. Kennan," especially pp. 240–42. Reagan's broadcasts on NSC-68 are in Skinner, Anderson, and Anderson, *Reagan, In His Own Hand*, pp. 109–11.

31 Reagan Diary, February 15, 1983, in Brinkley, ed., *Reagan Diaries*, p. 198; Shultz, *Turmoil and Triumph*, pp. 163–65.

32 GFK Diary, March 2, 1983.

33 Shultz, *Turmoil and Triumph*, pp. 246–67; Hayward, *Conservative Counterrevolution*, pp. 288–99. The speeches are in *Public Papers of the Presidents: Reagan, 1983*.

34 Committee on East-West Accord address, May 17, 1983, in GFK, *At a Century's End*, p. 86; Stephen S. Rosenfeld, "Prickly Prophet," *New York Times*, May 20, 1983; GFK Diary, May 17, 1983.

35 GFK, "Breaking the Spell," *New Yorker* 49 (October 3, 1983); GFK, "Inching Away from the Danger Zone," *Washington Post*, October 11, 1983; GFK Diary, September 30, 1983.

36 Lois Romano, "Regrets & Premises: U.S.-Soviet Relations At the Wilson Center," *Washington Post*, November 16, 1983.

37 Harriman to GFK, December 1, 1983; GFK to Harriman, December 6, 1983, GFK Papers, 19:3.

38 GFK Diary, January 15, 1984; Matlock to JLG, January 21, 2011, JLG Papers. Matlock did have authorization, but the calls went to all former ambassadors to the Soviet Union, as well as to certain senior academic experts.

39 Reagan Diary, January 6, 1984, in Brinkley, ed., *Reagan Diaries*, p. 305. The January 16 speech is in *Public Papers of the Presidents: Reagan, 1984*. Mrs. Reagan's astrologer also appears to have influenced the timing. See on this, and on the composition of the speech, Matlock, *Reagan and Gorbachev*, pp. 80–85.

40 GFK Diary, January 29, 1984.

41 Andrew and Gordievsky, *KGB*, pp. 581–98.

42 Reagan Diary, October 10, November 18, December 9, 1983, January 6, 1984, in Brinkley, ed., *Reagan Diaries*, pp. 273, 290, 297. See also Hayward, *Conservative Counterrevolution*, pp. 325–32; and Fischer, *Reagan Reversal*, pp. 120–38.

43 Reagan Diary, January 6, 1984, in Brinkley, ed., *Reagan Diaries*, p. 305.

44 Matlock, "George F. Kennan," p. 240; Matlock to JLG, January 21, 2011, JLG Papers.

45 GFK Diary, February 20, March 23, 1984.

46 Dobrynin, *In Confidence*, pp. 547–48; GFK Diary, August 26, 1984.

47 *Ibid.*, January 26, February 21, 1985.

48 Reagan Diary, March 11 and 16, 1984, in Brinkley, ed., *Reagan Diaries*, pp. 411, 434, 436; "Succession in Moscow: What the Specialists are Saying; Experts Differ on How Much of an Impact Gorbachev Will Have," *New York Times*, March 12, 1985. For Reagan's attempts to meet Chernenko, see Hayward, *Conservative Counterrevolution*, pp. 348–50.

49 GFK Diary, April 4, 21, 1985.
50 *Ibid.*, August 24, October 27, 1985; GFK, "First Things First at the Summit," *New York Times*, November 3, 1985 (emphasis added). The Norwegian ambassador was Dagfinn Stenseth, and the Houdini reference was from a James Reston column.
51 David Remnick, "The Day of the Soviet Watchers," *Washington Post*, November 8, 1985; Walter Pincus, "U.S., Soviets Near Positions for 'Real Negotiations' at Summit," *ibid.*, October 29, 1985; Minutes, Reagan-Gorbachev Second Private Meeting, Geneva, November 19, 1985, at www.gwu.edu/~nsarchiv/NSAEBB/NSAEBB172/Doc19.pdf.
52 GFK Diary, November 27, 1985; GFK to JLG, December 23, 1985, JLG Papers.
53 GFK to Dobrynin, March 9, 1986, GFK Papers, 11:9; GFK Diary, March 12, 1986. See also GFK Diary, October 27, and November 16, 1985, and February 5, 1986.
54 "Summit Aftermath: The View from Moscow," *New York Times*, October 15, 1986.
55 GFK Diary, October 15, 1986.
56 GFK to State Department, March 20, 1946, in *FRUS: 1946*, VI, 773. See also GFK Diary, December 23, 1986.
57 GFK Diary, December 9, 1987, quoted in GFK, *Sketches from a Life*, pp. 351–52; GFK interview, December 13, 1987, pp. 42–44. See also stories on the reception by Philip Taubman and David Remnick in *The New York Times* and *The Washington Post*, respectively, on December 9.
58 GFK to Eugene Hotchkiss, January 18, 1987, courtesy of Eugene Hotchkiss; GFK address, "The Marshall Plan and the Future of Europe," Berlin, June 25, 1987, GFK Papers, 289:5; GFK Diary, November 26, 1987.
59 GFK Diary, November 30, 1987.
60 Nitze to Halle, November 10, 1983, Nitze Papers, Box 29, Folder 5.
61 I have developed this argument more fully in *Strategies of Containment*, pp. 349–77.
62 GFK interview, June 10, 1996; also GFK to JLG, September 4, 1996, JLG Papers.
63 GFK Diary, April 3, 1989. See also GFK, "After the Cold War," *New York Times Magazine*, February 5, 1989; GFK, "The Last Wise Man," *Atlantic Monthly* 263 (April 1989). For the Bush policy review, see David Ignatius, "Life After 'Containment'—Muddling Through," *Washington Post*, April 9, 1989.
64 Mary McGrory, "Kennan—A Prophet Honored," *ibid.*; Peter Jenkins, "Vindication of a Western Prophet," *Independent*, April 13, 1989. See also Don Oberdorfer, "Revolutionary Epoch Ending in Russia, Kennan Declares," *Washington Post*, April 5, 1989.
65 Don Oberdorfer, "Bush Finds Theme of Foreign Policy," *Washington Post*, May 28, 1989; William Safire, "On Language: The Man With the Pictures," *New York Times*, June 18, 1989. Bush's May 13 speech is in *Public Papers of the Presidents: George Bush, 1989*. The conference was held at Ohio University in October 1988.
66 GFK Diary, June 29 and July 4, 1989.
67 *Ibid.*, July 8, 1989; GFK to Eugene Hotchkiss, August 20, 1989, GFK Papers, 23:8.
68 GFK Diary, April 16, May 11, June 2, July 29, and August 7, 1989. See also GFK, *Fateful Alliance*.
69 GFK Diary, November 14, 15, 1989; GFK, "This Is No Time for Talk of German Reunification," *Washington Post*, November 12, 1989.
70 GFK Diary, July 8, November 18, December 3, 1989.
71 *Ibid.*, June 1, 1990.
72 The best recent account is Sarotte, *1989: The Struggle to Create a Post–Cold War Europe*.
73 GFK Diary, October 8, 1990.

TWENTY-FIVE • LAST THINGS: 1991–2005

1   GFK Diary, December 12, 1979.
2   *Ibid.*, June 30, 1980, August 2, 1982, July 25, 1982, May 9, 1983. The first George Kennan in fact died on May 10, 1924.
3   GFK Diary, January 10, 13, 1983.
4   *Ibid.*, September 13, 1983.
5   Ullman interview, p. 15. Nitze's tribute is in his papers, Box 5, Folder 29. See also Thompson, *Hawk and the Dove*, pp. 1–2.
6   GFK Diary, February 20, 1984.
7   *Ibid.*, March 9, 1984; Christopher Kennan conversation with JLG, April 30, 2010.
8   GFK Diary, June 9, 10, 1983.
9   *Ibid.*, September 24, December 28, 1982, January 13, September 3, 1983; also GFK to Eugene Hotchkiss, December 11, 1984, and September 7, 1987, Eugene Hotchkiss Papers.
10 GFK Diary, July 16, 1983.
11 *Ibid.*, April 29, 1993, March 24, 1994.
12 JLG Diary, June 28–29, 1985, JLG Papers; Goodman interview, p. 16; Dilworth interview, p. 2; GFK Diary, February 5, 1977, July 20, 1979, November 27, 1982, August 7, 1992. The actual passage, from the "Witches'

Kitchen" scene in *Faust*, has Mephistopheles saying, in Lewis Filmore's 1847 translation: "If you the means would hold / Without physician, sorcery, or gold, / Betake yourself forthwith into the field, / And hack and dig—the spade and mattock wield."

13 GFK Diary, October 11, 1982, April 5, 9, 1989.

14 Clinton, *My Life*, p. 151; Talbott, *Russia Hand*, pp. 132–34; GFK Diary, October 14, 1994.

15 *Ibid.*, April 4, 8, May 6, 1995.

16 *Ibid.*, October 31, November 5, 1996; Talbott, *Russia Hand*, pp. 220, 232; George F. Kennan, "A Fateful Error," *New York Times*, February 5, 1997.

17 GFK Diary, August 5, 1997. The passage is from *Richard II*, Act II, Scene 1.

18 GFK Diary, April 7, 1993.

19 Constance Goodman memorandum to GFK, February 11, 1985, GFK to Nancy Bressler, December 20, 1983, copies in JLG Papers.

20 C. Ben Wright, "Mr. 'X' and Containment," *Slavic Review* 35 (March, 1976), 1–31; "George F. Kennan Replies," *ibid.*, 32–36; C. Ben Wright to JLG, March 24, 2011, JLG Papers. For a fuller account, see Thompson, *The Hawk and the Dove*, pp. 254–57. Wright's dissertation was "George F. Kennan, Scholar-Diplomat: 1926–1946," University of Wisconsin, 1972.

21 See, for example, GFK Diary, November 27, 1983. The voluminous correspondence relating to the biography is in the GFK Papers, Boxes 14–16.

22 GFK Diary, November 18, 1982, September 17 and November 23, 1986, April 24, 1992; GFK to JLG, December 16, 1986, and April 23, 1992, JLG Papers.

23 GFK to JLG, November 13, 1987, October 1, 1993, May 28, 1997, *ibid.*; GFK Diary, December 12, 1987, and February 12, 1989.

24 Barton Gellman, *Contending with Kennan: Toward a Philosophy of American Power* (New York: Praeger, 1984), p. 18.

25 GFK Diary, January 21, February 16, 1981. See also GFK, *Around the Cragged Hill*, p. 11.

26 GFK to Gellman, March 28, 1983, courtesy of Barton Gellman; GFK to JLG, February 20, 1985, JLG Papers.

27 I am indebted to Richard Ullman for suggesting the Platonic comparison, in a conversation prior to the publication of *Around the Cragged Hill*.

28 GFK, *Around the Cragged Hill*, pp. 17–52; GFK Diary, April 28, 1985, July 4, 1995, and May 3, 1998.

29 GFK Diary, January 4, 1995 [misdated 1994].

30 GFK, *Around the Cragged Hill*, p. 36; FKW interview, p. 11.

31 GFK Diary, July 24, 1983, May 13, 1985, January 2, June 15, 1988, April 26, 1994, April 28, 1996.

32 *Ibid.*, July 7, 1994, July 4, 1995, July 21 and December 26, 1996, May 13, 1997; GFK, *At a Century's Ending*.

33 GFK Diary, February 15, 25, March 3, 7, 1994; JLG Diary, February 15, 1994, JLG Papers. See also Chapter Twelve, above.

34 GFK Diary, January 31, 1995; GFK, *American Family*; Gordon S. Wood, "All in the Family," *New York Review of Books*, February 22, 2001. Copies of the bird poems are at the beginning of the GFK Diary for 1990.

35 GFK Diary, May 12, 14, 1998, November 29, 2000; JLG Diary, December 30, 2001, JLG Papers.

36 *Ibid.*, July 14, 27, 2001; JEK to JLG, March 19, 2011, JLG Papers.

37 JLG Diary, December 30, 2001, JLG Papers.

38 JEK to JLG, March 19, 2011, JLG Papers; GFK to JLG, November 18, 2002, *ibid.* For the interviews, see Albert Eisele, "George F. Kennan: At 98, Veteran Diplomat Declares Congress Must Take Lead on War with Iraq," *The Hill*, September 25, 2002; and Jane Mayer, "The Big Idea: A Doctrine Passes," *New Yorker*, October 14 and 21, 2002, p. 70.

39 JLG Diary, August 18, November 9, 2003, February 19, 20, 2004, JLG Papers.

40 Lukacs, *Kennan: A Study of Character*, p. 188; JLG Diary, March 6, 2005.

41 GFK interview, December 13, 1995, pp. 23–24. I have edited the passage slightly to avoid repetition, but have in no way changed the substance.

EPILOGUE • GREATNESS

1 Portions of this epilogue draw on my comments at the Princeton University George F. Kennan Centennial Conference, delivered on February 20, 2004, as well as, more briefly, on the 2005 edition of *Strategies of Containment*, p. 390.

2 Ziegler, *Mountbatten*, p. 701.

3 Kissinger, *White House Years*, p. 135.

4 Kennan, "Experience of Writing History," p. 214.

5 The Seeley Mudd Library at Princeton University, where Kennan's papers are housed, is currently arranging a published edition of his diaries under the editorship of Frank Costigliola.

BIBLIOGRAPHY

INTERVIEWS[1]

Adams, Ware:
   C. Ben Wright, September 30, 1970, Washington, D.C., Wright Papers.
Ball, George:
   JLG, October 12, 1987, Princeton, N.J.
Berezhkov, Valentin:
   JLG, September 21, 1991, Athens, Ohio.
Berlin, Sir Isaiah:
   JLG, November 29, 1992, Oxford, England.
Black, Cyril E.:
   JLG, November 24, 1987, Princeton, N.J.
Bohlen, Charles E.:
   C. Ben Wright, September 29, 1970, Washington, D.C., Wright Papers.
Bowie, Robert R.:
   JLG, December 10, 1987, Princeton, N.J.
Bradt, Constance Kennan:
   Joan Kennan, no date, Joan Kennan Papers.
   JLG, November 13, 1982, Rome, N.Y.
Bundy, McGeorge:
   JLG, December 17, 1986, New York, N.Y.
Bundy, William P. and Mary A.:
   JLG, December 6, 1987, Princeton, N.J.
Crawford, William A.:
   C. Ben Wright, September 29, 1970, Washington, D.C., Wright Papers.
Cumming, Hugh S., Jr.:
   JLG, April 17, 1984, Washington, D.C.
Davies, John Paton and Patricia:
   JLG, December 7–8, 1982, Asheville, N.C.
Davies, Richard T.:
   Peter Jessup, November 9, 1979, ADST Oral History Project.
Dilworth, J Richardson
   JLG, December 6, 1987, Princeton, N.J.
Durbrow, Elbridge:
   JLG, September 24, 1982, Washington, D.C.
Elliott, John H.:
   JLG, December 7, 1992, Oxford, England.
Fosdick, Dorothy:
   JLG, October 29, 1987, Washington, D.C.

---

[1]In each case, interviewers are listed under the names of interviewees. Unless otherwise indicated, copies of all JLG interviews are in the George F. Kennan Papers, Seeley G. Mudd Library, Princeton University. ADST is the Association for Diplomatic Studies and Training Foreign Affairs Oral History Project, available on-line through the Library of Congress American Memory Project.

Franks, Sir Oliver:
        JLG, August 1, 1987, Oxford, England.
Goodman, Constance:
        JLG, December 10, 1987, Princeton, N.J.
Green, Marshall:
        Charles Stuart Kennedy, March 2, 1995, ADST Oral History Project.
Harriman, W. Averell:
        JLG, September 24, 1982, Washington, D.C.
Henderson, Loy W.:
        Richard D. McKinzie, June 14, 1973, Washington, D.C., Oral History Collection, Harry S. Truman Library.
        JLG, September 25, 1982, Washington, D.C.
Hessman, Dorothy:
        C. Ben Wright, October 1, 1970, Washington, D.C., Wright Papers.
        JLG, September 24, 1982, Washington, D.C.
Hickerson, John D.:
        JLG, November 15, 1983, Washington, D.C.
Hotchkiss, Jeannette Kennan:
        Joan Kennan, November 2, 1972, Joan Kennan Papers.
        JLG, December 21, 1982, Highland Park, Ill.
Kennan, Annelise Sørensen:
        JLG, August 26, 1982; September 8, 1983; December 14, 1987; all Princeton, N.J.
Kennan, George Frost:
        Harry B. Price, February 19, 1953, Harry B. Price Papers.
        Forrest C. Pogue, February 17, 1959, Forrest C. Pogue Papers.
        Louis Fischer, March 23, 1965, Oral History Collection, John F. Kennedy Library.
        Joan Kennan, no date, Joan Kennan Papers.
        JLG, October 31, 1974, Washington, D.C., author's possession.
        JLG, February 2, 1977; August 24–26, 1982; September 7–8, 1983; September 4–5, 1984; December 13,
                1987; January 30, 1991; December 13, 1995; June 10, 1996, all Princeton, N.J.
        Patricia H. Labalme, August 30, 1989, and February 27, 1990, Institute for Advanced Study Archives.
Kennan, Kent Wheeler:
        JLG, December 29, 1982, Austin, Texas.
Kondrashov, Sergey N.:
        Vladimir Pechatnov, May 27, 1999, Moscow, Russia.
Link, Arthur S.:
        JLG, September 8, 1983, Princeton, N.J.
Mautner, Martha:
        JLG, September 24, 1983, Casper, Wyo.
Nitze, Paul H.:
        JLG, December 13, 1989, Washington, D.C.
Roberts, Sir Frank:
        JLG, March 15, 1993, London, England.
Rusk, Dean
        JLG, December 9, 1982, Athens, Ga.
Schlesinger, Arthur M., Jr.:
        JLG, December 17, 1986, New York, N.Y.
Smith, Janet:
        JLG, August 18, 1999, Hartford, Conn.
Taquay, Charles and Kitty:
        JLG, March 27, 1991, Washington, D.C.
Taplin, Frank
        JLG, December 5, 1987, Princeton, N.J.
Thompson, Kenneth W.:
        JLG, December 6, 1982, Charlottesville, Va.
Toon, Malcolm:
        Henry E. Maddox, June 9, 1989, ADST Oral History Project.
Tucker, Robert C. and Evgenia:
        JLG, September 4, 1984, Princeton, N.J.
Tufts, Robert:
        JLG, February 5, 1987, Oberlin, Ohio.

Ullman, Richard H.:
    JLG, September 30, 1987, Princeton, N.J.
Von Oppen, Beate:
    JLG, August 27, 1982, Princeton, N.J.
Willett, E. F:
    JLG, June 2, 1989, Bridgeport, Conn.
Worobec, Frances Kennan:
    Joan Kennan, no date, Joan Kennan Papers.
    JLG, June 28, 1984, South Lake Tahoe, Calif.
Yakovlev, Nikolay N.:
    Vladimir Pechatnov, November 13, 1994, Moscow, Russia.

OFFICIAL FILES

Canada. Ministry of External Affairs. Record Group 25, National Archives of Canada, Ottawa.
Great Britain. Foreign Office Records, FO 371, National Archives, London.
Russia. Presidential Archive of the Russian Federation, Moscow.
United States. Department of State. National Archives, Washington, D.C.
_____. _____. Executive Secretariat Files.
_____. _____. Inspection Reports, 1906–39.
_____. _____. Policy Planning Staff Records [PPS Records].
_____. _____. Record Group 59, Decimal File, 1910–29, 1930–39, 1940–44, 1945–49, 1950–54, 1960–63.
_____. _____. Record Group 84, Moscow Post Files, 1944–46, 1952.
_____. _____. Summaries of the Secretary's Daily Meetings, 1949–52.
_____. Federal Bureau of Investigation. George Kennan File, FBI Records, Washington, D.C.
_____. National War College Archives, Washington, D.C.

MANUSCRIPT COLLECTIONS

Acheson, Dean G.: Harry S. Truman Library, Independence, Mo.
_____: Sterling Library Manuscripts and Archives, Yale University.
Alsop, Joseph, and Stewart Alsop: Library of Congress.
Ayers, Eban A.: Harry S. Truman Library, Independence, Mo.
Bohlen, Charles E.: Library of Congress.
    : Record Group 59, National Archives.
Bull, Mimi: privately held.
Bullitt, William C.: Sterling Library Manuscripts and Archives, Yale University.
Davies, Joseph E.: Library of Congress.
Dulles, John Foster: Seeley Mudd Manuscript Library, Princeton University.
Eisenhower, Dwight D.: Dwight D. Eisenhower Library, Abilene, Kans.
Elsey, George: Harry S. Truman Library, Independence, Mo.
Forrestal, James V.: Seeley Mudd Manuscript Library, Princeton University.
Gaddis, John Lewis: privately held.
Halle, Louis J.: Alderman Library, University of Virginia.
Harriman, W. Averell: Library of Congress.
Henderson, Loy: Library of Congress.
Hersey, John: Beinecke Library, Yale University.
Holmes, John W.: Canadian Institute of International Affairs, Toronto.
Hopkins, Harry: Franklin D. Roosevelt Library, Hyde Park, N.Y.
Hotchkiss, Eugene: privately held.
Hotchkiss, Jeanette Kennan: privately held.
James, Douglas: privately held.
Jessup, Philip: Library of Congress.
Johnson, Lyndon B.: Lyndon B. Johnson Library, Austin, Tex.
Jones, Owen T.: Harry S. Truman Library, Independence, Mo.
Kennan, George F.: Seeley Mudd Manuscript Library, Princeton University.
Kennan, Joan Elisabeth: privately held.
Kennan, Kossuth Kent: Wisconsin State Historical Society, Madison.
Kennedy, John F.: John F. Kennedy Library, Boston, Mass.
Kissinger, Henry A.: Telephone Conversations, 1969–1977, Digital National Security Archive.

Leopold, Richard W.: Northwestern University.
Lippmann, Walter: Sterling Library Manuscripts and Archives, Yale University.
Murphy, Robert: Hoover Institution, Stanford University.
Nitze, Paul: Library of Congress.
Oppenheimer, J. Robert: Library of Congress.
Price, Harry B.: George C. Marshall Library, Lexington, Va.
Pogue, Forrest C.: George C. Marshall Library, Lexington, Va.
Strauss, Lewis: Herbert Hoover Library, West Branch, Iowa.
Truman, Harry S.: Harry S. Truman Library, Independence, Mo.
Webb, James E.: Harry S. Truman Library, Independence, Mo.
Wright, C. Ben: George C. Marshall Library, Lexington, Va.

UNPUBLISHED MATERIAL

Hotchkiss, Jeanette Kennan. "Memoirs for Two." Typescript. Edited by Eugene Hotchkiss, January 4, 1996. JEK
   Papers.
Kennan, Joan. Unpublished, undated memoir. JEK Papers.
Kennan, Kossuth Kent. Handwritten reminiscences, no date but probably 1933. KKK Papers, Wisconsin State
   Historical Society, Madison.
Morgan, Michael David. "The Origins of the Helsinki Final Act." Ph.D. dissertation, Yale University, 2010.
Schmidt, Michael Reed. "Present at the Creation and Beyond: Thucydides in the Cold War." Department of
   History Senior Essay, Yale University, 2008.
Seegert, Frederick C., Jr. Oakwood Bay Centennial: The Way We Were, 1882–1982. Typescript, July 1987.
Vogel, Theodore F., Jr. Sauce for the Gander (Wisconsin Style). Undated typescript.
Wright, C. Ben. "George F. Kennan, Scholar-Diplomat: 1926–1946." Ph.D. dissertation, University of Wiscon-
   sin, 1972.

PUBLISHED DOCUMENTS

Blum, John Morton, ed. The Price of Vision: The Diary of Henry A. Wallace, 1942–1946. Boston: Houghton
   Mifflin, 1973.
Brinkley, Douglas, ed. The Reagan Diaries: January 1981–January 1989, 2 vols. New York: HarperCollins, 2009.
Bullitt, Orville H., ed. For the President: Personal and Secret: Correspondence Between Franklin D. Roosevelt and
   William C. Bullitt. Boston: Houghton Mifflin, 1972.
Chandler, Alfred D., Jr., et al. The Papers of Dwight David Eisenhower, 21 vols. Baltimore: Johns Hopkins Uni-
   versity Press, 1970–2001.
Crossman, Richard. The Diaries of a Cabinet Minister: Secretary of State for Social Services, 1968–1970. New
   York: Holt, Rinehart, and Winston, 1977.
Etzold, Thomas H., and John Lewis Gaddis, eds. Containment: Documents on American Policy and Strategy,
   1945–1950. New York: Columbia University Press, 1978.
Ferrell, Robert H., ed. Off the Record: The Private Papers of Harry S. Truman. New York: Harper and Row, 1980.
Harlow, Giles D., and George C. Maerz, eds. Measures Short of War: The George F. Kennan Lectures at the
   National War College, 1946–47. Washington, D.C.: National Defense University Press, 1991.
Institute for Advanced Study. Report of the Director, 1948–1953. Princeton, N.J.: Institute for Advanced Study,
   1954.
Jensen, Kenneth M., ed. The Origins of the Cold War: The Novikov, Kennan, and Roberts "Long Telegrams" of
   1946. Washington, D.C.: United States Institute of Peace, 1993.
Karalekas, Anne. "History of the Central Intelligence Agency." U.S. Congress, Senate, Select Committee to Study
   Government Operations with respect to Intelligence Activities, Final Report: Supplementary Detailed Staff
   Reports on Foreign and Military Intelligence: Book IV. Washington, D.C.: Government Printing Office, 1976.
Lukacs, John, ed. George F. Kennan and the Origins of Containment, 1944–46: The Kennan-Lukacs Correspon-
   dence. Columbia: University of Missouri Press, 1997.
_____, ed. Through the History of the Cold War: The Correspondence of George F. Kennan and John Lukacs.
   Philadelphia: University of Pennsylvania Press, 2010.
McLellan, David S., and David C. Acheson. Among Friends: Personal Letters of Dean Acheson. New York: Dodd,
   Mead, 1980.
Millis, Walter, ed. The Forrestal Diaries. New York: Viking, 1951.
Moorehead, Caroline, ed. Selected Letters of Martha Gellhorn. New York: Henry Holt, 2006.
Public Papers of the Presidents of the United States. Washington, D.C.: Government Printing Office, 1961– .
Schlesinger, Arthur M., Jr. Journals: 1952–2000. Edited by Andrew Schlesinger and Stephen Schlesinger. New
   York: Penguin, 2007.

Skinner, Kiron K., Annelise Anderson, and Martin Anderson, eds. *Reagan: A Life in Letters*. New York: Free Press, 2003.
————. *Reagan, In His Own Hand*. New York: Free Press, 2001.
Sulzberger, C. L. *A Long Row of Candles: Memoirs and Diaries, 1934–1945*. New York: Macmillan, 1969.
————. *The Last of the Giants*. New York: Macmillan, 1970.
United States. Atomic Energy Commission. *In the Matter of J. Robert Oppenheimer*. Washington, D.C.: Government Printing Office, 1954.
————. Congress. House of Representatives, Committee on Foreign Affairs. *Foreign Policy and Mutual Security*. Washington, D.C.: Government Printing Office, 1956.
————. ————. Senate. *Legislative Origins of the Truman Doctrine*. Washington, D.C.: Government Printing Office, 1973.
————. ————. ————. Committee on Foreign Relations. *Historical Series: Economic Assistance to China and Korea*. Washington, D.C.: Government Printing Office, 1974.
————. ————. ————. *Historical Series, IV*. Washington, D.C.: Government Printing Office, 1976.
————. ————. ————. ————. *Supplemental Foreign Assistance Fiscal Year 1966—Vietnam*. Washington, D.C.: Government Printing Office, 1966.
————. Department of State. *Foreign Relations of the United States [FRUS]*. Washington, D.C.: Government Printing Office, 1862– .
————. ————. *The State Department Policy Planning Staff Papers, 1947–1949*. New York: Garland Publishing, 1983.

Books

Abramson, Rudy. *Spanning the Century: The Life of W. Averell Harriman*. New York: William Morrow, 1992.
Acheson, Dean. *Present at the Creation: My Years in the State Department*. New York: Norton, 1969.
Adams, Brooks. *America's Economic Supremacy*. New York: Macmillan, 1900.
Adams, Henry. *The Education of Henry Adams: An Autobiography*. Boston: Massachusetts Historical Society, 1918; reprinted Boston: Houghton Mifflin, 1946.
Aldrich, Richard J. *The Hidden Hand: Britain, America and Cold War Secret Intelligence*. London: John Murray, 2001.
Alliluyeva, Svetlana. *Only One Year*. Translated by Paul Chavchavadze. New York: Harper and Row, 1969.
Alsop, Joseph W., with Adam Platt. *"I've Seen the Best of It": Memoirs*. New York: Norton, 1992.
Anderson, Harry H., and Frederick I. Olson. *Milwaukee: At the Gathering of the Waters*. Milwaukee: Milwaukee County Historical Society and Continental Heritage Press, 1981.
Andrew, Christopher, and Oleg Gordievsky. *KGB: The Inside Story*. New York: HarperCollins, 1990.
Arbatov, Georgi. *The System: An Insider's Life in Soviet Politics*. New York: Random House, 1992.
Axtell, James. *The Making of Princeton University: From Woodrow Wilson to the Present*. Princeton, N.J.: Princeton University Press, 2006.
Bassford, Christopher. *Clausewitz in English: The Reception of Clausewitz in Britain and America, 1815–1945*. New York: Oxford University Press, 1994.
Behrman, Greg. *The Most Noble Adventure: The Marshall Plan and the Time When America Helped Save Europe*. New York: Free Press, 2007.
Beisner, Robert L. *Dean Acheson: A Life in the Cold War*. New York: Oxford University Press, 2006.
Beschloss, Michael R. *The Crisis Years: Kennedy and Khrushchev, 1960–1963*. New York: HarperCollins, 1991.
Bird, Kai. *The Color of Truth: McGeorge Bundy and William Bundy: Brothers in Arms*. New York: Simon and Schuster, 1998.
————, and Martin J. Sherwin. *American Prometheus: The Triumph and Tragedy of J. Robert Oppenheimer*. New York: Knopf, 2005.
Bohlen, Charles E. *Witness to History: 1929–1969*. New York: Norton, 1973.
Botti, Timothy J. *The Long Wait: The Forging of the Anglo-American Nuclear Alliance, 1945–1958*. New York: Greenwood, 1987.
Bowie, Robert R., and Richard H. Immerman. *Waging Peace: How Eisenhower Shaped an Enduring Cold War Strategy*. New York: Oxford University Press, 1998.
Brent, Jonathan, and Vladimir P. Naumov. *Stalin's Last Crime: The Plot Against the Jewish Doctors, 1948–1953*. New York: HarperCollins, 2003.
Brinkley, Douglas. *Dean Acheson: The Cold War Years, 1953–71*. New Haven, Conn.: Yale University Press, 1992.
Brodie, Bernard, ed. *The Absolute Weapon: Atomic Power and World Order*. New York: Harcourt, Brace, 1946.
Brownell, Will, and Richard N. Billings. *So Close to Greatness: A Biography of William C. Bullitt*. New York: Macmillan, 1987.

Bullock, Alan. *Ernest Bevin: Foreign Secretary, 1945–1951.* New York: Norton, 1983.

Bundy, McGeorge. *Danger and Survival: Choices About the Bomb in the First Fifty Years.* New York: Random House, 1988.

Burdick, Charles B. *An American Island in Hitler's Reich: The Bad Nauheim Internment.* Menlo Park, Calif.: Markgraf Publications, 1987.

Butterfield, Herbert. *The Whig Interpretation of History.* London: Bell, 1931.

Callahan, David. *Dangerous Capabilities: Paul Nitze and the Cold War.* New York: HarperCollins, 1990.

Cannon, Lou. *President Reagan: The Role of a Lifetime.* New York: Simon and Schuster, 1991.

Cassella-Blackburn, Michael. *The Donkey, the Carrot, and the Club: William C. Bullitt and Soviet-American Relations, 1917–1948.* Westport, Conn.: Praeger, 2004.

Chekhov, Anton. *The Steppe and Other Stories.* Translated by Ronald Hingley. Oxford: Oxford University Press, 1991.

Chen Jian. *China's Road to the Korean War: The Making of the Sino-American Confrontation.* New York: Columbia University Press, 1994.

Chester, Eric Thomas. *Covert Network: Progressives, the International Rescue Committee, and the CIA.* Armonk, N.Y.: M. E. Sharpe, 1995.

Churchill, Winston S. *Painting as a Pastime.* New York: Whittlesey House, 1950.

Clausewitz, Carl von. *On War.* Edited and translated by Michael Howard and Peter Paret. Princeton, N.J.: Princeton University Press, 1976.

Clifford, Clark, with Richard Holbrooke. *Counsel to the President: A Memoir.* New York: Random House, 1991.

Clinton, Bill. *My Life.* New York: Random House, 2004.

Cohrs, Patrick O. *The Unfinished Peace After World War I: America, Britain, and the Stabilization of Europe, 1919–1932.* New York: Cambridge University Press, 2006.

Congdon, Lee. *George Kennan: A Writing Life.* Wilmington, Del.: ISI, 2008.

Corke, Sarah-Jane. *U.S. Covert Operations and Cold War Strategy: Truman, Secret Warfare and the CIA, 1945–53.* New York: Routledge, 2008.

Craig, Gordon A., and Francis L. Loewenheim, eds. *The Diplomats: 1939–1979.* Princeton, N.J.: Princeton University Press, 1994.

Darling, Arthur B. *The Central Intelligence Agency: An Instrument of Government, to 1950.* University Park: Pennsylvania State University Press, 1990.

Davies, John Paton, Jr. *Dragon by the Tail: American, British, Japanese, and Russian Encounters with China and One Another.* New York: Norton, 1972.

Davies, Joseph E. *Mission to Moscow.* New York: Simon and Schuster, 1941.

DeSantis, Hugh. *The Diplomacy of Silence: The American Foreign Service, the Soviet Union, and the Cold War, 1933–1947.* Chicago: University of Chicago Press, 1980.

de Silva, Peer. *Sub Rosa: The CIA and the Uses of Intelligence.* New York: Times Books, 1978.

Divine, Robert A. *Second Chance: The Triumph of Internationalism in America During World War II.* New York: Atheneum, 1967.

Dobrynin, Anatoly. *In Confidence: Moscow's Ambassador to America's Six Cold War Presidents (1962–1986).* New York: Random House, 1995.

Earle, Edward Mead, ed. *Makers of Modern Strategy: Military Thought from Machiavelli to Hitler.* Princeton, N.J.: Princeton University Press, 1943.

Eisenberg, Carolyn. *Drawing the Line: The American Decision to Divide Germany, 1944–1949.* New York: Cambridge University Press, 1996.

Engerman, David C. *Know Your Enemy: The Rise and Fall of America's Soviet Experts.* New York: Oxford University Press, 2009.

_____. *Modernization from the Other Shore: American Intellectuals and the Romance of Russian Development.* Cambridge, Mass.: Harvard University Press, 2003.

Fischer, Beth A. *The Reagan Reversal: Foreign Policy and the End of the Cold War.* Columbia: University of Missouri Press, 1997.

Fitzgerald, F. Scott. *This Side of Paradise.* New York: Scribner's, 1920.

Fitzpatrick, Sheila. *Everyday Stalinism: Ordinary Life in Extraordinary Times; Soviet Russia in the 1930s.* New York: Oxford University Press, 1999.

Ford, Richard, ed. *The Essential Tales of Chekhov.* Translated by Constance Garnett. Hopewell, N.J.: Ecco Press, 1998.

Gaddis, John Lewis. *The Cold War: A New History.* New York: Penguin, 2005.

_____. *The Long Peace: Inquiries into the History of the Cold War.* New York: Oxford University Press, 1987.

_____. *Russia, the Soviet Union, and the United States: An Interpretive History,* 2nd ed. New York: McGraw-Hill, 1990.

_____. *Strategies of Containment: A Critical Appraisal of American National Security Policy During the Cold War.* 2nd. ed. New York: Oxford University Press, 2005.

_____. *The United States and the Origins of the Cold War, 1941–1947*. New York: Columbia University Press, 1972.

_____. *We Now Know: Rethinking Cold War History*. New York: Oxford University Press, 1997.

Gains, M. G. *Five Acres and Independence: A Practical Guide to the Selection and Management of the Small Farm*. New York: Greenberg, 1940.

Garthoff, Raymond L. *Détente and Confrontation: American-Soviet Relations from Nixon to Reagan*. Rev. ed. Washington, D.C.: Brookings Institution, 1994.

Gellhorn, Martha. *A Stricken Field*. New York: Duell, Sloan, and Pearce, 1940.

Gellman, Barton. *Contending with Kennan: Toward a Philosophy of American Power*. New York: Praeger, 1984.

Gellman, Irwin F. *Secret Affairs: Franklin Roosevelt, Cordell Hull, and Sumner Welles*. Baltimore: Johns Hopkins University Press, 1995.

Gibbon, Edward. *The Decline and Fall of the Roman Empire*, 3 vols. New York: Modern Library, 1977.

Gilbert, Martin. *"Never Despair": Winston S. Churchill, 1945–1965*. London: Heinemann, 1988.

Gladwell, Malcolm. *Blink: The Power of Thinking Without Thinking*. New York: Little, Brown, 2005.

Goldman, Eric F. *The Tragedy of Lyndon Johnson*. New York: Knopf, 1969.

Goncharov, Sergei N., John W. Lewis, and Xue Litai. *Uncertain Partners: Stalin, Mao, and the Korean War*. Stanford, Calif.: Stanford University Press, 1993.

Gregory, John G. *History of Milwaukee, Wisconsin*. Milwaukee: S. J. Clarke, 1931.

Grose, Peter. *Gentleman Spy: The Life of Allen Dulles*. New York: Houghton Mifflin, 1994.

Halle, Louis J. *The Cold War as History*. New York: Harper and Row, 1967.

Hamby, Alonzo L. *For the Survival of Democracy: Franklin Roosevelt and the World Crisis of the 1930s*. New York: Free Press, 2004.

_____. *Man of the People: A Life of Harry S. Truman*. New York: Oxford University Press, 1995.

Harbutt, Fraser J. *The Iron Curtain: Churchill, America, and the Origins of the Cold War*. New York: Oxford University Press, 1986.

Harper, John Lamberton. *American Visions of Europe: Franklin D. Roosevelt, George F. Kennan, and Dean Acheson*. New York: Cambridge University Press, 1994.

Harriman, W. Averell, and Elie Abel. *Special Envoy to Churchill and Stalin, 1941–1946*. New York: Random House, 1975.

Hayward, Steven F. *The Age of Reagan: The Conservative Counterrevolution, 1980–1989*. New York: Crown Forum, 2009.

Heinrichs, Waldo. *American Ambassador: Joseph C. Grew and the Development of the United States Diplomatic Tradition*. Boston: Little, Brown, 1966.

_____. *Threshold of War: Franklin D. Roosevelt and American Entry into World War II*. New York: Oxford University Press, 1988.

Hellman, Lillian. *An Unfinished Woman: A Memoir*. Boston: Little, Brown, 1969.

Henderson, Loy W. *A Question of Trust: The Origins of U.S.-Soviet Relations: The Memoirs of Loy W. Henderson*. Edited by George W. Baer. Stanford, Calif.: Hoover Institution Press, 1986.

Herken, Gregg. *Brotherhood of the Bomb: The Tangled Lives and Loyalties of Robert Oppenheimer, Ernest Lawrence, and Edward Teller*. New York: Henry Holt, 2002.

Herring, George C., Jr. *Aid to Russia, 1941–1946: Strategy, Diplomacy, the Origins of the Cold War*. New York: Columbia University Press, 1973.

Hersch, Burton. *The Old Boys: The American Elite and the Origins of the CIA*. New York: Scribner's, 1992.

Herwarth, Johnnie von, with S. Frederick Starr. *Against Two Evils: Memoirs of a Diplomat-Soldier During the Third Reich*. London: Collins, 1981.

Hill, Charles. *Grand Strategies: Literature, Statecraft, and World Order*. New Haven, Conn.: Yale University Press, 2010.

Hixson, Walter L. *George F. Kennan: Cold War Iconoclast*. New York: Columbia University Press, 1989.

Hochschild, Adam. *Half the Way Home: A Memoir of Father and Son*. New York: Viking, 1986.

Hoffmann, George F. *Cold War Casualty: The Court-Martial of Major General Robert W. Grow*. Kent, Ohio: Kent State University Press, 1993.

Hogan, Michael J. *A Cross of Iron: Harry S. Truman and the Origins of the National Security State*. New York: Cambridge University Press, 1998.

_____. *The Marshall Plan: America, Britain, and the Reconstruction of Western Europe, 1947–1952*. New York: Cambridge University Press, 1987.

Holloway, David. *Stalin and the Bomb: The Soviet Union and Atomic Energy, 1939–1956*. New Haven, Conn.: Yale University Press, 1994.

Hoopes, Townsend, and Douglas Brinkley. *Driven Patriot: The Life and Times of James Forrestal*. New York: Knopf, 1992.

Hughes, Emmet John. *The Ordeal of Power: A Political Memoir of the Eisenhower Years*. New York: Atheneum, 1963.

Immerman, Richard H., ed. *John Foster Dulles and the Diplomacy of the Cold War*. Princeton, N.J.: Princeton University Press, 1990.

Isaacson, Walter, and Evan Thomas. *The Wise Men: Six Friends and the World They Made*. New York: Simon and Schuster, 1986.

James, D. Clayton. *The Years of MacArthur*, 3 vols. Boston: Houghton Mifflin, 1970–85.

Jones, Joseph M. *The Fifteen Weeks (February 21–June 5, 1947)*. New York: Viking, 1955.

Kahn, E. J., Jr. *The China Hands: America's Foreign Service Officers and What Befell Them*. New York: Viking, 1975.

Kennan, George. *E. H. Harriman: A Biography*. Boston: Houghton Mifflin, 1922.

————. *Siberia and the Exile System*. New York: Century, 1891.

————. *Tent Life in Siberia*. New York: G. P. Putnam, 1870.

Kennan, George F. *American Diplomacy: 1900–1950*. Chicago: University of Chicago Press, 1951.

————. *An American Family: The Kennans; The First Three Generations*. New York: Norton, 2000.

————. *Around the Cragged Hill: A Personal and Political Philosophy*. New York: Norton, 1993.

————. *At a Century's Ending: Reflections, 1982–1995*. New York: Norton, 1996.

————. *The Cloud of Danger: Current Realities of American Foreign Policy*. Boston: Little, Brown, 1977.

————. *The Decline of Bismarck's European Order: Franco-Russian Relations, 1875–1890*. Princeton, N.J.: Princeton University Press, 1979.

————. *Democracy and the Student Left*. Boston: Little, Brown, 1968.

————. *The Fateful Alliance: France, Russia, and the Coming of the First World War*. New York: Pantheon, 1984.

————. *From Prague After Munich: Diplomatic Papers, 1938–1940*. Princeton, N.J.: Princeton University Press, 1968.

————. *The Marquis de Custine and His Russia in 1839*. Princeton, N.J.: Princeton University Press, 1971.

————. *Memoirs, vol. I, 1925–1950*. Boston: Atlantic–Little, Brown, 1967.

————. *Memoirs, vol. II, 1950–1963*. Boston: Atlantic–Little, Brown, 1972.

————. *The Nuclear Delusion: Soviet-American Relations in the Atomic Age*. New York: Pantheon, 1983.

————. *On Dealing with the Communist World*. New York: Harper and Row, 1964.

————. *Realities of American Foreign Policy*. New York: Norton, 1966. Originally published by Princeton University Press in 1954.

————. *Russia, the Atom and the West*. New York: Harper, 1958.

————. *Russia and the West Under Lenin and Stalin*. Boston: Little, Brown, 1961.

————. *Sketches from a Life*. New York: Pantheon, 1989.

————. *Soviet-American Relations, 1917–1920: The Decision to Intervene*. Princeton, N.J.: Princeton University Press, 1958.

————. *Soviet-American Relations, 1917–1920: Russia Leaves the War*. Princeton, N.J.: Princeton University Press, 1956.

Kennan, Kossuth Kent. *Income Taxation—Method and Results in Various Countries*. Milwaukee: Burdick and Allen, 1910.

Kershaw, Ian. *Hitler: 1936–45: Nemesis*. London: Allen Lane, 2000.

Kirk, Lydia Chapin. *Postmarked Moscow: An American Ambassador's Wife Looks at Life in Russia Today*. New York: Scribner's, 1952.

Kissinger, Henry A. *The Troubled Partnership: A Re-appraisal of the Atlantic Alliance*. New York: McGraw-Hill, 1965.

————. *White House Years*. Boston: Little, Brown, 1979.

Kofsky, Frank. *Harry S. Truman and the War Scare of 1948: A Successful Campaign to Deceive the Nation*. New York: St. Martin's Press, 1995.

LaFeber, Walter. *Inevitable Revolutions: The United States in Central America*. New York: Norton, 1984.

Lees, Lorraine M. *Keeping Tito Afloat: The United States, Yugoslavia, and the Cold War*. University Park: Pennsylvania State University Press, 1997.

Leffler, Melvyn P. *For the Soul of Mankind: The United States, the Soviet Union, and the Cold War*. New York: Hill and Wang, 2007.

————. *A Preponderance of Power: National Security, the Truman Administration, and the Cold War*. Stanford, Calif.: Stanford University Press, 1992.

————, and Odd Arne Westad, eds. *The Cambridge History of the Cold War*. Cambridge, U.K.: Cambridge University Press, 2010.

Lettow, Paul. *Ronald Reagan and His Quest to Abolish Nuclear Weapons*. New York: Random House, 2005.

Levering, Ralph B., Vladimir O. Pechatnov, Verena Botzenhart-Viehe, and C. Earl Edmondson. *Debating the Origins of the Cold War: American and Russian Perspectives*. New York: Rowman and Littlefield, 2002.

Lilienthal, David. *The Journals of David E. Lilienthal*. Vol. II, *The Atomic Energy Years, 1945–1950*. New York: Harper and Row, 1964.

Lippmann, Walter. *The Cold War: A Study in U.S. Foreign Policy*. New York: Harper and Row, 1972 (first published in 1947).

————. *U.S. Foreign Policy: Shield of the Republic*. Boston: Little, Brown, 1943.

Lukacs, John. *George Kennan: A Study of Character*. New Haven, Conn.: Yale University Press, 2007.

MacDonald, Betty. *The Egg and I*. Philadelphia: Lippincott, 1945.

Machiavelli, Niccolò. *The Prince*. Translated by Harvey C. Mansfield. 2nd ed. Chicago: University of Chicago Press, 1998.

MacLean, Elizabeth Kimball. *Joseph E. Davies: Envoy to the Soviets*. Westport, Conn.: Praeger, 1992.

McLellan, David. *Dean Acheson: The State Department Years*. New York: Dodd, Mead, 1976.

Masarik, Hubert. *Le dernier témoin de Munich: Un diplomate tchécoslovaque dans la tourmente européenne, (1918–1941)*. Translated from the Czech by Antoine Marès. Lausanne: Éditions Noir sur Blanc, 2006.

Mastny, Vojtech. *The Cold War and Soviet Insecurity: The Stalin Years*. New York: Oxford University Press, 1996.

Matlock, Jack F., Jr. *Reagan and Gorbachev: How the Cold War Ended*. New York: Random House, 2004.

May, Ernest R., ed. *American Cold War Strategy: Interpreting NSC 68*. Boston: St. Martin's, 1993.

Mayers, David. *Cracking the Monolith: U.S. Policy Against the Sino-Soviet Alliance, 1949–1955*. Baton Rouge: Louisiana State University Press, 1986.

————. *George Kennan and the Dilemmas of U.S. Foreign Policy*. New York: Oxford University Press, 1988.

Merry, Robert W. *Taking on the World: Joseph and Stewart Alsop—Guardians of the American Century*. New York: Viking, 1996.

Messer, Robert L. *The End of an Alliance: James F. Byrnes, Roosevelt, Truman, and the Origins of the Cold War*. Chapel Hill: University of North Carolina Press, 1982.

Miller, James Edward. *The United States and Italy: The Politics and Diplomacy of Stabilization*. Chapel Hill: University of North Carolina Press, 1986.

Miscamble, Wilson D., C.S.C. *From Roosevelt to Truman: Potsdam, Hiroshima, and the Cold War*. New York: Cambridge University Press, 2007.

————. *George F. Kennan and the Making of American Foreign Policy, 1947–1950*. Princeton, N.J.: Princeton University Press, 1992.

Mitchell, I. N., ed. *Quarter Centenary of the Milwaukee State Normal School, 1886–1911*. Milwaukee: no publisher, 1911.

Montefiore, Simon Sebag. *Stalin: At the Court of the Red Tsar*. New York: Knopf, 2004.

Morgan, Ted. *Reds: McCarthyism in Twentieth-Century America*. New York: Random House, 2003.

Morgenthau, Hans J. *Politics Among Nations: The Struggle for Power and Peace*. New York: Knopf, 1948.

Newman, Robert P. *The Cold War Romance of Lillian Hellman and John Melby*. Chapel Hill: University of North Carolina Press, 1989.

Niebuhr, Reinhold. *The Children of Light and the Children of Darkness: A Vindication of Democracy and a Critique of Its Traditional Defense*. New York: Scribner's, 1944.

————. *Moral Man and Immoral Society: A Study in Ethics and Politics*. New York: Scribner's, 1932.

Nitze, Paul H. *Tension Between Opposites: Reflections on the Practice and Theory of Politics*. New York: Scribner, 1993.

————, with Ann M. Smith and Steven L. Rearden. *From Hiroshima to Glasnost: At the Center of Decision—A Memoir*. New York: Grove Weidenfeld, 1989.

Orum, Anthony M. *City-Building in America*. Boulder, Colo.: Westview Press, 1995.

Oshinsky, David M. *A Conspiracy So Immense: The World of Joe McCarthy*. New York: Free Press, 1983.

Ouimet, Matthew J. *The Rise and Fall of the Brezhnev Doctrine in Soviet Foreign Policy*. Chapel Hill: University of North Carolina Press, 2003.

Parker, Ralph. *Conspiracy Against Peace: Notes of an English Journalist*. Moscow: Literaturnaya Gazeta, 1949.

Pechatnov, Vladimir. *Stalin, Ruzvel't, Trumen: SSSR i SShA v 1940-x gg*. Moscow: Terra-Knizhnyi Klub, 2006.

Pflanze, Otto. *Bismarck and the Development of Germany: The Period of Unification, 1815–1871*, 2nd ed. Princeton, N.J.: Princeton University Press, 1990.

Pickett, William B., ed. *George F. Kennan and the Origins of Eisenhower's New Look: An Oral History of Project Solarium*. Princeton, N.J.: Princeton Institute for International and Regional Studies, 2004.

Pipes, Richard. *Vixi: Memoirs of a Non-Belonger*. New Haven, Conn.: Yale University Press, 2003.

Pisani, Sallie. *The CIA and the Marshall Plan*. Lawrence: University Press of Kansas, 1991.

Pogue, Forrest C. *George C. Marshall: Statesman, 1945–1959*. New York: Viking, 1987.

Poundstone, William. *Prisoner's Dilemma: John von Neumann, Game Theory, and the Puzzle of the Bomb*. New York: Doubleday, 1992.

Regis, Ed. *Who Got Einstein's Office? Eccentricity and Genius at the Institute for Advanced Study*. New York: Addison-Wesley, 1987.

Reston, James. *Deadline: A Memoir*. New York: Random House, 1991.

Richie, Alexandra. *Faust's Metropolis: A History of Berlin*. New York: Carroll and Graf, 1998.

Rhodes, Richard. *Dark Sun: The Making of the Hydrogen Bomb*. New York: Simon and Schuster, 1995.

Roberts, Frank. *Dealing with Dictators: The Destruction and Revival of Europe, 1930–70*. London: Weidenfeld and Nicolson, 1991.

Roberts, Geoffrey. *Stalin's Wars: From World War to Cold War, 1939–1953*. New Haven, Conn.: Yale University Press, 2006.

Rosenthal, Joel D. *Righteous Realists: Political Realism, Responsible Power, and American Culture in the Nuclear Age*. Baton Rouge: Louisiana State University Press, 1991.

Ruddy, T. Michael. *The Cautious Diplomat: Charles E. Bohlen and the Soviet Union, 1929–1969*. Kent, Ohio: Kent State University Press, 1986.

Salisbury, Harrison E. *A Journey for Our Times: A Memoir*. New York: Harper and Row, 1983.

Sanborn Map Company. *Insurance Maps of Milwaukee, Wisconsin*, vol. I. New York: Sanborn Map Company, 1910.

Sarotte, Mary Elise. *1989: The Struggle to Create Post-Cold War Europe*. Princeton, N.J.: Princeton University Press, 2009.

Saul, Norman E. *Concord and Conflict: The United States and Russia, 1867–1914*. Lawrence: University Press of Kansas, 1996.

————. *War and Revolution: The United States and Russia, 1914–1921*. Lawrence: University Press of Kansas, 2001.

————. *Friends or Foes? The United States and Russia, 1921–1941*. Lawrence: University Press of Kansas, 2006.

Saunders, Frances Stonor. *The Cultural Cold War: The CIA and the World of Arts and Letters*. New York: New Press, 1999.

Schaller, Michael. *Douglas MacArthur: The Far Eastern General*. New York: Oxford University Press, 1989.

Schell, Jonathan. *The Fate of the Earth*. New York: Knopf, 1982.

Schilling, Warner R., Paul Y. Hammond, and Glenn H. Snyder. *Strategy, Politics, and Defense Budgets*. New York: Columbia University Press, 1962.

Schlesinger, Arthur M., Jr. *A Thousand Days: John F. Kennedy in the White House*. Boston: Houghton Mifflin, 1965.

Schwartz, Thomas Alan. *America's Germany: John J. McCloy and the Federal Republic of Germany*. Cambridge, Mass.: Harvard University Press, 1991.

————. *Lyndon Johnson and Europe: In the Shadow of Vietnam*. Cambridge, Mass.: Harvard University Press, 2003.

Selverstone, Marc J. *Constructing the Monolith: The United States, Great Britain, and International Communism, 1945–1950*. Cambridge, Mass.: Harvard University Press, 2009.

Sheng, Michael M. *Battling Western Imperialism: Mao, Stalin, and the United States*. Princeton, N.J.: Princeton University Press, 1997.

Shultz, George P. *Turmoil and Triumph: My Years as Secretary of State*. New York: Scribner's, 1993.

Simpson, Christopher. *Blowback: America's Recruitment of Nazis and Its Effects on the Cold War*. New York: Weidenfeld and Nicolson, 1988.

Sivachev, Nikolai V., and Nikolai N. Yakovlev. *Russia and the United States*. Translated by Olga Adler Titlebaum. Chicago: University of Chicago Press, 1979.

Smith, Gaddis. *The Last Years of the Monroe Doctrine, 1945–1993*. New York: Hill and Wang, 1994.

Smith, Jean Edward. *Lucius D. Clay: An American Life*. New York: Henry Holt, 1990.

Smith, Walter Bedell. *My Three Years in Moscow*. Philadelphia: Lippincott, 1950.

Spykman, Nicholas John. *America's Strategy in World Politics: The United States and the Balance of Power*. New York: Harcourt, Brace, 1942.

Steel, Ronald. *Walter Lippmann and the American Century*. Boston: Little, Brown, 1980.

Steneck, Nicholas H. *The Microwave Debate*. Cambridge, Mass.: MIT Press, 1984.

Stephanson, Anders. *Kennan and the Art of Foreign Policy*. Cambridge, Mass.: Harvard University Press, 1989.

Stueck, William. *The Korean War: An International History*. Princeton, N.J.: Princeton University Press, 1995.

————. *Rethinking the Korean War: A New Diplomatic and Strategic History*. Princeton, N.J.: Princeton University Press, 2002.

Suri, Jeremi. *Power and Protest: Global Revolutions and the Rise of Détente*. Cambridge, Mass.: Harvard University Press, 2003.

Talbott, Strobe. *The Master of the Game: Paul Nitze and the Nuclear Peace*. New York: Knopf, 1988.

————. *The Russia Hand: A Memoir of Presidential Diplomacy*. New York: Random House, 2002.

Thayer, Charles W. *Bears in the Caviar*. Philadelphia: J. B. Lippincott, 1951.

Thomas, Daniel C. *The Helsinki Effect: International Norms, Human Rights, and the Demise of Communism*. Princeton, N.J.: Princeton University Press, 2001.

Thomas, Evan. *The Very Best Men: Four Who Dared; The Early Years of the CIA*. New York: Simon and Schuster, 1995.

Thompson, Nicholas. *The Hawk and the Dove: Paul Nitze, George Kennan, and the History of the Cold War*. New York: Henry Holt, 2009.

Thoreau, Henry David. *A Week on the Concord and Merrimack Rivers*. New York: Thomas Y. Crowell, 1911.

Tolstoy, Leo. *War and Peace*. Translated by Richard Pevear and Larissa Volokhonsky. New York: Knopf, 2007.

Trachtenberg, Marc. *A Constructed Peace: The Making of the European Settlement, 1945–1963*. Princeton, N.J.: Princeton University Press, 1999.

Travis, Frederick F. *George Kennan and the Russian-American Relationship, 1865–1924*. Athens: Ohio University Press, 1990.

Vassiltchikov, Marie. *Berlin Diaries, 1940–1945*. New York: Knopf, 1987.

Wala, Michael. *The Council on Foreign Relations and American Foreign Policy in the Early Cold War*. Providence, R.I.: Berghahn Books, 1994.

Wallace, Robert, and H. Keith Melton. *Spycraft: The Secret History of the CIA's Spytechs from Communism to Al-Qaeda*. New York: Dutton, 2006.

Weil, Martin. *A Pretty Good Club: The Founding Fathers of the U.S. Foreign Service*. New York: Norton, 1978.

Weiner, Tim. *Legacy of Ashes: The History of the CIA*. New York: Doubleday, 2007.

Westad, Odd Arne. *The Global Cold War: Third World Interventions and the Making of Our Times*. New York: Cambridge University Press, 2005.

White, Graham, and John Maze. *Henry A. Wallace: His Search for a New World Order*. Chapel Hill: University of North Carolina Press, 1995.

Williams, William Appleman. *The Tragedy of American Diplomacy*. Cleveland: World Publishing Company, 1959.

Wittner, Lawrence S. *Toward Nuclear Abolition: A History of the World Nuclear Disarmament Movement, 1971 to the Present*. Stanford, Calif.: Stanford University Press, 2003.

Wohlforth, William Curti. *The Elusive Balance: Power and Perceptions during the Cold War*. Ithaca, N.Y.: Cornell University Press, 1993.

Wolverton, Mark. *A Life in Twilight: The Final Years of J. Robert Oppenheimer*. New York: St. Martin's, 2008.

Woods, Randall Bennett. *Fulbright: A Biography*. New York: Cambridge University Press, 1995.

Wright's Directory of Milwaukee for 1903. Milwaukee: Alfred G. Wright, 1903.

Ybarra, Michael J. *Washington Gone Crazy: Senator Pat McCarran and the Great American Communist Hunt*. Hanover, N.H.: Steerforth Press, 2004.

Yergin, Daniel. *Shattered Peace: The Origins of the Cold War and the National Security State*. Boston: Houghton Mifflin, 1977.

Ziegler, Philip. *Mountbatten*. New York: Harper and Row, 1985.

Zubok, Vladislav M. *A Failed Empire: The Soviet Union in the Cold War from Stalin to Gorbachev*. Chapel Hill: University of North Carolina Press, 2007.

ARTICLES

Begley, Adam. "The Lonely Genius Club." *New York*, January 30, 1995, 61–67.

Berger, Marilyn. "An Appeal for Thought" (interview with GFK). *New York Times Magazine*, May 7, 1978.

Berlin, Isaiah. "Political Ideas in the Twentieth Century." *Foreign Affairs* 28 (April 1950), 351–85.

Bridges, Peter. "George Kennan Reminisces About Moscow in 1933–1937." *Diplomacy and Statecraft* 17 (June 2006), 283–93.

Bullitt, William C. "What Should We Do About Russia?" *U.S. News & World Report*, June 29, 1956, 69–72.

Bundy, McGeorge, George F. Kennan, Robert S. McNamara, and Gerard Smith. "Nuclear Weapons and the Atlantic Alliance." *Foreign Affairs* 60 (Spring 1982), 753–68.

Cassels, Louis. "Mr. X Goes to Moscow." *Collier's*, March 15, 1952.

Costigliola, Frank. "'Unceasing Pressure for Penetration': Gender, Pathology, and Emotion in George Kennan's Formation of the Cold War." *Journal of American History* 83 (March 1997), 1309–39.

Dulles, John Foster. "A Policy of Boldness." *Life* 32 (May 19, 1952), 146–60.

Gaddis, John Lewis. "The Gardener." *New Republic* 235 (October 16, 2005), 26–32.

_____. "The Unexpected John Foster Dulles: Nuclear Weapons, Communism, and the Russians." In Richard H. Immerman, ed., *John Foster Dulles and the Diplomacy of the Cold War*. Princeton, N.J.: Princeton University Press, 1990.

"Global Nuclear Stockpiles, 1945–2006." *Bulletin of the Atomic Scientists* 62 (July–August, 2006), 64–66.

Hammond, Paul Y. "NSC-68: Prologue to Rearmament." In Warner R. Schilling, Paul Y. Hammond, and Glenn H. Snyder, eds., *Strategy, Politics, and Defense Budgets*. New York: Columbia University Press, 1962.

Harkins, Philip. "Mysterious Mr. X." *New York Herald Tribune Magazine*, January 4, 1948.

Lucas, Scott, and Kaeten Mistry. "Illusions of Coherence: George F. Kennan, U.S. Strategy and Political Warfare in the Early Cold War, 1946–1950." *Diplomatic History* 33 (January 2009), 39–66.

Kennan, George F. "After the Cold War." *New York Times Magazine*, February 5, 1989.
_____. "Breaking the Spell." *New Yorker* 49 (October 3, 1983), 44–53.
_____. "Commentary [on the Novikov Dispatch]." *Diplomatic History* 15 (Fall 1991), 539–43.
_____. "Disengagement Revisited." *Foreign Affairs* 37 (January 1959), 187–210.
_____. "The Experience of Writing History." *Virginia Quarterly Review* 36 (Spring 1960), 205–14.
_____. "Foreword." In *The State Department Policy Planning Staff Papers, 1947–49*. 3 vols. New York: Garland, 1983.
_____. "A Fresh Look at Our China Policy." *New York Times Magazine*, November 22, 1964, 27, 140–47.
_____. "Hazardous Courses in Southern Africa." *Foreign Affairs* 49 (January 1971), 218–36.
_____. "History as Literature." *Encounter* 12 (April 1959), 10–16.
_____. "How New Are Our Problems? The National Interest of the United States." *Illinois Law Review* 45 (January–February 1952), 718–42.
_____. "Interview with George F. Kennan." Conducted by Charles Gati and Richard H. Ullman. *Foreign Policy* 7 (Summer 1972), 5–21.
_____. "Introduction." In Orville H. Bullitt, ed., *For the President: Personal and Secret: Correspondence Between Franklin D. Roosevelt and William C. Bullitt*. Boston: Houghton Mifflin, 1972.
_____. "Is War with Russia Inevitable? Five Solid Arguments for Peace." *Reader's Digest* (March 1950), 1–9.
_____. "Japanese Security and American Policy." *Foreign Affairs* 43 (October 1964), 14–28.
_____. "The Last Wise Man." *Atlantic Monthly* 263 (April 1989).
_____. "Let Peace Not Die of Neglect." *New York Times Magazine*, February 25, 1951, 10ff.
_____. "The Passing of the Cold War." *International House of Japan Bulletin* 14 (October 1964), 49–74.
_____. "Report, the Internment and Repatriation of the American Official Group in Germany, 1941–1942." *American Foreign Service Journal* 18 (August 1942), 422–26, 456–59.
_____. "The Sisson Documents." *Journal of Modern History* 28 (June 1956), 130–54.
_____. "The Sources of Soviet Conduct." *Foreign Affairs* 25 (July 1947), 566–82.
_____. "Training for Statesmanship." *Atlantic* 191 (May 1953), 40–43.
_____. "The United States and the Soviet Union, 1917–1976." *Foreign Affairs* 54 (July 1976), 670–90.
Mackinder, Sir Halford J. "The Geographical Pivot of History." *Geographical Journal* 23 (April 1904), 421–44.
Matlock, Jack F., Jr. "George F. Kennan." *Proceedings of the American Philosophical Society* 151 (June 2007), 234–42.
Messer, Robert L. "Paths Not Taken: The United States Department of State and Alternatives to Containment, 1945–1946." *Diplomatic History* 1 (Fall 1977), 304–19.
Miner, Steven Merritt. "His Master's Voice: Viacheslav Mikhailovich Molotov as Stalin's Foreign Commissar." In Gordon A. Craig and Francis L. Loewenheim, eds., *The Diplomats: 1939–1979*. Princeton, N.J.: Princeton University Press, 1994, 65–100.
Moskin, J. Robert. "Our Foreign Policy Is Paralyzed [interview with George F. Kennan]." *Look* 27 (November 19, 1963), 25–27.
Nelson, Anna Kasten. "Introduction." *State Department Policy Planning Staff Papers*. New York: Garland, 1983.
Nichols, Lewis. "Visit with George Kennan." *New York Times*, October 29, 1967.
Nitze, Paul H. "A Plea for Action." *New York Times Magazine*, May 7, 1978.
Norris, Robert S., and Hans M. Kristensen. "Nuclear Notebook: Global Nuclear Stockpiles, 1945–2006." *Bulletin of the Atomic Scientists* 62 (July–August 2006), 64–66.
Pechatnov, Vladimir O., and C. Earl Edmondson. "The Russian Perspective." In Ralph B. Levering, Vladimir O. Pechatnov, Verena Botzenhart-Viehe, and C. Earl Edmondson, *Debating the Origins of the Cold War: American and Russian Perspectives*. New York: Rowman and Littlefield, 2002.
Rostow, Eugene V. "Searching for Kennan's Grand Design." *Yale Law Journal* 87 (June 1978), 1527–48.
Rovere, Richard. "Letter from Washington." *New Yorker*, May 17, 1952.
Salisbury, Harrison. "The View from Mokhovaya Street." *New York Times Magazine*, June 1, 1952.
_____. "When Russia's Revolution Was Young." *New York Times Book Review*, August 26, 1956.
Schilling, Warner R. "The Politics of National Defense: Fiscal 1950." In Warner R. Schilling, Paul Y. Hammond, and Glenn H. Snyder, eds., *Strategy, Politics, and Defense Budgets*. New York: Columbia University Press, 1962.
Trask, Roger R. "George F. Kennan's Report on Latin America." *Diplomatic History* 2 (Summer 1978), 307–11.
Urban, George. "From Containment to . . . Self-Containment: A Conversation with George F. Kennan." *Encounter* 47 (September 1976), 10–43.
Wood, Gordon S. "All in the Family." *New York Review of Books*, February 22, 2001.
Wright, C. Ben. "Mr. 'X' and Containment." *Slavic Review* 35 (March 1976), 1–31.

INDEX